Our Towns

Our Towns

Saskatchewan Communities from Abbey to Zenon Park

UNIVERSITY OF REGINA

CANADIAN PLAINS
RESEARCH CENTER

2008

David McLennan

Canadian Plains Research Center
University of Regina
Regina, Saskatchewan S4S 0A2
Canada
Tel: (306) 585-4758
Fax: (306) 585-4699
E-mail: canadian.plains@uregina.ca
http://www.cprc.uregina.ca

Library and Archives Canada Cataloguing in Publication
McLennan, David, 1961-
        Our towns : Saskatchewan communities from Abbey to Zenon Park / David McLennan.

(Trade books based in scholarship, ISSN 1482-9886 ; 23)
Includes bibliographical references.
ISBN 978-0-88977-209-0

        1. Saskatchewan--History, Local. I. University of Regina. Canadian Plains Research Center. II. Title. III. Series.

FC3661.M45 2007   971.24   C2007-906182-6

Printed and bound in Canada

Book design and layout: Donna Grant, Canadian Plains Research Center
Cover and title page designs: Duncan Campbell, Regina, Saskatchewan

The Canadian Plains Research Center acknowledges the financial support of the Government of Canada through the Book Publishing Industry Development Program (BPIDP) for our publishing activities.

We acknowledge the support of the Canada Council for the Arts for our publishing program.

We also wish to acknowledge financial support from the following, without which the publication of *Our Towns: Saskatchewan Communities from Abbey to Zenon Park* would have been impossible:
• Community Initiatives Fund
• Saskatchewan Heritage Foundation
• Cultural Assistance Program
• Cultural Industries Development Fund

for Jenny

and dedicated to the memory of

Albert Rodney Barnes 1911-1982
born Coventry, England
died Winnipeg, Manitoba

&

Janet McCairns Colvin (née Conway) Barnes 1916-2001
born Glasgow, Scotland
died Broadview, Saskatchewan

CONTENTS

PREFACE

This book contains information on 725 Saskatchewan communities: 273 villages, 172 organized hamlets, 147 towns, 42 hamlets, 39 resort villages, 13 cities, 13 northern villages, 11 northern settlements, 9 northern hamlets, the three communities that comprise the one municipal district in the province (the District of Katepwa), 2 northern towns, and the portion of Flin Flon that lies within the province. Lists of communities by type may be found in Appendix B. A brief discussion of community types may be found in Appendix C.

The general criterion for inclusion in this book was that a community was listed in the *Saskatchewan Municipal Directory* at some time between the 2001 Census of Canada and the end of June 2007. The status of each community in *Our Towns* reflects its status as of the end of June 2007. Thus, villages that have been dissolved and that have reverted to hamlet status since the 2001 Census of Canada have been included. Hamlets have been included in *Our Towns* if they are the headquarters of a rural municipality, and Flin Flon, Saskatchewan, somewhat of an anomaly, has been included because it is well-known.

Although the intention has been to be comprehensive, this book does not include a number of communities because they do not meet the above criterion: First Nations reserve communities, Hutterite colonies, hamlets that are not RM headquarters, and ghost towns are not included in this book. Nor are villages or organized hamlets that reverted to hamlet status prior to 2001. Some communities that are essentially ghost towns, or that are almost ghost towns, have been included if they still had legal standing in the *Municipal Directory* during the time frame mentioned above.

Population figures for most communities are based upon Statistics Canada's censuses; population figures for organized hamlets for 2006 were mainly courtesy of the Community Planning Branch of the Department of Saskatchewan Government Relations (in a few instances figures were provided by the rural municipality). Population figures for organized hamlets in the 1960s and 1970s were gleaned from the Government of Saskatchewan's directories of hamlets, settlements, and other unincorporated areas, which were published by the then Department of Municipal Affairs. Population figures for organized hamlets in the 1980s were found in Saskatchewan Rural Development's listing of organized hamlets produced in 1992. Unfortunately, the most recent population figures available for northern hamlets and northern settlements are from 2001. Population figures for the 2006 and 2001 Censuses of Canada are indicated in the first sentence of each community profile using the form: pop 412 (2006c), 485 (2001c). School enrollment figures were provided courtesy of Saskatchewan Learning and are current as of the fall of 2006; school closures are current as of the summer of 2007. Further information on source materials used to compose the community profiles on the following pages can be found at the end of this book in Appendix A.

Contributors of photographs are acknowledged within the book, as are artists who gave permission to reproduce their work. Unless indicated otherwise, photographs have been taken by the author.

Finally, both kilometres and miles, likewise metres and feet, are used to refer to distances and lengths. This may depend somewhat upon historical context; miles are used at times to help the reader accurately identify exactly where a locale might be, or may have been, given that our municipal (grid) road network is based upon imperial measures. The word "today" in the entries means as of the beginning of 2008.

ACKNOWLEDGEMENTS

My first expression of thanks must go to the many people I encountered as I travelled across Saskatchewan researching this book. Several hundred residents of this province gave freely of their time and knowledge, fielding my questions over the past five years, touring me through their communities, letting me into their homes, and allowing me to scour through their photo albums. The administrators of many of our towns, villages, and rural municipalities assisted with this project, as did the mayors of a number of communities. Countless teachers, principals, and school secretaries answered questions about schools; and the volunteers who take care of our many small community museums throughout the province are to be commended for their contributions; without exception, all dropped what they were doing to assist with my research. Many economic development personnel, people on coffee row, storekeepers, farmers, etc., also provided invaluable insights and knowledge.

At the University of Regina, Brian Mlazgar, the publications coordinator at the Canadian Plains Research Center (CPRC), must be thanked, first, for believing in this project, and also for his vision, patience, and unfailing support over the past few years. Editorial Assistant Donna Grant must be commended for her design and layout work, her editorial skill, her guidance and suggestions, and patience, as well. I also must thank Dr. David Gauthier, the former executive director of the Canadian Plains Research Center (currently the University of Regina's Vice-President / Research & International), and Dr. Harry Diaz, the current director of the Center, for their leadership, and for fostering and nurturing an environment where work such as this book can be produced. I must also thank the greater CPRC family — Lorraine Nelson, Diane Perrick, Anne Pennylegion, and Jeff Morman — for their great work, camaraderie, and general support. To all of you at the CPRC, my deepest appreciation.

The University of Regina itself must also be recognized for its role in building a better Saskatchewan, and for its continuing support of the Canadian Plains Research Center and the province's sole accredited university press. I also must thank the University for providing me with what I regard as an excellent education.

Beyond the University, there are a number of individuals I must mention by name for their contributions: the late Ken Aitken and the staff at the Prairie History Room at the Regina Public Library for their general assistance; Bob Ivanochko for proofreading a portion of the manuscript, and for his suggestions and his interest in the project over the years; Kristine Douaud for also proofreading the manuscript; Tim Novak at the Saskatchewan Archives Board for his always courteous help; Garth Pugh at the Saskatchewan Heritage Foundation for his belief in the project, and for his support and patience as the project took longer to develop than had been imagined; and Michael Hayes, formerly with the Community Planning Branch of the Department of Saskatchewan Government Relations. Michael graciously answered many questions over the years and arranged for me to access a number of government records. To Duncan Campbell my sincere thanks for his inspired cover and title page designs. My dear friend Nigel Francis must be thanked for riding shotgun on a number of forays around the province; and Tasha Wiebe of Fleming, Saskatchewan, with whom I became acquainted in a Moosomin restaurant in the fall of 2003, I would like to thank for providing me with information on Fleming and Moosomin, as well as her continued friendship (even though she now resides in Manitoba!).

To my family and friends I offer my deep and sincere thanks for putting up with and understanding my absenteeism over the years while I worked on this book.

Lastly, but most importantly, I owe a debt I can never repay to Jenny MacDonald, my partner in life. Without her support, understanding, patience, and belief in this project, its completion would have been impossible. Jenny accompanied me on numerous road trips throughout our great province, recording field notes and making many observations of things that I would otherwise have missed. She was also a great sounding board for me as this project developed. Further, Jenny also spent many weeks, evenings and weekends alone while I worked on this book, often managing our household without my assistance. This book would not have been possible without her.

INTRODUCTION

There are two parts to the story of how *Our Towns* came to be. The first part, the incunabula, dates to my childhood. My mother had a thing for packing us kids up in our big 1960s American car and driving out of Regina to explore the grid roads. Often there wasn't a destination, and often we'd get a little lost — but that was a part of the fun. Sometimes we'd end up in Lumsden or Craven; other times we'd go out to Regina Beach, perhaps Fort Qu'Appelle, or Qu'Appelle, after relatives had moved there. The men in my family were also great fishermen, and I remember that my first trip up to La Ronge was over a gravel road when I was about five. A love of rural Saskatchewan was born in those days — a love of gravel roads, bulrushes in the ditches, red-winged blackbirds, the song of a meadow lark, and trains. I grew to be fascinated with prairie towns — their general stores, gravelled Main Streets, old hotels, grain elevators, churches, and, usually, interesting folk. The second part of the story of how *Our Towns* came to be happened much later.

In 2003, through good fortune, and perhaps some ambition, I became involved with the development of the *Encyclopedia of Saskatchewan*, working on writing entries on the province's communities. As I got deeper into the research I realized there was much more that could be said about our towns than could included in an encyclopedia entry, which are by necessity rather brief, and rather general. I got it into my head that a book based solely upon Saskatchewan's communities might be worth pursuing — especially since it seemed it would fill a void. I had always liked to read any books I could find on Saskatchewan, but what was beginning to niggle at me was that there was not a singular handy, reliable source, no comprehensive guide, that I could go to for concise information on one community or another in the province. E.T. Russell and Bill Barry had produced books on the origins of place names; there were books on historic sites, canoe routes, wildflowers, and birds. I *could* go to the Saskatchewan Archives or the Prairie History Room at the Regina Public Library and browse through their hundreds of locally-produced histories (which is indeed fascinating), but I *could not* pick up just *one* book for an informative profile of, say, Elbow or Porcupine Plain. I presented my idea about a book on our towns to Brian Mlazgar, the

publications coordinator at the Canadian Plains Research Center, and he believed the project had merit.

My goal was to provide the reader with the general history of a community up until the present. The subjects I chose to address include the geographic location of a place, the settlement period of an area and the ethnic origins of the settlers, transportation (where applicable, the coming of railways and rail line abandonment), a community's beginnings and the origin of its name, the development of businesses, industry and the economy, schools and churches, boom times and decline, sports and recreation, the development of community services (such as the establishment of electrical, natural gas, and water and sewer systems), and major events and disasters (fires wiped out substantial portions of many communities in the days of all-wooden structures and little or no fire-fighting equipment). I also chose to look at population statistics, landmarks, attractions, heritage properties, and some community sons and daughters who have had notable careers and accomplishments. Generally speaking, the availability of information on these topics (not the community's size or status) has been the determining factor in the length of each community profile. (The exception to this is that the profiles of the province's cities are deliberately relatively brief, since a wealth of information about the cities is readily available in a variety of other sources.)

Additionally, I wanted to include a good selection of historical and contemporary photographs — a visual narrative, as it were, to accompany the written profiles of each community. Not every community is represented in photos, but many are, and many shared aspects of life in this province appear in the more than one thousand images. Thus, for example, early photos of Clement's Store in Esterhazy or Sample Bros. Store in Kerrobert provide a glimpse of that most common of pioneer businesses — the general store; images of Missinipe and Patuanak show the largely untouched natural beauty surrounding communities in the province's north; the demolition of the grain elevator in Grenfell speaks to the sense of loss that many in communities have felt as they witnessed a part of their history disappear; the fund-raising parade in Neilburg and the "World's Longest Hockey Game" in Moosomin (another fund-raiser) illustrate the community pride and spirit that are still very much alive throughout our province. The historical photographs that appear in *Our Towns* came from a variety of sources: from small community museums, village offices, and people's photograph albums. Their acquisition was often due to serendipity, to my stumbling across someone who had a treasure trove of historical photographs and was willing to share it, and I am grateful for what these images have added not only to this book but also to our understanding of the early days of the province. Many of these photographs were damaged: they were torn or had water marks, or faded from being too long in the sun. In a number of cases, writing on the back had bled through to the front. As such, liberty has been taken to digitally restore many of these images: some scratches and rips have been "repaired," and we have tinkered with the contrast of some of the photographs as well.

With regard to my own photographs that appear in *Our Towns*, I consider them more documentary in nature than an art form. Of course, one of the challenges of photographing the province as I did was that I had to work with whatever light and weather there was at the time I happened to be in any one location. Sometimes I would be in a place at midday, say in July, and the light would be harsh; at other times, I was fortunate to have the early morning light (see the photograph of the Prud'homme cemetery). The evening proved to be a rewarding time to photograph grain elevators (see Grand Coulee) and architectural structures in general (see Battleford). An overcast sky often resulted in some rather drab photographs, but sometimes it would provide for an element of drama (see the photograph of the grain elevators in Kenaston). In the later summer of 2003, I was often frustrated by hazy skies in the western part of the province, the result of smoke from the forest fires ravaging the interior of British Columbia that year. At times, however, these smoky skies added to the mood of a photograph (see the picture of Grasslands National Park accompanying the piece on Val Marie). Like many, I'm more comfortable driving through our province in months other than winter; however, I did find braving the elements could be rewarding (see the churches in Dysart).

The greatest difficulty I faced while working on *Our Towns* was sorting through misinformation — and reams of it. Sources, however seemingly reliable on their own, were often contradicted by others that I came across. Government publications, encyclopedias, local histories, newspaper articles, etc., were often rife with errors, and many times these errors had been repeated over and over again throughout the years to the point that the untruths had come to be considered facts. Given this challenge, I adopted a research strategy I describe as methodological eclecticism. That is, I tried looking at Saskatchewan communities from as many angles and perspectives as I could. What my work really required, however, was getting out there, hitting the road, visiting communities and talking to people. I estimate that I covered approximately 55,000 kilometres in Saskatchewan while working on this project. I endeavoured to corroborate the details presented in *Our Towns* two, three, or even four or more times — and, as such, I hope that I have been able to debunk some long-established fallacies. Any errors that do remain in this volume are solely this author's responsibility, and I would welcome any comments, queries, and constructive criticism. Correspondence may be directed to my attention at the Canadian Plains Research Center at the University of Regina.

One final, but important, point — while my intention was to be an unbiased voice in the writings on the following pages, I do hope that in some way my love and respect for all of these places, big and small, shines through. We live in a great province.

David McLennan
February 23, 2008

Our Towns

ABBEY, village, pop 130 (2006c), 137 (2001c), is located in southwest Saskatchewan, northwest of Swift Current on Hwy 32. The community is situated between the South Saskatchewan River and the Great Sand Hills. By the late 1890s, a handful of ranching operations had been established in the district, but after the winter of 1906-07 devastated the cattle industry, the area was opened up to homesteaders. By 1908, settlers were busy breaking and fencing land. The majority were of Scandinavian or British origin, with many of the Scandinavians arriving via the United States. In the early days, to obtain supplies or to deliver grain, area residents would have to journey south to Gull Lake or Swift Current, the nearest railway points. In 1912, however, the CPR approached from the southeast with the construction of its "Empress Line," and Abbey had its beginnings. By the time the first trains arrived in 1913, a number of businesses and homes dotted the previously barren townsite. On September 2 that year, the village was incorporated. In the early years, Abbey was plagued with fires. Many businesses were lost and, twice, due to a lack of proper fire-fighting equipment, much of the commercial district burned to the ground. One of the buildings that survived is the Abbey Fire Hall. Built in 1919, it also served as a jail, and the building was designated a heritage property in 2001. Despite the fires, though, the village continued to grow and it reached a peak population of 336 in 1961. In recent decades Abbey has experienced a steady decline, the population dropping with each successive census. The village still retains a core of essential businesses and services, though; and Abbey School provides K-12 education to approximately 75 community and area students. While agriculture (a combination of grain and livestock production) remains the main industry in the region, the recent discovery of large reserves of natural gas near Shackleton has proven somewhat of a boon, providing some off-farm employment. The Abbey district is popular for hunting, as deer, antelope, ducks and geese are found in abundance. The nearby South Saskatchewan River provides opportunities for fishing and recreation. Abbey serves as the administrative centre of the RM of Miry Creek No. 229.

ABERDEEN, town, pop 527 (2006c), 534 (2001c), is located approximately 32 km northeast of Saskatoon, off Hwy 41. Settlers began arriving in the area in the late 1890s: "Easterners," people of English and Scottish stock who were born in eastern Canada, were first to come to the district; Russian Mennonites, who came to the region via Manitoba, arrived in the early 1900s; and Ukrainian settlers, who established what became known as the Fish Creek Colony in 1898-99, would also frequent Aberdeen, rounding out the cultural milieu. The hamlet of Aberdeen was founded in 1904, the CNR arrived in 1905, and the community was incorporated as a village in 1907. By the 1930s, the population was close to 300. In 1937, during the peak of the Depression, and after years of poor crops, disaster struck the community. A fire destroyed much of Main Street and many businesses were lost, never able to re-establish themselves. Increasingly easy access to shopping and services in Saskatoon contributed to an economic decline and years of stagnation. Beginning in the 1970s, however, Aberdeen slowly began to grow again and, in 1988, the community attained town status. Its proximity to Saskatoon has resulted in the development of new residential subdivisions, and this in turn has led to the establishment of new businesses in the town. In 2003, the community received a major boost with the announcement that a multi-million-dollar cultural and recreational complex would be built. While many residents of Aberdeen commute to work in Saskatoon, local employment opportunities are found in agricultural-based industries and small businesses. Aberdeen Composite School has a staff of 38 and provides K-12 education to close to 350 students from the town and the surrounding district. Aberdeen serves as the administrative centre of the RM of Aberdeen No. 373.

ABERNETHY, village, pop 197 (2006c), 213 (2001c), is located east of Fort Qu'Appelle on Hwy 22 in the rolling countryside north of the Qu'Appelle Valley. Settlers began arriving in the area in 1882, the first travelling overland with oxen, teams of horses, and wagons from Brandon, Manitoba, in the months before the CPR was built into present-day Saskatchewan. Many would ford the Qu'Appelle River north of Wolseley at the site that would become known as Ellisboro. A large number of those taking up homesteads were of British origin, coming from both eastern Canada and overseas. One of the

▶ **LANARK PLACE** was the name W.R. Motherwell gave to his farm, now known as the Motherwell Homestead, a National Historic site located 4 kilometres south of present-day Abernethy. He chose the name to remember his birthplace, Lanark County, Ontario. Motherwell came west in the spring of 1882 to claim his homestead; after he gradually expanded his original quarter section into a large, prosperous farm, he was ready to build his now-famous estate. Over the years, Motherwell had collected fieldstone from his fields and the nearby Pheasant Creek coulee, and in 1896 he hired a local stone mason, Adam Cantelon, to build a stone stable. In 1897, Cantelon constructed Motherwell's large Italianate-style house, replacing an earlier home made of logs. The massive superstructure of the red, Ontario-style barn in the left of the photograph (taken October 4, 2003) was erected upon the stone stable in 1907.

earliest settlers in the Abernethy district was William Richard Motherwell, who would become the province's first minister of Agriculture, and a founder of the Territorial Grain Grower's Association. The Motherwell Homestead, just south of Abernethy, is now a National Historic Site. For the first couple of years, travel south across the Qu'Appelle River to the CPR main line was often a wet, muddy, and difficult undertaking, a situation which was much improved with the construction of the first bridge in the summer of 1884. This still did not alleviate the travel distance necessary to deliver grain or obtain supplies, however, and residents of the Abernethy district would petition authori-

▲ **HEADQUARTERS OF THE RURAL MUNICIPALITY:** The RM of Abernethy No. 186 was incorporated on December 11, 1911. This office building sits at the northeast corner of Main Street and Qu'Appelle Avenue. Photograph taken October 3, 2003.

▶ **BUILT IN 1905**, Knox United Church (originally Knox Presbyterian) stands on the corner of Qu'Appelle Avenue and Burton Street in Abernethy. Photograph taken October 3, 2003.

ties for many years for rail service. Meanwhile, though, the settlers went about building the foundations of their community. The post office was established in 1884, Christ Anglican Church was built in 1886 (two kilometres south of Abernethy until 1904 and now a municipal heritage

◀ **THE "OLD STONE CHURCH,"** located approximately 4 kilometres west of Abernethy, was built with volunteer labour for the area's Presbyterian congregation in 1892. Photograph taken October 3, 2003.

property), and schools were popping up in the countryside from the mid-1880s. In 1903, the CPR built the railway grade through the district and the townsite was established. Buildings were moved in from the country, and many new buildings were erected. In 1904 as the first trains rolled in, Abernethy was incorporated as a village. Within months, the population was 300, and it hovered around that mark until the mid-1980s. At the end of WWI, citizens of the community decided to construct a memorial to those from the area who had served and died for their country. The Abernethy and District Memorial Hall was completed in 1921 to accommodate social, cultural, and recreational activities and was considered at the time to be the finest facility of its kind in the region. Designated a heritage property in 1985,

this distinct local landmark is still in use today. The Abernethy Nature-Heritage Museum houses a collection reflecting both the community's pioneering era and the region's natural history. For fishing enthusiasts, the museum also includes a display of Len Thompson's famous fishing spoons, 30 million of which have been produced since Thompson made his first lure in Abernethy in 1929. Thompson constructed a factory in Abernethy, but relocated to Lacombe, Alberta, in 1958. In July 2004, the Village of Abernethy commemorated its centennial with a successful homecoming celebration. Abernethy serves as the administrative centre of the RM of Abernethy No. 186.

ADMIRAL, hamlet, pop 30 (2006c), 25 (2001c), is a picturesque former village located east of Shaunavon off Hwy 13. It sits between the former communities of Scotsguard, to the west, and Crichton, to the east: both once-busy centres, both non-existent today. Admiral, like many of the towns and villages in the province's southwest, had its largest population and celebrated its heyday between the time the railroad came through the region and the onset of the drought and the Great Depression of the 1930s. Settlement of Admiral district had begun in the early 1900s and, although the early arrivals were of diverse origins, there developed a significant Scandinavian (primarily Swedish) presence in the area. In 1913, as the CPR was building westward from Assiniboia, the townsite of Admiral was established, and in 1914 the new community was incorporated as a village. Fittingly, the community's streets were named after naval figures such as Drake, Nelson, and Frobisher. By the mid-1920s, Admiral had reached a peak population of around 250; however, the 1930s broke the spirit of many in the region, and the village lost close to one-third of its residents by the end of the decade. Subsequently, Admiral never recovered its population, nor the level of commercial activity seen in its earlier years. Each successive decade saw fewer and fewer people living in the village, and the once vibrant business district was slowly reduced to a handful of enterprises. Today, the Admiral Branch of the Shaunavon Credit Union, situated in an old two-storey red brick building, remains; as does a unique small business, the Svensen Toboggan Company. The toboggan business started in 1989 after the owner, Lloyd Garthus, made a durable plastic toboggan for his son for Christmas which quickly became a hit with neighbourhood children. Several thousand of the brightly coloured units have been produced and sold since, and the company has expanded into the production of combine auger downspouts. Admiral relinquished village status on August 17, 2006, and Admiral School, a K-7 facility that had 15 students enrolled in the fall of 2006, was scheduled to close at the end of June 2007. Admiral is situated in the RM of Wise Creek No. 77. Agriculture, a combination of grain and livestock production, is the major industry in the area.

▲ ▼ **ADMIRAL'S BUSINESS SECTION** (above) during the community's heyday. Saskatchewan Archives Board R-A18349. The building in the far right of the photograph still stands and remains in business as the Admiral Branch of the Shaunavon Credit Union (pictured below, left). The photograph below, right, shows a portion of the same street from the opposite direction. Photographs below taken on June 22, 2003.

AIR RONGE, northern village, pop 1,032 (2006c), 955 (2001c), is located on the west shore of Lac la Ronge, on Hwy 2, across the mouth of the Montreal River from the town of La Ronge. The village is also nestled between the reserve lands of the Lac la Ronge Indian Band. The combined population of these area communities is approximately 6,000. Air Ronge, as the name indicates, was for many years the location of one of the major airstrips serving northern Saskatchewan. With increasing air traffic through the region, however, a major airport was built north of La Ronge, and today much of the area of Air Ronge's old airstrip has been converted into a residential subdivision. The community has experienced rapid growth over the past few decades, being established as a Local Community Authority (LCA) in 1977 and becoming incorporated as a northern village in 1983. In addition to its residential areas, Air Ronge contains commercial, institutional, and industrial developments. Employment opportunities are sought at local area businesses, as well as with northern mining companies, government agencies, educational institutions, in construction work and in the area of health care. The growing and harvesting of wild rice provides some seasonal employment. Tourism is important to the regional economy, with fishing, hunting, camping, canoeing, snowmobiling, cross-country skiing, and the northern scenery the primary attractions. Air Ronge has a K-6 school with over 200 students; grades 7-12 attend high school in La Ronge, where medical and police services are also located.

ALAMEDA, town, pop 308 (2006c), 311 (2001c), is situated in the southeast corner of the province, 60 km northeast of Estevan and 40 km north of the U.S.

border. It is an area of mixed farming and oil field development. The community is located just off the junction of Hwys 9 and 18. Settlers of Scottish and English origins from Ontario began arriving in the district in the early 1880s, and the first businesses and buildings — a store and post office, a blacksmith shop, and a church — were located a few kilometres south of the present townsite. Mail arrived once a week from Moosomin. In 1892, when it was discovered that the CPR would run through

to the north, everything, including the cemetery, was relocated to meet the line of steel. Beginning in 1897, German settlers from Michigan began homesteading in the district. Alameda was legally established as a village in 1898 and in the next several years experienced rapid growth. The population went from 104 in 1904, to 333 by 1906. In the spring of 1907, Alameda was incorporated as a town. But it was not to be a good year for the community. That fall the grain crop was severely

damaged by rust, and then a fire in the town claimed thirty buildings. The community rebuilt and, although its numbers fluctuated somewhat over the periods of the two World Wars, the population has remained essentially stable for the past half-century. In 1993, the Alameda Dam about three kilometres east of the town was opened. The reservoir created by the dam is approximately 26 kilometres long and today provides a stable water supply and greater recreational opportunities for area residents. Alameda serves as the administrative centre of the RM of Moose Creek No. 33.

ALBERTVILLE, village, pop 110 (2006c), 132 (2001c), is located northeast of Prince Albert, a few km south of Hwy

▲ **HOMETOWN HEROES:** The Alameda Hockey Team, 1922-23. Back row left to right: Arnold (Sam) Hopper, Ed Slack, Sid Barker, Art Gibson. Middle row left to right: Claud Hopper, Earl Davidson, Stan Boyle, Sid Truscott, Harry Truscott. Front: Else Gorham. Photograph courtesy of the Ralph Allen Memorial Museum, Oxbow, Saskatchewan. Donated by Mrs. Herman Martens, Alameda, Saskatchewan.

◀ **LONG GONE:** This school (pictured in May 1952) was dismantled and replaced by a newer facility. A model replica of this building now stands outside of the new school along with the old school bell. Today's Alameda School is a K-9 institution, which had 86 students enrolled in the fall of 2006. Photograph courtesy of the Ralph Allen Memorial Museum, Oxbow, Saskatchewan. Donated by Mr. W. McNeil, Alameda, Saskatchewan.

▲ **ST. JAMES CHURCH** is known locally by its French name, Paroisse St. Jacques d'Albertville. The church was built in 1922-23, and the steeple, approximately 46 metres (150 feet) high, is one of the highest in Saskatchewan. Photograph taken September 23, 2003.

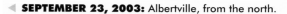

355. The small community is dominated by St. James Church, the oldest existing structure in Albertville. The community's beginnings date to 1910 when French-Canadian settlers arrived from Plessisville, Quebec. Originally settling just west of Albertville, they established the hamlet of Henribourg. But by 1913 many more French settlers had arrived in the district, taking up land further east. A need for a larger, more centrally located church resulted in the location of present-day Albertville being chosen. In 1916, the village became home to La Caisse Populaire d'Albertville, Saskatchewan's first credit union, twenty years before the province adopted the Credit Union Act. Another interesting early business established in the community was the Albertville Cheese Factory. Begun in 1918, it was in operation for approximately 25 years. The village was incorporated on January 1, 1986, and it straddles the boundary between the RM of Garden River No. 490 and the RM of Buckland No. 491.

ALICE BEACH, resort village, is one in a string of resort communities located on the west side of Last Mountain

Lake. Founded in the late 1960s, Alice Beach was established as an organized hamlet in 1977 and was incorporated as a resort village in 1983. There were 68 permanent residents in 2006; however, the population varies greatly depending on the season. Alice Beach is situated within the boundaries of the RM of Sarnia No. 221.

ALIDA, village, pop 106 (2006c), 117 (2001c), is situated in the extreme

southeast corner of Saskatchewan, north of Carnduff on Hwy 318. The first settlers began arriving in the region in the 1880s, some travelling by ox cart or horse from Winnipeg, while others brought their belongings as far as they could by rail, to Moosomin, or to Deloraine, Manitoba, both roughly 90 kilometres away. Access to the Alida district became easier after the railroad reached Carnduff in 1891, and by 1892 the first homesteaders settled on the land where Alida is now located. The railway reached Redvers and Manor, to the north, in 1902, and in the following few years a large influx of settlers began arriving from eastern Canada, the U.S., and Europe. In 1911, the townsite of Alida was surveyed, and in 1912 the CPR laid track into the small emerging hamlet. In 1913, the post office was established, the first store was built, elevators were erected, and the first telephone was installed in the CPR station. In March 1926, Alida was incorporated, with a population of 89 people. Grain and livestock production originally formed the basis of

the economy. Since the 1950s, however, the oil and gas industry has become significant, providing some opportunity for off-farm employment. Initially, the discovery of oil and gas led to a rapid growth of the area population. Between 1951 and 1966, the population of Alida nearly tripled, reaching close to 300 persons. This boom, however, proved to be short-lived, for as quickly as the community grew, it began to decline. In April 1976, a flood on the Souris River in Manitoba washed out a bridge on the CPR track, and rail service was never resumed. Alida's grain elevators were closed. In the fall of 2004, Alida School, a K-9 facility, had 31 students enrolled (students attended grades 10-12 in either Carnduff or Oxbow), but the following June Alida School's doors were permanently closed. The community retains a small core of businesses and basic recreational facilities; village residents seek most goods and services in the region's larger centres. Alida serves as the administrative centre of the RM of Reciprocity No. 32.

ALLAN, town, pop 631 (2006c), 679 (2001c), is located 58 km southeast of the city of Saskatoon on Hwy 397. Two things dominate the Allan skyline, both impressive in their own way: St. Aloysius Roman Catholic Church in town, built in 1922; and the Potash Corporation of Saskatchewan's (PCS) Allan mine, which looms over the community to the northwest. The first group of homesteaders in the area were of German origin, arriving from the U.S. in 1903. Originally, a general store, a post office, and a Roman Catholic church were constructed southwest of the present town. In 1906, the Grand Trunk Pacific

▲ **ALIDA, EARLY MORNING, AUGUST 22, 2003:** Looking north up Centre Street from Prairie Avenue.

Railway began work on the line that would run through the future townsite of Allan and, by the time the trains were running in 1908, several businesses, including stores, a grain elevator, and a hotel, were established. With the coming of rail service, the population of the community diversified. Entrepreneurs of British origin arrived from eastern Canada. The village was incorporated in 1910. By 1911, most of the available land in the district was occupied. The population of Allan that year was 139. By the mid-1920s, the population was well over 300, and it would remain stable until the early 1960s, even though the town's business community had dwindled as more people were shopping and seeking services in Saskatoon. In the mid-1960s, the construction of the potash mine at Allan began, and it had a major impact on the community. As many as 1,000 workers were employed building the mine and bringing it into operation. Some remained in Allan, and the community attained town status in 1965. The population was 337 in 1956; by 1971, it was 712. Today, the PCS Allan Division's mine employs approximately 300 workers. Similarly, the Colonsay mine, begun a couple of years later, is also a large area employer. The district surrounding Allan also supports a strong agricultural industry. The main crops grown in the area are wheat, canola, barley, oats, rye, and some specialty crops such as lentils and peas. The average yield for wheat is approximately 30 bushels per acre. Cattle, hogs, sheep, and buffalo are also raised in the district. A number of Allan's residents commute to work in Saskatoon and, while the town's business community is small given its proximity to the city, Allan's recreational facilities and the school are substantial and modern. The community centre has rinks for skating, hockey, and curling, and Allan has a golf course and an outdoor swimming pool. Allan Composite School provides K-12 education for approximately 175 students. Allan is situated in the RM of Blucher No. 343.

▲ **MATCH POINT** did not seem to be taken too seriously during a volleyball game held at the Vacation Bible School held at the Allan Parkland Hall during the summer of 2004. Photograph taken July 22, 2004.

◀ **ST. ALOYSIUS ROMAN CATHOLIC CHURCH**, Allan, Saskatchewan. The congregation held services in the church's covered basement from 1915 until 1922, the year the church was completed. Its cornerstone was blessed by Joseph-Henri Prud'homme (1882-1952), the Bishop of Saskatoon and Prince Albert, and a document bearing his signature, along with the names of 17 of Allan's early residents, is buried in the foundation. An annual fall supper at St. Aloysius attracts about 600 people each year. Photograph taken July 22, 2004.

ALSASK, village, pop 129 (2006c), 178 (2001c), is, as the name suggests, located just inside the Alberta-Saskatchewan border. It is situated west of Kindersley on Hwy 7 and was once well-known for its Cold War era military installation. Settlement of the district began around 1909 as the railway was being built westward from Rosetown. In 1910, Mennonite and Jewish settlements were established in the Alsask area. In the same year, the new emerging community of Alsask was incorporated as a village. In 1912, Alsask was elevated to town status, and by 1916 the population was over 300. The 1930s hit the region hard: by WWII, the town had lost a third of its citizens. On January 1, 1947, Alsask reverted to village standing, and the community was well in decline. In 1959, the village's fortunes changed when RCAF Station Alsask was conceived. It was part of an early warning radar system deemed integral to North American air defence against Soviet missiles and bombers. Construction of the 418-acre military facility adjacent to the north side of the village began in 1961, and in early 1963 the long range radar unit, 44 Radar Squadron, was operational. The station later became known as CFD (Canadian Forces Detachment) Alsask. The base included three radar domes, housing, a school, a swimming pool, and the first cable television in the province. It was staffed by 125 service personnel (many of whom lived on site with

their families) and 60 civilian employees. Alsask was transformed by the activity, and the population grew to over 800 by the early 1970s. The village provided not only civilian labour to the base, but shopping, banking, postal services, and additional recreational opportunities to the military personnel and their families. Joint water supply and sewer systems were developed. When the station was disbanded in 1987, it had a major impact on Alsask, as hundreds of people were gone within months. An attempt to turn the abandoned facility into something of a seniors' village has met with limited success, and few businesses remain in the community today. The one remaining radar dome, built in 1961, was designated a heritage property in 2002. Alsask is situated in the RM of Milton No. 292. Agriculture and oil and gas are the major industries in the area.

ALTA VISTA, organized hamlet, is a resort community on the east side of the south end of Last Mountain Lake, approximately 4 km west of the village of Silton. The 2006 Census recorded 33 permanent residents; however, the population varies widely depending on the season. The first summer homes were built in the 1930s, but the land was subdivided for the resort in 1961. Alta Vista was established as an organized hamlet in 1979 and it is located in the RM of McKillop No. 220.

ALVENA, village, pop 55 (2006c), 86 (2001c), is located northeast of Saskatoon on Hwy 41. Ukrainian pioneers settled the region in 1898, one of the early mass settlements of Ukrainians in what is now Saskatchewan. The settlement became known as the Fish Creek Colony. Alvena itself was no more than a small hamlet, essentially a couple of stores, until the railway came through in 1929. The community then began to grow, and in 1936 Alvena was incorporated as a village. Agriculture was the basis of the village and area economy, and Alvena reached a peak population of 220 in 1961. By the mid-1960s, however, the population began to decline. By 1976, as the number of residents had dropped to nearly 100, the village council took the decision to sell lots in the community for one dollar providing the purchaser built a house within a year. The population continued to dwindle, though, and community institutions, such as the school, were slowly lost. In 1980, CN ceased rail service to the community, with the result that all of the grain elevators were subsequently closed. Today, Alvena is in the advanced stages of decay. Dilapidated former businesses and homes line overgrown sidewalks. The community's churches, however, are maintained and cared for by volunteers and retirees. Alvena is situated in the RM of Fish Creek No. 402.

AMSTERDAM, organized hamlet, pop 19 (2006c), 25 (2001c) is located in east-central Saskatchewan, north of Canora, off Hwy 9. The district began to be settled in the early 1900s, particularly after the Canadian Northern Railway reached Kamsack and Canora in 1903-04. The

▲ **RELICS OF DAYS GONE BY:** A former schoolhouse on 1st Street East (left) and the Alvena Hotel on Railway Avenue (right). Photograph taken on August 9, 2004.

hamlet of Amsterdam began to develop with the construction of the rail line from Canora north to Sturgis in 1915-16. Stores and grain elevators were built, and a post office opened in 1917. In the 1930s, the large number of Ukrainians in the community established a cultural and educational centre, complete with a library of Ukrainian language books. By the late 1960s/early 1970s, however, the community was in decline. The school, post office and store closed, leaving a small and quiet residential community. Amsterdam is located within the boundaries of the RM of Buchanan No. 304.

ANEROID, village, pop 45 (2006c), 56 (2001c), is located roughly halfway between the towns of Assiniboia and Shaunavon on Hwy 13. The area economy is based upon mixed agriculture. Settlement of the district began several years prior to WWI, but it was in 1913, as the CPR was building westward through the area, that the townsite of Aneroid was established. The new community was incorporated the same year. The village

was apparently named by a survey party who had lost an aneroid barometer in the vicinity and, subsequently, the community's streets were given the names of other surveyor's instruments, such as Sextant, Transit, and Gunter. For a number of years, Aneroid grew rapidly, becoming an area trading centre. By the mid-1920s, the population was well over 300. The 1930s, however, broke the spirit of many in the region, and the village lost close to 100 of its residents by the middle of the decade. When WWII broke out, no fewer than 121 men and women from the Aneroid district joined the armed forces, many enlisting with the village's own unit, the 60th Field Battery RCA. After the war, Aneroid recovered both its economy and its population, the latter reaching 350, the community's peak, in 1956. But by the early 1960s, Aneroid began to rapidly decline: each successive census recorded fewer and fewer people living in the village. The once vibrant business district was slowly reduced to a handful of enterprises, and community institutions such as the school, which closed in 1997, were eventually lost. The Aneroid United Church, originally a Meth-

odist church built between 1913 and 1926, was designated a municipal heritage property in 1985. Aneroid is located in the RM of Auvergne No. 76.

ANNAHEIM, village, pop 218 (2006c), 217 (2001c), is located in central Saskatchewan, northeast of Humboldt on Hwy 756. Settled by German Catholics in the early 1900s, Annaheim became an organized hamlet in 1967, and achieved village status a decade later, on April 1, 1977. The name Annaheim means "Ann's home" in German, after St. Ann's Parish, which was established by the Benedictines in 1903. The economy of the Annaheim area is based primarily on agriculture; however, a strong industrial sector has developed, the most significant company being Doepker Industries Ltd., a manufacturer of highway semi-trailers with a market across Canada. The company employs about 250 people from the surrounding region and has twice been named the province's business of the year by the Saskatchewan Chamber of Commerce. Today, approximately 50 per cent of Annaheim's labour force is employed in this and other industries. The village of Annaheim also has several smaller local businesses, a library, a church, and Annaheim School, which provides K-12 educa-

tion to approximately 100 students. Recreational facilities in the village include sports grounds, a skating rink, a bowling alley, a playground, and a community centre. Additionally, there are several regional parks in the vicinity. Annaheim also has a seniors' centre and is home to a number of retirees from farms in the surrounding area. Annaheim serves as the administrative centre of the RM of St. Peter No. 369.

ANTLER, village, pop 40 (2006c), 45 (2001c), is located in the southeast corner of the province, in a gently rolling landscape at the southern fringe of the province's parkland. The community is situated on Hwy 13, just inside the Saskatchewan-Manitoba border. The first settlers arrived in the Antler area in 1892, and were primarily French and Belgian. They had come anticipating the arrival of the railroad, which was then being constructed westward toward the district from Manitoba. These early settlers, however, were to be disappointed for some years. The CPR initially built the line only as far as Reston, Manitoba, approximately 30 kilometres east, and so subsequently the Antler region developed slowly and the homesteaders faced hard times. It was not until 1900 that the line was completed to Antler and then was continued westward to reach Arcola in 1901. Rapidly then, a large number of homesteads were taken up in the region, with additional French settlers as well as people with British and Scandinavian origins, too, arriving. Within a year of the railway's arrival, the first grain elevator was built, and businesses were established at the townsite. In April 1905, the Village of Antler was incorporated, five months before Saskatchewan became a province. By 1926, the village reached its peak population: 171. Over

◀ **ANEROID CONSOLIDATED SCHOOL:** The main, two-storey, four-room structure (left side of photograph) was built in 1915, replacing a two-room school that had opened in 1913. Two rooms were added to the rear of the school in 1928 to accommodate a burgeoning student population. The school was closed in 1997. Photograph taken October 6, 2003.

▲ **ANTLER, AUGUST 21, 2003:** Abandoned businesses and vacated homes dot the townsite. The top of the former Saskatchewan Wheat Pool elevator can be seen just over the roof of the house in the photograph.

the ensuing years, Antler remained a trading and social centre for the district but, by the 1960s, the community's fortunes began to change as rural populations were in decline, and better roads were allowing access to the wider array of goods and services offered in larger centres. Businesses in Antler closed and, at the end of June 1969, the last classes attended Antler School. The village is situated in the RM of Antler No. 61.

AQUADEO, resort village, is located approximately 50 km north of North Battleford, at the north end of Jackfish Lake, one of several resort communities which circle the lake's shores. The area has been popular for fishing, hunting, swimming, and boating since the early 1900s. During the 1950s, the biggest rodeo in Saskatchewan was held at the village site and, this, along with the aquatic activities in the area, are the source of the community's name. Aquadeo Beach was established as

an organized hamlet in 1965, and the resort village of Aquadeo was incorporated in 1988. There were 62 permanent residents in 2001, and 123 in 2006; however, with approximately 350 cottages and 140 house trailers at Aquadeo, the summer population is estimated to reach over 1,000. Aquadeo is situated in the RM of Meota No. 468.

ARBORFIELD, town, pop 329 (2006c), 411 (2001c), lies northeast of Tisdale on Highway 23, on the western edge of the Pasquia Hills just south of the Carrot River. The first settlers cut trails into the heavily treed area of Arborfield in 1908. Several families had come from Ontario via rail to Tisdale that spring, and after having established a temporary camp just north of there, the men headed northeast seeking suitable land on which to permanently settle. The first house was built that summer, and the first woman joined her husband that fall. In 1909, land was cleared and broken, the first fields of grain were sown, and more houses were under construction. With timber plentiful, most homes and buildings were built of logs. In 1910, a large group of French Canadians came from New Bedford, Massachusetts, where they had been employed as factory workers, and the Arborfield Post Office was established the same year. In 1911, more settlers arrived, the school was built, a sawmill started operation, and roads into the area were developed. The local history records that the first car

made its appearance in 1912. The settlers had expected a railway would soon serve the district; however, by 1919, there were still no signs of construction. A delegation was chosen to travel to Ottawa to petition authorities, and they were promised a railroad in the near future. It was 1929 when the first train arrived. Over the following few years, more people streamed into the region from the drought-ravaged areas of the province's south. Arborfield was incorporated as a village in 1933 and achieved town status in 1950. At that time, the population was over 500 and growing. The main industry in the area is farming. Grains, lentils, hay, and cereal crops are grown. The types of animals raised in the Arborfield district are diverse and include leaf cutter bees, honey bees, hogs, cattle, horses, sheep, goats, elk, wild boar, and chinchillas. A large subsidiary to the agricultural industry is alfalfa dehydration and processing. Arborfield Dehy Limited, which was established by a group of local farmers in the early 1970s, is a large area employer. The company processes alfalfa hay into feed pellets and has a large export market in Japan. It now also owns a second plant near Aylsham. Shipment of

▲ **THE ROYAL HOTEL** and the elevator of the Arborfield Grain Producers Ltd. ▲ **ARBORFIELD DEHY LTD.:** The alfalfa dehydration and processing plant began production in 1971. Photographs taken August 13, 2004.

the product by rail was in jeopardy when CN planned to abandon the line in 1999; however, in 2001, area municipalities succeeded in purchasing the line, ensuring continued rail service. Arborfield area grain producers then purchased the unused United Grain Growers' elevator, so now grain cars, too, move regularly on the line. Another area project currently being researched is the viability of extracting shale oil from the Pasquia Hills. Although shale oil is controversial for environmental reasons, there is the potential that many jobs could be created and that there would be a significant boost to the area economy. The Pasquia Hills, beyond their resource potential, are also home to an abundance of wildlife, and provide opportunities for hiking, horseback riding, snowmobiling, and cross-country skiing. Outfitters are available to guide hunters. Pasquia Regional Park, a fifteen-minute drive northeast of Arborfield, has a swimming pool, a golf course, a campground, and a trail to the site where fossilized remains of a 90 million-year-old, 6-metre-long (20 ft.) crocodile were discovered. The town of Arborfield is an important centre in the area, with a wide range of businesses, a health centre with a special care home, a K-12 school with approximately 100 students, a community hall, skating and curling rinks, four churches, and a volunteer fire department. Police service is provided by the Carrot River RCMP detachment. Arborfield also serves as the administrative centre of the RM of Arborfield No. 456.

ARCHERWILL, village, pop 185 (2006c), 215 (2001c), is located just southwest of Greenwater Provincial Park on Hwys 35 and 349. The community developed later than most in Saskatch-

ewan, being established in 1924 when the CPR ran a line north through Wadena to Tisdale. Archerwill was incorporated as a village in 1947 and had a peak population of 340 in 1961. The Métis Nation of Saskatchewan has a regional office in the village. The major industry in the area is agriculture, a combination of grain and livestock production; however, since the community borders the parklands region, tourism is also a factor. Nearby recreational areas popular for camping and fishing include Kipabiskau Regional Park to the northwest, Marean Lake and Greenwater Lake to the east, and Barrier Lake to the northeast. Fishing in these areas takes place year-round, and during the winter months snowmobiling is also popular, as there are hundreds of kilometres of groomed trails in the region. Archerwill has a small but varied business community, a library, three churches, a seniors' centre, and Archerwill School, a modern K-9 facility which had 80 students enrolled in the fall of 2006. Grades 10-12 attend school in Rose Valley. Archerwill also serves as the administrative centre of the RM of Barrier Valley No. 397.

ARCOLA, town, pop 504 (2006c), 532 (2001c), is located just south of Moose Mountain Provincial Park, west of Carlyle on Hwy 13. The first settlers arrived in the area in 1882 and, within a few years, churches, schools, post offices, and stores were scattered about the countryside. Arcola had it beginnings in early 1900, when it was announced the CPR was constructing a branch line from south-western Manitoba into the area. As soon as the location of the townsite was determined, and before it was even surveyed, businessmen flocked to Arcola, and by 1901, as the first trains arrived, the community was al-

ready large enough to be incorporated as a village. Arcola would remain at the end of the rail line for the next few years and prospered as an important link during this period of large-scale immigration and westward expansion. On November 20, 1903, Arcola became a town and, reputedly, it was one of the larger communities in Saskatchewan by the end of the decade. The population was climbing to well over 800, and the town also served many in the countryside. Such was the rapid development of Arcola that city status was imagined. Many fine buildings were erected in the community in the early years, and a good number of them are still standing, with five having been declared heritage properties. The fact that Arcola possessed well-preserved early-twentieth-century buildings typifying the quintessential prairie town led filmmakers to choose the community as the setting for the filming of W.O. Mitchell's *Who Has Seen The Wind* in 1976. Arcola is also distinguished by another literary link: Sinclair Ross worked in the town between 1929 and 1933, and it is believed that during this time he be-

Arcola Architecture...

▶ **THE MERCHANT'S BANK OF CANADA BUILDING** (presently an office building) was built in 1905 (top, facing page).

▶ **ALSO BUILT IN 1905**, from locally manufactured bricks, is the former Arcola town hall which originally housed town offices, council chambers, a fire hall, and an opera house. Today, the building is home to a bar and restaurant (middle, facing page).

▼ **THE ARCOLA LAND TITLES BUILDING** (inset, below), erected in 1911-12, was designed by notable Regina architects Storey and Van Egmond. In 1961, the Arcola land titles district was merged into the Regina district, and subsequently the Arcola School Division purchased the building. It housed their business office until 1998. The building then became the home of an art gallery and tourist information centre.

▶ **ALONG THE EAST SIDE OF MAIN STREET** stand more of Arcola's historic buildings (bottom facing page). The building on the far left was also made from local brick and it originally housed the offices of H.A. Archer's legal firm. Archer, however, was killed in WWI; a junior partner, Peter McLellen, returned from overseas and continued a law practice from the building. At the onset of the twenty-first century, the building housed a pottery studio.

Photographs taken August 20, 2003.

gan work on his Canadian classic, *As For Me and My House.* The economy of the Arcola area has been traditionally based upon agriculture, typically mixed farming, and the district became well-known for its quality livestock quite early. One producer, Isabelle Rogers Bryce, came to the Arcola area in 1883 from Ireland and she later became an internationally acclaimed breeder of heavy horses. She was Canada's only woman exhibitor at the International Livestock Exposition at Chicago in 1924, and she won a grand championship with her Clydesdale mare, 'Doune Lodge White Heather.' It was the first time in the history of the show that the prize went to a woman, and it was one of many awards Bryce would earn over the years. Arcola's population began to level off by the mid-1920s — the railway had long since moved on — and then during the 1930s, the town lost about a quarter of its residents. Arcola recovered its numbers after WWII. The town developed into a stable community, and since 1989 the oil industry has become a significant part of the local economy. Pumpjacks dot the district. Arcola has an accredited hospital and a K-12 school, with approximately 225 town and area students. Both the hospital and the school are large employers in the area. The town also has a modern community centre with a seating capacity for 400, as well as a public library, a theatre, a museum, a skating rink, running track, ball diamonds, and tennis courts. Each summer, Arcola hosts an Annual Rodeo and Fair. Arcola is situated in the RM of Brock No. 64.

ARDILL, organized hamlet, is located south of Old Wives Lake, approximately 10 km east of Mossbank, off Hwy 2. Never a large community, Ardill had been incorporated as a village in 1920 and had a peak population of 82 in 1941. In 1972, the village was dissolved, and the community became an organized hamlet. The 2001 Census recorded no persons living in Ardill; however, there were three people living there in 2004. A hotel with a licensed beverage room remains and is the sole business in the community. Ardill is situated in the RM of Lake Johnston No. 102.

ARELEE, hamlet, pop 15 (2001c), is located west of Saskatoon just southwest of where Eagle Creek flows into the North Saskatchewan River. It is situated in the RM of Eagle Creek No. 376. The region was settled in the late 1890s by immigrants from Russia, and the community later became significant for its Russian Mennonite Brethren Church. The townsite developed in the 1920s with the arrival of the CPR, and interestingly the village was

▲ **ARELEE MENNONITE BRETHREN CHURCH**, built in 1946. Photograph taken August 28, 2004.

▲ **SET FOR DEMOLITION:** Remnants of Arelee's business section, August 28, 2004.

ARLINGTON BEACH, organized hamlet, is a resort community on the east side of the north end of Last Mountain Lake. Settlement of the district began in the early 1900s, and a post office and a school were shortly established. For a few years, Arlington Beach was a stopping place for the William Pearson Co.'s steamer *S.S. Qu'Appelle*, and in 1910 Pearson built a resort and a hotel on the lakeshore. It became a popular centre for social gatherings and community picnics during the 1920s and 1930s. In 1942, the Canadian Sunday School Mission purchased the 70-acre site, and in 1960 the property was bought by the Free Methodist Church and converted into a camp and conference centre. Arlington Beach was established as an organized hamlet in 1992. There are a small number of permanent residents; however, the population varies greatly depending on the season. Arlington Beach is located in the RM of Last Mountain Valley No. 250.

ARRAN, village, pop 40 (2006c), 55 (2001c), is located on Hwy 49 between the village of Pelly and the Saskatchewan-Manitoba border, just south of the Swan River and north of Duck Mountain Provincial Park. Early ranching operations had developed around Forts Pelly and Livingston, and by the late 1800s there were a number of ranchers in the district around what would become Arran. These were primarily of British stock. In 1899, 2,400 Doukhobors settled in the Pelly and Arran

incorporated in 1946, dissolved in 1950, and reincorporated in 1952. By 1961, Arelee had a population of 125, with six stores, lumber yards, machine agencies, a bank, a drug store, and a butcher shop. By the 1970s, however, the community was in decline, and area residents were moving to Saskatoon, working their farms from the city. The rail line was abandoned in the early 1980s and the elevators were removed. Today, few buildings remain in Arelee and, of these, a number are now scheduled for demolition as they are considered fire hazards. The village was dissolved for the last time on March 21, 2002.

▶ **ARLINGTON BEACH HOUSE** was built in 1910 as a hotel by William Pearson. It was a destination for early travellers on the steamer the *S.S. Qu'Appelle*. Last Mountain Lake is in the background. Photograph taken June 28, 2004.

▲ **BUILT IN 1918**, the Ukrainian Greek Catholic Church of St. John the Baptist. Arran, Saskatchewan, July 13, 2003.

districts on 69,000 acres of land reserved for their use. The Doukhobors cleared the forest, planted grain fields, and established about 20 communal villages in the area. They built a brickworks and a sawmill, gristmills, blacksmith shops, granaries, and barns. By 1918, however, the reserve was closed and the Doukhobors relocated to British Columbia or to individual homesteads. In the early 1900s, particularly after the railway was running through Kamsack in 1904, another wave of settlers had begun taking up land in the district. They were of various origins, but predominantly Ukrainian. Arran itself came into being with the arrival of the Canadian Northern Railway in 1909. The post office was established in 1911 and the first school was built in the spring of 1915. The community was named after a township in Bruce County, Ontario, which in turn was named for the island of Arran in the Firth of Clyde, Scotland. In 1916, the Village of Arran was incorporated, and

by 1951 Arran had reached a peak population of 223. The community's population and business sector began to decline in the 1960s, and by 1994 with fewer than 60 residents in the village, Arran's school was closed. Arran serves as the administrative centre of the RM of Livingston No. 331. Recently, there have been contentious debates in the district over the possible large-scale development of hog barn operations. Agriculture, a combination of grain and livestock production, is the main area industry.

ASQUITH, town, pop 576 (2006c), 574 (2001c), is located on Hwy 14 approximately 33 km west of Saskatoon. Settlers began arriving in the district around 1902, and in 1903 the townsite was established. A construction boom began in 1906, and in 1907 Asquith was incorporated as a village. A year later Asquith attained town status and both the CPR and the CNR

had come through by 1909. Beautification of the community was a concern of early residents, and a by-law was passed permitting tree-planting in lieu of paying taxes. Many of the trees planted in the town's early years still stand today. Sports always played an important role in the community, and over the years Asquith earned an enviable reputation in both baseball and hockey circles. Mixed farming and dairying became the economic backbone of the community; however, today many residents either commute to work in Saskatoon or are employed in nearby potash mines. Asquith has also become the retirement home of many area farmers. The town has two stores which together offer groceries, hardware, banking services, and a Sears Catalogue outlet; a farm and ranch supply store that caters to the area's farming community; two restaurants; and a hotel which has accommodations, a beverage room, and a liquor outlet. Asquith's recreational facilities include ball diamonds, a riding arena, and skating and curling rinks. The community hosts an annual rodeo in July and a Craft Fair in November. Lord Asquith School is a K-12 institution that had 306 town and area students enrolled in the fall of 2006. Asquith is situated in the RM of Vanscoy No. 345.

ASSINIBOIA, town, pop 2,305 (2006c), 2,483 (2001c), is located approximately 105 km southwest of Moose Jaw at the junction of Hwys 2 and 13. The town is named after the former district of the North-West Territories and the community serves primarily as an agricultural service centre for the surrounding region. The area was largely settled by people of English and French origin, although there were smaller numbers of Romanians,

Scots, and Scandinavians. Assiniboia's beginnings date to the construction of the rail line from Weyburn to Lethbridge and, specifically, October 12, 1912, when the CPR put 980 lots up for sale at the Assiniboia townsite. People stood in line overnight to buy their lots, and the community rapidly sprang up on the previously barren prairie. By December, Assiniboia was already large enough to be incorporated as a village, and by January all of the original parcels of land had been sold. It is estimated that over 1,000 people moved into Assiniboia in 1913 and that the population had risen from roughly 400 to 1,400 within the year. On the first of October, 1913, just under 12 months after the community was started, Assiniboia attained town status. A quarter of a million bushels of grain were shipped out of five brand new elevators that fall. The growth of the community was inhibited by the Depression, but forward-looking town officials planned for the future, employing out-of-work men to construct the town's sewer system, which it could not afford to operate until 1948. After WWII, prosperity returned to the area, and Assiniboia resumed growing at a steady rate. By the mid-1950s, the population was over 2,000 and climbing, peaking at 3,001 in 1986. Today, Assiniboia has a wide variety of businesses, including a number of agricultural equipment dealers and manufacturing companies. High-throughput grain handling facilities handle a majority of the grain grown in the region, and Assiniboia has one of the country's largest livestock auction yards. The community was dealt somewhat of a blow in April 2006, when the Prairie Rubber Corporation, which had begun operations in 2000, was permanently closed. It had been Saskatchewan's largest tire recycling plant and had employed up to 42 workers, but the com-

ASSINIBOIA

From bald prairie to boomtown: the development of a community...

▲ **BUILDING THE GRADE** for the CPR's Weyburn to Lethbridge line circa 1911-12. The railway company chose Assiniboia as a divisional point (the junction of the Assiniboia and Shaunavan subdivisions), and as such the community was guaranteed to grow rapidly and into a sizable town.

▼ **OCTOBER 24, 1912 — FOURTEEN DAYS OLD.** Centre Street, Assiniboia, looking south.

▲ ▼ **SOME OF THE FIRST** businesses in Assiniboia, mid-1910s. Note the right hand steering wheels on the automobiles.

▲ **THE CPR ROUNDHOUSE** at Assiniboia under construction.

▼ **A PANORAMIC VIEW** of Assiniboia's business district, July 1923.

▲ **LEAVING FOR THE FRONT:** Men of Assiniboia heading to serve in WWI, August 1914.

▲ **BANKERS** coping with flood waters in 1916.

▶ **WHITE'S BARBER SHOP:** Ernie White (left) opened a barber shop in the El Prado Hotel in Assiniboia in 1921. The shop had three barber chairs and there were large inset mirrors in the front. Ernie's son Jim (right) worked with him. On June 8, 1935, Assiniboia voted for beer by the glass and the hotel required the barber shop space for the beer parlour. Ernie moved his shop across the street. He enjoyed playing pool and installed three pool tables in his shop. After Ernie's death, Jim White, who had returned from Fort San, took over the shop. He found it was too much for him to handle both the barber shop and the pool room, so he partitioned off half of the building and sold the pool tables to Walter Sanftleben. Walter operated the tables in the other half of the building for a few years. Jim, with the help of Henry Peters, operated the barber shop until Jim retired in 1975.

All Assiniboia photos courtesy of the Assiniboia and District Museum.

Assiniboia Sask July 1923.

pany had been losing $2 million per year and it failed to convince the provincial government to raise tire recycling fees by $1 to help cover its operating costs. The town has a wide range of medical services including a hospital and a special care home. Schools provide K-12 education and accommodate approximately 530 town and area students; a regional college offers some post-secondary courses and special interest classes. Assiniboia has an RCMP detachment and a volunteer fire department. Town landmarks include St. Andrew's Presbyterian Church, completed in 1920, and the Assiniboia Court House, built in 1930 and designed by Provincial Architect Maurice Sharon. Its placement at the head of the community's main business avenue, Centre Street, greatly adds to the aesthetic appearance of the town. Both the church and the courthouse have been designated heritage properties. In 2001, the Prince of Wales turned the sod for a new cultural and recreation centre which bears his name, and, down the street, the Assiniboia District Museum is an excellent facility, featuring displays relating to the area's pioneer history. A new, major attraction is the Shurniak Art Gallery which opened in 2005. The collection of more than 500 works by Canadian and international artists, as well as the $1-million building it is housed in, was donated to the community by Bill Shurniak, a retired banker who grew up near Limerick, and whose successful career took him all over the world. Assiniboia serves as the administrative centre of the RM of Lake of the Rivers No. 72.

ATWATER, village, pop 25 (2006c), 30 (2001c), is located northwest of Esterhazy, a few km north of Kaposvar Creek. Settlement of the area began in the mid-

▲ **ATWATER SCHOOL DISTRICT NO. 2311** is commemorated by this marker at the school site in the village. Photograph taken October 21, 2003.

1880s and continued through into the early 1900s. Czechs, Hungarians, people of British origin, and Norwegian Lutherans via the United States took up land in the Atwater district. The Grand Trunk Pacific Railway came through in 1907-08, the post office was established at the beginning of March 1909, Atwater School was founded that year, and on August 12, 1910, the Village of Atwater was incorporated. The community was never particularly large, having reached a peak population of 106 in 1956. Atwater's population began to decline dramatically through the 1960s, and in 1979 the school was closed. In 1991, the post office closed its doors. In 2003, a service station remained the sole business operating in the village. A community landmark, Kristiania Lutheran Church, completed in 1920, was designated a heritage property in 1986. It is thought the name 'Kristiania' honours the former name of the Norwegian capital of Oslo. The basis of the Atwater district economy is agriculture and potash mining. Atwater is situated in the RM of Fertile Belt No. 183.

AVONLEA, village, pop 381 (2006c), 412 (2001c), is located 82 km southwest of the city of Regina at the junction of Hwys 334 and 339. The Dirt Hills loom along the skyline to the southwest. In 1882, the first of a number of ranches were started in the region, and for the next 20 years cattle and horses would dominate a wide open range. Homesteaders began to arrive in large numbers around 1902-03, and within short order the first store and post office were established in the area. The addition of a school, a blacksmith shop, and a butcher created a small settlement a few kilometres north of present-day Avonlea, which came to be known as New Warren, after Warren, Minnesota, the hometown of a number of the early settlers. While some supplies and services could be obtained locally, grain and coal still had to be delivered to and obtained from Rouleau, a one-day trip each way. In 1911, New Warren disappeared, as the Avonlea townsite came into being with the construction of the Canadian Northern Railway line from Radville to Moose Jaw. In 1912, the railway station was built, and Avonlea was incorporated, taking its name from the fictional Prince Edward Island home of Lucy Maud Montgomery's *Anne*

of Green Gables. With the addition of a rail line west to Gravelbourg in 1913, the village's station bustled with passengers and freight. By the 1920s, Avonlea's population was over 300, and, unlike many of Saskatchewan's smaller communities, the village has maintained its numbers and has slowly grown since its inception — this in spite of its distance from a major highway. The community functions primarily as a service centre for the surrounding agricultural district: a large percentage of the area's farms are mixed operations, producing a combination of cereal grains and cattle, as well as pulse crops and some oilseeds. A farm implements and auto dealer and a pulse crop processor are two of the community's major employers, with approximately 40 and 28 employees respectively. Avonlea also has a good range of other businesses providing consumer and commercial goods, as well as a number of tradespeople and professional services. The village has an RCMP detachment, modern skating and curling rinks among other recreational facilities, and Avonlea School, which provides K-12 education to approximately 130 students. The former CN station (withdrawn from active use in 1976) has been declared a heritage property and now houses an excellent museum. A mural of the famous

▼ **MAIN STREET, AVONLEA**, circa 1912.

MAIN ST. AVONLEA, SASK

Views of Avonlea and area...

▲ **LIVINGSTON AND BALL'S THRESHING CREW** working in the Avonlea area in 1912. The crew is posed in front of the cook car; Evie Barlow, the cook, stands in the door.

▲ **BUILT IN 1912**, the CNR Station was, for many years, the focal point of the village, and it served as a home to nine station agents and their families. In 1976 the CNR withdrew the station from active use, and it was subsequently purchased by the village and the local museum board to be converted into a museum. The building was designated a municipal heritage property in 1981 and is today known as the Avonlea and District Museum – Heritage House.

▽ **HAMILTON'S SHOP AND HOME** with members of the Hamilton family out front. John and Nettie Hamilton and three of their four children, Keitha, Phyliss, and Jack came to the Avonlea district from Carleton Place, Ontario in 1910. Daughter Norma was born in Avonlea in 1918. John Hamilton built his home and a machine shed in the village, sold farm equipment and bulk oil, before expanding his business to include sewing machines, pianos, and cream separators. He became the mayor, was a member of the school board, and was an undertaker. The family sold the business in 1926 and went back to Ontario, intending the make their home in Hamilton. However, they realized their love of the prairies and returned to Saskatchewan the same year, settling in Regina.

▲ **THE AVONLEA CREEK BADLANDS**, located just east of the village, exhibit natural landforms of 70-million-year-old rock, Cretaceous shales characteristic of what is known as the Bearpaw Formation in southern Saskatchewan. Photograph taken March 24, 2007.

▽ **FORE!** The Long Creek Golf and Country Club just east of Avonlea is an 18-hole championship course with 300-year-old Maple and Ash trees gracing fairways in a beautiful valley setting. The course has been deemed one of the finest in Saskatchewan. Photograph taken August 7, 2003.

NWMP march west, painted by local artist Paul Geraghty, is among many interesting exhibits. The Avonlea district also offers many attractions for tourists, including the nearby badlands (a rugged landscape of exposed 70 million-year-old rock and hoodoos), the Claybank Brick Plant, Dunnet Regional Park with its 300-year-old ash and maple trees, and the Long Creek Golf and Country Club, with an 18-hole championship course, reputedly one of the most challenging and beautiful in the province. The village of Avonlea serves as the administrative centre of the RM of Elmsthorpe No. 100.

AYLESBURY, village, pop 45 (2006c), 50 (2001c), is located southeast of Craik on Hwy 11. The rail line upon which the community sits was built from Regina through Saskatoon to Prince Albert in the late 1880s, with trains running the distance in 1890. But for more than a decade after its completion, the line merely served as a bridge between the southern and central regions of the province.

In 1902, at the urging of the Canadian government, Colonel Andrew Duncan Davidson formed the Saskatchewan Valley Land Company and began aggressive campaigns to promote immigration to the area. The first homesteaders arrived in the Aylesbury district that year. Within a few years, stores, a post office, a lumberyard, a farm implements dealership, and a number of other businesses were in operation. A school was built in 1908, opening in 1909. Aylesbury was incorporated on March 31, 1910, and by that time most of the available homesteads in the area were occupied. By 1916, five grain elevators lined the tracks in the village. For a number of years, Aylesbury had a successful stone crushing plant which employed several local people: Bitulithic and Contracting Ltd. set up operations in 1907, and the crushed rock was shipped out by rail cars to be used for road construction in Regina and Winnipeg, among other centres. Aylesbury was never particularly large: it had a peak population of 180 in 1956, but beginning in the 1960s the village's numbers steadily declined.

The school was closed in 1970, and students have subsequently been bused to Craik. Today, the village's old hotel is about the only business remaining in the community. Aylesbury is situated in the RM of Craik No. 222.

AYLSHAM, village, pop 92 (2006c), 106 (2001c), is a very pretty, quiet community located southeast of Nipawin in the Carrot River Valley. The district began to be settled around 1911. Since the land was wet and heavily wooded, every acre had to be cleared by axe and saw and with back-breaking labour. During WWI, settlement of the Aylsham area came almost to a standstill, although the clearing and breaking of land continued. After the war, many servicemen came to the district. When the railway finally arrived at the end of 1930 (it had been built as far as Ridgedale in 1921) the newly-surveyed townsite of Aylsham began to be built up. The community took its name from the Aylsham Post Office, which had been established in 1921, and which itself was

named after Aylsham, England. With rail service, the hamlet developed rapidly. Stores and grain elevators and other businesses were established, and more people began arriving in the area, many fleeing drought-ravaged farms on the southern plains. Aylsham was incorporated as a village in 1947, and by the early 1950s the population had grown to over 400. More rapidly than the village had grown, however, it began to decline. More than 150 people had moved out of the community by 1961. Businesses were folding, and eventually the school was closed, with students subsequently being bused to Nipawin. Today, a post office, a restaurant and bar located in the old hotel, and an agricultural products supplier remain. Aylsham also has a community centre with a hall and a skating rink, a seniors' drop-in centre (perhaps the busiest place in town), and a United Church. An alfalfa dehydrating plant, located in nearby Carlea, is an important area employer and produces alfalfa feed pellets which are marketed as far as Europe and Japan. Aylsham is situated in the RM of Nipawin No. 487.

▲ **ALTHOUGH THE SECOND-STOREY** rooms haven't been used in years, the Aylesbury Hotel is where one picks up the mail or comes for a cup of coffee or a beer. The bar features a large and unique collection of elephant figures and images gathered from around the world. Photograph taken July 22, 2003.

▼ **UNTIL A FEW YEARS AGO** the Aylsham Welding and Machine shop (far right) had a reputation for excellent work. It is now closed as are most of the businesses that once operated in the community. The Aylsham Community Complex and the village office are located within the buildings in the background in the left of the photograph. Photograph taken August 13, 2004.

BALCARRES, town, pop 598 (2006c), 622 (2001c), is situated northeast of Fort Qu'Appelle and is served by Hwys 10, 22, and 310. The first few pioneering settlers began arriving in the area in advance of the CPR in the early 1880s, leaving the railhead at Brandon with oxen and carts, with some then fording the Qu'Appelle River north of Wolseley at the site that would become known as Ellisboro. After the railway reached Indian Head in 1882, greater numbers began to arrive and, although the population would diversify over the subsequent decades, a large number of the first taking up homesteads in the Balcarres area were of British origin, from eastern Canada as well as from overseas. Before a railway was built into the district, supplies had to be obtained in Fort Qu'Appelle or Indian Head, the latter point being where grain was hauled to for many years. Initially, travel south across the Qu'Appelle River to the CPR main line was often a wet, muddy, and difficult undertaking, a situation that was much improved with the construction of a bridge over the river in the summer of 1884. That year, the Balcarres Post Office was established, named after Robert Balcarres Crawford, who was the postmaster in Indian Head, the point from which mail was hauled into the district. Travel distance remained an issue with Balcarres area residents for over two decades, and it hindered the development of the region: there were many petitions over the years to authorities for rail service. In 1903, the CPR was building westward north of the Qu'Appelle Valley toward Lipton, and the townsite of Balcarres was established. Buildings were moved in from the country, and many new buildings were erected. The arrival of the first trains in 1904

THE NEW SCHOOL BALCARRES SBSK.

brought many more people and greater development to the area, and Balcarres was incorporated as a village on November 21 that year. In 1911, Balcarres became the junction of two competing railroads, as the Grand Trunk Pacific line (later CN) was completed from Yorkton through Fort Qu'Appelle to Regina. With two railroads serving the community, some residents imagined Balcarres someday gaining city status. In 1951, Balcarres attained town status, and in 1966 the community reached a peak population of 751. The economic base of the area is agriculture, and a number of the town's businesses and services cater to the industry. Terminal 22, just west of Balcarres on Hwy 10, is a state-of-the-art facility managed by Cargill Ltd. that serves several area communities. The terminal has a storage capacity of 32,000 tonnes, and the ability to handle over 400,000 tonnes annually. It can load 112 rail cars with product cleaned and ready for export. It was the first inland facility in western Canada to be certified under internationally recognized standards. Just to the northeast of Balcarres, four First Nations communities (Little Black Bear, Star Blanket, Okanese, and Peepeekisis) occupy a large block of

land in the File Hills and, with a combined population of over 900, contribute to the town's economy and social fabric. Balcarres has a large and modern hospital with an attached special care home, an RCMP detachment, and Balcarres School, which provides K-12 education to close to 450 town and area students. The town's recreational facilities include parks, baseball diamonds, skating and curling rinks. Balcarres has a number of churches, service clubs, and community organizations, and is situated in the RM of Abernethy No. 186.

BALGONIE, town, pop 1,384 (2006c), 1,239 (2001c), is situated approximately 24 km east of Regina on Hwy 1 at the junction of Hwy 10. In 1881, CPR surveyors staked their route through the area, and in 1882 the tracks were in place and the trains were running. The Balgonie Post Office was established in 1883, named after the fourteenth-century Balgonie Castle in the County of Fife, Scotland. While Scots did settle in the Balgonie area from the 1880s, large numbers of English from

◀ BALGONIE WAS HOME to one of Canada's pioneers in aviation. During the first years of the twentieth century while the Wright brothers were experimenting with their own heavier-than-air aeroplane, William Wallace Gibson, also known as the "Balgonie Birdman," was building a four-cylinder, air-cooled engine for an aircraft he was designing. He worked in privacy and tested his model airplanes in the early morning hours to avoid ridicule from sceptical neighbours. Gibson built the first Canadian-made aircraft engine and installed it in an aircraft of his own design, which he successfully flew in Victoria in 1910. It was the first completely Canadian-built aircraft. Gibson (pictured here in 1905 standing behind one of his engines) has been the subject of both an animated short film produced by the National Film Board of Canada and a 60-minute documentary produced by the Regina-based film and video production company, Partners in Motion. Saskatchewan Archives Board R-B628.

BALONE BEACH, organized hamlet, est. 1974, is a resort community in central Saskatchewan, approximately 12 km east of Wakaw on the northwest shore of Wakaw Lake. It lies adjacent to Wakaw Lake Regional Park and is one of a number of cottage communities which surround the lake. Balone Beach has a small number of permanent residents; however, the population varies widely depending on the season. Balone Beach is situated in the RM of Hoodoo No. 401.

BANGOR, village, pop 50 (2006c), 48 (2001c), is located northwest of Esterhazy. In the mid to late 1880s, a few homesteaders of English and Scottish origins began arriving in the area from eastern Canada and the U.K., while to the south Hungarians and Swedes were taking up land; however, it was in 1902 that the district just north of Bangor was largely settled by Patagonian Welsh. These were

both eastern Canada and Great Britain also took up land in the district, together with a significant population of Germans from eastern Europe and southern Russia. Construction in the community was steady throughout the 1890s: in 1891, a school was built, followed by stores, a hotel, livery stables, a blacksmith shop, and grain elevators. Balgonie was incorporated as a village in 1903 and achieved town status in 1907. The economy developed around agriculture, particularly, the large-scale production of wheat. The population of Balgonie was approaching 400 by the end of the first decade of the twentieth century, but the construction of rail lines, south through Davin in 1908, and north through Edenwold in 1911, drew business and people away from the town. Balgonie's numbers had dropped by half by 1921. The community's population further plummeted during the 1930s and early 1940s, and only 121 people were left by 1946. Post-WWII, the community began to recover, and the completion of the Trans-Canada Highway in the late

1950s ushered in a period of significant growth. During the 1970s, substantial residential development began, and today construction of new subdivisions continues as Balgonie further develops into a bedroom community for people who commute to work in Regina. Balgonie's small core of businesses provides some local employment as do its schools. A key community business is a manufacturer of custom-designed homes. The district also has a strong dairy industry. Balgonie's schools provide K-12 education and had a combined student population of 1,056 enrolled in the fall of 2006; in addition to educating the town's schoolchildren, the schools accommodate students from surrounding farms and the communities of Kronau, White City, Pilot Butte, Edenwold, and the Muskowpetung First Nation. Balgonie's recreational facilities include a swimming pool, skating and curling rinks, and baseball diamonds. There are nearby campgrounds and golf courses. One of the oldest remaining buildings in Balgonie is the former United Church. A stone struc-

ture built in 1901 for the community's Presbyterian congregation, the building was designated a heritage property in 1987 and most recently has served as a community museum and heritage centre. Balgonie serves as the administrative centre of the RM of Edenwold No. 158.

▲ BANGOR HERITAGE DAY, July 21, 2002. In the foreground on the cart being pulled by the Shetland pony is Albert Abdai of Esterhazy (left) and Clarke Crow of Otthon. Photograph courtesy of Leona Bisch, Grayson, Saskatchewan.

people who had emigrated from Wales to Argentina in 1865, but who, after facing many difficulties in South America, re-migrated to Canada. They were followed by settlers who came directly from Wales. After the Grand Trunk Pacific Railway came through in 1907, these settlers requested that the railway company name their station Bangor, after the cathedral and university city in Wales. The Bangor Post Office was established in 1909 and the Saskatchewan community grew up around the railway station. The village was incorporated in 1911 and had a peak population of over 130 in the late 1940s/early 1950s. Bangor today retains a post office, a Catholic Church, and a community centre; there are also seniors' housing units in the village. Bangor Heritage Day is an annual event held each July. Bangor is located in the RM of Fertile Belt No. 183.

BANKEND, organized hamlet, pop 10 (2006c), 15 (2001c), is located southeast of the Quill Lakes on Hwy 35. Although the first few pioneers entered the district in the 1880s, it was in the early 1900s that large numbers of settlers took up land in the region and Bankend had its beginnings. Bankend School opened in 1906, just north of the present community, and was named after Bankend, Scotland, the home of one of the school district's founders. In addition to settlers of British origin, the Bankend area was also settled by Ukrainians and Scandinavians among others. It was an active district: there was a men's football team by 1906 and, in 1907, there was the Bankend Ladies Ball Team. Alexander James McPhail, who homesteaded in the Bankend area in 1906, was a zealous advocate for farmer's rights and cooperative marketing, and he became the first president of the Sas-

katchewan Co-operative Wheat Producers (later renamed the Saskatchewan Wheat Pool) in 1924. The hamlet of Bankend emerged in the late 1920s when the CPR began construction of its line from Foam Lake to Wishart. Soon four grain elevators were erected (considerably reducing the distance area farmers had to travel) and a new school was built at the townsite. Stores, garages, restaurants, and a hotel were constructed, and Bankend thrived as a mid-point on the road (highway by the late 1940s) between Leross and Elfros. The population was approximately 125 in 1955 and remained over 100 until the early 1970s. Today, there are a number of vacant lots in the community and a few abandoned businesses situated on the highway. The school is long gone. The Bankend Co-op, however, remains an important business, providing district residents with groceries, hardware, auto parts, and farm supplies. Bankend is situated in the RM of Emerald No. 277.

BARRIER FORD, organized hamlet, is a resort community on the east

end of Barrier Lake, roughly 20 km south of Bjorkdale, just west of Greenwater Lake Provincial Park. The community's name refers to an early nearby crossing of the Barrier River. Barrier Ford has a small number of permanent residents (there were 40 recorded in 2006); however, the population of the resort varies widely depending on the season. The area is popular for fishing, boating, camping, and swimming, and there is a nine-hole golf course nearby. Barrier Ford was established as an organized hamlet in 1986 and is situated in the RM of Bjorkdale No. 426.

BATTLEFORD, town, pop 3,685 (2006c), 3,820 (2001c), is located halfway between the cities of Saskatoon and Lloydminster on the Yellowhead Hwy (No. 16). The historic former capital of the North-West Territories, Battleford sits on a high plateau across from the city of North Battleford, on the south side of the North Saskatchewan River near its confluence with the Battle River. Fur trading activity in the area dates to the later 1700s. In the early-1870s, the route for the CPR was

▲ **AUGUST 12, 2004:** Boats docked in the early morning light at Barrier Ford.

surveyed across the northern plains and along the south banks of the river, through the site of the future community. Permanent settlement began at the location in the middle of the decade. A station was established as the telegraph line was being built westward from Winnipeg to Edmonton, and the locale was chosen to be the site for the capital of the North-West Territories. The name Battleford was selected after a nearby ford of the Battle River. In 1876, Fort Battleford was established as a NWMP post and, in the same year, construction of Government House, the first permanent residence of the lieutenant governor, began. The settlement developed rapidly. A post office and the Battleford Land Registry Office were opened in 1877, and in 1878 the first newspaper in what is now the province of Saskatchewan, the *Saskatchewan Herald*, was begun by Patrick Gammie Laurie. That same year, the first meeting of the Territorial Council, under Lieutenant Governor David Laird, took place at Government House. As the capital, Battleford appeared to have a bright future, and merchants, homesteaders, and ranchers were drawn to the area by the promise of the railway. But in 1881 the community's destiny was altered with the federal government's abrupt decision to change the route of the trans-continental railroad to cross the southern plains, with the consequence that the territorial capital was officially transferred to Regina in 1883. Battleford remained of strategic importance, however, for in 1885 it was the scene of significant events during the North-West Resistance. Approximately 500 people were sheltered within the fort's stockade during the weeks of unrest. On November 27, 1885, the largest mass hanging in Canadian history took place within the fort's walls, and to possibly thwart future uprisings, students from the nearby Indian Industrial School were forced to attend as eight Aboriginal men were publicly hanged. A mass grave, unmarked for years, serves as their final resting place. Despite the destruction caused during the Resistance, and despite being by-passed by the railway, the community continued to grow. The CPR had reached Swift Current in 1883, 300 kilometres due south of Battleford, and this opened up a new trading route (the Battleford-Swift Current Trail) which substantially cut down the time it took to bring in food and other supplies. Freight rates were cut in half, thus reducing the cost of living in the community. Regular freighters plied up and down the trail, and a much more frequent mail service was inaugurated. Battleford was incorporated as a village in 1899 and gained town status in 1904 — in spite of another disappointment: the community was by-passed by yet another railway survey. In 1905, the Canadian Northern Railway built its line en route to Edmonton on the opposite side of the river. North Battleford was launched into being and soon became one of the fastest growing centres in the west. It quickly surpassed the older community in size and importance and gained city status in 1913. Battleford would be somewhat compensated however: substantial public buildings were erected to administer government services. In 1907-08, a new Land Titles Building and the Court House (still in use) were constructed and, over the next few years, the Post Office, the Town Hall/Opera House, and a number of impressive homes were built. These structures, among numerous others dating from the 1870s though to about 1912, give Battleford perhaps the finest collection of period architecture and heritage properties in the province. In 1907-08, rail and road links from North Battleford

Buildings of Battleford
...a small sampling

▶ Believed to be the oldest existing court house in Saskatchewan still in use, the **BATTLEFORD COURT HOUSE** is one of the public buildings promised to Battleford as a part of a quid pro quo compensation package when the Canadian Northern Railway built its line on the other side of the North Saskatchewan River. With dark beamed ceilings, oak wainscotting, and a graceful interior staircase, the building, designed with a Georgian flavour by the Regina architectural firm of Edgar M. Storey and William Gysbert Van Egmond, is considered to be one of the finest examples of classical architecture in the west.

▶ Situated on a parcel of land overlooking the North Saskatchewan River, the **FRED LIGHT MUSEUM** houses artifacts related to the early history of the Battlefords area and the North-West Mounted Police. Originally, the St. Vital Roman Catholic Public School, the building was constructed in 1911 to replace an earlier school on the same parcel of land that had dated to 1886-87. Constructed of locally manufactured brick, it reflects a modified Second Empire architectural style, which, although largely out of fashion by the 1890s, continued to be used by the Roman Catholic Church for its convents and schools. St. Vital School closed in 1974 and at some point in the late 1970s the brick exterior was covered with the stucco finish that remains in place today.

▶ Built in 1912, the **BATTLEFORD TOWN HALL AND OPERA HOUSE** cost $40,000 at the time to complete. In addition the town offices and the auditorium, the building also housed an RCMP detachment, jail cells, the library, the Parks and Recreation Department, and the offices of the RM of Battle River No. 438. The top floor opera house/auditorium was used for school plays, high school graduations, live theatre, musical talent nights, Christmas concerts, and fireman's balls until it was gutted by fire in 1965. The building was repaired, but the opera house was subsequently closed. Today, the landmark structure contains the town office, council chambers, and the mayor's office. The Battleford Town Hall and Opera House was designed by the Saskatoon architect Walter W. LaChance.

Photographs on this page taken August 12, 2003.

◀ **THE BATTLEFORD POST OFFICE** is the oldest operating post office in Saskatchewan, being established in the 1870s. This red brick, Georgian-style building was erected in 1911; the town clock at the top was installed in 1914. Photograph taken August 12, 2003.

▼ The seat of the government of the North-West Territories from 1877-1882, **GOVERNMENT HOUSE** (below) in Battleford is pictured here in its original form circa 1877. (Photo courtesy of the North Battleford NHP Library.) More than two-thirds of Canada's geographical land mass was administered from Battleford until the Territorial capital was moved to Regina in 1883. From 1883 until 1914 the building housed an Indian industrial school, the first in western Canada, established to teach aboriginal children trades and agriculture. It was also an instrument for the federal government's policy of assimilation. Seventh Day Adventists then used the building as an academy until 1931; the Oblates of Mary Immaculate followed, operating a boarding school and a seminary until 1972, and a novitiate until 1984. Unfortunately, Battleford's 126-year-old Government House was completely destroyed by fire on June 7, 2003. Only the chimney and portions of the foundation were left standing (inset left). Photograph taken August 11, 2003.

were also completed. The twin spans built across Finlayson Island in the North Saskatchewan River in 1908 comprise the oldest existing highway bridge in the province, and the longest of its type. (There are currently plans to close the bridge to all but cyclists and hikers.) From 609 residents in 1901, Battleford's population was approaching 1,500 by 1916. By this time, rail connections from the community south to Biggar and west to Cut Knife had been completed. Battleford, however, was in financial trouble. It was bankrupt due to over-zealous municipal spending in anticipation of expansion which never came, and the debts were not cleared until 1959. The community's population fell during the 1920s and the 1930s, and the community languished until after WWII. Improvements to water and sewer systems in the 1950s, the introduction of natural gas and, in the 1960s, a modern highway bridge built on Hwy 16 giving easier access to North Battleford together ushered in a period of rapid growth. Battleford's population more than doubled in the years between 1961 and 1981, increasing from 1,627 to 3,565. Today, Battleford is an agricultural service centre that has a strong manufacturing sector. While the community has a wide range of businesses, services, and facilities, residents also have ready access to the city of North Battleford. Tourist attractions in the community include the Fort Battleford National Historic Site, which showcases the role of the North-West Mounted Police in the development of the Canadian West. Abandoned by the force in 1924, the fort now draws thousands of visitors each summer. Additionally, the Fred Light Museum houses one of the most comprehensive collections of firearms and military paraphernalia in western Canada: flintlocks, matchlocks, muzzleloaders, as well as

swords, bayonets, and military uniforms are on display. Battleford is also home to the Saskatchewan Baseball Hall of Fame. Unfortunately, Battleford's Government House was burned to the ground on June 7, 2003. Battleford serves as the administrative centre of the RM of Battle River No. 438.

BAYARD, organized hamlet, pop 5 (2006c), 10 (2001c), is located roughly 50 km southeast of Moose Jaw, nestled between the Dirt and Cactus Hills just southwest of the historic Claybank Brick Plant. German Catholics dominated area settlement in the early 1900s, establishing what was known as the Bayard Colony. The Bayard Station Post Office operated from 1914 to 1966 and the population by the latter year was 24. The organized hamlet was established in 1961 and is situated in the RM of Terrell No. 101.

BAYVIEW HEIGHTS, organized hamlet, is located north of North Battleford and is one of several resort communities that circle Jackfish Lake. There are a small number of permanent residents; however, the population varies significantly depending on the season. Bayview Heights was formally established in 1986 and is situated in the RM of Meota No. 468.

BEAR CREEK, northern settlement, pop 47 (2001c), is located between Buffalo Narrows and La Loche on Hwy 155. Other than a small K-6 school with about 10 students, Bear Creek is essentially a residential community. Businesses and services are located in the nearby centres.

BEATTY, village, pop 61 (2006c), 79 (2001c), is located 14 km northwest of Melfort on Hwy 3. The community takes its name from Reginald Bird Beatty, who came to the district with his wife and family in 1884. The former Hudson Bay Company employee settled on land just southeast of Melfort and received his patent on his homestead in 1888. The Beattys were the first and only settlers in the Melfort region for several years and the name Melfort honours Mrs. Beatty's family home in Scotland. The first settler in the immediate area of the present-day village of Beatty arrived in 1892, and the community slowly built up following the construction of the railway en route to Prince Albert in 1904. Trains were running in 1905. The first store in Beatty was built in late 1907 by George S. Wallace, who became the first postmaster in 1908, the same year the first of five grain elevators was erected. In 1918, a proper railway station was built, replacing the boxcar which had been used to serve the purpose. The Village of Beatty was incorporated on March 31, 1921; the population at the time was hovering around 100. In 1923, a school was built in the village. Previously, children from Beatty had attended Louisa School, somewhat to the west. In 1936, the community had a peak population of 153. It dropped by about a third during the war years, but recovered somewhat thereafter before beginning to steadily decline in the early 1960s. As the rural population dwindled and travel to nearby Melfort became commonplace, Beatty's economic and social institutions declined. High school students began to be bused to the city or to Kinistino in 1957, Beatty's railway station was closed to service in 1962, and at the end of 1967 Beatty School closed its doors for good. People began commuting to work in Melfort. The community's churches closed. Today, only a small store with a post office serves the community, and there are a number of vacant lots and homes for sale. The one remaining elevator is in private hands. Beatty is situated in the RM of Flett's Springs No. 429.

▲ **RELICS IN A LANDSCAPE OF ABANDONMENT:** Building in the foreground: unknown. The sole remaining elevator in Beatty, formerly operated by the Saskatchewan Wheat Pool, stands in the background. The elevator itself dates to 1958, the crib annexes on either side date to the 1930s and 1940s. Photograph taken August 24, 2004.

BEAUBIER, organized hamlet, pop 25 (2006c), 35 (2001c), is located south of Weyburn, east of Lake Alma off Hwy 18, a short distance north of the Canada-U.S. border. The community's origins date to the arrival of the CPR in the area in 1927, and the Beaubier Post Office was established that year. The hamlet was named in honour of a young school teacher from Manitoba, Eleanor Beaubier, who died after caring for many district residents during the flu epidemic of 1918-19. Beaubier was set up as an organized hamlet in 1949 and had a population of 90 in 1966. The community's numbers were down to 50 by 1972. Farming, ranching, and some oil are the main industries in the area. Beaubier is situated in the RM of Lake Alma No. 8.

BEAUVAL, northern village, pop 806 (2006c), 843 (2001c), is located southeast of Ile-a-la-Crosse on Hwy 165. Immediately to the east, at La Plonge, lies one of the reserve holdings of the English River First Nation. Beauval is situated in truly one of the most magnificent settings of any community in the province, overlooking the beautiful Beaver River Valley—hence, the community's name. The origins of Beauval date to the beginning of the twentieth century and are associated with the founding of a Roman

▲ **THE BEAVER RIVER VALLEY, BEAUVAL:** The community sits upon the west bank of the river (homes are situated immediately behind where the photographer was standing) and the name Beauval is French, meaning "beautiful valley." Photograph taken September 21, 2003.

Catholic mission and a residential school. The area has a history of trapping, freighting, commercial fishing and forestry, the latter two activities gaining prominence in the 1930s as the fur trade declined. An estimated 66 persons lived in the Beauval area in 1921; by the end of WWII, the community had grown to approximately 350. Northern roads were beginning to be developed, and, while for many years they were simply wagon trails and then gravel, eventually there was a paved highway from Meadow Lake. In 1969, the Beauval Local Community Authority was established, giving local residents the power to govern their community through an elected council, which had the authority to collect taxes, provide services, and create bylaws under the Northern Administrative District Act. Beauval was incorporated as a northern village in 1983. The community has a health centre, an RCMP detachment, and a complex for recreational activities. The village also has a gas station, a grocery store, banking facilities, a pre-school, and

a restaurant. A number of lodges in the area cater to tourists, fishers and hunters. The predominantly Metis community has grown rapidly over the past two decades (the population was 436 in 1971) and the average age is just over 21 years old. Valley View School provides K-12 education to close to 300 students. Economic opportunities are currently limited to some commercial fishing, some work in mines, a little trapping, and work in local businesses or the school. Tourism, particularly as it relates to fishing, provides some seasonal income and the economy is bolstered by local and provincial government subsidies, grants, and programs.

BEAVER CREEK, organized hamlet, pop 121 (2006c), 138 (2001c), is an upscale bedroom community located just south of the city of Saskatoon off Hwy 219. Beaver Creek was established as an organized hamlet in 1988 and is situated in the RM of Corman Park No. 344. The

community takes its name from the nearby Beaver Creek Conservation Area, one of few uncultivated short-grass prairie sites in the province.

BEAVER FLAT, resort village, is located on the south side of Lake Diefenbaker, east of Saskatchewan Landing Provincial Park. Development began in 1968 as the lake, a reservoir created by the construction of the Gardiner Dam, was nearing capacity. A cottage subdivision was planned for the new lakeshore, which had been previously farmland. The name Beaver Flat had been in use in the district since the early 1900s (the Beaver Flat School District was organized in 1918, and the Beaver Flat Post Office was established in 1923) so when the resort village was incorporated in 1981, residents chose to honour this heritage by perpetuating the name. Today, there are approximately 100 cabins at Beaver Flat; there are a small number of year-round residents and the population varies depending on the season. Beaver Flat is situated in the RM of Excelsior No. 166.

BEECHY, village, pop 243 (2006c), 295 (2001c), is located in the rolling landscape of the south and eastern slopes of the Coteau Hills southwest of Lucky Lake on Hwy 342. Lake Diefenbaker and Prairie Lake Regional Park lie 20 km to the south. In the early 1900s, the district was range land for huge ranching operations and the area remained basically unsettled until ferry services across the South Saskatchewan River opened the region to homesteaders. A ferry in the area of today's Riverhurst Ferry opened in 1908, but it was the inauguration of the Herbert Ferry to the south of Beechy in 1910 that

really opened up the district. This ferry was north of the community of Herbert on the CPR main line, and for the first few years Herbert was the market town for those in the Beechy district. Grain had to be hauled to Herbert, and coal and other provisions had to brought back from there, north across the river. The round trip could take four days. By 1912, most of the available land in the Beechy area was occupied. In 1913, a rail line was running to the north though Dinsmore and Wiseton, which gave Beechy area residents access to trading centres, albeit still distant, without having to cross the river. In 1919, surveyors staked the line for the railway into the Beechy area from Dunblane to the north, giving impetus to the development of the townsite. The first streets and lots were surveyed in 1920, and the first buildings were erected. That same year, the railroad reached Lucky Lake. In the spring of 1922 as the first trains rolled into Beechy, the beginnings of the community were well underway. The CNR named the community after Frederick William Beechey (why the different spelling is a mystery), a British Naval officer and an Arctic explorer who served with Franklin and Parry in the quest to discover the Northwest Passage. By early 1925, Beechy had a population of over 100, and it was incorporated as a village that May. The community grew steadily (although there was a downturn in the surrounding farming population during the 1930s), and Beechy reached a peak population of 428 in 1966. The population stabilized at around 300 in the early 1980s and has remained steady since. Today, the community has a diversity of businesses, several of which cater to the area's crop-growing and ranching industries. Beechy has financial institutions, accommodations, restaurants, grocery stores, a post office, a library, four churches, and a variety of professional services. The village also has a health centre, an ambulance service, and a volunteer fire department. Beechy School, a K-12 facility, had 101 students enrolled in the fall of 2006. The village's recreational facilities include skating and curling rinks and a large community hall. Beechy has a number of service clubs, community organizations and sports teams. The surrounding area is popular for hunting, and Lake Diefenbaker offers opportunities for boating, swimming, fishing and camping. An area attraction, and one of the province's most spectacular scenic wonders, is the Sandcastle on Lake Diefenbaker, a steeply-sloped hog's back with deep ridges resembling castle-like spires. Beechy hosts a number of annual events, the largest, a three-day Canadian Cowboy's Association approved rodeo attracting participants from across western Canada. A local drama group, the Snakebite Players, also stages productions each year. Beechy serves as the administrative centre of the RM of Victory No. 226.

BELLE PLAINE, village, pop 64 (2006c), 70 (2001c), is located on the Trans-Canada Hwy and the CPR main line, approximately halfway between the cities of Regina and Moose Jaw. The first homesteaders began arriving in the area in 1883 and 1884, and by 1905 most of the available land in the district was settled. It is possible that the community had a grain elevator as early as 1896, as records indicate farmers from Stony Beach, to the north, were bringing their harvests to Belle Plaine at that time. The Western Elevator Company was operating in the community in 1899. Over the next decade, Belle Plaine saw considerable growth: the first sports day was held in

1902, the post office opened and a church was built in 1903, the CPR station was constructed in 1908, and that year the Bank of Hamilton (operating until 1916) opened its doors. The village was incorporated on August 12, 1910. The senior room of the Belle Plaine school closed in 1946 with the students then being bused to Moose Jaw, and in 1974 the school in the village was closed. Today, most of Belle Plaine's population work in the nearby industries — IMC Kalium, Saskferco, and Canadian Salt — or commute to work in Regina or Moose Jaw. Belle Plaine is situated in the RM of Pense No. 160.

BELLEGARDE, organized hamlet, pop 45 (2006c), 40 (2001c), is located in the southeast corner of the province, approximately 10 km from the Saskatchewan-Manitoba border, southeast of Redvers on Gainsborough Creek. In the late 1880s, a young Roman Catholic priest from France, Mgr. Jean-Isidore Gaire, founded a mission in Grande Clairière, in south-western Manitoba, and in 1891 he travelled west into the North-West Territories, to an area then known as the "Fourth Coulee," the site of present-day Bellegarde. In 1892, Gaire led families from Belgium and France to the area, establishing the parish of St. Maurice. In a few years the community would come to be known as Bellegarde. (Mgr. Gaire was also responsible for founding a number of other French-speaking communities in what is today the province's southeast.)

Bellegarde's first homesteaders would later be joined by other French settlers from Quebec. At the turn of the century, as the CPR was laying track westward five kilometres to the north, there were more than 100 people established in the settlement, with the Catholic Church the foundation of the community. The first church and rectory were built around 1899, and in 1905-06 the first convent was built. By the 1960s, however, the small community began to decline. The once competitive hockey team folded in the early 1970s due to a lack of players, and by 1982 Bellegarde residents found themselves without a store. Today, the church, La Maison Culturelle de Bellegarde, and the school remain and together are the backbone of the community. L'École de Bellegarde,

▲ **BELLEGARDE LANDMARKS:** The Bellegarde cemetery (above, left) flanks the west side of the hamlet; the Roman Catholic Church (top right) sits at the east end of Avenue Mgr Jean Gaire. La Maison Culturelle de Bellegarde (bottom right) is situated in the centre of the community. Photographs taken September 13, 2006.

with approximately 70 students, provides K-12 education, one of just 12 schools in Saskatchewan's only Francophone school division. Bellegarde is situated in the RM of Storthoaks No. 31.

BENGOUGH, town, pop 337 (2006c), 401 (2001c), calls itself the "Gateway to the Big Muddy." Located in south-central Saskatchewan on Highway 34, the community lies just north of the famous valley and badlands — submarginal tracts primarily suited for ranching, where lands formerly utilized for crop production have been returned to pasture. Land nearer Bengough itself supports mixed farming as well as ranching operations. Wheat, durum, barley and oats are the main crops, with lentils and peas increasingly grown. The Bengough district was originally settled between about 1905 and 1913. Before a bank was established in Bengough, the bank manager in Willow Bunch rode the 50 or so kilometres once a week with the cash necessary to handle local transactions in his saddlebags. The railroad arrived in the fall of 1911 amidst a flurry of construction at the new village site, and the next spring, on March 15, 1912, Bengough was incorporated. The community was named in honour of John Wilson Bengough (1851-1923), one of Canada's most brilliant, prolific, and popular political cartoonists, and the founder of the satirical magazine *Grip*. One of the first buildings in Bengough was the hotel, which would come to serve the community in ways unimagined when it was built. In the winter of 1916, villagers had to move into the hotel to keep warm as trains could not get through with the coal people needed to heat their homes. Later, the flu epidemic of 1918-19 necessitated the hotel being turned temporar-

ily into a hospital. During the flu, those who were able volunteered as nurses, and 14 or 15 people died. The hotel, a local landmark, burned down in 1978. The drought years of the 1930s hit Bengough hard, and a good number of people left the village and the surrounding area. After WWII, the community witnessed an unprecedented period of prosperity, and the population grew. Bengough was incorporated as a town in 1958. By the mid-

1960s, 700 people called the community home. Bengough today provides an array of businesses and services to the district. The town has an RCMP detachment, a health centre and a special care home, a volunteer fire department, and a K-12 school that had 133 students enrolled in the fall of 2006. There are a range of facilities for social and recreational activities in the community, including the Bengough and District Regional Park, adjacent to the

▲ **GATEWAY TO THE BIG MUDDY:** This photograph was taken on September 3, 2003, just a few kilometres south of Bengough on Hwy 34, looking west.

◄ **LOOKING SOUTH UP MAIN STREET:** Bengough, September 3, 2003. Railway Avenue in the foreground.

town, which facilitates camping, swimming and golf. Each year Bengough hosts amateur and professional rodeos, a horse show and summer fair. A notable recent event was when Bengough and district schoolchildren accompanied palaeontologists from the Royal Saskatchewan Museum into the Big Muddy Valley to uncover the remains of a 55-million-year-old crocodile. The rare fossil is one of only a few known to exist in the world. Bengough serves as the administrative centre of the RM of Bengough No. 40.

BENSON, hamlet, pop 95 (2001c), is located in southeast Saskatchewan, 37 km north of Estevan on Hwy 47. Land in the area was surveyed in 1881-83, but it was not until 1911-12 with the construction of the Grand Trunk Pacific line from Regina to Lampman that the townsite was laid out and businesses were established at the location. In 1928, Benson was incorporated as a village, and in 1956 it had a peak population of 164. Agriculture, consisting of grain farming and livestock production, formed the basis of the area economy. Benson's proximity to Estevan meant that many of the village's businesses and services would eventually be superseded by those in the larger centre. High school students began to be bused to the city in the late 1960s, and in June 2004 Benson's K-6 school permanently closed its doors. On August 12, 2003, the village was dissolved, and Benson reverted to hamlet status. The community remains the administrative centre of the RM of Benson No. 35, which was established in 1909.

BETHUNE, village, pop 369 (2006c), 380 (2001c), is located a little over 50 km northwest of Regina on Hwy 11. The Qu'Appelle Valley lies a short distance to the south. The first few settlers began arriving in the region around the mid-1880s, establishing ranching operations based in the Qu'Appelle and Arm River valleys. Although the railroad connecting Regina, Saskatoon, and Prince Albert was running through the location of present-day Bethune by 1890, settlement northwest of Lumsden progressed slowly. It was not until 1903 that the first homesteads were claimed in the Bethune area, but by

1904 settlers were arriving in droves and the village developed. The post office was established in 1905, the school opened in 1906, and within a few years a number of businesses and homes lined the community's streets. The village was incorporated on August 2, 1912 (its name honouring C.B. Bethune, a railroad employee), and the population, other than during the 1930s and the following war years, has mainly grown. The area economy is based upon agriculture, although today a large percentage of the community's workforce commutes to work in Regina. Village businesses and services provide some local employment, as does Clive Draycott School, a K-8 facility with approximately 90 students. High school students attend classes in Lumsden. Bethune serves as the administrative centre of the RM of Dufferin No. 190.

BIENFAIT, town, pop 748 (2006c), 786 (2001c), is located approximately 14 km east of Estevan on Hwy 18. Coal mining has been a part of the community since its beginnings, and today many of Bienfait's residents still work in the area's coal mining operations. Many others, however, now work in the city of Estevan; for these people, Bienfait is in many ways a bedroom community. Agriculture, the oil and gas industry, and power generation contribute to a diversified economy and provide further employment. Sask-Power's Shand Power Station and Shand Greenhouse are located southwest of the town. People began arriving in the Bienfait area in the 1890s, and the first viable coal mine was established a few kilometres south at Roche Percee in 1891. The CPR came through from Brandon to Estevan in 1892 and the Soo Line was running though Estevan in 1893, providing easy

BIENFAIT ...Coal Country

▲ **GOING UNDERGROUND:** Workers of Bienfait Mines Ltd. in 1915. Note the "pit pony" in the centre of the rear of the picture. These animals were stabled underground and used for hauling coal in the mines. Some rarely saw the light of day. Photograph courtesy of Bienfait Coalfields Historical Society Museum.

▲ **YOUTHFUL FACES** appear among these underground miners in 1926. Photograph courtesy of Bienfait Coalfields Historical Society Museum.

▶ **THIS CANADIAN PACIFIC STEAM LOCOMOTIVE** (facing page) was built in 1907 and was one of the last to operate in Canada. It was donated to the Town of Bienfait by the Manitoba and Saskatchewan Coal Company Ltd. in 1968. A plaque dedicates the locomotive, which now sits in the town's business section, to "the memory of the mine workers, both deep seam and strip, who worked the lignite coal seam in the Bienfait-Coalfields area since the turn of the [twentieth] century."

▲ **ANNIE BULLER**, one of the founding members of the Communist Party of Canada and an ardent promoter of radical trade unionism, addressing a crowd in Bienfait two days before the Estevan Riot. Buller was asked to go to Bienfait to offer support and encouragement to the miners after mine owners refused to recognize their union and enter into negotiations. Buller spoke of the terrible living and working conditions of the miners and their inadequate wages. Two days later, the miners and their families marched into Estevan in protest. Following the ensuing melee, Buller was arrested, tried and convicted of participating in an unlawful assembly and inciting a riot. She was fined $500 and sentenced to a year of hard labour and solitary confinement at the Battleford Jail. Saskatchewan Archives Board R-A32584.

▲ **A FUNERAL FOR THREE:** Authorities estimate that as many as 1,500 mourners attended the funeral in Bienfait for the miners killed in the Estevan Coal Strike. Saskatchewan Archives Board R-A18508.

▲ **UNITED IN A CAUSE AND THEN UNITED IN DEATH:** the final resting place of the miners killed in the northwest corner of the Bienfait cemetery. Over the years, authorities had vandalized the tombstone, removing "R.C.M.P." It was always repainted. Photograph taken August 22, 2003.

▶ **COAL MINING IN THE MODERN ERA** is done with mammoth machinery such as this drag line working on the outskirts of Bienfait on August 26, 2003.

▼ **THE PLAQUE ERECTED** at the gravesite in 1997. Photograph taken August 22, 2003.

access to the area for many settlers coming from the United States, who were substantially of European origins. Although the Palliser Expedition noted coal along the Souris River in 1857, quantities had been thought too insubstantial to warrant development. It was decades before the extent of the coal beds was realized, and the first lignite mined in the area was by individual entrepreneurs and small-time operators. In the early 1900s, the CPR started Bienfait Mines Ltd., and soon more mines were opened in the area. Many local farmers used coal-mining income to help them establish their farms. The community had a second rail line by 1911 as the Canadian Northern Railway extended tracks south-westward from Carlyle, and Bienfait, one of a number of coal mining communities that had sprung up in the area, was incorporated as a village in 1912. In 1922, the only murder ever associated with Saskatchewan's illicit liquor trade with the United States took place in Bienfait. The population of the community grew rapidly in the early 1900s as people of many diverse nationalities flocked to the area, from 245 in 1916 to well over 500 in 1931. That same year, Bienfait coal miners joined the Mine Worker's Union of Canada and went on strike to try to force mine owners to recognize their union and to restore wages that had been cut. When the owners proved intransigent, miners held a protest march on September 29 in Estevan to gain community support for their cause. Estevan's mayor called on the RCMP to help the local police quash the demonstration, and in the ensuing pandemonium three miners were killed and many were injured. A contentious memorial at the men's gravesite in Bienfait attributes their deaths to murder by the RCMP. The Depression years hit the coal mining industry hard, but another

development which was to significantly affect miners was the beginning of surface 'strip' mining by electric shovels. Originally, all mining operations had been underground, but by 1956 a six-decade era of underground coal mining had come to an end — and with it a lifestyle and a good many jobs. Today, some of the world's largest mining equipment is operated in the Bienfait area, and coal mined in the district, as well as at Coronach, is used to generate 75 per cent of Saskatchewan's power. Bienfait attained town status in 1957 with a population of just over 800. While the community today has a small core of essential businesses and services, residents benefit from the easy access to the amenities and services that the city of Estevan has to offer. Bienfait's school provides K-9 education to approximately 200 students, while grades 10 to 12 are bused to the city. Bienfait has skating and curling rinks, a covered swimming pool operational during summer months, as well as baseball diamonds and a soccer field. Woodlawn Regional Park south of Estevan has an 18-hole golf course and the renowned outdoor Souris Valley Theatre. The Boundary Dam and Rafferty reservoirs provide excellent opportunities for boating and fishing. The coal mining industry and its role in the development of Bienfait has been commemorated in a museum, formerly the CPR station built in 1907. A vintage steam locomotive used by the Manitoba and Saskatchewan Coal Company is also displayed at the north end of the town's main street. Bienfait serves as the administrative centre of the RM of Coalfields No. 4.

BIG BEAVER, organized hamlet, pop 15 (2006c), 20 (2001c), is located south of the Big Muddy Valley, just off the

junction of Hwys 18 and 34. Coronach, approximately 28 km west, and Bengough, 35 km north, are the nearest trading centres. There is a small regional park adjacent to the community, and the Port of Big Beaver, a customs house on the Saskatchewan-Montana border, is located a little over 10 km to the south. Cattle ranching along with grain farming are the predominant industries in the area. There were few homesteaders in the region prior to 1910. However, the district was settled rapidly afterwards, and with the construction of the CPR eastward from Coronach in 1928 the community of Big Beaver developed. The rail line was to have been completed to Minton but, with the onset of the Depression, was never finished. In its heyday, Big Beaver supported a school, four grain elevators, three churches, a hotel, two grocery stores, a lumberyard, a bank, a restaurant, a couple of garages, a Massey Harris dealership and a John Deere dealership. Big Beaver was established as an

organized hamlet in 1949. Never a large community, Big Beaver had a population of a little over 100 in the 1960s. The surrounding rural municipality, once home to 1,800 people, today has 174 residents. In the mid-1980s, Big Beaver lost its rail line, its elevators, and its school. Today, Aust's General Store with its coffee shop is the hub of the community and, other than a small bed and breakfast, is Big Beaver's sole remaining business. The store's slogan is, "If we don't have it, you don't need it." This community landmark, however, is destined to close. Ron and Gail Aust are nearing retirement, and it is unlikely anyone will take the store over. Big Beaver serves as the administrative centre of the RM of Happy Valley No. 10.

BIG RIVER, town, pop 728 (2006c), 741 (2001c), is located approximately 135 km northwest of Prince Albert, just to the west of Prince Albert National Park.

▲ **EARLY SAWMILL OPERATIONS IN BIG RIVER.** The burner in the right of the photograph was erected in 1909 and stood as a community landmark until the early 1970s. Photograph courtesy of the Lashburn Centennial Museum.

▲ **WEYERHAEUSER OPERA-TIONS**, approximately 7 kilometres south of Big River, September 22, 2003. Four years later, in 2007, the facility was under new ownership.

◀ **YOU CAN FISH RIGHT OFF THE END OF MAIN STREET** in Big River. Looking west, Cowan Lake appears at the edge of the town, where campsites are also located. Photograph taken September 22, 2003.

The community is situated overlooking the southern end of the long and narrow Cowan Lake, which was created in 1914 by the damming of the Big River, from which the community derives its name. The town is located in a transitional area, between the southern more populated areas of the province and the wilderness of the north, and other than some land cleared for farming and a few natural meadows, Big River sits amidst a landscape of hundreds of lakes and boreal forest. Around 1908-09, commercial fishing operations began in the Big River area, with substantial catches being hauled in from the large Dore and Smoothstone Lakes to the north. The industry would remain significant until around the mid-1900s. Big River itself, however, began as a logging company town. In 1908, William Cowan built the first sawmill at Big River while, simultaneously, the Canadian Northern Railway began construction of a line into the area from Shellbrook. Equipment for the mill was brought in by horse and wagon, since the railroad was not completed to Big River until 1910. In 1911, the Big River Lumber Company was operating what was, reportedly, the largest sawmill in the British Empire. It had the capacity to produce one million board feet of lumber every 24 hours. The mill, as well as the work in the bush, provided employment for over 1,000 men. Newspapers in eastern Canada ran articles about the booming industry in Saskatchewan's northern frontier, and Big River soon became a boomtown with a population estimated to have been over 3,000. The logging company owned the entire townsite and built row upon row of identical tenement houses to accommodate the workers and their families. The company also built the school, the post office, and a hospital, and operated a store and other businesses. In 1914, the Big River Lumber Company sold the entire 'town' to American interests. In the summer of 1919, disaster struck the community. An enormous forest fire swept through the area, eventually completely surrounding the town. It was necessary to evacuate. A special train carried women and children south, while the men remained behind to battle the flames. The fire eventually burnt itself out and, miraculously, even though the countryside was blackened and scorched almost as far north as Green Lake, the townsite remained unscathed. However, Big River was a mill town, and with most of the area's timber gone, the community's future looked bleak, and the possibility of it becoming a ghost town seemed very real. Small patches of trees that survived the fire allowed the mill to operate on a limited scale for another couple of years, but then the company began to dismantle the operation, shipping the equipment out to be used at mills in The Pas, Manitoba, and British Columbia. All that was left was the burner that had been erected in 1909. Until it was dismantled in 1970-71 and sold for scrap metal, it had stood as a community landmark, a memorial to Big River's boomtown days. The absence of a major sawmill left most of the population unemployed, and many moved on. Some took a chance and remained, turning to homesteading, fishing, freighting, and trapping. The operators of small privately-owned sawmills scavenged the countryside for what timber was available. Five men were determined to see the community survive and purchased the townsite from the lumber company for a sum of $20,000. Without the aid of company funds, though, and lacking the ability to collect taxes, running the community was a difficult task. The burden of financing the operation of the school fell on the shoulders of the remaining businessmen. Realizing the limits of the situation, the community petitioned the provincial government for village status, and Big River was incorporated on August 18, 1923. The era of economic prosperity was over, and the community entered an economic slump that was to last for years. For decades, train travel was the preferred means in and out of the community. The dirt road that had been developed was often impassable in poor weather. In the 1940s, however, roads began to be improved. In 1942, a rough road was bulldozed north to Green Lake, and in 1943 the road between Big River and Prince Albert was gravelled. Other roads began pushing their way into fishing camps and areas of forest that fires had spared. In 1946, the Saskatchewan Timber Board decided to rebuild the lumber industry in the village. In 1948, a new planer mill was in operation, and by 1950, when the Saskatchewan Timber Board Mill was officially opened, the town once again had a booming industry. The population of Big River nearly doubled in five years: from 502 in 1946 to 901 in 1951. In 1966, Big River attained town status. Today, Big River is a vibrant community with a diverse array of businesses and services. The town has a hospital, a special care home and an RCMP detachment, and Big River's elementary and high schools provide K-12 education to close to 300 students. Big River has curling and skating rinks, 9-hole and miniature golf courses, approximately 160 kilometres of snowmobile trails, a ski hill, rodeo grounds, baseball diamonds, and a football and soccer field. The Canadian Northern Railway Station, built in 1910, is one of the oldest buildings in the community. Used as a railway station for almost 70 years, the building has been designated a heritage property

and rehabilitated for various community uses, including as a senior citizens centre. Tourism has been steadily developing in the region, as there are a number of resort destinations. Hunting and fishing, snowmobiling, camping, and boating are popular activities. The Big River area has also become home to a significant artistic community. Potters, photographers, writers, sculptors, and painters have made the area home. The Ness Creek Music Festival features musicians from across North America and draws audiences from across western Canada. Forestry, however, remains the backbone of the local economy, and recently a strong Canadian dollar and the protracted softwood lumber dispute with the U.S. have hurt the industry. Weyerhaeuser, Big River's largest employer, had been trying to sell its operations in Big River, Hudson Bay and Carrot River, and had cut back its workforce at the Big River mill. There had been temporary shutdowns at the operation, which normally employed roughly 200 people. Domtar Inc. acquired the complex in 2007. Big River serves as the administrative centre of the RM of Big River No. 555.

BIG SHELL, resort village, is located approximately 100 km west of Prince Albert on Shell Lake, southwest of the village of the same name. The locale was developed in the early 1970s and was incorporated in 1982. Today, there are a small, but growing, number of year-round residents; the population reaches about 75 to 80 during the summer months. Big Shell is located in the RM of Spiritwood No. 496.

BIGGAR, town, pop 2,033 (2006c), 2,243 (2001c), is located 93 km west of

THE MAJESTIC THEATRE, located at the corner of 4th Avenue and Main Street in Biggar, has been a community landmark since it was built in 1911. From 1914 until 1986, the theatre was operated by the Shepherd family. The building was substantially enlarged in 1916, and again in 1929 when it was also completely renovated. When the theatre closed in 1986 it sat unused until 1991 when a non-profit corporation, The Biggar and District Theatre Project, was established to purchase and update the building. A two-level addition was added to the rear of the building to provide meeting rooms and a kitchen was also added. The theatre re-opened in 1995 and it is now used for a variety of community events such as live theatre performances, music and carol festivals, school programs, as well as weekly movies. The photographs below and on the facing page, right, depict early live theatre productions that involved many local Biggar residents.
Photographs courtesy of the Biggar Museum and Gallery.

▲ The cast of this play, dating to 1911 or 1912, were, from left to right: Miss Maitland, Marnie Frampton, John Porteous, Miss Maude Flemming (Porteous), George Porteous, Jim Flemming, Jim Porteous.

Saskatoon at the junction of Hwys 4, 14, and 51. To the south and southwest lie the Bear Hills. The town is famous for its slogan "New York is Big, But This is Biggar"; local legend has it that an early survey crew had too much to drink one night and wrote the famous phrase on the town's sign as a prank. Evidently, the townspeople liked the slogan and adopted it. The Biggar district began to be settled around 1905, and with the arrival of the railroads the com-

munity had its beginnings. The CPR came through in 1907, and in 1908 the Grand Trunk Pacific (GTP) arrived. In 1909, Biggar was incorporated as a village, its name derived from William Hodgins Biggar, general counsel of the GTP. That same year, the community's weekly newspaper, the *Biggar Independent* (still in business) was started. In 1910, the GTP decided to establish Biggar as a divisional point on its line, which sparked both a construction

▲ This 1919 theatre production featured Frankie Ferguson, Mae Davidson, Aileen Lewis, Ruby Hanway, Kay Drummond, Lenore Miller, and Hazel Brown.

▲ "Babes in the Woods," a production dating to the mid-1920s featured, from left to right: George Porteous, Mrs. Farrell, Jack Miller, Dr. Saich.

boom and population growth. A roundhouse was built, and Biggar's station was, reportedly, one of the largest in the Canadian west, boasting an all-night restaurant. As a home terminal where train crews were changed, the community's population jumped to over 600, and in 1911 Biggar was incorporated as a town. Over the next few years rail lines were extended north to Battleford and southwest through Dodsland to Alberta. Biggar grew rapidly and the population exceeded 2,000 by the mid-1920s. This number remained fairly stable until the 1950s, when Biggar experienced a period of additional growth. At this time, CN (who took over the GTP in 1919) employed up to 500 local people. The population of Biggar peaked at 2,755 in 1966. Today, the railway still employs approximately 150 people; however, with the decline of CN as an employer, Biggar's economy is more reliant on agriculture and related industries. Some of the lands in the district, however, are somewhat marginal, comprised of sandy and alkali soils, and the past few years have also brought the scourges of drought, grasshoppers, hail, and unseasonable frosts. Repercussions have been that farming-related businesses (like grain elevators and farm dealerships) have cut back staff. As well, the Alberta oilfields have attracted the younger generations of farm families, with the result that the average age of the Biggar district's farming population is rising. The strength of local businesses and other industries help stabilize the district's economy, and there is significant employment in the fields of education and health care. Prairie Malt Limited exports to markets around the world and employs roughly 70 people, while Biggar Transport, which benefits from the business generated by Prairie Malt, has a fleet of over 50 trucks and has 60 full-time employees. Saskatchewan's largest greenhouse is also located at Biggar; it covers eight acres of land and employs up to 95 people during peak production. A manufacturer of environmentally-safe containment tanks for petroleum, chemicals, and other hazardous materials has a workforce of approximately 65. The province's second largest turkey producer, a sodium sulphate plant, agricultural suppliers, and an otherwise strong retail sector offer additional employment and add diversity to the town's economy. In total, Biggar has over 100 commercial enterprises. The town also has two schools: a K-9 separate school which provides a Catholic education to approximately 130 students; and a K-12 public school with an enrollment close to 400. Additionally, Prairie West Regional College offers programs and services for adult learners. The community also has a hospital and a special care home, an RCMP detachment, a volunteer fire department, and an airport. Community attractions include the Biggar Museum and Gallery, Roger Martin's Homestead Museum, and Sandra Schmirler Olympic Gold Park, established in honour of the Canadian and Olympic curling champion who was born and raised in the town. Biggar also has a full range of facilities for sports and recreation, including a stadium with an ice rink, a community hall, an aquatic centre, curling rinks, tennis courts, ball diamonds, a football and soccer field, and a running track. Biggar has public parks, cross-country ski trails, and a regional park with a nine-hole golf course and a trout fishing pond. Annual events include Biggar Rodeo Days and musicals presented each spring in the historic Majestic Theatre, a community landmark since 1911. The Biggar area was also home to the 'Hanson Buck,' a world record white-tailed deer pursued and shot by a local hunter in November of 1993. Biggar serves as the administrative centre of the RM of Biggar No. 347.

BIRCH HILLS, town, pop 935 (2006c), 957 (2001c), is located approximately 38 km southeast of Prince Albert at the junction of Hwys 3 and 25. Fur traders had plied the South Saskatchewan River north of the community since the latter half of the eighteenth century, and the

▶ **SERIOUS CONTENDERS:** The Birch Hills girl's hockey team of 1947 won a championship at the local arena when they defeated Kinistino in overtime 3 to 2 to take the final game of a four team tournament. Kinistino girls defeated Star City 2 to 0; Birch Hills defeated Melfort 7 to 1, and then defeated Kinistino to win the championship. Betty Brown scored nine of the ten goals for Birch Hills, and the other goal was scored by Betty Dunn. Members of the Birch Hills Girls' Hockey Team included Pat Vinnell, June Webb-Bowen, Pat Webb-Bowen, Betty Dunn, Lucille Gordon, Shirley Braaten, Margaret Stobbs, Ruth Hoiland, Betty Brown, Shirley Pushie, and Joy Webb-Bowen. The coach was Gordon Vinnell.

Some of the team members are pictured here. From left to right: Pat Webb-Bowen, Betty Dunn, June Webb-Bowen, Betty Brown, Pat Vinnell.

◀ **THE BIRCH HILLS LIVERY, FEED AND SALE STABLE** (date unknown) was typical of livery stable businesses in towns and villages throughout Saskatchewan.

Birch Hills photographs courtesy of the Birch Hills Historical Society.

origins of Birch Hills date to the 1880s, when settlement of the district began. A collection of farms belonging to the Harper family, who came to the area via ox cart from the Red River district, became first a stopping place and then, in 1894, the location of a school. First known as Harperview, the small settlement formed the nucleus of what would become the present community of Birch Hills. In 1895, the Birch Hills Post Office was opened, its name derived from the area hills which had long provided a source of birch bark for the construction of canoes. In 1905, the Canadian Northern Railway came

through the area, constructing its line from Melfort to Prince Albert, and new settlers began to pour into the district. They came from Ontario, the United States, Scandinavian countries (predominantly Norway), and other areas of Europe. The townsite developed rapidly: stores were set up, the first hotel was built, grain elevators were erected, and Birch Hills was incorporated as a village in 1907. By 1917, the population was approximately 250, and the district surrounding the community was proving to be some of the finest agricultural land in Saskatchewan. That year, according to local records, 200,000

bushels of wheat, 138 railcars of livestock, and 130,000 pounds of butter produced by the local creamery (close to 60,000 kg) was shipped out of the district. By the 1950s, the population of Birch Hills was over 500, and in 1960 the community attained town status and was continuing to grow. Birch Hills is one of the few rural communities in Saskatchewan not to have significantly declined over the past few decades, and over the past ten years the community's real estate market has been strong, with new residential subdivisions created and a total of about 40 new homes either built or in the works. Part of this

is due to the community's proximity to Prince Albert and the viability of commuting. The Birch Hills commercial sector consists of approximately 90 businesses and services, and the town has a health centre with a special care home, an RCMP detachment, and a fire department. The Birch Hills Flying Club plays an active role in managing the community's modern airport. Birch Hills School is a K-12 facility that had 375 students enrolled in the fall of 2006, which included high school students from the nearby reserve of the Muskoday First Nation. The community also has its own weekly newspaper, as well as numerous clubs, organizations, and church denominations. Recreational facilities include curling and skating rinks, a nine-hole golf course, parks, picnic areas, ball diamonds, campgrounds, and a seniors' recreation centre. The Civic Centre houses the Town and RM offices, as well as a community hall and a library. Birch Hills serves as the administrative centre of the RM of Birch Hills No. 460.

BIRD'S POINT, resort village, is located in the eastern Qu'Appelle Valley, southwest of Esterhazy on the north shore of Round Lake. The resort is named for the Bird family who settled at the lake in the 1890s. In 1961 'Bird Point' was established as an organized hamlet, and in 1981 Bird's Point was incorporated as a resort village. The 2006 Census recorded that there were 88 permanent residents; however, the population varies greatly depending on the season. Bird's Point is accessible via Hwy 247 and is situated in the RM of Fertile Belt No. 183.

BIRSAY, hamlet, pop 53 (2001c), is located south of Outlook on Hwy 45 west of Lake Diefenbaker. Settlement of the region was well underway by 1910, and when word spread in 1919 as to where the rail line would run and where the nearest townsite would be established, various outlying businesses and new entrepreneurs moved to the present location of the community. By 1921, development was substantial enough for Birsay to be incorporated as a village. The village secretary appointed that year, Don Cameron, would serve in the position until 1964, a period

▼ **THE FORMER SASKATCHEWAN WHEAT POOL ELEVATOR** in Birsay was built in 1960 (the crib annex dates to 1957). It is the sole elevator left standing in the community; there once were three. Photograph taken July 20, 2004.

▲ **A COMMUNITY LANDMARK SINCE 1928**, the Birsay United Church was designated a heritage property in 1997. It incorporates the bent peak characteristic of Nordic or Lutheran churches and a corner entrance typical of Methodist buildings. Triple side windows are reminiscent of Anglican designs, yet are rectangular rather and lack the usual Gothic arches. The interior of the church has open beams such as those used in Anglican churches and a fan-shaped seating arrangement common to Methodist buildings. The church was built for a total of $14,000. Photograph taken July 20, 2004.

of 43 years. Over the decades, Birsay had an active Co-op, CNR station, and school. There was a Royal Bank in the early years and, in the 1930s, a short-lived hospital. The community had a peak population of 177 in 1961, but, as its numbers began to fall, businesses and community institutions, such as the school, closed. The village was dissolved January 1, 2004. Birsay continues to serve as the administrative centre of the RM of Coteau No. 255. Agriculture is the main industry in the area.

BJORKDALE, village, pop 201 (2006c), 229 (2001c), is located roughly halfway between Tisdale and Porcupine Plain on Hwy 23, in a transitional area where rolling hills and parklands give way to the boreal forest. Bjorkdale lies between two of Saskatchewan's drainage basins: creeks and streams just north of the community flow into the Carrot River, while those just south flow into the Red Deer River. The community sits in a valley setting, with homes situated up the hillsides. The first wave of settlers began penetrating the once heavily-forested and swampy area in 1904, and Bjorkdale derives its name from one of the district's first arrivals, Charlie Bjork, a Swede who explored the region while working on the railway then being built between Hudson Bay and Tisdale. Many of the first settlers in the area found work with the railway or

in the region's rapidly developing logging industry. For many years, summers were spent clearing land on the homesteads, while winters were spent working in the forest. The first arrivals in the Bjorkdale area squatted on the land, as quarter sections were not surveyed until 1907. The Rural Municipality of Bjorkdale No. 426 was incorporated in 1913; however, no great development occurred in the area until mechanical land clearing equipment became available, the heavy bush being difficult to clear. Logging and work in area sawmills remained the chief occupation of those in the region until around the late 1920s; in the 1930s, most of the remaining marketable timber in the area was harvested, bringing an end to an era. There were no roads into the region for a number of years. Even when the railway arrived in 1928, the only other access into the district was via a trail from Crooked River that included a roughly-hewn section of corduroy road over a swamp. Any wheat grown on lands cleared had to be hauled to Tisdale, where the nearest grain elevator was located; oats and hay were taken to lumber camps to feed work animals. It was 1927 when survey crews working for the CNR plotted the route for the railway from Crooked River to Reserve (south of Hudson Bay), and with trains running in 1928 the townsite of Bjorkdale began to be built up and settlement of the district intensified. The first grain elevator was built right after the tracks were laid, and over the next few years stores and other businesses were established. Bjorkdale developed steadily; however, it remained under the management of the rural municipality until April 1, 1968, when the village was incorporated. By 1986, the population was 301. Today, a diversified agricultural industry forms the basis of the area economy: grain and cattle are produced, and bi-

son, llamas, katahdin sheep, long-horn cattle, and elk are raised. Bjorkdale has a wide array of businesses and services, a number of which cater to the district's agricultural sector. As well, tourism is a developing industry in the region. Resorts at Barrier and Marean lakes lie just to the south, as does Greenwater Lake Provincial Park. The immense provincial forests of the Porcupine and Pasquia hills lie to the east and northeast respectively. The village has a range of recreational facilities and community-based organizations. The nearest hospitals are located in Tisdale and Porcupine Plain, as are the closest RCMP detachments. The village has a volunteer fire department. Bjorkdale School, a K-12 facility, had 87 students enrolled in the fall of 2006. The community hosts snowmobile rallies, curling bonspiels, and a summer fair. The Bjorkdale district faced a significant challenge in the late 1990s when CN decided to abandon the rail line that ran through Bjorkdale, Porcupine Plain, and the village of Weekes. Adverse effects were elevator closures, lost

tax revenues, increased pressure on area roads, and changing trading patterns. The former Saskatchewan Wheat Pool elevator in Bjorkdale is now in private hands and grain is now trucked out of the district.

BLACK POINT, northern settlement, pop 47 (2001c), is a Dene community located south of La Loche, on the southeast side of Lac La Loche. The Clearwater River Dene Nation's reserve No. 221 lies just to the south and west. Black Point was legally established as a northern settlement under the Northern Municipalities Act in 1983, and between 1988 and 1990 a road was built linking the community to the provincial highway system.

BLADWORTH, village, pop 70 (2006c), 67 (2001c), is located between Davidson and Kenaston on Hwy 11. Although the railroad connecting Regina, Saskatoon, and Prince Albert was running

through the location of present-day Bladworth by 1890 (the community's name honours a railway official), for more than a decade after its completion the line merely served as a bridge between the southern and central regions of the province; much of the vast tract of land between had been deemed unsuitable for agriculture. But in 1902 at the urging of the Canadian government, Colonel Andrew Duncan Davidson formed the Saskatchewan Valley Land Company and began aggressive campaigns to promote immigration to the area. By 1904, settlers were arriving in droves, and the hamlet of Bladworth developed. People arrived from eastern Canada, the U.S., Britain, and eastern Europe. A substantial number of Croatians took up homesteads in the district. In 1906, Bladworth was incorporated, and the village school was established. The years up to the drought and the Depression were to be the community's heyday; the district population and the village had continued to grow until that time. Bladworth reached its peak population of 215 in 1926. The village lost nearly half of its residents during the 1930s, and fires in 1933 and 1941 claimed most of the business area, the latter blaze costing a num-

ber of families their living quarters and worldly possessions. Although there was some return to prosperity following WWII, the community never regained its previous vigour. By the 1960s the village was, again, steadily declining. The population fell from 190 in 1961 to 125 by 1971. In the early 1970s the school was closed, and in 1977, after suffering damage during a storm, Bladworth's CNR station, built in 1908 but unused for some time, was bulldozed into a pit. The population of the village has further plummeted over the past 15 years, and today only a couple of businesses remain. Just northeast of Bladworth, the magnificent former Johnston Residence, built circa 1911 by John Frederick Johnston, a long-serving Member of Parliament and the Canadian Senate, stands as a testimony to Bladworth's more prosperous times. Bladworth is situated in the RM of McCraney No 282.

BLAINE LAKE, town, pop 472 (2006c), 508 (2001c), is located 80 km north of Saskatoon at the junction of Hwys 12 and 40. Although there was some settlement in the area as early as the 1880s, it was in 1899 with the arrival of the Doukhobours that significant numbers of people settled the district. Within a few years, they were joined by French people from Brittany and Eastern Canada, and still others coming northward from the United States. Within ten to fifteen years, the communal villages of the Doukhobors were largely abandoned, as many had moved on to colonies in eastern Saskatchewan or to British Columbia. Those that remained in the area became independent landowners, and the town of Blaine Lake and the district today still reflect a strong Doukhobor heritage. The Blaine Lake townsite was established by the Canadian Northern Railway in 1910, and even before the tracks from Prince Albert via Shellbrook were laid into the new community in 1911, a number of businesses and a grain elevator had been built. The next year, 1912, Blaine Lake was incorporated as a village. By the 1920s, the population of the community was approaching 500, by the 1930s, 600. In 1954, Blaine Lake achieved town status, and by the late 1960s the population was peaking at close to 700. Today, the town is the major trading centre in the district, with a wide array of businesses and services. Several firms cater to agricultural operations, while others focus on tourism. The town has medical services, an array of recreational facilities, an RCMP detachment, and Blaine Lake Composite School, which provides K-12 education to approximately 135 students. Heritage properties in the community include the Canadian

◄ **FRANZ HOFFMAN, NOTARY PUBLIC**, in his office. Hoffman served as the Blaine Lake Village Secretary 1913-1914. Photograph courtesy of the Town of Blaine Lake. Donated by Alex P. Postnikoff, Mayor of Blaine Lake, 1983-85.

▼ **BLAINE LAKE, SASKATCHEWAN, SEPTEMBER 1970.** Looking south up Main Street. Photograph courtesy of the Town of Blaine Lake.

► **THE COMMERCIAL HOTEL**, built circa 1914, is situated on the southwest corner of Railway Avenue and Main Street. Photograph taken July 25, 2003.

Northern Railway Station, built in 1912 and now a library and a museum, and the Doukhobor Prayer Home, constructed in 1931, which serves as a meeting hall, library and cultural centre, while remaining a place of worship. Area attractions include the Doukhobor Settlement Caves, temporary riverbank dwellings constructed in 1899, and the Popoff Tree, reputedly

Saskatchewan's largest tree, with a girth of 4.9 metres (16 ft. 1 inch). There are also a number of regional parks in the district, and a variety of artists' studios dot the countryside. The town of Blaine Lake serves as the administrative centre of the RM of Blaine Lake No. 434.

BLUMENTHAL, organized hamlet, pop 74 (2006c), 44 (2001c), is located northeast of Saskatoon, between the town of Hague and the South Saskatchewan River. One of a number of Mennonite villages that were established in the region, Blumenthal was founded by Mennonite farmers from Manitoba in the late 1890s. Fertile soil, an abundance of water, and easy access to markets via the railway then linking Saskatoon to Prince Albert were reasons for settling in the region. Blumenthal today retains the layout of a traditional Mennonite village. The community was established as an organized hamlet in 1961 and is situated in the RM of Rosthern No. 403.

BORDEN, village, pop 223 (2006c), 225 (2001c), is located 50 km northwest of Saskatoon on Highway 16. A few kilome-

tres southeast of the village, the historic concrete, arched Borden Bridge (a make-work project completed in late 1936) and modern twin highway bridges span the North Saskatchewan River. Settlers to the Borden district were of diverse origins. Doukhobors had established a village in the area in 1900, but by 1907 the colony had moved to east-central Saskatchewan. Permanent district settlers included people of British origin (Quakers arrived in the area in 1903-04) and Ukrainians and Mennonites from southern Russia. Among one of the early homesteading families in the Borden district were the Diefenbakers, whose son John (the future prime minister) attended an area country school when the family lived in the district from about 1904 to 1909-10. But perhaps the first settlers in the immediate area of present-day Borden were a William Shepherd and his wife who came from the United States around 1902-03. They had named the locale Baltimore, but in 1905,

as the railway was being built from Langham to North Battleford, the name Baltimore was rejected, and the fledgling community was renamed Borden in honour of Sir Frederick William Borden (1847-

1917), who served in Laurier's cabinet as the Canadian minister of militia and defence from 1896 to 1911. Following the arrival of the railway, people flooded into the district and the community grew rapidly. Grain elevators were erected and many other businesses were established. In 1907, Borden was incorporated as a village, and by the mid-1930s the population was settling at around 200. Interestingly, even as the number of businesses in the community has declined over the decades (largely giving way to those in Saskatoon), Borden's population figures have remained fairly stable, and Borden was one of few villages in Saskatchewan to have an increase in population recorded during the 2001 Census. People are moving into Borden and are commuting to work in Saskatoon. Cheaper taxes, gas prices, the four-lane highway, a K-12 school, and rural living are making the community an attractive alternative to the city. The village's commercial sector provides most services, and a number of businesses support the district's agricul-

tural industry. Borden has a health centre, a personal care home, and a volunteer fire department; police service is provided by the Radisson RCMP detachment. Borden has facilities for indoor and outdoor recreation and has established a heritage park (the Borden Museum), which is comprised of a number of older buildings gathered from the village and the surrounding area. A feature is a replica of the Diefenbaker homestead. The original was lifted from its site by the provincial government in 1967 and transported to Wascana Centre in Regina, restored and rebuilt, and at the request of John Diefenbaker was opened as a memorial to the pioneers of the province. (In 2002, the Wascana Centre Authority closed the homestead to the public, and after it sat neglected for more than two years, the structure was relocated to the Sukanen Ship Pioneer Village Museum south of Moose Jaw.) In the spring of 2004, Borden experienced a population explosion, as hundreds of new residents literally flocked to the village. An odd visitation of cliff swallows descended upon the community's streets, building nests on the roofs of Borden's businesses. Their appearance was a boon for birders, since the swallow's population has been declining over the decades due to the proliferation of the house sparrow, which competes for food and often usurps the swallow's nests. By the fall, though, Borden's visitors were off to the tropics. Borden serves as the administrative centre of the RM of Great Bend No. 405.

BRABANT LAKE, northern settlement, pop 102 (2001c), is located 172 km northeast of La Ronge on gravel Hwy 102, amidst the forests and lakes of the Precambrian Shield. The small community is situated just north of the lake from which it derives its name. The population is predominantly Cree. The 2001 Census recorded 102 permanent residents; more recent estimates, however, put the number closer to 70. Trapping, fishing, guiding, some construction work, and mining provide some employment, much of which is seasonal. The community has a store and a local outfitter, and mail is delivered twice a week from La Ronge. Brabant Lake has cable television, internet access, and Ospwakun Sepe School, which had 9 students enrolled in grades K-6 in the fall of 2006. Older students live in La Ronge while they take classes. In the late 1990s, a significant archaeological discovery was made on the southwest shore of Brabant Lake after forest fires exposed campsites and artifacts which indicated people have lived in the area for at least 2,500 years; non-indigenous clays and stone materials revealed travel and contact with other areas, and evidence of ceremonial activity was also found. Artifacts discovered included pottery, stone tools, and the metal parts of a flintlock gun dating to about 1850. Brabant Lake was legally established as an unincorporated northern settlement under the Northern Municipalities Act in 1983.

BRACKEN, village, pop 25 (2006c), 35 (2001c), is located between Climax and Val Marie on Hwy 18. The region was the domain of ranchers when it was opened up to homesteaders in 1909, and over the next few years many arrived. A good proportion of the first were of Norwegian and Swedish origin, many of whom came to Canada via Minnesota. Until the CPR arrived in Shaunavon in 1914, the closest point on the Canadian side of the border to deliver grain and obtain lumber, coal, or other goods was Gull Lake, almost 100

▲ **BUILT IN 1976**, this elevator at Bracken was the first Saskatchewan Wheat Pool high-throughput grain elevator in the province. Photograph taken September 5, 2007.

kilometres north. As customs regulations were not rigidly enforced at the time, many cross-border transactions occurred, including a significant covert trade of grain into Montana. Even after 1914, the trips north to the rail line towns could take three to five days. In 1924-25, the CPR continued eastward from Climax toward Val Marie, and the community of Bracken began to develop at its predetermined point along the track. In 1926, Bracken, named after John Bracken, premier of Manitoba 1922-43, was incorporated as a village. An agricultural community, Bracken had a peak population of 165 in 1931; its numbers began to decline dramatically in the late 1960s, falling from 122 in 1966 to 64 by 1971. Bracken is situated in the RM of Lone Tree No. 18.

BRADWELL, village, pop 182 (2006c), 156 (2001c), is located southeast of the city of Saskatoon, just south of Hwy 16. Settlement of the district began around 1903-04. Within a few years, the first store, post office, and school were established. The year 1907 was an important one in the development of the community, as the Grand Trunk Pacific Railway was completing its line from Watrous to Saskatoon. The townsite was surveyed, and new businesses were established; the first railcars of wheat were loaded from the railway siding that December. Settlers continued to arrive, and in 1912 the Village of Bradwell was incorporated. By 1913, three grain elevators lined the tracks, and the community had approximately two dozen businesses. While it was initially thought that Bradwell might develop into a larger centre, it was not to be. The population hovered somewhat over 100 until the 1970s, at which point it began to increase. The nearby potash mines at Allan and Colonsay were in production creating area employment, and homes out of Saskatoon were becoming more attractive to those willing to commute. There are few businesses in Bradwell today, given its proximity to the city, and schoolchildren are bused to classes in Allan. The Bradwell National Wildlife Area, located just south of the community, provides nesting habitat for several species of waterfowl, shorebirds, songbirds, and hawks. Bradwell serves as the administrative centre of the RM of Blucher No. 343.

▲ **CANADIAN PACIFIC RAILWAY YARDS**, Bredenbury. Photograph taken July 12, 2004.

BRANCEPETH, organized hamlet, pop 50 (2006c), 35 (2001c), is located between Birch Hills and Kinistino, 2 km north of Hwy 3. The first people began taking up land in the area in the 1880s, and the Brancepeth Post Office was established in 1891, although about five kilometres southwest of the present community. Settlers came from Manitoba and eastern Canada, the U.S., and Europe; there were a significant number of Norwegians and Swedes. The railroad to link Melfort and Prince Albert was built through the district in 1905-06, greatly aiding the settlement and the development of the area. Brancepeth developed into a small centre for local business and social exchanges. At one time there were stores, a grain elevator, an active school, and community sports teams. Today Brancepeth is a residential community only; there are no services. Brancepeth was established as an organized hamlet in 1978 and is situated in the RM of Birch Hills No. 460.

BREDENBURY, town, pop 329 (2006c), 354 (2001c), is located roughly halfway between Yorkton and the Saskatchewan/Manitoba border on the Yellowhead Hwy (No. 16). The district began to be settled in the 1880s, with large numbers of people of British and Icelandic origins arriving after the middle of the decade. The Manitoba and Northwestern Railway (later taken over by the CPR) came through en route to Yorkton in the late 1880s, and by May 1911 Bredenbury had grown large enough to be incorporated as a village. Two years later, in May 1913, the community attained town status. Major employers are the CPR in Bredenbury and the IMC Kalium potash mines near Esterhazy. A manufacturer of semi-trailers provides additional employment, and the district surrounding Bredenbury sustains a combination of crop and livestock production. Many residents of the community also commute to work in Yorkton, and in recent decades Bredenbury has become somewhat of a bedroom community. Children attend school in Saltcoats until grade 8, and then travel to Yorkton for high school. Bredenbury has a doctor's clinic once a week and a volunteer fire department. A nine-hole golf course is maintained by local volunteers, and Bredenbury is well known for its elaborate displays during the Christmas season. Bredenbury is situated in the RM of Saltcoats No. 213 and had a peak population of 569 in 1966.

BRIERCREST, village, pop 117 (2006c), 113 (2001c), is located southeast of Moose Jaw on Hwy 339. The Cactus Hills lie to the southwest. In the 1880s, the first of a number of ranches were started in the region, and for the next 20 years cattle and horses would dominate an open range. Settlers began to arrive in large numbers around 1902-03, and during the summer of 1903 the Briercrest Post Office was established several kilometres northeast of the present community. The name Briercrest was coined by the wife of Charles Jaques, the first postmaster, it being the name she had given their homestead farm, upon which wild brier roses evidently grew, either on the crest of a small rise or around the edge of a small lake. The Jaques' daughter, Edna (1891-1978), became a well-known prairie poet, author, and lecturer. In 1909, a delegation of Briercrest district farmers met with Premier Walter Scott to discuss the possibility of a railway through the area, presenting the premier with a petition with 2,153 signatories requesting rail service. In 1911 the Canadian Northern Railway purchased the townsite, and by the end of the year trains were running and a number of businesses were established. The village was incorporated in 1912. Although Briercrest was predominantly an agricultural community, a number of the villagers worked at the Claybank Brick Plant. Briercrest is also where the Briercrest Bible Institute had its humble beginnings in 1935; the school relocated to the abandoned RCAF base in Caronport in 1946, when climbing enrollment necessitated a larger facility. A secular K-12 school remained in the village; however, after enrollment dropped to just 28 students in the fall of 2006 (down from 77 in 2003), the decision was taken to close Briercrest School in June 2007. Briercrest retains a small number of businesses which provide supplies and services to the area's agricultural industry. The community had a peak population of 223 in 1931 and it is situated in the RM of Redburn No. 130.

BROADVIEW, town, pop 611 (2006c), 669 (2001c), is located on the Trans-Canada Hwy and the CPR main line, approximately 155 km east of Regina and 80 km west of the Saskatchewan-Manitoba border. To the south lies the valley of the Pipestone Creek; to the north, bordering the south side of the eastern

Qu'Appelle Valley, lie the reserves of the Sakimay, Cowessess, Kahkewistahaw, and Ochapowace First Nations. The foundations of Broadview date to 1882 with the construction of the trans-continental railway across eastern Saskatchewan. The CPR designated the site to be the divisional point between Brandon and Moose Jaw because of its location and ample supply of good water. For many years, the railway was the economic backbone of the community, and despite mechanization the railway long remained a major employer in the town. The Broadview Post Office was established in 1882, and by the fall of 1883 the townsite had been surveyed and a four-stall roundhouse, coal dock, station, section house, dining hall, and stores built. Broadview developed rapidly as a distribution and service centre for a large trading area. In 1885 the RCMP set up a division in the community. Broadview was incorporated as a village in 1898, and in 1907 Broadview attained town status. A brick-making plant was established in 1906; reportedly, 165,000 bricks manufactured in Broadview were used in the construction of the Saskatchewan Legislative Building. The population of Broadview peaked at over 1,000 from the mid-1950s

▲ **DECEMBER 15, 1917:** First Nations members from the Crooked Lake area haul wood into Broadview to sell. Saskatchewan Archives Board R-B7336.

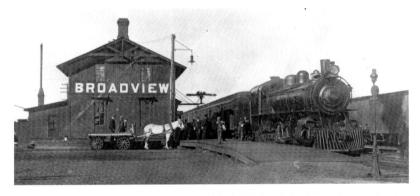

▲ **ALL ABOARD!** The CPR station at Broadview, circa 1915. Saskatchewan Archives Board R-A 18896.

▼ **KING GEORGE VI AND QUEEN ELIZABETH**, parents of our present Queen, visiting Broadview in 1939. Photograph courtesy of the Grenfell Museum.

▲ **SASKATCHEWAN'S MOST FAMOUS GOAT:** Sergeant Bill left his hometown of Broadview to serve as the mascot of the Fifth Canadian Battalion in France during WWI. Bill was gassed, wounded, and decorated (his medals included the 1914 Star, the General Service Medal, and the Victory Medal) before he safely returned to Canada, finishing his years out to pasture in his hometown. After his death, plans were to display him in the province's proposed War Memorial Museum. Instead, Bill resided briefly during the 1920s in the reading room of the Saskatchewan Legislative Building (the area where he stood in the reading room became a designated meeting place), and then returned to Broadview, where he is now honoured in the Broadview Museum. Saskatchewan Archives Board R-A10210-1.

through the 1960s, and in recent years the community has undertaken a number of economic development initiatives to help reverse the subsequent decline. Today, Broadview has a varied business community, a hospital and a special care home, an RCMP detachment, and a volunteer fire department. Broadview School is a K-12 facility with 137 students enrolled in the fall of 2006. The town also has a range of recreational facilities, including an ice-skating and hockey rink, a curling club, ball diamonds, tennis courts, rodeo grounds, a bowling alley, and a nine-hole golf course. Less than a half-an-hour drive from Broadview, the Cowessess First Nation operates one of the most picturesque and challenging 18-hole championship-level golf courses in the province, and the Ochapowace Ski Resort offers some of Saskatchewan's finest runs and facilities. The town of Broadview also has a number of community service clubs and organizations. Among them are the Lions, Kinettes, a senior citizens club, the Historical Society, and the Horticultural Society. The community has six churches. The extensive Broadview Museum site houses a collection of heritage buildings and

pioneer artifacts and a display honouring Saskatchewan's most famous goat, Sgt. Bill. Broadview serves as the administrative centre of the RM of Elcapo No. 154.

BROCK, village, pop 115 (2006c), 130 (2001c), is located between Rosetown and Kindersley, just south of the junction of Hwys 7 and 30. The first homesteaders began breaking land in the district around 1906, somewhat to the disdain of ranchers, who felt good ranching country was being spoiled and who warned the new landholders that they would go broke, that the area was too dry for farming grain. With the construction of the railway from Rosetown through to Alberta at the end of the decade, Brock was founded, and in 1910 the settlement gained village status. The community's name honours Major-General Sir Isaac Brock (1769-1812), who commanded the forces of Upper Canada during the War of 1812 and who was killed at the Battle of Queenston Heights on October 13 that year. The population of the village of Brock was 117 in 1911. With steady growth, the community was approaching 200 by the end of the 1920s.

▼ **THE BROCK HOTEL**, at the northwest corner of Main Street and 1st Avenue North. Photograph taken September 11, 2003.

In the early 1950s, a burgeoning oil and gas industry was developing in the region, and drilling in the Brock gas field produced one of the first successful wells. In 1950, the only natural gas service in the province was provided by local independent operators in Lloydminster, Unity, and Kamsack; however, in 1952 Brock and the nearby town of Kindersley were the first communities in Saskatchewan to be connected to the beginnings of a provincially-owned distribution system. In 1953, the network was extended to neighbouring communities and the city of Saskatoon. The 1950s were good years for Brock; the community reached a peak population of 240 in 1956. Over the past few decades, businesses, services, and village institutions, such as the school, have been lost to the larger centres in the region; however, Brock retains a core of essential businesses and is a well-kept and pleasant community, with many of the amenities of the nearby larger centres. Agricultural and oilfield industries form the basis of the regional economy. Brock is situated in the RM of Kindersley No. 290.

BRODERICK, village, pop 77 (2006c), 83 (2001c), is located on Hwy 15, approximately 10 km east of Outlook and the South Saskatchewan River valley. Settlement of the region began around 1903-04. Many of these early homesteaders disembarked the train at Hanley. Until the railroad through the Broderick area was built, Hanley was where district residents often went to obtain supplies and deliver grain, a distance of roughly 50 kilometres. As the railway approached Broderick in 1908, there came a steady stream of settlers of diverse origins: one of the largest concentrations of Norwegians in Saskatchewan settled in the region, together with

Czechs, Poles, English, and Scots, among others. With rail service, the townsite developed rapidly: elevators, stores, lumber yards, and other businesses sprang up, and Broderick attained village status on September 13, 1909. Community institutions were established: a school was built and churches erected, and for a few years Broderick had its own newspaper, *The Broderick Advocate.* Progress was steady until 1929, when a fire destroyed half of the community's businesses. The damage was extensive since Broderick's small fire engine was malfunctioning at the time. The 1930s resulted in some of the community's population moving; however, after WWII a level of prosperity returned, and in 1961 Broderick reached a peak population of 141. In the following years, though, the village began to quickly decline. Community churches shut their doors toward the end of the 1960s. In 1972, the school was closed, with children subsequently being bused to Outlook. In 1976, the administrative office for the RM of Rudy No. 284, which had been established in Broderick in 1909, moved to the town of Outlook as well. One by one commercial establishments began to go out of business. Today, most residents of the village who are in the workforce find employment either in Outlook or in the district's agricultural industry. Large storage facilities for the area's potato and hay crops are located on the outskirts of Broderick, as is a crop production centre, a joint venture between district farmers and Agricore United. The Broderick reservoir, just south of the village, has excellent year-round fishing. The Honourable Mr. Justice John Sopinka (1933-1997) was born in the Broderick area, and in 1988 he became the first Canadian of Ukrainian heritage to serve with the Supreme Court of Canada.

BROOKSBY, hamlet, is located north of Star City on Municipal Road No. 681. Settlement of the area began around 1900, and among the first to take up land in the region were people of British, Slavic, Scandinavian, and Jewish origins. In the late 1930s and early 1940s, Ukrainians migrated to the district from southern and central areas of the province. Brooksby developed along the rail line that was built north-eastwards from Melfort to Ridgedale in the early 1920s — the line was extended to Carrot River a decade later. The Brooksby Post Office was established on December 1, 1922, replacing the Willow Springs Post Office which had operated a couple of miles to the southwest since 1913. The hamlet that grew up around the railway point was never very large: the population was estimated to be 66 in 1966. By 1972, though, it was down to 36. Today, there are two seed farms at Brooksby and the office of the RM of Willow Creek No. 458. A landmark is a former Saskatchewan Wheat Pool elevator. Nine kilometres north of Brooksby stands the Beth Israel Synagogue, the only rural synagogue left in Saskatchewan. Built circa 1908, the building served as a place of worship until 1964. The synagogue, adjacent cemetery and surrounding wooded area have been declared a historic site.

BROWNLEE, village, pop 50 (2006c), 55 (2001c), is located northwest of Moose Jaw on Hwy 42. The available land in the Brownlee area was largely occupied by 1904-05, but until the railway came through, trips had to be made to places such as Caron on the CPR main line to obtain supplies. Flour was ground in Moose Jaw and wood for fence posts and building construction was gathered in the Qu'Appelle Valley. As the railway was being built into the area, several small businesses sprang up on the Brownlee townsite. Trains were running in 1908, and the fledgling community was incorporated as a village on December 29 that year. The village was named after James Brownlee (1859-1912), CPR superintendent at Moose Jaw from 1903-07. By the end of the 1920s, close to three dozen businesses lined Brownlee's streets and the population of the village stood at approximately 150, with substantially more people living in the surrounding countryside. In 1929, on the eve of the Depression, disaster struck the community. A large portion of the main business thoroughfare (Herbert Street) burned to the ground. The fire was seen for miles. One of the biggest losses to the community was the hotel. Built in 1909, it had contained a bowling alley, dance floor, restaurant, and bar. Because of the Depression, the village did not regain many of the enterprises that were lost in the blaze, and Brownlee never recovered its previous level of commercial activity and prosperity. One building to survive the flames was that of the Bank of Commerce, built in 1919. The bank itself, however, did not survive the 1930s, and the Brownlee village council took over ownership of the property in the 1940s. Still standing, the building was designated a heritage property in 1990. Over the past couple of decades the village of Brownlee has substantially declined. The fair-sized school, built in the mid-1960s, has been boarded up; the last church sits closed; and a number of abandoned businesses line the streets. A lone farm equipment repair shop and parts dealer remains. Most of the residents of the Brownlee area are engaged in farming, primarily grain and oilseed production, along with some livestock. The district is also popular with hunters, as it is home to good populations of deer, antelope, and waterfowl. Grant Devine, the premier of Saskatchewan from 1982-1991, graduated from Brownlee high school in 1962. Brownlee is situated in the RM of Eyebrow No. 193.

BRUNO, town, pop 495 (2006c), 571 (2001c), is located approximately 90 km east of Saskatoon, 7 km north of Hwy 5. The area terrain is gently rolling, with about 80 per cent of the land farmed, and the remainder aspen groves, wetlands, and prairie. The community is named for its founder, Reverend Bruno Doerfler, a Benedictine Father who came to the area in 1902 with a small number of German Catholic families from Minnesota. In 1903, more German American settlers arrived at the fledgling religious colony, and after the railway was completed in 1905 homesteaders poured into the district. In addition to the German population, largely from the U.S. but also from Europe, the Bruno area would also come to be comprised of people of French and Ukrainian backgrounds. The Village of Bruno was incorporated on March 9, 1909. On the eve of World War I, as convents in Germany were being taken over by the government for military use, a number of Ursuline Sisters sought refuge in Canada and, upon Father Doerfler's urging, a group eventually settled in Bruno. An Ursuline convent was opened in 1919, followed by St. Ursula's Academy in 1922. The community, however, like many other early prairie

▲ **SOME OF THE ABANDONED BUSINESSES** that now line Herbert Street in Brownlee. Photographs taken October 7, 2006.

▲ **THE URSULINE CENTRE IN BRUNO.** During the 1960s, it is estimated that there were more the 100 Ursuline Sisters based in the community. Photograph taken August 9, 2004.

settlements, would experience its growing pains. In 1916, a fire destroyed half of the businesses on Bruno's main street, which compelled the village council to make two decisions: first, an order that all persons have brick chimneys; and second, the purchase of fire fighting equipment. The Bruno village council would also have more mundane chores to deal with over the years. As automobiles became common, as they were by 1919, a bylaw was enacted setting the speed limit at 12 mph; interestingly, though, this came to be deemed to be too fast for, in 1924, the speed limit was lowered to 10 mph. The village continued to grow steadily over the years. On January 1, 1962, Bruno gained town status. The community has always had a somewhat diversified economy: in addition to the convent and the Academy, Bruno also had a clay works for a number of years. The primary economic base of the area, however, has always been agriculture, which today involves grains, oil seeds, hogs, cattle, and turkeys. The pot-

ash mines at Colonsay and Allan provide additional employment. Bruno also has a number of local businesses, a range of recreational facilities, and Bruno School, a K-12 facility, which had a staff of 16 and 166 students enrolled in the fall of 2005. The community has a volunteer fire department; policing is provided by the Humboldt RCMP detachment. Bruno has a seniors' housing complex with offices for medical practitioners who visit the community once a week. The nearest hospitals are located in Humboldt and Saskatoon. In 1999, community hopes were high when the University of Saskatchewan took over management of the Ursuline Academy, which had closed in 1982 due to a lack of personnel. The facility became the U. of S. Bruno Ursuline Campus, but after five years of trying to overcome operating deficits reaching up to $100,000 annually, the University pulled out, returning the campus to its original owners, the Ursuline Sisters. The complex has been renamed the Prairie Ursuline Centre;

however, its economic viability and future remain uncertain. Bruno had a peak population of 784 in 1986. The community serves as the administrative centre of the RM of Bayne No. 371.

B-SAY-TAH, resort village, is spread out along the south shore of Echo Lake on Hwy 210, between Fort Qu'Appelle to the east and Echo Valley Provincial Park to the west. B-Say-Tah Point is a major feature of the lake. Structures began to appear along the beachfront in the early 1900s and B-Say-Tah was incorporated in 1915. Development, however, has substantially increased since the 1970s. The 2001 Census recorded 177 year-round residents, and the 2006 Census, 206; however, the summer population can be significantly higher. As such, many area services are seasonal operations. The fish hatchery at B-Say-Tah, begun in 1913, is open to the public from May to the Labour Day long weekend. The station produces a wide range of native and exotic species and distributes 40 to 50 million fish per year in

over 200 bodies of water throughout Saskatchewan. The hatchery plays a major role in the province's fisheries resource, helping to support more than 3,400 jobs in the commercial and sport fishing industries. Over the years, the hatchery has stocked provincial waters with more than 2 billion fish. B-Say-Tah is situated in the RM of North Qu'Appelle No. 187.

BUCHANAN, village, pop 225 (2006c), 233 (2001c), is located 25 km northwest of Canora at the junction of Hwys 5 and 47. Good Spirit Lake lies to the south. The district began to be sparsely settled in the 1880s, and Buchanan derives its name from Robert Buchanan, a prominent early rancher. In 1899, Doukhobors arrived and began establishing a number of communal villages in the district; however, most of these would be abandoned within several years and the Doukhobors who remained in the area then became independent farmers or businessmen. Ukrainians also began settling the region toward the end of nine-

▲ **AFTER A MORNING RAIN:** Central Avenue, Buchanan, July 27, 2004. In 1955, four grain companies — the Saskatchewan Wheat Pool, the Federal Grain Co., the National Grain Co. (two elevators), and Ogilvie Flour Mills — were in business in the village. Today, only the Saskatchewan Wheat Pool remains, maintaining a farm service centre.

teenth century, and significant numbers of Polish settlers began arriving in the immediate area of Buchanan in 1901; Norwegians and Swedes would round out the cultural milieu a few years later. The Canadian Northern Railway reached the site of Buchanan in 1905; grain elevators were built, and in 1906 the community post office and school were established. Buchanan was incorporated as a village on June 11, 1907. The community continued to develop and grow into the 1950s, reaching a peak population of 538 in 1951, with a business sector serving a much more populous countryside; the community had five grain elevators at this time. The village population began to drop dramatically in the late 1970s, and in recent years Buchanan's school was closed; students now attend classes in Canora. The community's existent businesses provide groceries, automotive and financial services to area residents, and a number cater to the district's agricultural industry. The area surrounding Buchanan supports the production of cereals, oilseeds, and specialty crops, as well as livestock operations. Village recreational facilities include skating and curling rinks, a community centre, and a seniors' club. There are four churches in Buchanan. The nearest medical and police services are located in Canora, while fire protection is provided by the fire department in Sturgis. Lois E. Hole, prominent gardener, writer, speaker, and Alberta's fifteenth lieutenant governor, was born and raised in Buchanan. Buchanan serves as the administrative centre of the RM of Buchanan No. 304.

▶ **IN THE WATERS OF LAST MOUNTAIN LAKE** just off the beach at Buena Vista. Photograph taken mid-July, 1999.

BUENA VISTA, village, pop 490 (2006c), 397 (2001c), is a rapidly developing community located on Last Mountain Lake immediately southeast of Regina Beach. Homesteaders were making incursions into the area in the 1880s and, by the early 1900s, the locale that came to be known as Buena Vista — Spanish, meaning a good or beautiful view — was gaining popularity as a summer resort destination. With the CPR running through Buena Vista and Regina Beach in 1912, the area became more accessible to residents of Regina, and for many years the railroad ran excursion trains from the city to the lakeshore resorts. Swimming, picnicking, fishing, sailing, and dancing were the popular area attractions. Buena Vista was subdivided for cottage development in the 1920s, and from 1930 to 1954 a post office operated during the months of July and August. In the 1920s, and again in the 1950s and 1960s, a church group ran summer camps at the beach. Buena Vista was incorporated as a resort village in 1970 and was elevated to village status in 1983. Over the past few decades

the number of year-round residents has increased dramatically. The permanent population was 28 in 1971, 112 in 1981, 276 in 1991. Today, in addition to the permanently-inhabited residences, there are over 150 seasonally-occupied properties. There are no commercial businesses in the community; people utilize the amenities of Regina Beach and the city of Regina. Children attend elementary school in Regina Beach and high school in Lumsden, and a significant number of those in Buena Vista's workforce commute to work in the city. Buena Vista is situated in the RM of Lumsden No. 189.

BUFFALO NARROWS, northern village, pop 1,081 (2006c), 1,137 (2001c), is located in north-western Saskatchewan between the communities of Ile-a-la-Crosse and La Loche on Hwy 155. Buffalo Narrows is situated on the channel or "narrows" between Peter Pond and Churchill lakes, and prior to the establishment of a permanent settlement, the area was an ancient hunting site that provided a bottleneck into which Aboriginal hunters could drive wood bison or "buffalo." Aboriginal people had also long come to the narrows to catch and dry fish during the summer months, and in the 1790s the first fur trading posts were established in the area. The first people to settle permanently at Buffalo Narrows arrived in 1895, but for many years the locale was frequented only by transient trappers and fishermen, and the settlement developed very slowly. After WWI, and through the 1930s, there was an influx of people — many Norwegian, German, and Scottish — who came to work in commercial fishing operations and to trap. People also relocated to the district from the communities of Ile-a-la-Crosse and La Loche; oth-

ers moved in from scattered and remote outlying sites so their children could get an education and so that they could be closer to other services which were slowly being developed. A school was established at Buffalo Narrows in 1934, and a post office in 1936. The settlement began to grow, and from a population of fewer than 100 in 1935 Buffalo Narrows had grown to a community of over 200 by 1942. In addition to an economy based on fishing, trapping, and intermittent logging operations, mink ranching was developed in the area on a large scale. By 1950-51, there were 13 mink ranches in the vicinity of Buffalo Narrows, with several stocking over 1,000 animals. By the late 1960s, however, the price of mink pelts fell dramatically while input costs were going up; operators began going out of business, and by 1975 there were no mink ranches left in the area. The end of the industry was a devastating blow to the local economy and resulted in increasing unemployment and a reliance on welfare. Trapping also was in decline and the local commercial fishing industry had peaked during the 1960s and 1970s. From the 1940s until 1965, the Department of Natural Resources had administered the community, but then local government was established and, through the 1970s, community infrastructure was greatly improved. Better homes were built, long distance telephone service was introduced, a new airport capable of handling small jets was opened, and in 1980 a bridge across the narrows was opened, finally linking the community to the provincial highway system. The bridge replaced the ferry service begun in 1957 when the first road reached toward the community. Buffalo Narrows was incorporated as a northern village in 1983 and, subsequently, has developed into a significant regional centre providing government and commercial

▲ ▶ **WATER WORLD:** For many years access to Buffalo Narrows (above) was primarily by water. Later, float planes (such as the one pictured to the right) and then wheeled aircraft, became the dominant means of transportation. Only in recent decades has travel by road into Buffalo Narrows been possible. Photographs taken September 19, 2003.

services to the northwest of the province. The population is largely comprised of people of Cree, Dene, and European origins; the community's Metis population is estimated to be between 80 and 90 per cent. The median age is just over 25, while the average age in Saskatchewan is close to 37. There are small numbers of non-Aboriginal, non-Metis people, including some of Asian origin. Government offices and services are significant employers, as are businesses in the areas of mining, forestry, construction, fishing, and wild rice harvesting. Tourism is also important, and there are a number of local outfitters and airlines. There are a number of small businesses, and many people are employed in the service industry. Yet, while the economy is diverse, the

unemployment rate was last recorded at 19.8 per cent, compared to 6.3 per cent for the province. Thus, economic development is high on the community's agenda. The Buffalo Narrows Friendship Centre helps to seek solutions to socio-economic problems facing residents, and provides cultural, recreational, educational, and social programs for all ages and all people of the community. Buffalo Narrows has a pre-school and a daycare centre. The K-12 school had 310 students enrolled in the fall of 2006, and Northlands College offers programs and services for adult learners. Buffalo Narrows also has its own radio station, an RCMP detachment, and a community health centre. In the fall of 2004, controversy erupted when a sign was erected on the village outskirts declar-

ing Buffalo Narrows a Metis community; it was an issue of local politics that made national headlines.

BULYEA, village, pop 104 (2006c), 107 (2001c), is located southeast of Strasbourg on Hwy 20, approximately 20 km east of Last Mountain Lake. The beginning of settlement in the area dates to 1882-83, with people of Scottish, English, and Irish origins arriving from eastern Canada and Britain. By the mid-1880s, large numbers of people of German origin had settled in the surrounding districts, largely to the north and east. Many area residents had anticipated that a railway would be constructed up the east side of Last Mountain Lake toward Prince Albert in the not-too-distant future, so when the line was instead routed west of the lake, some of the early settlers moved on. For years, grain would have to be hauled either to Craven or Lumsden, and even Regina served as a market centre for Bulyea district residents. It would not be

until 1905 that the CPR finished its line between Lipton and Strasbourg, and with rail service an influx of new settlers began to stream into the area. Many Norwegians rounded out the cultural mosaic. With the advent of the railway the village developed, and by 1908 Bulyea had a variety of businesses, including a hotel and three grain elevators. The village was incorporated in 1909 and was named after George H.V. Bulyea, who had served in the Territorial Assembly before becoming Alberta's first lieutenant governor in 1905. In 1911, the village of Bulyea received a substantial boost when the rail line connecting the community to Regina was completed; the first run into Bulyea was inaugurated with a band playing and speeches given by local spokespeople and visiting dignitaries from the city. In the coming decades, Bulyea and the surrounding area would become noted for two developments of historical significance to both the province and the country. On July 1, 1925, the Saskatchewan Wheat Pool opened its first elevator in the village (it still stands), and in the late

▲ **CHEERS!** The interior of the first bar in Bulyea, circa 1912. Saskatchewan Archives Board R-B10842.

▲ **A PIECE OF PRAIRIE HISTORY:** Saskatchewan Wheat Pool No. 1 sits in the middle of the adjoining structures pictured here. Built in 1925, it was converted into a crib storage annex in the late 1960s. On its left is a frame annex constructed in 1955; the large wood crib elevator on the right went into operation in 1968. Photograph taken July 10, 2003.

1930s a municipal health care system was introduced by the district reeve, Matthew S. Anderson, which served as a model for plans later developed both provincially and then nationally. A marker just south of Bulyea commemorates Anderson's contributions. Today, Bulyea is an attractive and quiet community that provides supplies and services to the district's farmers, and Bulyea's school provides K-6 education to village and area students, with 43 enrolled in the fall of 2006. Older students attend classes in Strasbourg. A local village sign crafter, Don Renwick, a grandson of one of the district's earliest pioneers, makes signs that honour recipients of the province's Century Family Farm Award. Bulyea had a peak population of 193 in 1961 and is situated in the RM of McKillop No. 220.

BURGIS BEACH, organized hamlet, is a long-established resort community located on the east side of Good Spirit Lake. There are more than 200 cottages and an increasing number of year-round residents: the 2001 Census recorded a permanent population of 45; the 2006 Census counted 90. There are campsites and a community hall at Burgis Beach and a store which operates during the summer months. Canora and Yorkton are the nearest major centres. Burgis Beach is situated in the RM of Good Lake No. 274.

BURR, hamlet, is located approximately 18 km south of Humboldt on Hwy 20. The locale owes its name to J.C. Burr, who established the Burr Post Office on March 1, 1906, several kilometres west of the present hamlet. Burr remained the postmaster until he resigned in 1924, after which the post office was closed for several years. The office re-opened at its present location in 1931 after the CPR came through the area linking Lanigan and Humboldt. The population of Burr was never very large — it was approximately 37 in 1966, but it was down to about 14 by 1972. The rail line through the community was abandoned in the early 1990s. Today, the hamlet has only a few residents, yet the post office remains operational, and Burr continues to serve as the administrative centre of the RM of Wolverine No. 340.

BURSTALL, town, pop 315 (2006c), 388 (2001c), is located southwest of Leader, just inside the Saskatchewan-Alberta border on Hwy 321. Situated in the heart of a large natural gas–producing region, Burstall lies within close proximity to a number of huge gas plants and compressor stations. The community's name honours Sir Henry Edward Burstall (1870-1944), a Canadian military commander of great distinction who served in both the Boer and First World Wars. Settlers began trickling into the Burstall district around 1907-08 (there had been a few ranchers earlier), and by the outbreak of the First World War most of the available land in the area was taken up for homesteads. The village itself began with the CPR's decision to build a railway branch line into the area from Leader in the early 1920s. Businessmen began arriving and setting up shops, and Burstall was incorporated as a village May 31, 1921. The railway was operational in 1923, and within a few years it would be extended further south to Richmound and Fox Valley. Until the 1950s, Burstall, like many other Saskatchewan communities that sprang up along rail lines, was an agricultural service centre. Its population remained fairly stable at around 200. However, since construction of the Trans-Canada Pipeline began near Burstall in 1956, the natural gas industry has been a dominant area employer. By 1963, both the new industry and the community's population were booming. On November 1, 1976, Burstall was incorporated as a town, and the population that year was recorded at 548. That same year another notable event took place a few kilometres east of the town. Excavation work for the laying of another pipeline unearthed evidence of a prehistoric human settlement. The subsequent archaeological dig revealed evidence of a culture dating back roughly 5,000 years. Today, Burstall is a modern town with a diverse business community and wide, tree-lined, paved streets. There is a volunteer fire department and a team of volunteer first responders; police service is provided by the RCMP detachment based in Leader. Recreational facilities in-

▼ **PACIFIC DRIVE IN RESIDENTIAL BURSTALL** looks much like suburbia in any modern city. Photograph taken August 30, 2003.

clude an indoor swimming pool, a skating arena and a curling rink, a bowling alley, fitness centre, ball park, golf course, and a community hall for social occasions. Burstall School provides K-12 education to approximately 75 students. In fall, the area is popular with hunters. Burstall serves as the administrative centre of the RM of Deer Forks No. 232.

CABRI, town, pop 439 (2006c), 483 (2001c), is located approximately 65 km northwest of Swift Current on Hwy 32 and 60 km north of Gull Lake via Hwy 37. The community is situated between the South Saskatchewan River and the Great Sand Hills. In the late 1800s, only a handful of ranchers were operating in the district; however, the days of the wide open range were numbered, particularly after the winter of 1906-07 devastated the cattle industry. The area was then being opened up to homesteaders. By 1908 settlers were breaking and fencing the land. The village of Cabri had its beginnings in 1911 as the CPR was building its line from just west of Swift Current north-westward toward Empress, Alberta. Entrepreneurs flocked to a barren townsite, and by the time the first scheduled train pulled into Cabri in 1912, a couple of dozen businesses were already in operation, and the village was incorporated on May 13 that year. Growth was rapid and within five years, on April 16, 1917, Cabri gained town status. By 1918, an impressive string of nine grain elevators lined the railway tracks. By 1921, the population had reached 532. But the community was to have its trials and tribulations. In 1924, Cabri suffered a debilitating economic blow when the Home Bank closed its doors and 659 people lost their savings. The town council petitioned the Federal Government for protection for the depositors, but to no avail. Another problem the community faced was with water or, rather, a lack of it. Numerous wells were dug over the years, but it would not be until 1981 and the completion of a pipeline from Lake Diefenbaker that Cabri attained an adequate water supply. Water has also often been a problem for the area grain growers, and crop failures have been common. The low precipitation the region receives discouraged farmers for years, but the thirties were simply too much for some people and many left the area. In 1931, Cabri's population was 552; but by 1936 it was 394. Brightening the community's spirits over the years, however, was the Cabri Brass Band. It came to be renowned throughout the province, and one of its members, Bobby Gimby (1919-98), later gained national attention through the 1940s and 1950s with the cast of CBC Radio's 'Happy Gang.' Gimby is today best remembered as the composer of the 1967 Centennial song "Canada" ("One little two little three little Canadians…"), and he received the Order of Canada for his contribution to the country's national identity. Post-WWII, Cabri entered a period of unprecedented prosperity and growth. Agricultural technology had improved, and with fertilizers, herbicides, and some irrigation the heavy clay gumbo produced higher yields. With the discovery of oil in the region in the early 1950s, and the construction of the Trans-Canada Pipeline a few kilometres from town in 1956, came more people and exciting times. By 1971, the community had grown non-stop since the end of the war, and the census that year recorded that the town's population had swollen to 737. How large Cabri might grow then seemed uncertain. In subsequent decades, however, with improved roads, fewer people farming the countryside, and the abandonment of

CABRI ...on the Empress Line

Historical photographs are courtesy of the Cabri Museum.

▲ **CABRI FROM THE EAST**, August 29, 2003.

▲ **CABRI'S FIRST BUILDINGS**, December 3, 1911.

▲ **JACK T. MUNDELL** with his team of horses, circa 1917. Mundell hauled water to the residents of Cabri from a well south of town. He went house to house, selling water for five cents a pail.

▲ **SEVEN OF NINE ELEVATORS** can be seen in this 1928 photograph of Cabri; Archie Livingston's McCormick-Deering farm equipment dealership is in the foreground.

◄ **CABRI BAND, 1932.** Fourth from the left in the front row, holding a coronet, was Bobby Gimby, later known as "The Pied Piper of Canada." The boy seated in front of the drum was Milburn Trembath, who played drums with the band for nearly 78 years until his passing in 2007.

▼ **ON THE 60TH ANNIVERSARY** of Cabri's attaining town status, celebrations took place June 30 to July 3, 1977. A feature was a vocal performance by Clarice Redmond, Brenda Fahselt, Shirley Hoogeveen, and Joan McGuigan (front row); and Olive Telke, Betty Goddard, and Teri Forrest (back row).

▲ **AN EARLY RESIDENT OF CABRI** was Woo Sing, who arrived in 1913, a tailor by trade. For the next 55 years, he worked mainly as a tailor in the community, with dry cleaning as a sideline. He left Cabri in 1969.

rail service, the population returned closer to the community's historic average. Although agriculture and its subsidiary activities remain the backbone of the district, the recent discovery of large reserves of natural gas in the area has proven a bit of a boon, putting some dollars in the local economy and providing some off-farm employment. Today, Cabri remains an important centre in the district, providing shopping and services, accommodations, restaurants, banking, a library, and churches. There is an RCMP detachment, a health care centre, a seniors' centre, and a playschool. The community also has an active theatre group, the Prairie Players, as well as an impressive museum. Cabri School provides K-12 education to roughly 100 students. Recreational facilities include a skating and curling complex, ball diamonds, a tennis court, a fitness club, and an outdoor swimming pool. Nearby are both the Miry Creek Golf Course and Cabri Regional Park (located on the South Saskatchewan River), which provides opportunities for camping, fishing and other water sports. The Cabri region also attracts hunters from across North America. Pronghorn antelope, and mule and whitetail deer are found in abundance, as are a variety of geese and as many as 20 species of duck. Cabri is situated in the RM of Riverside No. 168.

CACTUS LAKE, organized hamlet, is located in west-central Saskatchewan, southeast of Macklin on Hwy 317. Settlers first began arriving in the district in 1906-07, but it was not until 1930 and the construction of the CNR line between Unity and Bodo, Alberta, that the community of Cactus Lake began to develop, its name derived from a body of water immediately to the northwest, along which several varieties of cacti grow. The hamlet of Cactus Lake had a peak population of about 75 in the mid-1930s, and the community once boasted three grain elevators, stores, a café, a hardware and a garage business, the office of the rural municipality, a blacksmith shop, a flour mill, and a dance hall. Cactus Lake even had a competitive hockey team. In 1950, a rural school (Edenview School) was moved into the community, and in 1951 Cactus Lake was established as an organized hamlet. But by the mid-1960s the community was in decline. The school was closed in 1965, and children were subsequently bused to either Macklin or Denzil to attend classes. In early 1966 the RM office was relocated to Luseland. The population at the time was then hovering around 40. In the 1970s, there was a reduction in the number of elevator agents working in the hamlet, and by the end of the decade the community had fewer than 10 residents. In the mid-1990s, the rail line was abandoned. Only two people were reportedly living in Cactus Lake by 2004. There is still a post office operating to serve the district, and there are a few homes which are used seasonally by American hunters. Cactus Lake is situated in the RM of Heart's Hill No. 352, and the RM shop remains in the hamlet.

CADILLAC

CADILLAC, village, pop 80 (2006c), 95 (2001c), is located 18 km west of Ponteix at the junction of Hwys 4 and 13. The first few homesteaders began arriving in the area in 1907-08, and over the next few years the district was increasingly dotted with settlers' shacks. Settlers to the area were largely a combination of English and French speaking people. The first arrivals

▲ **ROOMS AND A WATERING HOLE:** The original Cadillac Hotel was built in 1914; it was three stories high and had over thirty rooms. It burned down in 1946 and the present hotel was erected on the same site in 1947. It is still in business. Photograph taken June 22, 2003.

travelled to Swift Current by train and then ventured south overland from there. After the railway reached the village of Neville in 1912, the trek was cut by more than half. The Cadillac Post Office was established in 1911, about 2.5 kilometres east of the present community, its name derived from Cadillac, Michigan—Michigan being where the first postmaster, Claude Ive Bristol, was born. A school (originally known as Elmwood School) began serving the Cadillac district children in 1912. The CPR determined the location of the townsite in 1913 as the railroad was progressing westward toward Shaunavon. Entrepreneurial adventurers arrived and set about establishing a number of businesses, "squatting" until the townsite was surveyed and they could gain titles for their properties. The post office was moved in from the countryside in 1914, and the community adopted its name. The Village of Cadillac was incorporated on July 2 that year. The population grew to somewhat over 200 by the 1920s and hovered around that mark until the 1950s, when Cadillac experienced another period of growth. In 1956, the village reached a peak population of 300. In recent decades,

as the community's numbers have fallen, Cadillac's original business district has very much deteriorated, and the few active businesses are now located on the highway. The train station was closed in 1969, and recently the former school building (the school itself closed a few years ago) has been converted into an artist's studio. The major industry in the area is agriculture, largely a combination of grain and livestock production. Cadillac is situated in the RM of Wise Creek No. 77.

CALDER

CALDER, village, pop 80 (2006c), 109 (2001c), is located east of Yorkton, south off Hwy 10, approximately 13 km west of the Saskatchewan/Manitoba border. Settlement of the region began as early as the mid-1880s with people of Icelandic, German and British origins taking up land generally to the south and east of the present village site. Many arrived via the railway points at Saltcoats and Langenburg. In 1897, large numbers of Ukrainians began settling the Calder area. In 1908 the townsite was surveyed, and in 1910 the railway came through. The village was incorporated on January 18, 1911, and was named after James Alexander Calder (1868-1956), teacher, school inspector, member of the Territorial Government under Frederick Haultain, a key Cabinet Minister in Walter Scott's government, and a member of the House of Commons and then the Senate. The village of Calder became a trading centre in a region of mixed agriculture and grew to a peak population of close to 300 in the early 1950s. In recent decades many

▲ **THE EAST SIDE OF MAIN STREET**, looking south, Calder, Saskatchewan, July 12, 2004. The building with the Canadian flag is the community hall.

of the village's businesses and services have been superseded by those in the nearby city of Yorkton, and the rail line through Calder was abandoned in 1997. Calder School, however, remains an important community institution, providing elementary level education to village and area students. Calder is situated in the RM of Calder No. 241.

CAMSELL PORTAGE, northern settlement, pop 37 (2001c), is Saskatchewan's northernmost community, situated roughly 40 km northwest of Uranium City as the crow flies. Camsell Portage is located on a beautiful site, nestled in a secluded clear-water bay on the north shore of Lake Athabasca, surrounded on three sides by large Precambrian rock hills thinly covered with shallow-rooted trees. One of the province's most remote communities, Camsell Portage is accessible only by air or by water, or by snowmobile from Uranium City during winter. The community developed as a trappers' settlement in the early 1900s and is named for a nearby historic portage which connects Lake Athabasca to the great lakes of the Northwest Territories. The portage itself was named after Dr. Charles Camsell (1876-1958), the son of a Hudson's Bay Company factor who became recognized as a visionary geologist, map-maker, and explorer. Camsell served with the Geological Survey of Canada and the Department of Mines and Resources, and was a member of the National Research Council and the Commissioner of the Northwest Territories; he was also the founder and first president of the Royal Canadian Geographical Society. The population of Camsell Portage was once approximately 250 (largely Metis of Cree, European and Euro-Canadian ancestry who hailed from the

▲ **SASKATCHEWAN'S NORTHERNMOST COMMUNITY:** Camsell Portage, late 1940s. Saskatchewan Archives Board, Saskatchewan Photographic Services Agency collection, R-PS3228. Vern Kent, photographer.

areas of Lac La Biche and Fort Fitzgerald, Alberta), but with the creation of Uranium City in 1952 many people and services moved. Work in the area's 45 now-abandoned mines provided some employment for those remaining (the population was 87 in 1972), but the closure of the mines in the early 1980s caused the settlement's numbers to further decline. The community today engages in traditional activities such as fishing, hunting and trapping; and seasonal resources, such as the Beverly Caribou Herd, add to the settlement's self-sufficiency. Camsell Portage has a Northern Settlement Office, an airstrip, a store, a community hall, an outdoor skating rink, and a small school which had only two students enrolled in the fall of 2006. A log church is a community landmark. Camsell Portage has satellite TV and internet services.

▼ **RAILWAY AVENUE**, Candiac, October 15, 2003.

CANDIAC, organized hamlet, pop 20 (2006c), 25 (2001c), is located in a mixed farming district approximately 15 km east of Montmartre on Hwy 48. Scots were homesteading just to the north and east as early as 1885, and in 1893 settlers from France settled the district, primarily at Montmartre. Poles and Ukrainians from Galicia settled in the Candiac area beginning in 1896. The community developed with the arrival of the Canadian Northern Railway in 1908, and the post office was established at the settlement in 1909. Once a bustling little community (it was established as an organized hamlet in 1949 and the population was close to 100 in the late 1960s), Candiac today resembles a ghost town, as numerous abandoned buildings line the quiet streets. Of interest is the Candiac Calvary Religious Shrine site constructed in 1940 by the area's Roman Catholic community; the landscaped grounds include the 14 Stations of the Cross. Candiac is situated in the RM of Montmartre No. 126.

▲ **CANDLE LAKE:** The lake was so named because a mysterious light can sometimes be seen on its surface. The Cree who traversed the area believed the light to be associated with an evil spirit; the modern scientific view is that the phenomenon is the result of ignis fatuus, the flickering phosphorescent light seen above marshy or swampy areas believed generated by the spontaneous combustion or release of gas (methane) from decomposing organic matter. Photograph taken September 23, 2003.

CANDLE LAKE, resort village, pop 792 (2006c), 503 (2001c), is a massive, rapidly-developing and increasingly upscale resort community located 77 km northeast of Prince Albert off Hwy 120. The resort village is situated at the south end of the large lake from which it derives its name. The resort area is comprised of approximately 2,000 cottages and permanent homes; thus, the temporary summer population can far exceed the permanent population cited above, and numerous subdivision developments continue to be built. Candle Lake Provincial Park, which includes approximately 300 campgrounds, also encompasses much of the lake's shore. Candle Lake possesses an array of stores, restaurants, lodgings, and services. Commercial fishing and trapping in the area date to as early as around 1912; people were permanently settling in the area in the 1920s; the post office was opened in 1936; and tourism began to develop in the late 1940s. Candle Lake was incorporated in 1977 and is situated in the RM of Paddockwood No. 520.

CANDO, hamlet, pop 102 (2001c), is a former village located roughly halfway between Biggar and the Battlefords on Hwy 4. Two First Nations — the Red Pheasant First Nation and the Mosquito, Grizzly Bear's Head, Lean Man First Nation — lie just to the north. Settlers began arriving in the area in the early 1900s, and one of them, Charles Alexander Edwards from Cando, North Dakota, established a post office on his homestead in January 1909, naming it after his home town. Edwards lived several kilometres southwest of the present community (at NW18-39-16-W3), but with the construction of the railway from just west of Biggar north toward Battleford the location of the townsite was established, and in 1913 the post office was relocated to serve the community just beginning to develop on the rail line. By 1966, the population had grown to 300, and Cando was established as an organized hamlet that year. In 1968, the community was incorporated as a village. The population began to decline rapidly thereafter, however, and as it did the community's businesses began to disappear. By 1976, Cando's numbers had fallen to 144, less than half of a decade earlier. CN abandoned the railway into the community at the end of 1989, and Cando relinquished village status on December 31, 2005. Today, the focal point of the community is the school, a K-12 facility that had 191 students enrolled in the fall of 2006. Students are from the hamlet, surrounding farms, and the neighbouring First Nations communities. Agriculture is the main industry in the area and there is a large hog production operation a few kilometres south of Cando. Cando is situated in the RM of Rosemount No. 378.

CANNINGTON LAKE, organized hamlet, is a small resort in the southeast corner of the province, just east of Moose Mountain Provincial Park near Cannington Manor Provincial Historic Park. The resort was developed in the 1970s around a bay on the east end of the lake from which it derived its name; the bay has since dried up and now only a few cabins are occupied during the summer months. The resort had offered camping, rental cabins, boat rentals, and miniature golf. Cannington Lake is located in the RM of Moose Mountain No. 63.

▼ **ALL SAINTS ANGLICAN CHURCH AND CEMETERY** at Cannington Manor Provincial Historic Park was built in 1884 and is one of the major attractions in the area of Cannington Lake. Today, the church is property of the Diocese of Qu'Appelle, and it is still used by the local congregation. Photograph taken September 13, 2006.

The heart of Good Spirit Country... Canora

CANORA, town, pop 2,013 (2006c), 2,200 (2001c), is located 48 km due north of Yorkton at the junction of Hwys 5 and 9. The district began to be settled just at the end of the nineteenth century. Doukhobors began establishing villages just to the east and west of the present townsite in 1899, and Romanians settled in the immediate area of Canora in the early 1900s. Most significant, however, was the Ukrainian population, arriving largely between 1897 and the outbreak of WWI. Canora was a creation of the Canadian Northern Railway which laid steel through the area in 1904. That same year, the post office and local school district were established. In 1905, Canora was incorporated as a village, its name derived from a combination of the first two letters of each word in Canadian Northern Railway. The community grew extremely rapidly. Canora attained town status in 1910 with a population of around 400, and by 1921 its citizenry numbered over 1,200. The population remained fairly stable over the next few decades (even through the Depression), but it began to rise again after WWII, reaching a peak of 2,734 in 1966. Canora benefits from its location at the corners of four adjacent rural municipalities which constitute a trading area of approximately 15,000 people in a district well-suited to successful crop and livestock production. Additionally, Canora is situated in a parkland setting surrounded by several lakes and parks, including Crystal Lake, Good Spirit Provincial Park, and Duck Mountain Provincial Park. There are numerous golf courses in the region, and tourism is also bolstered by the proximity of the nearby National Doukhobor Heritage Village, the grotto at Rama, and the sites of Fort Pelly and Fort Livingstone. Canora has one of the highest highway traffic counts in the province. Canora is also situated on VIA Rail's transcontinental line and is the rail link to Churchill, Manitoba, with its beluga whale and polar bear tours. The town's 1904 railway station remains the oldest operating station of its type in the province; it also houses a museum. Canora has a wide range of businesses and services, health

▲ **DOUKHOBORS MEET** in Canora in 1911 to welcome Peter Verigin to the town. Courtesy of the Canora CN Station House Museum.

▶ **PUTTING UP CANORA'S FIRST STREET SIGNS**, June 25, 1947. The men in the photograph from left to right are: John Frinuik, John Funk, Mayor Jim Parker, Frank Wasylkiw (town utility manager), and George Stratechuck (councillor). Courtesy of the Canora CN Station House Museum. Donated by Walter Mysak.

"Milestones" in Canora's Early History

1884 First ranchers arrived

1896 Area surveyed by Dominion Government

1897 First homesteaders, including 180 families from Western Ukraine

1904 Canadian Northern Railway laid tracks through Canora, station built and part of original townsite surveyed

1905 Incorporated as a village

1910 Incorporated as a town

1912 Canora Chamber of Commerce established

▲ **A POSTCARD** showing Canora in 1929. Courtesy of the Canora CN Station House Museum. Donated by Walter Mysak.

CANWOOD, village, pop 337 (2006c), 374 (2001c), is located in the parklands 24 km northwest of Shellbrook on Hwy 55; the reserve lands of the Ahtahkakoop Cree Nation lie a short distance to the west. The first settlers began arriving in the area around 1904; however, it was not until 1910 when the Canadian Northern Railway line was being built north from Shellbrook to Big River to bring lumber out of the area that significant settlement and development took place. Norwegians and Swedes were predominant among those coming into the district. Canwood was incorporated in 1916—its name a contraction of CANadian WOODs, paying homage to the area's logging industry. The timber trade was the key economic activity for many years, but by the end of WWII much of the brush and heavy bush in the district had been cleared and agriculture was becoming the primary economic concern. In 1951, one million bushels of grain were shipped out of Canwood's four elevators, and by the early 1960s area farms were producing one and a half million bushels of grain annually and about 5,000 head of cattle were being raised in the district. During the 1930s, Canwood's population took

care facilities and practitioners. Protection services are provided by the local RCMP and a 21-member volunteer fire brigade, which provides fire and rescue service to the town and three of the adjoining rural municipalities. Canora's junior elementary and composite schools together provide K-12 education to close to 400 students, and a regional college provides a range of programs for adult learners. The town's recreational facilities include curling and ice-skating rinks, tennis courts, ball diamonds, soccer fields, a swimming pool, parks and playgrounds, cross-country ski trails, many kilometres of snowmobile trails, and a serviced campground. A walking tour of the community between its several museums, heritage sites, and other attractions has also recently been developed. A Canora landmark unveiled in 1980 by Edward Shreyer, then Governor General of Canada, is "Lesia," a 15-foot statue of a Ukrainian woman dressed in traditional clothing who symbolically offers visitors to the community bread and salt, a customary sign of welcome among Ukrainians and other eastern Europeans. In 2003, Canora was

judged to have the best-tasting municipal drinking water in Canada at the 13th annual Berkeley Springs International Water Tasting Awards competition held in West Virginia. Saskatchewan's first woman lieutenant governor, Sylvia Fedoruk, was born in Canora in 1927. Canora serves as the administrative centre of the RM of Good Lake No. 274.

▼ **IN THE SECOND HALF OF THE TWENTIETH CENTURY**, as land was increasingly cleared, agriculture became the dominant industry in the Canwood district. This farm is located on the northeast edge of the village. Photograph taken September 22, 2003.

▼ **LOOKING SOUTHWEST ALONG THE NORTH SIDE OF MAIN STREET** in Canwood. From right to left: 3D Accounting Services and the Canwood Hotel. The elevator sits across Railway Avenue (Highway 55). Photograph taken September 22, 2003.

somewhat of a downturn—falling from 259 in 1931 to 204 in 1936—but in the decades following through to the present, Canwood experienced slow, but fairly steady, growth. Today, the area's agricultural output also includes bison and wild game such as elk and boar, and forestry still remains important to the economy as many Canwood and area residents are employed at the sawmill operations at Big River. Canwood has a small core of local businesses, a nursing home, and a K-12 school which had 146 students enrolled in the fall of 2006. Canwood Regional Park, five kilometres east of the community, has ball diamonds, a golf course, and camping facilities. Canwood serves as the administrative centre of the RM of Canwood No. 494.

CARIEVALE, village, pop 241 (2006c), 254 (2001c), is located in the extreme southeast corner of the province, 12 km east of Carnduff at the junction of Hwys 8 and 18. It is approximately 20 km west of the Manitoba border, and 20 km north of the International Boundary. Estevan, roughly 100 km to the west, is the nearest city. Settlers began arriving in the Carievale district in 1884 and were largely of British origin. A small settlement developed a few kilometres northwest of the present village, and mail was initially hauled in by horse and buggy from Goodlands, Manitoba. In 1890, the Carievale School District was formed, and after the CPR surveyed the route for its Brandon-Estevan branch, the village site was moved to its current location. Freight began to arrive by rail in 1891, and passengers in 1892; that same year the first grain elevator was erected alongside the tracks. On March 14, 1903, the Village of Carievale was incorporated. The region's

OF THE ROUGHLY 500 TRADITIONAL GRAIN ELEVATORS remaining in Saskatchewan, two are standing in Carievale. The elevator in the foreground was formerly operated by the Saskatchewan Wheat Pool; Patterson Grain still conducts business at the other. This photograph, from the west, was taken August 21, 2003.

IN 2003, CARIEVALE CELEBRATED 100 YEARS of incorporation as a village; the community's origins, however, date to the 1880s. Photograph taken August 21, 2003.

soils would prove well-suited for farming and ranching, and in more recent decades the area has also seen significant oilfield exploration. Today, a number of Carievale's businesses provide oilfield services or are related to the industry. Carievale's school provides K-8 education (there were 59 students enrolled in the fall of 2006); high school students attend classes in Carnduff, where the nearest RCMP detachment is also located. Carievale has a volunteer fire department; health care facilities are located in the nearby village of Gainsborough. Holy Trinity Anglican Church, built in 1905 of local fieldstones, was designated a municipal heritage property in 1995. Carievale is located within the RM of Argyle No. 1.

CARLYLE, town, pop 1,257 (2006c), 1,260 (2001c), is located just south of Moose Mountain Provincial Park and the White Bear First Nation at the junction of Hwys 9 and 13. After the region was surveyed in 1881 and opened to homesteaders in 1882, settlers from Manitoba and Ontario began moving into the district, and up until around the First World War most of these homesteaders were of British descent. The name Carlyle was chosen by the first postmaster, J.G. Turriff, who opened the post office in 1883. The name honours the Scottish historian and essayist, Thomas Carlyle, and Turriff's inspiration was that the niece of the famous Scot, Annie Marie Yeoward, had settled in the district with her family. Around the Carlyle Post Office, which was located in Turriff's general store, were constructed livery barns, a blacksmith shop, a boarding house, and stables for horses belonging to the NWMP. The location would come to be known as "Old Carlyle," since the settlement moved somewhat north and east as the route for the railway was surveyed. The first Moose Mountain Agricultural Society Fair was held at "Old Carlyle" in 1885. In 1900, the CPR established a tent town in the vicinity of the present townsite for the railway construction crews then building the line from Manitoba westward toward Arcola; trains were running through the new site of Carlyle in 1901. Carlyle became a boomtown and was incorporated as a village on March 13, 1902. The census of 1901 had recorded a population of a scant 23 at the townsite, but by 1906 it was approaching 400, and Carlyle attained town status on January 1 that year. In 1909, the construction of a second railroad through the community was underway, as the Canadian Northern Railway was progressing

In the shadow of Moose Mountain...
CARLYLE

Historical photographs of Carlyle courtesy of the Rusty Relics Museum, Carlyle, Saskatchewan.

▲ ◄ FROM THE EARLY DAYS OF SETTLEMENT, the woods and lakes of the Moose Mountain plateau provided Carlyle district residents with opportunities for sport and recreation. Photo above: Canadian Girls in Training swimming in Carlyle Lake (now White Bear Lake) in 1923. Photo left: G.A. Marsh and S.A. Porteous, pioneer businessmen of Carlyle, with eagles and ducks they shot north of Carlyle in the Moose Mountain area circa early 1920s. The larger eagle measured seven and a half feet from wing tip to wing tip, and 39 inches from head to tail.

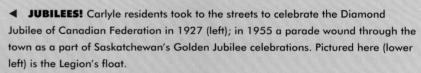

◄ JUBILEES! Carlyle residents took to the streets to celebrate the Diamond Jubilee of Canadian Federation in 1927 (left); in 1955 a parade wound through the town as a part of Saskatchewan's Golden Jubilee celebrations. Pictured here (lower left) is the Legion's float.

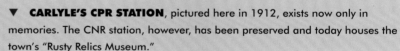

▼ CARLYLE'S CPR STATION, pictured here in 1912, exists now only in memories. The CNR station, however, has been preserved and today houses the town's "Rusty Relics Museum."

south-westward from Maryfield en route to the coalfields in the Bienfait-Estevan area. Following WWII, Carlyle experienced a second surge in its population. The town had still had around 400 residents in 1941, but by 1956 the number had grown to 829. Subsequently—and uniquely for a smaller community in Saskatchewan—Carlyle's population has slowly, but steadily, continued to climb. Traditionally, the area economy had been largely based upon agriculture; however, in recent decades the oil industry has become increasingly significant. Additionally, Carlyle is an important centre for tourists as it benefits from its proximity to Moose Mountain Provincial Park and Kenosee Lake, as well as the casino and resort at White Bear Lake and the championship golf courses in both locations. As well, Cannington Manor Provincial Historic Park is just a short drive northeast of the town. Carlyle has approximately 100 businesses; a wide array of recreational facilities; health care and emergency services; elementary and high schools; and a number of churches, service clubs, youth groups, and other community-based organizations. The former CNR train station now houses the town's museum. Each December, Carlyle hosts its premier annual event, the Dickens Village Festival. The entire town adopts a Victorian theme, and the festival features live stage productions and lighted parades at dusk. Carlyle serves as the administrative centre of the RM of Moose Mountain No. 63.

CARMICHAEL, village, pop 10 (2006c), 20 (2001c), is located west of Gull Lake, just south of Hwy 1; the Cypress Hills are prominent on the southern horizon. The CPR came through in 1883, and a railway siding named Cypress was established at or near the present village site sometime afterward. For the next two decades ranching operations dominated the area. Around 1906, homesteaders, many of German origin, began arriving in the district and the community began to take shape. The village was incorporated in 1917. Carmichael was never very large; the population peaked at 102 in 1931, and after the Trans-Canada Hwy bypassed the community in the mid-1950s, its numbers began to plummet. Today, only a few homes remain, as well as a small museum located in an old country schoolhouse dating from around 1911 which is opened by appointment. The village is located in the RM of Carmichael No. 109.

CARNDUFF, town, pop 1,012, (2006c), 1,017 (2001c), is located on Hwy 18 in the extreme southeast corner of Saskatchewan, 32 km west of the Manitoba border and 20 km north of the International Boundary. Estevan, an hour's drive west, is the nearest city. The first settlers arrived in the Carnduff district, primarily from Ontario, in the early 1880s. In 1884, the first post office was established, and Carnduff was named after the first postmaster, John Carnduff, who served in the position until 1900. In the mid-1880s, the nearest rail connections were at Moosomin and Deloraine, Manitoba, both approximately 120 kilometres away, and as this was then the horse and buggy era, Carnduff's blacksmiths and harness shop owners prospered. It was not until the fall of 1891 that the CPR's Brandon-Estevan branch line reached the Carnduff area. On March 29, 1899, the community legally attained village status, and on August 12, 1905, just weeks before Saskatchewan became a province, Carnduff was incorporated as a town. Until the 1950s, the town

▲ **ELEVATOR ROW**, the CPR station and water tower in Carnduff, circa 1910s. Saskatchewan Archives Board R-A228-2.

▲ **VOLUNTEERS** form the Carnduff and RM #2 Fire Department. Here, on the evening of August 21, 2003, an engine receives maintenance outside of the fire hall.

▼ **JUST BEFORE SUNDOWN:** The east side of Broadway Street, Carnduff, looking south from Railway Avenue. Photograph taken August 21, 2003.

had a widely fluctuating population. After that, the community experienced rapid growth, doubling in size by the 1970s, and then the population stabilized. Agriculture and oil production are the main industries in the area. The sandy loam land around Carnduff is used mainly for mixed farming, and many of the family farms in the district date back to the homestead era. Since there are several hundred producing oil wells in the region, a number of companies in the industry have offices in the town. Carnduff has a full range of businesses, services, and recreational facilities, including one of the province's longest 9-hole golf courses, situated in the small Antler River Valley. Moose Mountain Provincial Park, roughly 100 kilometres northwest, provides additional recreational opportunities. Carnduff also has a medical clinic, ambulance service, a fire department, and an RCMP detachment; the community's school provides K-12 education to more than 300 students. Carnduff also has the distinction of being the birthplace of Ernest C. Manning (1908-96), who served as the Premier of Alberta from 1943 to 1968 and who was the father of Preston Manning, the founder of the Reform Party. Carnduff serves as the administrative centre of the RM of Mount Pleasant No. 2.

CARON, organized hamlet, pop 125 (2006c), 120 (2001c), is located 26 km west of Moose Jaw just south of Hwy 1. The neighbouring community of Caronport lies just to the east, and the hills of the Missouri Coteau rise on the horizon to the southwest. Caron's origins date to its establishment as a railway siding in 1882, and the community's name is generally considered to honour Joseph Philippe René Adolphe Caron, a member of parliament from 1873 to 1900, who was the Minister of Militia and Defence at the time the railway was built across what is now southern Saskatchewan. In 1883, settlers, mostly from Ontario, began taking up land in the area, and in 1884 the Caron Post Office was established. By the beginning of the twentieth century, Caron was becoming a thriving trading centre for the surrounding farming district, and in January 1904 the community was incorporated as a village. People from eastern Canada continued to pour into the area, but they were joined by many from the United States and others from overseas (largely Scotland and England). By 1905, Caron had three grain elevators, two general stores, two lumber yards, two livery and feed barns, a hardware store, a blacksmith shop, a furniture store, a barbershop, a harness shop, a hotel, a butcher shop, a boarding house, a flour and feed store, and the post office. Thirty students were enrolled at the school. In 1906, the Bank of Hamilton opened a branch in the community and grain was being hauled to Caron from as far away as Gravelbourg for shipment. Also in 1906, Caron attained town status, and by 1916 the population was 254. Over the following years, however, several major fires, the Depression (Caron's population fell from 242 in 1926 to 156 in 1936), as well as improved transportation and changing population trends, significantly impacted the community. The result was that at midnight New Year's Eve, 1946, Caron reverted to village status. Five years later, in 1951, the village was dissolved and the community's administration was taken over by the rural municipality. In the 1970s, as the population continued to fall, the school was closed, as were the last businesses. In 1978, Caron was established as an organized hamlet. Today, the community is home largely to retirees and people who commute to work in Moose Jaw. Caron serves as the administrative centre of the RM of Caron No. 162.

CARONPORT, village, pop 919 (2006c), 1,040 (2001c), is located about a 15-minute drive west of Moose Jaw on Hwy 1. Caronport's beginnings date to WWII when a British Commonwealth Air Training Plan base was established three km east of the town of Caron (now an organized hamlet). At its peak, personnel at the base numbered about 700 and training involved around 100 aircraft. More than 1,800 pilots were trained at the CARON airPORT (the basis of the community's name), including ten airmen who lost their lives during training exercises and who are now buried in the local cemetery. The base was closed in 1944, and in 1946 the Briercrest Bible Institute, rapidly outgrowing its facilities in the village of Briercrest southeast of Moose Jaw, purchased the abandoned air base. Today, Caronport largely consists of the extensively developed 160-acre campus of the Briercrest Family of Schools, made up of a college, a seminary, and a Christian high school. Together, these had a combined enrollment of close to 1,100 students in 2004; additionally, there is a K-8 elementary school in Caronport that currently accommodates about 175 children. As such, these institutions are the community's largest employers and provide Caronport's economic base. The centrepiece of the village is the 2,400-seat Hildebrand Chapel, named in honour of Henry Hildebrand, founder of the Briercrest Bible Institute and long-serving principal. Built in 1988, it has the largest church auditorium in Saskatchewan. Caronport was incorporated as a village on January 1, 1988. Caronport is situated in the RM of Caron No. 162.

CARROT RIVER, town, pop 941 (2006c), 1,017 (2001c), is located southeast of Nipawin on Hwy 23, 10 km north of the river from which the community derives its name—a derivation of the Cree phrase meaning "the river of wild carrots." The first homesteaders crossed to the north side of the river in 1911; however, as the land was wet and heavily wooded, little development occurred before the CNR penetrated the region in 1931. A large number of those who took up homesteads in the area between 1925 and 1930 were Mennonites from the Rosthern area, and in 1927 they built the first church in the district. The railway brought in eastern-Canadian settlers as well as people from the drought-stricken regions of southern Saskatchewan. During the 1940s, conditions in the area were improved by road building, the drainage of vast tracts of land, and the establishment of dozens of sawmills which provided work. Carrot River was incorporated as a village in 1941 and attained town status in 1948. The community prospered following WWII, and the population jumped from 223 in 1946 to 801 by 1951. Over the next couple of decades, electricity, natural gas, and water and sewer systems

CARROT RIVER'S TOWN CREST

▲ **BILL POMEROY AND ERLE PEVERETT**, Carrot River pioneers, arrived in the district in the early 1930s, having given up lives in the drought-stricken regions of southern Saskatchewan. They are pictured here in front of Pomeroy's garage, where he fixed machinery and cars and did millwork. The Carrot River local history recounts that Pomeroy repaired "anything but broken hearts." Peverett took up land in the Battle Heights area, northeast of the town. Photograph taken in the late 1940s, courtesy of Jim Barnett, Carrot River.

were installed in the town. In the 1980s, the construction of many new public facilities was undertaken. These included a new hospital, seniors' housing, a library, a community hall, and curling and skating rinks. Today, Carrot River has a large and varied array of businesses and services, many of which cater to the district's agricultural industry. Several outfitters provide services to hunters in search of the abundant game in the area. The town has a health centre with an attached special care home, and an assisted-living housing complex. There is a local RCMP detachment, a volunteer fire department, and an ambulance service. Carrot River's elementary and high schools provide K-12 education — 320 town and area students were enrolled in the fall of 2006. Educational programs for adults are available through a regional college. Carrot River has a wide range of facilities for sports and recreation, and social and cultural events. The area economy, although large-

ly dependent on agriculture, is somewhat diversified. The harvesting and processing of peat moss provides approximately 70 jobs, and an industrial machine and welding shop, a trucking company, and seed processors are also located in the community. The district's agricultural output includes cattle, hogs, lamb, elk, leaf cutter bees, alfalfa, and honey, in addition to the high-quality oil seed and cereal grain crops produced. The Weyerhaeuser sawmill, which had employed approximately 120 local residents, was permanently closed in 2008. Carrot River serves as the administrative centre of the RM of Moose Range No. 486.

CASA RIO, organized hamlet, pop 247 (2006c), 229 (2001c), is a very upscale bedroom community located just south of the city of Saskatoon. Established as an organized hamlet in May 2002, Casa Rio is situated in the RM of Corman Park No. 344.

CATHEDRAL BLUFFS, organized hamlet, pop 135 (2006c), 78 (2001c), is located north of the City of Saskatoon, above the west side of the South Saskatchewan River near Wanuskewin Heritage Park. Largely a community of

commuters, Cathedral Bluffs is situated in the RM of Corman Park No. 344.

CEDAR VILLA ESTATES, organized hamlet, pop 135 (2006c), 139 (2001c), is a bedroom community located immediately southwest of the CN rail yards in the city of Saskatoon. Cedar Villa Estates was established as an organized hamlet in 1990 and is situated in the RM of Corman Park No. 344.

CENTRAL BUTTE, town, pop 372 (2006c), 439 (2001c), is located approximately 42 km north of Chaplin at the junction of Hwys 19 and 42. The Riverhurst ferry, which crosses the south arm of Lake Diefenbaker, operates to the northwest. The name of the community dates to the years prior to homesteading, when the region had been entirely devoted to ranching. The district has three large hills and, according to local lore, at round-up time the central butte became the most convenient landmark for all to converge. Homesteaders began arriving in the area around 1905-06. The early settlers were largely of British, German, and Scandinavian origins, with the majority of the latter two groups coming to Canada via the United States. Around 1926-27, a number of Mennonite families also moved into the region. The Central Butte Post Office and school were established in 1907 and 1908 respectively, both at separate locations within a few kilometres of the present townsite. After the arrival of the railroad from Moose Jaw in 1914 and the establishment of the townsite, these were moved into the fledgling community. Amidst much construction, Central Butte was incorporated as a village in 1915. The population was 122 in 1916 and grew fair-

◄ **TOURISM IS GAINING INCREASING IMPORTANCE IN CARROT RIVER** since the town is situated near Tobin Lake and Pasquia Regional Park. The latter location is the site of the recent discovery of a 92-million-year-old fossil of a crocodile-like sea dweller that lived during the Cretaceous period. Nicknamed "Big Bert," the remains found along the banks of the Carrot River are one of only four such fossils found in North America. Numerous other prehistoric marine fossils have also been found in the area, an interpretive centre has been established, and the location has been declared a provincial heritage site because of its palaeontological significance. This Big Bert cancellation stamp is put on all mail leaving the Carrot River Post Office.

▲ **CENTRAL BUTTE:** Looking south up Main Street from 2nd Avenue, September 5, 2003.

▲ **AUGUST 27, 2003:** A part of Ceylon's small business section.

ly steadily until the mid-1960s, at which point it levelled off, just shy of 550. Central Butte attained town status on July 1, 1967, the day the country celebrated its Centennial. The population of the town remained stable until 1996, the year the rail line through the community was abandoned. Subsequently, the Central Butte's numbers have fallen fairly dramatically. The community has a varied core of businesses and services, including a number related to the district's agricultural industry. Central Butte has a hospital, a variety of medical practitioners, a special care home, ambulatory service, and a fire department. The community is patrolled by the RCMP. The town has a range of recreational facilities, churches, a number of service clubs and community organizations, and a library. Central Butte School is a K-12 facility, which had 127 town and area students enrolled in the fall of 2006. Central Butte serves as the administrative centre of the RM of Enfield No. 194.

CEYLON, village, pop 90 (2006c), 105 (2001c), is located on Hwy 6, 110 km due south of Regina and 50 km north of the Canada-U.S. border. Radville is 23 km east on Hwy 377, and the Missouri Coteau rises to the southwest. The first homesteaders began arriving in the area in 1905, although it was not until the railroad was being built through the district in 1910 that Ceylon had its beginnings. Initially about a dozen businesses were set up on the north side of the rail line; however, in the spring of 1911 the townsite was surveyed on the south side of the tracks and all of the buildings had to be relocated to the present village site. Amidst a flurry of construction the community was incorporated as a village that September. A number of Ceylon's standing architectural landmarks, including the hotel built in 1912, date to the community's early years. In 1922, in the early morning hours

of Wednesday, September 27, the most notorious event in the village's history occurred: armed thieves used explosives and a fast get-away car to rob the Bank of Montreal of about $16,000 worth of cash, securities, and bonds. One theory is that the thieves knew the bank's vault would house the proceeds of the illegal liquor trade going on in the area at the time. The brazenness of the theft and the fact that the Union Bank in Moosomin was robbed the same night caused news of the robberies to capture provincial headlines for days. The culprits were never apprehended. In quieter times, Ceylon has served as a trading centre for the surrounding mixed farming and ranching district. The crop base in the region is quite diverse: wheat, durum, peas, canola, mustard, flax, and corn are grown. As well, cattle and horses are bred in the area, and there are a number of P.M.U. (pregnant mare urine) barns in the district. A small percentage of the area economy relates to oil and gas development. During the 1950s, when the village and area population was at its peak (the Village of Ceylon had a population of 355 in 1956), about 50 es-

tablishments in the community offered a variety of businesses and services. Far fewer businesses remain today, although tax incentives have been successful in attracting a seed-cleaning operation and an organic fertilizer manufacturer. A further community initiative has been the recent development of a 6,000-head feedlot for cattle, which will be expanded to accommodate 20,000 animals over time. Ceylon serves as the administrative centre of the RM of The Gap No. 39.

CHAMBERLAIN, village, pop 108 (2006c), 89 (2001c), is located approximately 80 km northwest of Regina on Hwy 11 at its junction with Hwy 2. The community is hemmed into a narrow strip of land by the CN rail line along the village's southwest and by the Arm River Valley which runs along Chamberlain's northeast side. The railway from Regina through Saskatoon to Prince Albert was built in the late 1880s, with trains running the distance in 1890. But for more than a decade after its completion, the line merely served as a bridge between the

AT THE CROSSROADS OF HWYS 2 AND 11: While Chamberlain's development has been hindered by its tight geographical location, this location is precisely what has kept the village's local businesses viable. The No. 11 Hwy between Regina and Saskatoon is the province's busiest north-south corridor, and the otherwise twinned route must narrow to a single-lane roadway for three kilometres as it passes through the village. Numerous service stations, restaurants, and convenience stores line the strip, catering to truckers, salesmen, tourists, and other travellers.

METAL SCULPTURES ALONG HWY 11, designed and fabricated by Don Wilkins who lives near Girvin, Saskatchewan, include this surveyor and Red River cart in Chamberlain. Wilkin's sculptures stand in a number of communities along Hwy 11, which was recently dubbed "The Louis Riel Trail."

Chamberlain photographs (left and below) taken July 8, 2003.

southern and central regions of the province. In 1902, at the urging of the Canadian government, Colonel Andrew Duncan Davidson formed the Saskatchewan Valley Land Company and began aggressive campaigns to promote immigration to the area; the first homesteaders arrived in the Chamberlain district over the next couple of years. The Chamberlain Post Office was established in 1904, and by 1911 the community had grown large enough to be incorporated as a village. Chamberlain developed into a trading centre for the district whose economy is based upon mixed farming. The community reached a peak population of 201 in 1966. Chamberlain is situated in the RM of Sarnia No. 221.

CHAPLIN, village, pop 235 (2006c), 292 (2001c), is located roughly halfway between Moose Jaw and Swift Current on the Trans-Canada Highway. Highway No. 19 leads north-eastward to Central Butte, while the provincial gravel Highway No. 58 leads south though the saline flats of Chaplin Lake, onward across the Missouri Coteau to the communities north of Gravelbourg. At the beginning of the twentieth century, Chaplin was no more than a point for the CPR's trains to take on coal and

RARELY SEEN: This view of Chamberlain is from the northeast, across the Arm River valley. Motorists passing through the village on the highway often have no knowledge that the community is bounded by this pretty setting. In the upper right is St. Anne's Roman Catholic Church; to its left, Chamberlain's sole remaining grain elevator, built by the Saskatchewan Wheat Pool in 1966.

◀ **ONE OF THE OLDEST BUILDINGS IN CHAPLIN** is the former Bank of Toronto building. Prefabricated at a woodworking mill in British Columbia in 1915, it was disassembled, shipped to Chaplin by rail and reassembled. It served as the Bank of Toronto until 1936 when it became a general store with living quarters upstairs. In 1961 the Royal Bank occupied the building, and in 1965 it became a credit union. It became Chaplin's village office in 1980 and continues to serve that function today. The building was declared a heritage property in 1981, the first Municipal Heritage Property designated under the province's Heritage Property Act.

◀ **SASKATCHEWAN MINERALS'** sodium sulphate plant at Chaplin.

Chaplin photographs taken August 28, 2003.

water. There was a box car station and a section house for railway crews, but otherwise the district was essentially unsettled. Within a few years, however, homesteaders began pouring into the region, and by 1906 the village of Chaplin had started to grow, with the establishment of a general store, a livery barn, a dray service, a restaurant, and a machine shop. The Chaplin Post Office was established in 1907, and the first school was built in 1908. Chaplin was incorporated as a village on October 8, 1912, and, reportedly, the longest wooden bridge in Canada was built over Chaplin Lake the same year. In 1913, the community hosted its first annual sports day, a tradition which is still continued.

Chaplin's population hovered around 200 until the late 1930s, at which point it began slipping toward 150. The dominant industry had been agriculture, but in 1948 the mining of sodium sulphate began in the Chaplin Lake basins, spurring a period of substantial growth for the community. From the mid-1950s through the early 1960s, Chaplin had a population approaching 500. The Saskatchewan Minerals operation is, today, one of the leading producers of sodium sulphate in North America. Additionally, a brine shrimp processing plant, in business for over 30 years, produces freeze-dried shrimp to be used as fish food. Agriculture remains important to the Chaplin area economy, and

it has become increasingly diversified: cereal grains, oilseeds, pulse crops, cattle, and bison are produced. Ecotourism, particularly bird-watching, has been a growing industry in the area. In 1997, Chaplin Lake, Reed Lake, and Old Wives Lake together were designated a Western Hemisphere Shorebird Reserve. Environment Canada, the Saskatchewan Wetland Conservation Corporation, and Saskatchewan Environment had nominated the site. An interpretive centre has been established at Chaplin, observation decks have been constructed over-looking the lake, and bus tours around the lake are available. Since 1997, over 150,000 people have visited the Chaplin Nature Centre. Chaplin has a small core of businesses, skating and curling rinks, a swimming pool, golf course, a campground, and a commu-

nity hall. Chaplin School is a K-12 facility which had 52 students enrolled in the fall of 2006, down from 74 students in the fall of 2003. Chaplin School is scheduled to close in 2009. Chaplin serves as the administrative centre of the RM of Chaplin No. 164.

CHELAN, organized hamlet, pop 45 (2006c), 52 (2001c), is located 10 km west of Porcupine Plain at the junction of Hwys 23 and 38. Before settlement, the region had seen logging and sawmill operations which had begun in the early 1900s. Homesteaders arrived in two main surges. The first occurred in the early 1920s and was comprised of veterans of WWI, who had had lands set aside for them. The second wave, about a decade later, consisted of refugees fleeing the dust bowl of southern Saskatchewan. Mixed in with both waves were immigrants from Europe. The railway was built through the area in 1928-29, and Chelan developed along the line. The cordwood industry was the backbone of the economy for years, until sufficient land was cleared and agriculture became the dominant enterprise. Chelan's population was 117 in 1966; however, like many smaller Saskatchewan communities, it has seen both its population and businesses lost to larger centres. The rail line was abandoned in 1999. Chelan is situated in the RM of Bjorkdale No. 426.

CHITEK LAKE, resort village, is located 56 km northwest of Spiritwood on Hwy 24, on the east side of the pine-encircled deepwater lake of the same name. The community is situated between the reserve lands of the Pelican Lake First Nation (Chitek Lake No. 191) to the south and the Chitek Lake Provincial Recreation Site to the west. The resort village had a year-round population of 219 tallied during the 2006 Census of Canada, but realizes a substantial increase in population with the arrival of cottage owners, vacationers, tourists, and campers during the summer months. These seasonal visitors provide the main sources of revenue for the community, as cabin rentals, houseboat rentals, stores, motels, restaurants, a gas station, and a golf course are among the village's key businesses. The area is also gaining in popularity as a winter recreation site, and grain farming and cattle ranching in the district, primarily to the south of the village, contribute to the local economy. Prior to the 1930s, there were not many non-Indian people in the area (other than trappers and fur traders), but the construction of the railroad from Debden to Meadow Lake early in the decade brought settlers who engaged in work in logging and sawmills, commercial fishing, and mink and fox ranching. After WWII, the first vacation cabins were built and, by the mid-1950s, a tourist trade was thriving. In the late 1960s work began on the golf course, and in the 1970s the Pelican Lake First Nation began its own major resort developments in the area. Chitek Lake was incorporated as a resort village on July 1, 1978 and is situated in the RM of Big River No. 555.

CHOICELAND, town, pop 346 (2006c), 370 (2001c), is located 42 km northwest of Nipawin, immediately north of the junction of Hwys 6 and 55. The CPR also serves the town. Choiceland is situated in the forest fringe of the northernmost agricultural region of eastern Saskatchewan. Narrow Hills Provincial Park and the beginnings of the Hanson Lake Road are located north of the town. Settlement of the area began in the early 1920s, the first arrivals being primarily of British origin. As the community developed it became somewhat cosmopolitan, as people of German, Ukrainian, Polish, and Chinese descent arrived. Schools and a post office were established in the district in the late 1920s; however, with the arrival of the railroad in 1932, the post

office relocated to the newly-established townsite and a new school was then built in the burgeoning community. Choiceland was incorporated as a village in 1944 and became a town in 1979. The community has a number of businesses and services, some of which are involved with the district's agricultural industry. Choiceland has a library, a museum, three churches, and a volunteer fire department. Policing is provided by the Smeaton detachment of the RCMP; the nearest hospital is located in Nipawin. Choiceland's William Mason School is a K-12 facility which had 129 students enrolled in the fall of 2006. Town recreational facilities include a curling rink, an indoor arena, ball diamonds, a campground, a paddling pool, and a community hall. The Wapiti Valley Ski Area, 25 kilometres south of Choiceland on the Saskatchewan River, offers 90 vertical metres of skiing, with runs well over a kilometre long. Choiceland has a large number of service clubs and community organizations, and the community is situated in the RM of Torch River No. 488.

CHORNEY BEACH, resort village, is situated on the southwest shore of Fishing Lake, approximately 22 km north of the town of Foam Lake via Hwy 310. There are a small number of permanent residents; however, the population fluctuates significantly depending on the season. Chorney Beach has over 70 private properties. The area is substantially developed as Fishing Lake's shores are comprised of several resort communities and public recreation areas, as well as the Fishing Lake First Nation, located on the lake's west side. Over the years, Fishing Lake's water levels have proven somewhat problematic, being susceptible to both drought and flooding. Its two basins were separated during a dry spell over a century ago, and in the 1930s levels also significantly receded. In the mid-1990s, and again in 2006 and 2007, area resorts, cottages, and district roads sustained considerable flood damage as waters reached unprecedented heights. Chorney Beach was incorporated in 1991 and is situated in the RM of Foam Lake No. 276.

▲ **ST. MARK'S LUTHERAN CHURCH** and the Senior Citizens' Community Hall (right) occupy the intersection of 1st Street and 1st Avenue in Choiceland. Two other churches in the town serve Roman Catholic and United congregations.

◄ **CHOICELAND, FROM THE SOUTHEAST.** The businesses on the right side of the picture are situated on the north side of Railway Avenue. The Saskatchewan Wheat Pool's farm supply centre is on the left.

Choiceland photographs taken July 18, 2003.

CHORTITZ, organized hamlet, pop 26 (2006c), 16 (2001c), is located southeast of Swift Current on Hwy 379. Established in 1905 by the Reinland Mennonite Association, Chortitz is one of a number of Mennonite communities that were established in the district. Chortitz still had a population of 76 in 1969, and it was established as an organized hamlet a decade later, in 1979. Chortitz is situated in the RM of Coulee No. 136.

CHRISTOPHER LAKE, village, pop 215 (2006c), 230 (2001c), is located approximately 40 km north of Prince Albert on Hwy 263, just southeast of the lake from which the community derives its name. The name honours Christopher Gravel, the brother-in-law of J.E. Morrier, a Dominion Lands surveyor who surveyed the area of Christopher, Oscar, and Emma Lakes; the latter Morrier named for his wife. A post office was established at Christopher Lake in 1925, and the community grew slowly, largely in conjunction with the cottage developments around the area lakes. Christopher Lake was established as an organized hamlet in 1977 and was incorporated as a village on March 1, 1985. For years, a dinner and dance club on Bell's Beach at Christopher Lake, "The Big Dipper," was home to Saskatchewan's Cottonpickers band, a provincial music industry institution for a quarter of a century, who recorded eight albums. Today, the village of Christopher Lake is continuing to grow, prospering as a service and supply centre to the area resort communities: there is a sportsplex, an outdoor skating rink, a number of restaurants and cafés, and a beverage room, credit union, grocery store, post office, insurance deal-

er, hair salon, and gas station. Christopher Lake has a K-8 school which had 120 students enrolled in the fall of 2006. Christopher Lake serves as the administrative centre of the RM of Lakeland No. 521.

CHURCHBRIDGE, town, pop 704 (2006c), 796 (2001c), is located approximately 54 km southeast of Yorkton and 31 km northwest of the Saskatchewan-Manitoba border at the junction of Hwys 16 (the Yellowhead) and 80. The district began to be settled in the mid-1880s. Settlers of German and Icelandic origin took up land in the area, and Churchbridge was founded by English settlers who were sponsored by the Anglican Church. In 1888, the Manitoba and Northwestern Railway was running trains into the fledgling hamlet, and in 1903 Churchbridge was incorporated as a village. The community developed as a small agricultural service centre; however, the development of the K1 potash mine south of Churchbridge in the late 1950s/early 1960s had a profound effect on both the area economy and the community. Churchbridge's population jumped from 257 in 1956 to 914 by 1966. Churchbridge attained town sta-

Views along Vincent Street...
CHURCHBRIDGE

Colour photographs are courtesy of Ruth Swanson, Churchbridge. Black-and-white photographs are courtesy of the Churchbridge Historical Society.

▲▼ **NORTH SIDE** of Vincent Street, Churchbridge, circa 1905-06.

▼ **VINCENT STREET IN THE 1940S.**

▲ **THE CHURCHBRIDGE SCHOOL BAND** had its beginnings in 1966. Here they are performing on Vincent Street on Band Day, 1973.

◄ **LANDMARKS OF CHURCHBRIDGE'S PAST:** Alongside Vincent Street are the CPR tracks. The two elevators were owned by the Saskatchewan Wheat Pool (foreground) and United Grain Growers. The latter was demolished in 1988; the Pool went down in 1989. No elevators are left standing in the town today.

tus in 1964, and today the majority of the community's workforce are employed at the K1 and K2 sites. Churchbridge serves the area with a variety of businesses and services, recreational facilities, a volunteer fire department, a number of churches, and a K-12 school that had 172 town and area students enrolled in the fall of 2006. Community attractions include a number of murals that depict various aspects of pioneer life on the prairies, as well as a monument featuring an enormous replica of the 1992 $1 coin which commemorated the country's 125th anniversary of confederation. The Royal Canadian Mint had held a design competition for the special edition coin, and the entry submitted by local artist Rita Swanson was selected from hundreds of entries from across the country. Churchbridge serves as the administrative centre of the RM of Churchbridge No. 211.

CLAVET, village, pop 345 (2006c), 357 (2001c), is located just southeast of the city of Saskatoon on Hwy 16. The district began to be settled in the early 1900s, and in 1907 as the Grand Trunk Pacific Railway was completing its line from Watrous to Saskatoon, the townsite began to be developed. In 1908, the community was first incorporated as the Village of French, but in 1909, for reasons unknown, the name was changed to Clavet. The new village struggled to manage its own affairs: the population was very small; council members moved away; the secretary-treasurer resigned; and the remaining residents of the community were disinterested in running a village. The provincial ministry of Municipal Affairs urged dissolution. The population was barely above two dozen in the early 1920s, and in 1927 the Village of Clavet was formally dissolved. For the next 40 years the affairs of the community were managed by the RM of Blucher No. 343. In the mid-1960s, Clavet was established as an organized hamlet, and in the 1970s the population of the community began to grow at a rapid rate, as Saskatoon residents began seeking homes outside of the city. Clavet grew from a population of 60 in 1972 to 234 in 1981 and 335 in 1986. The community achieved village status again in 1978. The rapidity of the development, and perhaps a lack of adequate planning, has led to the evolution of a rather unattractive bedroom community uncomfortably straddling a major highway. Large homes on small lots line characterless cul-de-sacs, and in one part of the village a large wall acts, unsuccessfully, as a sound barrier. Virtually nothing of the older village remains. Clavet has a small number of local businesses, but these are mostly conveniences such as a gas station and a confectionary, as people travel to Saskatoon for most of their shopping and services. Most people also work in the city, or in the district's agriculture-related industries or the region's potash mines. Clavet Composite School provides K-12 education to approximately 525 village and area students.

▲ **AN EARLY PHOTOGRAPH** of the brick plant in Claybank. Claybank brick lined the fireboxes of the steam locomotives that brought settlers to the prairies and were used in the construction of many provincial and national landmarks such as the Gravelbourg religious complex, Saskatoon's Bessborough Hotel, and the Chateau Frontenac in Quebec City. During World War II they were used to line the boilers of the corvettes and destroyers built in Canada's shipyards. Come the space age, the bricks were used in the construction of NASA's rocket launch pads at Cape Canaveral, Florida. Saskatchewan Archives Board R-A890(2).

CLAYBANK, organized hamlet, pop 20 (2006c), 20 (2001c), is located approximately 16 km west of Avonlea on Hwy 339 at the foot of the Dirt Hills. The community takes its name from the rich hillside clay deposits found in the area and is well known for its historic brick plant. In 1886, an early resident of the Moose Jaw area, Thomas McWilliams, ventured south into the hills and discovered the deposits of the excellent refractory clay. He began extracting it for sale to brick manufacturers in Moose Jaw, and for the next two decades he hauled the clay by horse and wagon there from the Dirt Hills, a distance of approximately 50 kilometres. Clay from Claybank was used in the construction of a number of Moose Jaw's early landmarks. Around 1902-03, large numbers of settlers, predominantly German Catholics, began arriving in the Claybank area, and with the construction of the railroad into the district in 1910-11 a local brick plant became viable. The plant began to be developed in 1912 and became operational in 1914. As the railway and the plant were built, so too was the community of Claybank. A post office was established in 1912, and the first Roman Catholic Church was built in 1913. Eventually there was a store, a poolroom and barber shop, a butcher, and from the 1930s through the 1950s there was a Saskatchewan Wheat Pool elevator at Claybank. Many of the people who lived in the community worked at the brick plant, and Claybank reached its peak around the mid-1930s and into the 1940s. Subsequently, the community declined. The population fell from 67 in 1969 to 35 in 1972, and by 1983 one of the concerns of the hamlet board was the removal of old buildings no longer in use. In 1989, the brick plant closed, yet it is still in operating condition today. The plant was declared a National Historic Site in 1994 and it remains one of Canada's finest examples of early twentieth-century industry. Claybank is situated in the RM of Elmsthorpe No. 100.

CLEMENCEAU, organized hamlet, pop 10 (2006c), 5 (2001c), is located southwest of Hudson Bay and is accessible via Hwys 9 and 23. The railway from Sturgis to Hudson Bay came though the area in 1928-29 and the railway siding established was named after the recently deceased French statesman, Georges Clemenceau (1841-1929), who served as the prime minister of France from 1906-09 and from 1917-20. Clemenceau led his country triumphantly through the last years of WWI and was one of the key framers of the Treaty of Versailles. In 1937, settlers began arriving in the Clemenceau district, primarily to work in the timber industry and then farming as land was cleared. The Clemenceau Post Office was established in 1938. By the 1950s, Clemenceau's population was around 150 and the community had a school, stores, a café, a pool hall, garages, sawmills, the CNR station and section house, and a grain elevator. But by the 1960s, the community was in decline. The population had fallen to 60 by 1969; the post office was closed in 1970; and by 1972, Clemenceau's numbers had

▲ **ORIGINALLY CONSTRUCTED BY THE SEARLE GRAIN COMPANY**, this grain elevator in Clemenceau was later purchased by the Federal Grain Company. Next to it was the grain buyer's house.

▼ **IF THESE WALLS COULD TALK:** Clemenceau's community hall.

Clemenceau photographs taken August 11, 2004.

dwindled to 28. Today, a few houses, the community hall, and the abandoned grain elevator and grain agent's house remain. Clemenceau is situated in the RM of Hudson Bay No. 394.

CLIMAX, village, pop 182 (2006c), 206 (2001c), is located in south-western Saskatchewan, 53 km south of Shaunavon, at the junction of Hwys 18 and 37. Cypress Hills Provincial Park is to the northwest, Grasslands National Park to the east, and the Port of Climax, at the Canada-U.S. border, is 23 km south. From the late 1800s through the first decade of the twentieth century, ranching operations, some on a huge scale, were working in the region. When the area was opened to homesteaders in 1909, the days of the wide open range drew to an end as land in the region was being fenced and broken for grain production. A substantial proportion of the first settlers in the district were Norwegians from Minnesota, and an early area post office was named Climax after a community in the American state, which, interestingly, had been named after a chewing tobacco company. Until the CPR arrived in Shaunavon in 1913, the closest point on the Canadian side of the border to deliver grain, obtain lumber, coal, or other goods was Gull Lake, almost 100 kilometres north. As customs regulations were not rigidly enforced at the time, many cross-border transactions occurred, and there was a significant covert trade in grain into Harlem, Montana. Then in early 1923, as the CPR approached from the west, a townsite was established and

▲▼ **MAIN STREET, CLIMAX, SASKATCHEWAN:** The photograph at top shows "Squatters Row" — buildings ready to be moved to surveyed locations on the townsite. The photograph immediately above shows the development of Main Street before the end of 1923. Both photographs courtesy of the Climax Community Museum. The photograph below was taken of the west side of Main Street on September 5, 2003.

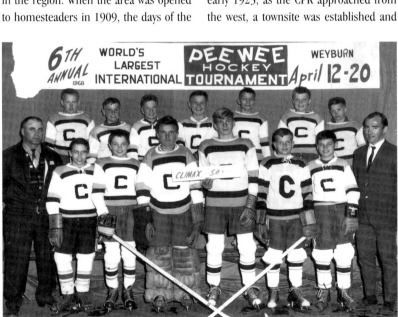

▲ **THE CLIMAX HOCKEY TEAM IN WEYBURN, 1968.** Back row left to right: Larry Jensen, Willie Desjardins, Rany Syrenne, Bryan Trottier, Reggie Smith, Donnie Larson, and Rex Mory. Front row left to right: Paul Desjardins (Manager), Michael Kirk, Grant Goodall, Joe George, Leslie Mything, Kim Laidlaw, Marcel Bellefeulle, and Phil Turnor (Coach). The team won the tournament. Photograph courtesy of the Climax Community Museum.

the village rapidly began to take shape. The quarter section set as the site for the new community had previously had one homesteader's shack and a small barn on it; within three weeks over twenty places of business had been erected. By the end of the year, on December 11, 1923, the Village of Climax was incorporated. Over the next couple of years five grain elevators were built and, until the railway reached Val Marie, a lot of grain was brought into Climax from areas to the east. In 1925, *The Weekly Climax* first went to print. The community newspaper would be published for 40 years, the last issue at Christmas in 1965. During the first year of the village, local businessmen formed a board of trade, and over the years it proved integral to the community's development. The hospital and community hall, the gravelling of the streets, recreational facilities, and annual events were all supported or initiated by this group. The 1950s and 60s were times of prosperity and growth for the village, and by 1961 the population had reached 425. Today, the community retains a core of essential businesses and services, including a health centre and a doctor's clinic. In the fall of 2006, school children attended grades K-9 in the village; grades 10-12 were bused to Frontier. At the end of June 2007, grades 6-9 were terminated at Climax School. The school is scheduled to close at the end of the school year in 2008. The community has an excellent museum and archives, and hosts an annual sports day each July 1st. The district economy is primarily based on farming and ranching, although a farm equipment manufacturer and a specialty crop processing plant, both located in Frontier, employ a large number of people. In 2000, the CPR line along which Climax was built was sold to Great Western Railway (GWR), a B.C.–based com-

pany. However, at the beginning of 2004, GWR was looking to sell, and by the fall a group led by farmers in south-western Saskatchewan succeeded in purchasing the line. The Climax RCMP detachment was closed in 2005. Climax serves as the administrative centre for the RM of Lone Tree No. 18.

COCHIN, resort village, is located 36 km north of North Battleford on Hwy 4, on the east side of Jackfish Lake. Cochin is one of a number of resort communities that encircle Jackfish and neighbouring Murray Lakes, and it is also situated in close proximity to the reserve lands of the Moosomin and Saulteaux First Nations, as well as The Battlefords Provincial Park. The area where Cochin sits today, between Jackfish and Murray Lakes, had been known as The Narrows (or Les Detroits) and was the southern terminus of what was known as the Cochin-Green Lake Trail, over which traders, missionaries, and the North-West Mounted Police travelled. The police patrolled the trail extensively during the North-West Resistance, and one of the more prominent mission-

aries working in the region was Father Louis Cochin, an Oblate born in France, who came west in the early 1880s. Père Cochin established missions in the region to serve the Indian and Metis populations and died in the community that came to be named for him in 1927. Immigrants from France had taken up land around Jackfish Lake by 1907, and shortly before WWI stores and other businesses began to be established. The Cochin Post Office opened in 1915. During the 1920s, families from North Battleford, Wilkie, Saskatoon, and other areas began leasing land around the lakes for their summer vacations. Soon cabins began to dot the area and Cochin began to steadily develop as a summer resort destination. Also during the 1920s, commercial fishing operations began, as did the development of market gardens. Businesses such as the Ternier family's Prairie Garden Seeds carry on the

latter tradition to this day. In 1978, Cochin was established as an organized hamlet, and on January 1, 1988, the community was incorporated as a resort village. The 2006 Census recorded 208 permanent residents; however, there are 550 properties in Cochin and the summer population may easily surpass 1,000. Factoring in all of the neighbouring resort areas, the district population can easily reach several thousands during the peak season. Cochin's economy is largely based on tourism, but also benefits from the surrounding agricultural industry. Camping, fishing, boating, hiking, and golf are key attractions, and amenities in the village include hotel and bed and breakfast accommodations, restaurants, stores, a service station, two churches, a community hall, a fire hall, a library, campgrounds, and a public beach. Cochin is situated in the RM of Meota No. 468.

▼ **AHOY!** A unique feature in Cochin, and indeed in Saskatchewan, is the province's only lighthouse. Built high on a hill overlooking the village and Jackfish Lake, the lighthouse — a project initiated in 1988 by Tom Archdekin, the community's first mayor — has a revolving beacon that can be seen for miles. Photograph taken July 23, 2003.

◁ ▲ **CODERRE: BUSINESSES PAST AND PRESENT.** The Coderre Hotel (top left) remains in business; however, the Coderre Store (left) has long been closed. The former Saskatchewan Wheat Pool elevator (dating to the 1950s) (above), is now owned by the Coderre Seed Cleaning Co-op. Photographs taken September 17, 2005.

CODERRE, village, pop 40 (2006c), 50 (2001c), is located northeast of Gravelbourg off Hwy 363, to the west of Old Wives Lake. French settlers arrived in the area around 1908-10, and the post office established in 1910 was named for the first postmaster, E. B. Coderre, who served in the position until 1956. The railway reached Coderre in 1924, and in 1925 the village was incorporated, retaining the post office name. The district economy grew to be based on farming and ranching. By 1941, the population of Coderre was 224, and it remained around that number until the mid-1960s. By 1971, it had fallen to 161; by 1981, it was down to 114. The rail line was abandoned in 1989. Coderre is situated in the RM of Rodgers No. 133.

CODETTE, village, pop 221 (2006c), 237 (2001c), is located about 7 km south of Nipawin on Hwy 35. The first settlers began making incursions into the area around 1906 and the village began to develop in the summer of 1924 when the CPR, en route to Nipawin from Wadena, purchased land for the development of a townsite. Soon buildings were constructed and the Codette Station Post Office opened in 1925. On March 9, 1929, the village was incorporated, its name (although a misspelling) honours a Metis fur trader for whom nearby rapids on the Saskatchewan River had been named. The rapids were submerged with the construction of the Francois-Finlay dam in the 1980s. Subsequently, Codette Lake (the reservoir created by the dam) has provided for recreational activities such as fishing, boating, and swimming. Codette had developed as an agricultural service centre and its population remained at somewhat less than 200 until the mid-1970s, at which point it began to climb, reaching a peak of 293 in 1991. Today, the town of Nipawin (pop 4,275) provides Codette's residents with many amenities, including shopping and services, as well as employment opportunities. Codette retains a Co-op gas station and bulk fertilizer dealership, an Agricore United elevator, a car wash, a hotel/bar, a woodworking business, and the post office. The village also has a private seniors' care home. Codette serves as the administrative centre of the RM of Nipawin No. 487.

COLE BAY, northern village, pop 156 (2006c), 161 (2001c), is a picturesque Métis community located in northwestern Saskatchewan, approximately 60 km west of Beauval on the southwest shore of Canoe Lake. It is situated near the junction of gravel Hwys 903 and 965, and it is located in close proximity to the reserve holdings of the Canoe Lake Cree First Nation, signatories to Treaty 10 in 1906. As well, Cole Bay's sister communities of Jans Bay and Canoe Narrows, which are also situated on the lake, lie just to the east. A traditional economy of hunting, trapping, and fishing prevailed until 1954 when the creation of the Cold Lake (Primrose Lake) Air Weapons Range encompassed vast tracts of traditional Aboriginal and treaty areas. Today, logging and tourism are the main sources of employment. The community has a store, a post office, a community hall, a church, rental cabins and facilities for camping. Lakeview School in Cole Bay is a K-8 facility, which had 44 students enrolled in the fall of 2006. Students attend high school at Canoe Narrows, where there is also a health clinic, a daycare centre, an indoor

arena with artificial ice, additional stores and gas. Cole Bay (previously known as Canoe Lake) was established as a northern hamlet in 1983 and was incorporated as a northern village on January 1, 1990.

COLESDALE PARK, organized hamlet, is one in a string of resort communities situated on the east side of Last Mountain Lake. Development began in 1960 and the organized hamlet was established in 1979. Colesdale Park is located in the RM of McKillop No. 220, and its population varies with the seasons.

COLEVILLE, village, pop 248 (2006c), 313 (2001c), is located on Hwy 307 roughly halfway between Kindersley and Kerrobert. Settlement of the area began in the early 1900s, and the beginnings of the village date to the construction of the railroad through the district in 1912-13. The name Coleville honours Malcolm Cole, who in 1908 established a post office by that name on his farm several kilometres southeast of the present village. After the railway arrived, the post office was relocated to the townsite and its name was adopted for the community. Agriculture dominated the regional economy until oil was discovered in 1951. The following boom brought many people to the area, and in 1953 the Village of Coleville was incorporated. By the early 1960s, its population was over 500. Today, several businesses servicing and supplying the surrounding oilfields are located in the village. Coleville also has a grocery store, a liquor vendor, a hotel, a credit union, a post office, and a library. Recreational facilities include skating and curling rinks, ball diamonds, and a golf course. Rossville School provides K-7 education, while grades 8-12 are bused to Kindersley. Jeni Mayer, an award-winning author of mystery books for young adults, was born in Coleville and resides there today. Coleville serves as the administrative centre for the RM of Oakdale No. 320.

COLLINGWOOD LAKE-SHORE ESTATES, organized hamlet, is a resort community situated west of Strasbourg on the east shore of Last Mountain Lake, within the RM of McKillop No. 220. Settlers were active in the area in the early 1900s and the name "Collingwood" appears as a "flag" stop on a 1910 timetable for the Wm. Pearson Co.'s *S.S. Qu'Appelle*. If signalled from shore, the steamer would dock, taking on passengers and freight. The current resort is largely of recent development, the land being subdivided in 1983, with the organized hamlet being established in 2003. There are only a few permanent residents; however, the population varies depending on the season. There are approximately 30 developed properties.

COLONSAY, town, pop 425 (2006c), 426 (2001c), is located 55 km east of Saskatoon on Hwy 16. The name of the community, as well as many of its streets, are named after islands off Scotland's west coast. The area was settled around 1905 and the beginnings of the village date to 1907-08 with the construction of the CPR line from Lanigan to Saskatoon. The first store was located on the townsite in 1907, and in 1908 the post office was established. Colonsay was incorporated as a village in 1910 as the population was approaching 100. In 1911, Colonsay became the junction of a second rail line as the CPR built a track north from Regina (this line was abandoned piecemeal over the past 30 years). By the early 1920s, the population of Colonsay was around the 200 mark, and it remained at that level for the next few decades. With the construction of the potash mine at Colonsay in the latter years of the 1960s, the community's numbers significantly increased. By 1971, the population was 526; in 1977, Colonsay attained town status. Although employment at the mine remains highly important (about 300 hundred people from area communities are employed there), many people commute to work in Saskatoon. Agriculture also contributes significantly to the local economy; a variety of crops and livestock are produced in the area. The Saskatchewan Wheat Pool (SWP) sells fertilizers, herbicides, pesticides, and seed products at Colonsay; however, in April of 2002, the town's SWP elevator was demolished, superseded by the ever larger inland terminals established in the region. Colonsay School's grade nine English class documented the demolition process and interviewed community members to gather their personal reflections on the loss of the landmark. Colonsay School is a K-12 facility which had 137 students enrolled in the fall of 2006. Colonsay has a small core of essential businesses and services; the many offerings in the nearby city of Saskatoon are readily accessible. Colonsay has an RCMP detachment, a volunteer fire department, a weekly doctor's clinic, home care services, and a Meals on Wheels program. Recreational facilities include a sports centre with skating and curling rinks, a nine-hole golf course, an outdoor swimming pool, ball diamonds, a tennis court, and a community hall. A community theatre group puts on an annual performance, and there are dance and gymnastics clubs in the town. Colonsay has a library, three churches, and a seniors' centre; there are several service clubs in the community. Colonsay serves as the administrative centre of the RM of Colonsay No. 342.

CONGRESS, organized hamlet, pop 28 (2006c), 36 (2001c), is located approximately 14 km north of Assiniboia on Hwy 2. The area was opened up to homesteaders around 1906-07, and settlers of English, German, Swedish, and Norwegian origin took up land in the Congress district, a number coming via the United States. The community's name honours the national legislative body of the United

States, and Congress's streets are named after American presidents — Washington, Wilson, Roosevelt, and Taft. The school was built in 1911. In 1912 a Baptist congregation was organized, although, until 1919 when the church was constructed, services were held in either the school or in people's homes. A Lutheran congregation was organized in 1914, but it was not until 1929 that they built their church, which was closed in 1962. The railway came through Congress in 1917 and grain elevators, stores, and other businesses were quickly established at the townsite. By 1919, the community was booming. At one time, there were four grain elevators in the community; however, with the advent of better roads and automobiles, Congress began to decline. From a population of 125 in 1966, the community's numbers had dwindled to 50 by 1972. The school closed in 1967 and students were thereafter bused to Assiniboia. Congress is situated in the RM of Stonehenge No. 73.

CONQUEST, village, pop 167 (2006c), 163 (2001c), is located about 20 km northwest of Outlook, north off Hwy 15. In the spring of 1904 the first settlers began to arrive in the Conquest area and, for the most part, the district was pioneered by people from Ontario and Manitoba, with a few arriving from the British Isles. Mail was initially taken to and picked up in Hanley (a round-trip of close to 130 kilometres), until an area post office (Fertile Valley) was opened in November of 1906. Obtaining supplies also meant a tedious journey to Hanley or Saskatoon, so

▶ **CONQUEST'S ELEVATORS** on the north side of Railway Avenue, looking west. Photograph taken September 12, 2003.

settlers usually purchased enough to last them six months. The year 1910 brought major developments as both the CPR, coming east from Kerrobert toward Outlook, and the Canadian Northern Railway, proceeding south from Saskatoon, were surveying routes through the area. On May 2 the CPR purchased NW32-29-9-W3 for a townsite, and prior to the lots being surveyed that September, the first buildings and businesses began to be erected (a store and a carpenter's shop) and a doctor's office was moved in from the country. As the town of Outlook had appeared on the map in 1908 and was now serviced by the CPR running out of Moose Jaw, lumber for construction at Conquest was bought in Outlook and transported across the South Saskatchewan River by ferry (the railway bridge across the river would not be completed until 1912). In the spring of 1911 the first mail addressed to the "Conquest Post Office" arrived, followed shortly thereafter by the Canadian Northern Railway, which succeeded in beating the CPR to the fledgling community. By the fall Conquest had developed fairly substantially, and on October 24, 1911 the Village of Conquest was incorporated. By the early 1920s the population of the village was just under 300, and in 1922 Peter Hugh Kennedy, now regarded as the father of field shelterbelts on the prairies, planted the first rows of trees around his section of land. In the 1930s, Kennedy petitioned for a federal government program to support tree planting, and he helped organize the Conquest Field Shelterbelt Association. From 1948 to 1960, Kennedy operated his farm as an experimental research station under contract to the federal Department of Agriculture, and by 1964 over 1,600 kilometres of shelterbelts had been planted in the Conquest area using about 7 million seedlings and covering an area of approximately 705 square kilometres. Over the years, representatives from departments of agriculture from countries such as Australia, New Zealand, the United States, India, and Pakistan, as well as other parts of Canada came to study the shelterbelt project and Conquest came to be known as the "Caragana Capital of the World." The village had lost about one third of its population during the 1930s, but in the years following WWII the community rebounded, recouping the numbers lost. However, beginning in the early 1960s, the community's fortunes began to change again. In 1963, the CPR discontinued passenger service after 51 years of continual operation — the first passenger train had arrived in Conquest in the fall of 1912 — and in 1966 the railway closed the station, curtailing the transport of freight via rail. In 1967, the Anglican and Catholic churches closed their doors due to diminishing congregations, and that same year students in grades eleven and twelve began to be bused to school in Outlook, followed by the grade tens in 1968. On the up side, however, community spirit and fund-raising initiatives had enabled thirty-four Conquest students and their chaperones to travel to Montreal for a week to visit Expo 67. At the end of the school year in 1996, though, Conquest School finally closed its doors to all grades. Today, the community retains a small core of essential businesses and services; the nearby town of Outlook offers a substantial commercial sector, as well as a range of health care services. The Conquest United Church, a 1916 structure unique architecturally, was designated a heritage property in 1985. Conquest serves as the administrative centre of the RM of Fertile Valley No. 285.

CONSUL, village, pop 93 (2006c), 91 (2001c), is located in the extreme southwest corner of the province, south of the Cypress Hills, on Hwys 13 and 21. In the early 1900s, only a few ranchers were operating in the district; however, the coming of the railway from Assiniboia via Shaunavon in 1913-14 brought an influx of settlers to the region and the rapid establishment of townsites. The Consul site was surveyed and began to develop in 1914, and in 1917 the village was incorporated. The rail line was to have continued on to Lethbridge, Alberta, but after WWI began the CPR was unable to obtain the necessary steel, and all railroad expansion in the province was severely limited for several years. The 1920s were times of prosperity and much activity, particularly involving renewed railway construction. In the early 1920s, the CPR began work on the Notukeu subdivision, heading southeastward from the Consul area toward what would become the future villages of Frontier, Climax, and Val Marie; and, in

THE CONSUL HOTEL **AND CAFE** on Railway Avenue (above) and the former Saskatchewan Wheat Pool facility at Consul (left). The small annex in the foreground of the elevator photograph was built as a stand-alone elevator in 1928; it became an annex to the larger, newer elevator in 1972. Photographs taken August 30, 2003.

1922, the railway to Lethbridge was completed as the gap between the Saskatchewan border and Manyberries, Alberta, was closed. Many farm families left the province's southwest during the drought and the Depression, but in the years following WWII the population began to increase again and Consul began to receive the modern amenities long taken for granted by Saskatchewan's city dwellers. In the late 1950s, SaskPower brought an end to the local light plant, bringing 24-hour service to people's homes; in the late 1960s, water and sewer systems were put in, and party lines came to an end when SaskTel began servicing the village. Over the past few decades, though, Consul's population has steadily fallen, and in 1989 the same year as the community celebrated its 75th birthday, the rail line beyond Consul through to Lethbridge was abandoned. In 2000, the line along which Consul was

built was sold to the Great Western Railway (GWR), a B.C.–based company; however, at the beginning of 2004, GWR was looking to sell, and that fall a group led by south-western Saskatchewan farmers succeeded in purchasing the line. Today, Consul remains an important centre in a sparsely populated region. The school is an active and modern K-12 facility, with approximately 90 students attending from the village and the surrounding countryside, and Consul has a small core of essential businesses and services to serve the region. The community's RCMP detachment was closed in 2005, and the nearest health care facilities are located in Eastend and Maple Creek. Consul had a peak population of 227 in 1966. Consul serves as the administrative centre for the RM of Reno No. 51.

CORNING, organized hamlet, pop 43 (2006c), 30 (2001c), is located north of Stoughton off Hwy 47. Moose Mountain Provincial Park lies to the southeast. The district was well-settled by the time the hamlet was established with the construction of a short railway subdivision south from Peebles in 1924. The Corning Post Office was set up in 1925, replacing the Glenada Post Office established in 1909, some distance to the southwest. Corning was erected as an organized hamlet in 1948, and in 1969 the community had a population of 77. CN abandoned the rail line into Corning at the end of 1989. Corning serves as the administrative centre of the RM of Golden West No. 95; the area economy is based on agriculture and some oil production.

CORONACH, town, pop 770 (2006c), 822 (2001c), is located due south of Moose Jaw on Hwys 18 and 36; 19 km north of the Canada-U.S. border. The area landscape is one of gently rolling hills underlain by substantial deposits of lignite coal. The land supports livestock production and grain farming, particularly red spring wheat. The region is sparsely populated and only began to be settled between 1908 and 1914, and development in the area was slow. Homesteaders came from Ontario, the Dakotas, and Minnesota. For years the nearest railway point was Bengough, over 40 kilometres northeast across the desolate badlands of the Big Muddy Valley. Area pioneers long petitioned authorities for a railroad; however, it was not until the mid-1920s that the CPR began construction of a line south from just west of Assiniboia. The community had its beginnings in 1926, and an official of the CPR named Coronach after the horse that won England's Epsom Derby that year. Regular rail service was inaugurated in 1927, and in 1928

Coronach was incorporated as a village. But just as the district's prospects seemed brighter, the Depression and drought hit and the population of the area and the village dropped. The post-war era brought people and a level of prosperity back to the community, but by the early 1970s the village was again in decline. Then came a pivotal moment in Coronach's history: although coal had been mined in the area since the early 1900s, it was not until the mid-1970s that the significance of the resource was realized. The richness of the coal seams was the determining factor in SaskPower's decision to locate a major new power-generating station and coal mine in the immediate vicinity of the community. Within a few years, the village of just over 300 mushroomed into a bustling business centre with a population of over 1,000. The community experienced a construction boom, and in 1978 Coronach gained town status. Many of the community's homes are subsequently modern, and Coronach has a wide range of businesses and services as well as a full array of recreational facilities. Coronach School provides K-12 education, and an integrated health care centre serves the town and surrounding district. There is a local RCMP detachment. The community hosts an agricultural fair in July and the Poplar River Indoor Rodeo in September, which attracts cowboys from across Canada and the United States. Recently there have been efforts to develop tourism in the Coronach area: from the town one can tour the natural and historic sites of the badlands of the Big Muddy Valley, the power station, and the coal-mining operations. The Poplar River Power Station and the Poplar River Coal Mine employ approximately 300 people today. Coronach serves as the administrative centre of the RM of Hart Butte No. 11.

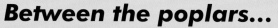

▲ **MEMBERS OF AN AREA DELEGATION** that travelled to Toronto in 1918 to petition for a railroad south of Willow Bunch. Later some of these men went to Ottawa. Delegates represented the RM of Hart Butte No. 11, the RM of Poplar Valley No. 12, and the RM of Willow Bunch No. 42. Back row left to right: Dave Whitlaw (Hart), Chas Craig (Big Beaver), A.M. Sorsdahl (Luella), Thomas Thompson (Poplar Creek). Front row left to right: Dr. Godin (Willow Bunch), Treffle Bonneau (Willow Bunch), Rev. D.N. Buntain (manse, south of Coronach), Jack Dangerfield (Fife Lake), Garnet Elliot (Fife Lake), Abel James Hindle (MLA for Assiniboia), T.W. Bennett (Willow Bunch), and Amil Katsmarski (Fife Lake). Photograph taken in front of the Walker House Hotel in Toronto. Photograph courtesy of the Coronach District Museum.

▶ **DOCTOR PESACH COODIN AND FAMILY**, Coronach, c. 1929. Dr. Coodin worked in the community from 1929 to 1932. Photograph courtesy of the Coronach District Museum.

▼ **CORONACH SCHOOL** burned to the ground in 1976. The building was only 13 years old, having opened in 1963. A new school was built in 1977. Photograph courtesy of the Coronach District Museum.

▲ **MRS. PEARL GOUDIE** in front of her new sod house, Coronach district, 1916. Family still reside in the area. Photograph courtesy of the Coronach District Museum.

▼ **THE POPLAR RIVER POWER STATION**, 10 kilometres southeast of Coronach, generates approximately 4 billion kilowatt hours of electricity annually. To put this figure into perspective, the average residential customer in the province uses about 7,600 kilowatt hours each year. The stack on the Power station rises 122 metres (slightly over 400 feet); the diameter at the base is 7.62 metres (25 feet). Photograph taken September 3, 2003.

COTEAU BEACH, resort village, is located on Lake Diefenbaker, northeast of Birsay. There are approximately 30 year-round residents; however, there are more than 130 cabins and homes, so the population varies greatly, depending on the season. Coteau Beach is located in the RM of Coteau No. 255, and was incorporated in 1982.

COURVAL, organized hamlet, pop 5 (2006c), 10 (2001c), is located southwest of Moose Jaw on Hwy 363, just west of Old Wives Lake. The Wood River, which drains into the lake, flows just south of the community. Courval was named

▲ **THE VIEW FROM COTEAU BEACH**, looking northwards up the lake. Photograph taken July 20, 2004.

for its founder, Louis Poulin De Courval (1854-1940), a Canadian Government surveyor from Quebec, who worked in the area of Old Wives Lake in the late 1800s, at which time only a few ranchers were operating in the region. Courval enticed French-Canadians from his home province to settle in the district with him beginning in 1908, and when a post office was established that year, it was named in his honour. A public school was opened in 1911 with instruction in French, but due to the objections of English-speaking settlers arriving in the area, classes were taught in English the next year. In 1916, a Roman Catholic separate school was opened to accommodate the French-speaking settlers' children, thus ending disagreements that had erupted over the language of instruction. Although the railway had reached the neighbouring community of Coderre (about 10 kilometres west) in 1924, it was another five years before the line was completed through the location of present-day Courval. The route surveyed necessitated the relocation of

◄ **ST. JOSEPH'S ROMAN CATHOLIC CHURCH**, Courval. Photograph taken September 17, 2005.

the small community that had developed, as it had grown up a short distance north of where the track would be laid. In the early 1950s the public school closed and all students were then taught at the separate school, with classes in both French and English. A decade later, high school students were transferred to Coderre, and in 1967 Courval's school was closed and all the community's children were transferred to Coderre. Courval's population at the time was then hovering around 100, but it was falling. By 1969, it was 65; by 1972, it had slipped to 46. The rail line was abandoned in 1989, and the community's grain elevators were demolished the next year. One fading landmark remains. St. Joseph's Roman Catholic Church, with its once-handsome entrance and octagonal bell tower, was built in 1927, furnished over the winter, and blessed in 1928. A memorial monument erected in honour of the Courval district pioneer families unveiled in 1965 stands in the grass out front. Courval remains the administrative centre of the RM of Rodgers No. 133.

CRAIK, town, pop 408 (2006c), 418 (2001c), is located roughly mid-way between Regina and Saskatoon on Hwy 11. Although the Qu'Appelle, Long Lake & Saskatchewan Railway was running between Regina, Saskatoon, and Prince Albert in 1890, the Craik district was not really settled until the early 1900s. The majority of those who arrived in the area were of British origin, either from eastern Canada or overseas; there were also people of German background and a fair number of Norwegians who came to the country via the United States. Craik was incorporated as a village in 1903 and attained town status in 1907. The town has a range of businesses and services,

Photographs on facing page, clockwise from top left:

PRIME MINISTER SIR WILFRID LAURIER visits Craik en route to Saskatoon in 1910. Laurier is descending the stairs on the right hand side of the back of the train.

CRAIK LIVERY, SALE AND FEED STABLE, CIRCA 1920: The dray teams are dressed to meet the train. The "Chinese" laundry is in the background to the right.

THE METHODIST'S ANNUAL PICNIC, Craik area. The photograph would predate 1921, the year of the union of Methodist and Presbyterian churches in Craik.

FORDS, FORDS, AND MORE FORDS. There was a brisk business in automobile sales in Craik in the 1920s.

THE CRAIK ECO-CENTRE. Photograph taken September 9, 2004.

LOOKING EAST UP 3RD STREET: The 1913 town hall is on the left (with the bell tower); the former Saskatchewan Wheat Pool elevator in the background dates to the late 1950s. Photograph taken July 19, 2004.

SASKATCHEWAN'S GOLDEN JUBILEE in 1955 was celebrated with a parade in Craik. The parade route wound from the school yard to the fairgrounds.

Historical photographs of Craik courtesy of the Craik Archives and Oral History Society Inc.

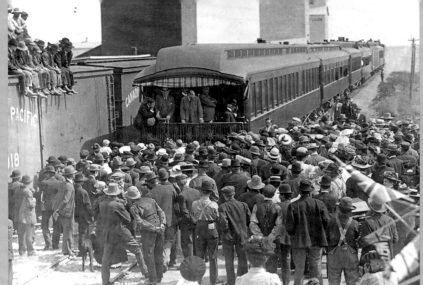

"The Friendliest Town by a Dam Site!"

CRAIK

CRAIK LIVERY
SALE AND FEED STABLE

CO-OP

MORE FORDS, FOR CRAIK SASK.

a number of which cater to the district's agricultural industry. Craik has a health centre with an attached special care home, a local detachment of the RCMP, a volunteer fire department, two churches, and a weekly newspaper. Craik School is a K-12 facility, which had 134 students enrolled in the fall of 2006. Community recreational facilities include skating and curling rinks; across the highway from Craik are the Craik and District Regional Park, the Craik Golf Course, and the Craik Dam across the Arm River, which has created a reservoir used for fishing and boating. The Craik Community Archives and Oral History Society is an impressive organization located in a 1913 building which originally housed the town hall, opera house, and fire hall. The Craik Prairie Pioneer Museum site includes a collection of pioneer artifacts housed in an assembly of heritage buildings. A significant town venture in recent years has been the development of the Craik Sustainable Living Project: this is a long-term community-based initiative aimed at advancing the local use of ecologically sound technologies by presenting viable alternatives related to land use, food and fibre production, energy generation and conservation, shelter, recycling, water and waste management. Through the recently completed Eco-Centre, the development of an Eco-Village, and outreach and education programs, it is hoped the project will stimulate socio-economic revitalization in the community. In July 2004, the town and the surrounding rural municipality announced they would provide 80 acres of prime industrial property as an incentive for Hemptown Clothing Inc., the world's largest hemp T-shirt apparel brand, to establish a multi-million-dollar fibre-production mill in the community. Production was expected to begin in mid-

2007, and the intention is for the company to source its hemp requirements from local area farmers. Over the past few years, Craik has been the site of a unique summer festival, an innovative two-day event that takes place in the middle of a hemp field and combines music and performance with workshops on sustainable agriculture and renewable energy for both area farmers and the general public. Craik had a peak population of 607 in 1956 and serves as the administrative centre of the RM of Craik No. 222.

CRANE VALLEY, organized hamlet, pop 20 (2006c), 40 (2001c), is located south of Moose Jaw on Hwy 36. The Cactus Hills and the Dirt Hills are visible to the north and northeast respectively. Settlers began arriving in the area in the early 1900s; however, it was not until the mid-1920s, with the coming of the railway, that the townsite was surveyed and began to be built up. For years people in the district had hoped for a railroad, as they had had to haul grain to the rail points at Galilee or Spring Valley to the north, or south to Readlyn, Verwood, or Viceroy. Groceries, coal, and things such as Eaton's catalogue purchases had to be brought back the same distance. When the first train arrived in Crane Valley in August 1926, it was thought Premier Dunning (1922-1926) had much to do with it. He was the MLA for the constituency and had considerable influence with the CPR. The post office, which had hopped from farm to farm for more than two decades was relocated to the townsite. Stores, lumberyards, a garage, and elevators were constructed, and Crane Valley developed into a trading centre for district. Unfortunately, during the construction of the Victoria Company elevator, a carpenter fell

and was killed. The drought and Depression of the 1930s hit the district hard, and many area farmers left for regions further north in the province. Crane Valley would never quite recover its previous vitality. In the past few decades, the population of the small community has dropped even further. It was 117 in 1969. The rail line into Crane Valley was abandoned in 1998 and the K-12 school remained the focal point of the community. Due to declining enrollment, however, Crane Valley School was closed at the end of June 2007. The economic basis of the area is grain farming and livestock production. Crane Valley is situated in the RM of Excel No. 71.

CRAVEN, village, pop 274 (2006c), 264 (2001c), is nestled in the Qu'Appelle Valley, northeast of Lumsden, where Last Mountain Lake tapers into the Qu'Appelle River. The community is served by Hwys 20 and 99. Settlement in the Craven area

dates from 1882, when the first few homesteaders made incursions into the district. The first store was established in 1883, and on February 1, 1884, the Craven Post Office opened (although originally in the area of Valeport). The name Craven honours William Craven (1606-97), Earl of Craven, a military man and an ardent English royalist. Leslie H. Hoskins, appointed the Craven postmaster in 1886, served in the position until his death in 1941, a term of over 55 years, thought perhaps to be the longest served by any postmaster in Canada. Interestingly, his successor, Agnes Rose (Torrie) Clatworthy held the position until 1976, a period of 35 years, and thus Craven had only two postmasters over a 90 year period. In 1885-86, a railway branch line was built from Regina to Craven (the terminus of the line was named Sussex); the idea was that another rail line would be built from Prince Albert to the north end of Last Mountain Lake and that the near-100-kilometres length

▲ **ST. NICHOLAS ANGLICAN CHURCH**, in the valley east of Craven, is reputedly Saskatchewan's most photographed church. Photograph taken circa 1999-2000.

▲ **NESTLED IN THE QU'APPELLE VALLEY** just south of Last Mountain Lake: Craven, from the southwest, July 10, 2003.

▲ **THE FORMER SASKATCHEWAN WHEAT POOL FACILITY** (SWP B) in Creelman consists of three parts: on the far right was a Lake of the Woods Milling Company elevator built in 1906; centre is an early crib annex; the elevator on the left dates to the mid-1960s. The facility has been purchased by Fill-More Seeds Inc., based in Fillmore, Saskatchewan. The company processes chickpeas, lentils, and edible peas.
Photograph taken August 19, 2003.

of the lake would be traversed by steamboats, linking the two lines. That the lake could be frozen for almost six months of the year apparently had not been factored into the scheme, and the rail line saw little use over the following years. By 1890, the Qu'Appelle, Long Lake, and Saskatchewan Railroad had completed a track through Saskatoon to Prince Albert, and with the completion of the CPR line from Regina through Craven to Lanigan in 1911, trade on the old "Sussex Branch" dwindled to almost nil. The last train trundled over the oldest railway branch line in what is now the province of Saskatchewan in 1927. The development of railways on both the east and west side of Last Mountain Lake also effectively killed the steamboat traffic on the lake, and Craven never became the transportation hub some imagined it could be. The small community did continue to slowly develop, however, and on April 11, 1905, the Village of Craven was incorporated. The population was recorded at 83 in 1906, and the community only grew very little over the next several decades. In the 1970s, though, following the twinning of Hwy 11 and the Qu'Appelle Valley becom-

ing more attractive to commuters, Craven began to grow at an unprecedented rate. Today the community is widely known for its summer music festivals, which began in 1983 with The Big Valley Jamboree, a widely-acclaimed country music extravaganza. In 1998, the format of the Craven concerts was changed to rock and roll, but after several years the focus became more on partying than music, and in 2005 the decision was made to return to the more family-oriented country music format. Other attractions in the Craven area include several market gardens where farmers sell vegetables and fruit. Roughly eight kilometres north of the village, on the shore of Last Mountain Lake, is the site of Last Mountain House, a short-lived Hudson's Bay Company post which operated from 1869 to 1871. Craven is situated in the RM of Longlaketon No. 219.

CRAWFORD ESTATES, organized hamlet, pop 60 (2006c), 50 (2001c), is a fairly recently developed residential subdivision located east of Regina, north of Hwy 1 on the Pilot Butte access road. Largely a bedroom community for people who work in Regina, Crawford Estates was established as an organized hamlet on January 1, 2002, and is situated in the RM of Edenwold No. 158.

CREELMAN, village, pop 81 (2006c), 85 (2001c), is located 27 km northwest of Stoughton on Hwy 33. The village had its beginnings with the construction of the railway between Stoughton and Regina in 1903-04. The post office was established in 1904, and in 1906 the Village of Creelman was incorporated. The community was named by the CPR, after A.R. Creelman, a lawyer working for the

railroad at the time. The village developed as a small agricultural trading centre and had a peak population of 215 in 1956. While today there is some local employment in Creelman, residents also commute to work in Weyburn, Stoughton, or Fillmore. Fillmore has the nearest health centre and RCMP detachment, as well as a K-12 school. Creelman School was closed in 1995. Each fall, for close to 30 years, the Creelman Drama Club puts on a dinner theatre that draws people from a wide area and that sells out year after year. Another popular annual event is the Creelman Agricultural Society Fair: the 100th anniversary of the event was in 2004. Acclaimed Saskatchewan artist Richard Widdifield was raised in the Creelman district and graduated from Creelman School in 1979. Creelman is situated in the RM of Fillmore No. 96.

◄ **CREELMAN'S UNIQUE GLASS BRICK WAR MEMORIAL** commemorates local people who died in World War I and World War II. Photograph taken August 19, 2003.

CREIGHTON, northern town, pop 1,502 (2006c), 1,556 (2001c), is located in north-eastern Saskatchewan near the Saskatchewan-Manitoba border, three km southwest of Flin Flon. Situated almost at the 55th parallel, it lies within the Precambrian Shield and is one of only two municipalities with town status in northern Saskatchewan (the other is La Ronge). By road, Creighton is accessed via Hwy 106 (the Hanson Lake Road) or, on the Manitoba side, by Hwy 10 from The Pas. Highway 167, leading south from Creighton, gives access to Denare Beach and picturesque Amisk Lake, the south end of which was the scene of Saskatchewan's first and little-known gold rush, which occurred between 1914 and 1918. Creighton had its beginnings in the 1930s after the Department of Natural Resources built a road from Flin Flon to Amisk Lake. People began to settle along this road, and after WWII a townsite was surveyed and lots were made available for residential and business development. Many servicemen returning from overseas came to the area, and in 1952 the community was incorporated as a village. Creighton attained town status in 1957. The community was named after Tom Creighton, whose prospecting discoveries in 1915 were largely responsible for the development of mining operations at Flin Flon. Today, the

Hudson Bay Mining & Smelting Company is by far the largest employer in the area, producing zinc, copper, and gold. Other economic activities are based on forestry and tourism. While Creighton has its own small commercial sector, a K-12 school, an RCMP detachment, and a number of government services, the city of Flin Flon provides many amenities and is a significant source of employment.

CROOKED RIVER, hamlet, pop 64 (2001c), 78 (1996c), is located east of Tisdale at the junction of Hwys 3 and 23. Begun as a sawmill settlement in the early 1900s, Crooked River takes its name from a twisting waterway that winds northward through the area. The first lumber companies began operating at Crooked River about 1905 (the post office was established that year) as the railroad from Hudson Bay (then known as Etoimami) to Prince Albert was nearing completion. People from many parts of Canada and from overseas came to work in the mills and the forests, and as the bush was cleared, many began to engage in agriculture. In the 1920s a grain elevator was built at Crooked River, and the community became a key grain handling point until late in the decade when railway branch lines were built from Crooked River southeast through Porcupine Plain and north to Arborfield. Following WWII, agriculture replaced lumbering as the main industry in the region, as most of the heavy timber had been harvested. The shutdown of sawmill operations at this time had

the effect of reducing the population, for many workers followed the mill as it was relocated to British Columbia. Those who stayed began clearing the remaining tree stumps, opening up every available acre of land for farming. By the mid-1950s, crop yields averaged a consistent 40 bushels an acre. By the 1960s, though, Crooked River was in serious decline. The population was 154 in 1966, but by 1972 it had fallen to 96, and thereafter the community's numbers continued to dwindle. The small core of businesses, too, began to disappear, largely superseded by those in neighbouring Tisdale. Crooked River's curling rink was last used in 1987, and a couple of years later the outdoor rink was flooded for the last time. At the end of the school year in 1989, Crooked River School was closed, with area students thereafter being bused to Tisdale, Arborfield, or Bjorkdale. The only businesses left in the community today are home-based enterprises such as a cabinet maker and a small equipment repair service. From 1977 until 2006 Crooked River had the status of an organized hamlet; the community remains the administrative centre of the RM of Bjorkdale No. 426, as it has been since 1937.

CRUTWELL, organized hamlet, pop 37 (2006c), 77 (2001c), is located roughly halfway between Prince Albert and Shellbrook on Hwy 3. In the early 1900s, there were several cordwood and railway tie cutting camps in the district, and with the opening of the railroad from Prince Albert to Shellbrook in 1910, Crutwell became a collection and shipping point for wood harvested from a considerable district. It was named for a Canadian Northern Railway official. Crutwell also became a grain handling point, and for many years a ferry

operated on the North Saskatchewan River just south of the hamlet, which gave farmers in the Lily Plain district across the river access to Crutwell's elevators. A post office opened in the hamlet in 1923; it closed in 1985. In 1947, a school was opened in the community; however, it was only in operation for a few years. In the 1950s and 1960s, the Saskatchewan Penitentiary at Prince Albert operated a work camp for inmates in the area between Crutwell and the neighbouring hamlet of Holbein — land was cleared, wood was cut, and chickens and horses were raised. Crutwell was formally established as an organized hamlet in 1978, and over the years it had developed into a largely Metis community. Beginning in 1982, a popular winter festival was held in the hamlet, which featured traditional activities such as dogsled races and competitions in trapping and forestry skills. In 1992, the Saskatchewan Wheat Pool began construction of a large high throughput terminal at White Star (a little more than 10 kilometres north of Prince Albert) and subsequently began closing grain elevators in communities throughout the region. The rail line between Prince Albert and Shellbrook was then abandoned, and with the discontinuance of grain handling activities in the communities along the line, much of their lifeblood was sapped. Crutwell today remains as a weary collection of boarded-up houses, a few house trailers and other homes scattered along a sandy road in the trees. Crutwell is situated in the RM of Shellbrook No. 493.

CRYSTAL BAY-SUNSET, organized hamlet, is located in west-central Saskatchewan, east of St. Walburg, and it is one of several resort communities situated on Brightsand Lake. The resort,

which began to be developed in the 1960s, became an organized hamlet within the RM of Mervin No. 499 in 1991. The population varies depending on the season, reaching approximately 125 during the summer months.

CRYSTAL LAKE, organized hamlet, is a resort community in east-central Saskatchewan, southeast of Sturgis, off Hwy 9. The first homesteaders arrived in the area in the early 1900s, and soon the lake, surrounded by spruce and poplar trees, became popular for fishing and swimming. In the 1930s, significant development took place: beach areas were developed and cottages, a store, and a golf course were built. A youth camp was established by Ukrainian Orthodox churches in the area. In the mid-1960s, a drive-in theatre became an added attraction. Crystal Lake was set up as an organized hamlet in 1987. There were 74 permanent residents in 2006; however, the population varies

greatly depending on the season. Crystal Lake is located in the RM of Keys No. 303.

CRYSTAL SPRINGS, organized hamlet, pop 23 (2006c), 25 (2001c), is located southeast of Birch Hills on Hwy 20. In the late 1890s and the early 1900s, settlers began taking up land in the area. They were French, Ukrainian, Hungarian, and Anglo-Saxon; Norwegians settled slightly to the north. The Crystal Springs Post Office was established in the district in 1909, the name derived from the French "Bonne Eau" meaning "good water." French Roman Catholic priests had established a mission on what is now known as Tway Lake prior to the North-West Resistance, and it is likely the name originates with them. The present community of Crystal Lake, however, developed with the construction of the railway from Humboldt to Prince Albert, which arrived in the area in 1929-30. Crystal Springs was established as an organized

▼ **CRYSTAL LAKE**, July 27, 2004.

hamlet in 1952. The population was 87 in 1966, but by 1972 it was down to 65. Subsequently, both the community's numbers and small core of businesses have continued to dwindle. Crystal Springs serves as the administrative centre of the RM of Invergordon No. 430.

CUDSASKWA BEACH, organized hamlet, is a resort community located approximately 12 km east of Wakaw, on the northwest shore of Wakaw Lake. It lies adjacent to Wakaw Lake Regional Park and is one of a number of cottage communities that surround the lake. Cudsaskwa Beach was established as an organized hamlet in 1974. It has a small number of permanent residents; however, there are roughly 100 cottages, so the population varies widely depending on the season. Cudsaskwa Beach is situated in the RM of Hoodoo No. 401.

CUDWORTH, town, pop 738 (2006c), 766 (2001c), is located south of Wakaw on Hwy 2 in the Minichinas Hills, an area of rolling aspen parkland. Ukrainian and French settlers began taking up land to the west and south of present-day Cudworth in the late 1890s, and the district population was significantly bolstered by German American Catholics who began establishing what came to be known as St. Peter's Colony in 1902. As Cudworth developed, it came to be comprised largely of people of Ukrainian, German, and French origins. In 1911, the village of Cudworth was established, as the railway was to be built north through the area, eventually to connect with Prince Albert in 1917. Cudworth developed at a steady rate (other than a slight slump experienced during the Depression) until the early

▲ **PUBLIC AND HIGH SCHOOL**, Cudworth. The left side of the school including the central tower was built in 1914; the right side was added in 1922 to accommodate a growing student population.

◄ **THIS PLAQUE** on the southeast edge of Cudworth commemorates the founding of St. Peter's Colony in 1902. Photograph taken August 10, 2004.

CUDWORTH
...the "Gateway to St. Peter's Colony"

► **THE FIRST CUDWORTH BAR**, circa 1914. The man standing in the front is John Wickenhouser. Photograph courtesy of the Watson and District Heritage Museum.

▼ **MAC METROPOLIT** (Cudworth town councilman for 14 years) as Santa Claus in 1954 in the first Santa Claus Day Parade, which he organized.

▼ **GRAIN TRUCKS LINED UP** at Cudworth's elevators, date unknown. Only one of the four elevators pictured here remains standing today.

Historical photographs of Cudworth, unless otherwise indicated, are courtesy of Audrey Cherneski, Cudworth, Saskatchewan.

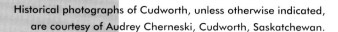

▲ **EMPLOYEES OF THE CUDWORTH RURAL TELEPHONE COMPANY**, circa 1964-65. The company merged with SaskTel in 1977.

▲ **TRAIN DERAILMENT** south of Cudworth in 1966.

◄ **SCHMIDT STORE AND HOTEL FIRE**, Cudworth, March, 1973. The fire started in the hotel.

▼ **PILGRIMAGE:** A few kilometres south of Cudworth, the Shrine of Our Lady of Sorrows, with its chapel and stations of the cross, draws large numbers of people during an annually conducted pilgrimage. This pilgrimage took place in 1999.

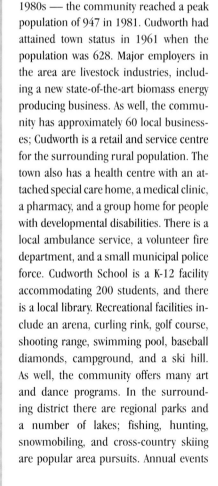

1980s — the community reached a peak population of 947 in 1981. Cudworth had attained town status in 1961 when the population was 628. Major employers in the area are livestock industries, including a new state-of-the-art biomass energy producing business. As well, the community has approximately 60 local businesses; Cudworth is a retail and service centre for the surrounding rural population. The town also has a health centre with an attached special care home, a medical clinic, a pharmacy, and a group home for people with developmental disabilities. There is a local ambulance service, a volunteer fire department, and a small municipal police force. Cudworth School is a K-12 facility accommodating 200 students, and there is a local library. Recreational facilities include an arena, curling rink, golf course, shooting range, swimming pool, baseball diamonds, campground, and a ski hill. As well, the community offers many art and dance programs. In the surrounding district there are regional parks and a number of lakes; fishing, hunting, snowmobiling, and cross-country skiing are popular area pursuits. Annual events hosted by the community include a fair held in July. Cudworth's former CNR station, built in 1925, has been declared a heritage property and has recently been converted into a museum which features German and Ukrainian pioneer artifacts. Cudworth has a number of volunteer and service organizations. The community is provided with bus and rail services and has a municipal airport. Cudworth serves as the administrative centre of the RM of Hoodoo No. 401.

CUMBERLAND HOUSE,

northern village, pop 810 (2006c), 632 (2001c), is situated 163 km northeast of Nipawin at the end of Hwy 123. Although Cumberland House is remote in terms of access by land, historically the community was centrally located in terms of water-based travel. During the fur-trade era, Cumberland House served as a key transportation hub and supply depot as waterways led north and northwest to the fur-rich Churchill and Athabasca regions, east to Hudson Bay, and southwest onto the plains and the herds of bison that provided the pemmican that fed the fur-trading brigades. Cumberland House became an important collecting and distribution centre for the staple. Situated on an island which separates Cumberland Lake from the Saskatchewan River, the community was established in 1774 by Samuel Hearne for the Hudson's Bay Company. It was the company's first inland trading post, the purpose of which was to compete with Montreal traders who were effectively intercepting North-West furs before they could reach Hudson Bay. The post was named for Prince Rupert, the Duke of Cumberland, who was the first governor of the Hudson's Bay Company. Cumberland House became the oldest permanent

settlement in Saskatchewan and western Canada. In 1781-82, smallpox took a devastating toll on the indigenous population; yet, while many died, the community survived. In 1840, an Anglican mission was established at Cumberland House by catechist Henry Budd, a Swampy Cree, who later became the first ordained minister of First Nations ancestry. Following the Red River insurrection in 1870, a number of Manitoba Métis came to the Cumberland district, and a Roman Catholic mission was established to serve these newcomers. The Cumberland House Cree Nation, whose reserve lands are located southeast of the village, signed an adhesion to Treaty No. 5 in 1876. Between 1874 and 1925, Cumberland House was an important centre for the steamboat traffic on the Saskatchewan River systems. The remains of the *S.S. Northcote*, which was involved in the battle at Batoche in 1885, are today

▲ **CUMBERLAND HOUSE**, February 1974. Saskatchewan Archives Board, Saskatchewan Photographic Services, 73-1843-116. Photographer: D. Varley.

▼ **REMAINS OF THE NORTHCOTE**, Cumberland House, August 20, 2004. The Northcote was permanently beached at Cumberland House in 1886.

situated in a park at Cumberland House. Between 1900 and the beginning of WWI, a second wave of Métis people arrived from St. Laurent, Manitoba. During both World Wars, many of the community's young men left Cumberland House to serve overseas, which had a great social, economic, and psychological impact on the entire community. A number never returned. As the twentieth century progressed, fewer people were making a living off of the land, and more were settling in the community. Not only had the demand for furs substantially declined, but developments in Cumberland House enticed individuals to lead a more sedentary life. In the 1940s, a hospital was built in Cumberland House, the provincial government started a local sawmill, initiated farming operations, and assumed full responsibility for the community's school. Family allowance payments conditional upon a child's attending school added an additional incentive to settle in the village. Outlying settlements in the district disappeared as Cumberland House grew. Both positive and negative developments followed: in 1966, an all-weather road was built into the area, giving residents a new connection with the outside world; however, it stopped at the south shore of the Saskatchewan River, necessitating reliance on a seasonal ferry service. The construction of the Squaw Rapids (now E. B. Campbell) Dam in the 1960s adversely effected the traditional livelihoods of many in the area: it dramatically altered water levels, significantly impacting animal populations and the navigation of the area waterways; in addition, the dam's reservoir caused mercury levels in fish to increase. In 1976, the community and the neighbouring Cumberland House Cree Nation sued the Saskatchewan Power Corporation and SaskWater for damages;

it took 13 years before a settlement was reached. In 1989, a compensation package worth an estimated $23 million was agreed upon. The Cumberland House Development Corporation was established to administer the funds. In 1996, a bridge was built across the Saskatchewan River; no longer were people reliant on the seasonal ferry service, and no longer were hazardous river crossings necessary when the ferry was unusable. Today, the combined population of the northern village and the adjacent reserve totals approximately 1,200 persons. Together they comprise one of Saskatchewan's principal Metis communities. The Cree heritage is particularly strong, as many people speak a dialect of Swampy Cree as well as English. Unemployment is a problem for this remote community, and many find it necessary to rely on government assistance. Some income, as well as food, is still derived from the traditional activities of trapping, hunting, and fishing, and a number of outfitters and guides accommodate hunters from all over North America each fall. Logging, cattle raising, wild rice harvesting, and the production of maple syrup provide additional opportunities. Some residents of Cumberland House are employed at northern uranium mines. Teaching positions, policing, administrative and clerical work, and work in health care also provide some employment. Cumberland House has a small core of local businesses, an airstrip, an RCMP detachment, and a health centre. Charlebois School provides K-12 education; it had 225 students enrolled in the fall of 2006. A small museum contains artifacts and photographs related to the community's unique and long history. Notable people from Cumberland House include Keith Goulet, Saskatchewan's first Metis cabinet minister; Judge Gerald

M. Morin of the Saskatchewan Provincial Court; and Solomon Carriere, a four-time world marathon canoeing champion.

CUPAR, town, pop 566 (2006c), 602 (2001c), is located 21 km east of Southey on Hwy 22; Fort Qu'Appelle lies approximately 45 km to the southeast. Settlers began arriving in the late 1800s and the early 1900s, and the community developed to be truly multi-cultural. Prior to the turn of the century, settlers were largely of Scottish, English, and Irish descent; afterwards, many came from eastern Europe, particularly, the historic polyglot province of Bukovina (now split between Romania and Ukraine). A significant number were Hungarian, but there was also a small quotient of Romanian Jews who settled in the district around 1906. The townsite was established with the CPR's construction of the rail line through the area in 1905, and Cupar was incorporated as a village in 1906. Named after Cupar, Fife, Scotland, the community developed into a significant service and trading centre for the surrounding agricultural district, growing steadily from the time of its inception until about the mid-1970s, at which point the population stabilized around its current level. Cupar attained town status in 1961 and is an attractive community with curbed paved streets, tree-lined boulevards, and well-kept yards and homes. The community has a range of businesses which include automotive, banking, legal, and financial services, and a number of enterprises which cater to the area's agricultural industry. Cupar has a health centre, a special care home, ambulance service, and a volunteer fire department. The community is patrolled by the RCMP. Cupar School is a K-12 facility, which had 184 students enrolled in the fall of 2005.

The town has one of the more impressive museums in rural Saskatchewan. Recreational facilities include an indoor arena, an outdoor swimming pool, ball diamonds, a golf course, and sports grounds dedicated to the Shore family of Cupar. Cupar was the home of Eddie Shore, legendary defenseman with the Boston Bruins, Stanley Cup champion, and inductee into the NHL Hall of Fame. His father, T. J. Shore, financed the first enclosed rink in Cupar in 1911. The town's main annual event is the "Cupar Gopher Drop," devised as a community fund-raising event in 1993. Residents purchase tickets on numbered stuffed facsimiles of the rodent which are then dropped from a hot air balloon. Prizes are awarded according their landing in proximity to target gopher holes. The event is the highlight of a day-long celebration which includes sporting events, concessions, rides, and an evening dance. Cupar serves as the administrative centre of the RM of Cupar No. 218.

CUT KNIFE, town, pop 532 (2006c), 556 (2001c), is located 50 km west of the Battlefords on Hwy 40. The Little Pine, Poundmaker, and Sweet Grass First Nations are situated north and east of the community. The name Cut Knife was derived from Cut Knife Hill (now Chief Poundmaker Hill) on the Poundmaker reserve. The hill was named for a Sarcee chief whose name was roughly translated to "Cut Knife" and who was slain near the location during a skirmish with the Cree in the 1840s. Cut Knife Hill was also the location of Colonel Otter's encounter with, and retreat from, Chief Poundmaker's forces during the North-West Resistance. When settlers of European origin arrived in the district in the early 1900s, they adopted the name for their community. In

▲ **WETTLAUFER'S FORD DEALERSHIP**, Cut Knife, 1921. Courtesy of the Clayton McLain Memorial Museum, Cut Knife.

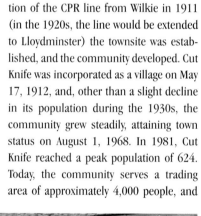

▲ **PUPILS AND TEACHERS** of Cut Knife School, 1923-24 term. Courtesy of the Clayton McLain Memorial Museum, Cut Knife.

1952, Governor General Vincent Massey unveiled a cairn erected by the Historic Sites and Monuments Board of Canada at Cut Knife Hill that memorializes the heroism on both sides of the 1885 conflict and pays tribute to Chief Poundmaker for restraining his men from slaughtering Otter's troops during their retreat. Homesteaders began arriving in the Cut Knife district around 1903-04, and the community would come to be comprised of British, Italian, Ukrainian, and Scandinavian people, as well as members of the Aboriginal population. With the construction of the CPR line from Wilkie in 1911 (in the 1920s, the line would be extended to Lloydminster) the townsite was established, and the community developed. Cut Knife was incorporated as a village on May 17, 1912, and, other than a slight decline in its population during the 1930s, the community grew steadily, attaining town status on August 1, 1968. In 1981, Cut Knife reached a peak population of 624. Today, the community serves a trading area of approximately 4,000 people, and grain farming and cattle ranching form the basis of the regional economy. The oil and gas industry, however, is becoming increasingly significant. Cut Knife has a health centre and a special care home, an RCMP detachment, banking services, hotels, restaurants, a library, churches, and a range of recreational facilities. The town's elementary and high schools provide K-12 education to approximately 270 students. A community park features a campground, an impressive museum consisting of several heritage buildings, and a tourist attraction described as "the world's largest tomahawk." There is a regional park just northeast of Cut Knife and slightly farther is the Table Mountain ski resort. Cut Knife serves as the administrative centre of the RM of Cut Knife No. 439.

◄ **SUMMER STUDENTS** Casey Gaw (left) and Andrea Waters (centre) employed at the Clayton McLain Memorial Museum in Cut Knife, August 13, 2003. At right is their friend Anna Weikle.

▼ **THE "WORLD'S LARGEST TOMAHAWK."** Perched upon a 9-metre-high teepee in Cut Knife's community park, the tomahawk sculpture was erected in 1971 as a part of Saskatchewan's Homecoming celebrations, and was built to symbolize unity and friendship between the area populations. Photograph taken August 13, 2003.

DAFOE, village, pop 10 (2006c), 15 (2001c), is located just southwest of Big Quill Lake on Hwys 6 and 16. Wynyard, 24 km east, is the nearest larger centre. There was significant settlement of the area by Icelanders beginning in 1905, and German settlers beginning in 1906, and with the construction of the CPR line from Wynyard to Lanigan in 1909-10 the townsite of Dafoe was established. The village was incorporated in 1920, and, although it was never a large community (it had a peak population of 131 in 1926), it grew into a service and trading centre for the area's mixed-farming community. At one time, Dafoe had five grain elevators, about 20 other businesses, and a well-attended school. As provincial roads and highways were developed, Dafoe was positioned at the intersection of major north-south and east-west crossroads. About one third of the community's population was lost during the 1930s; however, the advent of WWII was to have a significant impact on the Dafoe area. In 1941, a British Commonwealth Air Training Plan base, No. 5 Bombing and Gunnery School, was opened just north of the village. The base and the adjacent community, "Boomtown," which sprang up overnight, housing civilians and married military personnel and their families, grew to have a combined population of approximately 1,400. Dafoe area farmers, businessmen, and labourers provided a variety of services, and goods such as dairy products and meat. Dafoe's theatre, curling rinks, and dance halls were actively patronized. The base ceased operations in early 1945, and local lore has it that many an unexploded bomb dropped during training exercises lay beneath the waters of Big Quill Lake. By the late 1950s, Dafoe was in decline.

Businesses and services closed or moved to larger centres, and the population began to plummet. Today, other than a seed processing plant, there are no services in the village. There is, however, a service station with a restaurant and convenience store a few kilometres north at the highway junction. Dafoe is situated in the RM of Big Quill No. 308.

DALMENY, town, pop 1,560 (2006c), 1,610 (2001c), is located 24 km northwest of Saskatoon on Hwy 305. The district began to be settled in the early 1900s, most significantly by a large Mennonite population. A Mennonite Brethren Church was built at Dalmeny in 1901. With the arrival of the Canadian Northern Railway in 1904-05, the townsite developed. In 1906, the post office opened, the first grain elevator was built, and a general store was established. Named after Dalmeny, Scotland, the community was incorporated as a village in 1912, but re-

linquished this standing in 1914. However, in 1919, Dalmeny once again acquired village status. The community grew slowly but steadily until the 1960s, having developed into a service centre for the surrounding farming population. Beginning in the 1970s, though, Dalmeny began to attract people who worked in Saskatoon, but chose to live in a smaller community. Young professionals and their families sent the village's population from 417 in 1971 to 1,064 a decade later. In 1983, Dalmeny attained town status. Dalmeny has a small core of essential businesses; however, residents largely benefit from the employment opportunities, services, and amenities that Saskatoon has to offer. Dalmeny's two schools provide K-12 education to over 500 students, and the town has a library, its own municipal police service, a fire department, and a special care home. Recreational facilities include a new community complex with a rink for hockey and skating. Dalmeny is situated in the RM of Corman Park No. 344.

DARLINGS BEACH, organized hamlet, is a resort community located southwest of Swift Current on the east side of Lac Pelletier. It is bordered to the north and south by Lac Pelletier Regional Park and is one of several developed areas on the lake's shores. Lac Pelletier has been popular for swimming and fishing since the early 1900s; Darlings Beach was established as an organized hamlet in 1968. There are a small number of permanent residents; however, the population varies greatly depending on the season. Darlings Beach is situated in the RM of Lac Pelletier No. 107.

DAVIDSON, town, pop 958 (2006c), 1,035 (2001c), is located roughly midway between Regina and Saskatoon on Hwy 11. The railway through the area, which today's highway parallels, was built in the late 1880s. Trains were running the

▼ **DALMENY, CIRCA 1920s.** Third Street from Railway Avenue to Wakefield Avenue, looking north. Shown on left are an agricultural implement store, the post office, and A.R. Friesen's general store. Shown on far right is J.G. Williams and Son's General Store. Saskatchewan Archives Board S-B11730.

distance from Regina through Saskatoon and on to Prince Albert in 1890, but for more than a decade after its completion the line served merely as a bridge between the southern and central regions of the province. The first residents of the Davidson area were the Meshen family. Charles Meshen was a section foreman for the railroad, and between 1899 and 1902 he and his family spent the summer months living out of a boxcar just south of the present townsite. The location was then known as Finsbury. Mr. Meshen spent his days seeing to the maintenance of the track through the area, a region deemed to be nothing more than a desert-like wasteland. In 1902, at the urging of the Canadian government, Colonel Andrew Duncan Davidson formed the Saskatchewan Valley Land Company and began aggressive campaigns to promote immigration to the area. As much of Davidson's advertising was aimed at Americans, his marketing strategy included naming some of the townsite's streets after former U.S. presidents. Washington, Lincoln, Grant, and Garfield were among those such honoured. Colonel Davidson was immensely successful. The first few settlers arrived in 1902, but in 1903 waves of home-

steaders began pouring into the region. The Meshens built a house in town that year, the post office was established, and by early 1904 about 15 businesses were in operation (although many of these were in makeshift shacks). The population around the fledgling community at the time numbered close to 100, and on March 7, 1904, Davidson was incorporated as a village. Two years later the population of the community was over 500, and on November 15, 1906, Davidson became a town. Davidson became the trading centre for a large area that included the Watrous, Long Lake, Elbow, and Outlook districts in the years before rail lines were built into those regions, and very early on Davidson earned the nickname "The Midway Town" because of its location centred between the cities of Saskatoon, Regina and Moose Jaw. Today, Davidson serves a trading area of approximately 10,000 people, and the town has a wide array of businesses providing a variety of goods and services. Davidson is also one of the province's major grain handling points and agricultural service centres. Additionally, the town's health centre and volunteer fire department provide emergency services for a large surrounding area.

Policing in the community is provided by the Craik RCMP detachment. Elementary and high schools in Davidson provide K-12 education to approximately 220 town and area students. The community also has a pre-school. Post-secondary education and a variety of programs for adults are available through the Carlton Trail Regional College. Community recreational facilities include an outdoor heated swimming pool, a campground, a community centre with skating and curling rinks, a bowling alley, and a nine-hole golf course. Davidson has a number of churches, service clubs and community-based organizations, youth groups, and sports programs. The community has a library and a weekly newspaper, the *Davidson Leader*, established in 1904. Because of the town's central location, it has become established as a meeting place for business people and a variety of organizations from Saskatchewan's major cities. The community provides accommodations and facilities for conventions and banquets. Additionally, Davidson's centrality has led to the development of a 40-acre industrial park for industries wishing to be strategically located. Davidson serves as the administrative centre of the RM of Arm River No. 252.

DAVIN, organized hamlet, pop 49 (2006c), 50 (2001c), lies roughly 35 km southeast of Regina on Hwy 48. A few settlers from eastern Canada were making their way into the Davin region by the late 1880s, but beginning in the early 1890s German Lutherans from southern Russia and areas that are today in Austria and Romania began settling the district in significant numbers. Although an area post office by the name of Davin existed from 1890, the townsite of the present commu-

nity was not developed until the railroad came through in 1907-08. The name Davin honours Nicholas Flood Davin, who founded the *Regina Leader* in 1883 and who was the Conservative MP for Assiniboia West from 1887-1900. Before the arrival of the railroad, Davin area farmers often did their business in Qu'Appelle; mail was brought into the post office once a week from Balgonie. In 1905, Emmaus Lutheran Church was built on the homestead of Peter Brandt, immediately northwest of the present-day Davin; it was later moved into the hamlet. For a number of decades, Davin was a small service centre for the surrounding farming district; however, in recent times the hamlet has developed into a bedroom community for people who work in Regina. The community's school closed in the early 1970s, and children have subsequently attended classes in Balgonie. Davin was established as an organized hamlet in 1977 and is situated within the boundaries of the RM of Lajord No. 128.

DAY'S BEACH, organized hamlet, is located north of North Battleford, on the east side of Jackfish Lake — it is one of several resort communities in the area. In 1927, George Day, who owned lakefront property, opened up his land to develop a summer resort — hence, the community's name. Today, there are approximately 50 year-round residents and dozens of cottages, and the population varies greatly depending on the season. Day's Beach is situated in the RM of Meota No. 468.

DEBDEN, village, pop 348 (2006c), 355 (2001c), is located on Hwy 55, 93 km northwest of Prince Albert, between the communities of Canwood and Big River.

Debden developed as a French-Canadian settlement, and although the community evolved over the years to become comprised of people of many different backgrounds and cultures, the village today still retains a distinctive French flavour. People of French origin still comprise approximately two-thirds of Debden's population. Around 1909, French-Canadian labourers were drawn from Quebec and New England to work in the logging and pulp mill industries then developing at and around Big River. By 1912, many French-speaking families had settled the Debden district, many led to the region by Father Philippe Antoine Bérubé, who had been the parish priest at Vonda and who had been asked to help settle French families in the Debden-Victoire area. Bérubé Lake, the site of a provincial game preserve just southwest of Debden, is named in his honour. In 1910, the Canadian Northern Railway line was built north from Shellbrook to Big River to bring lumber out of the area, and the locale where Debden now stands was first known only as "Siding No. 4." When a post office was to be established in 1912, it was time to give a proper name to the

emerging hamlet, and railway officials chose the name Debden, after a village in England, in spite of the preponderance of French people in the district. That same year, the parish of St. Jean Baptiste at Debden was founded. The local school district was organized in 1914, and in 1915 Debden School opened its doors. As the area pioneers worked to clear the land, they sold or traded cordwood in order to obtain provisions. Additionally, homes were built from wood harvested in the area, as was furniture — tables, chairs, cupboards, and beds. Saw mills did a brisk business. Once cleared, the land proved rich and fertile; gardens were planted to provide individual families with food, and grain crops began to be produced. The first grain elevator was built in Debden in 1916. Interestingly, there is evidence that the infamous outlaw, Sam Kelley, having taken an early retirement from his first profession, turned over a new leaf and was homesteading in the Debden area around this time. A local legend is that Kelley and an adversary once squared off for a gun fight on a Debden street, but after circling each other and staring

each other down, both withdrew without a shot being fired. By 1920, Debden had developed substantially. Numerous businesses were operating, including three grain elevators, and an impressive Roman Catholic Church and a rectory had been built. On June 7, 1922, the Village of Debden was incorporated. The community had become the supply and service centre for a considerable territory; farmers who had travelled a long distance to Debden to sell their wheat and wanted to spend the night found a hotel, numerous rooming houses, restaurants, and a livery stable. Only after 1931, when the CPR completed a line west-northwest from Debden to Meadow Lake, did the community lose some of its importance as a shipping and receiving centre, as farmers along that line were then able to ship produce from and receive freight in their own respective communities. By WWII, however, Debden was again prospering and its population was growing. In 1942, Sisters of the Presentation of Mary arrived to teach school and conduct other community work, and in 1954 the near-monumental edifice of the new St. Jean Baptiste Roman Catholic Church rose above the village streets, replacing the 1918 structure that had burned down in 1951. In the mid-1950s, the community's then almost exclusive French culture began to be tested, as area rural schools started closing. With rural students being bused into the village, suddenly French students were becoming a minority at Debden School. Over the ensuing decades, however, several measures were undertaken to ensure the preser-

vation of Debden's French culture and heritage. A French Immersion program was put in place at Debden School, and a focus on French culture was integrated into the academic curriculum. A bilingual public library and bilingual street signs also bolstered the French language. In 1986, a large community facility which partially serves as a French cultural centre was built; French music, videos, greeting cards, etc., are available there. The building also houses a museum that honours the community's pioneers. Various village organizations, such as a French-language pre-school, also work toward preserving Debden's unique heritage. Today, the community has a wide range of businesses and services; it also has a health clinic and home care available. The nearest hospitals are in Big River and Shellbrook, where the nearest RCMP detachments are also located. The Debden area economy is based primarily upon agriculture, with much livestock, including exotic game, being raised, and upon lumbering, particularly at the mill operations near Big River. Debden is situated in the RM of Canwood No. 494.

◄ **CENTRE COMMUNAUTAIRE DE DEBDEN / DEBDEN COMMUNITY CENTRE**, east side of 2nd Avenue East. Photograph taken September 22, 2003.

DELISLE, town, pop 898 (2006c), 884 (2001c), is located approximately 40 km southwest of Saskatoon at the junction of Hwys 7 and 45. Settlers began taking up land in the area in the first few years of the twentieth century, and by 1905 a small semblance of a village had begun to appear a few kilometres south of the present townsite. A post office was established that year, taking its name from the first postmaster, John Amos Delisle. A few years later, as the railway was being built from Saskatoon to Rosetown, the fledgling community relocated to its present location to be situated on the rail line. Delisle was in-

▲ **DOWNTOWN DELISLE ON A SATURDAY AFTERNOON.** The west side of 1st Street West; post office on the left.

▼ **THE VALLEYVIEW GOLF COURSE** in Delisle opened in 2002. The nine-hole grass green course winds along, and into, the north end of the town.

Photographs taken August 28, 2004.

corporated as a village in 1908 and became a town in 1913. The community developed primarily as an agricultural service centre until a potash mine was opened just to the north in 1969. The mine boosted the local economy by providing a large number of well-paying jobs. While Delisle's economy is still based largely on agriculture and mining, the town is also increasingly becoming a bedroom community for a number of people who commute to work in Saskatoon. Large local employers in Delisle are the schools, a trucking company, and a significant food processing operation which specializes in producing salads for fast food restaurants and major grocery stores across Saskatchewan and Alberta. Delisle also has a range of businesses providing a variety of goods and services. The community has an RCMP detachment, a volunteer fire department, and first responders to assist with emergency situations. A community health centre provides a number of medical services. Delisle's elementary and composite schools provide K-12 education to close to 550 town and area students, and the town has a pre-school for three- and four-year-old children. Recreational facilities include skating and curling rinks, ball diamonds, a senior citizens' centre, and a beautiful golf course which partially winds through the community, adding much to the aesthetic appearance of the town. As well, Pike Lake Provincial Park is just a short drive to the east. Delisle also employs a full-time recreation director who coordinates programs for all ages. Delisle is well-known in curling circles: over the years, both women's and men's teams have won numerous provincial championships. In 2003, the community's composite school football team captured its second provincial championship, having played two complete seasons without a loss. Delisle was also the hometown of NHL hockey legends, Max and Doug Bentley, both inductees into the Hockey Hall of Fame. The community's hockey legacy may have been the inspiration for the 1973 filming of a B-movie in Delisle, "Paperback Hero," the story of a local hockey hero and womanizer who leads a fantasy life as the town gunslinger. Delisle is situated in the RM of Vanscoy No. 345.

DELMAS, organized hamlet, pop 116 (2006c), 112 (2001c), is located approximately 30 km northwest of the Battlefords off of Hwy 16, the Yellowhead Hwy. The origins of Delmas date to 1889 and the arrival of Father Louis Cochin, an Oblate missionary who had been in the North West for several years, ministering to Aboriginal and Métis populations. Delmas, named after Father Henri Delmas, the local priest at the time the railway went through in 1905, became a centre of Roman Catholic activity in the region, and there was a Roman Catholic "Indian" Residential School in Delmas from 1901 until 1948. The school, St. Henri of Thunderchild, which had grown into a sizable complex that dominated the townsite, burned to the ground on January 13, 1948. It was suspected, but never proven, that students had deliberately set the fire. Applications to rebuild were submitted to the government, but were denied. When the Canadian Northern Railway came through the Delmas area, surveyors laid out a townsite at what was the original reserve of the Thunderchild First Nation. These lands were relinquished for sale and exchanged for a reserve northeast of Turtleford in 1908. With more land opened up for homesteading, Father Delmas, an ardent promoter of French settlement, was increasingly successful in attracting settlers from France as well as French Canadian families to the area. In 1910, Delmas was incorporated as a village, and the same year a local school district was established to accommodate the education of "whites." In early 1912, St. Jean Baptiste de la Salle opened its doors, and for the next several decades the Sisters of Assumption oversaw the education of the school's pupils. In the 1920s two grain elevators were erected in Delmas, saving farmers having to shovel grain directly into railway freight cars. The population of the village at the time hovered around 200. By the mid-to-late 1930s, however, there was talk of disorganizing the village and having its affairs completely under the auspices of the R.M. Community members saw no advantage to being incorporated and believed they would save paying a significant amount of taxes. On April 1, 1942, Delmas relinquished village status and reverted to being a hamlet. In 1970, the community decided to organize a hamlet board to determine how the taxes allotted to Delmas from the municipality would be spent. The population of Delmas and the surrounding district began to decrease steadily in the late 1950s, and in the fall of 1967 high school students began to be bused to the Battlefords. In 1969, the Sisters of Assumption left, and by 1976 St. Jean Baptiste de la Salle School was down to one room, with only grades one to four being taught. On June 30, 1979, pupils walked out of the school for the summer, and Mrs. A. Gonda, the teacher, locked the door — the school was permanently closed. The next year the railway station was demolished, its remains buried a few metres away from where the structure had stood for 75 years. One of the former Saskatchewan Wheat Pool elevators remains standing, and a few abandoned businesses dot the townsite. Today, residents of Delmas drive to the Battlefords for shopping, services, employment, and entertainment. Delmas is situated in the RM of Battle River No. 438.

DEMAINE, organized hamlet, pop 20 (2006c), 20 (2001c), is located just east of Beechy in the RM of Victory No. 226; the community is accessed via municipal road No. 737. The origins of the hamlet date to 1910 when an early area settler, E. J. Demaine, established a post office on his homestead just west of the present community. The Demaine School opened somewhat south in 1911. The townsite itself developed with the construction of the railway from Lucky Lake to Beechy in the early 1920s, and Demaine developed into an area trading centre with a number of businesses. The community was very active in sports and hosted many annual events. The population was 118 in 1969, but began to decline sharply thereafter. In 1991 an area farmer lost a battle with CN to keep the siding open at Demaine to load producer cars. The Demaine Hotel, built in the early 1920s, remains in business today and is the centre of many community events. The hamlet has a riding club and an arena where horse shows are held, and another community group organizes scenic wagon treks though the area.

DENARE BEACH, northern village, pop 785 (2006c), 784 (2001c), is located 19 km southwest of Creighton on the northeast part of Amisk Lake. Although there was fur trade activity in the area from the latter 1700s, then prospecting activity and even a small gold rush at the lake in the early 1900s, and the development of commercial fishing after that — the community of Denare Beach did not get its start until the 1930s. Local legend, prospector and amateur archaeologist Harry Moody started the first store at the site in a tent in 1931. Two years later, the provincial **De**partment of **Na**tural **Re**sources initiated a resort project in the area; hence, the community's name. In 1937 the subdivision of the present community site took place, and a road from Flin Flon was also finished that year. With

▲ **THE ROCKY VIEW OTA** lodge at Denare Beach, perched above Amisk Lake, offers what is perhaps one of the most spectacular views in Saskatchewan.

▼ **AMISK LAKE** from the Rocky View OTA lodge Denare Beach. Amisk is the Cree word for Beaver.

Photographs taken August 18, 2004.

the completion of the road, resort facilities were further developed, and people began building cottages and an increasing number of permanent residences. Many who live at Denare Beach today are employed in the communities of Flin Flon or Creighton, a number with the Hudson Bay Mining & Smelting Company. The Denare Beach region abounds with archaeological and historic sites, many of which are featured in the community's museum, and the area's geological wonders include unique formations such as the deep limestone crevices near the lake's southeast shore. Today, Denare Beach retains its resort atmosphere, and tourists will find an excellent beach, lodgings, camping facilities, restaurants, and convenience stores. With the arrival of cabin owners during the summer months, the population of the community approximately doubles. Denare Beach was incorporated as a northern village in 1984.

DENHOLM, village, pop 61 (2006c), 79 (2001c), is located approximately 20 km southeast of North Battleford on Hwy 16. The North Saskatchewan River passes about 8 kilometres to the south of the community. The Canadian Northern Railway came through the area in 1905, and the Denholm Post Office was established on April 1, 1906. The local school district was organized the following year. On June 25, 1912, Denholm was incorporated, attaining village status, and in 1913 the community became the junction (the western terminus) of the rail line running through Blaine Lake to Prince Albert. The community's population was 105 in 1926, and it hovered close to that level until the 1960s. Denholm School closed in 1970; the population of the village in 1971 was 71. Today, a few

abandoned businesses and homes dot the townsite, and many village residents travel to the Battlefords for shopping, services, employment, and entertainment. The major industry in the Denholm area is agriculture, a combination of both grain and livestock production. Denholm is situated in the RM of Mayfield No. 406.

DENZIL, village, pop 142 (2006c), 161 (2001c), is located near the Saskatchewan-Alberta border, 27 km southeast of Macklin on Hwy 31. Denzil is situated in what was known as St. Joseph's Colony, a vast German Catholic settlement that developed between 1905 and 1910 in an area bounded by Landis and Handel in the east, Kerrobert to the south, the Alberta border and Macklin to the west, and Unity and Wilkie in the north. The settlers were mainly from the region of the Black Sea; many of the first to arrive (1905-08) had come to Canada after having first settled in the Dakotas; those that followed (1908-10) mainly came directly from southern

Russia. Smaller numbers of Norwegian, Scottish, and English settlers were also among those who homesteaded in the Denzil area. Denzil itself had its beginnings in 1910, as the construction of the Canadian Pacific Railway proceeded between Kerrobert and Macklin. The CPR station at Denzil was built that year. The Denzil Post Office was established on March 1, 1911, and the village was incorporated just over two months later, on May 3. Also by 1911

the first school in the village had been built, as had a hotel. The Catholic parish of Sacred Heart was established at Denzil in 1915, and the church remains active today, a focal point in the community. A Union Church was organized in Denzil about 1924, but lasted only into the 1930s. By the mid-1920s, Denzil had about two dozen business establishments and over 200 residents. Six grain elevators lined the railway tracks. The village experienced

▶ **SACRED HEART ROMAN CATHOLIC CHURCH** (top) in Denzil. This church was built in 1986 to replace the earlier structure that was destroyed by fire. The church is as impressive inside as that in any of the province's cities.

AT RIGHT are two of the church's beautiful stained glass windows.

Photographs taken August 14, 2003.

a downturn when the Canadian National Railway built a line from Unity to Bodo, Alberta, in 1930-31, resulting in the construction of elevators seven miles south of Denzil at Hearts Hill and seven miles east at Donegal. This reduced the amount of grain delivered to Denzil, and adversely impacted farm equipment suppliers and other local businesses. The competing rail line, along with the Depression, took its toll on the village as the population fell and two grain elevators went out of business. A Protestant separate school was established in the village in the mid-1930s, but it only lasted about ten years. Denzil rebounded following WWII, and in 1961 the community reached a peak population of 328. The village's numbers hovered at close to 300 until the early 1970s, after which they began to steadily decline. By the mid-1980s, Denzil was down to two grain elevators, both of which were by then owned by the Saskatchewan Wheat Pool. Today, one elevator remains standing (it dates to the 1920s), although it is now in private hands. Denzil Sacred Heart School, a K-12 facility, had recently experienced several years of declining enrollment (there were 47 students enrolled in the fall of 2005), and on June 30, 2006, the school was permanently closed. Denzil retains a small core of businesses, a seniors' centre, skating and curling rinks, a ball park, a children's playground, camping facilities, a trout pond, a community hall, and its church. The village holds an annual fall fair each October. The nearest medical facilities and RCMP are located in Macklin. Agriculture has historically been the economic backbone of the community; however, the production of oil and gas, and its related service industries, have increasingly become an important part of the area economy. Denzil is situated in the RM of Eye Hill No. 382.

DESCHARME LAKE, northern settlement, pop 42 (2001c), is a remote Dene community located in north-western Saskatchewan, approximately 85 km north of La Loche. The community is situated on the shore of the lake from which it derives its name, and it is accessible via gravel road No. 955, also known as the Semchuk Trail. The people of the settlement have no running water (residents get their drinking water from the lake), and in 2002 they rejected an offer from the province to move everyone an hour south to La Loche, where they would be guaranteed access to safe water and where new fully-serviced homes would be built. Descharme Lake residents feared the move would cost them their traditional way of life (based in trapping, hunting, and fishing) and increase access to alcohol, drugs, and gambling, which are problematic in La Loche. Descharme Lake's one-room elementary school had 4 students enrolled in the fall of 2006; communication with the community is via satellite telephone. The area is somewhat of a haven for cross-country skiing enthusiasts, as it features high-relief eskers running through old-growth forest and many lakes and streams.

DILKE, village, pop 80 (2006c), 70 (2001c), is located 10 km west of Last Mountain Lake, approximately 76 km northwest of Regina on Hwy 354. The name of the community honours Sir Charles Wentworth Dilke (1843-1911), a British statesman, author, and member of William E. Gladstone's Liberal government. Although a few settlers made incursions into the Dilke region in the 1880s and 1890s, the vast majority arrived in

▲ **ST. LUCY'S ANGLICAN CHURCH**, Dilke, is a quaint little stone church built in 1914 and a community landmark. It was designated a municipal heritage property in 1995.

▼ **THE DILKE HOTEL**, built in 1909, remains in business today.

Photographs taken July 9, 2003.

the early 1900s. They were mainly of English, Scottish, and German origins. The site for the village was chosen in 1909 and surveyed in 1910. Stores and other businesses immediately began to be established. In 1911, the CPR came through connecting Regina to Colonsay, the Dilke Post Office was established, and a school opened. Dilke was incorporated, attaining

village status, on December 30, 1912. That year, the community held its first annual Sports Day, and the first grain elevator was erected. Predominantly an agricultural community, commercial fishing, too, was an integral part of the local economy from the early 1900s until the 1970s. Many people were employed at Dilke's fish processing plants, worked transporting fish

from the lake to the plant, or cut ice from the lake for packing the fish. Dilke's population stabilized at a little over 100 in the mid-1920s, and it remained close to that level until after WWII when the village underwent a period of growth and prosperity. Dilke's numbers rose from 107 in 1941 to 155 by 1951, and in 1961 the community reached a peak population of 187. By 1971, however, the population was down to 130. Dilke's high school students began to be bused to Holdfast in 1963-64; ten years later, Dilke School was closed. In the 1970s the rail line running southeast of Dilke was abandoned after the waters of Last Mountain Lake rose and completely washed out the track bed across the lake to Valeport. The rail line running northwest of Dilke was abandoned in the 1990s. Dilke is situated in the RM of Sarnia No. 221.

DINSMORE, village, pop 269 (2006c), 337 (2001c), is located on Hwys 42 and 44, in the gently rolling farmland 40 km west of the Gardiner Dam. Settlers began to take up land in the district around 1905, coming from eastern Canada (Ontario, Manitoba, Quebec, and the Maritimes), as well as from the British Isles and the United States; in 1910, significant numbers of people of Finnish origin arrived in the area, forming a large bloc settlement southeast of the present community. In 1907, a post office was established in the district and given the name Dinsmore. The name likely honoured an early area homesteader, although certain scholars of Saskatchewan toponymy have suggested the name may have been inspired by the nineteenth-century Elsie Dinsmore series of books. When the Canadian Northern Railway came through in 1913, the post office was moved to the newly established townsite and the name Dinsmore was adopted for the community. With the arrival of the railway Dinsmore grew rapidly, and on November 3, 1913, Dinsmore was incorporated. The village has suffered numerous serious fires over the years — in 1916, 1931, 1935, and 1949 — during which many businesses were destroyed. However, the Dinsmore Hotel, built in 1913, remains a community landmark to this day. The village grew fairly steadily from its beginnings until the mid-1960s: the population was 71 in 1916, 171 in 1921, 256 in 1931, and 215 in 1941 (this decline is likely attributable to enlistments in the armed forces during WWII); by 1951 the community numbered 301. In 1966, the population of Dinsmore peaked at 510. The village grew to become the hub of a productive grain growing area, and in the early 1940s the community's seven grain elevators handled the district's first million-bushel crop, and Dinsmore came to earn the moniker, the "Buckle of the Wheat Belt." Grain farming remains the main industry in the region today, augmented by the raising of cattle and bison. Dinsmore has a good range of local businesses, recreational facilities, a health centre and a special care home, a K-12 school (100 students), a community museum, and a library. The administrative office for the neighbouring rural municipality of King George No. 256, to the south, is located in the village; Dinsmore is situated in the RM of Milden No. 286, which has its headquarters in the village of Milden, to the north.

DISLEY, village, pop 62 (2006c), 62 (2001c), is located approximately 40 km northwest of Regina, just off Hwy 11. The Qu'Appelle Valley lies about three km south of the community. Named after an English village, Disley became the site of a siding on the Qu'Appelle, Long Lake & Saskatchewan Railway in 1890, and in 1899 a post office, located a few miles south, opened and adopted the name. The village began to develop after 1903, as settlers began to pour into the district. A school was built in 1905, and Disley was incorporated on June 24, 1907. The village had its peak population early in its history: 99 in 1911. By 1936 the community's numbers had fallen to 53, but following WWII the village experienced a period of growth, and Disley had 82 residents by 1951. In the mid-1950s the community boasted two grain companies (the Saskatchewan Wheat Pool and the Patterson Grain Co.), a 15-room hotel, two garages, two general stores, and two churches (Anglican and United). Active clubs and organizations included the Ladies Aid, the Homemakers Club, a curling club, and a local baseball team. Today, Disley consists of 32 private dwellings; the only business left is an auto repair shop. The post office closed in 1970. Working residents of the village commute to work in Regina; schoolchildren attend classes in Lumsden. Disley is situated in the RM of Lumsden No. 189.

◄ **DINSMORE SENTINELS** from the west. Photograph taken September 12, 2003.

▲ **THE OLD WATERING HOLE.** The Dodsland Hotel is one of the village's oldest buildings. It is situated on the north side of 1st Avenue. Photograph taken September 10, 2003.

▲ **ONLY THE BIRDS SING HERE NOW.** More than a quarter century has now passed since the last services were held at this church in Dollard. Photograph taken June 22, 2003.

DODSLAND, village, pop 207 (2006c), 211 (2001c), is located on Hwy 31 in the gently rolling landscape southeast of Kerrobert. The area began to be settled about 1906; however, it was the arrival of the railroad in 1912 that brought substantial numbers of people to the district and brought about the establishment of the village, which was incorporated in 1913. Agriculture, primarily grain farming, and oil and gas, discovered in the 1950s, are the major industries in the region. In 1971, Dodsland had a peak population of 404. Dodsland retains a small core of businesses and services, including a health clinic; however, in June 2004, the elementary school was closed, and subsequently all schoolchildren are bused to the nearby village of Plenty. Dodsland serves as the administrative centre of the RM of Winslow No. 319.

DOLLARD, hamlet, pop 35 (2001c), is situated on the leeward side of the Cypress Hills, southwest of Shaunavon on Hwy 13. The highway closely follows the route travelled by Métis hunters, and later the NWMP, heading in and out of the Cypress Hills. Between 1908 and 1910, French Canadians and French-Europeans began settling in the area, and with the arrival of CPR survey crews in 1913 the townsite of Dollard was established. The community was incorporated as a village in 1914. Besides its French population, its constituents would also come to be comprised of Norwegians and English-speaking people from eastern Canada, the U.S., and Britain. The small fledgling community had fully expected to be chosen as a divisional point on the CPR's Weyburn-Lethbridge line, but was usurped when railroad company officials instead chose Shaunavon. Dollard residents suspected that prominent people in the Shaunavon district had lobbied, and been favoured by, CPR officials, and the railway company's decision was a subject of debate around Dollard for a number of years. However, the village continued to grow and was given a boost when oil was discovered in the area in 1952. The community's population nearly doubled within five years, growing from 108 in 1951 to 193 by 1956. Slowly though, due to changes in agricultural technology and transportation, as well as the community's proximity to Shaunavon, the village's population and business sector began to decline. Oil production reached a peak in 1962, and by the middle of the 1960s the oil company which had its headquarters in Dollard relocated to Shaunavon. Around the same time, the village's school was closed, and in 1981 the last public institution carrying on the French culture — the church — shut its doors. The village was dissolved New Year's Day, 2002. Dollard is located in the RM of Arlington No. 79.

DOMREMY, hamlet, pop 124 (2006c), 135 (2001c), is located 17 km north of Wakaw, one km east of Hwy 2. The community had its beginnings when settlers from France arrived in the district in the mid-1890s, thus adding to the significant numbers of ranchers, squatters, Métis, and French Canadians already present in the general region. The newcomers arrived at Duck Lake by train and pushed on to the district through St. Louis with horses. The new arrivals named their settlement after Domrémy-la-Pucelle, France, the birthplace of Joan of Arc. When a small chapel was built in 1895 and a parish organized, it was named after the famous saint. In 1896, the Domremy Post Office was established. A vote on forming a school district was taken in 1895, but it wasn't until 1904 that a school was in operation. The Daughters of Providence, from St. Brieuc, Brittany, arrived on December 31, 1903, to take charge. The nucleus of the original settlement of Domremy was about two miles north of the present village, but with the construction of the Grand Trunk Pacific Railway's line through the area beginning on the eve of the First World War, a new townsite was established on the rail line, and the community and the mission were relocated. In 1915, a new school district centred on the village was established. The Sisters, however, chose to remain

◄ **AUGUST 24, 2004:** Domremy, from about one kilometre west (Highway 2).

at the old location; finding themselves isolated and facing declining enrollment at the rural school, they left the area in 1916. Meanwhile, the district was growing to become comprised of people of Norwegian, Ukrainian, and Scottish descent. Domremy, though, would largely retain its distinct French character. The village was incorporated on March 31, 1921. By 1925, five grain elevators had been built, and by 1931 the population of the community was 195. In 1928, the Daughters of Providence returned, accepting the invitation of the local priest to assume responsibility for the village school. They retained the principalship of Domremy School until 1967; the last three teaching Sisters left in 1979. Following WWII, the population of Domremy reached its peak — 241 in 1951 — but beginning in the mid-1960s it started to slowly decline. In 1965, five grain elevators (Pioneer, National, Federal, UGG, and Pool) were still serving the district; in the 1980s, however, they began to come down. Two are standing today: a former Saskatchewan Wheat Pool elevator, and one operated by Belle Pulses, Ltd., based in nearby St. Isidore-de-Bellevue. Also in the 1980s, parents who wanted their children to have more of a French education began sending their children to St. Isidore-de-Bellevue. By 1991, enroll-

ment at Domremy School had declined to the point that grades seven through twelve were curtailed, and in 1992 Domremy School was closed. The community, which relinquished village status on December 31, 2006, retains a small core of businesses and services. Domremy is situated in the RM of St. Louis No. 431.

DORE LAKE

DORE LAKE, northern hamlet, pop 27 (2001c), is located approximately 115 km north of Big River, off Hwy 55, at the north end of gravel Hwy 924. The small community is situated on the south shore of the 61,000-hectare lake from which it derives its name. Although the area had long been traversed by First Nations and Métis people, and had seen the occasional camp of a trapper, there was no permanent settlement at Dore Lake before 1909. With the construction of the railroad into Big River, access to the region was greatly improved; new immigrants to Canada and many farm labourers from southern Saskatchewan came north seeking winter employment in logging, trapping, freighting, and fishing. In 1909, a trail was cut from Big River into Dore Lake, and in the years prior to WWI a number of Scandinavians and Icelanders — perhaps because of their familiarity with a cold climate and

rugged bush — came to the lake and pioneered a commercial fishing industry. (Fishing was also a traditional occupation in their original homelands.) By 1911-12, there were 23 licensed fishermen with camps established on the lake's numerous islands. Fish were hauled by horses and sleighs to Big River, where they were loaded onto trains and shipped to national and foreign markets. As there were yet no roads and air travel was in its infancy, freighting fish south and bringing supplies north developed into a substantial occupation of its own. Between 1909 and the 1940s, the population of Dore Lake fluctuated considerably due to the seasonality of the work. In 1945, a refrigerated filleting plant was built at the lake. This allowed fishing in the summer, and subsequently fishermen could be employed throughout the year. Other occupations were also developing at Dore Lake, however. Logging activity was intermittent, but mink ranching was at one time firmly established, and by the mid-1950s tourism in northern Saskatchewan was beginning to emerge from its infancy. Fishing lodges and campgrounds were built in the area, and a beach was developed. As a permanent population grew, basic services were sought. A post office was set up, a government wharf was built, and in 1949 construction of a road to Dore Lake began. Prior to 1960 the only education available was through a correspondence school, but that year the first school was established in the Department of Natural Resources' garage at the south end of the lake, which was as far as the road had been built. Several families moved their homes (and mink ranches) to the loca-

tion, and the permanent site of the community was established. At first, students in the new 'school' used picnic tables for desks. By 1966, the population of Dore Lake was 147. In 1967, a community hall and a curling rink were built as Centennial projects, and in 1974 a form of local government was instituted. In 1977, an out-of-control forest fire threatened the very existence of the community. It destroyed 7,772 acres of forest, and took 189 firefighters five days to bring under control. In recent decades, the population of Dore Lake has dropped significantly, and the school, which once had over 30 students, only had four enrolled in the fall of 2004. It has since closed. There is an airstrip at Dore Lake, and two area outfitters accommodate summer and winter fishers, hunters, snowmobilers, and eco-tourists.

DORINTOSH

DORINTOSH, village, pop 127 (2006c), 125 (2001c), is situated 34 km northwest of Meadow Lake on Hwy 4, six km south of the main eastern entrance to Meadow Lake Provincial Park. The Beaver River passes to the south of the community; the Waterhen River (in the park) passes to the north. The first mail to come into the district was via the post office at Barnes Crossing on the Beaver River, which was established in 1925. By the early 1930s much of the available land in the area had been taken up, and Dorintosh began to develop in 1937 when a right of way was cleared to extend what is today Highway 4 further north. This was mainly done by farmers working off relief. The road allowance cut north-south through the centre of four sections of land, and at the intersection of the four developed a crossroads upon which the first buildings began to appear. Joe Dunavon started a store on the southwest corner in 1937, and F.L. McRae built a large dance hall and a café on the northeast corner in 1938. Other buildings soon followed, and the local history recounts that the locality was originally referred to simply as "the corners." By 1940, the hamlet had three stores, the dance hall and café, a gas station, a blacksmith shop, curling and skating rinks, a livery barn, and other small places of business. The Dorintosh Post Office was established on December 1, 1940 — the name honours two area pioneers who became politicians: Cameron Ross McIntosh, the Liberal Member of Parliament for the region from 1925 to 1940, and Dorise Winifred Nielsen, the Unity candidate who defeated him and who sat in the House of Commons from 1940 to 1945. The first syllable of the name Dorise was combined with the last syllables of the name McIntosh to form Dorintosh. By 1947 the first hotel in the hamlet was constructed, and a local school had been started. In the early 1950s a United Church was moved in from about six miles west, and a Catholic Church was built. When the land in the Dorintosh area was first homesteaded, it was covered with dense spruce and poplar growth and was cleared mainly by hand. Many farmers supplemented their income by logging and working in sawmills, or by trapping, working in commercial fishing or road construction, or running mink or fox ranches. By the 1940s mechanized land clearing resulted in the bush and forest in the Dorintosh district giving way to fields of grain. Dorintosh was established as an organized hamlet in 1975 and attained village status on January 1, 1989. Today, many Dorintosh residents travel to Meadow Lake for shopping and services, medical attention, employment, and entertainment. However, the village has a small core of businesses and services,

including a hotel and beverage room, a motel, restaurants, the post office, a laundromat and showers, and a general store that sells auto insurance, liquor, gas, hardware, and groceries. The village also has a United Church, a community hall, a seniors' centre, a curling rink, an outdoor paved skating rink, and ball diamonds. The K-8 school had 56 students enrolled in the fall of 2006; high school students are bused to Meadow Lake. Annual events in Dorintosh include a fall supper in November, a seniors' supper in December, an ice fishing derby and a winter festival, both held in March. Meadow Lake Provincial Park and the vast tracts of wilderness in the region attract many vacationers, and a number of Dorintosh area outfitters cater to bear, deer, and bird hunters. Dorintosh is situated in the RM of Meadow Lake No. 588.

DRAKE, village, pop 232 (2006c), 248 (2001c), lies west of the Quill Lakes, 13 kilometres south of Lanigan on Hwy 20. In 1903 there were only a few settlers scattered throughout the district, but over the next few years a large influx began. Beginning in 1904, substantial numbers of General Conference Mennonites from Ontario, Kansas and Oklahoma began settling in the region. In 1906, Russian-German Lutherans began to take up land over a considerable area toward the east and north. People of English and Scottish origins, from both eastern Canada and Britain, also dotted the countryside. The largest influx of settlers took place during 1905 and 1906. With the construction of the CPR line from Strasbourg (then spelled Strassburg) to Lanigan in 1907, the village of Drake had its beginnings. It was named by the CPR after Sir Francis Drake (c.1540-96), the Elizabethan

◄ **SOME OF THE FINEST** sausage and beef jerky in the province is made by Drake Meat Processors. Norman Ediger (right in photo) and his wife Louise started managing the Drake Locker Plant in 1958 and purchased the business in 1962. Their son Kelly (left in photo) purchased the company in 1980. After fire destroyed the business in 1982, a new plant was built (completed in 1983) and Kelly renamed the company Drake Meat Processors. Photograph taken August 4, 2004.

privateer and explorer, who was the first Englishman to circumnavigate the earth (1577-80) and who is also noted for his role as vice-admiral in the defeat of the Spanish Armada in 1588. The village of Drake's main street is named Francis; Norreys, Gilbert, Howard, and Hawkins streets are all named after Drake's crew members. In 1907, the first structures appeared at the Drake townsite: the first grain elevator, a railway section house, and a boxcar which served as a station until a proper one was built in 1912. In 1908, the Drake Post Office was established, and in 1909 the boundaries of the Drake School District were approved. A one-room school was built in 1910, and the village was incorporated on September 19 that year. Several businesses now dotted the townsite. From a population of 66 in 1911, Drake grew steadily until the 1950s — the community numbered 232 in 1956

— and, subsequently, the population has remained fairly stable. In the 1920s, Mennonites fleeing Russia added to the district population; however, in the 1940s many Mennonite families left the area for British Columbia. In the early 1940s, the Saskatchewan Power Commission began supplying the village with electrical power, replacing the local power plant. After water and sewer systems were connected to the village's businesses and residences in the late-1960s and Drake gained dial telephones and became a part of the SaskTel system, the community then had most of the modern conveniences enjoyed by the province's city dwellers. At the same time, however, Drake was facing challenges: the CPR removed the railway station in 1968, and in the 1970s business began to drop off at the Drake Co-op leading to its ceasing operations and liquidating its assets in 1979. Where the Saskatchewan Wheat

▲ **DRAKE "HOMECOMING" PARADE, 1995.** Photograph courtesy of the Village of Drake.

Pool elevators and annexes stood on the west side of town in the 1980s, nothing remains today. The community has been buoyed, however, by the presence of two key industries: Bergen Industries, a manufacturer of agricultural implements for more than 50 years, which employs a staff of approximately 30; and Drake Meat Processors, which began as a co-operative locker plant in 1949. Owned by the Ediger family since 1962, Drake Meat Processors now employs over 80 people from the area and markets products throughout western Canada. Today, other businesses in Drake include a credit union, a grocery store and postal outlet, gas sales, an insurance broker, and a number of home-based small enterprises. Drake also has a Sportsplex, a ball park, a seniors' centre and seniors' housing, a library, and a volunteer fire department. North Star Mennonite Church occupies the northeast corner of Cadiz Avenue and Francis Street. Drake School

is a K-8 facility which had 64 students enrolled in the fall of 2006. High school students attend classes in Lanigan. Drake is situated in the RM of Usborne No. 310.

DRINKWATER, village, pop 65 (2006c), 80 (2001c), is situated on Hwy 39 and the CPR Soo Line, approximately 30 km southeast of Moose Jaw and 20 km northwest of the town of Rouleau. The community is named after Charles Drinkwater, a secretary to John A. Macdonald and then the first corporate secretary of the CPR. The railroad was completed from North Portal to Moose Jaw in 1893, but until the early 1900s few communities had been established along the line. Shortly after the turn of the century, with people arriving in droves, the Drinkwater townsite began to be developed. A store and post office were operating by 1902, and the community progressed rapidly in its early years. Numerous entrepreneurs eagerly plied their trades or wares, and lumberyards did a flourishing business. Construction of a Presbyterian Church began in early 1903; in 1904, the year the

hamlet gained village status (June 7), the Grand View Hotel was constructed, the first grain elevator went up (the first of several), and the first school — a wooden schoolhouse — was built. The Canadian Bank of Commerce erected an impressive edifice on Main Street and opened in 1907. Numerous farm implement dealers went into business, and, with the advent of the automobile, car dealerships were established — there were McLaughlin-Buick and Ford agencies. The population of the young community jumped from 58 in 1906 to 203 by 1911, the year the Methodist church was completed. Drinkwater would reach its peak population — 238 — in 1921, but its numbers thereafter averaged very close to 165 until the later 1960s. Like many smaller villages in the province that sprang up in the land rushes of the early 1900s, Drinkwater had its heyday prior to the Depression. After that came WWII, and after that, the world had changed. Drinkwater hung on, but by the 1970s the village was clearly in decline: it was losing its people. While the population of the village has been below 100 only since the early 1980s, the demise of the business community had begun in the 1930s. The Canadian Bank of Commerce closed in 1936 (the building was later purchased by the Masons, who in turn sold it in 1988), and by the time people again had money in their pockets, better roads and automobiles afforded easy access to the array of services, merchandise, and employment opportunities that Moose Jaw or Regina had to offer. With the consolidation of schools, Drinkwater children began to be bused to Briercrest; by 1962, only grades 1-8 remained in the village. In 1968, the school was closed entirely, and in 1969 the former railway station was removed by the CPR after a failed attempt by the village council to obtain the landmark

for another purpose. The school building was used as a community club for a number of years, then sold and, in 1987, torn down. That year, the Saskatchewan Wheat Pool closed its two elevators in Drinkwater, and they were subsequently demolished. Where several elevators once stood, none remain today. The skating and hockey rink, too, are long gone — as is the post office. There were, however, times of some progress in the past few decades, with varying degrees of lasting impact. In the 1960s and 1970s, while one by one Drinkwater's businesses were folding, Marshall Brown, and then his son Martin, established a manufacturing plant that originally produced farm equipment and then moved into the large-scale production of fibreglass caps and tonneaus for pick-up trucks. A large manufacturing plant was built on the east side of Drinkwater, where up to 52 people were employed. By the 1990s, Brown Industries had evolved into one of North America's leading manufacturers of truck caps and tonneaus, but the company's days in the village were numbered. In recent years, the company was sold to buyers from the United States, and in December 2005 the Drinkwater plant was closed and all operations were transferred to Moose Jaw. The Moose Jaw plant now employs 220 people — more people than have lived in Drinkwater since the early 1920s. The most lasting positive development in the village in recent times has been, after decades of frustration, running water in people's homes. A good local supply of water had eluded the village since its inception, and an adequate source was only obtained in the spring of 1990 with the completion of a pipeline north through Belle Plaine that tapped into the Buffalo Pound water line running to Regina. Drinkwater is situated in the RM of Redburn No. 130.

DUBUC, village, pop 55 (2006c), 80 (2001c), is located 32 km west of Esterhazy and about 18 km north of the Qu'Appelle Valley on Hwys 9 and 22. The community's name honours Sir Joseph Dubuc (1840-1914), an eminent lawyer, judge, newspaperman, and politician. Dubuc had arrived in Manitoba in 1870 from Quebec at the request of Louis Riel and became a strong supporter of Riel's Provisional Government. Through the mid-1870s, Dubuc served as a member of the Council of the North-West Territories; at the end of the decade he represented the Manitoba constituency of Provencher in the Canadian House of Commons. He was appointed the chief justice of Manitoba in 1903, and throughout his career he worked to ensure French Canadian and Métis equality in that province. In the early 1900s, the location of present-day Dubuc, Saskatchewan, was nothing more than a hay field where some of the district's early settlers cut their winter hay. Over 1903-04, as the CPR was building its line through the region, the village had its beginnings. The post office was established in 1904, and that year the local school was established. The Village of Dubuc was incorporated on May 29 the next spring, and businesses operating by 1905 included general stores, a meat market, a harness shop, a livery barn, a lumberyard, and a hotel. The first resident doctor, W.C. Arnold, arrived in 1905, and in 1907 the first skating rink was built. In 1910, the first bank, the Northern Crown Bank, opened, and that year the first issue of the community newspaper, *The Dubuc Enterprise*, was published by Thomas Brown. The village and area were populated by a rather cosmopolitan assortment of peoples — among them were Swedes, Norwegians, Hungarians, German-speakers, and people of English and Scottish origins, both from eastern Canada and the British Isles. From 70 village residents in 1906, Dubuc grew to reach a peak population of 250 in 1931. The community then numbered approximately 200 until the 1960s, when both its population and business community, began to steadily decline. Businesses operating today include a Co-op providing fuel sales and farm supplies, a credit union, and a hotel/bar. There is no longer a school in Dubuc, and the median age of the population in 2001 was just over 65; that of all Saskatchewan residents was 36.7. Dubuc has a community hall, a recreation association, an active seniors' centre, and a small seniors' housing complex. CP abandoned the rail line through the community in 1996, and no grain elevators are left standing in the village today. Dubuc is situated in the RM of Grayson No. 184.

▲ **DUBUC, CIRCA 1912-14**, Saskatchewan Archives Board R-A9501(1).

DUCK LAKE, town, pop 610 (2006c), 624 (2001c), is located 88 km northeast of Saskatoon and 44 km southwest of Prince Albert at the junction of Hwys 11 and 212. The Beardy's and Okemasis First Nation lands and the North Saskatchewan River are located just to the west of the community; the South Saskatchewan River lies just to the east. To the north of Duck Lake is the vast wilderness of the Nisbet Provincial Forest. The name of the town was taken from a body of water immediately southwest of the community, which was long known to the indigenous population of the area as a significant stopping place for migratory waterfowl. The community of Duck Lake is situated in a region of great historic importance. Within a short drive from the town is the Batoche National Historic Site, the Battle of Fish Creek National Historic Site, the historic site of the Battle of Duck Lake, Fort Carlton Provincial Historic Park, Our Lady of Lourdes Shrine at St. Laurent, and the Seager Wheeler Farm National Historic Site. Within the town is the 1890s NWMP jailhouse in which Almighty Voice was imprisoned, an 1890s Anglican church, and a 1914 school which, when established, was situated in one of the first two Protestant Separate School districts organized in Saskatchewan. All three of these buildings have been designated heritage properties. The Carlton Trail passed by Duck Lake, and Red River Métis established temporary camps in the area from which to pursue the bison as the herds moved further westward. In 1870, following the Red River Rebellion, there was an influx of Métis settlers to the Duck Lake area, and, subsequently, the beginning of a permanent settlement. Over the ensuing decades, not only was Duck Lake at the centre of events at the beginning of the North-West Resistance, it also became a hub of a burgeoning pioneer society: substantial numbers of French settlers were among those who came to the area. Duck Lake was incorporated as a village in 1898, and in 1911 the community attained town status. For many years, Duck Lake was an important provisioning centre, and settlers would haul grain to the town from as far as 60 to 80 kilometres away. However, as time went on, railways and roads were built to the east and west of the North and South Saskatchewan Rivers, and Duck Lake's importance as a trading centre was significantly diminished. In recent years, the community has undergone something of a renaissance, as aggressive tourism marketing focusing upon the history of the First Nations, Metis, and pioneer societies of the area has met with significant success. Tourism has developed into a major industry for the town, and the Duck Lake Regional Interpretive Centre, opened in 1992, now draws several thousand visitors a year. Additionally, the town has become a massive outdoor gallery of murals depicting the history of the region. To date, eleven large and colourful works have been completed. An additional community attraction is the gallery of notable Saskatchewan artist, Glen Scrimshaw. Town amenities include

Historical photographs courtesy of the Duck Lake Regional Interpretive Centre.

Contemporary photographs taken August 26, 2004.

◀ **VIEW FROM THE NORTH.**

DUCK LAKE

Frontier of First Nations, Métis, and Pioneer Society, 1870–1905
Frontière des sociétés autochtone, métisse et pionnière, 1870–1905

◀ **PIONEER ENTREPRENEURS.** One of Duck Lake's earliest businessmen in front of his establishment. A boot and shoe repair business was operated out of the shack in the background to the right.

◀ **NORTH-WEST MOUNTED POLICE** in front of the jail that housed Almighty Voice. The building is still standing in the town. Photo taken circa 1895.

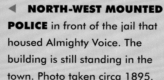

◀ **THE KING'S HOTEL** in Duck Lake, circa 1904.

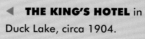

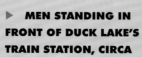

▶ **MEN STANDING IN FRONT OF DUCK LAKE'S TRAIN STATION, CIRCA 1905.** The railway to Prince Albert was completed in 1890 and Duck Lake became a point of disembarkation for many pioneers venturing out onto the land. The sign above the door reads, "Regina: 211 miles; Prince Albert: 38 miles."

ALMIGHTY VOICE: Duck Lake bills itself as being "Home of One of the World's Largest Outdoor Art Galleries." This mural of Almighty Voice, painted on the 1914 Victoria School (it now houses the library), is one of nearly a dozen murals in the town.

THE TOWN OFFICE, on the east side of Front Street, is located in a former Bank of Montreal building.

THE DUCK LAKE REGIONAL INTERPRETIVE CENTRE houses a gallery, a 64-seat theatre, a visitor's centre, a gift shop, and a museum collection of over 2,000 artifacts including elaborately beaded Indian costumes, 100-year-old crosses from St. Laurent, tools used in the buffalo hunt, and a gold watch presented to Gabriel Dumont by sympathizers in New York.

a variety of businesses offering both goods and services, a medical clinic and a special care home, a pharmacy, curling and skating rinks, a library, and a number of churches. A recent addition to the business community is a pea processing plant, which employs 10 people and ships product worldwide. Duck Lake's elementary and high schools provide K-12 education. The town has a volunteer fire department; policing is provided by the Rosthern RCMP. There are a number of major annual events which take place both within the community and in the surrounding area. A three-day powwow is held in late August, and the Duck Lake Métis Society hosts a rodeo on the Labour Day weekend. As well, Back to Batoche Days and two pilgrimages to the St. Laurent Shrine each summer draw thousands of people to the area. Duck Lake serves as the administrative centre of the RM of Duck Lake No. 463.

DUFF, village, pop 30 (2006c), 40 (2001c), is located 23 km southwest of Melville on Hwy 10. Settlers took up homesteads in the Duff region in bursts between 1882 and 1911. Those who arrived in the early 1880s were largely of English stock, primarily from Ontario, and many were members of the Primitive Methodist Church who came west with the encouragement of the Primitive Methodist Colonization Company. In the 1890s and early 1900s, German Protestants from eastern Europe and southern Russia arrived in the district. Duff's beginnings date to 1909 when the first stage of the Grand Trunk Pacific Railway's branch line from Melville to Regina was being built (the line was completed in 1911). The community was named after A.E. Duff, Chief Passenger Agent at Winnipeg for the railway company's Western Division. The Duff Post Office was established on September 1, 1910. The first grain elevator was erected in 1911, and that year the Duff School District boundaries were established. The school opened in 1912 with 14 pupils enrolled. The Grand Trunk Pacific Railway station was built in 1913. Duff was incorporated as a village on May 28, 1920, and the population recorded in 1921 was 111. The community's numbers peaked at 122 in 1931, and from the mid-1930s through to the early 1970s Duff's population hovered around the 100 mark. In the 1950s, the village had three garages, a blacksmith, two general merchants, electrical appliance sales and service, hardware supplies and a lumberyard, two grain companies, a hotel and restaurant, an International Harvester implement dealership, and coal suppliers. There were also three churches: United, Lutheran, and Anglican. Over the ensuing decades, however, the community began to decline, in no small part due to its proximity to the larger centres of Melville, Neudorf and Lemberg. The high school and elementary school closed in 1964, and businesses began to disappear. In 1975, the railway station was sold and moved to the city of Melville, where it is now featured at the Railway Museum. By 1981 the population of Duff was down to 76; by 1991 it was 52. Today, other than the post office, there are no services left in the community. The Duff Community Heritage Museum, located in a former church, is run by volunteers and opened by appointment. Duff is located in the RM of Stanley No. 215.

DUNDURN, town, pop 647 (2006c), 596 (2001c), is located about a 20-minute drive south of Saskatoon on Hwy 11. Canadian Forces Detachment Dundurn oc-

▲ **WORLD WAR ONE:** A store front in Dundurn in 1918. Photograph courtesy of Harry Friesen, Dundurn district, Saskatchewan.

▲ **SCHOOLCHILDREN PARTICIPATE** in a "Field Day" parade in Dundurn, circa 1922-23. Photograph courtesy of the Wilson Museum, Dundurn.

▼ **WORLD WAR TWO:** Military vehicles on the streets of Dundurn in the 1940s. Photograph courtesy of Harry Friesen, Dundurn district, Saskatchewan.

The streets of Dundurn... *during war and peacetime and war...*

cupies approximately 90 square kilometres just to the west and northwest of the town. While there were a few pioneering ranchers in the region in the 1880s, and a railway running past the site of Dundurn by 1889-90, the origins of the town date to 1902. Much credit for the founding of Dundurn is given to Emil Julius Meilicke and his sons, German immigrants from Minnesota. E. J. Meilicke was an enterprising entrepreneur who had served in the state senate, and he was successful in inducing a number of his fellow Americans to settle in the Dundurn area. The Meilickes established a lumberyard and machinery business at Dundurn and built a number of homes, four of which are still standing. By 1903, settlers were arriving in the Dundurn district in droves. Adding to the German component were people of British origins, both from eastern Canada and overseas. A few Barr colonists abandoned that group in Saskatoon to come to the Dundurn area. In 1924, Mennonites would arrive. As the Dundurn district filled with settlers, businesses arose in the new community to fill their needs, and by 1905 the community had developed sufficiently enough to be incorporated as a village. In 1906, the population was 213. Dundurn developed largely as an agricultural community; however, as the military base developed (its origins date to 1927), many residents found employment there. Today, many of its facilities and programs are available to the citizens of the town. In recent decades, Dundurn has also become home to a number of people who commute to work in Saskatoon. This latter development led to an increase in Dundurn's population beginning in the

1970s, and in 1980 Dundurn attained town status. Dundurn has a small core of businesses, a library, three churches, a museum, recreation facilities, and a volunteer fire department and a team of first responders to deal with emergency situations. The town has sports, figure skating, and dance programs, a number of annual events and celebrations, and a community of local artists and writers. Dundurn School, an International Reading Award recipient in 1997, is a K-6 facility, which had 126 students enrolled in the fall of 2006. Students are bused to the neighbouring town of Hanley to attend grades 7-12. Blackstrap Provincial Park and the Blackstrap Ski Hill are located just southeast of the community. Three buildings in Dundurn — the Northern Bank building built in 1906, the Moravian Brethren Church built in 1910, and a former school built in 1916 — have all been designated heritage properties. Dundurn serves as the administrative centre of the RM of Dundurn No. 314.

DUVAL, village, pop 94 (2006c), 103 (2001c), is located 10 km north of Strasbourg on Hwy 20, approximately 20 km east of Last Mountain Lake. Last Mountain, the height of land from which the lake's name is derived, rises to the southeast of the village. Duval is situated in what was known as the Neu Elsass Colony, which had its beginnings in 1884-85, and which was the first bloc settlement of German-speaking people in what is now Saskatchewan. Protestant, mainly Lutheran, these settlers initially came from Germany; in the years after 1900, more settlers

of German origin arrived, but these came mainly from southern Russia or via the United States. After the CPR reached Strasbourg (then spelled Strassburg) in 1905, the area population became more diverse — settlers came from eastern Canada and the British Isles, while there were others of Norwegian stock — but in 1971, 40 per cent of the people in Duval still claimed German ancestry. The village of Duval had its beginnings as the railroad was being built north from Strassburg to Lanigan in 1907. A post office by the name of Mountain Side had been established some distance east of the present community in 1906, but in 1908 it was

relocated to the village site and renamed Duval — the name honouring Edward William Du Val, then a superintendent with the CPR. During WWI, Du Val was a lieutenant with the Princess Patricia's Canadian Light Infantry (Eastern Ontario Division); he was killed in action July 2, 1918, at age 33, and is buried in Bellacourt Military Cemetery, Rivière, France. Originally, the CPR had selected land a few kilometres north of the present community for the development of the village (a store operated briefly at this location), but the locale proved to lie too low, prompting the move to higher ground. A boxcar served as the Duval railway station until 1911, when a proper structure was built (this was removed in 1968). The Village of Duval was incorporated on December 21, 1910, and in 1911 its population was 81. The community's numbers grew to 172 by 1926, but they fell to 111 by 1936 due to the Depression. Post-WWII, Duval experienced renewed growth and prosperity — the village had a peak population of 218 in 1956 — but beginning in the early 1960s the community's population and the number of businesses in the village began to dwindle. Five grain elevators lined the railway tracks in 1971; only one elevator and its two annexes still stand today. Despite the community's decline in the 1960s and 1970s, Duval's baseball teams remained formidable contenders, winning a number of league championships. Local businesses in the village today include the Duval Hotel and Restaurant, two garages, a pottery studio (located in the former school), refrigeration services, and financial services. Duval also has ball diamonds, a community hall, and an indoor community skating rink. Schoolchildren are now bused to the town of Strasbourg. Duval is situated in the RM of Last Mountain Valley No. 250.

DYSART'S CHURCHES: Ukrainian Catholic Church of the Holy Eucharist (above left) and St. George Romanian Greek Orthodox Church (above right). Photographs taken January 2005.

DYSART, village, pop 198 (2006c), 210 (2001c), is located about 18 km north of the Qu'Appelle Valley, specifically Pasqua Lake, between Cupar and Lipton on Hwy 22. The first few homesteaders arrived in the area south and east of the present village in the mid-1880s, and more came through the 1890s. The greatest influx of settlers into the district, however, was between 1900 and 1910. Those who took up land in the region were of many origins and included people of English, Scottish, Ukrainian, Polish, German, Romanian, Hungarian, and Irish descent. The village itself began to develop with the construction of the CPR line through Lipton to Strasbourg, and it was named at that time after Dysart in the County of Fife, Scotland. The Dysart townsite was surveyed in 1904, the rail line completed in 1905. In 1905 a school district centred on the village was established and businesses began to spring up, among them the Dysart Hotel. The Dysart Post Office

was established on September 15, 1906, and that year the first grain elevators were erected. Dysart was incorporated on April 6, 1909. The community grew from a population of 61 in 1911 to a peak of 341 in 1956. Through the 1950s and 1960s, the village served a surrounding trading area of approximately 750 persons. Thereafter, both the rural and community populations began to decline, as did the number of businesses in the village. The railway station was demolished in 1972. By 1996, enrollment at Dysart School had declined to the point that the school was closed, but only after an unsuccessful court battle between the local school board and the Cupar School Division. In June 2000, three of Dysart's grain elevators, which had served the district for close to 90 years, were demolished, then burned. Today, remaining businesses and services that cater to the district's mixed farms and livestock producers include a farm equipment dealer-

ship with parts and service, a construction company specializing in farm equipment, a machine shop, a credit union, and an insurance agency. The Dysart Co-operative Association runs a business that has automotive services and sells agricultural products, hardware, and regular and bulk fuels. The Co-op also operates a grocery store. Dysart also has a butcher shop, a postal outlet, a bar, a car wash, and a café. A community centre houses a fitness club, banquet facilities, a gymnasium and a stage; as well, Dysart has a hockey arena, a bowling alley, a playground and campgrounds. Fire protection is provided by a volunteer fire brigade; the nearest RCMP detachments are in Southey and Fort Qu'Appelle. There is a hospital in Fort Qu'Appelle and a health centre in Cupar. Dysart has three designated heritage properties: St. George Romanian Greek Orthodox Church, built in 1906 and featuring unusual circular transepts, one of

the oldest existing structures in Dysart; a building that was built by the Royal Bank in 1928 but operated as such for only two years and is now a private residence; and the former Dysart School, built in 1917 and expanded in 1927. This last building served all grades until 1960 when a new school was built on the west side of the village; grades 7-12 then moved to the new facility and grades K-6 were taught at the old location until 1983, after which all grades were taught in the new building. In 1987, the old school became the Dysart and District Museum, and a decade later the new school, too, was closed. Other notable Dysart landmarks are the twindomed Ukrainian Catholic Church of the Holy Eucharist, dating to 1957, and the village's sole remaining grain elevator, formerly a Saskatchewan Wheat Pool elevator that dates to 1950 (the annex to 1958), which is now privately owned. Dysart is situated in the RM of Lipton No. 217.

EAGLE RIDGE COUNTRY ESTATES, organized hamlet, is a bedroom community located east of the city of Saskatoon, between Hwys 5 and 41. Established as an organized hamlet in 2004, the community has an estimated population of 109 and is situated in the RM of Corman Park No. 344.

EARL GREY, village, pop 264 (2006c), 292 (2001c), is located east of Last Mountain Lake, between Southey and Strasbourg on Hwy 22. The community is situated in a mixed farming area which produces grains, oilseeds, specialty crops, and cattle. Although there were settlers in the general region in the mid-1880s, it was not until the early 1900s and the arrival of the CPR that Earl Grey had its beginnings. The local history recounts that the first resident of the community spent the winter of 1903-04 in a dugout carved out of a hillside. In 1905, trains were running through the fledgling community, the post office was established and the first grain elevator was built. In 1906, a large group of German Protestant settlers arrived in the area, and on July 27, 1906, Earl Grey was incorporated as a village. The name of the community honours Canada's Governor General at the time, Sir Albert Henry George Grey, 4th Earl Grey. Settlers of British and Scandinavian extraction also came to the district, and the village developed into a trading and cultural centre for the area, with an elevator, stores, livery barns, a flour mill, a hotel, churches, and a newspaper. By the early 1920s, the village's citizenry was numbering close to 300, and unlike many other Saskatchewan communities Earl Grey has maintained a fairly stable population over

IN 1924, the Earl Grey Hotel burned to the ground. Photograph courtesy of the Village of Earl Grey.

THE ROYAL CANADIAN LEGION HALL on Main Street, Earl Grey. The plaques to the right of the door commemorate those who served in both World Wars. Photograph taken August 6, 2003.

the decades. Today, however, a significant percentage of residents commute to work in Regina. Earl Grey School, a K-8 institution that had 50 students enrolled in the fall of 2006, closed in June 2007. High school students had attended classes in Southey for a number of years. Earl Grey serves as the administrative centre of the RM of Longlaketon No. 219.

EASTEND, town, pop 471 (2006c), 576 (2001c), is located in the Frenchman River Valley 33 km southwest of Shaunavon on Hwy 13. The Eastend area is rich in history, geologically fascinating, and rife with archaeological and palaeontological sites. In the mid-1880s as bison populations were being decimated on the eastern plains, the area became an increasingly important hunting ground for the animals, and Indian tribes to the east and west of the territory regularly fought over the essential resource. A Métis settlement developed (c. 1860s) just to the north of Eastend, and in the early 1870s the Hudson's Bay Company had a post at the location. The post, however, lasted only a season due to hostilities between the Assiniboine and Blackfoot peoples, and perhaps because of competition from independent traders selling whiskey. Many years later, the site would come to be known as Chimney Coulee, the name derived from the remnants of the stone chimneys that had been built in the Métis homes. In the mid to late 1870s, the NWMP established a satellite detachment of the newly-built Fort Walsh at the Chimney Coulee site, which they dubbed East End because of its location at the east end of the Cypress Hills. When the Mounties moved to the vicinity of the present townsite years later, the name persevered. The first ranch was established in the Eastend

103

EASTEND

...in the "Valley of Hidden Secrets"

Photographs on this page courtesy of the Eastend Historical Museum.

NWMP POST at East End, 1878.

McDonald Riding Parson East End Sask.

▲ EASTEND'S FIRST STAMPEDE, July 17-18, 1914.

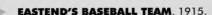
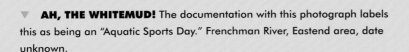

▶ EASTEND'S BASEBALL TEAM, 1915.

▽ AH, THE WHITEMUD! The documentation with this photograph labels this as being an "Aquatic Sports Day." Frenchman River, Eastend area, date unknown.

▽ OVER THE WINTER OF 1951-52, a record amount of snow fell in the Eastend area, and then extremely warm spring temperatures caused the snow to melt within three days, causing the dam above the community to wash out on April 15. The entire valley was flooded and Eastend had to be evacuated. After the water receded, it was discovered that many community records, business documents, and photographs had been lost. Subsequently, a dike and a new dam were constructed to prevent such an occurrence from happening again.

▲ **THESE GUYS LOOK HUNGRY!** Displays at the T.rex Discovery Centre.

▼ **THE FRENCHMAN RIVER VALLEY** between Eastend and Ravenscrag. The river was formerly known as the Whitemud because of the white mud clay deposits in the upper reaches of its banks. In the early 1950s, a ceramics course was offered in Eastend with the purpose of stimulating interest in developing a local industry; today, Eastend artisans utilize local clay to produce both decorative and utilitarian pottery.

Photographs taken September 2, 2004.

area around 1883, and from that point until the turn of the century numerous others were begun in the Eastend-Ravenscrag area. A ranch house built at Eastend in 1902 was the community's first residence, and it remains occupied to this day. Ranching operations, a number of them huge, started to give way to homesteaders and crop production, and in 1914 the CPR built the railway through the area and the village of Eastend (originally East End) was incorporated. The townsite grew and expanded, businesses developed to serve the growing district population, and in 1920 the community attained town status. In 1921, the population was 427 and Eastend was growing steadily. By 1966, the population of the community had grown to a peak 866. Today, Eastend's economy is driven by agriculture, oil and gas, and tourism. The agricultural industry is based on a combination of ranching and grain production; the oil and gas industry includes two major pipelines. Tourism has developed substantially in recent years, following the discovery in 1991 of one of the few Tyrannosaurus rex skeletons ever found in the world. Although pre-historic fossils had been unearthed in the region for over a century, the find, made by local school principal Robert Gebhardt, made history and led to the opening of a palaeontological interpretive centre and research station at Eastend. The T.rex Discovery Centre, opened in May 2000, now hosts several thousand visitors a year. Additional Eastend attractions include the Wallace Stegner House, the boyhood home of the Pulitzer Prize-winning author best known to Saskatchewan residents for his 1955 book, *Wolf Willow*, in which the early years of the community of Eastend are graphically documented. The Stegner home, designated a heritage property, was opened in 1990 as a retreat for writers and artists. Also in Eastend is one of the few observatories open to the public in western Canada. The Wilkinson Memorial Observatory was founded by Jack Wilkinson, a blacksmith who built his own telescopes and hand-ground his own lenses. When he died in 1953, the community took over maintenance of the observatory, which is located on top of one of the valley hills and features an 11-inch (28 cm) Celestron telescope. The museum in Eastend houses additional palaeontological specimens (collected by the community's legendary Harold 'Corky' Jones), as well as artifacts and exhibits relating to the town's early history. As a trading centre for a large surrounding district, Eastend has a number of businesses offering a variety of goods and services; it also serves the region with a health centre, a special care home, ambulance service, and a volunteer fire department. The local RCMP detachment was closed in 2005. Eastend School is a K-12 facility and had 125 students enrolled in the fall of 2006. Community recreational facilities include skating and curling rinks, a nine-hole golf course, campgrounds, an indoor swimming pool, tennis courts, ball diamonds, and rodeo grounds. There is a regional park just northeast of the community, and the two blocks of Cypress Hills Provincial Park lie to the west. The Eastend area is also home to writer Sharon Butala, who became an Officer of the Order of Canada in 2002. Eastend serves as the administrative centre of the RM of White Valley No. 49.

EATONIA, town, pop 449 (2006c), 474 (2001c), is located 44 km southwest of Kindersley at the junction of Hwys 21 and 44. For decades, Eatonia's slogan has been "the Prairie Oasis," as tree-planting efforts led by the community's first doc-

tor resulted in the early beautification of the town. The first settlers began arriving in the Eatonia district around 1906 and were primarily of British and Norwegian origins. They travelled north from the CPR main line and crossed the South Saskatchewan River. After 1910, the majority of those coming to the district were of German origin, a number hailing from the settled areas of eastern Saskatchewan. A significant German settlement developed south of the present site of Eatonia. With the advent of rail lines through Kindersley to Alsask (c. 1910-11) and south of the river to Leader (1913), larger numbers of people began to arrive in the region. Settlement was interrupted by WWI, but resumed through the 1920s. Ukrainians added to the cultural milieu. In 1918, as the railway progressed westward from Eston toward the Alberta border, the townsite of Eaton (Eatonia's original name) was established. Businessmen began erecting buildings, even though the townsite lots would not be surveyed until 1919, and people from the German settlement to the south began relocating to the new community. That same year a weekly newspaper, the *Eatonia Enterprise*, first went to print (it was absorbed by the *Kindersley Clarion* in 1965). In 1920, the village of

Eaton was incorporated, its name honouring the family of the famous Canadian retailers, the T. Eaton Company. The name of the community was changed to Eatonia in 1921 to avoid confusion with the community of Eston, some 50 kilometres to the east. Other than a setback experienced during the 1930s, the village grew steadily and in 1954 was incorporated as a town. From the late 1950s through to the early 1970s, Eatonia had a population of over 600. Today, Eatonia is a trading centre for a region whose economy is largely based upon grain farming, ranching and hogs, with some oil production occurring to the northwest. The community has a variety of businesses providing goods and services, a health centre with an attached special care home, ambulatory service, a team of first responders, and a volunteer fire department. Eaton School is a K-12 facility, which had 129 students enrolled in the fall of 2006. The town has three churches, a range of recreational facilities, and many service clubs and community-based organizations. The Eatonia area is popular for duck and goose hunting, and there are a number of archaeological and historic sites in the region. Eatonia serves as the administrative centre of the RM of Chesterfield No. 261.

EBENEZER, village, pop 139 (2006c), 147 (2001c), is located approximately 18 km north of the city of Yorkton on Hwy 9. The first few settlers began arriving in the district in 1885, and in 1887 large numbers of German-speaking Protestant settlers began taking up land around the present village site and westward. Many of these early arrivals converged in Winnipeg, then rode the rails to Whitewood and headed north from there. By 1889 a Baptist congregation had been formed, as had a school district; in 1891 a post office was established. All adopted the name Ebenezer, of Biblical origin. Also in 1891, the Manitoba and Northwestern Railway had reached Yorkton, significantly reducing travel distance and bringing even more settlers into the region. The 1901 Census recorded the population of the district to be comprised of 357 people of German origin, 134 Ukrainians, and 71 people of British stock. The hamlet of Ebenezer emerged as the Grand Trunk Pacific Railway was constructing its line north from Yorkton in 1909-10. The townsite was purchased and surveyed by the railway company in 1910, and, in the same year, the first grain elevator, blacksmith shop, livery stable and machine shop were built. In 1948, Ebenezer was incorporated as a village. Today, Ebenezer is somewhat of a bedroom community to Yorkton, and many of the village's businesses and services have been superseded by those in that city. Ebenezer is situated in the RM of Orkney No. 244.

ECHO BAY, resort village, is located approximately 100 km west of Prince Albert, on Shell Lake, southwest of the village of the same name. The resort was developed in the early 1970s and was incorporated in 1982. Today, there are several dozen year-round residents; however, the summer population may be significantly higher. Echo Bay is situated in the RM of Spiritwood No. 496.

EDAM, village, pop 399 (2006c), 429 (2001c), is located in the parklands 26 km southeast of Turtleford on Hwy 26. The district was settled in the early 1900s. Settlers were primarily of Dutch, French, Scottish, and English origins; many of the original Dutch settlers came from Edam, in the province of North Holland, Netherlands (famous for its pale yellow cheese coated in red paraffin) — hence, the community's name. Today, the village's slogan is, "A Little Bit of Holland in Saskatchewan," and a 6.7 metre-high (22 ft.) windmill stands in the village alongside the highway, erected in honour of the district's original Dutch settlers. At first, area residents had to haul goods into the district, often by oxen, from North Battleford, a distance of approximately 65 kilometres. After the Paynton Ferry opened in 1907, the distance to the nearest railway point was cut by more than half. The Edam Post Office was established on May 1, 1908, somewhat north of the present village. In 1910, the townsite began to develop as the railway was being built into the district, and the post office was relocated. The Canadian Northern Railway arrived in Edam in 1911 en route from North Battleford to St. Walburg. The first grain elevator was erected that year, and

Edam was incorporated on October 12, 1911. Edam remained the end of the rail line for a few years, and the entire stretch of track was not completed to St. Walburg until 1921. Construction began on the Lady Minto Union Hospital in 1916, and it opened its doors in 1917, the same year the village's second grain elevator went up. By the 1920s the population of Edam was over 200, and the community boasted close to 30 places of business. In the 1950s, Edam's population began to grow again, reaching over 300 by the early 1960s. By the 1980s the community numbered more than 400. Cattle and crop production had dominated the area economy, and remain significant still, but since the late 1970s the oil and gas industry has become increasingly important. By 1980 over 100 wells had been drilled in the area west of Edam toward the North Saskatchewan River; to date, there are several hundred. The industry employs many people in the area and sustains several businesses in the community. Today, Edam has a wide range of businesses and

services, an airstrip, a volunteer fire department, first responders, and a public library. The Lady Minto Health Care Centre has an attached special care home. The nearest RCMP detachment is located in Turtleford. H. Hardcastle School in Edam, named for a long-time teacher and principal, is a K-12 facility that had 192 students enrolled in the fall of 2006. Village recreational facilities include a community centre with skating and curling rinks, a five-diamond ball park, and a nine-hole golf course. There are many miles of groomed cross-country ski trails in the area, and there are a number of regional and provincial parks within close range. The Edam Fall Fair is the community's premier annual event. Two village landmarks, both among the oldest extant buildings in Edam, have been declared municipal heritage properties: the Canadian Northern Railway Station, closed in 1979 and bought by the village in 1981, has served as a community centre, a play school, and a meeting place for the local Lions Club; the other property is what was

for many years the Edam Café. Built in 1915, the business at one time consisted of the café, a hotel, and an adjacent ice cream parlour, and it was considered to be one of the most elegant establishments of its kind in the region. Its owner, Charlie Chan, had come from China in 1910, and was originally only a partner in the café. Later he bought the business, and his family operated it until 1986. In 2003, it was moved from its original location on Main Street to the Lions Heritage Village situated on East Railway Avenue. A feature attraction of the Heritage Village is the Washbrook Museum. Originally operated as a private museum by Harry and Mildred Washbrook, based on a private collection they had accumulated over years, the museum is now managed by the Lions Club, and was in recent years moved into the former Saskatchewan Wheat Pool elevator. Three floors of the annex have been converted into showrooms to display a vast array of local pioneer era items and First Nations artifacts. Edam serves as the administrative centre of the RM of Turtle River No. 469.

EDENWOLD, village, pop 242 (2006c), 226 (2001c), is located 44 km northeast of Regina in a rolling setting characterized by frequent poplar bluffs. In the early 1880s, a few individual pioneers from Ontario and Britain began taking up land in the area, but it was German Protestants who came to be predominant in the Edenwold district. German Baptists from the Dobruja area of Romania were the first to arrive in 1885, followed by settlers from Bukovina who began to take up land in the district in 1889. The Bukovinian Germans would come to make up the majority of the pioneers in the Edenwold area. A few settlers would also come from

Germany itself, and, after a lull in immigration through the late 1890s, a second wave of settlement began in the early 1900s, consisting of German-speaking peoples from Poland, Galicia, and southern Russia. In 1907, the first German Catholics began to settle in the district. In 1886, the Baptist settlers formed the first German Baptist congregation west of Winnipeg, and in 1887 they organized to build their first church, which was located about seven kilometres south of the present community (the cemetery remains at the site). The settlement in the Edenwold district was originally known as New Tulcea, or Neu Tulcea, after the county of Tulcea in northern Dobruja. The New Tulscha school district (spelling varies) was established on July 12, 1887, and the Baptist Church doubled as the first school. The name Edenwold (originally Edenwald) — an amalgamation of the words Eden, after the biblical garden, and *wald*, the German word for forest — emerged with the establishment of an area post office in 1890. When the railway came through and the village site was determined, the name was adopted for the community. By 1893, the Lutheran presence had grown to the point that the congregation had established a cemetery and had built their first church a couple of kilometres west of the Baptist church on a small hill overlooking the surrounding countryside. The first church on the site was replaced by a more substantial and impressive structure in 1919. It was designated a heritage property in 1985, and regular worship services continue to be held there. In 1911, with the completion of the Grand Trunk Pacific rail line from Melville through Fort Qu'Appelle to Regina, life in the Edenwold district was transformed. A townsite was located, surveyed, and thereafter the present village began to develop rapidly. A rail-

▼ **MAIN STREET, EDAM**, looking west. Photograph taken July 24, 2003.

▲ ▼ **ORIGINS OF EDENWOLD:** The Edenwold Baptist Cemetery (above), established circa 1887, is located about seven kilometres south of the village. St. John Lutheran Church (below), built in 1919 to replace the smaller original structure, is located somewhat west of the cemetery; construction of the first Lutheran Church on the site was begun in 1891. Photographs taken May 22, 2006.

way station was constructed in 1911, and in 1912 the post office was relocated from the countryside to the village site and a new school was built in the community. The village was incorporated on October 3, 1912. Never a particularly large village — the population was 134 in 1916, 176 in 1931, down to 128 by 1946, up to 190 by 1956, and back down to 129 by 1971 — Edenwold was for many years, though, a hub in the district. With the coming of the railroad, elevators were constructed, and the other essential businesses — dray services, lumberyards, liveries, and stores — emerged. Seventh-day Adventists established a church, and there was from the early 1920s until 1957 an Apostolic Mission in the community. Lutherans built St. Paul Church in the village in 1916, and the community's Catholics erected St. Mary's in 1937. In 1949, the Baptists built a new church in the village as the country church had burned to the ground a few years earlier. Unfortunately, this church, too, burned in 1967, and thereafter the congregation disbanded to attend services in either Balgonie or Regina. In 1931, the Village of Edenwold won a $1,000 first prize in a competition sponsored by the Canadian National Railway that focused on the progress of communities with a population at least 70 per cent continental European in origin. Developments in education, agriculture, social welfare, co-operation, and the arts were all judged, and in each category Edenwold scored high. The prize money went to making improvements to the village hall. Following something of a post-war boom in the 1950s, the community slipped into a period of decline. Businesses were folding, as the amenities of Regina became increasingly accessible due to better roads and automobiles. The Edenwold railway station was closed in July 1963, and in

1974 the building was sold and dismantled. But just as one era in the community was ending, another was beginning. By the early 1970s the village's population had reached an all-time low; however, the installation of sewer and water systems at the end of the 1960s precipitated the construction of new homes and lured people into the community who would commute to work in Regina. The population of Edenwold has since continued to grow to the point where, today, it has reached an all-time high. A new school was built in the community in 1987, replacing the 1919 red brick structure which has since been converted into a private residence. Edenwold Elementary School, a K-6 facility, had 54 students enrolled in the fall of 2006. Students in grades 7 through 12 attend school in Balgonie. St. Paul Lutheran Church remains active (St. Mary's closed in the early 1990s), and Edenwold has a pre-school, a seniors' centre, a post office, the village office, and a bar. The village has skating and curling rinks, and a soccer field. The grain elevators were closed in June 2000, then demolished and burned. Edenwold lies within the boundaries of the RM of Edenwold No. 158.

EDGELEY, organized hamlet, pop 41, is located 20 km southwest of Fort Qu'Appelle, just off Hwy 10. The first settlers to arrive in the Edgeley district came from the Guelph, Ontario, area in early 1882. A work train would transport people as far as Broadview, and from there they trekked the rest of the distance. That same year, English brothers by the name of Sykes purchased 18 sections of land in the district, establishing one of the largest farming operations of its kind in the Territories. They named the operation Edgeley Farm, after their hometown, which is

▲ **FAMILY AND FRIENDS** gather for the christening of two babies at the Anglican Church in Edgeley, circa 1913. Saskatchewan Archives Board R-A20271.

▼ **EDGELEY UNITED CHURCH.** Photograph taken August 5, 2007.

situated in the Manchester area. Edgeley Farm was managed by Mr. and Mrs. William C. Cameron until 1903, when it was divided into smaller parcels and sold. The Camerons retired to Kelowna. Over the years, many settlers arriving from eastern Canada and England learned the basics of agriculture working at Edgeley Farm, and it developed into a centre for the district's social activities, meetings, and church services. The headquarters of the farm were some kilometres southeast of the present community, and in October 1884, a post office named Edgeley Farm was established, with Mr. Cameron serving as the postmaster until his retirement (the name of the office was shortened to Edgeley in 1897). In 1883, a Methodist Church was built to the northwest (about two and a half kilometres south of the present community), and in 1885 a school was constructed somewhat to the east of that. The Edgeley Football Club took on the task of building a community hall just northwest of the Edgeley Farm post office in 1896, and in 1899 St. Thomas Anglican Church (still standing and today a heritage property) was built at NE32-18-15-W2, roughly halfway between present-day Edgeley and the village of McLean. One winter, during the 1890s, an outbreak of diphtheria ravaged the district and many children died. One family, the Craigs, lost three. In 1911, with the construction of the Grand Trunk Pacific Railway line between Melville, Fort Qu'Appelle and North Regina, the location of the present community was determined. Around the station site, a hamlet, which adopted the name Edgeley, began to form and expand. Edgeley Hall was moved in from the countryside in 1912, and the post office was also established at the new site. In 1919, a tender was accepted to have a new school built in the community, and in 1924 the Methodist Church was moved in from the country. It became a Union Church and, later, the United Church. This remains in use, and is reputedly the province's oldest continually active Protestant church. The building was designated a heritage property in 1983. Edgeley developed into an active community with competitive sports teams and a curling club, a 4-H Club, a jazz band and a choir. Until 2001, when the last grain elevator was demolished, it was also a grain-handling point for the district's farmers. High school students had begun to be bused to Fort Qu'Appelle to attend classes in 1963, and on June 30, 1967, due to declining enrollment, Edgeley School was closed. The post office closed in 1988. Today, some of the community's residents commute to work in Regina. Edgeley was established as an organized hamlet in 1976 and is situated in the RM of South Qu'Appelle No. 157.

ELBOW, village, pop 294 (2006c), 298 (2001c), takes its name from its position at the elbow of the South Saskatchewan River, which was flooded with the creation of Lake Diefenbaker. The first known written use of the term "elbow" for the location was recorded in 1804 in the journal of John Macdonald of Garth, a trading partner with the North West Company. The first known settler in the area was James Middagh, who arrived via Moose Jaw in 1898 and engaged in ranching just southeast of the present resort village of Mistusinne. Extensive settlement of the area, however, began about 1903, and by the end of the decade much of the land in the Elbow area was occupied. Those who came to the region were largely of English and Scottish origins, from eastern Canada or overseas; others were Norwegians, most of whom arrived from the United States. Some came to the district through Moose Jaw; many took the train as far as Davidson and disembarked there. The townsite of Elbow was established in 1908 as the CPR line from Moose Jaw to Outlook was being built, and the line was completed in 1909. Much of the village was built up that year: the area post office, known as River View (established in 1906 a few kilometres to the north), relocated to the townsite and was renamed Elbow; stores moved in from the countryside; a townsite school district was organized; and many new businesses were started. A popular slogan of the day was, "Fifty years ago Palliser slept here, nobody is asleep here now!" On April 6, 1909, the village was incorporated, and Elbow flourished

THE FEARY. ELBOW

◄▼ **THE FIRST FERRY** across the South Saskatchewan River at Elbow in 1905. The service was discontinued after the Dunblane viaduct was built in the mid-1920s.

Photographs courtesy of the Elbow Museum.

Once upon a bend...
ELBOW

through the first number of years and grew to have a population of about 300 by the outbreak of the Depression — during which the community's numbers fell by half. From 1905 to 1926, there had been a ferry service across the river, connecting settlers on both sides; then the CNR's Dunblane viaduct, a mammoth combination road and rail bridge, was opened and the ferry was no longer needed. As railroads were completed to Dunblane, Birsay, and Beechy, west of the river, and to Lawson, Riverhurst, and Grainland, south of Elbow, Elbow's trade from these districts dwindled and the community's development was stalled until the late 1950s. In 1958 the agreement between the federal and provincial governments to build the Gardiner Dam was signed, and in 1959 construction began. The South Saskatchewan River Project brought an influx of workers and their families to the region, and Elbow's population almost doubled during the decade. From 281 residents in 1956, the community's numbers skyrocketed to 470 by 1966. By

◄ **BEFORE THE DAMS.** Elbow from the north. The Dunblane viaduct is shown on the right. Saskatchewan Archives Board R-B5154(2).

▲ **ON THE BEACH** just below the village. Photograph taken July 22, 2005.

▶ **ELBOW HARBOUR.** Photograph taken July 30, 2003.

▼ **A LOCAL HERITAGE PROPERTY** in Elbow is the former Canadian Bank of Commerce building, built circa 1908, which now houses the village office and remains a landmark on Elbow's main street. Photograph taken July 30, 2003.

the mid-1970s, however, Elbow's population was back down to its pre-project level. The year 1967 was an exciting one for the community: Elbow's curling team of Doug Wankel and Art, Gay, and Elmer Knutson were the Saskatchewan Brier champions, and were narrowly defeated at the national competition in Ottawa that year; as well, both the Gardiner and the Qu'Appelle Valley Dams became operational — the latter constructed to prevent the rising waters of the emerging lake from flowing into the valley. The result of the South Saskatchewan River Project has been manifold and mixed. Some farms and pasture lands were flooded; the Dunblane viaduct was dismantled and their across-the-river neighbours (and customers) suddenly became rather like strangers across the deep waters of Lake Diefenbaker; favourite picnic and camping areas disappeared. But in this drought-prone region, communities, irrigators, and industrial users now had a stable supply of water; and with the creation of the lake,

▶ **SWEET TREATS ICE CREAM PARLOUR** in Elbow is popular with both locals and tourists and does a brisk business during the summer months. Photograph taken July 30, 2003.

and then the establishment of Danielson and Douglas Provincial Parks, tourism and recreation slowly began to replace agriculture (largely wheat production and cattle ranching) as the dominant industries in the area. Due to this, Elbow has been undergoing a period of substantial growth in recent years. Two major attractions include a deep-water marina and an 18-hole championship golf course and country club with a spectacular view over the lake. Retirees are moving to Elbow, and new housing subdivisions have been and are being built. As well, people are purchasing properties for seasonal use, and during the summer months the village population is significantly higher than the number of year-round residents cited above. The village also hosts a number of annual events including a three-day rodeo, fishing derbies, a dinner theatre, a car show and street dance, and a craft fair and trade show, all of which draw many people. A local family creates an elaborate corn maze each year, and invites the public to their lakeside property. Another attraction is the Elbow Museum which includes a fully furnished replica of an early twentieth-century sod house. Additionally, the community recently announced that its sole remaining grain elevator (no longer in use) will be saved and preserved. Elbow has a library, a fitness centre, a civic centre, an arena, three churches, and a wide range of clubs and organizations. Local businesses include a hotel, B&Bs, lakeshore condominium and suite rentals, an RV park and campgrounds, restaurants, a miniature golf course, grocery stores and a liquor vendor, artists' studios, an antique shop, and a range of specialty stores. Commutron Industries, located in the former school, is a locally-owned company which assembles electronic circuit boards and employs as many as 30 people during

peak production. Area businesses include a seed cleaning and processing plant, and the Gardiner Dam Terminal grain elevator. Elbow has an RCMP detachment, a team of first responders, and a volunteer fire department. The nearest hospital is in Central Butte; schoolchildren are bused to the neighbouring village of Loreburn, 13 kilometres to the north (Elbow School was closed in 1993). Elbow is situated in the RM of Loreburn No. 254, which benefits considerably from revenues generated by oil and gas pipelines running through the area.

ELBOW LAKE, organized hamlet, est. 1987, is a small resort community situated in the Porcupine Hills in east-central Saskatchewan. The resort is a part of the Woody River Provincial Recreation Site and the population varies depending on the season. Elbow Lake is located on provincial road No. 980 in the RM of Hudson Bay No. 394.

ELDERSLEY, organized hamlet, pop 30 (2006c), 40 (2001c), is located 16 km east of Tisdale, just north of Hwy 3. The rail line through the area became operational circa 1904-05, and a few years later the community had its beginnings as a major supply and distribution centre for the north-eastern area of the province. The Pas Lumber Co. built a warehouse at the site (which had become known as Osgood Siding) to provision their logging camps. As well, a rail spur was built for loading boxcars and flatcars with cordwood and lumber. In 1913, a Mr. Theodore Will built a house and established a store, and in 1914 he opened a post office which he named Eldersley after the surrounding rural municipality. (The

name of the RM of Eldersley No. 427 was changed to the RM of Tisdale No. 427 in 1921.) The RM had been named after Elderslie, a community in Renfrewshire, Scotland; however, somewhere along the line a spelling mistake was made and never corrected. The name Osgood Siding was changed to that of the post office in 1921. In 1916, the Canada West Grain Co. built an elevator at Osgood Siding, and grain was hauled to it from as far as the Zenon Park and Arborfield areas. A sawmill was also established at Osgood Siding about 1920. Eldersley was incorporated as a village on June 8, 1922, and throughout the decade, as a great influx of new farming families arrived in the district, many a boxcar of settler's effects — household furniture, farm implements, cattle, and horses — were unloaded in the community and transported to their respective homesteads. Eldersley boomed as a supply, distribution, and transportation hub, and a wide range of businesses were established in the community. The village's trade suffered somewhat as a result of the CP line being built from Wadena through Tisdale to Nipawin in the mid-1920s, but Eldersley's economy sustained a major blow when CN constructed lines north and southeast from Crooked River in 1929, to Arborfield and Reserve respectively. Some businesses in the village closed or relocated elsewhere. Eldersley lost about one third of its population during the five years between 1926 and 1931 — down from 159 to 105 — and in 1935 the village council wrote to the Department of Municipal Affairs in Regina to have the community's incorporation revoked and have the management of its affairs returned to the auspices of the RM. The Village of Eldersley was legally dissolved on January 1, 1936, and the community reverted to hamlet status. In 1956, the

railway station was closed, and in 1960 students in grades nine through twelve began to be bused to classes in Tisdale. By the spring of 1969 only 34 students were enrolled at Eldersley School, and the school was closed at the end of the school year in June. The post office was closed in 1970, and the last store in the community operated until 1974. The population of the community at that time had fallen to about 60. Eldersley is situated in the RM of Tisdale No. 427.

ELFROS, village, pop 110 (2006c), 161 (2001c), is located 25 km east of Wynyard on Hwys 16 and 35. Elfros developed in what is known as the Vatnabyggd Icelandic settlement, which had its beginnings in 1891. The settlement eventually

▼ **THE VATNABYGGD MEMORIAL STATUE** in the Centennial Park in Elfros. Photograph taken August 4, 2004.

stretched from Foam Lake to the Kandahar-Dafoe area, and north to Fishing Lake and the Quill Lakes. Vatnabyggd is Icelandic and means "Lakes Settlement." After the turn of the twentieth century the origins of the region's population began to diversify (Swedes were among the mix), yet today Icelanders and other Scandinavians still make up more than a third of Elfros' residents. Icelanders took up land in significant numbers in the Elfros district in 1903; the village began to develop five years later with the coming of the railway. The name Elfros is said to be derived from an Icelandic term referring to the wild roses that grew in the area. The first building — a store — appeared on the Elfros townsite in 1908, and the next year trains were running through from Yorkton to Wynyard. The Elfros Post Office was established on April 1, 1909, and Elfros was incorporated on December 1 that year. The population of the village in 1911 was 103; by 1926 it was 260; and in 1956 the community reached a peak population of 308. At this time, the village had close to two dozen business, two grain elevators, a resident doctor and a druggist. In the 1970s the population of Elfros began to decline; since 1991, when the community numbered 181, it has fallen substantially. The school closed in 1999. Today, only a few businesses remain in Elfros, including the Co-op, which sells groceries, gas, and hardware, a credit union, and the hotel/bar. The Elfros Union Church, built in 1934-35 when local Presbyterian and Lutherans decided to merge together to finance the construction of a church, is a village landmark and was designated a municipal heritage property in 2000. Another landmark is a memorial to the region's Icelandic pioneers commissioned by the Vatnabyggd Icelandic Club of Saskatchewan. The memorial, located in the village's Centennial Park, includes information on the first Icelanders to move into the Vatnabyggd settlement, murals of Iceland in the late 1800s, the voyage to Canada and the prairies, and Vatnabyggd then and now. The memorial also includes a bronze statue created by renowned Saskatoon sculptor Hans Holtkamp, which depicts a young Icelandic couple in turn-of-the-century Icelandic dress. Elfros serves as the administrative centre of the RM of Elfros No. 307.

ELROSE, town, pop 453 (2006c), 517 (2001c), is located 38 km south of Rosetown on Hwys 4 and 44. The area was largely settled between 1909 and 1912, and it was during the latter year that the CNR completed the railway grade into the district. Along the line a hamlet sprang up, which was originally known as LaBerge, after Albert LaBerge, one of the first settlers and businessmen in the area. In 1913, the townsite was surveyed, and, as the first trains rolled in, the name Elrose (derivation unknown) was chosen as the permanent name for the community. Elrose was incorporated as a village in October that year. In 1915, the railroad was extended westward from Elrose to Eston. Elrose grew rapidly until the beginning of the 1930s, then experienced a substantial loss of population during the decade, which it did not recover until after WWII. In 1951, Elrose achieved town status, and by the mid-1980s the town's population was close to 700. The basis of the regional economy was, and remains, agriculture; however, in recent years oil and gas production has become an increasingly important factor. The town has a number of suppliers and services which cater to the agricultural industry, as well as financial and professional services, recreational facilities, and cultural institutions. There is a health centre, and fire and ambulatory services. Policing is provided by the Rosetown RCMP detachment. Elrose Composite School provides K-12 education; there were 126 students enrolled in the fall of 2006. Elrose serves as the administrative centre for the RM of Monet No. 257.

▼ **THE END OF A LANDMARK:** Built in 1913 and originally known as the LaBerge Hotel, the Elrose Hotel (the name was changed in 1926) burned to the ground in September 1994. Photograph courtesy of Catharina Smith, Elrose, Saskatchewan.

ELSTOW, village, pop 91 (2006c), 97 (2001c) is situated approximately 40 km east of Saskatoon and 14 km west of Colonsay on Hwy 16. The first few settlers took up land in the Elstow area in 1902; more arrived in 1903. The village of Elstow had its beginnings in 1906 when CPR surveyors staked out a townsite on SE10-35-01-W3, the homestead of James Nicholas Harvie. Harvie relinquished his homestead for sale and received one half of the surveyed lots as payment. It is believed a CPR official was reading John Bunyan's *Pilgrim's Progress* at the time and dubbed the townsite "Elstow" after the author's birthplace, Elstow, Bedfordshire, England. The first building on the townsite — a store — went up in the spring of 1907, and by the fall a number of new businesses and other buildings had been erected. The railway grade was completed in 1907, and some freight service was offered that year. In 1908 the CPR station was built and passenger service was inaugurated. The Elstow Post Office was established on December 15, 1907, and the Village of Elstow was incorporated on December 17, 1908. In 1910 a school that had been constructed just northeast of Elstow in 1906 (originally known as Athens School) was moved into the village. By 1918, four grain elevators had been erected; by 1921, the population of Elstow was 146. This, however, would begin to dwindle by the 1930s. The construction of the Allan Potash Mine in the mid-1960s, and its becoming operational in 1968, brought somewhat of a boon to the village — the population rose from 98 in 1961 to 150 by 1971 — but other forces were beginning to have a major impact on the community. In 1960, the last passenger train passed through the village, and in 1961 the CPR withdrew their station agent. The station was sold for removal from the CPR right-of-way in 1973. In 1963, Elstow's school was downsized, and subsequently only grades one to six were taught locally. Older children then went to Colonsay, Clavet, or Allan. In 1969 Elstow School was closed. Also in the 1960s, Elstow's United and Anglican churches closed, and in the early 1970s the Elstow Co-op, which had been in operation for 58 years, went out of business, a victim of the trend toward shopping in Saskatoon. When the Saskatchewan Wheat Pool elevator was struck by lightening on August 5, 1979, and destroyed by fire, it brought an end to grain handling in the village. The post office in Elstow closed on August 15, 1986. Today there are no businesses or services in the village; residents either work in area potash mines, the region's agricultural supply and service businesses, or commute to work in Saskatoon. Elstow is situated in the RM of Blucher No. 343.

ENDEAVOUR, village, pop 118 (2006c), 154 (2001c), is located north of Preeceville, south of the Porcupine Provincial Forest, just west of Hwy 9. It is an area of the province where the northern parklands meet the southern timber zone. As such, the logging industry is an

▲ **ENDEAVOUR**, early morning, looking east, July 29, 2004.

ENGLEFELD, village, pop 227 (2006c), 245 (2001c), is located nine km west of Watson on Hwy 5. Humboldt, 32 km west of Englefeld, is the nearest city. Settlers came to the district in 1902-03, as a large tract of land from Watson through Humboldt to the Cudworth area began to be settled by German Catholics from the northern and mid-western United States. The area was known as St. Peter's Colony, and Englefeld developed as one of a number of communities within the settlement. St. Peter's Colony was founded and colonized by the German-American Land Co. in conjunction with Minnesota Benedictines, and Englefeld was named after Abbot Peter Engel (why the spelling was altered is unknown) of St. John's Abbey

important part of the regional economy, as is agriculture; farmers in the area are engaged in grain and livestock production. A few settlers were in the district as early as 1907, with more homesteads being taken up after the railway reached Sturgis, to the south, in 1911. However it was in 1928, when the railway was being built north to Hudson Bay, that the townsite of Endeavour was developed. In the late 1920s and early 1930s, a majority of those settling in the area were refugees fleeing the drought and dust storms then sweeping the southern plains. By 1953, the population of Endeavour was approximately 200, and the community was incorporated as a village that year. Today, Endeavour has a small number of active businesses and quiet residential streets. A handful of abandoned homes and vacated businesses are sprinkled throughout the community. The village has curling and

skating rinks, sports grounds, churches, a community hall, and a seniors' centre. John Palagian's Museum, on the east edge of the village, has a large array of historic McCormick-Deering farm equipment. A village institution, Endeavour School, closed in June 2006, after enrollment had dropped to 23 students the previous fall. In 1996, one student, then in grade two, had written a letter which brought a famous visitor to the community. Rene Jakubowski wrote children's author Robert Munsch about the playhouse her father had built. Munsch was so charmed by the girl's letter that, in 2000, he visited the girl's family farm. Inspired, Munsch published the book "Playhouse" in 2002, and the illustrations in the book are based upon the photographs he took during his visit with the Jakubowski family. Endeavour is situated in the RM of Preeceville No. 334.

▲ **THE MID-WAY CO-OP ELEVATOR** in Englefeld was built by the Saskatchewan Wheat Pool in 1986. It was sold to the Co-op in 2002 and the company now buys, stores, cleans, and sells agricultural grain, seed, fertilizers, and chemicals.
Photograph taken August 6, 2004.

◀ **TOURISTS** taking a photograph in front of Englefeld's Hog. The community's premier annual event is a two-day extravaganza known as "Hog Fest," which has attracted as many as 1,600 people. Begun in 1971, Hog Fest is an important community fundraiser featuring baseball games, a car show, rides for children, a dinner, a dance, and fireworks. As many as 16 spit-roasted pigs are prepared for Hog Fest, as well as hundreds of pounds of potatoes. In addition to raising considerable sums of money for their community, Englefeld residents, on a per capita basis, have long been among the largest contributors to the Saskatchewan Kinsmen's Telemiracle. Photograph taken August 6, 2004.

in Collegeville, Minnesota. Construction of the Canadian Northern Railway was proceeding through the district in 1904, and in 1905 trains were running from Kamsack to Humboldt. In 1906, a general store and a lumberyard were built in Englefeld, and on February 1, 1907, the post office opened. In 1909, Matthew and Gerry Herriges built a hotel, but in 1911 tragedy struck the establishment when there was an outbreak of diphtheria in the building, and Matt Herriges' two children and a woman working there died. The first grain elevator in Englefeld was erected in 1910, and a railway station — a fourth-class structure — was operational in 1912. On June 13, 1916, the Village of Englefeld was incorporated and it grew slowly but steadily over the years. Today, three industries in the village together employ approximately 150 people. Englefeld successfully thwarted an attempt to have its school closed in the late 1990s. The community realized that the school would be an important drawing card for any potential new families. The companies in Englefeld manufacture farm equipment and industrial machinery, moulded plastic products, and windmills. Englefeld School is a K-12 facility, which had 101 students enrolled in the fall of 2006. Other businesses in Englefeld today include a hotel, a motel, two restaurants, a service station, a post office, and a credit union. Recreational facilities in the village consist of a park with a picnic shelter and barbeques, basketball and volleyball courts, skating and curling rinks, bowling lanes, ball diamonds, and a soccer pitch. The community has a volunteer fire department of twelve members. Englefeld is situated in the RM of St. Peter No. 369.

ERNFOLD, village, pop 35 (2006c), 50 (2001c), lies 11 km northeast of the town of Morse, nestled between the east and west-bound lanes of Hwy 1. Railway sidings, or "stopping-off" points, had existed in the area for some years, but the present location of the village was established when the CPR straightened its tracks through the region in 1905. The name Ernfold is believed to have originated with the railroad, but its derivation is not known. The first few settlers began trickling into the area in 1903-04, but by 1907-08 the real influx had begun. Homesteaders largely came from eastern Canada, the United States, and the British Isles. The Ernfold Post Office was established on March 23, 1908, and in 1910 a school, a one-room affair, was built for the district's children. Ernfold was incorporated on December 4, 1912, and by this time the village boasted a hotel, livery stables, a restaurant, stores, a lumberyard, and farm implement dealers. By 1913, the first church was completed and a proper railway station had replaced the boxcar that was originally used for the purpose. For a number of years, until railway branch lines were built north and

south of the CPR main line, farmers from a considerable distance hauled their grain to the Ernfold elevators. Through into the 1920s, the village was built up. In 1917, a building was erected to serve as the local headquarters for the newly-formed Saskatchewan Provincial Police (the force disbanded in 1928 and the building became the telephone office), and in 1919, to accommodate a burgeoning student population, a new two-room, red brick schoolhouse was built. In 1926, the community reached a peak population of 167. People moved away during the Depression, but during the post-war period the community largely recovered. In 1956, Ernfold had 156 residents, but from that point forward the population steadily declined to its present level. In 1963, the CPR buildings — the station and section house, the freight shed and coal dock — were sold, torn down, or moved away. Ernfold was wired into the province's growing electrical grid in the late 1940s; natural gas became available to village residents in 1954, but it was not until 1968 that water works were completed and the homes had running water. In 1958, high school students began to be bused to Morse, and in 1972, due to the small numbers of children enrolled, Ernfold School was closed,

ERNFOLD SCHOOL: After its closure, the 1919 building was subsequently purchased and renovated for use as a Baptist church, but in 1989 membership in the congregation had dwindled to the point that the church, too, was closed. In 1990, the landmark structure was designated a municipal heritage property; however, today it sits derelict in disrepair. Photograph (facing page) taken August 28, 2003.

with all students then travelling to Morse for their education. In the 1970s, Ernfold still had a population of around 100 and several businesses, including three elevators, in operation. Today, village residents travel to larger centres for supplies and services. Ernfold is situated in the RM of Morse No. 165.

ERWOOD, organized hamlet, pop 63 (2006c), 68 (2001c), is located about 15 km east of the town of Hudson Bay on Hwy 3, 35 km west of the Saskatchewan-Manitoba border. At the beginning of the twentieth century, the Canadian Northern Railway reached the site of the present community as it proceeded from Swan River, Manitoba, en route to Melfort and Prince Albert. Until a bridge was built over the Red Deer River in 1903 allowing trains to travel westward, the location, named for E. R. Wood, a railway company official, was the end of the line. Along this stretch of line there were no towns or villages at the time, only a string of logging centres that were just springing up. Thousands of men were employed working in the bush, and by about 1910 Erwood had a small number of businesses and several dwellings. This early settlement, however, was temporary, as most of the area mill towns were. As logging timber became scarce, much was dismantled and moved away. The post office closed and only seasonal forest workers and the odd trapper remained in the district. In 1926 the area was opened up to homesteaders, and slowly a small farming community began to emerge. However, it was not until the 1940s and the arrival of bulldozers to clear the land that agriculture became significant. In 1931, a school was built somewhat east of Erwood, and in 1932 postal service was re-established in a

building near the school, relocating to the present community location a couple of years later. During the 1930s businesses developed slowly; since the country was sparsely populated, there was little incentive for commercial ventures. Until 1939, when the first elevator was built at Erwood, grain was hauled overland during the winter months to Hudson Bay (then known as Hudson Bay Junction). It was not until the 1940s that a school was established in the hamlet, relieving the community's schoolchildren of the approximately four-kilometre walk east to the country school. A few graded roads began to appear in the district, and in the 1950s Hwy 3 was completed as far as Erwood, linking the community with the rest of the province. In the latter decades of the twentieth century, Erwood's businesses, services, and school were superseded by those in the neighbouring town of Hudson Bay — Erwood's post office closed in 1970 — and today, Erwood is essentially residential, somewhat of a bedroom community to the larger centre. The rail line through the hamlet was abandoned in 1990. Erwood is situated in the RM of Hudson Bay No 394.

ESTERHAZY, town, pop 2,336 (2006c), 2,348 (2001c), is located southeast of Melville at the junction of Hwys 22 and 80. The area was first settled by English homesteaders in 1882, who established what was known as the Sumner colony, named after the postmaster, just north of the present town. A few years later a large Swedish settlement was founded to the west; to the southwest, Czech settlers took up homesteads. Germans and Scandinavians would also come to round out the region's cultural milieu. In 1886, a man known as Count Paul Oscar

d'Esterhaz settled the first 35 Hungarian families just south of Esterhazy, establishing what came to be known as the Kaposvar Colony. After initial hardships, the settlement flourished, and its success helped publicize the agricultural viability of the region to later waves of immigrants. The construction of the CPR line from Tantallon up the steep ascent through the Kaposvar Valley was pivotal to the development of the Esterhazy townsite, which was named to honour the community's Hungarian benefactor. The first buildings were erected as the tracks were being laid, and Esterhazy was incorporated as a village on December 3, 1903. The first train rolled through in 1904. The community grew steadily, from a population of 231 in 1906 to 652 in 1951. The development of the potash industry in the late 1950s and early 1960s then had a dramatic impact on Esterhazy's progress. International Minerals and Chemicals Corp. (IMC) began construction of the world's largest potash mine, K1, which became fully operational in 1962. A second mine, K2, was finished in 1967, and, although at the surface the two mines are approximately 10 kilometres apart, they are linked underground. The workforce required at these mammoth enterprises had an astounding effect on Esterhazy's population. By 1966, it had reached 3,190. Esterhazy attained town status on March 1, 1957. No longer just a farming community, Esterhazy became one of the bigger and more modern rural communities in Saskatchewan, with all the facilities and amenities of a larger urban centre. Today, the area potash mines employ approximately 800 people. Agriculture, too, remains important to the economy, with district farms growing wheat, canola, and flax, as well as raising cattle. Esterhazy has a broad range of locally-owned businesses, as

"Salt of the Earth"
ESTERHAZY

▲ **THE CPR** was a part of life in Esterhazy for over 90 years. Trains served the community from 1904 until the line was abandoned in 1996. During the era of steam locomotives, the water tower in the background in the right of this photograph was supplied with water pumped overland from Kaposvar Creek.

◄ **ESTERHAZY, 1911.** The Central Hotel, in the left of the photograph, was the first building constructed on a surveyed lot in Esterhazy in 1903. It is now known as the Old Central Hotel, and it is still in business today.

▲ **THE ESTERHAZY OBSERVER OFFICE, 1911.** The paper began publishing in 1907. The man on the left is Arthur Ford, the editor; on the right is Fred Barker, identified as the "printer's devil." A printer's devil is an historical term for an apprentice, or an errand boy, in a printing establishment who performed a number of tasks, such as mixing tubs of ink and fetching type.

▼ **MAIN STREET**, looking north in the 1930s.

▼ **CLEMENTS' STORE, ESTERHAZY**, was a pioneering retail firm operated by several generations of the Clements family. The company was recognized with a Master Retailers Award.

Photographs on this page courtesy of the Esterhazy Community Museum.

THE KAPOSVAR HISTORIC SITE is a 10-acre religious complex that includes the magnificent Our Lady of Assumption Roman Catholic Church pictured here, a ten-room rectory, stations of the cross, and a grotto. The church, which dates to 1906-07, was constructed of large stones hauled to the site by the early Hungarian pioneers. Since 1961, it has only been used for an occasional wedding, funeral, or special mass, but the site continues to be the location of a traditional annual pilgrimage. Photograph taken on July 12, 2003.

IN ESTERHAZY HISTORICAL PARK are located both the town's museum and the impressive Esterhazy Flour Mill, which dates back to 1906-07. The mill was closed in the mid-1980s, but its equipment and machinery remain intact, providing a unique snapshot of the province's industrial past. Photograph taken on October 18, 2003.

K-1. October 18, 2003.

VOLUNTEERS refurbishing the 1910 residence of William Howland Blyth, a prominent Esterhazy businessman, for its new role as the Esterhazy Community Museum, July 2003. Photograph courtesy of the Esterhazy Community Museum.

ESTERHAZY, SASKATCHEWAN, SATURDAY, OCTOBER 18, 2003, 9:30 A.M. John Putko of John Putko Auction Service conducts an auction.

well as franchises of national companies. Esterhazy also has a full array of medical practitioners and services, including a 21-bed hospital and a special care home. There is an RCMP detachment, and an award-winning volunteer fire department. Esterhazy's schools provide K-12 education to approximately 570 town and district students. The town also has a wide range of recreational facilities. Attractions include Esterhazy Historical Park and the Esterhazy Flour Mill, as well as the Kaposvar Historic Site just south of the town. Esterhazy is also the hometown of some notable Canadians: Dana Antal, who was a member of the Canadian women's hockey team that defeated the U.S. team to win a gold medal at the Salt Lake City Olympics in 2002; and Guy Vanderhaeghe, who has twice won the Governor General's Literary Award for his writing. Esterhazy is situated in the RM of Fertile Belt No. 183.

ESTEVAN, city, pop 10,084 (2006c), 10,242 (2001c) is situated in the southeast corner of the province, on the north side of the Souris River Valley, approximately 200 km southeast of Regina and 16 km north of the border with North Dakota. Settlement of the Estevan area dates to 1892, when the CPR completed their line into the area from Brandon, Manitoba. That spring, Estevan had its beginnings as a "tent town" — as the summer progressed the tents were replaced with tar paper shacks, and before the year's end some fifty buildings of various types had been constructed and occupied. The Estevan Post Office was established on September 1, 1892, its name honouring Sir George Stephen, the first president of the CPR. "Estevan" was his cable name, or his "registered telegraphic address." In 1893, the Soo Line was extended from North

◄ **4TH STREET, ESTEVAN, 1903.** Saskatchewan Archives Board R-B756.

▼ **GOING UNDERGROUND.** Coal miners in the Estevan area beginning a day's work, 1914. Saskatchewan Archives Board R-A5996(1).

Portal to Moose Jaw, accelerating the pace of settlement and bringing many Americans into the area. Estevan attained village status on November 2, 1899, and became a town on March 1, 1906. The population that year was recorded as being 877, up from just 141 five years earlier, in 1901. By WWI, Estevan was a regional agricultural service centre, a railway divisional point, and the centre of intensive coal mining operations. The first viable coal mine in the area had been established in 1891; within a few years dozens of mines were in operation, and many area settlers used coal mining income to help them establish their farms. Estevan grew steadily through the twentieth century, largely because of its increasing role as an electric

power-generating centre, and the exploitation of the coal and oil resources in the area. The Estevan Generating Station, fired by local lignite, began operations in 1930; the Boundary Dam Power Station was commissioned in 1960; and the Shand Power Station was commissioned in 1992. The development of the oil industry in the 1950s, however, is what transformed the community. From a population of 3,935 in 1951, Estevan grew to number 7,728 a decade later. Estevan attained city standing on March 1, 1957, becoming the province's ninth city. Today, there are several thousand oil and gas wells in the area. Agriculture, too, is important to the economy: red spring wheat and durum are the predominant cereal crops grown in the

region, and canola, mustard, flax, pea and lentil acreages have been increasing in recent years. Also key to Estevan's economy is its continuing role as a regional service centre in government, education, medical, retail, automotive, recreation and tourism sectors. Feature attractions of the city include Woodlawn Regional Park and its 18-hole golf course, the Souris Valley Theatre, and the Estevan Art Gallery and Museum. Heritage properties in Estevan include the 1883 Wood End NWMP post and the Estevan Court House. Events of national significance for which Estevan is known include the Estevan Coal Miner's Strike of 1931, during which three miners were killed, and the crash of a military aircraft in 1946 that killed 21. More positively, Estevan is also know as the "Sunshine Capital of Canada," as the city receives an average of approximately 2,500 hours of sunshine per year. Environment Canada also makes the distinction that Estevan has the clearest skies year-round, with an annual average of 2,880 hours. Estevan serves as the administrative centre of the RM of Estevan No. 5.

ESTON, town, pop 971 (2006c), 1,048 (2001c), is located in western Saskatchewan, southeast of Kindersley on Hwys 44 and 30. The South Saskatchewan River and Eston Riverside Regional Park lie 23 km south of the town. The Eston area was opened to homesteaders in 1906, and settlers arrived from Eastern Canada, the U.S. and the British Isles. The community emerged in the spring of 1914 as the CNR progressed westward from Elrose. The townsite had been surveyed and the first businesses began to appear along the railroad's right-of-way at what would become Main St. and Railway Ave. Trains were running into Eston in 1915, and by the end of the year five grain elevators had been built. In 1916, Eston achieved village status. Growth of the community was rapid, and in 1928, with a population climbing above 500, Eston was incorporated as a town. Progress continued unabated, and in 1961 the population of Eston was at 1,695. By 1984, close to 600 students attended school in the community. Then, however, began a period of decline and challenges. The population began dropping, the hospital was closed, and CN announced plans to abandon the rail line. Community leaders reacted with a series of successful locally-based initiatives and economic development strategies. A health clinic, doctor's services, and advanced seniors' care were

secured. Community-based agri-business ventures were started, and the rail service was saved. Modern facilities for recreation and cultural pursuits were built. These measures helped stabilize the population, create employment, and enhanced the quality of life in the town. The area economy remains based upon agriculture — the production of a wide variety of cereal grains and specialty crops, as well as cattle, bison, and elk — and Eston has a number of services and suppliers catering to the agricultural industry. Eston also has

Pioneering women in the Eston district...

◄ **MRS. MCGILL**, a local doctor's wife, treating Ernest and Lucy Jane Fish to cake outside of her homestead shack (packing cases for settlers effects still outside), Eston area, circa 1915. The portion of the building in the foreground is covered in tar paper. Photograph courtesy of the Prairie West Historical Centre, Eston. Donor: Hazel McCloskey.

◄ **MRS. ANNIE FISH BAKING BREAD** in Brust's cook car, Eston district, 1915. Photograph courtesy of the Prairie West Historical Centre, Eston. Donor: Ethel Marjerison.

▼ **MAKING RAG RUGS.** A grandmother shows her granddaughter how to tear rags and then sew the strips together to make hooked rugs, 1928. Photograph courtesy of the Prairie West Historical Centre, Eston. Donor: Hazel McCloskey.

▲ **THE CORONATION OF KING GEORGE VI AND QUEEN ELIZABETH** in 1937 being celebrated in Eston. The view is of Main Street, looking north. Photograph courtesy of the Prairie West Historical Centre, Eston. Donor: Mrs. E. Babin.

◄ **AUCKLAND AND MCALLISTER'S SNOW SERVICE** in Eston, circa late 1930s. Photograph courtesy of the Prairie West Historical Centre, Eston. Donor: Beatrice McAllister.

an RCMP detachment, banking, shopping, and a weekly newspaper. Eston Composite School provides K-12 education to approximately 200 students each year, and the Full Gospel Bible Institute is a post-secondary college. Annual events in Eston include an indoor rodeo, the "World Super Gopher Derby," and the "Communities in Bloom" competition. Eston serves as the administrative centre for the RM of Snipe Lake No. 259.

ETTERS BEACH, resort village, is located on the west side of the north end of Last Mountain Lake, east of Stalwart. The community is named for the Etter family who homesteaded the land in 1905 and who began development of the resort in 1924. A large dance hall, restaurant, boat house, and cabins were built, and a large boat ran excursions across the lake. In the 1930s, few people had money to spend at the resort, so the dance hall was torn down and the lumber put to other uses. Post-WWII, development of the resort resumed, and in 1965 Etters Beach was incorporated as a resort village. Today, there are a small number of permanent residents; however, there are 123 cabins and the population can swell to over 300 during the summer months. The adjacent provincial recreation site, with over 100 campsites, brings additional people to the area, and ice fishing is a popular draw in the winter. Etters Beach is situated in the RM of Big Arm No. 251.

EVERGREEN ACRES, organized hamlet, est. 1989, is located in west-central Saskatchewan and is one of several resort communities situated northeast of Turtleford on Turtle Lake. Initially developed around 1980, Evergreen Acres lies within the RM of Mervin No. 499. There were 15 permanent residents in 2006; however, the population varies greatly depending on the season, reaching several dozen during the summer months.

EVERGREEN BRIGHTSAND, organized hamlet, est. 1991, is located in west-central Saskatchewan and is one of several resort communities situated east of St. Walburg on Brightsand Lake. The resort, initially developed in the 1970s and 1980s, has a population which varies depending on the season, reaching approximately 140 during the summer months. There were 43 permanent residents reportedly living at the locale in 2006. Evergreen Brightsand is located within the RM of Mervin No. 499.

EXNER'S TWIN BAYS, organized hamlet, is a resort community located in the Qu'Appelle Valley on Crooked Lake; the number of residents varies greatly depending on the season. Situated within the RM of Grayson No. 184, Exner's Twin Bays was established as an organized hamlet in August 2006.

EYEBROW, village, pop 135 (2006c), 136 (2001c), is situated 24 km east of Central Butte and 70 km northwest of Moose Jaw, on Hwy 42. The Qu'Appelle Valley lies to the north. The name of the community is believed to be derived from First Nations' terms for area landmarks — a low lying range of hills, or a particular hill within the range. Captain John Palliser's map of his travels through the area in 1858 shows Eyebrow Hill and Eyebrow Hill Ridge. The Cree word *miýêsâpiwinân* means Eyebrow, and it may well have had a local application. A post office established about nine miles south of the present village in 1904 was initially called Eyebrow Hill. When the CPR line from Moose Jaw to Outlook was being built through the area between 1906 and 1909, today's townsite was determined and a new post office there, established on January 1, 1908, was known as Eyebrow Station for the first six months. On June 1 that year, the name was shortened to simply Eyebrow, and at the same time the Eyebrow Hill Post Office, to the south, was renamed Eskbank. In 1901, there were only a few homesteaders in the Eyebrow area, but with the coming of the railroad they began to arrive in droves. The first were largely of British origin; in the late 1920s, Mennonite families who had succeeded in fleeing the Soviet Union also came to settle in the area. The first two stores were erected on the Eyebrow townsite in 1907, the year before the tracks were laid through the community. The merchants travelled to Mortlach on the CPR main line to obtain their wares. In 1908, with trains running, many more businesses sprang up including the first two grain elevators. Two more elevators were constructed in 1909, and another in 1910 brought the total to five. The Village of Eyebrow was incorporated on January 8, 1909, and that year the Union Bank opened for business. The bank was taken over by the Royal Bank in 1925, and it remains in operation today. Also in 1909, the first school was built

in the village, and two newspapers began serving the community: the short-lived *Eyebrow-Eyeopener*, published out of Caron; and the locally produced *Eyebrow Herald*, last published in 1943. Disastrous fires in 1914 and 1915 dealt the village a setback, as all but one business on the west side of Main Street were destroyed. The community rebuilt and continued to grow, however, and from a population of 182 in 1911, Eyebrow grew to have just under 300 residents by the mid-1920s. The Depression then took its toll on the community — by 1941, the population had fallen to 161. In the 1950s, Eyebrow experienced boom times again; from the middle of the decade through to the mid-1960s, the community once more numbered close to 300 people. By this time,

though, even as modern conveniences were being introduced (sewer lines were installed in 1962 and natural gas became available in 1973), changes were taking place that would limit, and ultimately reverse, the village's growth — largely the decline of the rural population and a trend toward shopping in Moose Jaw. In the 1950s, Eyebrow had served a district containing about 1,500 people; by the early 1970s the number was at 600 and falling — today, the population of the surrounding RM is 305. By 1951, the highway north of the city of Moose Jaw was paved as far as the village of Tuxford, and better and faster automobiles were giving people easy access to the goods, services, and other amenities that the city had to offer. Eyebrow's population fell by almost

100 between 1966 and 1971. In recent years, there have been a couple of significant positive developments: in the mid-1990s, the Saskatchewan Wheat Pool built a large concrete grain handling terminal and farm supply centre at Eyebrow; and the lone remaining wooden elevator (formerly the Pool elevator) was converted into a seed cleaning plant a few years ago. Other businesses in Eyebrow today include the branch of the Royal Bank, the post office, an insurance agency, a general store, a café, a construction company, and a custom matting and framing shop. An ice cream shop and a nursery operate seasonally. Eyebrow has a K-12 school that had 63 students enrolled in the fall of 2006, and there are three churches in the community — the Eyebrow Mennonite Church, the Free Methodist Church, and Eyebrow United. There had been an Anglican Church in the village, but the congregation dwindled to the point that services were not held regularly. The building was sold to the Coronach parish in 1982, and it was moved to Coron-

▼ **MURALS BY LOCAL ARTIST JANE BUECKERT** adorn the side of Hohner's General Store (below, left) and Eyebrow's Memorial Hall (below, right). The mural on the Hall depicts Main Street circa 1912.

Photographs by the author (taken July 30, 2003); used with the permission of Jane Bueckert, Eyebrow, Saskatchewan.

ach in the spring of 1983. Eyebrow has a curling rink and an outdoor skating rink, sports grounds, a seniors' centre, and an attractive, well-maintained electrified free campground. The nearest hospital and special care home are in Central Butte; the closest RCMP detachment is in Elbow. Yearly events in Eyebrow include the Town Fair held during the first week in July, the Terry Fox Run in September, and the United Church Fall Supper each October. A recreational hockey league is organized every winter. Fall brings many hunters to the area, particularly to the Qu'Appelle Valley, as deer, antelope, and waterfowl are found in abundance. Grain, oilseed, and livestock production forms the basis of the district economy. Eyebrow serves as the administrative centre of the RM of Eyebrow No. 193.

FAIRHOLME, organized hamlet, pop 20 (2006c), 20 (2001c), is located northwest of Glaslyn on Hwy 3. The post office was established in 1923, and in 1924 the railway from Turtleford was running. The community was named after Fairholme, Ontario, the hometown of Alfred James Brand, who had homesteaded the quarter section upon which the townsite was established. In 1926, significant numbers of Mennonites began arriving in the area; Saskatchewan writer Rudy Wiebe was born in the district in 1934, his parents among the Mennonite families who settled in the area. A Mennonite Brethren church existed to the northeast at Speedwell until 1948; the congregation of the Bruderthaler Mennonite Church in Fairholme was dissolved in 1961 or 1962. In the 1930s and 1940s Fairholme had a range of businesses and services (Fairholme was established as an organized hamlet in 1949), but these dwindled as

better cars and roads allowed people to travel further afield. In 1966, the population of Fairholme was 50; the rail line was abandoned in the late 1970s. Today, residents seek services in Glaslyn, Turtleford, or North Battleford. The district economy is based on cattle and grain production, logging, and resort-based commerce. There is a community pasture at Fairholme for area residents. Fairholme is situated in the RM of Parkdale No. 498.

FAIRLIGHT, village, pop 40 (2006c), 45 (2001c), is located in southeast Saskatchewan, 19 km from the Saskatchewan-Manitoba border and 31 km south of Moosomin at the junction of Hwys 8 and 48. Land in the district was surveyed beginning in 1880, and on the heels of the survey crews the first settlers began arriving in the area. Initially, they were principally from Ontario and the British Isles; later, they would be joined by large numbers from the U.S. For the first year or two, as the CPR main line was being built westward, settlers travelling from the east by train would disembark at the end of steel at Brandon, and later Oak Lake, Manitoba, then travel overland to reach the district. After 1900, settlers also entered the region from the south as the railway was constructed from Souris, Manitoba, to Arcola. The name "Fairlight" began to be used in the early 1890s, when a post office and a school were established and named Fairlight after the English hometown of the first postmaster, Henry Hyde. The site that would become the Village of Fairlight was surveyed by the CPR around 1905 as the railway company proceeded westward with the construction of its line from Reston, Manitoba, to Wolseley. The track through Fairlight became operational in 1906, and the little mixed

train that ran back and forth on the line eventually became affectionately known to local residents as the "Peanut." In 1907, the Canadian Northern Railway came through Fairlight, building a line parallel to the CPR's, but which ran directly to Regina. With the railways came a construction boom: grain elevators were erected, businesses established, and the Village of Fairlight was incorporated October 5, 1909. Gone were the long years of travelling to Fleming or Moosomin to deliver grain or to obtain supplies. The two railroad companies became major employers in the community and were a dominant influence in the village until the 1950s, when Fairlight's population was close to 200. Then, beginning in 1960, came major changes. The CPR abandoned its line, and the track was lifted. The population of the village began to steadily decline. Passenger and freight volumes decreased on CN's lines, and in 1974 the station was removed. Businesses closed, and Fairlight continued to lose many of its landmarks and institutions. The Fairlight Hotel, built in 1906, burned in 1978, and in 1983

the school was closed and students were bused to Maryfield. Subsequently, only a small core of the village remains. Agriculture, a mixture of grain and livestock production, remains the major industry in the region. Fairlight is situated in the RM of Maryfield No. 91.

FAIRY GLEN, organized hamlet, pop 35 (2006c), 25 (2001c), is located 25 km north of Melfort, about one km south of Hwy 6. Settlement of the district began in the early 1900s, mainly after the Canadian Northern Railway reached Star City and Melfort in 1904-05. Scandinavian settlers — Norwegians and Swedes — predominated in the Fairy Glen area; however, there were also large concentrations of people of Slavic origin — Ukrainians and Poles — as well as settlers of British origin taking up land in the region. The Fairy Glen post office was established on an area farm in 1909, and the same year

▼ **HALL, FAIRY GLEN**, August 24, 2004.

a local school district was established. The CPR built north from Melfort to Gronlid in 1927, and the following year the post office was relocated to the townsite. The year after that, the country school was moved into the hamlet. The first grain elevators in Fairy Glen were erected in 1927, and in 1928 the railway station was built and the first crops were shipped out via rail that year. A core of essential businesses and services were established and, for a number of years, the community prospered. Fairy Glen, however, was never a particularly large community, and in 1965 the school was closed. The population of the hamlet was then around 60. In 1977 the last grain elevator went out of business, and the rail line was abandoned in 1982. Today, with Melfort being only a few minutes drive away, Fairy Glen's commercial activity has been reduced to a Co-op and a couple of home-based businesses. The production of grain and specialty crops forms the basis of the area economy. Fairy Glen is situated in the RM of Willow Creek No. 458.

FENWOOD, village, pop 35 (2006c), 48 (2001c), is located 16 km northwest of Melville on Hwy 15. With the arrival of the Grand Trunk Pacific Railway in 1907-08 the townsite was established, its name likely chosen simply to fit the alphabetical sequence of naming communities along the rail line: Fenwood, Goodeve, Hubbard, Ituna, Jasmin, Kelliher, and Leross. The Fenwood Post office was established on August 1, 1908, and a hotel was built that year. The village was incorporated on June 30, 1909; unfortunately, municipal records prior to 1920 were destroyed in a council chamber fire. The population grew from 51 in 1911 to 170 by 1931, and in the post-WWII period

Fenwood enjoyed its heyday. Fenwood residents were mainly of German and Ukrainian descent. The population peaked at 191 in 1956; at the time, three churches served the community — Baptist, Lutheran, and Seventh Day Adventist — as did three elevators and approximately two dozen other businesses. There was a two-room elementary school and a one-room high school. By the 1960s, however, the population began to plummet: it was down to 127 by 1966 and 112 by 1971. As it fell, Fenwood's businesses, services, and institutions, such as churches, began to disappear, mainly giving way to those in Melville, then Yorkton. Fenwood School closed in the early 1990s, and schoolchildren are now bused to Melville. A few individuals remaining in Fenwood run small businesses. Fenwood is situated in the RM of Stanley No. 215.

FIFE LAKE, organized hamlet, pop 40 (2006c), 46 (2001c), is a former village located in south-central Saskatchewan, approximately 20 km east of Rockglen, north off Hwy 18. The community is named after the large body of water 11 km to the northwest. The first settlers began applying for homesteads in the area around 1906; however, it was in 1909 and 1910 that large numbers of people arrived. In the mid-1920s, when the CPR began building the line south from Ardwick Junction, just west of Assiniboia, a construction boom began at the site that would become the village of Fife Lake. In 1927, regular rail service came to the young community, and in 1928 Fife Lake attained village status. The community reached a peak population of 166 in 1956; however, since the 1960s, the village's numbers have steadily declined. The school closed in 1969, and Fife Lake's

businesses and services have been superseded by those in the area's larger centres. The regional economy is based upon grain and livestock production, as well as employment at the coal mine and power station near Coronach. Fife Lake, which relinquished village status on January 27, 2005, is situated in the RM of Poplar Valley No. 12.

FILLMORE, village, pop 193 (2006c), 246 (2001c), is located approximately 100 km southeast of Regina on Hwy 33. Weyburn lies roughly 50 km to the southwest, and Stoughton, 40 km to the southeast. Fillmore serves as the shopping, banking, and service centre for the surrounding farming district. The village has a K-12 school which had 100 students enrolled in the fall of 2006, and the community has an RCMP detachment, a

volunteer fire department, a health centre with an attached special care home and an ambulance service. A recreation centre houses curling and skating rinks, and the community has sports grounds, camping facilities, and a nearby nine-hole golf course. There are two churches: Roman Catholic and United. Fillmore has a museum, several service clubs and community-based organizations. The Fillmore district had been surveyed in the early 1880s; however, settlement mainly occurred in the early 1900s. As the CPR progressed with their line from Arcola to Regina, Fillmore had its beginnings. Businesses began to appear near the present townsite in 1903, and after the village lots were surveyed later that year, the enterprises were relocated to present Main Street. In 1904, the railway was in operation to Regina and the post office was established. The village was incorporated in 1905, and in

▲ **THE FILLMORE UNION HEALTH CENTRE** houses a special care home, observation/convalescent beds, a palliative care unit, a laboratory, and an ambulance service. The facility opened in 1987, replacing a hospital that had been built in the late 1940s. Photograph taken August 19, 2003.

1906 the community numbered 156 residents. Fillmore grew slowly but steadily over the ensuing decades, its population hovering close to 400 from the mid-1960s through to the early 1980s. On June 26, 1933, at a convention of the Farm-Labor party in Fillmore, a resolution asking that the name of the group be changed to "The Co-operative Commonwealth Federation (CCF), Saskatchewan Section," was given endorsement. That evening, a packed hall listened to a speech given by the Rev. T. C. Douglas of Weyburn. During this time, Fillmore also had a hockey star. Hometown hero, Frank (Buzz) Boll, was a Memorial Cup champion with the Regina Pats in the 1920s, and during the 1930s and 1940s he had an NHL career with the Toronto Maple Leafs and the Boston Bruins. Also a Stanley Cup champion, Boll, known as the "Fillmore Flash," was inducted into the Saskatchewan Sports Hall of Fame in 1978. Fillmore is also home to another sporting member of the Boll family: Rod Boll, Buzz Boll's nephew, is a world-class trap shooter who was on Canada's National Team at the Atlanta Olympics in 1996. Yet another Fillmore citizen of note is Leo Carteri, a long-time teacher at Fillmore's school. In 1995 Prime Minister Jean Chretien awarded Carteri the Prime Minister's Award for Teaching Excellence in Science, Technology, and Mathematics. That same year, the village of Fillmore was struck by a violent tornado which caused over $1 million worth of damage. Fortunately, there were no injuries or fatalities. Fillmore serves as the administrative centre of the RM of Fillmore No. 96.

FINDLATER, village, pop 49 (2006c), 62 (2001c), is located approximately 70 km northwest of Regina on Hwy 11, between the villages of Bethune and Chamberlain. Although the Qu'Appelle, Long Lake & Saskatchewan Railway was built through the area in the late 1880s, it was not until around 1908 that the village began to develop. That year, a boarding house, a blacksmith shop, and a livery barn were started; on May 1, 1908, the Findlater Post Office was established. More development followed over the next few years. A school opened in 1909; the first grain elevator was built in 1910; and second and third elevators were erected in 1915 and 1922-23. A hotel was built in 1912. Findlater was incorporated on September 27, 1911, and on October 9 nominations for the election of the first village councillors took place. Sixteen bylaws were passed in 1912 regulating the procedures of council, prescribing the duties of the village overseer and the secretary-treasurer, regulating billiards, bowling alleys, dogs running at large, hawkers and peddlers, the slaughter of horses, and cruelty to animals, among other things. Findlater developed into a small agricultural service centre and grew to number 102 residents by 1931. The community experienced a downturn through the 1930s and the 1940s — the Depression forced the hotel to close and the population fell to just 60 by 1946 — but the village rebounded in the 1950s to reach a peak population of 128 in 1961. By this time, however, major changes to Findlater's small business district were beginning to take place: in the late 1950s the Findlater Store and the lumberyard closed; in 1964 the café closed when the owner retired; Madson's Garage and the Red & White Store burned down in 1965 and 1966 respectively; and in 1966, CN removed their station agent. The station was sold and lifted from its site in 1977; it now sits on a private vacation farm in the Qu'Appelle Valley. The only business left at Findlater today is a gas station on the highway. The last grain elevator came down in the late 1990s. In 1970, Findlater School closed, and subsequently area schoolchildren have been bused to either Bethune or Lumsden. Findlater is situated in the RM of Dufferin No. 190.

FISKE, organized hamlet, pop 81 (2006c), 96 (2001c), is located between Rosetown and Kindersley on Hwy 7. Homesteaders began occupying land in the region over 1906-07, and as the Canadian Northern Railway was building its line between Rosetown and Kindersley through 1909-1910, Fiske began to develop. The railway station was built in 1910, and that year much of the townsite was built up. Among the first businesses established were an implement dealership, two stores, a blacksmith shop, livery barn, lumberyard, poolroom, bakeshop, barbershop, the post office, and a hotel. The community school district was established in 1910, and the school itself, Valley City, was built in 1911. By 1913, Fiske was fielding a competitive baseball team; by 1914, three grain elevators had been erected. For three years, from 1913-16, Fiske was incorporated as a village. Subsequently, however, the community's affairs were managed by the RM, until 1966 when Fiske was established as an organized hamlet with a small degree of independent political and financial power. The community's population has remained fairly stable since the mid-1960s, but its businesses and other institutions have largely given way to those in the region's larger centres. The last regular services were held at the United Church in 1968; the school closed in 1972. Fiske Mennonite Church remains active. Fiske is situated in the RM of Pleasant Valley No. 288.

FLAXCOMBE, village, pop 111 (2006c), 128 (2001c), is located in a small, picturesque valley 30 km west of Kindersley on Hwy 7. The streets of the community are lined with cottonwood and spruce trees. Flaxcombe had its beginnings as the railroad that would connect Saskatoon and Calgary was being built westward from Kindersley. In 1909 the rail bed was graded and the townsite was surveyed. Lots were put up for sale in 1910, and that year the first businesses — a general store, a hardware store, a livery, and a restaurant and bake shop — were established prior to the tracks being laid late in the summer. With the rails in place, the Beaver Lumber Company brought in carloads of lumber to fuel a building boom. When a local post office was established on January 1, 1911, it was initially named Harwell, after Wesley H. HARvey, an early area settler, and Alfred Ernest BusWELL, a pioneer storekeeper and the first postmaster. When the community was incorporated as a village on June 4, 1913, it was under the name Harwell, but in September that year the names of both the post office and the village were changed, evidently at the request of Canadian postal authorities, who claimed there was some difficulty with the mail due to confusion with another Saskatchewan post office having a similar name, that being Howell (later known as Prud'homme). The name Flaxcombe had been put forward by George Langrish, the railway company pumpman, it being a combination of the words "flax" and "combe": thousands of acres of flax were being grown on the newly-broken land in the district, and "combe" was derived from an Old English word meaning valley. In 1911, a drug store, a farm implement dealership, and a Methodist Church were built, the latter wherein the first school was begun; by 1913, the first grain elevator had been erected, as had the Silver Hotel. Over the next several years the village continued to be built up: a telephone company, a "Chinese" laundry, more elevators, a bank, a curling rink, and a garage were among the further enterprises established. Through the decades, Flaxcombe has retained a fairly stable population, even during the 1930s. On average, the community has numbered slightly under 115 residents since its beginnings, and from the early 1990s to the present the population has remained steady. The village, however, has become something of a bedroom community to Kindersley. Flaxcombe retains a small core of businesses, while nearby Kindersley, with a population approaching 5,000, offers a full range of amenities including a hospital. A number of Flaxcombe's residents either commute to Kindersley to work or are employed in the region's oilfields. The last village elevator, a Pool, which had been converted to a high through-put facility with a 90,000-bushel annex in 1980, is now privately owned. Flaxcombe's schoolchildren attend Westcliffe Composite School in the nearby village of Marengo. Flaxcombe's high school students had begun to be bused to Marengo in the 1950s, and in 1967 Flaxcombe School closed its doors. The building was torn down in 1976, and the school property has been turned into a residential area. The median age of Flaxcombe residents was 29 in 2001; the Saskatchewan average was just under 37. Flaxcombe is situated in the RM of Kindersley No. 290.

FLEMING, town, pop 75 (2006c), 95 (2001c), is located 6 km west of the

▲ **FLEMING, CIRCA 1904**, from the west. Saskatchewan Archives Board R-A19026.

Saskatchewan-Manitoba border on Hwy 1. Moosomin, 14 km northwest, is the nearest larger centre (pop 2,257 in 2006). The spring of 1882 brought the arrival of both the CPR main line and settlers to the district. The first settlers were primarily from Ontario and Great Britain; later, during the 1930s, Mennonites would also settle in the Fleming area. In 1884, the Fleming post office opened, its name honouring Sir Sandford Fleming (1827-1915), the country's distinguished engineer, surveyor, and inventor of standard time. The main thoroughfare in the young community is named Sandford Street. In 1885, the Fleming Protestant School District was established, and the community's first teacher began instructing classes the next year. Fleming developed into a service centre for the surrounding mixed farming district, and on July 2, 1896, Fleming was incorporated as a village. In 1901, the population was 160; in 1906 it was 260; and on June 15, 1907, Fleming gained town status. In 1916, Fleming reached its peak

▲ **THE FLEMING GRAIN ELEVATOR** is a Provincial Heritage Property on South Railway Street adjacent to the CPR right-of-way in the town of Fleming. It is significant because it is the oldest standing grain elevator on its original site in Canada. Constructed in 1895, it is a 32,000-bushel capacity, wood-crib, hip-roof grain elevator, with an attached receiving shed and office building. It was one of several built by the Lake of the Woods Milling Company to supply its Ontario-based flour mills. It is currently being restored to its original appearance. Photograph taken October 17, 2003.

population, 310. In 1954, a view of Fleming first appeared on the back of the Canadian one-dollar bill — a quintessential vista of a small prairie town under a magnificent sky that would be familiar to Canadians for years. As the decades passed, Fleming would increasingly be overshadowed by Moosomin. With the rationalization and centralization of services, Fleming's institutions, business sector, and population declined. In 1960, high school students began to be bused to Moosomin, and, gradually, grade by grade, students were transferred to the larger centre. In June 1975, after almost 90 years, Fleming's school was closed for good. Today, most Fleming residents in the work force are employed in Moosomin, while a smaller percentage engages in farming. Moosomin also has the nearest health care facilities and RCMP detachment. Fleming residents shop either in Moosomin or in Virden, Manitoba. Fleming has produced its share of notable personalities over the years: Clarence Campbell, president of the National Hockey League from 1946-77, was born in Fleming in 1905, and it was his controversial suspension of Maurice "Rocket" Richard from the 1955 playoffs that sparked a riot in Montreal. Fleming has also been the home of at least two heroes. In 1958, eight-year-old John Wiebe rescued a younger boy near Wawota who was badly burned by a live wire at a high voltage transformer. Master Wiebe was subsequently awarded a medal for his heroism, presence of mind, and courage in dangerous circumstances. In 1995, volunteer fire chief Doug Van De Kerckhove risked his life attempting to rescue another man who had been overcome by noxious fumes and had fallen down a well. Van De Kerckhove spent weeks in intensive care recovering from hydrogen sulphide gas poisoning, and received the

Governor General of Canada's Medal for Bravery in 1996. Fleming is situated in the RM of Moosomin No. 121.

FLIN FLON is a mining city straddling the Saskatchewan-Manitoba border within the Precambrian Shield near the 55th parallel. By road, Flin Flon is accessed via Hwy 106 (the Hanson Lake Road) or, on the Manitoba side, by Hwy 10 from The Pas. Highway 167, leading south through the neighbouring northern town of Creighton, gives access to Denare Beach and picturesque Amisk Lake, the south end of which was the scene of Saskatchewan's first and little-known gold rush, which occurred between 1914 and 1918. Tom Creighton's prospecting discoveries in 1915 were largely responsible for the development of mining operations at Flin Flon. Today, the Hudson Bay Mining & Smelting Company is by far the largest employer in the area, producing zinc, copper, and gold. Only a small portion of the city of Flin Flon is in Saskatchewan: the Manitoba population was 5,594 in 2006, while only 242 residents lived on the Saskatchewan side of the border.

FOAM LAKE, town, pop 1,123 (2006c), 1,218 (2001c), is located southeast of Wynyard at the junction of Hwys 16 and 310. The first family of settlers in the region arrived in the early summer of 1882 and, for the next ten years, they lived practically isolated, with only the odd white traveller and the region's indigenous inhabitants passing by their home. The Irish Milligan family had travelled north from Fort Qu'Appelle and had settled several miles northwest of the present-day town of Foam Lake, engaging in ranching. The Milligan's named a shallow

▲ **THE FIRST STORE** in Foam Lake in 1907. It was owned and operated by Robert Cain.

▼ **HOWE LIVERY AND FEED BARN** with attached photography studio, Foam Lake, 1914.

Photographs courtesy of the Foam Lake Museum.

body of water in the region Foam Lake, as a froth often developed along its shores — hence, the origins of the community's name. With the railroad arriving at Saltcoats in 1888 and at Yorkton a couple of years later, a few more settlers began

trickling into the area; however, before 1900, there were still only a small number of people in the Foam Lake district. Ranching was the major activity, and it was not until the early 1900s that substantial tracts of land were broken for the purpose

▲ **THE FOAM LAKE POST OFFICE**, situated on the southeast corner of Main Street and Bray Avenue, was built in 1938. Photograph taken July 15, 2004.

▼ **THE SASKATCHEWAN WHEAT POOL** grain terminal and farm supply centre just west of Foam Lake on Hwy 16. Photograph taken August 5, 2004.

of crop production. The first Icelanders came to the district in 1892, and during the first decade of the twentieth century many Ukrainians arrived to take up land. As well, people of British origins rounded out the cultural milieu. Settlement of the area was greatly hastened by the arrival of the railway at Sheho in 1904; three years later, as the CPR was pushing westward again, the townsite of Foam Lake was established. The first buildings were erected in 1907, and in 1908 the fledgling com-

munity was incorporated as a village. By the early 1920s, the population was well over 400, and in 1924 Foam Lake attained town status. It became the major service and distribution centre for the surrounding agricultural district. Today, the community has a wide array of businesses and services, medical facilities, an RCMP detachment, a volunteer fire department, recreational facilities, churches, and elementary and high schools. Town and area attractions include the Foam Lake Museum, housed in the community's former 1926 town hall; the 1915 Douglas Heritage House; and the Foam Lake Heritage Marsh, an important staging area for migratory birds. During the summer of 2006, Foam Lake suffered a significant blow when, within a period of just over a month, two major fires claimed four businesses on Main Street and a grain elevator. Foam Lake serves as the administrative centre of the RM of Foam Lake No. 276.

FORGET, village, pop 40 (2006c), 40 (2001c), is situated about 11 km east of Stoughton, off Hwy 13. The Moose Mountain plateau rises on the northeast horizon. Forget's origins date to 1892 when, through the efforts of the missionary-colonizer, Monseigneur Jean-Isadore Gaire, settlers from Belgium and France, particularly from the regions of Lorraine and Dauphiné, came to settle in the district of the present-day village. The area would also attract French-speaking people from Quebec. Travelling missionaries served the community's spiritual needs for the first several years, but in 1899 La Salette priests arrived from France to administer the parish, and they continued to serve the community's needs for the next 46 years. The first church and rectory were built in 1899, about two and a

half kilometres southwest of the present village, and by the time the railway arrived in 1904 a flourishing, largely Catholic community with a well-developed mercantile life had evolved. The Forget post office was established on September 1, 1904, and on November 21 that fall the village was incorporated. The name of the community honours Amédée Emmanuel Forget (1847-1923), then lieutenant governor of the North-West Territories (1898-1905), soon to become the first lieutenant governor of Saskatchewan (1905-10). In 1905, on invitation of the La Salette priests, several Sisters of Our Lady of the Cross came to Forget from France, and in 1906 the Sisters opened a convent with a bilingual school, later named St. Joseph's Academy. It accommodated both boys and girls, both boarders and day-students. The Sisters also taught in the village's Catholic public school. A Protestant separate school was established in Forget in 1916; it closed in 1948. In the 1920s, work began on the Our Lady of La Salette Shrine in the village, to which annual pilgrimages were made for a number of years. Forget thrived during the first three decades of the twentieth century: hotels, automobile dealerships, farm implement agencies, a bank, and a local newspaper were among the numerous businesses that lined the village's busy streets, and the community's population hovered at close to 300 from 1911 until the early-1930s. The Depression, though, exacted a heavy toll on the village, and Forget never recovered its earlier vibrancy. Today, Forget little resembles the community of yesteryear, and the village's history presents one of the most dramatic stories of decline in the province. When St. Joseph's Academy closed in 1964, it was yet another blow, and the effect on the community was profound. Forget's population plummeted from 220 in 1961 to 118 a decade later, in 1971. The village's public school closed in 1969. By 1976, the community numbered only 74 residents. In 1985, Forget's last grain elevator closed, and in 1990 the rail line through the community was abandoned. The tracks were torn up and now only the remains of the rail bed runs along the south side of Railway Avenue. The magnificent Church of Our Lady of La Salette, however, remains in weekly use, and Forget retains a post office, a credit union, and a motor vehicle licence issuer. The former Catholic rectory (1904), located next to the church, has been beautifully renovated and is now home to a non-profit organization that works to support the arts in southeastern Saskatchewan. Numerous performances are held at "Ananda Arthouse" throughout the year, and for several years now the organization has hosted the successful Forget Summer Festival, an outdoor event featuring a range of musical performers and craftspeople, food booths and beer gardens. Forget is situated in the RM of Tecumseh No. 65.

▲ **ST. JOSEPH'S ACADEMY, FORGET**, date unknown. Photograph courtesy of the Stoughton and District Museum.

▼ **THE ACADEMY CLOSED** in 1964; today, only portions of the foundations remain at the site of the once-bustling institution. Photograph taken August 20, 2003.

The Rise and Fall of a Prairie Village: Forget's Population Figures Since Incorporation	
Year	Population
1906	200
1911	267
1916	278
1921	257
1926	312
1931	280
1936	192
1941	152
1946	162
1951	165
1956	166
1961	220
1966	139
1971	118
1976	74
1981	70
1986	81
1991	68
1996	62
2001	40
2006	40

FORT QU'APPELLE, town, pop 1,919 (2006c), 1,940 (2001c), is situated in the Qu'Appelle Valley 70 km northeast of Regina between Echo and Mission Lakes. The community is served by Hwys 10, 22, 35, 56, and 210. Named for the Qu'Appelle River, Fort Qu'Appelle was the crossroads of a number of historic trails that traversed the North-West Territories. An Anglican mission was established in 1854, and the Hudson's Bay Company built a post at Fort Qu'Appelle in 1864. After 1870, there was an influx of Métis from Red River. Cree and Saulteaux peoples signed Treaty No. 4 at Fort Qu'Appelle in 1874, followed somewhat thereafter by the establishment of a NWMP post. Chief Sitting Bull and a party of Sioux travelled to Fort Qu'Appelle from Wood Mountain in 1881 to secure provisions and to negotiate with Superintendent James Walsh in a last-ditch effort to remain in Canada. A post office was established at Fort Qu'Appelle in 1880; settlers began to appear and the homesteading era began in earnest. At least a dozen businesses had been established by 1882. On April 6, 1885, General Middleton marched out of Fort Qu'Appelle en route to Batoche. As the fur trade waned and the district became increasingly settled, agriculture came to play a significant role in the expansion of the community. Fort Qu'Appelle was incorporated as a village on June 25, 1898. Shortly after the province of Saskatchewan was formed, Fort Qu'Appelle, along with several other communities, vied to become the new provincial capital; however, Premier Scott was unswayed and the seat of government remained at Regina. Significant development of Fort Qu'Appelle occurred in the years prior to WWI as the railway came through the valley. The rec-

THIS SIGN ON HIGHWAY 10 on the south side of the Qu'Appelle Valley greets visitors to Fort Qu'Appelle today. Photograph taken October 3, 2003.

FORT QU'APPELLE
...between the Calling Lakes

◀ **FORT QU'APPELLE, 1890**, view from the cemetery (southeast). Saskatchewan Archives Board R-B7353.

▲ **THE TREATY 4 MONUMENT**, Fort Qu'Appelle. Photograph taken December, 2001.

▼ **CONSTRUCTING THE HUDSON'S BAY COMPANY STORE**, Fort Qu'Appelle, 1897. Saskatchewan Archives Board R-B9979.

THE TREATY 4 GOVERNANCE CENTRE completed at Fort Qu'Appelle in recent years; it houses administrative and educational offices for the 34 Indian bands that comprise the Treaty 4 First Nations. The facility also includes an archives, a museum, and a cultural centre, and a striking feature of the building is the Legislative Council Chamber, designed in the form of a large contemporary teepee. Photograph taken October 3, 2003.

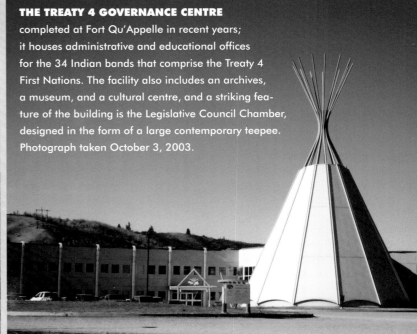

reational potential of the district began to be exploited, and numerous cottages began to appear on the area lakes. In 1913, construction began on a fish culture station near Fort Qu'Appelle and, to date, the facility has supplied more than 2 billion fish to stock water bodies throughout the province. Construction began on the Fort Qu'Appelle Sanatorium (Fort San) for tuberculosis patients in 1912, though wartime exigencies delayed its opening until 1917. Fort Qu'Appelle experienced steady growth and, on January 1, 1951, the community attained town status. The population that year was 878 and the town continued growing until the early 1980s, at which point the population stabilized close to its current level. Today, Fort Qu'Appelle is a shopping, service, and institutional centre serving the surrounding farming community, neighbouring resort villages, cottagers and summer vacationers, as well as several area First Nations reserves, the nearest of those being the Standing Buffalo and Pasqua First Nations. Fort Qu'Appelle also serves the area with a full range of health care facilities, educational institutions, and recreational opportunities. Perhaps the single most important issue facing Fort Qu'Appelle today is that of an aging population. The median age of Fort Qu'Appelle residents is over 45 years, while the provincial average is under 39. Additionally, the unemployment rate in Fort Qu'Appelle is higher than the provincial average, and the median family income is substantially lower. Full-time jobs are scarce. Upon graduation, high school students are increasingly leaving the community and, in recent years, attempts to create new full-time employment opportunities have failed to be realized. The former Hudson's Bay Company store in Fort Qu'Appelle, built in 1897, remains a community landmark, as does the 1911

Grand Trunk Pacific Railway station. Fort Qu'Appelle serves as the administrative centre of the RM of North Qu'Appelle No. 187.

FORT SAN, resort village, pop 215 (2006c), 239 (2001c), is located northwest of Fort Qu'Appelle along several kilometres of the north and east shore of Echo Lake. The community is served by Hwy 56, and a scenic walking path, a part of the Trans Canada Trail, runs the length of the village. Fort San derives its name from the Fort Qu'Appelle Sanatorium, which operated to treat Saskatchewan tuberculosis patients from 1917 to 1972. Area cottage development began in the early 1900s, particularly after the completion of the Grand Trunk Pacific rail line through Fort Qu'Appelle in 1911. The most significant development, however, has taken place since the 1960s. The resort community today is comprised of both the homes of permanent residents and the cabins of city dwellers and residents of other communities in the province. Construction of the Sanatorium, situated on 230 acres, began in 1912, but due to the exigencies of World War I the facility was not opened until 1917. Because of the highly contagious nature of tuberculosis, the centre

was developed to be almost completely self-sufficient: it had its own powerhouse, stables, poultry ranch, pigs, and a five-acre garden. World War I veterans established an extensive library, and patients — almost 360 at one time — engaged in activities and pursuits that included a jazz band, a drama club, and an internal radio program. Over the decades, thousands of patients spent months, even years, at "Fort San," and a post office by that name was opened at the institution in 1926. By the 1960s, tuberculosis was ceasing to be a public health problem, and with the support of the Thatcher Liberal government Fort San was extensively renovated for use as a summer arts school run by the Saskatchewan Arts Board. The provincial government terminated funding for this program in 1991. The facility was then revamped for use as a conference centre run by the Saskatchewan Property Management Corporation (SPMC), to be used by government departments, private businesses, unions, and special interest groups. Additionally, in a partnership with the Department of National Defence, the institution also became a summer home for sea cadets in training. In 2004, after years of absorbing losses, the SPMC announced the centre's closure and 43 part-time and eight full-time personnel were

issued pink slips. The Resort Village of Fort San lost a major tax contributor (the centre had provided almost 10 per cent of the community's revenue), and local officials estimated a loss of approximately $3 million to the local economy. Today, the future of the sprawling historic institution is in doubt: the property is up for sale and there are some who believe that all of the buildings on the property, which includes close to 1,900 feet of lakefront, should be levelled to make room for an up-scale housing subdivision. The Resort Village of Fort San is situated in the RM of North Qu'Appelle No. 187.

FOSSTON, village, pop 55 (2006c), 55 (2001c), is situated 11 km south of Rose Valley on Hwy 35. In 1908, five brothers, Arnie, Carl, John, Martin, and Oscar Rustad, immigrated to Canada from Fosston, Minnesota, and settled about six and a half kilometres north of the present village. They established a post office in 1911 with Oscar as the postmaster and named the office after their former hometown. When a school was established in the vicinity of the post office in 1914, it, too, was given the name Fosston and thus the community had its beginnings. Early settlers to the district came from eastern Canada, the British Isles, and the United States, and were of Swedish, Norwegian, Polish, Ukrainian and Scottish origins. In the early 1920s, the CPR came through the district and the present site of the village of Fosston was established. Grain elevators and a hotel were built as the rail bed was being laid in 1923; the line became operational in 1924, and a livery barn, stores, and various other businesses began to line Fosston's streets. The post office moved into a store at the townsite, a boxcar railway station was set up, and

▲ **THE SASKATCHEWAN SANATORIUM, "FORT SAN," 1918.** Courtesy of the Lung Association of Saskatchewan.

a new school was built in the burgeoning community. In the years following, many more businesses were established — among them a drug store, a hardware store, a butcher shop, and a poolroom — and Fosston flourished. An addition to the school, and then a new building, was necessitated, and Fosston's schools were filled to capacity during the forties, fifties, and sixties. In 1925-26, the Roman Catholic Church, Mary Queen of Poland, was started, and the Polish Hall became the centre of Polish culture and social life. In 1932, the Elim Evangelical Free Church was built; in 1933, the Ukrainian Orthodox Hall was erected. A Ukrainian Greek Catholic Church was built in 1937, and in 1956 the Ukrainian Orthodox Church was constructed. Fosston was established as an organized hamlet in 1952, and on January 1, 1965, the community attained village status. Fosston's growth, however, had reached its peak. The community began losing population. In 1966, students in grades seven through twelve began to be bused to Rose Valley to attend classes, and a few years later Fosston's school was closed. Over the subsequent decades, the number of businesses in the village has been significantly reduced. Fosston is situated in the RM of Ponass Lake No. 367; agriculture is the major industry in the region.

FOX VALLEY, village, pop 295 (2006c), 326 (2001c), is located west of the Great Sand Hills, roughly halfway between Maple Creek and Leader, off Hwy 21. The region began to be settled in 1907 by large numbers of Germans from Russia, but it was not until the CPR constructed the Burstall subdivision from Leader in the mid-1920s that the townsite of Fox Valley was established. The village

▲ **LOOKING EAST UP RAILWAY AVENUE**, Fox Valley, August 30, 2003.

▼ **FROM THE SOUTHWEST:** Fox Valley, August 30, 2003.

was incorporated on August 30, 1928. Fox Valley was situated at the end of the rail line, which meant the community was an important centre to all those who lived beyond. By the end of the 1920s, half a dozen grain elevators lined the tracks in the village. Agriculture, a combination of grain and livestock production, was the

major industry in the area for a number of decades. In 1967, however, Saskatchewan Minerals opened one of the most modern sodium sulphate plants in North America at Ingebrigt Lake, approximately 24 kilometres southeast of the village. The plant became the largest employer in the area, and the population of Fox Valley grew to

over 500. The bubble would burst when, in the late 1980s, the provincial Tory government sold Saskatchewan Minerals to private interests. The Crown Corporation had assets estimated at $30 million, and had contributed profits of over $50 million to provincial coffers. However, the Devine government, then running a $3.4 billion deficit, sold the industry for a quick $16 million. The operation declined, and the plant was later closed. Today, the Fox Valley area is increasingly becoming dotted with gas wells and compressor stations; however, there has been considerable debate in recent years over how to further develop the industry and still maintain the integrity of the natural environment, particularly that of the Great Sand Hills. Fox Valley has nine oilfield-related companies, three agriculture-based companies, and a small number of other businesses. Many people travel to Leader or Maple Creek for shopping and services or for medical attention. Fox Valley has a volunteer fire department; policing is provided by the Leader RCMP. Fox Valley School provides K-12 education and had 123 students enrolled in the fall of 2006. The village serves as the administrative centre of the RM of Fox Valley No. 171.

FRANCIS, town, pop 148 (2006c), 172 (2001c), is located approximately 60 km southeast of Regina on Hwy 33, and 50 km north of Weyburn on Hwy 35. First settled around 1900 by Scots from the historic Glengarry County, Ontario, Francis grew to include a significant population of German-speaking people with origins in southern Russia. The majority of these were Catholics; a smaller percentage were Lutherans. Francis, named after James Francis, who donated the land for the townsite, was incorporated as a village in

village in 1904, the same year the CPR had trains running between Arcola and Regina. Two years later, in 1906, Francis attained town status. The community had a peak population of 263 in 1911, but its numbers have hovered roughly around the current level since the early 1920s. The basis of the area economy is agriculture, largely a combination of grain and livestock production. Francis has a small business community, consisting mainly of farm suppliers and services. Agricore United retains a fertilizer sales centre in the community. Francis School, a K-6 facility that had 51 students enrolled in the fall of 2006, officially closed on August 15, 2007. Students now attend grades K-8 in the neighbouring village of Sedley; high school students travel to Vibank. Francis has indoor rinks for skating and curling, and three churches. Francis serves as the administrative centre of the RM of Francis No. 127.

FRENCHMAN BUTTE, organized hamlet, pop 64 (2006c), 74 (2001c), is located 18 km northwest of Paradise Hill on Hwy 797; historically, the Carlton Trail passed by this location, connecting Forts Garry, Carlton, and Edmonton. The community is perched on the north bank of the North Saskatchewan River and takes its name from the nearby historic site of Frenchman Butte. The name refers to a large area hill and has origins in the early 1800s; it is attributed to the murder of an unknown Frenchman at the hill, likely a fur trader, who, for reasons unknown, somehow displeased local First Nations and was killed. Palliser's map from his 1857-60 expedition refers to the hill as the "French Knoll." In 1885, the locale was the site of an indecisive skirmish between Cree warriors led by Wandering Spirit and the forces of General Strange. The dedication of the Frenchman Butte National Historic Site took place on June 29, 1965. Although settlers had been in the district for a number of years, today's community had its origins just prior to the railway being built into the area in 1928-29, and an important part

of the hamlet's early economy was cutting and hauling railway ties for the line's construction. The first store opened at Frenchman Butte in 1927 and, like the other early buildings in the settlement, it was situated down the hill from the present community, near the ferry crossing. A ferry service ran from 1913 until the late 1960s, when a bridge was built a few miles downstream; interestingly, the ferry

▲ **FRENCHMAN BUTTE** overlooks the North Saskatchewan River. View from the northwest.

▼ **THE FORMER CANADIAN NATIONAL RAILWAY STATION** at Frenchman Butte is now a part of the museum site.

Photographs taken July 23, 2003.

◄ **BUCHTA BROS. STORE**, Frenchman Butte, was built in the late 1920s, and the Buchta brothers — Adolf, Otto, and Charlie — took over the store following WWII. Charlie left to take a job as an elevator agent for the National Grain Company; Adolf and Otto ran the store into the 1980s. The store closed around 1987. Photograph taken July 23, 2003.

was originally known as the Yankee Bend Ferry due to the number of settlers from the United States in the area. Two grain elevators were erected in 1928 while the railway was being built, and by 1929 trains were running into Frenchman Butte and the settlement had relocated to the tracks up the hill. A hotel was also built in 1929. Schoolchildren attended Big Hill School in the country until 1935, when a school in the hamlet was established. Classes, however, were conducted in various locations until a school was built in 1944-45. In 1959, Frenchman Butte was established as an organized hamlet; in 1969, the population was recorded as being 111. The grain elevators were both closed by 1973, and the track from Paradise Hill was formally abandoned a few years later. In 1980, Frenchman Butte School closed. The community's museum overlooks the North Saskatchewan River valley and is an impressive complex featuring the former CNR station, a blacksmith shop, a rural schoolhouse, a log cabin teahouse, arrowheads, rifles, and pioneer artifacts. Guides are available to give tours of the Frenchman Butte National Historic Site and nearby Fort Pitt Provincial Historic Park. The district economy was long based upon grain and cattle production, with cattle being predominant; in recent decades the oil and gas industry has come to the fore. The community is situated in the RM of Frenchman Butte No. 501.

FROBISHER, village, pop 145 (2006c), 149 (2001c), is located in the extreme southeast corner of the province, west of Oxbow, on Hwy 18. The village, incorporated in 1904, also sits at the junction of CP and CN rail lines. The original settlers to the area came largely from Ontario, and in the early days Frobisher was one of the most populous and active communities in the district. The village was particularly well-known in sporting circles. In 1908, the Frobisher Football Club won the Southern Saskatchewan Cup, and narrowly lost the provincial finals. One of the team members, James Garfield Gardiner, went on to become the premier of Saskatchewan (1926-29, 1934-35), and later the federal Minister of Agriculture (1935-57). Frobisher was primarily a farming community, although many residents found employment in the coalfields in the Bienfait area. In 1954, however, the fortune of Frobisher changed, with the discovery of oil in the region and the subsequent flurry of activity. The population doubled during the decade, reaching

▲ **THE FIRST BAKERY AT FROBISHER.** It was operated by Jack Collins and Mrs. Collins (his mother), pictured here in 1902. Photograph courtesy of the Ralph Allen Memorial Museum, Oxbow, Saskatchewan. Donated by Mr. Wm. McNeil, Alameda, Saskatchewan.

▲ **THE LAST STORE IN FROBISHER?** This photograph, taken August 22, 2003, shows the former Lucky Dollar Foods on the northeast corner of Third Street and Railway Avenue. A photograph in the local history book, dated 1907, shows the same building as a banking and insurance establishment.

a peak 335 in 1961, and a thriving and varied business community emerged as a number of oil companies based their operations in the village. Today, only a few oilfield services remain, and the community's other businesses have been superseded by the shopping and services offered in the nearby towns of Oxbow and Bienfait, as well as in the City of Estevan. One of the village's few remaining institutions is Frobisher School, a K-6 facility which had 25 students enrolled in the fall of 2006. Grades 7-9 attend classes in Bienfait, and 10-12 students are bused to Estevan. Frobisher is located in the RM of Coalfields No. 4.

FRONTIER, village, pop 283 (2006c), 302 (2001c), is located in the southwest corner of the province, on Hwy 18. The international border is 22.5 km to the south; the Cypress Hills are situated to the northwest and Grasslands National Park to the east. Large ranching operations had been active in the region since

the late 1800s; however, the first records of homesteading in the area date to 1908-09 when the region south of the Frenchman River was opened for settlement. Between 1910 and 1914, there was an influx of settlers into the area. A large percentage were Norwegian, who came to Canada via Minnesota, although others from England, Sweden and eastern Canada also took up homesteads in the Frontier district. Before the CPR arrived in Shaunavon in 1914, the closest points in Canada to deliver grain or obtain lumber, coal, or other goods were Gull Lake or Maple Creek, almost 100 kilometres to the north. As customs regulations were not rigidly enforced at the time, many cross-border transactions occurred. Until 1913, most of the area grain crop was sold in Harlem, Montana. The next year, the railroad at Shaunavon was open for business, and it was hoped that in the near future a line would be built south of the Frenchman River to the Frontier district. However, the country would soon be at war, and construction of the railway would be delayed for several years. Finally,

in early 1923, as the CPR approached from the west, a townsite was chosen, and rapidly the village began to take shape. Buildings were moved in from the countryside, and soon five grain elevators dominated the skyline. The boom times would be short-lived, though. By 1930, the year the village was incorporated, the drought and the Depression were deepening. Many became discouraged and left the area. The government offered new homesteads further north in the province, or in Alberta, and covered freight expenses for those wanting to relocate. Many of Frontier's businesses closed. For those who hung on, however, the decades following WWII were years of unprecedented prosperity, even though a fire on Main Street in 1946 claimed several buildings. The village rebuilt and, while grain and livestock production continued to be the major industries in the area, beginning in the 1970s, farm equipment manufacturing on a large scale began in the community.

As the industry grew, so did the number of available jobs. By 1981, the population of Frontier had climbed to 619. Soon, however, the factory was in trouble, and in 1984 the company was sold. During the 1980s, other manufacturers started up, but most lasted only a few years. Honey Bee Manufacturing, however, which relocated to Frontier from Bracken in 1987, remains a growing success, employing approximately 140-150 people from the area. A specialty crop processor also provides local jobs. Frontier has a wide range of businesses to serve the district, as well as a full array of facilities for recreational, social and cultural activities. Each May, the village holds a Norwegian Day celebration. Frontier has a K-12 school with approximately 130 students. The nearest health centre is located in the nearby village of Climax. In 2000, Frontier faced a serious problem: the CPR line along which the village was built was sold to Great Western Railway (GWR), a company based in Brit-

▼ **HANGING AROUND.** High school students at lunch time, Frontier, September 5, 2003. Some of the students are from farms in the Climax and Bracken areas.

ish Columbia, but almost immediately the Saskatchewan Wheat Pool announced it would shut down all of its elevators on the line, thus undermining its economic viability. Private interests began purchasing the elevators; however, by the beginning of 2004, GWR was looking to sell. That fall, a group led by south-western Saskatchewan farmers succeeded in purchasing the line. Recently, an interesting development has been taking place to the west of Frontier. Over 13,000 acres of the Old Man On His Back Plateau has become part of a conservation project to protect and restore the short-grass prairie. Purebred Plains Bison have been reintroduced to the area and are again roaming their natural habitat for the first time in over 100 years. Frontier serves as the administrative centre of the RM of Frontier No. 19.

FURDALE, organized hamlet, pop 192 (2006c), 195 (2001c), is a decades-old residential subdivision located immediately south of the city of Saskatoon. Furdale was declared an organized hamlet in 1988 and is situated in the RM of Corman Park No. 344.

GAINSBOROUGH, village, pop 250 (2006c), 286 (2001c), is one of the oldest incorporated villages in what is now the province of Saskatchewan. It was incorporated on May 25, 1894, with a recorded population of 29. Situated upon the pretty Gainsborough Creek, the village is located in the extreme southeast corner of the province, on Hwy 18, 6 km west of the Saskatchewan-Manitoba border, and 23 km north of the International Boundary. Estevan, 115 km to the west, is the nearest city. The first homesteaders began arriving in 1882. They believed a railway would

soon be built through the region because by the mid-1880s rail lines were being extended into south-western Manitoba, as well as the northern reaches of North Dakota. However, it was not until 1891 that the CPR laid tracks into the Gainsborough area, and it was August 1, 1892, when the first passenger train arrived on the line. A post office was established in 1884, and the first school was built in 1892. In 1889, the Anglican Mission was founded, and in 1897 parishioners built Christ Church, which stands to this day. Between seeding and harvest that year, farmers had hauled fieldstones from all directions for its construction, and when the church was consecrated that November not a cent was owing on the building. The church has since been in continuous use, and it was designated a municipal heritage property in 1988. The land around Gainsborough proved well-suited to farming and ranching over the years; in the 1930s, tons of hay were shipped out of the Gainsborough area to the dried-out regions of the province. Weather would, though, wreak havoc

▲ **FALSE FRONTS:** (top) Buildings along the south side of Railway Avenue in Gainsborough.

▲ **MOVIELAND IN GAINSBOROUGH** (above), situated on the east side of Bruce Street.

◀ **GAINSBOROUGH ELEVATORS**, north side of Railway Avenue from the west. The elevator in the foreground was demolished toward the end of 2005; the other was still standing in the summer of 2007 and was privately owned.

Photographs taken on August 21, 2003.

from time to time. A cyclone to the north of Gainsborough in 1909 killed three people, injured 30, and damaged a number of buildings and killed livestock. Floods were a recurring problem, as heavy snowfalls would cause the creek and area rivers to overflow. Gainsborough grew steadily until the 1960s, by which time the population had reached just over 400. Today, grain and livestock production, along with oil, are the major industries in the area, and village businesses serve both agricultural and oilfield operations. Gainsborough has a volunteer fire department, as well as a health centre and a special care home; policing is provided by the RCMP detachment in Carnduff. Gainsborough School closed in 2005. Gainsborough serves as the administrative centre of the RM of Argyle No. 1.

GARRICK, organized hamlet, pop 30 (2006c), 30 (2001c), is located on Hwy 55 between the town of Choiceland and the village of Love. Garrick is situated on what remains of the CPR line that was built from Nipawin to Prince Albert in the early 1930s; only the line from Nipawin to Choiceland remains operational today. Settlers began arriving in the Garrick district in the 1920s, and until the road deck on the CPR bridge over the Saskatchewan River at Nipawin was opened to traffic in 1930, supplies were freighted into area: horses and wagons crossed the river at Nipawin by ferry in summer, sleighs were used over the frozen river in winter. With the coming of the railroad into the Garrick district, townsites began to be located and established; Garrick began to develop around 1929 with the opening of the first stores. The Garrick Post Office was established on March 16, 1930. The 1930s brought more settlers into the area, many

fleeing the drought-ravaged southern plains. Numerous places of business were established in Garrick during the decade, and the community was flourishing in the 1940s with a population the local history estimates was at about 200. Forestry originally dominated the district economy, and it was not until the fall of 1938 that the first grain elevator was erected in the community. By the late 1940s, area timber stands were being depleted, and with more and more land being cleared by bulldozer, mixed farming began to replace logging as the area's pre-eminent industry. The Garrick School District had been established in 1933 (previously informal education had been provided by a Lutheran student minister in various homes and a shack in the community), and by 1951 Garrick School had three teachers and 65 students. By the mid-1950s, there were five teachers and over 100 students, as country schoolhouses in the surrounding district had been closed. But by 1957, however, the consolidation of the province's schools was to have an impact on Garrick itself. Grades 11 and 12 were no longer taught in the community, and those students then attended William Mason School in Choiceland. Grades nine and ten followed in 1964, and in 1967 grades seven and eight. Grades one to six were taught in Garrick until 1987, when the Nipawin School Division closed the community's school. By this time, Garrick was well in decline. The population of both the rural area and the hamlet had been falling for years — Garrick's population was down to about 100 in the mid-1960s — and many businesses had closed. The community suffered a significant blow when, on February 24, 1988, the Garrick Hotel, a community landmark since 1938, was completely destroyed by fire. By 1990, the hamlet was reduced to

a store, an auto body shop, the post office, a Pool elevator, and a coffee shop in the curling rink. Garrick is situated in the RM of Torch River No. 488.

GARSON LAKE, northern settlement, pop 34 (2001c), is located in the boreal forest, 48 km by road southwest of La Loche, just inside the Saskatchewan-Alberta border. The community is situated on the southeast shore of a lake of the same name. The name dates to 1911, and honours C.N. Garson, a manager of the Hudson's Bay Company post at Onion Lake. Garson Lake's mainly Dene inhabitants have traditionally engaged in the activities of hunting, fishing, and trapping for a living. The settlement was long remote and difficult to access; it had been primarily a fly-in community, and for most of the year supplies had to be brought in via air. Eventually, a winter road was developed that served the settlement for a window of time each year after freeze-up. In recent years, Garson Lake has been connected to the provincial highway system with an all-weather road, giving people greater access to services, and greater mobility in general. It is also recognized that the road has the potential to change the nature of living at Garson Lake. Completing the road to Fort McMurray, Alberta, and its lucrative oil sands extraction-based industry will likely create more employment and economic opportunities for area residents. Further, forestry, tourism, commercial fishing, and mining, as well as oil and gas, are all industries in north-western Saskatchewan seen to have growth potential.

GERALD, village, pop 124 (2006c), 159 (2001c), is located east of Esterhazy, off Hwy 22. The first settlers began taking

up homesteads in the region in the early 1880s, and in 1898 a concentration of Czech settlers arrived in the immediate area of the future village. They erected St. Wenceslaus Church in 1919. Gerald had its beginnings with the construction of the Grand Trunk Pacific Railway line through the district in 1907-08. A small agricultural community emerged, and in 1953, with a population hovering around 100, the Village of Gerald was incorporated. The development of potash mining in the area in the late 1950s and early 1960s led to somewhat of a boom period for the community; the population grew from 98 in 1956 to 231 a decade later. Today, both potash mining and agriculture form the basis of the district economy. A large farm equipment manufacturer in Gerald, Bridgeview Manufacturing, employs approximately 70 people in the area, and the company's owner and president, Kevin Hruska, received the "1997 Entrepreneur of the Year" award for agricultural services. Gerald's proximity to Esterhazy has resulted in many of the village's businesses and services being superseded by those in the larger centre; schoolchildren attend classes in Esterhazy, where the nearest police, fire, and medical services are also located. Gerald is situated in the RM of Spy Hill No. 152.

GIRVIN, hamlet, pop 25 (2001c), is a former village located 13 km south of Davidson, very close to mid-way between Saskatoon and Regina on Hwy 11. Today, other than having a few inhabited residences, Girvin has the appearance of a ghost town. The name of the community honours John Girvin, a Winnipeg contractor who was responsible for the construction of many railway stations across western Canada. The Qu'Appelle, Long Lake

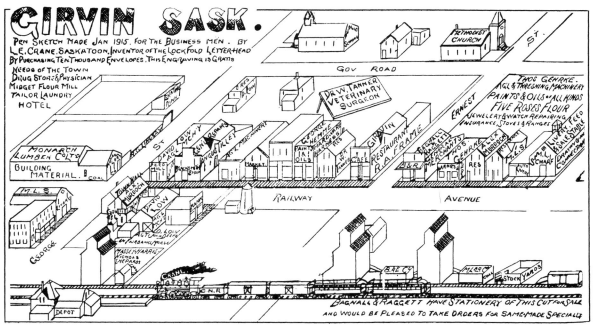

Postcard map.

▲ **A PEN SKETCH POSTCARD** of Girvin made in 1915 for the community's businessmen, by L.E. Crane of Saskatoon. Postcards such as this were a common way to promote a community.

◀ **THE GIRVIN PUMP HOUSE** was built in 1906 to provide water for horses hauling grain into the community. A gas engine (later electric) ran a pump that filled a tank in the top of the pumphouse. Pulling a rope released water into a horse trough at the front of the building. The pump house went out of regular service when horses were no longer the standard method of transporting grain. This is the only known pumphouse in Saskatchewan. Photograph taken July 21, 2004.

& Saskatchewan Railway built their line through the location of Girvin in the late 1880s; however, it was not until the early years of the twentieth century that settlement of the district took place and the village had its beginnings. The majority of the settlers came from Ontario, starting to arrive about 1902. As the district became increasingly populated over the next few years, Girvin emerged to become a trading centre for the area. The first development began in 1904 — the cemetery was laid out that year — but it was over 1905 and 1906 that much construction took place. The Girvin Post Office was established on April 1, 1905, and a local school district was established that year. Girvin was incorporated as a village on March 1, 1907, and businesses started within the community's first few years included a Massey-Harris dealership, stores, a restaurant, a veterinary service, a lumber yard, a livery stable, a blacksmith shop, a butcher shop, and a bank. A three-storey hotel was built complete with a bar, pool tables, a barber's chair, and a sitting room with a piano. Three grain elevators lined the tracks by 1915. Early on, Girvin had a hockey team, and baseball and football clubs; harness racing became popular in the 1920s, declined in the 1930s, but again became a preoccupation in the late 1960s. Curling was started in Girvin around 1930. By 1926, the village had grown to number 151 residents, but by 1941 the population had fallen to 93. The community experienced a resurgence in the 1950s — the population rose to over 140 — but beginning in the early 1960s, Girvin declined, steadily through the 1960s and then rapidly from the 1970s to the present. The school closed in 1970. When a new Highway 11 was built between Saskatoon and Regina, district people began to go to larger towns and the cities for their needs, and businesses in Girvin began to disappear. By the early 1980s, the last small grocery store had closed and only a gas station and a garage remained. There are no businesses or services in Girvin today; by 2004, the skating rink had collapsed, and dilapidated homes and former businesses dotted the townsite. Girvin relinquished village status on December 19, 2005, and is situated in the RM of Arm River No. 252.

GLADMAR, village, pop 53 (2006c), 45 (2001c), is located 142 km almost due south of Regina, and 10 km east of Minton off Hwy 18. The Saskatchewan-Montana border lies approximately 18 km to the south. Homesteaders began taking up land in the area in 1908-09; they were from many backgrounds, but a significant number were of Norwegian origin who had first settled in the United States. Some of the first settlers in the Gladmar area worked at a now long-defunct coal mine. In 1911, a post office was established a few miles north of the present village; the name was chosen by the first postmaster, James Edgar Black, who took the first letters of his children, Gladstone and Margaret, to concoct the name Gladmar. Black served for many years as the reeve of the RM of Surprise Valley and was instrumental in urging the CPR to build into the district. The first church services in the area were held in a building on the Black farm; when the first school in the district was built in 1913, it was also located on Black's land. It, too, was named Gladmar. The first store in the area had been established in 1912. In 1929, the railway arrived and buildings were moved to the new townsite, which adopted Gladmar as its name. In 1929, the Saskatchewan Wheat Pool built the first grain el-

evator; Parish and Heimbecker erected theirs in 1930. In the 1940s, the mining tradition in the area was continued when the Sybouts Sodium Sulphate Company began operations about 13 kilometres south of the community. At its peak, the mine provided full-time employment for as many as 35 people; it closed in the 1980s. By 1968, Gladmar had grown large enough to be incorporated as a village, and in 1971 it reached a peak population of 131. Almost immediately, however, Gladmar's numbers began to decline. Today, the community retains a Co-op store, a two-lane bowling alley, a seniors' centre, and an attractive park. The key feature of the village is Gladmar Regional School, which in 2006-07 provided K-12 education to 111 students from the community, the village of Minton, and the surrounding area. There is some oilfield activity in the region; however, agriculture, a combination of grain and cattle production, is the major industry in the district. Gladmar is situated in the rolling hills and coulees of the RM of Surprise Valley No. 9.

GLASLYN, village, pop 369 (2006c), 375 (2001c), is located approximately 70 km north of the Battlefords, and about 50 km east of Turtleford, at the junction of

Hwys 3 and 4. The first few settlers entered the district in 1908, among them the Hoskins family, who settled where the village now stands. Edwin D. Hoskins, of English parentage, and his Welsh wife had resided in Wales before coming to

▲▼ **THE GLASLYN AND DISTRICT MUSEUM** is housed in the restored 1926 CNR station on Railway Avenue (above). The site also includes a CNR caboose and the CNR water tower (below), one of only a few railway water towers remaining in the province. Also situated on the museum grounds is the Glaslyn War Memorial, built in 1922 to commemorate the district's Great War veterans. Photographs taken July 22, 2003.

Canada with their eight children, and when Hoskins succeeded in establishing a post office on January 1, 1911, he named it Glaslyn — Welsh for "clear water" — after the Glaslyn River in Wales. He may have been inspired by a small lake near his farm. The rail line from North Battleford was built as far as Edam in 1911, and Turtleford by 1914, but Glaslyn district residents remained about 30 miles (50 kilometres) from the nearest rail point for many years. The railway reached Glaslyn in 1926, and when the hamlet that had emerged became an incorporated village on April 16, 1929, the name Glaslyn was adopted. In the 1930s, the community grew, as homesteaders flocked to the area from the dried-out southern plains. From a population of 148 in 1931, Glaslyn grew steadily to number over 400 by the 1980s. Today, the village has a range of businesses and services including banks, grocery stores, farm suppliers, automotive services, contractors, accommodations, and restaurants. A wood products plant employs approximately 50 full-time people. The village also has recreational facilities, churches, seniors' housing, a seniors' centre with bowling lanes, a library, a museum, and a K-12 school which had 140 students enrolled in the fall of 2006. The community has a medical clinic, an RCMP detachment, and a fire and rescue fleet, and supports minor hockey and baseball programs and a figure skating club. The economy of the area is based in wood products, tourism, resort-based commerce, and agriculture, a combination of grain and cattle production. Several agricultural businesses, logging companies, resorts, and outfitters operate within the district. Little Loon Regional Park is located just east of Glaslyn; the major resort areas at Turtle and Brightsand Lakes are about a half-hour's drive to the north-

west; Meadow Lake Provincial Park is an hour to the north; and Jackfish Lake and The Battlefords Provincial Park are about a half-hour's drive to the south. Glaslyn serves as the administrative centre of the RM of Parkdale No. 498.

GLEN BAIN, hamlet, is situated approximately 35 km west of Gravelbourg. The first homesteaders arrived in the district in 1908, and by 1910 almost every available quarter section of land had been taken up. In the spring of 1911, a group of men headed by Richard B. McBain applied for permission to form a rural municipality. McBain, from Glengarry County, Ontario, became the first reeve, and the municipality was named in his honour. McBain was the postmaster of a short-lived post office named Glen Bain, which operated from 1912 to 1914. Mail was delivered on horseback from Gravelbourg. But the CPR had arrived in Vanguard, and then came through Meyronne and Kincaid to the south, so the mail was delivered by train to those points. For the first 25 years, the RM of Glen Bain had its office outside of its boundaries in the village of Vanguard. In the 1930s, as the CPR slowly built its line between Vanguard and Meyronne, thought was given to establishing the office in Glen Bain. A building was purchased and a lot located, and in 1936 the RM headquarters were relocated to their present site. The Glen Bain Post Office was re-established that year. With the coming of the railway, small businesses had begun to emerge at the hamlet site, and in 1935, despite it being the middle of the Depression, the Saskatchewan Wheat Pool and the Federal Grain Company each built grain elevators. By the 1940s an array of businesses had been established to serve the surrounding farming district.

However, as the rural population began to decline, so, too, did Glen Bain. In 1926, the population of the RM was 2,424; by 1966, it was down to 827; and in 2006, it was 232. The population of the hamlet in the mid-1950s was reported as being about 60; in the 1960s and 1970s the community numbered approximately three dozen residents; by 1988 there were only 11 inhabitants. At that time, the two grain elevators and the Co-op were the only remaining businesses. The CPR station had permanently closed in 1960. Today, the elevators are gone; the Co-op, however, still maintains a bulk fuel station. Glen Bain School closed in 1997. Glen Bain remains as the administrative headquarters of the RM of Glen Bain No. 105; the RM office, which had doubled as a high school from 1936 until 1944, was designated a municipal heritage property in 1986.

GLEN EWEN, village, pop 120 (2006c), 158 (2001c), is located in the extreme southeast corner of the province, just east of Oxbow on Hwy 18. The first settlers began arriving in the district in 1882 with the belief a railway would shortly be built through the region; by the mid-1880s, rail lines were being extended into south-western Manitoba, as well as the northern reaches of North Dakota. It was not until 1891, however, that the CPR laid tracks into the Glen Ewen area; the first train arrived in 1892. The railway brought increasing numbers of homesteaders: the district was largely settled by people of British origin, from both eastern Canada and overseas. A local post office was established in 1890 on the farm of Thomas Ewen and named Glen Ewen; hence, the origin of the community's name. In 1899,

▼ **AN EARLY SCENE AT GLEN EWEN**, date unknown. Photograph courtesy of the Ralph Allen Memorial Museum, Oxbow, Saskatchewan. Donated by John Hood, Oxbow, Saskatchewan.

the Glen Ewen school district was formed, and in 1904 the Village of Glen Ewen was incorporated. Little information about the early years of the community exists, as a devastating fire in November 1937 destroyed most of the village council's historical records. The community thrived until the 1930s; however, during that decade, a number of the village's businesses closed. While there was some recovery in the late 1940s and during the 1950s, the community slowly began to decline and stagnate economically as the neighbouring towns of Carnduff and Oxbow grew and prospered. In the early 1960s, the population of Glen Ewen was near 300; however, by 1976 it was down to 143. Dozens of businesses — including restaurants, general stores, implement dealers, hardware suppliers, a hotel, and a theatre — once lined the village's streets. Today, other than a store, virtually none remain. The grain elevators (there were once several) are gone, and the school closed in 1989. A quiet, somewhat decaying, residential community remains. Glen Ewen is located within the RM of Enniskillen No. 3, an area where the major industries are agriculture, and oil and gas.

GLEN HARBOUR, resort village, is one in a string of growing resort communities on the east side of Last Mountain Lake. The first settlers arrived in the area in the 1880s, and by 1910 Glen Harbour was a stopping place for the Wm. Pearson Co.'s steamboat, the *S.S. Qu'Appelle*. It was not until around the 1960s, however, that the development of the present resort community began. In 2006, the census recorded 73 permanent residents and, of these, approximately two-thirds commuted to work in Regina, about a 45-minute drive away. The summer population of the resort village reaches roughly 200. Glen Harbour was incorporated in 1986 and is situated in the RM of McKillop No. 220.

GLENAVON, village, pop 183 (2006c), 207 (2001c), lies southwest of Grenfell on Hwy 48. The village developed with the construction of the Canadian Northern Railway line from Brandon, Manitoba, through Maryfield and Kipling to Regina. The first buildings began to go up on the townsite in 1907, and in 1908 the first trains were running. The Glenavon Post Office was established on March 1 that year and the first shipments of wheat were manually loaded into rail cars as there was yet no grain elevator. In 1909, the first elevator was built and the Glenavon railway station was erected. The new village was incorporated on April 13, 1910, and that year a hotel was built and a branch of the Bank of Toronto opened. By 1912, three grain elevators lined the tracks in the village. Though the majority of the first settlers that came to the area were from England, Scotland, and Wales, a significant Polish presence developed in the district; as well, Ukrainian, German, French, Hungarian, Scandinavian and Chinese people came to call the village home. Glenavon's population grew from 130 in 1911 to 251 by 1936. The community's numbers fell significantly during the latter half of the 1930s — to 180 by 1941. During the post-war era, the community burgeoned. By the early 1960s, the population was approaching 400 and achieving town status seemed within the realm of possibility. However, Glenavon's proximity to the larger centres of Kipling, Wolseley, and Grenfell — not to mention Regina, less than an hour's drive away — had a negative impact on the village's business sector as people increasingly travelled outside the area to shop. Older people began moving away from Glenavon, as there was not any seniors' housing in the village, nor was there a resident doctor, pharmacy, or hospital in the community. A lack of economic diversity and employment opportunities also forced younger people to seek careers elsewhere. Steadily, Glenavon's numbers fell to their present level. Businesses serving the community and district today include grocery and fuel retailers, a beverage room and restaurant, auto body services, a post office, an insurance agency, a liquor outlet, and a Saskatchewan Wheat Pool farm supply centre. The village has an indoor arena and curling rinks, a ball park, churches, a library, and a park with camping facilities. Glenavon School, a K-12 institution that had 66 students enrolled in the fall of 2006, was closed in the summer of 2007. The Glenavon and District Agricultural Society holds an annual summer fair and sports day toward the end of July. The Village of Glenavon and the RM of Chester No. 125 share office space in the community, and the RM maintenance shop is also located in the village.

GLENSIDE, village, pop 86 (2006c), 63 (2001c), is situated 24 km east and south of the town of Outlook on Hwy 219. Settlers began arriving in the area around 1903. They came from eastern Canada (primarily Ontario), the United States, Great Britain and other areas of Europe; and they were of many extractions: largely Norwegian, Scottish, English, Czech, and Finnish. Most disembarked the train at Hanley with their household effects, machinery, and livestock before heading out across the country to their homesteads. Hanley was where supplies and mail were first obtained, and also where grain was hauled to before the construction of the

▼ **GLENSIDE**, July 21, 2004.

rail line though the Glenside district. The village of Glenside itself had its beginnings with the construction of the CPR rail line from Moose Jaw to Outlook. The track was built through the Glenside area in 1908, and by 1909 the length of the line had been completed. The Glenside Post Office was established on May 14, 1909. Grain elevators and many other businesses sprang up, the school was built in 1910, and the village was incorporated on March 30, 1911. A Presbyterian church (later United) was built in 1916 (services had been held in the school until then), and in later years Anglican and Alliance churches were also constructed. Approximately eight kilometres southwest of Glenside, the district's early Czech settlers built the John Huss United Church (originally the Bohemian Presbyterian Church). This church was still frequented by a small congregation in the mid-1970s; today, there is only the occasional funeral service and burial at the cemetery. Likewise, none of the village churches remain active today. However, the architecturally unique United Church building was designated a heritage property in 1987, and it remains a community landmark. Glenside's heyday was during its first two decades of existence — the population jumped from just 54 in 1911 to its peak population of 165 by 1921. The village's numbers plummeted by more than a third through the 1930s, and while Glenside rebounded somewhat from the mid-1950s through to the mid-1960s, it has since steadily declined. Although the community retains its post office, all other businesses have disappeared. The school was closed in the late 1970s. Four grain elevators still lined the tracks in 1987; today, two remain standing, although their former owners — United Grain Growers and the Saskatchewan Wheat Pool — have abandoned them. The Glenside townsite now consists of many vacant lots and abandoned buildings; people travel mainly to the nearby town of Outlook (pop. 1,938 in 2006) for employment, shopping and services, entertainment and recreation. Glenside is situated in the RM of Rudy No. 284.

GLENTWORTH, hamlet, pop 88 (1996c), is located in south-central Saskatchewan, west of Wood Mountain on Hwy 18. The east block of Grasslands National Park lies to the south. The area was settled after 1909, and when the CPR constructed its line from Wood Mountain to Mankota in 1928-29, the townsite of Glentworth was established. Glentworth was never a large community; incorporated as a village in 1945, its population peaked at 157 in 1966. In the late 1990s, rail service into the community was discontinued, and on September 6, 2000, the Village of Glentworth was dissolved. In 2003, the population was approximately 70. The hamlet continues to serve the district with a small core of essential businesses and services; Glentworth Central School provides K-12 education and had 117 students enrolled in the fall of 2006. The nearest health care facilities and police service are located in Mankota, approximately 30 kilometres to the west. Ranching and farming are the major industries in the Glentworth area. Glentworth serves as the administrative centre of the RM of Waverley No. 44.

GLIDDEN, hamlet, pop 48 (1996c), is located 26 km south of Kindersley on Hwys 21 and 44; the South Saskatchewan River lies 28 km to the south. The district began to be settled around 1906, and among the first in the area was Allan S. Newcombe for whom the RM of Newcombe

▲ **A FORMER SASKATCHEWAN WHEAT POOL GRAIN ELEVATOR** at Glentworth dates to 1980. Photograph taken September 3, 2007.

No. 260, in which Glidden is situated, was named. Newcombe led a group of men, women, and children from Boston, Massachusetts, to an area northeast of present-day Glidden, east of Cutbank Lake; the school they established in 1909 was named Bostonia after their former home. In the early years more settlers came from other areas of the United States (among these were a number of Norwegian origin), and there were many of English and Scottish origins who came from both the British Isles and eastern Canada (a significant number were from Ontario). After 1910, a large number of people of German extraction took up land in the area; in the 1920s Ukrainians and Mennonites further contributed to the district's ethnic fabric. In the early 1960s, Hutterites established a colony to the south of Glidden. The Canadian Northern Railway built the rail bed through the area around 1915, and a location for a townsite was chosen about a mile west of the present village. Laying the steel rails was delayed, though, due to wartime exigencies, and it was not until 1917 that the track into the area was laid. In 1916, the first buildings were erected at the first townsite, but the land proved to be too low-lying and the locale was flooded. The railroad then purchased 40 acres to the east from Chase Glidden for the development of the present townsite — hence, the community's name. Mr. Glidden had come to the region from DeKalb, Illinois, as a surveyor for the J.E. Martin Land Company; impressed by the land, he purchased several choice sections himself and encouraged others from his home state to follow suit. In 1917, construction commenced at the new townsite, and within a couple of years the community of Glidden had all the businesses one would have found in a village at the time, including a bank, a hotel, a drug store, and two "Chinese" restaurants. The Holbeck Post Office, established in 1909 about four miles west, was relocated to the bourgeoning community in July 1918 and renamed Glidden; on March 31, 1919, the village was incorporated. By this time four grain elevators lined the tracks. Also in 1919, an area schoolhouse — Kincora — was moved into the village. In 1920 a new, larger school was built in Glidden to accommodate a growing number of children. The rail line was completed through to Alsask in 1920; the link from Glidden north to Kindersley was built in 1928. The village grew to have a population that hovered around 100 until the post-WWII period, when Glidden experienced another period of growth, albeit somewhat brief. From a population of 94 in 1951, the community's numbers reached 145 by 1961, the village's all-time high. Since, however, Glidden has steadily declined. In 1964, the local branch of the Toronto Dominion Bank (opened in 1917 as the Bank of Toronto) closed to Kindersley. In

1966, the United Church also closed to Kindersley. Glidden's grade 12 students began to be bused to Kindersley in 1962, and by 1970 only grades one, two, and three were still being taught at the village school. The last store in Glidden closed in 1970; the school closed in 1973. The rail link to Kindersley was abandoned in 1978. The population of the community has been below 50 since the mid-1980s, and on October 19, 2000, Glidden relinquished village status. The administrative office of the surrounding RM remains in the hamlet.

GOLDEN PRAIRIE, village, pop 35 (2006c), 56 (2001c), is located west of the Great Sand Hills, 48 km northwest of Maple Creek on Hwy 728. German immigrants, many of whom came via North Dakota, began arriving in the region around 1907. Up until this time there had been only a few ranchers in the district, and initially there were some tensions as the newcomers began to fence and break the former grazing lands for farming. When the CPR built a branch north from the main line into the area in the late 1920s, the village quickly sprang up around the railway point established. But in the dry years of the 1930s, many people moved on. However, the community rebounded after the decade, and attained village status in 1942. After WWII, there was a period of prosperity, and by the mid-1950s the village reached a peak population of around 250 and had a thriving business community. Since the 1960s, though, the population and the commercial sector have steadily declined. By the fall of 2005 a small K-6 school in the community had only 12 students enrolled, and it was closed at the end of the school year in 2006. Caragana bushes are

now taking over abandoned lots in the village. Traditionally, grain and livestock production dominated the local economy, but in recent years many farmers in the area have been switching from cereals to drought-tolerant and more self-sufficient crops like chickpeas, feed peas and lentils. Today, the Golden Prairie region is increasingly becoming dotted with gas wells and compressor stations, and the natural gas industry now factors significantly in the area economy. Those living in Golden Prairie today are mainly seniors and oil field workers. Golden Prairie serves as the administrative centre of the RM of Big Stick No. 141.

GOOD SPIRIT ACRES, organized hamlet, is a growing, upscale resort community located north of the town of Springside, just south of Good Spirit Lake. The hamlet is essentially comprised of residential and seasonal properties set within an 18-hole golf course. Many of the permanent residents are retirees. The year-round population is approximately 125; however, in the summer it can reach far higher. There is a clubhouse and restaurant, and a confectionary/gas station. Canora and Yorkton are the nearest larger centres. Good Spirit Acres is situated in the RM of Good Lake No. 274.

GOODEVE, village, pop 50 (2006c), 70 (2001c), is located approximately halfway between Ituna and Melville on Hwy 15. Southwest lie the reserve holdings of the Little Black Bear, Star Blanket, Okanese, and Peepeekisis First Nations. In the early 1900s, settlers, mainly of Ukrainian, Polish, and German descent, came to the Goodeve area (among them were a few Anglo-Saxons), and with the arrival of

▲ **GOOD SPIRIT LAKE**, immediately north of Good Spirit Acres. Photograph taken July 13, 2003.

▲ **GOODEVE'S ORIGINAL SCHOOL HOUSE** with Holy Ghost Ukrainian Orthodox Church in the background. A new school was built in 1950 and expanded with an addition in 1964. This red brick schoolhouse has in recent times been used as a seniors' centre. Photograph taken July 14, 2003.

the Grand Trunk Pacific Railway in 1907-08 the Goodeve townsite was established and the village began to develop. The village's name was likely chosen simply to fit the alphabetical sequence of naming communities along the rail line: Fenwood, Goodeve, Hubbard, Ituna, etc. The Goodeve Post Office was established on December 1, 1909, and Goodeve was incorporated on August 18, 1910. During the latter year, a school district centred on the village was organized. Goodeve developed rapidly: its population jumped from 71 in 1911 to 219 by 1921, and in 1926 it reached a peak of 287. In the mid-1950s, the village boasted four churches, a number of active clubs, sports teams and other community-based organizations, as well as four grain elevators (Federal, Pioneer, Saskatchewan Wheat Pool, and Searle) and more than two dozen other places of business. From this point forward, however, Goodeve steadily declined: the population fell from 258 in 1951 to 212 by 1961, and thereafter plummeted even more dramatically. By 1971 it was down to 169; by 1981 it was 116. One by one the village's businesses closed, and today only the post office and one grain elevator remain in what was once a viable commercial centre. The only counter to the trend of decline in recent years was the development of a hog production facility in the Goodeve area operated by Big Sky Farms. Due to declining enrollment, Goodeve School closed its doors at the end of June 2003, after serving the community for close to a century. At the time, the school had 32 students registered; schoolchildren are now bused to Melville for their education. Landmarks in Goodeve include the Pioneer grain elevator (still in operation), St. Michael's Ukrainian Catholic Church, Holy Ghost Ukrainian Orthodox Church, and an old red brick schoolhouse that now houses a seniors' centre. A notable person born in Goodeve is the artist Russell Yuristy, well-known for his large animal sculptures, many of which are located in playgrounds. Through the fall of 2003 and into the spring of 2004, Goodeve was embroiled in political turmoil as villagers claimed the fall municipal election was invalid. They said ineligible voters had cast ballots, and they took the mayor to court over what they claimed was election fraud. A Yorkton judge agreed with the plaintiffs, threw out the election result and ordered that another election take place. The provincial government appointed an outside returning officer to oversee the voting, and on May 26, 2004, villagers ousted the mayor. Goodeve is situated in the RM of Stanley No. 215.

GOODSOIL, village, pop 253 (2006c), 284 (2001c), is located 75 km northwest of Meadow Lake, immediately south of Meadow Lake Provincial Park on Hwy 26. A few pioneering ranchers had moved into the district as early as 1912, but the majority of the settlers arrived between 1928 and 1932 to take up homesteads. These settlers were, for the most part, German Catholics. In 1926, Father Johan Schultz and Father F.J. Lange, both then with the Sacred Heart Parish at Denzil, Saskatchewan, scouted the area, as land was much needed for the expanding population of St. Joseph's Colony, as well as newly-arrived German-speaking immigrants from Europe and the United States. The goal was to create a new, highly homogeneous German Catholic settlement; Father Lange had more than twenty years' experience establishing German Catholic bloc settlements in Saskatchewan. In 1971 almost two-thirds of Goodsoil's residents still claimed German origins.

▲ **GOODSOIL GUS** is made of wood and reaches a height of 6.1 metres (20 feet). The lumberjack welcomes visitors to the village's tourist information centre.

▼ **THE GOODSOIL HISTORICAL MUSEUM** and the village's library are housed in the community's former stone schoolhouse. The school was built in 1945-46 of local stone cut and shaped by area craftsmen, under the guidance of John Weber, a stonemason by trade.

Photographs taken July 23, 2003.

In 1928, the few settlers that were in the area began working to establish the parish of St. Boniface; the Goodsoil Post Office was established on December 1, 1929; an RCMP detachment opened in 1931. As the land in the area was cleared, bush work was replaced with work in the fields, and the district became more agricultural. It was expected that the rail line that had reached St. Walburg in 1921 would be built north through Loon Lake and then extended to Bonnyville, Alberta (the CNR reached Bonnyville in 1928 from the other direction), but due to the Depression these plans were never realized. Goodsoil area farmers were left to haul their grain, livestock, and cream by horses, or trucks as they became more common, to the rail points at either Meadow Lake or St. Walburg, both considerable distances away. In 1940 a grain elevator was built just south of Goodsoil at Peerless — it would be a rather unique elevator in that it would never be served by rail. Farmers hauled their grain to the elevator in wagons or sleighs, and from there it was trucked out to the railheads. The elevator remained in operation until 1950; by this time most farmers had their own large trucks and chose to do the hauling themselves. The construction of Highway 26 in the late 1940s made transportation much easier and faster. By the late 1950s the hamlet of Goodsoil had grown to the point where residents decided their community should be elevated to having village status, and on January 1, 1960, the Village of Goodsoil was incorporated. Since 1961 when the community numbered 246 residents, the village's population has remained very stable; however, it is getting older and many are retirees. In 2006, the median age of community residents was 54.3, while that of all Saskatchewan residents was 38.7. The percentage of the population aged 15 or older was 86.3. Goodsoil has a business sector that includes automotive and agricultural services, a Co-op, a credit union, the post office, restaurants, a hotel, stores, a laundromat, and a pool hall/arcade. There is a community recreation complex and ball park, a library, a museum, a seniors' centre, and a miniature golf course. Eight kilometres west of the village, the Northern Meadows Golf Club has an 18-hole championship course; Meadow Lake Provincial Park offers many recreational opportunities. St. Boniface Church serves the area's Catholic worshipers; Goodsoil Central School, a K-12 facility, had 146 students enrolled in the fall of 2006. Goodsoil has an airstrip, a fire hall, and a health centre with an attached special care home. The RCMP detachment was closed in 2005 along with five other detachments in villages in the province's southwest. The nearest police services are now located in Pierceland and Loon Lake. Goodsoil is the hometown of Ron Greschner, the New York Rangers' high-scoring defenseman from 1974–90. Goodsoil is situated in the RM of Beaver River No. 622.

GOODWATER, village, pop 25 (2006c), 25 (2001c), is located south of Weyburn, approximately 10 km east of Hwy 35. The north end of the Rafferty Dam Reservoir on the Souris River lies to the east. People of British origin, and Norwegians via the United States, settled in the district in the early 1900s. With the arrival of the railroad in 1911, the village of Goodwater developed, and it was incorporated on May 8 that year. The village had a peak population of 123 in 1921; however, the community's numbers fell during the Depression and Goodwater never fully recovered afterward. The area economy has traditionally been based upon agriculture, a combination of grain growing and cattle production; however, in the 1950s, with the discovery of oil in the area, oilfield-related service industries developed. Although the oil industry burgeoned to the point where there are now over 1,100 wells in the region, the population of the area, and of Goodwater, has simultaneously decreased. Goodwater remains a small residential community of quiet tree-lined streets; businesses and services are sought in Weyburn. Goodwater is located in the RM of Lomond No. 37.

GOVAN, town, pop 232 (2006c), 274 (2001c), is located to the east of the north end of Last Mountain Lake, roughly mid-way between Strasbourg and Nokomis on Hwy 20. The first known settler in the area arrived in 1903, and by around 1906 all of the available homesteads in the area were occupied. Govan developed as a farming community with the construction of the railway from Strasbourg to Lanigan. The townsite was surveyed in 1906, and in 1907 Govan was incorporated as a village, its name honouring Walter Govan, one of the area's early settlers. The Canadian Museum of Civilization in Gatineau, Quebec, has an exquisitely rendered model depicting Govan at about the time of its incorporation — an example of a typical early prairie town. Govan attained town status in 1911, and in 1916 the community reached a peak population of 500. Today, the village is best known for hosting the Govan Old Tyme Fiddle Festival and the Saskatchewan Fiddlers Championships. The concurrent events, held the first weekend in July, have been running for over 20 years and draw competitors and fans from across North America. The Vintage Snowmobile Races, hosted by a local club, are also held annually in Govan. The machines must date to 1979 or before. Govan has a core of local businesses, four active churches, a library, skating and curling rinks, ball diamonds, sports grounds, and

▼ **WALTER THE WHOOPING CRANE** welcomes visitors to Govan. He has a wingspan of 6.4 metres (21 feet), is made of fibreglass and steel, and was built in 1987 to commemorate the 100th anniversary of the establishment of the nearby bird sanctuary on Last Mountain Lake, the first federal bird sanctuary reserved in North America. Photograph taken June 28, 2004.

▲ **THE GRAND FINALE** of the Govan Old Tyme Fiddle Festival and the Saskatchewan Fiddlers Championships in July 1998 included fiddlers aged 4 to 84. Photograph courtesy of Carolyn Mortenson, Govan, Saskatchewan.

a small golf course. The community has a K-9 school; students attend grades 10 to 12 in Strasbourg. In 1967, Govan's senior men's baseball team won the Western Canadian Baseball Championships and were subsequently inducted into the Saskatchewan Sports Hall of Fame. Govan serves as the administrative centre of the RM of Last Mountain Valley No. 250.

GRAND COULEE, village, pop 435 (2006c), 366 (2001c), is located 12 km west of Regina, four km north of the Trans-Canada Hwy. Essentially now a bedroom community, Grand Coulee has grown rapidly over the past few de-

▶ **FINAL DAYS:** This former Pioneer grain elevator at Grand Coulee was photographed in spring 1999. The last of a row of elevators that once stood in the village, it was demolished later that same year.

cades — the population was 131 in 1972 — and there is a strong potential for continued growth as affluent city workers increasingly choose to purchase properties in quieter rural settings. According to the 2001 Census of Canada, the median income for all Grand Coulee households was $71,587 for the year 2000, while Regina's was $46, 847. Settlement of the Grand Coulee district began in the early 1880s, just in advance of the construction of the CPR mainline through the region. The Grand Coulee post office was established in 1903. The community has twice been incorporated as a village: from 1908 to 1919, and again from 1984 to the present. From 1968 to 1984, Grand Coulee had the status of an organized hamlet. The community's proximity to Regina has negated any significant local commercial development, and the last remaining grain elevator was demolished in 2000. Children attend elementary school in Grand Coulee (Stewart Nicks School is a K-8 facility which had 90 students enrolled in the fall of 2006); high school students attend classes in Regina. The Grand Coulee Old Tyme Jug Band, long-time Saskatchewan entertainers, had their beginnings in the community in 1967. Grand Coulee is situated in the RM of Sherwood No. 159.

GRANDVIEW BEACH, resort village, is one in a string of growing resort communities located on the west side of Last Mountain Lake. In the 1920s, a hotel and dance hall were built and the resort became a popular getaway. Hunters and fisherman used it as a base. In the 1940s

▶ **A THRESHING CREW** on the farm of Toussaint Deaust, Gravelbourg area, 1926. Photograph courtesy of the Gravelbourg and District Museum.

Built on farming and faith...

GRAVELBOURG

OUR LADY OF ASSUMPTION Roman Catholic Co-Cathedral in Gravelbourg, built 1918-19. Photograph taken September 1, 2004.

▲ **ELEVATOR ROW AND RAIL LINES IN GRAVELBOURG, CIRCA 1950s.** Saskatchewan Archives Board R-B12269.

▼ **THE CONVENT OF JESUS AND MARY**, built in 1917, now houses Gravelbourg Elementary School. Photograph taken September 1, 2004.

and 1950s significant cottage development began, and Grandview Beach was incorporated in 1961. There are about three dozen permanent residents; however, the population varies greatly depending on the season. Grandview Beach is situated in the RM of Sarnia No. 221.

GRAVELBOURG, town, pop 1,089 (2006c), 1,187 (2001c), is located southwest of Old Wives Lake at the junction of Hwys 43 and 58. The confluence of the Wood River and the Notukeu Creek is a short distance northeast of the community. Gravelbourg was founded by Father Louis-Joseph-Pierre Gravel (1868–1926), a missionary colonizer, and his five brothers and a sister who settled at the location in 1906. On behalf of both the Canadian government and the Roman Catholic Church, Fr. Gravel encouraged Francophones in eastern Canada and New England to come west; he was also involved with the founding of the south-western communities of Lafleche, Val Marie, and Ponteix. Gravelbourg was incorporated as a village on December 30, 1912, and with the arrival of the railway in 1913 the community rapidly developed. Gravelbourg attained town status on November 1, 1916. Although settlers of various origins would settle in the community over the years (these would include German Lutherans and Irish Catholics), Gravelbourg would develop over the coming decades as a bastion of both the French culture and the Roman Catholic Church in Saskatchewan. In 1918, the Convent of Jesus and Mary and the College Mathieu were built, followed in 1919 by the construction of the Romanesque cathedral, which has a seating capacity for over 1,500 people. College Mathieu, which provides grade 8-12 education, is now the only French-language

residential school operating in western Canada. Additionally, École Beau-Soleil, located on the campus of College Mathieu, provides French-language education for children in grades K-7. The Centre Culturel Maillard, constructed in 1985, was established to ensure the preservation of the community's French language and culture. It houses a French language bookstore, as well as the offices of the Association Communautaire Fransaskoise de Gravelbourg and the Association Culturelle Franco-Canadienne de la Saskatchewan. Gravelbourg Elementary School offers two programs: an English program with Core French, and a French immersion program with an hour of English instruction each day. Gravelbourg High School also has a French immersion program, as well as an English curriculum. Gravelbourg remains a service centre for the surrounding agricultural region, which produces staple crops such as wheat, durum, and barley, as well as pulse crops such as peas and lentils. The town has over 100 businesses providing a wide range of goods and services, with a number of enterprises catering to the district's agricultural sector. An award-winning manufacturer of light commercial trailers in Gravelbourg employs about 120 people. Gravelbourg has a hospital with an attached special care home, an ambulance service, a dentist, and a range of additional health care services. The community has an RCMP detachment and a volunteer fire department, both of which serve the town and the surrounding area. Community recreational facilities include an arena for hockey and skating, a curling club, a fitness club, a bowling alley, ball diamonds, and a competition-size indoor pool at the College Mathieu Aquaplexe. Two regional parks in the area have golf courses, camping facilities, and opportu-

nities for fishing. Gravelbourg also has a library, a museum, a French language resource centre, and a completely restored 1946 theatre, now a heritage property, which houses two of the oldest movie projectors in Saskatchewan. Gravelbourg also has a professional French Canadian dance ensemble, Danseurs de la Rivière de la Vieille, and in 2003 the CRTC approved the licencing of Gravelbourg's first Francophone community radio station. There are many points of interest in the community, primarily its buildings, several of which have been designated heritage properties. The imposing ensemble of the cathedral, the former convent school, and the Bishop's residence is outstanding in scale and architectural refinement. The post office, the court house, and the Canadian Northern Railway station are other notable community landmarks. Gravelbourg hosts the annual Southern Saskatchewan Summer Solstice Festival, which features a diverse weekend of music as well as literary and performing arts programming. Gravelbourg serves as the administrative centre of the RM of Gravelbourg No. 104.

GRAY, organized hamlet, pop 89 (2006c), 106 (2001c), is located approximately 35 km southeast of Regina on Hwy 306. In 1883, the first few homesteaders began taking up land in the area west of present-day Gray. In 1889 larger numbers of settlers arrived in this district, and what became known as the community of Buck Lake began to develop. The name honoured Walter Buck, one of the original 1883 pioneers. Before the development of Milestone on the Soo Line in the early 1900s, the only market for grain and source for supplies was in Regina. A Methodist church was built at

Buck Lake in 1893, a school in 1894, and after 1906 there was a post office nearby. These were the main social centres of the district until 1912, when the Grand Trunk Pacific Railway came through the region and the hamlet of Gray was established. Settlers began taking up land closer to the hamlet site between 1900 and 1904, and in 1905 Iowa School, named for the home state of a number of the district's early settlers, was built somewhat southeast of the present community. Also in 1905, on December 1, the Gray Post Office, named after Gray, Audubon County, Iowa, opened just northeast of the school. Although a number of the district's settlers did hail from the American state of Iowa, others had origins in Illinois, eastern Canada, and Europe. By 1910-11, almost all of the available land in the Gray area had been claimed as homesteads. In 1911, the railroad grade was built, the townsite of Gray was surveyed (the name of the post office was adopted for that of the new community), and lots were put up for sale. The first general store was built that fall. In 1912, the rails were laid and the first train rolled through Gray. Two grain elevators were erected that year and a number of other businesses, including lumber yards, blacksmith and tinsmith's shops, a hardware and harness store, a pool room and a barber shop, were established. A café, a third grain elevator and a farm equipment dealership were constructed in 1913. In 1914, a Methodist church and the railway station were built; in 1915, a fourth elevator. The community continued to grow, and in 1921 a two-room brick school was built in Gray, replacing Iowa School which was then closed. By the end of the 1920s, a fifth grain elevator lined the tracks in the hamlet. Gray's population and business community declined significantly during the 1930s. Although the hamlet recovered during the post-War period, as the century progressed, Gray's businesses began to give way to those in nearby Regina, and in recent decades Gray has increasingly become a bedroom community for those who commute to work in the city. In the mid-1970s, construction began on a new complex to house skating and curling rinks and a seniors' centre. Gray was established as an organized hamlet in 1977, and in 1979 a sewer and water system were installed and a number of trees were planted on Main Street. A new United Church in the community was dedicated in June 1982. In 1983, five grain elevators still lined the tracks in the hamlet, but by the mid-1990s none remained. There had not been any traffic over the rail line in years, and in October of 2005 CN formally announced its plan to discontinue operation of the line. Today, there are no businesses or services left in Gray. Gray Elementary School was a K-6 facility which had 22 students enrolled in the fall of 2006; it closed the following summer. A

community landmark in the hamlet is the 1893 Buck Lake Methodist Church building. It is the oldest building in Gray, as it predates the community by almost two decades. The church had closed in 1918 and was moved into Gray in 1924 by the Masons, who occupied the premises until 1982, at which time they amalgamated with the Milestone Lodge. Gray is situated in the RM of Lajord No. 128.

GRAYSON, village, pop 179 (2006c), 210 (2001c), is located 33 km southeast of Melville on Hwy 22 and 15 km north of the Qu'Appelle Valley and the summer resort developments on Crooked Lake. In 1896, settlers began arriving, largely from the Austrian-administered areas of Bukovina and Galicia. Before the railway came through, the nearest town was Grenfell on the CPR main line. It took two days to make the round trip by ox cart. The trip was usually undertaken about once a month to obtain groceries or

other supplies; however, during harvest, grain had to be hauled the distance once a week. When construction of the railway began in the Grayson district in 1903, the townsite was established. In 1904, the first businesses in the community sprang up. In 1906, with a population of 74, Grayson was incorporated. Ursuline Sisters from Winnipeg arrived in the fall of

1915, and would for several decades tend to the needs of the village's large Catholic community. By the early 1920s the population of Grayson was well over 200; in the early 1950s it was nearing 400. By that time Grayson's population had grown somewhat more diverse: village residents then also included people of English, French, Swedish and Norwegian origins.

▼ **GRAYSON'S POLKA DOT PLAYERS DINNER THEATRE CAST** dressed for the performance of Nuncrackers — the Nunsense Christmas Musical, presented in November and December 2000.

▲▼ **GRAYSON POLKA FEST**, July 1999.
Grayson photographs courtesy of Leona Bisch, Grayson, Saskatchewan.

By the end of the 1950s, though, people began moving away from the community, and in the subsequent years the number of businesses and services in the village declined. Grayson retains its school, a K-9 facility which had 43 students enrolled in the fall of 2006. Until recently, Grayson had best been known for its summer festival. For two decades, the Grayson Annual Polka Fest drew up to 2,500 visitors each year from across western Canada and the United States. It was the community's most celebrated event. Another village tradition, which continues, is the annual dinner theatre held by the Grayson Polka Dot Players. Grayson serves as the administrative centre of the RM of Grayson No. 184. Agriculture, primarily mixed farming, is the major industry in the area.

GREEN LAKE, northern village, pop 361 (2006c), 498 (2001c), is located 49 km northeast of Meadow Lake at the junction of Hwys 55 and 155. Green Lake serves as a gateway to a number of communities further north. The village sits at the north end of a long, narrow lake from which it derives its name. Green Lake is predominantly a Métis community with

a history dating back to the late 1700s and the fur trade. In the 1870s, a Roman Catholic mission was established, and an ox cart road was hewn from Fort Carlton on the North Saskatchewan River to Green Lake. From Green Lake, freight could then be transported over water to Ile-a-la-Crosse, reducing the amount that had to come over the voyageur highway from Cumberland House. Through Green Lake much pemmican that would fuel the northern fur brigades was transported. By the 1890s, Green Lake's population was steadily increasing, and in 1901 a post office was established. In the twentieth century, forestry and farming began to dominate the Green Lake area economy. In 1939, the provincial government established farming operations to assist and train people in agriculture. In the 1940s, the Sisters of the Presentation of Mary arrived to provide education and medical services. The Sisters also oversaw the running of a cannery, and carpentry and sewing shops through which people could acquire trade skills. A sawmill was established at Green Lake, becoming a major community employer. Today, two unique features of the village are its community-owned businesses: Green Lake Métis

Wood Products Ltd., and Green Lake Métis Farms Ltd. Tourism is also an important, albeit seasonal, industry in the area, as the region is popular for hunting and fishing. Four outfitters work out of the community. There is also an expanding cottage development at Green Lake. Green Lake has a small core of businesses, an RCMP detachment, and a volunteer fire brigade. People travel to Meadow Lake for many services and to shop for larger purchases. The village school, St. Pascal, is a K-9 facility, which had 80 students enrolled in the fall of 2006. Until recently the school ran classes through to grade 12, but now high school students are bused to Meadow Lake. Green Lake's recreational facilities include a hockey arena, a community hall, and a curling complex. The village faces several challenges as it moves forward into the twenty-first century: The population has been slowly falling (thus, the downsizing of the school), and unemployment currently hovers at around 20 per cent. As well, the median family income in Green Lake is substantially lower than in the province as a whole. Green Lake was incorporated as a northern village in 1983.

GREENSPOT, organized hamlet, is a cabin subdivision located in the Qu'Appelle Valley on Crooked Lake. There are close to two dozen permanent residents; however, the number varies greatly depending on the season. Situated within the RM of Grayson No. 184, Greenspot was established as an organized hamlet in May 2005.

◄ **GREEN LAKE**, 1950.
Saskatchewan Archives Board
R-A11626(1).

GREIG LAKE, resort village, is a major, somewhat upscale, cottage development situated within Meadow Lake Provincial Park north of Dorintosh. Long established as a cottage community, Greig Lake was incorporated as a resort village in 1983. There is a popular campground at Greig Lake with over 150 campsites. Area services operate on a seasonal basis. The resort village itself has a small number of permanent residents; however, the population varies greatly depending on the season. Greig Lake is situated in the RM of Meadow Lake No. 588.

GRENFELL, town, pop 947 (2006c), 1,067 (2001c), is located roughly halfway between Regina and the Saskatchewan-Manitoba border at the junction of Hwys 1 and 47. The town of Wolseley lies to the west, Broadview to the east, and the Qu'Appelle Valley is about a 15-minute drive north. A service centre for the surrounding farming community, Grenfell had its beginnings in 1882 as the first settlers began arriving in advance of the railway. By the following spring, numerous shacks and tents dotted the townsite. The first settlers were mainly from the British Isles and eastern Canada; later, people of German origin would settle the Grenfell area. The Grenfell Post Office was established in 1883 — the name honouring Pasco du Pre Grenfell, a railway company official. Grenfell was incorporated as a village in 1894 and reached town status in 1911. Grenfell has a wide range of businesses, a significant number of which service the district's agricultural industry. The surrounding trading area has a population of approximately 6,000. Grenfell has a health centre, an ambulance service,

THE GRENFELL BRASS BAND is thought to be the second band organized in the North-West Territories. Back row left to right: Warren Hood, E. Thomlinson, Fred Griffin, R.B. Bennett, J. Dixon, and J.W. Jones. Front row left to right: W. Hodges, G. Faulkner, W. Faulkner, W. Thomlinson, A. Walters, R.B. Taylor, and Fred Chisholm. Photograph circa late 1800s/early 1900s.

▼ DESMOND STREET, CIRCA 1900.

Photographs courtesy of the Grenfell Museum.

A "main line" town...
GRENFELL

and a special care home. The community provides transportation for seniors and persons with disabilities. Grenfell's elementary and high schools had a total of 256 town and area students enrolled in the fall of 2006. The town has a good array of recreational facilities, many of which are situated at Grenfell Regional Park, adjacent to the town. Grenfell has several churches, a library, and a number of service clubs, sports teams, and other community-based organizations. The Grenfell Museum is located in a large and magnificent Queen Anne revival-style house, making it one of the best accommodated museums on the Trans-Canada Highway. Grenfell was the birthplace of William J. Patterson, premier of Saskatchewan from 1935 to 1944, and lieutenant governor of the province from 1951 to 1958. Grenfell is situated in the RM of Elcapo No. 154.

▶ LEAVING FOR THE FRONT: troops leaving Grenfell Station in 1915.

◀ THE "MADE-IN-CANADA EXHIBITION TRAIN," which was sponsored by the Manufacturers' Association of Canada, in Grenfell in 1912. The train went from Toronto to the west coast of Canada. There would be advertisements well ahead of the station stops, and there was all the hoopla of a circus coming to town. The train would pull into a siding, and a special feature was the showing of motion pictures on a sheet hung on the side of the boxcar.

▲ **DR. CHARLES WRIGHT** (seated behind the horse) was Grenfell's first veterinarian. Another of Grenfell's veterinarians was Dr. Ballard, who in the 1920s was canning a homemade dog food that became the basis of nationally produced product. "Dr. Ballard's" became a household name.

▲ **THE GRENFELL MINERAL WATER FACTORY** (foreground) and a view of Grenfell looking east, circa 1900. In 1896, the company advertised, "New Season, New Drinks: Champagne Cider, Lemon Sour, Ginger Beer, Lemonade, Ginger Ale, Sarsaparilla, etc."

▼ **DOG SLED RACES** in Grenfell, February 16, 1935.

▲▼ **SASKATCHEWAN WHEAT POOL "A"** coming down, Grenfell, Saskatchewan, n.d.

GRIFFIN, hamlet, pop 70 (2001c), 72 (1996c), is located 32 km east of Weyburn on Hwy 13. Settlement of the district began in 1905, and within a year both a post office and a school were established in the area. The townsite was surveyed by the CPR in 1907, and by 1908, as the first trains rolled through, the first businesses including a hotel and the first grain elevator were in operation. In 1909, Griffin attained village status. The Grand Trunk Pacific Railway built a line through the community in 1911-12, and the village then found itself at the junction of two competing railroads. The population grew until the beginning of the 1930s, at which point it was nearing 200. The Depression, though, would prove hard on the small community, as would the outward migration of young men to serve in WWII. The population had fallen to 106 by 1946, and Griffin would not afterward recover either its previous population or the level of commercial and social activity enjoyed in earlier times. In 1956, the village was dissolved, its affairs thereafter managed by the rural municipality. In 1981, Griffin was established as an organized hamlet, somewhat increasing the community's political voice — this status, however, was relinquished in 2006. Griffin School was down to 21 students in the fall of 2005; it closed at the end of the school year in 2006. The RM of Griffin No. 66 is administered from an office in the community. Agriculture is the main industry in the area.

GRONLID, organized hamlet, pop 60 (2006c), 70 (2001c), is located approximately 32 km north of Melfort at the junction of Hwys 6 and 335. The Saskatchewan River passes about 18 km to the north, and the Carrot River passes about 6 km to the south. Settlement of the district began in the early 1900s, particularly after the Canadian Northern Railway reached Star City and Melfort in 1904-05. Settlers of Slavic origins — Ukrainians and Poles — predominated in the Gronlid area; however, there were also large concentrations of people of Scandinavian origin — Norwegians and Swedes — as well as settlers of British stock taking up land in the region. Additionally, one of the province's few Jewish settlements was established southeast of Gronlid in 1906: today, the Beth Israel Synagogue, built in 1908, still stands (it was closed in 1964). As the area was increasingly settled, schools, churches, post offices, and stores were established to serve the needs of the people. The hamlet of Gronlid — named after Pastor H. O. Gronlid, who established the Beaver Creek Lutheran congregation in the district in 1912 — began to develop in advance of the railroad being built north from Melfort in 1927. The first grain elevators were erected, and in 1928 a number of new businesses were established in the hamlet, including the post office. In 1930, a two-room school was built in the community, as was an outdoor skating rink. Gronlid grew through the 1930s, and in 1940 a power plant was installed and the hamlet had its first electric lights. By 1966, the population of Gronlid had grown to 210 and the community could have sought village status. By 1972, however, the population had fallen to 138. With centres such as Melfort, Nipawin, and Tisdale within easy driving distance, Gronlid's businesses and services dwindled. Today, a small core of businesses remains, as does Gronlid Central School, a K-12 facility, which had 82 community and area students enrolled in the fall of 2006. Gronlid is situated in the RM of Willow Creek No. 458; the production of grain and specialty crops forms the basis of the area economy.

◀ **THIS ELEVATOR IN GRONLID** was built by the Searle Grain Company as the CPR was building its line north from Melfort. It was later purchased by the Federal Grain Company, and in 1972 it became a Saskatchewan Wheat Pool elevator after Pool purchased Federal's assets. Photograph taken August 24, 2004.

GUERNSEY, organized hamlet, pop 88 (2006c), 108 (2001c), is a former village located 11 km west of Lanigan on Hwy 16. The community is named after the island of Guernsey in the English Channel, and its streets are named after locations on the island, among them D'Icart, St. Peter, St. Martin, and Hanois. Homesteaders began arriving in the Guernsey district in 1905, mainly disembarking the train at Humboldt some 25 miles (40 kilometres) to the north, then the nearest railway point. The settlers were of various origins; Mennonites from Ontario settled in a bloc centred just south of present-day Guernsey in 1905. In 1906, as work began on building a railway through the region, the first building — a store — was erected on the townsite. Other businesses and residences followed in rapid succession. The Guernsey Post Office was established on November 1, 1907, and Harold Alexander Spence served as the postmaster from the office's inception until his death in 1956. In 1908, the CPR completed the rail line between Saskatoon and Lanigan, elevators were being erected (there would eventually be four), and the busy hamlet that had sprung up on the Guernsey townsite was incorporated as a village on July 8 that year. A school district centred on the village was established in 1909, relieving village children of a trip of more than two miles to a school in the country. By 1911, the population of Guernsey had grown to

173. By 1961, the village's numbers had dwindled to 79, but the development of a potash mine immediately south of Guernsey in the mid-1960s was to have a profound effect on the community's numbers for several years (the mine began production in 1968). By 1976, the village numbered 222 residents, and with the expansion of the mine in the 1970s the population of Guernsey remained close to 200 until the 1980s. Thereafter, the village's numbers began, once again, to fall rapidly. The school closed in 1997, and Guernsey relinquished village status on December 31, 2005. Today, only a couple of small businesses remain in the community; Guernsey is primarily residential. Most shop and seek services in the area's larger centres. Guernsey is situated in the RM of Usborne No. 310.

GULL LAKE, town, pop 965 (2006c), 1,016 (2001c), is located 56 km southwest of Swift Current at the junction of Hwys 1 and 37. It is believed the community's name is derived from explorer and naturalist John Macoun's translation of an Indian name for a small nearby lake — perhaps now dried up — which was frequented by gulls. It is believed that surveyors for the railway adopted Macoun's name for the area in 1883. The townsite of Gull Lake is situated on what was once part of the 76 Ranch, established in 1887. The 76 Ranch house, built in 1888, is still standing in Gull Lake and is currently used as the office for the Gull Lake School Division. It is one of south-western Saskatchewan's oldest existing buildings. The 10,000-acre 76 Ranch at Gull Lake was one of several massive ranches es-

tablished by Sir John Lister-Kaye's Canadian Agricultural, Coal and Colonization Company. By the early twentieth century, however, the company was suffering financial losses. Land was becoming more profitable for grain farming, and in 1905 the Gull Lake block was sold to American millionaire developers, Conrad and Price. They surveyed the townsite and put the lots up for sale. Interestingly, since the townsite was not determined by the railroad as others along the main line were, Gull Lake's layout is markedly different from other communities. Settlers began to pour in, and between 1906 and 1912 Gull Lake was booming. It was a company town, however, under the authority of Conrad and Price. It was up to individuals to bring about improvements or developments in the community. Toward the end of 1908 it was determined that a municipal authority and administration was necessary to manage the community's affairs. A petition was sent to the provincial government and, on January 12, 1909, Gull Lake was incorporated as a village. By 1911, the population was over 600, and the community attained town status on November 1 that year. In 1912, Gull Lake had a well-established school, many businesses and services, a doctor, a hospital, and a newspaper, *The Gull Lake Advance*. Established in 1909, the paper is still in business. In 1914, the first automobiles began to appear on Gull Lake's streets. After the initial rush of settlers and the building boom, development levelled off. In the early 1950s, the population was somewhat over 700. With the discovery of oil and gas in the region during the decade, however, Gull Lake's population jumped to over 1,000, and it has remained relatively stable since. Today, farming and ranching, and oil and gas form the basis of the economy, and many

of Gull Lake's businesses cater to these industries. Two massive grain handling facilities, one farmer-owned, the other a Saskatchewan Wheat Pool operation, are situated just to the east and the west of the community respectively; numerous oil pumpjacks, gas wells, and battery sites dot the landscape. Wind power is another energy resource that is being developed in the Gull Lake area: today, numerous graceful and high-tech wind turbines span the horizon around the town. In addition to the businesses mentioned above, Gull Lake's commercial sector provides town and area residents with a variety of goods and services. Further, the town serves the area with a health centre, a special care home, ambulance service, an RCMP detachment, and a volunteer fire department. Gull Lake has a range of facilities for sports and recreation. The town has a library, four churches, and a number of service clubs and community-based organizations. Gull Lake School is a K-12 facility which had 260 town and area students enrolled in the fall of 2006. Gull Lake serves as the administrative centre of the RM of Gull Lake No. 139.

HAFFORD, town, pop 360 (2006c), 401 (2001c), is located 65 km east of North Battleford, at the junction of Hwys 40 and 340. The town, situated in beautiful rolling countryside on the southern edge of the aspen parklands, is a service centre for a predominantly agricultural district. In the early 1900s, the region was populated by one of the largest block settlements of Ukrainians in Saskatchewan. As the railway was constructed through the area in 1912-13 the townsite developed, and Hafford was incorporated as a village in December of the latter year. The community grew rapidly, and although much of the business district was destroyed by fire in 1950, the village rebuilt and had a population of nearly 600 by the late 1960s. On January 1, 1981, Hafford became a town. Hafford today has a wide array of businesses and services including a hospital and special care centre, an RCMP detachment, and Hafford Central School, which provides K-12 education to approximately 150 students. The community also has modern facilities to accommodate recreational pursuits and cultural events. While most of Hafford's residents are employed in agriculture, small business, health, administration, and education, a small number commute to work in Saskatoon. Hafford's rich Ukrainian heritage is still very much in evidence: the town's street signs are in both Ukrainian and English, and a number of the community's annual events have Ukrainian themes. Hafford area attractions include Redberry Lake Regional Park and National Migratory Bird Sanctuary, which are a part of an international biosphere reserve designated by the United Nations in 2000. Also, located northwest of the town are the famous Crooked Trees, a strange and unusual grove of gnarled and twisted aspens whose appearance remains a mystery to science. Hafford is the administrative centre of the RM of Redberry No. 435.

HAGEN, organized hamlet, pop 39 (2006c), 41 (2001c), is located about 12 km southwest of the town of Birch Hills on Hwy 25. The first settlers came to the area at the beginning of the twentieth century, although the neighbouring Fenton and Birch Hills districts were settled years earlier. Before the railway arrived at Birch Hills in 1906, the nearest trading centre was Prince Albert. Many of those who came to the district were Norwegians from the United States; among the first was Andrew C. Hagen from Minnesota, who came to the area in the fall of 1902. When the CPR was building through the district in 1929 the station and the emerging hamlet were named in his honour. The first store was built in 1929 and the Saskatchewan Wheat Pool built a grain elevator as soon as sites were available. The rail line opened in 1930, and the Hagen Post Office was established on January 20, 1931. The Hagen Co-op was organized in 1938. The Church of the Nazarene was built on the south edge of Hagen in the late 1940s. It was later moved to St. Louis, Saskatchewan. The Bethel Lutheran Brethren Church was erected in 1951. In 1947, United Grain Growers took apart their elevator in Fenton and rebuilt it in Hagen (it closed in 1969). A two-sheet curling rink was built in 1949 and was well-used until a larger facility was built in Birch Hills and the Hagen rink was closed. The hamlet also had an open-air skating rink and sports grounds. In 1959, children in grades 11 and 12 began to be bused to Birch Hills to attend school; by 1967 grades 7 through 12 were transported to Birch Hills, and in 1969 the local school was closed. The population of the hamlet at this time was around 50. In 1978, Hagen was established as an organized hamlet. In the mid-1990s, the rail line through Hagen was abandoned, and the tracks have long since been removed. Today, other than the post office, the only business is a farm supply centre operated by Agricore United. Hagen is situated in the RM of Birch Hills No. 460.

▼ **THE FORMER SASKATCHEWAN WHEAT POOL ELEVATOR** in Hagen, built 1930. Photograph taken August 24, 2004.

HAGUE, town, pop 707 (2006c), 711 (2001c), is located approximately 45 km northeast of Saskatoon and 95 km southwest of Prince Albert on Hwy 11. The Hague Ferry crosses the South Saskatchewan River 12 km due east of the town. Hague is situated on the rail line which was completed by the Qu'Appelle, Long Lake & Saskatchewan Railway in 1890, linking Regina, Saskatoon, and Prince Albert; the community derives its name from a railway engineer who worked on the line. In the mid-1890s, large numbers of Mennonite settlers began arriving in the Hague district — the beginning of a massive bloc settlement of Mennonites in the region. The Hague post office was established in 1896, and by 1903 the small agricultural community had grown large enough to gain village status. The Ukrainian and Polish people who had settled to the east frequented the community's

business establishments. In 1905-06, a future prime minister of Canada, John Diefenbaker, attended school in Hague, as his father had been employed to teach at the village's one-room school. The population of the community at the time was approaching 300, and its numbers remained roughly around this level until after WWII, at which time the community experienced another period of growth, reaching over 400 by the mid-1960s. In the mid-1970s, a housing boom was spurred by people who worked in Saskatoon but wanted to live in a smaller community. Hague attained town status in 1991 with a population of 655. Additional residential subdivisions were completed in 1997 and 2003. While residents benefit from easy access to the employment opportunities, services, and amenities that Saskatoon has to offer, the town maintains a varied business community and the area economy is still agriculturally based. There is a significant dairy indus-

▲ **HAGUE STATION** area, circa 1910.

try in the district, as well as a number of producers of hogs and poultry. Businesses in Hague include an automotive dealership and auto services, grocery and hardware stores, restaurants, a lumberyard, a cabinet making shop, a tool and die manufacturer, and service stations. The town has elementary and high schools which provide K-12 education to close to 350 town and area students. Hague has a volunteer fire department and a team of first responders. Policing is provided by the Rosthern RCMP detachment. Hague operates a transit service for seniors and people with special needs, and, as well, new seniors' condominiums were built in 2003, complementing the existing seniors' housing. Recreational facilities in Hague include a sports complex with rinks

for hockey, skating, and curling. The community has lighted ball diamonds, tennis courts, and football and soccer fields. Annual summer events include community sports days, and a car show hosted by a local club each June. Each September, the Hague Thresherman's Club features events which recall the area's pioneer activities. A major attraction in the community is the Saskatchewan River Valley Museum: located on a three-acre site, the museum houses over 3,000 artifacts and includes a number of heritage buildings, among them an extremely rare Mennonite house-barn dating to 1908. Hague is situated in the RM of Rosthern No. 403.

◄ **HAGUE'S GRAIN ELEVATOR AND ONE OF THE FEW EXISTING RAILWAY WATER TOWERS REMAINING IN SASKATCHEWAN.** The tower holds about 40,000 gallons (about 180,000 litres), and was filled by a pump located at an old spring-fed well east of Hague. It is 54 feet high (about 16.5 metres) and consists of two separate structures. The 40,000-gallon inner tub is made of 3-inch-thick cedar and is supported by 16-foot square beams, 22 feet in the air. The height provided the gravity pressure needed to fill the steam locomotives. An outer shell, not attached to the tub, served as an insulating cover for the water. A stove was lit in the bottom of the building during cold months, warming space between the inner tub and the outer shell, preventing the water from freezing. Photograph, looking north, taken August 26, 2004.

▲ **HAGUE POOL HALL, BARBER SHOP, AND BOWLING ALLEY, 1912.**
The building was located on 2nd Street, and G. Mahnke was the proprietor. In the photograph Philip Penner is throwing what appears may be a strike; Henry Friesen, barely visible, is the pin setter. The men playing pool are unknown. Bachelors' living quarters were in the rear.

▼ **DR. BENJAMIN RALPH, A TRAVELLING RAWLEIGH PRODUCTS**
DEALER (right), shaking hands with Frank Duchain at a home in the Hague area circa 1917. Ralph, with his one-horse cab and stock, travelled from farm to farm throughout the Hague district selling liniments, salves, ointments, oils, pills, plasters, snake oil, wonder oil, "eclectric" oil, and toilette articles.

HALBRITE, village, pop 98 (2006c), 109 (2001c), is located 29 km southeast of Weyburn on Hwy 39. Halbrite is situated on the Soo Line, and it was this rail connection that allowed land seekers from the United States direct access to the area. A significant percentage of those who first settled in the Halbrite district came from the states of Minnesota and Iowa, and many were of Norwegian and Swedish origin. Others would come from eastern Canada and other areas of Europe. The first settlers began arriving at the townsite in 1902, and the community developed rapidly. The post office and school district were established in 1903, and in 1904 the Village of Halbrite was incorporated. By 1906, the community numbered close to 300 persons and boasted every type of business and profession. The years leading up to the 1930s were to be Halbrite's most bustling; never again would the community have the population nor the variety of commercial activity. Not only did the drought and Depression take their toll on Halbrite (the population had fallen to 105 by 1941), but a fire in the village in 1934 destroyed a large number of buildings which were never replaced. In the early 1950s, the discovery of oil in the area led to a temporary resurgence of activity and a short-term boost to the community's population. Although Halbrite's numbers have subsequently dwindled, revenue from the oil industry provides the major source of income for the village today. Two oil trucking companies are based in Halbrite and pumpjacks dot the area landscape. Agriculture, as well, remains important to the economy. In recent decades, however, the majority of Halbrite's businesses and services have been superseded by those in the city of Weyburn.

Features of Halbrite include St. Andrew's United Church, which was built around 1908 for the area's Presbyterian congregation. The building, which has trefoil gothic windows, an asymmetrical bell tower, and a "witch's-cap" steeple, has been designated a heritage property and today houses a craft store and country market that is open each summer. Approximately 18 kilometres south of Halbrite lies Mainprize Regional Park, named in honour of Midale's Dr. William Mainprize, who served the district (including Halbrite) for close to 50 years. The park has facilities for camping and golf, and offers excellent opportunities for fishing. Halbrite celebrated its centennial in 2004 and is situated in the RM of Cymri No. 36.

HANDEL, hamlet, pop 25 (2006c), 25 (2001c) is situated in a sparsely-populated district, 50 km west of Biggar, east of Tramping Lake. The community is named after George Frederick Handel (1685-1759), one of the great composers of the late baroque period. Streets in the hamlet are named Mozart, Wagner, and Schuman [*sic*]. The first settlers arrived in the district in 1905-06, and by 1910 most of the available homesteads had been taken up. The majority of those who came to the district were German Catholics. The parish of Our Lady of the Assumption was organized in 1906; by 1908, an area store, post office, and school had been established. In 1911, the CPR began construction of a branch line through the area and the locations of townsites along the line were determined. The line was in operation in 1912, and Handel sprang up quickly. The first businesses were started that year and the first grain elevator was erected. The Handel Post Office was established on May 1, 1913; Handel was incorporated as a village on August 16, 1913. That fall, construction of a Catholic Church began. A school was built in Handel in 1915, and a Methodist (later United) church was completed in 1919. By the mid-1920s, four grain elevators lined the tracks in the village; by 1931 the community reached a peak population of 135. During the 1930s, however, the population dwindled and a number of businesses closed. The bank closed in 1938 after almost twenty years of service. The village, although it rebounded somewhat in the following decades, never quite regained its former vitality. The population of both Handel and the surrounding rural area began to decline sharply beginning in the 1960s. Between 1961 and 1981 the community's numbers fell from 100 to 53. The United Church closed in 1966 as did the CPR station. There were, though, positive developments during these years. A new Roman Catholic Church was built in the mid-1960s, and a burgeoning student population due to the closure of rural schools led to an expansion of Handel's school — in 1966, the school population reached a peak enrollment of 187. In the late 1970s a new community complex with a new curling rink was built. The village suffered a major blow in the 1980s, however: the rail line was abandoned in 1983 and Handel's grain elevators were closed. About a year later the tracks were removed; in April of 1986 all four of the elevators were demolished. By 1991, Handel was down to 38 residents. The school managed to continue to operate until the early 1990s — it is now boarded up. Handel relinquished village status on January 31, 2007, and today sidewalks run along vacant lots, and a few long-closed businesses dot the townsite. The Handel Hotel remains, housing a bar, a postal outlet, and an insurance agency. Notable Sas-

katchewan politician Otto Lang was born in Handel in 1932. Handel is situated in the RM of Grandview No. 349.

HANLEY, town, pop 464 (2006c), 495 (2001c), is located 56 km southeast of Saskatoon on Hwy 11. In 1889-90, the Qu'Appelle, Long Lake & Saskatchewan Railway came through en route to Saskatoon from Regina, but it was more than a decade before Hanley had its beginnings. The first settlers in the district arrived in 1901, and in 1902 the first buildings began to appear on the townsite. One of the first business operations in Hanley was that of the Saskatchewan Valley Land Company, and as settlers began to pour into the district further enterprises arose to fulfill their needs. The Hanley Post Office

was established in 1903, and by 1904 the young community could boast of having a doctor, a dentist, a bank, a grain elevator, a hotel, and a butcher shop among numerous other businesses. In 1905, Hanley was incorporated as a village, and in 1906 the community attained town status. Although settlers arriving in the district were of diverse backgrounds (there were people from eastern Canada, the British Isles, and the mid-western United States), two large bloc settlements of people took up land in the Hanley area: Norwegians in 1903, and Mennonites in 1924. While many young Saskatchewan communities suffered devastating fires, Hanley seems to have weathered more than its share. Significant blazes occurred in 1912, 1929, 1935, and 1947, each with a number of properties lost. The conflagration of 1947

left a gaping hole in the community, and the cumulative result of the fires is that little of Hanley's original architecture survives. One community landmark that did survive the flames could not survive the wrecking ball. For decades, the Hanley Opera House, completed in 1914, served as a centre of cultural activity for a wide area reaching from Outlook to Watrous; but by 1982 it was dilapidated beyond repair, unsafe, and was therefore demolished. Today, Hanley has a core of essential businesses and services which includes restaurants, a grocery store, a hotel and bar, a bank, a post office, service stations, a hardware store, and a hairdresser. The town has an RCMP detachment, and a volunteer fire department. Hanley has a library, churches, a pre-school and, as well, Hanley Composite School, a K-12 facility

▼ **SASKATCHEWAN WHEAT POOL OPERATIONS** at Hanley, 1973. No grain elevators remain in the town today.
Photograph courtesy of Leona King, Montreal, Quebec (formerly of Hanley).

which had 243 town and area students enrolled in the fall of 2006. Recreational facilities include an arena for skating and hockey, curling rinks, ball diamonds, a seniors' centre, a nine-hole golf course, and facilities for camping. Additionally, Blackstrap Provincial Park and the Blackstrap Ski Hill are located a short distance north of the community. Slightly more than 25 per cent of Hanley's population is over the age of 65, and a small percentage of residents commute to work in Saskatoon. Agriculture, the production of both crops and livestock, continues to be the basis of the area economy. Hanley serves as the administrative centre of the RM of Rosedale No. 283.

HARRIS, village, pop 187 (2006c), 232 (2001c), lies approximately 70 km southwest of Saskatoon on Hwy 7, between the village of Tessier and the town of Zealandia. The name of the community honours Richard Elford Harris (1847-1919), who homesteaded two miles north of the present community in 1904. The Harris family home became a popular stopping place for travellers to rest overnight, have a hot meal, and shelter their animals. In 1906 the Harris Post Office was established, and Richard Harris served as the postmaster. A small hamlet developed at the site, which included a store and a Methodist Church. When the railway was being built from Saskatoon toward Rosetown in 1908, it passed to the south, and it was decided to move the post office, the church, and the store to the townsite then established on the rail line. This was done in early 1909, and the name of the post office was adopted as that for the newly-developing community. The Village of Harris was incorporated on August 10, 1909. In the summer of 1914, what was known as

COMMERCIAL HOTEL, HARRIS, SASK.

▲ **THE COMMERCIAL HOTEL IN HARRIS:** built 1909, destroyed by fire in 1924. It is thought that the proprietors of the hotel, the Gordon Brothers, may have been behind the Great Ruby Rush hoax, and cashed in on the two weeks of hysteria.

▶ **HARRIS JUNIOR HOCKEY CLUB**, 1912-13.

▼ **VE DAY PARADE IN HARRIS, 1945.**

Photographs courtesy of the Harris and District Museum.

the Great Ruby Rush was on: twenty miles northwest of Harris a road construction crew found some red stones in a rock near the road. The Saskatoon newspaper reported the find and for a period of about two weeks as many as 3,000 people were involved at the site, staking out claims, digging up stones, or profiteering in any way possible. Tents went up housing saloons and restaurants (one egg cost one dollar), and the hotel in Harris did a brisk

business. The owner of one of the three automobiles in Harris charged two dollars for a ride out to the claim site, five dollars for a ride back. The ruby rush was soon discovered to be a hoax, however, as the "rubies" were determined to be garnets of little value. In recent times the village has commemorated the event with the annual celebration of Ruby Rush Days in the summer. In quieter times, Harris has served the surrounding agricultural district as a trading centre. Today, five community landmarks dating back to Harris's earlier years have been designated municipal heritage properties: St. Brigitte Roman Catholic Church (built in 1909 and closed in 1996); the Royal Bank building (now a credit union), built in 1922; Harris United Church, completed in 1924; the Rural Municipality of Harris No. 316 office, constructed in 1927; and the octagonal CNR water tower built in 1934, one of fewer than ten such water towers remaining in the province. Violet McNaughton, an active agrarian feminist who was a leader of the Saskatchewan women's suffrage movement and the organizer of the Women Grain Growers in Saskatchewan, homesteaded in the Harris area in 1909. The village had a peak population of 305 in 1961. Harris serves as the administrative centre of the RM of Harris No. 316.

HAWARDEN, village, pop 75 (2006c), 57 (2001c), is located southeast of Outlook on Hwy 19. Settlers began arriving in the area about 1904: they were mainly people from eastern Canada (Ontario, Quebec, and New Brunswick); English and Scottish arrivals from Great Britain; and people of Norwegian origin from the central United States. With construction of the CPR rail line from Moose Jaw to Outlook, the village of Hawarden had its beginnings; the track was built through the Hawarden area in 1908, and by 1909 the length of the line was completed. That year, the Hawarden Post Office was established, a school district centred on the village was set up, the Canadian Bank of Commerce opened a branch, and on July 16 the community was incorporated. It was named after Hawarden Castle in Flintshire, Wales, the stately country residence of William Ewart Gladstone (1809-98), Queen Victoria's four-time prime minister. The main street of Hawarden, Saskatchewan, is named Gladstone; the two on either side are named William and Ewart. Other streets are named Ches-

ter, after an English city just across the border from Flintshire; and Dee, after a prominent river that forms part of the border between Wales and England, and which runs through Chester. By 1911, Hawarden, Saskatchewan, was fairly well established — the population was at 126 — but two weeks before Christmas that year, fire wiped out a half-dozen businesses. Still the community grew: a local light plant was providing some electricity by 1915; by 1926 the village numbered 262 residents and it looked as though it would reach 300. It is interesting to note that Edward L. Diefenbaker, youngest paternal uncle of Prime Minister John Diefenbaker, was the principal at Hawarden School from 1922-23. The 1930s were devastating years for the community as the population plunged by almost 100 over the decade. The village rebounded somewhat during the post-war period, and for several years through the early to mid-1960s while the dam-building and other work on the South Saskatchewan River Project was underway, Hawarden's population mushroomed as workers and their families

thronged to the area. Afterwards, however, there began a steady decline: from 267 residents in 1966, the village was down to 133 a decade later. By the end of the 1970s the school was down to being a K-9 facility: students in grades 10-12 were being bused 33 kilometres northeast to Kenaston. By the early 1990s, only grades K-6 were taught at Hawarden School, and in 1993 the school was closed. Most area students today attend school in Kenaston; some, though, travel south to the village of Loreburn. As though the loss of population and business and the down-sizing of the school were not enough to endure, a tornado ripped through the village on July 5, 1988 — it uprooted trees, knocked boxcars off the railway tracks, and caused extensive property damage throughout the village and area. With the demolition of the Pioneer grain elevator and its annexes in 1996, all that was left where six elevators once stood was the Pool elevator. But it only had a few years left and is gone now too. District farmers now haul their grain to the Gardiner Dam Terminal (south between the villages of Strongfield

and Loreburn); it is a 17,000-tonne high-throughput grain elevator jointly owned by area producers and Agricore United. Businesses remaining in Hawarden today, scattered amongst a number of abandoned buildings and vacant lots, include Perry Industries, a manufacturing company that produces products for the agriculture and construction industries; a trucking company that hauls grain; the Hawarden Hotel and coffee shop; and the post office. There are a small number of tradespeople with home-based businesses. The last place to buy groceries and other essentials closed in the early 1990s. Hawarden has a community hall (which was a Presbyterian church until 1927), a Mason's lodge (situated in a 1907 country schoolhouse), and a skating rink (in poor condition, but still flooded each winter). A few kilometres west of Hawarden a family runs a bed and breakfast in their 1913 farmhouse. The last regular services were held in Christ Anglican Mission Church in Hawarden in 1979, and the 1926 building was designated a heritage property in 1985. Hawarden United Church began to rely on

▶ **THE FORMER CANADIAN IMPERIAL BANK OF COMMERCE**, Hawarden, July 19, 2004. The Canadian Bank of Commerce opened a branch in the village in 1909, but a fire on December 12, 1911, destroyed almost all of the north side of Gladstone Street, including the bank. Money and documents were deposited in the lumberyard safe, and banking business resumed from a temporary office. In 1922, this structure was built and it was operated as the Canadian Bank of Commerce until June 1, 1961, when it merged with the Imperial Bank of Canada to form the Canadian Imperial Bank of Commerce. In 1986, the bank in Hawarden reduced its business hours to two days a week; in the early 1990s, the branch was closed. The building was designated a heritage property in 1987.

THE HAZEL DELL GENERAL STORE AND THE HAZEL DELL GOSPEL CHAPEL. Photograph taken July 29, 2004.

members of the lay ministry in 1997, and it closed its doors a few years later. Bethlehem Lutheran Church, approximately 11 kilometres north of Hawarden, remains active: the congregation was organized in 1909, and the extant church building was erected in 1914. Hawarden is situated in the RM of Loreburn No. 254.

HAZEL DELL, organized hamlet, pop 20 (2006c), 30 (2001c), is located approximately 24 km west of Preeceville, off Hwy 49. Settlers began arriving in the early 1900s, and after 1905 were aided by the fact that the Canadian Northern Railway was by then running roughly 15 kilometres to the south. Access to the Hazel Dell area was further improved after the railway reached Preeceville in 1912; however, further construction of the line was delayed because of WWI, and it was not until 1921 that trains were running through Hazel Dell. People of British stock from overseas, Ontario, and Manitoba came to the region, as did Ukrainians, Swedes and Poles; after about 1908 many Norwegians, a number of whom arrived via the United States, also settled in the district — Hazel Dell is named after a community in Minnesota. The 1930s brought more people to the area from the regions of southern Saskatchewan parched by the drought. In 1959, Hazel Dell was established as an organized hamlet, and by the mid-1960s the population was approaching 200. By the end of the decade, however, the number had fallen by about half. Today, the community's business sector has been reduced to the post office and a small general store; cracked sidewalks run along vacant lots. The district economy is primarily based on agriculture, a mixture of grain and cattle production. Hazel Dell is situated in the RM of Hazel Dell No. 335.

HAZENMORE, village, pop 57 (2006c), 71 (2001c), is located in south-western Saskatchewan, 27 km east of Ponteix, between the villages of Kincaid and Aneroid on Hwy 13. Settlers began taking up land in the Hazenmore district in 1908-09. The nearest rail line at the time was the CPR main line, and many pioneers came south from Morse or Herbert, or travelled southeast from Swift Current. These centres, in addition to being points of disembarkation, were the main centres for Hazenmore area pioneers to procure supplies until the railroad was built to Vanguard in 1912. The next year, 1913, the CPR's Weyburn-Lethbridge branch was being built across south-western Saskatchewan, and Hazenmore was put on the map. The village was incorporated on August 20 that year. The post office was established on November 1, 1913. Hazenmore was named after Sir John Douglas Hazen (1860-1937), the premier of New Brunswick from 1908-11, and the federal minister of Marine and Fisheries, as well as the Naval Service from 1911-17. Hazen left politics in 1917 to become the chief justice of New Brunswick. In the village of Hazenmore, during the years following the coming of the railway, the business community grew and prospered. Hazenmore School was built, and churches were established. By the early 1920s, six grain elevators were operating, and by 1926 the community reached its all-time peak population — 254. The drought and the Depression hit, and by 1936 the village's population had fallen to 156 and a number of businesses had closed. Hazenmore rebounded somewhat following the 1930s; an all-weather road was built through the region following WWII, and by the 1950s the population had climbed back to just under 200. By the early 1960s, however, it was clear the community was again in decline. The older grades at Hazenmore School began to be bused to the village of Kincaid, and in 1968 Hazenmore school was closed. Four years earlier, in 1964, the CPR station had closed, and then the trains only stopped to load grain at the village elevators. The station was sold and moved out of Hazenmore, and eventually the elevators, too, were gone. In 2000, the CPR sold four branch lines in the region to Westcan Rail Ltd., a railway salvage operation out of Abbotsford, B.C. However, local producers intervened, and the subdivisions were saved and operated under the name of the Great Western Railway. In November of 2004, the crop-dependent short lines were successfully purchased from Westcan by a large group of producers in the province's southwest. In the fall of 2005, after more than twenty years since a producer car was loaded at Hazenmore using the old wooden elevators, South West Terminal Ltd., who have headquarters near Gull Lake, opened a new producer car-loading facility at the village, and local grain was once again shipped from a local operation. The business also runs a retail warehouse for farm supplies. A few years earlier, another promising local development was the establishment of Red Coat Cattle Feeders' 10,000-head feedlot just southwest of Hazenmore. Other businesses in the community are a Co-op bulk fuel station and a Co-op grocery store with postal services. The village has a hotel, a community hall, and a seniors' centre. Hazenmore has an older population; the median age of its residents according to the 2006 Census was 57.5, while the median age of all Saskatchewan residents was 38.7. Two early church buildings in the village — St. James Anglican, built in 1915, and Hazenmore Community Church, built c. 1917-18 (originally a Methodist church, later United) — have both been designated municipal heritage properties. Hazenmore Community Church today houses the village's museum. Hazenmore is situated in the RM of Pinto Creek No. 75.

HAZLET, village, pop 85 (2006c), 126 (2001c), is located off the eastern edge of the Great Sand Hills, on Hwy 322. Swift Current, approximately 70 km to the southeast, is the nearest major centre. In the 1880s, an era of large ranching operations began in the region, but beginning around 1907 the first homesteaders began to arrive, fencing and breaking the land for crop cultivation. A post office, named Hazlet after an early settler, was established in 1911, and an area school adopted the name a few years later. The CPR reached Cabri, roughly 25 kilometres north, in 1912, and for a number of years, especially as motor vehicles were becoming available, many area residents travelled to that village for banking, supplies, the services of professionals such as lawyers, and for the daily train service. In 1928, things changed. The CPR began construction of the Pennant subdivision, and with the coming of the railway the lots of a surveyed townsite were put up for sale and the hamlet of Hazlet was born. A construction boom ensued, and five grain elevators were operating in time for the 1929 harvest. By 1930, close to three dozen businesses were established in the new community. Immediately, however, the drought and Depression hit, elevators closed, businesses folded, and never again would Hazlet see the level of activity it had in its formative years. A second boom, of sorts, began in 1952 when oil was discovered close to nearby Fosterton, and for the next few years Hazlet was home to a number of survey and drilling rig crews. On New Year's Day, 1963, the hamlet gained village status, and in 1966 the population stood at 219. In the 1970s, the population began to decline, and in the late 1990s CP abandoned the rail line into Hazlet. Today, agriculture still dominates the area economy, particularly durum wheat production; cattle are raised toward the Great Sand Hills. As well, significant oil and gas exploration is again taking place. The village has a small number of businesses and services, and recreational facilities which include curling and skating rinks, a ball park, and a golf course at the nearby regional park. Hazlet School provides K-

12 education, with 50 students enrolled in the fall of 2006. In May of 2005, Hazlet School launched its International Program, an English-immersion and farm-stay opportunity for students from non-English-speaking countries. In the spring of 2007, there were 14 students from 12 different countries enrolled at Hazlet School. Hazlet is the administrative centre of the RM of Pittville No. 169.

HENDON, organized hamlet, pop 10 (2006c), 25 (2001c), is located 16 km north of Wadena on Hwy 35. The hamlet came into being in 1924, a year after the CPR came through the district en route to Tisdale and Nipawin. The name of the community was suggested by Mrs. Herman Hyslop, who came to the area as a war bride from Hendon, England, a borough in Greater London. The Hendon, Saskatchewan, area first began to be settled around 1903, and it came to be comprised mainly of people of Swedish and Norwegian origins; settlers also came from Ontario, the British Isles and, later, central Europe. Hendon was never a very large community but it prospered for several decades serving the surrounding district. The population was 100 in 1969, and for many years an annual Lutefisk Supper was held in the community with great success — lutefisk being a traditional Scandinavian dish. The Scandia Lutheran Church, completed in 1915, still stands immediately east of Hendon and was designated a heritage property in 1985. It had been in use until 1970, at which time the congregation was facing either costly repairs and renovations, or amalgamation with another church. When the school in Hendon closed the same year, with children subsequently being bused to Wadena, church members purchased the

school building and renovated it for use as a new place of worship. Hendon is situated in the RM of Lakeview No. 337.

HEPBURN, village, pop 530 (2006c), 475 (2001c), is a steadily growing community situated in the Saskatchewan River Valley, approximately 50 km north of Saskatoon, 4 km west of Hwy 12. The North Saskatchewan River passes 12 km to the west. Mennonites began settling in the general region in the 1890s; around 1900, Mennonite Brethren with origins in southern Russia arrived via the United States and took up land in the district surrounding present-day Hepburn. Schmidtsburg School, a few miles north of where the village is now located, was established at the turn of the century, and churches were founded. Several years later, with the construction of the Canadian Northern Railway line into the

district from Dalmeny, the townsite was established with a variety of stores, grain elevators, a church, and a post office. In 1908 the first storekeeper went into business and two elevators were built (there were later four). The post office was established on March 20, 1909. The community derives its name from either the first postmaster, Rowat Hepburn (1909-10), or Gordon Hepburn, who donated the land upon which the village now sits. The history is unclear, and perhaps the community's name honours both men. The Mennonite Brethren built the first church in Hepburn in 1910. In 1912, the hamlet began to organize a school. Further businesses sprang up, the population of the community and the district grew, and Hepburn became an incorporated village on July 5, 1919. The population was 178 in 1921; 286 in 1941; 294 in 1961; 411 in 1981; and 485 in 2001. The Depression merely stalled the growth of the commu-

▲ **THIS FORMER SASKATCHEWAN WHEAT POOL ELEVATOR** in Hepburn dates to 1926. It now houses the Museum of Wheat. Photograph taken August 26, 2004.

nity: since the spread of bituminous and oil highways into the district area in the 1960s, Hepburn has developed considerably, in no small part due to its proximity to Saskatoon. The presence and success of Bethany College, an accredited, degree-granting Bible college, has also bolstered the village. Pioneered by the Mennonite Brethren in 1927, Bethany College has about 30 faculty and staff and attracts approximately 160 students during the fall and winter months. It has had the sponsorship of the Conference of Mennonite Brethren Churches in Alberta since 1968, and the sponsorship of the Saskatchewan Conference of Evangelical Mennonite Mission Churches since 1995. Despite the demolition of the railway station in 1982, the closure of Hepburn's grain elevators and the abandonment of the rail line from Dalmeny through Hepburn to Laird in the early 1990s, the village has benefited from a growing population and is likely to be seeking town status in the near future. The remaining elevator in Hepburn, built in the late 1920s by the Saskatchewan Wheat Pool, has been preserved and now houses the Museum of Wheat; here, one can learn how an elevator of the period worked and about the grain industry in Saskatchewan. The elevator has been designated a municipal heritage property, the first elevator declared as such in the province. Another of Hepburn's historic structures is the 1927 two-storey, four-room brick school still in use. Discreet wings have been built off the back of the school over the years to accommodate a burgeoning student population, but the 1927 building remains original. It is one of only a few remaining schools of its type in Saskatchewan still being used for its initial purpose. Hepburn has about a dozen businesses and services, a community arena, a community park, and a

bowling alley. The village has an annual fair in June; Bethany College hosts a dinner theatre each December. The public K-12 school has had a steadily increasing enrollment; 250 students were enrolled in the fall of 2006. The village has a volunteer fire department and a team of first responders. Hepburn is situated in the RM of Laird No. 404.

HERBERT, town, pop 742 (2006c), 812 (2001c), is located 45 km northeast of Swift Current on the Trans-Canada Hwy. The Herbert area began to be settled in the early 1900s, predominantly by Mennonites, but also by people of British and Scandinavian origins among others. Originally, their point of disembarkation was at a box car railway station with the name 'Herbert' posted on it — the name honouring Sir Michael Henry Herbert, a British diplomat. In 1904, the foundations of the village were established. Within

▲ **HERBERT STATION**, date unknown. Photograph courtesy of the Ralph Allen Memorial Museum, Oxbow, Saskatchewan.

months, a boarding house, livery stable, hardware and grocery store, lumberyard, implement dealer, and post office were in business. A school was being built, and one could buy seed grain, coal, bricks, and feed in the young community. The district was quickly settled, and in 1907 Herbert was incorporated as a village. By 1911, the population had grown to 559; by 1912, the community had grown sufficiently to attain town status. From 1916 to 1926, Ford Model Ts were assembled at a garage

▲ **MENNONITE LAND SEEKERS FROM MANITOBA** who arrived in Herbert in September, 1903. The CPR granted them a reduced fair of one cent per mile to come to the area, since the railway wanted to sell the land on either side of their right-of-way for $3.00 an acre. Saskatchewan Archives Board R-B10548-1.

in Herbert to be distributed to communities in the region, including Swift Current. Herbert developed as a service centre for the surrounding agricultural district, and from the late 1950s through to the early 1980s, the community's population remained fairly stable at around 1,000. Herbert's economy continues to be largely based on agriculture (a combination of crop and livestock production), and a number of the town's businesses and services cater to the industry. Additionally, the community's health care and educational institutions provide a good number of jobs. Herbert has a hospital, a medical clinic, special care homes, a pharmacy, and an ambulance service. Herbert School is a K-12 facility, which had 154 town and area students enrolled in the fall of 2006. Herbert also has a number of local businesses that provide an array of goods and services. The town has a volunteer fire department; an RCMP detachment is located in the neighbouring community of Morse. Recreational facilities include an outdoor swimming pool, ball diamonds, a nine-hole golf course, a park, playgrounds, and a sports complex with rinks for hockey, skating, and curling. To the north of the town on Lake Diefenbaker lies Herbert Ferry Regional Park, with opportunities for boating, fishing, and camping. Herbert hosts an annual rodeo at the beginning of August. The community has a number of churches, service clubs, community organizations, sports clubs, and youth groups. The town has a library, a weekly newspaper, and a museum located in the community's former CPR station, built in 1908 and now a heritage property. *Faspa* (a low-German term used to describe a late afternoon lunch put together for unannounced visitors) is served in the former station agent's quarters throughout the summer, honouring a tradi-

tional Mennonite custom. Other heritage properties in Herbert include two stately homes dating to 1912 and 1913, and St. Patrick's Roman Catholic Church, built in 1912, now a private property. The Herbert area has produced a number of people of note, among them Jack Wiebe, former Lieutenant-Governor of Saskatchewan and former member of the Senate of Canada; Don Wittman, the CBC Sports commentator; and Homer Groening (born in Main Centre, just northwest of Herbert), father of Matt Groening, creator of *The Simpsons*. Herbert is situated in the RM of Morse No. 165.

HERSCHEL, hamlet, pop 30 (2006c), 35 (2001c), is a former village located northwest of Rosetown, off Hwy 31, in the picturesque Eagle Creek Valley, an area important for its archaeological,

anthropological, ecological, and paleontological riches. Because of the hilly and rocky terrain, wooded coulees and winding creeks, the area was not substantially developed for agriculture, and much of the unique prairie habitat, ancient fossils, and archaeological sites were left undisturbed. The Ancient Echoes Interpretive Centre in the village (located in the school which closed in 1994) houses displays and artifacts highlighting the Aboriginal and natural history of the region. Tours can be arranged to tour sites which include petroglyphs, buffalo jumps, tipi rings, and a medicine wheel. Another unique feature of the Herschel area is the Twin Towers Ski Resort, located 3 kilometres south of the nearby hamlet of Stranraer. The village of Herschel was both established and incorporated as the railway came through in 1911. It had a peak population of 203 in 1956. The community relinquished vil-

lage status on December 31, 2006. Herschel is the administrative centre of the RM of Mountain View No. 318.

HEWARD, village, pop 20 (2006c), 25 (2001c), lies approximately 130 km southeast of Regina, 11 km northwest of Stoughton on Hwy 33. Heward's origins date to the first few years of the twentieth century, when the foundations of the community developed just to the northeast of the present village, on land owned by a Hamilton Caldwell. In 1903, stores, a lumberyard, and a livery stable were established at this site (NE22-09-09-W2), and the small settlement was briefly known as Caldwell. In early 1904, however, the CPR surveyed the current village setting (NW15-09-09-W2) for a townsite and the location of their station. The railroad rejected the name Caldwell for the new locale and instead chose the name Heward in honour of A.R.G. Heward, a

▼ **HERSCHEL**, from the northeast. Photograph taken September 10, 2003.

▲ **HEWARD'S BEAUTIFUL STONE CHURCH** on Whyte Street officially opened in 1921 as an Anglican church. It evokes the sense of optimism and community spirit that prevailed in the village in its early years. Modelled after Gothic Revival-styled rural churches in England, Heward's stone church, once a showpiece for the community, closed in 1968 due to diminishing attendance (it had become a United Church in 1961). It was declared a municipal heritage property in 1983; however, today it sits in a fairly poor state of repair. Photograph taken August 19, 2003.

CPR assistant secretary in Montreal. Although it was expensive and inconvenient, the businessmen from the Caldwell settlement relocated to the new site to enjoy the great advantages that came with the railway. No longer did area settlers have to haul their grain the 50 or so kilometres to either Arcola or Weyburn, nor would they have to travel these distances for supplies that could now be shipped in via rail. Heward flourished in its infancy: on April 1, 1904, the post office was established, and on November 21 that fall the young village was incorporated. Two years later, the 1906 Census of Canada recorded the community's highest ever population — 173. Heward had its heyday during the first decades of the twentieth century, and other than a brief resurgence during the post-WWII period, the village has subsequently declined. At one time, as many as three dozen businesses existed in the community — a number of general stores, bakeries and butcher shops, a jeweller, a hotel and a boarding house, a local newspaper, a bank, a doctor's office, lumberyards, livery barns, farm implement dealers, a laundry, and a real estate office were among the number of village enterprises. Three grain elevators and the CPR station were the hub of activity. A flour mill, reputedly a controversial venture, was erected, but it was reduced to rubble in a 1907 cyclone or wind storm and was never rebuilt. The local history recounts that owners of the flour mill viewed it as disadvantageous to share a water supply with the railway, which reportedly had plans to build from Heward toward Weyburn. This would have created a junction between routes at Heward, and with it the potential for continued growth and business development. It seems the mill owners, however, influenced area settlers against selling land to the CPR for the construction of the proposed line, and thus an opportunity was lost and Heward slipped into a slow but steady decline. The railway to Weyburn was completed from nearby Stoughton in 1908, and Stoughton became the dominant community in the district. By 1961, Heward's population had dropped to 136; by 1971 it was 79; and by 1981 it was only 54. Heward School, which had opened in 1905, closed in 1969. High school students had been bused to Stoughton for some years. By the mid-1980s, the only commercial ventures left in the village were the elevators and a couple of small trenching businesses — and the elevator's days were numbered. Today, a scattered handful of residences line streets that were busy decades ago. Heward is situated in the RM of Tecumseh No. 65.

HITCHCOCK BAY, organized hamlet, est. 1992, is a resort community located on Lake Diefenbaker, southeast of Birsay. The bay itself, upon which the resort sits, was created in the late 1960s as the waters of Lake Diefenbaker were reaching capacity. It was named for Jack Hitchcock, an early pioneer, whose 1903 cabin still stands. A museum at Hitchcock Bay houses displays relating to the local history of the area. Today, the hamlet has a small number of year-round residents; however, the population varies depending on the season. Hitchcock Bay has facilities for conventions, family reunions, retreats, and camping. Hitchcock Bay is situated in the RM of Coteau No. 255.

HODGEVILLE, village, pop 142 (2006c), 175 (2001c), lies approximately 78 km southeast of Swift Current at the junction of Hwys 19 and 363. The community is situated upon the Missouri Coteau at about 640 metres (2,100 feet) above sea level; Regina and its surrounding plains, by comparison, are at about 577 metres (roughly 1,900 feet) above sea level. The Hodgeville area landscape may be described as moderately rolling to somewhat hilly. In the early 1900s, the region was essentially the domain of ranchers — the Turkey Track Ranch, with headquarters to the west of present-day Hodgeville, was a massive operation with more than 30,000 head of cattle and hundreds of horses. However, after the killing winter of 1906-07 dealt a severe blow to Saskatchewan's cattle industry (the Turkey Track alone lost over 10,000 animals), the southwest was increasingly being opened to homesteaders and soon settlers' shacks were dotting the area around where Hodgeville would develop. The people that came to the district were of various origins: there were those of British and Scandinavian stock, but German-speaking people — Lutherans, Catholics, and Mennonites — came to the region in large numbers between 1907 and the beginning of WWI. Many were from settlements in the United States founded by earlier emigrants from the Old World; a number came directly from overseas, from southern Russia or Hungary. While the village of Hodgeville itself didn't formally develop until the early 1920s with the coming of the railroad, local government was established in the district when the Rural Municipality of Lawtonia was formed in 1910. The name Hodgeville originates with the establishment of a post office on July 1, 1908, about six and a half kilometres northeast of the present townsite. The name of the office is thought to have honoured an Ernest Hodges, who homesteaded somewhat further northeast, northwest of what became the hamlet of Kelstern. A few years later the post office was relocated to a general store run by a Daniel Kaufman, just east of what is now Hwy 19 where it runs through the village. That portion of the highway that passes through the community today was later named Kaufman Street to honour the pioneering businessman. The post office and store, and the growing cluster of settlers in the area, formed the nucleus of an emerging community. The region was given a boost after the CPR reached Vanguard in 1912, for then Hodgeville district farmers could choose between travelling to either Morse, on the CPR main line, or Vanguard to sell their crops. In the Hodgeville area, churches were built, a bank was set up to serve the district, and a blacksmith and a welder set up shops. Given the emerging amenities, the council of the rural municipality established their headquarters at Hodgeville. In the mid-teens, Hodgeville School was established a few kilometres east of the present townsite, but as the village developed it was moved there. In the early 1920s, the Canadian National line that ran from Mossbank through Gravelbourg pushed north-westward through the community. However, construction progressed slowly beyond Hodgeville, and the line would never quite be completed through to Swift Current as intended. The Village of Hodgeville was incorporated on June 22, 1921 — the population that year was 88; by 1926 it had grown to 220. Four grain elevators lined the railway tracks in the community. But then the village stopped growing and Hodgeville stagnated until the 1950s. The CPR had built a line north of Hodgeville creating competing grain-buying points (Vogel, only a few kilometres north had three elevators); the Depression set in, and the drought, and the direct rail link to Swift Current failed to materialize. Then, in the post-war years, the community experienced sig-

nificant growth and a period of modernization. The population almost doubled. The Saskatchewan Power Corporation took over control of the electrical grid in 1954; sewer and water systems were installed in the 1960s; and in the 1970s natural gas was hooked up, a swimming pool was built, and village streets were paved. Through the 1960s the population of the village peaked at around 400, and Hodgeville's businesses served a district of approximately 1,500 rural residents. Due to the closure of rural schoolhouses, Hodgeville's schools were accommodating close to 400 village and area students at the time. The elementary school alone had an enrollment of over 200. But a profound change was on the horizon: both the rural and village populations began to decline. By the mid-1970s, Hodgeville had lost a quarter of its citizenry, and today the entire population of the RM of Lawtonia, excluding Hodgeville, is down to 432. In 1969, the hospital was reduced to a health clinic, and around this time a number of businesses began closing. The newspaper folded in the late 1960s, a variety store closed, the pool hall followed in 1973, and by the mid-1970s, Beaver Lumber, too, was gone. By 1981, CN had abandoned most of the rail line running northwest of the community (through Neidpath to Burnham), and in 1985 the CPR took over the rail line that ran into the village, bringing an end to more than 60 years of CN service to the community. The CP line that ran to the north of Hodgeville — the portion of the Shamrock subdivision between Archive and Tyson — was abandoned at the end of 1989. A positive development in the community around this time, though, was the construction by the Saskatchewan Wheat Pool of a large, modern concrete grain handling and storage facility. It opened in the spring of 1990,

but thirteen years later, in May 2003, the terminal was closed, and the future of Hodgeville as a grain-handling point was then in doubt. The Pool reopened the facility in October 2005, however, and as of the spring of 2006 it was still in operation. The Pool also sells farm supplies from this location. Hodgeville also has a small core of other businesses and services today, including a credit union and the Pioneer Co-op, which deals in groceries, hardware, building materials, tires, fuel and oil. The village also has a volunteer fire department; policing is provided by the RCMP detachment out of the town of Morse. Hodgeville has a health centre offering inpatient and outpatient services; a clinical nurse is available twice a week, and a doctor and a massage therapist visit once a week. The nearest hospitals are located in the towns of Gravelbourg and Herbert (from where ambulance service is dispatched). Hodgeville has a veterinary clinic. Recreational facilities in the village include a community centre and a rink,

sports grounds and the swimming pool. A number of service clubs and other community-based organizations operate in the village, sponsoring annual events such as Oktoberfest, a trade show, a dinner theatre, and a dinner and dance. Village and area attractions include the community's museum and craft shop, and the nearby Hutterite colony. Hodgeville School is a K-12 facility which had 81 students enrolled in the fall of 2006. The economic base of the community remains agriculture and related services. Hodgeville serves as the administrative centre of the RM of Lawtonia No. 135.

HOEY, organized hamlet, pop 47 (2006c), 50 (2001c), is located between Wakaw and Prince Albert on Hwy 2. In the 1870s, Métis dominated the region; in the 1880s, French immigrants from Belgium and France settled in the Hoey area. The name of the community honours James Hoey (b. 1828), Member of

▲ **THE FORMER RM OFFICE IN HOEY**, built in 1917 and used until 1987 when a new building was constructed, now houses a seniors' drop-in centre. One of the oldest remaining buildings in the hamlet, it has been designated a municipal heritage property. Photograph taken August 24, 2004.

the Legislative Assembly of the North-West
Territories for the electoral division of Kinistino 1888-91. The RM of St. Louis No.
431 was incorporated in 1913, and Hoey
became, and remains, the administrative headquarters. During WWI, the Hoey
Post Office was established and the Grand
Trunk Pacific Railway came through the
area. Hoey was established as an organized hamlet in 1952, and through the
1960s the population hovered at around
100. Just north of the community the St.
Louis-Hoey grain elevator still stands (it
was formerly owned by the Saskatchewan
Wheat Pool); just south of Hoey, the Saskatchewan Wheat Pool maintains a farm
supply retail operation.

HOLBEIN, organized hamlet, pop
84 (2006c), 92 (2001c), is located 13
km east of Shellbrook and 31 km west of
Prince Albert on Hwy 3. The community
was built on what was once federal forest
reserve land and had its origins in 1909-
10 when the railway came through and a
siding was established. Building sites were
initially held by yearly permits. A camp
which produced railroad ties and cordwood was established at the siding, and
in one of the camp buildings a post office
opened in 1912. As the locale had yet to
be named, a Mr. John Miller suggested the
name Holbein, in honour of Hans Holbein
the Younger, a German Renaissance artist who became King Henry VIII's court
painter, and whose work Miller admired.
The name was accepted. Also in 1912, a
school was built, and in 1914-15 a ranger
station and an observation tower were
constructed. By 1920, the first grain elevator was erected and a small business community was emerging. Agriculture would
eventually come to replace logging as the
dominant area industry, as more and

more land was cleared. In 1927, a survey
plan for the hamlet was drawn up and approved by the Department of the Interior
in Ottawa; 80 acres were then withdrawn
from the forest reserve for the townsite of
Holbein. In 1952, Holbein was established
as an organized hamlet, but the next year
the school closed, and since then students
have been bused to Shellbrook. In the
late 1980s, the elevators at Holbein were
handling over a million bushels of grain
and oilseeds per year, but, faced with
the threat of branch line abandonment
and the impending demise of the freight
subsidy provided by the Crow's Nest Pass
Agreement, grain handling companies
began consolidating their operations. In
1992, the Saskatchewan Wheat Pool began
construction of a large high-throughput
terminal at White Star (a little more than
10 kilometres north of Prince Albert), and
in 1993 the Pool ceased their operations
in Holbein. The rail line through the community was then abandoned. Although
Holbein sustained a blow, and has seen
its business community decline over the
years, it has grown in recent decades as
people have been moving into the hamlet
and commuting to work in Prince Albert
or Shellbrook — Holbein's population
had been down to 37 in 1972. Today, residents enjoy modern homes well spaced
amongst trees in a forest setting. A gas station located on the highway sells groceries
and hardware, and a general store in the
hamlet proper also has gas pumps and
houses the post office. Holbein is situated
in the RM of Shellbrook No. 493.

HOLDFAST, village, pop 173
(2006c), 190 (2001c), lies west of Last
Mountain Lake off of Hwy 2, about 18 km
north of Hwy 11. The community is dominated by the impressive Assumption of

the Blessed Virgin Mary Roman Catholic
Church, built in 1920-21. Settlement of
the district began in 1904, although some
homesteaders had filed on their land the
previous year. They arrived via the Canadian Northern Railway line to the west,
detraining at Chamberlain or Aylesbury.
The majority were Germans from Russia
and were predominantly Catholics. Some
of these came to the district from earlier
settlements in the Kronau district southeast of Regina or from the United States;
a few came from South America; others
came directly from southern Russia. German Catholic families from the Banat
area of Hungary settled on the northern
fringes of the Holdfast district; German
Lutherans with origins in southern Russia
were scattered throughout the area, but
settled largely to the west of the present-
day village. English-speaking protestants,
too, appeared, hailing from Ontario and
the United States: they settled primarily in
the western part of the district. The German-speaking population remained by
far the majority, however; in 1971, most
residents of Holdfast still claimed German
descent. By 1910, eight district schools
had been established in the region and
the first Catholic church had been built
three miles east of present-day Holdfast,
where the community's cemetery is still
located. Also by 1910, most of the homesteaded land in the area had been broken,
but farmers still had to haul their grain
to Findlater, Chamberlain, Aylesbury, or
Craik, points where they could also obtain
supplies. The CPR built its line through
the region in 1910-11, and the village
developed quickly around the grain elevators and the railway station that were constructed. The rail line was operational in
1911 and soon the community had a wide
range of businesses. Holdfast was incorporated on October 5 that year. In 1912,

▲ **INTERIOR** of the Assumption of the Blessed Virgin Mary Roman Catholic Church, Holdfast. Photograph taken July 8, 2003.

the Holdfast Post Office was established, replacing the Frohlich rural post office that had been in operation since 1907. A village school was started in 1912. Lutherans built a church in the village in 1913; Catholics attended the country church until the present church in Holdfast was built. In 1915, fearful they would lose their doctor, Dr. Henry Joseph Schmitt, as he was having difficulty collecting fees, the rural municipality headquartered at Holdfast voted to pay him a salary out of tax dollars despite not having the legislative authority to do so. Dr. Schmitt agreed to the arrangement, and became the first contracted, full-time municipal doctor in Canada. It was an early step toward the development of medicare. The provincial government was forced to quickly amend the Municipalities Act in order to legalize the arrangement pioneered in Holdfast, and eventually there were 173 municipal doctors employed in the province. During the period of the First World War, Holdfast was growing rapidly. By the end

of the war, five grain elevators lined the tracks in the village. By 1921 the population was over 200 and nearing 300 by the end of the decade. In 1924, the Sisters of Charity of the Immaculate Conception arrived in Holdfast; they opened a convent and taught in the village until 1976. Schell School, a K-12 facility that had 102 students enrolled in the fall of 2006, was named after Sister Christina Schell, who spent 35 years (1933-68) as a teacher and principal at Holdfast. From the mid-1920s until the mid-1950s, the population of the village remained fairly stable. Between the mid-1950s and the early 1970s, however, the population mushroomed: the "baby boom," together with retiring farmers who were moving into the village, pushed the community's numbers to a peak of 446 in 1966. The population began to decline dramatically in the 1970s, and today the median age of the village population is almost ten years older than the provincial figure: in 2006 the median age of Holdfast residents was 48.5, while that of all

Saskatchewan residents was 38.7. In the 1970s the rail line running southeast of Dilke was abandoned after the waters of Last Mountain Lake rose and completely washed out the track bed across the lake to Valeport; in the late 1990s the rail line running north of Holdfast was abandoned. Now, where five grain elevators once stood, only the former Saskatchewan Wheat Pool elevator, built in 1979-80, remains standing. Today, the community retains a small core of businesses and services, its school, its church, a library branch, ball diamonds, and a nine-hole sand-green golf course. In the late 1980s, the Sarnia Community Complex was built: it has an artificial ice surface, a canteen, and a mezzanine. The facility accommodates hockey games, skating, curling bonspiels, reunions, and other social functions. Holdfast United Church (the congregation purchased the Lutheran Church in 1960) closed in the summer of 2007. Renowned Saskatchewan artist David Thauberger was born in Holdfast in 1948. Holdfast serves as the administrative centre of the RM of Sarnia No. 221.

HORSESHOE BAY, organized hamlet, est. 1991, is one of several resort communities situated northeast of Turtleford on Turtle Lake. The 2006 Census recorded 62 permanent residents; however, the population varies greatly depending on the season, reaching close to 300 during the summer months. Originally developed during the 1960s and 1970s, Horseshoe Bay lies within the RM of Mervin No. 499.

HUBBARD, village, pop 43 (2006c), 38 (2001c), is situated 10 km southeast of Ituna on Hwy 15. Factoring significantly

among those who settled in the district were Ukrainian and Polish settlers who began arriving about 1903-04 respectively. The village had its beginnings with the arrival of the Grand Trunk Pacific Railway in 1907-08, and among the first businesses licenced to serve the community were implement dealerships, a lumberyard, a blacksmith shop, liveries, general merchants, a butcher shop, and a grain elevator. It is believed Hubbard may have been named after an employee with the railway, but whatever the origins of the name, it was certainly chosen to fit the alphabetical sequence of communities along the rail line: Fenwood, Goodeve, Hubbard, Ituna, etc. The Hubbard Post Office was established in March 1909, replacing a country post office, Drumague, which had operated a couple of miles to the southwest since 1906. The first postmaster in Hubbard, Sydney Chipperfield, was one of the village's first storekeepers, and he served on the village council for close to twenty years. It was in his role as village overseer that Chipperfield greeted King George VI and Queen Elizabeth on June 6, 1939, during their whistle stop in the community. Hubbard was incorporated on June 11, 1910, and in 1911 a country schoolhouse that had operated for a few years, originally known as Marland, was moved into the village and renamed Hubbard School. The village's population grew fairly slowly until the mid-1920s, at which point it hovered around 100; but in the years following, even through the Depression, the community began to experience a period of renewed growth that lasted through to the mid-1960s. The village reached a peak population of 187 in 1956. In the latter half of the 1960s, however, Hubbard started slipping into decline. Once several families lived in the village who had men working for the rail-

▲ **HUBBARD LANDMARKS:** the Church of the Holy Spirit and the sole remaining grain elevator, the latter formerly operated by the Saskatchewan Wheat Pool. Photographs taken July 14, 2004.

way, but with less freight being moved and the discontinuance of passenger service — in 1965 the village council protested the closing of the railway station — the jobs of the station agents and operators and the section foreman and crew were lost. Businesses were closing in the late 1960s, and by 1975 enrollment at Hubbard School was falling. By 1979, only grades one to six were being taught in the village; older children were being bused to Ituna. Hubbard's population plunged by half between 1966 and 1976 — from 180 to 90. While the school was still open in 1984, it eventually closed. In 1975, the village council wrote the CNR asking them to remove the abandoned station as it was considered a public hazard. Today, other than the post office, there are no services left in the community. Long-closed churches, closed businesses, and vacant homes and lots now dominate the streets of the once-thriving village. Hubbard is situated in the RM of Ituna Bon Accord No. 246.

HUDSON BAY, town, pop 1,646 (2006c), 1,783 (2001c), is located 116 km east of Tisdale, nestled in the Red Deer River valley between the Pasquia and Porcupine Hills. The community is situated at the junction of Hwys 3 and 9, 50 km west of the Saskatchewan-Manitoba border. The immediate area encompassing the town consists of farmlands surrounded by vast tracts of forest wilderness. Fur trading activity in the area dates to the latter half of the 1700s, and at least one trading post was established just south of Hudson Bay at the confluence of three area rivers. The Canadian Northern Railway entered the district from Manitoba in the first years of the twentieth century, and the beginnings of today's community were that of a railway siding that developed largely to serve logging interests. In 1907, the Village of Etoimami (the community's original name, of Cree origin) was incorporated; a fairly magnificent hotel built that year is

still in business. In 1909, the name of the community was changed to Hudson Bay Junction for its position as the starting point for the on-again off-again Hudson Bay Railway to Churchill, Manitoba, which was not completed until 1929. For many years, logging and railway work were the primary occupations in the district, but in the 1920s agriculture began to develop when areas of the surrounding forest reserves were opened for settlement by soldiers who had served in WWI. Land then became available to civilians, and in 1928 the community's relative isolation became somewhat less so with the arrival of another rail line from Canora via Sturgis. The 1930s saw increasing settlement of the district and a simultaneous growth of the village as people moved north, fleeing the drought-ravaged southern plains. It was not until the late 1930s and early 1940s that the first roads began to be built into the region. In 1946 the community attained town status, and in 1947 the word "Junction" was dropped from its

name. In 1948, the first plywood plant in Canada was built at Hudson Bay, followed in 1961 by a waferboard plant, a joint venture between private industry and the Saskatchewan government. The latter operations, sold to MacMillan Bloedel in 1965, were purchased by Weyerhaeuser Ltd. in 1999. Until recently, Weyerhaeuser operated both the plywood and the OSB plants. (OSB, oriented strand board, is the successor to wafer, or particle, board.) The development of these facilities spawned a building boom in Hudson Bay, and the population grew from 793 in 1946 to 1,957 in 1966. The railroad was still employing about 100 people in the mid-1960s; however, as that workforce was reduced over the following years, agriculture and especially forestry became the community's economic mainstays. A wide range of crops are grown in the valley: locally grown alfalfa enables Hudson Bay Dehydrators to process 10,000 tonnes of alfalfa pellets annually for local and export markets. Currently, there are concerns in the forestry sector, however. Weyerhaeuser has been embroiled in labour disputes at all of its Saskatchewan operations for the past couple of years, and in February 2008, the company announced its intention to permanently close its plywood mill in Hudson Bay. It had not helped that the protracted softwood lumber dispute with the U.S. and a strong Canadian dollar had been hurting the industry. Another factor in Hudson Bay's economy is tourism, particularly as it relates to big game hunting. Moose and elk are found in abundance in the region, and each hunting season many hunters utilize the services of the community's numerous outfitters. There are approximately 130 businesses in Hudson Bay, providing a wide array of goods and services. The town has a range of medical, educational, and recreational facilities, an

◀ **CHURCHILL STREET**, looking south, decorated for the Christmas season, circa 1940s. Photograph courtesy of the Town of Hudson Bay.

▲ **HUDSON BAY'S HERITAGE DAY PARADE, 1993.** Photograph courtesy of the Al Mazur Memorial Heritage Park, Hudson Bay.

"Moose Capital of the World"

HUDSON BAY

▶ **THIS CN CABOOSE**, due to be retired, was donated to the Al Mazur Memorial Heritage Park. It was renovated, and moved by railway equipment and track personnel to its new home on Thursday, June 24, 1982. Joe Jakubowski managed the move easily with his semi, while experienced crewmen laid new track and unloaded the caboose. Photograph courtesy of the Al Mazur Memorial Heritage Park, Hudson Bay.

▼ **DESROCHERS HOTEL**, at the corner of Railway Avenue and Churchill Street, has long been a community landmark. Photograph taken August 11, 2004.

◀ **SUMMER STUDENTS** employed at the Al Mazur Memorial Heritage Park work on refurbishing one of the buildings at the 16-acre site. Photograph taken August 11, 2004.

RCMP detachment, a fire department, and an ambulance service, as well as a local radio station and newspaper, a number of churches, service clubs and other community-based organizations. Community attractions include the Hudson Bay Museum, housed in the original 1911 public school, and the Al Mazur Memorial Heritage Park. The 16-acre park consists of a recreated village depicting Hudson Bay Junction in 1909, and has a large collection of restored vintage tractors, and a small train that provides rides and circles the site. Hudson Bay serves as the administrative centre of the RM of Hudson Bay No. 394.

HUMBOLDT, city, pop 4,998 (2006c), 5,161 (2001c), is located approximately 113 km east of Saskatoon and 230 km north of Regina at the junction of Hwys 5 and 20. Established with the arrival of the Canadian Northern Railway in 1904, Humboldt was named for the nearby Dominion Telegraph station established on the Carlton trail in 1876. The station had been named for the German scientist, explorer, and author Baron Alexander von Humboldt (1769-1859). Humboldt became the largest centre in St. Peter's Colony, a 50-township tract of land roughly from Cudworth to Watson settled

by German Catholics, most of whom came via the northern and mid-western United States. The settlement was established by the German-American Land Company in conjunction with priests of the Order of St. Benedict and the Catholic Settlement Society of St. Paul, Minnesota. Before the railway came through Humboldt, many of the settlers arrived via Saskatoon or Rosthern. The first homesteads were filed on in the fall of 1902. Many people arrived in 1903; after the railway came through, settlers poured into the district. Humboldt prospered from being a divisional point on the rail line, and a judicial, administrative, and agricultural service centre. Today, a number of manufacturing firms in the district not only serve local agricultural needs, but export markets as well. The city has a 25-acre industrial park. Humboldt is also situated in the largest hog-producing region in the province. Humboldt attained village status on June 30, 1905; town status on April 1, 1907; and became Saskatchewan's thirteenth city on November 7, 2000. Humboldt has a 45-bed hospital, two public and two Catholic schools, and a broad range of recreational and cultural facilities. Based upon its German heritage (in 1971 approximately half of the residents still claimed German origins), Humboldt adopted a German theme in 1991. German-themed events

such as Polkafest in July and Oktoberfest in the fall are held annually; one can learn about the area's history at the Willkommen Centre and the Humboldt and District Museum and Gallery. A number of murals in the city depict the German history of the area. Nearby St. Peter's Cathedral and St. Peter's Abbey in Muenster are other district attractions. Heritage properties in the city include the pre-WWI post office and the WWII-era water tower, the latter being one of only four similar structures remaining in Saskatchewan. Another heritage property is the Provincial Court House completed in 1920. Humboldt serves as the administrative centre of the RM of Humboldt No. 370.

HYAS, village, pop 111 (2006c), 131 (2001c), is situated 11 km west of Norquay and about 20 km east of Sturgis off Hwy 49. Settlers began arriving in the area toward the end of the nineteenth century, and as the Canadian Northern Railway line was being built from Pelly to Preeceville in 1911-1912, the small settlement of Hyas emerged. The townsite was surveyed in 1911 and construction followed rapidly. The Hyas Post Office was established in 1912. The predominantly Ukrainian and Scandinavian settlement was incorporated as a village on May 23, 1919: the population of the community was then about 100. Hyas grew steadily until the mid-1950s — at which point the population was approaching 300 — and the village was a busy and bustling centre that supplied the material and social needs of the surrounding farming district. The basis of the area economy was, and remains, agriculture, a combination of grain and livestock production. In recent decades, both the village's population and the number of businesses has dwindled. Hyas serves as the administrative centre of the RM of Clayton No. 333.

▼ **MAIN STREET, HYAS, LOOKING SOUTH.** Photograph taken July 27, 2004.

ILE-A-LA-CROSSE, northern village, pop 1,341 (2006c), 1,268 (2001c), is located in north-western Saskatchewan, southeast of Buffalo Narrows, 21 km off Hwy 155. The community is situated upon a peninsula that juts into an expansion of the upper Churchill River, called Lac Île-à-la-Crosse. The name of the village and of the surrounding lake originates with early French fur traders' observations of the game of lacrosse being played on a nearby island. The voyageurs had come to know the game as la crosse, because the sticks used to play it resembled a bishop's crozier or *crosse*. Although the current name of the community has long been in use, it is still referred to as "Sakitawak," derived from the Cree term for "the place where the rivers meet." To the regularly visiting Dene, it is called "Kwoen," meaning "a place where people stay" or "a village." Ile-a-la-Crosse became the hub of much activity and competition during the fur trade due to its strategic location. To the north, via Methy Portage and the Clearwater River, lay the vast and fur-rich Athabasca region; from the south, pemmican, the fuel of the fur trade, could be brought to Ile-a-la-Crosse from the plains via the

NOTE: The spelling of Ile-a-la-Crosse has changed over the years. In earlier times the name of the community was spelled like that of the lake, with both French accents and hyphens. Toward the end of the twentieth century the accents and the hyphens had pretty much been dropped and the name was often spelled Ile a la Crosse. However, the hyphens have gained favour again, and the village currently uses the hyphenated form, but without the accents. At present, government publications are inconsistent.

Photographs this page courtesy of Ovide and Irene Desjarlais, Ile-a-la-Crosse.

◄ **MR. AND MRS. MICHEL BOUVIER**, early Métis settlers at Ile-a-la-Crosse, circa late 1890s. Descendants of the Bouviers still live in the community.

"Sakitawak"

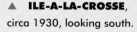

ILE-A-LA-CROSSE

▲ **ILE-A-LA-CROSSE**, circa 1930, looking south.

► **BISHOP LAJEUNESSE** arriving in Ile-a-la-Crosse in 1946.

◄ **BISHOP LAJEUNESSE AND THE GREY NUNS** in Ile-a-la-Crosse, circa 1940s.

◄ **ILE-A-LA-CROSSE, 1946**, looking south. Saskatchewan Archives Board R-B5900.

▼ **SOUTH BAY WAR VETERANS' PARK**, Lac Île-à-la-Crosse, July 20, 2005. Photograph courtesy of Jenny MacDonald, Regina, Saskatchewan.

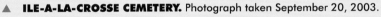

▲ **ILE-A-LA-CROSSE CEMETERY.** Photograph taken September 20, 2003.

▼ **THIS PAINTING OF ILE-A-LA-CROSSE BY ROGER JEROME** of Air Ronge hangs in the Ile-a-la-Crosse village office. Another of Jerome's works adorns the rotunda of the Saskatchewan Legislative Building. Jerome won the commission to paint the 2005 Centennial Mural in the building, which was unveiled by Queen Elizabeth II that year. Photograph taken September 20, 2003; reproduced with the permission of Roger Jerome, Air Ronge, Saskatchewan.

Beaver River. Heading back east down the Churchill, traders could head for Hudson Bay or Montreal. It was Montreal-based fur traders who established the first trading post at Ile-a-la-Crosse in 1776, making the village Saskatchewan's oldest continually inhabited community after Cumberland House. Rival posts were set up with varying degrees of success in subsequent years, including one set up in 1885 by Alexander Mackenzie. The Hudson's Bay Company tried to establish a footing at Ile-a-la-Crosse in 1799, but were initially largely thwarted by fierce competition from the North West Company. After the merger of the companies in 1821, Ile-a-la-Crosse became the headquarters for the Hudson's Bay Company's operations in the territory. In 1846, Father Alexandre-Antonin Taché (later Bishop) and Father Louis-François Richer Laflèche (for whom the southern Saskatchewan town is named) arrived from St. Boniface to establish the first Roman Catholic mission in what is present-day Saskatchewan. In 1860, Sisters Agnes, Pepin, and Boucher founded a convent, bringing medical services, education, and Western culture to the community. Around the Hudson Bay Company post and the mission, a growing settlement developed, comprised of the

Métis descendants of the fur trade. Louis Riel's paternal grandparents were married in Ile-a-la-Crosse and his sister, Sara Riel, worked at the convent and is buried in the community's cemetery. Although a few men still voyage into the bush to trap each winter, the economy of Ile-a-la-Crosse has changed. A landing strip was built in the late 1940s; in the late 1950s an all-weather road was built to the community. Today, a modern highway runs from Ile-a-la-Crosse. Commercial fishing, forest fire fighting, forestry, wild rice harvesting, and work at the hospital and the school provide jobs. Additional employment is found in local and provincial government offices and many people work in northern uranium mines, being flown in on a "week in/week out" basis. The natural splendour of the community's location also gives rise to increasing tourism. The community's former newspaper editor and mayor, Buckley Belanger, was born in Ile-a-la-Crosse, and has held several provincial cabinet portfolios, including the Ministry of Northern Affairs, since his election to the legislature in 1995.

IMPERIAL, town, pop 321 (2006c), 339 (2001c), is located approximately 37 km south of Watrous, off Hwy 2. The north end of Last Mountain Lake and the Last Mountain Lake National Wildlife Area lie about 10 km to the east. Homesteaders began taking up land in the district in 1903, and for a number of years before the railway was built through the area, much of the transportation of people and freight into the region was by water. The Wm. Pearson Company established a "port of call" for its barges and steamer, the *S.S. Qu'Appelle*, on the lake to the east of present-day Imperial, at a location known as Watertown. In 1910, as

the railway approached, businesses from Watertown and other areas moved to the rail line, and the first structures began to appear on the Imperial townsite. The rail line was constructed several kilometres west of the lake in order to maximize the amount of agricultural land on either side. The name of Imperial fits the pattern of names given to other communities established along the line — such as Holdfast, Stalwart, and Liberty — reflecting the ideological traits and glory associated with the British Empire. Many of Imperial's beautiful tree-lined streets further the theme, with names such as King, Queen, Prince, and Princess. The community's main thoroughfare is Royal Street. The railway arrived in 1911, and Imperial was incorporated as a village that year. By the late 1950s, the population was approaching 600, and Imperial attained town status in 1962. The area economy is based on agriculture, and, accordingly, Imperial has a number of businesses related to the industry — a major manufacturer of agricultural machinery with about 50 employees and a crop processing plant among them. Additional businesses provide a variety of goods and services, and Imperial serves the district with an integrated health centre and special care home, and a K-12 school. The town also has four churches, a library, and facilities for recreational activities. For a number of years, the community has hosted successful dinner theatres and has sponsored an ice-fishing derby on Last Mountain Lake. Imperial is situated in the RM of Big Arm No. 251.

INDIAN HEAD, town, pop 1,634 (2006c), 1,758 (2001c), is located approximately 70 km east of Regina on Hwy 1; Hwy 56 leads north from Indian Head

▲ **ELEVATOR ROW, PAST AND PRESENT.** The first grain elevator built in what is now the province of Saskatchewan was likely in either Moosomin or Indian Head. The oldest remaining elevator in Saskatchewan, built in 1895, is in the town of Fleming. It is believed that Indian Head may have had the highest number of traditional wooden country elevators: in the undated photograph above, ten are visible (Saskatchewan Archives Board R-B133-5). The Indian Head local history published in 1984 states that "in 1905 Indian Head had twelve elevators and a flour mill, which adds up to 13."

▼ ▶ Today, N.M. Paterson & Sons' high-throughput concrete elevator (in the right of the photograph below) shares the railway right-of-way with the elevator built by Parrish & Heimbecker in 1949 (left foreground), and the former N.M. Paterson & Sons elevator shown in the photograph on the next page. Colour photographs taken October 15, 2003.

to the Qu'Appelle Valley and Katepwa Lake. The community's name is believed to be derived from First Nations peoples' phrases or terms for a nearby hill, or range of low-lying hills, somewhat to the south. Indian Head had its beginnings in 1882 as the first settlers, many of Scottish origin, pushed into the area in advance of the railroad, most travelling by ox-cart from Brandon. The Indian Head Post Office was established that year, as well as a large-scale farming enterprise, the Bell Farm. Conceived of and managed by Major W. R. Bell of Ontario, the farm consisted of over 50,000 acres and was run like a military operation. Although the enterprise experienced some success, poor crops in the middle of the decade, as well as the settlers' preoccupation with the North-West Resistance resulted in the farm's failure. The need for agricultural research in the west was recognized by the federal government, and in 1887 an experimental farm was established at Indian Head. Development in the young community was slow at first — although a school and churches were established — but after 1900 settlers began arriving in droves. Indian Head attained town sta-

▶ **UKRAINIAN GREEK ORTHODOX CHURCH OF THE DESCENT OF THE HOLY GHOST**, Insinger, July 15, 2004.

tus in 1902, and by the outbreak of WWI it was a thriving agricultural service centre with a population of over 1,200. Some of the province's largest wheat shipments were passing through the Indian Head elevators. The research farm at Indian Head remains to this day, as does the Prairie Farm Rehabilitation Administration (PFRA) Shelterbelt Centre, which had its origins at the beginning of the twentieth century. Today, both operations are major community employers. A significant number of Indian Head residents are also employed in the area of health care: a hospital, a special care home, a medical clinic, dentist's and optometrists' offices, and an ambulance service. The town also has a chemical dependence rehabilitation centre, homecare programs, and an abilities van for the convenience of the elderly and the disabled. Indian Head has elementary and high schools, as well as an office of the Southeast Regional College, through which post-secondary classes and a variety

of educational programs may be pursued. Protective services are provided by the Indian Head RCMP detachment and a volunteer fire department. The community has a wide range of recreational facilities, a library, a theatre, a number of service groups, community-based organizations, and sports teams. The town has several churches. Indian Head is home to the Orange Home and Orange Home Farm. Started by the Orange Benevolent Society, the homes have provided safe and secure shelters for children experiencing family stress or turmoil since 1923. Indian Head has a range of professional services and tradespeople, financial institutions, and a large number of retail establishments. The community serves as the administrative centre of the RM of Indian Head No. 156.

INDIAN POINT — GOLDEN SANDS, organized hamlet, was established in 1985 as the result of a merger of two resorts. Situated northeast of Turtleford on Turtle Lake, it is one of several resort communities in the area. Sixty-five permanent residents were recorded living in the hamlet in 2006; however, the population varies greatly depending on the season. The community is situated in the RM of Parkdale No. 498.

INSINGER, hamlet, pop 20 (2001c), is located southeast of Foam Lake on Hwy 16, roughly halfway between the villages of Sheho and Theodore. The first few settlers began arriving in the region in the early 1890s, and the community and the surrounding rural municipality are named for Fredrik Robert Insinger (1862-1946), a Dutch settler, successful rancher, and politician, who homesteaded adjacent to where the village of Willowbrook (west of Yorkton) is today. Insinger served as an MLA in the Territorial government from 1892-97. With the extension of the railway from Yorkton to Sheho over 1903-04, there was an influx of new settlers into the district (of various origins, but largely Ukrainian), and the townsite of present-day Insinger began to develop. Prior to this time the nearest market centre had been Yorkton. Insinger was incorporated as a village on May 14, 1921, and that year a school was built in the community, relieving schoolchildren of the walk to the rural school they had previously attended. From the early 1930s through to the mid-1960s the village had a population of over 100 (the peak was in 1956 when the community numbered 135 residents), and in it heyday (the 1950s) Insinger's business section was comprised of four general stores, two garages, a hotel, a café, a community hall, municipal office, post office, churches, a skating rink, and the school. By the late 1960s, though, the community was advancing into decline; the population was down to 72 by 1971, 56 by 1976, and only 39 in 1981. Through the 1980s the business section was abandoned. The school in Insinger was closed in 1967 (a reunion of former students was held in 1998). In 1999, the community's two grain elevators were demolished. On September 11, 2003, the Village of Insinger was dissolved, becoming a hamlet under the jurisdiction of the RM of Insinger No. 275, for which it serves as the administrative centre. The Ukrainian Greek Orthodox Church of the Descent of the Holy Ghost, built in 1942, is a community landmark. It was designated a municipal heritage property in 1988.

INVERMAY, village, pop 262 (2006c), 284 (2001c), is located in east-central Saskatchewan, roughly halfway between Wadena and Canora on Hwy 5. Two lakes, Saline and Stonewall, lie just south of the community; to the southwest lies Whitesand Lake, the headwaters of the Whitesand River, which flows east into the Assiniboine River at Kamsack. Ranching activity was recorded in the Invermay area in the mid-1890s, and among the first ranchers was Walter Tulloch, who arrived in 1895. These early ranchers were squatters and were free to pasture their stock wherever they pleased. The first settlers, though, began to arrive to take up homesteads in 1902-03, and the days of the open range quickly came to an end. People of many different origins settled the district, ranging from Scots to Ukrainians to Finns. Tulloch took up a homestead about 5 kilometres south of the present

▲ **THE SIGN THAT WELCOMES VISITORS** to Invermay was erected in honour of the community's pioneers. Photograph taken July 29, 2004.

community and established a post office there in March of 1904. The Invermay townsite also began to be developed that year as a service and supply centre for the surrounding farming community as the Canadian Northern Railway was building through the region en route from Kamsack to Humboldt. Work had begun on the line in 1903; the Invermay station was built in 1904; and the railway was opened to traffic in the spring of 1905. The post office was relocated to the community early that summer. For a number of years Invermay served as a coal supply depot for all of the trains travelling the line. With the coming of the railway, there was an influx of settlers and a great deal of building on the village site. A school was opened in 1905, and on September 1, 1908, the Village of Invermay was incorporated. In 1912, a disastrous fire struck. A lack of fire-fighting equipment and the fact that the town

well was frozen up at the time resulted in the loss of the butcher shop, harness shop, drug store, general store, and an implement shed. Shortly afterward, fire-fighting equipment was purchased. Despite the setback, Invermay continued to grow steadily. From a population of 93 in 1911, the community's citizenry climbed to number 200 by 1936 and 300 by 1956; it reached a peak of 444 in 1966. The last passenger train stopped in Invermay on May 18, 1963, and freight service was discontinued on December 31, 1980, when the station was closed. The landmark building was purchased and moved off its site in 1984. The community remains a vital and important trading centre in the district, however; its businesses include hardware and grocery stores, restaurants and a liquor outlet, automotive services and a used car dealer, a hotel, a gas bar and confectionary, a farm supply centre, a post office, an insurance broker, and a Royal Bank. The village also has a community hall, a library, a seniors' centre, churches, skating and curling rinks, and ball diamonds. Invermay has a number of service clubs and minor league sports teams. Annual events include a dinner theatre performed by a local troupe, the Invermay Agricultural Society Fair, a winter festival, and the Vesna Ukrainian Dance Club recital each spring. Invermay has a health centre with an attached special care home, and a volunteer fire department that, in addition to serving the village, serves the neighbouring community of Rama as well as the surrounding RM. Police service is provided by RCMP detachments located in the larger centres in the region. Invermay School is a K-12 facility that had 119 students enrolled in the fall of 2006. Invermay serves as the administrative centre of the RM of Invermay No. 305.

ISLAND VIEW, resort village, is located just south of Rowan's Ravine Provincial Park on the east side of Last Mountain Lake. The first land for the resort community was purchased in 1959 and was originally known as Strasbourg Beach, after the nearby town. By the early 1980s over 100 cottages and some permanent homes had been built, with the majority of the owners from Regina. In 1989, the community was established as an organized hamlet, and in 1991 the name was changed to Island View. In 1994, Island View was incorporated as a resort village. The 2006 Census recorded 88 year-round residents; however, more recently, local authorities have stated that the number is closer to 40 and that the population varies greatly depending on the season. Island View is situated in the RM of McKillop No. 220.

ITUNA, town, pop 622 (2006c), 709 (2001c), is located 55 km northwest of Melville on Hwys 15 and 310. Highway 52, just north of the community, runs east to Yorkton. Although the first few settlers arrived in the area in the 1880s and 1890s, it was not until the first years of the twentieth century that a wave of people of British origins began to take up homesteads in the district. With the construction of the Grand Trunk Pacific Railway through the region in 1907-08, the townsite began to develop. The railway brought an influx of Ukrainian settlers to the district, who would come to significantly enrich the community with their cultural heritage. The Ituna Post Office was established in 1909, and in 1910 the young community was incorporated, its name the archaic Celtic name for the Solway Firth in Scotland. Ituna developed

Early views along Main Street Ituna...

Town Hall photograph courtesy of the Town of Ituna; Main Street photographs courtesy of the Ituna and District Museum.

▲ **MAIN STREET**, looking south, circa 1910.

▼ **ITUNA, 1911.** Ituna's first postmaster, S.A. Veals, is in the wagon with two horses in the centre of the photograph. Buildings in the background include, from right to left, the Ituna Livery Stable, the hardware store (with the staircase-shaped roof), the post office (with veranda), the Bank of British North America, and the pool room (with sign visible).

▲ **ITUNA TOWN HALL AND COUNCIL**, 1911.

▼ **ITUNA, MAIN STREET**, 1913. From left to right: the pool room, the Bank of British North America, the post office, and the Ituna Hardware Store.

as the major distribution and service centre for the surrounding agricultural district, and in 1961 the community gained town status. Five years later, in 1966, Ituna reached a peak population of 975. Agriculture remains the basis of the Ituna area economy, and two grain companies and numerous trucking services handle agricultural exports. A variety of crops are grown in the district, and cattle and hog operations add diversity to the area's agricultural production. Ituna has a variety of local businesses and services, and the town serves the district with a health centre and special care home, housing for independent living, and a range of medical practitioners and services. As well, the town has an RCMP detachment, a volunteer fire department, an array of recreational facilities, four churches, a library, and a museum. The community's K-12 school had 171 students enrolled in the fall of 2006. Ituna serves as the administrative centre of the RM of Ituna Bon Accord No. 246.

▲ LOOKING NORTH up the main road in Jans Bay, September 21, 2003.

JANS BAY, northern village, pop 181 (2006c), 198 (2001c), is located in north-western Saskatchewan, west of Beauval on gravel Hwy 965. It is situated on the southeast shore of Canoe Lake. Jans Bay is a Metis community located in close proximity to the reserve holdings of the Canoe Lake Cree First Nation, signatories to Treaty 10 in 1906. As well, Jans Bay's sister communities of Cole Bay and Canoe Narrows, which are also situated on the lake, lie just to the west. A traditional economy of hunting, trapping, and fishing prevailed until 1954, when the creation of the Cold Lake (Primrose Lake) Air Weapons Range encompassed vast tracts of traditional Aboriginal and treaty areas. Today, logging and tourism are the main sources of employment for those in the workforce. Jans Bay has one of the youngest populations of any community in Saskatchewan; the median age is 14.7, while the average age of all provincial residents is 36.7. Jans Bay has a K-8 school, which had 46 students enrolled in the fall of 2006; students can complete high school at Canoe Narrows, where there is also a health clinic, a daycare centre, an indoor arena with artificial ice, stores and gas. Jans Bay was established as a northern hamlet in 1983 and was incorporated as a northern village on October 1, 1988.

JANSEN, village, pop 140 (2006c), 158 (2001c), lies 23 km east of Lanigan on Hwy 16, to the southwest of Big Quill Lake. The district was largely settled between 1904 and 1910, with the greatest influx coming in through 1905-07. Two brothers, Peter and John Jansen, American Mennonites, were significant for their colonizing efforts. They assisted in bringing a number of other Mennonites from the United States to the region. More numerous, however, were German Lutherans from the Volhynia and Volga colonies of Russia; as well, good numbers of people of British extraction, both from eastern Canada and overseas, settled in the Jansen area. The village itself began to develop as the CPR was working on the line between Wynyard and Lanigan. The first construction at the townsite evidently began in 1907, and on July 1, 1908, the Jansen Post Office was established. The Village of Jansen was incorporated on October 19, 1908. A local school district was formed in 1909, and in 1910 classes began at Jansen School. The population of the village was 111 in 1916, and 181 by 1931; but then through the Depression and the War, the community languished. However, through the boom years of the 1950s and 1960s Jansen prospered, its population soaring from 154 in 1946 to 282 by 1966. Simultaneously, though, services and schools were slowly becoming centralized, the rural population was falling, and better roads and automobiles allowed people to travel to larger centres to shop. In the late 1950s and early 1960s, high school students were transferred to Lanigan; in 1989, the grade eights followed. In 1991, due to declining student numbers and tough economic conditions, Jansen School was closed after 82 years in operation. Through the last few decades the village population has steadily declined and its business district has dwindled. Today, businesses in Jansen include a garage and bulk fuel dealer, a credit union, the post office, and a grocery store. Village organizations include the Kinsmen and Kinettes, the Community Club, and Baptist and Lutheran churches. Recreational facilities include a community centre, a bowling alley, and campgrounds. There is also a local library. Lanigan has the nearest hospital, ambulance service, and RCMP detachment; Jansen has its own volunteer fire department. Annual community events include a snowmobile rally, Canada Day celebrations, and a fall supper; bi-annually, community members organize a dinner theatre. For years, there were three grain elevators in Jansen; none remain today. But agriculture continues to play a major role in the economy: Pound-Maker Agventures Ltd., an integrated feedlot and ethanol plant located north of Esk, and Stomp Pork Farms' intensive hog operations at Leroy are key district employers. Other employment is found at PotashCorp's Lanigan Division mine at Guernsey, which is currently undergoing a 300-million-dollar expansion. When completed in 2007, the mine will provide close to 500 jobs, up from the current 350. In June 2006, Jansen area residents received exciting news when it was announced that BHP Billiton, an Australian-based company known for its 80 per cent stake in the Ekati Diamond Mine in the Northwest Territories, was seriously studying the village area as a potential site for a completely new potash mine in Saskatchewan, the first in decades. World demand for potash is increasing, largely to keep up with food production in growing Asian economies. Agrium Inc., who operate the potash mine at Vanscoy, are also looking at building another mine in the province. If the Jansen area project gets the go-ahead, seismic work and feasibility studies could take five years, and the mine could take five years to build. Jansen serves as the administrative centre of the RM of Prairie Rose No. 309.

JASMIN, organized hamlet, pop 0 (2006c), 5 (2001c), is a former village situated just northwest of Ituna on Hwy 15. Although some people made incursions into the Jasmin area in the late 1800s, the district was largely settled in the early 1900s, with most of the available land homesteaded between 1904 and 1906. Settlers were of many nationalities: English, Irish, Scottish, French, Swedish, Ukrainian, and Polish. Jasmin was largely French in the early days; as the years passed, however, the district became predominantly Ukrainian. The first settlers in the area detrained at Qu'Appelle, travelled north through Fort Qu'Appelle, east through Lebret, then north through Patrick to the Jasmin district. The majority of the homesteaders, though, travelled southwest from Sheho after the CPR reached that point in 1904. Jasmin itself began to develop between 1906 and 1908 as the Grand Trunk Pacific Railway was building its line from Melville through Watrous to Biggar. The community was so named (Jasmin is a subtropical flowering shrub belonging to the olive family) because it was situated on the Grand Truck Pacific's "alphabet line." Stations heading northwest out of Melville were named Fenwood, Goodeve, Hubbard, Ituna, Jasmin, and so on. The Jasmin Post Office was established on March 1, 1909, and Jasmin was incorporated as a village on August 10 that year. The next several years would be boom times. By 1910, the community boasted a grand hotel; by 1911, the population was 130, the community's peak; and by the outbreak of WWI, Jasmin offered a wide range of businesses: a rooming house and restaurants, a lumberyard, stores, a livery barn, dray service, hardware store, a printing company, bakery, implement dealership, blacksmith shop, notary public, real estate office, billiard parlour, butcher shop, tinsmith, grain buyer, flour mill, and an electric light plant. A quick succession of fires, though, took all but the rooming house — with the exception of the flour mill, which had earlier been moved to Kelliher. The Jasmin Hotel burned to the ground in 1920. The businesses lost were not rebuilt and many people left the community. The village was then overshadowed by its neighbours. Jasmin once had churches, a dance hall, a drama club, and football and baseball teams. But the population was down to 70 by 1956. 1965 was a bad year: the one remaining elevator burned to the ground, and at the end of the school year, the school closed and students were thereafter bused into Kelliher. By 1971, the population of Jasmin had fallen to 30, and on July 1, 1973, the village was dissolved and

Jasmin became an organized hamlet. The post office closed in 1982. By 1986, the population was 13. Today, you could drive by Jasmin and never know there had been a community there. Jasmin is situated in the RM of Ituna Bon Accord No. 246.

JEDBURGH, hamlet, pop 20 (2001c), 13 (1996c), is a former village located northwest of Yorkton (south of Theodore), midway between Hwys 16 and 52. Early residents were primarily Scottish; later, the community became predominantly Ukrainian. In the early 1900s there was a rapid influx of settlers into the district, and with them the demand for mail service grew. On September 1, 1909, a post office was established about five kilometres southwest of the present community and mail was brought in twice a week from Theodore by Peter Hoy, the mail carrier, who travelled by horse and democrat. The name of the post office was chosen to honour Hoy's birthplace, Jedburgh, Roxburghshire, in the borders area of Scotland. The rural municipality in which the post office was located, Garry No. 245, was established in 1913. In 1926 the RM council began to petition for a rail line to be built into the area from Willowbrook, and in 1928 the Canadian National Railway came through the Jedburgh district, extending its line as far as Parkerview. With the arrival of the CNR the Jedburgh Post Office was relocated to a townsite on the rail line, and the developing hamlet adopted its name. The CNR built a station, a foreman's house, a bunkhouse, and a tool shed. The first business started in Jedburgh was a small store, but soon four grain elevators were erected and Jedburgh became an important grain delivery point — four elevators operated until the 1970s. A one-room

▲ **THE JEDBURGH COMMUNITY HALL** narrowly escaped destruction in 1984, when the Jedburgh Hotel that was to the left of the building burned to the ground.

▲ **ALL THAT IS LEFT** of Jedburgh's once-busy business section is this cluster of buildings. The post office, second from the right, remains in operation.

▶ **ST. PETER AND PAULS UKRAINIAN CATHOLIC CHURCH**, Jedburgh, built 1946.

Jedburgh photographs taken July 14, 2004.

school was built in 1930 and 41 pupils were enrolled; following WWII a burgeoning student population necessitated the construction of new two-room school. Jedburgh once boasted a livestock yard, a blacksmith shop that manufactured snowplanes, a lumber yard, farm equipment agencies, a pool room, a general store, garages, a café, a curling rink, community hall, and sports grounds. A three-domed church still stands as a testimony to a once-active community. In 1947, the Jedburgh Hotel was built. On May 1, 1948, Jedburgh gained village status, and in 1951 the population of the community was 92. At the time, the population of the surrounding RM was close to 2,000 (in 2006 the RM of Garry No. 245 had a total of 426 total residents). Jedburgh's decline was clearly evident in the 1960s, even though electricity and water supplies had been vastly improved, and by 1971 the village numbered only 64 residents. In 1977, United Grain Growers, which by then owned three of the elevators, ceased operations in Jedburgh, and that year CN abandoned the rail line from Jedburgh to Parkerview. The Saskatchewan Wheat Pool closed it doors in 1978, and the rail line from Willowbrook to Jedburgh was officially abandoned in 1979. Jedburgh School, which had seen its senior grades begin moving to Ituna in the late 1950s, closed in 1983 after the last teacher, Anne Chyz, retired. It was another blow to the community when, on September 25, 1984, a fire that had started in the basement of the Jedburgh Hotel went unnoticed until well advanced, claiming the local landmark despite all possible efforts to save it. By 1986 the village numbered 21 residents. On August 3, 2000, Jedburgh relinquished village status. It remains the administrative centre of the RM of Garry No. 245.

KAMSACK, town, pop 1,713 (2006c), 2,009 (2001c), is located approximately 80 km northeast of Yorkton at the confluence of the Whitesand and Assiniboine Rivers and the junction of Hwys 5 and 8. Canora lies 40 km to the west, and Duck Mountain Provincial Park and Madge Lake are a short distance to the northeast via Hwy 57. The region was traversed by fur traders for many years dating back to the late 1700s; in the late 1800s, the name *Kamsack* was derived

from that of a well-known First Nations man in the area. The CPR was pushing its way north-westward toward Yorkton in the mid- to late 1880s, and it was during this decade that the first settlers began working their way north to the Kamsack area. Doukhobors came to the district in large numbers in 1899. During the first years of the twentieth century, with the approach of the railway, settlers poured into the area from eastern Canada, the United States, and Europe. A large num-

▲ **BUSINESSES SUCH AS THIS STORE, CIRCA 1908**, sprang up to serve the needs of the community's growing population. Saskatchewan Archives Board R-A4093.

KAMSACK
...gateway to Duck Mountain

▶ **THE PARKINSON BOYS** delivering newspapers in Kamsack, circa 1918. Saskatchewan Archives Board R-A4106.

▼ **LINED UP OUTSIDE THE CAPITOL THEATRE** for the 1954 film *Magnificent Obsession*, starring Jane Wyman and Rock Hudson. Clearly, Wyman (married to Ronald Reagan 1940-48) was the larger draw.

Unless otherwise indicated, photographs are courtesy of the Kamsack Powerhouse Museum.

THE MORNING AFTER: Kamsack residents survey the damage wrought by the "Kamsack Cyclone."

ber were Ukrainians. The Canadian Northern Railway was at Kamsack in 1904, and the first businesses were springing up on the townsite. By 1905, the district was well settled and Kamsack was incorporated as a village; it became one of the province's fastest growing and most progressive communities. Kamsack attained town status in 1911, and in 1914 construction began on an electric light plant, the waterworks, and a sewage system. By the early 1920s, the population was over 2,000. The community suffered somewhat of a setback during the 1930s, but the establishment of a petroleum company in the town in 1936 proved somewhat of a boon. In 1937, Kamsack became one of only three communities in Saskatchewan with their own natural gas system, prior to SaskPower being given the authority in the 1950s to begin establishing a province-wide utility (Lloydminster had natural gas in 1934, and Unity's system was in place in 1944). At its peak, the petroleum company in Kamsack had a minimum of 60 employees. On August 9, 1944, a tornado tore through the town. Locally referred to as the "Kamsack Cyclone," it damaged or destroyed 400 homes and 100 businesses, leaving three people dead and scores injured. The military was despatched to Kamsack to clean up the debris and help restore services. With the help of veterans returning from overseas, the biggest building boom in the community's history ensued; with the provincial trend toward urbanization, Kamsack's population was nudging 3,000 by the early 1960s. In 1962, however, the community faced another setback. The CNR had employed approximately 200 people in its roundhouse and shops at Kamsack, but that year the railway abandoned the town as a divisional point; many railway company employees had to leave the community

to find work, while those who remained had to seek new occupations. From that point on, the community's population has slowly declined. Today, Kamsack serves primarily as an agricultural service centre for the surrounding district with an array of businesses and services. Kamsack has a hospital with an attached special care home, a nursing home, a medical clinic, and an additional range of medical services and practitioners. Kamsack has a seven-member RCMP detachment and a 20-member volunteer fire department. The community has two schools, which together provide K-12 education to about 500 town and area students. The town's recreational facilities include a nine-hole golf course and clubhouse, campgrounds, sports grounds with three ball diamonds, and a complex which houses rinks for curling, skating, and hockey, as well as facilities for banquets and conventions. A seniors' centre provides recreational activities for the community's older residents. Duck Mountain Provincial Park, a few minutes drive away, affords opportunities for snowmobiling, cross country skiing, hiking, horseback riding, mountain biking, hunting, and fishing. Kamsack has a number of churches, service clubs, sports clubs, youth groups, and other community-based organizations. Annual community events include a weekend festival in August and an indoor rodeo each October. The Kamsack Historical Museum is located in the town's 1914 power plant, now a heritage property; the Kamsack Playhouse (also a heritage property), provides a venue for cinema, live theatre, and concerts. The National Doukhobour Heritage Village is a few kilometres west at Veregin. Kamsack has a 2,500-foot paved and lighted airstrip, and is one of only a few communities on the prairies that still has passenger rail service. Notable town landmarks are the two water towers which dominate the skyline. The original 1915 tower has been designated a heritage property and is one of only a handful of its kind in existence in Saskatchewan. Kamsack serves as the administrative centre of the RM of Cote No. 271.

KANDAHAR, organized hamlet, pop 25 (2006c), 15 (2001c), is located immediately south of Big Quill Lake and 12 km west of Wynyard on Hwy 16. A potassium sulphate manufacturing plant lies on the lake shore just to the east. There was significant settlement of the area by Icelanders beginning in 1905, and with the construction of the CPR line from Wynyard to Lanigan in 1909-10 the townsite of Kandahar was established. The community was named to commemorate a nineteenth-century British military victory in the ancient Afghan city. Kandahar, Saskatchewan, gained village status in 1913 and had a peak population of 125 in 1931. The community once boasted a number of stores, restaurants, two banks,

▼ **KANDAHAR, BEFORE 1919.**
Saskatchewan Archives Board
R-B10077.

a hotel, three grain elevators, and an active school. Today, other than a few homes surrounded by decaying ruins, virtually nothing remains. The village was dissolved at the end of 1970, and the community was reduced to organized hamlet status in 1971. Kandahar is situated in the RM of Big Quill No. 308.

KANNATA VALLEY, resort village, inc. 1966, is located on the east side of the southern end of Last Mountain Lake. The community had a year-round

▲ **FERRY CROSSING THE QU'APPELLE RIVER** near Katepwa, 1905. Saskatchewan Archives Board R-A9838-2.

▼ **KATEPWA LAKE** in the Qu'Appelle Valley, 1939. Saskatchewan Archives Board R-A17482.

population of 133 in 2006; this swells to 350 or more in the summer months. Kannata Valley is situated within the RM of Longlaketon No. 219.

KATEPWA BEACH is the common name for a resort area located in the Qu'Appelle Valley, on the northeast side of Katepwa Lake, on Hwy 56. The locale encompasses Katepwa Point Provincial Park. Settlers arrived in the area in the 1880s and the first cottages were built in the early 1900s. Katepwa Beach was incorporated as a resort village in 1957. The most significant development, however, has occurred over the past two or three decades. The Census of Canada recorded 45 year-round residents in 1981; today, the number is over 300. There are 550 cottages and homes at Katepwa Beach, and during the summer months the population can easily reach 1,000. In 2004, Katepwa Beach and the neighbouring resort villages of Katepwa South and Sandy Beach amalgamated, forming the District of Katepwa. The restructuring agreement was negotiated to enhance the administration and delivery of community services.

KATEPWA SOUTH is the common name for a resort area located in the Qu'Appelle Valley, on the southwest side of Katepwa Lake, north of Indian Head, off Hwy 56. There has been development in the area for roughly a century; however, the most rapid growth has taken place over the past couple of decades. Katepwa South was incorporated as a resort village in 1990. The 2001 Census recorded 44 permanent residents, although during the summer months the population can easily number 300. In 2004, Katepwa South and the neighbouring resort villages of Katepwa Beach and Sandy Beach amalgamated, forming the District of Katepwa. The restructuring agreement was negotiated to enhance the administration and delivery of community services.

KAYVILLE, organized hamlet, pop 5 (2006c), 15 (2001c), is located south of Avonlea on Hwy 334. Between 1905 and 1908, large numbers of Romanian settlers arrived in the district, forming the foundations of the community of Kayville and of the now vanished hamlet of Dahinda. The influence of these Romanian pioneers is still evident in the architecture of Kayville's churches. A post office and a school were established in 1912 and 1913 respectively. With the arrival of the CPR in 1924, the townsite was formally established and Kayville developed into a once-thriving centre of culture and business serving the surrounding agricultural district. Kayville became an organized hamlet in 1951, and in the early 1970s the population was still over 100. Subsequently, however, Kayville slowly declined. The school was closed in the early 1990s, and in 1998 the rail line was abandoned.

▲ **HOLY TRINITY RUSSIAN ORTHO-DOX CHURCH**, immediately west of Kayville on a small rise, was built in 1923. The cemetery, with many plots enclosed with iron fences, lies just behind the church.

▲ **ST. PETER AND PAUL ROMANIAN ORTHODOX CHURCH**, built 1908.

▲ **A THIRD CHURCH** in Kayville has seen better days.

Photographs taken April 11 ("Easter Sunday") and April 23, 2004.

KAYVILLE *Once upon a time...*

◄ ► **ABANDONED BUILDINGS** along the east side of Kayville's main street.

▼ **ABANDONED HOMES** such as these below are scattered about the Kayville townsite. The house with the second-floor balcony (far right) burned to the ground shortly after the photograph was taken.

▼ **THE KAYVILLE CO-OP**, with origins in the late 1930s, closed about 2004.

▼ **THE FORMER SASKATCH-EWAN WHEAT POOL ELEVATOR** dates to 1973.

▼ **DESPITE KAYVILLE'S SMALL POPULATION** (down to just five in 2006), the former Georgian Hotel, now known as the "Dodge City Saloon," was still in business in the fall of 2007.

Businesses have closed and many abandoned homes line the streets. Kayville is situated in the RM of Key West No. 70.

KEELER, village, pop 5 (2006c), 15 (2001c), is located 44 km northwest of Moose Jaw on Hwy 42, between the villages of Marquis and Brownlee. The Qu'Appelle Valley lies approximately 14 km to the north. The name Keeler honours Joseph Paul Keeler Sr., who is considered the founder of the community. Keeler was born in England in the 1850s and had moved to Winnipeg (Fort Garry) as a boy. In the early 1900s, Keeler induced a number of people to move west with him, and in 1904 when a post office was established about five miles north of the present village, it was named Keelerville in his honour. Keeler's current mayor, Duncan Keeler, is the great-grandson of the community's founder. In 1905, a school built a couple of miles to the southeast of the post office was also named Keelerville. Settlers to the district largely came from Manitoba, Ontario, England, and Scotland, or from the states of Minnesota, Wisconsin, and Iowa. Until the railroad was built through the area, Keelerville district residents had to haul their grain to Caron, on the CPR mainline, where they could also obtain supplies. When the railway built their branch line from Moose Jaw to Outlook through the area between 1906 and 1909, it passed several miles south of the Keelerville district, and a townsite for a new community was surveyed. The name Keeler was adopted, and beginning about 1908 the first buildings began to appear at the village site. The post office would move to the new locale and shorten its name to Keeler, and the postmaster, William Francis Fowle, would serve in the position from 1904 until 1948. Shortly after the railroad

arrived at Keeler, four grain elevators lined the tracks. A Presbyterian church (later United) was built circa 1909-10, and the village was incorporated on July 5, 1910. In 1911, a local village school district was established, and classes commenced at Keeler School in 1912. The Keelerville School, to the north, remained in operation until 1959; however, it had been closed from 1942 to 1951 due to a lack of pupils. Excerpts from the Village of Keeler minutes, recounted in the local history, shed light on some of the more colourful aspects of life in the community during its heyday: for a brief time during the 1920s it was rumoured that the laundry run by a

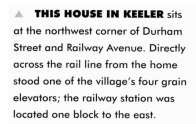

certain Sam Hing also served as a brothel. "Ladies of the evening" from Moose Jaw reportedly "visited" between trains. Another excerpt from 1927 states that the Village sought to communicate with the Saskatchewan Provincial Police in Moose

▲ **THIS HOUSE IN KEELER** sits at the northwest corner of Durham Street and Railway Avenue. Directly across the rail line from the home stood one of the village's four grain elevators; the railway station was located one block to the east.

Keeler photographs taken July 9, 2003.

Jaw to assist with the problem of the bootlegging industry in the community. Another entry, recorded in 1941, recounts that the Village requested the floor manager at local dances to restrict the dance known as the "jitterbug" to two such dances per evening. Elsewhere in the local history, it is stated that the village doctor, a Dr. Redmond, who worked in Keeler from 1916-20, "disappeared mysteriously." Keeler reached a peak population of 115 in 1926, but the community's numbers declined sharply during the Depression and the outbreak of WWII, to the point that, by 1941 the village population was down to 60. Honour rolls listing the Keeler district's veterans who served in both World Wars total 59 men and women. During the post-war period, Keeler rebounded somewhat, and the population was up to 90 by 1956. Since that time, however, the village has been in steady decline; there have been fewer than 50 people in Keeler since 1981. Keeler's grade 11 and 12 students began to be bused to Brownlee to

▲ **THIS SCHOOL** was built in Keeler in 1921 and served the community until its closing in 1970. It is now the residence of the village mayor, Duncan Keeler.

▼ **THE KEELER HOTEL** began its life in 1908 when it was built by Oliver George and operated as "The People's Store." In 1935, it was converted into a hotel with a beverage room. It was still a local watering hole in the 1980s, but it has now been vacant for many years.

attend school in 1958, followed by grades 9 and 10 in 1960. The grade 8 class was transferred to Brownlee in 1968, and in 1970 Keeler School was closed. The United Church closed in 1971. The indoor hockey and skating rink was used until the 1970s, when it was closed for safety reasons. In 1988, the rink was demolished. Five years later, the post office closed. The first of Keeler's elevators came down in 1978; two were torn down in 1986, and the last was demolished several years ago. Today, there are no businesses or services remaining in the community, and Keeler has the appearance of becoming a ghost town, as many buildings stand in various states of disrepair. In 2006, the community was in the news, after the Saskatchewan Government took the Village to court for violating the provincial Water Act by failing to put chlorine in its drinking water. A judge ruled in favour of the Province, and the Village was fined $750 and ordered to buy a chemical pump that would automatically add chlorine. Keeler residents argued that their well water was fine, that they didn't want chlorinated water, and that the cost of a chlorination system was too expensive and would bankrupt the community. Keeler requested that Saskatchewan Environment reclassify its water supply as off-limits for drinking, which would make it unnecessary for the Province and the courts to further financially penalize the village. The area economy is based on crop production and cattle ranching; a Saskatoon berry farm located just south of Keeler provides summer employment for about 10 area students. Keeler is situated in the RM of Marquis No. 191.

KELFIELD, hamlet, pop 5 (1996c), is located 36 km east of Kerrobert on Hwy 51. The Kelfield Post Office was es-

tablished on September 1, 1909, on the farm of David H. Kelly, which was located somewhat east of the present hamlet (the name Kelfield is short for "Kelly's field"). Kelly served as the postmaster until 1913, when the post office relocated to the newly-established townsite. The CPR completed a line into Kelfield from Wilkie in 1912. With the arrival of the railway, businesses sprang up, including a three-storey hotel, and Kelfield became an incorporated village on February 26, 1913. In 1918, there was a building boom: a new brick school was built, several new houses were completed, and the office for the surrounding rural municipality (est. 1911) was moved into the village from the country (it remains in Kelfield today). The population of Kelfield rose from 45 in 1916 to a peak of 132 in 1926. In 1931, the village numbered 105 residents and, according to the local history, the community was comprised of 24 people of English origin, 13 Irish, 49 Scots, 10 Germans, 1 Russian, 7 Ukrainians, and 1 Chinese. Along religious lines there were 3 Anglicans, 3 Baptists, 2 Lutherans, 21 Presbyterians, 7 Roman Catholics, 68 United Church members, and 1 other. During the late 1920s and through the 1930s, many businesses in the community closed; those that survived were mostly gone by the 1950s. By 1956, the population of Kelfield was down to 60; by 1961, it was 32. In 1959, high school students began to be bused to the village of Springwater, 21 kilometres to the east; Kelfield School closed in 1964. The CPR station closed in 1966, although trains serviced the elevators until the early 1980s when the rail line was abandoned. By 1981, the population of Kelfield was down to 16 members of three families. Kelfield relinquished village status in 2000; it remains the administrative centre of the RM of Grandview No. 349.

KELLIHER, village, pop 257 (2006c), 317 (2001c), lies 24 km northwest of Ituna on Hwy 15, a few km east of its junction with Hwy 35. In the 1880s, a few enterprising cattle ranchers were operating in the district, having come over the trails leading to the Touchwood Hills trading post and Fort Carlton. After about 1903, homesteaders began to arrive, coming by way of the railway points at Yorkton or South Qu'Appelle (today, the town of Qu'Appelle). A couple of years later the nearest railway points were at Sheho, to the northeast, and Lipton, to the south, and many settlers came to the Kelliher area from those points. The district would come to be settled mainly by people of Swedish, Ukrainian, and English origins. The village of Kelliher had its beginnings as the Grand Trunk Pacific Railway was building its line between Winnipeg and Saskatoon, and it was named after B.B. Kelliher, the railway company's chief engineer — the name chosen to fit the alphabetical sequence of naming commu-

nities along the rail line: Ituna, Jasmin, Kelliher, Leross, etc. The grading for the rail line was finished in 1907, and in 1908 the steel rails were laid and the Kelliher townsite was chosen. The Kelliher Post Office was established on November 1, 1908, and a number of other businesses were started that year. On April 27, 1909, the burgeoning hamlet was incorporated as the Village of Kelliher; by May that year a school had been built; and by 1911, the community numbered 220 residents. By the 1920s, the population was over 300; it was well over 400 through the 1950s; and in 1966 a peak population of 503 was recorded. At this time, approximately three dozen businesses served the community and surrounding area, as did five churches — United, Ukrainian Catholic, Roman Catholic, Anglican, and Swedish Lutheran. The village served a trading area of about 1,250 people. Kelliher benefited from a diversified economy — not one entirely dependent upon grain production. While cereal crops were important — three grain elevators once served the community — cattle production, which included

▲ **KELLIHER, JULY 14, 2004.** Second Avenue, looking east from Main Street.

a good number of purebred herds, pigs, sheep, poultry, and a creamery which employed about 20 people were also going concerns. More than 75 per cent of the area farms had dairy herds in the 1950s. At one time fur farms were numerous in the district and played an important role in the economy — there were about 80 in total, raising mainly fox and mink — but by the 1960s most of these operations had been curtailed. Since the mid-1960s, Kelliher and the surrounding district have been steadily losing population. The village experienced a dramatic loss between 1966 and 1976, when its numbers fell from 503 to 411 over the course of the decade. The population then remained fairly stable for the next 10 years, but since the mid-1980s it has again steadily declined. Between 1996 and 2006, Kelliher again lost significant numbers as the population fell from 338 to 257, a drop of close to 25 per cent. The community retains a broad range of businesses and services, however, as well as four churches, recreational facilities, a library, and a number of community-based organizations and sports clubs. Kelliher hosts an annual rodeo in June. Kelliher Motors, a Ford dealership, has been family owned and operated for about 40 years. The community has a volunteer fire department; there is a hospital 20 kilometres to the east in the village of Lestock; the nearest RCMP detachment is based in Ituna. Kelliher's school is a K-12 facility which had 143 village and area students enrolled in the fall of 2006. One of the oldest commercial buildings existing in Kelliher, built around 1910, and formerly known as Goddard's Dry Goods, is a designated heritage property which now houses the Kelliher and District Heritage Museum. The false-front, two-storey building had been a store until the 1990s, and throughout its history it was used to sell a variety of products including groceries, meats, liquor, clothing, and, of course, dry goods. Today, agriculture remains the main industry in the Kelliher area, with grain, cattle, and buffalo being raised; a number of agriculture-related businesses operate in the district, including seed cleaning plants and seed processors, farm supply outlets, machinery fabricators, a livestock auction service, and an abattoir, among others. Kelliher is situated in the RM of Kellross No. 247.

KELVINGTON, town, pop 866 (2006c), 1,007 (2001c), is located in east-central Saskatchewan, south of Greenwater Provincial Park, on Hwy 38 just north of its junction with Hwy 49. The town's economy is largely based on agriculture, with area farms producing grain, cattle, and exotic livestock. The first settlers arrived in the district around 1900, and in 1906 and 1907 the Kelvington post office and the first general store were opened respectively. It was after WWI, however, and through the 1920s, that most of the land in the area was taken up. In 1921, CN's line from Preeceville was completed, and Kelvington was incorporated as a village in November that year. The community's location at the end of the line greatly contributed to its development, as it became an important grain handling point and distribution centre (prior to the arrival of the railway, area farmers had to travel to Wadena to deliver grain and obtain supplies). The population of Kelvington skyrocketed from 370 in 1926 to 698 in 1946. Kelvington became a town in 1944, and by the mid-1970s the population was over 1,000. In the late 1980s, a potential problem for the community developed

▲ **GRONSDAL MOTORS, KELVINGTON, 1949.** The business burned down in 1964, and a new garage was built in 1965. It later became a Bumper to Bumper auto parts dealership. Photograph courtesy of Heritage Place, Kelvington.

"Canada's Hockey Factory"
KELVINGTON

▼ **FIVE OF THE SIX KELVINGTON SONS** who have played in the National Hockey League stand in front of their respective hockey cards, erected as a tribute to them at the entrance to the community. Left to right: Barry Melrose, Joey Kocur, Wendel Clark, Kerry Clark, and Kory Kocur. (Missing from the photograph is Lloyd Gronsdahl whose hockey card is at the far left.) Photograph courtesy of Donald Link, Kelvington.

▲ **PARTICIPANTS** at Kelvington's 81st Annual Agricultural Fair and Race Meet (Light Horse Division).

▲ **ELEVATOR ROW** in Kelvington was saved when the CPR built a line into the community after CN abandoned its track from Preeceville.

▼ **KELVINGTON'S FORMER CN STATION**, built in 1922, is now a heritage property, serving as a tourist information centre, a gift shop, and a museum.

Photographs taken July 30, 2004.

when CN decided to abandon its line between Kelvington and Preeceville. The solution came when CP constructed a 23-kilometre link west from the town to its line, thus ensuring continued rail service to Kelvington's grain elevators. Today, the town has several dozen varied businesses and services, a number of which cater to the agricultural sector. Kelvington has a hospital, a medical centre, an extended care facility, ambulance service, a volunteer fire department, and a local RCMP detachment. The town has a library, four churches, and elementary and high schools which provide K-12 education to over 300 students. Kelvington also has a full range of recreational facilities including two parks, a golf course, a swimming pool, baseball diamonds, tennis courts, a bowling alley, and a seniors' activity centre. The community also has curling and hockey rinks, and Kelvington dubs itself "Canada's Hockey Factory," having had six players achieve success in the NHL. A large mural on the south edge of town depicts the players' hockey cards. The number of parks and lakes in the Kelvington region offer additional recreational opportunities and also attract tourists. Hunting and fishing are popular area activities, as is cross-country skiing. A local snowmobiling club maintains a few hundred kilometres of groomed trails. The town also hosts an annual summer hockey tournament and a hockey school in July; a fair and sports day are held in August. Kelvington serves as the administrative centre of the RM of Kelvington No. 366.

KENASTON, village, pop 259 (2006c), 282 (2001c), is nicknamed the "Blizzard Capital of Saskatchewan," and is situated approximately 70 km south of Saskatoon at the junction of Hwy 11 and Hwy 15. The Qu'Appelle, Long Lake and Saskatchewan Railway reached the site of the present community from Regina in 1889 (the track was completed through to Prince Albert the next year), but there was not any permanent settlement in the area until after 1902. In this year, at the urging of the Canadian Government, the Saskatchewan Valley Land Company was formed. Colonel Andrew Duncan Davidson (for whom the town of Davidson is named) was the president, and F.E. Kenaston was the vice-president, and they began aggressive campaigns to promote immigration to the area. By 1903, waves of homesteaders were pouring into the region. Among those who first came to the area around Kenaston, which was originally known as Bonnington Springs, were Croatians, Czechs and Slovaks, and Scandinavians, mainly Norwegians. The first store on the townsite was built in 1903; the next year a hotel was constructed. The Bonnington Post Office was established in 1904 (the name was changed to Kenaston at the beginning of 1906); in 1905 the Kenaston School District was formed. The first grain elevator was erected in 1906, and the first telephone was installed in the community in 1909. Kenaston became an incorporated village on July 18, 1910. By 1926 the population was 243 and it remained at close to that level until after WWII. From the mid-1950s through to the beginning of the 1970s, Kenaston's numbers mushroomed: the community had a peak population of 466 in 1966. Today, Kenaston has a good array of businesses and services, and an active Chamber of Commerce; Saskatoon, a 45-minute drive away, affords village residents easy access to all the amenities of a city. Kenaston has three churches and a Jehovah's Witnesses' Kingdom Hall, a number of volunteer organizations, sports teams,

and other community groups. Kenaston Place auditorium and community centre has a theatre-style performance stage and, with a capacity to accommodate 500 people, can facilitate functions such as trade shows, graduations, and conferences. Kenaston has ball diamonds, a seasonal indoor swimming pool, a social centre for seniors, and a hockey arena — home to the Kenaston Blizzards senior hockey team. The Bonnington Springs campground has hot shower facilities and walking trails. The village has a volunteer fire department; the nearest hospital is in Davidson; the closest RCMP detachment is in Hanley. Kenaston School is a K-12 facility, which had 125 students enrolled in the fall of 2006. The village's CN water tower remains standing, as do three of Kenaston's five grain elevators, including the first all-steel elevator in western

Canada, built in 1960. The elevators are now independently owned by farmers who have developed them into private business ventures. Kenaston serves as the administrative centre of the RM of McCraney No. 282.

KENDAL, village, pop 59 (2006c), 83 (2001c), is located 13 km west of Montmartre and roughly 80 km southeast of Regina on Hwy 48. The reserve of the Carry the Kettle First Nation lies a short distance to the northeast. The Kendal district was largely settled between 1898 and 1909 by French, English, and German speaking pioneers. The French came from France or Quebec; the English-speaking settlers were mostly from Ontario, although some came from the United States; people with Germanic roots came from areas of Poland, Hungary, and Austria, and the Odessa region of southern Russia. The English-speaking people were largely Protestant; the French and Germans, Roman Catholic. The German settlers in the district were predominant. The village of Kendal itself — the origin of the community's name is unknown — began to develop between about 1905 and 1907 as the Canadian Northern Railway line was being built from Brandon, Manitoba, through Kipling to Regina. Prior to the coming of the railroad, district settlers had had to travel to Indian Head for staple items such as flour, sugar, lumber, and clothing. The Kendal Post Office, originally known as Kendal Station, was established on January 17, 1910 (the name was shortened in 1957), and in March that year a school, named Silver Hills after a low range of hills in the area, was completed in the village. The initial enrollment was 37 students. From 1909 to 1919, Kendal was a hamlet administered by the RM of

Montmartre No. 126, but on February 17, 1919, the Village of Kendal was incorporated and thereafter could manage its own affairs. In the early years, there was a great deal of trade and interaction between the villagers and members of the Carry the Kettle First Nation: younger reserve residents were prominent players on Kendal's hockey and baseball teams. Kendal had a population of 155 by 1926, and although the community's numbers fell somewhat during the 1930s and WWII, Kendal recovered during the 1950s. In 1961, Kendal numbered 161 residents. The early 1960s, however, marked the beginning of a steady decline for the village. Students in grades 11 and 12 began to be bused to school in Montmartre, and in 1970 Kendal's school was closed — then all of the community's schoolchildren were bused to the neighbouring centre. In the 1970s — the population was down to 90 by 1971 — the railway station, too, was closed: it was sold and removed in 1977. Thereafter trains stopped in Kendal only to load grain at the elevators. Today, though, where four elevators once stood, none remain, and the village has essentially been reduced to an assemblage of well-kept and attractive residences. A community landmark is St. Ignatius Church, built in 1919 and renovated in 1965. Tragedy struck the St. Ignatius congregation during the night of June 1, 1951, when a fire of electrical origin started in the rectory kitchen and Reverend Aloysius Beechey, the parish priest, succumbed to smoke inhalation and died. His name (albeit spelled incorrectly), along with the other priests who served the community, is commemorated on a cross in the St. Ignatius churchyard. The church holds an annual bazaar each November, and other yearly events in the village include a summer sports day and a snowmobile rally held in January or

February. Kendal residents seek medical attention, and shopping and services in Montmartre, where there is also an RCMP detachment, a team of First Responders, and a fire department.

KENNEDY

KENNEDY, village, pop 187 (2006c), 243 (2001c), is situated due north of Moose Mountain Provincial Park, 23 km southeast of Kipling on Hwy 48. The district surrounding Kennedy was settled by people of diverse origins who arrived via eastern Canada, the United States, and Europe. These included people of British, French, and Belgian origin, who began arriving in the 1880s, and settlers of German and Hungarian stock, who arrived in the early 1900s. The Hungarians largely took up homesteads a few kilometres west of present-day Kennedy, forming a settlement centred at what became known as Bekevar. From the mid-1880s mail was hauled into the area from Whitewood. The Montgomery post office, to the north of present-day Kennedy, was established in 1884, and the Fletwode post office, to the southwest, began operating in 1895. There was a post office at St. Hubert in 1900. When Nelson A. Reid established a post office on his farm on August 1, 1904, just west of where Kennedy lies today, he chose the name Kennedy to honour the mail carrier at the time, Findlay Kennedy, who covered the route from Whitewood to Fletwode on horseback or with a team and buggy. Shortly thereafter, the CPR surveyed a route for a line that would connect Reston, Manitoba, with Wolseley, and the location for a townsite was established just east of the Reid farm. In 1906, the post office was relocated to the townsite, and the name Kennedy was adopted for the developing community. The track through the district was completed that year, and the little mixed train that came to run back and forth on the line eventually became affectionately known to local residents as the "Peanut." In 1907-08, the Canadian Northern Railway built a line roughly five kilometres north of Kennedy. It ran parallel to the CPR track from the Manitoba border through Langbank to Kipling, but ran directly on to Regina after Peebles. Meanwhile, Kennedy had continued to develop. A general store, a lumberyard, a hotel, a shoemaker's shop, and an implement dealership were among the businesses operating by 1906, and on November 5, 1907, the Village of Kennedy was incorporated. That year, a branch of the Bank of Toronto was established and a local school was started, with classes carried on in various locations until a schoolhouse was completed in 1909. The Kennedy Union Church was built in 1907, and in 1912 the first Roman Catholic church was constructed. In 1908, the Kennedy Agricultural Society sponsored its first summer fair, and by that time the first grain elevator had been erected, relieving farmers of the long haul to Whitewood. Although crop production would be integral to the area economy, over the years it was for award-winning purebred herds of cattle that the Kennedy area would come to be known. By 1921, Kennedy's population had reached 247, and, somewhat surprisingly — despite the Depression, rail line abandonment at the outset of the 1960s, and the concurrent elevator closure — the village's population has remained almost perfectly stable over the decades, fluctuating very little. The rural population, however, has significantly declined over the years, and with the ease of travel, Kennedy's business district has been greatly reduced, superseded by offerings in larger centres (for a short period of time in the mid-1990s, the village found itself without a grocery store or a service station). Today, other businesses operating in the community include a beverage room and a restaurant, a hardware store, a credit union, a shoe repair and leather sales shop, and the post office. As well, there are a handful of tradespeople and home-based businesses. The village has a library, United and Catholic churches, a community hall, and rodeo grounds. The Moose Mountain Rodeo, held annually in Kennedy, had its beginnings in 1934, and became part of the professional rodeo circuit in 1987. The Saskatchewan Power Corporation brought 24-hour electricity to Kennedy in 1953, sewer lines were installed in 1963, natural gas became available in 1971, and by 1986 most of the village streets were paved. In 1984, a new skating arena opened, replacing the first covered rink which had been built in 1949. In 1985, Kennedy and Langbank schools amalgamated, with grades K-6 being taught in Langbank and grades 7-12 in Kennedy. In 2001, the school in Langbank was closed. All grades were subsequently taught in Kennedy. The school was renamed Kennedy Langbank School and 103 students were enrolled in the fall of 2006. In the spring of 2007, it was announced the school would be losing grades 9-12. Subsequently there ensued a bitter fight over where, Montmartre or Wolseley, high school students would be bused. Kennedy is the hometown of Colleen Sostorics, who plays defence with the Canadian National Women's Hockey Team. Sostorics captured her first Olympic gold medal in Salt Lake City in 2002 and her second at the Winter Games in Torino, Italy, in 2006. Prairie Avenue in the village has been renamed Colleen Sostorics Avenue in her honour. Kennedy is located within the boundaries of the RM of Wawken No. 93.

KENOSEE LAKE

KENOSEE LAKE, village, pop 194 (2006c), 182 (2001c), is a resort-based community situated 22 km north of Carlyle off Hwy 9, adjacent to the boundary of Moose Mountain Provincial Park. The reserve of the White Bear First Nation is located a few kilometres to the south. The village lies on the northeast shore of the lake from which it derives its name. The lake, originally known as Fish Lake, is the largest in the region, and the word "Kenosee" is derived from the Cree word for fish. The area known as Moose Mountain is a wooded plateau dotted with lakes, which rises as much as 200 metres above the surrounding plains. The resort potential of the area was exploited shortly after the first homesteaders began taking up land on the peripheral prairie in the 1880s-90s. They initially came to the Moose Mountain uplands for many of the same resources that had earlier brought Aboriginal peoples, hunters and trappers to the region — wood for fuel, logs for buildings, and a good supply of fresh fish and game. In the 1890s, a cluster of cabins developed in the area of the present village of Kenosee Lake, and what became known as the Christopher Trail (today an extant road) was hewn in from the settled plains to the east, an area known as the Glen Adelaide district. Charles Frederick Christopher, for whom the trail was named, was instrumental in its construction, and he and his wife, Harriet, were largely responsible for the beginnings of the resort development. Up until 1913, they provided cabin, tent, and boat rentals, and sold fishing tackle and other supplies. The federal government designated much of the area a forest reserve in 1906, and in 1931, following Saskatchewan gaining control of its natural resources a

▲ **THE FIELDSTONE CHALET IN MOOSE MOUNTAIN PROVINCIAL PARK** was built in the early years of the Depression as a relief project. It originally housed a hotel; today, the building houses the park's visitors centre and the park office — it sits just to the west of the boundary of the village of Kenosee Lake. Photograph courtesy of Michael and Anna Clancy, Saskatoon.

◄ **STILL OPERATIONAL**, this wood-clad, standpipe water tower in Kerrobert is a landmark in the town. Only ten such water towers were built in Saskatchewan — this is one of the remaining four. Erected in 1914, the original cost to build the tower was $49,000. Designed to resemble a coastal lighthouse, it has a capacity of 156,000 gallons (709,191 litres). It was declared a municipal heritage property in 1981. Photograph taken August 14, 2003.

KERROBERT
"The Town on the Old Tote Road"

year earlier, Moose Mountain Provincial Park became one of first provincial parks established in the province. At the outset of the Depression, the construction of infrastructure in the park provided relief employment: the highway was developed, and, over 1931-33, a pier, a golf course, a clubhouse, and a stone chalet (today the park's visitors centre) were built. Thereafter, however, as the economic situation worsened and the country became involved in war, the park system in the province was largely ignored. Rebuilding and investment followed in the decades after, however. Big Bands played at Kenosee Gardens and a drive-in theatre was built. The area became one of the most popular tourist destinations in Saskatchewan, and to this day the population of the Moose Mountain area swells to many thousands during the summer months. The village of Kenosee Lake was originally incorporated as the Resort Village of We-Non-Cha in 1978; the name was changed to the Resort Village of Kenosee Lake in 1981. On October 1, 1987, Kenosee Lake became a village proper. Today, major area attractions include a luxury hotel and confer-

ence centre, two 18-hole golf courses, a waterslide park, horseback riding stables, hiking and biking trails, miniature golf courses, and a casino. The Moose Head Inn, a restaurant and nightclub complex in the village, has long been rumoured to be haunted, and it has been the subject of a number of media reports in recent times. The Inn has subsequently become the site of an annual psychic fair. A short drive to the southeast is Cannington Manor Provincial Historic Park. It is a partially restored late-nineteenth-century village, where English aristocrats attempted to maintain the social customs of Victorian England in a utopian agricultural settlement on the Canadian prairie. The community failed, however, and Cannington Manor was abandoned at the beginning of the twentieth century. The village of Kenosee Lake lies within the boundaries of the RM of Wawken No. 93.

KERROBERT, town, pop 1,001 (2006c), 1,111 (2001c), is located in the west-central region of the province, north of Kindersley at the junction of Hwys 21,

▲ **THE GROCERY DEPARTMENT OF SAMPLE BROS. STORE**, the first store in Kerrobert, circa 1912-13. Photograph courtesy of the Kerrobert Museum.

◀ **THE KERROBERT BLOOMERS**
girls' baseball team, 1917. Saskatchewan
Archives Board R-A15554.

▶ **KERROBERT'S LACROSSE TEAM**
were the provincial champions in
1918. They are pictured here with their
championship trophy. Photograph courtesy
of the Kerrobert Museum.

▼ **CHILDREN IN COSTUME**
parade through Kerrobert to advertise
a Chautauqua, date unknown.
Saskatchewan Archives Board R-A23724.

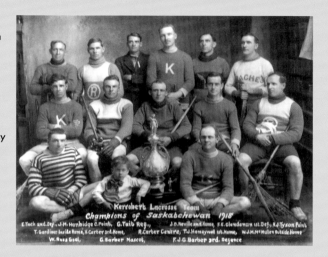

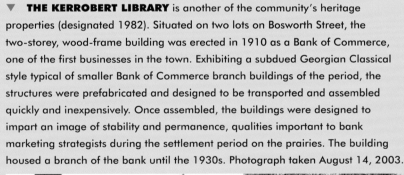

▼ **ALLEN'S BARN**, originally a piggery, was once the home to legendary barn
dances. Located just on the west side of town, it is now covered each year after
high school graduations with the signatures of a new generation. Photograph
taken August 14, 2003.

▼ **THE KERROBERT LIBRARY** is another of the community's heritage
properties (designated 1982). Situated on two lots on Bosworth Street, the
two-storey, wood-frame building was erected in 1910 as a Bank of Commerce,
one of the first businesses in the town. Exhibiting a subdued Georgian Classical
style typical of smaller Bank of Commerce branch buildings of the period, the
structures were prefabricated and designed to be transported and assembled
quickly and inexpensively. Once assembled, the buildings were designed to
impart an image of stability and permanence, qualities important to bank
marketing strategists during the settlement period on the prairies. The building
housed a branch of the bank until the 1930s. Photograph taken August 14, 2003.

▼ **THE KERROBERT COURT HOUSE**, built in 1919-20, was one of a series
of ten courthouses designed by Provincial Architect Maurice Sharon. Neo-
Classicism is still evident in the building's pediment and the columns surrounding
the entrance; largely, however, the structure exhibits a transition from Beaux-Arts
Classicism to a Colonial Revival style. The Kerrobert Court House was designated
a municipal heritage property in 1982. Photograph taken August 14, 2003.

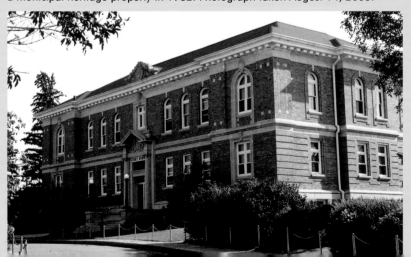

31, and 51. Saskatoon is 180 km to the east; the Saskatchewan-Alberta border, 65 km to the west. The first few settlers began taking up homesteads in the district in 1906; beginning in 1907, however, a great land rush was on, as word spread that the CPR would be constructing a line through the district. People largely of British and German origins came to the area: the former from eastern Canada and Great Britain; the latter, from the United States and southern Russia. By the summer of 1910 a cluster of tents and shacks containing a number of businesses had developed just north of the proposed townsite. Mail for the area was handled through a post office still further north, named Hartsburg. Established in 1908, the office, located in a sod house, would close to the Sample store in Kerrobert in the coming fall. On September 1, 1910, surveying of the townsite began, and at 9:00 a.m. on September 14 the hillside lots were put up for sale. The auctioneer was Tobias C. Norris, who would become the premier of Manitoba in 1915. On November 9, 1910, the fledgling community was incorporated as a village, its name honouring Robert Kerr, a CPR traffic manager based in Montreal who had retired that year. By Christmas, work trains were bringing freight into the community, and, as reported in the first issue of *The Citizen* published that month, over 50 places of business had been established. Within a year, on November 1, 1911, Kerrobert attained town status. As a CPR divisional point and a trading centre for a large district, it was initially envisioned that Kerrobert would grow to perhaps rival Swift Current or North Battleford in size. The community's beginnings were as a major handling point for shipments to the grain-buying markets in eastern Canada and the United States. Additional land around the

town was purchased for future development, and infrastructure and institutions were established in anticipation of a substantial boom which did not materialize. An ambitious waterworks system was created and imposing buildings such as the 1920 court house, designed by provincial architect Maurice Sharon, were constructed. A major factor, however, in limiting the town's future growth had to do with area land not being as productive as had been imagined. As well, there were changing patterns in prairie wheat shipments, as much grain traffic was being re-routed to the major terminals constructed in the port of Vancouver. Although Kerrobert did not mushroom to the proportions projected, the community did continue to grow and prosper. The development of the oil and gas industry in the 1950s diversified the area economy, and the industry continues to be important. Five pipelines run through the district, and a major pumping station with three large collection systems that gather and store oil from area fields is located at Kerrobert. Grain and livestock production, however, remains vital to the economy. Kerrobert serves the area with an array of businesses and services, a range of medical facilities and related services, an RCMP detachment, a volunteer fire department, recreational facilities, churches, and a K-12 composite school, which had 258 town and area students enrolled in the fall of 2006. A community attraction is the Kerrobert Museum, and a landmark in the business district is the Hanbidge Building, which once housed the offices of Robert and Jack Hanbidge's law firm. Robert Leith Hanbidge served on Kerrobert's town council before becoming mayor, and he later went on to become the Lieutenant-Governor of Saskatchewan from 1963 to 1970. Heritage properties in Kerrobert include the former 1911 CPR

station; the library, housed in a Bank of Commerce building dating to 1911; the 1914 water tower, visible for miles, still in use, and one of only a few of its kind left in Saskatchewan; and the 1920 court house, situated in a beautiful park-like setting. The courthouse, which now holds the town offices, as well as the offices of a number of professional services, is rumoured to be haunted. The story is that a ghost, related to a skull that was once locked in the building's evidence room, roams the court house halls in the early hours of the morning. The skull was used as evidence in a 1931 murder trial at which, reportedly, John G. Diefenbaker served for the defence. Kerrobert is situated in the RM of Progress No. 351.

KETCHEN, organized hamlet, pop 15 (2006c), 10 (2001c), is located 13 km northwest of Preeceville on Hwy 49. Settlers, many of Scandinavian and Ukrainian origins, began taking up land in the district in the early 1900s. Access to the area increased after the railway reached Preeceville from the east in 1912; however, further construction westward was de-

layed because of WWI, and it was not until 1921 that trains were running through Ketchen. After the railway arrived, a post office was moved in from the country and the small hamlet developed. The population of Ketchen hovered around 30 in the 1960s and early 1970s. Ketchen was established as an organized hamlet in 1981, and is situated in the RM of Preeceville No. 334.

KHEDIVE, hamlet, pop 15 (2001c), is approximately 46 km west of Weyburn, off Hwy 13. The district began to be settled around 1906, and with the construction of the railway from Weyburn to Assiniboia through the area in 1911 the townsite began to develop. Within a few years, Khedive had grown into a small, but thriving community. Three grain elevators, three churches, a school, a hotel, and a variety of businesses were established, serving the surrounding farming population. In 1916, Khedive was incorporated as a village. For a number of years, Khedive station was a busy place, with two passenger trains daily and special return-trip trains arranged on occasion to take

▼ **THE REMAINS OF THE OPEN-AIR RINK** in Khedive where many hockey games were played. Khedive Public School, in the background, was opened in 1921, and closed in 1976. Photograph taken August 31, 2004.

residents to hockey games in Weyburn. In 1956, Khedive had a peak population of 153; however, by the mid-1960s, centralization and rural depopulation began to negatively impact the village. Businesses began to close, the school closed, the churches closed, the rail line was abandoned and the tracks torn up, and the elevators were closed and then demolished. On January 1, 2002, the village was dissolved. Khedive is situated in the RM of Norton No. 69 and, today, very much resembles a ghost town.

KILLALY, village, pop 77 (2006c), 91 (2001c), is located approximately 20 km south of Melville on Hwy 22, just west of the junction with Hwy 47. The pretty Pearl Creek winds through a small valley on the west side of the village en route to the Qu'Appelle Valley, roughly 12 km to the south. The district began to be settled in the mid-1890s, when settlers began moving north across the Qu'Appelle Valley. The majority of those who took up land in the area were of German Catholic origin. The village began to develop with the construction of the railroad from Esterhazy to Balcarres in 1904. That year, the first store opened in Killaly and the first grain elevator was built. In 1905, the Killaly Post Office was established, a hotel was built, and houses began to spring up on the townsite. Shortly after, a community school was established, and in 1909 Killaly attained village status. Its name honours a construction engineer with the railway. The community continued to grow through the 1920s, but suffered a major setback when a spectacular fire in 1932 destroyed a substantial part of the village. Many businesses were lost. The years following WWII through to the mid-1960s were the community's most prosperous. The population peaked during this period when it was steady at over 200. Beginning in the late 1960s, however, the community began to decline, with many of the village's businesses and services superseded by those in the city of Melville. In the mid-1990s, the rail line was abandoned and the school was closed. Today, an active seniors' club and a Roman Catholic church remain. Killaly is situated in the RM of Grayson No. 184.

KINCAID, village, pop 135 (2006c), 161 (2001c), is located southwest of Gravelbourg at the junction of Hwys 13 and 19. Homesteaders began to come to the area in 1908-09. The district population came to be largely comprised of people of British, Scandinavian, French, and German origins. Kincaid, like most prairie communities, had a string of Chinese businessmen, and, additionally, one of Saskatchewan's pioneering Lebanese families, the Haddads, who became prominent in the village as owners and operators of a large general store and the hotel. A post office opened about a half-dozen miles south of the present village in 1910, but closed as Kincaid itself began to develop with the construction of the railroad between Assiniboia and Shaunavon in 1913-14. The Village of Kincaid was incorporated on July 19, 1913, and the community's local history attributes the name of Kincaid to that of a CPR official. A school opened in the village in 1914, and by 1915 numerous businesses had been established and Kincaid was booming. Many transient workers passed through the community, and bootlegging, gambling, and the occasional fight on a Saturday night were not out of the ordinary. People would come up from the United States and ride their horses right into the pool room — at least, according to local lore. During the first decades, Kincaid, like many Saskatchewan communities, was plagued with fires. In 1922, a livery barn burned to the ground and 22 horses were lost; in 1926, a fire that started in another livery barn got out of control, swept down the block and claimed a café, a bank, a poolroom, a lawyer's office, and furniture and hardware stores. In the late 1920s, a restaurant, a tinsmith shop, a garage, and a barbershop were lost in another blaze. In 1928, a cyclone hit the town, tearing the roof off the school and damaging a number of other structures. In spite of these losses, Kincaid was a major grain handling point and commercial centre for a considerable territory in the early days. The construction of railway branch lines in the region, however — from Wood Mountain to Mankota in 1929, and from Vanguard to Meyronne in 1935 — took a good deal of business away from Kincaid, and matters were only made worse by the years of drought and the Great Depression. Seven grain elevators had lined the CPR tracks at Kincaid, but by the 1950s there were four. Kincaid's population had jumped from 125 in 1916 to 300 by 1926, but it fell during the 1930s, and during this period a number of the village's businesses folded. Many of Kincaid's sons and daughters also left during the war years, but by the mid-1950s through to the early 1970s the village population was again hovering at around 300. In the years following, however, both the population and the number of businesses in the community began to decline. A particularly big blow was the loss of the farm machinery dealerships. The Massey-Ferguson dealership left Kincaid in the late 1960s, and by the end of the 1980s Co-op Implements, John Deere Ltd., and J.I. Case International were also gone. There was a period when Kincaid was without the basic services of a grocery store, a gas station, and a financial institution. But the village has experienced a certain level of revitalization in recent years. The community convinced the Mankota Credit Union to establish a branch in Kincaid, and the village itself now owns and operates its own grocery store. Further, the gas station/car wash was reopened. Other businesses operating in the community today include a hotel, coffee shop, hardware store, post office, automotive services, insurance agent, hair salon, and one remaining grain elevator. The village has a 21-unit seniors' home, and a health centre with a doctor and a lab technician available on certain days of the week. Kincaid School is a K-12 institution that accommodates close to 100 students, including those from four surrounding communities. Recreational facilities in the village include a baseball diamond, a seniors' centre, and a community sports facility with artificial ice for skating and curling and a banquet room. Additionally, Thomson Lake Regional Park, the first regional park in Saskatchewan, is about a half hour's drive to the northeast. It has facilities for camping, golfing, swimming, and boating. Kincaid also has a library and a museum, located in the former Apostolic Church, which contains local pioneer artifacts. The village has a number of service clubs and other community-based organizations, such as the Lions, the Legion, and the United Church Women. Together, they host and finance many sporting, cultural, and entertainment activities. Agriculture remains the major industry in the region, and the district has recently received somewhat of an economic boost with the establishment of a 10,000-head feedlot for cattle near the village of Hazenmore. Kincaid serves as the administrative centre of the RM of Pinto Creek No. 75.

1st Boarding House in Kindersey Aug 1909

KINDERSLEY SASK.

▲ **KINDERSLEY IN 1909 WAS A TENT TOWN.** This photograph was taken about the time the Canadian Northern Railway established the location for the townsite.

▲ **A CANADIAN NORTHERN RAILWAY STEAM LOCOMOTIVE** at Kindersley station, circa 1912.

KINDERSLEY *...images from before yesterday*

◀ **OX TEAMS** drawing high-wheeled wagons loaded with bagged grain. Kindersley, circa 1912.

▼ **BY 1915** in Kindersley, horses were replacing oxen as the preferred method of hauling grain; as well, the first automobiles were making their appearance.

KINDERSLEY. SASK. 1915

Photographs courtesy of the Kindersley
and District Plains Museum.

▲ **THE KINDERSLEY FIRE DEPARTMENT** in the mid-1950s.

▼ **LEN AND LLOYD'S BARBER SHOP** was one of the popular places in
Kindersley to get a haircut in the early 1960s.

KINDERSLEY, town, pop 4,412 (2006c), 4,548 (2001c), is located in the province's west-central region, between Rosetown and the Saskatchewan-Alberta border at the junction of Hwys 7 and 21. The first settlers began arriving in the district in 1907. In July 1909 the grade for the Canadian Northern Railway line from Saskatoon was nearing what would be the future site of the community — a small tent town emerged that summer, as entrepreneurs anticipated the coming of the rails. When the tracks were laid into the area, loads of lumber were shipped in for the building boom that would ensue. The townsite was surveyed in September, and in October lots were put up for sale. Five lumber companies were soon doing a thriving business. In December 1909, the post office was established, and on January 10, 1910, the village of Kindersley was incorporated, named after Sir Robert Kindersley, a major shareholder in the Canadian Northern Railway. Within 10 months, on November 1, Kindersley attained town status. The community, whose fortunes depended on grain farming, had a population of just over 1,000 by the early 1920s, and it remained around that mark until after WWII. In the early 1950s, major discoveries of oil and gas in the region, near the villages of Coleville, Smiley, and Brock, ushered in an era of rapid development and a surge in Kindersley's population. Numerous companies moved in to exploit the resources, and soon dozens, then hundreds, of oil and gas wells dotted the landscape. The town's population soared from 990 in 1941 to 1,755 in 1951 to 2,990 in 1961. Prosperity in the oil and gas fields also more than offset the declining railway company payroll, which, next to agriculture, had been the community's

second largest source of income (up until the 1950s, CN had approximately 140 employees in the town). Kindersley is the main shopping, service, and administrative centre for a trading area population of approximately 40,000 people. Strategically located on the main highway between Saskatoon and Calgary, the community also benefits from an annual traffic count of over 5 million vehicles. Kindersley has a complete range of businesses and services, with approximately 75 companies involved with the region's oil and gas industry. Numerous businesses in the town also operate in support of the region's agricultural industry. Kindersley also serves the area with a full range of medical facilities, services, and practitioners, as well as an RCMP detachment, a volunteer fire department, and an emergency response team. Educational facilities include elementary and high schools, the privately-funded K-12 Kindersley Christian Academy, and the Prairie West Regional College, which offers a broad range of vocational, avocational, and academic upgrading programs. The town has an array of recreational facilities, including Berard Field, a semi-pro ball diamond with night lighting and bleacher seating for 5,600. The facility hosts regional, provincial, and national tournaments, and in 1984 was the site of the World Youth Baseball Championships. Kindersley also has a museum, a library, a number of churches, and dozens of community-based organizations. Community landmarks — the water tower constructed in 1912-13 and the 1935 post office — have been designated heritage properties. Area attractions include the Addison Sod House and the Great Wall of Saskatchewan. Built between 1909 and 1911, the Addison house is the oldest continuously inhabited sod building in the province. The "Great Wall," three kilometres west

KINISTINO SASK.

of Smiley, was built by Albert "Stonewall" Johnson entirely of stones without the use of cement or mortar. Built purely as an artistic expression, the wall is roughly a kilometre long, three metres wide, two metres high, and took Johnson about 30 years to complete. In 2004, Kindersley was in international headlines when it was announced that the town would be the site of Canadian da Vinci Project's space launch. Project members were vying for a $10-million prize, which was to be awarded to the first team to put a privately-owned, manned craft into space twice within a two-week period. A U.S. team, funded by Microsoft billionaire Paul G. Allen, won the award, and the da Vinci Project's launch was put on indefinite hold. Kindersley serves as the administrative centre of the RM of Kindersley No. 290.

KINISTINO, town, pop 643 (2006c), 702 (2001c), is located 30 km northwest of Melfort on Hwy 3. The Saskatchewan River Forks are 30 km north of the community. The Kinistino district is one of the oldest areas settled in Saskatchewan for the purpose of basing a life on agriculture. Prior to the construction of the railway across the southern plains in 1882-83, settlers preferred the "fertile belt" of the parklands over the open, more arid prairie. In the 1870s, what was known as the Carrot River Settlement developed just to the south of today's community. In 1883, a post office was established and given the name Kinistino in honour of the Saulteaux chief, Kinistin. The settlement developed slowly for the first 25 years, however, until the construction of the Canadian Northern Railway through the area in 1905. With the arrival of the railway, both the settlement and the name Kinistino shifted to the present

Kinistino, circa 1940s...

▲ **MAIN STREET.**

▼ **THE BANK OF NOVA SCOTIA.**

▲ **THE KINISTINO POST OFFICE.**

▼ **ELEVATOR ROW.**

Photographs courtesy of Lorraine Hovdebo, Birch Hills, Saskatchewan.

townsite, and Kinistino was incorporated as a village on July 30, 1905. Settlers to the area largely included people of Scottish, English, and Norwegian origins, and one Black man, who would become one the district's most-respected citizens. Alfred Schmitz Shadd came to the Kinistino area from Ontario in 1896 to teach school and was likely the only Black educator out of approximately 400 employed in the territories at the time. He was also certainly the first Black person many people in the district had ever seen. Shadd had studied medicine and, seeing the great need for doctors in the area, he returned to Ontario and completed his medical degree in 1898. He returned to Kinistino and set up a medical practice, quickly earning the admiration of both the area's settlers and the indigenous population. He later moved his practice to Melfort where he set up a drug store, became the editor of the newspaper, and served on the town's council. He ran unsuccessfully in the territorial election in 1901, and in 1905 came within 52 votes of becoming the first Black ever elected to a provincial legislature. Kinistino grew steadily over the decades, attaining town status in 1952, and it reached a peak population of 861 in 1966. For the past 10 years, the population has remained stable at close to 700. Kinistino is the main trading centre in the district, and agriculture, a combination of both grain and livestock production, is the major industry. The town's two largest businesses are farm equipment dealerships. Kinistino has a special care home and a medical clinic, as well as a library, a museum and several service clubs and community-based organizations. Businesses include restaurants, grocery stores, auto services, a bulk oil agent, a post office, an insurance agent, and a number of home-based businesses operated by tradespeople, hair dressers, and a massage therapist among others. A bank and a credit union have automated services in the town. Kinistino School is a K-12 facility, which had 297 town and area students enrolled in the fall of 2006. Recreational facilities include rinks for skating, hockey, and curling, and ball diamonds, playgrounds, and halls, which accommodate both social and business functions. Additionally, the town is situated in close

proximity to a summer resort popular for boating, fishing, swimming, and camping. Kinistino serves as the administrative centre of the RM of Kinistino No. 459.

KINLEY, village, pop 35 (2006c), 40 (2001c), lies approximately halfway between Saskatoon and Biggar, just south off Hwy 14. The first store on the townsite was built in 1907 as railways were being built through the district. Both the Grand Trunk Pacific Railway and the Canadian Pacific Railway came through in 1908. The tracks were separated by about a mile: the CPR's was to the north at what locals called North Kinley; the Grand Trunk Pacific line (now CN) passed to the south through the main part of the townsite. Two grain elevators were erected on the CPR's line; four went up on the southern track. The name of the community honours Reverend H.J. Kinley, a Methodist minister who settled in the district. The post office took his name when it was established in 1908, and Kinley served as the second postmaster in 1909-10. In 1908 an Anglican Church was constructed and a school district was set up; the school was built the next year. Kinley became an incorporated village on January 7, 1909. Methodists conducted services in a variety of locations until the United Church was built in Kinley in 1926. During the community's formative years, a number of businesses including a hotel and a bank were started, and Kinley's population grew to hover at around 100 until the mid-1960s. Its peak population was 119 in 1961. By the 1960s, however, the Anglican Church had closed, and many businesses had disappeared. The school closed at the end of June in 1966 (students were then bused to Perdue), and by the end of the decade the only businesses remaining in the village were a store and

the post office. Today, older homes remain scattered amongst vacant lots, and a former Saskatchewan Wheat Pool elevator (c. 1968) remains standing. Kinley is situated in the RM of Perdue No. 346.

KIPLING, town, pop 973 (2006c), 1,037 (2001c), is situated southwest of Whitewood on Hwy 48. The city of Regina is approximately 150 km to the northwest, and Moose Mountain Provincial Park is just a short drive to the southeast. The community was named in honour of Rudyard Kipling, the renowned British poet and author. Although the district was settled for a good number of years before railways arrived, the present community developed as the Canadian Northern Railway came through in 1907-08 en route from Mary-

field toward Regina (the CPR had passed just to the south about a year earlier). Kipling was incorporated as a village in 1909 and grew steadily as an agricultural service centre until the 1930s, at which point the community experienced a substantial decline. The population of Kipling plunged from 470 in 1931 to 321 by 1941. A return to prosperity began during WWII, and, in the decades since, Kipling has been one of the limited number of communities in rural Saskatchewan to experience fairly continuous growth. On January 1, 1954, Kipling attained town status. As the largest community in the region, centrally situated amidst a half-dozen rural municipalities, Kipling serves a substantial trading area. The economy is largely based upon agriculture, a combination of grain and livestock production. There are

▼ **THE ELEVATOR** formerly operated by the Saskatchewan Wheat Pool in Kipling. Photograph taken October 15, 2003.

▲ **JACK KEITH'S THRESHING OUTFIT** at the Elias Cumming farm in the Kipling area in 1896. Elias Cumming is driving the wagon in the foreground. Photograph courtesy of the Kipling and District Historical Society Museum.

▼ **CANADA DAY–MUSEUM DAY** celebrations in Kipling in 2003 included entertainment from local performers. Left to right: Allan Palmer, Arnold Daku, and Vince Waynert. Photograph courtesy of the Kipling and District Historical Society Museum.

a good number of mixed farming operations in the district. The livestock industry has been significantly bolstered by the development of several large hog operations in recent years. Kipling has become the headquarters for one of the world's leading companies conducting research on swine genetics, and the swine industry in Kipling generates an annual payroll of approximately $2.75 million for the community and surrounding area. Additionally benefitting the economy is increasing oil patch exploration and the development of related services. Kipling is also becoming the major centre for health care in the district. Educational facilities in the community include a play school, a K-12 school that accommodates approximately 300 town and area students, a library, and a museum. Health care facilities include a hospital, a special care home, an ambulatory service, and a dentist. A chiropractor and an optometrist visit the community on a regular basis. Kipling has an RCMP detachment and a volunteer fire department, and the town has a lighted and licenced airstrip. There are eight churches in Kipling, a variety of service clubs, sports clubs, youth groups, and other community-based organizations. Recreational facilities include an arena complex with rinks for skating, hockey, and curling, as well as a four-diamond ball park, a park with a children's playground, tennis courts, a swimming pool, a nine-hole golf course, campgrounds, and community and seniors' centres. Heritage properties in the community include Kipling's former CN station, built circa 1909, and the rural municipality office, built in 1919. Additionally, the Kipling and District Historical Society Museum occupies a large site featuring an impressive collection of the region's earliest buildings. Just to the south of Kipling stands the unique Bekevar Church, which was constructed by the district's Hungarian settlers circa 1911-12. Kipling serves as the administrative centre of the RM of Kingsley No. 124.

KISBEY, village, pop 185 (2006c), 199 (2001c), is situated southwest of Moose Mountain Provincial Park, 14 km west of Arcola on Hwy 13, the Red Coat Trail. The Moose Mountain Creek flows

▼ **THE FORMER CANADIAN NORTHERN RAILWAY STATION** built in 1909 is a Kipling community landmark situated in its original prominent position in the town — on Railway Avenue at the north end of Main Street. Photograph taken October 15, 2003.

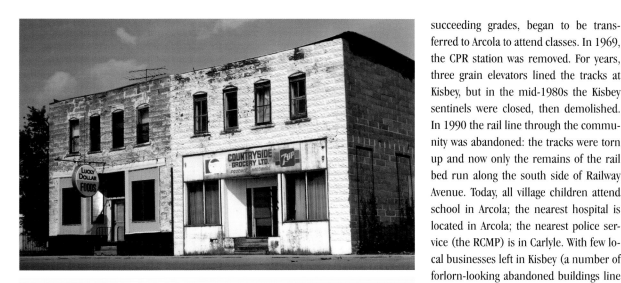

▲ **CLOSED.** Many businesses in Kisbey folded, such as these on the north side of Railway Avenue, as people began shopping in the region's larger centres. Photograph taken August 20, 2003.

approximately 2 km south of the village en route toward the Alameda Dam, and then on to its confluence with the Souris River near Oxbow. The Pheasant Rump First Nation has small land holdings immediately to the north and the south of the community. The name of the village honours Richard Claudius Kisbey who, with his brother, William Dennington Kisbey, emigrated to Canada from Ireland in 1881. They took the train to Brandon, where they purchased a yoke of oxen before travelling via Cannington Manor to settle in the area southeast of present-day Carlyle. Richard Claudius Kisbey invested in land in the region, and, after the CPR extended its line between Arcola and Stoughton in 1904, it was a tract owned by Kisbey that was purchased for a townsite. The steam locomotives that began running through the locale took advantage of an abundant water supply, a supply which continues to be an asset to the village. An interesting perk of living in Kisbey is that residents do not pay for water, as each household has its own

well. Shortly after the coming of the railway, the townsite was surveyed. The post office was established on May 1, 1905; the first school opened for classes in July that year; a Board of Trade was organized in 1906; and on May 8, 1907, the Village of Kisbey was incorporated. One of the first tasks of local officials was grading streets, as most of the townsite at the time was still natural prairie. A major improvement to the appearance of Kisbey took place in the spring of 1920 when 1,000 trees were planted along the village streets. While the community's population peaked at close to 400 around 1916, it levelled off at close to 300 in the 1920s, and it remained close to that mark until the mid-1960s, at which point it slowly, but steadily, began to decline. Modern transportation, the consolidation of rural services, and changing shopping trends would slowly lead to the erosion of the local business community, and would present challenges to village residents' sense of social cohesion. In 1964, high school students, the first of

succeeding grades, began to be transferred to Arcola to attend classes. In 1969, the CPR station was removed. For years, three grain elevators lined the tracks at Kisbey, but in the mid-1980s the Kisbey sentinels were closed, then demolished. In 1990 the rail line through the community was abandoned: the tracks were torn up and now only the remains of the rail bed run along the south side of Railway Avenue. Today, all village children attend school in Arcola; the nearest hospital is located in Arcola; the nearest police service (the RCMP) is in Carlyle. With few local businesses left in Kisbey (a number of forlorn-looking abandoned buildings line the streets), many residents shop in these centres, or the town of Stoughton, 26 kilometres west. Kisbey retains a branch of the Stoughton Credit Union, a trucking company, the post office, an insurance broker, an Anglican Church (1914), and a United Church (1927). The community has a volunteer fire department. Village facilities include a recreation centre and rinks for skating, hockey, and curling, as well as a playground and a park. Moose Mountain Provincial Park, a short distance to the northwest, provides Kisbey residents with a wide range of recreational facilities and opportunities. Crop production, ranching, and oilfield-related businesses provide the basis of the area economy. Pump jacks dot the farmland surrounding the village. Kisbey serves as the administrative centre of the RM of Brock No. 64.

KIVIMAA-MOONLIGHT BAY, resort village, is located in west-central Saskatchewan, and is one of several growing resort communities situated northeast of Turtleford on Turtle Lake. Kivimaa-Moonlight Bay was incorporated in 1989 as the result of the merger of

two separate resorts which had begun to develop in the 1960s. The 2006 Census recorded 126 permanent residents; however, the population varies greatly depending on the season, reaching close to 500 during the summer months. The community is situated in the RM of Mervin No. 499.

KOPP'S KOVE, organized hamlet, est. 1989, is located in west-central Saskatchewan, and is one of several resort communities situated northeast of Turtleford on Turtle Lake. The 2006 Census recorded 54 permanent residents; however, the population varies greatly depending on the season, reaching over 200 during the summer months. First developed in the 1970s, Kopp's Kove lies within the RM of Mervin No. 499.

KRONAU, organized hamlet, pop 209 (2006c), 196 (2001c), is located 25 km southeast of Regina on Hwy 33. Settled in the 1890s by a German population, Kronau had been incorporated as a village from 1907 to 1917. It was reconstituted as an organized hamlet in 1971, at which point the population hovered at around 60. Growth over the past few decades is attributed to the community's proximity to Regina and its development as a bedroom community. Kronau had a K-6 elementary school which had 33 students enrolled in the fall of 2006; the school closed in the summer of 2007. Kronau is situated in the RM of Lajord No. 128.

KRYDOR, village, pop 25 (2006c), 25 (2001c), is located northwest of Saskatoon, 14 km west of the town of Blaine Lake on Hwy 40. In the early 1900s, the

▲ **BOARDED UP.** The former Krydor Café on the east side of Main Street.

▼ **KRYDOR ORTHODOX CHURCH.** A Ukrainian settlement near Blaine Lake, Krydor was named for Peter Krysak and Teodor Lucyk, early Ukrainian pioneers in the area. Krydor is the birthplace of Stephen Worobetz, the province's first Lieutenant-Governor of Ukrainian ancestry.

Photographs taken August 25, 2004.

region was populated by Doukhobors, Poles, and one of the largest bloc settlements of Ukrainians in Saskatchewan. With the arrival of the railway in 1913, the village had its beginnings, and Krydor was incorporated in August 1914. The community became a thriving service centre for the surrounding agricultural district, and by 1961 the village had a population of close to 200. Subsequently, however, the community has steadily declined, and today vacant businesses, vacant houses, and an abandoned school give the village the appearance of a ghost town. Krydor is situated in the RM of Redberry No. 435.

KUROKI, organized hamlet, pop 65 (2006c), 74 (2001c), is located 22 km southeast of Wadena, at the junction of Hwys 5, 38, and 310. Fishing Lake and its surrounding resort communities lie a few kilometres to the south. Kuroki was named after the Japanese general Tamemoto Kuroki (1844-1923), who distinguished himself during the Russo-Japanese War. In the 1890s, the district was home to only a handful of ranching operations, but after 1900 homesteaders began to arrive in numbers, and the Kuroki district would become truly a melting pot of cultures. In addition to a significant concentration of Polish settlers, there were Ukrainians, Norwegians, Swedes, Germans, and British. In 1926-27, Czechoslovakians settled in the area, further diversifying the cultural milieu. The hamlet had its beginnings with the construction

▼ **FORGET MUSKOGEE!** This sign erected at the entrance to Kuroki puts a twist on the old Merle Haggard standard. Photograph taken August 4, 2004.

of the Canadian Northern Railway north-westward from Canora in 1904. In 1905, trains were running through Kuroki and the post office was established. Within a few years, a small business community had developed, and a school and the first church were built. The economy then, as now, was predominantly based on agriculture, a combination of grain and livestock production. In 1919, Kuroki was incorporated as a village; however, a mere seven years later, in 1926, for reasons the local history does not relate, the village was dissolved, and Kuroki reverted to "unorganized" hamlet status. The community prospered after WWII, and in 1949 Kuroki was established as an organized hamlet. At the beginning of the 1970s, the population of Kuroki was over 200. Subsequently, however, the community's businesses and services began to be superseded by those in Foam Lake, Kelvington, and, particularly, Wadena. The population of Kuroki began to slowly decline, and at the end of June 1979, after over seven decades of serving the community, the school was closed. Today, only a few businesses remain in Kuroki; the community serves as the administrative centre of the RM of Sasman No. 336.

▲ **IN 1964, THE REMAINS OF A WOOLLY MAMMOTH** were found by road workers 5 kilometres west of the town of Kyle. The bones were estimated to be about 12,000 years old, and, to commemorate the find, a concrete replica of the mammoth, approximately three metres high, was erected in the community. Photograph taken September 8, 2003.

KYLE, town, pop 423 (2006c), 478 (2001c), is located approximately 69 km northwest of Swift Current, north of the South Saskatchewan River and Saskatchewan Landing Provincial Park. Clearwater Lake Regional Park is situated just northeast of the town. Kyle is served by Hwys 4 and 342. Ranchers had been operating in the district as early as 1883, but it was in 1906 that the area was opened to homesteaders. In 1909, area residents began picking up their mail at a post office named Kyleville, at the farm of Jerry Kyle, a few kilometres west of the present town. In 1923, the railway came through the district and the townsite of Kyle was established. The railway made life much easier for the area settlers who previously had to haul their supplies from Elrose to the north, or from Success and Pennant across the river to the south. In 1926,

Kyle was incorporated as a village with a population of 93. The community grew steadily until the 1950s, at which point the population stabilized at around 500. In 1959, Kyle attained town status. The Kyle area economy has traditionally been based upon agriculture; however, in recent years, oil and gas production has become quite important. A number of Kyle's businesses are involved in both the agricultural and the oil and gas industries. The town also has health care services, an RCMP detachment, a volunteer fire department, a municipal airport, modern facilities for cultural and recreational activities, and a variety of businesses and services, churches, clubs and organizations. Kyle Composite School provides K-12 education to approximately 100 students. The community hosts a number of annual events, and the area is a popular destination for hunting and fishing. Kyle is situated in the RM of Lacadena No. 228.

KYLEMORE, organized hamlet, pop 37 (2006c), 56 (2001c), is located 12 km southeast of Wadena, on Hwy 5. Lands belonging to the Fishing Lake First Nation lie immediately to the south. In the 1880s and 1890s, a few ranching operations were established in the area; however, after 1900, homesteaders of various European backgrounds began arriving. In 1905, the Canadian Northern Railway was running through the district, and in 1909 the Kylemore Post Office was established. The small settlement developed slowly, and, as there were rural schools operating in the district, the first school in Kylemore was not built until 1920. In 1917-18, Doukhobor leader Peter Verigin purchased large parcels of land around Kylemore, totalling 11,362 acres. He brought 250 colonists from British Columbia, who established 14 communal villages in the district and who constructed a central storehouse, a prayer home, a blacksmith shop, granaries and barns. At Kylemore, they also built what was reported to be the largest grain elevator in Saskatchewan. During the 1920s, Kylemore was a thriving community. But by 1938, the Doukhobors, like many, were in financial difficulty. Creditors foreclosed and most of the colonists returned to British Columbia, leaving a few, however, who re-established themselves as independent farmers. Subsequently, as roads improved and services became centralized, Kylemore's businesses and institutions were eventually superseded by those in Wadena. In the late 1950s, Kylemore School was closed, and students were subsequently bused to the neighbouring larger centre. By the 1960s, the population of Kylemore was less than 40, and by 1996 it had fallen to a mere 11. The population has grown in recent

years as people from the Fishing Lake First Nation have taken up homes in the community. A convenience store and gas bar located on the highway is Kylemore's only business. Kylemore is situated in the RM of Sasman No. 336.

LA LOCHE, northern village, pop 2,348 (2006c), 2,136 (2001c), is located in north-western Saskatchewan near the Saskatchewan-Alberta border, northwest of Buffalo Narrows and just south of Clearwater River Provincial Park on Hwy 155. The community sits on the east side of Lac La Loche and immediately to the north is the main reserve of the Clearwater River Dene Nation. Although Aboriginal peoples had traversed the area for generations, the origins of today's community began with the arrival of fur traders and, later, missionaries. Lac La Loche is one of the headwaters of the Churchill River, and in 1778 Indian guides led Peter Pond over Portage La Loche, or Methy Portage, to the Clearwater River. The 20-kilometre portage bridged the height of land between the Hudson Bay and Arctic Ocean drainage basins and opened up the vast Athabasca region and its untold riches in furs. *La loche* is French for the burbot, a variety of freshwater cod, and the word "methy" is derived from the Cree term for the same fish. Rival fur trading posts operated on Lac La Loche over the decades following Pond's "discovery," and from the mid-1800s a community centred around a Hudson's Bay Company post began to develop on the west side of the lake. About the same time, Catholic missionaries from Ile-a-la-Crosse began working in the area. In 1895 a mission was established at the site of the present community. Hudson's Bay Company competitors started operating at La Loche in the early 1900s,

▲ **LA LOCHE, MARCH 1964.** Saskatchewan Archives Board, Saskatchewan Photographic Services, R-PS63-398-09. Photographer: Alan Hill.

▼ **MORNING RECESS** at La Loche Community School in La Loche, September 19, 2003. Lac La Loche is in the background; the land visible in the distance is a peninsula named Big Point, which almost divides the lake in half.

and after the HBC post at West La Loche burned down in 1936, the company relocated to the present townsite. Families at the western settlement also began to relocate to the east side of the lake, and West La Loche eventually disappeared. In 1943, the Grey Nuns arrived at La Loche, bringing Western education and nursing to the community. In 1962-63 a road from the south was built to the village, but it was not until 1974 that dial telephone services were available. In 1976, the community received television. Sewer, water, and electrical systems were developed in the 1970s, and in 1983 La Loche was incorporated as a northern village. The population is largely Métis and non-treaty Dene and is very young compared to the rest of the province. Approximately half of the population are children. The median age was 20.5 in 2006; that of all Saskatchewan residents was 38.7. La Loche Community School provides K-12 educa-tion to close to 1,000 students and has 50 full-time teachers and a support staff of an additional 50 people, making it the largest employer in the community. Since the demise of the fur trade, La Loche has struggled with high unemployment (close to 50 per cent in 2001), as self-sufficiency was transformed into dependency. An economy substantially based on welfare was created, and La Loche struggles with issues of economic and social well-being to this day. The median family income in 2001 was between $17,000 and $18,000 per year — the median income for all Saskatchewan families in 2001 was over $49,000. In addition to its educational facilities, La Loche has a hospital with a special care home, an RCMP detachment, a small core of businesses, some government offices, and an air strip.

LA RONGE, northern town, pop 2,725 (2006c), 2,727 (2001c), is located near the geographical centre of the province, 237 km north of Prince Albert on Hwy 2 at the southern edge of the Canadian Shield. La Ronge is located on the west shore of scenic Lac La Ronge, Saskatchewan's fourth largest lake, which encompasses over 1,300 islands. La Ronge is the largest community in northern Saskatchewan, and along with the neighbouring northern village of Air Ronge and the First Nations communities of the Lac La Ronge Indian Band, the total area population numbers several thousand. La Ronge is a major service and transportation centre for the northern part of the province. Originally inhabited by Cree, the area began to see the incursions of fur traders in the latter 1700s. Numerous competing posts were operated intermittently on the lake throughout the 1800s. In the 1850s some activity began to be centred at what is now

◀ **LA RONGE**, September 1979. Saskatchewan Archives Board, Saskatchewan Photographic Services, R-PS79-1453-138. Photographer: B. Weston.

▼ **AIRBORNE** with pilot Doug Chisholm over Lac La Ronge Provincial Park, early August, 2001.

known as Stanley Mission, as Reverend Robert Hunt oversaw the construction of Holy Trinity Anglican Church, and the Hudson's Bay Company established a post at the site. The church at Stanley Mission is now Saskatchewan's oldest standing building. In the early 1900s, trading posts, an Anglican church and an associated residential school were built where the community of La Ronge now sits. Parents usually spent the winters working traplines and returned to the settlement in summer where they grew gardens and fished. In 1911, postal service was established. In the 1930s, La Ronge began to develop as a fly-in fishing resort, and after the road was built from Prince Albert in 1947-48 tourism expanded. About the same time, the provincial government introduced resource management and conservation officers to the area. Local government came to the community in 1955 when La Ronge gained village status with a population of around 400. Over the following decades the community grew rapidly, reaching a population of 933 by 1966. It was almost double that a decade later, in 1976, with a population of 1,714. In 1983, La Ronge was proclaimed a northern town. La Ronge today is a base of governmental, institutional, industrial, and commercial activity, and its business sector provides a wide range of goods and services. A number of mining companies have offices in the town. La Ronge has a hospital and a special care home, an ambulance service, a volunteer fire department, and an RCMP detachment. The community has a wide range of recreational facilities and a public library. Bus service to and from La Ronge is provided by the Saskatchewan Transportation Corporation, and the community has regularly scheduled air services. La Ronge's schools provide K-12 education, and post-secondary institutions offer a wide range of services and programs. Today's economy is based on tourism, forestry, mining, commercial fishing, trapping, fur trading, dried meat products, mushroom and berry picking, and the wild rice industry. Lac La Ronge Provincial Park has an international repu-

tation as a wilderness paradise, offering full-service campgrounds, boat launches, and hiking trails. The park encompasses the lake, Precambrian Shield, boreal forest, and muskeg, and there are more than 30 documented canoe routes in the area.

LACADENA, hamlet, pop 4 (2007 approximation), is located northwest of Kyle on Hwy 342. The area began to be settled around 1906; the development of the hamlet dates to the early 1920s with the construction of the railway into the area from Eston. Lacadena served as a small commercial service centre and grain handling point, and from 1949 to 1997 the community had the legal standing of an organized hamlet. The population plummeted from 138 in 1969 to 76

in 1972; rail service into the community was discontinued in the late 1990s. Today, Lacadena is comprised of a few homes, a church, a post office, a community centre, and the administrative office and shop for the RM of Lacadena No. 228.

LADY LAKE, organized hamlet, pop 25 (2006c), 30 (2001c), is located just north of Preeceville on Hwy 9. Settlers, many of Ukrainian and Scandinavian origins, began taking up land in the district in the early 1900s. In 1928, the Canadian National Railway came through the area and the hamlet of Lady Lake developed. In March 1929 the post office opened, and in 1952 Lady Lake was established as an organized hamlet. The population was 57 in 1969; the post office closed in 1970.

Immediately west of the hamlet lies Lady Lake Regional Park, situated on the small lake from which the community derives its name. Lady Lake is situated in the RM of Preeceville No. 334.

LAFLECHE, town, pop 370 (2006c), 446 (2001c), is located south of Gravelbourg at the junction of Hwys 13 and 58. Lafleche is named after Louis-François Richer Laflèche (1818-98), a Roman Catholic missionary to Rupert's Land from 1844 to 1856, and the bishop of Trois-Rivières, Quebec, from 1867 to 1898. The Lafleche district began to be settled around 1905-06 and, prior to the arrival of the railway in the area, the beginnings of a settlement emerged a short distance from the present community. When the CPR came though in 1913, the settlement was relocated to the townsite established by the railway company, and on September 3 that year the young community was incorporated as a village. People of British and German origins settled the district, and a large number of French settlers took up land in a vast area extending from west of Old Wives Lake, south through Gravelbourg to Lafleche, and west toward Ponteix and down to Val Marie. In 1922, Ste. Radegonde Roman Catholic Church was built in Lafleche, becoming the most dominant architectural landmark in the town. Its exterior was faced with brick from the Claybank Brick Plant, and today it is both a heritage property and the oldest existing church in the community. Lafleche developed as a service and distribution centre for the surrounding agricultural district, and on June 1, 1953, the community attained town status. In 1961, Lafleche had a peak population of 749. Generally, grain production is the major activity to the north of the community, while mixed farms and ranching operations are dominant to the south. Lafleche's business community provides a range of goods and services, and the town has a K-12 school, a library, and a museum. Lafleche has a health centre, a special care home, and a volunteer fire department. Recreational facilities which include a curling club and an arena for hockey and skating are augmented by the community's proximity to Thomson Lake Regional Park, where there is a golf course, a swimming pool, camping facilities, and opportunities for boating and fishing. Lafleche also has a hockey team that plays in the NHL — the Notukeu Hockey League. Lafleche serves as the administrative centre of the RM of Wood River No. 74.

LAIRD, village, pop 207 (2006c), 236 (2001c), is located 24 km northwest of Rosthern; the North Saskatchewan River passes approximately 10 km to the west. The community is named after David Laird (1833-1914), the first resident Lieutenant-Governor of the North-West Territories (1876-1881). Mennonites detraining at Rosthern settled the district in the 1890s; after the turn of the century, large numbers of German Lutherans arrived. The present townsite was developed with the construction of the Canadian Northern Railway line from Dalmeny in 1909-10, and Laird became a railway point for the agricultural community in the rich farmlands of the surrounding area. Laird became an incorporated village on May 4, 1911. The population that year was 195; by 1926 it was 302, and it remained close to 300 until the mid-1960s. Four grain elevators erected in Laird stood into the 1980s; however, the rail line was abandoned in the early 1990s, and now none of the landmarks remain standing. Today, Laird has about 18 places of business, several of which cater to the district's agricultural industry. The village has an arena and curling rink, a community hall, a seniors' centre, an arboretum, a library, and a museum. Laird School, a K-8 facility, had 51 students enrolled in the fall of 2006. Three churches serve the community: Laird Mennonite Church, Tiefengrund Rosenort Mennonite Church, and St. John's Lutheran Church. Laird is situated in the RM of Laird No. 404.

LAJORD, hamlet, is located approximately 40 km southeast of Regina on Hwy 33. The settlers who arrived in the district in the late 1800s were predominantly of German origin; in the early 1900s a number of Norwegians arrived. One of them, P.E. Thompson, owned the land where the hamlet now sits when the CPR came through in 1904, and it was after his home in Norway that the community was named. On March 1, 1905, the Lajord Post Office was established; on December 13, 1909, the RM of Lajord No. 128 was incorporated, with the hamlet as its headquarters. The Lajord Hutterite colony, several kilometres to the north, was established in the mid-1970s. Notable Lajord area residents were Ellert Olaus Hanson and Helmer Hartman Hanson, who are represented in the Saskatchewan Agricultural Hall of Fame. The two brothers, who came to Canada from Iowa, were leading innovators in the design of farm equipment in the 1920s. They initiated the era of swath threshing in the province and their inventions were mass produced by such leading industry manufacturers as Case, John Deere, and the International Harvester Company.

LAKE ALMA, village, pop 30 (2006c), 35 (2001c), is situated in a sparsely-populated area of rolling hills

▲ **LAFLECHE, CIRCA 1930s.** Drawing courtesy of Rollie Bourassa, Regina, Saskatchewan.

▲ **A FORMER SASKATCHEWAN WHEAT POOL GRAIN ELEVATOR**
at Lake Alma. Smoke from forest fires in British Columbia hangs in the air.
Photograph taken August 27, 2003.

south of Radville, at the junction of Hwys 18 and 28, about 16 km north of the Canada-U.S. border. Settlers of predominantly Norwegian and Swedish origin began arriving in the area in the early 1900s, with many coming via the United States. Smaller numbers of people with German and British backgrounds also settled the district. For many years, communities in Montana and North Dakota, as well as Radville, were the nearest points to obtain supplies, and trips to these centres for Lake Alma district residents could take three days or more. Coal was often dug out of the region's hillside seams to heat homes in the winter. In 1925, there was news of a railway. In 1926, the first buildings were constructed on the townsite, and in 1927 trains began to run through the fledgling community toward Minton. However, just as life for the district's pioneers was becoming somewhat easier, the drought and Depression hit the area hard. During the 1930s, relief supplies had to

be freighted in to sustain both families and their livestock. Things improved in the 1940s, and in 1949 the Village of Lake Alma was incorporated. In the mid-1950s, SaskPower brought electricity to the community, and in 1967 household water and sewage systems were established. In 1971, the population of Lake Alma reached a peak of 173. Subsequently, however, the community's numbers began to plummet. By 1981, the population was 101; by 1991, it was 66. Businesses closed. In the late 1990s, the community was dealt two devastating blows when the school was closed and CP abandoned the rail line through the village. There are virtually no services left in the community today, and Lake Alma is on the verge of disappearing. The nearest medical facilities and police services are located in Radville. Farming, ranching and some oil are the main industries in the area, and Lake Alma serves as the administrative centre of the RM of Lake Alma No. 8.

LAKE LENORE, village, pop 306 (2006c), 314 (2001c), is located approximately 33 km northeast of Humboldt on Hwy 368, just south of Lenore Lake. The district began to be settled in 1903, largely by German Catholics from Minnesota. Lake Lenore is situated in the heart of St. Peter's Colony, a vast 50-township area extending roughly from Cudworth to Watson, established under the spiritual leadership of the Benedictines of Collegeville, Minnesota, and St. Peter's Monastery at Muenster. Most of the early settlers to the area arrived via Rosthern and, until the railway was completed through Humboldt in 1905, travel to Rosthern was necessary to obtain supplies. Originally, the community began to develop a mile north of the present village — the first store was opened in 1905 — and when George Gerwing established the post office in 1906 it was given the name Lenora Lake after the nearby body of water. Lenora Lake, now Lenore Lake, had been named in the 1890s by a government surveyor after his daughter, Lenora. Before the railway arrived in the area in 1919-20, a number of stores, a pool room, a harness shop, a few homes, and St. Anthony's Church and a rectory had been built at the original hamlet site. When the CNR arrived from Humboldt en route to Melfort, they selected the homestead of Peter Wolsfeld, to the south, on which to build the railway siding and station. Wolsfeld was thus given the honour of naming the siding and station, and chose Lenora Lake. However, due to a mix up somewhere, the railway company named the locale "Lake Lenore," and Lake Lenore it remained. The post office, though, continued as Lenora Lake until 1939 when its name was finally changed to coincide with that of the village. At

some point in time, the lake itself became known as Lenore Lake. With the railway being built south of the original settlement, most of the businesses relocated to the new townsite. The local history recounts that the bank continued to accept deposits and handle withdrawals even as it was being moved southward to its new location. In December 1920, the first train carrying freight and goods arrived in Lake Lenore from Humboldt, but had to return the way it came as the track was still being laid north of the community. The Village of Lake Lenore was incorporated on April 28, 1921. In the fall of 1921 the first scheduled train ran through to Melfort. With the arrival of the railway, the community developed rapidly: elevators were being erected even before the tracks were laid, stock yards were built along the rail siding, and a variety of businesses sprang up, creating a significant trading centre for the surrounding agricultural district. From a population of 119 in 1921, Lake Lenore grew to number close to 250 souls by the outbreak of WWII. Following the War, brush in the area continued to be cleared and land broken, and by the mid-1950s five grain elevators in Lake Lenore were shipping almost one million bushels of grain out of the district annually. A local generator supplying power to the business district had become obsolete in 1949, as SaskPower took over the distribution of electricity, rewiring the entire village and installing street lights. Sewer and water systems were completed in 1968, and natural gas was available to residents in 1975. Despite this progress, though, the village also began to simultaneously experience a reversal of fortune. From a peak population of 460 from the mid-1950s to the mid-1960s, the village's numbers steadily declined to 290 by 1996. The railway discontinued passenger service to the

village in 1965, and freight service ended on August 31, 1979, when the station was closed. The number of businesses in Lake Lenore also declined, and the local history book refers to the Main Street of 1985 as being "rather desolate" compared to the bustling business sector of earlier times. In recent years, however, Lake Lenore has been on a bit of an upswing. Between the 1996 and 2001 Censuses of Canada, the community's population rebounded, growing by 8.3 per cent. Lake Lenore School, a K-12 facility, had 170 students enrolled in the fall of 2006. Today, approximately 25 businesses serve the community, and the village's facilities include curling and skating rinks, sports grounds, a community hall in which the library is located, a seniors' drop-in centre, and a recreation centre with a bowling alley, a fitness centre, and banquet facilities. Lenore Lake, just north of the village, has a beach and camping facilities and is a popular destination for anglers. It is a three-section body of water, the site of a migratory bird sanctuary, wildlife refuge, and a walleye rearing pond. Lake Lenore has a number of community service clubs and volunteer groups which include the Catholic Women's League, the Knights of Columbus, the Lake Lenore Wildlife Federation, the Senior Citizens' Club and the Lions and Lionesses. St. Anthony's Roman Catholic Church is a community landmark, as is the Memorial Grotto across the street. The latter was erected in honour of those who served in WWII, including five young Lake Lenore men who never returned from overseas. Lake Lenore is situated in the RM of St. Peter No. 369.

LAKEVIEW, organized hamlet, est. 1990, is located north of North Battleford, one of several resort communities that circle Jackfish Lake. Development may have begun as early as the 1930s. There were 49 permanent residents in 2006; however, the population varies greatly depending on the season. Lakeview is situated in the RM of Meota No. 468.

LAMPMAN, town, pop 634 (2006c), 650 (2001c), is situated approximately 50 km northeast of Estevan on Hwy 361. The first settlers arrived in the district about 1890, and after 1900 there was a substantial influx of German-speaking people into the region. Lampman developed with the construction of the CNR line from Carlyle to Estevan in 1909. In 1910, the Lampman Post Office was established and, amidst the construction of elevators and the establishment of new businesses, Lampman was incorporated as a village that year. In 1913, Lampman became the junction of two rail lines, as the track linking Regina to the Port of Northgate on the Canada-U.S. border was completed. The community grew slowly but steadily (except for a slight downturn during the 1930s) until the 1950s, when development of the area's oil industry began. A frenzy of activity followed the drilling of the first successful wells in the district, and Lampman's population jumped from approximately 250 at the end of WWII to 637 by 1961. A gas processing plant built at nearby Steelman in the late 1950s became a large area employer, and drilling rigs dotted the countryside. Lampman gained town status in 1963, and in 1971 the community's population peaked at 830. The community's numbers stabilized thereafter, and Lampman's population has hovered around its current level for the past two decades. Lampman has a full range of businesses and services, many of which cater to the oilfield and agricultural industries which form the basis of the regional economy. The town has a modern health centre with an integrated care home, a wide range of recreational facilities, a K-12 school that serves over 200 students, a library, a volunteer fire department, four churches, a number of

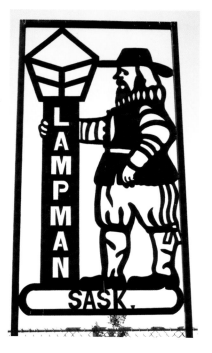

community clubs and organizations, and a local airstrip. Recently, a new housing subdivision has been developed. In 1984, the community hosted one of its most successful events with the Lampman and District Homecoming: over 5,000 people attended, and past and present residents of the area contributed recipes for a cookbook which was published for the occasion. The book is now in its eighth printing, with over 11,000 copies sold to date. The Town of Lampman and the RM of Browning No. 34 share an office space and administrators.

LANCER, village, pop 65 (2006c), 75 (2001c), is situated on Hwy 32 approximately 100 km northwest of Swift Current. It is one in a string of communities that sprang up with the construction of the CPR's Empress Line, which ran from a point just west of Swift Current to Empress, Alberta. The Lancer Ferry crosses the South Saskatchewan River approximately 20 kilometres to the north of the village, and the Great Sand Hills lie about 10 kilometres to the south. Only a handful of ranchers had established themselves in the district when the first homesteaders began arriving around 1907, and, until the railway came through, people had to make the long trip to Gull Lake or Swift Current, on the railway company's main line, to obtain supplies or deliver grain. By 1912, almost all of the available land in the Lancer district was occupied. In early 1913, as the railway proceeded north-westward from Cabri, the site of Lancer was established. Buildings were erected, and when the railway arrived later that year, the nucleus of the village had already developed. Lancer was incorporated on September 11, 1913. The next year, there was almost a total crop failure

▲ **TWO SEASONS OF THE CHOKECHERRY** are depicted with this metal sculpture which stands 21 feet (6.4 metres) high. Located on Lancer's main street, it was unveiled by Lieutenant-Governor Sylvia Fedoruk on October 8, 1988, during the village's annual Chokecherry Festival, to commemorate the community's 75th Anniversary. The sculpture was designed and constructed by George Jaegli of Cabri, Saskatchewan. Photograph taken August 29, 2003.

in the area due to a severe drought, but in 1915 the harvest was bountiful and the community prospered. Lancer grew steadily until the end of the 1920s, but the 1930s devastated the area, and half of the village's surrounding farm population abandoned their lands: in 1937, cattle sold for only one cent a pound, and number one wheat sold for only 19 cents a bushel. In the 1940s, there was an influx of new people to the district who took up the farms abandoned in the 1930s. The area was again prosperous, and by 1966 Lancer had a population of 254 and five grain elevators lined the railway tracks. The village had a wide variety of businesses and services. Subsequently, however, the village has suffered the same fate as many small Saskatchewan communities: the population has steadily fallen, and many businesses have closed. Today, there is a credit union, a grocery store,

a café, a hotel, and a post office. Lancer Elementary School was closed in June 1999, and the last remaining grain elevator was demolished a couple of years ago. Yet, a community spirit remains: Lancer hosts two major annual events — a rodeo in early summer, and the Chokecherry Festival held every Thanksgiving. An additional attraction is the Lancer Centennial Museum, which, open seasonally, has exhibits featuring the natural history and settlement of the area. Agriculture, a mixture of grain and livestock production, remains the major industry in the region, although the oil industry and the recent discovery of large reserves of natural gas near Shackleton has proven somewhat of a boon. Lancer is located in the RM of Miry Creek No. 229. The area is popular with hunters as pronghorn antelope, mule and white-tailed deer, geese and ducks are found in abundance.

LANDIS, village, pop 119 (2006c), 161 (2001c), is located 34 km northwest of Biggar on Hwy 14. Landis is situated on the eastern edge of what was known as St. Joseph's Colony, a vast German Catholic bloc settlement (77 townships) started in 1905. Most of the settlers were from the Black Sea region: many who arrived between 1905 and 1908 had first settled in the Dakotas; those who came over the next few years mainly came directly from southern Russia. By the outbreak of WWI, an estimated 7,000 to 8,000 people of German origin had settled in St. Joseph's Colony. The townsite of Landis began to develop in 1908 with the construction of the Grand Trunk Pacific Railway line from Biggar to Wainwright, Alberta. The community was named after Kenesaw Mountain Landis (1866–1944), an American federal judge who later became the first commissioner of organized professional baseball. In 1908, the first businesses on the townsite were established: E.E. Bent moved a store into Landis and became the community's first postmaster. Landis was incorporated on May 17, 1909, and that year the hotel (still standing) was built, a bank opened, and a school was started in the village. For a few years, Landis businesses served the districts of Leipzig, Handel, and Kelfield, until the railway came through those areas and the towns were built. Landis grew from a population of 127 in 1911 to close to 250 before the outbreak of the Depression. The community languished somewhat subsequently, its numbers falling to 161 by 1951; from the mid-1950s through to the mid-1980s, however, Landis prospered. Throughout the period the population neared 300. Significant developments in Landis and the area over the years were formation

◀ **LANDIS, FROM THE SOUTH** (grid road No. 656). Photograph taken August 27, 2004.

▼ **THE LANDIS HOTEL** was built in 1909 by contractors Lee, Hope, and Meldrome. Like many hotels built around this time, the Landis Hotel once had a covered balcony on the second floor on the front of the building. As it was made of wood, however, it eventually became unsafe and was removed. In 1935, the hotel's beverage room was opened; in 1960, women were allowed in. Photograph taken August 27, 2004.

of the Landis Co-operative Association in 1929, the establishment of a sodium sulphate plant at nearby Palo in the 1930s, the opening of the Landis and District Savings and Credit Union in 1942, the creation of natural gas caverns and the construction of the Landis Power station by the Saskatchewan Power Corporation in the 1970s, and the establishment of a manufacturing firm in 1990 that produces chemical handling systems for agricultural applications among other products. Today, Landis retains a small core of businesses and services (most Co-op ventures), and two significant grain elevator complexes remain standing: one facility is operated by Agricore United; the other, a former Saskatchewan Wheat Pool facility, was purchased by the Landis Producer Co-op in 2001. The village has a skating arena, a curling club, a Roman Catholic church, a library, and a community hall. Landis School is a K-12 facility that had 84 students enrolled in the fall of 2006. Village residents seek medical services in Wilkie or Biggar. The loss of population between 2001 and 2006 represented a drop of 26.1 per cent. Landis is situated in the RM of Reford No. 379.

LANG, village, pop 172 (2006c), 189 (2001c), lies 13 km southeast of Milestone on Hwy 39 and the CPR's "Soo Line." Regina is a little over 60 km north-north-west; Weyburn, about 45 km southeast. The community's name honours an early railway company employee. Although the railway was completed from North Portal through Estevan and Weyburn to Moose Jaw in 1893, it was not until after the beginning of the twentieth century, and the arrival of significant numbers of homesteaders, that Lang was established. Settlers to the district came from Ontario, the United States, and Europe. English and German would become the languages commonly spoken in Lang, although a number of Norwegians also settled in the region. To serve the influx of settlers pouring into the Lang area in the early 1900s, it was essential to establish a townsite. The railway company had originally contemplated a location about five kilometres southeast of the present community, at a point more equidistant between Milestone and Yellow Grass. However, a prominent area land owner, Bernard Larson, often referred to as the founder of Lang, persuaded (one account says "bribed") a CPR official to locate the railway siding on his land, the site of present-day Lang. Larson donated lots for the construction of churches and the school, and became a successful businessman in the community. He was also elected to the Saskatchewan Legislature as a Liberal MLA for the electoral division of Milestone in the 1912, 1917, and 1921 elections. Bernard Larson died in 1923 and, interestingly, was laid to rest in what is now one of the province's most unique municipal heritage properties — the Larson Mausoleum. Located in Lang's cemetery, this Tyndall-stone structure was commissioned by Larson in the early 1920s as a tomb for the Larson family, and it was designed by the renowned Regina architectural firm of Storey and Van Egmond. In 1904, with the railway siding at the Lang townsite in place, the first businesses began to appear. A post office was established in May that year, a hotel was constructed, and the first stores were built and opened for business. In 1905, the first of several grain elevators that would come to line the tracks at Lang was erected (only one remains standing today), and by 1906 the community was booming. Lang was legally established as a village on July 27 that year. The Presbyterian Church was built in 1906, and in 1907 the newly-constructed Methodist and Lutheran Churches were dedicated. Until the mid-1950s, the services in the Lutheran church were predominantly conducted in German. In 1908, a new four-room brick school was constructed to accommodate a burgeoning student population, replacing a one-room schoolhouse built a few years earlier. The old school was then taken over by the community's Anglican congregation for use as their church. The Lang Board of Trade was also organized in 1908, and by 1911 the population of the village had surpassed the 300 mark. The CPR provided passenger service both ways twice daily, and Lang flourished in the first decades of the century. The 1930s took a toll, however, on some of Lang's businesses. Then, with the advent of faster automobiles and better highways, village merchants faced increasing competition from the cities, and commercial activity in Lang waned, never regaining its former vibrancy. After the mid-1950s, the population of the community slowly dropped from around 300 to its present level. Improvements, however, were still being made in the village: natural gas was installed in 1960, and water and sewer systems were connected in 1965. By the early 1980s, some village residents had become commuters, driving to work in Regina, Weyburn, or Wilcox. Businesses operating in Lang today include a grocery store which contains the post office, a Co-op bulk sales and hardware dealer, a branch of the Weyburn Credit Union, a beverage room and restaurant in the old hotel, farm equipment sales and service (also auto service), an outfitter that accommodates waterfowl and upland game hunting, and a coffee shop at the local ice rink. The rink offers figure skating and hockey, although the season can be quite short at times as the facility relies on natural ice. Lang also has an active baseball team, which has won several league championships over the years. A community centre in the village accommodates weddings and cabarets and an annual fowl supper in October. Service clubs and community-based organizations active in Lang include the Lions, Lang Helping Hands,

a community club, a karate club, and a club for seniors. The village has United and Lutheran Churches; members of the Catholic parish attend bi-weekly services held at the community centre. In recent years, Lang School had accommodated students in grades K-5, while older children attended classes in Milestone. But after enrollment had dropped to only 11 students registered in the fall of 2006, Lang School was slated to close at the end of the school year in 2007. Lang residents travel to either Weyburn or Regina for medical services; Milestone is where the nearest RCMP detachment is located. Lang is situated in the RM of Scott No. 98, and agriculture, largely grain farming with a few livestock operations, is the major industry in the district.

LANGBANK, organized hamlet, pop 30 (2006c), 35 (2001c), is located about 35 km south of Whitewood on Hwy 9. The town of Kipling lies to the northwest, Moose Mountain Provincial Park to the south. For a community with a population of only 35, Langbank is a fairly well-equipped farm service centre, closely tied to the neighbouring village of Kennedy, just a few kilometres to the southwest. The area began to be settled in the early 1880s; however, it was over 1907-08 with the construction of the Canadian Northern Railway line through the district that the hamlet of Langbank began to develop. The name Langbank is presumed to originate with an area settler, who suggested that a low range of hills in the vicinity reminded him of Langbank, Scotland, which is in the Glasgow area. Within about five years, Langbank, Saskatchewan, became a thriving community with a train station, a grain elevator, stockyards, and an array of other businesses and services.

Over the years the Langbank area would come to be known for its award-winning purebred herds of cattle. The Langbank Post Office was established on January 1, 1910, and the first school was built in 1911. The population of the community peaked in the 1920s, and, evidently, in 1928, Langbank even boasted a tennis court. The population was roughly 80 from the mid-1960s through to the early 1970s, but began to steadily decline thereafter. In 1985, Langbank and Kennedy's schools amalgamated, with grades K-6 being taught in Langbank and grades 7-12 in Kennedy. In 2001, the school in Langbank was closed to Kennedy where all grades were subsequently taught. The school was renamed Kennedy Langbank School, and 103 students were enrolled in the fall of 2006. In the spring of 2007, however, it was announced the school would be losing grades 9-12. Subsequently there ensued a bitter fight as to where — Montmartre or Wolseley — high school students would be bused. Businesses operating in Langbank today include a Cargill grain elevator, a seed-cleaning plant, a Co-op (feed, fuel, and food), an automotive and machine shop, the post office, a café, and a hair salon. There is also a United Church in Langbank. A few kilometres north of the community is a good-sized farm equipment dealership; a few kilometres to the west is Enbridge Pipelines' Langbank pumping station. Langbank was established as an organized hamlet in 1978, and is situated within the boundaries of the RM of Silverwood No. 123.

LANGENBURG, town, pop 1,048 (2006c), 1,107 (2001c), is located 15 km inside the Saskatchewan-Manitoba border at the junction of Hwys 8 and 16. Yorkton, 70 km northwest, is the nearest city. The

Langenburg area began to be settled in the mid-1880s by people who were predominantly of German origin and was named after Prince Hohenlohe-Langenburg, who had visited south-eastern Saskatchewan in 1883 and who had recommended the area for German settlement. In 1888, the Manitoba and Northwestern Railway was running trains into the fledgling hamlet, and by the turn of the century Langenburg had developed into a thriving agricultural community. Langenburg was incorporated as a village in 1903. The discovery of potash south of the community in the late 1950s brought about a period of unprecedented growth and prosperity, and Langenburg's population doubled between 1966 and 1976, growing from 668 to 1,269. Langenburg achieved town status in 1959. Today, the community has a comprehensive array of businesses and services, as well as health care and recreational facilities, fire, ambulatory, and police services. Langenburg's two schools provide K-12 education to approximately 320 students. Carlton Trail Regional Park and Golf Course, located 18 kilometres south of Langenburg, as well as Asessippi Provincial Park, across the border in Manitoba, provide Langenburg residents with additional recreational opportunities and attract tourists to the area. Langenburg is the administrative centre of the RM of Langenburg No. 181. (See Langenburg photographs on page 212.)

LANGHAM, town, pop 1,120 (2006c), 1,145 (2001c), is located approximately 30 km northwest of Saskatoon on the Yellowhead Highway. The North Saskatchewan River lies a few kilometres to the north and west. Doukhobor families began settling in the region in 1899, followed by Mennonite settlers

LANGENBURG...
LANIGAN...
LASHBURN...

Langenburg photographs (this page) courtesy of the Langenburg & Area Homestead Museum. Lanigan photographs (facing page) courtesy of the Lanigan & District Heritage Centre. Lashburn photographs (facing page) courtesy of the Lashburn Centennial Museum.

LASHBURN

LANIGAN

LANGENBURG

◀ **PULLING OUT** of the Echo Milling Company elevator in Langenburg, perhaps 1900-01.

▼ **THE IMPERIAL HOTEL** (below) in Langenburg was built in 1902. As new towns and villages sprang up across the province, most had a hotel and bar. Bars were common gathering places for men, whether they were businessmen or farmers. By the early 1900s, bars had become a flashpoint for the growing temperance movement. The photograph (bottom left) shows the bar at the Imperial Hotel in 1911. Behind the bar: George Felling (left) and Richard Berger. Left to right: three unknown, Pete Olson, unknown, John Betz, Sr., E. Naffziger, Franz Hoffman, Karl Bechman, Sr., John Skaar.

▲ **THE LANGENBURG JUNIOR HOCKEY CLUB OF 1935-36** made the play-offs in Moose Jaw that season. Back row left to right: V. Slugoski, W. Gyuricsko, C. Kerr, H. Crich, J.G. Becker (coach and manager), S. Caul, E. Patzer, C. Berger, H. Schoepp. Front row: G. Anderson, J. Gray, W. Mitschke, A. Mitschke, J. Cook.

▼ **A CANADIAN PACIFIC RAILWAY SECTION CREW** in Langenburg, date unknown.

▲ **CANADIAN PACIFIC RAILWAY STATION** and trackage at Lanigan, date unknown. The station was built in 1908 for a cost of $10,000 and other features of the Lanigan rail yards included a water tower, a coal dock, eight side tracks, and a four-stall roundhouse. Lanigan was an important railway divisional point, and for many years almost everything that passed in and out of the Lanigan district came through this station. Passenger service, which started in Lanigan on November 25, 1907, was eventually discontinued; the station, however, remained in business until 1994. The building was then moved, restored, renovated, and officially opened to the public on July 3, 1996, as the Lanigan and District Heritage Centre.

▲ **THE WEST SIDE OF MAIN STREET, LANIGAN,** looking south, circa 1910.

▶ **THE FIRST TENNIS COURTS** in Lanigan were located on Railway Avenue, across from the Lanigan Hotel. Photograph circa early 1940s.

...three towns along the Yellowhead

▲ **LASHBURN DURING THE WINTER OF 1906-07.** The Canadian Bank of Commerce is under construction in the foreground to the right.

▼ **LASHBURN MAIN STREET, CIRCA 1930s.** At the end of the street is the high school built in 1927.

▲ **NURSES IN THE OPERATING ROOM** at the hospital in Lashburn in 1913. Officially opened in 1909, the 12-bed Lashburn Cottage Hospital was built for $15,000 and was considered one of the most up-to-date and best-equipped hospitals of its size in western Canada at the time.

▼ **CANADIAN NORTHERN RAILWAY TRAIN WRECK** at Lashburn in 1915.

emigrating from the United States as well as people from eastern Canada and Great Britain. With the construction of the Canadian Northern Railway through the area toward Edmonton in 1904-05, the Langham townsite began to develop, its name honouring an employee with the railway. The first businesses appeared in 1904, and in 1905 the post office was established. Langham became an incorporated village in 1906; the population of the community that year was 246, and Langham was a boomtown. It attained town status the next year, in 1907. By the 1920s, the community's population was over 400; however, after the initial rush of settlement it began to decline, slipping to 305 by 1951. This trend was reversed a decade later, in the 1960s, when the Yellowhead Highway was routed from Saskatoon directly to Langham, reducing the driving time between the communities to about 20 minutes. Young professionals and business people began locating their families in Langham and commuting to work in the city. What was once a service centre for the surrounding agricultural district mushroomed into a burgeoning bedroom community for a number of people. From a population of 433 in 1966, Langham had grown to a community of 729 ten years later. By 1986, the town had 1,193 residents. New residential subdivisions continue to be developed today. Langham has a core of essential businesses; however, residents largely benefit from easy access to the employment opportunities, services, and amenities that Saskatoon has to offer. Langham's two schools provide K-12 education to approximately 400 students, and the community has a range of recreational facilities including an arena, sports grounds, a curling club, a BMX bike track, a skateboard park, and a community hall. Additionally, there is a

golf course situated overlooking the river just north of the town. Langham has a 20-member volunteer fire department and a team of first responders. A medical doctor has a part-time office in the town and there is a special care home. The community has a library, a museum, a number of churches, athletic groups, service clubs, and other community-based organizations. Langham is situated in the RM of Corman Park No. 344.

LANIGAN, town, pop 1,233 (2006c), 1,289 (2001c), is located west of Big Quill Lake, and south of Humboldt, on Hwys 16 and 20. Lanigan developed with the arrival of the CPR from Strasbourg (then Strassburg) in 1907. The small cluster of shacks which sprang up on the townsite quickly gave way to more substantial structures, and Lanigan was incorporated as a village on August 21, 1907. On April 15, 1908, the community attained town status, and by the end of the decade, rail lines connected it to Saskatoon to the west and Wynyard to the east. By the end of the 1920s, rail lines were spreading in five directions as tracks had been completed to the northeast through Watson to Melfort, and north through Humboldt to Prince Albert. As a service and distribution centre for the surrounding agricultural district, Lanigan's population had grown to just over 500 by the early 1960s. In the mid-1960s, it received a substantial boost to both its population and its economy as the Alwinsal Corporation established a potash mine 11 kilometres west of the community. By 1971, Lanigan's population had jumped to 1,430; by 1981, the community numbered 1,732 residents. The potash mine, which was purchased by the Potash Corporation of Saskatchewan in 1977, today employs approxi-

mately 325 people, many of them Lanigan residents. Agriculture remains the other component in the area economy, and an integrated feedlot and ethanol plant is located eight kilometres east of the town. The feedlot has the capacity to hold close to 30,000 head of cattle, and the ethanol plant produces over 10 million litres of ethanol each year; the operation has about 50 full-time employees. Additionally, large-scale hog operations are located northeast of the community near the town of Leroy. Lanigan serves the area with an array of businesses and services, a range of medical facilities and related services, an RCMP detachment, a volunteer fire department, recreational facilities, churches, a day care, a pre-school, and elementary and high schools. The schools' combined student population numbers close to 400. The community has a library, and a museum situated in the town's 1908 CPR station, one of only a handful of its type left standing in Saskatchewan. Lanigan serves as the administrative centre of the RM of Usborne No. 310. (See Lanigan photographs on page 213.)

LANZ POINT, organized hamlet, is located in west-central Saskatchewan, north of North Battleford, one of a number of resort communities on Murray Lake. There have been cabins at the point for several decades; the resort was established as an organized hamlet in 1981. There were 35 permanent residents in 2006; however, the population varies greatly depending on the season. Lanz Point is situated in the RM of Meota No. 468.

LAPORTE, organized hamlet, pop 5 (2006c), 5 (2001c), is located in west-

central Saskatchewan, 8 km west of Eatonia on Hwy 44; the South Saskatchewan River lies a little over 30 km to the south. There had been some ranching activity north of the river for a few years before the first few settlers began arriving in 1906. These travelled north from the CPR main line, disembarking at Swift Current or Maple Creek, and were largely English-speaking Protestants from eastern Canada, the British Isles, and the United States. A number of Norwegians from the United States who re-migrated to Canada were also among the earlier arrivals. After 1909-10, the majority of the settlers were of German origin: some came from the United States, others from Manitoba and areas of earlier German settlement in Saskatchewan, particularly the Melville, Neudorf and Lemberg districts. Ukrainians, too, added to the mix. Settlement in the region of Laporte greatly accelerated once rail lines were completed to Kindersley (Canadian Northern, 1910) and through Prelate and Leader south of the river (CPR, 1913). In the district south of present-day Laporte, the Martin Land Company purchased a tract of land and established a large farm; most of the employees came from La Porte, Indiana, so when an area post office was established in January of 1914, the name Laporte (as one word for some reason) was adopted. When the railway came through, the name was then given to the townsite. The Laporte School District was established in 1917, with the school originally about one and a half miles north of where the hamlet would develop. The CNR built the railway through the area over 1918-20, and with its advent construction commenced at the present site of Laporte. Four elevators, a lumberyard, hardware and grocery stores, a hotel and café, a butcher shop and a poolroom, and a bank were among the community's early businesses. In the early 1920s, tennis was a popular activity — and an important part of the social life of the district — and in addition to tennis courts, Laporte also boasted a golf course, a curling rink, and a baseball diamond. Laporte also hosted Chautauquas and Annual Sports Days, where one memorable year Laporte's girls' softball team, who had never played together, beat what had been acclaimed as a very professional team from the village of Glidden. Laporte was established as an organized hamlet in 1959; the population was still 80 in 1966, but by 1972 it was down to 44, and by 1986 it was at 23. The Laporte Community Hall was designated a heritage property in 2004. Laporte is situated in the RM of Chesterfield No. 261.

LASHBURN, town, pop 914 (2006c), 783 (2001c), is located 32 km southeast of Lloydminster on Hwy 16. Settlement of the Lashburn area began in the spring of 1903 when a number of the Barr Colonists took up land. Additional settlers from eastern Canada arrived in 1904, and in January 1905 a post office in a store was established just northwest of the present community. The Canadian Northern Railway came through the district in 1905, and the location for the townsite of Lashburn was chosen. The first tent was erected on the site in December, the post office was soon relocated from its original location, and by December 1906 the fledgling community had developed sufficiently enough to be incorporated as a village. The name Lashburn is a combination of the word "Lash" (honouring a railway company solicitor, Z. A. Lash) and "burn," a Scottish word for a small stream. After incorporation, Lashburn grew steadily as additional settlers contin-

ued to pour into the region; they included a significant number of Mennonite families and, in the 1930s, people from the dried-out regions of southern Saskatchewan. By the mid-1960s, the community's population passed the 500 mark, and in 1979 Lashburn attained town status. The major industries in the area are oil and agriculture: more than 1,600 oil wells dot the district's rich agricultural lands. The town's business sector provides an array of goods and services, and the community's educational facilities accommodate more than 300 children from play school through to grade 12. Lashburn has a number of churches, a range of recreational facilities, and a museum. There are RCMP detachments in the neighbouring communities of Maidstone and Lloydminster, where major health care facilities are also located. Today, Lashburn residents benefit greatly from the community's proximity to Lloydminster, a city of 24,000 people which provides Lashburn residents with employment opportunities, amenities and services not locally available. The Lashburn Bluebirds dominated women's softball at both the provincial and national levels from the mid-1970s to the mid-1980s. One exceptional player to come out of Lashburn was Brenda Staniforth. An inductee into the Saskatchewan Sports Hall of Fame and Softball Canada's Hall of Fame, Staniforth has played and coached Canadian women's softball at the international level. Another Lashburn resident was Augustus Kenderdine, who arrived there to farm in 1907 and who went on to become perhaps the most significant painter in Saskatchewan before 1950. Trained in England and France, Kenderdine (1870-1947) began recording prairie life in his paintings, and in the mid-1930s he established the summer art school at Emma Lake. Lashburn is situated in the

RM of Wilton No. 472. (See Lashburn photographs on page 213.)

LEADER, town, pop 881 (2006c), 914 (2001c), is located 30 km east of the Saskatchewan-Alberta border, just south of the South Saskatchewan River at the junction of Hwys 21 and 32. Only a few ranchers were in the area when it was opened up to homesteaders, who began arriving in large numbers in 1907. Although there were a few from Ontario, the British Isles, Ukraine, and Norway, the vast majority were Germans from southern Russia, many of whom arrived in Saskatchewan via the United States. The German population was so significant that at least until the mid-1930s one of the qualifications for working in the local RM office was the ability to speak the language. Prior to the construction of the railway through the Leader district, early settlers had to make the three-day trip to Maple Creek on the CPR main line, to obtain supplies or to deliver grain. In 1911, the CPR purchased a quarter section of land for the Leader townsite, and soon enterprising businessmen were acquiring lots and setting up shop in anticipation of the coming railway. In 1913, the railway arrived, and in September that year the Village of Prussia (Leader's original name) was incorporated, another in the string of communities that grew up along the "Empress Line" as it progressed northwestward toward Alberta from just west of Swift Current. By 1917, the population of the community was over 500, and in May that year Prussia attained town status. Since Canada was at war with Germany at the time, some in the community believed such a strong German name for the town was inappropriate. Deliberations took place, and on November 1, 1917, the name Prussia

was changed to Leader. At the same time, the town's original German street and avenue names were changed to numbers. In the mid-1920s, a railway subdivision was built southwestward from Leader through Burstall to Fox Valley. After WWII, Leader's population skyrocketed, reaching a high of 1,236 in 1966. Today, Leader's several dozen business establishments provide a wide range of goods and services for a trading area which includes at least three rural municipalities. Many of the town's businesses operate in support of the region's grain and cattle industries; the Great Sandhills Terminal just east of town is a major grain handling facility, with a total storage capacity of over 20,000 tonnes and the ability to accommodate 56 rail cars. Leader also serves the region with a hospital, a medical clinic, and a special care home, a fire department, ambulance service, and an RCMP detachment. There are five churches in the town. Recreational facilities in Leader include an arena, a curling rink, an outdoor swimming pool and a bowling alley, and there is a golf course just north of town. A community centre and a seniors' centre facilitate social activities. Leader has a library, its own newspaper, and Saskatchewan's first and only reptile zoo. Leader Composite School provides K-12 education (242 students in the fall of 2006), and college courses are available via satellite. Additionally, St. Angela's Academy, 10 kilometres east in the village of Prelate, is an independent Catholic girls' residential school which offers a curriculum for grades 9-12. The Leader region is dotted with numerous points of interest including a number of historic sites, and tourism has been a developing industry for the community. The nearby Estuary Hutterite Colony offers tours by appointment, and Leader is surrounded by a unique and spectacular countryside

Black-and-white photographs courtesy of the Kindersley and District Plains Museum. Colour photographs taken August 30, 2003.

LEADER

...between sand bars and sand hills

▲ **THE LEADER FERRY** on the South Saskatchewan River, 1919. A ferry service operated in the area from 1910 until 1971, when the Chesterfield Bridge was completed.

▼ **THE LARGEST BARN EVER BUILT IN NORTH AMERICA** was constructed by W.T. Smith northwest of Leader in 1914. The building was 400 feet long, 128 feet wide, and 60 feet high (122 by 39 by 18 metres). Building materials included 875,000 board feet of fir lumber from British Columbia, 60,000 square feet of roofing, 30,000 sacks of cement, and one and a half railcar loads of nails. The barn took 100 men five months to build, and when completed it could house 600 head of cattle. Smith died only fours years after the barn's completion and in 1921 the structure was dismantled. The concrete foundation still remains at the site.

◄ ▼ **AS A TRIBUTE TO THE REGION'S FAUNA**, Leader has erected a number of larger-than-life wildlife sculptures throughout the town. They include burrowing owls (below) and Ord's kangaroo rats (left), as well as a red-headed woodpecker, a mule deer, a lake sturgeon, ferruginous hawks, and a western meadowlark.

▼ **EARLY MORNING LIGHT** illuminates buildings on 1st Street West.

of varied ecosystems, ranging from the riparian woodlands of the South Saskatchewan River Valley to the Great Sand Hills. The region supports an abundance of wildlife, including mule and white-tailed deer, pronghorn antelope, and over 200 species of birds during spring and fall migrations. The region is popular with both photographers and hunters. Leader serves as the administrative centre of the RM of Happyland No. 231.

LEASK, village, pop 418 (2006c), 447 (2001c), is located in central Saskatchewan, approximately 35 km southwest of Shellbrook, on Hwy 40. Leask was named after Robert Leask, on whose land the townsite was located. Originally from Ontario, Leask homesteaded in 1903, and in 1911, as the Canadian Northern Railway was pushing through from Prince Albert to North Battleford, his land was selected as a station site. Immediately, elevators, stores, livery barns, banks, rooming houses, a school, and a post office were built, forming a new settlement. In 1912, Leask was incorporated. By the 1920s the population was over 200, by the late 1940s it was nearing 300, and

in the 1960s Leask's population levelled off at close to 500. Leask is situated in a mixed farming district, and a number of the village's businesses cater to the agricultural industry. Leask has health care facilities including a special care home, fire and ambulance services, recreational facilities, a number of churches, clubs and community organizations, as well as a diverse sector of businesses and services. Policing is provided by the Blaine Lake and Shellbrook RCMP detachments, and Leask Community School provides K-12 education to close to 350 students. Leask serves as the administrative centre of the RM of Leask No. 464.

LEBRET, village, pop 203 (2006c), 207 (2001c), is located in the Qu'Appelle Valley on the northeast shore of Mission lake, 6 km east of Fort Qu'Appelle on Hwy 56. In 1864, Bishop Alexander Taché of St. Boniface passed through the Qu'Appelle Valley on his way home from Ile-a-la-Crosse. Seeing the opportunity for a Catholic presence, he returned to the area in 1865, and selected the site of present-day Lebret for a Catholic mission. In 1866 Abbé Ritchot arrived to open the mission,

building a simple combined house and chapel made of logs with a thatched roof. It was one of the earlier Roman Catholic missions established in what would become the province of Saskatchewan. The building burned in 1869 and was replaced by a larger wood frame structure in 1870. The mission became the main centre of Catholicism for the Métis and First Nations people in the region and a base for Oblate priests who travelled the southern plains to points such as Wood Mountain

▲ **ANNUAL CORPUS CHRISTI PROCESSION** in Lebret, circa 1950. Sacred Heart Church is on the left; Sacred Heart Scholasticate is visible on the far side of the lake. Saskatchewan Archives Board R-B2769.

▼ **THE INTERIOR OF SACRED HEART CHURCH IN LEBRET.** Photograph taken June 1, 2007.

▼ **LEASK, CIRCA 1920s.** Saskatchewan Archives Board R-B10311.

▼ **OVERLOOKING THE QU'APPELLE VALLEY FROM THE SMALL CHAPEL ABOVE LEBRET:** Below, to the right, is Mission Lake; in the distance to the left lies Katepwa Lake. Photograph taken mid-May, 1999.

and the Cypress Hills. In 1884, a residential school financed by the federal government was started, with Father Hugonard as the principal. In 1886, the parish priest, Father Louis Lebret, became the first postmaster of the community and, although he only held the position for a little more than six months, the office was named Lebret and the name became that of the community. Also in 1886, a rectory was built — it stood until 2005 when it

was demolished as it had fallen into disrepair. In 1899, the Sisters of Our Lady of the Missions arrived and began work in the community. In 1906, they founded Saint Gabriel's Convent. The Village of Lebret was incorporated on October 14, 1912. By the early 1920s the growing parish, substantially Métis, required a larger edifice, and in 1925 the impressive fieldstone Sacred Heart Church was built. In 1929, the landmark stations of the cross and the small chapel shrine on the hill overlooking Lebret were erected. In 1966, the wooden cross at the top of the hill was replaced with a metal one, which is illuminated at night and visible from across the valley. Until the latter half of the twentieth century Lebret was an important religious and educational centre. In addition to the residential school and the convent, there was a public school, and the Oblates established a theological training centre, Sacred Heart Scholasticate, on the south side of Mission Lake. The public school closed to Fort Qu'Appelle in 1980; the convent, as well as the scholasticate, closed in the 1960s. The residential school was signed over to a First Nations school board in October 1973, at a ceremony presided over by then Minister of Indian Affairs, Jean Chrétien. The school, which eventually became known as White Calf Collegiate, closed in 1998. Today, Lebret remains a picturesque, yet very quiet, community. The population is aging (85 per cent were the age of 15 or older in 2006), and there are no banks or restaurants in the village. There is a shop that sells antiques and collectibles, and a lone grocery store still exists. Lebret's Sacred Heart parish is now the responsibility of a lay administrator, and an Ursuline nun runs a second-hand store which doubles as a community gathering place. Lebret is situated in the RM of North Qu'Appelle No. 187.

LEMBERG, town, pop 255 (2006c), 306 (2001c), is located southwest of Melville on Hwy 22 between the villages of Abernethy and Neudorf. There was some settlement in the district in the early 1880s: one group known as the Primitive Methodists, a nineteenth-century splinter group from mainstream Methodism, took up land in the Pheasant Forks area. Many early settlers, however, would leave within a number of years, owing to the promised railway not arriving and difficulties encountered in farming. Intensive settlement of the Lemberg area occurred in the 1890s, as both Protestant and Roman Catholic Germans arrived. Ukrainians followed in 1902. Two years later, trains were running through the area and the townsite was developing rapidly. Lemberg was incorporated as a village on July 12, 1904, its name the German form of L'viv (today, an industrial centre in western Ukraine). By 1906 the population of the community was 365, and in 1907 Lemberg attained town status. In 1911, James Garfield Gardiner, future Premier of Saskatchewan and federal Minister of Agriculture, became the principal of Lemberg School, a position he retained until 1914, the year he first became an MLA. Gardiner bought a farm just outside of Lemberg and served as the community's mayor in 1919-20; he retired to his farm at Lemberg in 1958, passing away in 1962. His son, J. W. Gardiner, was the town's secretary-treasurer in the 1950s, at which point the town had reached a peak population of over 500. Lemberg continues to be a trading centre for the surrounding agricultural district, where grain and livestock production and a number of seed farms form the basis of the area economy. Lemberg has a 7-12 school (111 students in the

▲ ▶ LEMBERG LANDMARKS: St. Michael's Roman Catholic Church, above, and Trinity Lutheran Church, right.

Photographs taken October 3, 2003.

fall of 2006); the neighbouring village of Neudorf has a K-6 school (95 students in the fall of 2006). A shuttle bus transports students between the two communities. There is also a health centre in Neudorf; Balcarres has the nearest hospital, as well as an RCMP detachment. Community landmarks at Lemberg include: Trinity Lutheran Church, built in 1926 using an estimated 83,000 bricks; St. Michael's Roman Catholic Church, dating to 1901; and the former Weissenberg School, a fieldstone structure built in 1900 and named for a Galician village. The latter two structures were constructed before the present townsite was established and lie just to the east of the community. Lemberg is situated in the RM of McLeod No. 185.

LEOVILLE, village, pop 341 (2006c), 343 (2001c), is located 32 km north of

Spiritwood on Hwy 24. The community lies within the northernmost reaches of the province's agricultural lands; a short distance north of Leoville, farms give way to forest and innumerable lakes and streams. Northeast of the village rise the Leoville Hills. The first settlers came to the Leoville district when it was heard that the CPR was going to build a railway through the area — a line surveyed to run from Debden to Meadow Lake. The first settler credited with homesteading in the area of Leoville was Leo Charpentier (Carpenter) who arrived in 1927, and it was in his honour that the community was named. Over the following few years more people began arriving in the district and, through the 1930s, many came from the southern regions of the province, driven north by the drought. A large percentage of the original settlers at Leoville were French speakers who came from the Wil-

low Bunch district. In 1930, as the railway was under construction, the area of the townsite was cleared of brush, and area pioneers began building shacks at Leoville even before it was surveyed into lots. On April 1, 1930, the Leoville Post Office was officially established, although it was in a home a couple of kilometres out of the hamlet until 1931, the year the rail line through to Meadow Lake was opened. No longer were the long trips to Debden, later Rabbit Lake or Medstead, the nearest railway points, necessary to deliver grain or to obtain supplies. With the arrival of the railway, Leoville grew rapidly. Elevators were erected and numerous businesses were soon established. In 1932, both the school and a Roman Catholic Church opened their doors. Initially, the area economy was largely based in forestry: sawmills, pulpwood producers, and firewood cutters were major employers until

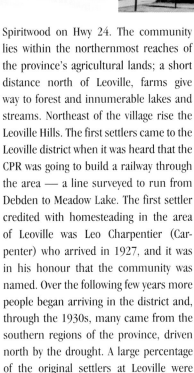

farming came to the fore as more and more land in the district was cleared. After the railway arrived, many thousands of railway ties were produced in and shipped out of the Leoville district. During the winter months, many early area settlers also engaged in commercial fishing or trapping (primarily of muskrats, foxes, and minks), which brought in enough money to help carry them through the summer while they worked clearing and breaking their lands. The Village of Leoville was incorporated on June 26, 1944. Today, the economy is primarily based on agriculture — mixed farming, grain and cattle production — with forestry a smaller contributing factor. A number of district residents also travel to work in the oil and gas fields of Alberta and west-central Saskatchewan. Leoville has a small core of local businesses which includes a grocery store, a restaurant, a convenience store, gas stations, the post office, an insurance broker, and a credit union. The village also has a library, a seniors' drop-in centre, a fire hall, and a health centre with an attached special care home. The nearest RCMP detachment is located in the town of Spiritwood. Leoville Central School is a K-12 facility which had 166 students enrolled in the fall of 2006. Community recreational facilities include skating and curling rinks, ball diamonds, and a town hall where functions such as weddings and dances are held. Additionally, Chitek Lake, a short distance to the northwest, is a popular year-round resort and recreation destination. Leoville has a number of service clubs, sports teams, and other community-based organizations. A key annual event in the village is the Leoville Trail Riders Rodeo, an amateur rodeo that features events such as steer riding, team roping, calf roping, chicken racing, mutton busting for children, ladies' calf throwing, and two nights with outdoor dances. Leoville is situated in the RM of Spiritwood No. 496.

LEROSS, village, pop 42 (2006c), 59 (2001c), is situated approximately 60 km north of Fort Qu'Appelle between the villages of Lestock and Kelliher on Hwy 15, just west of the junction with Hwy 35. The area topography is gently undulating, dotted with poplar bluffs and a profusion of sloughs and small lakes. Some ranching interests were active in the region beginning in the 1880s; the homesteading era began about 1903, with the period of the most intensive settlement in the district taking place over 1905-06. The largest number of the first homesteads in the area were taken up to the south of the present-day villages of Lestock, Leross, and Kelliher. Early settlers arrived from Ontario, Central Europe, and the British Isles; Swedes took up land around the neighbouring village of Kelliher and to the north of Leross; Hungarians settled in the district, largely to the south and east, beginning in 1906. Later, Ukrainians added to the cultural milieu. Besides those of European origins who came to the region, First Nations people resided in the area: the reserve holdings of the Muskowekwan First Nation (originally surveyed in 1883) lie approximately nine kilometres to the west, adjacent to the village of Lestock. Additionally, there were a number of Métis at Lestock. In 1908, the Grand Trunk Pacific Railway came through the district and Leross had its beginnings — its name, chosen to fit the alphabetical sequence of naming communities along the line (Ituna, Jasmin, Kelliher, Leross), honours L.E. Ross, a paymaster with the railway company. The first general stores were erected on the townsite in 1908, followed shortly by a lumberyard, a hardware store, a livery barn, and a blacksmith shop. The Leross Post Office was established on March 1, 1909; Leross School officially opened in May 1909 (with 26 pupils enrolled); and Leross was incorporated on December 1, 1909. Thirteen business establishments were reportedly operating in the community by year's end. Two grain elevators were built in 1911 and 1912 (these were closed in 1973 and later demolished), and during the latter year construction began on what would become a 24-room hotel, run by a manager, a bartender, a cook, a waitress, and a chamber maid at the height of its operation. The population of Leross had grown to 114 by 1911 and the community enjoyed boom years through to the early 1920s, after which the village experienced a period of decline — a cooperative store begun in the early part of the decade failed, and the population of the village was down to 73 by 1931. Post-WWII, the community rebounded — a new four-room school was built in 1958 — and Leross reached a peak population of 117 in 1961. Water and sewers systems were installed in the village in 1969, followed by natural gas in 1973. In 1969, the Leross railway station, which had closed a few years earlier, was sold and moved to a farm where it then was used for storing fertilizers and chemicals. A second co-operative venture begun in Leross in 1946 prospered for a period, but it, too, failed in 1970. Due to a shrinking congregation, the Roman Catholic church closed in 1976, and due to declining enrollment Leross School closed in 1978. In 1980, the area received a boost, as the Cargill Grain Company began construction of a 145,000-bushel grain elevator and farm supply warehouses immediately southwest of Leross. The facility was officially opened in August 1981, with 800 area farmers in attendance for a celebratory dinner and an evening's entertainment. The mayor of Leross at the time, George Kish, performed the ribbon-cutting ceremony, declaring the business open. Cargill, however, sold out a few years ago and the facility now operates as Tri-Way Fertilizer, Ltd. Other businesses operating at Leross today include an auction service, and an abattoir and hide processor. Leross has experienced a dramatic loss of population over the past two decades: its numbers fell from 103 in 1986 to 82 by 1996, and have subsequently dropped by half. Leross serves as the administrative centre of the RM of Kellross No. 247.

LEROY, town, pop 412 (2006c), 413 (2001c), is located southwest of Watson, 13 km west of Hwy 6. The area economy is based on agriculture. Settlers to the district were largely of English, Scottish, Irish, Scandinavian, and German origins. In 1907, the first school, named Bogend, and in 1909, a post office, named Bog End, were established within about a kilometre and a half of where Leroy is now situated. With the construction of the CPR line between Lanigan and Watson in 1920-21, the present townsite was established and the name Leroy adopted for the community. The name was chosen to honour John Leroy, the son of one of the first families to settle in the district, who lost his life during the First World War. After the railway arrived, more people and businesses moved into the area and Leroy was incorporated as a village in 1922. During WWII, airmen from all over the British Commonwealth made Leroy a bustling place, as they prepared and trained for the war effort at No. 5 Bombing and Gunnery School just west of Big Quill Lake.

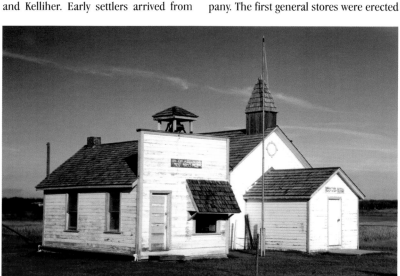

▲ **LEROSS HERITAGE PARK** contains an old rural schoolhouse, formerly Granatier School, built in 1907 about six miles southwest of Leross, and the original RM of Kellross office building constructed circa 1910 (left). Adjacent to these structures is the Leross and District Swimming Pool and a civic centre that houses the village office and a seniors' club. Photograph taken October 22, 2003.

The years following WWII were prosperous times, and Leroy's population more than doubled within ten years, growing from 213 in 1946 to 514 in 1956. Leroy attained town status in 1963. Beginning in the late 1960s, however, the community entered a period of continuous decline. Between 1980 and 1990, the population of the town fell by 17 per cent, and that of the surrounding rural municipality fell by 25 per cent. As the retail and service sector of the community was declining, some began to wonder if the community could completely disappear. Part of the problem was that Leroy is rather isolated, as it is not situated on either a major highway or a major rail line. What has happened subsequently, however, has been a small-town success story. Proactive community leaders in Leroy vigorously pursued initiatives, innovations, partnerships, and new co-operative ventures, and have realized a significant degree of success in building a sustainable future. Volunteerism and productive and creative fund-raising events led to the revitalization of social, cultural, and recreational facilities, bolstering Leroy as an attractive place to live. Commu-

▲ **LEROY ADMINISTRATION BUILDING** at the corner of Aspen Street and 1st Avenue. Photograph taken August 5, 2004.

nity-rooted business ventures, such as the Leroy Watson Co-op's establishment of an integrated farm supply service for fertilizers, crop protection and seed, as well as the significant furthering of the area's hog industry, have led directly to the creation of at least 100 new jobs in the community since 1990. In recent years, the Saskatchewan Government's Action Committee on the Rural Economy (ACRE) named Leroy a model community in terms of contemporary economic development strategies for rural Saskatchewan. Leroy serves as the administrative centre of the RM of Leroy No. 339.

LESLIE, hamlet, pop 20 (2006c), 30 (2001c), is a former village located 13 km northwest of Foam Lake on Hwy 16. People who settled in the district were mainly Icelandic; others were Ukrainian and British in origin. The CPR reached

the Leslie townsite from Sheho in 1908. The post office, known as Leslie Station until the name was shortened to Leslie in 1962, was established on June 1, 1909. The community was named after John Leslie, comptroller for the CPR. Leslie was incorporated as a village on November 16, 1909. The first school was built in 1912. By 1921 Leslie's population had reached 162 (the all-time high), and in its heyday the village had grocery stores, a hardware store, a bank, a drugstore, a doctor, two churches, farm implement dealerships, a hotel, a railway station and station agent, a pool hall and barber shop, a livery barn, and several other businesses. The community had a choir known throughout the region, and Leslie hosted a midwinter gathering called "Thorrablot," a traditional Scandinavian feast dating back centuries. People from Foam Lake to Dafoe attended the celebration. Two major fires, though, took their toll on the community, as did the Depression, and in the latter half of the twentieth century, Leslie steadily declined. In 1953, high school students began to be bused to Foam Lake; in the early 1960s, Leslie School was closed. By 1969, only the grain elevators, the Co-op store and fuel sales, a church, and the village office remained. The Co-op is still in business; the church building is now privately owned. The last grain elevators in Leslie were demolished in 1993, and the community relinquished village status on July 17, 2006. Leslie is situated in the RM of Elfros No. 307.

LESLIE BEACH, resort village, is located approximately 22 km north of the town of Foam Lake, on the southwest shore of Fishing Lake. The resort takes its name from the nearby village of Leslie. Leslie Beach had its beginnings in 1952

after district residents held several years of annual fundraisers, which enabled them to buy 171 acres of lake front property and begin development of a recreation area. Camp sites, a concession booth, change rooms, and a play area were established, and in 1978 the public facilities came under the jurisdiction of the Fishing Lake Regional Park Authority. Adjacent to this, a substantial cottage subdivision also developed, which today is comprised of over 131 private dwellings. There are close to a few dozen permanent residents; however, the population fluctuates significantly depending on the season. The resort village was incorporated in 1999. Fishing Lake's shores are now highly developed and are encircled by several resort communities and public recreation areas, as well as the Fishing Lake First Nation situated on the lake's west side. Fishing Lake's water levels have proven somewhat problematic over the decades, being susceptible to both drought and flooding. Its two basins were separated during a dry spell over a century ago, and in the 1930s levels also significantly receded. In the mid-1990s, and again in 2007, area resorts, cottages, and district roads sustained considerable flood damage as the lake's water level reached unprecedented heights. Leslie Beach has one of the longest and finest sand beaches in the province and is situated in the RM of Foam Lake No. 276.

LESTOCK, village, pop 138 (2006c), 226 (2001c), is approximately halfway between the towns of Raymore and Ituna on Hwy 15. The reserve holdings of the Muskowekwan First Nation border the western side of the village, and Touchwood Hills Post Provincial Historic Park lies further along the highway to the northwest. Homesteaders began taking up land in the area around 1903 and extensive settlement of the district occurred over 1905-06. Hungarians arrived in significant numbers during the latter year and they occupied large holdings from the Lestock area toward the south and west. The Grand Trunk Pacific Railway came through in 1908 and a hamlet sprang up at the pre-determined townsite — the beginnings of present-day Leross. The locale was to have been named Mostyn (the railway station was originally known as such) in order to fit the alphabetical sequence of naming communities along the rail line (Ituna, Jasmin, Kelliher, Leross, Mostyn, etc.). But Canadian postal authorities rejected the name as it was too similar to another post office, Mosten, in the Wiseton-Dinsmore area. Subsequently, the community was named for John Lestock Reid (1841-1911), who had served with the Midland Battalion during the 1885 Resistance, and who had been a member of the Legislative Assembly for Prince Albert West from 1894-97 before becoming a government land surveyor. The post office, originally known as "Lestock Station," was established on July 1, 1911, and the Village of Lestock was incorporated on April 17, 1912. The community grew very rapidly: its population was somewhat under 300 by the 1920s, remained steady through the Depression, and soared following WWII to reach over 400 by the early 1960s, hitting a peak of 452 in 1971. Notable in the history of Lestock were the services of the Oblate Fathers and the Grey Nuns who had been working among the area's Saulteaux and francophone Métis population. It is worth noting that for many years the Muskowekwan Reserve population were banned from Lestock after sundown, and that destitute Métis lived in shantytowns on the community's periphery. The Oblate Fathers were instrumental in the es-

tablishment of a Roman Catholic parish at Lestock, and the Grey Nuns established St. Joseph's Hospital, now known as St. Joseph's Integrated Care Centre, today a 16-bed facility offering acute care, emergency, long-term, respite, and adult day care services. The Sisters left Lestock in the early 1980s; as of 2007 an Oblate Father was still working out of the village. Since the 1980s, Lestock has been rapidly declining, and at a rate perhaps greater than that faced by many of the province's smaller communities in recent decades. From the 452 residents the community numbered in 1971, the population was down to 369 by 1986, and 301 by 1996. Over the past decade, that number has been cut by more than half. Today, boarded-up homes and businesses outnumber those occupied and operating. Lestock School closed in 1999 — enrollment had declined by almost 40 per cent since 1993. The student population, 50 per cent of whom were bused in from neighbouring First Nations communities, now mainly attend classes at the modern facility built on the Muskowekwan Reserve or go to the public school in the village of Kelliher, 18 kilometres to the southeast. There were three grain elevators in Lestock in 1965; the last was demolished around 2003. The health care centre and a small core of businesses remain. Lestock is situated in the RM of Kellross No. 247.

LIBERTY, village, pop 73 (2006c), 94 (2001c), is located on Hwy 2 just southwest of Big Arm Bay on the west side of Last Mountain Lake. The hamlet of Stalwart lies to the north; the village of Penzance, to the south. Land seekers first arrived in 1903; the first few settlers began taking up homesteads in the Liberty district in 1904. Many came from

the United States: they detrained at Craik, or came via the steamer on Last Mountain Lake. The first school in the district, Wolff Valley, was built in 1906, and the first post office, Wolffton, was established in 1907. Both were named after William Wolff, one of the first settlers in the area. The schoolhouse served as a place for religious services, public meetings, and dances. Supplies such as lumber had to be hauled from Craik, or brought in by barge on the lake. The village of Liberty itself had its beginnings with the construction of the CPR line up the west side of Last Mountain Lake in 1910-11. It is believed the community may have been named after Liberty in New York state, the hometown of early settler Ben Wolff. The first two businesses — a general store

and a blacksmith shop — were started at the townsite in the fall of 1910. In 1911 the rails were laid and Liberty was developing rapidly. A hotel was built that year, the post office was established, and the Northern Crown Bank opened for business. By the end of 1911 the community had grown sufficiently to warrant incorporation, and petitions were sent to provincial authorities. Liberty officially became an incorporated village on January 23, 1912. In 1912, the first grain elevators were erected and a school that had been built a mile south in 1908 was moved into the village. With many Americans in the district, baseball became a passion, and for many years Liberty was known as "The Baseball Town" — its teams had a reputation for being formidable competitors, not

Liberty Directory

Auto Supplies	General Merchants	Oil Company
Pontiac — D. Ruether	Liberty Co-op Ass'n. — C. B. Moore	Liberty Co-op Ass'n. Ltd. — C. B. Moore
Plymouth — M. Nelson	Martin's Store — J J. Martin	Painter & Decorator
Bank	**Grain Companies**	F. Castell
Royal Bank of Canada — F. C. McMillan	Sask. Wheat Pool — C. Schultz	**Restaurants & Cafes**
Barber	United Grain Growers — J. Stratton	Liberty Hotel
A. M. Comba	Searle Grain Co. — P. Downison	W. & M. Store
Blacksmith	**Hardware Supplies**	**School**
P. Dupron	Liberty Hardware — Ross Wm. Cowen	W. A. Wheatley, Principal
Contractor	Liberty Co-op Ass'n.	**Shoe Repairs & Sales**
L. A. Dickson	**Hotel**	F. Balicki
Dray and Transport	Liberty Hotel — Mrs. E. Gutgsoll	**Wood-Coal**
H. Clow	**Insurance & Real Estate**	Security Lumber — A. E. Bishop
Electrical Appliances	A. E. Bishop	Searle Grain — P. Downison
Sales & Service	**Implement Dealers**	**Mayor**
Liberty Co-op Ass'n.	I.H.C. — E. Obregewitsch	J. Park
Ed's Hardware — E. Obregewitsch	Minneapolis-Moline — Nelson's Garage	**Secretary-Treasurer**
Garages	Massey-Harris — Liberty Service Garage	A. E. Bishop
Liberty Service Garage — D. Ruether	John Deere — C. E. Tannanhill	**Councillors**
Nelson's Garage — M. Nelson	**Meat Market**	D. H. Stuart, B. Brightwell
E. Obregewitsch	Liberty Meat Market — Wm. E. Henderson	**Board of Trade President**
C. E. Tannanhill	**Lumber & Building Supplies**	F. C. McMillan
	Security Lumber Co. — A. E. Bishop	

332   SASKATCHEWAN BUSINESS DIRECTORY

▲ ▼ **THE DIFFERENCE 48 YEARS MAKES.** In 1955, the village listed several dozen businesses in the Golden Jubilee Edition of the Saskatchewan Business Directory, above. By July 8, 2003, when the photograph below was taken, the townsite was characterized by abandoned buildings and vacant lots. Pictured here are the former bank and fire hall. The fire hall is no longer standing.

accustomed to losing. By 1931 the population of the village was 172, but that year the Searle grain elevator closed after two years of poor crops. The post-WWII era was a time of prosperity for Liberty — the community's population peaked at 182 in 1956. In the 1960s, however, the village began to slowly decline. In 1962 high school students began to be bused north to the town of Imperial to attend classes; in 1971 grades seven and eight followed; and by 1977 grades four, five, and six were also riding the school bus out of the village. Liberty School was closed in 1981. In the 1970s, flooding on Last Mountain Lake severed the rail link to the south; in the 1980s, CN took over the line through Liberty; and in the late 1990s, the line was abandoned. A few years later the track was torn up and the rails were sold to American buyers; area farmers were left to haul their crops as far as Moose Jaw or the Mid-Sask grain terminal south of Watrous. Roads in the area deteriorated. In the 1980s about a dozen businesses were still operating in the village; today, the Co-op and the Liberty Motor Hotel are about the only commercial ventures remaining. One of the former Saskatchewan Wheat Pool elevators still stands. Liberty is situated in the RM of Big Arm No. 251.

LIMERICK, village, pop 130 (2006c), 146 (2001c), is located in south-central Saskatchewan, 21 km west of Assiniboia at the junction of Hwys 13 and 358. Among the first settlers in the district were members of the Lossing family from Ontario, who arrived in the west between 1906 and 1908. They took up homesteads just northeast of the present village, and Edward Lossing, who arrived in 1907, was asked to install a telegraph key in his house, as it was situated along the telegraph line that ran between Moose Jaw and Wood Mountain. He was given the honour of naming the station and he chose "Limerick" after Limerick, Ireland, the home of his grandmother. The name was then given to the post office when Edward's neighbouring brother Frank became the first postmaster on July 15, 1908. For a number of years, supplies had to be brought from Moose Jaw using horses or oxen and wagons, but in 1912 as the railway was being built from Assiniboia toward Shaunavon, a location for a townsite was established and the name Limerick was chosen for what would quickly become a new village. The Irish theme was carried on with the naming of the streets — Connaught, Shannon, Galway, and Killarney among them. It is interesting to note, however, that by the outbreak of WWI, Romanians were possibly the most numerous settlers in the district. Trains were running through Limerick in 1913, bringing in large numbers of settlers and supplies, and businesses were rapidly springing up to serve the newcomers' needs. Some eager entrepreneurs, though, had began construction even before the townsite was surveyed, and had to relocate once the streets and lots were laid out — the foundations of the first elevators had to be repoured further east from where they had originally been laid. Limerick was incorporated on July 10, 1913, and by the end of the year the area country school (which was a couple of kilometres north) had been relocated to the village. The community grew extremely fast in the early years but was almost wiped off the map in 1915 when a prairie fire blew in from the west. Women and children were evacuated while the men frantically ploughed fire guards and set a back fire. The prairie fire was brought under control only at the outskirts of the

▲ **A SCHOOL BUS BEGINS ITS MORNING ROUNDS** in Limerick, September 1, 2004. Three years later the school in the village was closed.

village. Limerick had its heyday during the "roaring twenties," when the population was over 400 and approximately 50 places of business were in operation. But the furious expansion of the community was not without its down side. Transient labour formed a significant part of the population, and rowdiness and drunkenness were a nagging irritant for the village council. In 1928, Limerick lost some business, particularly at the grain elevators, when the CPR built a branch line that passed about 12 kilometres south of the community en route to Wood Mountain and Mankota. But a more ominous threat to Limerick's well-being came in 1929, when the first dust storm rolled in off the plains. In its wake came the drought, the grasshopper plagues, and the long years of the Great Depression. Businesses closed and many families moved away. Then in 1939 war was declared and 300 young men and women from the village and the surrounding rural municipality joined the armed forces — almost three times as many as had gone to serve in WWI. Twenty sons never returned after the First War; 22 did not make it back after the Second. The years following WWII were a time of prosperity, but Limerick did not regain its former population, nor the previous level of business activity. The population was down to 240 by 1951, and has more or less declined steadily since. Further, better roads and automobiles were taking people to Assiniboia, Gravelbourg, or Moose Jaw to shop for services and supplies. There were, however, a number of positive developments in the community: a new high school was built in 1966, a rink was built as a Centennial project, a new Saskatchewan Wheat Pool elevator was erected and annexes were built onto the older elevators, sewer and water systems were upgraded, and the community's streets were paved. Even so, vacant lots and vacant buildings were slowly beginning to outnumber occupied ones, and today only one elevator (a Paterson) is left standing and operating. Limerick School, a K-12 facility, had remained an important community institution; however, after enrollment fell to only 48 students in the fall of 2006 (down from 67 in 2003), the school was scheduled to close at the end of the school year in 2007. Businesses remaining in the village include the post office, a branch of the Conexus Credit Union, an insurance agency, a Lucky Dollar grocery store, auto body and automotive repair shops, a beverage room in the old hotel, and a seed cleaning plant. An important community employer is the Limerick Co-op bulk station. Recreational facilities in the village include a baseball diamond, an arena, a community centre and a seniors' centre, and a playground. Limerick has a volunteer fire department; policing is provided by the Assiniboia RCMP. The nearest hospital is also located in Assiniboia. Limerick serves as the administrative centre of the RM of Stonehenge No. 73.

LINTLAW, village, pop 145 (2006c), 187 (2001c), is located 25 km southeast of Kelvington on Hwy 49. The first settlers began arriving in the district around 1904-05, aided by the fact that the Canadian Northern Railway was beginning to run roughly 15 kilometres to the south, from Canora through Wadena and westward. For a number of years, mail and

supplies were obtained in Margo and Invermay, the nearest points on the line. Settlers to the Lintlaw area were of diverse origins: British from overseas, or from Ontario and Manitoba; also Ukrainians, Swedes, and Poles; and after about 1908 many Norwegians, most coming to Canada from the United States. Shortly, school districts were organized. The Lintlaw Post office was established a few kilometres southwest of the present townsite in 1910, and the first store in the area opened in 1912. However, until the railway surveyed the townsite and put the steel through in 1919-20, Lintlaw was little more than a small collection of shacks. With the arrival of the railway came more settlers and businesses, and by the end of 1921 Lintlaw was large enough to be incorporated as a village. From around 1917 to 1933-34, logging and lumber production, generally northeast of Lintlaw, employed many men. The 1930s brought more people to the area from regions of southern Saskatchewan parched by the drought,

and through the next two decades, particularly after WWII, the population of the village continued to grow, reaching close to 350 by 1956. Today, for a village its size, Lintlaw has a surprisingly diverse array of businesses, services, and community organizations. The village has a library, a recreation centre for sports and social occasions, seniors' housing and a seniors' centre; there are three churches, as well as volunteer organizations, including the fire department. Lintlaw also has a number of craftspeople, carpenters, a photographer, a welding shop, and a plumbing and heating business. There are restaurants, grocery stores, a hotel, a credit union, a meat market, and the Co-op, which has groceries, hardware, farm supplies, and postal services. The community had a K-9 school that had 50 students enrolled in the fall of 2005; this, however, was closed in 2006 and the village's schoolchildren are now bused to classes in Kelvington. The Lintlaw area economy is predominantly based on agriculture — traditionally, a combination of grain and livestock production — however, there are now significant hog production operations within a few kilometres of the village, and area farms are now raising exotic livestock. Lintlaw is situated in the RM of Hazel Dell No. 335.

◁ **LINTLAW IS WELL KNOWN TO THE PROVINCE'S SNOWMOBILE ENTHUSIASTS.**
The Lintlaw Bush Bandits Snowmobile Club maintains 235 kilometres of groomed trails through the Porcupine Forest, and each March the community hosts a snowmobile derby which draws 400 to 600 participants. Here, Lane Foster catches some air during the event in March 2000. Photograph courtesy of Coleen Foster, Lintlaw.

LIPTON, village, pop 342 (2006c), 331 (2001c), is located approximately 18 km north of Fort Qu'Appelle, on Hwy 22, just west of Hwy 35. The name of the community honours Sir Thomas Johnstone Lipton (1850-1931), the Scottish merchant who created the famous Lipton tea brand, and who was also a famous yachtsman, one of the most persistent challengers in the history of the prestigious America's Cup sailing regatta. In the 1920s, the village's Great War Veteran's Association wrote to Sir Lipton informing him that the community had been named in his honour and requested a photograph. The request was granted and a signed portrait of Lipton has hung in a place of honour in the village since 1925. People of many ethnic groups from many parts of the world came to settle in what became known as the Lipton district: a few Scots were among the first in the early 1880s; in 1883 a group of young Englishmen sponsored by a wealthy patron in their home country, one L. Hogg, settled to the north of present-day Lipton; beginning in 1901, with the assistance of the Jewish Colonization Association, Jews settled in an area from east of Dysart to the northeast of Lipton toward Ituna. Romanian Jews came first and mainly established farms; Jews from Russia gravitated to the new village of Lipton, where they were merchants and artisans constituting approximately one third of the community's early population. Slovaks and Czechs, too, settled in the Lipton area after 1905, and, just north of Lipton, between 1904 and 1912, there developed one of Saskatchewan's more unique settlements: deaf-mute settlers, a number of whom had attended a school for deaf-mute people in Belleville, Ontario, took up land in the district with

▲ **JEWISH SETTLERS FROM ROMANIA**, Samuel and Hanna Schwartz (on right) with daughter Simma and her husband, Lipton district, circa 1903. Saskatchewan Archives Board R-B1781.

▲ **LIPTON, CIRCA 1907.** Saskatchewan Archives Board R-B1830.

▽ **IN 2000, IT WAS ANNOUNCED THAT LIPTON WOULD LOSE THREE GRAIN ELEVATORS**, two owned by the Saskatchewan Wheat Pool, the other by United Grain Growers. The village faced a loss of 21 per cent of its tax base, and local businesses lost the support of area grain haulers. The last Lipton elevator, built in 1984 and pictured here, was demolished in 2004. Photograph taken October 22, 2003.

their families, and engaged in farming or work in various trades. German Lutherans were also numerous throughout the district, and after many of the area's Jewish settlers had left by the mid-1930s, the population remaining at Lipton had predominantly German origins. With the construction of the railway through the district — the line from Neudorf to Lipton opened in 1904, and was completed through to Bulyea the following year — the village developed rapidly. Surveys for the townsite of Lipton — described in the local history as a slough-ridden area — were conducted over 1903-04, and businesses and services, at first in tents and shacks, sprang up to serve not only the increasing number of homesteaders in the countryside, but also the railway construction workers camped in the area. Work on a three-storey hotel and the first grain elevator commenced in 1903. The Lipton Post Office was established on April 24, 1905, and the village was incorporated on May 15 that year. The date set for the election of the first village overseer was May 29. Also in 1905, a school district

centred on the village was established. In 1906, the population of Lipton was 160 and the Royal Bank of Canada opened a branch in the community. The village numbered close to 300 residents by 1911 and Lipton prospered over the following two decades. One momentous occasion in Lipton's history was the 1925 visit by Lord and Lady Byng — the Governor General of Canada and his wife. A setback was the loss of several businesses along Railway Avenue to a fire in 1929. By 1931, the village population had grown to 353. Lipton lost 10 per cent of its population through the 1930s — a drop, but not nearly as significant as that experienced by other communities in the more dried-out areas of the province. In 1934 a new "town" hall was built, and in 1938 the Village entered into a contract with the Roxy Theatre company to show motion pictures in the hall. Following WWII, the community experienced steady growth until the mid-1960s. Lipton had six churches and a synagogue in the 1950s; it reached a peak population of 453 in 1966, and at this point the community boasted nearly three dozen

businesses. Subsequently, both the population and the business community began to slowly decline. The loss of population was somewhat buoyed by area farmers moving into Lipton to retire (in 2001 the median age of village residents was 46.6, ten years older than the average age of all Saskatchewan residents). Today, Lipton retains a small core of local services and its school, a K-12 facility which had 126

village and area students enrolled in the fall of 2006. The stately brick Brinkworth Residence, built in 1907 at 1108 Erin Avenue, was designated a municipal heritage property in 1995, and another area heritage site, located approximately 15 kilometres northeast of Lipton, is the Lipton Hebrew Cemetery, all that remains of the once-viable Jewish settlement in the area. The last interment appears to have taken place in the early 1940s. Lipton serves as the administrative centre of the RM of Lipton No. 217.

LISIEUX, organized hamlet, pop 15 (2006c), 20 (2001c), is located in south-central Saskatchewan, on Hwy 2 north of Rockglen. The district around Lisieux had originally been known as Kantenville, after Andrew Kanten, a Norwegian who from 1912 ran a post office from his homestead. Beginning in 1915, a hamlet emerged a few kilometres to the west, which became known as Joeville, after Joseph Prefontaine, who, along with a number of other French settlers, homesteaded near the site. When the CPR line was built from Assiniboia through the area in 1926, grain elevators were erected somewhat north of Joeville, and a conflict then erupted in the community as to whether or not to relocate to the elevators' location. Joeville consequently became divided. Twenty-six buildings were moved to Rockglen, and the remainder were relocated to the site of the new elevators. The new community was renamed Lisieux, after a city in France. In 1964, Lisieux was established as an organized hamlet; however, today, not much remains of what was once a thriving community. Lisieux School closed in 1969. Lisieux is situated in the RM of Willow Bunch No. 42.

▼ **LISIEUX SCHOOL CLOSED IN 1969.** The cupola on the ground in front of the building had surmounted the front part of the roof (in front of the chimney) and had held the school bell. Photograph taken May 15, 2005.

LITTLE FISHING LAKE, organized hamlet, est. 1988, is a resort community located north of Paradise Hill on Hwy 21. It is situated within the Bronson Forest Recreation Site, a large area of land specifically designated for recreational use. One of the most unique attractions of the area is a herd of about 60 wild horses. Little Fishing Lake lies within the RM of Loon Lake No. 561. The resort has about two dozen permanent residents; however, the population varies depending on the season.

LITTLE SWAN RIVER, organized hamlet, est. 1993, is a resort area located within the Porcupine Provincial Forest off provincial road No. 982, roughly halfway between the towns of Norquay and Hudson Bay. It consists mainly of seasonal hunting cabins and has only a few permanent residents. Little Swan River is situated in the RM of Hudson Bay No. 394.

LIVELONG, organized hamlet, pop 95 (2006c), 93 (2001c), is located 26 km northeast of Turtleford, off Hwy 3. In the 1800s, the Hudson's Bay Company had fur trade posts a few kilometres north of the present community on Turtle Lake; prior to the district being surveyed, ranchers made use of the grazing lands in the area for their cattle. After homesteaders began to arrive around 1905, many of the cattlemen moved on. The early settlers detrained at North Battleford, then drove wagons to their homesteads; after the rail line reached Turtleford in 1914, settlers poured into the district. In the winter months, many men found employment fishing on Turtle Lake, and a large-scale fishing industry soon developed. The Livelong Post Office was established on July 1, 1917, about a mile south of the present community. In 1924, the CNR line from Turtleford came through the district; the post office was subsequently relocated to the townsite, and two grain elevators were built in Livelong in 1925-26. A local school district was organized in 1926 and a school was built, opening in January 1927. A hotel was built in 1929. In 1951, Livelong was established as an organized hamlet, and in 1969 the population was approximately 165. In the 1960s, high school students began to be bused to Turtleford; Livelong School closed in 1994. In the late 1970s, the rail line was abandoned and both of the community's grain elevators were closed. Today, a small core of local businesses includes a grocery store, the post office, and a licenced restaurant. The economy of the area is based upon mixed farming, oil and gas, tourism and resort-based commerce. Livelong is situated in the RM of Mervin No. 499.

LLOYDMINSTER, city, pop 8,118 in SK and 15, 910 in AB (2006c), 7,840 in SK and 13,148 in AB (2001c), is a continuously growing community located northwest of the Battlefords on the Saskatchewan-Alberta border. Known as "the Border City," Lloydminster had its beginnings in 1903 with the arrival of the Barr Colonists — approximately two thousand English "greenhorns." The mastermind of the great scheme was Reverend Isaac Barr, an Anglican minister who lost favour with the colonists during their journey to their new homes: a crowded ship, a lack of food, and completely inadequate arrangements once in Canada led to the leadership of the venture being turned over to their chaplain, Reverend George Exton

Lloyd (1861-1940). Lloyd coordinated the final stages of the trek to the new colony, securing funds and convincing the Canadian Northern Railway to build its line through the settlement. Initially, the new settlers dubbed the colony "Britannia" to honour their British heritage; shortly afterward, the main settlement to develop was named Lloydminster. "Lloyd" honoured Reverend Lloyd; "minster" is the church of a monastery or a large important church — as such, the name in essence means "Lloyd's church." Lloydminster was incorporated as a village in the North-West Territories on November 25, 1903; when the provinces of Alberta and Saskatchewan were formed in 1905, and the fourth meridian was chosen as the provincial boundary, the young community was legally split in two. The result was a duplication of all municipal functions: two separate municipal councils, two municipal offices, two fire departments, etc. This situation prevailed for twenty-five years. The Alberta portion of Lloydminster was incorporated as a village in that province on July 6, 1906; the Saskatchewan portion was incorporated as a town on April 1, 1907. In 1929, a major fire destroyed most of downtown. The following year, in May 1930, through acts of legislation in both provinces, the two communities were amalgamated into a single municipality with a single administration — the Town of Lloydminster. On January 1, 1958, propelled by a booming oil and gas industry, the Town of Lloydminster received its charter as the City of Lloydminster, becoming the tenth city in both provinces. Lloydminster was one of the first places in Saskatchewan to have its own natural gas system — years before the provincial utility franchise was created. Husky Oil began production in the region's oilfields in 1946; their refinery

▲ **BARR COLONISTS** unloading freight from barges at what was known as Lloydminster Landing on the North Saskatchewan River, no date. Saskatchewan Archives Board R-B3850.

▲ **IMMIGRATION HALL AT LLOYDMINSTER, 1905.** Prior to selecting their homesteads, many immigrants sought assistance from government officials. Saskatchewan Archives Board R-B2750.

▼ **THE BIRTH OF AN INDUSTRY:** The first trainload of oil to leave the Husky refinery in Lloydminster was in the spring of 1947. Saskatchewan Archives Board R-A9297-5.

became operational in 1947; and in 1992 a $1.6-billion-dollar plant was completed to upgrade heavy crude. Today, more than 4,000 people are employed in companies active in the region's oil and gas industry. Husky completed a $95-million ethanol plant in Lloydminster in 2006, generating an additional 25 jobs and creating a demand for significant quantities of wheat grown by local producers. Agriculture, a combination of crop and cattle production, is the region's second largest industry, and Lloydminster's economy also benefits from strong service, retail, construction, manufacturing, and transportation sectors. The city serves a trading area in excess of 115,000 people: about 58 per cent reside in Alberta; close to 42 per cent live in Saskatchewan. Downtown Lloydminster has more than 250 businesses and services; Lloyd Mall has over 40 stores; and, increasingly, "big box" stores are making their imprint on the cityscape. Residents of the entire city of Lloydminster are exempt from paying Provincial Sales Tax. Major city attractions include: Bud Miller All Seasons Park, a 200-acre site featuring a ten-acre man-made lake, hiking trails, a skateboard park, tennis courts, a miniature golf course, a fitness centre, and indoor waterslides and a wave pool; the Barr Colony Heritage Cultural Centre, situated in a complex that includes a museum, the Fuchs Wildlife Display, the OTS Heavy Oil Science Centre, and the Imhoff Art Collection; and Lloydminster's Golf and Country Club, which has a course ranked as one of the best in both provinces. City landmarks include four 100-foot-high border markers, and the old post office situated on Meridian Avenue. Completed in 1931, the post office building replaced a structure lost in the 1929 fire. It features stone-corbelled pilasters and a metal-clad dome surmounting a clock tower. The

Saskatchewan half of Lloydminster is situated within the boundaries of the RM of Britannia No. 502.

LOCKWOOD, hamlet, pop 25 (2001c), is a former village located 15 km north of Nokomis and 22 km south of Lanigan, just west off Hwy 20. Homesteaders began arriving in the district in 1905, and by 1907 most of the available land in the area was taken. The early settlers came by train to Davidson, Strassburg (later spelled Strasbourg), or Humboldt, and then travelled over land to the Lockwood district. Those who settled in the area were of diverse origins and came from many places: from eastern Canada, the British Isles, the United States, and Russia. After 1906, Mennonites settled in significant numbers to the west of Lockwood and to the north (around Drake), while Russian-German Lutherans took up land over a considerable area toward the northeast. With the construction of the CPR line from Strassburg to Lanigan

in 1907, the community of Lockwood — named after one of the railway company's passenger agents — had its beginnings. In 1907, the railway station was built, the first grain elevators were erected, and the first other few businesses began to spring up on the townsite. The Lockwood Post Office was established on March 14 the following year. (The first post office to serve the district was established in 1905 and was several kilometres southeast of the present community; it was named Macfarlane after the postmasters.) Lockwood was incorporated as a village on August 18, 1908, and that year the school was built, as was the Lockwood Hotel (which burned down in 1951). In 1909, the Northern Crown Bank opened a branch in the community. Presbyterians erected the first church in Lockwood in 1911, and at that time the village numbered about 100 souls. By the 1920s, the community had its own band, football team, baseball club, and hockey team. The village reached a peak population of 150 by 1931. Following WWII, Lockwood's population began

to slowly decline; in the late 1960s, it began to fall rapidly — from 89 in 1966 to 60 by 1971. In 1967, the community still had Pool and Federal grain elevators, a general store, a garage and implement dealership, a bulk oil station, and a school with two teacherages; and Lockwood also had active sports teams, a community hall, a Legion hall, a curling rink, and an indoor skating arena completed that year as a Canadian Centennial project. On June, 30, 1967, over 700 people attended the community's Centennial celebrations. But during the 1960s, the village's churches began to close due to declining memberships, and rooms at Lockwood School were closed due to declining enrollment — high school students were being bused to Lanigan to take classes. Lockwood School's days were numbered, and one by one the village's businesses began to close. By 1981, the village was down to 38 residents. The last grain elevator was demolished in 1999 and today Lockwood is verging on becoming a ghost town. Sidewalks now run along vacant lots or in front of abandoned businesses and homes. The community relinquished village status on January 1, 2002, and its affairs are now under the management of the RM of Usborne No. 310.

LONE ROCK, organized hamlet, pop 83 (2006c), 87 (2001c), is situated 34 km southeast of Lloydminster and is accessed via Hwy 17 just across the Saskatchewan-Alberta border. The Battle River passes to the southeast. The arrival of the Barr Colonists in the Lloydminster area in 1903 gave impetus to the settlement of the Lone Rock district, and by 1908 practically all of the available homesteads in the area were occupied. Settlers came from the British Isles,

eastern Canada, and the United States. In 1912, the Lone Rock School District was formed, with the school originally being about three miles southeast of the present community. The name was derived from a large lone glacial erratic that stood by the school gate; formerly used by bison as a rubbing stone, the monument was moved into the hamlet in 1967 as a Centennial project. In 1914, a post office was established somewhat to the northwest (yet still south of the present-day community), and it was named Lone Rock after the school. In the mid-1920s, the CPR resumed construction of its line from Wilkie (the line had not progressed beyond Cut Knife since 1911); by 1924 the track snaked through Jones Coulee north of Marsden, reaching to the Battle River at Unwin. In 1925, a bridge was built across the river, and by 1926 the line had climbed up out of Buzzard Coulee on the opposite shore and was completed to Lloydminster. The townsite of present-day Lone Rock was surveyed in 1926, and soon three grain elevators were built, along with a hardware store, a confectionary, implement dealers, Fong's café and dance hall, a blacksmith, a livery barn and a dray service, a lumberyard, a butcher, a pool hall, and a barber shop. Over 1927-28, a community hall was erected. It quickly became evident that, with school-aged children moving into the hamlet, the travel distance to the old Lone Rock School to the south and another school, Strathmore, to the north was unacceptable. A new school was then built in the hamlet and given the name Strathrock, a name it retained until after the original Lone Rock school closed — at which point the hamlet school adopted the name. For a number of years, Lone Rock hosted a summer sports day; people would come from Lloydminster, Marshall, Lashburn, Unwin, and nearby places in

▲ **"LOCKWOOD MOTORS,"** south side of Main Street, August 3, 2004.

Alberta to participate in a ball tournament and other athletic contests, enjoy ice cream and lemonade served from a concession stand, and later a supper and a dance at the community hall. Lone Rock once had competitive softball and hockey teams, a number of musical groups, and a Dramatic Society that put on a series of successful plays. In 1949, Lone Rock was established as an organized hamlet, and it was around this time that the oil and gas industry was rapidly beginning to have a significant impact on the area economy. The boon would be short-lived, however, as Lone Rock was doomed as a business centre almost from its beginnings. In the late 1920s, the CPR built a branch line from Furness west into Alberta, along which other communities developed, and business in Lone Rock was reduced to a fraction of what it had been. Later, an all-weather road was built along the provincial boundary to Lloydminster, and the amenities of that centre were then easily accessible. These, along with other factors, made it increasingly difficult for the hamlet's businesspeople to make a living, and one by one they closed their doors. Eventually, all of the elevators came down too. The school fell victim to centralization and area children now attend school in either Lloydminster or the village of Marshall. Lone Rock's population dropped from 158 in 1966 to 109 by 1986. Today, the community retains a tea house/convenience store and the post office. Lone Rock is situated in the RM of Wilton No. 472.

LOON LAKE, village, pop 306 (2006c), 318 (2001c), is located in a rolling terrain amidst lakes, woodlands, and land opened for agriculture, approximately 50 km north of St. Walburg and 60

◄ **THE LOON LAKE HOTEL**, beverage room, and liquor vendor. Photograph taken July 23, 2003.

km west of Meadow Lake. The community is served by Hwys 26 and 304. Its name is derived from nearby Makwa Lake — Makwa being the Cree word for "Loon." The Makwa Sahgaiehcan First Nation has land holdings and community infrastructure adjacent to the village; 800 members were residing on-reserve in 2006. Just west of Loon Lake is Makwa Lake Provincial Park; about ten kilometres west of the village is Steele Narrows Provincial Historic Park, a site commemorating the last engagement of the North-West Resistance. The Dominion of Canada began its survey of lands in the Loon Lake area in 1909; non-indigenous people began settling in the district in 1912. The pioneering period lasted until about 1932, when most of the cultivable land had been settled. Because of the immediate timber resources, log cabins stood on almost every quarter section. Sawmills, trapping, and some commercial fishing provided early employment. In the great northern fire of 1919 some early settlers lost their homes and animals — some, all of their possessions. Settlement of the region progressed slowly at first as the nearest rail line was at North Battleford — after the railway reached

Turtleford in 1914, then St. Walburg in 1921, the pace accelerated. During the first years of the Depression and the prairie drought, many came to the district from the southern areas of the province. A relief settlement established in the Loon Lake region in 1931 was known as "Little Saskatoon," due to the number of people that had come north from that city. At the outbreak of the WWII some of those who had struggled to hew an existence out of the area left, finding employment opportunities with the war effort. Others, however, came to settle in the district, such as socialist-leaning Sudeten Germans escaping Nazi persecution in 1939. An historical irony is that some of them took up land northeast of Loon Lake vacated by Germans who were Nazi sympathizers and who, fed up with a decade of the rigours of life in northern Saskatchewan, opted to return to Germany. In the late 1920s, the Canadian National Railway proposed a route through the Loon Lake area — an extension of their line into St. Walburg that would connect to Bonnyville, Alberta. The railway offered employment and work began in 1928. Grades were built, a right-of-way was cleared, a townsite surveyed,

and culverts installed. New businesses sprang up while others relocated from the countryside. The new locale was initially called Loon Lake Siding to distinguish it from the nucleus of the Loon Lake settlement that had developed approximately six miles to the southeast. There, a post office and a school had existed since the early 1920s — Old Loon Lake School closed in 1956. By the time the railway abandoned the St. Walburg to Bonnyville project in the early 1930s, the new Loon Lake townsite had developed sufficiently enough to sustain itself. Although the railway never came — the closest station remained 30 miles away — the community persisted. A school district centred on the fledgling hamlet was established in 1932. The earthen road from St. Walburg to Loon Lake was gravelled in the early 1940s, and the Village of Loon Lake was incorporated on January 1, 1950. Power lines were erected in 1957 and water and sewer systems were completed by 1966. Natural gas was hooked up in 1974. Loon Lake has an RCMP detachment and a hospital with an attached special care home. Ernie Studer School is a K-12 facility which had 202 students enrolled in the fall of 2006. Loon Lake serves as the administrative centre of the RM of Loon Lake No. 561.

LOREBURN, village, pop 113 (2006c), 143 (2001c), is located 45 km west of Davidson, 13 km north of Elbow, off Hwy 19 just south of its junction with Hwy 44. Settlers began arriving in the early 1900s, hailing from the Maritime provinces, Ontario and Manitoba, England

and Scotland, and Norway and Denmark (many of the Scandinavians came via the U.S.). A few came from what is today Ukraine. Loreburn began to be built up over 1908-09 as the CPR line from Moose Jaw to Outlook was being built. The Loreburn Post Office was established on November 21, 1908, with Edward T. Child as the first postmaster; the Village of Loreburn was incorporated on May 20, 1909. The community was named by the CPR after Robert Reid, 1st Earl of Loreburn (1846-1923), a notable British parliamentarian and jurist. In 1910, a school that had been established in 1908 somewhat to the north of what became Loreburn was moved to the village site. It was known as Oxford School until 1916, when its name was changed to that of the community. In 1911, the population of the village was 135, and it grew to reach just under 200 before the onset of the 1930s, during which Loreburn's numbers fell by about

30 per cent. The post-war years brought a period of recovery, and Loreburn's population leapt to over 300 through the first several years of the 1960s while the Gardiner and Qu'Appelle Valley Dams were being built — workers and their families flooded into all the communities in the area while the South Saskatchewan River Project was under way. In the years subsequent, though, Loreburn's population has fallen through each consecutive census period. What sustains the community is that it has retained a small core of businesses and its school. Loreburn Central School is a K-12 facility which had 126 village and area students enrolled in the fall of 2006, and more than a dozen people are employed at the institution. Loreburn has a small Ford dealership with gas pumps, a grocery store, motel and restaurant, a credit union, post office, an insurance broker, a skating arena, a ball park, a library, a United Church, and a seniors'

centre. Two remaining grain elevators (formerly Pool and UGG) are privately owned by area farmers — in the 1920s there had been seven company-owned elevators lining the track along the community's west side. Important area businesses today include a seed cleaning and processing plant, and the Gardiner Dam Terminal, a 17,000-tonne high-throughput grain elevator jointly owned by area farmers and Agricore United. Revenues from oil and gas pipelines that run through the district contribute substantially to the rural municipality's coffers. Loreburn serves as the administrative centre of the RM of Loreburn No. 254.

LOVE, village, pop 55 (2006c), 71 (2001c), is situated about halfway between Nipawin and Choiceland on Hwy 55, in a swath of agricultural land north of the Saskatchewan River. The Torch River Provincial Forest lies just northeast of the village; Fort à la Corne Provincial Forest is to the southwest. Although local folklore has suggested that the community's name stems from an early area romance, the village in fact was named after F.S. Love, a CPR passenger bureau chief in Winnipeg. The village of Love was originally built by lumbermen, and the logging industry was greatly spurred by the opening of the CPR rail line between Nipawin and Prince Albert in the early 1930s. The railway brought in people and goods and hauled out wood and lumber. The forests that once covered the Love area consisted of white spruce, black spruce, jack pine, tamarack (larch), white poplar (trembling aspen), black poplar, and white birch. The white spruce, which was the mainstay of the area industry, takes 80 to 120 years to reach maturity, and with a diameter reaching nearly a metre, these trees could

yield 300 or more board feet of lumber. Numerous logging camps, sawmills and planer mills operated in the Love area, and the local history recounts that as much as four million board feet of lumber would be stacked in Love at one time, ready to be run through the large planer mill in the village. This mill would at times operate day and night, particularly during WWII, when lumber production boomed. Although the railway came through at the beginning of the 1930s, Love was merely a railway siding largely serving forestry interests until 1935 when William George Sears built a general store and established the Love Post Office on the north side of the CPR tracks (Sears would remain the postmaster until 1965). In 1936, a second general store was established. With local mills running throughout the year, quite a few families began building homes in the fledgling settlement, although, as no lots were yet surveyed, people just built where they could find room on what was then government land. The community grew with the lumber industry, and the people who came to the Love area were of diverse backgrounds — they had origins in the British Isles, Europe, Russia, what is today Ukraine, and China. In 1939, as the informal collection of homes and businesses began to mature into something of a cohesive community, the government decided to advertise approximately 35 acres of land at Love for sale by tender. The settlers, wanting title to the lots and security for the structures they had developed, met and agreed to bid on the parcel under the auspices of what they called the Love Development Company. Shares in the company were sold for $25 each, and the company successfully purchased the 35 acres of crown land for $1,200. The company then had the area surveyed and anyone who had already built on a lot

▲ **LOOKING FOR LOVE IN ALL THE WRONG PLACES?** Photograph taken July 18, 2003.

was given the first option to purchase the land. In 1942, more land was added to the Love townsite, and on June 2, 1945, the Village of Love was incorporated. This was the community's heyday. Love not only had mills operating within or near its boundaries, there were logging operations throughout the countryside. The village's numerous stores, garages, cafés, and other enterprises did a brisk business supplying goods and services to the industry, its employees and their families. The population of Love was nearing 300 — the Census of Canada recorded 274 in 1946 — but it would never be as high again. The timber berths were being depleted and mills were moving north and to larger towns. Following WWII, both markets for lumber and the regulations governing the industry changed to the disadvantage of Love area firms. Agriculture became dominant as the district trees disappeared, but the newly cleared farmland varied in quality. Agriculture was also an industry becoming increasingly mechanized and less labour-intensive, with the result that farms became larger and fewer people were living on the land. Many lumber mills kept operating in the Love area for a time, but by 1956 the popula-

tion of Love was 148, almost half of that a decade earlier. Over the ensuing decades, the population of the village continued to decline, as did that of many other smaller Saskatchewan communities. The curling rink closed down in the mid-1960s due to declining use, and at the end of June 1977, the last classes were taught in the village school. Today, Love is a picturesque, quiet village that retains a small handful of local businesses and a church. The post office receives numerous requests from far and wide to have items such as wedding invitations, Mother's Day and Valentine's Day cards mailed through the office and marked with the village's unique cancellation stamp. Love has a volunteer fire department; policing is provided by the RCMP detachment in Nipawin, where the nearest medical facilities are also located. The village hosts a gospel jamboree in early July and a winter festival in February. Love has a fully-serviced campsite. Mixed farming now dominates the area economy: cereal grains, canola, and forage seed are common crops grown, and livestock producers raise bison, elk, fallow deer, and miniature horses. District outfitters accommodate hunters, and a few companies in the region are still engaged

in the logging industry. Love is situated in the RM of Torch River No. 488.

LOVERNA, hamlet, pop 5 (2001c), is located just inside the Saskatchewan-Alberta border, northwest of Kindersley in the RM of Antelope Park No. 322. Incorporated as a village in 1913, the community reached a peak population of 221 in 1926. After WWII, however, Loverna steadily declined. The rail line was abandoned in 1979, and the village was officially dissolved in 2003.

LUCKY LAKE, village, pop 295 (2006c), 354 (2001c), is situated southwest of the Gardiner Dam, at the junction of Hwys 42 and 45; the Riverhurst Ferry crossing on Lake Diefenbaker (the South Saskatchewan River) lies 18 km to the southeast; to the north of the village lies Luck Lake, from which the community derived its name. According to the local history, Luck Lake itself was named by an early area pioneer who was able to successfully retrieve a team of oxen that had

ventured into the lake's marshy quagmire. Settlers began taking up land in the Lucky Lake district in the early 1900s, crossing the South Saskatchewan River to get to their homesteads. A ferry was operating at the elbow of the river in 1905, and in 1908 one was put in service where the Riverhurst Ferry now operates, where previously scows were used to make the crossing. On March 28, 1908, a post office named Lucky Lake was established about a half-mile east of the present townsite, and, amusingly, the first two postmasters were men named King and Lear. Charles C. King held the position from the office's founding until 1916, and Andrew Lear was in charge from 1916 to 1919. The rural post office was also the location of a store, where groceries, clothing and other essentials could be purchased — it was the hub of the surrounding district until 1919-20, when the railway came through and the present village had its beginnings. As soon as the location of the townsite was determined, businessmen began setting up shops. The rail line was completed into Lucky Lake in 1920 and the village was incorporated on November 23 that

◄ **A PRODUCER CAR LOADING SYSTEM** under construction in Lucky Lake. This is one of four built by West Central Road and Rail, a producer-owned company based in Eston, that allows farmers to ship their own grain on producer cars. Others facilities have been built in Eston, Laporte, and Beechy. Photograph taken September 8, 2003.

year. The first grain elevator was erected in 1920; by 1922, there were four. In 1921 the school was built and the population of the village was 112; by 1931, the community numbered just under 300, and Lucky Lake served a district population of English, Scottish, Norwegian, Finnish, and Mennonite settlers. (A village street sign noted in 2003 read, "Caution, Norwegian Crossing.") The community's population decreased only slightly during the Depression, and in the years following, Lucky Lake prospered. The village numbered 432 residents by 1956 and the population remained close to this number until the late 1960s. The community went into something of a slump in the early 1970s — paved roads had been completed from Outlook and Saskatoon — and as people began doing their business and shopping further away, a number of businesses in Lucky Lake closed. The village population settled at close to its current level by the middle of the 1970s, and it has remained fairly stable since that time. The community retains a core of businesses and services, a health centre with an attached special care home, and a K-12 school which had 145 village and area students enrolled in the fall of 2006. One of the community's historic buildings, now a heritage site and Lucky Lake's Museum, is the former newspaper office and print shop. The original part of the building was built in 1920, it was enlarged in 1928, and it was later the village's post office before becoming the museum building in 1974. Lucky Lake area attractions include Palliser Regional Park on the east side of Lake Diefenbaker; an aquaculture operation that produces steelhead trout, also on the lake; and the Luck Lake Heritage Marsh, about eight kilometres north of the village. A historically inconsistent marshland in terms of water level, Luck Lake's water supply was stabilized in 1988 through a major project involving Ducks Unlimited. A pressurized pipeline system that supplies area irrigators now also feeds the lake, and today the 6,000-acre marshland provides nesting stations, and moulting and staging areas for an average 48,000 ducks and a number of species of geese. The area attracts hunters from across North America. Lucky Lake serves as the administrative centre of the RM of Canaan No. 225.

LUMSDEN, town, pop 1,523 (2006c), 1,596 (2001c), is located in the Qu'Appelle Valley, 25 km northwest of Regina at the junction of Hwys 11 and 20. The first settlers arrived in 1881 and the area came to be colloquially known as Happy Hollow. In 1884, one of the first settlers, Edward Carss, established a post office just west of present-day Lumsden, at the confluence of Wascana Creek and the Qu'Appelle River. In 1889, the Qu'Appelle, Long Lake, and Saskatchewan Railway came through the site of today's community en route to Saskatoon and Prince Albert, and the name Happy Hollow was changed to honour Hugh Lumsden, a senior engineer with the railway. Thomas Hill opened a general store and had a post office at Lumsden in 1892, and a blacksmith shop and an implement agency were soon established. Other businesses followed. Grain elevators were erected — the first run by horsepower — and in 1897 Lumsden had its first doctor. On December 29, 1898, the settlement had developed significantly enough to be incorporated as a village. The first newspaper began publishing in 1900, and in 1904 a flour mill was opened and did a thriving business until it burned down in the 1920s. Lumsden attained town status on March 15, 1905. After the boom period prior to WWI, Lumsden's population settled at around 500 and the community functioned primarily as a thriving farm

▼ **A BASEBALL GAME NEAR LUMSDEN, CIRCA 1890s.** Walter Scott, who became the first premier of Saskatchewan, was among the players. Saskatchewan Archives Board R-B1859.

▼ **THE LUMSDEN FLOOD OF 1904** was one of the worst in the community's history. The tracks through the valley were washed out, causing many difficulties for settlers travelling north. Saskatchewan Archives Board R-A9646.

▲ **BUSINESSES ON THE EAST SIDE OF JAMES STREET** in Lumsden, April 3, 2004.

◄ **ONE OF THE MANY MARKET GARDENS** in the Lumsden area. Photograph taken September 30, 2007.

the beginning of a period of major population growth. Today, although town businesses, schools, administrative positions, and health care facilities provide a base of local employment, Lumsden is increasingly becoming a bedroom community for commuters to Regina. Once dubbed "the prettiest town in Saskatchewan," Lumsden is witnessing subdivision developments of upscale homes — previously uninterrupted vistas of the valley are becoming a thing of the past. Lumsden serves as the administrative centre of the RM of Lumsden No. 189.

LUMSDEN BEACH, resort village, pop 40 (2006c), 0 (2001c), is located on the west shore of the south end of Last Mountain Lake, southeast of Regina Beach. The resort had its beginnings in 1905 as a summer camp run by the Methodist Church. In the early years, most people came to the camp by taking the train to Lumsden; from there, a local livery stable provided transportation. Others came across the lake on the steamboat *S.S. Qu'Appelle*. By 1912, however, the CPR had completed the line that ran up the southwest shore of the lake. Lumsden Beach was incorporated on July 22, 1918, and from 1914 to 1966 a post office was operated during the months of July and August. As of 2006, there were about 90 private dwellings in the village, but it has only been in the past couple of years that people have been residing at Lumsden Beach as permanent, year-round residents. A few of the summer cottages built in the 1920s are still in use today, and the summer camp, now run by the United Church, is now at the beginning of its second century of operation. Lumsden Beach is situated in the RM of Lumsden No. 189.

service centre until the mid-1960s. With the construction of the four-lane divided highway through the valley early in the decade, people who worked in Regina began to establish homes in the community. Artists were attracted to Lumsden's quiet country lifestyle and picturesque setting, and city dwellers came to frequent the area's developing market gardens. The community, however, was beset regularly by floodwaters (major floods occurred in 1892, 1904, 1916, 1948, and 1969), and in 1974 the highest water levels in the town's history were recorded. Schoolchildren from Regina, including the author, came to help with the sandbagging. The town subsequently undertook the development of a major flood protection project, straightening the river's channel and building substantial dikes. This marked

▲ **LUSELAND'S MEN'S BASEBALL TEAM, 1912.**
▶ **LUSELAND SCHOOL, 1928.**
Photographs courtesy of the Luseland
and Districts Museum.

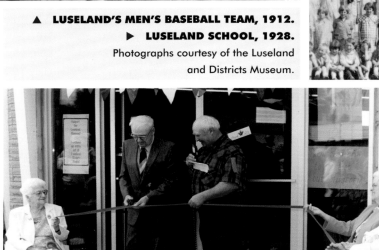

◄ **THE OFFICIAL RIBBON-CUTTING CEREMONY** for the opening of the
Luseland and Districts Museum on July 1, 1992. From left to right: Gladys
Detert; Bob Hoddinott, who donated the building (cutting the ribbon); Jack
Krupka (an excellent yodeller); Lena Hohman; Mary Honeker.
Photograph courtesy of the Luseland and Districts Museum.

LUSELAND, town, pop 571 (2006c), 602 (2001c), is located in the west-central region of the province, between the town of Kerrobert and the Saskatchewan-Alberta border on Hwy 31. Settlers began arriving in the district in the spring of 1906, with more coming the subsequent year. It was in the following years, however, that the district came to be substantially settled. The Luse Land and Development Co. of St. Paul, Minnesota, acquired 100,000 acres of land in the area, and successfully attracted large numbers of German settlers from the mid-western United States. The CPR was building its line through the district in 1910 and, on December 10 that year, Luseland (name derivation apparent) was incorporated as a village. Developing as a service centre for the surrounding farming district, Luseland grew steadily, attaining town status on January 1, 1954. Through the 1950s and the 1960s the community grew substantially, as rural populations shifted to urban centres, and the development of the oil and gas industry in the area boosted and diversified the economy. By 1966, Luseland had a population of 826. From 1953 to 1965 the number of homes in the community rose from 160 to 300 and, during the same period, the town was modernized with streets paved and sewer and water systems installed. Today, Luseland has a variety of businesses and services, a health clinic with doctor's services, a museum (complete with a yodelling curator), a library, churches, seniors' housing, an ambulance service,

◄ **GRAIN HANDLING FACILITIES IN LUSELAND.** The first modern
concrete grain terminal built in the province by the Saskatchewan Wheat Pool
was constructed in Luseland in 1987 (centre), and at the time it was the largest
facility of its kind in western Canada. The Pioneer elevator on the left dates to
1981; the Wheat Pool elevator on the right dates to 1967. Photograph taken
August 14, 2003.

and a volunteer fire department. Luseland is one of only a few towns in the province with its own municipal police. Luseland School is a K-12 facility, which had 184 town and area students enrolled in the fall of 2006. The community has a wide range of recreational facilities and a large number of service clubs, youth organizations, sports associations, and groups involved with artistic and cultural activities. The Luseland Social Community Hall and Theatre, built in 1920, has been designated a heritage property, and for 87 years the dual-function facility has been a centre of community activity. Agriculture continues to dominate the area economy and consists of both crop and cattle production. Crops grown in the district include cereal grains, canola, mustard, canary seed, and lentils, and a number of area farms are mixed operations. The oil and gas industry continues to gain in importance in the region, and five pipelines now run through the district. Luseland serves as the administrative centre of the RM of Progress No. 351.

MACDOWALL, organized hamlet, pop 123 (2006c), 136 (2001c), is located 30 km southwest of Prince Albert on Hwy 11. The Nisbet Provincial Forest lies just west of the community. Scots had settled in Prince Albert under the leadership of the Presbyterian missionary James Nisbet as early as 1866; in the ensuing years their settlement extended southwestward into the area of present-day MacDowall. In the 1880s, a post office and a school were established in the district, both originally named Willoughby, in honour of a prestigious pioneer doctor who had been present at the Battle of Batoche. Willoughby later served as a Regina councilman and then mayor of Regina, before becoming a successful Saskatoon businessman. In 1890, the Qu'Appelle, Long Lake & Saskatchewan Railway was completed through the area of present-day MacDowall from Regina; the first train arrived in Prince Albert on September 4 that year. The nucleus of a community began along the rail line, and in the early 1900s, with the establishment of the post office at the hamlet site, the name Mac-Dowall was adopted for both the post office and the locale (the school, however, would remain as Willoughby until 1929). The name MacDowall honours Day Hort Macdowall (1850-1927), a Prince Albert lumber merchant and sawmill operator, born in Carruth House, Renfrewshire, Scotland. Macdowall served on the Council of the North-West Territories for the District of Lorne from 1883-85, and was a conservative Member of the House of Commons for the District of Saskatchewan from 1887-96. In 1902, the Western Elevator Company built a grain elevator at MacDowall, relieving area farmers of having to load grain themselves into railway cars at the siding (the elevator was taken over by the Saskatchewan Wheat Pool in the late 1920s). Additionally, pens and loading facilities for livestock were built along the tracks, and MacDowall had a number of businesses over the years — general stores, service stations, hair salons and barber shops, restaurants, and a hotel and café — these, though, came to be superseded by all that Prince Albert had to offer. In the early days, community residents were mainly employed in agriculture and forestry, or worked on the railway. Nowadays, most either commute to work in Prince Albert or farm in the district. The Saskatchewan Power Corporation brought electricity to MacDowall in the 1950s; Saskatchewan Telecommunications began providing telephone service to the hamlet in the 1970s; and in the 1980s, natural gas became available to the community. The local grain elevator was closed in 1975, and the railway station was demolished in 1977. MacDowall School had 54 students enrolled in the fall of 2006; it closed at the end of the school year in 2007, after having served the district for 120 years. MacDowall was established as an organized hamlet in 1966 and is situated in the RM of Duck Lake No. 463.

MACKLIN, town, pop 1,290 (2006c), 1,330 (2001c), is situated just inside the Saskatchewan-Alberta border, approximately 110 km south of Lloydminster. The community is served by Hwys 14, 17, and 31. Settlers first began arriving in the district in 1906-07, and in 1908 a post office was established a short distance from the present community. Within a couple of years the railway came through, the townsite was established, a settlement developed, and, on November 8, 1909, the Village of Macklin was incorporated. The name of the community honours E. H. Macklin, a chief business manager with the Winnipeg *Free Press*, whose paper had chronicled the development of the railway. Developing a theme, the community's streets were named after famous newspapers: Times, Herald, and Tribune, among others. By 1911, the population of Macklin was well over 300 and, on November 1, 1912, the community attained town status. Macklin has experienced continuous growth since its beginnings, initially

◄ **MANY WHO CAME TO THE MACKLIN AREA WERE GERMAN CATHOLICS** from southern Russia and the United States; they brought with them the unique game of bunnock which has become enthusiastically embraced by the community over the years. The game, a kind of a cross between bowling and horseshoes played with 52 horse ankle bones (today, synthetic), is thought to have been developed by Russian soldiers posted in northern Siberia more than 200 years ago. Bones are set in two straight rows 10 metres apart and opposing teams toss other bones ("throwers") to knock them down in a certain order. Today, Macklin hosts the World Championship Bunnock Tournament, which draws as many as 250 teams each August. To commemorate Macklin's sport of choice, this 10-metre-high bunnock (an exact replica of a horse's ankle bone enlarged 98 times) stands at the entrance to the town. Illuminated at night, it can be seen for miles around. Photograph taken August 13, 2003.

MACKLIN

No bones about it —
"Home of the World Championship Bunnock Tournament"

◄ **CANADA'S 50TH JUBILEE** in 1927 was celebrated with a parade through Macklin's streets. Photograph courtesy of the Macklin and District Museum.

▼ **AN EARLY STREET SCENE** in Macklin, no date. Photograph courtesy of the Macklin and District Museum.

▲ **MACKLIN HOCKEY TEAM, 1930s.** Back row, left to right: Art Warrin, William Hillis, Barton Kidd, E.V. Lanford, Al Crabtree, Atch Kidd, Dodger Wilkie, Wilbur Thomson. Middle row, left to right: Fred Foster, William Stang, Pete Prediger, Jack Lee, Pat Ivor, Ross Kidd. Front, left to right: Johnny Buchner, Scotty Allen. Photograph courtesy of the Macklin and District Museum, donated by Jack Block, Victoria, British Columbia.

▲ **THE MACKLIN AND DISTRICT MUSEUM.** Housed in the stately 1919 home of the town's first bank manager, the museum features artifacts and displays pertaining to Macklin's early development. Photograph taken August 14, 2003.

developing as a trade and service centre for the surrounding agricultural district. The agricultural industry remains important today, with mixed farming operations producing traditional crops such as wheat, as well as peas and sunflowers. The livestock industry has become increasingly diversified, as animals such as bison and ostriches are raised in addition to cattle. Increasing exploration and development in the area's gas and oil fields has resulted in significant economic growth for the town in recent years; hundreds of oil and gas wells, and a number of batteries and compressor stations surround the community. A number of large oil companies operate in the district, and about a dozen companies have been established in the town to provide oilfield services. Up until the last census, the town's population had been steadily rising, and close to 70 per cent were under the age of 45 in 2001. The median family income for Macklin residents in 2001 was $54,488 compared to the provincial median of $49,264. The community's prosperity is evident as educational, recreational, and health care facilities are all fairly modern and well-equipped. Macklin has a health centre with an attached special care home, ambulance service, local RCMP, and a fire department. Educational facilities include a pre-school, a library, and Macklin School, a K-12 institution, which had 444 town and area students enrolled in the fall of 2006. The community's substantial recreational facilities are augmented by a regional park adjacent to the town, which features a lakeside golf course and a new club house. Macklin serves as the administrative centre of the RM of Eye Hill No. 382.

MACNUTT, village, pop 80 (2006c), 85 (2001c), is located 5 km inside the Saskatchewan-Manitoba border, 32 km north of Langenburg on Hwy 8. Settlement of the region began in the mid-1880s; however, it was in the early 1900s that the village had its beginnings. In 1909 the townsite was surveyed, and in 1910 the railway came through. The village was incorporated in 1913; its name honours Thomas MacNutt, MLA for Saltcoats 1902-08, MP for Saltcoats 1908-21, and the first speaker of the Legislative Assembly of Saskatchewan after the province was formed. Despite the Scottish name, the population of the village was largely of German origin. MacNutt became a trading centre in a region of mixed agriculture and grew to a peak population of close to 250 in the early 1950s. Subsequently, the village has slowly declined. A fire claimed a number of businesses in 1960, the lumberyard was torn down and, in 1969, a long-standing business institution, the creamery, also burned to the ground. Many of the village's businesses and services have since been superseded by those in the nearby towns of Langenburg or Roblin, Manitoba, as well as the city of Yorkton, approximately 75 kilometres northwest. Further, in the late 1990s, the rail line through MacNutt was abandoned and the community's school was closed. MacNutt is situated in the RM of Churchbridge No. 211.

▲ **MAIN STREET, MACNUTT**, looking southwest.

▼ **NOW IN PRIVATE HANDS**, this former Saskatchewan Wheat Pool grain elevator dates to 1982. The crib annex (an older elevator) dates to 1948.

Photographs taken July 12, 2004.

MACOUN, village, pop 168 (2006c), 170 (2001c), is located 27 km northwest of Estevan on Hwy 39. The village was named after John Macoun (1831-1920), the Canadian botanist and explorer. Originally, the community of Macoun had been nothing other than a boxcar station and living quarters for the rail crews who tended that section of the CPR's Soo Line, constructed in 1893. This connection to Minneapolis allowed land seekers from the U.S. direct access to the area, and a good number would come from the states of Minnesota and Iowa. Many were of Norwegian and Swedish origin. Others would come from eastern Canada and other areas of Europe. The first homesteads in the Macoun district were filed on around 1901, and over the following few years an influx of settlers arrived. Before the Macoun post office was established in 1903, mail was handed out from the mail cars of the stopping trains. Within a couple of years, Macoun developed into a trading centre which, because of its strategic position on the rail line, serviced settlers moving into a large outlying region, particularly to the southwest. Mail was hauled from Macoun as far as Minton, almost 100 kilometres away. By October 1903, the community had grown large enough to be incorporated as a village, and the following two decades were to be Macoun's most active. Its train station bustled with the comings and goings of passengers, its businesses were varied and numerous, and a row of grain elevators lined the tracks. By 1916, the population of the village was approaching 300. Not all developments were positive, however. While almost every pioneer community suffered the hazards of fires with only volunteer bucket brigades to fight them, Macoun seems to have weathered more

than its share. The most tragic occurred April 20, 1914, when a gas explosion in the hotel triggered an instant inferno that left 13 dead and a number injured. One residence and three other businesses were also lost in the blaze. The 1930s also took a toll on the community; by 1941 the population of the village had fallen to 129. The discovery of oil in the region in the early 1950s brought a return to prosperity and diversification to an economy that had previously been solely based on agriculture. It was neighbouring Midale, however, that would reap the greatest benefit from the boom — its population more than doubled, reaching close to 800, while Macoun's only climbed back to near the 200 mark. Today, Macoun is essentially a residential community. The city of Estevan's businesses and services have largely superseded those in the village, and a number of Macoun's residents commute to work in the city. Macoun School, however, remains a long-standing community institution. It is a K-8 facility, which had 51 students enrolled in the fall of 2006. High school students attend classes in Estevan. St. Paul's United Church in Macoun, built in 1907 as a Presbyterian church, and the town hall, built circa 1903 and Macoun's oldest building, are community landmarks. One of Macoun's more prominent sons is Leonard J. Gustafson; born in Macoun in 1933 and raised in the community, Gustafson became a farmer and businessman before being appointed to the Senate of Canada in 1993. Macoun is located in the RM of Cymri No. 36.

MACPHEAT PARK, organized hamlet, is one in a string of resort communities located on the east side of Last Mountain Lake off Hwy 322. Plans for the resort were drawn in the early 1980s;

however, development has been fairly recent. To date, about two dozen properties have been established; the locale became an organized hamlet on March 24, 2004. MacPheat Park is situated in the RM of McKillop No. 220, and its population varies depending on the season.

MACRORIE, village, pop 78 (2006c), 96 (2001c), lies just northwest of the Gardiner Dam and Danielson Provincial Park, approximately 20 km south of Outlook, west of the South Saskatchewan River. Macrorie is served by Hwys 44 and 45. The community's name may possibly honour William Campbell McQuarrie, who homesteaded about two miles southeast of the present village. Why the

name of the village would be spelled differently is unknown. Settlers began entering the district in 1904; in 1905 there were a reported 57 people living in the township where Macrorie would be established. Among those who settled in the district were many Scandinavians — Norwegians, Finns, and Swedes — as well as people of Scottish and British origin. Mail and supplies were originally brought in from Hanley; after the CPR reached Outlook in 1908, the hauling distance was greatly reduced. With the construction of the Canadian Northern Railway line south from Delisle, the village of Macrorie had its beginnings. The townsite was surveyed in 1911, and the first trains arrived before the end of the year. Macrorie was incorporated on February 8, 1912, and that year

▼ **MACRORIE PUBLIC SCHOOL.** Completed in 1917, the school served the community for 71 years until its closure in 1988. During the 1918 Spanish flu epidemic, the building served as a hospital. In the middle of the twentieth century when most rural schools were closed, Macrorie School remained open, becoming the central school for the district. Photograph taken July 20, 2004.

the first grain elevators were erected, and a number of businesses, including a bank, were established. The village school district was set up in 1915; classes were held in a rented hall until the school was completed in 1917. The community prospered from its beginnings though the 1920s; the years of drought and depression, however, nearly cut the community's population in half. Macrorie's numbers fell from 183 in 1931 to 101 by 1941. The community only somewhat recovered afterward, but the construction of the Gardiner Dam brought an influx of temporary residents to the village. From a population of 123 in 1951, Macrorie grew to number close to 200 by the mid-1960s; the school had a peak enrollment of 150 students over the 1963-64 school year. When the dam was finished, though, the workforce moved away, and Macrorie was down to 120 residents by 1971. The population was a bit higher in the early 1980s, but it has since steadily declined. The school closed in 1988, and, today, the 1917 two-storey structure (designated a municipal heritage property in 2000) houses a fitness centre and some of the village's museum collection. Other buildings in the village also house museum displays, and Macrorie has a CN caboose and jigger at the end of Main Street. One grain elevator was still standing in the village in 2001; it has since been demolished. Today, the Macrorie District Co-op is the community's main business, selling groceries, fuel, agricultural supplies, hardware, fishing and camping gear, etc. The village has Lutheran and United Church organizations, a number of service clubs, and a volunteer fire department. The nearest medical practitioners and facilities, RCMP detachment, and schools are located in Outlook. Macrorie has a senior men's hockey team, curling and figure skating

clubs, a 4-H club, a seniors' centre, and a small golf course. In 2004, the Macrorie Mavericks senior men's baseball team overpowered Kindersley to become the Coteau Hills Baseball League Champions. The Macrorie Music Medley is an annual outdoor, day-long music festival held each July at the village sports grounds. One of the Macrorie district's most interesting characters was Tom Sukanen (Damianus Sukanen in the homestead records), a Finnish immigrant who spent much of the 1930s building a ship that he intended to sail home to Finland via the South Saskatchewan River and Hudson Bay. Impoverished, and physically and mentally exhausted, Sukanen suffered a breakdown in the early 1940s and died in the Battleford Asylum in 1943. His ship, the *Dontianen*, now rests at the Sukanen Ship Pioneer Village and Museum south of Moose Jaw. Macrorie is situated in the RM of Fertile Valley No. 285.

MAIDSTONE, town, pop 1,037 (2006c), 995 (2001c), is located between the Battlefords and Lloydminster at the junction of Hwys 16 and 21. Many of the first settlers in the Maidstone area were Barr Colonists, who arrived in the spring of 1903. With the construction of the Canadian Northern Railway through the region in 1905, the townsite was established and settlement of the area increased dramatically. The community developed rapidly and, on July 19, 1907, Maidstone was incorporated as a village. It was named after Maidstone, Kent, England. In the coming years, Blacks from Oklahoma settled just north of Maidstone, and a significant number of Mennonites would eventually come to take up land in the district. While both groups faced the same hardships many early settlers on the prairies faced,

the Black settlers' search for equality in Saskatchewan was met with suspicion and paranoia. Local politicians obstructed the pioneers' attempts to establish a school for a number of years, for fear area white students might possibly attend classes with Black children. The Black settlers, who had hoped for an open, integrated system, were forced to accept a segregated school. As years passed, however, and the district became increasingly settled, white children did begin attending the school, and slowly hostility toward the Black settlers mellowed. Among the Maidstone district's early homesteaders was John Henry "Jack" Wesson, who took up land near the young community in 1907. Wesson went on to become one of the province's foremost farm leaders; among other accomplishments, he became the first president of the Canadian Federation of Agriculture in 1936 and the president of the Saskatchewan Wheat Pool in 1937. As a trading centre for the surrounding agricultural district, the village of Maidstone grew steadily over the decades and attained town status in 1955. In the 1970s, the developing oil industry came to have a tremendous influence on the economy of the community, causing the town's population to grow from less than 700 at the beginning of the decade to over 1,000 by 1981. Today, with an expanding gas industry, close to 2,000 wells dot the surrounding countryside, while canola, grains, and purebred cattle dominate the district's agricultural output. Maidstone's business community serves a trading area population in excess of 7,500 and, additionally, the town has a hospital, a special care home, an RCMP detachment, and a fire department which serves the district. As well, Ratushniak Elementary School and Maidstone High School together provide K-12 education to close to 400 town

and area students. Maidstone has six churches, a library, and a number of service clubs, sports clubs, and youth groups. Recreational facilities include an arena, a curling rink, and a bowling alley; there are numerous golf courses in the district. On the east side of Maidstone, Delfrari-Victoria Park covers 40 acres, a site comprised of a museum, campgrounds, walking paths, a trout pond, ball diamonds, and tennis courts. The museum consists of a number of heritage buildings assembled together to recreate a pioneer village. A Maidstone area attraction is the Shiloh Baptist Church, built by the district's Black community around 1911. The building was abandoned after 1940, rediscovered in the early 1970s and restored. The church and the adjacent cemetery were designated a heritage property in 1991. Maidstone serves as the administrative centre of the RM of Eldon No. 471.

MAIN CENTRE, organized hamlet, pop 0 (2006c), 5 (2001c), is situated 25 km northwest of Herbert, roughly 15 km south of Lake Diefenbaker and Herbert Ferry Regional Park. Main Centre developed in the middle (hence the name) of a large area of Mennonite settlement that had its beginnings in 1903. The Bethel Mennonite Brethren congregation was established at Main Centre in 1904, and by 1906 the first school had been built. A mail route from Herbert to the area had been established by the end of 1904, although the Main Centre post office itself was not in operation until 1912. A ferry service was established to cross the South Saskatchewan River in 1910, opening up the Beechy area for settlement, and Main Centre became an overnight stopping place for the farmers north of the river who hauled grain to, and got supplies from, Herbert or Rush Lake. The first store opened in Main Centre in 1911, followed by another retail operation the next year, and then livery stables and a hotel. Eventually, garages and farm implement dealers, too, were set up. By the early 1920s, Beechy had its own rail service, but it was not until 1930 that the CNR laid the track from Mawer (just southeast of Central Butte) into the Main Centre area. The line, however, was laid about three-quarters of a kilometre north of the community, and as this is where the station, grain elevators, and stockyards would be located, a "New Main Centre" developed. Businesses moved to the rail line from the old locale, but the school, the church, and a number of residents remained at "Old Main Centre," so essentially the community spanned two sites in close proximity to one another. A local board of trade was formed in 1935; a Co-op store opened in 1937; and Main Centre was established as an organized hamlet in 1949. Subsequently, considerable developments took place. Streets were gravelled, street lights were installed, trees were planted, and an indoor skating rink was built, the latter endeavour fairly unique for a Saskatchewan hamlet. Main Centre was well-placed as the business, social, and religious centre of the surrounding farming community. By the 1960s, though, rural depopulation, modern transportation, centralization of services, and shopping trends were contributing to the hamlet's decline. High school students were now being bused to classes in Herbert. The creation of Lake Diefenbaker in the 1960s signalled the end of the Herbert Ferry and, although area residents protested, the service was terminated in 1968. In the early 1970s, the Main Centre Co-op boasted grocery and hardware sections, gas and oil sales, a service bay, the postal outlet, and veteri-

nary supplies, but by 1979, business had fallen off to the point that the store was closed. The year was a very bad one for the community. The school also closed, the grain elevator closed, and the rail line was abandoned. Within two or three years only four families were left living at Main Centre. Today, a postal outlet remains, and there is a museum containing artifacts and memorabilia which reflect the community's history. In July 2004, roughly 500 people turned up in Main Centre to celebrate the 100th anniversary of the Mennonite Brethren Church. Main Centre is situated in the RM of Excelsior No. 166.

MAJOR, village, pop 67 (2006c), 81 (2001c), is located approximately 37 km west of Kerrobert just off Hwy 51, approximately 30 km east of the Saskatchewan-Alberta border. Settlement of the area began around 1905. Significant numbers of people of German origin arrived from the U.S. and southern Russia, while others of British origin also took up land in the area. With the construction of the CPR line from Kerrobert west into Alberta around 1911-12, the townsite of Major developed and the population of the area grew rapidly. In 1914, the village was incorporated. The military name of the community was chosen by the railway, and the military theme was carried on in the naming of the village's streets: Trooper Street, Recruit Street, and Sergeant Avenue are among them. Major is located within the RM of Prairiedale No. 321, where agriculture and the oil industry form the basis of the economy. Major has a small core of essential businesses and services, an indoor rink, and Major School, a K-12 facility which had 63 students enrolled in the fall of 2006. CP abandoned the rail line in the 1990s, and now a branch of the Trans

Canada Trail follows the gravel roadbed of the tracks which used to run through the village. The community had a peak population of 179 in 1961.

MAKWA, village, pop 96 (2006c), 101 (2001c), is situated approximately 40 km southwest of Meadow Lake and about 15 km east of Loon Lake on Hwy 304. The settlement era began in the region in the years just prior to WWI, but the district was sparsely settled until the land rush took place in the late 1920s and early 1930s. Many came north driven by the Depression and the drought in the south. A good number of those who came to the district were French. The area population was diverse, however; many people of German origins, too, settled in the region. In 1926, a post office named Makwa — Makwa being the Cree word for "Loon" — opened somewhat north of the present community. In 1939, a post office named "South Makwa" opened where the present village is now located, and at this time the more northerly post office became "North Makwa." When "North Makwa" closed

in 1957, the name of "South Makwa" was changed to simply "Makwa," and it remains this today. The Village of Makwa was incorporated on June 1, 1965. Cattle and grain farming are the primary basis of the economy; however, many Makwa residents have found employment in the forestry industry, particularly at the pulp and saw mills in Meadow Lake. Seasonal work is also found at area parks and resorts. Makwa has a Co-op store, a hotel/beverage room, a restaurant, and a library. Recreational facilities include a bowling alley, a curling rink, a skateboard park, and an outdoor skating rink. The village's schoolchildren are bused to Loon Lake; medical services are provided in Meadow Lake. Makwa is situated in the RM of Loon Lake No. 561.

▼ **NESTLED BETWEEN MID-BOREAL UPLANDS** to the north and south, Makwa sits within the Meadow Lake plain, a part of the province's boreal transition ecoregion. View from the community's east side taken July 23, 2003.

▲ **MANITOU BEACH**, circa 1924. Saskatchewan Archives Board R-A16897-2.

▲▼ **MANITOU BEACH LANDMARKS:** Danceland (above, photographed July 22, 2004), and Camp Easter Seal (below, photographed August 9, 2004).

MANITOU BEACH, resort village, pop 233 (2006c), 212 (2001c), is located approximately 5 km north of Watrous on Hwy 365. The resort developed early in the twentieth century when the district's settlers discovered the mineral waters of Little Manitou Lake, long known to the region's indigenous population. The resort village was incorporated in 1919, and excursion trains brought vacationers and those seeking renewed health from across the prairies to the lake and the spas that developed. Danceland, built in 1928, became famous for its 5,000-square-foot maple dance floor, cushioned by a thick layer of horse hair. In the 1930s, as a relief project, the provincial government began the development of a provincial park at the lake and constructed the beautiful fieldstone buildings which were later taken over by the Saskatchewan Abilities Council, becoming Camp Easter Seal. The wheelchair-accessible resort now provides summer vacation opportunities for special children. Manitou Beach declined during the Depression and subsequent years, but entered a period of substantial growth in the 1980s and 1990s due to a renewed interest in the putative healing powers of mineral waters. With a multi-million-dollar investment infusion, Manitou Beach has again become a major centre for spa tourism. Manitou Beach is situated in the RM of Morris No. 312.

MANKOTA, village, pop 238 (2006c), 248 (2001c), is located in southern Saskatchewan on Hwy 18, centrally situated north of the East and West Blocks of Grasslands National Park. The NWMP trail connecting Wood Mountain with Fort Walsh ran close to the present village site. Beginning in 1910, settlers from Manitoba and the Dakotas began arriving in the district; hence, the name "Mankota." In 1928, as the railway was being built westward from McCord, the village site

▲ **KOURI'S MARKET** on the east side of Main Street in Mankota has been a fixture of the village's business community for many years. Photograph taken September 4, 2003.

developed. Six grain elevators, a hotel, a bank, and a variety of other businesses were quickly opened, and in 1929 the CPR line was completed. This was of tremendous benefit to the people of the area, as previously the nearest trade centres were Hazenmore and Kincaid, both roughly 30 kilometres (19 miles) to the north. However, just as things were looking brighter for the community, the dry years that followed created tremendous hardships, and many people were on relief. As well, railway development in this region of the province was forever altered. The CPR line that ended in Mankota was originally intended to continue on to connect with the track in Val Marie, thus creating a loop in southwestern Saskatchewan, but it was never built. Mankota would remain the end of the line. In 1941, the Village of Mankota was incorporated, and there began a period of increasing prosperity and growing population. By the late 1950s, nearly 500 people called Mankota home. In the following decades, the population levelled off at about 400, until the 1990s, when significant numbers of people started to move away. Rail service was abandoned at the end of the decade, although the CPR station had been closed since 1970; the building had originally been relocated to the village of Kincaid where, for a time, it served as a restaurant. Ranching and farming remain the major industries in the Mankota area, and the village continues to provide a range of businesses and services to the district. Mankota School provides K-12 education to approximately 90 students, and the community has a health centre, as well as facilities for sports and recreation. The community's RCMP detachment was closed in 2005. The village serves as the administrative centre of the RM of Mankota No. 45.

MANOR, village, pop 312 (2006c), 305 (2001c), lies in the south-eastern corner of the province, about 14 km east of Carlyle and approximately 50 km west of the Saskatchewan-Manitoba border on Hwy 13, otherwise known as the Red Coat Trail. The village of Manor, like the majority of southern Saskatchewan's communities, developed as a creature of the railway — in this case, the CPR. The community takes its name from Cannington Manor, some 14 km north. Cannington Manor had been established in 1882 by Captain Edward Michell Pierce and his four sons, who came to Canada from England. Following on the heels of the Dominion

▲▼▶ **BORN AND RAISED IN MANOR**, Ron Kyle, above, had a career as a pharmacist in Regina and Fillmore, Saskatchewan, prior to retiring back to his hometown. He now spends much of his time constructing stone walls and other features on his property on the northwest corner of Newcombe Street and Railway Avenue, adorning them with his unique metal sculptures.

Photographs taken August 20, 2003.

▶ **KNOX UNITED CHURCH**, on the southeast corner of Mountain Avenue and Newcombe Street in Manor, was built in 1905 for the community's Presbyterian congregation. Photograph taken August 20, 2003.

Lands surveyors that had surveyed the Manor district in 1881, they sought to establish a utopian English settlement which would attract aristocrats, landowners, and businessmen. The community survived for about two decades. A number of agricultural business enterprises were initiated and a number of grand buildings were erected, but after Pierce's sudden death in 1888, the young Englishmen, many bachelors, largely amused themselves by participating in numerous social events. They played tennis, cricket, and billiards; they hunted, drank, caroused, and chased women, including some who were, reportedly, married. For a period the "gentlemen" of Cannington Manor exchanged visits with the French counts at St. Hubert, south of Whitewood, and, although English and French, Protestant and Catholic, they were drawn to each other by the bonds of class, and together rode to the hounds. However, excess, a lack of leadership, and isolation from markets led to Cannington Manor's decline. When the CPR decided to build the long-anticipated branch line a distance south of Cannington Manor to avoid the hills and lakes of the Moose Mountain area, it was the death knell for the community and the locale was shortly abandoned. The present site of today's village of Manor was determined when the railway company chose a location for a station on the highest point of land between two creeks, so that trains running in either direction would start with a downhill run. The townsite was surveyed into blocks and lots in 1900, and the railway being built from the east was completed as far as Arcola that year. The line to Regina via Stoughton was opened in 1904. With the railway came an influx of settlers from the United States, England, Ontario, and Manitoba. French-speaking people from France, Belgium,

and Quebec rounded out the district's cultural milieu. The years 1900 to 1907 were boom times for Manor: carpenters had no shortage of employment as another prairie town sprang into being. The Manor Post Office was established on April 1, 1901, and on May 9 the same year the Manor Public School District was officially formed. Classes were held in a rented hall until January 1903, when a one-room schoolhouse was opened. By 1908, a new four-room brick school was necessitated to accommodate a rapidly bourgeoning student population. At a public meeting in January 1902, local ratepayers had voted unanimously to send a request to the Department of Municipal Affairs in Regina asking that the young community be established as a village. On April 15, 1902, the Village of Manor was incorporated, and its rapid growth ensured it became a significant centre for services and supplies for the developing mixed farming district. Manor had had a population of just 27 in 1901, but by 1911 the community numbered close to 300. After losing about one-third of its population by 1936 due to the Depression and the drought, the village recovered during the post-WWII period, and its population peaked between the mid-1960s and the mid-1980s when it was hovering around 400. Oil was discovered in the district in the 1950s, and, today, oil wells and oilfield-related services are important factors in the regional economy. In 1948, a permanent and stable supply of electricity was provided to village residents; in 1965 a sewer and water system was installed; and in 1966, gas lines were extended to the community. In 1974, the first thoroughfare in Manor, Main Street, was paved. In 1975, low-rental housing was built to accommodate senior citizens, and in 1977, nine new homes for young families were built with government assis-

tance. Today, Manor School, a K-12 facility that had 104 students enrolled in the fall of 2006, is a focus of village activity. Moose Mountain Provincial Park, a short distance to the northwest, provides Manor residents with a wide range of recreational facilities and opportunities. A landmark in the village is the Manor Museum. It is located in a simplified Queen Anne-style home built circa 1904-05 for the Dagleish family, prominent community residents. The building is situated on landscaped grounds and features mahogany flooring, stained glass windows, and decorative woodwork. It was designated a municipal heritage property in 1982. Another unique structure in Manor, situated on the west side of Main Street, is a two-story brick and stone edifice constructed in 1906 as the Northern Bank. The building presents a western Canadian interpretation of early twentieth-century Canadian banking architecture. Built in a Classical Revival style, the structure features a broad sweeping arch over the front entranceway with two sculpted buffalo heads above on either side. The building has long served as Manor's post office and has an identical twin in the town of Qu'Appelle. Manor is situated in the RM of Moose Mountain No. 63.

MANTARIO, hamlet, pop 10 (2006c), 10 (2001c), is a recently-dissolved village located in west-central Saskatchewan, 26 km west of Eatonia on Hwy 44. The first few settlers began trickling into the region over 1906-07, having travelled north from Maple Creek on the CPR main line. Settlement in the district greatly accelerated after the Canadian Northern line was built westward from Kindersley through Alsask into Alberta over 1910-11. The Mantario Post Office was established

on March 1, 1912, a little southeast of the present townsite. The name was evidently chosen because of the precedent set by the naming of nearby Alsask, near the provincial border. That name is an amalgamation of the words ALberta and SASKatchewan, and as a number of early Mantario area residents hailed from MANitoba and OnTARIO, they combined the names of their home provinces following Alsask's lead with the amalgamation theme. With the completion of the railway between Glidden and Alsask in 1920, the Mantario townsite was established, and the post office was relocated to serve the emerging village. Mantario was incorporated as a village on May 28, 1923, but the community remained fairly small. Its population was only 50 by 1926, and it had only reached 71 by 1946. During the post-War boom years, Mantario enjoyed its heyday: from the early 1950s through to the mid-1960s the village numbered more than 100 residents – its population peaked at approximately 135 in the mid-1950s. The community boasted cement sidewalks, two churches, a community hall, an open-air skating rink, a curling rink, two general stores, a hardware store, the post office, two garages, two bulk fuel outlets, a lumberyard, telephone office, fire hall, and, eventually, four grain elevators. By 1971, however, the village was down to 48 residents (the school closed in the mid-1960s), and today Mantario is on the verge of becoming a ghost town. The post office was closed in the early spring of 1986, and Mantario relinquished village status on June 30, 2007. Mantario is situated in the RM of Chesterfield No. 261.

MAPLE CREEK, town, pop 2,198 (2006c), 2,270 (2001c), is located 40 km east of the Saskatchewan-Alberta border

▲ **A CATTLE ROUNDUP** on the Greeley and Parsons ranches southeast of Maple Creek, 1897. The writing on the bottom left of the photographs informs, "Stretching a steer to examine a brand." The man on horseback holding the rope in the centre of the photograph is identified as Bill Hammond. The photograph was taken by Geraldine Moodie, the wife of John Douglas Moodie, an officer with the North-West Mounted Police.

▲ **A CAMP OF COWBOYS** during a roundup, 1887.

Historical photographs unless otherwise indicated are courtesy of the Southwestern Saskatchewan Oldtimers Association Museum and Archives, Maple Creek.

The Old Cowtown... MAPLE CREEK

▼ **THE PIONEER STORE OF THE DIXON BROTHERS**, circa 1880s. John Dixon is the man with the black beard third from the right; Chester Dixon is at the extreme right; the man sitting on the crate is G.O. Beesley. The others are unidentified.

▶ **GOW'S LIVERY BARN**, circa 1900. The proprietor is likely the suited man on the right; Sam Clay (left), and Jack Dennis (centre) are presumably the stable hands identified.

▼ **DINING AT THE MAPLE LEAF HOTEL, 1914.**

► **MAPLE CREEK, CIRCA 1918.** Cattle-loading facilities and grain elevators are visible to the left of the tracks. The CPR station and water tower are visible in the centre of the photograph. To the right is Pacific Avenue. Photograph courtesy of Saskatchewan Archives Board R-B9116-1.

▼ **CROWDS COME OUT TO GREET THE ROYAL TRAIN** carrying King George VI and Queen Elizabeth, Maple Creek, May 26, 1939. Photograph courtesy of the Jasper Cultural and Historical Centre, Maple Creek.

"The Royal Train"
Maple Creek, Sask.
May 26/39

▼ **BRICK HOMES AND BUILDINGS** are a feature of the town. Pictured below is the Maple Creek Post Office. Photograph taken September 3, 2004.

▲ **THE GATEWAY TO THE CYPRESS HILLS.** Approximately 250,000 tourists travel through Maple Creek each year to the Cypress Hills. Photograph taken September 2, 2004.

▼ **VISITORS** examine the small civilian cemetery located on a hill just above Fort Walsh. Photograph taken September 6, 2007.

on Hwy 21, 8 km south of the Trans-Canada Hwy. Maple Creek serves as a gateway for an estimated 250,000 tourists each year heading to the Cypress Hills Interprovincial Park, Fort Walsh, and the historic site of the Cypress Hills Massacre. The town got its name and its beginning in the fall of 1882, when construction of the trans-continental railway was halted and workmen spent the winter on the banks of a small creek lined with Manitoba Maples — the creek which flows northward along the west side of the present town. In 1875, prior to significant settlement in the North-West Territories, the NWMP established Fort Walsh in the Cypress Hills approximately 50 kilometres southwest of the location. But with the coming of the railway in 1883, Fort Walsh was abandoned and the NWMP detachment, "A" Division, relocated to new barracks near what was called Maple Creek. The Maple Creek Post Office was established that year. With the police came the pioneers and businessmen who had been established at the village that had developed at Fort Walsh, while others came to the new community via the railway. Within a few years, community institutions such as a school and churches were established. Ranching developed into the main industry in the area, and on April 28, 1896, Maple Creek was incorporated as a village. By April 30, 1903, the community had grown sufficiently to attain town status. However, as more settlers arrived, the vast ranching empires began to give way to fences, homesteads, and crop production — particularly after the winter of 1906-07 devastated the ranching industry. Maple Creek would become a community of firsts: in 1907, a gravity-fed water system was established, with water piped into the community from springs several kilometres to the southeast; a few years later, a sewage

system was installed and an electric light system was established; and Maple Creek became one of the first communities of its size in the province to have most of its streets paved. While today agriculture remains the substantial contributor to the town's economy (generally speaking, crop production to the north and ranching to the south), gas exploration and production, tourism, various small manufacturing enterprises, and service industries provide a significant degree of economic diversity. Maple Creek has a substantial business community providing a wide range of goods and services to both town residents and an additional trading area population of close to 4,000 people. Maple Creek has four physicians and a 21-bed hospital which provides acute care, 24-hour emergency service, treatment and diagnostic services, laboratory and x-ray services, and obstetric, pediatric, and palliative care. A special care home facilitates long-term and respite care, and houses an adult day care service. The community has an ambulatory service with emergency medical technicians, as well as a variety of health care practitioners. A daytime vocational and life skills program, combined with residential services, assists adults with disabilities. The community retains its long-established RCMP detachment, and has a volunteer fire department. Maple Creek's elementary and high schools together provide K-12 education to approximately 600 students. Additionally, the community has a play school, and programs and classes are available to adults through the Cypress Hills Regional College. Community recreational facilities include skating, hockey, and curling rinks, an outdoor swimming pool, a skateboard park, ball diamonds, tennis courts, a golf course, and playgrounds. The community also has a library, a number of churches,

service clubs and community organizations. Maple Creek has two impressive museums: the Oldtimers Museum, established in 1926, houses artifacts and an extensive collection of photographs documenting the 1870-1910 frontier period of the region; and the Jasper Cultural and Historic Centre, which features theme exhibits depicting different aspects of pioneer life. Maple Creek, living up to its long-established moniker "The Old Cowtown," hosts five or six rodeos over the course of the year, as well as the Cowboy Poetry Gathering and Western Art and Cowboy Gear Show, which is held each September. Sheep dogs test their skills at the Stock Dog Trials held in October. Additionally, the Cowtown Livestock Exchange is one of the most important livestock auction rings in the country. Located in Saskatchewan's "banana belt," Maple Creek also enjoys the warmest annual average temperature

▼ **COCKSHUTT IMPLEMENTS,**
Marcelin, likely shortly after
the village was established.
Saskatchewan Archives Board
R-B10370-1.

in the province and, subsequently, the largest number of frost-free days. Maple Creek serves as the administrative centre of the RM of Maple Creek No. 111.

MARCELIN, village, pop 169 (2006c), 167 (2001c), is located in west-central Saskatchewan, northeast of Blaine Lake, on Hwy 40. The origins of the community date to 1902, when Antoine Marcelin, originally from Pont Chateau, Quebec, purchased 1900 acres of land near the present townsite. In the following years, Marcelin actively recruited French settlers to the district from eastern Canada and France. In the summer of 1911 the railway came through; in September, the village was incorporated. During the late 1920s and early 1930s the village was at its peak, having a population of close to 400. The district had been further settled by immigrants from Russia, Ukraine, Poland, and Hungary, which resulted in giving Marcelin's school a distinctly cosmopolitan feel for many years. The village's population began to drop significantly in the 1970s, and institutions such as the

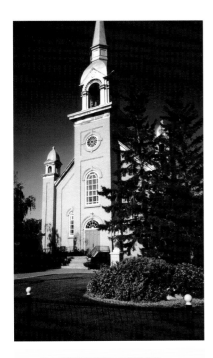

school and a number of businesses were inevitably closed. Today, a focal point in the community is St. Joseph's Roman Catholic Church. Constructed in 1922-23, the building was declared a heritage property in 1984. Marcelin is situated in the RM of Blaine Lake No. 434.

MARENGO, village, pop 51 (2006c), 47 (2001c), had three different names within the first few years of its existence. As the railway came westward from Kindersley in 1910, the village was first incorporated as Melbourne. Then, in 1911, the name was changed to Fuller, and in 1914 the name Marengo was finally settled upon. The name honoured the Illinois hometown of one of the district's pioneers — Marengo, Illinois, had been named after the June 14, 1800, Battle of Marengo in Italy, during which Napoleon roundly defeated Austrian forces. Marengo, Saskatchewan, is located just off Highway 7, a short distance from the Alberta border. The community houses a joint office for the village, the RM of Milton No. 292, and the neighbouring RM of Antelope Park No. 322, to the north. The office had also, for nearly 40 years, administered the Village of Loverna until it was dissolved in March 2003. A key institution in the community is Westcliffe Composite School, which provides K-12 education to approximately 120 students from the village and the surrounding area. Agriculture (grain and livestock) and oil production are the major industries in the area. Marengo had a peak population of 163 in 1961.

MARGO, village, pop 90 (2006c), 106 (2001c), is located northeast of Foam Lake on Hwy 5. A handful of ranchers were operating in the area in the 1890s; shortly after 1900, homesteaders began to arrive in numbers. Up to 1905, most were of British extraction (either from overseas or eastern Canada), or were Norwegian or Finnish (many of whom came to Canada via the United States). After 1908, when more land in the district was opened up for settlement, Ukrainian, German, and French homesteaders also settled the region. In 1927, Czechoslovakians, settling just north of the village, rounded out the cultural milieu, delighting many with their never-seen-before demonstrations of calisthenics and gymnastics. The village of Margo had its beginnings with the construction of the Canadian Northern Railway north-westward from Canora in 1904. In 1905, trains were running through Margo, the post office was established, and the business community was growing. The name Margo is believed to have been derived from a nearby body of water that was once known as Margot Lake. According to one of the district's first settlers, Bob Reid, who settled near the lake in the 1890s, area trappers, fur traders, and early settlers called the lake Margot Lake after a young Métis girl who had been murdered near its shores. In 1911, the Village of Margo was incorporated, the population was 83, and the economy then, as now, was predominantly based in agriculture, a combination of grain and livestock production. Post-WWII, Margo experienced a period of growth, and from the mid-1950s to the mid-1960s the population was over 250. Subsequently, however, even as the villager's lives were improved with the installation of water, gas, and sewer, the population and the business community of Margo fell into a slow but steady decline. The older grades that attended Margo School began to be bused to Invermay or Wadena for classes, and in the mid-1990s the school was closed. Today, only a small core of businesses remains, which includes a Co-op, a credit union, the post office, a hair salon, gas stations, a restaurant, and a construction company. In late summer 2004, the hotel was open, but up for sale. A community landmark, St. Paul's Anglican Church, built in 1912, was designated a municipal heritage property in 1998. It is open for visitations by tourists and is still used for occasional marriages, funerals, and services. Margo is situated in the RM of Sasman No. 336.

MARKINCH, village, pop 59 (2006c), 67 (2001c), lies between the towns of Southey and Cupar on Hwy 22; a picturesque small valley etched by Loon Creek runs immediately northeast of the community. The district was settled by Scottish-Canadians from Ontario, many German Lutherans, and people from the British Isles; with the coming of the railway, the village of Markinch developed. The CPR opened the line between Lipton and Strasbourg in 1905. The first grain elevator was built in Markinch in 1906, and on October 1 that year the post office was established. The community was named after Markinch, Fife, Scotland. A school district centred on the village was erected in 1907 and the Beaver Lumber Company started in business the same year. Soon Markinch boasted a store, a harness shop, a livery barn, blacksmith shops, implement dealers, a billiard hall, and a flour mill. By 1909, the rate of settlement in the district was such that the RM of Cupar No. 218 was established to improve the management of the area's affairs. Until recently the RM office was located in Markinch; it is now, however, located in the town of Cupar, although a maintenance shop remains in Markinch. By 1914, five grain elevators lined the tracks at Markinch station, and in 1916 the population of the village was 129. The local history recounts, however, that the population of the surrounding RM at this time was well over 3,000. (The 2006 Census of Canada recorded the population in the RM of Cupar at 502.) Methodists organized a congregation at Markinch in 1910 and built their church, which later became the United Church, in 1914. Lutherans formed a local congregation in 1920. The village was incorporated on February 16, 1911, and by 1913 a bank was in business and the impressive three-storey Maple Leaf Hotel had been built on the northwest corner of Railway Avenue and Royal Street (this burned to the ground in the late 1920s). Markinch reached its peak population — 172 — in 1921. The bank closed at the onset of the Depression, and through the 1930s the community's population significantly declined. Following the Depression, the village never regained its former vitality. Beaver Lumber ceased operations at the beginning of the 1940s. Subsequently, the village population dwindled with each successive decade, as did the number of businesses. The United Church was closed in 1953 due to declining membership, and the building was moved to Fort Qu'Appelle. Water and sewer systems were established in the village in 1966; sidewalks were paved in the late 1950s and the main street was paved in 1973. The railway station was closed in 1968 and was demolished in 1970. Markinch School was closed in 1969 and students then went to either Southey or Cupar. Today, the only visible business in the village is the Markinch Hotel (bar) and Steak Pit. In 1971, three-quarters of the community's population claimed to have German origins.

MARQUIS, village, pop 71 (2006c), 94 (2001c), is located 33 km northwest of Moose Jaw on Hwy 42, between the villages of Tuxford and Keeler. The Qu'Appelle Valley lies to the north, Buffalo Pound Lake to the east. The first few settlers in the region settled in or near the valley in the 1880s, wanting to have easy access to water, as well as wood for building material and fuel. With the rapid construction of railway branch lines in the early 1900s prior to WWI, the land rush was on and most of the Marquis district was homesteaded during this period. With the construction of the CPR line from Moose Jaw to Outlook between 1906 and 1909, the present village had its beginnings. The townsite was surveyed in 1907, and by 1908, with trains running, a handful of businesses were in operation. The railway named the locale, yet whether the

name refers to a nobleman's ranking or Charles Saunders' newly-developed strain of wheat is unclear. The Marquis Post Office was established on July 1, 1907; the first postmaster, George T. McFadden (after whom one of the community's streets is named), came to the district in 1902 from Ontario, settling on what is now the village site. He travelled to Caron to pick up the mail until the railway arrived. Marquis was incorporated on March 21, 1910, and that year a Presbyterian church (later United) was built in the community. The first Catholic church was completed circa 1915-16. As the number of school-age children in Marquis grew, it was decided to move the country school, established in 1903 about a mile west, into the village. In 1915, a Roman Catholic separate school, St. Mark's, was opened. Two orders of nuns taught at St. Mark's over the years: the Sisters of Service from the later 1930s into the early 1940s; then, beginning in the 1950s, the Sisters of Charity of St. Louis taught for many years. Marquis had grown to have a population of 135 by 1926, but the village's numbers declined through the Depression and during the subsequent war years, when many young people left to find employment in larger centres or joined the armed services. In the 1950s the community rebounded, and its population peaked at just under 200 in the mid-1960s. By this time, however, the village's proximity to Moose Jaw was leading to the closure of local businesses and the loss of community institutions; as these began to disappear, so, too, did Marquis's population. It has, however, remained fairly stable over the past 20 years. In 1969, Marquis Public School was closed; some students then attended St. Mark's, but most were bused to Moose Jaw. In 1970, the CPR station, built in 1910 replacing a temporary structure, was sold

and demolished; and in 1971, the United Church was closed. The elevators began to come down in the mid-1970s — the last was torn down several years ago. St. Mark's grade 11 and 12 students began to be bused into Moose Jaw to attend classes in 1966, followed by the grade 9 and 10 classes in 1972. In 1979, St. Mark's Roman Catholic Separate School became a public school — it was closed in 2001. The Marquis area economy is based in agriculture: cereal grains, pulse crops, and oil seeds are grown; and cattle ranching is a major source of farm income. Several seed cleaning plants in the area have become important assets, somewhat filling the void left by the closure of the local elevators. Today, a number of Marquis residents commute to work in Moose Jaw. Businesses in the village today include a

general store with a liquor outlet, a service station, the post office, a credit union, and a sandblasting and painting company. Religious services are provided by St. John the Evangelist Roman Catholic Church. The community hosts an annual sports day on July 1, and a curling bonspiel in January. Marquis serves as the administrative centre of the RM of Marquis No. 191.

MARSDEN, village, pop 234 (2006c), 276 (2001c), lies 60 km south of Lloydminster and 60 km west of Cut Knife, on Hwy 40 about 10 km from the Saskatchewan-Alberta border. Manitou Lake lies just to the southeast. Settlers from eastern Canada, the British Isles, and the United States began taking

◄▼ **MARSDEN SKYSCRAPERS:** The main portion of this former Saskatchewan Wheat Pool facility (left) was built in 1967 as is evidenced by the Centennial emblem on the cupola. The attached crib annex dates to 1948. Cargill's concrete facility (below) at the north end of Centre Street dates to 1984. Photographs taken August 13, 2003.

up land in the area in 1905. The Marsden Post Office was established on June 15, 1907, a little more than a kilometre northeast of the present village site. The name Marsden was chosen by the wife of the first postmaster, Mrs. Alexander Ferguson Wright, after her birthplace, the town of Marsden in Yorkshire, England. Before the railway was built through the district, farmers had to travel to either Artland or Lashburn both for supplies and to deliver their grain and stock for shipment. When the construction of the CPR branch line from Wilkie to Lloydminster was resumed in the mid-1920s (the line had not progressed beyond Cut Knife since 1911), new village sites were established along the line — Marsden, in 1923, one of them. Businessmen originally believed that the Marsden townsite was to be developed on the north side of the railway tracks, and four eager entrepreneurs set up establishments there before the railway intervened, explaining that the side tracks that would serve the elevators would have to be laid on the south side of the main line, on the outside of the curve that passed through the townsite, in order to allow oncoming trains an unobstructed view of the tracks from both directions. Three businessmen relocated their operations then to the south side of the tracks, while a fourth packed up and moved up the line to Neilburg. Marsden was built up over 1923-24, and while schools had existed in the countryside since shortly after the first settlers arrived, in 1925 the first school was built on the townsite. In 1926, and again in 1930, fires swept through the community, each time claiming a number of businesses. Marsden rebuilt, however, and on April 24, 1931, the community gained village status. In spite of the Depression, Marsden residents undertook a number of major initiatives: a community

hall was built in 1933, a village barn was constructed and a community bee was organized to gravel Main Street in 1934, and in 1935 a curling rink was erected. Through WWII, the village's population hovered at somewhat over 100; after the War, Marsden experienced a long period of growth and prosperity. From a population of 129 in 1946, the village grew to number 176 by 1956, and 255 by 1966; and other than somewhat of a downturn in the mid-1970s, Marsden's numbers have remained fairly stable over the past 40 years. The railway station was closed in 1970 and dismantled in 1973, and in the early 1990s the senior grades at Marsden Jubilee School began to be bused to the neighbouring community of Neilburg. Marsden's school remains a K-6 institution today, and there were 48 students enrolled in the fall of 2005. The major industries in the area are based in oil and agriculture. There are hundreds of oil wells in the surrounding area and a number of oil batteries. Wheat, canola, oats, barley, peas, and flax are grown; and prize-winning purebred cattle are raised — the breeds include Charolais, Hereford, Simmental, and Angus. One of the district's leading cattlemen was John Stanley Palmer, who settled in the Marsden area in 1909. Palmer came to be

widely recognized as a leading breeder of Hereford cattle, and he served as the president of both the Saskatchewan and Canadian Hereford Associations, the president of the Saskatchewan Cattle Breeders Association, and as a member of the Senate of the University of Saskatchewan. Palmer was inducted into the Saskatchewan Agricultural Hall of Fame in 1976. Marsden area attractions include the regional park on Manitou Lake, which has a nine-hole, sand-green golf course, campsites, and baseball diamonds. Manitou Outfitters offers trail rides through 130,000 acres of the Manitou Sand Hills, an area that is home to approximately 145 resident and migratory species of birds, and 400 native plant species. Marsden serves as the administrative centre of the RM of Manitou Lake No. 442.

MARSHALL, town, pop 608 (2006c), 633 (2001c), is located approximately 16 km southeast of Lloydminster on the Yellowhead Hwy. As such, its origins and development are tied to the arrival of the Barr Colonists in 1903. A mile northwest of the present town of Marshall, on NW6-49-26-W3, a Barr Colonist by the name of Lewis Stringer homesteaded with his sons. On December 1, 1904, a post of-

▲ **THIS LARGE OIL TANK** on the highway on the north side of Marshall welcomes visitors to the community, and informs one of the importance of the oil industry to the area economy. Photograph taken August 12, 2003.

fice was established here, operating under the name Stringer. It was here, too, that the first church in the Colony was built, an Anglican Church known as St. George's on the Trail. Other men set up a store, and it is said a blacksmith worked in the locale as well. When the Canadian Northern Railway came through in 1905, the location of the present community was

▲ **MARSHALL'S BUSINESS DISTRICT CIRCA 1907.** The Savoy Hotel (left foreground) was built in 1906. Photograph courtesy of the Lashburn Centennial Museum.

▲ **MARSHALL'S 75TH ANNIVERSARY?** Vehicles get in line for a celebratory parade in 1988; however, that celebrations were held that year is somewhat odd. The townsite was established in 1905 and the community was incorporated as a village on January 21, 1914! Thus it would seem the intention was to celebrate the community's incorporation as a village. It is probable that someone referred to the petition for the erection of the village, which very likely was held in 1913, and that is the reason why the celebration took place a year early. Photograph courtesy of the Town of Marshall.

▼ **MARSHALL'S FORMER SASKATCHEWAN WHEAT POOL GRAIN ELEVATOR.** Photograph taken August 12, 2003.

determined, and the church, the post office, and the other businesses relocated to the site. Over the next few years, a number of new businesses were started. The emerging hamlet was named Marshall, although the origin of the name is uncertain. The Stringer Post Office officially adopted the name on August 1, 1906. The first school in Marshall was built in 1907. By the beginning of 1914, the community had developed sufficiently enough to warrant incorporation, and the Village of Marshall was legally constituted on January 21 that year. In 1916, the population was 81, and for the first half of the twentieth century the community grew very little and its population remained fairly stable. In 1951, the village numbered 98 residents. In the following decades, however, Marshall grew substantially, propelled by a booming oil and gas industry. By 1961,

the population was 161; in 1981 it was 453; and by the mid-1990s the community numbered more than 600. Marshall attained town status on October 26, 2006. Work in the oil fields and related services, as well as agriculture, form the basis of the regional economy; however, many who live in the town commute to work in Lloydminster, and Marshall has developed into a flourishing bedroom community due to its proximity to the city. Local businesses in Marshall include a credit union, a restaurant, a hotel and a bar, the post office, a store, and several other small, home-based businesses. The community has a library, two halls, a skating rink, ball diamonds, and a skateboard park. Marshall School is a K-9 facility, which had 142 students enrolled in the fall of 2006. Marshall is situated in the RM of Wilton No. 472.

MARTENSVILLE, town, pop 4,968 (2006c), 4,365 (2001c), is located about eight km north of Saskatoon on Hwy 12. The community developed on land which had been owned by area farmer Isaac Martens and his son, Dave Martens, who saw an opportunity to subdivide their property for residential development. Substantial growth occurred in the 1960s as Saskatoon was undergoing a period of significant expansion and suburbanites were looking for lower land prices and new homes. In 1966, Martensville was incorporated as a village; it attained town status in 1969. After water and sewer systems were completed in 1976, Martensville began to grow rapidly: between 1976 and 1981, the population grew from 960 to 1,966; ten years later, in 1981, the community had over 3,300 residents. At its current rate of growth, Martensville is poised to gain city status. Largely a bedroom community, the town thrives on the economic base provided by Saskatoon; Martensville residents benefit from easy access to the amenities and services that the city has to offer, without having to pay Saskatoon city taxes. Further, according to the 2001 Census, the median income for Martensville households was $58,683, while Saskatoon's was $41,991. Martensville is situated in the RM of Corman Park No. 344.

▼ **SUBURBIA.** Martensville is characterized by large new homes on small lots, with two-car garages facing each other across the streets. Photograph taken August 27, 2004.

MARTINSON'S BEACH,

organized hamlet, est. 1983, is located north of North Battleford, and is one of several resort communities that circle Jackfish Lake. There were 39 permanent residents in 2006; however, the population varies greatly depending on the season. Martinson's Beach is situated in the RM of Meota No. 468.

MARYFIELD,

village, pop 347 (2006c), 359 (2001c), is located approximately 43 km southeast of Moosomin, 7 km west of the Saskatchewan-Manitoba border on Hwy 48. The Pipestone Valley lies northeast of the village. Land in the district was surveyed beginning in 1880, and on the heels of the survey crews the first settlers began arriving in the area. Initially, they were principally from Ontario and the British Isles; later, these were joined by large numbers from the United States. For the first year or two, as the CPR main line was being built westward, settlers travelling from the east by train would disembark at the end of steel at Brandon and, later, Oak Lake, Manitoba, and then travel overland to the Maryfield region. The name Maryfield dates to 1883 and was originally the name of an early

pioneer's farm, which he had named after his sister. After 1900, settlers also entered the district from the south as the railway was constructed from Souris, Manitoba, to Arcola. The site that would become the village of Maryfield was surveyed by the CPR around 1905, as they proceeded westward with the construction of their line from Reston, Manitoba, to Wolseley. The track was built as far as Peebles by 1906, and was completed through to Wolseley in 1908. The little mixed train that ran back and forth on the line eventually became affectionately known to local residents as the "Peanut." With the railway came a construction boom, and the Village of Maryfield was incorporated August 21, 1907. That same year, the Canadian

Northern Railway had come through Maryfield building a line parallel to the CPR's, but which ran directly to Regina. Within two years, Canadian Northern began construction of another line running southwest from Maryfield through Carlyle toward Estevan, and with business booming on the railways, there was talk of building a roundhouse and of Maryfield becoming a railway centre of great importance. The two railway companies did become major employers in the community, and they were a dominant influence in the village until the 1950s, when Maryfield's population was close to 500. Beginning in 1960, however, came major changes. The CPR abandoned its line and the track was removed. Passenger and freight volumes decreased on CN's lines, and in the early 1980s the last employee of that company worked in the village. Maryfield's days as a rail centre were over. Furthering the community's misfortunes was the pro-

◄ KATIE ROBINSON WAS GETTING MARRIED and friends posted notice of her bridal shower on Maryfield & District Lions Club's community announcement board. Photograph taken August 21, 2003.

vincial government's decision in 1969 to withdraw funding for Maryfield's hospital. Residents took their objections to the provincial legislature, but to no avail. The effects of these changes, among others, became evident as the business community fell into decline. Many businesses were closed, and a great number of the village's buildings were eventually torn down. Maryfield's population was slowly, but steadily, falling. While many residents now shop and seek services in Moosomin, or across the border in Virden or Brandon, Manitoba, Maryfield retains a small core of essential businesses and has a volunteer fire department, ambulance service, and health clinic. Two seniors' residences, one for independent living, the other a special care facility, accommodate Maryfield's aging population. According to Statistics Canada, the median age of village residents was close to 50 in 2006 — the median age for all Saskatchewan at the time was 38.7. Maryfield has three churches and a library, and recreational facilities which include curling and skating rinks and a fitness centre. Maryfield Auditorium houses a movie theatre, concert stage, dance hall, and banquet facilities. The community hosts an indoor rodeo as well as a fair each summer. Maryfield School provides K-12 education, and had 87 students enrolled in the fall of 2006. Agriculture, a mixture of grain and livestock production, remains the dominant industry in the region. Maryfield serves as the administrative centre of the RM of Maryfield No. 91.

MAYFAIR, organized hamlet, pop 30 (2006c), 48 (2001c), is located approximately 45 km south of Spiritwood and 55 km northeast of North Battleford on Hwy 324. Ukrainians and Poles settled in significant numbers to the east and south in the early 1900s; French settlers were scattered to the east as well; in the late 1920s, many Mennonites settled in the Mayfair district spreading to the northwest. Mayfair, however, owes its name to an Englishman. The community derives its name from the Mayfair School District established in 1916; the school was built about three miles northwest of the present community. The name for the school was chosen by William Clease, whose homestead was located on an adjacent quarter section. Clease emigrated to Canada from Bristol, England, in 1908 and initially lived in the Mayfair district that is now a part of Saskatoon. When a post office was established a couple of miles to the southeast of the school on September 1, 1919, it adopted the Mayfair name. The development of the hamlet of Mayfair began in 1928 with the construction of the CNR line through the area. The townsite was surveyed that year, the first businesses were built, and the post office moved in from the country. Within a short period of time, a lumber company, hardware store, general stores, real estate office, café and rooming house, blacksmith shop, livery stable, garage, pool room and barber shop were in business. The Bank of Toronto established a branch, and a ten-room hotel was built. A community hall was constructed in the fall of 1929, and a Ukrainian Hall was erected. By 1931, the community was well-established and three grain elevators lined the railway tracks. That year, however, disaster struck: a fire originating in one of the stores destroyed that store, along with the post office, bank, café and rooming house, and another store before it was brought under control. In 1930, a school district centred on the hamlet had been set up; the school was originally named Redleaf to distinguish it from the rural Mayfair School. The country school closed in 1956 (the year Mayfair was established as an organized hamlet), and in 1960 the name of Redleaf School was changed to Mayfair Central School. In 1967, a covered arena was completed in the hamlet, largely through volunteer labour, ushering in an era of organized minor hockey. Mayfair's hockey teams, as their baseball teams had been in earlier times, were competitive for a number of years. Mayfair proper numbered 134 residents in 1972, and its population still hovered at close to 100 in the mid-1980s. In recent decades the community has declined — in terms of both its population and its business community. Mayfair Central School closed in 2004, and by that year the post office and a confectionery were the only viable commercial entities remaining. A former Saskatchewan Wheat Pool elevator, dating to 1928, still stands, as does the newer arena, completed in the mid-1980s. Grain production dominates the area economy, although some livestock are raised. Mayfair serves as the administrative centre of the RM of Meeting Lake No. 466.

MAYMONT, village, pop 130 (2006c), 164 (2001c), is located approximately 45 km southeast of North Battleford and about 90 km northwest of Saskatoon on the Yellowhead Hwy. Highway 376 runs north of the community through the village of Richard; south of Maymont, it runs across the North Saskatchewan River through the hamlet of Sonningdale. Glenburn Regional Park is located 12 km south of Maymont on the north shore of the river, where the Maymont Ferry ran until the bridge was constructed in the mid-1970s. Settlement in the Maymont area began in the early 1900s, and the community developed with the construction of the Canadian Northern Railway through the district in 1905. The townsite was named in honour of May Montgomery, a niece of Sir William Mackenzie, a partner in the railway company. The Maymont Post Office was established on November 1, 1905; the local school district was established in 1906; and the first school was completed the following year. The village was incorporated on June 24, 1907. The community enjoyed a heyday in its first two decades: until the CPR built its line northwestward from Asquith into Sonningdale (c. 1923) and Baljennie (1931), Maymont was the main trading centre for the settlers in the district south of the river. From a population of 121 in 1911, Maymont grew to number about 200 residents by the 1930s, and the population remained fairly stable until the early 1990s. The village's peak population was 239 in 1961. Today, the community retains a small core of businesses and its school. There were once three grain elevators in the village; none remain. Maymont Central School is a K-12 facility that had 183 students enrolled in the fall of 2006. The student population has been substantially bolstered since the fall of 2004 as a result of the closure of the school in the town of Radisson to the southeast. Maymont's school had only 96 students enrolled in the fall of 2003. The current school was completed in 1996, replacing a building that dated to the early 1960s. Adjoining the new school is a multipurpose facility housing an ice rink; the complex is jointly used by the school's students and the rest of the community. The Maymont district economy is based in grain and livestock production; some residents of the village commute to the cities of North Battleford and Saskatoon to work. The nearest medical facilities are in North Battleford; the nearest RCMP detachment is in Radisson. Maymont serves as the administrative centre of the RM of Mayfield No. 406.

MAYMONT BEACH, organized hamlet, is located north of North Battleford, and is one of a number of resort communities on Murray Lake. There are a small number of permanent residents; however, the population varies greatly depending on the season. Maymont Beach is situated in the RM of Meota No. 468.

MAZENOD, hamlet, pop 26 (2001c), is a former village located southwest of Old Wives Lake, 25 km east of Gravelbourg off Hwy 43. Settlers had been in the region a few years when, on April 1, 1909, a post office named Mazenod was established roughly 9 kilometres south of the present community. After the railway came through the district and established a location for a new townsite, the post office, and the name along with it, were transferred to the locale. The name Mazenod had been chosen by the missionary colonizer Father Louis-Joseph-Pierre Gravel (1868-1926), for whom the town of Gravelbourg was named; Gravel was the priest for the Roman Catholic community in the district and chose the name to honour Charles Joseph Eugene de Mazenod (1782-1861), the Bishop of Marseille, who, in 1826, founded the Oblates of Mary Immaculate (the Oblate Fathers). The Canadian Northern Railway surveyed the route for the railway through the area in 1911, and in 1912 the rail bed was graded and the townsite for Mazenod was purchased from a homesteader, William Galloway. A small hamlet began to develop, and in 1913 the tracks were laid through the district and the first grain elevator was built in the community. Eventually, there would come to be six. The railway station was built in 1914, the first doctor arrived, and the local school was established (it was known as Edward Grey School until the name was changed to Mazenod in 1937). Mazenod hosted its first agricultural fair in 1915. Early businesses included a general store, a drug store, a hardware store, dray services, a boarding house, farm implement dealers, a Bank of Toronto, lumber yards, harness and blacksmith shops, a pool hall and barber shop, livery stables, a laundry, a photographer, a dressmaker, and a hotel with a dining room. Churches were built. On June 22, 1917, Mazenod was incorporated as a village. In the early 1920s, the population reached its all-time high, when it was hovering around 180. The community's numbers dropped during the 1930s and 1940s, and not nearly as many businesses were left operating afterwards. But by 1956 the population had risen to 173. By the mid-1960s, however, the population was below 100, and thereafter it steadily declined. The railway station was closed in 1967, and as the 1970s opened, the school, too, was closed. In 1979, Mazenod still had two elevator companies, two churches, a Co-op service station, two mechanics, a gravelling business, a community hall, a curling rink, a fire hall, and the post office. But at this time, the population was falling fast. It was 70 in 1976; by 1981 it was 43. Today, the Co-op bulk station remains, as does the postal outlet and the community hall. Sidewalks now run along many va-

▶ **MCCORD UNITED CHURCH.** Photograph taken September 4, 2003.

cant lots; no elevators are left standing. The school building, now long empty, still stands. On January 1, 2002, the Village of Mazenod was dissolved; the community's affairs have since been managed by the RM of Sutton No. 103.

MCCORD, organized hamlet, pop 40 (2006c), 45 (2001c), is situated in south-central Saskatchewan, just off Hwy 18, north of the East Block of Grasslands National Park. The NWMP Wood Mountain-Fort Walsh Trail ran just south of the community. The first homesteads in the area were filed on in 1909; in 1910, the country began to be occupied. Over the ensuing years a small hamlet about a mile north of present McCord emerged, known locally as "Four Corners," where a store, stopping place, a blacksmith shop, a livery stable, and a few other businesses became established. While other post offices had been operating in the region for a number of years, in 1917, those at Four Corners decided they should have their own. On June 1 that year, the McCord Post Office was established at the locale, its name honouring the landowner. In 1928, as the CPR survey was taking place for the line that would run from Wood Mountain to Mankota (the original plan was to connect with Val Marie), the businesses at Four Corners moved south to where the rail line would be built. The first grain elevators were erected in 1928 and 1929, and by the latter year, trains were running and a local school district centred on the new hamlet was established. Five grain elevators lined the tracks by 1930. McCord once had a peak population of about

150, and was established as an organized hamlet in 1960. The community's numbers began to declined significantly in the 1960s; by 1972, the population was down to 72. By 1986, McCord had only 47 residents. The CPR abandoned the rail line in the late 1990s; the last train went through in 1998, and the tracks were lifted in 1999. In 2000, McCord's school was closed; on June 24 that year, the community gathered for the closing ceremonies. The former CPR station now houses a museum dedicated to the life of the area pioneers. Built in 1928, the station had been in use until its closure in 1970. It was purchased and renovated by the McCord Museum Committee, and has since been designated a municipal heritage property. Another community landmark is the former Saskatchewan Wheat Pool elevator dating to 1928. It was sold by the Pool in 1992 and is now privately owned. The United Church in McCord was still active in 2007. McCord is located in the RM of Mankota No. 45; farming and ranching are the main industries in the region.

MCLEAN, village, pop 275 (2006c), 271 (2001c), lies halfway between the towns of Balgonie and Qu'Appelle on Hwy 1. With the construction of the CPR main line through the region in 1882, the first homesteaders began taking up land in the McLean district. On April 1, 1884, the McLean Post Office was established, its name honouring William J. McLean, who had been the Hudson's Bay Company factor at Fort Qu'Appelle. W. J. McLean was later the factor at Fort Pitt during the North-West Resistance. He successfully negotiated the surrender of his family and the fort's other civilians to Big Bear's followers who had surrounded the fort, thus allowing the hopelessly outnumbered NWMP detachment to withdraw to Fort Battleford. W. J. McLean later became an inspector with the Department of Indian Affairs. The McLean Post Office closed temporarily between 1889 and 1893. In 1895, there were reportedly only four buildings at McLean — a railway section

▲ **THE MCLEAN POST OFFICE, 1928.** Mrs. Charlie Cates is sitting in the car; Avis Elizabeth Smith, the postmistress from 1920 to 1945, is sitting on the steps. Saskatchewan Archives Board R-B7926.

▼ **BEAVER LUMBER OFFICE AT MCLEAN, 1911.** B.D. Smith is behind the counter. Saskatchewan Archives Board R-B8843.

house, a schoolhouse (the school district was established in 1886), a log house, and a shack. Over time, farmers established a number of granaries along the track at the locale in which to store wheat prior to shovelling it into freight cars. As railway branch lines were not built north or south of the CPR main line for many years, crops were hauled to McLean from over a considerable area. In the early 1900s, McLean began to develop more rapidly. Businesses were established and the box car used as a station was replaced in 1906 with a proper station house. In 1911, McLean became the meeting place for the council of the Rural Municipality of South Qu'Appelle, but by the end of 1916 the council had moved back to the town of Qu'Appelle for their meetings. McLean was incorporated as a village in 1913; however, as the community's population plummeted over the following years to a point where there were only a handful of resident ratepayers, a petition was sent to the Department of Municipal Affairs requesting the dissolution of the village. In 1919, the community reverted to hamlet status, its affairs again under the auspices of the rural municipality. In the 1930s, about two hundred cans of milk were shipped from McLean to Regina each morning, and CPR personnel began to refer to the community as "Cow Town," because of the volume of milk that was produced in the district. The dairying industry was important to the community for many years, and after rail shipments were curtailed in 1955, milk was then trucked into Regina. In November 1951, Canada's first and only outbreak of foot-and-mouth disease originated on a McLean farm. The case was officially diagnosed the following spring, but by then infected animals had been shipped to a Regina meat-processing plant, whose effluent contaminated farms along Wascana Creek. The United States immediately placed an embargo on the importation of cattle and meat products. Strict quarantine measures were enacted; farms, vehicles, and all potential carriers of the highly contagious virus were meticulously disinfected, and roughly four thousand animals had to be destroyed before the outbreak was brought under control. In 1957, the completion of the Saskatchewan section of the Trans-Canada Highway had a direct and lasting impact on McLean. Increasingly, village residents were seeking the goods and services available in Regina, and, simultaneously, city workers were seeking rural living. On September 1, 1966, McLean was once again incorporated as a village. Running water improved community living in the late 1960s, and in 1976 a sewage system was installed. McLean's businesses were closing, though, superseded by those in the city, and a number of buildings were either demolished or moved away. Today, a large number of those living in McLean, or on acreages in the surrounding countryside, commute to work in Regina. McLean School is a K-8 facility, which had 60 students enrolled in the fall of 2006. Students attend high school at Greenall School in Balgonie. There are three active churches in McLean, and the hotel has a bar and a restaurant. A community landmark that would have been noted by passing travellers for many years was the towering coal dock built in 1920. It was in continuous use until steam locomotives were replaced by diesels and, in April 1961, it was demolished. McLean is situated in the RM of South Qu'Appelle No. 157.

MCTAGGART, village, pop 114 (2006c), 126 (2001c), is situated 11 km northwest of Weyburn on Hwy 39 and the CPR's "Soo Line." The community's name honours an early railway employee. Although the railway, following a line from the United States, was completed from North Portal through Estevan and Weyburn to Moose Jaw in 1893, it was not until about 1898 that the first settlers took up land in the McTaggart area. The actual beginnings of McTaggart date to about 1904 when the first businesses began to emerge. The McTaggart Post Office was established on June 1, 1904. That year, the first grain elevator — the first of four that once stood in McTaggart — was also erected. A school was opened in 1905, and in 1906 the railway station was built. McTaggart was incorporated on October 5, 1909, and during these early years the community flourished. Numerous stores and shops, a large hotel, a bank, a drug store, implement dealerships, and lumberyards were among the businesses operating before the 1920s. By 1912, McTaggart boasted four churches, and the population of the village proper was approaching 150, with many more living in the surrounding farming district. McTaggart also had a skating rink and a competitive hockey team, which played against rivals up and down the Soo Line. Two major fires in the early 1920s, however, destroyed a good portion of the community's business district; it was never rebuilt. Another fire in 1935 further decimated the village, and this, coupled with the effects of the Depression, reduced McTaggart's numbers significantly — the population had fallen to 64 by the time the Census was taken in 1941. In the late 1950s, due to declining enrollment, the senior grades from McTaggart School began to be bused to Weyburn, and in 1963 McTaggart School was closed entirely. In 1964, the CPR station was closed, the building sold and moved

out of town. Also, in the mid-1960s, the last of the village churches — the United and the Catholic — closed their doors. The rebuilding and expansion of Hwy 39 in 1967 was also to have a dramatic impact on the community: all the buildings along Railway Avenue were either demolished or moved, and a number of large trees which had lined the thoroughfare were uprooted and destroyed. With the development of the new highway, and with the installation of a modern community water system in 1975, McTaggart began to experience renewed residential growth. Commuting to work in Weyburn from the village became a popular option for some. At the same time, however, what were almost the only remaining businesses in the community — the elevators — were facing their demise as farmers began hauling their crop to the newly-constructed inland terminal in Weyburn. McTaggart was no longer the commercial hub of the local farming district. Today, the community retains its post office, but other than a couple of home-based businesses, there are no other services or stores in the village. Weyburn provides McTaggart residents with a full range of amenities: shopping, employment opportunities, educational institutions, recreational facilities, entertainment, and medical and police services, and McTaggart is now largely a bedroom community to the city. McTaggart is situated in the RM of Weyburn No. 67.

MEACHAM, village, pop 70 (2006c), 90 (2001c), is situated northeast of Colonsay, approximately 60 km east of Saskatoon on Hwy 2. Settlement of the region began in the early 1900s. Meacham's origins date to the survey for the rail line through the area c. 1912. The village was incorporated on June 19,

▲ **THE GRAIN ELEVATOR AT MEACHAM**, August 9, 2004.

1912, and the Meacham Post Office was established on August 1 that year — the origins of the community's name are unclear. Trains were running within a couple of years, and in 1914 a local school district was established. From a population of only 44 in 1916, Meacham grew to number 221 residents by 1931, but the 1930s took their toll on the community. The population had dropped to 148 by 1941, but subsequently rose again to a peak of 245 in 1961. Since that time, the village's numbers have steadily declined. Today, the community retains only a small number of businesses, which include a hotel/bar, the village office, the post office, a construction company, and a branch of the Colonsay Credit Union. The Meacham Co-op offers bulk fuel sales. A significant artistic community has developed in the village: potters, musicians, and actors call Meacham home. The Hand Wave Gallery represents and sells the works of several dozen artists working in a variety of media, and the Dancing Sky Theatre

company presents several productions a year in a converted community hall with seating for about 100. Pre-show dinners in the facility are an option. The rail line south of Meacham was abandoned in the late 1970s, and the line north in the late 1990s. Although the tracks have since been torn up, a former Saskatchewan Wheat Pool elevator dating to 1950 still stands as a village landmark. The Meacham area economy is based upon agriculture and the potash industry. Crops grown in the district include red spring wheat, barley, oats, flax, canola, mustard, lentils, and peas; there are area cattle producers and intensive dairy and hog operations. Potash mines are located near Young, Allan, and Guernsey. Meacham is situated in the RM of Colonsay No. 342.

MEADOW LAKE, town, pop 4,771 (2006c), 4,582 (2001c), is located 160 km north of North Battleford on Hwys 4 and 55. The history of Meadow Lake dates from the fur trade. In 1799, Peter Fidler, working for the Hudson's Bay Company, travelled south along the Beaver River from Ile-a-la-Crosse, then entered the Meadow River and followed it to its source, a lake that would become known as *Lac des Prairies*, or "Meadow Lake." He and his companions constructed a log building as a company post, naming it Bolsover House, after Fidler's birthplace in England. Although the post did not flourish and shortly closed, Fidler was a master surveyor and Meadow Lake was now on the map. As the fur trade increased dramatically along the western Churchill River during the 1880s, a route was established from Ile-a-la-Crosse south through Green Lake and then southeast toward Fort Carlton. Small settlements sprang up along the way. Eventually, people migrated westward to the Meadow Lake area, and around 1879 Cyprien and Mary Morin from Ile-a-la-Crosse became the first to settle permanently at the site of the future community. Other Métis families followed in the coming years. Preliminary surveys were made in the district, and soon reports of the agricultural possibilities of the area surfaced. In 1888, the area directly west of the lake was surveyed for a future townsite, and in 1889 Cree signatories to Treaty Six assumed title to a reserve just north of the lake. They are now known as the Flying Dust First Nation. Cyprien Morin established a Hudson's Bay Company Post at Meadow Lake, traded in furs, and raised horses and cattle. The first Roman Catholic Church was built on the Morin's land. Although the Métis families who settled at Meadow Lake prospered, it was not until 1907-08 that subsequent settlers began to arrive in the area. In 1919, a massive forest fire swept through the region, and the waning fur trade in the Meadow Lake region was decimated. From Green Lake to Big River the earth was blackened, the lumber industry devastated. The community of Big River almost did not recover. Land was, however, further opened up for homesteads and agriculture. The pace of settlement quickened, and by the end of the 1920s most of the prime agricultural land was taken. The remaining marginal lands were taken up by dust bowl refugees from southern Saskatchewan. As the railway approached at the beginning of the decade, an economic boom began, and Meadow Lake was incorporated as a village on August 24, 1931. By 1936, the population of the community was 800, and on February 1 that year, Meadow Lake attained town status. Ten years later, in 1946, the population was 1,456 and, in another decade, approaching twice that. Forestry, fishing, and farming dominated the economy, with the area's agricultural output ever increasing. By the mid-1950s, more grain was shipped out of Meadow Lake than from any other point in rural Canada. Meadow Lake continues to grow, and at its current rate the town is poised to gain city status in the near future. It is somewhat of a younger community, the average age being close to 32 in 2006, while the median age for all Saskatchewan residents was just under 39. Meadow Lake serves an additional trading area population of 15,000 people; the primary industries in the region continue to be forestry and agriculture and, increasingly, tourism. Meadow Lake serves as the administrative centre of the RM of Meadow Lake No. 588.

◄ **MEADOW LAKE TOWN HALL.**
Constructed in 1938 by the federal government, this public building served as the community's post office until 1980. The upper floor housed offices for the RCMP from 1938 until 1954. After a new post office was built in Meadow Lake in 1979, the older building was then acquired by the Town for use as a town office. In 1992, it was designated a municipal heritage property. Photograph taken July 23, 2003.

MEATH PARK, village, pop 179 (2006c), 204 (2001c), is located approximately 40 km northeast of Prince Albert near the junctions of Hwys 55, 120, and 355. The origins of Meath Park were about six and a half kilometres south of the community's present location — the first Meath Park post office was established in 1913 on NW7-51-23-W2. While settlers in the district included people of British origins — the name Meath Park is derived from that of the county of Meath in Ireland — the area was most significantly settled by people of Ukrainian and Polish stock, who began to arrive in 1906-07. In the early 1930s, as the railway was being built to link Prince Albert with Nipawin, the CPR established a location for a station at the present village site, and the name Meath Park was eventually adopted for the community that sprang up at the locale. The old Meath Park post office was renamed Janow Corners in 1938, the same year as the Village of Meath Park was incorporated. The community developed as a service centre for the surrounding agricultural district, and its population grew from 130 in 1941 to a peak of 298 in 1976. The population has subsequently steadily declined, and in the 1990s the rail line through the community was abandoned. Now, no grain elevators are left standing in the village. Meath Park School, however, remains a key community institution. It is a K-12 facility which had 328 students enrolled in the fall of 2006. The village also retains a small core of businesses which includes a grocery store, a café, a tavern, a credit union, and the post office. The former CPR railway station, now a heritage property, houses a daycare centre. Today, Meath Park residents largely access the amenities that the city of Prince Albert has to offer, and find recreational opportunities close at hand with Candle Lake Provincial Park just a short distance to the north, and Prince Albert National Park not far to the northwest. An annual community event held in the village is the Meath Park Polka Festival, which takes place in August. Meath Park serves as the administrative centre of the RM of Garden River No. 490.

MEDSTEAD, village, pop 148 (2006c), 144 (2001c), lies in the parklands 46 km west of Spiritwood and about 80 km north of the Battlefords on Hwy 794. About 20 km north of Medstead, agricultural lands give way to forest. The first settlers in the district began arriving about 1907-08, and the community takes its name from an area post office established on January 1, 1911. The Rural Municipality of Medstead was formed in 1913. Sources differ as to where the name Medstead comes from: several state that it was to have been Medford, after

the United States hometown of the first postmaster, but that this was rejected by postal authorities as being too similar to Melfort, and thus the name was revised to Medstead; another source claims the name honours a place of the same name in England. In the spring of 1926, the CNR cut the right-of-way through the present townsite and the tracks were laid that fall. A grain elevator was built, and in 1927 trains were coming in from North Battleford via Speers, and the post office moved in from the country. Soon other businesses sprang up, the population of the new hamlet grew, and on April 23, 1931, Medstead became an incorporated village. That year, a school district centred on the community was established. The railway had been connected to Prince Albert in 1929, ran south through Hatherleigh to North Battleford the following year, and in 1931 the CPR built a line from Medstead that connected with its Meadow Lake subdivision. For many years, close to 30 trains a week passed through the village, and in the early years, as land in the area was being cleared, a good amount of cordwood was shipped out of the community. Even in the 1950s, a large portion of the land surrounding the village had not been broken for crop production; a large number

of area farmers relied on beef and dairy herds, as well as hogs and sheep, to provide a living. In 1946, a DC power plant was established in Medstead; up until that time only a few buildings such as the hotel and a few homes had their own battery-run power supplies. Ten years later, in 1956, the Saskatchewan Power Corporation arrived and then everyone on area farms had electricity. Also by 1956, Medstead had reached a peak population of 202. Today, local businesses in Medstead include a grocery store, a credit union, a service station, a hotel, the post office, a construction company and home-based tradespeople; additionally, a number of businesses service the area's agricultural industry. These include a feedlot, a farm supply dealer, and various custom operations offering grain cleaning, processing, hauling, and silage harvesting. Medstead also has a K-12 school which had 166 village and area students enrolled in the fall of 2006; as well, the village has an arena, a curling rink, a library, churches, and a community hall. The school is a major employer. Residents of Medstead travel to North Battleford or Spiritwood for larger purchases and health services. Medstead serves as the administrative centre of the RM of Medstead No. 497.

MELFORT, city, pop 5,192 (2006c), 5,559 (2001c), is a leading agricultural service centre in northeastern Saskatchewan, 96 km southeast of Prince Albert at the junction of Hwys 3, 6, and 41. Melfort dubs itself "the City of Northern Lights," due to the aurora borealis frequently observed in the night skies for much of the year. Among the first settlers in the district were Reginald Beatty, formerly with the Hudson's Bay Company, and for whom the village of Beatty was named, and his wife Mary. The Beattys took up land about three miles south of present-day Melfort in 1884, and for several years the Beatty home was prominent among the very few in the area. In 1892, more settlers began arriving and a post office was set up, named Melfort after Mary Beatty's family estate and birthplace in Scotland. By the beginning of the 1900s what was locally referred to as the Stoney Creek settlement had developed significantly. The Canadian Northern Railway surveyed the townsite of present-day Melfort in 1902; the first structures went up that year and development was rapid. People moved to the rail line locale and, on November 4, 1903, even before the rail line was completed, Melfort was incorporated as a village. The railway came through in 1904 and the first grain elevator was erected. Within a few years Melfort had grown into a sizable community; it attained town status on July 1, 1907. That year, the Lady Minto Hospital opened — one of the driving forces behind the hospital was Dr. Alfred Schmitz Shadd. Shadd had come to the Kinistino area from Ontario in 1896 to teach school, and was likely the only Black educator out of approximately 400 employed in the territories at the time. He was also certainly the first Black person

many people in the district had ever seen. Shadd had studied medicine and, seeing the great need for doctors in the area, he returned to Ontario and completed his medical degree in 1898. He returned to Kinistino and set up a medical practice, quickly earning the admiration of both the area's settlers and the indigenous population. He later moved his practice to Melfort, where he set up a drug store, became the editor of the newspaper, and served on the town's council. He ran unsuccessfully in the territorial election in 1901, and in 1905 came within 52 votes of becoming the first Black ever elected to a provincial legislature. His funeral in Melfort in 1915 is said to have been the largest the community has ever had. By 1909, five grain elevators lined the railway tracks in Melfort, and about 1,000,000 bushels of grain were shipped out of the community that year. A creamery built in 1910 was producing up to 240,000 pounds of butter per year by 1917. By 1921, the population of the town was 1,746; by the early 1950s it was nudging 3,000; and by the opening of the 1960s it was over 4,000. In the 1950s, Melfort served a trading area population of tens of thousands, rail lines emanating out of the town in seven directions carried at least 70 passenger trains weekly, and each week about the same number of buses passed through. In the early 1960s, hundreds of properties were developed, and Melfort had become Saskatchewan's largest town. On September 2, 1980, Melfort attained city status, becoming the province's twelfth city. It had a peak population of 6,078 in 1986, but the community has been struggling with a decline ever since. Today, as it has been from the beginning, the Melfort economy is largely sustained by agriculture: the Agriculture and Agri-Food Canada Melfort Research Farm develops sustainable crop

production technologies for the black and grey soil zones of the northern prairies; meat processing, seed-cleaning plants, feed mills, the distribution of farm chemicals, and grain storage and handling are key economic components; and the sale and service of agricultural equipment and supplies factor heavily into the city's annual retail activity. The current trading area population numbers approximately 60,000. Within the Melfort region, approximately 1,000 people are employed in manufacturing and processing; transportation, service, health care, and education sectors are additional significant employers. Tourism is another major industry — several millions of dollars are spent by travellers in the Melfort area annually. There are currently high hopes in the region that the diamond exploration activities taking place in the Fort à la Corne Provincial Forest north of Melfort will lead to the development of economically viable mining operations. Melfort has four elementary schools, and a large high school, which combined had a student population of more than 1,200 enrolled in the fall of 2006. Cumberland Regional College offers a range of programs and post-secondary courses for adults. The community is served by an RCMP detachment and a volunteer fire department, both of which have close to two dozen members. Melfort has a full range of health care practitioners and facilities, including the largest hospital in the region. The Northern Lights Palace in Melfort is home to the Melfort Mustangs hockey team and is a multi-purpose facility used for concerts and trade shows. It also houses a wave pool/water slide/swimming complex. Major media outlets in Melfort are the *Melfort Journal* and Radio CJVR. Several buildings in the city have been designated heritage properties: the Spence residence (1907), the

▲ **MAIN STREET, MELFORT.** Farmers have come into town to market their grain, likely in the 1910s. Saskatchewan Archives Board R-A219.

▼ **THE CARROT RIVER VALLEY FLOUR MILL AND ELEVATOR** in Melfort opened in 1904. The first sack of flour produced was presented to Mary Beatty. Saskatchewan Archives Board R-A228-4.

▼ **THE MELFORT BAND** in 1910 at Tisdale, where they performed at the community's sports day. Saskatchewan Archives Board R-B723.

1912 brick power plant (now housing a museum), the 1916 water tower (originally at the Prince Albert Penitentiary), the McKendry residence (1918), the provincial telephone building (1922), and the court house (1928). Melfort is situated in the RM of Star City No. 428.

MELVILLE, city, pop 4,149 (2006c), 4,453 (2001c), lies 43 km southwest of Yorkton and 144 km northeast of Regina at the junction of Hwys 10, 15, and 47. It is the smallest city in Saskatchewan, smaller than a number of towns, yet it serves a trading area population of approximately 50,000 people. Although the district had been well-settled for years, Melville had its beginnings in 1907-08 with the construction of the Grand Trunk Pacific Railway line through the area. This would be part of a second trans-continental railway, a line that ran from Winnipeg through Melville, to Saskatoon and Edmonton, terminating at Prince Rupert, which offered western farmers an alternative route for shipping grain. Melville's future as a larger prairie town, perhaps a city, was determined with the railway company's decision to establish the locale as a divisional point on the line. This would guarantee a good amount of infrastructure and would ensure many jobs. Melville was named after Charles Melville Hays (1856-1912), general manager, and later president (1909), of the Grand Trunk Pacific Railway, who died in the *Titanic* disaster. Land for the townsite was purchased in 1906, the first in a flood of new businesses started in 1907, and the rail line opened in 1908. Melville was incorporated as a village on December 21, 1908, and became a town on November 1, 1909. By 1911, the population was nudging 2,000. The years leading into WWI saw major developments: coal docks were

▲ **PASSENGERS AT THE CNR STATION IN MELVILLE, 1976.**
Saskatchewan Archives Board R-B11756-2. Courtesy of Charles Bohi, White River Junction, Vermont, U.S.A.

erected, a power plant was built, a hospital was built, the Melville Milling Company commenced operations, a creamery was established, Luther Academy (now Luther College in Regina) had its beginnings, and the community's hockey team, the *Melville Millionaires*, were Allan Cup champions in the 1914-15 season. It was a highlight in the community's formative years. Another of the most celebrated events in Melville's history was the June 3, 1939, stop made by King George VI and Queen Elizabeth during their cross-country tour. Although scheduled only for a 10-minute whistle stop, their Majesties lengthened their stay into almost an hour in view of the magnitude of the crowd that greeted them. An estimated 60,000 people had arrived at Melville Station, including 10,000 schoolchildren waving flags. They had come by car, on open trucks, and by horse and buggy, overwhelming the town of Melville which then had a population of about 4,000. By the beginning of the 1960s, Melville numbered more than 5,000, and it attained city status on August 1, 1960, becoming the eleventh city in the province. In 1966, Melville had a peak population of 5,690. For the first half of the twentieth century the railway

(which had become Canadian National in 1919) was by far the largest employer in the community. By 1911, another rail line bisected Melville running from Yorkton to Regina. The multi-million-dollar payroll of railway company employees, who

numbered in the hundreds, made its impact felt in the economic life of the city. As the century passed, the importance of the railway became less paramount. While agriculture, particularly grain production, was a key part of the area economy, Melville also developed into a processing hub for growing dairy and poultry industries. Small manufacturing companies also emerged. Today, the city has approximately 200 stores and services. It is home to the head office of the provincial government's Saskatchewan Crop Insurance Corporation, as well as plants operated by industrial leaders such as Babcock & Wilcox and Century Glass. The Canadian National Railway remains a major employer; others include St. Peter's Hospital and St. Paul Lutheran Home. The city has a full range of medical facilities and practitioners, four elementary schools and one high

▼ **TUESDAY, JULY 31, 2001.** A fire which began just before midnight the previous day destroys a Saskatchewan Wheat Pool elevator in Melville. Nobody was injured in the blaze. Photograph courtesy of Leona Bisch, Grayson, Saskatchewan.

school. Together, the five schools had a total enrollment of 957 students in the fall of 2006. Parkland Regional College offers a range of programs and post-secondary courses for adults. Melville has an array of facilities for recreation: Melville Stadium is home to the *Melville Millionaires*; the Merv Moore Sportsplex houses a second ice surface; an 18-hole golf course bounds the city's northern perimeter; fair grounds and a regional park lie at the city's northeast. There are six neighbourhood parks in Melville and two museums: the Melville Railway Museum and the Melville Heritage Museum. Melville Community Works is a complex dedicated to arts, culture, and recreation; it includes gallery, studio, and performance spaces and facilitates artistic workshops for youth and adults in a variety media. Melville has a number of service clubs, sports organizations, and groups involved in artistic, cultural, and recreational activities. There are numerous churches serving many denominations in the community: five churches have been designated municipal heritage properties. The city has many fine examples of early-twentieth-century architecture — no fewer than 10 of Melville's landmark properties have been designated heritage properties over the years. Melville is served by the *Melville Advance*, a weekly newspaper published each Wednesday. Melville serves as the administrative centre of the RM of Cana No. 214.

MELVILLE BEACH, resort village, inc. 1983, is located in the eastern Qu'Appelle Valley, southwest of Grayson on Crooked Lake. There are approximately 40 permanent residents, although the population reaches up to 250 during the summer months. Cottages date to the 1930s. Melville Beach is situated in the RM of Grayson No. 184.

MENDHAM, village, pop 35 (2006c), 40 (2001c), is located southwest of Leader, 8 km west of Hwy 21 and 26 km east of the Saskatchewan-Alberta border. Agriculture, a mixture of grain and livestock production, is the major industry in the district, although there has been increasing development in the area gas fields. Only a few ranchers were in the region when homesteaders began arriving in 1908. These were predominantly Germans from southern Russia, although a small percentage were Scottish, Irish, and English. The first crops were harvested in 1909 and, prior to the arrival of the railway in Leader in 1913, area residents would have to make the long three-day trip to Maple Creek on the CPR main line to deliver grain or obtain supplies. The village of Mendham itself began to take shape with the construction of the Burstall railway subdivision in the early 1920s. By the time the line reached Mendham in 1923, four grain elevators had been constructed and a small business community was established. By 1930 the community numbered over 100 people, and on April

▲ **THE COMMUNITY HALL** in Mendham, built circa 1944-45. Photograph taken August 30, 2003.

1 that year the Village of Mendham was incorporated. Mendham reached its peak in the years following WWII. In the early 1950s the area produced bumper crops and Mendham's elevators were overflowing; the village had a population of over 200 from the middle of the decade through to the mid-60s. However, since the early 1970s, the population has plummeted, the largest decline occurring between the 1986 and 1991 censuses when the population fell from 103 to 43 over the five-year period. Today, most of the former businesses on Main Street stand abandoned. Mendham is located in the RM of Happyland No. 231.

▼ **THIS MURAL IN MENDHAM** commemorates the 1995 balloon landing near the village of the famous American aviator, sailor, and adventurer, Steve Fossett. Fossett had taken off from South Korea and became the first person to make a solo balloon flight across the Pacific Ocean. In 2002, he became the first person to fly solo, non-stop around the world in a balloon. In September of 2007 Fossett went missing in a single-engine aircraft in the rugged high country of northwestern Nevada, and by late November 2007, he still had not been found and was presumed dead. The Mendham mural was painted by "the Kurtz Girls" in 2003. Photograph taken August 30, 2003.

MEOTA, village, pop 297 (2006c), 293 (2001c), sprawls along the southwest shore of Jackfish Lake, about 37 km northwest of North Battleford, on Hwy 26. The land is gently rolling, covered with bluffs of aspen and willow. Situated at Meota is Meota Regional Park, with a wide array of recreational amenities; immediately to the east is the organized hamlet of Lakeview, one of the many resort communities that encircle both Jackfish and nearby Murray Lakes. With its expensive lakefront homes, well-treed streets, golf courses, sailing and curling clubs, beach, boat launch, ball diamonds, sand volleyball courts, and horseshoe pits, Meota has become something like the kind of place the board of trade formed in 1911 dreamed of. They envisioned Meota as the Coney Island or Newport of Saskatchewan, and subsequently the village has always been tied to the resort industry and the resort areas it serves. Summers have brought a brisk trade as several generations of cottage owners have come to the area. Meota became an incorporated village on July 6, 1911, but its history predates that by a number of years. Familiar to travellers between Forts Carlton and Pitt, the area attracted the attention of at least one enterprising rancher in the early 1880s — Robert Wyld, formerly with the NWMP. Others followed after the 1885 Resistance. In 1889-90, Québécois and a few Batoche-area Métis settled at Jackfish Lake. By 1894, most of the district land was surveyed, but the greatest influx of settlers came after 1900. Within a few years, all available homesteads were occupied. Those who settled the area were of diverse origins: Métis, French, Scottish, English, Irish, Scandinavian, and a sprinkling from various other regions of

▶ **BUILDING BOOM.** Once only rustic cabins lined the shores of Jackfish Lake. Increasingly, expensive luxury homes are being built, such as these in Meota. Photograph taken July 24, 2003.

Europe. In 1894, a post office by the name of Meota was established at the south end of Jackfish Lake (about where present-day Metinota is located) — the name is derived from a Cree phrase referring to a good place to camp. By the early 1900s, a few homesteaders were established on the land where the village of Meota now stands; with the advent of a railway coming north from North Battleford, some entrepreneurs began to recognize the resort potential of the locale. The Canadian Northern Railway began work on the roadbed from North Battleford in 1909, and before the line through to Edam was opened in 1911 Meota was already fairly well established. A post office set up in 1910 had operated for several months under the name of Beachview; however, when the railway company bought the townsite and a name for it had to be decided upon, older settlers pressured for the name to be Meota, and the name was adopted. Between 1910 and 1915 there was a flurry of activity. First a store and then a hotel were built; shortly, the village had a wide range of businesses to cater to not only summer vacationers, but the growing agricultural district as well. The first grain elevator was built in 1912; in time there would be three. In 1921, a dance pavilion opened on the lakeshore; outside, boats offered pleasure cruises on the lake. The pavilion was a popular destination for decades, and some of the last performers were Buddy Knox, the Checkers, and Bobby Curtola. The land-

mark was destroyed by fire in July 1963. Other business ventures established early in Meota's history included a local brick plant (Meota's first school erected in 1914 was built of local brick, and a number of homes in the district built of Meota brick still stand); additionally, there was a cement block factory, which lasted until the village council halted operations due to the depletion of beach sand; a flour mill was constructed in 1924. Another, more long-lived business venture was commercial fishing. It began in the 1890s and lasted for several decades — "Meota Whites" were shipped frozen to New York City at one time — and the industry greatly augmented the incomes of many people in the district. Today, Meota lacks the commercial activity of earlier times — the proximity of North Battleford lures many for shopping and services — and the townsite barely resembles that of yesteryear. Besides the loss of the pavilion, fires have claimed many community landmarks over the years, including the 1911 two-storey Edward Hotel, which once boasted hot and cold running water, gas lights, and a telephone in every room. It burned to the ground in 1928. Today, village businesses offer basic amenities such as groceries, gas, liquor, a hotel and café, a credit union and an insurance broker; additionally, Meota has Anglican,

Catholic, and United Churches, a community hall and library. Meota Elementary School remains as a K-3 school that had 13 students enrolled in the fall of 2006. High school students began to be bused to North Battleford in 1967; by 1978, grades 7 and 8 were as well. The Meota Municipal Office, built in 1924, was designated a heritage property in 1982. Meota has a team of first responders and a volunteer fire department; the nearest RCMP, ambulatory service and hospital are located in North Battleford. While tourism has always been important to the economy, agriculture (a combination of grain and cattle production) and, increasingly, petroleum are the key area industries. The first area oil wells were drilled in the early 1970s. The 2006 Census of Canada recorded the village's highest-ever year-round population; the numbers during the summer months can be significantly greater. Today, Meota has partially become a bedroom community for a number of homeowners who commute to work in the Battlefords. Meota serves as the administrative centre of the RM of Meota No. 468.

MERRILL HILLS, organized hamlet, pop 79 (2006c), 72 (2001c), is a residential subdivision, essentially a bedroom community, located just southwest of the city of Saskatoon. It was established as an organized hamlet on January 1, 2003, and is situated in the RM of Corman Park No. 344.

MERVIN, village, pop 228 (2006c), 146 (2001c), is located 8 km southeast of Turtleford on Hwy 26. In the fall of 1906, Archibald and Mabel (Stewart) Gemmell left Manitoba and took up a homestead at SW24-50-21-W3, three miles west and a little south of the present village of Mervin. Their home became a stopping place for incoming settlers, and in 1908 when they established a post office, "Archie" named it Mervin, after a son from a previous marriage. It was near the Gemmell's home that the Clover Lake School District was established in 1908, and on the Gemmell's property that the first two stores to serve area settlers were started. A cemetery was established somewhat to the north. When the Canadian Northern Railway proceeded north from Edam toward St. Walburg in 1913, it was realized the track would pass to the east of the Gemmell's, and one of the stores relocated to "New Mervin," the townsite surveyed on the rail line. The other store-keeper relocated north to where Turtleford was developing. In 1914, trains were running and the post office was relocated to the townsite, bringing the name Mervin along with it. The name was adopted for the developing hamlet, and the nucleus of the old community was then known as "Old Mervin" for a number of years. Mervin developed rapidly following the arrival of the railway: three grain elevators were erected, a school was started, and numerous businesses were set up. A "town" hall was constructed in 1915, as was a sawmill, and a creamery was built in 1919. On March 17, 1920, the Village

of Mervin was incorporated. In 1921, the population was 126, and around this time the Standard Bank of Canada opened a branch. The community grew to number more than 200 by the end of the decade, and the population remained around that level until the 1970s, when it started to decline — the peak had been 231 in 1966. Mervin's grade 12 students began to be bused to Turtleford in 1962, and by 1980 the school was down to only one K-6 classroom. As Mervin's population fell, its business community was superseded by establishments in Turtleford, St. Walburg, and North Battleford. Today, most Main Street businesses are closed — the school and a hotel are boarded up. There is a Co-op, a post office, and a community complex that houses the village office and the library. There are also auto repair and excavating and trenching businesses. Mervin has an arena and a golf course with irrigated fairways and greens. The nearest RCMP detachment is in Turtleford, where there is also a health centre; the closest hospitals are in North Battleford, Paradise Hill, and Maidstone. Mixed grain and cattle farming (with raising cattle being predominant) remain key to the economy; logging, outfitting, and commercial guiding are other area occu-

pations. As well, Mervin benefits from the influx of tourists and cottagers that pass through each summer en route to Turtle and Brightsand Lakes. Most significant, however, is the increasing activity by the oil and gas industry in the region in recent years. The industry now employs a number of area residents and sustains several local businesses, and Mervin's population gains over the 2001-2006 period represents an increase of 56.2 per cent. Mervin is situated in the RM of Mervin No. 499.

MESKANAW, organized hamlet, pop 18 (2006c), 20 (2001c), is situated about 32 km southwest of Melfort on Hwy 41. The origins of Meskanaw date to the arrival of William Edward Traill (1842-1917), the district's pioneering settler. Formerly with the Hudson's Bay Company, Traill came to the area in the late 1890s to ranch, and his home — no doubt in part due to the presence of popular daughters — became a frequented stopping place for newcomers to the district. When it came time to set up a post

office to serve the area, people thought the name should be Traill, to honour the early pioneer. Since there was already a post office named Trail in British Columbia, this was rejected, and so the Cree word for a trail, or a path, *mêskanaw* was chosen instead. The post office was established on February 1, 1908, with W.E. Traill the postmaster until his death. An Anglican church had been built on Traill land (about a mile east of today's community) and the foundations of Meskanaw began at this locale. In 1929, with the construction of the Canadian National Railway line through the area, the present townsite was established. Meskanaw was set up as an organized hamlet in 1954, and in the mid-1960s had a population of about 100. By the early 1970s, however, the population was rapidly declining, and Meskanaw School closed in 1973. The rail line was abandoned at the beginning of the 1980s. Today, a combination grocery store/confectionary/post office/liquor vendor/coffee shop remains situated on a service road along the highway. Meskanaw is situated in the RM of Invergordon No. 430.

▼ **BUILT IN 1929**, the McCloy Creek Trestle, just west of Meskanaw, is the longest wooden structure left standing in the province. Photograph taken, looking east, August 10, 2004.

METINOTA, resort village, pop 89 (2006c), 69 (2001c), is situated on the south shore of Jackfish Lake, 33 km north of North Battleford. The name of the community, like that of nearby Meota, is derived from a Cree phrase meaning "a good place to camp." The origins of Metinota date to 1887 and the arrival of Henry Arthur Mannix, a military man who saw action during the Fenian raids, the Red River Resistance, and the North-West Resistance. Mannix homesteaded where Metinota is now situated and built a home for himself, his wife Helen, and their five children. He established a post office at the locale in 1894. In the early 1900s, with his family grown and his health failing, Mannix sold his property to land developers, and in 1909, 87 lots were put up for sale. People of means from North Battleford and other locales bought them up and made plans for summer homes. Metinota remained largely a summer destination until recent decades; increasingly, it is becoming somewhat of a bedroom community for a number of homeowners who commute to work in the Battlefords. Commercial enterprises were never developed at the resort, as people either brought supplies with them from the city or went to the nearby village of Meota to shop. The 2006 Census of Canada recorded the village's highest-ever year-round population; however, the numbers during the summer months can be significantly greater. Metinota was incorporated as a resort village on August 19, 1924, and is situated in the RM of Meota No. 468.

MEYRONNE, hamlet, pop 35 (2006c), 35 (2001c), is a former village situated in southern Saskatchewan, roughly midway between Assiniboia and Ponteix just south of Hwy 13. Pinto Creek flows just to the south of the community, merging into the Wood River a short distance to the east. The district was opened to homesteaders in 1908, but many squatters had arrived somewhat earlier. Settlers to the district were largely of British or French origin, from eastern Canada, or from England and the French-speaking countries of Europe. Smaller numbers of people of German and Norwegian backgrounds also settled in the region, most of these coming via the United States. These early pioneers often travelled to the Meyronne district overland from Moose Jaw (some walking), while others took the train as far as Morse before heading south. The Meyronne post office was established on June 1, 1909, a little northwest of the present community, but the village itself began to develop in 1913 with the construction of the railway between Assiniboia and Shaunavon. The Village of Meyronne was incorporated on October 21 that year. From its inception through to the beginning of the Depression, Meyronne developed rapidly, serving as a centre for commodities, services, grain handling, and social activities. The population jumped from 109 in 1916 to 357 in 1926, the community's peak. The completion of the Wood Mountain railway subdivision through to Mankota to the south in 1929 took business away from Meyronne, but it was the 1930s that really took a toll on the community — the village had lost 100 citizens by 1941. In the years following WWII, the population continued to steadily decline (it has been below 100 since the mid-1970s), and, today, a large percentage of the community's citizens are middle-aged to older people — a number are retirees. Meyronne's United Church was dissolved in 1969, the public school was closed in 1970, the separate school was closed in 1981, and the last grain elevator was demolished in 1987. Sidewalks now run along vacant lots; however, for a community of its size, Meyronne still retains important businesses and amenities. Village businesses consist of a Co-op bulk station and hardware store, a post office, and a credit union. There is a Catholic church, community and seniors' centres, a bowling alley, a playground and a campground. Groceries are obtainable in the village of Kincaid, some 14 kilometres west, where children also attend school. Kincaid also has the nearest rink for winter activities. Assiniboia, approximately 65 kilometres to the east, provides a larger shopping and service centre. Meyronne relinquished village status on September 5, 2006, and is situated in the RM of Pinto Creek No. 75.

MICHEL VILLAGE, northern hamlet, pop 70 (2001c), is located on the western shore of Peter Pond Lake, 87 km by road from Buffalo Narrows at the end of gravel road No. 925. Immediately south of Michel Village lies the reserve of the Buffalo River Dene Nation, headquartered at the community of Dillon. The on-reserve population is approximately 600. The residents of Michel Village (name derivation uncertain) are mainly non-treaty Dene, and while retention of the Denesuline language is low, many pursue traditional activities including trapping, fishing, and hunting as a part of their culture and a way of life. The hamlet of Michel Village is a relatively recent entity. Although people have lived in the locale for a number of decades, by the mid-1970s no businesses or services of any kind had been established, and the only access to the area was over a winter road. Communication with the outside world was via two-way radio. Michel Village began to develop somewhat during the 1970s when the population began to grow. By 1983, an all-weather road and power lines reached the community,

▼ **AN AERIAL VIEW OF MICHEL VILLAGE**, September 1979. Saskatchewan Archives Board, Saskatchewan Photographic Services, R-PS79-1453-405. Photographer: B. Weston.

and on November 1 that year Michel Village was formally established as a northern hamlet to meet the needs of managing community affairs and infrastructure. In the mid-1980s, Michel Village numbered between 110 to 125 people. A Catholic church, a community hall, a hamlet office, and a school became the core of the settlement. The school was closed in June 2003. Most goods and services are obtained in Dillon or Buffalo Narrows.

MIDALE, town, pop 462 (2006c), 496 (2001c), shares the distinction with the town of Yellow Grass as having had the highest temperature ever recorded in Canada. On July 5, 1937, the mercury in both communities hit a blistering 45°C (113°F). Located about midway between Weyburn and Estevan on Hwy 39, Midale is situated on the Soo Line, and it was this rail connection that allowed land seekers from the United States direct access to the area. A significant percentage of those who first settled the Midale district came from the states of Minnesota and Iowa. Many were of Norwegian and Swedish origin. Others would come from eastern Canada and other areas of Europe. The first homesteads in the district were filed on in 1901. Midale itself was established in the spring of 1903, when three new arrivals from the United States formed a partnership, establishing the Midale Mercantile Company and the first businesses on what would become Main Street and Railway Avenue. Many settlers arrived that year, and on June 12 the first baby was born in the burgeoning settlement. In 1907, Midale was incorporated as a village, with a variety of business, three grain elevators, a doctor, churches, and a school in operation. With the opening of the Canadian Northern Railway line between Lampman and Radville in 1911, Midale became a junction for passengers and goods transferred between the railways. Abandonment of the east-west line in the early 1950s was hastened by the flood waters of the Souris River, which had undermined the integrity of much of the track. The discovery of oil in the Midale area in 1953 not only diversified the economy, which had been based solely upon agriculture, but also led to a doubling of the village population. In 1951, the population of the community was 400; by the mid-1960s, during the main years of oil exploration and drilling operations, Midale's numbers peaked at just under 800. Midale attained town status in 1962. Although the population subsequently levelled off, the oil industry has come to be the predominant contributor to the area economy, and today pumpjacks dot the landscape. Agriculture continues to include grain and cattle production. The town has a health centre with an attached special care home and a K-12 school, which had 145 students enrolled in the fall of 2006. The community houses an exceptional museum, boasting over 17,000 antiques and pioneer artifacts. The collection was begun by Maynard Moser, Midale's barber for 42 years. Roughly 15 kilometres west of Midale lies Mainprize Regional Park, named in honour of another of Midale's long-time residents, Dr. William Mainprize, who served the area for close to 50 years. The park has facilities for camping and golf and offers excellent opportunities for fishing. Midale has a small commercial core; the nearby cities of Weyburn and Estevan provide a full range of services. In the summer of 2003, Midale celebrated its centennial. Notable personalities from the Midale area are Ken and Brad Johner. The multi-award-winning performers were voted 'Entertainers of the Decade' by the Saskatchewan Country Music Association in the 1990s and received national and international acclaim. Brad Johner has since embarked on a successful solo career. Midale serves as the administrative centre of the RM of Cymri No. 36.

MIDDLE LAKE, village, pop 277 (2006c), 300 (2001c), is located in a picturesque parkland setting 45 km northwest of Humboldt off Hwy 20. The community, which sits adjacent to Lucien Lake Regional Park, is named after nearby Middle Lake (so named for its position between Basin Lake and Lake Lenore). Settlement of the area began around 1905-06. Immigrants were mostly of German and Hungarian origins, migrating from the United States and Europe, and the beginnings of the community of Middle Lake were nearer the lake from which the present village derives its name. Thus it was to the northeast of today's community that a post office, school, store, farm implement shops, a municipal office, and a pool room were first established. In 1907, the construction of the CPR branch line from Lanigan toward Prince Albert had been given the go-ahead, and in 1909 a proposed route was approved. The line was to run in a north-westerly direction from Humboldt to Wakaw, on a path about 10 kilometres west of the present community. This would have bypassed a number of the developing hamlets southwest of the three lakes. Petitions were put forth with force, and changes to the route were made in 1913. Construction was put on hold due to WWI, and then following the War it was still another 15 years before work proceeded. Finally, in the summer and fall of 1929, work on the rail bed was undertaken; however, no provision had been made for a townsite between Pilger and St. Benedict — the residents of Middle Lake vigorously pressured authorities for one in between. The battle was won, and the grading for the Middle Lake elevators and siding was done in October that year. In the spring of 1930, the first building was dragged in from the northeast using two tractors and 16 horses. Soon elevators, a number of stores, and various other businesses sprang up, creating a trading centre for the surrounding agricultural district. Regular rail service

▶ **MIDALE HERITAGE VILLAGE** features a streetscape of preserved area buildings, which reflect the history of south-eastern Saskatchewan from the turn of the century to the 1930s. Photograph taken August 27, 2003.

began in 1930. Farmers could then haul their grain to local elevators and commercial necessities could be obtained locally. No longer necessary were long journeys by cart or sled to Cudworth, Wakaw, or Lake Lenore, previously the nearest railway points. Because of its location alongside Lucien Lake, Middle Lake was a preferred work camp for the rail gangs. The lake was a good source of drinking water for both the men and their horses, and it provided a much-needed place to bathe. As long as their work sites were within travelling distance, the workers' camp remained at Middle Lake. The work crews provided a source of extra income for area farmers, as eggs, meat, milk, and butter were in great demand. Homemade wine and other spirits, the local history recounts, were also lucrative commodities. With the arrival of the railway, Middle Lake prospered, and by the 1950s it was a thriving village with new churches, businesses, and homes. On January 1, 1963, the Village of Middle Lake was incorporated. Today, the community has approximately 30 businesses, regular medical clinics, churches, a seniors' drop-in centre, and a special care home, which is a major employer in the area. Three Lakes School, a K-12 facility, had 188 village and district

students enrolled in the fall of 2006. Recreational facilities include a skating rink, ball diamonds, a community centre, and a bowling alley. Additionally, Lucien Lake Regional Park, immediately adjacent the village's west side, has a popular beach, a boat launch, facilities for camping, a miniature golf course, an extensive playground, and a concession. Middle Lake has a number of service clubs, youth groups, and other community-based organizations. The Three Lakes Area Volunteer Fire Department, located in Middle Lake, provides fire protection for the community and the surrounding area, while policing is provided by the Humboldt RCMP detachment. Ambulance service is also dispatched from Humboldt, although on occasion the service may be sent from Wakaw. Middle Lake serves as the administrative centre of the RM of Three Lakes No. 400.

MIKADO, organized hamlet, pop 56 (2006c), 55 (2001c), is located 13 km east of Canora on Hwy 5. Ranching activity was recorded in the area in the mid-1880s, as herds were driven into the district from Manitoba and the Qu'Appelle Valley, areas then struck by serious

drought. Homesteaders began arriving in the Mikado district in the late 1890s. Most had taken the Manitoba and Northwestern Railway to Yorkton, then either walked or travelled in wagons drawn by oxen purchased in Yorkton. Settlers travelled to their homesteads following the trails of

fur traders and ranchers. So rapidly was the Mikado area settled that by the time railways were built through the district much of the available land was already occupied. The Mikado area was pioneered by Ukrainians, Doukhobors, Poles, and people of British origins. In 1904, the Canadian Northern Railway was building through the district, providing a great deal of employment to settlers. Along the line, Mikado, its neighbouring communities to the east, Veregin, and Canora, to the west, developed. Because the Russo-Japanese War was raging at the time and the Japanese were allies of Britain, the name "Mikado" — the traditional title of the Emperors of Japan — was chosen for the new prairie community. The post office opened in 1908; the local school district was established in 1912; and by 1920, according to the local history, Mikado con-

▼ **THE MIKADO GENERAL STORE** was built by Sam Korney following World War One. Korney, a prominent member of the community and a school board trustee, also sold bulk gas and oil, delivering gas in 45-gallon barrels and oil to farmers in their fields. He also sold fuel at the store; at one time a British American (B/A) gas pump stood at the corner in front of the store, a few feet from the door. Korney sold the business in 1941 to Mike and Elsie Zielinsky who in turn sold out to Reney Zimmerman, who operated the store into the 1980s. Photograph taken July 27, 2004.

sisted of six grain elevators, three general stores, two lumber yards, one poolroom, a Bank of Montreal, the railway station, the school, a Ukrainian National Home, a livery barn, and a number of houses. The estimated population was 80. In later years, churches, the Polish Parish Hall, a hotel, service stations, cafés, and skating and curling rinks would be built. For several decades Mikado hosted district social, religious, and recreational activities and functioned as a centre for obtaining services and supplies. Up until the 1960s, the community's elevators were shipping out almost as much grain as the facilities in Canora. Toward the end of the 1960s, though, Mikado's population was beginning to decline — it fell from roughly 150 during the middle of the decade to 90 by 1972. The school closed in 1970, and subsequently the community's children left for Canora every morning. People were also increasingly shopping in Canora and Kamsack, and businesses in Mikado began to close their doors. In the mid-1990s, the post office closed, and shortly thereafter the last grain elevator was demolished. Mikado remains the administrative centre of the RM of Sliding Hills No. 273; a new RM office was built about a decade ago. The former RM office (which was originally the Bank of Montreal from its construction in 1920 until the Depression, when it closed) was declared a municipal heritage property in 1982, but now sits derelict and crumbling. Its days — like those of other community landmarks of the past—are likely numbered.

MILDEN, village, pop 172 (2006c), 196 (2001c), lies about halfway between Outlook and Rosetown on Hwy 15. In 1905, the first settlers began taking up land in the area; in 1906, there was an influx.

The settlement period generally extended to about 1912. Settlers were mainly from eastern Canada, a few were from Europe (there were some Czechs and Slovaks), and some came from the United States. They unloaded their supplies at the rail points at Hanley or Saskatoon, and trips back to these locations were necessary to obtain mail and supplies. Saskatoon was more often the destination, since the South Saskatchewan River had to be crossed to get to Hanley. On February 1, 1907, Charles Edward Mills established a post office on his homestead, about four miles east of the present village. Its name was a concoction of the first three letters of his last name and the last three letters of the last name of his neighbour to the north, Robert Bryden (the local history recounts that the name actually honours their wives). Charles Mills would serve as the Milden postmaster until his death in 1935. In 1908, the first store in the Milden district, operated by Andrew Shatilla, opened within a couple of miles of the post office. At this time, supplies could be obtained much closer, in Zealandia, as Canadian Northern's line from Saskatoon to Kindersley had been built that far. The CPR surveyed the present townsite of Milden in 1909; the line would run from Moose Jaw to Macklin and on to Edmonton, via a bridge over the South Saskatchewan River at Outlook. In 1910, the grade was completed and townsite lots were put up for sale. Charles Mills moved in to open a hardware store, bringing the Milden Post Office with him, and, evidently, after a little debate, the name was adopted for the emerging community. At first, rail service was only from the west, since the Outlook bridge was not opened until 1912. With the railway, a building boom was ushered in that would last for several years. Milden was incorporated on July 20, 1911. That

year, a local school district was established and the Milden Hotel was completed. In 1912, the Royal Bank set up a branch in Milden, the first of the grain elevators was erected, and the first church, an Anglican church, was built. Over the years, it was followed by United, Roman Catholic, and Alliances churches. The first electric lights were installed in the skating and curling rinks in 1919; the Saskatchewan Power Commission (SaskPower) took over responsibility for the village's electricity in 1930-31. In 1924, the CPR completed a line from Milden to McMorran, threaded between two of CN's tracks to the north and south. (This was abandoned in the 1980s.) In 1948, the sizable Memorial Arena was built in the village; Interprovincial Pipeline established its continuing presence in the community in 1950. Today, Petro-Canada's pumping station just outside of the village delivers gas and diesel products to a refinery in Saskatoon. In the mid-1950s and into the early 1960s, Milden's population was nudging toward 400 — the peak was 390 in 1956, but the community's numbers have been declining steadily since. Following the closure of Milden's hospital in 1993, a committee was struck to find an alternative use for the facility, and in 1996 the Bridgepoint Centre for Eating Disorders was established. In July 2005, high winds knocked over a power line in Milden, which started a fire in a lumberyard. Before the blaze could be brought under control, the local fire hall, medical clinic, and a car wash were destroyed. Fire crews from neighbouring communities, as well as area Hutterites and farmers pitched in to assist. Today, Milden retains a small core of local businesses, churches, a library, golf course, subsidized housing units, its school, and a museum. The school is a K-12 facility. Plagued by decreasing enroll-

ment, it has been on the brink of closing for a few years. There were 48 students registered in the fall of 2006, down from 89 enrolled in the fall of 2003. The Milden Community Museum, situated in a 1917 rural schoolhouse brought in from the country, houses pioneer artifacts, wildlife displays, and items relating to the area's local history. The village's feature event is Thresherman's Days, a bi-annual Thanksgiving celebration featuring demonstrations of heritage agricultural equipment. Milden serves as the administrative centre of the RM of Milden No. 286. The main industries in the area are grain farming, cattle and bison.

MILESTONE, town, pop 562 (2006c), 542 (2001c), is located between Regina and Weyburn on Hwy 39, with both cities being just over a half-hour's drive away. The town is situated near the junction of two of the province's major highways (Nos. 6 & 39), which enhances its position as an area trading centre. Agriculture is the major industry in the region and consists of a combination of grain, specialty crop, and livestock production. Seed cleaning, pulse crop processing, and small manufacturers add diversity to Milestone's economy. The origins of Milestone date to 1893, when the CPR constructed the Soo Line connecting Moose Jaw to Minneapolis. Milestone was one of the few stations on the line in Saskatchewan, and for a number of years nothing else existed at the site; the only residents were CPR employees. By the mid-1890s, a few ranchers had established themselves in the district, and in 1896 the first sod was broken in the area by a rancher seeding a few acres to oats. In 1898, two CPR section men filed on the first homesteads in the area; then, around 1900, significant

▲ **THE HOTEL IN MILESTONE** has long been a community landmark and remains popular for its bar and restaurant — the latter is often packed during the lunch hour. The building once featured an enclosed wooden balcony around the far corner of the second floor. Photograph taken August 1, 2003.

▼ **MILESTONE'S ST. ALOYSIUS ROMAN CATHOLIC CHURCH**, completed in 1920, stands at the corner of Main Street and Martin Avenue; it was designated a municipal heritage property in 1982. Until the town got its own resident priest in 1928, it was a mission of the Wilcox parish. In 1927, Father Athol Murray of Wilcox looked after the Milestone congregation, and later he compiled a record of all baptisms, marriages, and deaths from 1913 to 1931. Photograph taken August 1, 2003.

▲ **A SECOND WATERING HOLE** in Milestone is situated adjacent to the campground. Photograph taken August 1, 2003.

▼ **HOMECOMING CELEBRATIONS** and Saskatchewan's Centennial were celebrated at Milestone on July 8, 9, and 10, 2005. A parade took place on the last day. Photograph courtesy of Lorraine Nelson, Regina, Saskatchewan.

settlement began, with settlers primarily hailing from eastern Canada, the British Isles, continental Europe, and the U.S. By 1903, a substantial community had developed, and Milestone was incorporated as a village on March 14 that year. In 1906, with a population of 244, Milestone gained town status. In the subsequent decades, the community experienced steady growth and, unlike many Saskatchewan communities, Milestone has had a relatively stable population since the mid-1950s. Today, Milestone has an array of amenities and services. Milestone School is a K-12 facility, which had 182 students enrolled in the fall of 2006. The town has a library, an RCMP detachment, volunteer fire and ambulance services, a number of churches, and a variety of businesses. An industrial park is located on the south side of the town. There is a senior citizens' housing complex and a seniors' drop-in centre. The Milestone Recreation Complex, a multi-purpose facility, houses skating and curling rinks and is the centre of many community events, including the annual Milestone Indoor Rodeo held each April. Other recreational facilities include an outdoor swimming pool and a playground, which are located adjacent to grounds for camping, and a sports park with five baseball diamonds. There are a number of regional parks in the area. Milestone residents look to the city of Regina for medical care. As well, many of them commute to Regina, or to Weyburn, to work. Milestone is the administrative centre of the RM of Caledonia No. 99.

MINTON, village, pop 60 (2006c), 95 (2001c), is located 148 km due south of Regina, 19 km north of the Saskatchewan-Montana border on Hwy 6. Minton is situated in a stark, yet sublime, landscape of rolling hills, coulees, saline lakes, and badlands, over which are scattered centuries-old teepee rings, buffalo (bison) jumps, and rock effigies. Settlement of the district began around 1908-09. People came from eastern Canada and the United States. Many of the settlers were German; others were of British and Scandinavian origin. By 1916, a number of small schoolhouses dotted the countryside. The village of Minton itself had its beginnings in 1929, when the CPR purchased land for the townsite. Rail service from Estevan began in 1930. The townships just south and southwest of Minton had only recently been opened up for homesteaders. Two grain elevators were erected in the hamlet as the rail line was nearing completion, and a number of businesses began to be established. The economy developed around grain production and ranching. In 1951, Minton was incorporated as a village, and in 1966 the community reached a peak population of 219. Beginning in the 1970s, the population of the community began slowly falling, and in the 1990s the community faced the challenges of its school closing, the rail line being abandoned, and the subsequent closure of its grain elevators. Schoolchildren now attend classes in the village of Gladmar, and grain is trucked out of the district. Minton retains a small core of businesses, including a credit union, an insurance agency, an implement dealership, a bar and liquor vendor, a hair salon, a massage therapist, a ranching supplier, and a Co-op store and service station. The community has a curling rink, an outdoor skating rink, a heated swimming pool, and a rodeo arena. Minton hosts an annual rodeo and a fall fair. The village has a community hall and a number of clubs and volunteer organizations. A particularly interesting episode in Minton's

history occurred in 1945, although little was known of it at the time. A Japanese balloon released several bombs over the community; however, as there was no loss of life, media outlets cooperated with the government and withheld the information. Minton serves as the administrative centre of the RM of Surprise Valley No. 9.

MISSINIPE, northern hamlet, is a resort community located within the Canadian Shield, 80 km northeast of La Ronge off Hwy 102, an all-weather gravel road. Missinipe is situated in Walker Bay, which is the westernmost arm of Otter Lake, one of the Churchill River's medium-sized, slower and deeper lakes. To the northeast, across the lake from Missinipe, lies Grandmother's Bay, a reserve established in the early 1970s for members of the Lac la Ronge Indian Band. The name Missinipe is derived from the Cree name for the Churchill River, mâhtâwi-sîpiy, which literally means, "difficult, wondrous river." During the winter

months, the hamlet of Missinipe is a quiet place, home to about 40 permanent residents. In summer, the area population can number many hundreds, as fishers, canoeists, and other tourists flock to the Churchill River and pass through to the further reaches of northern Saskatchewan. Missinipe had its beginnings in the 1960s, after the all-weather road was built to Otter Rapids and the area became more accessible. Early in the decade, the first bush was cleared at the present townsite, and shortly thereafter tourist camps were operating, soon establishing Missinipe as one of North America's sports fishing destinations. A store/café/gas station was opened in 1968; air charter service was introduced in 1972. With the advent of tourism, the area's indigenous population began to shift to an economy wherein they relied upon earning wages. The need to administer and oversee the development of community infrastructure led to Missinipe's establishment as a northern hamlet on February 1, 1984. Subsequently, streets were built and a water treatment

plant and sewer system were put in place. Today, tourism remains the basis of the economy. Originally, outfitting, sports fishing and fishing camps predominated, but Missinipe now is one of Saskatchewan's premier canoe trip bases, and it has the province's largest canoeing outfitter. The community also offers guides, air charter services into northern fishing camps, accommodations including cabin rentals, boat and canoe rentals, stores, "upscale" dining, a community hall and library, a gallery, camping facilities, a public beach and a government dock. The community recently acquired over 450 acres for expansion.

MISTATIM, village, pop 89 (2006c), 104 (2001c), is located on Hwy 3, about 56 km east of Tisdale and 64 km west of Hudson Bay. Situated in the boreal transition ecoregion, Mistatim's economy has been primarily based upon forestry and agriculture, some trapping, and, until WWII, a limited amount of fox-ranching.

▼ **A CANOEIST'S PARADISE:** Missinipe in August 1971 (left), and a closer view three years later in August 1974 (right). Saskatchewan Archives Board, Saskatchewan Photographic Services, R-PS71-756-182 and R-PS74-868-153 respectively. Photographer: D. Varley.

Logging activity began when the Canadian Northern Railway pushed through from Hudson Bay to Prince Albert during the early years of the twentieth century, and agriculture began to develop significantly after the area was opened for homesteading in 1926. Much of the land in the district was first taken up by people who had been employed in the surrounding forest industry. In the 1930s, families from southern Saskatchewan moved into the area, escaping the drought then ravaging the open prairie. Settlers to the Mistatim district were of diverse origins: among them, Scandinavians, Scots, Irish, English, French, Germans, and Hungarians. The Arpad United Church in Mistatim, named for the founder of the dynasty that brought proto-Hungarians to present-day Hungary in the late ninth century, had services originally conducted in Hungarian. The building was designated a municipal heritage property in 1984. The Village of Mistatim was incorporated on July 1, 1952; the name Mistatim comes from the Cree word for horse, and it was first applied to an area post office that opened in 1907. The village had a peak population of 215 in 1966, although in the first decades of the twentieth century, when logging activity and sawmill operations were at their peak, thousands of men worked in the region and Mistatim was originally comprised of cook shacks, bunk houses, and barns, which accommodated men and horses that worked in the bush. The first store was constructed on the present village site in the fall of 1923, doing a brisk business with the lumberjacks and trappers, and in 1929 the first school was built in the hamlet. Today, the community has a small core of businesses, which includes a post office, a hotel, a garage, and a general store with an insurance agency and a liquor vending licence. The

village also has a library, a seniors' centre, churches, camping facilities, a playground, an arena and curling rink, and a community centre located in the former school, which closed to classes in the last few years. The oldest standing building in the village is the Canadian National Railway section house, built in 1925. The district is popular for hunting and fishing, and there are hundreds of kilometres of groomed snowmobile trails throughout the region. Mistatim is situated in the RM of Bjorkdale No. 426.

MISTUSINNE, pop 56 (2006c), 31 (2001c), is a resort village located 8 km southeast of the village of Elbow off Hwy 19, on the northeast shore of the Gordon McKenzie Arm of Lake Diefenbaker. The name Mistusinne is derived from the Cree word *mistasiniy*, meaning "big stone," which referred locally to a large glacial erratic that was left lying on the floor of the Qu'Appelle Valley just east of the elbow of the South Saskatchewan River after the last ice age. The stone, thought to resemble a resting buffalo, is estimated to have weighed 400 tons and was a sacred site for millennia — not only to the Plains Cree, but also to other First Nations who traversed the prairies. Two legends are associated with the stone's origins: one tells of an eagle soaring in the sky clutching a giant buffalo. The eagle suddenly dropped the buffalo to earth, and when people arrived, only the rock, shaped like the buffalo, was to be found. The other legend, recounted by Deanna Christensen in *Ahtahkakoop: The Epic Account of a Plains Cree Head Chief, His People, and Their Struggle for Survival 1816-1896*, is that the stone was once a man who had been raised by buffalo. As a baby, he had fallen unnoticed from his Cree parents' travois,

only to be found and saved by a herd of the large mammals, who then looked after the infant until he was an adult. One day, when his buffalo father lay dying after a Cree hunting party had descended upon the herd, the young man vowed he would not flee the hunters anymore, and he was able to transform himself, first into a buffalo, and then into a rock, which grew to a tremendous size. The stone became regarded as sacred, and people travelled great distances to the site; it became the setting for ceremonies such as the Sun Dance. In the late 1850s, Henry Youle Hind visited the area and measured the rock, determining it to be 79 feet (24 m) in circumference at three feet above the ground; a tape stretched over the highest point from one side to the other measured 46 feet (14 m). Hind also recorded that there were offerings to the Creator (*mâmaw-ôhtâwîmâw* in Cree) left at the rock — among these tobacco, beads, fragments of cloth, and other objects. During the 1960s, when it became apparent that the stone would be submerged by the rising waters of Lake Diefenbaker, efforts were made to save the mistasiniy. A long campaign led by the late Zenon S.

Pohorecky, a professor of anthropology and archaeology at the University of Saskatchewan, to move the rock to higher ground ultimately proved unsuccessful. Many believe a "quiet" decision was made to quell the lobby: on the morning of December 1, 1966, a crew from the PFRA (Prairie Farm Rehabilitation Administration) arrived with a reported 60 sticks of dynamite and reduced the millennia-old stone to rubble. Fragments were later incorporated into a cairn at Elbow Harbour and a memorial to Chief Poundmaker on the Poundmaker Cree Nation reserve in the Cut Knife area. The remainder now lies submerged. With the advent of Lake Diefenbaker as a recreation area, the present resort village, incorporated on August 1, 1980, began to develop. Today, the community of Mistusinne has 245 privately-owned properties, the majority for seasonal use, as well as a nine-hole golf course, a boat launch, and miles of sandy beach. Other than the golf course, there are no commercial developments at Mis-

▼ **"MISTASINIY"** prior to being reduced to rubble. Photograph courtesy of the Elbow Museum.

▲ **MISTUSINNE BEACH TODAY.** Photograph taken July 30, 2003.

tusinne; the nearby village of Elbow offers a range of goods and services. The above population figure is that of the permanent, year-round residents; the number is many times higher during the peak summer months. Mistusinne is situated in the RM of Maple Bush No. 224.

MOHR'S BEACH, organized hamlet, is one in a string of resort communities located along the east side of Last Mountain Lake. The organized hamlet was established in 1985 and is situated in the RM of McKillop No. 220. There are a small number of permanent residents; however, population varies depending on the season.

MONTMARTRE, village, pop 413 (2006c), 465 (2001c), is situated approximately 90 km southeast of Regina on Hwy 48. The reserve of the Carry the Kettle First Nation lies just to the north of the community; to the south lie what are known as the Chapleau Lakes, the headwaters of Moose Mountain Creek. In the spring of 1893, the first small group of French Catholic settlers disembarked the train at Wolseley, headed southwest and took up land in the district. They had

come from France and chose to name their new settlement Montmartre, after what is now a major and famous district in the northern part of Paris. The name means "mountain of the martyrs," and it originally referred to the high hill in the Parisian district where leading church figures were executed around 250 CE. Between 1893 and 1903 more French settlers, including French Canadians, arrived in the area of what is now Montmartre; as well, the district came to be settled by Ukrainians, Poles, Germans, Scots, Irish, and English — although the population of the village would come to be predominantly French and Ukrainian. The Montmartre Post Office was established on September 1, 1894. With the construction of the Canadian Northern Railway line from Brandon, Manitoba, through Maryfield and Kipling to Regina, the present townsite was established, and in 1908 the first scheduled trains were running. On October 19, 1908, the Village of Montmartre was incorporated. The Rural Municipality of Montmartre No. 126, for which the community serves as headquarters, was established in 1909. The population of the village was 201 in 1911 and 395 by 1951; in 1966, Montmartre had a peak population of 566. Community landmarks today include the Roman Catholic

Sacred Heart Parish Church built in 1918 (the parish was founded in 1903), and Sts. Peter and Paul Ukrainian Catholic Church, constructed between 1950-52. The major industry in the Montmartre area is agriculture (mostly grains, some cattle), and a number of related businesses, including a large John Deere dealership, a fuel company, and a fertilizer and chemical company, are situated in the village. There were 22 oil wells located within the Rural Municipality of Montmartre in 2003; however, there is only a small amount of local economic benefit from this industry. Other businesses in Montmartre include two grocery stores, a bank, a credit union, restaurants, and several service-related enterprises. There are companies dealing in gravel aggregates, crushing, and concrete, although these are largely seasonal operations. The community has a K-12 school that had 189 students enrolled in the fall of 2006, and Montmartre has a health centre with an attached special care home. The village also has a detachment of the RCMP. Located on the edge of the village is Kemoca Regional Park, which features an outdoor heated swimming pool, camping facilities, ball diamonds, a children's playground, horseshoe pits, a canteen, and a walking trail. The name Kemoca is derived from the first two letters of the three communities in the area: Kendal, Montmartre, and Candiac. In close proximity to the park is a nine-hole golf course. Montmartre has an arena and a seniors' centre, and the community hosts a popular biweekly farmers' market. A recently constructed complex in Montmartre houses the village office, the library, and an office for a unique and innovative regional arts and continuing education centre. Major employers in Montmartre are the school, the health centre, and the Co-op.

MOOSE BAY, organized hamlet, est. 1979, is a resort community located in the eastern Qu'Appelle Valley south of Grayson on Crooked Lake, adjacent to Crooked Lake Provincial Park. There are a small number of permanent residents; however, the population varies greatly depending on the season. Moose Bay is situated in the RM of Grayson No. 184.

MOOSE JAW, city, pop 32,132 (2006c), 32,131, (2001c), lies 71 km west of Regina on the Trans-Canada Highway. The city, the province's fourth largest, lies on the eastern flank of the Missouri Coteau, at 550 metres (1,800 feet) above sea level. The escarpment of the Coteau separates the flat Regina Plain to the east, and the gently rolling landscapes of the Alberta Plateau, or third prairie level, to the southwest. Thunder Creek joins with the Moose Jaw River in a valley setting in the city. First Nations people long used the sheltered locale, and from about the mid-1880s, Métis *hivernants* frequented the area as well. There have been a number of theories over the years as to the origins of the community's name, but it is now believed the name is derived from a misinterpreted Cree phrase referring to a warm place by the river, or warm breezes, and that the Cree pronunciation of a part of the phrase was incorrectly thought to sound like "Moose." The city's beginnings date to 1881, when the route for the CPR main line was being surveyed across southern Saskatchewan. Because of its abundance of fresh water, this location was a desirable one for a town site and the land was secured. The railway arrived in 1882 and permanent settlement began. The CPR's decision to establish a divisional point at the location, and the completion of the Soo Line from Minneapolis and Chicago in 1893, secured Moose Jaw's future as a major centre, its growth closely tied to the development of cereal crop agriculture. Moose Jaw became an incorporated town on January 19, 1884. In 1891, a major fire destroyed 17 businesses and a church on Main Street, and this, along with earlier fires, prompted town officials to make brick or stone construction mandatory. A local brickworks flourished, and the bylaw is part of the reason why there are so many red brick heritage properties in downtown Moose Jaw today. In fact, as of 2007, there are 29 designated heritage properties in the city. Moose Jaw attained city status on November 20, 1903, and for the first two decades of the twentieth century grew rapidly. From a population of 1,558 in 1901, the city expanded to number just under 20,000 by the beginning of the 1920s. During this period, commerce and industry boomed, and Moose Jaw became an important retail, service, wholesale, and distribution centre. The processing of agricultural products and numerous manufacturing industries helped drive the economy. Growth then slowed until after WWII, after which there was another period of expansion. By the 1980s, however, Moose Jaw was suffering with a sluggish economy, and the downtown was decaying, as suburban malls and big box stores on the city's periphery drew business away from the city's core. Over the past 10 to 15 years, though, Moose Jaw has rebounded significantly as a boom in tourism has spurred dramatic changes. The development of the Temple Gardens Mineral Spa Resort Hotel, Casino Moose Jaw, and the Tunnels of Moose Jaw tourist attraction, which plays on the city's prohibition-era gangster activity, have all been met with success and together have

spurred a period of revitalization in the city centre. More long-established attractions in Moose Jaw include: the Western Development Museum, opened in 1976, which features "The History of Transportation"; the Festival of Words (eleventh season in 2007), which celebrates and promotes the imaginative use of language to entertain and enlighten an audience; and Crescent Park, a 28-acre site in the centre of the city. Amidst an abundance of

MOOSE JAW SIGHTS, clockwise from top:

MOOSE DETAIL on the Fourth Avenue Viaduct.
ST. ANDREWS CHURCH, completed 1912.
MAIN STREET, looking north.
THE RAIL YARDS, as viewed from the Fourth Avenue Viaduct, looking east.

Photographs taken October 29, 2007.

trees, shrubs, and flower beds, the park contains an Olympic-size swimming pool, tennis courts, lawn bowling greens, an outdoor amphitheatre, and the Centre in the Park, which houses a library, art gallery, museum, and auditorium. While tourism has given Moose Jaw a boost in recent years, the city's primary industries remain based in the agricultural, manufacturing, service, retail, and transportation sectors. The main businesses in the city and area are CP Rail, XL Foods, Mosaic Company, the Canadian Salt Company, Saskatchewan Minerals, Bombardier Aerospace, Doepker Industries Ltd., General Cable, the Moose Jaw Refinery, and SaskFerco Products. Moose Jaw's

main employer for decades has been 15 Wing Moose Jaw (formerly CFB Moose Jaw). With beginnings as a British Commonwealth Air Training Plan base during WWII, the facility is now home to the NATO Flying Training in Canada Program, as well as the Canadian Forces Snowbirds flight aerobatics demonstration team. Approximately 800 people are employed at the base. There are a total of 20 primary and secondary schools in Moose Jaw; the Saskatchewan Institute of Applied Science and Technology (SIAST) provides a range of post-secondary programs. Moose Jaw Union Hospital is the city's main medical facility, and Moose Jaw has two radio stations (Country 100 and CHAB), and a newspaper, *The Moose Jaw Times-Herald*. The city also has a Western Hockey League (WHL) team, the Moose Jaw Warriors. Moose Jaw serves as the administrative centre of the RM of Moose Jaw No. 161.

MOOSOMIN, town, pop 2,257 (2006c), 2,361 (2001c), is located 16 km west of the Saskatchewan-Manitoba border at the junction of Hwys 1 and 8. Settlers, predominantly of English and Scottish origin, began arriving in the Moosomin area around 1881 in advance of the CPR's push westward across the plains. Some of these first arrivals acquired land in the district walking from rail points established in Manitoba, thereby getting a jump on the wave of settlers that would ensue with the arrival of the rails. Before the railway arrived in 1882, these settlers would have to occasionally make the long trek back to centres such as Brandon for staples such as flour, sugar, salt, and tea. The Moosomin Post Office was established in the fall of 1882, the name derived from the Cree word for the "mooseberry," or high bush cranberry. By 1884, the com-

▲ **A ROYAL VISIT.** Mayor Lloyd H. Bradley welcomes Queen Elizabeth II to Moosomin in 1959. Bradley served as the town's mayor 1955-61, 1964-71, and 1974-84.

▶ **STEER WRESTLING** at a rodeo, 1964.

▼ **WRIGHT'S DRUG STORE**, 1966.

MOOSOMIN

Black-and-white photographs courtesy of the Town of Moosomin.

Colour photographs taken October 16, 2003.

COUNTRY LEGEND WILF CARTER proudly examines a display of his records in a Moosomin business in 1964.

SHIFTY MORGAN, a band made up of Moosomin and area musicians, entertain the crowd during the "World's Longest Hockey Game." The quintet was named the Group of the Year by the Saskatchewan Country Music Association (SCMA) in 2004; in 2006, "You Belong Here," composed by the group's songwriter, Anthony Kelly (centre), won the SCMA award for Song of the Year.

▲ ▼ **TAKIN' IT TO THE STREETS:** Above: Freshie Day, 1961. Below: Members of the Chamber of Commerce cleaning streets, 1966. Bottom: A tug-of-war in the centre of town took place during the Centennial celebrations in 1967.

▼ **THE MOOSOMIN MOOSE** battle exhaustion during the "World's Longest Hockey Game," October 2003.

munity boasted five hotels, five general stores, two blacksmiths, two livery stables, nine implement dealers, a doctor, a lawyer, and a butcher. Additionally, a newspaper was established in Moosomin that year, which evolved into the *World-Spectator*, still publishing. On March 20, 1889, the Town of Moosomin was incorporated. Prior to the development of railway branch lines, Moosomin served an area reaching from the Qu'Appelle Valley to the Souris River district. Stagecoaches provided communications and freight and passenger transit with far-flung points throughout the North-West. Bertram Tennyson, the Poet Laureate's nephew, was one of the drivers. It may be that no other town in the eastern North-West Territories sent so many homesteaders and businessmen out onto the plains. In 1905, when the Province of Saskatchewan came into being, Moosomin's population was already around 1,000 and growing. Moosomin's economy is largely tied to the region's agricultural industry, which has long consisted of mixed farming, with the production of traditional crops. Spring wheat is the mainstay, but some barley and oats are grown, with oilseeds making up less than 10 per cent of the acreage seeded. A small amount of rye and winter wheat is also grown in the district, and many livestock producers grow forage crops to provide winter feed for their stock. Many agri-businesses which supply and service the region are located in the town. Other significant area employers are the PCS Rocanville mine; TransCanada Pipelines, which has a pumping station northeast of Moosomin; the Government of Saskatchewan, which has several regional offices in the community; and the oil and gas industry, which has been making incursions into the region. Moosomin also has a substantial local business commu-

nity that provides a wide range of goods and services to a trading area population calculated to be at about 20,000. Moosomin also benefits from its location on the Trans-Canada Highway, as it is estimated that over a million people pass through the community each year. Many hotels, motels, restaurants, and service stations accommodate the traveller. The community also serves the district with a hospital and special care housing among the town's wide range of medical services. Moosomin is a judicial centre and has an RCMP detachment and a volunteer fire department. MacLeod Elementary School and McNaughton High School together provide K-12 education, and had a combined student population of 505 in the fall of 2006. Gordon Thiessen, formerly Canada's chief banker and monetary policy maker as the governor of the Bank of Canada, is a Moosomin high school graduate. Recreational facilities in the community include a major regional arena that facilitates public skating, figure skating, and a number of hockey programs, and which in the past couple of years has been the site of an ambitious community fundraiser. The Moosomin Moose, a recreational hockey team, has raised over $500,000 toward the construction of a new $20-million integrated health care facility that was scheduled to open in late 2006 or early 2007. The team played three marathon hockey games, each temporarily a world record — the last, 130 hours long. Moosomin also has a curling club, with origins dating to the 1880s, an outdoor swimming pool, numerous ball diamonds, tennis courts, an 880-metre oval track, gymkhana and rodeo arenas, a bowling alley, and a seniors' drop-in centre. Moosomin and District Regional Park, 14 kilometres southwest at Moosomin Lake in the Pipestone Valley, facilitates swimming, camping, boat-

ing, and fishing, and there is a golf course in the vicinity. One of the community's most notable citizens was General Andrew George Latta McNaughton, an army officer, scientist, and diplomat. He was born in Moosomin in 1887, and went on to become the president of the National Research Council of Canada, the senior Canadian officer in the United Kingdom during WWII, the Canadian minister of national defence, and, among other portfolios, was the Canadian representative on the United Nations Atomic Energy Commission, as well as the president of the Atomic Energy Control Board of Canada. Moosomin serves as the administrative centre of the RM of Moosomin No. 121.

MORSE, town, pop 236 (2006c), 248 (2001c), is located approximately 60 km east of Swift Current on the Trans-Canada Highway and the CPR main line. The community was a product of the railway and the expansion of agriculture into the west. The first setter at Morse was a railway company employee, responsible for the maintenance of the track in the area. In 1896, he moved his family into the section foreman's house, one of only two buildings then at the townsite. A 14-

foot-square wooden station, a water tank and a windmill were the only other structures. The townsite was surveyed in 1902, and between 1906 and 1908 carloads of settlers, their household effects, and livestock were unloaded from the rails at the locale. Mainly Mennonites, English, and Scottish people would come to comprise the populace. In 1906, the post office was established, followed by the school district in 1907, and the construction of the school in 1908. By 1909, approximately 100 people were residing in the community, and in 1910 Morse was incorporated as a village. The community was named for Samuel Morse, the inventor of the electric telegraph and originator of Morse code. The population of the village was 298 in 1911, and in 1912 the community attained town status. The same year, Morse was reportedly the third largest grain marketing point in the province, and in 1915 a record-setting two and a quarter million bushels of wheat were shipped out of the community. By 1921, Morse reached a peak population of 559 people. However,

▼ **THE LIVERY BARN IN MORSE, 1911.** Photograph courtesy of the Morse Museum and Cultural Centre.

▲ **MORSE BOY SCOUTS, 1934.** Back row: B. Evans, R. Foster, R. Evans. Middle row: H. Angott, R. Rainer, A. Wunsch, Eric Dobbs, R. Janzen, B. Van Wyck. Front row: Dave Wunsch, Robert Steinhauer, Morley Cornwell, Harold Roberts, H. Mackay, Tom Jordon. The scoutmaster was J.R.V. Deyell, and the troop leader was Morley Cornwell, assisted by H. MacKay. Photograph courtesy of the Morse Museum and Cultural Centre.

as other towns and villages developed in the surrounding region, Morse's population slowly declined, although it was still over 400 in the early 1980s. Agriculture remains the main industry in the area today, with the focus being on grain, oilseed, and beef production. Ranching takes place to the north toward Lake Diefenbaker. The town has a core of essential businesses and services, a number of which are agriculturally based. Morse has an RCMP detachment and a fire department; there is a hospital, a special care home, and an ambulance service located 14 kilometres to the west in the neighbouring town of Herbert. Morse School is a K-12 facility, which had 77 students enrolled in the fall of 2006. A feature of the town is the Morse

Museum and Cultural Centre, housed in a large and majestic red-brick schoolhouse built in 1912. A community landmark, the building was in use as a school until 1961; in 1981 it was saved from demolition by being declared a heritage property. With grants for its restoration obtained, it was re-opened to the public in its current capacity in 1986. The facility houses an elaborate museum, a craft and gift shop, a Victorian tea room, and a gallery which hosts local and travelling art exhibits. Rooms are rented for meetings, and the building retains its function as a learning institution as school tours and activities are common. Morse serves as the administrative centre of the RM of Morse No. 165.

MORTLACH, village, pop 254 (2006c), 241 (2001c), is located 40 km west of Moose Jaw on Hwy 1. Within a couple of years of the CPR coming through the Mortlach area in 1882, ranching operations began to develop, but it was not until the early 1900s that significant areas of land began to be broken and fenced with the arrival of homesteaders. With the re-routing of the CPR mainline somewhat south of its original course in 1904, Mortlach came into being. The townsite was established on land originally homesteaded in 1902 by Khamis Michael, who came to Canada from what is now known as Iraq. A building boom ensued, as people from eastern Canada, the United States, and overseas began pouring into the area. A good number of them were of Scottish, English, Norwegian, and Swedish origins. By 1905, the post office was established, a member of the Royal North West Mounted Police was stationed in the young community, a school was under construction, and the business district was developing. In

1906, Mortlach was incorporated as a village, and in 1913 the community attained town status. In 1916, the community had a peak population of 456, but in the decades following, Mortlach's numbers steadily declined, falling to 218 by 1951. The 1930s had been particularly hard on the community, and on January 1, 1949, Mortlach reverted to village status. In 1954, a landmark archaeological excavation was undertaken in the Mortlach area. On the heels of amateur arrowhead collectors and diggers, Boyd Wettlaufer, with the Museum of Natural History in Regina, conducted the first scientific archaeological dig in Saskatchewan, at what came to be known as the Mortlach site (this is actually just slightly east of the community, adjacent to the Besant campground). Wettlaufer was the first in Canada to use radiocarbon dating, and he established that several cultures had occupied the Mortlach area dating back to 1445 BC, roughly 3,500 years. The work established a chronological framework for archaeology, not only in Saskatchewan, but across the Great Plains. The 1950s through to the

▼ **MORTLACH**, prior to 1912. Photograph courtesy of the Mortlach Museum.

▲ **THE EAST SIDE OF ROSE STREET**, Mortlach, looking south.

▼ **LOOKING SOUTHWEST ACROSS SECOND AVENUE**, Mortlach. The building at the right with the bell tower was originally the Mortlach Fire Hall, built in 1910. The main floor housed the fire-fighting equipment as well as a jail; the second floor housed a court room and jury room, and was used for village council meetings. Today, the building houses the Mortlach Museum and a seniors' drop-in centre.

mid-1960s were times of renewed growth and prosperity for Mortlach (the population had climbed to 331 in 1966), but since, the village's numbers have again slowly declined. Mortlach retains a number of essential businesses, a K-12 school, churches, a library, a museum, and a recreational facility that houses rinks for skating, hockey, and curling. There are a number of community organizations in Mortlach, a youth drop-in centre, a seniors' club, and musical groups that include a community choir and the Mortlach Old Time Fiddlers. A community attraction and recent village beautification project is a three-acre community fruit orchard, an undertaking of the village's environmental committee assisted by the Prairie Farm Rehabilitation Administration (PFRA). The orchard will comple-

▼ **DETAIL FROM A MURAL ON THE WAGONS WEST COOKHOUSE** on the corner of Rose Street and Second Avenue in Mortlach, painted by D. Holmes in 2001.

Mortlach photographs taken August 28, 2003.

ment the development of a wildlife habitat shelterbelt begun in 1998. Another community attraction, and one of Mortlach's oldest structures, is the former Bank of Hamilton building, built in 1911. The village landmark was designated a heritage property in 1986. Mortlach serves as the administrative centre of the RM of Wheatlands No. 163, whose primary industry is agriculture — the production of cereal and pulse crops, oilseeds, livestock and livestock feed. Mortlach celebrated its centennial in 2006.

MOSSBANK, town, pop 330 (2006c), 379 (2001c), is located just south of Old Wives Lake, approximately 70 km southwest of Moose Jaw and 35 km north of Assiniboia off Hwy 2. The Mossbank area was first settled around 1907. People of British, Scandinavian, and German origins took up land in the district and with the construction of the Canadian Northern line between Avonlea and Gravelbourg in 1913, and CP's track from Moose Jaw en route to Assiniboia coming through the following year, the community of Mossbank developed. In 1915, Mossbank was incorporated as a village. The name was coined by Robert Jolly, a homesteader from Scotland. In 1909, he had named a post office established on his farm Mossbank, and when the railways came through, the service was moved to the townsite and the name was adopted for the community. As a growing service centre for the developing mixed farming district, Mossbank's population almost doubled in the five years between 1916 and 1921, jumping from 164 to 303. During WWII, the village population soared (from 358 in 1936 to 606 in 1941) as a British Commonwealth Air Training Plan base was established just east of the communi-

ty. Work began on the site in 1939 and the facility closed in 1944. In 1946, one of the aircraft hangars was moved into the community to become what was known locally as "the longest school in Saskatchewan." Mossbank's population remained stable after the War and, in 1959, the community attained town status. Through to the mid-1960s, Mossbank prospered. Then, however, began a period of decline, with which the community continues to struggle. Between 1966 and 1976, the town lost a quarter of its population, as its numbers dropped from 596 to 444 over the ten-year period. The same scenario was taking place in the countryside, and in 1969 Mossbank's hospital was downgraded to a health centre. The community's pharmacist left shortly thereafter. Businesses began closing, the CN line from Avonlea was abandoned in the mid-1980s, the number of students attending school was dwindling, an oriental noodle factory failed, and "for sale" signs were popping up in people's yards all over the town. By the early 1990s, where three grain elevators once competed for business, only one remained. Today, young people leave the community after completing high school as there is little work for them in the area, leaving a substantial percentage of Mossbank's population over retirement age. The median age of the town's population was recorded at just under 50 in the 2001 Census, while the median age in Saskatchewan was somewhat over 36. The community retains a small core of local businesses, a variety of recreational facilities, a library, a museum, and a K-12 school, which had 106 town and area students enrolled in the fall of 2006. The town, the surrounding RM of Lake Johnston No. 102, and the neighbouring RM of Sutton No. 103 are jointly administered from an office in the community.

◄ **ON MAY 20, 1957**, Mossbank became the scene of one of Saskatchewan's most famous political debates as Premier Tommy Douglas and Liberal candidate Ross Thatcher squared off over the issue of the province's Crown corporations. An overflow crowd came to the community hall for the debate, spilling into the basement to listen in on loudspeakers, while hundreds of others sat in their cars outside and listened to the debate on radio. The popular consensus was that Thatcher equalled, perhaps bested, his eloquent rival. A sign on the top of a car in the right of the photograph asks, "Where's that dam Thatcher?" — likely in reference to the South Saskatchewan River Project. Saskatchewan Archives Board, West's Studio Collection R-WS15172, courtesy M. West, Regina.

◄ **EVENING DESCENDS ON THE EAST SIDE OF MAIN STREET**, Mossbank, August 31, 2004.

MOWERY BEACH, organized hamlet, est. 2003, is located in west-central Saskatchewan and is one of several resort communities situated east of St. Walburg on Brightsand Lake. There are a small number of permanent residents; however, the population varies greatly depending on the season. Mowery Beach is situated in the RM of Mervin No. 499.

MOZART, organized hamlet, pop 34 (2006c), 40 (2001c), is located south of Little Quill Lake in a mixed-farming district, 14 km east of Wynyard, just off Hwy 16. The ethnic origins of the community were largely Icelandic and Ukrainian; Icelanders were predominant in the community's formative years, arriving in 1903-04 from North Dakota and Manitoba. With the construction of the CPR's line south of the Quill Lakes westward toward Wynyard in 1909, the village of Mozart had its beginnings. Men working for the railway boarded with an area family, the Lunds, and gave the honour of naming the townsite to Julia Lund, whom they had discovered was an accomplished pianist. She chose "Mozart" in recognition of her favourite composer, and then followed the theme naming the community's streets — from east to west: Schubert, Haydn, Wagner, Liszt, and Gounod. In 1909, T.S. Laxdal moved in the post office he had established in 1907 a few miles northeast of the community, changing the name from Laxdal to Mozart in the process. With the arrival of the railway, construction followed rapidly and a number of businesses were started: hardware stores, general stores, confectionary, pool room and barber shop, blacksmith, lumberyard, three or four implement dealerships, and a livery stable; the Bank of Montreal based in Wynyard came to Mozart once a week for people to do their banking; four grain elevators were erected along the railway tracks. The Mozart School District was organized in 1911, and the school was built in 1912. The Mozart Co-op had its beginnings in 1935, and Mozart was established as an organized hamlet in 1949. In 1966, the Jubilee Centennial Hall was officially opened, replacing the 1909 community hall that had fallen into disrepair. Mozart's population had peaked in the 1920s and the decade had been the community's heyday; in the mid-1960s, the hamlet's population was still 85, but it was declining. High school students had been bused to Wynyard since 1954; Mozart School closed in 1965. By the 1970s, only two grain elevators remained; these were bulldozed, burned, and buried in 2001. In 1991, which marked the 200th anniversary of the death of Wolfgang Amadeus Mozart (1756-91), approximately 2,000 philatelists and music-lovers from around the world sent self-addressed, stamped envelopes to the Mozart postmaster, Jean Halldorson, requesting the community's unique postmark, which they received along with the postmaster's special cachet. Halldorson then had the idea of inviting the Regina Symphony's Chamber Orchestra to play "Mozart in Mozart," and they played to a sell-out crowd of more than 200 in the community hall that year. Mozart still retains its Co-op, which sells groceries, hardware, agricultural supplies, and fuel; the Elfros-Mozart Credit Union operates three days a week. Mozart is situated in the RM of Elfros No. 307.

MUENSTER, village, pop 342 (2006c), 379 (2001c), is located about 8 km east of Humboldt on Hwy 5. The history of Muenster dates to 1903 with the arrival of the first German Catholic homesteaders in the area, along with a number of Benedictine monks. The monks came from the priory of Cluny near Wetaug, Illinois, and St. John's Abbey in Collegeville, Minnesota, and, likewise, many of the settlers in what came to be known as St. Peter's Colony, a broad swath of land extending from Cudworth through Humboldt to Watson, came from the northern and mid-western United States. Among the Benedictines was Fr. Bruno Doerfler, for whom the Saskatchewan town of Bruno is named, and it was Doerfler who in 1902 scouted the territory, deeming it ideal for the establishment of a large German-Catholic settlement. On May 16, 1903, a contingent of monks led by Prior Alfred Mayer left Rosthern (then the nearest railway point), arriving on May 21 near the banks of the Wolverine Creek just south of present-day Muenster. The group celebrated mass on the spot (which is today marked by a cairn), before heading further north along the creek to a point not far from where St. Peter's Cathedral now stands. By fall, quarters for the monks — the monastery — was erected, as was a small church made of logs. Other buildings were soon put up, and the priory, now named St. Peter's in honour of Abbot Peter Engel of St. John's Abbey in Minnesota, became the spiritual centre of the region. In 1904, the Canadian Northern Railway line was being built just to the south of the St. Peter's Priory buildings, and along the track the village of Muenster began to develop. The name Muenster, like the English word "minster," is derived from the Latin word "monasterium." With the arrival of the railway, the district around Muenster began to be settled rapidly (by 1906 there were 6,000 settlers in St. Peter's Colony). A post office had been established in the young community, a school district was set up, and soon stores, a livery barn, a blacksmith shop, and grain elevators, among other businesses, were constructed to serve the burgeoning populace. A hotel built in 1903-04 is still standing. In 1907, work began on a new church, St. Peter's Cathedral, which officially opened in 1910 and which is today a heritage property. In 1919, Count Berthold Von Imhoff, a German-born artist who had become friends with then Abbot Bruno, painted the interior of the cathedral with 80 life-sized figures and frescoes that now are a major tourist draw. The Village of Muenster was incorporated on August 18, 1908, and the Benedictine monks' influence in the community would continue over the years. They founded parishes and parish schools throughout the district; established the majestic landmark, St. Peter's College, just off the southeast edge of the village in 1921, which today is a fully affiliated

▶ **ST. PETER'S CATHEDRAL**, Muenster, completed in 1910.

▼ **MICHAEL HALL**, St. Peter's College, Muenster, completed in 1921.

Photographs taken August 5, 2004.

College of the University of Saskatchewan; and set up a press, publishing Catholic newspapers — the German-language *St. Peter's Bote* (1904-47) and the English paper, *The Prairie Messenger* (1923-present). The monks also engaged in mixed farming, establishing a model farm where, during the 1930s, agricultural field days were held for area farmers with demonstrations of good farming practices being given. The monastic community of St. Peter's Abbey reached its zenith in the 1960s when over 60 monks were in residence. Over the decades, the monks were aided in their work, particularly in the area of education, by the Ursuline Sisters who had originally come to Canada on the eve of WWI. Muenster itself grew slowly from its beginning until WWII (the population had reached only 117 by 1941), but following the War the community's numbers began to significantly increase. By 1961, the population was 182; by 1971, it was 280; and from the early 1980s until the beginning of the twenty-first century, the population hovered around 400. The village today has a variety of retail and service businesses, including a grocery store and gas bar, a post office, a restaurant, a meat shop, a candle shop, a credit union, and a beverage room. Additionally, there are a number of tradespeople and home-based businesses in the community. As well, the nearby city of Humboldt provides residents with a wide range of goods, services, medical facilities and practitioners, and police protection. Muenster has a local volunteer fire department and a K-12 school which had 194 students enrolled in the fall of 2006. The village and St. Peter's College combined provide residents with a full range of recreational facilities. Muenster is situated in the RM of St. Peter No. 369; the main industry in the area is agriculture.

MULLINGAR, organized hamlet, pop 5 (2006c), 5 (2001c), is located south of Spiritwood in the Thickwood Hills. Settlers began taking up land in the area in 1906. Among the first were the Comerford family, who established a post office in the district in 1907. They named it Mullingar, after Mullingar, County Westmeath, Ireland, evidently to honour their Irish heritage. Three Comerford brothers, Mark, Charles, and Frank, served as postmasters between 1907 and 1912. Andrew Haldane McLeod then operated the Mullingar Post Office in conjunction with a small store on his homestead about three miles south of the present townsite. About a mile northwest of his farm, Mullingar's first school was built in 1908. This was burned down when the teacher was burning rubbish in the schoolyard one day, and so a second school had to be built in 1909. A prairie fire that September claimed that building, too. Classes were then held in an area home for the next four years. In 1926, a couple of years before the railway came through, large numbers of Mennonite families began settling in the region, over a swath of land that extended roughly from Mayfair northwest to the Fairholme area. A Mennonite Brethren church and cemetery were established about a mile from the McLeod farm. The congregation was dissolved in the years following WWII, however, due to people moving out of the district. In 1928, with the construction of the CNR line through the area, the Mullingar hamlet site was chosen, and McLeod relocated his store and the post office to the locale (McLeod served as the Mullingar postmaster until 1948). A community hall was soon erected and, with rail service, two grain companies built elevators — the Saskatchewan Wheat Pool and

▲ **THE NAICAM ORCHESTRA**, 1939-40. Photograph courtesy of the Naicam Museum.

Searle — and other businesses were established. At one time, Mullingar had two stores, two garages, a livery stable, blacksmith shop, café, rooming house, and a very active stockyard. In 1934, a school in the hamlet was started. The community had a hockey team and a baseball team, and a sports day became an annual event. A curling rink was built in 1950 and was well utilized for a number of years. Mullingar had Homemakers and 4-H clubs, and in 1956 the community was established as an organized hamlet. In 1966, the population was 50. But by 1972 it had fallen to 33, and in 1986 only 18 people were counted as residing in Mullingar. The school closed in the 1970s; the post office closed in 1987. Today, a couple of abandoned buildings and sidewalks running along vacant lots are about all that is left at the townsite. A sizable cemetery gives testimony to the fact that there was once a viable community in the area. Mullingar is situated in the RM of Meeting Lake No. 466.

NAICAM, town, pop 690 (2006c), 761 (2001c), is located between Watson and Melfort at the junction of Hwys 6 and 349. The community is situated in an area of rich farmland dotted with numerous small lakes and patches of wetland wilderness. It is an area where the aspen parklands blend into the boreal transition ecoregion. The first settlers began taking up land in the district in 1904 and, with the Canadian Northern Railway soon running through Watson, settlement of the area intensified over the following years. Many who came to the Naicam area were of Norwegian and Swedish origin, but, additionally, there were people of English and German origins, among others. By 1910, a post office and a school had been established in the vicinity of the present community. In late 1918, the CPR purchased land for a townsite from Mrs. Ingeborg Knutson, and in 1919 the first couple of businesses appeared, followed by more

the next year as the railway drew nearer. In December 1920, the first work train arrived in Naicam, and Ingeborg Knutson had the honour of driving a ceremonial spike. On April 28, 1921, Naicam was incorporated as a village, its name derived from the first three letters of the names of two railway contractors, Naismith and Cameron. The population that year was 119. By the 1950s, the population was over 500, and on September 1, 1954, Naicam attained town status. Today, Naicam serves a trading area population of approximately 4,600 people within about a 30-kilometre radius, and a number of the community's businesses operate in support of the district's agricultural industry. Naicam has a medical clinic, a pharmacy, home care services, seniors' housing, and an ambulance service. Additionally, the community has an RCMP detachment and a volunteer fire department and rescue unit. Educational facilities include a pre-school, a K-12 school, which accommodates close to 300 town and area students, and a library. The community has a weekly newspaper, churches, service clubs, sports and youth groups, and other community-based organizations. Recreational facilities include a sports complex with rinks for skating, hockey, and curling, and the town has ball diamonds, lighted tennis and basketball courts, a seniors' centre, and a nine-hole golf course. Hunting and fishing are popular in the area and there are two regional parks in the district. Community attractions include the Naicam Museum, located in the 1923 Pioneer School, and the town's original CPR station, which now houses a licenced dining room. During the summer months, the town's floral displays are an added attraction and, for two years running, Naicam has been the provincial winner in its category in the nationally acclaimed Communities in Bloom competition. Saskatchewan singer-songwriter Stan Garchinski's musical career began with a family dance band called the Cavaliers in Naicam, and it was Garchinski's song that was chosen as the official song of the Saskatchewan Centennial in 2005. Naicam serves as the administrative centre of the RM of Pleasantdale No. 398.

NEILBURG, village, pop 394 (2006c), 366 (2001c), is located on Hwy 40, approximately 100 km west of the Battlefords, and 75 km southeast of Lloydminster. Manitou Lake lies just south of the community. Settlers began moving into the area around 1905, and Neilburg derives its name from a post office established in 1908 at the home of Clifford O'Neil, who lived southwest of the present site of the village. That same year, a local school district was established. With the construction of the CPR branch line from Wilkie to Lloydminster being resumed in the mid-1920s (the line had not progressed beyond Cut Knife since 1911), new village sites were established along the line, Neilburg, in 1923, being one of them. By 1924, four elevator companies were buying grain, and a hotel and numerous other businesses were in op-

▼ **THE "PIONEER PARADE" IN NEILBURG**, June 24, 2000, was a community fundraising event organized to raise money to build a local museum. Photograph courtesy of the Manitou Pioneers Museum, Neilburg.

Naicam Sask. 1922.

eration. That year, the post office was relocated to the townsite, and in 1925 children began attending a school established in the community. From the late 1920s through the ensuing decades, Neilburg's baseball teams — first the All-Stars, and then the Monarchs — were a dominant force in the province, winning numerous trophies and championships. On January 1, 1947, Neilburg attained village status, and the community prospered through the 1950s. The population of Neilburg stabilized at close to its current level in the mid-1970s. The major industries in the area are in agriculture, and oil and gas. Cereal grains, canola, peas, flax, lentils, and canary seed are grown; cattle, including purebred herds, are raised, as are hogs. There are over 600 oil wells in the surrounding rural municipality. Manufacturers in Neilburg supply products to the area's oil and gas industry, and the village has two farm supply centres and a veterinary clinic. The village also has a heath centre, a credit union, a volunteer fire department, a community hall, a library, the Manitou Pioneers Museum, a bowling alley, a hair salon, a hotel, cafés, and grocery stores. Neilburg Composite School is a K-12 institution, which had 185 students enrolled in the fall of 2006. The regional park at Manitou Lake has ball diamonds, campsites, and a nine-hole, sand-green golf course. In September 1999, interesting formations of crop circles were discovered in the Neilburg district. Neilburg serves as the administrative centre of the RM of Hillsdale No. 440.

NESSLIN LAKE, organized hamlet, est. 1989, is a small resort area located 25 km northeast of Big River near the western boundary of Prince Albert National Park. The area is popular for fishing, hunting, photography, and camping, and the cottage community's beautiful setting has also been the subject of paintings by the noted Saskatchewan artist Glen Scrimshaw. Nesslin Lake has a small permanent population and is situated in the RM of Big River No. 555.

NETHERHILL, village, pop 30 (2006c), 35 (2001c), is located approximately 21 km east of Kindersley on Hwy 7. The first settlers began arriving in the district in 1906, and one of them, John Craig, established a post office he named Netherhill in March of 1908. Craig, who served as the postmaster until his death in 1936, was a Scot, and the name Netherhill refers to a place where he had lived in the country of his birth. The Canadian Northern Railway came through the Netherhill district circa 1909, and with its arrival the community developed. Netherhill was incorporated as a village on April 28, 1910. Netherhill reached a peak population of 133 in 1941, and the village's numbers hovered at a little over the 100-mark until the mid-1960s. Subsequently, the community has steadily declined. Netherhill is situated in the RM of Kindersley No. 290.

NEUANLAGE, organized hamlet, pop 143 (2006c), 141 (2001c), is located between Osler and Hague, just off Hwy 11. One of a number of Mennonite villages that were established in the area, Neuanlage (meaning 'new settlement' in German) was founded by Mennonite farmers from Manitoba in 1895. Fertile soil, an abundance of water, and easy access to markets via the railway then linking Saskatoon to Prince Albert were reasons for choosing the site. While many left for Mexico in the 1920s over the issue of English schooling, simultaneously, many more Mennonite immigrants arrived, fleeing the Soviet Union. Today, the traditional village layout remains and is situated in an agricultural setting; a number of residents commute to work in Saskatoon. The focal point of the hamlet is the active Neuanlage Grace Mennonite Church. Until the 1950s, worship services were conducted in German. Neuanlage was legally established as an organized hamlet in 1984 and is situated in the RM of Rosthern No. 403.

NEUDORF, village, pop 281 (2006c), 304 (2001c), is situated southwest of Melville, between the town of Lemberg and the village of Killaly on Hwy 22; the Qu'Appelle Valley lies approximately a dozen kilometres to the south. Settlement of the district occurred between 1890 and 1900 with the arrival of Russian and Galician German Lutherans. The name Neudorf — German for "new village" — dates to the establishment of the Neudorf Post Office on July 1, 1895. The name was chosen by Ludwig Wendel, Sr. (1842-1909), the first postmaster, after his home town of Neudorf in Galicia, crown land of the Austro-Hungarian monarchy until 1918. Wendel later donated the land upon which the village now sits, on the condition that the name Neudorf was adopted for that of the community. Prior to the arrival of the railway, trips to either Grenfell or Wolseley were necessary to sell grain or purchase many supplies, and the Neudorf Post Office was served through Grenfell, with couriers making the trip twice a week. The present village dates to the construction of the CPR rail line through the district in 1904, and for the first half of the twentieth century the railway played a major role in the community. Neudorf was chosen by the CPR as a divisional point, and the railway company became, by far, the village's major employer. Rail yards with about two miles of track, a six-stall roundhouse and a turntable for locomotives, a station, a storehouse, a coal dock, a water tower, and a bunkhouse were constructed. The CPR also established a park and garden around the station site. Several train crews, locomotive foremen, the station agent, section men, mechanics, shop and yard hands, coal men, telegraph operators, a timekeeper, a storeman, etc. — all had homes and families in Neudorf. In 1904, Neudorf had the post office, two stores, livery barns, a liquor outlet, and about a half-dozen log houses; within a few years there was a hotel, dance halls, a theatre and a bowling alley, churches, a village school, a doctor, implement agencies, blacksmiths, barbers, carpenters, a tailor, a shoemaker, and a butcher. The first skating rink — an outdoor surface — was built in 1908. The Union Bank of Canada (later acquired by the Royal Bank) opened for business in 1910. The Village of Neudorf was incorporated on

April 25, 1905, and the population grew from 159 in 1906 to 500 by 1921. The local history published in 1980 recounts that during WWI there was an RNWMP detachment in Neudorf, reportedly established because of government anxiety over people of German ancestry possibly endeavouring to sabotage the Canadian war effort. There was no trouble. In the 1920s, a large slough just north of Neudorf, known locally as Wendel's Lake, was a popular spot for swimming. The slough covered about 150 acres during wet years, and people built diving platforms, rafted, and had picnics there. For a few years, until a pipeline from the Qu'Appelle Valley was completed, water from the "lake" was also pumped into Neudorf for railway use. Wendel's Lake dried out during the 1930s and was completely dry by 1942; by the time it filled up again in the 1950s, better roads and cars had given people easy access to the lakes in the Qu'Appelle Valley, and the old swimming hole was not visited any more. Neudorf experienced a loss of population and economic hardship during the Depression; however, the community recovered for a period during the post-WWII boom. In 1948, an indoor hockey arena was erected, and the Neudorf Union Hospital was built in 1949. In the early 1960s natural gas was piped into the community, and water and sewer systems were installed. As the village entered the latter half of the twentieth century, however, it had begun to witness the end of an era — the end of its days as a railway town. The first blow came during WWII, when the roundhouse was reduced from its six original stalls to two. These would eventually be closed, too; then the rail yards, buildings, and the heavy machinery were removed, and with the advent of diesel locomotives the coal dock and the water tower were no longer necessary

▲ **JULY 12, 1905:** a fair at the picnic grounds in Neudorf. Note the swing to the right.

▲ **THE WEDDING OF MIKE SCHMIDT AND BERTHA FRYER** at a Neudorf area farm, circa 1913.

▼ **MAIN STREET, NEUDORF**, facing southwest, circa 1927. Within months of this photograph being taken, the large general store in the right foreground burned down.

and they were demolished. First passenger, then rail freight, services were terminated, as were the last jobs with the CPR. All-weather roads, and modern cars and trucks precipitated changing times. Travel to Yorkton, Melville, and even Regina for business and shopping became routine and led to a deterioration of local services. In 1969, despite a large protest at the Provincial Legislative Building, the Neudorf Union Hospital was closed — there remained a community health centre, but Neudorf never again had a resident doctor. Other Saskatchewan towns and villages that had their hospitals downgraded that

year included Quill Lake, Leroy, Maryfield, and Hodgeville. By 1980, many of the businesses that once existed in Neudorf were gone. The Federal Grain elevator had closed, as had the United Church, and the post office was downgraded, resulting in a reduction in hours of operation. Older schoolchildren began to be bused to Lemberg. From a population of 506 in 1966, Neudorf's numbers were down to 425 by 1981, and they have continued to fall over each consecutive census period. The median age of Neudorf residents in 2001 was 55.5, while that of all Saskatchewan residents was 36.7. The rail line from Ester-

hazy to Neudorf was abandoned in 1996, and Neudorf's remaining grain elevators were demolished in 2001. In spite of the decline in the community's fortunes over the past decades, Neudorf residents still demonstrated unity and a co-operative spirit: in the mid-1970s the indoor rink was destroyed in a wind storm, but through volunteerism and donations a new rink complex with three sheets of curling ice and a regulation-size hockey arena were constructed. The same kind of effort went into the building of a new community hall and the production of a local history book to coincide with Saskatchewan's 75th an-

niversary celebrations in 1980. Neudorf produced an updated history book for the province's Centennial in 2005. Today, the community hosts a number of annual events, including a snowmobile derby and a fall supper. Neudorf has six ball diamonds and a well-maintained and attractive golf course. The local golf club hosts a tournament in June. Hockey, curling, figure skating, softball and fastball are seasonally pursued. Neudorf has two co-operatives: one sells fuels and hardware and provides auto servicing; the other sells groceries and liquor, and has a Sears outlet and movie rentals. The community has a credit union, a restaurant, a general store and café, a hair salon, and several other local businesses. The village has three churches, a library, a seniors' centre, a daycare, and a volunteer fire department. The nearest RCMP detachment is in Melville. North Valley Elementary School in Neudorf is a K-6 institution which had 95 students enrolled in the fall of 2006: children attend grades 7 through 12 in Lemberg. One of Neudorf's more notable sons was Henry Taube (1915–2005). Born in Neudorf, Taube received the Nobel Prize in Chemistry in 1983. Neudorf serves as the administrative centre of the RM of McLeod No. 185.

118 MAIN STREET. This fieldstone house in Neudorf was built in 1905. Photograph taken October 20, 2003.

Other than the fieldstone house, all Neudorf photographs on this and facing page courtesy of Murray J. Hanowski, Mayor of Neudorf and Administrator of the RM of McLeod No. 185.

LAST TRAIN leaving Neudorf in June 2001. The grain elevators came down shortly afterward. Photographed by Murray J. Hanowski, Neudorf.

NEUHORST, organized hamlet, pop 126 (2006c), 135 (2001c), is located north of Warman on Hwy 305. One of a number of Mennonite villages that were established in the area, Neuhorst was founded by Mennonite farmers from Manitoba in the late 1890s. Fertile soil, an abundance of water, and easy access to markets via the railway then linking Saskatoon to Prince Albert were among the reasons for settling in the region. While many left for Mexico in the 1920s over

the issue of English schooling, simultaneously, many more Mennonite immigrants arrived, fleeing the Soviet Union. Today, the traditional village layout remains. Neuhorst was legally established as an organized hamlet in 1961 and is situated in the RM of Corman Park No. 344.

NEVILLE, village, pop 65 (2006c), 70 (2001c), is situated 46 km south of Swift Current on Hwy 43. Homesteaders began coming to the district around 1907, and, with the CPR laying the groundwork for a branch line to run southeast from Swift Current (the route was surveyed in 1910 and track was beginning to be laid in 1911), Neville had its beginnings. Land for the townsite was purchased from homesteaders Hugh Graham and Edward Payne. The local history records that the first train coming into the townsite in February of 1912 got stuck in the snow and had to be shovelled out. There were reportedly only two buildings at Neville at this time, but after the arrival of the railway Neville developed rapidly and, within a year, perhaps as many as three dozen businesses were in operation where previously was prairie. The CPR station was built in 1912 as was the Methodist (later United) Church, and Neville was incorporated as a village on July 5 that year. In 1913, a school was started in the community and Neville boasted a band and even a newspaper. By 1916, the population of the village was 179; a decade later, in 1926, it was 232. On May 24, 1917, a future premier of Saskatchewan, Ross Thatcher, was born in Neville, where his father, Wilbert, ran a hardware and dry goods store and his mother, Marjorie, taught school. The first several years in the village were boom times; the 1920s were halcyon days. Neville even boasted a rather unique attrac-

tion for a prairie village of its size — a roller-skating rink. The community lost a significant portion of its population, though, through the Depression, the drought, and the war years — its numbers had fallen to 143 by 1946 — but the village prospered again during the 1950s and early 1960s. The population was again over 200 by 1961. Subsequently, however, the community's numbers began to decline to their present level and businesses in the village began to close, largely superseded by the array of Swift Current's offerings. A major community landmark in Neville, the Royal George Hotel, built circa 1912, burned to the ground in 1964 and, that year, the older grades at Neville School began to be bused to classes in Swift Current. Today, Neville retains a post office, the United Church, and the skating rink; the Pioneer Co-op has a keylock fuel facility in the village from where gasoline may be obtained. The one remaining grain elevator is now privately owned and is served by the Great Western Railway. Neville is without a grocery store or a restaurant. The community school was a K-9 facility, which had 19 students enrolled in the fall of 2006; it closed in June 2007. Neville residents travel to Swift Current for medical services, and the village is policed by the RCMP detachment out of Ponteix. Neville lies just within the western boundary of the RM of Whiska Creek No. 106; less than a kilometre to the west begins the RM of Lac Pelletier No. 107. The latter RM has its administrative office in the village.

▲ **BUSH WORK** in the Nipawin area, late 1940s. Third from the left is Fred Lundgren; in the centre is Pete Ferguson; others unknown.

▲ **A STERNWHEELER** being unloaded at Nipawin circa 1920.

▼ **FERRY SERVICE AT NIPAWIN**, date unknown. Photograph courtesy of the Drake Village Office.

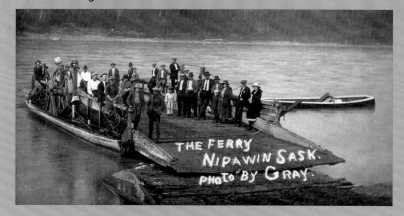

Unless otherwise indicated, photographs are courtesy of the Nipawin and District Living Forestry Museum.

NIPAWIN
Once upon a river...

Canadian Pacific Bridge Construction Nipawin. Sask.

▲▼ **BRIDGE-BUILDING.** Work on the Canadian Pacific Railway's bridge at Nipawin began in 1928. Early stages of construction are pictured above. Work continues, below. During the peak of construction, between 450 and 500 men worked on the project.

Rapid Transit across the Saskatchewan River. 1017 Nipawin. Sask.

▲ **RAPID TRANSIT IN A BUCKET, 1919.** This was the method of transportation used to cross the Saskatchewan River when it was partially frozen and unsafe to travel over.

NIPAWIN, town, pop 4,061 (2006c), 4,275 (2001c), is located northeast of Melfort on Hwys 35 and 55. The Saskatchewan River passes just to the west of the community. The first settlers began making incursions into the area around 1906. By 1910, Nipawin's original townsite was developing about six and a half kilometres south of the present community. In 1924, the CPR arrived in the area from Tisdale and, subsequently, announced its intention to establish a village at the community's present location. Within weeks, using teams of horses, everything from the old townsite was relocated to the rail line. In May 1925, the village of Nipawin was incorporated. In 1928, a bridge to facilitate rail and road traffic west across the river was begun, which, when completed, would bring an end both to the ferry service and to the cable car operation that was used to cross the river when neither open water nor ice accommodated crossing. A diverse economy based on forestry, trapping, agriculture, and business allowed the community to develop rapidly. In 1936 the population was 892, and in 1937 Nipawin acquired town status. By 1951, the population was over 3,000. In the early 1960s, the Squaw Rapids (now E. B. Campbell) Dam was completed, forming the large body of water now known as Tobin Lake northeast of the community; in 1986, the Francois-Finlay Dam was completed, creating Codette Lake to the town's southwest. Subsequently, tourism has become an important part of Nipawin's economy, and the area has become a virtual Mecca for sports fishing. Many record fish have been caught in Tobin Lake over the years, and on January 4, 2005, a world record was set when Father Mariusz Zajac of Carrot River landed the largest walleye ever caught ice-fishing. The catch weighed 8.3 kgs or 18.3 lbs. When asked whether he has a special fishing tip, Father Mariusz suggested reciting the prayer in Luke 1:46-55. Today, Nipawin has a diverse economy, with approximately 400 businesses and services providing for virtually every need. Nipawin has a complete range of medical facilities, related services, and practitioners, as well as an RCMP detachment and a volunteer fire department. The community has daycare and pre-school facilities, elementary and high schools (which had a combined enrollment of over 1,000 in 2006-07), a post-secondary Bible college, and a secular regional college that provides an additional range of post-secondary programs. Its complete array of recreational facilities is further augmented by numerous parks in the area, including a regional park located 2 kilometres from the town. The community has a number of churches, service clubs, athletic associations, cultural organizations, and youth groups. The town has a library and a museum complex which occupies a 14-acre site. Agricultural-based industries are significant employers, and Nipawin is one of the country's leading producers of honey. A 200-acre nursery produces trees and shrubs, which are sold across western Canada, and innovative businesses such as fish farming and manufacturing fishing tackle have developed in recent years. Forestry, as well, remains an important component of the area economy. The longest highway bridge in the province is located at Nipawin, crossing the Saskatchewan River. Two of Saskatchewan's most creative minds — author Sharon Butala and painter Arthur (Art) Fortescue McKay, of Regina Five fame — were born in the community. Nipawin is located in the RM of Nipawin No. 487.

NOKOMIS, town, pop 404 (2006c), 436 (2001c), is located just to the northeast of the north end of Last Mountain Lake on Hwys 15 and 20. The first homesteads were established in the Nokomis area around 1904, and the community developed a few years later at the junction of two competing railways as they came through the area. The north-south CPR line reached Nokomis in 1907, followed shortly thereafter by the east-west Grand Trunk Pacific (now CN). Nokomis developed rapidly at the intersection of the tracks and was incorporated as a village on March 5, 1908. Just over five months later, on August 15, the commu-nity attained town status. The name Nokomis had been chosen in 1906 by Florence Mary Halstead for a post office she started southeast of the present townsite. Nokomis was Hiawatha's grandmother in Longfellow's famous epic poem, and, according to local history, Halstead, who had recently arrived from England, chose the name because, to her, the west represented the romantic domain of the Indian. By 1916, the town had a population of 508 and had developed into a substantial service centre for the surrounding agricultural district. Notable Canadian author Max Braithwaite was born in Nokomis in 1911. Agriculture remains the basis of the Nokomis area economy today, and a number of the town's businesses are related to the

▲ **AN EARLY VIEW OF NOKOMIS**, lumberyard in foreground. Saskatchewan Archives Board R-B362.

▼ **NOKOMIS AND DISTRICT MUSEUM.** Photograph taken June 28, 2004.

industry. Nokomis has a health centre and special care home and a volunteer fire department. Policing is provided by the Lanigan RCMP detachment. Nokomis has a K-12 school, four churches, and a library. Its museum features the community's former CN train station, as well as wildlife dioramas and a re-creation of a 1907-era business district. Nokomis has a number of service clubs, sports teams, and other community-based organizations. A recreation centre houses rinks for skating, hockey, and curling, and the town has a nine-hole golf course. The community's Bank of Commerce building, built circa 1907-08 and immaculately preserved, has been designated a heritage property and now houses a bed and breakfast. Area attractions include the Last Mountain Lake National Wildlife Area. Established in 1887, it was the first federal bird sanctuary in North America and is regarded as a wetland of international importance. Nokomis serves as the administrative centre of the RM of Wreford No. 280.

NORQUAY, town, pop 412 (2006c), 485 (2001c), is located northwest of Kamsack, approximately 35 km from the Saskatchewan-Manitoba border, on Hwys 8 and 49. The community is situated between the Assiniboine and Swan Rivers in a parkland setting, and cultivated land gives way to forest, lakes, and streams north of the town. During the first half of the twentieth century, logging was a key part of the area economy. Today, the district surrounding Norquay sustains grain and livestock operations. Settlement of the area began in the late 1800s and increased in the early 1900s as railways began to approach the region. Ranchers, homesteaders, lumbermen, and farmers were followed by storekeepers, black-

▲ **STEAM ENGINE AND TRAIN** at Norquay Station, date unknown. Photograph donated by Carol Jorgesson, courtesy of Paulette Nygren, Norquay.

▲ **MAIN STREET, NORQUAY**, circa 1940s. Photograph donated by Nelda Graham, courtesy of Paulette Nygren, Norquay.

smiths, teachers, and doctors. Although few at first, settlers increased in numbers after the Manitoba and Northwestern Railway began running trains into Yorkton in 1891, and the Canadian Northern Railway had lines built to Swan River, Manitoba, in 1898-99, and Kamsack in 1904. The Canadian Northern line was built into Norquay in 1911. Settlers in the Norquay district were of diverse origins: the first ones came from eastern Canada, particularly Ontario, and from the British Isles; later arrivals were from the U.S. and continental Europe. Doukhobors disembarked the train at Yorkton and headed north; many Scandinavians from both the U.S. and northern Europe arrived around 1906-08. Large numbers of Ukrainians arrived prior to WWI and again in the 1920s. Then, in the 1930s, people from the dried-out regions of southern Saskatchewan came to settle the forest fringes north of Norquay. With the arrival of the railway, the townsite developed and Norquay was incorporated as a village in 1913. The name of the community honours John Norquay, premier of Manitoba from 1878 to 1887. The village grew to have a population of just over 300 by the early 1940s; following WWII, however, Norquay developed significantly. By the early 1960s, the population was over 500 and, in 1963, Norquay attained town status. The community had a peak population of 575 in 1986. Today, the median age of Norquay's population is 54.3, while the average age of Saskatchewan residents is 36.7. Slightly more than 42 per cent of Norquay's residents are over the age of 65. The town has a range of businesses and services, a number of which are involved with the district's agricultural industry. Norquay has a health centre with an attached special care home, a medical clinic, home care services, and an ambulance service. Protective services are provided by a local volunteer fire department, the Pelly RCMP detachment, and area emergency measures organizations operated in partnership with the communities of Sturgis and Canora. Norquay School provides K-12 education to over 200 town and area students, and post-secondary classes and programs are available through the Parkland Regional College. The town also has a pre-school and a library, and there are a number of churches, clubs and organizations. A community recreation complex houses rinks for skating, hockey, and curling, and has a hall with a stage, dance floor, and a seating capacity for roughly 550 people. The town has sports grounds and campgrounds, and a local snowmobile club maintains 322 kilometres (200 miles) of trails. Hunting for bear, moose, elk, and white-tailed deer is popular in the area, as is fishing for pike, perch, walleye, and trout in both summer and winter months. The Norquay Wildlife Federation works with the provincial government to manage the region's wildlife, developing and preserving habitat areas. A unique business in the town of Norquay is an award-winning magazine publishing company. *Prairies North* magazine, founded in 1998 as *Saskatchewan Naturally Magazine* by Michelle and Lionel Hughes, has been nationally and internationally recognized for its journalistic and photographic portrayals of life in Saskatchewan. Norquay is situated in the RM of Clayton No. 333.

NORTH BATTLEFORD, city, pop 13,190 (2006c), 13,692 (2001c), is situated on the north side of the North Saskatchewan River opposite the town of Battleford, approximately 140 km northwest of Saskatoon and 140 km southeast of Lloydminster. Founded by the Canadian Northern Railway in 1904-05, North Battleford is today served by a municipal airport and five highways: the Yellowhead Highway, and Hwys 4, 26, 29, and 40. It had been fully expected that the Canadian Northern Railway would construct their line across the province through the well-established community of Battleford on the south side of the river; however, history once again passed Battleford by when the railway was surveyed to run along the river's north side, and a new townsite was surveyed. North Battleford was launched into existence, becoming one of the fastest growing centres in the west. To the indignation of the established south shore town, the new site was named "North Battleford," and it quickly surpassed the older community in size and importance. With a history dating to the 1870s, Battleford, once the Territorial capital, was left to remain a modest town, while North Battleford gained village status on March 21, 1906, became a town within four months, and became the province's fifth city on May 1, 1913 — the first city declared as such by the Government of Saskatchewan. Growth in the countryside was equally as dramatic: over 1905-06, homestead entries in the district were filed at the rate of about 400 per month. By the early 1920s, however, the boom period was over and North Battleford's population remained level at somewhat under 5,000 for the

next 25 years. In the 15 years following WWII, the population then doubled, and through the 1960s, 1970s, and 1980s the city continued to grow. Today, approximately 20 per cent of North Battleford's residents are of First Nations or Métis ancestry. Over the course of its history, North Battleford has grown to become a key service, distribution, and receiving centre for the province's northwest. Agriculture, lumber, and fishing were the traditional components of the economy; oil and gas production is of increasing importance, and today a number of companies in North Battleford provide services to the industry. At the beginning of the twenty-first century, the Battlefords were witnessing a record number of new construction projects: no fewer than 17 condominium and housing subdivisions were underway in 2007, and during the first years of the millennium "big box" retailers such as Wal-Mart and Canadian Tire, and major national franchise ventures such as Staples and Boston Pizza, were either building brand-new operations or expanding existing ones. Battlefords Union Hospital, the Saskatchewan Hospital, and the Battlefords Mental Health Centre are the city's major medical facilities, and North Battleford has nine elementary schools and three high schools. Northwest Regional

College offers post-secondary programs and first-year university classes. Centennial Park, an 80-acre site in the heart of the city, is a hub of recreational and sporting activities. The park consists of the Lions Stadium baseball complex, a civic centre and an aquatic centre, track and field facilities, soccer and horseshoe pitches, lawn bowling greens, and tennis courts. North Battleford attractions include the Western Development Museum, the Chapel Gallery, the Golden Eagle Casino, the North Battleford Golf & Country Club, and the internationally-recognized collection at the Allan Sapp Gallery, situated in a former Carnegie-funded library, one of only 13 built in western Canada and the only remaining in Saskatchewan. On the North Saskatchewan River lies Finlayson Island, an area of protected native flora and fauna. Across the river, in Battleford, is the Fort Battleford National Historic Site. A half-hour's drive north of the city on Jackfish Lake is The Battlefords Provincial Park; about a half-hour's drive west is Table Mountain, which accommodates downhill skiing and snowboarding with a 110-metre (360-ft.) vertical drop and a longest run of 1,100 metres (3,600 ft.). The 500-acre complex sees 65–75,000 skiers and snowboarders each year. North Battleford made national headlines in the

spring of 2001 when more than 7,000 people fell ill when the town's water supply became tainted with the cryptosporidium bacterium. The outbreak was traced to the city's water treatment plant and an official inquiry was launched. Both the City and the Province agreed to an out-of-court compensation package for those who had become ill. Fortunately, no one died as a result of the contamination. North Battleford serves as the administrative centre of the RM of North Battleford No. 437.

NORTH COLESDALE PARK,

organized hamlet, is one in a string of resort communities situated along the east shore of Last Mountain Lake. It is located in the RM of McKillop No. 220. Originally a part of the resort community of Colesdale Park, North Colesdale Park became independently established in 1987. There are a small number of permanent residents; however, the population varies greatly depending on the season.

NORTH GROVE, resort village,

inc. 1989, is located on the northeast shore of Buffalo Pound Lake. The community stretches for several kilometres along the lake's shore and is accessible via Hwy 2. There is a year-round population of 68 (2006c); however, there are approximately 120 cabins and permanent residences, so the summer population may reach well over 200. A number of people commute to work in Moose Jaw. North Grove is situated in the RM of Dufferin No. 190.

NORTH PORTAL, village, pop

123 (2006c), 136 (2001c), is located on Hwy 39, 37 km southeast of Estevan, astride the Canada-U.S. border; as is indicated by its name, the community serves as an international port of entry. In 1893, the CPR's Soo Line connecting Moose Jaw and Minneapolis was built through the community and, in the same year, the customs house was established. In 1903, the village was incorporated. During the prohibition era, North Portal was a centre of the illegal trade in liquor, with rum-runners bottling booze in the basement of

▼ **COMING INTO CANADA:** a CP train about to cross the international boundary at North Portal. Photograph taken August 26, 2003.

the Grandview Hotel. The building, built in 1903 and now a municipal heritage property, also served as a nightstop for many early immigrants to Saskatchewan who were arriving via the United States. Another unique feature of the village is that it is home to the only golf club in North America located in two countries. While the course is primarily in Saskatchewan, the 9th hole and the club house are in North Dakota. A modern visitor's centre in North Portal welcomes travellers to Saskatchewan and Canada, and customs houses and brokerage firms provide some local employment. The border crossing is open 24 hours a day. North Portal is located within the RM of Coalfields No. 4.

NORTH SHORE FISHING LAKE

, organized hamlet, is a resort community located approximately 22 km southeast of Wadena on Fishing Lake, south of Hwy 5. The area became a popular summer vacation spot in the early 1900s as early settlers from the Wadena and Kuroki areas would tent, swim, picnic, and fish there during the summer. By the 1920s, the area featured a dance pavilion, a bathhouse, boathouses, cottages, wharfs, and diving platforms. The lake's water levels, however, are susceptible to both drought and flooding. Its two basins were separated during a dry spell over a century ago and, in the 1930s, levels also significantly receded. In the mid-1990s, resort areas, cottages, and district roads were substantially damaged by rising water. Fishing Lake's shores are now highly developed and are comprised of several resort communities. A regional park authority oversees public recreation areas and a golf course. The 2006 Census recorded 106 permanent residents at North Shore Fishing Lake; however, during the summer months, the population may be substantially higher. The community was established as an organized hamlet in 1988 and is situated in the RM of Sasman No. 336.

NORTH WEYBURN

, organized hamlet, pop 72 (2006c), 51 (2001c), is situated just northeast of the city of Weyburn and is the site of the Weyburn Airport. The Weyburn Airport was constructed in late 1941 as a British Commonwealth Air Training Plan base and was operated as such from 1942 to 1944, during which time 1,055 pilots received their wings. The base was abandoned in June 1944 and the site was quiet for a few years. Then, due to overcrowding at the Saskatchewan Hospital in Weyburn, some of the former armed forces buildings were converted into a medical facility and hundreds of mentally-handicapped patients were moved to the site. The hospital community was relocated to Moose Jaw in 1955, and in 1957 the Western Christian College then occupied the buildings, remaining in North Weyburn until their departure in 1989. Also in the late 1950s, as the Weyburn area was beginning to attract a number of industries, the former airport, with its numerous buildings and aircraft hangars, became the logical place for the development of an industrial park. Over the following decades, numerous manufacturers and other businesses were established at the site — the Saskatchewan Power Corporation had a training centre there — and around 1957, the Weyburn Flying Club began the first aviation operation at the former air base since the War. By the early 1960s, private and commercial aviation was becoming increasingly important at the Weyburn airport. Runway lights were installed in 1965 and, in addition to the numerous industrial concerns, crop-spraying services, an aircraft maintenance business, pilot training, charter services, aerial surveying, and air ambulance services were among the operations becoming based in North Weyburn. In 1981, to address the need for upgrading area infrastructure, residents sought a degree of political power and North Weyburn was established as an organized hamlet. North Weyburn is located in the RM of Weyburn No. 67.

NORTHSIDE

, organized hamlet, pop 25 (2006c), 48 (2001c), is located about 35 km north of Prince Albert at the junction of Hwy 2 and the access road to the village of Paddockwood. The name Northside was originally that of a post office established several kilometres south of the present community in 1915. In 1937, after several moves, the name became that of the post office in a store at the present hamlet's location and, subsequently, the name became that of the community. Northside was established as an organized hamlet in 1978 and is situated in the RM of Paddockwood No. 520.

NUT MOUNTAIN

, organized hamlet, pop 15 (2006c), 15 (2001c), is located just southeast of Kelvington on Hwy 49. The first settlers began arriving around 1904-05, largely aided by the fact that the Canadian Northern Railway was beginning to run roughly 15 km to the south, through Margo and Kuroki. Country schoolhouses began to spring up, and in 1908 the Nut Mountain Post Office was established somewhat northeast of the present community. The railway from Preeceville came through Nut Mountain en route to Kelvington in 1921, and much of the land in the district was taken up

◀ ▲ **ONCE HOMES, NOW JUST HOUSES.** Two former dwellings in Nut Mountain. Photographs taken July 29, 2004.

over the next decade. The townsite had developed with the coming of the railway. Agriculture, a mixture of grain and livestock production, became the major industry in the area. The community was established as an organized hamlet in 1949 and had a population close to 150 in the mid-1960s. The rail line was abandoned in 1990 and, today, the former Saskatchewan Wheat Pool elevator is privately owned. The community's old hotel was up for sale in the summer of 2004, and only a few houses scattered about the townsite remained occupied. Nut Mountain is on the verge of becoming a ghost town. It is situated in the RM of Sasman No. 336.

ODESSA, village, pop 201 (2006c), 242 (2001c), is located about 60 km southeast of Regina on Hwy 48. The area was predominantly settled by German Catholics, along with some people of British and French backgrounds. The first German settlers arrived between 1901 and 1904, many coming from the Odessa area of what was then southern Russia — hence the community's name. Before the village developed with the coming of the railway, Indian Head and Qu'Appelle were the main trading centres for the Odessa area residents. With the construction of the Canadian Northern Railway line from Brandon, Manitoba, progressing from Kipling to Regina in 1907, the townsite was established and surveyed, and in 1908 a good deal of development took place as general and hardware stores, an implement dealership, a livery barn, a lumber company, and a hotel all opened. The first Catholic church was built the same year. Within a few years, four grain elevators had been erected. A post office, which opened as Magna in 1908, changed its name to Odessa Station in 1910, and the Village of

▲ ▶ **HOLY FAMILY CHURCH**, built in 1953 and situated at the north end of Main Street in Odessa, dominates the community. A large, impressive, and colourful mosaic depicting Jesus, Mary, and Joseph graces the main entranceway. Photographs taken July 31, 2003.

Odessa was incorporated on March 14, 1911. The population of the community that year was 77. In 1914, a school was opened in the village (there had been a rural school district established as early as 1904), and in 1920 Ursuline Sisters came to teach at Odessa Village School, remaining a part of the teaching staff until 1975. By 1921, the village population had risen to 254, and other than a couple of fluctuations over the decades, Odessa's population has remained relatively stable compared to other Saskatchewan communities. The village's numbers dropped somewhat during the Depression — to 207 by 1941 — and through the 1930s several businesses — including the Bank of Toronto, the Massey Harris equipment dealership, a grain elevator, and the meat market — closed. The 1940s found the community engaged in the war effort, and the tensions between German-speaking people and non-Germans in the Odessa area that had existed during the First World War were largely nullified as scores of young men of all backgrounds hastened to recruiting depots to offer their services to their country. One Odessa family, the Deutschers, had eight sons — Ralph,

Henry, Mike, Tony, Bert, Adam, Joe, and John — serving in the R.C.A.F. Tribute was paid to the Deutscher family in the Canadian House of Commons, and the parents were honoured in a special ceremony held in Moose Jaw. Miraculously, given the life-expectancy of those who served in the Air Force, all of the Deutscher sons survived the War. Three other Odessa men, however, never came home. Following the War, Odessa's population recovered — it peaked at 281 in 1951 — but the 1950s were disastrous as far as the village's business community was concerned. At the beginning of the decade there were five farm implement dealerships in the village, but as the companies began to consolidate and concentrate their businesses in larger centres, all the enterprises in Odessa were closed. In the 1960s, water, sewer, and natural gas systems were installed in the community, but passenger service on the CNR line was discontinued. The station was closed, and the number of businesses in the village continued to decline as, increasingly, people were driving to Regina to shop and to work. Today, a good number of Odessa's residents are commuters and only a few businesses re-

main in the village. There is a bar, a Co-op gas and service station, a credit union, and a small company that sells grain bins and hoppers. The one remaining grain elevator is privately owned. Odessa has a community hall, an arena, and a seniors' centre. The K-9 school, which had 50 students enrolled in the fall of 2006, was closed at the end of June 2007. Students had attended grades 10 through 12 in Vibank since 2002. Odessa is situated in the RM of Francis No. 127.

OGEMA, town, pop 304 (2006c), 292 (2001c), is located approximately 110 km south of Regina, midway between Weyburn and Assiniboia on Hwy 13. The district began to be settled between 1906 and 1908, with people arriving from eastern Canada, areas of Europe, and the United States. With the advent of the railway the foundations of the townsite were established. The Ogema post office opened in 1910, and in 1911 the railway came through and Ogema was incorporated as a village. The population that year was recorded as being 171. By 1913, Ogema acquired town status. The community prospered through

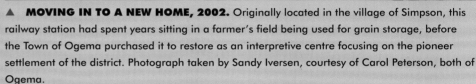

▲ **MOVING IN TO A NEW HOME, 2002.** Originally located in the village of Simpson, this railway station had spent years sitting in a farmer's field being used for grain storage, before the Town of Ogema purchased it to restore as an interpretive centre focusing on the pioneer settlement of the district. Photograph taken by Sandy Iversen, courtesy of Carol Peterson, both of Ogema.

◄ **AN OGEMA CURLING TEAM, 1915.**

Curling team photograph and the photographs of the fire and aftermath are courtesy of the Deep South Pioneer Museum.

Deep South Country... OGEMA

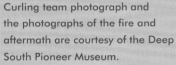

▲ **IN JANUARY OF 1915**, a fire destroyed the east side of Ogema's Main Street (3 photos above), and although firewalls were an uncommon and costly proposition at the time, town councillors decided that to ensure against future disasters they would construct across the west side of the street a wall that was 70 feet long, 28 feet high, and sunk 8 feet into the ground. On the east side, a fire hall was built with one of its walls constructed to act as the opposite firewall. This unique pair of structures remain features of Ogema's Main Street to this day (photos right and left). Interestingly, the contractor who built them was Robert John Lecky, who had been the construction superintendent during the erection of Saskatchewan's Legislative Building. Photographs of the firewall and the fire hall taken September 3, 2003.

the 1920s, witnessed an exodus during the 1930s, and saw a return to prosperity and growth during the post-WWII period. It was a typical Saskatchewan community with an economy based on mixed farming and ranching. By the 1980s, however, rationalization and consolidation were leading to a massive loss of infrastructure, and Ogema, which had developed as a hub for the surrounding communities in terms of providing basic services, was rapidly beginning to be overshadowed by the larger centres of Weyburn, Assiniboia, and Regina. In the mid-1990s, SaskPower closed its office in the town to Radville; CP abandoned and tore up the rail line from Weyburn to Pangman, and was planning on ceasing operations on the line running west through Ogema to Assiniboia; local elevators were closing; and with the number of students at the school falling below 100 (there had been 300 in the 1970s), there was fear the town would lose that institution. Ogema's population had hovered around 450 from post-WWII until the mid-1980s, but by the 1990s it was clear the community was in decline. What resulted subsequently, however, has been a small-town success story. Proactive community leaders in Ogema and other area communities sought initiatives and partnerships, and advanced the concept of a regional economy. When the hospital in the neighbouring village of Pangman was to be closed, Ogema residents rallied in support of the community to help retain local medical services. A health centre with a resident physician, an attached personal care home, and an ambulance service were successfully established, and this set the stage for future regional business ventures. In 1999, members of various communities completed negotiations to purchase the CP branch line that ran from Pangman to Assiniboia, and Red

Coat Road and Rail became the first community-owned short line in the province. Ogema area farmers also purchased the town's former Saskatchewan Wheat Pool (SWP) elevator and developed a producer car-loading facility; similarly, small groups and individuals along the line bought other SWP elevators, ensuring the continuation of local service as well as the short line's success. Community leaders also enticed Big Sky Farms to establish a 5,000-sow farrow-to-finish hog operation in the Ogema area, the first of that size in Canada. The facility created more than 60 new jobs. The economic momentum generated by these projects also led to both the expansion and the establishment of small manufacturing companies in the area, and the cumulative result has been a significant degree of success in building a sustainable future. In recent years, the Saskatchewan Government's Action Committee on the Rural Economy (ACRE) named Ogema a model community in terms of contemporary economic development strategies for rural Saskatchewan. Ogema School continues to provide K-12 education to town and area students. The Deep South Pioneer Museum, situated on a 12-acre site, is one of the largest in the province and contains a complete townsite comprised of over 50 historic buildings; the site has been used for the production of films. Ogema also has a well-preserved British American service station, which is thought to date to the WWI era, and a 1911 CPR train station situated at the end of Main Street. Ogema has a wide range of recreational facilities, most notably the regional park on the south side of town, where there is another unique community landmark, the Ogema Grandstand, which dates to the mid-1920s. Ogema serves as the administrative centre of the RM of Key West No. 70.

OKLA, organized hamlet, pop 25 (2006c), 35 (2001c), is located 32 km west of Preeceville on Hwy 49. The first settlers arrived roughly between 1906 and 1911, largely aided by the fact that by then the newly-completed Canadian Northern Railway line was running roughly 20 km to the south. In 1917, the one-room Okla School opened, named after the U.S. state of Oklahoma, from where a number of the first district families had come. In 1918-19, the flu epidemic claimed several lives in the area. Trains were running through Okla in 1921, and shortly thereafter the first store was opened at the townsite. A community hall was built, and the Okla Post Office opened in 1923. With rail service, many more people arrived in the district and the area came to have a diverse population: British from overseas or from eastern Canada, as well as Ukrainians, and many Norwegians. The early 1930s brought more people to the Okla area from regions of southern Saskatchewan parched by the drought; however, their migration northward was to offer little reprieve from hardship, as the Depression by then was deepening. In

the winter of 1935, an appeal was made to the province to provide food and clothing, but no help was available. Furthering the hardship was an outbreak of polio in 1936. The school was forced to close and one child died. During the 1940s, Okla's fortunes changed and the small community thrived. The cordwood industry that dominated the area economy was giving way to agriculture, new businesses were started, and a gravel highway made travel much easier. In more recent decades, though, the community has been in decline. Most businesses have closed and the population of Okla has not been above 50 since the 1960s. The school closed in 1970. Today, Okla remains the administrative centre of the RM of Hazel Dell No. 335; the area economy is primarily based on agriculture, a mixture of grain and cattle production.

ORKNEY, organized hamlet, pop 0 (2006c), 5 (2001c), is located southwest of Val Marie on Hwy 18, a few km west of the West Block of Grasslands National Park. Homesteaders began taking up land in the area around 1909, and Orkney developed with the construction of the rail-

▼ **ORKNEY** as photographed September 5, 2003. The N.M. Paterson & Sons grain elevator in the background dates to 1976 and was the company's first high-throughput elevator in Saskatchewan. Both the store and the elevator were still standing in September 2007.

way from Climax to Val Marie in 1924-25. The Orkney post office was established in 1924, and by 1928 the community had grown large enough to be incorporated as a village. The area economy grew to consist of grain and livestock production. The population of Orkney peaked at 121 in 1956; however, by the 1960s the community's numbers began to drop. The village was dissolved in 1968, and by 1972 Orkney numbered 52 persons. Today, despite the community's legal status as an organized hamlet, the townsite has been largely abandoned. A few dilapidated buildings dot the streets and the remnants of concrete sidewalks run along vacant lots. The post office closed in 1991 and the rail line through the community was abandoned in 2002. Orkney is situated in the RM of Val Marie No. 17.

ORMISTON

ORMISTON, organized hamlet, pop 15 (2006c), 35 (2001c), is located approximately 72 km south of Moose Jaw, just east of Crane Valley. The region today is sparsely populated and Ormiston sits in a sublime setting, nestled between the Dirt Hills and the rise of the Missouri Coteau. Settlers from eastern Canada, eastern Europe, and southern Russia began arriving in the area around 1910. They were primarily of British, Romanian, and German origins respectively. The Ormiston Post Office was established in 1911, although some kilometres southwest of the present community. At first, settlers would make annual treks to Moose Jaw or Rouleau to obtain supplies; however, within a couple of years the travel distance was significantly cut, with the opening of the railway from Weyburn to Assiniboia and the establishment of communities along that line. Ormiston began to develop in 1925 as the railway was being

▲ **ON EASTER SUNDAY**, April 11, 2004, a service was held at the Ormiston Baptist Church. The church had been a Lutheran church situated in Assiniboia before it was purchased by Ormiston's Baptist congregation in 1959. Previously, services had been held in Ormiston's community hall.

built into the district. The first train pulled into Ormiston in 1926 amidst much construction. Businesses were being started, and elevators erected. A community hall was completed in 1928, and, gradually, a school, churches, and skating and curling rinks were built. A sodium sulphate mine at Shoe Lake, just east of the community, was established, and for many years it employed a good number of Ormiston's residents. The mine, at one time the largest in the province, added diversity to an economy based on grain and livestock production. In the 1930s, despite the drought, forward-thinking residents of Ormiston began planting poplars, Manitoba maples, and elms which, today, give the community its attractive appearance. By the late 1960s, the population of the hamlet was over 200. In the 1970s, however, the community was sinking into decline. Businesses and services were being superseded by those in Moose Jaw and Assiniboia, the population began to decline, and the school was closed. Schoolchildren now attend classes in Crane Valley. In the late 1990s, the sodium sulphate mine closed and the rail line was abandoned. The community's Baptist Church remains active. Five kilometres north of Ormiston is Oro Lake Regional Park, the site of an

annual rodeo. Ormiston is situated in the RM of Excel No. 71.

OSAGE

OSAGE, village, pop 20 (2006c), 25 (2001c), is located approximately 50 km northwest of Stoughton on Hwy 33. The community developed with the construction of the CPR line from Arcola to Regina in 1903-04. The Osage Post Office was established in 1903, and the village was incorporated in 1906. The community was named after Osage, Iowa, the hometown of the settler upon whose land the

▲ **OSAGE HOCKEY TEAM, CIRCA 1930s.** Photograph courtesy of James H. Lynch, Osage.

▼ **OSAGE SCHOOL** opened in 1905 and closed in 1969. For 25 years, Mary Lakeman and her family performed the janitorial work. Photograph taken August 19, 2003.

townsite was located. An agricultural community, Osage had a population of 108 in 1961; subsequently, however, the village's numbers began to plummet and the small business community began to disappear. Osage School was closed in 1969, with students thereafter being bused to the neighbouring village of Fillmore. Osage is situated in the RM of Fillmore No. 96.

OSLER, town, pop 926 (2006c), 823 (2001c), is located about a 15-minute drive north of Saskatoon on Hwy 11. Named for Sir Edmund Boyd Osler, a wealthy financier and railway contractor, Osler had its beginnings in 1890 as the Qu'Appelle, Long Lake & Saskatchewan Railway was completed, linking Saskatoon and Prince Albert. The post office was established in 1891, the same year as advance members of what would become a substantial bloc settlement of Mennonites began to arrive in the region. A small agricultural community developed, and by 1903 Osler had a number of stores, a lumber yard, and a grain elevator. By the 1920s, three grain elevators lined the railway tracks in the community, and these, along with the railway station, were the centre of Osler's economic activity. In 1928, the Osler Mennonite Church was built. Osler's legal status changed numerous times over the years. In 1904, Osler was incorporated as a village. In 1918, the village was legally dissolved, reduced in status to that of a hamlet. In 1949, it was established as a organized hamlet (giving it a small degree of political power), and in 1968 Osler again attained village status. It would become a town in 1985. Osler remained a small agricultural trading centre until the late 1970s, at which point the community began to experience rapid growth when it became an attractive

location for people who wanted to live outside of Saskatoon yet continue to work in the city. From a population of 225 in 1976, Osler grew to have 594 residents by 1986, and the community is still growing. New residential subdivisions and business lots continue to be developed. Osler has a varied business community; however, town residents also benefit from easy access to the employment opportunities, services, and amenities that Saskatoon has to offer. Osler has a K-9 school; children attend grades 10 to 12 in the neighbouring town of Warman. Additionally, a private K-12 school, Valley Christian Academy, is located just outside of Osler. The community has a volunteer fire department and a team of first responders; policing is provided by the RCMP detachment in Warman. Medical attention is largely sought in the city of Saskatoon. Osler has a public library, a community hall, a museum, and four churches. There are a range of facilities for recreational activities. The community hosts an annual sports day, and a notable area attraction is The Barn Playhouse. A multi-faceted enterprise, the Playhouse is the home of a community theatre group that puts on various productions including dinner theatres. The Barn also features a craft shop, a place for weddings, banquets and conferences, horse-drawn wagon rides, food booths, and live music performances. Osler is centred in the midst of a healthy dairy farming industry, with approximately 250 dairy-producing farms located within a 24-kilometre radius. Osler is situated in the RM of Corman Park No. 344.

OTTHON, organized hamlet, pop 56 (2006c), 56 (2001c), is located between Yorkton and Melville on Hwy 10. A Hungarian colony founded in 1894 by

Reverend Janos (John) Kovacs, a minister of the Hungarian Reformed Church in Pennsylvania, Otthon attracted immigrants largely from the United States, although a number of families did come directly from Hungary. At the suggestion of Stephen Balint, one of the original settlers of the colony, the name Otthon — which means "home" in Hungarian — was chosen for the community. A post office was established in 1896, and in 1911 Otthon was incorporated as a village. The community was never very large — the Census of Canada taken in 1921 recorded a peak population of 72 — and on January 1, 1951, the Village of Otthon was dissolved and the community's affairs were then managed by the rural municipality. In 1979, Otthon was established as an organized hamlet. Otthon is situated in the RM of Cana No. 214.

OTTMAN-MURRAY BEACH, organized hamlet, is a resort development located north of the town of Foam Lake, on the east side of Fishing Lake off Hwy 310. A long-established cottage community, Ottman-Murray Beach is becoming highly developed and increasingly consists of luxury summer homes. It is also one of several resort communities and public recreation areas now lining the shores of Fishing Lake. Ottman-Murray Beach has a small number of permanent residents; however, during the summer months the population can reach into the hundreds. The resort was established as an organized hamlet in 1989 and is situated in the RM of Sasman No. 336.

OUNGRE, organized hamlet, pop 15 (2006c), 15 (2001c), is located 60 km west of Estevan and 58 km south of

Weyburn at the junction of Hwys 18 and 35. The Port of Oungre on the Canada-U.S. border is 16 km to the south. People of German, Norwegian, and British origins began arriving in the early 1900s; Jewish settlers arrived in the area in 1905-06, establishing what were called the Sonnenfeld and Hoffer colonies. When the railway arrived in 1927, a townsite was surveyed and the name Byrne was initially chosen for the station, the name honouring Philip Byrne, an early area postmaster. The district's Jewish settlers, however, wanted to honour Dr. Louis Oungre, the director of the Jewish Colonization Association, and so a deal was struck wherein the name Oungre would be adopted in exchange for a $500 contribution toward the construction of a community hall. As such, Oungre may be the only name of a Saskatchewan community that was purchased! During the drought and the Depression of the 1930s, however, many of the Jewish settlers abandoned their farms and left the area. This would not be the community's last exodus, though. In the late 1960s and early 1970s, the population again fell dramatically, from 88 in 1966 to 22 by 1972. Today, the centre of the small community is Lyndale School, which provides K-12 education to roughly 70 students from the surrounding district. Another focal point is Oungre Memorial Regional Park. Located just north of the hamlet on Long Creek, it is a popular venue for many of the region's recreational and social activities. Oungre serves as the administrative centre of the RM of Souris Valley No. 7. Agriculture is the main industry in the area.

OUTLOOK, town, pop 1,938 (2006c), 2,129 (2001c), is located approximately 90 km southwest of Saskatoon, about 30 km downstream from

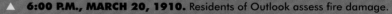

▲ **6:00 P.M., MARCH 20, 1910.** Residents of Outlook assess fire damage.

▲ **SEPTEMBER 25, 1912.** The landmark CPR bridge nears completion.

◄ **THE SKY TRAIL.** Beginning in September 2003, the 33rd Field Engineer Squadron from Calgary began work on Outlook's railway bridge's refurbishment; the work was done under a national "Bridges for Canada" program which celebrated the centennial of the military engineers. Crossing more than a kilometre of river at a height of close to 48 metres (156 feet), the bridge was officially reopened to pedestrian traffic by the Honourable Dr. Lynda Haverstock, Lieutenant Governor of Saskatchewan, on May 15, 2004.

OUTLOOK

...more than a point of view

Black-and-white photographs courtesy of the Outlook & District Heritage Museum.

Colour photographs taken July 20 and 21, 2004.

◄ **ANOTHER OF OUTLOOK'S LONG-STANDING LANDMARKS** is the former highway bridge across the South Saskatchewan River which was opened to traffic in 1936 (upper left). It remained in service until a new bridge was opened in 1998 (lower left).

► **THE PRESENT GIRLS' DORMITORY** at the Lutheran Collegiate Bible Institute. The building dates to 1915 and was the first building erected on the campus.

the Gardiner Dam on the east side of the South Saskatchewan River. The community is served by Hwy 15. Settlers had begun entering the district in the early 1900s, a few years before the CPR announced it would be developing a townsite above the river. On August 26, 1908, in advance of the coming railway, the townsite lots were put up for sale. The railway named the location Outlook for its spectacular vantage over the river valley. Land buyers had hauled in loads of lumber from Hanley, and the day after the sale the foundations of buildings were being squared and structures were quickly beginning to take shape. Within a month, a sizable community had come into existence. On November 23, the first train rolled into Outlook, and on December 19, 1908, the new community was legally established as a village; less than a year later, on November 1, 1909, Outlook attained town status. Within five months, however, on March 20, 1910, residents were standing in the streets staring at smouldering ruins: a fire had claimed a good portion of the business district. The community rebuilt, and by 1911 the population had reached 685. In 1912, the community's landmark railway bridge was completed across the river. The Depression took its toll on the area, and Outlook's population fell by more than 200 over the decade. Subsequently, Outlook and area residents were at the forefront of the campaign for the construction of a dam across the South Saskatchewan River, extolling the value of irrigating the semi-arid region. Today, the district has a diversified agricultural base, producing sunflowers, corn, potatoes, and vegetables, in addition to more traditional crops. The Canada-Saskatchewan Irrigation Diversification Centre, located on the outskirts of the town, is a major leading research facility that promotes crop di-

versification and sustainable irrigation practices. Outlook is the main service and shopping centre for a large district. The community has a wide range of health care facilities and practitioners, a special care home, and seniors' housing; plans are underway for a new state-of-the-art integrated health centre. Educational facilities include elementary and high schools, the Lutheran Collegiate Bible Institute, and a library. Outlook is the school division headquarters, and an office of the Prairie West Regional College facilitates a wide range of courses for adults. Offices of both the Regional Economic Development Authority and the Community Futures Development Corporation provide assistance to entrepreneurs with regard to financing, business planning, and community projects. Outlook has extensive and modern facilities for recreation, significantly augmented by the regional park located adjacent to the community on the river. The park, situated under a canopy of 800-year-old American elm trees, has campsites, hiking trails, a junior-size Olympic swimming pool, and one of the province's most picturesque golf courses. The South Saskatchewan River, nearby Lake Diefenbaker, and Danielson Provincial Park provide a further range of recreational opportunities. Outlook's arts community includes two theatre groups and a gallery, and a number of town businesses display the work of local artists and craftspeople. The Outlook and District Heritage Museum is housed in the town's former 1909 CPR station. Outlook's main attraction is the Sky Trail, part of the Trans Canada Trail, and Canada's longest pedestrian bridge; it spans the former 1912 CPR railway bridge, which had been closed for a number of years. Outlook serves as the administrative centre of the RM of Rudy No. 284.

OXBOW, town, pop 1,139 (2006c), 1,132 (2001c), is located approximately 60 km east of Estevan on Hwy 18, just northeast of where the Moose Mountain Creek flows into the Souris River. The name of the town was derived from the large oxbow bend in the Souris River, which passes along the community's south side. Settlers, largely of English, Irish and Scottish origin (from Ontario and the British Isles), began homesteading in the district in 1882. In 1891, the CPR's Brandon-Estevan line was being built through the area and the townsite was established. In 1892, the first trains were running into Oxbow and a number of dwellings and businesses were emerging in the new community. That same year, the first Jewish settlers arrived in the district. In 1899, Oxbow was incorporated as a village. The community grew very rapidly: the population was 230 in 1901,

▲ **DESPITE OXBOW'S RATHER RUSTIC APPEARANCE** during its formative years, it was not a community without culture. Musical ensembles were particularly popular...

▶ **OXBOW CITIZENS' BAND, 1906**, facing page, centre. Back row, left to right: unknown, unknown, Sam Nix, unknown, unknown, Bill McBride. Second row from back: Bert Davies, unknown, Jack Armstrong, G.S. Hames (bandmaster), George Riddell, Bert Winteringham, (first name unknown) Bernstein. Third row from back: Bert Hill, Frank Walsh, Alf. Hames, Rev. Dyke-Parker, unknown, unknown, unknown, Dave Clark (with the large drum). Front row: W. Hulbert, unknown, unknown, J.K. Buelley, unknown, Albert Earl Hames (with cymbals).

All photographs courtesy of the Ralph Allen Memorial Museum, Oxbow. Street scene above donated by Isobel Osten, Oxbow; photographs of musical ensembles donated by Mrs. Grace Quinn, Oxbow.

"Queen of the Scenic Souris"
OXBOW

▲ **OXBOW METHODIST CHURCH CHOIR, 1898.** Back row, left to right: George Hames (leader), Miss Powell, Ed. Thompson, Bert. Hames, Alice Hames. Front row, left to right: Mrs. McHaffie, Mrs. Chas. Walsh, Carrie Hames, Lily Jackson.

▼ **OXBOW LADIES' SILVER BAND, 1909:** The band had its beginnings in 1908 and continued for about three years under the guidance of George S. Hames, a prominent figure in Oxbow's music scene for 40 years.

Oxbow achieved town status in 1904, and by 1916 the number of residents was 678. The population took somewhat of a dip during the 1930s; however, it recovered after WWII. In the mid-1950s, significant development began in the area's oilfields, and for several years the region experienced boom times as drilling rigs, industry-related services and personnel moved into the area. The housing situation in Oxbow became critical. The town had had a population of 688 in 1951; by the mid-1960s, however, it had grown to close to 1,600. Hotel rooms were full, residents took in boarders, house trailers were parked in farmers' yards throughout the countryside, and before long several trailer courts had sprung up around the town. Today, oil and gas, as well as agriculture, drive the regional economy, and several of Oxbow's businesses cater either to oilfield operations or to the agricultural industry. Oxbow has a health centre and a special care home, and Oxbow's schools provide K-12 education to approximately 340 students. Policing is provided by the Carnduff RCMP detachment. The *Oxbow Herald*, the weekly newspaper, has been published since 1903. Highlights of the Oxbow area include the new Moose Creek Regional Park and Golf Club, the Alameda Dam, Bow Valley Park (from where one can take a riverboat ride on the *Lady Souris*), and the Ralph Allen Memorial Museum, named after the locally-raised and renowned Canadian journalist, war correspondent, and author. Another of the town's famous sons is the hockey player Theoren Fleury, who was born in Oxbow in 1968 and who was the first player in the history of the NHL to score three short-handed goals in one game. He also won the Stanley Cup with the Calgary Flames in the 1988-89 season and a gold medal with the Canadian men's hockey team at the Salt Lake City Olympics in 2002. Oxbow serves as the administrative centre of the RM of Enniskillen No. 3.

PADDOCKWOOD, village, pop 125 (2006c), 171 (2001c), is located in an attractive parkland setting approximately 36 km northeast of Prince Albert on municipal road No. 791. During the summer of 1911 the first few settlers began venturing into the Paddockwood area, then thickly covered in bush — black and white poplar, spruce, jack pine, and the odd birch. From 1911 to 1919 there was a gradual but steady stream of people coming into the area taking up homesteads, and cordwood was the economic mainstay of the district until the land was cleared. Then crops began to be sown and the bucolic sound of cowbells began to ring across the countryside as people started introducing cattle to the area. Whitefish harvested from Candle Lake and then freighted through Paddockwood to Prince Albert also put some dollars in the pockets of the hardy and adventurous. The first settlers into the district were largely of British origin; later, central Europeans, mostly Ukrainians and Poles, arrived in numbers. The name Paddockwood dates to 1912, when an application for an area post office was made. Mrs. Frances Pitts, the wife of the first postmaster, Frederick Pitts, had been born in Paddock Wood, Kent County, England, and the honour of choosing the post office name, subsequently the township name, had been given to her. The Paddockwood Post Office was officially established on January 1, 1913. Fred Pitts enlisted to serve overseas during WWI and was killed in action. Of the 28 men from the Paddockwood area who had enlisted, Pitts was one of eight who failed to return. Following the War, there was an influx of returned servicemen and their families into the Paddockwood district, claiming lands which had been set aside for veterans under the Soldier Settlement Act. In October 1920, the first Red Cross Outpost Hospital in the British Empire was built in Paddockwood. This hospital, the forerunner of more than 200 eventually established in Canada (often in soldier settlement districts) was part of a Red Cross initiative to bring medical care to remote communities that were unable to afford such facilities and services. The hospitals were built and maintained by the communities and then staffed and provisioned by the Red Cross. Also in 1920, students began attending the first classes at Paddockwood School. In 1924, the railway was built north from Prince Albert through Henribourg, terminating at Paddockwood. The first grain elevator was erected and by the time the first train rolled into the fledgling community a number of enterprising homesteaders were making plans to become businessmen. Stores were built, and in 1929 a hotel was erected and the Paddockwood Coop was incorporated. In 1931, a telephone system was installed. Through the 1930s, another migration into the Paddockwood area took place as farmers abandoned the drought-stricken southern plains and resettled in the parkland fringes. A community hall built in 1935 still stands and was designated a municipal heritage property in 2000. World War II drew 341 volunteers from the Paddockwood district, and on January 1, 1949, the Village of Paddockwood was incorporated. The electrical grid was set up in 1952, and in 1972 the access road into the village was blacktopped, as was Railway Avenue. In 1975, individual residences were connected to the village's newly completed sewer and water system. It was about this time that the economy

of the Paddockwood area had come full circle — forestry was again providing employment. Many village residents found work at the new pulpwood plant built near Prince Albert in the late 1960s, while others worked in the forests themselves. In recent decades, Paddockwood has become a quieter, largely residential community. Only a handful of businesses remain, as accessing the amenities of Prince Albert has become commonplace. Paddockwood does retain, however, a Co-op, beverage room, credit union, insurance broker, post office, library, museum, and the community hall. Paddockwood School has now been closed for a number of years, and village students attend classes in Meath Park. In 1992, the Saskatchewan Wheat Pool began construction of a large high-throughput terminal at White Star (a little more than 10 kilometres north of Prince Albert) and in 1993 the Pool closed its operations in Paddockwood. The rail line into the community was then abandoned. Paddockwood serves as the administrative centre of the RM of Paddockwood No. 520.

PALMER, hamlet, pop 20 (2001c), is a former village located 13 km east of Gravelbourg, and about 2 km south off Hwy 43. In 1907, brothers Talmage and Beacher Palmer, from Freeland, Prince Edward Island, filed on homesteads a few kilometres north of the present community. They operated a small store and, on October 1, 1910, established a post office named Palmer with Talmage as the postmaster. After the railway came through, the post office was moved to the new townsite and the name Palmer was adopted to be that of the fledgling community. In 1911, the Canadian Northern Railway surveyed the route for the line

through the district; in 1912 the rail bed was graded; and in 1913 the track was laid and Palmer began to develop. Until the mid-1920s, the community grew steadily. An elevator was erected even before the trains were running, and businesses in Palmer in the early years included general stores, a hardware store, farm machinery dealerships, a bank, pool hall and barber shop, a hotel, a lumber yard, dray services and a livery stable, a blacksmith shop, a butcher shop, and restaurants. A Roman Catholic Church was built in 1916; a Methodist Church in 1918; and an Anglican congregation was formed in 1924. The Village of Palmer was incorporated on May 12, 1920. In 1921, a new two-room school was completed in the village, replacing a rural schoolhouse which had been located a distance south of the community. In 1926, the population of Palmer was 75, but the community's numbers fell significantly during the 1930s, and during this time a number of businesses folded. By 1941, the population had dropped to just 47. The post-War years were a time of renewed and exceptional growth for the village, and in 1961, Palmer reached its all-time high population — 104. Thereafter, however, it again steadily declined, and with the exodus of residents, too, went the business community. At the beginning of the 1970s, the school closed, and by the end of the 1970s, there was no commercial activity whatsoever left in the village. On January 1, 2002, the Village of Palmer was dissolved; the community's affairs are now managed by the RM of Sutton No. 103.

PANGMAN, village, pop 200 (2006c), 255 (2001c), is located approximately 90 km due south of Regina, on Hwy 13, just west of the junction with Hwy

6. Weyburn, 56 km east, is the nearest major centre. Homesteaders began arriving in the area around 1906 and, for the first few years, would have to make long wagon trips to Yellow Grass or Milestone, on the Soo Line, to deliver their grain during harvest. The round trip would take at least a couple of days. In 1910, as CPR construction crews came through the area working from Weyburn toward Assiniboia, Pangman had its beginnings. Businesses were set up, grain elevators erected, and on May 17, 1911, the Village of Pangman was incorporated. For a number of years, Pangman was, in a way, a risky place to do business. Fire after fire after fire claimed many buildings over the decades, and, today, few of the community's early structures remain. On Christmas Eve, 1978, even the fire engine was lost in a blaze. Pangman's population grew slowly but steadily up to the mid-1950s, and remained fairly stable until the last few years. In the mid-1990s, the village faced a potential turning point as the hospital was to be closed and CP announced its intention to abandon the rail line. Proactive community initiatives, however, overcame both problems. A regional health centre with an adjoining personal care home and ambulatory service was created, and after CP tore up the rails between Weyburn and Pangman, individuals from the village and other communities along the track running west to Assiniboia formed a cooperative and raised the funds to purchase the line. Red Coat Road and Rail was born. Today, in addition to the health centre, the village also has a small core of businesses, a library, four churches, and recreational facilities. Pangman School provides K-12 education; 65 students were enrolled in the fall of 2006. Pangman serves as the administrative centre of the RM of Norton No. 69.

PARADISE HILL, village, pop 483 (2006c), 486 (2001c), is located approximately 24 km southwest of St. Walburg and 40 km east of the Saskatchewan-Alberta border on Hwy 3. The Carleton Trail passed directly through the locale, and this is commemorated by a larger-than-life ox and a Red River Cart at the entrance to the community. The village is nestled against the northern flank of a plateau that extends south toward the North Saskatchewan River. The plateau had been dubbed "Paradise Hill" by one of the area's earliest settlers, Ernest Beliveau. Ernest and his brother Alphonse had been among the few ranchers in the area prior to 1900 and had come back after a perilous and fruitless journey to the Klondike. The plateau or "hill" apparently seemed like paradise after all they had been through, and Ernest evidently concocted the name "Hill of Paradise" or "Paradise Hill" for the area. In 1903, the townships of the plateau were surveyed and opened up for homesteaders: a few of the Métis familiar with the area were among the first to take up land, and over the following years other French-speaking arrivals formed a settlement focused at Butte St. Pierre, southeast of present-day Paradise Hill. People of German origin settled north and toward St. Walburg, people of English backgrounds homesteaded throughout the district, and a contingent from Indiana and Illinois came to "the hill" as well. The land rush had become a flood around 1910. The name Paradise Hill was applied to a district post office in 1911, and became that of an area school in 1914. When the CNR, en route from south of St. Walburg to Frenchman Butte, established the location for a townsite in 1928, they were persuaded to adopt the

▲ **MAIN STREET**, Paradise Hill, looking east, July 23, 2003.

name for the locale. The country post office relinquished the name to a post office then established in the hamlet; and in 1934, when a school district was formed in the hamlet, the rural Paradise Hill School surrendered its name too. Classes in the hamlet were held in the United Church, however, since a school was not built in Paradise Hill until 1942. Within a few years of the railway arriving, a business community emerged and three grain elevators were built. A hospital was opened in 1941, and Paradise Hill became an incorporated village on January 1, 1947. No longer were the community's affairs managed by the surrounding rural municipality. In 1951, the population of the village was 234; by 1971 it was 344; and in 1991 Paradise Hill numbered 455. The area economy was dominated by agriculture for many years, particularly cattle ranching; in more recent times the oil and gas industry has come to heavily impact the district. Many farmers now supplement their farming incomes with oilfield services and trucking, and the industry is keeping younger people in the region — the median age of village residents in 2006 was 34.2, al-

most five years younger than that of the province as a whole. The village appears prosperous: it is clean and attractive and has modern homes, paved streets and street lights. A large farm machinery and automobile dealership in Paradise Hill is a major source of employment, employing as many as 45 people. Other businesses in Paradise Hill include restaurants, a hotel, credit union, gas stations, garages, a grocery store, a liquor vendor, and hair dressers. The city of Lloydminster, about 70 kilometres to the southwest, provides more specialized services and shopping. Paradise Hill has a volunteer fire department and a 17-bed hospital with a pharmacy; the nearest RCMP detachment is located in St. Walburg. Paradise Hill School is a modern (1991) K-12 facility that had 262 students enrolled in the fall of 2006. The community also has four churches, a library, a range of recreational facilities, a community centre, and a number of service clubs, sports groups, and other community-based organizations. An attraction in Paradise Hill is the Roman Catholic church decorated by Count Berthold Von Imhoff in 1929. The church, which originally stood at Butte St. Pierre, was moved into Paradise Hill in 1973. On the edge of a marsh adjacent to the village, an obser-

vation deck has been constructed for bird-watching enthusiasts. Paradise Hill serves as the administrative centre of the RM of Frenchman Butte No. 501.

PARKLAND BEACH, organized hamlet, est. 1991, is one of several resort communities situated northeast of Turtleford on Turtle Lake. Parkland Beach was originally developed in the late 1970s and is located in the RM of Mervin No. 499. The population varies depending on the season, reaching roughly 70 during the summer months.

PARKSIDE, village, pop 129 (2006c), 130 (2001c), is located 57 km west of Prince Albert, on Hwy 40. The district began to be settled in the late 1800s and early 1900s, and the village derives its name from Parkside House, Yorkshire, England, the hometown of an early area settler, who homesteaded in 1903. Other settlers came to the Parkside district from Britain, and from eastern Canada, primarily Ontario; however, it was Scandinavians, who began arriving in 1904, that largely settled the district. Many came directly from Sweden or Norway, while many others were people who had originally emigrated to the U.S. around the 1880s. By 1907-08, most of the available land in the Parkside region was occupied. In 1911, as the Canadian Northern Railway was pushing through from Prince Albert to North Battleford, the townsite of Parkside was established. By the time the first trains rolled through the next year, several businesses were either operating or under construction. The village was incorporated in 1913. The community grew until the mid-1930s, at which time the population neared 200. After WWII, however, Park-

▲ **PARKSIDE SCHOOL.** Photograph taken August 25, 2004.

side's fortunes began to change. In 1961, the village suffered a catastrophic fire that claimed many businesses, including Parkside's most prominent landmark, the hotel, a three-storey structure built in the early days of the village. Both business-wise and aesthetically, the fire was a devastating blow for the community. Over the years, the population had also begun to decline, and by the mid-1970s it had fallen to 100. In 1979, due to declining enrollment, Parkside's school was closed. Built as a two-room facility in 1920 and expanded to four rooms in 1954, the building has been designated a heritage property, as has the Saskatchewan Wheat Pool elevator, built in 1959. Today, Parkside retains a small number of businesses and has a seniors' housing development. The community hosts an annual demolition derby and ball tournament. Parkside is situated in the RM of Leask No. 464.

PARKVIEW, organized hamlet, is one of a number of resort communities situated on Buffalo Pound Lake. It lies on the southwest shore immediately west of Buffalo Pound Provincial Park, and is accessible via Hwy 202, north of Moose Jaw. Land for the resort subdivision was surveyed in 1960; Parkview was established as an organized hamlet in 1985. There are approximately 86 properties developed with homes and cottages. The 2006 Census recorded 45 year-round residents; however, the population may reach roughly 200 during the summer months. Ice fishing is popular in the winter. Parkview is located in the RM of Marquis No. 191.

PARRY, organized hamlet, pop 18 (2006c), 20 (2001c), is located southwest of Milestone, 8 km west of Hwy 6. Agriculture, a combination of grain and livestock production, is the basis of the area economy. Around 1900, homesteaders began arriving in the Milestone area, but as available land there was taken up, settlers began moving further to the south and west, homesteading in the Parry area around 1903-04. Many had come to Saskatchewan riding the Soo Line from the U.S. and were of German and Danish origin. Others came from eastern Canada, while a few came from England and continental Europe. For several years, to obtain supplies or to deliver grain, people had to travel the distance to Milestone, the nearest railway point. The railway came to Parry in 1911, and by 1912 a number of businesses had been established and two grain elevators had been erected. For decades, the small community prospered, and Parry hosted popular annual sports days and curling bonspiels. But by the mid-1960s, centralization and rural depopulation began to impact the hamlet. The community's population fell from 120 in 1969 to 67 in 1972. High school students were bused to Pangman followed by elementary school students during the 1970s. At the end of the decade, CN abandoned the track south of Parry, and in 1989, sold the line running northwest to Avonlea to the farmer-owned Southern Rails Cooperative (SORA). Unfortunately, in 1999, that track was washed out during a storm and never repaired. Subsequently, the lone remaining elevator in Parry closed. In 2000, the last store also closed, and, today, the only businesses remaining are the post office and a bowling alley open only during the winter months. Parry is situated in the RM of Caledonia No. 99.

PASQUA LAKE, organized hamlet, est. 1985, is largely a resort community in the Qu'Appelle Valley which stretches several km along the north shore of the lake of the same name. The 2006 Census recorded 224 permanent residents; however, local authorities claim the number is much lower. In either case, there are approximately 300 developed properties, and population varies greatly depending on the season. Pasqua Lake is situated in the RM of North Qu'Appelle No. 187.

PATUANAK is a Dene community that stretches along the eastern side of a large peninsula that extends into the Churchill River system, 95 km north of Beauval at the end of gravel road No. 918. To the west of the peninsula lies Lac Île-à-la-Crosse; to the north lie the Shagwenaw Rapids, and to the east of the peninsula lies Shagwenaw Lake, upon the shore of which Patuanak sits. The name Patuanak is derived from the Cree term wâpâciwanâhk, meaning "where the white water is." Although in essence one community, Patuanak is comprised of two legal entities. The southerly, smaller part, sometimes referred to as "Little La Ronge" by local residents, has the legal status of a northern hamlet; the northern, more populous and main part of the community is reserve land held by the English River First Nation. The hamlet population was 72 in 2001; accounts of the reserve's numbers vary widely, ranging from 500 to 800 people. The majority of area residents, though, whether living in the hamlet or on the reserve, are members of the English River First Nation and hold treaty status. The main religious denomination at Patuanak is Roman Catholic, and a major figure in the community's history was Father Louis Moraud. From 1916 until his death in 1965, Moraud served the people along the river in the area, and he was responsible for the construction of the church in Patuanak in 1937. He is buried in the churchyard. The Patuanak area economy evolved around the fur trade and later concentrated on commercial fishing. For many years Patuanak's permanent population remained small, as the region's people were highly nomadic, travelling from one place to another to hunt, fish, and trap. Patuanak was mainly a fur-buying centre and a seasonal stopping place until a number of factors began to induce people into settling into a more sedentary existence. The advent of commercial fishing operations at Shagwenaw Lake and the development of a provincial welfare system were influences, but it was the opening of a school in Patuanak in 1968 that drew many people in from the surrounding region so that their children could receive an education locally (prior to this, some children had been sent to residential schools in Beauval and Ile-a-la-Crosse while their families worked in the bush). Additionally, snowmobiles began to be commonplace, allowing people to reside longer in the community while still working their far-flung traplines; an all-weather road was built to Patuanak; and local businesses and infrastructure were increasingly developed. By the 1970s, most of the Dene who had lived scattered throughout the area had settled in the community. Today, local employment is found in the band and hamlet offices, a medical clinic, the local radio station, a general store with fuel sales, and the school; many, however, still engage in seasonal pursuits and traditional activities such as hunting, fishing, berrypicking, and the making of handicrafts. The English River First Nation also operates a successful fishing camp, and some Patuanak residents work out of the community in the northern forestry and mining industries. Patuanak has an RCMP detachment, an airstrip, a youth centre, a community hall, an arena, a fire hall, and a small business community that offers a range of products and services. The Patuanak Post Office was established in 1949.

PAYNTON, village, pop 151 (2006c), 172 (2001c), is located northwest of North Battleford on the Yellowhead Hwy, 27 km east of Maidstone. The Paynton Ferry crosses the North Saskatchewan River a short distance to the east; the Battle River passes about 12 km south of the village, and along the river lie reserve holdings of the Little Pine and Poundmaker First Nations. The first settlers in the Paynton district were former members of the NWMP who took up land in the area a few years after the North-West Resistance. One of these was Peter Paynter, and the name "Paynton" is likely derived from the first four letters of his last name and the last three letters of the name Grafton. Many of the American settlers who arrived in the district in the early 1900s were from Grafton, North Dakota. In addition to the Americans, Barr Colonists also took up land in the area in the early twentieth century. The Paynton Post Office was established by Arthur Morley Black on his homestead about two miles northeast of present-day Paynton on September 1, 1904. It was relocated to the present village after the railway came through and the townsite location was established. The village had its beginnings in 1905 with the construction of the Canadian Northern

▼ **PATUANAK, SEPTEMBER 1976.** Saskatchewan Archives Board, Saskatchewan Photographic Services, R-PS76-1183-298. Photographer: G. Leggett.

▲ **PAYNTON, CIRCA 1905-06.** Saskatchewan Archives Board R-A5972.

Railway line between North Battleford and Lloydminster. The first grain elevator was erected that year, and the Paynton School District was established. The school was completed in early 1906. Businesses also began to appear on the townsite in 1905-06, and the Village of Paynton was incorporated on May 2, 1907. By 1911, the population was 121, and in 1956 Paynton had a peak population of 241. The community still numbered more than 200 in the 1980s, but by the early 1990s the population was in decline. The school closed in 2002 due to decreasing enrollment, and, today, a few abandoned buildings line Main Street. The village retains a credit union, the post office, and a service station with a store. Paynton also has a community hall, a library and a seniors' centre. Crop farming and cattle ranching remain the main industries in the area; oil and gas has become somewhat of a factor in the economy in the past few years. Paynton serves as the administrative centre of the RM of Paynton No. 470.

PEBBLE BAYE, resort village, is located approximately 100 km west of Prince Albert, southeast of the village of Shell Lake, off Hwy 12 on Iroquois Lake. The resort was developed in the late 1970s and was incorporated in 1983. Today, there are roughly 90 cottages and homes. There are a small number of year-round residents (27 in 2006); however, the population varies depending on the season. Pebble Baye is located in the RM of Leask No. 464.

PEEBLES, organized hamlet, pop 20 (2006c), 20 (2001c), is located west of Kipling on Hwy 48. The history of the hamlet of Peebles dates to 1906 and the arrival of the CPR at the site. The area, however, began to be settled in the 1880s, significantly by large numbers of Scots. A second large group — German Catholics — began homesteading in the district

east of Peebles over 1902-03. Others, too, came to the area — eastern Canadians, Scandinavians, and people from the British Isles. When a post office was established in the district in 1905, it was originally called Glenwell; but in 1907, due to the large German presence, the name was changed to Kaiser. In 1916, the post office was relocated to the railway siding and, with anti-German feelings running high at the time, the office adopted the name Peebles after Peebles, Scotland, a town south of Edinburgh. Although Peebles would develop as a service centre for the surrounding agricultural district, the community's fortunes over the years would be tied mainly to railway developments. The CPR line, which was built from Reston, Manitoba, was continued through to Wolseley in 1908, and, that same year, the Canadian Northern Railway came through Peebles en route from Kipling to Regina. In 1924, CN built a line from the hamlet south through Corning to Handsworth. Many people who came to live in Peebles worked for the railways, and in its heyday the hamlet was a busy little place, with a school, grain elevator, stores, a blacksmith, farm equipment dealerships, a Co-op Association, hotel and café, curling rink, church, and a hall for dances and other social functions. Peebles was established as an organized hamlet in 1950. In 1960, the CPR abandoned the Reston-Wolseley line, and in 1961 the rails were taken up. In 1965, with the population of the hamlet hovering around 60, Peebles' high school students were transferred to the neighbouring village of Windthorst, and in 1970 Peebles School was closed. In 1972, the last regular services were held at the community's church. In the 1980s, CN abandoned its line south through Corning. In 1989 the railway closed their siding at Peebles, after tornado-speed

winds and golf ball-size hail on July 8 that year severely damaged the Pool elevator, and it was announced it would not be replaced. Today, there is a Co-op gas station in Peebles and a postal outlet. Peebles is situated in the RM of Chester No. 125.

PELICAN COVE, organized hamlet, is a resort community located southeast of the village of Shell Lake, off Hwy 12, on Iroquois Lake. The 2006 Census recorded 30 permanent residents; however, the population varies greatly depending on the season. The resort has existed for decades and was originally established as an organized hamlet under the name of Iroquois Lake in 1984. The name of the community was changed in 1989. Pelican Cove is located in the RM of Leask No. 464.

PELICAN NARROWS, northern village, is located 120 km northwest of Creighton via the Hanson Lake Road and gravel Hwy 135. The community is situated near the narrows that join Mirond and Pelican Lakes, which lie between the Sturgeon-Weir and Churchill River systems. Pelican Narrows is the administrative centre for the Peter Ballantyne Cree Nation, and the majority of the townsite is reserve land. The Peter Ballantyne Cree Nation is the province's second largest First Nation; it has a total population of about 6,700, with roughly 2,500 living in the Pelican Narrows area. Oral history places the Cree at the site around 1730; summer camps where women and children stayed were established while men travelled to Hudson Bay to trade furs. Both the North West Company and the Hudson's Bay Company had trading posts established in the area by the late 1700s, but after the merger of the

▲ **PELICAN NARROWS, FEBRUARY 1974.** Saskatchewan Archives Board, Saskatchewan Photographic Services, R-PS73-1843-256. Photographer: D. Varley.

▼ **REFUELLING AT PELICAN NARROWS, CIRCA 1925.** Float planes such as this were long the only means, other than by water, of accessing many of the province's northern communities, fishing camps, and mine sites. Saskatchewan Archives Board R-B2679.

companies in 1821 there was not a post at Pelican Narrows for several decades. In 1874, the Hudson's Bay Company established a permanent post at Pelican Narrows, which became the Northern Store in 1987. In the early 1900s, rival fur-buying operations were established. Roman Catholic missionaries were traversing the area from the mid-1800s and established a permanent mission in 1878. Anglican missionaries arrived in the late 1890s and built a church in 1911. Schoolchildren were sent away to residential schools for a number of years. In 1967, an all-weather road was built into the community and other services followed. Today, Pelican Narrows has a health centre with a dental clinic, two schools, an RCMP detachment, a provincial government resources office, churches, a main store, confectionaries, a number of outfitters with cabins and restaurants, and the Peter Ballantyne Cree Nation administration centre, which houses the post office.

PELICAN POINT, organized hamlet, est. 1981, is located north of North Battleford, and is one of a number of resort communities on Murray Lake. There were 34 permanent residents in 2001; however, the population varies greatly depending on the season. Pelican Point is situated in the RM of Meota No. 468.

PELICAN POINTE, resort village, is one in a string of resort communities on the east side of Last Mountain Lake. In 1910, Pelican Pointe was a stopping place for the Wm. Pearson Co.'s steamboat *S.S. Qu'Appelle*; however, it was not until recent decades that the development of the present community began.

The 2006 Census recorded 23 permanent residents; however, the population varies greatly depending on the season. Pelican Pointe was incorporated in 1987 and is situated in the RM of McKillop No. 220.

PELICAN SHORES, organized hamlet, is a resort community located in the eastern Qu'Appelle Valley, northeast of Broadview on the north shore of Round Lake. The resort, established in the mid-1980s, was formerly known as Espeseth Cove. There are a small number of permanent residents; however, the population varies greatly depending on the season. Pelican Shores is accessible via Hwy 247 and is situated in the RM of Fertile Belt No. 183.

PELLY, village, pop 287 (2006c), 303 (2001c), is situated on Hwys 8 and 49, 32 km north of Kamsack, 24 km west of the Saskatchewan-Manitoba border. The village is located near the sites of two historic forts: Fort Pelly, from which the community takes its name, was a Hudson's Bay Company post from 1824 to 1912; and Fort Livingstone, an early NWMP headquarters, was briefly the capital of the North-West Territories over the winter of 1876-77. Before 1900, there was some ranching activity in the Pelly area; however, settlers began arriving and the land was soon broken up for farming. In 1899, large numbers of Doukhobors arrived in the area. While many would move on to British Columbia, those remaining would abandon their communal villages to take up individual homesteads. After 1900, and particularly after 1903, when the railway reached Kamsack, many settlers began arriving in the Pelly district. They were of diverse backgrounds, including from

FORT PELLY, 1907. The Hudson's Bay Company Post was located approximately 13 kilometres (8 miles) southwest of the present village of Pelly at the elbow of the Assiniboine River. From 1824 until 1856 it was situated on low-lying ground prone to flooding; a move to higher ground was then undertaken, and the post at the new location, pictured above, remained in operation until 1912. This overgrown marker (right) stands at the site of the first fort.

Historical photographs courtesy of Fort Pelly Livingstone Museum.

Photographs of the fort markers taken July 27, 2004.

PELLY
...from Forts to Founding

ABANDONED FOR SEVEN YEARS. Men stand outside of a derelict Hudson's Bay Company building at Fort Pelly's second location in 1919.

THE LOCATION OF FORT LIVINGSTONE, about 6.5 kilometres (4 miles) northwest of Pelly above the Swan River, is today marked by this cairn and is a National Historic Site. Constructed in 1874, the fort once consisted of at least 16 buildings which could house as many as 185 men and their horses. Abandoned in 1882, Fort Livingstone was destroyed by fire in 1884.

▲ **THE COMING OF THE RAILWAY.** A man and two horses carefully negotiate a corner while building the railway grade in the Pelly region in the summer of 1908.

▲ **ALL THE LIVELONG DAY.** Pounding the spikes through the rails in the fall of 1908.

▲ ▼ **RAPID DEVELOPMENT** followed the arrival of the railway; many businesses and institutions such as churches and the school were established: the school is pictured here under construction in 1912 (above, left), and among the community's early businessmen were Charlie Skunk, shown here in front of his laundry circa early 1920s (below, left). Cecil F. Heming, pictured here in his Main Street drug store (date unknown) (above, right), operated his business for more than 25 years, selling out in 1946. By the time this photograph of the Homemakers' Club in front of the Legion Hall was taken (circa 1924-25) (bottom, right), Pelly was a thriving village of about 250 people.

English, Ukrainian, German, and Scandinavian origins. The village itself began to develop with the coming of the railway. In 1909, the Canadian Northern Railway arrived, and in 1911 Pelly was incorporated with a population of 82. The community grew rapidly, reaching a population close to 300 within ten years. By the mid-1950s and through to the mid-1960s, the population hovered close to 500, and Pelly had become an important service centre catering to the agricultural industry of the region. Today, Pelly has a core of essential businesses and services, recreational facilities, churches, and Fort Livingstone School, which provides K-12 education to close to 120 students. The village also has two heritage properties: the Fort Pelly-Livingstone Museum site, which includes Pelly's former school and CNR station; and St. Alban's Anglican Church, which was originally a school built south of Pelly in 1907-08. During the winter of 1955-56, Pelly received 386 cm (12.7 ft.) of snow, an amount which stands as the highest snowfall ever recorded in Saskatchewan in a single season. Pelly serves as the administrative centre of the RM of St. Philips No. 301.

PENNANT, village, pop 119 (2006c), 150 (2001c), is located approximately 46 km northwest of Swift Current on Hwy 32. Saskatchewan Landing Provincial Park on the shores of Lake Diefenbaker lies a short distance to the northeast; to the west lie the Great Sand Hills. Only a few ranchers were in the region when the first homesteaders began to arrive around 1905-06. A good number came from the United States, others from eastern Canada and Europe. They were largely of Norwegian, Scottish, and English origins. A few pioneering Chinese businessmen were

▲ **FIVE GRAIN ELEVATORS**
stood at Pennant in 1916; today, only this solitary former Saskatchewan Wheat Pool elevator (dating to the mid-1950s) remains. Photograph taken August 29, 2003.

also among the first in the village as it was established. In the early days, to obtain supplies or to deliver grain, people in the district travelled to either Swift Current or Webb, the nearest railway points on the CPR main line. Pennant had its beginnings in 1911, with construction of the CPR's Empress line through the region. Rapidly, a number of businesses and residences were established on the townsite, and on July 29, 1912, the Village of Pennant was incorporated. By 1916, five grain elevators lined the tracks. By the end of the 1920s, the population of the village was approximately 200. In 1928-29, the CPR built a branch line from just west of Pennant, which ran 40 kilometres south through Hazlet. It increased the trade and traffic through the village. In the early 1950s, Pennant received another boost: oil was discovered at nearby Fosterton. Many Pennant residents found work connected with the oilfields, and, for a number of years, the village was dotted with house trailers belonging to survey crews and people working the drilling rigs. New homes were also being built in the community and, by the mid-1950s, Pennant's population had grown to over 300. However, from

the late 1960s, with fewer people farming the countryside, the abandonment of passenger rail service, and with improved roads and the community's proximity to Swift Current, the village's population and business sector began to slowly, yet steadily, decline. Today, almost all of Pennant's commercial sector has been superseded by that in the nearby city. On July 20, 1983, a powerful tornado struck Pennant. Damage to the community and area farms was extensive. Buildings were completely destroyed — these included a church, the skating rink, and a number of homes. Trees in the town were torn up from their roots, and power and telephone lines were down. Two grain elevators were extensively damaged and huge pumpjacks in the area's oilfields were ripped out of the ground. Despite the level of destruction, there was no loss of life nor any severe injury. The community rallied to clean up and repair the damage. Today, the Pennant area economy is largely based upon grain and cattle production; however, the increasing importance of the oil and gas industry is evident as pumpjacks dot the district. The former Pennant School, a four-room red-brick classic built in 1928, has been designated a municipal heritage property, as schoolchildren now attend classes to grade nine in the village of Success, and finish high school in Swift Current. Pennant is situated in the RM of Riverside No. 168, and has served as its administrative centre since 1915.

PENSE, village, pop 507 (2005c), 533 (2001c), is situated between Regina and Moose Jaw just north of the Trans-Canada Highway. Settlement of the general district began in 1881, the year before the CPR mainline was built through the region. In advance of the railway, the first few pioneers came to the area, travelling with wagons and oxcarts from Brandon, Manitoba, which was then the end of the rail line. The first settlers were largely of British stock, either from Ontario or overseas; later, particularly after the turn of the century, many came via the United States. The naming of Pense took place at the end of August 1882. An excursion party, including a number of newspapermen following the construction of the railway, arrived at the location of the present village, then the westernmost reach of the CPR on the prairies. The party decided to christen the spot with a champagne celebration, naming it Pense in honour of Edward Baker Pense, president of the Canadian Press Association, who was present with the group. The railway brought steadily increasing numbers of people into the district, but for several years development at the village site was very slow. Settlement of the region initially followed the area coulees and creeks, such as the Cottonwood Creek that flows north to Wascana Creek, for in these areas settlers could easily obtain water, perhaps some shelter, and wood for fuel. As well, the heavy clay land in the vicinity of Pense, typical of the Regina plain, was at first largely avoided, deemed too heavy to be effectively broken with the ploughs at the time. North of Pense, the soils change gradually into a looser clay loam, which was initially more attractive. For a short time after 1882, Pense remained a fairly insignificant sid-

▲ **ALL SAINTS ANGLICAN CHURCH, PENSE.** Built in 1909 and still in use, this red brick structure replaced a wooden building constructed in the late 1880s. The steeple of the present church was originally somewhat higher.

▼ **SASKATCHEWAN WHEAT POOL FACILITY, PENSE.**

Photographs taken October 29, 2007.

▲ **A BARN-RAISING BEE** at Herb Keith's farm in the Cottonwood district north of Pense, 1912. Saskatchewan Archives Board R-B12988.

ing. The Pense Post Office, for several years located a few kilometres north of the present community, was established November 1, 1883. During the 1880s, a boarding house and general store, a livery stable, a warehouse for grain, and the first church were built; in 1892, the first grain elevator. The land adjacent to Pense came to be significantly and rapidly settled only after 1900, and its productivity was quickly realized. Until 1911 when the GTP line

(now CN) was built about six kilometres north of Pense, the community, with its five elevators, was a major shipping point for wheat. In 1903, the first school was built in the community, and on March 7, 1904, Pense was incorporated as a village. The population was just over 100, and 36 buildings, not including the grain elevators, were subject to taxation. Also in 1904, a 30-room, three-storey hotel, the Carlton, was built (it was demolished in

1943 and the wall of mirrors that had hung over the bar was salvaged for use in the village's barber shop). In the years following incorporation, settlers poured into the district and the village grew steadily until the Depression. Pense's population rose from 185 in 1906 to 236 by 1911, and by the mid-1920s it was nudging 300. A setback for the community occurred during the winter of 1912-13, when the village was plagued by a succession of suspicious and devastating fires, including one which claimed a livery stable and 14 horses. In total, several buildings were destroyed, but the losses could have been worse. Fires were started at a number of other locations, including the hotel on a night when most of the rooms were occupied, but these never got out of control. It was apparent that an arsonist was at work. It was later discovered to be one Rod McIntyre, who was brought to trial in the Pense Hall on May 15, 1913, and sentenced to several years in the Saskatchewan Penitentiary in Prince Albert. Like many Saskatchewan communities, Pense

declined somewhat during the 1930s and it was not until after WWII that the community began to recover. From a population of 266 in 1951, the village's numbers climbed to 374 by 1961, and then to 472 by 1981. Today, many in the community's workforce commute to work in either Regina or Moose Jaw, or to nearby industries: Mosaic Potash, SaskFerco Products, and Canadian Salt, located close to the village of Belle Plaine. Businesses in Pense include a bar and restaurant, an insurance agency and financial consulting service, agricultural chemical sales, seed cleaning and sales, automotive services, a hair salon, a reflexologist and massage therapist, and a food and liquor store with a gas bar and coffee shop. Additionally, the village has a number of trades and craftspeople. Pense has a playschool and a K-8 facility that currently accommodates about 90 children. High school students are bused to Regina. The Pense Recreation Board, the Pense Fundraising Committee, and the local Lions coordinate and finance a variety of community projects and programs, and the village has a number of sports teams and clubs. Recreational facilities include skating and curling rinks, ball diamonds, a driving range, a playground and a water park. Pense has a volunteer fire department and a team of first responders; policing is provided by the RCMP. A Pense landmark, All Saints Anglican Church, has been designated a municipal heritage property. A once longtime resident of Pense, internationally acclaimed sculptor Joe Fafard, retains a commercial foundry in the village, Julienne Atelier, where he produces his famous limited-edition bronze sculptures. Pense serves as the administrative centre of the RM of Pense No. 160.

PENZANCE, village, pop 30 (2006c), 41 (2001c), is a tiny village located west of Last Mountain Lake, approximately one half km off Hwy 2, between the villages of Liberty, to the north, and Holdfast, to the south. The hills surrounding Last Mountain Lake are visible on the eastern horizon. The first few homesteaders arrived in the area in 1902; between 1903 and 1909 much of the land in the district was occupied. Most settlers came from the United States or eastern Canada. They were of many backgrounds, including German, Norwegian, Swedish, English, Scottish, and Irish. Most came via the railway at Craik, and Craik was where supplies could be obtained and where most farmers would haul their crops to. Some farmers living closer to Last Mountain Lake would haul to Strasbourg when the lake was frozen. Between 1905 and 1907 the first area school districts were established; in 1905, Nathan Foote established the Foote Post Office about two miles northwest of present-day Penzance. In 1910, CPR surveyors were establishing

the route for a line to run up the west side of Last Mountain Lake, and the location for the present village was chosen. It was named after Penzance, a resort town in west Cornwall, England, perhaps at the suggestion of early district residents from that area. The rail line was completed in 1911, and within a year or so of Penzance coming into being all manner of businesses were in operation: general stores, a blacksmith shop, station depot, lumberyards, livery barn, farm implement agencies, barbershop and poolroom, and a hotel. In 1912, the Foote Post Office was moved in and its name was changed to Penzance. Over the winter of 1911-12, farmers loaded grain directly into boxcars, as there were no grain elevators yet in operation. But in 1912, three grain elevators were in business; a fourth one was erected in 1922. Other business ventures in Penzance over the years included a millinery, bulk oil agencies, and a hardware store. On July 13, 1912, Penzance became an incorporated village. In 1913, a school district centred on the community was established and a one-room schoolhouse

was completed in time for classes to begin in January 1914. A two-room brick school was built in 1924. The community became active in sporting circles: the first village hockey team was organized in 1913, and that year a baseball league was organized, largely through the efforts of those who had come to the country from the United States. In 1919, two tennis courts were built on the village's main street. Agriculture was, and remains, the basis of the district economy, but for many years commercial fishing was a viable occupation for some. Fish were shipped to New York, Chicago, and Newark, New Jersey; "Long Lake Whites" were in big demand. Never a large community, Penzance grew from a population of 60 in 1916 to number 108 by 1926. The drought and the Depression then hit and some people were forced to leave the district (the present Highway 2 was built as a government-organized work program to provide relief), and then young men left to serve in WWII. The village also sustained a serious blow in 1941 when the hotel and a number of other buildings were lost in a fire. By 1946, the population

of the village was down to 70. During the boom years following WWII, the community entered a second heyday, rebounding to reach a peak population of 122 in 1956. The heyday would not last, however, as rural depopulation, upgraded highway connections and the community's proximity to Regina and other larger centres mitigated the sustainability of businesses in Penzance. The consolidation of schools would have an effect as well. In 1961, high school students began to be bused to Holdfast. The last classes held in Penzance School were in June 1970; subsequently, all of the village's schoolchildren were bused to the neighbouring community. Penzance School stood for seven more years, but in 1977 the community landmark burned to the ground, the victim of arson. By 1965, businesses remaining in Penzance were a general store, a garage, the post office, and the elevators. As well, two churches, the Legion, a sports club, and the Chamber of Commerce were still active. Improvements had been made to the village infrastructure in the 1960s and 1970s — water and sewer systems, natural gas, and a hard-surfaced main thoroughfare were the major changes — and in the early 1980s, a new community hall (still standing) was built. But the population of Penzance continued to fall. The community numbered 74 people by 1981; ten years later, in 1991, the population was down to 52. There were still four grain elevators standing in the village in the 1980s; in the late 1990s the rail line was abandoned and the last elevator was demolished. A couple of years later the tracks were torn up. Today, about two dozen homes, the United Church building, and the community hall are about all that remain of Penzance. Not one business remains in the community today. Penzance is situated in the RM of Sarnia No. 221.

▼ **PENZANCE UNITED CHURCH** was built in 1916 as a Presbyterian Church. It originally had a square, flat-topped Elizabethan-style steeple over the entrance; this, however, proved problematic when it rained, and the present Gothic steeple with a pointed spire was built to replace the original structure in the late 1920s. In 1969, a company from New York filmed a Red Rose Tea commercial in the basement of the United Church; it was a scene depicting a typical fowl supper in a small village on the Canadian prairies.

PERCIVAL, organized hamlet, pop 4 (2006c), 15 (2001c), is situated between the towns of Broadview and Whitewood on Hwy 1. About eight kilometres to the north lies the reserve of the Ochapowace First Nation. Several explanations as to the origins of Percival's name have been put forward over the years — none, however, are conclusive. Settlers, largely from eastern Canada, began arriving in the district in the 1880s, but it was Swedes, the first of whom arrived in 1897, that came to be dominant in the area. They constructed Immanuel Evangelical Lutheran Church at Percival in 1899. On May 15, 1902, the Percival Post Office was established. Percival School opened in 1908, and in the early years, the local history recounts, more Swedish was spoken on the playground than English, due to the preponderance of Scandinavians in the area. In 1913, an elevator at Percival was constructed by the Co-operative Elevator Company, which was taken over by Saskatchewan Pool Elevators in 1926. A larger, 35,000-bushel facility replaced the structure in 1940. In its heyday, the community had four stores including a hardware and a lumber operation, as well as a pool room and a barber shop, gasoline and oil dealers, and the services of a blacksmith, a shoemaker, a tailor, a dressmaker, carpenters, and a stonemason. Many Percival men found work constructing Pool elevators in various communities, and in their free time many engaged in sports. The Percival Tigers baseball team was well-known as a competitive force in the 1920s. Women concerned themselves with hamlet affairs through participation in several organizations such as the Lutheran Ladies Organization, the Temperance League, the Literary Society, the

▲ **THE CONGREGATION OF THE SWEDISH IMMANUEL EVANGELICAL LUTHERAN CHURCH** at Percival, 1912. Saskatchewan Archives Board R-A20868.

Little Theatre Group, and the Percival Hospital Auxiliary. In the 1920s, the CPR built stockyards near the grain elevator in Percival (prior to this, area cattlemen had driven their herds to Whitewood), and, as late as the 1950s, people from the surrounding region drove their cattle to Percival for shipment. The Percival Co-op store was established in 1935 and the Percival Credit Union was established in 1948. In 1947, it was determined that the Lutheran church had become structurally unsound, and services were then held in the parsonage and later a store until 1957. In 1958 the congregation transferred its membership to Grace Canadian Lutheran Church in Broadview. In 1957, the Percival Credit Union amalgamated with that in Broadview, and in 1961 the Co-op closed and the building was dismantled. On June 30, 1965, Percival School was closed. The population of the community at that time was about 50. On July 31, 1972, the Pool elevator in Percival closed, and on May 9, 1973, that long-standing landmark was

demolished. In 1975, the garage in Percival closed when Ed Sundquist, the proprietor since 1946, retired. At the end of December 1987, with the retirement of the postmaster, Julius Muszty, who had served in the position since 1957, the post office, too, was closed. The building, along with some of the postal scales, was donated to the Broadview Museum, where it still stands. A resurrected Percival landmark, one which would have been noted by passing travellers for many years, is a unique 1905 windmill located on the western outskirts of the hamlet, adjacent to the Trans-Canada Highway. Restored in 1995 and declared a municipal heritage property, the windmill had provided Percival residents with a good supply of water for many years. The technology of its design is unusual in that the orientation of the blades guides the windmill to face into the wind without the need of a vane, and, as well, the circumference of the wheel holding the blades expands through centrifugal force as wind speeds increase,

allowing more air to pass through the blades, thus slowing the wheel's rotation — century-old technology more efficient than that of traditional windmills on the prairies. Percival was established as an organized hamlet in 1981 and is situated within the boundaries of the RM of Willowdale No. 153.

PERDUE, village, pop 364 (2006c), 372 (2001c), is located 31 km east of Biggar, and approximately 55 km west of Saskatoon on Hwy 14. A low range of hills is visible to the west; to the north of Perdue lies a small lake. The first settlers began arriving in the area in 1903, and for a few years Saskatoon was the nearest market for crops and place to obtain supplies. The first development of the village of Perdue occurred in 1907 in anticipation of the coming railway. When the CPR came through in 1908, the townsite was named in honour of William Edgerton Perdue, then a prominent Manitoba lawyer. Perdue was the secretary and president of the Manitoba Law Society and was named Chief Justice of the province in 1918. A second railway came through the Perdue district in 1908; the Grand Trunk Pacific passed by about a mile to the south, where the village of Leney developed (Leney was incorporated 1910-71). The Perdue Post Office was established on March 23, 1908; the first postmaster, Frank Reid, served in the position until his death in 1941. Perdue was incorporated on July 15, 1909, and by 1910 could boast of a wide range of businesses, two churches, and an agricultural society. In 1911, a country school that had operated southeast of Perdue for two years was moved into the village. The population in 1911 was 155 and predominantly of English origin. In 1912, Perdue had a band and the first closed-in skating rink was built. There were four grain elevators in the village in the earlier years, but later there were only two. By the end of the 1920s, the village's population was nearing 400; by the outbreak of WWII, however, it had fallen to less than 300. During the post-War period the community flourished, reaching a peak population of 455 in 1966. Today, Perdue retains a good range of businesses, services, and other amenities despite its close proximity to the larger centres of Saskatoon and Biggar. Businesses include a grocery store, hardware, garages, gas stations and confectionaries, an insurance agency, bar, hotel, hair dresser, credit union, post office, restaurants, bulk fuel and farm supply outlets. Larger businesses include automobile and farm equipment dealerships, and E-zeeWrap, a manufacturer of plastic-wrap dispensers and other kitchen products. Recreational facilities in Perdue include a hockey arena, curling rink, ball diamonds, fairgrounds, a campground, and a seniors' centre. A community recreation complex houses a large hall, meeting rooms, banquet facilities, a library, and a bowling alley. A mile west of the village is the newly-opened Perdue Oasis Golf and RV Resort; it had 20 of 27 holes open for play in 2007. Senior and minor hockey, and figure skating are organized at the Perdue Arena. The village has a library, a museum, a number of service clubs and other community-based organizations, and an active United Church. Years prior to becoming the premier of Saskatchewan, Lorne Calvert served the pastoral charge at Perdue. Perdue School is a K-12 facility which had 111 students enrolled in the fall of 2006. Saskatoon is within commuting distance and provides all of the amenities and services of a major centre. Perdue serves as the administrative centre of the RM of Perdue No. 346.

PHILLIPS GROVE, organized hamlet, is a resort community located northeast of Big River toward the southwest end of Delaronde Lake. It was established as the organized hamlet of Phillips Beach in 1989; the name was officially changed in 1995. There are a small number of permanent residents; however, the population varies depending on the season. Phillips Grove is situated in the RM of Big River No. 555.

PIAPOT, hamlet, pop 55 (2001c), is a former village located northeast of Maple Creek just south of Hwy 1. Just northwest of the hamlet, Bear Creek flows into Piapot Creek, which in turn flows north into Crane Lake. The name of the community honours Chief Piapot, the Cree leader who temporarily blocked the construction of the CPR main line near the site in 1883. In the 1880s, massive ranching operations began to dominate the region; however, as grain farming became more profitable, and as the killing winter of 1906-07 devastated the cattle industry, ranchers found profits in parcelling out their lands for settlement and crop production. In 1910, a parcel of land was sold that would become the townsite of Piapot. Over the next two years, carloads of settlers unloaded their effects at the railway siding and businesses sprang up to serve the newcomers' needs. The post office was established on January 1, 1911, and the village was incorporated on December 6, 1912. The first grain elevator was erected in 1913. Piapot grew steadily until the 1930s, when the population peaked at around 300. The community's numbers dropped to roughly 250 by the 1940s, and hovered at around that level until the

▲ ▼ **PIAPOT TODAY LARGELY RESEMBLES A GHOST TOWN**, as empty and derelict buildings, cracked and overgrown sidewalks, and vacant lots line the once-busy streets. Photographs taken September 3, 2004.

early 1960s. It was during the post-WWII period that the community served a district population of close to 1,000 (by 2001 the population of the surrounding RM was down to 369), and during the 1950s there were approximately three dozen varied businesses, including four grain elevators, three churches, a bank, and a K-12 school in the village. Crop production, and cattle and sheep ranching were the economic backbone of the area at this time; sheep ranching, though, had practically disappeared by the mid-1960s. When the Trans-Canada Highway was built to the north of the village in the 1950s, bypassing community businesses that had previously profited from tourist and other traffic, it symbolized a new era in

Piapot's history. With the advent of faster automobiles and better highways, village merchants also faced increasing competition from larger centres such as Maple Creek and Swift Current, and commercial activity in Piapot steadily diminished. By the early 1960s, the population of the community had begun to plummet. From 246 residents in 1961, the village's numbers dropped to 160 by 1971, and 101 in 1981. By this time, all of the community's churches had closed. By the mid-1960s, children in grades 11 and 12 were being bused to Maple Creek to attend school. In 2005-06, the school was still open, but only grades K-6 were taught and only 16 students were enrolled. The school was closed in the summer of 2007. The Village of Piapot was dissolved June 6, 2003, its affairs thereafter under the auspices of the surrounding rural municipality. In recent years, the landscape surrounding Piapot, particularly to the north, has become dotted with natural gas wells. Interestingly, though, there is no indication of there being any positive economic spin-off for the community. There remains a branch of the Chinook Regional Library in Piapot, a postal outlet, a curling rink, and a Legion hall. A branch of the Cypress Credit Union closed in 2004, and the hotel was closed not long after that. Businesses in the district include a seed cleaning plant and gas field-related services. Piapot serves as the administrative centre of the RM of Piapot No. 110.

PIERCELAND

PIERCELAND, village, pop 498 (2006c), 449 (2001c), is located south of the west end of Meadow Lake Provincial Park, 16 km east of the Saskatchewan-Alberta border on Hwy 55. The community derives its name from Pierce Lake, to the north, which was reportedly named for an early area settler, but nothing seems to be known about this individual. The first few non-Native settlers began arriving in the region about 1911, but it was not until the late 1920s and the early

▼ **PIERCELAND UNDER OVERCAST SKIES**, July 23, 2003. View looking north up Main Street.

1930s that significant settlement of the area took place. It was around this time that development at Pierceland began. It had been expected that the Canadian National Railway would extend their line from St. Walburg through the district to Bonnyville, Alberta, but although work began, the Depression put the plans on hold for good. The Pierceland Post Office was established in 1932, and a number of business ventures were started during the decade. Also in the 1930s, a Red Cross Outpost Hospital was established. By the mid-1930s much of the available land in the district was occupied. People were initially lured to the area by the good fishing and trapping; later, lumbering, cattle, and crop production became livelihoods. By the late 1940s, resort activity had begun to develop on the lakes to the north of the community. Today, many Pierceland area residents find employment working in the oil and gas industry, both in the province and in Alberta. By the 1960s, Pierceland had developed into a sizable community, and on January 1, 1973, Pierceland became an incorporated village. In 1976, the population was 358. During the summer months, the community benefits from tourist traffic heading north to the provincial park — many Pierceland residents also spend their summer months at cabins in the area — and during the winter months there is still some commercial fishing at Pierce Lake. Pierceland has a range of businesses and services, three

churches, a library, a community hall, a recreation centre, an RCMP detachment, and a volunteer fire department; there is a health centre in Goodsoil. Pierceland School is a K-12 facility, which had 211 students enrolled in the fall of 2006. Pierceland serves as the administrative centre of the RM of Beaver River No. 622.

PILGER

PILGER, village, pop 74 (2006c), 85 (2001c), is located about 34 km northwest of Humboldt on Hwy 20. The district began to be settled in 1903, largely by German Catholics from Minnesota, as well as from other northern and mid-western states. Pilger is one of the German Catholic settlements that formed St. Peter's Colony, a vast 50-township area approximately from Cudworth to Watson, established by the German-American Land Company in conjunction with priests of the Order of St. Benedict and the Catholic Settlement Society of St. Paul, Minnesota. Most of the settlers to the area arrived via Rosthern, and, until the railway was completed through Humboldt in 1905, travel to Rosthern was necessary to obtain supplies. The foundations of the community of Pilger were laid some kilometres east of the present village with the construction of St. Bernard Church in 1907 and the beginning of a parochial school. The Pilger Post Office was also established in this area in 1908, and the name "Pilger," German for Pilgrim, was selected by Pius Mutter, the first postmaster. Construction of a new and much larger St. Bernard Roman Catholic Church was begun in 1918, about two and a half kilometres north of the first church, followed by the building of another school with increased capacity for a growing student population. In 1929, as the CPR was building from Lanigan toward Prince Albert, the present townsite

for Pilger was established, and as work on the rail bed proceeded, elevators, general stores, a hotel, and other various businesses sprang up, providing a trading centre for the surrounding agricultural district. In 1930, trains were running and the post office was moved in from the country. Farmers could then haul their grain to local elevators, relieving them of the longer journeys to Cudworth or Lake Lenore, previously the nearest railway points. In 1935, due to an increasing number of children in Pilger, a country school was also moved into the community. For a number of years, before a chapel was built in Pilger, people would still venture out to St. Bernard's Church to attend services. In 1948, a basement for a church was built in the community, which, covered, served as a chapel until 1964, when the upper portion of the church was finally completed. Pilger was established as an organized hamlet in 1958, and on January 1, 1969, Pilger was incorporated as a village. In 1971, over 80 per cent of the population still claimed German ancestry. A natural gas system was installed in 1974, and in 1975 sewer and water lines were put in place. In 1981, the village had a peak population of 150. The rail line was abandoned in the mid-1990s and Pilger School has now been closed for several years. The village today retains a store with postal service, a licensed beverage room, a curling rink, a community hall, a library, and the Catholic church. Pilger is situated in the RM of Three Lakes No. 400.

PILOT BUTTE

PILOT BUTTE, town, pop 1,867 (2006c), 1,850 (2001c), is located just east of Regina between Hwys 1 and 46. The community's name is derived from an area hill, which had long been used as a lookout point. With the construction of the railway through the region in 1882, the area's sand and gravel deposits were extensively utilized, and in the following years, as settlers began farming in the district, Pilot Butte developed. Brickyards became major local employers, and within several years the community boasted a number of businesses, churches, and a school. In 1913, Pilot Butte was incorporated as a village. The brickyards closed during the First World War, however, and with automobiles facilitating easy transportation into Regina, Pilot Butte began to lose its population, a trend that would continue for years. In 1923, the village was dissolved due to the loss of residents. The new Trans-Canada Highway was completed in the late 1950s, and in the subsequent decade living in Pilot Butte began to become a popular option for those who wanted to commute to work in the city. Pilot Butte re-acquired village status in 1963. In 1966 the population was 405, and between 1976 and 1981 the community's numbers jumped from 585 to 1,255 over the five-year period. Although Pilot Butte is largely a bedroom community, the growth has spurred the development of recreational facilities and essential business services, particularly home-based enterprises. A modern school provides K-8 education; high school students attend classes in Balgonie. Other than one or two older houses, there are virtually no reminders of the community's formative years, as most early structures have been destroyed. In 1995, a severe storm struck the community, damaging many modern homes. Pilot Butte is situated in the RM of Edenwold No. 158.

PINEHOUSE, northern village, pop 1,076 (2006c), 1,038 (2001c), is a relatively young community situated in a

sparsely settled and forested area on the fringe of the Canadian Shield. Pinehouse sits on a gentle rise overlooking the western shore of Pinehouse Lake (previously Snake Lake), a part of the Churchill River system approximately halfway between Lac Île-à-la-Crosse and Lac la Ronge. By air, the community is about 95 kilometres northwest of La Ronge; by road, it is 340 kilometres north of Prince Albert, the last 160 of which are gravel. The road (No. 914) that passes by Pinehouse continues north to the Key Lake Mine. The first missionaries visited the district in the late 1890s, and at that time the people who inhabited the area were Denesuline; they had, for much of the nineteenth century, replaced the district's earlier Cree inhabitants. Sometime after the beginning of the twentieth century, however, the small Dene population at Pinehouse Lake was evidently decimated by an epidemic, and most of those who survived relocated. Over the ensuing years, people of Cree and Cree Métis heritages began moving into the area to trap and fish, mainly from the districts around Lac Île-à-la-Crosse and Lac la Ronge, and they settled at various locations around Pinehouse Lake. Although many of the people in the northern village today hold treaty status and are affiliated with either the Canoe Lake First Nation or the Lac la Ronge Indian Band, all have strong Métis roots. Cree remains the first language of the community; English is the second. The present village of Pinehouse had its beginning toward the end of the 1930s, when area peoples decided that moving together to a central location would have benefits. Following WWII, several factors fostered the growth of the community: the establishment of a permanent school was an incentive for people to adopt a less migratory existence so that their children could receive a for-

▲ **AN AERIAL VIEW OF PINEHOUSE** taken in August 1980. Saskatchewan Archives Board, Saskatchewan Photographic Services, R-PS80-1400-128. Photographer: P. Stepaniuk.

mal education (a requirement if parents wanted to collect recently introduced Family Allowance payments); the economy at the lake was shifting to commercial fishing; a Roman Catholic mission was built and a priest regularly travelled from Ile-a-la-Crosse to conduct services and mass; the provincial government set up a store to sell merchandise and buy furs; and a post office was established. In the 1960s, modern homes began to be built under government programs, gradually replacing older dwellings. In 1976, an airstrip was built, and within the next two years the community experienced the advent of television and the construction of the first all-weather road linking Pinehouse to the south. On October 1, 1983, Pinehouse was established as a northern village under the Northern Municipalities Act, giving the community greater autonomy. In 1984, the village was connected to the provincial power grid, eliminating dependency on diesel fuel generators which had supplied the community with electrical power since about the early 1970s. Over time, Pinehouse residents have relied on

the fur trade, commercial fishing, government-funded programs, the development of local businesses, forestry, firefighting, some guiding, wild rice harvesting, and work in the northern mining industry for income. Significantly, too, people have retained close ties to the land and still engage in traditional activities such as hunting, fishing, berry picking, and trapping, as means by which to earn extra cash as well as to maintain a level of self-sufficiency. Community facilities and businesses in Pinehouse today consist of a Co-op café/gas bar/post office, a Co-op store, a confectionary, a medical clinic, an RCMP detachment, a community hall, and the Catholic church. Additionally, Minahik Waskahigan School in Pinehouse is a K-12 facility, which had 423 students enrolled in the fall of 2006. The school is a large, modern, fully-equipped school where learning snowmobile maintenance is a part of the Industrial Arts program. The median age of the population at Pinehouse was recorded as being 18.5 in 2006, while that of all Saskatchewan residents was 38.7.

PLEASANTDALE, village, pop 85 (2006c), 98 (2001c), is located north of Naicam, off Hwy 6. The name of the community — which is simply descriptive — originates with that of an area post office established in an early settler's store in 1909. Bert Sheere, who arrived in the district in 1906 and who was the first postmaster, became the secretary of the local improvement district in 1909 and that of the Rural Municipality of Pleasantdale No. 398 when it was formed in 1911. Sheere served in the position until 1923. Between 1920 and 1923, as there were whispers of a railway coming through, a sizable hamlet consisting of several businesses developed a couple of kilometres east of the present townsite. The Pleasantdale Post Office was located here during this period. When the CPR arrived in the area in the fall of 1923, building from Naicam to Melfort, the railway company established the present townsite, and immediately plans were made to relocate the various businesses to the railway. Large steam tractors were used to move the buildings, and the name Pleasantdale found its permanent home. With the coming of the steel, three elevators were built, much to the relief of area farmers who previously had to endure long trips by team and wagon or sleigh to Watson or Melfort to sell their grain. In the years following WWII, the number of residential homes in the community increased, but there began to be fewer places of business, as accessing the amenities of larger centres became increasingly convenient. By the 1960s and early 1970s, more than 150 people were living in Pleasantdale, and in 1982 it was established as an organized hamlet. On January 1, 1987, Pleasantdale gained village status. The CPR ended passenger service to the community in 1960, and freight service in 1973, when the station was closed. In 1975, Pleasantdale's three elevators were also closed, and in 1977 they were demolished. In 1983, the rail line through the community was abandoned, and more recently, one of the community's few remaining businesses, the Co-op store, also became a thing of the past. A key remaining institution was Pleasantdale Central School, a K-12 facility that had 77 students enrolled in the fall of 2005; it was closed in the summer of 2006 and students now attend classes in either Naicam or Melfort. Pleasantdale is situated in the RM of Pleasantdale No. 398.

PLENTY, village, pop 126 (2006c), 147 (2001c), is located southeast of Kerrobert on Hwy 31, and just west of Opuntia Lake, an important migratory bird sanctuary. A number of Aboriginal heritage sites dot the area, including turtle effigies and a medicine wheel. Settlers began arriving in the district between about 1905 and 1910, and with the arrival of the railway in 1911 the village was established and incorporated. Plenty is situated within the RM of Winslow No. 319, where grain production and oil and gas are the major industries. The village has a small core of businesses and services, and a modern school, which provides K-12 education to approximately 135 students from the community, the surrounding countryside, and the neighbouring village of Dodsland. A unique heritage building in Plenty predates the village itself. Originally built as a country store in 1910, the structure was moved to the new townsite in 1911, and over the subsequent years served as an Anglican Church, a Roman Catholic Church, and, later, a hall used by the Legion and the Scouts. In 1998, Prairie West Terminal Ltd. opened a facility a few kilometres west of Plenty, which has a capacity for storing over a million bushels of grain. Plenty had a peak population of 250 in 1966.

PLUNKETT, village, pop 75 (2006c), 75 (2001c), is located 3 km west of Lanigan, and 34 km north of Watrous, at the junction of Hwys 16 and 365. Plunkett came into being in 1908 as the Canadian Pacific Railway was building their line between Yorkton and Saskatoon. The locale was named after a prominent Irishman, Viscount Horace Plunkett. Settlers to the area were of varied origins; significant, however, were the large number of Hungarians who settled in the district the year the railway went through. The Plunkett Post Office was established on May 1, 1909, and that year the first of three grain elevators that lined the tracks in the village was built. In 1910, a local school district was set up, and in January 1911 the completed school was ready for classes. By December 28, 1921, the community had grown large enough to be incorporated as a village. Prior to this, Plunkett's affairs had been managed by, first, the local improvement district, then, after 1909, the surrounding rural municipality. The population of the community grew to hover at about 100 from the 1920s until the 1950s; it then rose to 136 by 1961, and, spurred by the development of potash mines at Allan, Colonsay, and Lanigan (Guernsey), Plunkett's population hit a peak of 152 in 1971. Many village residents still work in the region's potash industry. Agriculture is the area's other major industry — it consists of the production of grains, pulse crops, and cattle. In the early 1980s, Plunkett still had several viable businesses; today, residents largely travel to Lanigan, Watrous, or Saskatoon for goods and services. The Plunkett Hotel Bar and Grill remains in business, and

▼ **WAITING OUT THE WINTER:** a young homesteader keeps warm inside his sod shack in the district between Plunkett and Young in 1909. Saskatchewan Archives Board R-A2321.

a manufacturer of honey extractors and beekeeping equipment is located in the former school. The community retains an active curling rink. Plunkett is situated in the RM of Viscount No. 341.

PONTEIX, town, pop 531 (2006c), 550 (2001c), is located southeast of Swift Current off Hwy 13. After a 1907 scouting mission, the community was founded by Father Albert Royer from the parish of Ponteix, in the region of Auvergne, France. In 1908 he came to Canada, establishing the French-speaking parish of Notre-Dame d'Auvergne north of the present community, across the Notukeu Creek. In 1913-14, as the CPR was building its line toward Shaunavon along the south side of the Notukeu, the community shifted to the townsite on the rail line, naming it Ponteix in honour of Father Royer's former parish. Ponteix developed as a bilingual community over the decades, yet today retains a distinct French culture. The community grew to meet the physical, social, and spiritual needs of the surrounding agricultural district, being incorporated as a village in 1914 and attaining town status in 1957. In 1961, the community's population was 887. Ponteix has a health centre with a special care home, an RCMP detachment, and a volunteer fire department. Educational institutions include Ponteix School, a K-12 facility; École Boreale, which provides French language education at the elementary level; and a library. Community recreational facilities include an arena with rinks for skating, hockey, and curling. A regional park, which lies adjacent to the community, has a nine-hole golf course, an outdoor swimming pool, a tennis court, and sites for camping and picnics. Community attractions include the Notukeu Heritage Museum at the Cen-

314 ←

PONTEIX

...a place by the Notukeu

▲ **THE TOWERS OF NOTRE DAME D'AUVERGNE CHURCH**, Ponteix, are visible from miles away. Construction of the church began in 1928 and the first mass was celebrated in the completed building on July 21, 1930. Photograph taken October 6, 2003.

▶ **MAY 24, 1929**, the church, then under construction, was all but completely demolished by a cyclone. Notre Dame Convent is in the left of the photograph.

▼ **LARGE CROWDS** attend the Eucharistic Congress held in Ponteix in June 1947.

Photographs right and below courtesy of Notre Dame d'Auvergne Church Archives, Ponteix.

HENRI LIBOIRON spent more than 50 years working as an amateur archaeologist assembling one of the largest recorded collections of First Nations artifacts in southwestern Saskatchewan and documenting numerous archaeological sites — including more than 650 tipi rings between 1980 and the early 1990s. He starting collecting artifacts in 1937 when severe wind erosion resulted in many being left exposed in area fields. Liboiron also immersed himself in First Nations culture, practising ethno-archaeology: making pemmican (top left), creating pottery, crafting arrowheads, and building a sweat lodge. His collection of arrowheads and other artifacts, once housed in a museum in his basement, are now housed in Notukeu Heritage Museum at the Centre Culturel Royer (left). In the 1990s, Liboiron, along with his good friend Bobby St. Cyr, was also instrumental in the discovery and excavation of the fossilized remains of a Plesiosaur in the area, remains which date back 70-75 million years. Henri Liboiron passed away in 1996 at the age of 67.

tre Culturel Royer. The museum features impressive displays of archaeological and palaeontological artifacts. The vast Henri Liboiron collection consists of locally-found arrowheads and other stone tools dating back several thousands of years, and the museum provides information on the 70 to75-million-year-old plesiosaur (a marine reptile) found in the area in 1993. Dominating the town's skyline is Notre Dame d'Auvergne Church, the largest column-free church in the province's southwest. Built between 1928 and 1930, the church houses a 500-year-old sculpture of the Virgin Mary holding the dead body of Christ in her lap. A gift to Father Royer, the oak pieta came from France, where, reportedly, it had survived the French Revolution hidden in a haystack. Other Ponteix landmarks include the Convent of Notre Dame and the former Gabriel Hospital. Both were founded by the Sisters of Our Lady of Chambriac, who joined Father Royer in Ponteix in 1913. The hospital, which was completed in 1918, was largely financed by the Michelin family, whose rubber- and tire-producing empire is headquartered in Auvergne, France; the contribution was made on the condition that the hospital be named Gabriel after a family son who had been killed in WWI. Ponteix serves as the administrative centre of the RM of Auvergne No. 76.

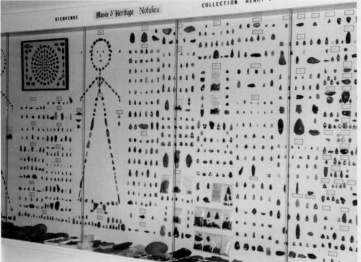

▼ **O CANADA!** At the invitation of Father Keith Heiberg students from the School of Journalism at the University of Regina travelled to Ponteix and the neighbouring village of Vanguard for a few days in October 2003. The purpose was to look for big stories in small towns. On the night of October 6 the students and the community attended an evening of lectures, theatrical performances, and music at the Catholic parish hall in Ponteix. The journalism students are shown here on stage doing their bit — singing O Canada in both French and English.

Photograph of Henri Liboiron courtesy of Le Centre Culturel Royer, Ponteix; other photographs on this page taken October 6, 2003.

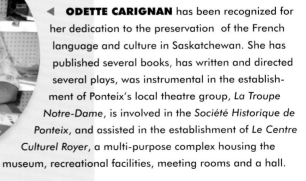

◄ **ODETTE CARIGNAN** has been recognized for her dedication to the preservation of the French language and culture in Saskatchewan. She has published several books, has written and directed several plays, was instrumental in the establishment of Ponteix's local theatre group, La Troupe Notre-Dame, is involved in the Société Historique de Ponteix, and assisted in the establishment of Le Centre Culturel Royer, a multi-purpose complex housing the museum, recreational facilities, meeting rooms and a hall.

PORCUPINE PLAIN, town, pop 783 (2006c), 820 (2001c), is located in east-central Saskatchewan, just northeast of Greenwater Lake Provincial Park on Hwy 23. The Porcupine Provincial Forest lies immediately southeast of the community and to the east loom the Porcupine Hills. During the first two decades of the twentieth century, prior to intensive settlement, the primary activity in the region concerned logging interests. After WWI, land was opened up for soldiers returning from overseas, and by the mid-1920s civilian settlers were taking up land. In 1921, a Red Cross Outpost Hospital, the second in the province, was opened northeast of the present hamlet of Carragana; soon, one-room schools and churches began to dot the countryside. However, prior to the completion of the rail line from Crooked River to Reserve, there were only a few families and a couple of bachelors within several kilometres of present-day Porcupine Plain. But with the arrival of the railway in 1928, the location for a siding was chosen, the townsite began to develop, and on April 1, 1929, the Porcupine Plain Post Office was established. As forestry was the primary basis of the economy for many years, Porcupine Plain became known as the cordwood capital of Saskatchewan. It was incorporated as a village on April 9, 1942, and, on January 1, 1968, the community attained town status. As the land was cleared, it was developed for the cultivation of crops, and, today, agriculture is the main industry in the region, forestry being second. Cereal grains and oilseeds are the main crops grown, and individual farmers also raise livestock. Over the past few years, intensive hog operations have been developed in the area, creating approximately 50 full- and part-time jobs.

► **THE SAME VIEW** of Porcupine Plain's business section two years apart, in 1947 (top) and 1949 (centre), and an aerial view of the town taken in 1974. Photographs courtesy of the Porcupine Plain and District Museum.

As the largest community in a considerable territory, Porcupine Plain is the main service, supply, and business centre for a substantial trading area population — many local businesses cater to the agricultural sector. The town also serves the district with a hospital, special care homes, ambulance service, an RCMP detachment, and a volunteer fire department with rescue and emergency extrication equipment. The Porcupine Opportunities Program provides vocational and life skills training for persons with special abilities and needs, assists with housing, and provides employment through a recycling depot, a laundromat, and other community services. Porcupine Plain's elementary and composite high schools provide K-12 education to over 300 town and area students. Community recreational facilities include an arena with a sports lounge, a curling rink, an outdoor pool, a community-owned and operated theatre, and three parks. Additionally, a lo-

► **CHUCKWAGON AND CHARIOT RACES** are held during the annual Porcupine Plain Community Sports Day each July 1 long weekend. Photograph courtesy of the Etomami Valley Regional Economic Development Authority.

cal snowmobile club maintains over 100 kilometres of groomed trails in the area and the region is very popular for hunting and fishing. There are a number of outfitters in the district. Further, nearby Greenwater and Marean Lakes are popular resort destinations. Porcupine Plain has a library, a substantial museum, and a number of churches, service clubs, sports teams, and other community-based organizations. The town faced a significant challenge in the mid-1990s when CN announced its intention to abandon the rail line that ran through the community. Despite farmers, municipal officials, and other citizens along the subdivision attempting to negotiate its purchase for a short-line railway, CN refused to negotiate and the line was abandoned in 1999. The result was elevator closures, lost tax revenues, increased pressure on area roads, and changing trading patterns. Porcupine Plain serves as the administrative centre of the RM of Porcupine No. 395.

POWM BEACH, organized hamlet, est. 1982, is one of several resort communities situated northeast of Turtleford on Turtle Lake. There were approximately 40 permanent residents in 2006; however, the population varies greatly depending on the season, reaching roughly 130 during the summer months. Developed in the 1970s, Powm Beach lies within the RM of Mervin No. 499.

PRAIRIE RIVER, organized hamlet, pop 35 (2006c), 30 (2001c), is located 40 km west of the town of Hudson Bay, 2 km north off Hwy 3. To the south lie agricultural lands, while immediately to the north is the vast expanse of the Pasquia Provincial Forest. The pretty

Prairie River, after which the community is named, runs along the southwest side of the hamlet. The Canadian Northern Railway was built through the area from Hudson Bay to Melfort in 1905, and in 1906 James and Thomas Shaw of Dauphin, Manitoba, began the operation of a saw and planing mill immediately west of the present community. In 1910, the brothers began construction of a logging railway that ran southwest to Bjork Lake; however, by 1917, the mill was closed and the rail line was abandoned. In 1911 a post office by the name of Bouvier was opened (a Shaw was the postmaster); but the office's name was changed to Prairie River in 1913. Following WWI, Prairie River became established as the nearest railway point and staging site for a developing soldiers' settlement to the south, stretching toward Weekes and Porcupine Plain. Stores, lodgings, and livery barns were built at Prairie River, and in 1920 the CN station was constructed. In 1925, a private community school was opened, and in 1935 the Prairie River School District No. 5094 was established. The community had a population of over 100 in the mid-1960s, but subsequently the hamlet's

numbers began to plummet. Today there are no businesses or services left in the community, other than a postal outlet and a library that is open twice a week; Prairie River students are bused to school in Hudson Bay. The track that runs through the community is now overgrown, although the station remains, housing a local museum that is opened upon request. The building was designated a heritage property in 1982. Prairie River is situated in the RM of Porcupine No. 395.

▼ **THE FORMER CNR STATION** that now houses the Prairie River Museum. Passenger and freight services were handled on the building's main floor; the station agent's living quarters were housed on the second. Photograph taken August 11, 2004.

PREECEVILLE, town, pop 1,050 (2006c), 1,074 (2001c), is located in the north-eastern parkland, roughly 105 km north of Yorkton at the junction of Hwys 9, 47, and 49. The vast area of the Porcupine Provincial Forest lies to the north, and Preeceville sits along the upper reaches of the Assiniboine River. Fur trading activity in the area dates to the late 1700s. Ranching activities, which had begun in the late 1800s, gave way to homesteads after the township was surveyed in 1900. The townsite of Preeceville was surveyed in 1911, as the Canadian Northern Railway progressed westward from Sturgis. In 1912, the railway arrived. On February 6 that year, the fledgling hamlet was incorporated as a village, its name honouring the Preece family upon whose land the community was built. With the arrival of the rails, settlement of the district increased, many settlers being of Scandi-

Photographs courtesy of Esther Paul, Preeceville, except the two "Main Street" photographs, which are courtesy of the Sturgis Station House Museum.

navian and Ukrainian origins. The community developed steadily over the next few decades and experienced a period of rapid growth during the 1940s, its population almost doubling over the decade. On November 30, 1946, Preeceville attained town status with a population of 540; it had a peak population of 1,272 in 1986. The area economy is based on agriculture, a combination of grain and livestock production; a large-scale hog operation provides many local jobs. Preeceville has a wide range of businesses and is a supply and service centre for a trading area population of approximately 5,500. There are two farm implement dealers in the town. Preeceville also serves the area with a hospital, a special care home, a pharmacy, and dental services. The community has an ambulance service and a volunteer fire department; policing is provided by the Sturgis RCMP. Preeceville School is a K-12 facility, which had 283 town and area students enrolled in the fall of 2006. The town has an array of recreational facilities including an arena with an NHL-size ice surface. Additionally, there are a number of regional parks, resort areas, and tracts of pristine wilderness in the area. The town has a library, and a number of churches, service clubs, sports teams, and other community-based organizations. Major annual events include the Preeceville Lions Trade Show each April; "Western Days," the summer fair held

▲ **MAIN STREET**, Preeceville, 1914 or earlier.

◄ **THE FIRST STATION AGENT**, James Lowie, with his family, circa 1912.

PREECEVILLE

... "Headwaters of the Assiniboine"

▶ **THE PREECEVILLE FARMERS SUPPLY CO.,** on the east side of Main Street, opened in 1911 and was owned by Sam Bricker (1886-1975). In 1917, he sold out to a cousin, another Sam Bricker, who carried on in business until 1932, when the store, the neighbouring Bank of Toronto, and the City Café were destroyed by fire. Photograph circa late 1910s or early 1920s.

▶ **DRAY MAN BILLIE BRIGGS** hauling lumber in Preeceville in 1919 with his mules Duke and Duit. Briggs operated the business from 1919 until 1948 when he sold out to Peter Maksymiw, who in turn sold out to Bill Maksymiw. The business was later sold to Lonko Horbachewski.

▼ **GOOD TRANSPORTATION IN WINTER.** The Wallis tractor, pictured here, was popular in the 1920s, and became the basis for the subsequently famous Massey-Harris tractors after Canada's Massey-Harris bought out the J.I. Case Plow Works of Racine, Wisconsin in 1928, acquiring the Wallis line. Massey-Harris had been selling the advanced Wallis tractor since 1927.

◀ **THE ROYAL NORTH-WEST MOUNTED POLICE** were stationed in Preeceville shortly after the community's founding. This photograph predates 1919, the year the name of the force was changed to the RCMP. The man in the left of the photograph is Percival Griggs, the builder of this home which stood on Railway Avenue which housed the Mounties for a time. Later, barracks, a courtroom, and a residence was constructed on Main Street. In the 1930s the detachment was moved to Sturgis, where it remains to this day. During the years the police were stationed in Preeceville, officers owned their own horses and were paid two cents per mile for patrols.

▼ **SOUTHWEST MAIN STREET**, Preeceville, circa late 1940s.

in July; and the Musher's Rendezvous, a major winter festival featuring world-class sled dog races that attracts competitors from as far away as Alaska, the Yukon, and Minnesota. Preeceville residents have also been actively involved in a number of community beautification projects over the past few years, winning high honours in the nationally-acclaimed Communities in Bloom competition. Preeceville serves as the administrative centre of the RM of Preeceville No. 334.

PRELATE, village, pop 126 (2006c), 164 (2001c), is located approximately 15 km south of the South Saskatchewan River, on Hwy 32, 10 km east of Leader. Settlers began arriving in large numbers in the region in 1909-10, and, although a few were from Ontario, the British Isles, Ukraine, and Norway, the majority were German Catholics from Russia, many of whom arrived via the United States. Before the railway came through, these early settlers would have to make the long three-day trip to Maple Creek on the CPR main line to obtain supplies or to deliver grain. However, with the arrival of the railway in 1913, Prelate quickly became another in the string of communities that grew up along the "Empress Line," and

◄ **AFTER 88 YEARS** in the community, the Ursuline nuns announced the closure of St. Angela's Academy in Prelate in the summer of 2007. The decision was based on rising costs, low enrollments (42 in 2006-07), and the age of the teaching sisters (most of the 12 living in Prelate were over the age of 75). With a staff of approximately 28, St. Angela's was a major employer in the area, and its loss is another substantial blow to the village.

◄ **THE FIRST GRAIN ELEVATOR** in Prelate was erected in 1914. The bumper crops of 1915 and 1916 necessitated the construction of four more, and soon eight elevators lined the tracks in the village. By 2008, this Paterson Grain elevator, built in the mid-1970s, was the only one left standing.

▼ **THE PRELATE FIRE HALL** at one time also housed the village office and a residence for local police constables.

Prelate photographs taken August 29, 2003.

the village was incorporated on October 25 that year. The community grew rapidly and was substantially bolstered in 1919 by the arrival of the Ursuline Sisters, who founded St. Angela's Convent and, later, St. Angela's Academy. By the end of the 1920s, the population of the village was over 500. However, in the following years, as the district was hit hard by the drought and the Depression, many people left, relocating to other parts of Saskatchewan or to Alberta or British Columbia. By 1940, the village was bankrupt and a large percentage of Prelate's population was on Relief. The provincial government stepped in, disbanded the village council and appointed an overseer to manage the community's finances, an arrangement that remained in place until the end of 1946. The post-WWII era was a period of unprecedented prosperity and growth. By 1956, the population had swollen to a peak of 632, dozens of businesses provided services to the grain-growing and ranching district surrounding the village, and several grain elevators lined the railway tracks. The community's athletic teams excelled. In the early 1960s, the Prelate Mustangs baseball team was a powerhouse feared throughout the province's southwest. Since the 1970s, however, the community has experienced a slow, but steady, decline. In 1985, the public school was closed, with schoolchildren subsequently being bused to Leader. The skating arena was condemned and the curling rink closed. Today, all but one of the grain elevators have disappeared, and only a couple of businesses are left in the village. With the economy surrounding agriculture questionable, the recent discovery of large reserves of natural gas near Shackleton has proven somewhat of a boon to the region, providing some off-farm employment. The Village of Prelate is situated in the RM of Happyland No. 231.

PRIMATE, village, pop 50 (2006c), 45 (2001c), is situated 11 km southeast of Macklin at the junction of Hwys 31 and 317. Primate was established on a Canadian Pacific Railway line that was built between Kerrobert and Macklin in 1910-11. The post office was established on September 1, 1911, and a number of businesses were started that year. Settlers had begun arriving in the district around 1906. Although some were of English and Scottish backgrounds, a large part of Primate's population was made up of German Catholics. St. Joseph's Colony, a vast 77-township settlement between Unity and Kerrobert, and Macklin and Landis, was largely peopled by German Catholics from the Dakotas and southern Russia. In 1971, more than 80 per cent of the residents of Primate still claimed German origins. German Catholics established the parish of St. Elizabeth at Primate during WWI; Anglican and Methodist ministers came from Macklin to attend to the community's Protestants. Primate was incorporated as a village on April 5, 1922; the Primate School District was set up in 1924. Previously schoolchildren attended

▲ **NOW STANDING ALONE**, this former Saskatchewan Wheat Pool grain elevator in Primate dates to 1960 and is one of approximately 500 of the traditional wooden structures remaining in the province. Photograph taken August 14, 2003.

rural schools that had been established between 1910 and 1913. Four grain elevators lined the tracks in Primate for many years, and the community's population hovered at approximately 120 from the 1920s until the early 1960s, with the exception of a slight downturn during the 1930s. The community's peak population was 129 in 1961. The village's population began to dwindle in the 1960s, and during that decade, students in grades 10, 11, and 12 began to be bused to school in Macklin. Primate School was still open in the early 1980s, but has now been closed for many years. The community's businesses have been superseded by those in Macklin, where there is also a health centre, special care home, ambulance service, RCMP, fire department, recreational facilities, and a K-12 school. Primate's post office closed in 1990; one former Saskatchewan Wheat Pool grain elevator, dating to 1960, remains standing. The oil and gas industry, and agriculture, form the basis of the district economy. Primate is situated in the RM of Eye Hill No. 382.

PRINCE, organized hamlet, pop 45 (2006c), 50 (2001c), is located approximately 27 km north of North Battleford, just south of Jackfish Lake on Hwy 26. The community is named after Benjamin Joseph Prince (1855-1920), who, along with his brother Alphonse, came west in the 1880s from Quebec. They became prominent early settlers in the Highgate area across the North Saskatchewan River to south of Prince. The brothers became businessmen in Battleford. Benjamin Prince served with the Battleford Home Guards in 1885, represented Battleford in the Territorial Assembly from 1898-1905, was the mayor of Battleford from 1907-09, and was appointed to the Senate of Canada on the advice of Wilfred Laurier in 1909, where he served until his death at age 65. The Prince district saw increasing settlement, mainly ranching activity, following the 1885 Resistance — travellers between Forts Carlton, Battleford, and Pitt were familiar with the area. By 1894, most of the district land was surveyed, but the greatest influx of settlers took place after 1900. With the construction of the Canadian Northern Railway line northwest from North Battleford, the Prince townsite was established. The line, which would eventually run to St. Walburg, ran as far as Edam by 1911. An area post office established

in 1904 and originally known as Meota, changed its name to Prince in 1911. The first grain elevator was built in 1912, and the railway station was built in 1913. A school was completed at the end of 1916, and classes commenced in January the next year. Prince developed into a small service centre for the surrounding agricultural district, and by the 1950s boasted a store and post office, garage, blacksmith and repair shop, railway station and section house, the school, a United Church, and two grain elevators (there had earlier been four; none remain today). The community's proximity to the Battlefords, however, would lead to changes: high school students began to bused to North Battleford in the mid-1950s; in 1965, grades 8 and 9 followed, as did grades 5, 6, and 7 in 1967. Grades 1-4 were taught for one more year at Prince School before it was closed in 1968. The railway station (closed for a number of years) had been hauled to the grounds of the Western Development Museum in North Battleford in 1967, and in 1970 the Prince Post Office was closed. By 1980, the United Church stood empty. In 1981, Prince was established as an organized hamlet; it was by this time, however, becoming somewhat of a bedroom community to the city. Today, there are no businesses left in the hamlet. Prince is situated in the RM of Meota No. 468.

PRINCE ALBERT, city, pop 34,138 (2006c), 34,291 (2001c), is the province's third largest city. It is situated on the North Saskatchewan River, 141 km northeast of Saskatoon. In 1776, Peter Pond built the first fur trading post in the area, to the west of present-day Prince Albert, where the Sturgeon River flows into the North Saskatchewan River. In 1862,

James Isbister established a small Métis settlement just west of today's city limits. Prince Albert's founding, however, is credited to James Nisbet (1823-74), a Presbyterian missionary. Nisbet was born in Scotland and came to Canada West with his family in 1844, settling at Oakville. He studied theology at Knox College in Toronto, graduating in 1849. In 1866, with the assistance of John MacKay and George Flett, Nisbet selected a site to establish a mission at what became Prince Albert. He named the locale in honour of Queen Victoria's late consort. Nisbet started a school and an industrial farm: by 1871, 40 acres of land were broken, and a threshing machine and a horse-powered grinding mill were in operation. About 300 English-speaking settlers were established on the south bank of the river by 1874; by about 1877 a steam-powered grist mill and a saw mill were evidence of continuing development. By the time the Prince Albert Post Office was established in 1879 the population of the community had almost tripled, and the Dominion government opened a land office at Prince Albert in 1881. Things did not look as rosy, however, after the CPR abandoned the planned northern route for the trans-continental railway, opting instead for a line across the southern plains. Nonetheless, Prince Albert was proclaimed a town on October 8, 1885, the Board of Trade was organized in 1887, and in 1890 a rail link, although it would be little used for years, was completed from Regina. By 1891, the population of Prince Albert was 1,009. By 1901, the community numbered 1,785, and on October 8, 1904, Prince Albert attained city status, becoming the province's third city. The following year, work began on the construction of sewer systems and a municipally-owned water supply. Shortly, electric street lights were erected. The

▲ **LEGALLY ESTABLISHED AS A TOWN IN 1885**, Prince Albert attained city status on October 8, 1904. The celebrations, however, took place on November 30, 1904, which was declared a public holiday. Events included a parade, a performance by the city band in front of city hall (pictured here), and a banquet attended by the Premier of the North-West Territories, Frederick Haultain. Saskatchewan Archives Board R-B1613.

city prospered and grew rapidly at the beginning of the twentieth century, due to an influx of settlers taking up the remaining agricultural lands in the region, the expansion of northern fisheries, and the establishment of numerous large lumbering operations. A wealth of fur, fish, and timber from the north was funnelled through the city. Prince Albert's sawmills fed the construction boom then occurring in the Canadian west. Optimism for the city's future remained high. By 1911, the city's population had grown to 6,254, and that year the federal penitentiary opened. Prince Albert would become well-known for its penal institutions in the years to come. In addition to the Saskatchewan

Penitentiary, men's and women's correctional centres, and a facility for young offenders would be built. In 1912, work began on the ill-fated La Colle Falls Dam project east of the city. It had been expected that the production of inexpensive hydroelectric power would attract industry, but escalating costs, among other factors, brought the half-completed project to a standstill in 1913 and the City of Prince Albert to the brink of bankruptcy — it was 50 years before the debts were finally paid off. The dam debacle, along with the 1912-13 recession, followed by the 1918 announcement by the Prince Albert Lumber Company that it was closing operations due to the fact that accessible

timber berths were exhausted, brought an end to the boom. Growth was slowed for decades. A bright spot came when William Lyon Mackenzie King lost his seat in York North during the 1925 elections. The MP for Prince Albert stepped aside to let the prime minister run in that constituency, which he won. The deal for the seat, though, came with a hitch: the creation of a new national park north of the city in the Sturgeon River Forest Reserve. Prince Albert National Park was officially established in 1927, and a new industry — tourism — had its beginnings. Prince Albert grew during the Depression, but this was largely due to people — many of them Métis — moving in from rural areas seeking work or some form of relief. It was not until WWII that the city's fortunes began to significantly turn around, mirroring the general era of prosperity then being enjoyed by the province as a whole. The population jumped from 11,049 in 1936 to 17,149 by 1951, and the city became firmly established as the major service, retail, and distribution centre not only for the region, but for Saskatchewan's north. Mining companies and the provincial government began to use Prince Albert as the base of operations for their interests in the northern half of the province. With the opening of a pulp mill in 1968, forestry became the second most important industry next to agriculture. In the early 1980s, the Peter Ballantyne Cree First Nation successfully established the Opawakoscikan Reserve in Prince Albert, the first urban reserve in Saskatchewan. Today, thirty per cent of the city's population claim an aboriginal heritage: about half of these identify themselves as First Nations; the other half report a Métis identity. Of the total city population, a large proportion (25 per cent in 2000) live below the Low Income Cutoff, or the "pov-

erty line," and a significant percentage are children. The city's population has slipped slightly over the past ten years — by 639 since 1996, but Prince Albert has seen major developments during the first years of the present century: the Cornerstone Centre, representing 240,000 square feet of new retail development, opened in 2001; the E.A. Rawlinson Centre for the Arts opened in 2003; and the Saskatchewan Forest Centre building was completed in 2004. Approximately one third of Prince Albert's residents find employment in health, education, and government sectors (work with government is found at the federal, provincial, and municipal levels); other employment is found in service industries, retail trade, agriculture and forestry, construction, and manufacturing and processing. In the spring of 2006, Weyerhaeuser closed its pulp and paper facilities in Prince Albert, putting several hundred people out of work, and as of the fall of 2007 there were no signs of the mills reopening. Subsequently, the city's leading employers, in descending order, are: the Prince Albert Parkland Health District, the Government of Saskathewan (not including Crowns), Government of Canada, Saskatchewan Rivers School Division, City of Prince Albert, Northern Lights Casino, Wal-Mart, Prince Albert Development Corporation, Saskatchewan Institute of Applied Science and Technology (SIAST), and the Real Canadian Superstore. Prince Albert's primary market area covers a large region, extending from Cudworth and Rosthern to the south, Tisdale and Carrot River to the east, Blaine Lake and Spiritwood to the west, and La Ronge to the north. This primary market area has an estimated population of close to 86,000 people. The city also serves a secondary market that includes most of northern Saskatchewan and an additional 17,000 people, bringing the total combined population in the market spheres to about 103,000. Prince Albert's educational facilities include public and separate elementary and high schools, the SIAST campus, First Nations University of Canada campuses, and a campus of the Gabriel Dumont Insitute. Among the city's many recreational facilities are the Kinsmen Water Park, the Cooke Municipal Golf Course (in the heart of the city), Riverbank and Little Red River Parks, and the Communiplex, home to the Prince Albert Raiders of the Western Hockey League. The E.A. Rawlinson Centre is a 600-seat, state-of-the-art visual and performing arts facility; the Prince Albert Arts Centre, situated in the 1893 Town Hall and Opera House, facilitates art exhibitions, and arts and crafts workshops. City museums include the Prince Albert Historical Museum (located in the city's 1912 fire hall), Diefenbaker House (once the home of the former Prime Minister), the Rotary Museum of Police and Corrections, and the Evolution of Education Museum. One of the city's more notable landmarks is known as the Keyhole Castle, built in 1913 by Sam McLeod, a local businessman and two-time mayor of Prince Albert. The unique and opulent home has been designated a National Historic Site. The *Prince Albert Daily Herald* (origins in 1894) is the city's daily newspaper; the city's premier annual event is the winter festival, which is held over a two-week period each February. The highlight of the festival is the Canadian Challenge Sled Dog Race, Canada's premier mushing event. Traditionally run from Prince Albert to La Ronge and back, the race covers approximately 500 kilometres (300 miles) and has a purse of over $20,000. Three Canadian prime ministers have served Prince Albert in the House of Commons: Wilfred

Laurier, William Lyon Mackenzie King, and John Diefenbaker. Prince Albert serves as the administrative centre of the RM of Prince Albert No. 461.

PRUD'HOMME, village, pop 167 (2006c), 203 (2001c), is located in a rolling setting approximately 55 km northeast of Saskatoon on Hwy 27. The community developed through the efforts of people mainly of French, Hungarian, and Ukrainian backgrounds. In 1897 Joseph Paul Marcotte, originally from Quebec, established a ranch in the area of the present village. The locale was known simply as Marcotte's Ranch, or Marcotte's Crossing, until the Canadian Northern Railway came through the area in 1904-05, building the section of their transcontinental main line between Humboldt and Warman. They established a townsite, which they named Howell, evidently in honour of a railway company employee, a surveyor. A post office by the name Howell was formally established in 1906, and when the hamlet had developed sufficiently enough, Howell became an incorporated village in the Province of Saskatchewan in 1908. The name of the village was changed to Prud'homme in 1922, in honour of Joseph-Henri Prud'homme (1882-1952), the Roman Catholic bishop of Prince Albert and Saskatoon. In 1923, the name of the post office was changed as well. By 1926, the population of Prud'homme was 268; the community reached its peak population in 1966, when it numbered 321. Four grain elevators lined the railway tracks at this time — none remain today. Businesses of note that operated in the village over the years included a cheese factory, egg candling station, furniture factory, and a mushroom growing operation. For many years, the Daughters of Providence

(les Filles de la Providence) operated a convent and taught school in the community. Today, Prud'homme has a credit union, general store, hotel and bar, post office, community hall, and a community complex that facilitates hockey tournaments, skating, and bowling, among other functions. Prud'homme has an active recreation board, a museum, and a library. Community landmarks include Sts. Donatien and Rogatien Roman Catholic Church, and St. John the Evangelist Ukrai-

▲ **STS. DONATIEN AND ROGATIEN ROMAN CATHOLIC CHURCH**, Prud'homme.

▼ **THE GENTLY ROLLING SETTING** around Prud'homme is evident in this photo of the town's cemetery, located on a hill on the north side of the village. View looking north.

Photographs taken August 10, 2004.

nian Catholic Church. The village was the birthplace of Jeanne Sauvé (1922-93), the first woman to serve as the speaker of the House of Commons (1980-84) and the first woman to be named Governor General of Canada (1984-90). Sauvé visited Prud'homme in her official capacity as the Governor General in October 1984. Agriculture forms the basis of the area economy (cereal crops, oilseeds, cattle, turkeys, chickens, sheep, and pigs are produced); however, some residents leave the area to work, since Prud'homme is within commuting distance to Saskatoon and Humboldt. Prud'homme is situated on the boundary of the RM of Bayne No. 371 and the RM of Grant No. 372.

PUNNICHY, village, pop 277 (2006c), 317 (2001c), is situated in the Touchwood Hills on Hwy 15, 20 km east of Raymore and approximately 13 km west of Touchwood Hills Post Provincial Historic Park. Four First Nations reserves are located in the vicinity: that of the Kawacatoose Band to the northwest; the Day Star Band to the north; the Muskowekwan Band to the east; and the Gordon Band to the south. In the decades prior to the development of the village, the area had an interesting history: to the north of Punnichy passed the Carlton Trail, connecting Fort Garry, Fort Ellice, Fort Carlton and Fort Edmonton; in 1849, the Hudson's Bay Company established their first trading post in the Touchwood Hills, and by this time Red River Métis had also developed a wintering, or "hivernant," camp in the area; the North West Mounted Police established one of their early posts in the vicinity; and, in 1883, a station on the Dominion Telegraph line was established northeast of present-day Punnichy, at a location where, in 1887, one of the earliest

△ ▽ **VIEWS FROM MONUMENT HILL IN PUNNICHY:** the first (above, Saskatchewan Archives Board R-A9869-1), circa 1920s, shows the north end of the village and the three grain elevators that once stood in the community; the second photograph (below), taken on October 22, 2003, from approximately the same location, shows the one remaining elevator.

post offices in what is now Saskatchewan was established — it was known as the Kutawa Post Office. General Middleton's column passed through en route from Qu'Appelle Station to the Fish Creek and Batoche district in 1885. It was in the vicinity of the Kutawa Post Office and telegraph station that Wolfe Armstrong Heubach established a store and stopping place during the 1880s, and it is after a Saulteaux nickname for Heubach that the village of Punnichy would later be named. Evidently, the Saulteaux thought the young Heubach looked like a young bird, either because of his hooked nose or because the sparse whiskers he grew while attempting to grow a beard resembled, it was thought, a fledgling's early feathers. Thus Heubach was given the name "Punnichy" — the spelling a translation of the Saulteaux word "panacay" — meaning fledgling bird. In 1908, the Grand Trunk Pacific Railway line was completed through the area, and Heubach relocated to the newly-surveyed townsite to become one of Punnichy's first storekeepers. The Punnichy Post Office was established on April 1, 1909, and the village was incorporated on October 22 that year. Also in 1909, the first village school was built. Several businesses were now in operation, and Punnichy's population grew from 73 in 1911 to 200 by 1921. The community continued to grow, even through the Depression, and its population soared during the decades following WWII to reach a peak of 451 in 1971. Although the village's numbers have subsequently fallen, Punnichy retains a good range of busi-

◀ **HANGING OUT.** Students from Punnichy High School enjoy a warm autumn day during lunch hour. Photograph taken October 22, 2003.

nesses and services (these are bolstered by a sizable area population). It also has a seniors' centre, a golf course, a curling rink, a library, and an RCMP detachment. Punnichy's elementary and high schools together provide K-12 education, and combined had over 350 students enrolled in the fall of 2006. Students are drawn from the village itself, the surrounding farms, and area First Nations reserves. Punnichy landmarks include "Monument Hill," located on the village's east side, and the former Saskatchewan Wheat Pool grain elevator (1956) and annex (1949), situated along the tracks (now CN) which run along the north side of the community. Monument Hill, so-named because of the war memorial erected on its crest after WWI, offers a good view of the surrounding countryside; the grain elevator (now privately owned) is the last of three which once stood in Punnichy and is one of the approximately 500 wooden grain elevators left standing in Saskatchewan. Punnichy is situated in the RM of Mount Hope No. 279.

QU'APPELLE, town, pop 624 (2006c), 648 (2001c), is located 50 km east of Regina just off Hwy 1 on Hwy 35. The Hudson's Bay Company had a trading post a short distance southwest of Qu'Appelle from 1854 to 1864; however, it was with the coming of the railway in 1881-82 that the community began to develop. The first post office established in 1882 was known as Troy, but the name was changed to Qu'Appelle Station in 1884. Qu'Appelle Station became the base for the telegraph line running north through Humboldt to Fort Battleford and Edmonton, as well as a major jumping-off point for settlers. An immigration agent was stationed in the young community, and passengers and

mail were carried by stagecoaches to Fort Qu'Appelle, Prince Albert, Fort Battleford and Edmonton. Freight was also transported northward by cart and wagon to the Saskatoon, Duck Lake, and Prince Albert areas. The community's prominence as a disembarkation and distribution centre led General Middleton in 1885 to establish an initial staging point at Qu'Appelle, before heading north for his rendezvous with history. The years of the 1880s were boom times for the community, and a number of structures dating to the era still stand in the town. Knox Presbyterian Church (United in 1925) was built in 1884, and in 1885 St. Peter's Anglican Church was constructed, becoming the pro-Cathedral church of the Diocese of Qu'Appelle for sixty years. The stone rectory next door, built in 1894, is now a private residence. Sadly, one of the town's landmarks, and one of Saskatchewan's oldest buildings, the Queen's Hotel, which officially opened in 1884, was lost in a suspicious early morning blaze on April 16, 2003. The completion of the Qu'Appelle, Long Lake, and Saskatchewan Railway in 1890, linking Regina, Saskatoon, and Prince Albert dealt a great blow to Qu'Appelle's economic fortunes, as Regina, and not Qu'Appelle,

▲ **THE QUEEN'S HOTEL** in Qu'Appelle, date unknown. Saskatchewan Archives Board R-A4117.

now delivered settlers and supplies to the northern territories. Yet businessmen continued to attempt to establish industries in the community — among them a flour mill, a creamery, and a felt and boot factory — and with the great influx of settlers into the District of Assiniboia in the early 1900s the community continued to grow. On February 20, 1904, the Town of Qu'Appelle was incorporated. The population of the community was 434 in 1901, but by the end of the first decade of the

twentieth century, it was reaching toward 1,000. Substantial department stores, hotels, and bank buildings lined the streets of the commercial district. Then, another blow. The Grand Trunk Pacific line was completed from Melville to Regina in 1911, and with the development of settlements along that line, and the erection of competing grain elevators in those communities, trade was again diverted from Qu'Appelle. Diminished somewhat in stature, the town nonetheless continued in its role as a service and supply centre for the surrounding agricultural district for many decades. The community was actively engaged in sports of all types, and plays, musical performances, and magic shows were enjoyed in the town hall/opera house. By the 1960s, though, Qu'Appelle was entering a period of general decline. The newly-constructed Trans-Canada Highway was completed in the

◄ **A DISPLAY OF CATTLE** at the Qu'Appelle Fair, 1898. Saskatchewan Archives Board R-A9937.

late 1950s, and with increasing mobility, people's shopping habits were changing — they were heading to the city. Long-time businesspeople were also retiring, and fewer and fewer people were stepping in to fill the voids. Many businesses closed for good. In 1966-67, Highway 10, the direct link from Balgonie to Fort Qu'Appelle was built, greatly reducing the traffic on Hwy 35 though Qu'Appelle to the valley. The hospital was closed and the CPR station was torn down by the end of the decade. By 1971, the town's population had fallen to 451, the lowest since the beginning of the century. However, over the course of the 1970s, the community's fortunes would begin to turn around as city dwellers — usually young couples with families seeking affordable housing and lower taxes — and retired farmers moved into the town. Although the number of businesses remained at a fraction of earlier times, the population was again on the rise. Jobs in Regina became the major source of employment and commuting became a part of townspeople's routines. Today, about 80 to 90 per cent of the town's workforce drive to and from the city each day. At present, only a small core of businesses remains in the community. There is a general store, a credit union, an insurance broker, a service station, a café, and a bar; as well, there are a few tradespeople who operate out of their homes. Additionally, there are three unique businesses in the town. A print shop has operated for many years, and a tattoo parlour, which also accommodates those interested in body piercing, is thriving. Microbiologist Sheila Blachford and chemist John Blachford have operated an analytical laboratory in Qu'Appelle for close to 15 years. The company is accredited in both Canada and the United States, and its services include microbial, toxin, biochemical, and chemical testing. Qu'Appelle also retains a K-9 school (131 students enrolled in the fall of 2006); students attend grades 10-12 in Indian Head. In addition to the aforementioned 1880s churches and the 1894 rectory, heritage properties in Qu'Appelle include the 1906 town hall/opera house and the former Royal Bank building (originally the Northern Bank) built the same year. Qu'Appelle serves as the administrative centre of the RM of South Qu'Appelle No. 157.

QUILL LAKE, village, pop 413 (2006c), 439 (2001c), is situated on Hwy 5, 20 km southeast of Watson and 34 km northwest of Wadena. The village lies just north of two of southern Saskatchewan's most prominent bodies of water, Big Quill and Little Quill Lakes — hence, the community's name. The lakes themselves were named for the abundance of goose and crane quills once gathered in the area nesting grounds and shipped in considerable consignments to Europe for use as pens. The origins of the village date to 1904 as the Canadian Northern Railway was progressing with the construction of the railway through the region. That year, R. A. 'Uncle Dick' Gordon, who homesteaded near the present community the year before, established a post office and requested that it be named Quill Lake. Also in 1904, the first school, a small log structure, was built. For a couple of years prior to the establishment of the post office, mail for the scattered settlers was dispatched from Yorkton to the Fishing Lake Post Office, which was operated by the Milligan family, who pioneered the area in 1882. The mail was then forwarded via surveyors, railway builders, or other settlers — anyone the Milligans believed reliable enough to carry the mail. After the rails were laid north of the Quill Lakes, the railway company apparently tried to name the present townsite Lally, after a railway official, but a successful request was sent to the government to name the fledgling community Quill Lake, the same as the new post office. In 1905, a number of businesses began to appear at the townsite and families started moving into the community. On December 8, 1906, the Village of Quill Lake was incorporated. By 1911, the population had grown to 163; by 1941, it was 350; and through the 1960s, when the population peaked, the community was nudging toward numbering 600. In the mid-1950s, there were no fewer than 50 places of business in Quill Lake, and five grain elevators lined the railway tracks. At this time the surrounding countryside was densely populated, and Quill Lake served a trading area of roughly 5,000 persons. Today, the population of the surrounding RM and the three nearest adjacent RMs combined is less than half that number. On May 18, 1963, the last passenger train stopped in Quill Lake, and in 1980 the landmark station was demolished. While the community's importance as a commercial centre has diminished over the years, it retains a range of retail and service businesses to serve its residents and the surrounding farming district. Additionally, the village has a health clinic; the Quill Lake Volunteer Fire Department and the Quill Lake First Responders provide fire protection and emergency medical services. The community's school is a K-12 facility, which had 163 village and district students enrolled in the fall of 2006. Recreational facilities in Quill Lake include sportsgrounds, curling and hockey rinks, a campground, a playground, a seniors' centre, and a nine-hole golf course. There is a seniors' housing complex, a library, and a park, and Quill Lake has a number of service clubs, youth groups, and other community-based organizations. There are four churches in the village, and St. Michael's Anglican Church, a community landmark built between 1907 and 1913 and one of the oldest existing buildings in Quill Lake, was designated a municipal heritage property in 2000. Agriculture is the main industry in the area and is largely based in grain farming; however,

▼ **QUILL LAKE CALLS ITSELF THE "GOOSE CAPITAL OF THE WORLD,"** and a giant goose statue is found at the end of Main Street along Highway 5. An annual "Goose Fest" in November features banquets and craft shows. Photograph taken August 5, 2004.

a number of farms raise livestock, such as cattle, bison, fallow deer, elk, and chinchillas. Another area industry of increasing importance is tourism, as ecotourism, particularly bird watching, becomes more and more popular. The shallow, saline Quill Lakes and the surrounding wetlands have been recognized as a region of international importance, since they are a stopover and breeding ground for tens of thousands of migrating birds, particularly shorebirds and waterfowl. Over 200 varieties of birds frequent the area, and Big Quill Lake has the province's largest breeding population of piping plovers. In addition to birdwatchers, the area has also drawn hunters for many years during the duck and goose hunting season. Quill Lake serves as the administrative centre of the RM of Lakeside No. 338.

QUINTON, village, pop 108 (2006c), 107 (2001c), is located between the town of Raymore and the village of Punnichy on Hwy 15. The Kawacatoose First Nation reserve lies 10 km to the north; the Gordon Band's holdings are to the southeast. Homesteads began to be taken up in the area in 1904 and the majority of the first settlers were German Catholics from the Banat region of Hungary. These first settlers came west on the CPR line as far as South Qu'Appelle (today, the town of Qu'Appelle), the nearest railway point, then made the remainder of the trip to their new home by oxen and wagon, or horse and wagon, or on foot. In 1906, a post office was established approximately six miles south of present-day Quinton and was named Wolfsheim (German for "Wolf's home") after Johann Wolff, an immigration officer who was instrumental in settling the early homesteaders in the district and who took up

land in the area himself. The Wolfsheim Post Office was serviced from the Kutawa Post Office, which had been established in 1887 along the Dominion telegraph line somewhat northeast of present-day Punnichy. As the Grand Trunk Pacific Railway completed its line through the district in 1908, the Quinton townsite was established; its name, honouring a railway company engineer, was chosen simply to fit the alphabetical sequence of naming communities along the rail line: Punnichy, Quinton, Raymore, Semans, etc. Businesses were started, and in 1909 a frame church and school were built. The Quinton Post Office was established on May 22 that year. The village was incorporated on March 1, 1910, and about that time the first railway station was built. This was destroyed in a fire in 1917, rebuilt the same year, and demolished in 1976. Quinton grew from 76 residents in 1911 to reach a peak population of 227 in 1966. The community's numbers declined somewhat over the next two decades — down to 168 by 1986 — but began to drop more sharply in the 1990s. The school closed in

the first half of the decade. A small core of businesses serve the community and surrounding area. Quinton is situated in the RM of Mount Hope No. 279.

RABBIT LAKE, village, pop 113 (2006c), 87 (2001c), is located in the Thickwood Hills 67 km northeast of North Battleford off Hwy 378. Settlers began arriving in the area in 1905-06 after the Canadian Northern Railway reached North Battleford. They came from eastern Canada, the United States, and Europe, and for two decades belongings and supplies were hauled north by horse and oxen the distance from the Canadian Northern line. In the mid-1920s, the railway came through the Rabbit Lake district and the

townsite quickly developed. In 1928, the Village of Rabbit Lake was incorporated, and around this time large numbers of Mennonites were settling in the district. Rabbit Lake grew to a peak population of 218 in 1966, and at one time had more than three dozen businesses serving the community and the surrounding area. In recent decades the number of businesses and services in the community has declined. In 1999, the K-12 school was downsized to a K-9 facility, which has been subsequently closed. For close to two decades, Rabbit Lake and the district community have hosted the Carlton Trail Jamboree, a large outdoor country music festival which takes place each July. Rabbit Lake serves as the administrative centre

▼ **THE RABBIT LAKE STORE AND TEA ROOM** is an important local business in the village. In the background of the photo are Rabbit Lake's two grain elevators. The red elevator is owned by Pioneer Grain, and grain is transported from the location by truck. The white elevator was formerly operated by the Saskatchewan Wheat Pool; it is now privately owned. Photograph taken August 25, 2004.

▲ THE FORMER RAILWAY STATION in Rabbit Lake now houses a museum and has been declared a heritage property. Photograph taken August 25, 2004.

of the RM of Round Hill No. 467; agriculture is the main industry in the area.

RADISSON, town, pop 421 (2006c), 401 (2001c), is located roughly halfway between Saskatoon and North Battleford at the junction of Hwys 16 and 340. The North Saskatchewan River lies 12 km to the south. Settlement in the area began in the early 1900s, and the first few businesses were built on the present townsite in 1904 in anticipation of the coming railway. The Canadian Northern Railway came through in 1905, and the local history states that that year some 65 buildings were erected, among them the railway station, a hotel, and the first grain elevator. The Radisson school district was formed in 1905, with classes held in temporary quarters until a school building was completed the following year. Radis-son was incorporated as a village in 1906 and attained town status in 1913. The community was named after Pierre-Esprit Radisson, the opportunistic and colourful explorer and fur trader, whose exploits led to the founding of the Hudson's Bay Company. The Radisson district economy is based on the cattle industry and diversified grain farming. The community has a core of businesses providing essential goods and services, and Radisson has an RCMP detachment and a volunteer fire department. The town has a library and a number of churches. Community recreational facilities include skating and curling rinks and a ball park. Radisson is situated in the RM of Great Bend No. 405.

RADVILLE, town, pop 755 (2006c), 735 (2001c), is located approximately 50 km southwest of Weyburn, on Long Creek, at the junction of Hwys 28 and 377. The topography of the surrounding area is one of level to gently rolling farmlands; to the south and west, the hills rising to the Missouri Coteau provide grazing lands for ranchers. The region was settled in the early 1900s, largely by French, British, and Scandinavian pioneers arriving from eastern Canada, the United States, and Europe. There was a small quotient of Lebanese immigrants as well. In 1909, the Canadian Northern Railway began advancing south-westward from Maryfield, just inside the Manitoba border, and by 1910, rail had been laid to the location of Radville. The townsite was surveyed and construction began immediately. Radville, the railway company had decided, was to be an important centre. They were looking to construct a roundhouse and railway yards about midway between Winnipeg and Lethbridge, and Long Creek provided the reliable source of water that was needed. In 1911, Radville was incorporated as a village, construction of the roundhouse began, and a wide range of businesses were started. Radville could soon boast three lumberyards, a livery, a photographer, a dental office, a surgeon, a jeweller, a bakery, a real estate office, and many other professions and services. In 1912, the village suffered a temporary setback when a serious outbreak of typhoid struck the community. There were about 80 cases, and seven people died. Radville, however, continued to prosper and grow at a rapid rate. It was incorporated as a town in 1913, and by the 1920s the population was over 1,000. Although the town's importance as a railway hub diminished substantially when the roundhouse was shut down in the 1950s, today, Radville remains an important commercial and cultural centre in the district. The town's population, however, has declined over the past 25 years — it was 1,012 in 1981. The town retains over 100 businesses, a number of which cater to the district's ag-

▼ FOR 100 YEARS the community of Radisson had its own school. The most recent building, pictured here (photo left), was a modern K-12 facility of which the town was justifiably proud. Seventy-two students were enrolled in the fall of 2003; however, after a controversial decision made by the Saskatoon (West) School Division, the school was closed after the end of the school year in June 2004. Two months later, on August 27, community members lined the streets (photo right) as their students left on buses to travel the 25 km to the village of Maymont.

Radville Landmarks...

▶ **THE EMPIRE HOTEL**, pictured behind the three-wheeled Bull Gas Tractor loaded with settlers' effects, was built in the fall of 1911, with the third floor being added in the spring of the following year. As of 2008, the hotel was still in business, housing the Long Creek Saloon. Saskatchewan Archives Board R-B13143.

▶ **THE RADVILLE SENIOR CITIZENS CLUB** is housed in what was originally a two-storey, 1912 building long associated with the town's social and cultural life. For many years townspeople enjoyed movies and live performances in the main-floor theatre (known as the Province Theatre until 1925 when the name was changed to the Princess Theatre), and on the second floor the Odd Fellows had their lodge. In 1943 a fire, which started in the projection room, caused extensive damage to the building, resulting in the subsequent removal of the second floor. The main-floor theatre survived the blaze and remained in use until 1961, after which the building remained vacant for a number of years. Purchased by the Radville Senior Citizens Club in 1974, it was renovated and converted for use as a meeting place and for other club-related activities and events. The structure is one of Radville's oldest surviving buildings.

▶ **BUILT IN 1911**, the Canadian Imperial Bank of Commerce stands at the southeast corner of Main Street and Healy Avenue in Radville. It is a prefabricated structure, manufactured by British Columbia Mills, Timber and Trading Company. Originally, it was a Canadian Bank of Commerce — the bank attained its current name through a merger with the Imperial Bank of Canada in 1961. The bank is one of the longest-serving businesses in the community.

Colour photographs taken August 31, 2004.

riculture and oil and gas industries, and a key business in Radville is Berkshire Management (TWC Financial Corporation before a recent business merger), which employs approximately 70 people in the community. Established in Radville in 1986, the mutual fund company grew into a national firm controlling close to $4 billion worth of assets. Radville also has an integrated health centre and special care home (another large employer), an RCMP detachment, and schools which provide K-12 education to close to 220 Radville and area students. The town also hosts several popular annual events, including the Long Creek Rodeo and the Kinsmen Mud Fling and Demolition Derby. Many of these activities take place at Radville-Laurier Regional Park. The park provides a full range of recreational facilities, including a golf course and campgrounds often used as a base for hunters who take advantage of the good pheasant, deer, and duck hunting in the area. Radville is a picturesque town: poplar and ash trees planted in the early 1930s line the streets, and three of Radville's earliest buildings have been designated heritage properties, including the Canadian Northern Railway Station, built in 1912. Radville serves as the administrative centre of the RM of Laurier No. 38.

RAMA, village, pop 75 (2006c), 90 (2001c), is located 43 km northwest of Canora on Hwy 5. Poles and Ukrainians from Galicia had settled in the district in 1901, and in 1905, after two years of construction, the Canadian Northern Railway line between Kamsack and Humboldt was opened to traffic. For the first couple of years, however, trains only stopped at Rama if they were flagged down. The first person credited with settling at the Rama

AN IMPRESSIVE GROTTO at Rama, a replica of the Our Lady of Lourdes Shrine in France, is the site of an annual pilgrimage that takes place on August 14 and 15. In years past, the event had attracted as many as 2,000 people. Polish settlers were largely responsible for the establishment of St. Anthony's parish in Rama in 1922, and they, under Father Anthony Sylla, began construction of the shrine in 1939. Only a small detail is pictured here. Photograph taken July 26, 2004.

▲ ▼ THE FIRST TWO BUILDINGS (photo, above) appeared on the east side of Main Street in Raymore in 1908. By 1911, the hotel had been built and a number of other businesses were in operation (photo, below). Immediately to the right of the hotel was a land office; to the right of that was a meat market. The lobby of the Hotel Raymore (photo, bottom) is shown as it was in 1913.

Raymore photographs this page and facing page courtesy of the Raymore Pioneer Museum.

townsite was John A. Berge, who became the first postmaster when the post office opened on April 9, 1908. In December of that year, area residents voted in favour of establishing a local school district, and on January 4, 1910, with construction of the school completed, classes began with 21 students enrolled. Rama was incorporated on December 18, 1919, and in 1921 the village population was recorded at 127. Rama's population peaked at 288 in 1961, and, at this time, close to 200 village and area children were attending Rama School. In the late 1960s the community's population began to dramatically decline, as did the number of business establishments. By 1976 the number of village residents had fallen to 163. In 1975, fire destroyed both of the village's grain elevators, but the following year they were replaced by an elevator moved in from the hamlet of Tuffnell (to the southwest) and an annex relocated from the neighbouring village of Buchanan. Today, the remaining grain elevator in Rama is in private hands. In the mid-1990s the village population fell below 100, and Rama School was

closed, with schoolchildren subsequently being bused to Invermay. Amenities and services in Rama today include a curling rink, community halls, a gas station and convenience store, a seniors' centre, a hotel, and a Co-op which deals in lumber, hardware, and groceries. The nearest police service is the RCMP detachment located in Canora, where there is also a hospital. The neighbouring village of Invermay (pop 262 and 12 kilometres west) has a health centre, and Rama receives fire protection through an agreement with this community. Agriculture, a combination of grain and livestock production, is the major industry in the area; in recent years, large-scale factory hog barns were established in the district by Big Sky Farms, in the midst of some considerable debate over the pros and cons of such operations. A community landmark in Rama is St. Michael's Ukrainian Greek Orthodox Church, built in 1936. It was declared a municipal heritage property in 1994. Another landmark is the Our Lady of Lourdes Shrine and Grotto. Rama is situated in the RM of Invermay No. 305.

RAYMORE, town, pop 581 (2006c), 625 (2001c), is located approximately 100 km north of Regina on Hwys 6 and 15. Four First Nations reserve lands lie a short distance to the northeast and the southeast of the community. The area was largely settled by people of German and British origins, and the community had its beginnings with the construction of the Grand Trunk Pacific Railway through the area. In 1908, the first small wooden structures began to appear on the stretch of prairie that would become Main Street. Raymore grew rapidly and was incorporated as a village in 1909. A three-storey hotel had been built by 1911, and by 1912 the business district had substantially developed and the Bank of British North America had established a branch in the community. The population of the burgeoning agricultural service centre grew steadily over the decades, climbing from 280 in 1921 to 378 in 1951; in 1963 the community attained town status, with a population of over 500. Raymore's numbers peaked at just under 700 in 1986; only in recent years has the number of residents declined. Mixed farming remains the basis of the area economy, and a number of farm equipment dealers are among Raymore's core of businesses. The town has a health centre and a special care home, and a K-12 school which had 282 town and area students enrolled in the fall of 2006. A community attraction is the Raymore Pioneer Museum. Housing an impressive collection of the district's historical artifacts, the museum is located in two adjoining buildings: a former Lutheran Church, built in the neighbouring village of Quinton in 1921; and Raymore's former St. Martin's Anglican Church, built in 1910. The museum site has been des-

ignated a heritage property. Raymore was situated in the RM of Kutawa No. 278; however, due to a shrinking assessment and a declining population, the RM and the neighbouring RM of Mount Hope No. 279 entered into a restructuring agreement that saw both RMs dissolved. A study had revealed potential savings from the elimination of duplicated services, and Raymore entered into an enlarged and newly incorporated RM of Mount Hope No. 279 on January 1, 2004.

▲ **DARBY AND TROSKEY** were early land agents and auctioneers in Raymore — pictured above is Claude Darby and his wife. Claude Darby died in 1917 at the early age of 41.

▼ **EARLY RAYMORE FIRE-FIGHTERS:** (left to right) William Tate, unknown, Harold Martin, August Kauth, Bert Humphries, unknown, and Ernest Greenaway.

REDVERS, town, pop 878 (2006c), 917 (2001c), is located in the southeast corner of the province at the junction of Hwys 8 and 13. It is situated 19 km from the Saskatchewan-Manitoba border, and 67 km north of the international boundary. French and British homesteaders began settling in the district in the 1890s, and during the first decade of the twentieth century a significant number of Danish people came to the area. Some Danes came directly from Denmark, but the majority came from North Dakota and other mid-western states. Surveyors arrived in the district in 1897-98 in advance of the railway, and the CPR line being built westward from Manitoba toward Arcola reached Redvers in 1900. The community was named for Sir Redvers Buller, a general and the commander of the British forces during the Boer War. The Redvers Post Office was established in 1902, and in 1904 Redvers was incorporated as a village. By 1911, the population was 200, and it remained around that number until after WWII. Subsequently, Redvers experienced a period of exceptional growth: during the 1950s and 1960s, it was one of the fastest growing communities in the province. In 1946, the population was 230; by 1971, it was 846. The population has been fairly stable since the mid-1980s. Redvers had attained town status on July 6, 1960. Redvers is an important commercial centre serving a large surrounding area, with a full range of businesses, services, professional and trades people, and an array of modern facilities. The Redvers Health Centre is an integrated health care facility with over 90 employees, providing acute care, long-term care, home care, and ambulatory and laboratory services, among others. Another large community employer

331

REDVERS

...Gateway to Saskatchewan's Red Coat Trail
La porte d'entrée du Red Coat Trail

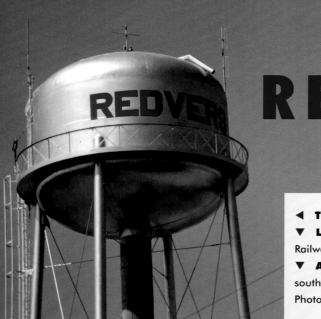

◄ **THE REDVERS WATER TOWER.**

▼ **LOOKING NORTH** up the east side of Broadway Street from Railway Avenue.

▼ **AGRICORE UNITED'S** large grain-handling facility on the southwest side of town.

Photographs taken August 21, 2003.

is Redvers School, which provides K-12 education to approximately 275 students. The Redvers Activities Centre provides life skills training to adults with developmental disabilities and/or chronic mental health problems. It also coordinates employment programs, enabling people to live independently in the community. Redvers also has exceptional facilities for sports and recreation. A recreation complex houses curling and skating rinks, as well as a swimming pool. Five baseball diamonds are located outside. The community also has tennis courts, a nine-hole golf course, and a fully-serviced campground. Additionally, Moose Mountain Provincial Park is located approximately 60 kilometres to the northwest. The Redvers Arts Centre provides a venue for dance performances and dramatic productions performed by both local and travelling companies. Redvers Library provides free internet services and has summer reading programs for various age levels. Redvers has a volunteer fire department; police service is provided by the Carlyle RCMP. A veterinary clinic is set up for both large and small animals. The town also has its own newspaper, *The Redvers New Opti-*

mist, which is published weekly. The Redvers and area economy is predominantly based upon agriculture: crops grown in the area include wheat, barley, flax, oats, and canola; livestock raised include cattle (beef and dairy), sheep, and hogs, as well as the less traditional elk, bison, wild boar, and emu. The town has two large agricultural implement and tractor dealerships, a large Agricore United plant, and several other businesses and services which cater to the agricultural industry. Oilfield operations and associated services add some diversity to the economy, as Redvers is situated on the fringe of south-eastern Saskatchewan's oil industry. A number of related businesses are located within the town. Redvers serves as the administrative centre of the RM of Antler No. 61.

REGINA, city, pop 179,246 (2006c), 178,225 (2001c), is the capital of Saskatchewan. It is located in the south-central region of the province on the Trans-Canada Highway, 160 km north of the Saskatchewan-Montana border. The city sits in a wide, flat alluvial plain, historically of moist mixed grassland, but dominated today by crop production. Regina covers over 118.87 square kilometres (almost 46 square miles), and sits at 577.4 metres (approximately 1,900 feet) above sea level. More than 300,000 hand-planted trees, many elms, now cover the city. Originally known as "Pile O' Bones" due to bison bones in the area, Regina was

▲ **THE SASKATCHEWAN LEGISLATIVE BUILDING IN REGINA.**
Photograph taken July 2002.

▲ **DOWNTOWN REGINA** as seen from the top of the Saskatchewan Legislative Building looking north across Wascana Lake. Photograph taken late July 2002.

REGINA
...the Queen City

▶ **GOVERNMENT HOUSE.** Prefabricated wooden structures first served as Government House in Regina after the Territorial capital was relocated from Battleford in 1883. Between 1889 and 1891 the present Government House was built, its design the work of the Dominion Architect Thomas Fuller. A new wing on the building was officially opened by Queen Elizabeth II in May 2005. Photograph taken late March 2003.

◀ **AS THE PROVINCIAL CAPITAL**, Regina has seen many protests, demonstrations, and celebrations over the years. On Monday, September 15, 2003, ranchers from across Saskatchewan brought about 250 cattle to the front of the Legislative Building to protest against what they saw as an inadequate federal response to the crisis of bovine spongiform encephalopathy (BSE), commonly known as mad cow disease.

▶ **BUFFALO DAYS**, a provincial exhibition held in Regina each summer, had its origins in 1884 when a two-day fair was held on the site that is now Victoria Park, in the city's downtown. Photograph taken during the first week of August 2000.

founded and named in honour of Queen Victoria in 1882 — thereafter it has been known as the "Queen City." The city is a creation of the Canadian Pacific Railway, its location determined when the CPR decided to reroute the construction of the trans-continental rail line across Canada's southern plains. The railway reached the site in 1882, and that year the NWMP made the locale their new headquarters. What began as a cluster of tents and shacks in 1882 became the capital of the North-West Territories on March 27, 1883. Regina was proclaimed a town on December 1 that year. Growth was subsequently steady, yet not spectacular: by 1901, the population was 2,249. On June 19, 1903, Regina attained city status — the first community in Saskatchewan to achieve the ranking — and, after the creation of the Province of Saskatchewan in 1905, Regina was named the capital. The ensuing years were boom times: by 1911, the city numbered more than 30,000 residents. The killer F4 tornado that struck the city on June 30, 1912 — which remains the worst in Canadian history in terms of deaths — was regarded as a mere setback, but the economic depression of 1913 and then WWI brought development to a near standstill. The population also declined for the first time since Regina's inception: it was down to just over 26,000 by 1916. It took some years after the War for the city to gain momentum again, but in the mid-1920s Regina was booming once more — its population soared to close to 50,000 before the onset of the Depression and the drought that would ravage the prairie. Relief projects were initiated in the city to provide employment: Wascana Lake was drained and deepened, and the Albert Memorial Bridge was built across Wascana Creek. In the middle of June 1935, a freight train originating in Vancouver arrived in Regina full of single, homeless, and unemployed men determined to reach Ottawa to put their situation to the Prime Minister. The Canadian Government had ordered the train stopped in Regina by RCMP, and, after a two-week stalemate, a public rally disintegrated into a pitched melee when police tried to arrest the trekkers' leaders. Two were killed, including a policeman, hundreds were injured, and downtown Regina sustained considerable damage. The event went down in history as the "Regina Riot." In 1939, the plight of Saskatchewan's farmers began to improve, and Regina's fortune's were renewed as well. Following WWII, the city once again experienced steady growth: the population more than doubled between 1946 and 1966, rising from 60,246 to 131,127 over the period. An economy dominated by agriculture became increasingly diversified, providing increased economic stability. People moving from farms to the city and a migration of Aboriginal peoples from reserves bolstered Regina's numbers. The momentum had waned by the early 1990s, and the city's population in 2006 was somewhat lower than it had been in 1996. Regina is the most important retail, distribution, and service centre in the southern part of the province, and its economy is largely driven by agriculture, oil and gas, employment with the provincial government, telecommunications, insurance, financial and data management services, telephone call centres, and the making and fabricating of steel. The production of film, video, and television shows has been increasing. The city's post-secondary institutions include the University of Regina, the Saskatchewan Institute of Applied Science and Technology, and the First Nations University of Canada. Public and Catholic school boards administer elementary and high schools; a third board, Division Scolaire Francophone, looks after the K-12 École Monseigneur de Laval. The major health care facilities are the Regina General Hospital, the Pasqua Hospital, and the Wascana Rehabilitation Centre. In addition to its situation on the Trans-Canada Highway, Regina is at the hub of a number of the province's other major roadways, and it is also served by the Canadian National and Canadian Pacific Railways. The Regina Airport is served by several airlines providing both regularly scheduled flights and charter services. Two bus lines serve the city; within Regina, a public transit system of approximately 100 diesel buses carries almost six million passengers annually. Water and sewer services in Regina are owned and managed by the city; SaskTel is the leading provider of telecommunications services; SaskPower and SaskEnergy provide electricity and natural gas respectively. The 930-hectare (2,300-acre) Wascana Centre is the city's most popular park: it is the site of the man-made Wascana Lake, the Saskatchewan Legislative Building, the Royal Saskatchewan Museum, the MacKenzie Art Gallery, the Saskatchewan Science Centre and Kramer IMAX Theatre, and the Conexus Arts Centre. Other Regina attractions include the RCMP Heritage Centre, Casino Regina, the Regina Plains Museum, and the Dunlop Art Gallery. New Dance Horizons is the city's leading contemporary dance company; the Regina Symphony Orchestra is Canada's oldest continuously performing orchestra; and the Globe Theatre has a nation-wide reputation for its professional theatre productions. The Canadian Football League's Saskatchewan Roughriders and the Western Hockey League's Regina Pats provide sports entertainment. The city's main annual events include the Canadian Western Agribition (an international agricultural exhibition), the Western Canada Farm Progress Show (North America's premier dryland farming technology show), Mosaic (a multicultural festival), Bazaart (Saskatchewan's largest outdoor arts and crafts sale), the Dragon Boat Festival on Wascana Lake, the Regina Folk Festival, the Cathedral Village Arts Festival, and Buffalo Days, a provincial exhibition held each summer. Regina is served by cable television providers, three English-language television stations, one French-language television station, numerous radio stations, a daily newspaper, the *Leader-Post*, a bi-weekly newspaper, the *Prairie Dog*, and a student newspaper produced at the University of Regina, *The Carillon*. Additionally, a weekly French-language newspaper that is circulated throughout the province, *l'Eau vive*, is published in the city. Regina's municipal government consists of a mayor and ten councillors: the mayor is elected at large by all voters; councillors are elected by ten specific city constituencies, or wards. Municipal elections take place every three years. In recent decades Regina has taken on some of the carbon-copy sameness of many North American cities, as American multinational and out-of-province retailers have built "big box" chain stores on the city's periphery, effectively branding the urban landscape at the expense of locally-owned businesses and the city core. Additionally, many of the city's long-standing buildings and public spaces have been branded with corporate names; for example, Regina Exhibition Park, established in 1895, is now known as IPSCO Place. In 1987, Regina was "twinned" with the City of Jinan, China, in order to foster exchanges and co-operation in matters of economy, trade, science and technology, education, culture, and city administration. Regina is surrounded by the RM of Sherwood No. 159.

REGINA BEACH, town, pop 1,195 (2006c), 1,039 (2001c), is a continually growing community located 58 km northwest of Regina on the west side of the south end of Last Mountain Lake. Homesteaders were making incursions into the region in the 1880s, and by the early 1900s the area that came to be known as Regina Beach was gaining popularity as a summer resort destination. With the CPR running through Regina Beach in 1912, the area was easily accessible to residents of Regina and, for many years, the railway ran excursion trains to the developing lakeshore resort. The Regina Beach Post Office was established in 1912. Along with swimming, picnicking, and fishing, sailing, too, was becoming very popular, and in 1913 the Regina Beach Yacht Club was established. In 1920, Regina Beach was incorporated as a village and recreational facilities and services included hotels, boathouses, dance pavilions, summer cottages, and boat excursions. Following WWII, the importance of the railway declined and the car became the primary mode of transportation to the lake. The last excursion train made its trip to Regina Beach in 1949 and regular passenger service ended in the 1960s. Accessibility by car precipitated further cottage development and boosted Regina Beach's position as a major day use area. For a number of decades, the population hovered around 300, but in the 1970s it began to increase, and in 1980 Regina Beach attained town status. Substantial construction occurred during the following decade and many new homes were built, as commuting to work in Regina became increasingly popular. The year-round population grew from 488 in 1966 to 921 in 1991 and, today, the population of the community more than doubles when seasonal residents arrive at their summer cottages. The annual Canada Day fireworks display over the lake is one of the town's premier events. Regina Beach is situated in the RM of Lumsden No. 189.

▲ **BUTLER'S BLUE BIRD CAFE**, popular for its fish and chips, has been a community fixture since 1928. Photograph taken in the beginning of July, 2003.

▼ **REGINA BEACH** attracts people throughout the year. Ice-fishing off the point at Regina Beach in the winter is very popular. Here, people enjoy hot air balloon rides during a winter festival in February 1999. The Regina Beach Yacht Club is visible in the background in the right of the photograph.

REWARD, hamlet, is located 30 km southwest of Unity on Municipal Road 675. It is situated in the heart of what was known as St. Joseph's Colony, an area of 77 townships settled largely, although not exclusively, by Black Sea German Catholics between 1905 and the beginning of the First World War. Some of the early settlers came to Canada after having first settled in the United States; afterwards, many came directly from southern Russia. Before the railway was built through the district, many of the settlers conducted business in Salvador, to the southwest, where the CPR had arrived in 1911. In 1929, Canadian National began work on a rail line that would run from Unity south-westward to Bodo, Alberta, and selected a location for a townsite. It was named Reward after a recently developed strain of rust-resistant wheat. In 1930, the rails were laid, the first store was started, and the first grain elevator was erected by the Saskatchewan Wheat Pool. William Payne started the Reward Post Office in 1931, and, that year, two more grain elevators and a dance hall were built. Additionally, the headquarters for the rural municipality was relocated to the hamlet from Salvador. In 1932, a large general store opened in Reward and a fourth grain elevator went up. Other businesses established in the early years were a poolroom and barber shop, harness and shoe repair shop, blacksmith shop, and a hardware store. In 1948, a school was built in Reward; previously, children had attended rural schools. Reward was established as an organized hamlet in 1952, a standing it retained until 1997. In the mid-1960s, the population of the community was approximately 100, but it was beginning to decline. The last store closed in 1969; the school closed in 1982. By the mid-1980s, fewer than two dozen people were left in the community. The rail line through the hamlet was abandoned in the mid-1990s; of the four grain elevators that once served the district, none remain. Holy Rosary Church and an associated shrine, two miles south of Reward, were designated heritage properties in 1998. The local parish was organized in 1911, and there is a cemetery at the site. The present church was built and decorated between 1918 and 1920; Count Berthold Von Imhoff painted the interior. There has been an annual pilgrimage to the locale since 1932. Reward serves as the administrative centre of the RM of Grass Lake No. 381.

RHEIN, village, pop 161 (2006c), 175 (2001c), is located approximately 34 km northeast of Yorkton on Hwy 309. The community is named after the River Rhine in Europe, "Rhein" being the German spelling of the name. In 1887, German Protestants from settlements along the Volga River in Russia began arriving in the area of present-day Ebenezer, to the west; by the early 1900s, their numbers had expanded to include the district of present-day Rhein. The first religious services were held in a schoolhouse just to the east of the present village in 1902. The growth of the huge Ukrainian settlement around Yorkton steadily encompassed the Rhein district; however, in 1971 close to

▼ **CHRIST LUTHERAN CHURCH**, built in 1920, sits in a picturesque location at the north end of Main Street in Rhein. Photograph taken July 13, 2004.

half of the village's residents still claimed German origins. The post office was established in 1905, and the railway came through in 1911. Rhein was incorporated as a village on March 10, 1913, and the community grew very rapidly: the population was over 400 by the 1920s, and it was close to 500 in the early 1940s. The village became a service centre in a district where agriculture, a combination of grain and livestock production, is the major industry. As the latter half of the twentieth century progressed, the community's businesses and institutions, such as the school, were gradually superseded by those in Yorkton. The village population declined significantly in the 1960s, somewhat in the 1970s, and has fallen steadily thereafter. A Pioneer elevator and farm service centre, hotel, credit union, bulk fuel dealership, post office and insurance agency are among the few businesses remaining in Rhein. The community has a seniors' centre and seniors' housing. The landmark Christ Lutheran Church remains active. Rhein is situated in the RM of Wallace No. 243.

▲ **SHULTZ BROS. HARDWARE & IMPLEMENTS** in Riceton was built in 1912 by Fred and William Shultz who came to the new community from Kronau (Fred Shultz is standing in front of the store). The business was later sold to Paul Aarness and was run by John Peck. It was lost to a fire on October 26, 1931. Saskatchewan Archives Board R-A10200.

RICETON, organized hamlet, pop 65 (2006c), 75 (2001c), is located about 45 km southeast of Regina on Hwy 306. The name honours James Seneca Rice who, in 1902 along with his wife, homesteaded on the land upon which the community would come to be founded. Many of the first settlers to the area arrived on the Soo Line running up from North Portal, disembarking at either Lang or Milestone. For several years, the pioneers of the Riceton district had to travel to these communities for supplies, or north to the German community of Kronau, on the CPR's Regina-Stoughton line. In 1911-1912, the Grand Trunk Pacific Railway drove a rail line right through the middle of the two CPR tracks, and upon this stretch Riceton developed. In 1911, the first store and the post office were established, as was a livery stable. A hotel with a restaurant, pool hall, and a barber shop followed.

In 1912, an area school was moved in from the country to the townsite. It had been founded in 1906 and was known as Denver School; the name was changed to Riceton School in 1933. A hardware store and a bank opened in 1912, and the first of four grain elevators was erected. The second elevator was built by George William Brown, Saskatchewan's Lieutenant Governor from 1910 to 1915, who had amassed considerable land holdings in the district, most of it Métis scrip, from which he made a sizable fortune. The first scheduled passenger train went through Riceton in 1913. An interesting feature of the community in the early days was a nine-hole golf course that started at the railway station and went completely around the townsite. Numerous businesses developed in Riceton over the years, including lumberyards, a café, and farm implement dealerships, but a number of these enterprises would fall victim to the Depression. Later, the community's

businesses would suffer further due to Riceton's proximity to Regina; the centralization of grain handling facilities and the consolidation of schools would also have a negative impact on the hamlet. In the fall of 1959, students in grades 9 to 12 began to be bused to Milestone to attend school, and in the fall of 1980 grades 7 and 8 followed. The Saskatchewan Power Corporation brought electricity to Riceton in 1952; natural gas was installed in 1960. Riceton was established as an organized hamlet in 1974, and water works were installed in the community's homes in 1978. In the same decade, however, a number of Riceton landmarks were lost: the community centre and rink to a fire in 1974; the CNR station to another fire in 1976. By the early 1980s only two grain elevators were left in the community — none remain today. The school has now been closed for several years, and the rail line has been abandoned. Today, a portion of those residing in Riceton commute to work in Regina. Riceton retains a credit union, a Co-op bulk station, and a postal outlet at the Main Street Market. Riceton is situated in the RM of Lajord No. 128.

RICHARD, village, pop 25 (2006c), 20 (2001c), is located 41 km east of North Battleford on Hwy 376. The area was settled in the early 1900s, and the Richard Post Office, named after an early area pioneer, was established in 1904. The railway came through in 1913, and in 1916 the Village of Richard was incorporated. The community was never particularly large, having a peak population of 151 in 1936. Fewer than 30 people have lived in the village since the mid-1970s. The basis of the district economy is agriculture; Richard is situated in the RM of Douglas No. 436.

RICHMOUND, village, pop 159 (2006c), 193 (2001c), is located west of the Great Sand Hills, 21 km east of the Saskatchewan-Alberta border on Hwy 371. The district began to be settled around 1910, and by about 1914 most of the available land in the area was occupied. Settlers came from eastern Canada, the United States, and Europe — a substantial number were German Catholics. Schools and churches were quickly established in the region; Richmound was originally the name of a post office established in 1912. The arrival of the CPR in the mid-1920s led to the development of the village and made life much easier for residents of the district. Scattered businesses were brought in from the countryside, new enterprises were begun, and soon four grain elevators were constructed. Before this, grain had to be hauled to, and supplies obtained from, Hatton or Maple Creek, the nearest railway points, about a three-day round trip. During the 1930s many people gave up on the Richmound area and abandoned

their farms; lineups for relief were a common sight on Richmound's streets during the decade. The 1940s were a period of recovery, and on May 5, 1947, the Village of Richmound was incorporated. In the 1950s, the Saskatchewan Power Corporation took over the supply and distribution of power in the village and began bringing service to area farms. Water and sewer systems were installed in the village in the 1960s. Natural gas was piped into Richmound from an area well in 1969, and, today, the region is increasingly becoming dotted with gas wells and compressor stations, to the point that the natural gas industry now dominates the local economy. Businesses related to oilfield operations are located in the village, providing local employment. The energy resource industry has also helped subsidize farming operations, as surface leases and pipeline right-of-ways generate significant income for landowners. Richmound area agricultural operations produce grains, oilseeds, pulse crops, and livestock. The community's five grain elevators, however, have all disappeared since 1989. Product is now hauled out of the district by truck to the giant concrete terminals at locations such as Leader or Dunmore, Alberta. Richmound has a small core of essential businesses, recreational facilities, a church, and a community centre. Businesses related to oilfield activities give the community somewhat of an industrial appearance. A K-12 school, which had 53 students enrolled in the fall of 2006, is scheduled to close in 2008. Richmound serves as the administrative centre of the RM of Enterprise No. 142.

RIDGEDALE, village, pop 66 (2006c), 85 (2001c), is located about 23 km north and 8 km west of Tisdale off Hwy 35. The Carrot River passes just to the north of the community. The townsite was surveyed by the CNR in 1919, and in 1920 the first building was erected. In 1921, the railway was laid into Ridgedale from Melfort, and on December 15 that year the Village of Ridgedale was incorporated. The name of the community was taken from an area post office which had opened in 1907. The arrival of the first passenger train was celebrated as a gala event, and Ridgedale was the end of the line until the railway was extended to Carrot River in 1931. Ridgedale grew rapidly during the first few years; however, the community suffered a significant loss on September 18, 1923, when seven buildings along Main Street were lost to a fire. In 1924, the community took another blow when the CPR inaugurated train service on the Sheho-Nipawin line and many residents left for Nipawin or other locations. The district continued to be settled, however, and by 1951, when the village had a population of 251, its trading area population numbered approximately 1,500. By 1953, four grain elevators and approximately twenty other businesses were operating in the community. However, by the end of the decade, it was evident the village population was declining; as the community's numbers dwindled, so, too, did its business community. The closure of rural schools in the area kept Ridgedale School active and growing for many years, but by the end of the school year in June 1998, with an enrollment down to 12 students, the school was closed. The sole remaining grain elevator closed shortly thereafter and the business community was reduced to a store, a hotel/bar, and the post office. Today, the village retains a curling rink, a community centre, and an active senior citizens organization. The landmark Ridgedale United Church, built in 1928, has been designated a heritage property, and is one of the oldest remaining buildings in the community. The farms in the surrounding area produce cereals, oilseeds, specialty crops, and alfalfa, and an alfalfa dehydrating plant located near Ridgedale employs several local people. Ridgedale is situated in the RM of Connaught No. 457.

RIVERHURST, village, pop 121 (2006c), 143 (2001c), lies approximately 30 km northwest of Central Butte on Hwy 42, just east of Lake Diefenbaker (the South Saskatchewan River) and the Riverhurst Ferry crossing. Homesteaders began arriving around 1905, and by the outbreak of WWI the district was well settled. The majority of those who came to the area in the early years were from Ontario, but there were also immigrants from England and Scotland. In later years, the population would become more diverse. Mennonites from the Soviet Union took up land in the region in the late 1920s, and established a Mennonite Brethren church in the nearby hamlet of Gilroy. By the time the Grand Trunk Pacific Railway began construction of its line north-westward into the district from Moose Jaw around 1913, country schools, small stores, and post offices dotted the region. Farmers still had to haul grain considerable distances, however, and obtaining lumber and other bulk supplies required long trips to rail lines as well. The townsite of Riverhurst was surveyed in 1914, and those in the area who had set up businesses in anticipation of the coming railway moved onto the village lots. Pioneering Chinese were among the first to establish businesses in Riverhurst when the village had its beginnings. So, too, was William Rode, born in Poland, who with his family came to the fledgling community in 1916 from Manitoba to open a shoe and harness repair shop. The Riverhurst Post Office was established December 1, 1914, its name an amalgam of the names of two earlier area post offices: **River**side (est. 1907) and Bolden**hurst** (est. 1909). By the outbreak of the First World War in 1914, however, construction of the rail line had stalled east of Riverhurst, at Gilroy. Construction continued at the townsite, but amidst concerns that the track might not be completed. It was two years later, in 1916, that the line finally reached into the young community. The village was incorporated on June 22, 1916, and the first of five elevators was erected that year. A school district centred in Riverhurst was also established in 1916, and in 1917 a two-room school was built. That year, the construction of Catholic and Protestant Churches was under way, a curling rink was erected, and the railway built a roundhouse where steam locomotives were to be serviced (this was dismantled in 1938). The Spanish Influenza epidemic of 1918-19 necessitated closing the school and converting it temporarily into a makeshift hospital, and several people in the village and surrounding district died, including the manager of the Canadian Bank of Commerce. In one issue of the local newspaper in December 1918, there were five obituary notices. Otherwise, however, these were boom times for the community: settlers from across the river came to shop in the village, and enormous shipments of wheat passed through the elevators during the first few years, as farmers from the Lucky Lake and Demaine districts hauled their crops to Riverhurst until the railway was built through their area in the early 1920s. The first several years were Riverhurst's heyday; the village gradually declined thereafter. The community's

▲ **THE RIVERHURST FERRY** on Lake Diefenbaker (shown here preparing to load vehicle traffic on the east side of the lake) is Saskatchewan's largest ferry. It is 35.6 metres (117 ft.) long, 14 metres (46 ft.) wide, and weighs 90.7 tonnes (100 tons). During winter months an ice road across the lake is laid out and maintained by the Saskatchewan Department of Highways and Transportation. Photograph taken September 8, 2003.

population was recorded at 330 in 1921, an all-time high. The number hovered very close to 300 through the decade, but during the Depression and the drought many businessmen and area farmers left in search of greener pastures. The exodus continued through the war years, and by 1951 Riverhurst's population was down to 218. The community rebounded for about a ten-year period from the mid-1950s through to the mid-1960s (there was much activity in the general region as a result of the South Saskatchewan River Project), and during the period Riverhurst somewhat recovered its population. Since that time, though, the village has steadily, and more rapidly, declined. In the late 1950s and early 1960s farm equipment agencies began to be discontinued, and increasingly the number of businesses began to dwindle. On September 13, 1962,

the last edition of the village newspaper, *The Weekly Courier,* rolled off the press in Riverhurst. It had been published continuously since November 3, 1914. The editor and proprietor, Fred T. Hill, had begun collecting area fossils, First Nations artifacts, rocks, guns and other weapons as a hobby early in his career, and these formed the nucleus of what became a substantial collection he amassed over the years. For many decades now, the Fred T. Hill Museum, which had its beginnings in the newspaper office, has been one of the community's main attractions. While Riverhurst has declined over the past four decades (its population fell from 301 in 1966 to 182 by 1976), there were also positive developments and good times. In the mid-1950s, the Riverhurst Memorial Rink, with curling and skating surfaces, was completed; new homes were built in

the early 1960s as area farmers moved into the village; water and sewer systems were installed in 1964; and the community's hockey teams were highly competitive: the Minor League and Seniors League teams were league champions in the early 1960s, and the Bantam team won the provincial championship for the 1964-65 season. With the creation of Lake Diefenbaker, nearby Palliser Regional Park became a major area attraction, and today it boasts hotel and convention accommodations, a golf course, a marina, camping facilities, and houseboat rentals, among other amenities. As of 2006, the village of Riverhurst retains a general store/service station with postal services, where one can purchase fuel, groceries, hardware, and liquor, and the Riverside Inn, which has accommodations and dining and beverage rooms. The village has a community

centre and a library branch. The school was closed in 1991, and students have subsequently attended Central Butte; the rail line into Riverhurst was abandoned in 1996. Since 1983, Riverhurst has served as the administrative centre of the RM of Maple Bush No. 224; previously, the office was situated in the village (now hamlet) of Lawson.

RIVERSEDGE, organized hamlet, pop 64 (2006c), is a bedroom community situated north of the city of Saskatoon, east of the South Saskatchewan River roughly opposite Wanuskewin Heritage Park. Established as an organized hamlet in 2004, Riversedge is located within the R.M. of Corman Park No. 344.

RIVERSIDE ESTATES, organized hamlet, pop 248 (2006c), is largely an upscale bedroom community in a country-residential setting south of the city of Saskatoon, on the east side of the South Saskatchewan River. The community was established as an organized hamlet in 1982, was disorganized in 1999, and then re-established in 2004. Riverside Estates is situated in the RM of Corman Park No. 344 and is located next to the exclusive Riverside Country Club, long considered one of Canada's most scenic and challenging courses.

ROBSART, hamlet, pop 15 (2001c), relinquished village status on January 1, 2002. Once a bustling frontier community, Robsart is located in the extreme southwest corner of the province, south of the Cypress Hills at the junction of Hwys 13 and 18. The Village of Robsart had been incorporated on November 2, 1914, as the

◀ **NAMED FOR AMY ROBSART**, the heroine of Sir Walter Scott's novel, *Kenilworth*, Robsart, Saskatchewan is on the verge of becoming a ghost town. Abandoned homes line the streets (top), businesses have long been closed and boarded up (centre), and the former hospital (bottom), has been closed for decades.

businesses were also lost to a fire. They were never rebuilt. As the drought and the Depression deepened, many farm families left the area. A period of recovery and a degree of relative prosperity followed WWII, but between 1961 and 1971 the village lost over half of its population. The last passenger train left Robsart in 1957. The community itself had always numbered around 100 residents; however, as the rural population declined, so, too, did the need for Robsart's services — hence, Robsart itself began to disappear. Except for a few homes, the small hamlet now resembles a ghost town. Robsart is located in the RM of Reno No. 51.

ROCANVILLE, town, pop 869 (2006c), 887 (2001c), is located 25 km north of Moosomin and 15 km south of the Qu'Appelle Valley on Hwy 8. The Saskatchewan-Manitoba border is 21 km via road to the east. Above the Qu'Appelle River northeast of the town lies the Fort Esperance National Historic Site, the location of two North West Company fur trading posts dating to the late eighteenth century. The name Rocanville dates to 1884, when a post office was established a few kilometres from the present townsite — it was named after the first postmaster, A. H. Rocan Bastien. In 1885, a school adopt-

ing the name Rocanville was established in the district. The name would be applied to the present townsite as it developed with the coming of the railway through the area. The townsite and the CPR station grounds were surveyed in 1902, and that year the Schwanz brothers' store became the first building in Rocanville. Records state that a necktie, purchased by one David Moran on August 20, 1902, was the first item bought at the store. With the advent of the railway, more businesses were set up, and on March 1, 1904, a one-room school opened in Rocanville. On March 24, 1904, the young community was incorporated as a village. The CPR station was built the same year. The community developed as a service and supply centre for the surrounding farming district, with grain and cattle production being the primary activities. In recent years, the area's agricultural industry has grown to include dairy, elk, and fallow deer producers, as well as several beekeepers. In 1924 a local entrepreneur, Ernie Symons, began mass production in Rocanville of an oil can he

▼ **THE WORLD'S LARGEST OIL CAN**, Rocanville. Photograph taken October 17, 2003.

CPR came through the area. Settlers had begun to settle the region around 1909-10, and a large number that came to the Robsart area were Norwegians immigrating to Canada after spending time in the United States. They engaged in dryland wheat farming and cattle ranching, and Robsart developed to support the emerg-

ing agricultural industry. Within its first few years, the community boasted over 30 places of business. In the years following WWI, the further construction of railways in the region generated substantial activity. In 1929, one of Robsart's grain elevators burnt down, and on Thanksgiving Day, 1930, a number of homes and

▲ **ALEX CAMERON'S STORE** in Rocanville, 1905.

▲ **ROCANVILLE HOCKEY CLUB, 1930-31.** Back row, left to right: R. Johnson, trainer; G. Wyatt, president; C. Chilton, exec.; E. Davis, manager; S. Cheesman, exec. Middle row: L. Goodman, right wing; K. McLeod, right defence; J. Beard, goal; M. Lockhart, left defence; D. Moffat, sub. Front row: G. McLeod, centre; C. Goodman, sub.; C. Hudon, left wing; J. Gray, sub.

designed for use on farm and industrial machinery. Symons Oilers proved to be the best of their kind, and a small shop turned into a factory. During WWII, the oil cans were greatly in demand for the maintenance of aircraft, tanks, and other military equipment; by the end of the war, over one million had been produced at

◄ **CUTTING SHEAVES** at the Logan farm near Rocanville for the Museum Threshing Day, which is held the second Saturday in September each year. Photograph circa 2000.

◄ **AN OLD-STYLE THRESHING DEMONSTRATION** at the Rocanville and District Museum, circa 1993.

Photographs on this page courtesy of the Rocanville and District Museum.

the Rocanville plant. On July 1, 1973, the community honoured Ernie Symons for 50 continuous years in business: the day was proclaimed Symons Day, and a giant scale-model oiler was erected on a base at the east entrance to the town. After Symons' death, the factory was purchased by another company which changed the oil can's design; it proved unsuccessful and the plant folded in the late 1980s. Recently, local residents have undertaken the restoration of the oil can factory, which was declared a heritage property in 1996. In the late 1960s, a potash mine was developed 16 kilometres northeast of Rocanville; acquired by the Potash Corporation of Saskatchewan in 1977, it continues to employ approximately 330 people, drawing an annual payroll worth close to $23 million. With the mine's development, Rocanville's population rose from 496 in 1961 to 891 by 1971; the community attained town status in 1967. In November 2007, the Potash Corporation of Saskatchewan (Potash Corp) announced a major mine and mill expansion; it is expected that an additional 190 jobs will be generated by 2012. In recent years, the oil industry has become more active in the area. Today, Rocanville has approximately 70 local employers; businesses provide a range of goods and services. Rocanville School, a K-12 facility, had 324 students enrolled in the fall of 2006. Town recreational facilities include an indoor swimming pool, a nine-hole golf course, skating and curling rinks, a seniors' centre, and cross-country ski trails. As well, the community is connected to hundreds of kilometres of groomed snowmobile trails. Rocanville has a small medical centre with doctors visiting three times weekly from Moosomin, where major medical facilities and a wide range of medical practitioners are located. The Moosomin RCMP detachment polices the Rocanville area; Rocanville has a volunteer fire brigade. The community has a home care program, seniors' housing, and a library.

The Rocanville and District Museum site has one of the province's most impressive assemblies of vintage tractors, as well as a collection of historic buildings, among them the Schwanz Store and the 1904 CPR station. Rocanville serves as the administrative centre of the RM of Rocanville No. 151.

ROCHE PERCEE, village, pop 149 (2006c), 162 (2001c), is located southeast of Estevan in the Souris River Valley. It is situated just off Hwy 39, a short distance from the Canada-United States border. The name of the community is derived from a unique landform, and landmark, long known to First Nations peoples who camped in the area. Their name for a large, hollowed sandstone outcropping was translated by Métis travelling through the region as *la Roche Percée*. James Hector of the Palliser Expedition, who visited the area in 1857, was the first to note coal along the Souris. The North-West Mounted Police made their first major camp here,

the Short Creek Camp, during their 1874 trek westward. The coal-mining industry, which gave life to the community, had its beginnings in the 1880s, when individual entrepreneurs and small-time operators began digging the coal, then transporting it by barge down the Souris River, into the Assiniboine River, and then on to Winnipeg, Manitoba. The first viable coal mine in the area was established in 1891. The CPR's Soo Line came through in 1893 and larger-scale mining operations were started in the decade. Within a few years, dozens of mines were in operation, and there were many men living at mining camps in the district. Local farmers used coal-mining income to help them establish their farming operations. It was a few years before the village proper developed; Roche Percee was incorporated on January 12, 1909. Although agriculture, consisting of grain and cattle production, were important in this sandy region, the community's fortunes have always been closely related to the coal-mining industry. Underground operations began to give way to surface "strip" mining by electric shovels in the 1930s and, by the mid-1950s, the era of underground coal mining in the region had come to an end. By the early 1960s, some operations in the Roche Percee area were mined out; today, there are only two companies mining coal in the Estevan-Bienfait area. Their huge dragline operations, however, produce an annual production of approximately 12 million tonnes. Today, Roche Percee

◄ **ALTHOUGH THE LARGEST ORIGINAL PIERCED ROCK** at Roche Percee has succumbed to the effects of time, weather, and vandalism, a number of hollowed sandstone outcroppings remain. Photograph taken August 26, 2003.

is essentially a residential community, as businesses, services, and the school have long given way to those in the nearby city of Estevan. Roche Percee is located in RM of Coalfields No. 4.

ROCKGLEN, town, pop 366 (2006c), 450 (2001c), is located on Hwys 2 and 18, 54 km south of Assiniboia and approximately 18 km north of the Canada-U.S. border. The community is located in a picturesque valley surrounded by hills topped with rock formations that have been given names such as Table Rock and the Queen's Chair — these formations inspired the town's name. Cattle and sheep ranchers began operating in the district in the late 1800s; as the area was opened for homesteading, people of British, French, and Scandinavian origin began to take up land, and the prairie began to succumb to crop production. In 1910, a number of German families from Winnipeg settled in the Rockglen district. While district schools and post offices began to be established, particularly after about 1912, it was not until the mid-1920s that Rockglen had its beginnings. That was when the CPR began construction of a line south from Ardwick Junction, just west of Assiniboia. Originally, and briefly, the small cluster of buildings gathered in anticipation of the railway was known as Valley City. The railway came through in 1926, and amidst rapid construction at the new townsite, the descriptive and somewhat romantic name of Rockglen was adopted for the burgeoning community. In 1927, the village was incorporated; in 1928, the CPR station was built and the future seemed bright. The 1930s, however, were extremely difficult times for the community; so many people were on relief that it was almost impossible to collect any

ROCKGLEN

...where the hills are frozen in time

CHANGING TOPOGRAPHY, about 4.5 kilometres east of Rockglen on Highway 18. Rockglen is situated amidst the Wood Mountain uplands: the higher elevations of the area, along with those in the Cypress Hills, were left unglaciated during the Wisconsinan period; thus, remnants of the Tertiary landscape remain. Lacking significant depths of glacial deposition, the Rockglen area hills have yielded many fossils of animals from the Paleozoic and Mesozoic eras. Imprints of tropical plants can be found between layers of sandstone and in the lignite coal seams of the area. Petrified wood is common.

A CIRCUS PARADE on Centre Street heading south toward Railway Avenue, June 11, 1929.

GOOD TIMES. Grant's Beach, now known as Rockin Beach, on nearby Fife Lake, has long been a place for recreation for Rockglen residents. Photograph circa 1927.

Historical photographs courtesy of the Town of Rockglen; colour photographs taken September 4, 2003.

HARD TIMES. Farmers line up for feed and seed distributed by the Saskatchewan Relief Commission, April 19, 1934. The Commission was created by the government of J.T.M. Anderson in 1931 to administer the province's relief programs.

ONE OF ROCKGLEN'S CHURCHES as seen from a hill on the north side of the town.

THE 1928 CPR STATION on the south side of Railway Avenue now houses a museum and a tourist information centre. The building served as a passenger station until 1962, housed railway company employees until 1973, and was sold to the Rolling Hills Historical Society in 1982 — that year, it was designated a municipal heritage property.

taxes. Local residents would work off their debts to the municipality by laying sidewalks or installing culverts, but in some cases authorities were forced to seize people's property. In the 1940s, a period of recovery, and then prosperity, began. The population of Rockglen was 239 in 1941, but by the mid-1950s it had grown to about 550. In 1957, Rockglen attained town status. The Saskatchewan Power Corporation brought round-the-clock electricity to the community in 1951, and by 1961, Rockglen had running water and a sewage system. In the 1970s, a lack of housing became a temporary problem, as many area farmers were choosing to retire to the community. Today, Rockglen provides the district with a range of businesses and services, as well as an array of facilities for social and recreational activities. These include a community hall, skating and curling rinks, a theatre, and a bowling alley. Rockglen School provides K-12 education to close to 150 students, and the community has a library, four churches, a volunteer fire department, a veterinary clinic, and a healthcare centre with a special care home. The town also hosts a number of popular annual events. In 2002, a local cooperative was formed that saved the Saskatchewan Wheat Pool elevator (which had closed two years earlier) from the wrecking ball. In 1998, the Pioneer elevators had been closed and then demolished. The community's CPR station, which provided passenger service until 1962, now houses a museum and has been declared a heritage property. Beyond Rockglen, there are a number of historic sites, regional parks, and Grasslands National Park, which is about a half-hour drive to the west. The area's valleys and hills abound with a profusion of wildlife, as well as wildflowers and many varieties of native trees. Further, native prairie grasses are still to be found in the region's vast tracts of uncultivated land. Rockglen serves as the administrative centre of the RM of Poplar Valley No. 12.

ROCKHAVEN, village, pop 20 (2006c), 30 (2001c), is situated 18 km southeast of Cut Knife, south of Hwy 40. The district was surveyed in 1903 and, although the first few homesteads may have been taken up as early as that December, most of the district's early settlers began arriving in 1904. In 1905 a post office by the name of Ovenstown was started about a mile southeast of the present village; in 1907 the Ovenstown School District was established. A schoolhouse was completed a little more than a mile southeast of the post office in 1908. The "Ovenstown" name was chosen to honour Dr. Robert Ovens from Ontario, who homesteaded in the district with a number of his family and who was the area's first medical practitioner. When the CPR entered the district, building their line from Wilkie to Cut Knife (a line that would eventually run on to Lloydminster), they enlisted the services of a Clayton Rorke, a real estate agent who had been operating out of the Ovenstown post office. When a new townsite was surveyed, the railway company gave the honour of naming it to Rorke, who chose Rockhaven, after his family's home in Ontario. The rail line was completed in 1911, and in 1912 there was a great deal of development at the Rockhaven townsite. The Ovenstown Post Office was moved in from the country and the name was changed, the CPR station was built, stores were established, both Clayton Rorke and Dr. Ovens moved their offices in from the country, a blacksmith shop and a lumberyard were set up, and the first two grain elevators were erected. In short order, the Northern Crown Bank (later the Royal Bank), a livery barn and other businesses were established. The Village of Rockhaven was incorporated on March 19, 1913. Schoolchildren attended country schools until 1916, when classes began to be taught in the village hall; a school was completed in 1917. Over the years numerous farm equipment dealerships were established and additional grain elevators were built — Rockhaven became a major grain handling and farm supply centre for a large region. Methodists, Presbyterians, Baptists, Anglicans, and Lutherans formed church congregations, football and hockey teams were started, and a curling rink was built. By the beginning of the 1930s the population of the village was close to 140. The bank was forced to close in 1933; however, it was in the 1940s that the community's business sector began to significantly decline, either as older businessmen retired and their operations were not continued, or because people were beginning to seek goods and services in larger centres. The lumberyard closed in 1940; the blacksmith died in 1950 and his shop was closed and the wares sold; the farm implement dealerships began folding in the late 1940s and were gone by 1964; the CPR station closed in 1960; and the last grocery store closed in 1978. While these changes were taking place the village population simultaneously declined. It had fallen from 124 in 1946 to only 60 by 1966, and in 1967 Rockhaven School was closed. In the early 1980s, Rockhaven remained an important grain handling and farm supply centre, serving customers over 480 square miles, yet the population was down to 42 and the only business other than the grain companies' operations was the post office. Over two million bushels were handled in Rockhaven in the 1979-80 crop year. Today, both the Saskatchewan Wheat Pool and Pioneer Grain maintain substantial operations in the community. Rockhaven is situated in the RM of Cut Knife No. 439.

ROSE VALLEY, town, pop 338 (2006c), 395 (2001c), is located in the east-central parklands, southwest of Greenwater Lake Provincial Park and 38 km north of Wadena on Hwy 35. Settlers

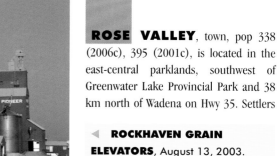

◄ **ROCKHAVEN GRAIN ELEVATORS**, August 13, 2003. Both operations were still in business in 2008.

▲ **ST. MARY'S UKRAINIAN CATHOLIC CHURCH OF THE ASSUMPTION**, built 1960, on the west side of Highway 35 at Rose Valley.

▼ **THE ROSE VALLEY HOTEL**, on the north side of Centre Street.

Photographs taken July 30, 2004.

began arriving in the district around 1904-05; most were of either Scandinavian or Ukrainian origins. The Rose Valley townsite was purchased by the CPR in 1923, and in 1924 construction of the railway from Wadena through the townsite to Tisdale was completed. Businesses began to be established in 1924, and the new community was named after a rural post office which was moved to the townsite the same year. In 1940, Rose Valley was incorporated as a village, and by 1961 the community had a peak population of 627. In 1962, Rose Valley attained town status.

Agriculture is the area's economic mainstay and is based upon grain and livestock production. Rose Valley serves the district with a core of businesses, a medical clinic and health centre, ambulance service, a pharmacy, an RCMP detachment, and a volunteer fire department. Additionally, the community has a public library, a museum, a seniors' centre, churches, community halls, skating and curling rinks, and a campground. There are a number of service clubs and community-based organizations. Rose Valley School is a K-12 facility, which had 143 town and area stu-

dents enrolled in the fall of 2006. Students from the village of Archerwill are bused to Rose Valley to attend grades 10 through 12. Scattered throughout the district are a number of pioneer churches, which have been designated heritage properties. The structures feature Scandinavian and Ukrainian motifs. Rose Valley serves as the administrative centre of the RM of Ponass Lake No. 367.

ROSETOWN, town, pop 2,277 (2006c), 2,471 (2001c), is located 115 km southwest of Saskatoon at the crossroads of two major Hwys: No. 4, following the historic north-south trail between Swift Current and the Battlefords; and east-west Hwy 7, linking Saskatoon, Kindersley, and Calgary. The first settlers arrived in the area in 1904-05, following what was known as the "Old Bone Trail" that ran southwest from Saskatoon and that was known as such for the bison bones which were collected along it and shipped to eastern Canada to be made

into lampblack and fertilizer. In 1907, a post office was established on an area farm and named Rosetown in honour of James and Ann Rose, from Lancashire, England, who had come to the district in 1905. With the arrival of the Canadian Northern Railway in the region in 1908-09, settlers began arriving in larger numbers, and in 1909 businessmen were quickly establishing themselves at the townsite. Rosetown was incorporated as a village in August that year, and on November 1, 1911, the community attained town status. A second railway, the CPR, came through, and with the completion of the bridge across the South Saskatchewan River at Outlook in 1912, Rosetown had direct rail access to Moose Jaw and the CPR main line. Along the two tracks separate rows of elevators developed, as large-scale grain farming had begun, and by the early 1920s Rosetown's population was approaching 1,000. At 11:00 p.m. on the night of June 16, 1923, the "Rosetown Cyclone" struck. Area farm buildings were tossed to the wind and Rosetown's busi-

▼ **HIGHWAY NO. 7** passing along the south side of Rosetown, looking west. The elevators stand along CN's track. CP's line runs along the north and west sides of the community. Photograph taken September 12, 2003.

▲ **ROSETOWN'S TOWN OFFICE** at the corner of Main Street and Fourth Avenue. Photograph taken September 10, 2003.

▼ **MAIN STREET, ROSETOWN**, looking south. Photograph taken September 12, 2003.

ness district was severely damaged, as was the community's hospital. However, the community quickly rebuilt and prospered as a transportation hub and distribution centre situated in traditionally productive croplands. Today, Rosetown continues as the main shopping, service, and administrative centre for a considerable territory. The community's 200 businesses serve a trading area population of over 8,100 people; numerous companies operate in support of the region's agricultural industry. Rosetown also serves the area with a range of medical facilities and services,

an RCMP detachment, a volunteer fire department, recreational facilities, churches, and elementary and high schools. Prairie West Regional College offers a wide range of post-secondary programs, and Rosetown has a 3,000-seat multi-purpose facility used for sports, entertainment, trade shows, and cultural events. The community has a museum, a library and archives, a local newspaper, and a radio station. Area attractions include the petroglyphs and other archaeological sites near the village of Herschel, and the Twin Towers Ski Resort, located 3 kilometres south

of the hamlet of Stranraer. Rosetown serves as the administrative centre of the RM of St. Andrews No. 287.

ROSTHERN, town, pop 1,382 (2006c), 1,504 (2001c), is located about equidistant between the cities of Saskatoon and Prince Albert at the junction of Hwys 11 and 312. Situated between the converging branches of the North and South Saskatchewan Rivers, Rosthern lies within close proximity to a number of historic sites: Batoche, Fish Creek, Duck Lake, and Fort Carlton are all within a short drive; as well, the National Historic Site of the Seager Wheeler Farm is just a few kilometres to the east. Rosthern benefits from the tourism these sites generate, and the community retains its traditional position as a service centre for the surrounding farming population, a position it has maintained for more than a century. The Qu'Appelle, Long Lake & Saskatchewan Railway was running through to Prince Albert in 1890, and Mennonite settlers began taking up land in the Rosthern district shortly thereafter. The Rosthern Post Office was established in 1893, and

by 1898 the community had developed sufficiently enough to be incorporated as a village. The population of Rosthern had grown to 413 by 1901, and in 1903 the community attained town status. By 1911, the town numbered well over 1,000 residents. Today, Rosthern has a substantial business community providing virtually every type of good and service. The town has a weekly newspaper, a library, a hospital, a special care home, ambulance service, and a variety of medical practitioners and services. The town has an RCMP detachment and a volunteer fire department with an emergency measures extrication team. The community also has a transit bus for persons with special needs. Rosthern is served throughout the work week by daily semi-trailer transport services, and the Saskatchewan Transportation Company runs six buses through the community daily. Rail service is operated by the Carlton Trail Railway over the former CN line. Rosthern has public elementary and high schools, providing K-12 education; additionally, Rosthern Junior College, a private residential Mennonite high school, offers a curriculum for grades 10-12. The community has several churches, and a large

▲ **ROSTHERN, CIRCA 1915.** Photograph courtesy of the Town of Rosthern.

number of service clubs and other community-based organizations. Rosthern has a broad range of recreational facilities, including an arena with curling and skating rinks, an outdoor pool, and a regional park with an 18-hole championship golf course that opened in the spring of 2004. The Station Arts Centre in Rosthern, located in the former 1902 railway station, houses a tea room and an art gallery and hosts a number of musical performances and theatrical events throughout the year. The Rosthern Mennonite Heritage Museum, located in one of the most prominent structures in the community, houses artifacts which pertain to the area's pioneer history and which offer unique insights into Mennonite folklore. The museum is housed in one of the number of heritage properties in the town, many of which are over a century old. An interesting bit of Rosthern trivia is that William Lyon Mack-

enzie King laid the cornerstone for the town's post office in 1928. Rosthern's premier annual celebration is the Town and Country Fair. A three-day event held each August, the fair has a very strong agricultural base, featuring livestock shows, horticultural exhibits, and a rodeo. Rounding out the festivities are fireworks, sporting events, a demolition derby, and a variety of entertainment. An interesting archaeological discovery was made in the Rosthern area in recent years: the well-preserved remains of a Métis *hivernant* village. Known as "Petite Ville," the site, which is believed to date the 1860s (thus predating permanent settlement at Batoche), was declared a provincial heritage site by ministerial order in February of 2005. It is the best preserved of only a few *hivernant* sites identified in the province. Rosthern serves as the administrative centre of the RM of Rosthern No. 403.

▲ **WEB SMITH'S HARDWARE STORE** in Rouleau, circa 1908. Smith is standing in the doorway in the background.

▼ **THE CPR STATION AND WATER TOWER** in Rouleau, date unknown.

▼ **THE ROSTHERN TOWN OFFICE**, on the southwest corner of Railway Avenue and Sixth Street, is located in a building that was originally built by the Imperial Bank of Canada, and that opened for business in 1903. It became the Canadian Imperial Bank of Commerce in the early 1960s after the merger of the Imperial Bank of Canada and the Canadian Bank of Commerce. Photograph taken August 26, 2004.

ROULEAU, town, pop 400 (2006c), 434 (2001c), is located 50 kilometres southeast of Moose Jaw on Hwy 39 and the CPR Soo Line. The Soo Line was completed in 1893, and the Rouleau Post Office opened in 1895, its name honouring Charles-Borromée Rouleau, a judge of the Supreme Court of the North-West Territories. Rouleau was incorporated as a village in 1903 and became a town in 1907.

Being situated on the productive soils of the Regina Plain, agriculture, particularly grain farming, has traditionally been the community's economic base, and Rouleau was reputed to be the province's first "million-bushel town." During the first decade of the twentieth century, Rouleau was booming as a trading centre for a large area; however, the construction of rail lines to the east and west of the community around 1911-12 drew some of the lifeblood out of the town's commerce, and

▲ **THE ROULEAU FAIR**, circa 1920s.

Historical photographs of Rouleau on this and previous page are courtesy of Roger and Fay Haig, Rouleau.

▼ **ON THE SET OF CORNER GAS**, August 7, 2003. Gabrielle Miller (Lacey Burrows), Brent Butt (Brent Leroy), and Nancy Robertson (Wanda Dollard) take a pause during filming. Special thanks to the cast and crew.

the loss of business cut inroads into the town's population. From a peak population of just under 700 in 1911, Rouleau's numbers fell to below 500 by 1916. Subsequently, however, the community has enjoyed a comparatively stable population; today, in addition to the traditional agricultural output of the area, crops such as lentils, canary seed, peas, chickpeas, and sunflowers are grown. Community-based businesses and services provide some local employment, but Regina, Moose Jaw, and industries near Belle Plaine also provide jobs for some Rouleau residents. In 2003, Rouleau became the location for the filming of the CTV hit comedy series *Corner Gas*, which stars Tisdale-born-and-raised comedian Brent Butt. As the fictitious town of "Dog River," Rouleau now bustles each summer with film crews. Another star in Rouleau in recent years has been Christina Beck, a student at Rouleau School: from 2002 to 2004, Beck was the winner of five provincial championships in the track and field events of shotput and discus. Rouleau School is a K-12 facility, which had 100 students enrolled in the fall of 2006. Rouleau serves as the administrative centre of the RM of Redburn No. 130.

RUDDELL, village, pop 20 (2006c), 25 (2001c), is located 30 km southeast of North Battleford, between the villages of Denholm and Maymont on Hwy 16. The North Saskatchewan River passes about four km south of the community. The first settlers began arriving in the district around 1903, and by 1907 most of the land available for homesteads in the area was taken up. Those that came to call Ruddell home were largely of British origins, mainly English, but there were some Irish and Scottish people as well. A few came from overseas, most came from Ontario, and a number were Canadians who had spent time in the United States. Ruddell began to develop in 1905 as the Canadian Northern Railway was building its transcontinental line toward Lloydminster. The community's name likely honours John Henry Ruddell (1859-1906), from Morden, Manitoba. Ruddell served on the Morden town council and was at one time the community's mayor; he also was a Conservative member of the legislative assembly of Manitoba from 1899-1903. The Ruddell Post Office was established on January 15, 1906, and through the year a building boom ensued. The first grain elevator was erected in 1906; the Cavan Presbyterian Church (later United) was completed that fall; and over the winter of 1906-07 the school was built. Town merchants had started a newspaper by 1907, and that year the first doctor arrived, a baseball team was organized, and a second elevator went up. A third would follow in the years to come. In 1912, a 25-piece brass band was started, playing many engagements, including the Battleford fair. The Village of Ruddell was incorporated on March 18, 1914. Around 1915, the Imperial Bank of Canada opened its doors, and in 1916 the population of Ruddell was 84. By 1926, it was 98, and that year a cenotaph was erected near the railway station with the names of 14 area men on it who never returned after the First World War. Two names were added after WWII, and two trees were planted at the gate of the Ruddell cemetery in honour of those men. In addition to the baseball team and the band, Ruddell had a number of other community-based organizations over the years: Oddfellows and Rebekahs, Masons, Ladies Aid (later United Church Women), a branch of the Legion, hockey, basketball, and curling clubs, Homemakers, and a wildlife conservation club. Equally diverse was the village's business community: not including the elevators, post office, and train station, Ruddell once had a number of general stores, a blacksmith shop, butcher shop, barbershop, bank, bakery, hotel, poolroom, livery stables, farm implement dealerships, and a veterinarian. The 1930s took a toll on the community from which it never really recovered, and this, along with the village's proximity to North Battleford, led to its steady decline. The population had fallen to 53 by 1951. In 1954, following the deaths of the owners of the hotel, the wares were sold, as was the building (built in 1907).

It was demolished and the lumber used to build a locker plant in Maymont. The United Church closed in 1966, although occasionally the premises were still used for funerals. High school students began to be bused to Maymont in 1967, and in 1972 Ruddell School was closed, sold, and dismantled. In 1972, the garage, fuel, and grocery business closed; in 1975, the community hall burned to the ground. The grain elevators were closed in the mid-1970s, and by 1980, a sign on the highway read, "Ruddell: No Services." Only the post office and about 25 residents remained. In the years following, Ruddell became home to several ceramic artisans and other artists, which helped sustain the village population. Ruddell is situated in the RM of Mayfield No. 406.

RUNNYMEDE, organized hamlet,
pop 15 (2006c), 28 (2001c), is located in a picturesque, rolling parkland setting 21 km southeast of Kamsack on Hwy 5. In 1903, the Canadian Northern Railway was approaching from the Manitoba border, and by 1904 had reached Kamsack. At this time German Lutherans were settling the district in significant numbers, and within a few years the small community of Runnymede began to develop. The hamlet was named after Runnymede Meadows in England, where it is believed King John signed the Magna Carta on June 15, 1215. A post office was established at Runnymede in 1908, and, a few years later, a school district. In 1912, the first grain elevator was built, and by 1918 a store, blacksmith shop, lumberyard, and additional grain elevators were in business. Runnymede was established as an organized hamlet in 1950 with about 125 residents, and the community's population hovered around 100 through the 1960s. The school was closed in 1968, however, and by the early 1970s, Runnymede's numbers were beginning to dwindle. In April 1982, a notable community landmark, the Runnymede Hotel, was lost to a fire. Today, Runnymede is a quiet and pretty collection of residences. A decaying Federal elevator stands alongside the railway track, a silent testament to busier days. Runnymede is situated in the RM of Cote No. 271.

▼ **RUNNYMEDE**, as viewed from the bridge over the railway tracks on Highway 5. Photograph taken July 13, 2004.

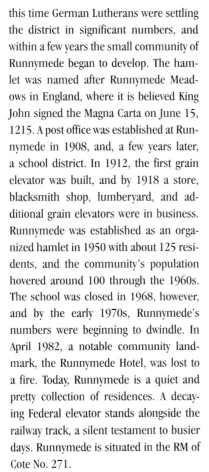

RUSH LAKE, village, pop 50 (2006c), 65 (2001c), is located approximately 30 km northeast of Swift Current just off Hwy 1. When the railway was built through the district in late 1882, the Rush Lake siding was established about three km north of the present village site, on the north shore of a lake from which the community derived its name. The Rush Lake Post Office was first established at this location on April 15, 1903. In 1905, the CPR drained the lake and straightened their track through the area, and the present site of the village was established. From the late 1880s, the district had come to be dominated by large-scale ranching operations — at Rush Lake, one of the legendary "76" ranches was established by the Canadian Agricultural, Coal and Colonization Company under the leadership of Sir John Pepys Lister-Kaye, a wealthy English baronet. In the early 1900s, entire trainloads of cattle were shipped from the Rush Lake stockyards. Grain farming, however, was becoming increasingly profitable, and after the killing winter of 1906-07 dealt the cattle industry a severe blow, ranchers increasingly found profits in parcelling out land for settlement and crop production. Mennonites scouted out the area north of Rush Lake in 1903,

▲ **RUSH LAKE SCHOOL**, closed in 1973. Photograph taken September 3, 2004.

and between 1904 and 1910 most of the available land in the area was taken up for homesteads. The developing community of Rush Lake itself came to be quite cosmopolitan, as people of various origins from eastern Canada, the United States, and Europe mingled in the streets. In 1908, Rush Lake had telegraph and post offices, a boarding house, a CPR agent, a butcher, blacksmith, tinsmith, an insurance broker, and hardware, lumber, and farm implement businesses. By the time the village was incorporated on October 16, 1911, the Rush Lake Board of Trade had been established. In 1912, the first of five grain elevators were erected and a branch of the Northern Crown Bank was established (it was taken over by the Royal Bank of Canada in 1919). Also in 1912, the first community sports day was held. In the 1920s, Rush Lake prospered and had all the facilities of a progressive village of the time. Farmers hauled grain into Rush Lake from considerable distances and returned home with supplies purchased in the community. The construction of the railway into Vanguard in 1912 may have had some impact on Rush Lake's economy, but the business community certainly suffered when lines were completed into Main Centre, to the north, and Burnham, to the south, in 1930. Then, through the dry years and the Depression, people moved away. By 1936, Rush Lake had lost about one third of its population, as its numbers had fallen to 102. That same year, the Board of Trade was disbanded. Following the 1930s, irrigation projects bolstered the area's agricultural economy, and during the post-war era into the early 1960s the community witnessed renewed growth, its population climbing to a peak of 213 in 1961. In 1966, a new community rink and civic centre was opened, its construction a Jubilee-Centennial project. But times were changing in rural Saskatchewan: in 1962 the CPR station at Rush Lake was removed, as highway travel had come into prominence; people were travelling to the town of Herbert or to Swift Current to shop and to work, as well as for medical and other services, and for entertainment. Further, the population in the Rush Lake trading area had significantly declined. Whereas there were close to 700 farms in the surrounding municipality in 1926, by 1976 there were far fewer than half that. Today, sidewalks run along vacant lots in Rush Lake, and there are a number of vacant homes and former businesses. The RM of Excelsior No. 166 office remains in the village, housing the library branch and the postal outlet. The former Rush Lake School building (the last classes were held there in the early 1970s) remains a community landmark.

RUTHILDA, village, pop 5 (2006c), 20 (2001c), is located 47 km southwest of Biggar, 5 km south of Hwy 51. The first homesteaders arrived in the district as early as 1905, and with the construction of the rail line through the area in 1910-

12 the townsite was established. Alexander and Elizabeth Goodwin from Ontario had filed on and broken land a couple of miles northeast of the present village site in 1909, but left the area for the first winter. When they returned in the spring of 1910, they found survey stakes for a rail line running across their land; railway crews ended up boarding at the Goodwin farm. In 1910 a site for a station and a townsite was surveyed, and a name for it had to be decided upon. Someone got the idea that putting together the names of the Goodwin's two daughters, Ruth and Hilda, would sound nice, and Ruthilda thus became the community's name. The Grand Trunk Pacific Railway built the grade for the track in 1911; in 1912, the rails were laid and the Ruthilda station was built. Prior to the completion of the line, the first enterprising storekeeper set up shop. The Ruthilda Post Office was officially established on November 1, 1912, and that year other new businesses began to be started. In 1914, Ruthilda School was built and two grain elevators were erected. On February 3, 1921, the Village of Ruthilda was incorporated; ten years later, in 1931, the community had its peak population of 114. The Saskatchewan Wheat Pool erected a third grain elevator in Ruthilda in the mid-1920s, and it was during this decade that the community fielded one of the province's most formidable baseball teams. In 1928, the United Church was built — previously, people had worshipped in homes, the lumberyard, the school, and the community hall. A second church — Glad Tidings Gospel — operated from 1936 until 1956. Ruthilda experienced several destructive fires over the years — in 1926, 1936, 1951, and 1959 — which claimed many buildings, dramatically altering the appearance of the village. One of the grain elevators was

dismantled in 1947. Ruthilda School was closed in 1964 and thereafter all schoolchildren were bused to Plenty; in the late 1960s, the community's population began to plummet, dropping from 85 in 1966 to 48 by 1971. Businesses were closing, as the declining population could no longer sustain them. Ruthilda still had two grain elevators in operation in the late 1970s; however, the rail line was abandoned in the mid-1980s and no elevators remain standing today. Ruthilda is situated in the RM of Grandview No. 349.

SALTCOATS, town, pop 467 (2006c), 494 (2001c), is located 27 km southeast of Yorkton on the Yellowhead Hwy, No. 16. The town is situated in an attractive setting, as a crescent-shaped lake forms the southern and eastern boundaries of the community. Anderson Lake was named after William Anderson, a Scot who settled in the immediate area in 1882, and the district was originally known as Stirling, after Stirling, Scotland. Though the first settlers were predominantly of Scottish and English origin, a walk through the historic Saltcoats cemetery reveals that Métis, Irish, Welsh, German, Hungarian, Ukrainian, Icelandic, and Scandinavian people also came to call the district home. Significant development began to occur in the area in the late 1880s as the railway was being built toward Yorkton. In 1887, the nucleus of a business community began to form, with the first entrepreneurs conducting their affairs out of tents. Later, lumber was hauled in from Langenburg by ox team and shacks were erected. As the townsite was not yet surveyed, the settlers took possession of the land by what was known as "squatter's rights." With the arrival of the Manitoba and Northwestern Railway in 1888 the name of the commu-

nity was changed to Saltcoats, after Saltcoats, Scotland, the birthplace of one of the major shareholders in the railway. The Saltcoats Post Office was also established in 1888, and on April 4, 1894, Saltcoats was incorporated as a village, the first community established as such in what is now Saskatchewan. In 1910, Saltcoats attained town status. Today, agriculture, manufacturing, the Esterhazy area potash mines, and the city of Yorkton provide employment; additionally, Saltcoats has a small core of local businesses. Saltcoats School is a K-8 facility, which had 119 students enrolled in the fall of 2006; students attend grades 9-12 in Yorkton. The community has a volunteer fire department, and a doctor visits on a weekly basis. The town has a special care home. The community has two active churches, and a former church houses the Saltcoats Museum. The town has skating and curling rinks and, on the southern shore of Anderson Lake, Saltcoats Regional Park has a beach, camping, and picnicking facilities. An arboretum and a nature trail are additional community features. A number of notable people have come from the town of Saltcoats. Thomas MacNutt served as a member of the Territorial Assembly from 1902 to 1905, and after the formation of the province, he became the first Speaker of the Legislative Assembly of Saskatchewan. He was also a member of the House of Commons in Ottawa from 1908 to 1921. Gordon Barnhart was Clerk of the Legislative Assembly of Saskatchewan from 1969 to 1989 and Clerk of the Senate of Canada from 1989 to 1994. He served as University Secretary of the University of Saskatchewan before becoming the province's twentieth lieutenant governor in 2006. Barnhart is also an author and editor of a number of books relating to Saskatchewan history. Saltcoats

▲ **HORSE AUCTION**, no date.

▼ **AN ASSEMBLY AT SALTCOATS STATION**, no date.

▲ **HIGH STREET**, no date.

▼ **SCHOOLYARD PLAY** at Saltcoats Protestant Public School, 1904.

The Saltcoats Museum is situated in a building that was built as a Presbyterian Church in 1890. It houses items that tell the story of the area's early settlers and of the community's founding. A region encompassing 21 former school districts is represented. The photographs shown here are but a small sample of those housed in the museum; they were digitally scanned on the museum premises on July 12, 2004.

Gleanings from the

SALTCOATS

Museum...

▼ **C.A. PARTRIDGE AND FAMILY.** Partridge was an award-winning grower of malting and brewing barley in Saskatchewan, no date.

▼ **THE BANK OF BRITISH NORTH AMERICA**, no date.

▼ **TWO YEARS AFTER ATTAINING TOWN STATUS**, a new town hall was under construction. Photograph: April 1912.

also celebrates being the hometown of Joan McCusker, who, with the famed Sandra Schmirler rink, became a Canadian, World, and Olympic curling champion. Saltcoats serves as the administrative centre of the RM of Saltcoats No. 213.

SAND POINT BEACH, organized hamlet, is one of a number of resort communities on Buffalo Pound Lake. It lies on the southwest shore and is accessible via Hwy 2, north of Moose Jaw. Land for the resort subdivision was surveyed in 1968 and Sand Point Beach was established as an organized hamlet in 1988. There are 88 properties developed with homes and cottages. There were 64 year-round residents in 2006; however, the population may reach up to about 200 during the summer months. Ice-fishing is a popular activity in the winter. Sand Point Beach is located in the RM of Marquis No. 191.

SANDY BAY, northern village, pop 1,175 (2006c), 1,092 (2001c), is a growing community located just inside the Saskatchewan-Manitoba border on the Churchill River, near the Island Falls Power Station. Sandy Bay lies 70 km northeast of Pelican Narrows via gravel road No. 135; Flin Flon, approximately a two-hour drive away, is the nearest larger centre. The residents of the community are predominantly Cree; approximately one quarter are members of the Peter Ballantyne Cree Nation. Although the area was occupied by Aboriginal peoples for hundreds of years, the present community of Sandy Bay came into being with the construction of the Island Falls hydroelectric station in the late 1920s. The facility was built to supply power for the smelters and mines in Flin

◀ **SANDY BAY, FEBRUARY 1974.** Saskatchewan Archives Board, Saskatchewan Photographic Services, R-PS73-1843-213. Photographer: D. Varley.

Flon, and it became operational in 1930. The original residents of Sandy Bay were families of the region's indigenous people, who came to work on the construction project as low-paid labourers. About a quarter of the 200-man labour force that was employed for the first number of years were Aboriginal people; the non-native workers who came to the area to work at the power station lived at a separate, specially built townsite closer to the dam, with modern homes, a hospital, a school, a store, and a community hall with a theatre. Sandy Bay, about 20 minutes away after a road was completed, came to be known as the "Indian village." While there were some employment opportunities for the Aboriginal population following the power station's construction, the majority of the better jobs were held by the Island Falls townsite residents. After the townsite was vacated in 1967 when the power station became a remotely-controlled operation, Sandy Bay residents lost a major employer, and by that time the development of the Island Falls project had dramatically altered traditional lifestyles that had been based in trapping, hunting, and fishing. SaskPower took over ownership of the province's oldest hydroelectric station in 1981. Today, traditional occupations re-

main a part of some Sandy Bay residents' livelihoods, but work in education, local businesses, health care, government offices, and outfitting and guiding provide most employment opportunities. Hector Thiboutot School, a major employer, is a fully-equipped, modern, K-12 facility, which had 509 students enrolled in the fall of 2005. Sandy Bay has a health centre which also functions as a dispensary for pharmaceuticals, a rehabilitation centre, an RCMP detachment, and air service. In 1965, Sandy Bay acquired a form of local government (a Local Community Authority), and in 1983, due to the increasing population and infrastructure, Sandy Bay was incorporated as a northern village. The population is very young and community concerns include low levels of employment and household income. The median age of Sandy Bay residents in 2001 was 18.5, while the average age of all Saskatchewan residents was 36.7. The village's unemployment rate the same year was 29.5 per cent; throughout the province it sat at 6.3. In 2000, the median family income in Sandy Bay was $27,200; the median income of all Saskatchewan families was $49,264. Notable residents of Sandy Bay have included actor/director/ playwright Kennetch Charlette, the artistic

director and co-founder of the Saskatchewan Native Theatre Company, and a drama teacher at the First Nations University of Canada in Saskatoon; and Angus Bear (1907-88), a highly respected elder in the community of Sandy Bay, who was hired as a guide in 1927 by the Churchill River Power Company (a subsidiary of the Hudson Bay Smelting and Mining Company) to lead the first team of engineers to the Island Falls dam site. Travelling by canoe and on foot, Bear located the most economical routes for supplies, machinery, and power lines, and for 38 years he made a vital contribution to the development of mining and hydro-electric power in the province's northeast, both as a guide and a worker. Bear also worked to help record the history of the hydro-electricity industry at Island Falls, as well as to preserve the oral history and traditions of the region's Cree people. Angus Bear received the Saskatchewan Order of Merit in 1987.

SANDY BEACH is the common name for a resort area located in the Qu'Appelle Valley, on the northeast side of Katepwa Lake, on Hwy 56. The first cottages were built in the early 1900s, and Sandy Beach was incorporated as a resort village in 1954. The most significant development, however, has occurred over the past two or three decades. There were only about a half-dozen year-round residents in the mid-1970s; today, the number is close to 90. There are 240 cottages and permanent residences at Sandy Beach, and during the summer months the population can easily reach 500. In 2004, Sandy Beach and the nearby resort villages of Katepwa Beach and Katepwa South amalgamated, forming the District of Katepwa. The restructuring agreement was negotiated to enhance the administration and delivery of community services.

SARNIA BEACH, organized hamlet, est. 1965, is a resort community located northeast of Holdfast on the west side of Last Mountain Lake. It is situated in the RM of Sarnia No. 221 directly across the lake from Rowan's Ravine Provincial Park. There were 27 permanent residents recorded during the 2006 Census; however, the population varies greatly depending on the season.

SASKATCHEWAN BEACH, resort village, pop 155 (2006c), 120 (2001c), is located on the east side of the south end of Last Mountain Lake, 11 kilometres northwest of Craven and approximately one kilometre south of the village of Silton. Saskatchewan Beach was the location of the original Silton Post Office, which opened on January 1, 1888, with Charles Benjafield, one of the earliest pioneers in the area (1883), as postmaster. For a few years in the early 1900s (c. 1905-13), the William Pearson Land Company serviced the "Port" of Silton with its steamboats, but with the completion of the rail line between Regina and Bulyea in 1911, train travel became the preferred means of accessing the area. The Silton Post Office was relocated to the present village site. What is now known as Saskatchewan Beach was then known as Lake View Park, until June 16, 1919, when the resort village was incorporated and the present name was adopted. Un-

til the 1970s there were only a handful of permanent residents at Saskatchewan Beach, but in recent times the number of year-round residents has been increasing rapidly, as people who work in Regina have been buying permanent homes at the lake and commuting. There were nine full-time residents recorded in 1971; 49 in 1981; and 99 in 1991. These population figures, however, were, and continue to be, greatly augmented during the summer months with the arrival of seasonal cottagers. Saskatchewan Beach Regional Park offers two beaches, a playground and picnic area, and a boat launch, and was the sailing venue for the 2005 Canada Summer Games. The Last Mountain Lake Sailing Club clubhouse is located in the park area. Saskatchewan Beach is situated in the RM of McKillop No. 220.

SASKATOON, city, pop 202,340 (2006c), 196,861 (2001c), is Saskatchewan's largest city — the total "metropolitan area" as defined by Statistics Canada had a population of 233,923 in 2006. The city lies 259 km northwest of Regina and 141 km southwest of Prince Albert; the Battlefords lie 138 km to the northwest, Humboldt 113 km to the east. The city is situated along the banks of the South Saskatchewan River, and seven bridges cross the river within the city limits. There has been a First Nations presence in the Saskatoon area for more than 6,000 years; however, it was not until 1883 that settlers first arrived and the present city had its beginnings. The name of the city is likely derived from an archaic Cree verb, manimisâskwatwân, referring to the activity of gathering saskatoon berry willows at the location — evidently for use as arrow shafts. The founding of Saskatoon dates to the early 1880s and an

opportunity presented by the Government of Canada: eager to settle the west, the government was offering incentives to colonization companies. Members of Toronto's Methodist community formed the Temperance Colonization Society in 1881, seeing a chance to escape the evils of Toronto's liquor trade with the formation of a temperance colony in the west. In the early summer of 1882, John Neilson Lake, a Methodist minister and the group's leader, scouted out a location for a settlement along the banks of the South Saskatchewan River. In 1883, the first settlers disembarked the train at Moose Jaw, still not much more than a cluster of tents and shacks, and trekked northward to the site of the present city. The Union Jack was raised, and the first streets were surveyed along the east bank of the river that year. Close to 60 settlers had arrived. Their efforts to maintain a community of abstinence, however, would come to be thwarted, as they had no legal means by which to prevent non-teetotallers from settling in their midst. The colonists had also hoped that steamboats would be able serve the settlement, navigating the South Saskatchewan River from the rail line at Medicine Hat. However, the many shifting sandbars and the river's shallow depth made the trip quite difficult. This, along with the unease caused by the 1885 Resistance, discouraged settlement, and Saskatoon grew slowly. In 1890, the Qu'Appelle, Long Lake and Saskatchewan Railway bridged the river at Saskatoon, connecting the locale to Regina and Prince Albert. The railway built its station on the more level ground on the west side of the river, and a new townsite was laid out. When the settlement on the west side of the river was incorporated as a village in 1901, it appropriated the name Saskatoon, and the original east side community then be-

came known as Nutana. In 1903, Saskatoon attained town status, and Nutana was incorporated as a village. In 1906, Saskatoon, the Village of Nutana, and the Village of Riversdale (inc. 1905), which had developed on the northwest bank of the river, amalgamated, with the understanding that there would be civic improvements, including a traffic bridge over the river. Together they formed the City of Saskatoon, which received its charter on May 26, 1906, becoming the province's fourth city. The traffic bridge opened in 1907, bringing an end to a somewhat despised ferry service. The arrival of the Barr colonists in 1903 proved to be a boon for Saskatoon merchants, and over the years leading up to WWI the city enjoyed vigorous boom times. By 1908, three railway bridges and the traffic bridge spanned the river, and Saskatoon became one of western Canada's important railway hubs and distribution centres. The railway village of Sutherland, founded by the CPR in 1908, began to develop on the city's northeast fringes (incorporated as a town in 1912, Sutherland became part of the City of Saskatoon on January 1, 1956). Although Saskatoon lost its bid to become the permanent capital of Saskatchewan after the province's inauguration, it did succeed in obtaining the provincial university in 1909. From a population of a mere 113 in 1901, the city's numbers soared to more than 21,000 by 1916. Saskatoon's growth slowed during the world-wide depression immediately following the First World War; during the 1920s, growth resumed: the population jumped from 25,739 in 1921 to 43,291 by 1931. The grandest construction project undertaken during the boom years of the late 1920s was the construction of the landmark Bessborough Hotel, begun in 1929. Throughout the 1930s, Saskatoon did not grow at all — the open-

21ST STREET EAST, circa 1940s. Saskatchewan Archives Board R-B7873.

AN AERIAL VIEW, 1959. Saskatchewan Archives Board R-B1882-3.

Then and now... **SASKATOON**

THE CITY OF SASKATOON TODAY with the South Saskatchewan River in the foreground. Photography courtesy of f:11 Photography/Marketing Den/Tourism Saskatoon.

ing of the Bessborough was delayed until 1935, and, indeed, the city lost a small percentage of its population. Following WWII, however, significant development resumed, as an economy largely related to agriculture began to become more diverse. In the 1950s, the population shift from Saskatchewan's rural areas to the cities made Saskatoon one of the country's fastest growing cities — by 1961, the city numbered more than 95,000. During the 1960s and 1970s, Saskatoon emerged as an industrial hub for the half-dozen potash mines developed in the region, as well as a base for mining operations developing in the province's north. The 1980s witnessed the emergence of high-tech industries. From a settlement founded by people from eastern Canada, then the United Kingdom and the United States, Saskatoon grew in the early twentieth century to include immigrants from many parts of Europe, particularly Ukraine and areas of the Austro-Hungarian empire. Mennonites also came to develop a significant presence in the city. The years following WWII saw war brides from England come to the city, as well as people migrating from farms. In the latter half of the twentieth century immigrants came from Pakistan, India, and China; in later years others came from the Philippines, Vietnam, and Latin America. The Aboriginal population has grown rapidly in recent times, as there has been a continued move from reserves to the province's urban areas — in 2001, approximately 10 per cent of Saskatoon's population was First Nations or Métis. Although a significant presence, the Aboriginal population remains marginalized, plagued with the problems of discrimination, poverty, substance abuse, violence, and prostitution — problems that have generated much national attention. Today, Saskatoon, more

than any other city in the province, faces the pains of unmitigated growth: traffic congestion is becoming common, as increasing numbers of commuters swarm in and out of the city each day. Dozens of bedroom communities have developed around Saskatoon and are continuing to be developed. Additionally, Saskatoon has become somewhat of a carbon copy of many North American cities in recent decades: suburbs of identical-looking housing continue to rim the city edges, and American multinational and out-of-province retailers have built "big box" chain stores, branding the urban landscape with their corporate logos, often at the expense of locally-owned businesses and the city core. Long-standing community institutions, such as the Centennial Auditorium, now have corporate names. The rapidly expanding population has put much pressure on the city's infrastructure — the police force has had to increase its staffing, and a new 90-million-dollar police station is now in the works. A new traffic bridge across the river on the city's south side is also planned. Saskatoon taxpayers are now facing a one per cent property tax hike for each of the next six years to cover the costs — a situation similar to that faced by Vancouverites in the late 1980s and 1990s, which forced many seniors out of their homes. The economy of Saskatoon today is diverse and is based on its continuing role as a retail and distribution centre, manufacturing to serve resource and agricultural sectors, health and educational services, food processing, transportation and warehousing, mining (two of the world's largest mining companies have head offices in the city), and advanced technology industries (life sciences, information technology, agricultural biotechnology, and telecommunications). The University of Saskatchewan's Colleges

of Agriculture and Bioresources, Medicine, and Veterinary Medicine have become recognized as world leaders. Research capabilities at the University of Saskatchewan are significantly augmented by the presence of the Canadian Light Source, a $173.5-million project and Canada's largest science research initiative in decades — it is one of the most powerful third-generation synchrotrons in the world. Additionally, Innovation Place has become one of North America's most successful and internationally recognized university-related research parks. Beyond the U of S, other educational institutions in the city include the Kelsey Campus of the Saskatchewan Institute of Applied Science and Technology, the Saskatoon Campus of the First Nations University of Canada, and the Saskatoon Public Library. In the realm of arts and culture, the city has a number of professional theatre companies, a symphony orchestra, and art galleries (the Mendel Art Gallery and the university's Kenderdine Art Gallery are notable). Annual festivals and events include the Saskatchewan Jazz Festival, Shakespeare on the Saskatchewan, the Saskatoon Fringe Theatre Festival, and the Saskatoon Exhibition (origins of which date to 1886). Ethnic celebrations include Folkfest and the Ukrainian Vesna Festival. City museums include the Western Development Museum, the Diefenbaker Canada Centre, and the Ukrainian Museum of Canada. Other notable Saskatoon attractions include the 60-kilometre Meewasin Trail system along the South Saskatchewan River Valley, the Saskatoon Forestry Farm Park & Zoo, and the 760-acre Wanuskewin Heritage Park just north of the city. Nineteen archaeological sites at Wanuskewin relate to the First Nations people of the northern plains and contain summer and winter campsites, tipi rings,

a medicine wheel, and bison kill sites. An award-winning interpretive centre is a major tourist attraction and is visited by an average of 14,000 schoolchildren each year. Saskatoon is served by a mayor and ten councillors, elected for three-year terms. Saskatoon is situated within the RM of Corman Park No. 344.

SCEPTRE, village, pop 98 (2006c), 136 (2001c), is known as the "Gateway to the Great Sand Hills." Sceptre lies 20 km east of Leader on Hwy 32, and is situated between the South Saskatchewan River, to the north, and the sand hills, which begin approximately 16 km south of the community. The area was opened up to homesteaders in 1908, and they came from far and wide: from Manitoba, Ontario, the United States, and from many parts of Europe, including Britain, Sweden, Norway, Russia, Ukraine, Romania, and Poland. By 1910, most of the available land in the district was occupied. Before the railway arrived, in order to obtain supplies or deliver grain, people would have to make the long trip to Swift Current or Maple Creek on the CPR main line, or take the ferry north across the river and travel to Kindersley. When the railway arrived in 1913, Sceptre quickly became another in the string of communities that sprang up along the "Empress Line." In April that year the village was incorporated. Among the first entrepreneurs in Sceptre were a small number of Chinese immigrants, who operated the café, the laundries and, later, the hotel. By 1921, Sceptre had a population of 266. The hardships of the 1930s claimed about a third of the community's population; however, as elsewhere, the post-WWII era was a period of unprecedented prosperity that lasted through the 1960s. Since the 1970s,

▲ **THE GREAT SAND HILLS**, south of Sceptre, are an ecologically-sensitive region, home to an abundance of rare plant and animal species. They are also an area coveted by the oil and gas industry, and since the early 1990s many studies have been conducted to assess the economic potential of the area as well as the impact of resource extraction upon this unique environment. Photograph taken August 29, 2003.

though, the community has experienced a slow, but steady, decline. The row of grain elevators that once lined the tracks at Sceptre have disappeared one by one, superseded by the huge concrete inland terminals constructed at larger centres, such as the Great Sandhills Terminal approximately 20 kilometres west at Leader. In the late 1970s, as the population of the village fell below 200, the school was closed, and, subsequently, children have been bused to Leader. The former school now houses the Great Sandhills Museum and Interpretive Centre. Opened in 1988, the facility was the beginning of efforts to develop the tourism potential of the Sceptre district. Other endeavours have included the construction of sculptures and the painting of numerous murals throughout the village. One mural pays tribute to Sceptre's illustrious baseball history. For a good many years the local team was a formidable powerhouse, whose achievements culminated in the winning of the semi-pro Canadian National Championship in 1951. Today, the village retains a small core of businesses serving a district of mixed agricultural operations. Sceptre also serves as the administrative centre for the RM of Clinworth No. 230.

SCOTT, town, pop 91 (2006c), 110 (2001c), is located just southwest of Wilkie and is Saskatchewan's second smallest town after Fleming. The Scott area was first settled around 1905, and a significant number of those who came to the region were of German Catholic origin, largely from Russia. With the construction of the Grand Trunk Pacific railway through the area the townsite of Scott developed. Scott was incorporated as a village in 1908 and attained town status in 1910. The community was named for Frank Scott, a railway company treasurer. The 1911 Census recorded a population of 420 in the town, the largest the community would ever have. Although the population hovered between two and three hundred from the 1920s through to the early 1970s, by the early 1950s, the town's commercial sector had been reduced to only a handful of establishments, superseded by the business communities in nearby Wilkie or Unity. Over the past few decades, Scott's numbers have plummeted. Over the five years from 1986 to 1991, the population fell from 202 to 118. The community is notable for the experimental farm established in the early 1900s. The Agriculture and Agri-Food Canada operation focuses on research related to oilseeds and cereal crops in the north-western region of Saskatchewan. Scott has a long and beautiful tree-lined central avenue and retains a small store and café. Scott serves as the administrative centre of the RM of Tramping Lake No. 380.

SCOUT LAKE, organized hamlet, pop 20 (2006c), 20 (2001c), is located in the centre of a small valley on Hwy 2 between Assiniboia and Rockglen. Settlers had been homesteading in the area since the early 1900s, and with the construction of the CPR line from Assiniboia through the area in the mid-1920s, a small centre with a variety of businesses and services

◄ **SCOTT TOWN HALL** (left) and a former business, Main Street and Third Avenue. Photograph taken August 15, 2003.

► **THE SCOUT LAKE CO-OP**, May 15, 2005.

emerged. Not all of these enterprises were legitimate, however. The local history recounts that a resident undertaking an informal census in Scout Lake's early years found that roughly 10 per cent of the community was involved in bootlegging. Over the following years, though, legitimate businesses, and the community of Scout Lake, thrived. By mid-century, however, as roads and vehicles improved, the community's businesses and services were being superseded by those in Assiniboia and Rockglen. The railway station closed, and then the school. A quiet hamlet remains. Scout Lake is situated in the RM of Willow Bunch No. 42.

SEDLEY, village, pop 319 (2006c), 322 (2001c), is located 50 km southeast of Regina on Hwy 33. The area was settled by German Catholics prior to the beginning of the twentieth century, and Sedley developed with the construction of the CPR line between Stoughton and Regina in 1903-04. French-speaking settlers arrived in the district around 1906, and Sedley was incorporated as a village in 1907. The basis of the area economy is agriculture, largely a combination of

▲ **A GIRLS' BOARDING SCHOOL IN SEDLEY** operated by the Sisters of Loretto from the 1920s until the 1960s, and then a residential treatment centre for troubled young women (the Roy Wilson Centre), this impressive building has been converted into a private residence in recent years.

▼ **A FORMER SASKATCHEWAN WHEAT POOL GRAIN ELEVATOR** in Sedley dating to 1955.

Photographs taken August 19, 2003.

grain and livestock production. Sedley has a small business community which includes farm suppliers. Sedley School was a grade 7-12 institution until 2007, but with the closure and restructuring of schools in the Prairie Valley School Division that year, Sedley School became a K-8 institution. Grades K-6 had previously attended Francis School, which was closed; high school students now travel to Vibank. Sedley has a magnificent Roman Catholic Church and an equally impressive former Roman Catholic boarding school, which has recently been converted into a private residence. In 1979, two community members, Joseph Helfrick and Edward Leier, were posthumously awarded the Star of Courage by the Governor General of Canada. Both were murdered while pursuing thieves after a robbery at their local church in 1976. Sedley is situated within the RM of Francis No. 127.

SEMANS, village, pop 195 (2006c), 267 (2001c), is located 13 km west of Raymore just off Hwy 15. Among the notable features of the village are the tall, old trees which line many of the community's streets; they were planted in the 1930s as

a make-work project for those on relief. Homesteaders began taking up land in the district in 1904 and, a few years later, with the construction of the Grand Trunk Pacific main line that would connect Winnipeg, Saskatoon and Edmonton, the village of Semans began to develop. The right of way for the rail line was surveyed through the Semans district in 1906; the grading of the roadbed, done with horse-drawn scrapers, was completed in 1907 (around this time the first store was built on the Semans townsite); and in 1908 the tracks were laid and, according to the Semans local history, reached a junction with the CPR line at Nokomis on April 20 that year. The townsite of Semans was reportedly named after the maiden name of the wife of a railway company official. The name, originally misspelled "Semons" (this is how the name first appeared on the station sign), was chosen to fit the alphabetical sequence of community names along the rail line: Quinton, Raymore, Semans, Tate, etc. The railway station and the first grain elevator were constructed by the fall of 1908, and the Semans Post Office was established on October 12 that year. The first postmaster, Louis Irwin Steenson, held the position until his retirement in 1950. Semans was incorporated on December 14, 1908, and a school district centred on the village was established in 1909. By this time, local businesses could supply all necessary commodities and services. In 1916, the Village erected a small building to house an electric power plant — two engines and two generators were bought second-hand from the Regina jail — and in 1917, after the village built its own distribution system, electricity was provided from dusk until midnight. This system was in operation until 1928: Canadian Utilities then erected a power line from Nokomis to Semans, bringing 24-

hour service to the community. Semans had grown to reach a population of 194 by 1911. By 1921 the number had swollen to 450, which would end up being an all-time high. The majority of the population were of British stock, having originated in about equal numbers from eastern Canada and the British Isles. From the mid-1920s through to the mid-1980s, the population of Semans levelled off, averaging approximately 365. For many years, the countryside around the village was noted for its exceptional wheat production: during some years in the 1950s, more than 2,000,000 bushels of wheat were shipped out of the Semans grain elevators, and Semans had more elevators than most communities its size. In 1955, the following grain companies were doing business in the village: Searle, National, Lake of the Woods Milling, Parish and Heimbecker, and the Saskatchewan Wheat Pool with elevators "A" and "B." Today, only the former Saskatchewan Wheat Pool elevator (1967) and its crib annexes (1956-57) remain. In 1999, the Saskatchewan Wheat Pool built a high-throughput terminal between Semans and Raymore at Booth Siding to serve the region's grain growers, but the downside was that farmer traffic into Semans was further reduced, and village businesses had fewer customers. The village had approximately 30 businesses and services in 1965; today there are only a few, and abandoned buildings now dot the once vibrant commercial area. Semans began to decline rapidly in the 1990s — the community still numbered 333 residents in 1991 — and the village population was getting older. In 2001, the median age of Semans residents was 50.9, while that of all Saskatchewan residents was 36.7. More than 90 per cent of Semans residents were over the age of 15 in 2001, and by the fall of 2003 enrollment

at Margaret McClumb School, a K-12 facility, was down to 38 students. The school had been named in 1962 in honour of a teacher, then principal, who had taught at Semans from 1921 to 1945. In 2004 the school was closed. A building which served as Semans' first public school (1909-18), then the Odd Fellows and Rebekahs' Hall (1921-82), was designated a heritage property in 1983 and now houses the Semans and District Museum. Notable people from Semans include Gordon Currie and Gordon MacMurchy. Currie, born in Semans on May 20, 1923, became an inspirational teacher and notable football and hockey coach. He led the football team at Balfour Technical School in Regina to eight provincial championships, their hockey team to three; he then coached the Regina Rams to six national titles and was named the Canadian amateur coach of the year in 1975. Currie became the principal of Campbell Collegiate in Regina and served as a member of the Saskatchewan Legislative Assembly from 1982-85. He was invested as a Member of the Order of Canada in 1979. Gordon MacMurchy, born in Semans in 1926, was a provincially recognized sports figure and served as a notable Saskatchewan MLA and prominent cabinet member in the government of Allan Blakeney from 1971 to 1982. He then served as the mayor of Semans from 1982 to 1997. A long-time advocate for farmers and rural issues, he received the Saskatchewan Order of Merit in 1999. MacMurchy died in 2005. Semans serves as the administrative centre of the RM of Mount Hope No. 279.

SENLAC, village, pop 45 (2006c), 50 (2001c), is a pretty, treed community situated in the beautiful rolling countryside northeast of Macklin, an area popular for

▲ **LOOKING SOUTH UP GODWIN STREET** in Senlac from Hastings Road. Early evening, August 13, 2003.

hunting. The community developed with the construction of the CPR line through the district in 1910, and Senlac gained village status in 1916. The community was named after Senlac Hill in England, where the Battle of Hastings was fought in 1066; Senlac's street names are also associated with the conflict. In the early 1920s, the first known production of salt in the province took place in the Senlac area. Although the Senlac Salt Company was only in operation for a couple of years, it was a precursor to an industry which remains important in the region. Senlac had a peak population of 136 in 1926, and its numbers remained fairly stable until the early 1990s. Traditionally, the area economy has been largely based upon mixed agricultural operations; however, in recent decades there have been substantial developments in the area's gas and oil fields. Oil batteries, compressor stations, and hundreds of wells surround the village; interestingly, though, as elsewhere in the province where the oil and gas industry looms large, the economic benefits

do not seem to trickle down to the local level. Only a small number of businesses remain in village. Senlac serves as the administrative centre of the RM of Senlac No. 411.

SHACKLETON, village, pop 10 (2006c), pop 10 (2001c), is situated roughly halfway between Swift Current and Leader on Hwy 32. Settlers began arriving in the area around 1907 and the village had its beginnings in 1913, as the CPR approached from the southeast from Cabri en route to Leader. The new community, named after the famous explorer, gained village status in 1919. Its streets honour other illustrious polar pathfinders, such as Scott, Amundsen, Franklin, Peary, and Cook. For twenty years the village of Shackleton grew rapidly. In the early 1920s, a tree-planting program was initiated to beautify the community, and the annual Shackleton Sports Days, featuring baseball tournaments, athletics, and horse races, were popular events. In the early

▲ **NO TIGER IN THE TANK HERE.** Gas pumps at an abandoned filling station, Shackleton. Photograph taken August 29, 2003.

1940s, a twenty-acre market garden at Shackleton produced flowers, vegetables, plums, and cherries. The village reached a peak population of 141 in 1931; however, since the early 1960s, the population has steadily fallen and the businesses have disappeared. Fewer than 30 people have lived in the village since the early 1980s. Today, other than a few homes scattered about the townsite, Shackleton resembles a ghost town. Recent discoveries of large reserves of natural gas in the area have proven somewhat of a boon to the region, providing some off-farm employment and a welcome boost to the area economy. Shackleton is located in the RM of Miry Creek No. 229.

SHAMROCK, village, pop 20 (2006c), 35 (2001c), is located 37 km north of Gravelbourg on Hwy 363. It is situated upon the Missouri Coteau; Chaplin Lake lies to the north, Old Wives Lake to the east. Settlers began arriving in the district in 1907-08; some were of English, Irish, and Scottish stock, coming from eastern Canada or overseas, while others were Norwegians, most of whom came through the United States; east of Shamrock settled people of French-Canadian

origin, and immediately to the west were many German-speaking settlers. Most rode the railway to Mortlach, Parkbeg, Ernfold, or Morse, the main jumping-off points for homesteaders coming to the Shamrock district. Some of the German-speaking settlers would travel the extra distance to Herbert, where they could converse in their own language while buying their supplies, as Herbert was predominantly a Mennonite settlement. Chaplin, the nearest community on the CPR main line where one could have detrained or could have bought provisions, was somewhat avoided for decades. From about 1912 the vast saline flats that form Chaplin Lake could be crossed only by means of a series of precarious wooden bridges; it was only in 1953 that road grades were built through the area. After the Canadian Northern Railway reached Gravelbourg in 1913, and later Bateman, some settlers came to the Shamrock district via those points. The Rural Municipality of Shamrock was established in 1912, and, ten

▶ **DOWNTOWN SHAMROCK:** a grocery store with a postal outlet is one of the few businesses remaining in the village. Photograph taken September 18, 2005.

years later, with the approach of the railway, the townsite was established by the CPR and thereafter the present village began to develop. One of the first buildings to be located in the fledgling community was the RM office. The first elevator was also built in Shamrock in 1922; by 1924, there were three. Shamrock was incorporated as a village on April 30, 1924, with approximately 20 places of business in operation, among them general stores, restaurants, a drug store, livery barns, a harness shop, poolrooms, a garage, a laundry, and a lumberyard. The Weyburn Security Bank opened a branch in Shamrock in 1926, and the population of the community that year was 72. In 1928, a village school was established, relieving schoolchildren of a trip to a country school roughly five kilometres to the north. By then, a number of implement dealers were doing a brisk business. Following the Depression through to the early 1970s, the population of the community remained fairly stable at around 100, peaking in 1961 at 126. For several years during this period, however, from December 31, 1953, to December 31, 1959, Shamrock had relinquished

its village status and had reverted to being a hamlet within the jurisdiction of the rural municipality. On January 1, 1960, Shamrock was incorporated as a village for a second time. During the 1950s, the Saskatchewan Power Corporation had taken over the supply of electricity to the community and had brought power to area farms. In 1965, Highway 363 was paved, and that year an indoor rink was opened in the village, the result of much volunteer labour. Gone were the days of hockey games and skating outside. By the mid-1970s, though, the population of both the village and the district were in decline and businesses in Shamrock were folding. People were increasingly seeking the amenities that Hodgeville, Gravelbourg, and Moose Jaw had to offer. Due to declining enrollment, Shamrock's school was closed in 1977. The last elevator in Shamrock closed at the end of the harvest in 1989, and at the end of the year the rail line through the region was abandoned. By June 1990, the track and ties, and the culverts from under the rail bed had been pulled up and removed. Shamrock's population fell by more than half over this

period — from 74 in 1986 to just 34 in 1991. According to the 2001 Census of Canada, there were 17 private dwellings left in Shamrock that year; today, a credit union, a Co-op bulk station, and a grocery store with the postal outlet are the only businesses remaining in the community. Situated to the southeast on the Wood River, Shamrock Regional Park remains an attractive, popular, well-maintained and well-equipped park, featuring a natural nine-hole golf course, an outdoor swimming pool, camping facilities, and ball diamonds. Livestock and crop production remain the basis of the area economy. The Village of Shamrock remains the administrative centre of the RM of Shamrock No. 134.

SHAUNAVON, town, pop 1,691 (2006c), 1,775 (2001c), seemed to explode into existence on the open prairie. Located in southwest Saskatchewan, 53 km south of Gull Lake, and 75 km north of the Canada-U.S. border, Shaunavon is situated in a level to gently rolling landscape. The brown loam soils traditionally supported mixed-grass prairie and there was nothing but open land until 1913. On September 17 that year, townsite lots were put up for sale by the CPR in Gull Lake. The railway had decided the barren piece of land would be a divisional point on its Weyburn-Lethbridge line. The very next day, the first issue of *Shaunavon Standard* proclaimed that 370 business and residential lots had been purchased within eight hours. A flurry of construction began and in exactly two months, on November 27, 1913, the community was incorporated as a village. At the same time, the first work train arrived carrying the steel rails to be laid as the railway progressed westward, and the commu-

nity already boasted a school, a church, a post office, the newspaper and about sixty other businesses. On November 1, 1914, Shaunavon was incorporated as a town, with a population of over 700 comprised of people of British, Scandinavian, French Canadian, and German origins. The same year, the first rodeo was held. This was cowboy country, and local lore recounts that until cowboys had the rodeo at which to express their particular skills, they would vent their energies by shooting up

the town or by riding their horses into hotel bars. Other aspects of the "wild west" were also evident in the early days. During the years of prohibition, bootlegging was commonplace, and even after prohibition was repealed in Saskatchewan, bootleggers turned to the U.S. market where alcohol would be illegal for several more years. Early settlers also dug lignite coal out of the hills around Shaunavon to heat their homes. Later, larger mines were established and coal was mined for profit. Over the decades, grain farming became perhaps as important as ranching, and

SHAUNAVON TOWN HALL, situated in the former 1927 court house. Photograph taken September 2, 2004.

SHAUNAVON

...boomtown in the Bone Creek Basin

LUMBER STACKED HIGH along Second Street in Shaunavon during the community's formative days attests to the rapidity of the building boom.

▼ DEVELOPMENT BY 1914.

◄ **FRONTIER DAY**, the forerunner of today's "Boomtown Days" and the Shaunavon Rodeo, 1916. The parade remains an annual event.

locally-produced wheat won top awards at international agricultural shows. Eight grain elevators lined the railway tracks in Shaunavon by the 1950s. With the discovery of oil in the region in 1952, Shaunavon again experienced a substantial rise in its population, coupled with a housing boom. The population jumped from 1,625 in 1951 to a peak of 2,318 in 1966. The oil industry remains important to this day. In 1981, another milestone in the development of the town was the construction of the Shaunavon Industrial Park, comprised of 65 acres of serviced land.

▲ **CENTRE STREET**, Shaunavon, 1946.

▲ **GRAIN ELEVATORS AT SUNSET.** Photograph taken September 1, 2004.

◄ ► **IN FEBRUARY 2004**, the town was the centre of national attention when visiting NHL personalities and the CBC produced a fifteen-hour live television broadcast entitled "Hockey Day in Canada," emphasizing Shaunavon's long hockey tradition (left). In attendance was Hayley Wickenheiser (right), who was born in the community and is an Olympic gold medallist and a member of Canada's national women's hockey team since 1995. Photographs courtesy of Gary M. Houston, Cypress Hills Interprovincial Park; scanned from the collection at the Grand Coteau Heritage and Cultural Centre, Shaunavon.

Today, Shaunavon has the appearance of a mature community. Three buildings have been declared heritage properties: the Shaunavon Court House, completed in 1927, which since 1958 has also served as the town hall; the Grand Hotel, built in 1929; and the Shaunavon Hotel, built in 1915. Tree-lined streets adorn attractive residential neighbourhoods. Shaunavon has three schools: public and Catholic elementary schools, and a high school which shares space and facilities with the Cypress Hills Regional College. There is a hospital, a special care home, two medical clinics, a pharmacy, and a variety of health care practitioners. Emergency services are provided by the Shaunavon and District Ambulance service and the Shaunavon and District Fire Department. Policing is provided by the local detachment of the RCMP. Shaunavon Airport has a 3,000-ft. lighted airstrip, and according to Statistics Canada there are over 200 businesses registered in the community. The town also has a wide range of facilities for recreation, as well as social and cultural events. The Grand Coteau Heritage and Cultural Centre houses a library, a museum, an art gallery, and a tourist information centre. There are a number of service clubs and church organizations. The Darkhorse Theatre group puts on successful performances each spring and fall, and, continuing the tradition begun in 1914, the Shaunavon Pro Rodeo is held each July. Shaunavon serves as the administrative centre for the RM of Grassy Creek No. 78.

SHEHO, village, pop 121 (2006c), 148 (2001c), is located 24 km southeast of Foam Lake on Hwy 16. The name Sheho is derived from the Nakota word for the prairie chicken. The influx of settlers

▲ **UNICK'S FOODS**, Sheho, Merle and Peter Unick proprietors. Photograph taken July 30, 2004. Peter Unick served on the Sheho village council from 1973 to 1976 and was the mayor of the community from 1977 until 2006.

▲ **ONE OF SHEHO'S EARLIEST BUSINESS VENTURES** was The Great West Trading Company. Photograph circa 1904, courtesy of the Foam Lake Museum.

▼ **PERFORMERS IN BLACKFACE IN SHEHO**, 1923 or 1924. Photograph obtained from Emil Sebulsky courtesy of Helen Wunder, Sheho area.

into the district began after the Manitoba and North Western Railway reached Yorkton in 1890. German Protestants in North Dakota were among the first attracted to the area (there were also some expatriate Canadians who came up from the United States); a large number of Ukrainians came to the district beginning in 1896. A post office, originally known as Sheho Lake, was established in 1891; a school district known by the same name was formed in 1892. Both were located about two and a half miles north of the present community, near the small lake from which their names were derived. Although the early settlers had been promised that the railway would shortly be extended from Yorkton into the district, it would be a decade before the line became a reality; long treks to Yorkton and back for supplies were a necessity for the district's early pioneers. In 1903, the long-awaited railway was finally being built into the area; the surveyed route, however, ran south of Sheho Lake. The first buildings began to appear on the townsite in 1903. The trains were running in 1904. That year, the railway station, the first grain elevator, hotel, general store, drugstore, and the first church (Methodist) were built, the local school district was formed, and a detachment of the Royal North-West Mounted Police was established. Sheho became an incorporated village on June 30, 1905; by 1907, the Crown Bank of Canada had established a branch, the *Sheho Standard* newspaper was being published weekly, and the Sheho Football (soccer) Team won a provincial championship. Sheho remained at the end of the rail line for a few years, serving as a springboard and early supply centre for a broad area until the railway pushed further westward in 1907-08. From a population of 120 in 1906, the village grew steadily (although

▲ **STUDENTS AT SHEHO SCHOOL**, October 1943. Photograph obtained from Emil Sebulsky courtesy of Helen Wunder, Sheho area.

▼ **SHEHO GRAIN ELEVATORS CIRCA 1963.** The last was torn down in about 1997. Photograph courtesy of Peter Unick, Sheho.

growth was stalled in the 1930s), and Sheho reached a peak population of 407 in 1956. Throughout the latter half of the twentieth century, though, the community steadily declined. Four grain elevators (the community's economic backbone) lined the railway tracks in the 1960s; the last was demolished about 1997. The school closed in 2000; today, students are bused to Foam Lake. The village retains a core of essential businesses and had two active churches (Ukrainian Catholic and Ukrainian Orthodox) in 2007. Sheho is situated in the RM of Insinger No. 275.

SHELL LAKE, village, pop 152 (2006c), 185 (2001c), is situated just north of the junction of Hwys 3 and 12, approximately 32 km east of Spiritwood and 90 km west of Prince Albert. The village is situated in a gently rolling landscape of forest, farmlands, and numerous lakes. The community lies adjacent to Memorial Lake Regional Park, and with several other regional parks, provincial recreation areas, and several hundred cottages also in the Shell Lake vicinity, tour-ism factors largely in the local economy. The Shell Lake district, named for a lake several kilometres southwest of the community, was well-settled for a number of years — the post office and a rural school district were established in 1913 — but it was not until the coming of the railway in the late 1920s that the present village began to take shape. For a period of time, Canwood, on the rail line running to Big River, had been the nearest railway point where farmers could haul grain to and pick up many supplies. However, in 1927, with the railway approaching from Spirit-wood, the townsite of Shell Lake sprang into being. The track into the community was laid in 1928. In 1929, the first grain elevators began to go up, and in 1930 the Canadian National Railway station, now a municipal heritage property housing a museum, was constructed. Shell Lake quickly grew to include stockyards, res-taurants, stores, a livery stable, a lumber-yard, numerous other small businesses, and homes. In the late 1920s and early 1930s, while the world economic crisis was beginning to take hold, there was a building boom going on in Shell Lake. Although the Depression and the drought did come to exact a toll on those in the Shell Lake area, people continued to move into the district, fleeing the dust-blown southern plains. By 1940, the community had grown large enough to attain village status, and Shell Lake was incorporated as such on October 18 that year. Continu-ing to grow steadily thereafter, the com-munity reached a peak population of 264 in 1966. Then tragedy struck. In the early morning hours of August 15, 1967, one of the saddest and most vicious mass mur-ders in Canadian history took place at a farmhouse just west of Shell Lake. James Peterson, his wife, Evelyn, and seven of their children, aged one to 17 years, were shot at close range and killed. Nearly all of the children were killed as they lay sleep-ing in their beds. One child, four-year-old Phyllis Peterson, sleeping between her siblings, survived. Mr. Peterson was found dead in the kitchen, and Mrs. Pe-terson and a one-and-a-half-year-old boy were found in the backyard. News of the tragedy quickly spread across the country, the continent, and abroad. A neighbour, Wildrew Lang, had discovered the lonely farmhouse killings at about 9 a.m. in the morning, when he had come to call on Mr. Peterson to begin haying operations. A few days later, the same day as the nine members of the Peterson family were laid to rest, the RCMP solved the crime and ar-rested Victor Ernest Hoffman, a 21-year-old, at his parents' home in Leask, about 65 kilometres southwest of Shell Lake. Thus ended a tragic, short chapter in the community's history. Hoffman had been released from a mental hospital just three weeks before the murders. Today, Shell Lake is a thriving, vibrant community that is the scene of a tremendous amount of activity throughout all seasons. A choir, a theatre troupe, and curling and figure skating clubs are among the many orga-nizations active in the village. Shell Lake is the home to a vibrant artistic commu-nity, and the village sits in the middle of what has become known as the Thick-wood Hills Studio Trail. Traversed by sev-eral hundreds of visitors each August, the "Trail" winds its way through the district's scenic backroads, linking the studios of a wide range of artists. Painters, sculptors, woodworkers, and clothing designers are among those featured, and the studio trail tour has won the Saskatchewan Tourism Award for Excellence. In 1999, volunteers built a gazebo in the village of Shell Lake specifically designed for craft demon-strations, and featured exhibitions have included blacksmiths, wood turners and wood carvers, craftspeople, and collectors who work with rocks, gems, and fossils. For a village of its size, Shell Lake also hosts an impressive array of annual festivities. During the winter months, there is an ice-sculpting event, a popular ice-fishing derby, a dinner theatre, and numerous curling bonspiels. Beginning in May, a weekly flea market is held in the Métis Hall, and in June the Shell Lake Métis Trail Ride takes place. Throughout the summer months, a number of golf tournaments are held, and in July the three-day Homecoming Homesteader Hey Days features entertainment, a parade, community breakfasts and a dinner, among numerous other activities. Shell Lake hosts an annual fall supper, in addition to Novemberfest, a gala dinner-and-dance event sponsored by the Lions Club. Additional district attractions include numerous lakes which support a wide range of fish species, trail rides, guest ranches and bed and breakfast accommodations, snowmobile rallies, and good hunting. Shell Lake is situated in the RM of Spiritwood No. 496.

SHELLBROOK, town, pop 1,215 (2006c), 1,276 (2001c), is located 44 km west of Prince Albert and is served by Hwys 3, 40, and 55. Settlers began arriving in the area in the late 1800s, and in 1894 a post office named after the Shell Brook was established. The Shell Brook (which is actually more of a river) passes just to the north of the present community, flowing east into the Sturgeon River, which in turn flows into the North Saskatchewan west of Prince Albert. The community is situated near the northern edge of agricultural settlement in the province. As the early settlers arrived, the land had to be cleared of the jack pine forests before

crops could be planted. The trees, however, provided an early cash crop, and logs were rafted into Prince Albert where many were converted into railway ties. Larger numbers of settlers began to arrive in the district in the early 1900s, with significant representation from people of British and Scandinavian origins. In 1909, the first buildings began to go up on the townsite as the railway approached, and on November 18 that year Shellbrook was incorporated as a village. By 1910, the Canadian Northern Railway was servicing Shellbrook from Prince Albert, and with the arrival of the railway the community developed as a service centre for the surrounding agricultural region. On April 1, 1948, the community attained town status. Today, approximately 50 businesses

▶ **THE SHELLBROOK HOTEL** on the northeast corner of Main Street and Railway Avenue, 1913. The hotel still stands, and is still in business, although the wooden balconies no longer exist.

▶ **FIRE!** Shellbrook businesses burst into flames on January 3, 1915. Fires plagued many Saskatchewan communities during the first decades of the twentieth century when fire-fighting equipment was either non-existent or inadequate to deal with the conflagrations generated by compact rows of wooden structures. Often, entire blocks of buildings were lost.

▶ **A SUMMER MORNING** in Shellbrook, July 25, 2004.

Historical photographs courtesy of the Shellbrook and District Museum.

provide a wide range of goods, services, and professional expertise. The community's largest employers are the educational institutions and the health care facilities. Two automobile dealerships and a construction company also provide a significant number of local jobs, although some community residents commute to work

in Prince Albert. Shellbrook's elementary and composite schools provide K-12 education to 500 town and area students, and the town has a hospital, medical clinics, a special care home, an ambulance service, an RCMP detachment, and a volunteer fire department. Shellbrook has six churches, and a variety of service clubs

and community-based organizations. The town has a library, and its museum is located in the former Canadian Northern Railway station built in 1909. Shellbrook has a range of recreational facilities, and the town's golf course is rated as one of the finest in the province. Additionally, Prince Albert National Park is just a short drive north of the community, and there are seven regional parks and numerous lakes in the district, accommodating fishing, swimming, boating and camping. A snowmobile club maintains groomed trails, and the Shellbrook Fish and Game Club has gun and archery ranges, helps restock area lakes, and works alongside Ducks Unlimited. Shellbrook hosts an annual agricultural fair in June. One of Canada's most respected writers, James Sinclair Ross, was born in the Wild Rose school district just northeast of Shellbrook in 1908. Shellbrook serves as the administrative centre of the RM of Shellbrook No. 493.

SHIELDS, resort village, is located just east of Dundurn on the northwest side of the Blackstrap Reservoir, more commonly known as Blackstrap Lake. The reservoir was formed in 1967 as part of a system of canals and reservoirs originating at Lake Diefenbaker and terminating at Little Manitou Lake. In 1968, the townsite of Shields was surveyed and lots were put up for sale. In 1978, Shields was established as an organized hamlet, and in 1981 it was incorporated as a resort village. The 2006 Census recorded 172 permanent residents; however, the population varies greatly depending on the season. A number of people who live in Shields commute to work in Saskatoon. Shields is situated in the RM of Dundurn No. 314.

SHIPMAN, organized hamlet, pop 15 (2006c), 15 (2001c), is located approximately 70 km northeast of Prince Albert on Hwy 55. Settlers began arriving in the area during the 1920s, and with the construction of the railway between Nipawin and Prince Albert in the early 1930s the hamlet began to develop. The Shipman Post Office was established on March 1, 1933. The school district was organized in 1934, and the school became operational the following year. Initially, the area timber stands were key to the local economy: a sawmill operation was located in Shipman, and cordwood was cut and hauled into the hamlet to be loaded into boxcars for shipment. As the bush in the district was cleared, however, mixed farming became the main industry in the area, and in 1935 the Saskatchewan Wheat Pool built its first elevator in the community. Fires plagued Shipman over the years, and numerous businesses burned, including three grocery stores, a restaurant,

a service station, a poolroom, the town hall, and a grain elevator and annex. Yet, despite the numerous setbacks, Shipman was once a busy place — trains came and went, sports teams in the hamlet competed with others in the district, and community picnics were held at Birch Bark Lake, just to the northwest. In the latter half of the twentieth century, however, the hamlet was to suffer a steadily declining population, the centralization of services, and the abandonment of rail service. In 1975, the school was closed, and students were then bused to Smeaton. In 1981 Shipman's elevator was closed. In the 1990s, the CPR abandoned the line that had earlier served the community. Shipman is situated in the RM of Torch River No. 488.

SILTON, village, pop 91 (2006c), 94 (2001c), is situated approximately 50 km northwest of Regina, a little east of the south end of Last Mountain Lake on Hwy 322. The settlers who began arriving

▲ **SILTON UNITED CHURCH.**
Photograph taken July 10, 2003.

in the area in the 1880s were mainly of English and Scottish origins; later, some of the German settlers who had taken up land in the Bulyea-Strasbourg area moved into the district, after the promised railway through that region failed to materialize. The Longlaketon Post Office was the first established in the Silton area, in 1884; in 1886 the Longlaketon Church was built; and in 1890 the Longlaketon School District was set up. In 1888, Charles Benjafield, who had first come to the area in

▲ **SHIPMAN TODAY** consists of a few homes, and a small white Presbyterian Church on an overgrown lot, above left. The boarded up Shipman Hotel, above right, sign swinging in the wind, sits along sidewalks cracked with weeds, a silent testimonial to the community's busier days. Photographs taken July 18, 2003.

1883, started another post office a little southwest of the present village of Silton, closer to the lake, which he named Silton after his previous home in Silton, Dorset, England. In the early 1900s, there was also a "port" of Silton, located where the resort village of Saskatchewan Beach is today; it was a regular stopping place for the steamboats and barges that transported passengers and freight on the lake until the coming of the railway. The CPR built its link between Regina and Bulyea in 1910-11; with its construction, the present-day townsite of Silton was established and began to be built up, its name taken from the Benjafield post office which was moved into the locale. Among the first businesses established were a hotel, lumberyard, general store, hardware store, and butcher shop. The first grain elevator was erected in 1911; a second went up in 1912. The Silton School District was established in 1912, and the school opened in early 1913. On July 2, 1914, Silton became an incorporated village. By 1926, the population was 102. A Catholic church was built in 1924; a United Church was constructed in Silton in 1928. From 1959 until 1968 there was also a Lutheran church in the community. Silton's population remained fairly stable from the 1920s until the early 1960s, then during the decade it dropped dramatically — from 97 in 1961 to only 59 by 1971. Grade 12 students began to be bused to Strasbourg in 1962; they were followed by grades 9, 10, and 11 in 1964. By 1968 only grades one to four were being taught at Silton School, and the school was closed in 1969. Grades one to six then went to Bulyea, seven through twelve to Strasbourg. The community languished through the 1970s — the population was still 59 in 1981 — but in the mid-1980s the community experienced a period of growth, as it began to fall within

the sphere of commuters working in Regina. Today, the village retains a small core of businesses selling gas, groceries, and meals. Silton is situated in the RM of Longlaketon No. 219.

SIMMIE, organized hamlet, pop 15 (2006c), 10 (2001c), is located southwest of Swift Current on Hwy 343. Immediately to the north lies the Duncairn Reservoir Migratory Bird Sanctuary. The district began to be settled around 1906-07 and grew to be comprised significantly of Norwegian and German-speaking populations. Simmie developed with the construction of a CPR subdivision from south of Swift Current in the early 1930s. The post office was established in 1933. The community had a school, and four grain elevators lined the tracks by 1942. Simmie was established as an organized hamlet in 1950 and had a population of 125 in 1969. The community's numbers and small business sector subsequently began to decline, and by 1996, the year the rail line was abandoned, the population had fallen to 25. Simmie is situated in the RM of Bone Creek No. 108.

SIMPSON, village, pop 118 (2006c), 194 (2001c), is located 25 km south of Watrous on Hwy 2, to the west of the north end of Last Mountain Lake. Settlement of the district began in 1903-04. Many were lured to the area by the efforts of the Saskatchewan Valley Land Company headed by Colonel Andrew Duncan Davidson, for whom the town of Davidson was named. Settlers were people of Scandinavian origin from the United States, expatriate Canadians who had spent perhaps a generation south of the border, and many from Ontario and the British Isles. In the

early days, supplies were hauled in from Davidson, then Nokomis or Watrous. With the construction of the CPR line up the west side of Last Mountain Lake in 1910-11, Simpson had its beginnings. The railway named the locale in honour of Sir George Simpson (c.1787-1860), governor of the Hudson's Bay Company 1821-60. Within a few months the townsite was surveyed, the lots were sold, and buildings were erected. The first businesses were started in 1910; the Simpson Post Office was established on April 1, 1911. On July 11, 1911, Simpson was incorporated; by November that year, trains were running. In 1912, the Simpson School District was formed; prior to this, students attended Seaforth School, located about a mile and a half east of the village. The first grain elevators were erected in 1912; there would eventually be six. In 1913, a newspaper, the *Simpson Recorder*, began publishing; by 1914, the village had more than twenty businesses. In 1916, the community numbered 161 residents; by 1926 the population was 228. The 1930s would prove to be trying, however. Businesses, including the Royal Bank, closed in the early 1930s; a fire in 1932 wiped out half of the main-street businesses; afterwards, only one of the businessmen affected remained in the community. The population of the village slipped somewhat, and only about 15 businesses were left by 1940. The Simpson Co-operative Association had been formed by necessity in 1938, but without a bank, residents were left to seek financial services elsewhere, until the Simpson Credit Union was established in 1960. The business section in the village changed very little during the 1940s, but the population of Simpson grew and continued to grow into the 1950s, reaching a peak of 371 in 1956. The increasing mechanization of farms, however, was leading

to larger and fewer farms, which meant less business for Simpson's merchants. In the early 1960s, two hardware stores, a general store, and a lumberyard closed. In 1961, the CPR discontinued passenger service, and the railway station was sold and moved to an area farm where it sat for years being used for grain storage (the station was saved in 2002, when the Town of Ogema purchased it and moved it into their community, where it has undergone a thorough restoration). By 1971, Simpson's population had fallen to 239, but it then stabilized until the 1990s, when it began to plummet. The loss of population between 2001 and 2006 represents a decline of almost 40 per cent. In the fall of 2003, Simpson's K-12 school was down to 45 students — the following summer the school was closed. A company that manufactures custom fibreglass speaker enclosures for automobiles purchased the building. CN took over the rail line in the late 1980s; a decade later, the line was abandoned and the tracks were then torn up. A sole remaining grain-handling facility is now privately owned. The Pioneer Grain Company retains a facility for selling agricultural chemicals; other businesses in the community today include a credit union, insurance broker, hotel/bar, café, welding shop, liquor vendor, post office, a Co-op store, and a Co-op service station. The community has an active United Church, a library, community hall, curling rink, skating arena, and ball diamonds. An archive and museum is located in the 1911 rural municipality office, now a heritage property. A new municipal office was built in 1980. The nearest hospital and RCMP detachment are in Watrous; there is a health centre in Imperial; Simpson has a volunteer fire department. Simpson serves as the administrative centre of the RM of Wood Creek No. 281.

SINTALUTA, town, pop 98 (2006c), 145 (2001c), is located 16 km southeast of Indian Head on Hwy 1. Sintaluta had its beginnings in the early 1880s as the first settlers began arriving in advance of the railway. They were mainly of British origin from Ontario. The first post office established in 1885 was named Carson after Michael J. Carson, briefly the first postmaster; however, the name was changed to Sintaluta in 1888, the name derived from a Lakota Sioux term referring to a fox tail, which in turn referred to the nearby headwaters of the Redfox Creek, which flows north to the Qu'Appelle River. Sintaluta developed as a service centre for the surrounding agricultural district and attained town status in 1907. By 1911, the population was approaching 400, seven grain elevators lined the tracks, and the town had a large school and a substantial commercial sector. As well, Sintaluta had become well-known as a centre of farmers' agitation for economic and political rights. In 1902, Sintaluta farmers took the CPR to court for failing to provide enough grain cars, as had been stipulated under the Manitoba Grain Act, and when the farmers won, Edward Alexander Partridge, who played an important role in the case, emerged as a leader for western grain producers. In 1905, Sintaluta-area farmers sent Partridge to Winnipeg to study the operations of the grain exchange, and he determined that growers should control the sale of their own crops through their own company. When the Grain Growers' Grain Company was established in 1906, he became the first president. Sintaluta remained an important trading centre through to the 1960s, but by the 1970s both the population of the community and the number of local businesses began to decline. Schoolchildren are now bused to Indian Head, and the town's two remaining grain elevators are now privately owned. Sintaluta has a number of fine brick and stone structures, many of them more than a century old. Sintaluta is situated in the RM of Indian Head No. 156.

▲ **THE OLD UNION BANK IN SINTALUTA**, on the northeast corner of Main Street and Durward, now houses the main collection of the Sintaluta Community Museum. Museum collections are also housed in an 1899 Anglican stone church in the town, as well as in the adjacent stone manse. Photograph taken October 3, 2003.

▼ **ORANGEMEN'S PARADE** in Sintaluta, 1910. The Union Bank is visible on the corner on the right hand side of the street. Saskatchewan Archives Board R-B7032.

SLED LAKE, northern settlement, pop 35 (2001c), is located 80 km north of the town of Big River, via 48 km of paved highway and then approximately 30 kilometres of gravel road. The community is situated at the mouth of a large bay (Appleby), on the southeast shore of Sled Lake, from which the settlement derives its name. The region is considered to contain one of the most pristine tracts of boreal forest remaining in the world today. The first known people to settle in the area were Métis from Ile-a-la-Crosse, who began arriving as early as the 1890s. Baptiste Mirasty, for whom a street in the settlement is named, and for whom nearby Mirasty Lake is likely named, arrived at Sled Lake in 1896. The Hudson's Bay Company established a fur-trading post at Sled Lake around 1908. In 1909, a trail was cut from Big River into Dore Lake, to the north of Sled Lake, and with the construction of the railway into Big River in 1910, access to the region was greatly improved. New immigrants to Canada and many farm labourers from southern Saskatchewan came north seeking winter employment in trapping, commercial fishing, logging, and freighting. A permanent settlement at the community's present location began to develop around the late 1930s and into the 1940s. Mink ranching was actively pursued for a number of years, and by the mid-1950s tourism was beginning to develop. Hunting and fishing lodges began to be established in the area, and, today, Sled Lake's outfitters are key to the local economy. Some residents of the community have maintained a traditional way of life based on harvesting, which includes hunting, fishing, trapping, and growing wild rice. Sled Lake was legally established as a northern settlement under the Northern Municipalities Act on October 1, 1983. A cottage subdivision bolsters the population with summer arrivals.

SLEEPY HOLLOW, organized hamlet, is located north of North Battleford, one of a number of resort communities on Murray Lake. It was established

as an organized hamlet in 1986. Twenty people claimed permanent residency in 2006; however, the population varies greatly depending on the season. Sleepy Hollow is situated in the RM of Meota No. 468.

SMEATON, village, pop 183 (2006c), 178 (2001c), is located 79 km east of Prince Albert and 63 km west of Nipawin just off the junction of Hwys 55 and 106. Smeaton sits in a narrow swath of agricultural land hewn between forests and lakes to the north and the Fort à la Corne Provincial Forest to the south. Highway 106, also known as the Hanson Lake Road, winds through a pristine wilderness north-eastward from Smeaton toward Creighton and Flin Flon. The first few settlers began arriving in the Smeaton area around 1923, but in the latter half of the decade, as plans were being formulated for the construction of a bridge across the Saskatchewan River at Nipawin, foreshadowing the construction of a rail line through the area to Prince Albert, many more people began arriving in the region. The CPR established the location of the Smeaton townsite in 1930, and development began immediately. General stores, a hardware store, a livery barn, a barber shop and pool room were built; the post office opened in 1931, and in 1932 the first grain elevator was erected. According to the local history, the locality had been known as Dorrit (no explanation is given as to why), but the CPR wanted the station to be called Smeaton, after Senator Richard Smeaton White, who had been appointed to the Senate by Prime Minister Borden in 1917 (Smeaton served until his death in 1936). Evidently, the community was told that if the name Smeaton was accepted, it might be given special consid-

erations. Smeaton did get the first station and section man on the line; however, it is possible that the community's central location on the stretch may have had much to do with it. The first scheduled train ran between Nipawin and Prince Albert in 1932, and that year the Smeaton School District was established. At the time, a flour and feed mill, a sawmill and a shingle mill were among the many businesses springing up. In 1933, in the midst of continuing construction, the RCMP detachment was established and the Women's Missionary Society of the United Church opened a hospital. On March 7, 1944, the Village of Smeaton was incorporated, and by 1946 the population had grown to 250. In the years following WWII, agriculture began replacing forestry as the dominant industry in the region. In 1951, the Smeaton Union Hospital opened, succeeding the Women's Missionary Society facility. At about the same time, the Saskatchewan Power Corporation took over the responsibility for supplying power to the community. In 1966, Smeaton reached a peak population of 335. In 1970 the CPR station was closed, and in 1973 tragedy struck the village when the landmark Smeaton Hotel burned and two young men lost their lives in the fire. The population of the village began to decline in the 1970s. A major community undertaking begun in 1977 was the construction of the recreation centre housing curling and skating rinks, a large auditorium/gymnasium, dressing rooms, a kitchen, and a club room. Although high school students had begun to be bused to Choiceland in 1963 — grades 11 and 12 at first, followed by grade 10 in 1967 and grade 9 in the mid-1970s — Smeaton School's enrollment remained stable at around 120 students from the mid-1970s to the mid-1980s. The school remained a K-8 facility

until the spring of 2004, but then, due to declining enrollment, grades 7 and 8 were sent to Choiceland that fall. In the fall of 2006, 39 students were enrolled in grades K-6 in Smeaton; at the end of the school year in 2007, Smeaton School was closed. Nonetheless, the community remains an important retail and service centre in the district. The village has a health centre with doctor's services, an adjacent special care home which is an important community employer, an RCMP detachment, a Saskatchewan Environment office, a credit union, post office, insurance agency, library, a modern hotel and restaurant, a craft store and tea room, a video store, and a Co-op store with a liquor outlet and a bulk fuel station, as well as a variety of home-based businesses. Key annual community events include a sports day at the end of June and a winter festival on the first weekend in March. Just northeast of Smeaton is a campground with a miniature golf course. Approximately 70 kilometres north of Smeaton on the Hanson Lake Road lies Narrow Hills Provincial Park, which has more than 1,780 campsites ranging from fully-serviced spots to isolated wilderness locations, and about 25 bodies of water which offer anglers the opportunity to fish for perhaps the greatest variety of fish species in the province. The Smeaton district's economy remains dominated by agriculture, with forestry remaining a factor. Regional mining developments, however, are becoming increasingly significant. Diamondiferous kimberlites were first discovered in the Fort à la Corne Provincial Forest in 1989, and it is now known that the area's diamond-bearing kimberlite clusters rank among the largest in the world. A consortium spearheaded by De Beers Canada Exploration Inc. and Kensington Resources Ltd. continues to explore the economic viability of

developing producing mining operations. Smeaton is situated in the RM of Torch River No. 488.

SMILEY, village, pop 50 (2006c), 55 (2001c), lies 40 km northwest of Kindersley on Hwy 307. The community's name honours one of the first homesteaders in the district, Ernest Everett Smiley (1877-1956) from Pettis County, Missouri, who took a homestead in the area in 1906. By the time the railway was built from Biggar to the Smiley townsite in 1912, the district was well-settled — the line was built through to Loverna on the Saskatchewan-Alberta border the following year. The Village of Smiley was incorporated on November 26, 1913; the post office was established on March 16, 1914, and that spring the school was built. The village developed as a small service and supply centre for the surrounding farming community, and the population grew to hover at a little over 100 until the early 1950s, when oil was discovered in the region and there was an ensuing boom. Then, for a period of about 10 years, Smiley could count over 200 residents (the peak was 232 in 1961), and the school was filled to such a capacity that a room in the basement had to be utilized. By the mid-1960s, however, the boom was over and the village population returned to its traditional level. By this time, though, Smiley's businesses were beginning to give way to centralization and the convenience with which one could access the goods and services offered in larger centres. Smiley School closed at the end of June 1982, and from the mid-1980s onward, Smiley's population has declined dramatically. Smiley ceased to be a grain-handling point when the rail line into the village was abandoned in the late 1990s. Businesses operating out of Smiley

◄ **AFTERMATH.**
On July 6, 1935, the village of Smiley was hit by an F3 tornado. Two were killed and damage to property was extensive. Photograph courtesy of the Kindersley & District Plains Museum.

today largely service the area oilfields. A major Smiley area attraction is the "Great Wall of Saskatchewan," located 1.6 kilometres west of the village. It was built over a 30-year period beginning in the early 1960s by Albert "Stonewall" Johnson, who had no idea what he was going to end up with when he began unearthing stones from an area he was excavating to enlarge a slough. Almost a half-mile long and 12 feet high in places (it averages about 6 feet in height), the wall has a base averaging about six to eight feet wide. It was deemed finished by its constructor in 1991 and is visible from space. Alongside the wall, adjacent to a picnic area, is a sod house "Bert" Johnson and others in the Smiley district built in 1986. Smiley serves as the administrative centre of the RM of Prairie-dale No. 321.

SNOWDEN, organized hamlet, pop 22 (2006c), 30 (2001c), is located north of the Fort à la Corne Provincial Forest between the village of Smeaton and the town of Choiceland, just north off Hwy 55. The first few settlers began arriving in the area in the early 1920s, but in the latter half of the decade, as plans were being formulated for the construction of a bridge across the Saskatchewan River at Nipawin, foreshadowing the construction of a rail line through the area to Prince Albert, many more people began arriving in the region to take up land. The first stores were established at what would become Snowden in 1929. In 1930, the CPR acquired the land for the townsite, and that year Robert English, one of the area's early homesteaders, became the first postmaster of the Snowden Post Office. English had named the location Snowden in memory of a Harry Snowden, a fellow homesteader who had reportedly been a good friend and who had drowned in the Saskatchewan River while working on the ferry at Nipawin. There has been some question as to the veracity of this story; however, a community profile published in 1955 recounts the tale and, as well, a history of the Nipawin district published in 1964 states that a "Mr. Snowden" had indeed worked on the ferry prior to 1930, when the service was discontinued as the bridge across the river had been completed. The hamlet of Snowden developed rapidly after regular train service began in 1932, and during the 1930s many more settlers began arriving in the region, a good number fleeing the drought-ravaged areas of southern Saskatchewan and Manitoba. The Star Hotel (still operating) opened in 1935, and that year schoolchildren began attending classes in the hamlet. They had previously attended Elkridge School, located several kilometres to the southeast. As Snowden developed, sports teams were organized: a competitive boys' hockey team, a girls' baseball team, and a championship-winning curling team among them. Logging had been the main industry in the Snowden area until enough land was cleared that farming became pre-eminent. Early photographs show that wood piles dominated the town landscape in 1937; but by 1938 agriculture had developed to the point that the first, and only, grain elevator was built — it closed in 1975. The community was in its prime during the 1930s, 1940s, and 1950s (it was established as an organized hamlet in 1951), but by the 1960s — the population was sitting at 100 in 1966 — it was apparent the community was beginning to decline. Steadily, people moved away. Businesses closed, churches closed, the school closed, and today, other than the hotel, a community hall and sports grounds, Snowden consists of only a small collection of homes, one of which houses the postal outlet. The small hamlet did, however, host a successful evening social, dance, pancake breakfast, and a family sports day in July 2005, as part of the province's centennial celebrations. Snowden is situated in the RM of Torch River No. 488.

SORENSON'S BEACH, organized hamlet, is one in a string of resort communities located along the east shore of the south end of Last Mountain Lake off Hwy 322. Development began in the 1960s, and Sorenson's Beach, named after an area farmer who was the original landowner, was established as an organized hamlet in 1980. There were approximately 30 year-round residents in 2006; however, the population varies depending on the season. There are currently about three dozen developed properties. Sorenson's Beach is situated in the RM of McKillop No. 220.

SOUTH LAKE, resort village, is one of a number of resort communities situated on the southwest shore of Buffalo Pound Lake. It is accessed via Hwy 2. According to the local history, the first permanent settlers in the area were a Mr. Charlie Nabess and family in the 1890s. At some point, Mr. Nabess started a dance hall and a summer concession, and in 1911 he began a ferry service to the opposite side of the lake. The ferry served farmers on the north side who wanted to haul their grain to the village of Tuxford, and it ran until the 1920s. A hunting lodge, which attracted hunters from the United States, was also started in 1911, and it was around this time that the first cottage development began to take place, with most renters or owners coming from Moose Jaw. However, the first major subdivision of individual lots at South Lake did not take place until 1958. In 1960, South Lake was established as an organized hamlet, and in 1989 it was incorporated as a resort village. In 2001, there were 47 year-round residents; in 2006, the number was 105. However, there are well over 200 property owners — as such, the population varies greatly depending on the season, reaching into the hundreds during the summer months. In winter, ice fishing is a popular activity. South Lake is located in the RM of Marquis No. 191.

SOUTH WATERHEN LAKE, organized hamlet, is a resort area situated within the eastern portion of Meadow Lake Provincial Park on the southwest shore of

Waterhen Lake. The main attraction is fishing. The lake itself is fairly large and consists of two sections divided by a narrows. The larger western half, upon which the resort is situated, is approximately 13 by 8 kilometres; the smaller section is about 6.5 by 5 kilometres. The lake is approximately 30.5 metres (100 feet) deep, producing firm northern pike and pickerel. There are cabin, boat, canoe, and kayak rentals at South Waterhen Lake, as well as campgrounds, a children's playground, a laundromat, and a store that has gasoline sales. There were only nine permanent residents at the resort in 2006; however, the population varies significantly depending on the season. South Waterhen Lake was established as an organized hamlet in 2005 and is situated in the RM of Meadow Lake No. 588.

SOUTHEND derives its name from its position at the south end of Reindeer Lake, 220 km northeast of La Ronge on Hwy 102, an all-weather gravel road. What is generally referred to as Southend actually consists of two separate legal entities: a mainland northern settlement and, on an island immediately east across a bridge, a far more populous First Nations reserve holding, Southend 200, one of several reserves held by the Peter Ballantyne Cree Nation in the region to the north and west of Flin Flon. The combined population at Southend is approximately 1,000. Chipewyan Dene (Denesuline) lived in the area until the advent of the fur trade, but as the fur traders moved in, so, too, did the Woods (or Woodlands) Cree, displacing the Dene. Both North West Company and Hudson's Bay Company posts were operating in the vicinity of the present community by 1800, and until recent years there was a Hudson's Bay Company store

at Southend. Although trappers and traders resided at the locale for many years (a post office was established at the Hudson's Bay Co. store in 1949), the population was quite nomadic until the 1960s, when a school was built. Until the 1970s, when the road was completed from La Ronge, Southend was either accessed by water or was a fly-in community. Today, commercial fishing, outfitting and guiding, the Noble Bay Graphite Mine, local businesses, and hunting and trapping provide most employment. Southend has a modern K-12 school, a community church, an RCMP detachment, a Saskatchewan Environment office and fire base, a local radio station, a confectionary with fuel sales, a restaurant, a campground, accommodations, area outfitters, and a sizable general store which supplies groceries, clothing, and miscellaneous items. Southend has air charter and local taxi services. The Arthur Morin Memorial Health Centre provides 24-hour emergency care and a range of programs including homecare, dental care, addictions counselling, mental health therapy, and approaches to holistic health. Doctors are flown in from La Ronge twice a week, from where ambulance service is based. Recreational activities in Southend include fishing, boating, hiking, swimming, hockey, cross-country skiing, and dog-sledding; the community hosts a range of annual events.

SOUTHEY, town, pop 711 (2006c), 693 (2001c), is located 55 kilometres north of Regina at the junction of Hwys 6 and 22. Settlers began arriving in the area around 1902-03, and by the time the Canadian Pacific Railway arrived in 1905 most of the available land in the area was taken up. The first building, a store, went up on the townsite in 1904 as railway

▲ **DRAYMEN** performed the important function of hauling goods in communities before the advent of truck transport. Pictured here, from left to right, is Southey drayman Frank Engel, with helpers Philip Zapf and Arnold McIlmoyl, 1926.

▼ **HERITAGE DAY**, July 7, 1990, at the Southey & District Museum, featured demonstrations of old methods of separating cream and washing clothes. Here, Jack Henshaw describes the procedure by which Doris Pycroft cleans a garment.

Photographs courtesy of the Southey & District Museum.

crews were working on the line coming along the north side of the Qu'Appelle Valley that would turn north at Last Mountain Lake and head on toward Lanigan. With the arrival of the railway the townsite was established, and one of the original settlers suggested the name Southey in honour of a favourite English poet, Robert Southey (1774-1843); subsequently, many of the community's streets were given the names of writers and poets, such as Coleridge, Burns, Browning, Kipling, and Keats. Southey was incorporated as a village on November 9, 1907. Homesteaders in the district were predominantly of German and Scandinavian origins, with lesser numbers of Romanians, Hungarians, and people hailing from the British Isles settling into the mix. The community developed rapidly in the years from 1905 to 1912, and in the ensuing decades Southey experienced steady growth, being incorporated as a town in 1980. Southey is situated on rich agricultural lands with a mixture of dark brown and black sandy loam and silty clay soils suitable for growing a variety of crops. Southey serves an area of about 1,500 people involved in mixed farming and the production of grain, specialty crops, and oilseeds. The town has a wide range of local businesses, with three automobile dealerships and two farm machinery dealers being significant employers. The dealerships are widely known and attract buyers from a considerable distance. The community also has an RCMP detachment, a volunteer fire department, a health centre, seniors' housing with special care considerations, and a team of first responders. Robert Southey School is a K-12 facility, which had 248 students enrolled in the fall of 2006. The town's original school, built in 1906, has been designated a heritage property and is now located on the town's museum

grounds. Southey has modern recreational facilities, a library, four churches, a seniors' club, and a number of service clubs and other community-based organizations. Some Southey residents commute to work in Regina. Southey is situated in the RM of Cupar No. 218.

SOVEREIGN, hamlet, pop 52 (2001c), is a former village located 24 km east of Rosetown on Hwy 15. The first settlers began arriving in 1905, many following what was known as the "Old Bone Trail" that ran south-westward from Saskatoon. The trail was known as such for the bison bones which were collected along it and shipped to eastern Canada to be made into lampblack and fertilizer. Others detrained at Hanley and crossed the South Saskatchewan River on the Rudy Ferry near present-day Outlook; a few forded the river. Those who came to the Sovereign district were largely English-speaking, hailing from eastern Canada, the United States, and Great Britain. The Canadian Pacific Railway came through in 1910-11, and with it the townsite developed. The railway gave Sovereign its regal-sounding name — the village council followed suit, naming the streets King,

▶ **THE LAST REMAINING GRAIN ELEVATOR** in Sovereign, dating to 1963, was formerly operated by the Saskatchewan Wheat Pool. Photograph taken July 20, 2004.

Queen, Monarch, Empress, Imperial, Prince, Regent, and Consort. The Sovereign Post Office was established on May 1, 1911, having moved in from the countryside, where it had been operating under the name of Haddington since 1907. Sovereign was incorporated as a village on March 29, 1912, and in 1913 the local school district was established. Classes were held in the Presbyterian church until the school was completed in 1914. The population of Sovereign was 148 by 1916, and in 1931 it reached 184, which would be the community's highest. The opening dance at the Sovereign Community Hall had been held on August 21, 1928. By 1941, the community's numbers had fallen to 127; during the 1940s the village rebounded — its population was up to 171 by 1951. In 1955, high school students began to be bused to Rosetown (a few years later they were sent to Milden), and in the late 1950s Sovereign's population began to decline. By the 1960s the village's businesses were closing to those in nearby Rosetown. A new three-room school was built in Sovereign in 1959, but by 1967 students in grades 7 and 8 were being bused to Milden. Enrollment further declined and Sovereign school was closed in 1969. By 1976, the village numbered

69 residents. On December 31, 2005, Sovereign relinquished village status, and today it is a residential community, somewhat of a bedroom community to Rosetown. A few long-abandoned businesses dot the townsite, and sidewalks run along vacant lots. The post office remains, as does a sole grain elevator, a former Saskatchewan Wheat Pool structure dating to 1963. Sovereign is situated in the RM of St. Andrews No. 287.

SPALDING, village, pop 237 (2006c), 261 (2001c), is located between Watson and Naicam on Hwy 6. The first settlers arrived in the district between 1904 and 1906, and Spalding had its origins a few kilometres northeast of its present location. In 1906, one of the early settlers, J. W. Hutchison, opened the first store and post office in the area, naming the office after his wife Pattie's birthplace, Spalding, England. The same year, Spalding School was opened at the same location. By the time the CPR came through in 1919-20, settlers of Norwegian, German, British, and French origins had taken up land in the district, and "Old Spalding" had developed into a sizable community with a bank, a café, a doctor's office, a blacksmith, a butcher, and a telephone system. However, with the rail line passing to the west, a move was necessitated and "Old Spalding" vanished as most everything was moved to the rail line. It appears the CPR may have had plans to name the townsite Magellan, but when the post office was moved in from the old settlement, the name Spalding was adopted for the new location. On March 11, 1924, the Village of Spalding was incorporated. Spalding became the service and supply centre for the surrounding agricultural district, and its population grew steadily

SPEERS, village, pop 74 (2006c), 71 (2001c), is located approximately 53 km east of North Battleford, off Hwy 40. The first few homesteaders began trickling into the district around 1902. The origins of the community date to 1903 when Reverend John Grenfell of Ottawa toured the area looking for land for his congregation. He was impressed by the district and, in 1904, brought a number of his parishioners westward to form the nucleus of a settlement known as "New Ottawa." Independent settlers also arrived, among them a large number of Ukrainians, and between 1905 and 1910 much of the

available land in the area was taken up for homesteads. In 1913, with the extension of the railway from Prince Albert to North Battleford, the townsite was formally established, and in 1914 it was renamed in honour of C. Wesley Speers, a prominent immigration official at the time. The Village of Speers was incorporated in 1915. Four grain elevators and a number of other businesses were established, and Speers became an area hub of commercial and social activity. In the mid-1920s, the Prince Albert Creamery Co. set up an operation in the village, and the creamery prospered and was an important community employer until it was destroyed by fire in 1950. Never particularly large, Speers

▲ ▼ **THE LEGION MEMORIAL HALL** (above) in Speers has been home to the Speers and District Museum since 1993. Also situated at the museum site in the village is this replica of a British American gas station (below). Photographs taken August 25, 2004.

▲ **SPALDING UNITED CHURCH**, at the west end of Centre Street, was built in 1926. The cornerstone of the church was laid by Joseph William Hutchison, using a trowel that his late wife's mother had used while laying the cornerstone of a church near Spalding, Lincolnshire, England. Pattie Hutchison died in 1920, leaving behind five sons and six daughters, the youngest of whom was only two years of age. Photograph taken August 6, 2004.

until the early 1960s, when it peaked at over 400. Today, residents have access to basic shopping and services within their community, but they travel to Naicam or Watson for additional needs or to Melfort or Humboldt for a full range of goods and services. Spalding has a health centre and a volunteer fire department; ambulance services are available from both Naicam

and Watson; police service is provided by the Naicam RCMP. The community has a library, a seniors' centre, skating and curling rinks, a bowling alley, and a number of service clubs and community-based organizations. In 2001, however, after 95 years in existence, Spalding School was closed. There are three local churches in the village, and Spalding United Church, built in 1926, was designated a heritage property in 1991. Also a heritage property is the former residence of Reynold Rapp. Rapp was elected to the Canadian House of Commons for the constituency of Humboldt-Melfort in 1958 and served in the Diefenbaker government. He also acted as the Progressive Conservative Party whip in 1967-68. Rapp donated his home to the village of Spalding in 1971 for use as a museum, which was officially opened by the Honourable John George Diefenbaker the same year. Spalding serves as the administrative centre of the RM of Spalding No. 368.

▲ **THE FAMOUS CROOKED TREES.** Northeast of Speers lies one of Saskatchewan's true oddities — a strange and unusual grove of gnarled and twisted aspens whose appearance long remained a mystery. Locals had conjectured that contaminated soils, a meteorite impact, and perhaps even an alien visitation was responsible for the deformity; it is now believed, however, that the peculiar trees are the result of a genetic mutation. Photograph taken August 25, 2004.

reached a peak population of 175 in 1961. Subsequently, however, the community has been in decline. In 1969, high school students began to be bused to the town of Hafford, the beginning of a slow end to Speers School. No elevators line the tracks of the village today, and the business community has virtually disappeared. Vacant lots now line the once-busy streets. The administrative office for the RM of Douglas No. 436, however, remains in the village. Today, essential goods and services are largely obtained in Hafford, roughly 15 kilometres to the east, where the nearest hospital and RCMP detachment are also located. The Battlefords, too, are only a short drive away. The major industry in the Speers area is agriculture, a combination of grain and livestock production.

SPIRITWOOD, town, pop 911 (2006c), 907 (2001c), is located 125 km west of Prince Albert and about 110 km northeast of North Battleford at the junction of Hwys 3, 24, and 378. The community is situated in a parkland setting, and as the largest community in the region, Spiritwood functions as the major supply, service, and administrative centre for a trading area population of several thousand, including four First Nations communities. Spiritwood's economy is derived from retail trade, government services, tourism, and the agricultural operations in the district. Mixed farming predominates and consists primarily of grain production followed by the raising of cattle. A Spiritwood company that focuses on pig genetics, producing breeding stock and commercial swine, has roughly 50 employees. There is some forestry in the region north of Spiritwood. The district began to be settled around 1911-12; however, growth in the area was slow until the

coming of the railway in the late 1920s. The first settlers engaged primarily in ranching. The Spiritwood Post Office was established in 1923 and was named after Spiritwood, North Dakota, the hometown of the first postmaster, Rupert J. Dumond. After the railway arrived, settlers of diverse origins poured into the district and many businesses were established. On October 1, 1935, Spiritwood was incorporated as a village, and by September 1, 1965, the community had grown large enough to attain town status. Spiritwood has a hospital with an attached special care home, a medical clinic, an ambulance service, and an additional range of health care facilities and practitioners. The town has an RCMP detachment and a fire department. There are a number of churches, service clubs and other community-based organizations. The town has a complete range of recreational facilities; additionally, there are six golf courses in the district, six regional parks, and about 35 lakes within an hour's drive. The region is popular for fishing and hunting, snowmobiling,

▲ **A RAINY MORNING.** Looking south up Main Street, Spiritwood.

◀ **"SPIRIT OF THE NORTH"** is the slogan adopted by the town of Spiritwood, and this statue of a howling wolf is situated at the community's visitors' centre.

Photographs taken July 25, 2003.

and camping. Spiritwood has public and Catholic K-6 schools, a public high school, and a library. Post-secondary classes and programs are available through the local office of the Northwest Regional College, and the Saskatchewan Communications Network (SCN) broadcasts televised credit courses from the province's universities and the Saskatchewan Institute of Applied Science and Technology (SIAST). Spiritwood serves as the administrative centre of the RM of Spiritwood No. 496.

SPRING BAY, organized hamlet, is one in a string of resort communities located along the east shore of Last Mountain Lake off Hwy 322. Initial development began in the late 1950s, and Spring Bay was established as an organized hamlet in 1981. By 2005 approximately 40 properties had been developed and there were a small number of year-round residents. Nineteen were recorded in 2006. The population, however, varies depending on the season. Spring Bay is situated in the RM of McKillop No. 220.

SPRING VALLEY, hamlet, pop 13 (2007, unofficial), 16 (1991c), is located approximately 70 km south of Moose Jaw, nestled between the Dirt and Cactus Hills. Settlers began arriving about 1905; among them were a significant concentration of German Catholics and a smaller number of German Lutherans. Spring Valley developed as the Canadian Northern Railway was constructing its line between Avonlea and Gravelbourg; the townsite of Spring Valley was bought from homesteader Martin Lorenz Beitel. The grade for the railway was built in 1911; in 1912 the rails were laid and construction trains were hauling in supplies; and in

▲ **THE HEADQUARTERS FOR THE RURAL MUNICIPALITY OF TERRELL NO. 101** are located in this building in Spring Valley.

▼ **EASTER SUNDAY** at Mater Dolorosa Roman Catholic Church in Spring Valley.

Spring Valley photographs taken April 11 (Easter Sunday), 2004.

▼ **THIS FORMER SASKATCHEWAN WHEAT POOL GRAIN ELEVATOR** in Spring Valley was originally located at the railway siding at Pickthall, Saskatchewan, in the Scout Lake area. It was moved into Spring Valley in 1963 to replace an elevator that had burned down.

1913 the line was opened for scheduled passenger service. A small settlement had begun to develop as soon as the location of the townsite had been determined, and there are two plausible, yet similar, sources for the community's name. One story holds that the first businessman on the scene, E.J. Reiman, who erected a small shed to sell International Harvester machinery, was given the honour of choosing a name and, inspired by the springs between the area hills, he simply chose the descriptive name "Spring Valley." A second explanation is that area ranchers and cowboys had known the area between the Dirt and Cactus Hills as the "spring valley" for years, and that the name simply stuck. The Spring Valley Post Office was officially established on August 1, 1913; Artesian School (an obvious play on the name) was established in 1914. Spring Valley Peace Lutheran Church was built in 1915; Mater Dolorosa Roman Catholic Church was constructed around 1917. On December 20, 1920, Spring Valley was incorporated as a village; in 1926 the population was 118. The community's numbers remained fairly stable at between 100 and 120 until the early 1970s, at which point the population began to quickly decline. From 94 residents in 1966, the village dwindled to number only 44 people by 1976. By 1981, the population had dropped to 31. The railway was abandoned in 1985, the village was dissolved January 16, 1991, the Lutheran church closed in 1993, and Artesian School was closed in 2002. There had been only nine students enrolled during the last school year. The Roman Catholic church remains in use, and Spring Valley continues to serve as the administrative centre of the RM of Terrell No. 101. There are no businesses or services in the community; a former Saskatchewan Wheat Pool elevator remains standing.

▲ **SPRINGSIDE SCHOOL** on the corner of Main Street and Taylor Avenue, is comprised of the 1919 structure, on the right, and a modern addition, left. Photograph taken July 12, 2004.

SPRINGSIDE, town, pop 494 approx. (2006c), 525 (2001c), is located 25 km northwest of the city of Yorkton at the junction of the Yellowhead Hwy (No. 16) and Hwy 47. The region began to be settled in the 1880s by Scottish, English, German and, later, Ukrainian homesteaders. Those that settled in the immediate vicinity of Springside were largely of British extraction, either from other regions of Canada or from overseas. The village came into being in 1903 as the railway was extended north-westward from Yorkton. Springside was incorporated in 1909. The name of the village was derived from nearby freshwater springs, which long were a watering stop on the old prairie trails system. Springside grew steadily, and by the 1950s, when bylaws were passed outlawing chickens and cows in the village, the population was over 300. Springside attained town status in 1985, and in 1986 the population was 603. The town has a small but varied business community, modern recreation facilities, seniors' housing, a library, churches, and a volunteer fire department. Yorkton pro-

vides additional shopping and services, employment, and medical facilities; police service is provided by the Yorkton RCMP. Springside Elementary School provides K-8 education to approximately 75 students; high school students attend classes in the nearby city. Good Spirit Lake Provincial Park and Whitesand Regional Park, both located a short distance north of the town, provide Springside residents with additional recreational opportunities. Springside is situated in the RM of Orkney No. 244.

SPRINGWATER, hamlet, pop 15 (2006c), 20 (2001c), is a former village located 35 km southwest of Biggar on Hwy 51. The community takes its name from Springwater Lake to the north, in the vicinity of which the post office was originally established in 1911. The locale was originally known as McMillan Coulee, after D. C. McMillan, who walked into the district from Saskatoon in 1905. Between about 1905 and 1909 very few settlers had ventured into the district, then people, mainly from Ontario and the United States, began to arrive in numbers. In 1911, the present

hamlet had its beginnings as the Grand Trunk Pacific Railway progressed through the area. The tracks were laid in 1912, and over the following few years a building boom ensued: Springwater attained village status on December 10, 1913, and that year a one-room school was built. The population rose from 48 in 1916 to 173, the community's peak, by 1931. Springwater once boasted a railway station, hotel, hardware store, general stores, pool room, blacksmith shop, butcher shop, beauty shop, barber shop, bank, lumberyards, implement dealerships, four grain elevators, a bulk fuel dealership, a laundry, jail, drug store, garages, a local Co-op store, and two churches. The heyday was in the 1920s: a four-room brick school was built in 1927, and that year a dance pavilion was constructed at Springwater Lake, where orchestras played for a number of years. Springwater once had hockey and baseball teams, a curling rink, a nine-hole golf course, and a tennis club. Businesses closed during the 1930s, and the population fell throughout that decade and through the following war years. By 1951, the community's numbers had fallen to 85 — less than half the number of twenty years earlier. The community then experienced somewhat of a rebound in the 1950s — the population had climbed back up to 120 by 1961. Thereafter, though, Springwater steadily declined. Springwater School closed in 1966 and was demolished around 1969-70; the pavilion at Springwater Lake was torn down in 1974; the last local place to buy groceries closed in the mid-1970s; and the post office closed in 1986, the same year that the rail line was abandoned. By 1986 the population of the village had plummeted to 24. On December 31, 2006, Springwater relinquished village status; today, none of the grain elevators remain standing, the

United Church stands in disrepair, and, other than a few homes, the former village looks like a ghost town. Springwater is situated in the RM of Biggar No. 347.

SPRUCE BAY, organized hamlet, is a resort community located southwest of Spiritwood on the north shore of Meeting Lake. It is one of a number of resort areas on the lake, including Meeting Lake Regional Park. The area has been a popular centre for recreational and social activities since early in the twentieth century, and for a number of years the park was the site of an annual fair. Spruce Bay has a very small number of permanent residents; however, the population varies depending on the season — approximately 40 properties have been developed. Spruce Bay, established as an organized hamlet in 1992, is situated in the RM of Spiritwood No. 496.

SPRUCE LAKE, organized hamlet, pop 46 (2006c), 70 (2001c), is located 14 km southeast of St. Walburg on Hwy 26, at the southern end of the lake from which it derives its name. There was some ranching activity in the district in the latter 1800s; after the railway reached North Battleford in 1905, then Lloydminster in 1906, the influx of homesteaders into the Spruce Lake area began. The Canadian Northern Railway had extended a line as far as Turtleford by 1914; a half-dozen years later, with its continuation through to St. Walburg, the townsite of Spruce Lake began to develop. The post office was established on November 1, 1919. Two grain elevators were built shortly after the railway tracks were laid (around 1920), and within a couple of years a core of essential businesses had been started.

The Standard Bank of Canada opened a branch in 1922; in 1923, Thomas J. Collins began publishing a newspaper, the *Spruce Lake Times*. During the 1920s the railway company's stockyards at Spruce Lake handled cattle from as far away as Meadow Lake. Schooling was conducted in the community hall until a two-room school was built in 1928; church services were held in various locations until congregations could afford to construct their own buildings: it appears that the Pentecostal Church was the first, being built shortly after the railway came through; Anglicans completed their church in 1925; and the United Church was built in 1935-36. Spruce Lake attained village status on August 26, 1929, and it was in 1936 that the community reached its peak population — 142. From the 1950s through the 1970s, Spruce Lake numbered approximately 100 residents; thereafter, the community's numbers steadily dwindled. In the 1960s, enrollment began to decline at Spruce Lake School, and high school students and then grades 7 and 8 began to be bused to St. Walburg. By 1971, only grades 1 to 6 were being taught in the village. The school hung on until 1993, when it was finally closed. The last Saskatchewan Wheat Pool elevator was lost to a fire in July 1983, and then the nearest points for area farmers to deliver grain were St. Walburg and Turtleford. Today, there are no businesses or services left in the community, the churches have all been closed, and Spruce Lake is essentially residential; those in the work force find employment outside of the community. Spruce Lake is situated in the RM of Mervin No. 499.

SPY HILL, village, pop 201 (2006c), 213 (2001c), is located 27 km south of Langenburg on Hwy 8. Settlement of the area began in the early 1880s. In 1907, as the Grand Trunk Pacific Railway was building its line through the district, the Paynter Brothers from Tantallon erected the first store on the Spy Hill site to provide railway construction crews with groceries and other supplies. In 1908, the townsite was surveyed, and Spy Hill was incorporated in 1910. The community grew slowly, but steadily, until the mid-1950s. Then, the discovery of potash in the region at the end of the decade brought about a period of unprecedented prosperity and growth. The population of Spy Hill grew from 172 in 1956 to 384 in 1971, and,

today, the potash mines at Gerald, Yarbo, and Rocanville provide many area jobs. However, agriculture, too, remains vital to the district economy. Spy Hill is also the hometown of the former NHL player, Jeff Odgers, who played with San Jose, Boston, Colorado, and Atlanta. A few minutes' drive north of Spy Hill is Carlton Trail Regional Park, which offers area residents fishing, golfing, camping, and swimming. A highlight of the village itself is the Spy Hill Museum. Its displays feature the history of the village and surrounding district from pre-settlement times to the present. Spy Hill has a volunteer fire department; the nearest medical and police services are located in Esterhazy. Schoolchildren attend classes in Langenburg. Spy Hill serves as the administrative centre of the RM of Spy Hill No. 152.

▼ **THE LORCH SNOWPLANE.** The village of Spy Hill is home to one of Saskatchewan's most important early inventions: In 1929, at the age of 19, Karl Lorch designed, built, and patented the propeller-driven snowplane. It became widely utilized across the Canadian prairies and the northern United States, and was often used by doctors to travel to rural patients during winter months, as well as by police, mail carriers, school teachers, geologists, and the armed forces at times when roads were impassable. This snowplane and a cairn were erected on the outskirts of Spy Hill in 1983 in recognition of Lorch's contribution to winter transportation. Photograph taken October 21, 2003.

ST. BENEDICT, village, pop 78 (2006c), 109 (2001c), is located in a beautiful, rolling parkland setting southeast of Wakaw off Hwy 20. Numerous lakes dot the landscape. In the latter years of the 1880s, ranching was carried out in the area by large cattle companies from Winnipeg; in 1899, the first settlers began to arrive in the district. The general region would come to be settled largely by French, Hungarian, German, and Ukrainian settlers, and by 1910 much of the land in the district was taken up. The name St. Benedict had its origins in the area in January of 1903, when Father Bruno Doerfler and Prior Alfred Mayer, both Benedictines, celebrated the first mass in the district at a location some kilometres west of the present community, at S21-41-25-W2. On the occasion, they named the district before them St. Benedict in honour of their patron saint, and the Benedictine monks who would provide spiritual support to the then burgeoning colony of St. Peter's. The colony, a broad swath of land extending from Cudworth through Humboldt to Watson, was settled by German Catholics largely from the northern and mid-western United States, primarily Minnesota. The first St. Benedict Post Office was officially established on September 1, 1907, about five kilometres south of the present village; in 1914, it was relocated to a site a few kilometres to the west, where the St. Benedict Roman Catholic Church, a parish school, and a country store were then located. It would still be a number of years before today's village was established. From the turn of the century until the late 1920s, area farmers had had to deliver their produce to Rosthern, then later Bruno, Cudworth or Wakaw; hauling was done during the winter months and was a tremendous hardship. Often unscrupulous elevator agents knew farmers would not want to haul their loads back home, so they would rate the produce two or three grades lower than the crop actually warranted. Eventually, representatives of the district were sent to Ottawa to petition CPR and government officials for the construction of a railway through the district. The effort proved a success, and in the spring of 1929 railway survey crews began work in the region. When it came time to determine the location of an area townsite, three names were bandied about: Basin Lake, after the large lake to the northeast; Budapest, after the capital city of Hungary; and St. Benedict. The CPR chose St. Benedict for the name of their station, and thus the name became that of the new village. With the coming of the railway in 1929 the first businesses began to appear even before the townsite was surveyed. In 1930, the first grain elevators were built, and by the end of the year approximately two dozen places of business were either in operation or under construction. Also that year, the first church was built in the community. In 1931, the post office opened at the townsite, and construction of the first school in the village was undertaken. After the lean years of the 1930s passed, the village prospered, growing through the 1940s, the 1950s, and into the 1960s. The Village of St. Benedict was incorporated on January 1, 1964, and in 1966 the population was recorded as 234. In the decades following, however, the community steadily began to decline. By 1976, the population had fallen to 164, and over the years businesses that had once thrived became no more. Buildings were demolished, giving way to vacant lots. In September of 1991, after a fierce battle to save the school, grades seven to twelve, along with chil-

dren from the village of Pilger, began to be bused to Middle Lake to attend classes. Kindergarten to grade six did continue to be taught in St. Benedict for a period of time. In the mid-1990s, the rail line into the village was abandoned and the tracks were subsequently lifted. Today, no grain elevators stand in St. Benedict and the business community has been reduced to a few enterprises interspersed among now derelict buildings. St. Benedict is situated in the RM of Three Lakes No. 400.

ST. BRIEUX, town, pop 492 (2006c) 505 (2001c), is located about 35 km southwest of Melfort and approximately 65 km northeast of Humboldt on Hwy 368. The region is characterized by rich farmland and boreal-transition parklands. The community of St. Brieux has a rich Francophone heritage with beginnings in 1904, when the settlement started developing with the arrival of about 40 families from St. Brieuc, Brittany, under the leadership of Father Paul LeFloc'h. The group had sailed from St. Malo, the same port from which Jacques Cartier sailed on his voyages of discovery to the New World. According to St. Brieux local history (and it may just be folklore), the new arrivals in the Canadian Northwest erected a cross on the shore of Lake Lenore in honour of the famous explorer. Somewhat thereafter, when an application was made to establish a post office, the settlers chose to honour their home community in Brittany by naming both the post office, and their parish, St. Brieuc. The fact that the 'c' was changed to an 'x' is thought to have been the result of a typographical error made by postal authorities. The St. Brieux Post Office was established on June 1, 1905. Settlers from France continued to arrive through to the beginning of WWI,

▲ **DR. BACHAND** (right) **AND HENRI HAMONIC** in the drug store in St. Brieux, circa 1940s. Photograph courtesy of the St. Brieux Museum.

and between the years 1908-1920 they were joined by immigrants from the United States, many of whom were of French Canadian origin, descendants of families who had earlier emigrated from Canada to find work south of the border. Hungarians also came to the district, primarily between the years 1911-1923. Hungarian settlement extended eastward from the Wakaw Lake area, and it was French priests from St. Brieux who ventured out to serve the Hungarian congregations. The influence of Hungarians in the district was still strong in 1954, as dancers in traditional Hungarian costume partook in the village's Golden Jubilee celebrations. A small number of Italian families also settled in the region of St. Brieux, and a fair number of English-speaking people, many from Ontario, came to the area as well. The settlers of French origin, however, followed by the Hungarian immigrants, constituted the largest ethnic group in the district. The actual town of St. Brieux had

its beginnings in 1913 when the railway from Melfort was being built into the area. The townsite lots were auctioned off by the Canadian Northern Railway in Melfort in April that year, and the fledgling community was incorporated as a village on November 11 that fall. For a number of years, St. Brieux was the end of the rail line, and, as such, the community enjoyed a certain importance, prospering as a trading centre for a considerable territory. Businesses begun in 1913 included general stores, a hotel, a livery barn, a lumberyard, and a restaurant. Farmers from as far away as the Lake Lenore and Pleasantdale districts hauled their grain to St. Brieux, and bought their supplies in the community. In the early 1920s, however, following the further development of rail lines in the region, St. Brieux went into a slump as competing businesses arose in newly developing communities. The situation for the village only worsened in 1924 when a fire destroyed many of

▲ ▼ **ST. BRIEUX'S GOLDEN JUBILEE** celebrations in 1954 included a parade (above) and a performance by these Hungarian dancers in traditional dress (below). Their instructor, Mrs. Jos. Zabos, is in the centre of the photograph.

the years following WWII, but it has now been reduced to not much more than a small collection of homes off the highway. St. Brieux has perhaps seen its greatest period of growth over the past decade and a half — the population was still hovering around 400 in the early 1990s. The population remains predominantly French in origin, and among the numerous community activities such as trade fairs, sports days, and golf and hockey tournaments is an annual Bilingual Christmas Pageant. St. Brieux has a range of businesses and services including a motel and a hotel, a credit union, a post office, a library, service stations, automotive and farm implement dealerships, restaurants, grocery stores, a health food store, and a meat market. Churches provide worship services, and the community has a seniors' centre, rental apartments, a special care home, and home care available for the elderly and others with special needs.

A number of service clubs, youth groups, sports teams, and other community-based organizations operate in the town. Also, a number of artists, craftspeople, and musicians reside in the community. St. Brieux School offers a K-12 program and had 195 students enrolled in the fall of 2006. Recreational facilities in the community include skating and curling rinks, a theatre, a bowling alley, and a library; throughout the year, residents are offered classes in areas such as music, dance, and karate. About one kilometre west of the town is St. Brieux Regional Park, which offers opportunities for swimming, boating, fishing, camping, and golf. The Roman Catholic rectory in St. Brieux, built in 1919, now houses a museum and has been designated a heritage property. St. Brieux was elevated to the status of a town on November 8, 2006, and serves as the administrative centre of the RM of Lake Lenore No. 399.

▼ **CANADA DAY CELEBRATIONS, 1997**, at the St. Brieux Museum, which is housed in the former Roman Catholic Rectory.

Photographs courtesy of the St. Brieux Museum.

the main street businesses, including the hotel. St. Brieux languished; its population fell and then remained fairly static, and it was not until after WWII that the community again showed any real signs of growth. Then, from a population of 177 in 1946, St. Brieux's numbers jumped to 411 by 1956, and were still above 400 in the mid-1960s, when again the village began realizing a downturn. Then, in 1973, at a time when many other small Saskatchewan communities were declining or disappearing, Frank Bourgault founded

Bourgault Industries in the village. Starting out in a small shop, Bourgault Industries has grown into a world-renowned manufacturer of agricultural equipment; a major area employer, it has added much to the district economy. From a population of 362 in 1976, St. Brieux once again numbered over 400 by the beginning of the 1980s. St. Brieux's prosperity was at the expense of smaller district communities, as rural populations, businesses and services became increasingly centralized. Pathlow to the northeast also thrived in

ST. GEORGE'S HILL, northern hamlet, pop 102 (2001c), is located just south and west of Peter Pond Lake, on the Dillon River, 67 km by road from Buffalo Narrows on gravel road No. 925. Immediately north of St. George's Hill lies the reserve of the Buffalo River Dene Nation, headquartered at the community of Dillon. The on-reserve population is approximately 600. The residents of St. George's Hill (name derivation uncertain) are mainly non-treaty Dene, and while retention of the Denesuline language is low, some pursue traditional activities including trapping, fishing, and hunting as a part of their culture and way of life. The hamlet of St. George's Hill is a relatively recent entity, dating to perhaps around the 1950s. But by the mid-1970s, no businesses or services of any kind had been established, and communication with the outside world was via two-way radio. In the early 1980s, an all-weather road and power lines reached the community and, on December 1, 1983, St. George's Hill was formally established as a northern hamlet to meet the needs of managing community affairs and infrastructure. In 2001, the median age of the population was 20 (the average age of all Saskatchewan residents was 36.7), and unemployment in the community rested at just under 60 per cent. St. George's Hill has a K-9 school that had 28 students enrolled in the fall of 2006; the community has little else in the way of services. Most goods and services are obtained in Dillon or Buffalo Narrows.

ST. GREGOR, village, pop 102 (2006c), 121 (2001c), is situated halfway between Humboldt and Watson on Hwy 5. St. Gregor is one of a number of communities which developed in what became known as St. Peter's Colony, a broad tract of land that extended from Watson through Humboldt to the Cudworth area, that was largely settled by German Catholics from the northern and mid-western United States. St. Peter's Colony had its beginnings in 1902-03, and was founded and colonized by the German-American Land Co. in conjunction with Minnesota Benedictines. Construction of the Canadian Northern Railway was proceeding through the St. Gregor district in 1904, and in 1905 trains were running from Kamsack to Humboldt. The arrival of the railway sparked an immediate increase in the regional population, and in 1906 the first general store was opened at what was developing as the St. Gregor townsite. On January 17, 1907, Father Bruno Doerfler founded the parish of St. Gregory, named for Pope Gregory I, and the community in turn was named after the parish — why the community ended up with a shortened version of the name, however, is a mystery. The St. Gregor Post Office was established on July 1, 1907, and a parochial school opened in the spring of 1908. A flourishing business community developed in the following years and included a grain elevator, a blacksmith shop, a bank, and the railway station. In 1912, the St. Gregor Grain Growers Association constructed a community hall where, over the years, many public meetings and social events took place. On March 26, 1920, the Village of St. Gregor was incorporated. In 1923, the community landmark, St. Gregory Church, was built, and today its 26-metre-high (86 ft.) tower remains the focal point of the village. St. Gregor reached a peak population of about 170 in the mid-1950s to the early 1960s, but shifting demographics, centralization, and improved transportation subsequently took a toll on the village, and many businesses and, eventually, the school were closed. Schoolchildren now attend classes in Muenster, but a degree of economic stability has returned to the community in more recent years with the establishment of two manufacturing firms. Other businesses in the village include a transport company, an agricultural products supplier, a seed processing facility, a bar, a credit union, a post office, a meat processor and retailer, and a restaurant. Policing in St. Gregor is provided by the Humboldt RCMP detachment, and fire protection is provided by departments in either Humboldt or the village of Annaheim, just to the north. As well, ambulance service comes from Humboldt, where the nearest hospital is located. St. Gregor also has a seniors' centre, a bowling alley, a library, and a curling rink. St. Gregor is situated in the RM of St. Peter No. 369.

▼ **THE VIEW FROM MANATINAW HILL** just east of St. Isidore-de-Bellevue. Photograph taken August 24, 2004.

ST. ISIDORE-DE-BELLEVUE, organized hamlet, pop 110 (2006c), 95 (2001c), is a francophone community located approximately 60 km south of Prince Albert, between Domremy and Batoche on Hwy 225. Métis families had settled in the district by the early 1880s and were followed by descendants of exiled Acadians who had resettled in Quebec, Québécois from the eastern townships and other areas of Quebec, French-Canadians who had settled in the United States, and a few families from France and Belgium. Originally, the area belonged to the parish of St. Antoine de Padoue at Batoche. In 1902, Father P. E. Myre founded the parish of St. Isidore-de-Bellevue — the name honours St. Isidore the Farmer, and the word "Bellevue" was inspired by the sweeping vista from nearby Manatinaw Hill, just east of the community. St. Isidore-de-Bellevue is one of the rare centres in the southern half of the province that survived in spite of the absence of a railway, or without the benefit of being located on a major highway. Established as an organized hamlet

in 1980, St. Isidore-de-Bellevue retains a strong francophone heritage bolstered by École St-Isidore de Bellevue, a K-12 facility that had 121 students enrolled in the fall of 2006, and Centre Le Rendez-Vous, which houses a cultural centre, archives, restaurant, boutique, and a seniors' centre, "Club d'age d'or." Additionally, all of the signs in the community are bilingual. The area economy is largely based upon agriculture, and St. Isidore-de-Bellevue is at the centre of one of the province's leading pulse crop-producing districts. Belle Pulses Ltd., founded by Ron Gaudet (1926-1994) and his sons in 1978, is one of the community's leading employers. St. Isidore-de-Bellevue is situated in the RM of St. Louis No. 431.

ST. JOSEPH'S, organized hamlet, pop 79 (2007 recount), pop 68 (2001c), is situated about six and a half kilometres east of Balgonie on Hwy 1. St. Joseph's developed as a German Catholic settlement after the first homesteaders arrived at Balgonie in 1886 from the small colony of Josephstal near Odessa, then in southern Russia. The first church built in 1887 of mud and stone also functioned as a school, and rooms added to it served as living quarters for the priest and the school teacher. By 1891, many more families had arrived in the area, and after going to their respective quarter-section homesteads and filling cultivation requirements, they decided to establish a hamlet, or *dorf*, in order to strengthen religious, social, and community ties. Thirty families occupied the original surveyed lots and in 1894 the hamlet, known to the local residents as the "Village of Josephstal," was officially recognized by the federal government. It later became known as St. Joseph's Colony. A number of the German Catholic parishes that developed south and east of the settlement were established with the assistance of the St. Joseph's colonists. The existent St. Joseph's Roman Catholic Church was built in 1897, and in 1903 a frame schoolhouse was built. Also that year, a three-storey fieldstone rectory, still standing, was constructed. In the mid-1930s, Ursuline Sisters from Vibank came to teach in the community, and they remained at St. Joseph's for the next 30 years. In the mid-1960s, high school students began to be bused to Balgonie, and in 1967 the colony school was closed. That same year, a new St. Joseph's Catholic Church was built in Balgonie, rendering the hamlet church largely unused thereafter. In 1968 the old colony school was moved into Balgonie to provide extra classroom space. The population of Saint Joseph's Colony was then down to about 30. In recent years, the community's population has grown, as affluent city workers have sought gentrified rural living — large houses on large lots and low taxes. Currently, new housing developments are under construction, and, today, St. Joseph's is largely a bedroom community for commuters to Regina. There are no businesses or services in the hamlet. The 1897 church, the 1903 rectory, and a 1928 community hall were all designated heritage properties in 1984. The church now houses a museum. St. Joseph's was established as an organized hamlet in 1986 and is situated within the boundaries of the RM of South Qu'Appelle No. 157.

ST. LOUIS, village, pop 431 (2006c), 474 (2001c), is located about 33 km south of Prince Albert on Hwy 2, on the south and east side of the South Saskatchewan River. A Métis settlement comprised of Red River exiles was developing just to the west of the present community by the early 1880s; soon Catholic clergy from France arrived. Originally, the St. Louis settlement was a mission of St. Laurent, across the river to the southwest; Oblate Fathers from Prince Albert began to minister to the settlement in 1884. The defeat of the Métis freedom fighters in 1885 was profoundly demoralizing and greatly upset the lives of those in the region — there was yet another diaspora,

homes were raided, animals were lost, a season of crop production was lost — however, the impoverished population managed to survive. Following the Resistance, Québécois and immigrants from France increasingly settled throughout the region. In 1886, a local school district was established, and in 1887 a homesteading missionary, Father Lecoq, helped to build the first church and rectory for the new mission. In 1897, a convent was built, as the Daughters of Providence from France arrived to teach school in the small parish, then comprised of a few French families and French- and English-speaking Métis. That year, Louis Schmidt settled at the site of the present village. The Grand Trunk Pacific Railway began construction of a line between Young and Prince Albert prior to the beginning of WWI; however, the war delayed its construction and the full length of the line did not open until the now famous bridge at St. Louis was completed across the river in 1917. With train service, there was an influx of settlers, and the settlement that had its nucleus to the west slowly shifted toward the rail line. Until traffic wings were added to the bridge in 1928, a ferry service was still required to cross the South Saskatchewan River, unless, of course, one was travelling by train. In 1919, a new Roman Catholic convent and boarding school, St. Joseph Academy, were built at the site of the newly-developing locale. Also in 1919, a Grain Growers' Hall was constructed; Anglicans held their first services there — an Anglican church was not completed until 1931. By the 1950s, St. Louis had grown to the point where residents were seeking political autonomy: St. Louis was established as an organized hamlet in 1956; on May 19, 1959, St. Louis was incorporated as a village. A Christian college, Notre Dame, operated in St. Louis from 1967 until 1974; it was then converted into the St. Louis Alcohol Rehabilitation Centre, which, in turn, closed in 2005. Enrollment was in decline at the convent by the early 1970s; its closure followed several years later. The rail line through the community (from Hoey to Prince Albert) was abandoned in 1983. Today, St. Louis has a core of small businesses and services; the nearby city of Prince Albert provides a full range of amenities, and a number of St. Louis residents commute to work in the city. The village has a community hall, skating and curling rinks, a seniors'

ST. LOUIS, 1955. Saskatchewan Archives Board R-B1474.

ST. LOUIS' FAMOUS BRIDGE. Photograph taken August 24, 2004.

centre (with bowling alley), seniors' care homes, a library, a volunteer fire department, service clubs, sports associations, and other community-based organizations including the Association Culturelle Coeur Franc and the St. Louis Métis Local No. 28. There are active Roman Catholic and Anglican Churches. St. Louis Community School is a K-12 facility, which had 219 students enrolled in the fall of 2006. Although English is the predominant language spoken in St. Louis today, there are still significant French and Métis populations. St. Louis is situated in the RM of St. Louis No. 431.

ST. VICTOR, hamlet, pop 49 (2001c), is perhaps best known today for the prehistoric and mysterious petroglyphs located just south of the community. Situated in south-central Saskatchewan, 26 km southeast of Assiniboia, the origins of St. Victor date to 1870 when Red River Métis, uncertain of their future in the new province of Manitoba, came west and established new settlements from which to hunt bison. As the bison disappeared from the area, some of the Métis moved on, while others began adopting a more sedentary life and engaged in ranching. In 1902, the first French Canadian settlers started to arrive, and they combined ranching with crop production. Within a few years, a post office was established, a school was opened, and the hamlet developed. In the 1950s, a small business, the Family Life Assurance Company, was begun in St. Victor, and in 1963 Family Life was federally chartered and the company became very successful, providing 30 local jobs. It was a tremendous boost to the community. In 1964, St. Victor was incorporated as a village; in 1966, the population was 100. In 1974, however,

381

◄ **A 100-MILE VIEW** from the site of the petroglyphs just south of St. Victor. The community is nestled in the trees in the centre of the picture; the steeple of the church just visible. Photograph taken August 31, 2004.

the local company was sold and, in 1977, it was relocated to Calgary. This had a devastating impact on the economy and life of St. Victor. The population declined and with it the use of the French language, once dominant in the community. By 1981 the community numbered only 54 residents, and the school was closed that year. In 1986, the Roman Catholic Church closed, and on February 26, 2003, the village was dissolved. Today, the Poplar River Power Plant, south of Coronach, provides the main source of employment. Not all is quiet in St. Victor, however, for each June, for three days, the hills resound with the roar of motorcycles as the St. Victor Biker's Boogie takes place at nearby Sylvan Valley Regional Park. In 2008, the event will have been running for 29 years. St. Victor is located in the RM of Willow Bunch No. 42.

ST. WALBURG, town, pop 672 (2006c), 667 (2001c), is located in northwestern Saskatchewan, approximately 90 km northeast of Lloydminster and 130 km northwest of North Battleford. The community is situated on Hwy 26 just northeast of the crossroads of Hwys 3 and 21. To the north lies the Bronson Provincial Forest and to the east lie the popular resort and vacation destinations of Brightsand and Turtle Lakes. Settlement of the area began in the early 1900s. In 1907 Rudolph and Walburga Musch, settlers from Minnesota, arrived, setting up a general store somewhat southeast of the present town. Stocking their store required a three-day round trip south across the North Saskatchewan River to the village of Paynton, on the recently completed rail line running from North Battleford to Lloydminster. In 1910, the Musches established the St. Walburg Post Office, with Rudolph becoming the first postmaster. Although the name obviously honours his wife, it also indirectly honours St. Walburga, an eighth-century Eng-

lish nun educated by the Benedictines, who was canonized for a life dedicated to evangelical work among the German people. The Musch store and post office became a hub of activity, not only a place to obtain mail and supplies, but also a place to socialize. A settlement developed at the location and included a blacksmith shop, a pool room, a café, a flour mill, and even a Bank of Commerce. In 1919, the rail line was being built into the area from Turtleford, but it was bypassing the

community. Since the railway was going to build its station to the northwest, the entire community packed up to relocate to the new townsite. The Canadian Northern Railway put the lots up for sale, and the buildings were dragged to the site on skids, leaving little at what would become known as Old St. Walburg. In 1921, the rail line was completed, and by 1922, the year the community was incorporated as a village, St. Walburg had three general stores, two livery stables, drug and hard-

▲ ▼ **MAIN STREET, ST. WALBURG, 1958 AND 2003**, showing the community's landmark church at the south end of the street. Black and white photograph: Saskatchewan Archives Board R-B8425; colour photograph taken July 23, 2003.

ware stores, and a 30-room hotel among its businesses. The area was comprised of a mix of settlers. There was a substantial population of people of German origin, as well as English, Scottish, Irish, French, and Scandinavian homesteaders. In 1939 a number of Sudeten Germans, who had been vocally opposed to Adolph Hitler, came to the area, having fled Czechoslovakia for their lives. Upon arriving at St. Walburg, the families were temporarily housed in boxcars in an encampment on the outskirts of the community before they moved out to area homesteads. Ironically, Sudeten Germans who settled in the Loon River area, roughly 60 kilometres north of St. Walburg, occupied lands vacated by earlier German settlers who had returned to Germany supportive of Hitler and the Nazi regime. St. Walburg's early economy was fairly diverse. While farming and ranching were developing to become the main industries, fish, fur, and railway ties were exported from the area in addition to agricultural products. For two decades district sawmills supplied railway ties for the province's expanding railways. Additionally, according to the local history, a significant underground industry in the manufacture of home brew augmented many a farmer's income. On February 1, 1953, St. Walburg attained town status, and in the early 1980s the community

had a peak population of just over 800. Today, the area economy is based upon cattle and grain production, as well as an oil and gas sector that has been continually expanding over the past couple of decades. Tourism continues to be a factor as regional resort areas develop. St. Walburg is the main centre in the region and has in excess of 65 businesses providing a range of goods and services. The town also serves the district with a health centre and a special care home, a medical clinic, an ambulance service, an RCMP detachment, and a fire department. St. Walburg School is a K-12 facility, which had 212 town and area students enrolled in the fall of 2006. A community complex houses skating and curling rinks and a bowling alley. A picturesque golf course and clubhouse are situated on the southern edge of the town, as is a campground. St. Walburg has five churches, a number of service groups, sports teams, and other community-based organizations, as well as a library and a museum housed in the community's former Roman Catholic church, a landmark dominating the southern end of the town's Main Street. A key area attraction is the former studio and home of Count Berthold Von Imhoff, located a short distance from the town. Born into nobility in Germany in 1868, the classically trained artist won the prestigious Art Academy

Award of Berlin at age 16 for a portrait of Germany's Prince Frederick William. Imhoff turned to painting religious subjects and moved to St. Walburg in 1914. By the time of his death in 1939 his work had come to adorn numerous churches throughout Saskatchewan and the United States. Today, approximately 200 of his paintings can be viewed at the Imhoff Museum. In 1998, the town honoured the famous artist with the installation of a life-sized bronze statue created by another renowned local artist, Susan Velder. Other works by Velder include a bust of T.C. Douglas at Saskatchewan's Legislative Building, and a statue of Queen Elizabeth II riding her favourite horse, Burmese, on the Legislative Building grounds, which was commissioned in honour of the Queen's Golden Jubilee. Key events in St. Walburg include an annual fair in July and the Annual Blueberry Festival, a combined craft sale and street festival that attracts in excess of 5,000 visitors each year. St. Walburg is situated within the RM of Frenchman Butte No. 501.

STALWART, hamlet, pop 20 (2007 approximation), is located about 10 km west of Last Mountain Lake on Hwy 2, between the town of Imperial, to the north, and the village of Liberty, to the south. Just to the east of the hamlet is the Stalwart National Wildlife area. Settlers began arriving in the district in 1903-04; when the CPR built the rail line up the west side of Last Mountain Lake in 1911, Stalwart had its beginnings. The Rural Municipality of Big Arm No. 251 was incorporated in December 1911, and Stalwart became the headquarters. In 1912, the Stalwart Post Office was established, a school opened, and the first store was moved in from the country. In the early years, Stalwart had a number of businesses: four grain elevators, an implement dealership, garage, blacksmith shop, lumberyards, shoe and harness repair shop, dray service and livery barn, hardware store, butcher shop, boarding house, a pool room and café. For a short period, there was a branch of

▲ **THERE WERE ONCE FOUR GRAIN ELEVATORS** in Stalwart; today only this former Saskatchewan Wheat Pool structure remains. The elevator dates to 1963; the crib annex (the peak of which is just visible in the background) dates to 1912. Photograph taken June 28, 2004.

the Royal Bank. There was a dance hall, an 18-hole golf course in the 1920s, annual sports days until the early 1940s, and a curling rink from 1954 until 1976. Stalwart had the standing of an organized hamlet from 1952 to 1969; the population in 1969 was close to 50. CN took over the rail line in the late 1980s; a decade later, the line was abandoned. Today, the post office is the only remaining business in the community; a remaining grain elevator is now privately owned. Stalwart remains the administrative centre of the RM of Big Arm No. 251.

STANLEY MISSION is located 80 km northeast of La Ronge on the Churchill River. Although it is located in an area long frequented by the region's indigenous people, Stanley Mission began as a settlement with the arrival of the Anglican Church. The Missionary Society of the church had already established a presence in Africa and South America when it started building missions in Rupert's Land

in 1822. The primary goal was to convert Aboriginal people to Christianity, but the Society also wanted to develop small, self-sufficient agricultural communities that would use hunting and fishing to supplement the food produced. In 1845, the Hudson's Bay Company, which controlled the territory (or tried to), granted permission to the Anglican Church to establish a mission in what was then known as the English River (now Churchill) district. Reverend Robert Hunt arrived at Lac La Ronge in 1850 and in 1851 chose a site on the north side of the Churchill River for the mission. The first buildings erected were the parsonage and a schoolhouse, followed by a warehouse, storeroom, barn, icehouse, and carpenter's shop. Between 1854 and 1860 Reverend Hunt oversaw the construction of the magnificent Holy Trinity Anglican Church, now the oldest building standing in Saskatchewan. The lumber was cut locally; however, the locks, hinges, and the thousands of pieces of coloured glass which would comprise the stained glass windows were shipped

and then freighted all the way from England. The name Stanley Mission honours Reverend Hunt's ancestral home, Stanley Park, Gloucestershire, England. Although the Hudson's Bay Company opened a trading post across the river in 1853, it was on the north side of the river, around the mission, that a thriving community developed. Through the 1860s and 1870s the farm land under cultivation was increased and a grist mill for grinding local wheat into flour was constructed. By the early twentieth century, though, the situation at the mission was changing. The mission and residential school at La Ronge were gaining greater importance at the expense of Stanley Mission and by 1905 had replaced Stanley Mission as the church headquarters in the district. Also, around 1919-1920, an epidemic, perhaps influenza, perhaps smallpox, claimed, according to one source, about 30 lives. As well, rival trading posts were competing with the Hudson's Bay Company on the south side of the river in the 1920s, creating additional activity in that area, and with the creation of an Indian reserve and the subsequent construction of houses, also on the south side, the population of Stanley Mission began to dwindle. By the early 1960s virtually all of the buildings were situated across the river from Holy Trinity Church. In 1978 an all-weather road was built from La Ronge and with it came all of the trappings of the modern age. Today, approximately 1,500 people live in the community. A small number live on the point of land across the river from the church, which is technically the Northern Settlement of Stanley Mission.

◀ **STANLEY MISSION AND HOLY TRINITY ANGLICAN CHURCH, 1964.** Saskatchewan Archives Board R-B11467.

The remainder, and bulk, of the population are members of the Lac La Ronge Indian Band who live on the adjacent reserve. Holy Trinity Anglican Church is a Provincial Heritage Property, a National Historic Site, and is incorporated into Lac La Ronge Provincial Park. It is accessible only by water.

STAR CITY, town, pop 428 (2006c), 482 (2001c), is situated equidistant between the communities of Melfort and Tisdale off Hwy 3. The first few settlers arrived in the area in 1898-99, and in 1902 one of the first couples in the area, Mr. and Mrs. Walter Starkey (homestead entry May 1, 1899), opened a post office in addition to the small store they operated out of their log home. The name Star City was chosen, honouring the Starkeys and reflecting the early pioneers' hopes for development in the area. The first settlers in the Star City district came via the railway to Prince Albert, and then travelled with horses or oxen and wagon from there. After the turn of the century, others came from Erwood, just east of Hudson Bay, as the Canadian Northern Railway was approaching from Manitoba. As the railway progressed westward, many would find work involved with its construction. In 1904, the Star City townsite was surveyed and lots were put up for sale. The Starkeys moved in from their homestead and built a substantial general store. In 1905, many more businesses were started. A hotel was built. The first school classes were held in another general store, and on April 6, 1906, Star City was incorporated as a village. The population was 109. Lumbering was big business as the parklands were cleared for agriculture. The community grew steadily, and, with a population of just under 600 in 1921, Star City attained

► **STAR CITY'S FORMER TOWN OFFICE BUILDING,** now housing the library, on the northeast corner of First Avenue and Fourth Street.

▼ **BUSINESSES** on the east side of Fourth Street in Star City.

Photographs taken in the early evening of August 12, 2004.

STENEN, village, pop 91 (2006c), 110 (2001c), is located in the parklands of east-central Saskatchewan, east of Sturgis, off Hwys 9 and 49. People began taking up homesteads in the Stenen area around 1902, and the district would come to be largely comprised of people of Scandinavian, Ukrainian, and English origins. In 1906, Johannes (John) Amundson Stenen, a Norwegian who came to Canada via the United States, settled where the village now stands. When the Canadian Northern Railway arrived in 1911, Stenen donated a parcel of land for a townsite, on the condition that the new community would bear his name. As the railway was being built through the area, the townsite was rapidly built up and among the first businesses established in 1911 were two grain elevators and the Toronto-Dominion Bank. On May 23, 1912, the Stenen School District was established, and on August 14 that year the Village of Stenen was incorporated. In 1916, the population was 99; by 1921, it was just shy of 200. The community thrived, functioning for several decades as a centre for obtaining services and supplies, and it hosted many district social, religious, and recreational activities. In 1956, Stenen had a peak population of 301. The village declined dramatically from the late 1960s through the

► **UKRAINIAN SETTLERS** at Stenen, 1929. Saskatchewan Archives Board R-A32763.

▼ **ST. DEMETRIOUS UKRAINIAN ORTHODOX CHURCH**, Stenen. Photograph taken July 28, 2004.

town status. The population remained fairly stable until the mid-1960s, at which point rural depopulation and the convenience of accessing the amenities of the nearby larger centres began to have an impact on the Star City business sector. Today, Melfort and Tisdale provide Star City residents with many sources of employment, goods, services, and recreational and cultural activities. Star City retains a small core of essential businesses and has paved, tree-lined streets throughout attractive and well-kept residential neighbourhoods. Additionally, the community has a public library, a museum, churches, and a number of active service clubs and community-based organizations. Star City School is a K-12 facility, which had 148 town and area students enrolled in the fall of 2006. Recreational facilities include skating and curling rinks, ball diamonds, sports fields, and an outdoor riding arena. Fourth Street features fine examples of pre-Depression era architecture. Star City serves as the administrative centre of the RM of Star City No. 428.

1970s, in terms of both population and the number of business establishments. Stenen School was closed at the end of the school year in 1989, and today the community is largely residential in nature. A notable village landmark is St. Demetrious Ukrainian Orthodox Church, built in the mid-1950s. Stenen is situated in the RM of Clayton No. 333.

STEWART VALLEY, village, pop 100 (2006c), 101 (2001c), is located roughly 30 km north of Swift Current on Hwy 4. Saskatchewan Landing Provincial Park on the shores of Lake Diefenbaker lies a short distance to the northwest. For several years following the completion of the railway into Swift Current in 1883, there was increasing traffic through the Stewart Valley district over the trail that ran to Battleford. The area became the domain of large-scale ranching enterprises until the first decade of the twentieth century, when the land was largely given over to homesteaders. Among the settlers, people of Scottish, English, and Norwegian stock numbered significantly. On October 1, 1908, a post office was established to the east of the present village, its name "Stewart Valley" honouring the first postmaster, John T. Stewart. In 1911, a school, adopting the name Stewart Valley, was built in the area, moving to the village site in 1930 after the railway had arrived. Celebrations commemorating the driving of the last spike at the village site were held in November 1928, and in 1929 the CPR branch line which ran from just east of Swift Current to Stewart Valley was opened to scheduled traffic. After years of long journeys, local farmers could haul grain to local elevators — at least until the late 1970s. The line into Stewart Valley was intended to extend north-westwards,

to cross the South Saskatchewan River and connect with the Matador subdivision running through Kyle, but the plan was never completed. Stewart Valley remained at the end of the line, and subsequently rail service into the community was fairly poor — in the early 1950s, trains only ran into the village on a once-weekly basis. District residents had long petitioned the provincial government for a bridge at Saskatchewan Landing to improve transportation in the region — many mishaps had occurred crossing the river both on ferries and over the ice through the years — so the 1951 ribbon-cutting ceremony presided over by Premier Douglas was a much-celebrated occasion. What was called the "million-dollar bridge" created a continuous highway link (albeit gravel) that ran from Val Marie through Swift Current, Rosetown, and the Battlefords, on to Meadow Lake. Nine months later, however, the bridge lay at the bottom of the South Saskatchewan River. An abnormal spring breakup on the river had led to the buildup of a huge ice jam and, despite army engineers' efforts using hundreds of pounds of dynamite to relieve the pressure, the ice continued to build up. It lifted the bridge deck up off its piers and, within seconds, the structure collapsed. Ferry service was resumed until the summer of 1953, when a new, higher bridge was then opened to vehicle traffic. Years of prosperity followed, and Stewart Valley attained village status on January 1, 1958. In 1961, the population was 181. In June of 1960, the community issued the first of what would become many protests over the possibility of the CPR abandoning the rail line into Stewart Valley, and in 1966 a direct appeal was made to Premier Ross Thatcher. The fight lasted until the late 1970s, but in December 1978 the line was abandoned, and in 1979 the track was torn up. In

1984, the Stewart Valley council made an application to have the CPR right-of-way property transferred to the village, and in 1986 the village received the titles to the land. The Pioneer elevator was levelled and burned; the other three elevators were torn down plank by plank by area farmers. After fifty years, local farmers once again had to travel outside the district to market their crops. Today, Stewart Valley largely falls within Swift Current's sphere of influence — consumer goods, health care, jobs, and entertainment are sought in the city. Stewart Valley has a K-8 school that had 49 students enrolled in the fall of 2006, and a key business in the village is the Co-op, which offers groceries, hardware, lumber, farm and veterinary supplies, postal services, and fuel sales. Saskatchewan Landing Provincial Park provides village residents with many recreational opportunities. Stewart Valley serves as the administrative centre of the RM of Saskatchewan Landing No. 167.

STOCKHOLM, village, pop 323 (2006c), 303 (2001c), is located 20 km west of Esterhazy at the junction of Hwys 9 and 22; Round Lake and the Qu'Appelle Valley lie approximately 16 km to the south. Swedish immigrants settled in the area to the south of the present community in the mid-1880s, and named their

colony *New Stockholm* after the capital city of their homeland. They established the first Swedish Augustana Lutheran congregation in Canada on October 3, 1889, at a meeting in the home of one Erick Hammerstrom. Their first church was built in the mid-1890s of logs hauled by oxen from the Qu'Appelle Valley; the present church, built of brick, was dedicated in 1921. At the beginning of the twentieth century the population of the area grew substantially with the arrival of many Hungarian settlers. These came to be predominant in the village, although the arrival of the railway also brought people of English and Scottish origins, from both eastern Canada and Great Britain. The CPR came through in 1903, the present townsite was surveyed, and the first thoroughfares — Railway Avenue, and Ohlen and Forslund Streets — were named. The fledgling village took its name from the New Stockholm Colony. Also in 1903, Dougald Lamont established the first business (a hardware store) and the Colonial Elevator Company erected the first grain elevator. In 1904, the Stockholm Post Office was established, and a Presbyterian church (later United) was built. It served

▼ **HEADQUARTERS.** The Rural Municipality of Fertile Belt No. 183 has its office in Stockholm. Photograph taken October 20, 2003.

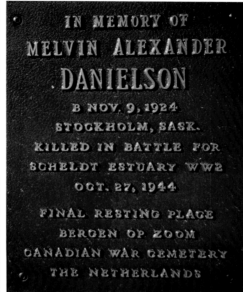

as a school until one was constructed. On June 30, 1905, the Village of Stockholm was incorporated, and that year construction of the first Roman Catholic church — St. Elizabeth of Hungary — began. (Lutherans would continue, and still continue, to attend the New Stockholm Lutheran Church in the heart of the old colony, 13 kilometres southeast of the village.) Stockholm's population grew from 70 in 1906 to number between 200 and 250 from the early 1930s through to the early 1960s — the population was 238 in 1961. By 1966, however, the village numbered 372 residents and the community reached a peak of 406 in 1986. The development of the potash industry in the region had spurred widespread development. Today, two area potash mines, agriculture (a combination of grain and livestock production), a highways maintenance centre, and several local businesses (including a Co-op, a grocery store, and a credit union) provide employment. Stockholm has a library, a community hall, a seniors' housing complex, an arena, and a ball park. Miniature replicas of Stockholm's railway station and three grain elevators mark the location of the originals. CP abandoned the rail line through the community in 1996. The village has a volunteer fire department and a team of first responders; the nearest hospital and RCMP detachment are in Esterhazy. Stockholm has a K-9 school that had 82 students enrolled in the fall of 2006; grades 10 through 12 are attended in Esterhazy. Active organizations in Stockholm include a branch of the Royal Canadian Legion, a Lions club, a senior citizens' club, a drama club that hosts an annual dinner theatre, and a number of recreational groups. Stockholm serves as the administrative centre of the RM of Fertile Belt No. 183.

▲ ◄ **NEW STOCKHOLM LUTHERAN CHURCH** (above, left) is situated in what was the heart of the old Swedish colony, about 4 kilometres north of the Qu'Appelle Valley, and 13 kilometres southeast of the village of Stockholm. This stained-glass window (left) adorns the north side of the sanctuary, and this plaque (above, right) at the building's front entranceway was placed in honour of a young member of the congregation who perished during World War II. Trooper Melvin Alexander Danielson, the son of Peter K. and Hildur C. Danielson of Stockholm, and the youngest of five brothers to enlist, served with the South Alberta Regiment, R.C.A.C. He was only 19 years old when killed, just under two weeks before what would have been his twentieth birthday. Danielson Bay on Nokomis Lake in northern Saskatchewan (west of Reindeer Lake) is named in his memory. Photographs taken October 21, 2003.

◄ **STONY RAPIDS**, September 1976. Saskatchewan Archives Board, Saskatchewan Photographic Services, R-PS76-1183-212. Photographer: G. Leggett.

STONY RAPIDS, northern hamlet, pop 189 (2001c), is located in the province's extreme north, approximately 80 km south of the Saskatchewan–Northwest Territories border, on the south shore of the Fond du Lac River between Lake Athabasca and Black Lake. Access to the area is primarily by aircraft, although in 2000, a 200-kilometre seasonal (primarily winter use) road was built connecting Stony Rapids to Points North Landing and gravel Highway 905, which leads south to La Ronge. The total distance to La Ronge is 665 kilometres. In late February/early March, if ice thickness exceeds 36 inches, an ice road is built from Stony Rapids through Fond du Lac to Uranium City. Immediately to the east of Stony Rapids lie the reserve lands of the Black Lake Denesuline First Nation, with a population of over 1,200. Many Black Lake members reside in Stony Rapids, and the closely intertwined communities are connected with an all-season road. Métis began settling at Stony Rapids in the 1920s (the post office was established in 1937) and the community began to grow through the 1940s and 1950s. Denesuline was once widely spoken in the community, but today its usage is not as prevalent as it is on the Black Lake reserves. Many aspects of Dene culture remain strong, however, and traditional activities such as fishing, hunting, trapping, and guiding remain a major source of income. Many people also use the area's abundant fish and wildlife to supplement their food supplies and offset the cost of food, which, due to high shipping costs, is locally very expensive. During the winter months, when barren-ground caribou from the Beverly and Qamanirjuaq herds migrate south from the Northwest Territories to their wintering grounds in the Athabasca basin, many participate in the caribou hunt. During the summer months, sports fishing is one of the mainstays of the area economy, and outfitting and guiding anglers is a major source of employment, as there are numerous fishing lodges and camps in the area which attract an international clientele. In winter, commercial net fishing provides an additional means of revenue. Besides fish and wildlife, another of the region's plentiful resources is minerals, particularly uranium and other heavy metals. Due to the increase in the prices of these commodities, exploration in the region has increased threefold over the past few years. At present, northern mines provide some employment for Stony Rapids and Black Lake residents, and there are plans for mineral exploration in the immediate area throughout 2007. Local employment in Stony Rapids is found in businesses and services which include the northern hamlet office, the post office, restaurants, accommodations, a Saskatchewan Environment office, construction companies, an air strip and a water base for aircraft, air charter services, an RCMP detachment, and general stores, which together provide clothing, household appliances, hunting equipment, groceries, hardware, snowmobiles, and a branch of the Prince Albert Credit Union. A new hospital, a key community employer, was built in 2003. Stony Rapids has a K-9 school that had 51 students enrolled in the fall of 2006 — the community of Black Lake, 17 kilometres southeast, has a K-12 institution. In June 2006, a forest fire on the north side of the Fond du Lac River threatened to jump the river and destroy the hamlet. As burning embers rained down upon the community, igniting spot fires, most residents (including patients at the hospital) were evacuated to Black Lake or to Prince Albert, while those who remained behind cleared a firebreak and kept the community's major buildings damp. While Stony Rapids escaped destruction and there were no injuries, several trappers' cabins on the north side of the river were lost. In November 2006, Stony Rapids and the Black Lake and Fond du Lac Denesuline First Nations gained access to high-speed internet services.

STORNOWAY, hamlet, pop 10 (2006c), 10 (2001c), is a former village located northeast of Yorkton, approximately 8 km north of Hwy 10. Settlement of the area began in the late 1800s and, with the arrival of the railway in 1911, the village was established and incorporated. The name of the community honours the town of Stornoway, on the Isle of Lewis, Scotland. The Village of Stornoway be-

▼ **STORNOWAY**, July 13, 2004.

came a small centre for trade and social activities, and its school educated children from the surrounding district. At the outbreak of WWII, the population was close to 150. There were about 100 people living in the village in the mid-1960s; however, by 1971, the population had plummeted to 37. Today, other than a few abandoned businesses and a number of vacant houses, very little remains of the community. Stornoway relinquished village status on December 31, 2006, and is located in the RM of Wallace No. 243.

STORTHOAKS, village, pop 82 (2006c), 99 (2001c), is located in the southeast corner of the province, south of Redvers on Hwy 361, about 15 km from the Saskatchewan-Manitoba border. In 1899, the first French settlers arrived. They had origins in Quebec, but had been working in the industrial centres of the United States when lured to western Canada by the prospects of owning their own land and farming. By 1903, there were approximately 40 French families in the district and most of the available homesteads had been occupied. The first crops were produced in 1901 and were hauled to either Redvers or Carievale. The parish of St. Antoine des Prairies was established, and a church was built in 1902 on the homestead of Father Apollinaire Ferland (NW28-5-31-W1), about three miles northwest of the present village. By 1905, two district schools — St. Edmond and St. Thomas — were in operation. St. Thomas School was about two miles west of present-day Storthoaks. The village itself had its beginnings in 1911-12 when the CPR was building its line from Lauder, Manitoba, to Alida. The townsite was surveyed in 1911; the honour of naming locales along the rail line was

given to Sir Harry Brittain, English author, barrister, and politician, and he named Storthoaks after his estate of Storth Oaks in Yorkshire, England. Between 1912 and 1914 a number of places of business were started in the emerging hamlet; in 1915, non-French Protestants erected a Methodist (later United) church in Storthoaks; by 1916, St. Thomas School, two miles away, was becoming overcrowded, so a new two-storey school was built in the community. The Storthoaks Protestant Separate School District was established in 1918; in 1919 the school opened about a mile to the west of the hamlet. This school lasted until 1951 when it was closed and ratepayers amalgamated with St. Thomas. In 1926, the Roman Catholic Church (built in 1911 to replace the original 1902 structure) was moved in from the country. Storthoaks became an incorporated village on June 5, 1940, and reached a peak population of 234 in 1956, up from 146 a decade earlier. The rise in the community's numbers during the 1950s was in part spurred by the development of the area's oil industry. The first well was drilled in 1953, and soon people found employment working as rig hands, truckers, battery operators, or on construction and maintenance crews. The activity was also a boon to Storthoaks' businesses. By the 1960s, however, the community was showing signs of decline — the population was falling and businesses were closing. An automobile dealership closed in 1966, a hardware and farm equipment business closed in 1972, one of the grocery stores closed in 1984, a café closed in 1987. In 1968, the United Church closed and the building was moved to Alida, high school students were bused to Carnduff, and the 16,000-square-foot skating and curling complex burned to the ground. Nine months later, however, a determined

▲ **CHILDREN STANDING IN FRONT OF DAVID CARDIN'S HOUSE** in Storthoaks, 1912. Saskatchewan Archives Board R-A24222.

▼ **THE FIRST OFFICE FOR THE RM OF STORTHOAKS NO. 31** was housed in this building built in 1927. It was replaced by a more spacious building in 1978 which houses the offices of both the village and the rural municipality, the road equipment garages, and the fire hall. Photograph taken August 21, 2003.

community had completed the construction of a new village rink. For many years, Storthoaks' hockey teams were formidable contenders, often league champions. In the spring of 1976, the rail line into Storthoaks was washed out during a flood on the Souris River in Manitoba; CP never repaired the track and it was officially abandoned in 1978. With the loss of rail service, the grain elevators were demolished. The Sisters of the Cross who had taught at St. Thomas School since 1966 were gone in 1982. Today, the Storthoaks Hotel, a farm equipment dealership, and a welding shop are about the only businesses left in the village; residents mainly shop and seek services in either Redvers or Carnduff. Storthoaks retains an active seniors' centre, Catholic church, and curling rink; St. Thomas School closed in June 2003; area children now attend schools in either Redvers, Carnduff, or Carievale. The nearest RCMP detachment is in Carnduff; there is a health centre in Gainsborough and a hospital in Redvers. Storthoaks serves as the administrative headquarters of the RM of Storthoaks No. 31; the RM and the village share office space in a building which also houses the fire hall. About half of the people in Storthoaks still claim French origins, grain farming continues to dominate the area economy, and oil fields and a pipeline contribute close to 40 per cent of the RM's tax revenues.

STOUGHTON, town, pop 653 (2006c), 720 (2001c), is located 60 km east of Weyburn and 60 km north of Estevan at the junction of Hwys 13, 33, and 47. Moose Mountain Provincial Park lies to the northeast. About three years prior to the CPR arriving in the district in 1904 a small settlement by the name of New Hope had begun to develop a short dis-

tance from today's community. When the railway surveyed and named the present townsite Stoughton after a surveyor, New Hope disappeared as people relocated to be on the rail line. Stoughton was incorporated as a village in 1904, with tracks running northwest to Regina and east into Manitoba. The line from Regina remains the longest straight stretch of track in North America and is the second longest in the world (the longest is in Australia). By 1908, rails were running west to Weyburn. The community was situated to become the distribution centre for a wide area, and by 1916 the population of Stoughton was 455. The community faced a significant downturn during the 1930s (the population was down to 302 by 1941), but in the years following WWII growth was steady, with the rate levelling off in the 1970s. Stoughton attained town status in 1960. The area economy is based mainly upon agriculture (grains, oilseeds,

▲ **THE DAVID DONNELLY HOMESTEAD, CIRCA 1900.** The Donnelly family's home, pictured here, was located at NE28-08-08-W2, where the town of Stoughton now stands. Donnelly became the village's first overseer in 1904. Donnelly family members included, from left to right: Stan Donnelly (out of focus and on the horse), Orville Donnelly, David and Annie Donnelly (in the buggy), Walter Donnelly, and Elizabeth Donnelly (in the upstairs window).

Photographs, other than of Taylor Park, courtesy of the Stoughton & District Museum.

At the "Crossroads of Friendship"...
STOUGHTON

▲ **DOMINION DAY**, Stoughton, 1927.

▲ ▶ **STOUGHTON MAYOR ALBERT LEVESQUE**
sawing a log with the help of mascot "Snowball" (above) and Sno-Pitch competitors (right) at the Wheatland-Souris Regional Winter Games held in Stoughton in 1980.

◀ **TAYLOR PARK**, named after Wilfred C. Taylor, the first mayor of the Town of Stoughton, lies just west of Main Street. Photograph taken August 19, 2003.

and pulse crops) and oil and gas production and related oilfield support services. One of the best known rinks in Canadian curling history, the Richardson rink, came from Stoughton. In 1959, the family team of two brothers (Ernie and Garnet) and two cousins (Arnold and Wes) became the youngest team to win the Brier, and they went on to capture four Briers in five years, and four Scotch Cups for the world championships, among numerous other championships and titles. Brier number four in 1963 was won with close family friend Mel Perry playing lead, as Wes Richardson was sidelined from the team with severe back problems. The Richardson rink was inducted into the Canadian Sports Hall of Fame, and skip Ernie Richardson was honoured with the Order of Canada in 1978. Stoughton serves as the administrative centre of the RM of Tecumseh No. 65.

STRASBOURG, town, pop 732 (2006c), 760 (2001c), is situated east of Last Mountain Lake, 80 km north of Regina on Hwy 20. Just northeast of the town rises the height of land from which the lake's name was derived. The history of Strasbourg dates to 1885 with the arrival of the first German settlers. Immigration literature which circulated in Germany called the area Neu Elsass, with the hope that a German name would attract settlers, and the colony that developed in the Last Mountain area came to be known as the Neu Elsass Colony. In 1886, a post office was established in the district which was named Strassburg, after the European city which had been annexed to Germany since 1870. The immigration literature had shown that a railway was to be built from Regina along the east

▲ **FAIR DAY IN STRASBOURG**, August 8, 1918, attracted a large crowd to the community's fair grounds. Saskatchewan Archives Board R-B7910.

side of Last Mountain Lake and north to Prince Albert, and the first settlers had expected the development within a few years. When the railway did not come, discouraged settlers left for less isolated locations. Those that remained faced a period of slow development, and prairie fires and bad weather which claimed many crops. Finally, in the early 1900s, the CPR was progressing toward the district. A townsite was established, followed by a building boom. The railway arrived in 1905, and on April 19, 1906, the village of Strassburg was incorporated. On July 1, 1907, the community attained town sta-

tus. The railway brought an influx of settlers of various origins, and the area began to develop a multicultural flavour. Rapid development occurred in the period prior to WWI. Following the war, the European Strassburg was re-annexed to France and the spelling of its name changed to Strasbourg. Amidst considerable controversy, the spelling of the name of the Saskatchewan town was changed to its present form in 1919. In 1921, the population of the town was 514, and it hovered around the 500 mark until the post-WWII period, when, again, the community experienced significant growth. From a population of

505 in 1951 the town's numbers rose to 636 by 1961 and 759 in 1971. Today, the town continues as a market, service, and cultural centre for a mixed farming district of roughly 2,500 square kilometres (1,000 square miles). Strasbourg also benefits from tourist traffic to Rowan's Ravine Provincial Park, the migratory bird sanctuary on Last Mountain Lake's north end, and the resort communities situated on the lake's east side. As well, hunters arrive in the fall. The town has a core of essential businesses, an RCMP detachment, a volunteer fire department, and an ambulance service, as well as a medical clinic with the services of a doctor, dentist, and chiropractor. William Derby School is a K-12 facility, which had 250 town and area students enrolled in the fall of 2006. Community recreational facilities include an arena, curling rinks, a fitness centre, and a new nine-hole golf course, the result of local fundraising and volunteer efforts. The town has four churches and a library. The Strasbourg and District Museum housed in the 1906 CPR station, now a heritage property, displays pioneer and First Nations artifacts. The building was purchased by the community in 1971 after the station had closed the previous year. Strasbourg serves as the administrative centre of the RM of McKillop No. 220.

STRONGFIELD, village, pop 47 (2006c), 42 (2001c), is situated on Hwy 19, 24 km north of Lake Diefenbaker, between the villages of Loreburn (to the south) and Hawarden (to the north). The first applications for homesteads in the Strongfield region were made in 1903; settlers began to arrive in 1904. Land in the district was largely taken up by a few main groups of people. More than a third came from Grey County, Ontario, led by George Whitfield Armstrong, who was a businessman from Markdale, Ontario, and an agent for the Saskatchewan Valley Land Company. Strongfield's name was derived by combining the second syllables of Armstrong's last two names, and the name was first applied to a post office established in 1906, two miles northwest of the present village. Another group that settled early in the region, to the east and west of the South Saskatchewan River valley, were Finnish farm families hailing from the Dakotas. Many of these who took up land in the Strongfield area moved on, however, to take up new homesteads to the west of the river where the majority of the Finns had settled. Another large group came to the Strongfield area from the central United States and were largely of Norwegian descent, mainly Lutherans. After a few years, a handful of the Norwegians gave up trying to make a life on the Saskatchewan prairie and returned to Norway; later, though, their numbers were replenished as relatives of those who remained came directly from their homeland to make a new life in the province. Adding to the Strongfield area mix were also arrivals from England. Most of the early settlers — the majority arrived in 1905 — came through Regina and detrained at either Bladworth or

▲ **AN AERIAL VIEW** of Strasbourg, circa 1960s. Saskatchewan Archives Board R-B1879-2.

▶ **MOUNTAIN STREET**, Strasbourg, looking east. Photograph taken July 10, 2003.

Hanley, then the nearest railway points. The village of Strongfield had its origins in 1908, as the CPR was constructing its line from Moose Jaw to Outlook. Evidently, the railway company wanted to name the location "Conan," but local influence was such that the name of the area post office was adopted. In 1909, the post office was relocated to the townsite, and a number of businesses and homes, a Methodist (later United) church, and three grain elevators were built. The CPR constructed a sta-

tion in 1910, and that year a local school district was formed. Children attended classes in the church until a school was built in 1911. The Village of Strongfield was incorporated on May 3, 1912, and the population of the community stabilized at approximately 100. Its business centre remained active until the late 1960s, at which point it began to be superseded by offerings in larger centres. In the period following WWII, Strongfield had prospered and its population began to increase; in

the early 1960s, with the construction of the Gardiner Dam underway, it briefly rose to over 200 as workers and their families temporarily made their homes in the community. By the mid-1960s, however, Strongfield's population was declining, and it has continued to do so through each consecutive census period to date. In the fall of 1961, high school students began to be bused to the neighbouring village of Loreburn to attend classes. At the end of the school year in 1993, Strongfield School, then down to a K-6 school with about 30 students, was closed. By the mid-1970s, only one grain elevator remained in operation; by the end of the 1990s, where a row of them had once stood, none remained. Today, Strongfield retains an agricultural chemical and fertilizer dealer and its skating and curling rinks. An important area business is the Gardiner Dam Terminal located south of the village. It is a 17,000-tonne high-throughput grain elevator jointly owned by area farmers and Agricore United. The Strongfield Café houses a postal outlet. A machine and welding shop is located in the former school, in front of which stands the cenotaph (impressive for a community the size of Strongfield) commemorating 11 sons who died in two world wars. Strongfield is situated in the RM of Loreburn No. 254.

and opened up to homesteaders and land purchasers, and over the following few years increasing numbers of settlers came to the district. People came from the United States, eastern Canada, England, the Scandinavian countries, Poland, and the Ukraine. The district was originally known as Stanhope, but when an area post office established in 1908 was given the name Sturgis, the name stuck and became that of the community upon the arrival of the railway. Sturgis, North Dakota, was likely the home of the first postmaster, F. C. Brooks, hence the name. With the approach of the Canadian Northern Railway from Swan River, Manitoba, through Pelly, the townsite was established and began to develop. The railway arrived in 1911, and by September 3, 1912, the fledgling community had grown large enough to be incorporated as a village. The line from the east continued on to Preeceville and eventually Kelvington. In 1916, another rail line, from Canora to the south, was built to Sturgis, continuing on to Hudson Bay in the late 1920s before being built through to Churchill, Manitoba. Sturgis thus became the junction of important east-west and north-south rail lines, and by the 1950s the community had become the largest cattle shipping centre in the eastern area of the province. The community grew to have a population of roughly 350 by the outset of WWII, and then in the post-war period Sturgis experienced rapid growth. From a population of 364 in 1946, its number grew to 640 by 1951, and on March 1 that year the community attained town status. By the early 1980s, the population of the town was just shy of 800. Today, the community and the surrounding region, including Preeceville, is home to roughly 5,500 people. The town's businesses provide a range of goods and services and include a farm machinery

▲ ◄ **THE STRONGFIELD CAFE** and postal outlet (above) and the village's war memorial (left). The inscription on the front of the memorial reads, "To the memory of the gallant men of Strongfield who laid down their lives on the field of battle while upholding the cause of freedom and justice." Photographs taken July 19, 2004.

STURGIS, town, pop 575 (2006c), 627 (2001c), is located in a rolling parkland topography 10 km east of Preeceville on Hwys 9 and 49. The town is nestled between hills to the north and south; a regional park, through which the Assiniboine River flows, forms the southern boundary of the town, greatly adding to the community's aesthetic appearance. In 1902, area townships were surveyed

▲ **THE WEST SIDE OF MAIN STREET**, circa 1915.

▼ **THE STURGIS BAND** in 1950.

STURGIS FIRE.

▲ **HAPPY HALLOWEEN?** A serious fire in the business section on October 31, 1949 destroyed five businesses and left four families homeless. The fire broke out at 10:00 in the morning in a boarding room over a print shop. An explosion of an airtight heater resulted in the destruction of Kolot's Café, the Lagasse Bake Shop, W. Holmberg's snack bar, Otto Reitlo's meat market, and the *Northeast Review* print shop (production of the newspaper had to be suspended until the end of February 1950 because of the blaze). A call for help over CJGX Radio brought responses from the Preeceville, Canora, Kelvington, and Hudson Bay fire brigades, and hundreds of people from far and wide arrived to work bucket brigades. A vacant lot stopped the fire from spreading further; Harold Ast, the druggist, administered first aid at the scene; Clark (Buster) Grass served coffee and sandwiches from his hotel for the firefighters; and five airplanes flew in from Yorkton and Kamsack carrying newspaper and radio reporters. The loss at the time was estimated at $75,000.

Home of Saskatchewan's largest one-day rodeo...

STURGIS

▼ **STURGIS STATION HOUSE MUSEUM.**

▲ **THE STURGIS COMPOSITE HIGH SCHOOL JUNIOR BASEBALL CLUB** in 1951 with what looks like a possible ringer from the village of Buchanan.

STURGIS SPORTS JUL. 1. 1959.

▲ **BILLED AS THE LARGEST EVENT OF ITS KIND** in Saskatchewan, Sturgis's Sports and Rodeo Days have been a long-standing tradition. The event is pictured here on July 1, 1959.

Historical (black-and-white) photographs courtesy of the Sturgis Station House Museum; colour photographs taken July 29, 2004.

▼ **THE ASSINIBOINE RIVER** winds through Sturgis and District Regional Park on the town's southern edge.

dealership. Agriculture is the major industry in the area and consists of grain production, cattle ranching, and an intensive hog operation that produces approximately 70,000 hogs annually. Timber and logging are an important secondary industry, and, recently, a Manitoba-based oil and gas company has been making exploratory incursions into the beautiful Porcupine Provincial Forest north of the town. Community services in Sturgis include an RCMP detachment and a volunteer fire department; a hospital and a range of medical services are located in nearby Preeceville. Sturgis has a nursery school, and the town's elementary and high schools provide K-12 education to approximately 200 students. The town has a library, six churches, a number of service clubs and other community-based organizations. The Sturgis Station House Museum is located in the former 1912 Canadian Northern Railway Station. Community recreational facilities include an arena, which accommodates public and figure skating as well as organized hockey. The town has a curling club and a bowling centre, and there is a ski hill with a tow bar at the regional park. As well, there are a number of lakes and resort areas in the region. The community's junior men's and junior women's lacrosse teams have won numerous medals and championships over the years. The town's premier event is a long-running sports day and rodeo, billed as "Saskatchewan's Largest," which takes place on July 1 each year in a sizable natural amphitheatre. Sturgis is situated in the RM of Preeceville No. 334.

SUCCESS, village, pop 40 (2006c), 51 (2001c), is located northwest of Swift Current on Hwy 32, in the RM of Riverside No. 168. Saskatchewan Landing Provincial Park on the shores of Lake Diefenbaker lies approximately 30 km to the north; to the west lie the Great Sand Hills. Only a few ranchers were in the region when the first homesteaders began arriving around 1905-06, and in the early years people travelled to Swift Current, or to Beverley, the nearest railway points on the CPR main line, to obtain their supplies or deliver grain. In 1911, when the railway came through, construction of the village began. The first grain was shipped via rail that fall and Success was incorporated a year later, on October 25, 1912. The years prior to the drought and Depression were to be Success's most active; numerous businesses served the surrounding region, and toward the end of the 1920s the village had a population nearing 200. With the hard times that followed, though, the population began to shrink, and through the 1940s the trend continued. The discovery of oil at nearby Fosterton in the early 1950s brought about somewhat of a resurgence; however, by then, improved roads, the community's proximity to Swift Current, and fewer people farming the surrounding countryside all contributed to the village's continuing decline. Today, little remains of the community's former business district. Success School, however, remains an important community institution, providing K-9 education. There were 76 students enrolled in the fall of 2006. Agriculture, and oil and gas are the major industries in the area.

SUMMERFIELD BEACH, organized hamlet, is located north of North Battleford, one of a number of resort communities on Murray Lake. It was established as an organized hamlet in 1996. By 2006 there were 40 permanent residents; the population, however, varies depending on the season. Summerfield Beach is situated in the RM of Meota No. 468.

SUN VALLEY, resort village, is one of a number of resort communities situated on the southwest shore of Buffalo Pound Lake. It is accessed via Hwy 2 north of Moose Jaw. The Sun Valley subdivision was surveyed in the early 1950s and was established as an organized hamlet in 1962. In 1985, Sun Valley was incorporated as a resort village. There was a year-round population of 128 in 2006; however, with permanent residences and cabins stretching for roughly 5 kilometres along the lake shore, the summer population may reach into the several hundreds. A number of people commute to work in Moose Jaw. Sun Valley is located in the RM of Marquis No. 191.

SUNSET BEACH, organized hamlet, is a resort community located in the eastern Qu'Appelle Valley, south of Grayson, on Crooked Lake. Sunset Beach lies 2 km east of Crooked Lake Provincial Park and is one of a number of resort areas surrounding the lake's shores. Established as an organized hamlet in 1953, the resort has a store, gas sales, cabin and boat rentals, and traditionally, a flea market held each Sunday through the summer months. The population of Sunset Beach varies depending on the season. Sunset Beach is situated in the RM of Grayson No. 184.

SUNSET COVE, resort village, is one in a string of resort communities on the east side of the south end of Last Mountain Lake accessed by Hwy 322. Developed in the 1960s, and incorporated in 1983, Sunset Cove had about two dozen permanent residents in 2006. The summer population may reach 125. Sunset Cove is situated in the RM of McKillop No. 220.

SUNSET VIEW BEACH, organized hamlet, is one of several resort communities situated northeast of Turtleford on Turtle Lake. It was developed during the 1950s and 1960s, established as an organized hamlet in 1985, and incorporated as a resort village in 1992. It reverted to organized hamlet status on January 1, 2005. There were 28 permanent residents in 2006; however, the population varies greatly depending on the season, reaching approximately 400 during the summer months. Sunset View Beach is located in the RM of Mervin No. 499.

SWAN PLAIN, organized hamlet, pop 15 (2006c), pop 15 (2001c), is located 27 km north of Norquay on Hwy 8. Swan Plain sits at the northern fringe of the parklands; just to the north and east lies the Porcupine Provincial Forest. The name of the hamlet refers to its location within the big bend of the Swan River. The first settlers ventured into the area around 1904-05, and settling the area was not easy. Most of the district was heavily forested, and the land had to be cleared by hand, with the axe the main piece of equipment. The majority of the early settlers were of Ukrainian descent. The region became fairly extensively settled during the first two decades of the century; however, the hamlet of Swan Plain did not come into existence until later. The school district was set up in 1911, but grocery stores, postal facilities (the Swan Plain Post Office was established in 1913), and other places of business were operated from individual farms, and it was not until 1922 that the first place of business — a general store — opened at the present hamlet site. In the 1930s, people from the parched southern areas of the province came through Swan Plain, settling the area to the north, and during the same period an Old Colony Mennonite settlement was established in the Swan Plain area. Swan Plain developed into a small, but busy and bustling centre that supplied the material and social needs of the surrounding district for several decades. There were 80 people living in the hamlet in 1966, but by then the population was rapidly falling. At the end of the school year in June 1969, the school was closed, followed in 1970 by the closure of the post office. By 1972, the population of Swan Plain had fallen to 51. There is still a grocery store in Swan Plain today, and two landmark churches remain, both of which have been designated heritage properties: St. Andrew's Church, a Ukrainian United Church built circa 1936; and Saint Peter and Paul, a Ukrainian Greek Orthodox Church, built in the 1940s. Swan Plain is situated in the RM of Clayton No. 333.

SWIFT CURRENT, city, pop 14,946 (2006c), 14,821 (2001c), affectionately known by many residents of Saskatchewan as "Speedy Creek," is located 245 km west of Regina, 168 km east of the Saskatchewan-Alberta border, and 152 km north of the Saskatchewan-Montana border at the junction of the Trans-Canada Hwy and Hwy No. 4. The Swift Current Creek, from which the community derives its name, flows northward through the city into the South Saskatchewan River. The origins of the community date to 1882-83 and the construction of the CPR main line through the region. The townsite was reserved in 1882, and the tracks were laid that fall. The post office was established on August 1, 1883. It was during these early years that the railway set up a depot, and the first entrepreneurs set up the first stores. With the completion of the railway, Swift Current became the southern terminus of an important overland transportation route to Battleford. Until the Qu'Appelle, Long Lake & Saskatchewan Railway was completed between Regina and Prince Albert in 1890 via Saskatoon, many people traversed, and much mail and freight was hauled over, the 309-kilometre (192-mile) Battleford–Swift Current Trail. During the North-West Resistance, Colonel Otter marched some 500 men up the trail from Swift Current toward defeat at Cut Knife Hill. Portions of the trail are still visible at Swift Current to this day. In 1887, Sir John Lister-Kaye purchased land at Swift Current for one of his massive "76 Ranch" operations, and, until the early twentieth century, ranching was the primary activity in the region. The country remained sparsely populated and Swift Current was a small settlement until after the turn of the century, when homesteaders began to arrive in droves. They came from eastern Canada, the United States, and Europe. Mennonites settled in large numbers in the region: a six-township colony south of Swift Current grew to be comprised of close to twenty villages. Swift Current was incorporated as a village on February 4, 1904, attained town status on March 15, 1907, and received its city charter on January 15, 1914, becoming Saskatchewan's seventh city. The population climbed from 121 in 1901 to 3,181 by 1916. While Swift Current grew steadily, serving a large ranching, mixed farming, and grain farming area throughout the first half of the twentieth century (other than a slight downturn during the Depression), the development of the region's oil indus-

▲ **FRONTIER DAYS PARADE IN SWIFT CURRENT**, looking north over Main Street, 1961. Saskatchewan Archives Board R-B5598-6.

try in the 1950s was a catalyst for significant growth. From a population of 6,379 in 1946, Swift Current's numbers rose to 14,485 by 1966. While the community's population has remained relatively unchanged for the past 40 years, the city has seen substantial investment in infrastructure and commercial developments in recent years. Today, the city's economy is based in agriculture, oil and gas, retail and service industries, and a growing manufacturing sector. The city serves a market area of approximately 55,000 people, and also benefits from the high volume of traffic along the Trans-Canada Highway: numerous motels, service stations, and restaurants have lined the stretch since it was rebuilt and rerouted out of the city centre in the 1960s. Swift Current has approximately 1,000 licensed businesses, manufacturers, and professionals; among these in 2007 were 255 retail firms, two large shopping malls, several strip malls, and businesses in a revitalized downtown shopping district. Swift Current's educational facilities include four elementary schools (one Catholic), three junior high schools (one Catholic), and two high schools; post-secondary studies are available through the Cypress Hills Regional College. The new Cypress Regional Hospital which opened its doors in April 2007 is the city's major health care facility — in the realm of health care, Swift Current gained the distinction of establishing the first universal, tax-supported hospital and medical insurance plan in North America in the mid-1940s, a pilot project that served as a model for the development of province-wide medicare. The RCMP provide Swift Current with policing services; the city has a municipal fire department. Thirty-one places of worship serve Swift Current's diverse religious communities; the city has two radio stations: CKSW and The Eagle 94.1 FM. The *Prairie Post* and *The Southwest Booster* are weekly newspapers; local television news is broadcast twice each weeknight by Southwest TV News on cable television. The city has a wide range of sports and recreation facilities: the Centennial Civic Centre, built in 1967 and recently expanded and branded with a corporate name, is home to the Swift Current Broncos of the Western Hockey League; the Indians Ball Diamond is home to the Swift Current Indians of the Western Major Baseball League. The city's artistic and cultural life is bolstered by the Art Gallery of Swift Current, the Southwest Artists' Guild, the Swift Current Allied Arts Council, Swift Current Little Theatre, and numerous annual festivals and multi-cultural events. The Swift Current Museum moved into a new facility in the spring of 2007; "Doc's Town" is a recreation of an early twentieth-century pioneer village; the Mennonite Heritage Village in Swift Current depicts the life and times of the Mennonite settlers who arrived in the region in the early 1900s. A 35-million-dollar casino and performing arts complex is scheduled to open in late 2008 or early 2009. Swift Current's city council is comprised of a mayor and six councillors elected for three-year terms. Swift Current serves as the administrative centre of the RM of Swift Current No. 137.

SYLVANIA, organized hamlet, pop 58 (2006c), 56 (2001c), is located about 17 km south of Tisdale, just east of Hwy 35. In the early 1900s, settlers, who were largely English speaking, began to arrive in the district, and by 1915 most of the available homesteads were taken. In the early years, many men found seasonal work in the logging camps in the region toward Hudson Bay. In 1909, a post office was established somewhat east of the present community, and given the name Sylvania, Latin for "beautifully wooded country." When the CPR built a branch line north from Sheho to Tisdale in 1923, the hamlet began to develop and the post office was soon moved in from the country. A hotel, stores, a livery and feed stable, three grain elevators, and a lumberyard were among the first businesses established. A Bank of Nova Scotia opened in 1926, but closed in 1932, a victim of the Depression. Children in the young hamlet first attended classes in a space in the eastern portion of the hotel, rented for $25 a month, and where the bar would later be located, until a proper schoolhouse was built in 1931. In the fall of 1941, the community was saddened to learn of the death of a former student of Sylvania School, Ross Stewart (Bud) Hambly, who had been well-liked, and active in junior hockey and other sports. Hambly had become a sergeant in the Royal Canadian Air Force and was shot down over the English Channel following a raid on shipping along the French coast. He was 21 when he died on September 18 that year, and his body was never recovered. He is commemorated at the Runnymede Memorial in England. Sylvania began to experience a slow decline in the years following WWII, as rural populations dwindled, transportation improved, and businesses, services, and institutions became centralized in larger centres. The Imperial Oil Company located in Sylvania moved to Tisdale, as did the Beaver Lumber Company in 1948. In the fall of 1955, high school students began to be bused to Tisdale, and over the following years the population of the community steadily fell. The service station, tennis court, pool room, barber shop, etc., disappeared. The population of Sylvania was still 125 in 1976 and new homes were still being built, but, today, residents of the quiet and attractive little hamlet largely look to Tisdale for businesses, services, employment, entertainment, and other amenities. Sylvania School was down to being a K-5 facility with 31 students enrolled in the fall of 2006; it was closed at the end of the school year in 2007. Sylvania is situated in the RM of Tisdale No. 427.

TADMORE, organized hamlet, pop 31 (2006c), 30 (2001c), is located north of Canora, a few km west of Hwy 9. The district began to be settled in the early 1900s, particularly, after the railway reached Canora around 1904-05 and then Sturgis, to the north, in 1911. The settlers were of various nationalities: there were Ukrainian, Polish, British and Scandinavian homesteaders in the Tadmore region.

When the rail line was being built north from Canora toward Hudson Bay in 1916, Tadmore was put on the map. Within a few years, a thriving and varied business community developed, which included everything from a pool hall to a shoe repair shop. There were three grain elevators. By the 1960s and 1970s, however, the community was in decline. Businesses closed, as did the school. In the early 1980s, the last of the grain elevators also closed, leaving what is today a small and quiet residential community. Tadmore is located in the RM of Buchanan No. 304.

TANTALLON, village, pop 105 (2006c), 110 (2001c), is situated in one of the most beautiful settings of any community in Saskatchewan. Located in the middle of the eastern Qu'Appelle Valley, Tantallon lies northwest of Rocanville, west of Hwy 8. The first settlers began arriving in the area in the 1880s, and later one of them, a Scot, James Douglas, named his farm Tantallon Farm after Tantallon Castle, which overlooks the Firth of Forth in Scotland. In 1897, Douglas ran the first Tantallon Post Office, and by that time the district was growing to include people of Finnish, Icelandic, and English origins. With the coming of the CPR in 1903-04,

the townsite was established. It developed rapidly, and on June 17, 1904, the Village of Tantallon was incorporated. The community was never tremendously large, fluctuating between approximately 100 to 150 people over the decades, but it did become a centre of commercial and social activity for the district. In the mid-1960s, the community experienced a short-lived boom after potash mining began in the region. The population grew from 145 in 1961 to 328 in 1966, before falling back to 174 by 1971. In 1993, Tantallon had two very interesting visitors. Two British canoeists, who were on a 21,000-kilometre trip from Alberta to Brazil, paddled down the Qu'Appelle River and made a stop at the village. After their voyage was complete, the canoeists wrote to the people they had met in Tantallon, filling them in

◄ **"TANTALLON: THE EARLY YEARS"** was designed and painted by Marlene Daniel of Tantallon with the assistance of Janet Scholz of Churchbridge, Saskatchewan. The work, created in 2001 and situated in a prominent location in the community, depicts the village's Main Street in the 1910s and early 1920s. Photograph by the author; used with permission of the artist.

Tantallan photographs taken October 17, 2003.

▼ **THE TANTALLON VILLAGE OFFICE** is located in what originally was a rural schoolhouse built in 1909. It was called Holar School and was constructed to replace an earlier 1894 building. The school was used until around the end of WWI, when the area was then absorbed into the Tantallon School District. The structure then became known as Holar Hall and was used as a community hall and a church. It was moved into Tantallon in 1985 and restored as a heritage property.

on the rest of their trip. The Tantallon of today has been described in stark but loving terms by Saskatchewan writer Trevor Herriott, who spent parts of his childhood there. In *River In A Dry Land*, Herriott describes Tantallon as "a dwindling assemblage of potash miners, retired farmers, and a few children waiting to grow up and move away." Indeed, the village has grown increasingly quiet. The elevators are gone, the rail line has been torn up, there is no more school, and, in recent years, one of the village's few remaining businesses, the old hotel, was put up for sale. In November 2007, however, the Potash Corporation of Saskatchewan (PotashCorp) announced a major mine and mill expansion at the nearby Rocanville mine; it is anticipated that an additional 190 new jobs will be generated by 2012. Tantallon is situated in the RM of Spy Hill No. 152.

TAYLOR BEACH, organized hamlet, is a resort community located on the southwest shore of Katepwa Lake. Although there was some initial activity in the area in the early twentieth century, it is in the past few decades that significant development has taken place. There are a few dozen permanent residents; however, the population may reach up to 150-200 during the summer months. Taylor Beach was established as an organized hamlet in 1972 and is situated in the RM of North Qu'Appelle No. 187.

TESSIER, village, pop 20 (2006c), 30 (2001c), is located 50 km northeast of Rosetown on Hwy 7. Goose Lake lies to the southeast; Eagle Creek passes about 5 km to the northwest. In the early 1900s settlers began heading southwest from the small settlement of Saskatoon on what

was known as the Old Bone Trail; by 1904-05, many were beginning to arrive in the area of present-day Tessier. Most were from eastern Canada, the British Isles, and the United States. One was Dr. Wilfred Onesime Tessier from Michigan, who arrived in 1904, homesteading along the trail about a mile south of the present village. Next to his home, Tessier built a shack he used as a doctor's office; adjacent to this was a sod store built by Alexander Shatilla; a butcher shop was established nearby. These were the origins of the community. In June 1906, an area post office that had been operating for about a month (known as Marshall) was relocated to the Shatilla store and renamed Tessier in honour of the doctor. In 1908, the Canadian Northern Railway came through the district en route from Saskatoon to Rosetown, and the townsite then established was given the name of the Tessier Post Office. In 1911, Gunner Hsorleifson Johnson became the postmaster; in the fall of 2007 (96 years later) the post office was still being run by the Johnson family. Tessier had become an incorporated village on August 24, 1909, and during the first two decades boasted a wide range of businesses and services, an active social life, and church groups. Implement agencies, garages, general stores, grain elevators, a bank,

drug store, undertaker, veterinarian, lumber companies, a blacksmith, livery and dray services, a butcher, bakery, barber shop and pool hall, a hardware store, a large hotel, oil companies, an insurance agency, restaurants, a laundry, and a co-op were among the early business concerns; dances, travelling minstrel shows, "pie socials," theatrical performances, and, later, homecoming celebrations were held in the Tessier Hall; a village United Church (originally Presbyterian) and a Catholic Church, south of Tessier, served area congregations. The Tessier School District was established in 1909. In 1931, the village had a peak population of 173, but the community had already witnessed its heyday. Businesses, including the bank and the hotel, were lost to the Depression, and by 1941 Tessier's population was down to 132. By 1956, the community numbered 104; by 1966, the population was 70. The railway station agent was removed in 1960; passenger service was discontinued in 1963; the station itself was removed from the townsite in 1980. In 1969, the school was closed. Today, the village is characterized by sidewalks along vacant lots and some long-abandoned homes and businesses. A former Saskatchewan Wheat Pool elevator remains standing; in 2007, the small Johnston Store containing

▼ **A CN TRAIN** rolls by Tessier's sole remaining grain elevator, which was built in 1957. Photograph taken August 28, 2004.

the post office was open only on weekday mornings. Tessier is situated in the RM of Harris No. 316.

THEODORE, village, pop 339 (2006c), 381 (2001c), is located approximately 40 km northwest of Yorkton on Hwy 16, the Yellowhead. Good Spirit Lake lies to the northeast; Whitesand Regional Park is about 5 km directly to the north of the community. The first settlers in the area arrived in the late 1880s and in the 1890s. Some had English, Scottish and Irish roots, others had Scandinavian and German origins. Most significant were Ukrainians. In the early 1890s, Richard Seeman established a large ranch based about three miles southeast of today's village; here a store was set up and, in 1893, a post office. It was named Theodore in honour of Seeman's wife, Theodora. A school by the same name was also established, and toward the latter portion of the 1890s a second store was started and a place for obtaining lodging and meals was begun. The present townsite began to develop in 1903-04 as the railway was being built from Yorkton to Sheho. The first new buildings were erected in 1903, and in 1904 the school, post office, and a store were moved in from the country. Rapidly, more people moved in and several businesses soon emerged. The new village of Theodore was incorporated on July 5, 1907. By 1911, the community numbered 193. The population increased steadily until the 1930s, having reached 371 by 1931; then it declined to 329 by 1946, before rising to a peak of 489 in 1966. Thereafter, the community's numbers remained stable until the early 1990s — Theodore still counted 473 residents in 1991. The decline in recent years is largely attributable to an aging population:

the median age of Theodore's residents in 2006 was 59.9, while that of the province as a whole was 38.7, a difference of over 21 years. There were only 32 students enrolled at St. Theodore School, a K-8 separate school, in the fall of 2006. Other schoolchildren attend the public school in nearby Springside; older children from both communities are bused to Yorkton to attend high school. Theodore has a health care centre and a special care home, a good range of businesses and services, community organizations and clubs, and a recreation complex that houses a hall, hockey arena, and a three-sheet curling rink. Two prominent village landmarks are the former Canadian Pacific Railway station, which now houses the community's museum, and Elim Evangelical

▲ **ONE OF CANADA'S LARGEST** manufacturers of Ukrainian pottery is located in Theodore. The business, now known as Diana May Clay 2004 Ltd., was started in the mid-1970s by Diana Budzinski and taken over in 2004 by the current proprietors, Stella Malanowich and Donna Makowsky. Pictured filling moulds is ceramicist Marty Napady. Photograph taken July 13, 2004.

▼ **ONE OF A KIND.** The Canadian Pacific Railway Station in Theodore, which now houses the community's museum as well as a seniors' centre, is the last remaining example of its kind (a Type 9 railway station) in Saskatchewan. It was designed by B.R. Pratt, a CPR architect, and was one of only five constructed in the province. It was closed as a railway station in the mid-1970s. Photograph taken July 12, 2004.

Lutheran Church built in 1916 by Swedish Lutherans who had settled in the district. Although the latter still stands, it was closed in the 1980s due to declining attendance. St. Paul's United Church, built in 1905 as a Presbyterian church, remains active, and, along with the railway station, is one of the oldest buildings standing in the village. Theodore is situated in the RM of Insinger No. 275.

THODE, resort village, is located just southeast of Dundurn on the west side of the Blackstrap Reservoir, which is more commonly known as Blackstrap Lake. Blackstrap Lake was formed in 1967 as part of a system of canals and reservoirs originating at Lake Diefenbaker and terminating at Little Manitou Lake. In 1968, the townsite of Thode was surveyed and lots were put up for sale. In 1978, Thode was established as an organized hamlet, and in 1981 it was incorporated as a resort village. The 2001 Census recorded 133 permanent residents; the 2006 Census, 156. However, the population varies significantly depending on the season. A number of people commute to work in Saskatoon. Thode is situated in the RM of Dundurn No. 314.

TIMBER BAY, northern hamlet, pop 108 (2001c), is located approximately an hour and a half's drive north of Prince Albert on the east side of Montreal Lake on gravel road No. 969. While the area was traditionally utilized as hunting and trapping grounds for the Cree, the present community did not develop until sometime between 1910 and 1920, when a horse trail was hewn between Prince Albert and La Ronge for freighting purposes, and a stopping place with a horse barn

and later a trading post developed. Eventually, a road was completed and traditional livelihoods based in hunting, fishing, and trapping shifted to an economy where logging, a sawmill in Weyakwin, commercial fishing, and construction were increasingly factors. For many years, the Mennonite Brethren operated a children's home in Timber Bay for children whose parents worked trap lines during the school term; today a Bible camp is run each summer by the Northern Canada Evangelical Mission. Until Highway 2 was completed along the west side of Montreal Lake in the early 1970s, Timber Bay lay on the main road from Prince Albert north. In 1965, a post office was established at Timber Bay; in 1971, power lines were extended into the region, bringing electricity to the hamlet; a community hall was built in 1977; and in 1979 a skating rink was completed. Today, Timber Bay School is a K-9 facility, which had 22 students enrolled in the fall of 2005. The community of Timber Bay is largely Metis and includes members of the Montreal Lake Cree Nation. The median age of the population in 2001 was 19.3, while that in all of Saskatchewan was 36.7. Timber Bay was officially established as a northern hamlet on October 1, 1983; its population was 174 in 1986.

TISDALE, town, pop 2,981 (2006c), 3,063 (2001c), is located 40 km east of Melfort on Hwys 3 and 35. The region is characterized by farmlands interspersed with stands of aspen, white spruce, and jack pine. People began settling the area around 1902, and before the railway arrived the locality was known as Doghide after the Doghide River, which flows along the town's east side. With the construction of the Canadian Northern Railway from Hudson Bay to Melfort in 1904, the

▲ **BOY SCOUTS** in Tisdale, circa 1912.

Photographs courtesy of the
Tisdale & District Museum.

▲ **THE TISDALE BRANCH** of the Canadian Legion, 1920.

Days on the Doghide gone by... TISDALE

▲ **NORTH-EASTERN SASKATCHEWAN FIRE BRIGADE**
Convention in Tisdale, September 26, 1934.

▲ **"IN OLD VIENNA."** The cast of a high school operetta
pose for a group photograph, March 1939.

▼ **THE PROVINCE'S GOLDEN JUBILEE** in 1955 celebrated with
a parade.

▼ **MAIN STREET**, circa 1920s.

townsite was named Tisdale in honour of Frederick W. Tisdale, a civil engineer with the railway. From a cluster of tents and shacks assembled in anticipation of the coming steel, Tisdale grew to gain village status on May 15, 1905. The first wave of settlers in the district came largely from eastern Canada, Great Britain, and the United States; through the 1920s people from continental Europe came to the area, most of them settling lands to the east of Tisdale; and, in the 1930s, people from the dried-out southern plains migrated to the region. Tisdale attained town status on November 1, 1920, and received an added boost in 1924 as the CPR line from Wadena to Nipawin came through. The community had grown fairly gradually at first, but with the advent of modern machinery the heavy bush in the region was cleared and its agricultural potential came to be realized. Tisdale, already established as the major supply and service centre for a sizable surrounding territory, developed extremely rapidly from the WWII era through to the mid-1970s, and came to be known as "the Land of Rape and Honey." Today, approximately one-third of the farmland in the region is cropped with canola, and the area is widely known for its honey production. The honey industry began to develop significantly in the 1940s; by the mid-1950s, 85 per cent of the almost three million kg of Saskatchewan honey produced annually came from apiaries in the Tisdale area. Presently, more than 4 million kg (9 million lbs) of honey — 10 per cent of that produced in Canada — comes from the district, worth several millions of dollars to the economy. Tisdale, from very early on, has possessed agriculturally related industries — at first, a flour mill and a creamery, and then the province's first honey processing co-operative. Today, the largest

pulse crop processing facility in Canada is located in the area, as is the largest alfalfa dehydrator in Saskatchewan. In the 1970s, Tisdale faced stagnation and began lumbering slowly into decline. Eventually, the population began shrinking. Seeing the fate of other Saskatchewan communities, strong, determined community leadership and a collectivist spirit fostered the development of creative counteractive and aggressive initiatives. Success bred success and local investment attracted outside capital. A city-sized shopping mall that is 100 per cent locally owned was built in the mid-1980s, attracting a Zellers and an OK Economy store. Maintaining a quality of life so that people would want to continue to live in Tisdale was a priority for the community's leadership, and subsequently an imaginative focal point for the community has evolved, receiving national attention for its integrated approach to providing a broad range of community services under one roof. The Tisdale RECplex has grown to include health care services, a day care, a preschool, middle and secondary schools, a community college, a library, a multi-purpose auditorium, a performing arts theatre, an aquatic centre, a regulation-size arena, a curling rink, a rifle, hand gun, and archery range, several meeting rooms, and a kitchen with the capacity to serve more than 500 meals. The Doghide River Trail system has also been developed over the years: it is a scenic route for walking, cycling, and cross-country skiing that runs along several sections of riverbank, passing though a wooded park and a natural wetland with a trout pond, boardwalk, and observation deck. Community leaders also aggressively pursued economic development. Tactical approaches to major grain companies resulted in the construction of four inland grain terminals between 1997

and 2000, and, today, five such facilities make Tisdale the largest grain handling centre in Saskatchewan. A major ethanol development is a current initiative and, in recent years, Tisdale's manufacturing sector has expanded substantially and many new jobs have been created. A number of new homes and commercial buildings are being built each year, and, until recently, Tisdale's growth rate has ranked among the province's highest. The number of Kindergarten classes has increased and Tisdale's schools currently accommodate approximately 900 town and area students. Tisdale's trading area population is estimated at around 53,000 people. The town's premier annual event is the Doghide River Festival, held during the last weekend in April. The festival celebrates arts and culture, featuring entertainers from the region, a dinner theatre, and local artwork. Other community attractions include the Tisdale Riverside Golf Course, the Tisdale and District Museum, a stock

car racing venue built in 2000, and the 1935 Falkon Theatre, which showcases cinema on what is reputedly the largest theatre screen in northern Saskatchewan. Tisdale is also the hometown of comedian/actor/writer Brent Butt, the star of the hit TV series *Corner Gas*, filmed in Rouleau, Saskatchewan. Butt was born in Tisdale on August 3, 1966, which was, as his biography points out, the very day that legendary comedian Lenny Bruce died. Tisdale serves as the administrative centre of the RM of Tisdale No. 427.

TOBIN LAKE, resort village, pop 87 (2006c), 45 (2001c), is located northeast of Nipawin on Hwy 255 and is situated on the southwest shore of the lake from which it derives its name. The village site was originally known as Pas Trail after its location along an old trail to The Pas, Manitoba. The first settlers arrived in 1929, and by the 1930s a store, post office,

▼ **TOBIN LAKE**, upon which the resort village of the same name is located, is bounded by miles of pristine sandy beaches and boreal forest. Photograph taken in mid-July 2006.

church, and school had been established. The resort developed, and the name was changed from Pas Trail, after Tobin Lake was created by the construction of the E. B. Campbell Dam (formerly known as the Squaw Rapids Dam) across the Saskatchewan River in the 1960s. The resort village was incorporated in 1973. Today, Tobin Lake is one of North America's premier walleye and pike fisheries, and on September 21, 1997, its waters yielded the largest walleye ever caught in Saskatchewan waters, weighing in at 8.2 kg (or just over 18 lbs). The resort provides guides, boat rentals, camping and cabins, and caters to both summer angling and winter ice-fishing seasons. Tobin Lake is situated in the RM of Moose Range No. 486.

TOGO, village, pop 100 (2006c), 143 (2001c), is a pretty community located in a picturesque rolling parkland setting, 35 km southeast of Kamsack on Hwy 5, just inside the Saskatchewan/Manitoba border. Settlers began arriving in the region in the 1880s, and, at first, consisted primarily of people of British descent coming from eastern Canada. By the beginning of the twentieth century, people of various European extractions were taking up land in the area, and toward the end of WWI, German Lutherans with origins in southern Russia also settled in the district. One early area homesteader was Reginald J. M. Parker, later Lieutenant-Governor of Saskatchewan from 1945 to 1948. Born in Cornwall, England, Parker emigrated to Canada at age 17 and worked for two years as a farmhand before settling in the Togo area and establishing a cattle ranch. When a local improvement district was established, Parker became the first councillor, and when the RM of Cote No. 271 was formed in 1910, he became the first

▲ **MAIN STREET**, Togo, July 13, 2004.

reeve, a position he held until 1930, the year after he was elected to the Saskatchewan Legislature as a Liberal MLA for the Pelly constituency. Parker is buried in the family plot at Togo. By the fall of 1903, the Canadian Northern Railway, proceeding westward, had constructed the line that would connect Winnipeg and Edmonton to a point about six kilometres northwest of the present village site. On September 23 that year, the first townsite lots were put up for sale, and by winter four businesses had been built and were in operation: two general stores, a drug store, and a hardware store. It was a males-only domain the first winter; no women arrived at the stripling community until the following spring. Originally, the small settlement was known as Pelly Siding, because of its nearness to the trail that ran between Fort Ellis, Manitoba, and Fort Pelly, then in the District of Assiniboia. Red River carts hauling tons of freight over the trail cut deep ruts over the years, scant remnants of which may still be seen just west of the village. As the young community was becoming more formally established it was to be given another name — Togo. The Russo-Japanese War of 1904-05 was mak-

ing world headlines at the time, and Pelly Siding was renamed to honour Admiral Heihachiro Togo, who decimated the Russian Baltic fleet in 1905 at the Battle of Tsushima. The next town east on the CNR line, just across the border in Manitoba, was named Makaroff after Vice Admiral Stepan Osipovich Makaroff (Makarov) of the Imperial Russian Navy. The young Saskatchewan community was incorporated as the Village of Togo on September 4, 1906; the population that year was recorded at 50. New businesses, homes, churches, and a school were established, and the population grew to 111 by 1911. By the outbreak of the First World War, five grain elevators were in operation. By the early 1920s, the village numbered 300 persons, and Togo had become the centre of a bustling mixed-farming district. The village prospered until the onset of the Depression. In 1929, the Union Bank withdrew from Togo and the community then went without a local financial institution for thirty years, until the Credit Union was established in 1959. Togo lost almost a third of its population during the 1930s, but through the 1940s the village began to grow again and it reached a peak popu-

lation of 320 in 1951. During the 1950s, rural schools in the surrounding area began to close, and a new school was built in Togo to accommodate the additional students. Also during the decade, SaskPower took over the job of providing electricity to the community, and in the 1960s a village sewer system was installed. With modernity, however, particularly much-improved roads and highways, Togo steadily began to decline, as accessing the goods, services, and employment offered in larger centres, such as Kamsack and Roblin, Manitoba, became increasingly feasible. In the early 1970s, the community's long-standing tradition of hosting an annual country fair was discontinued. The centralization of the province's schools would also have an impact on the village when, in 1966, Togo's high school students began to be bused to Kamsack. High school returned to Togo in 1968, but in 1970, the classes were again transferred to the larger centre, this time for good. In the late 1970s, students in grades seven and eight also began to be bused to Kamsack. Togo School remained as a K-6 facility for a number of years, but as the community's population continued to fall, eventually the school closed its doors entirely. Today, no grain elevators remain at Togo, and only a handful of businesses are in operation, among them the credit union, the hotel, the post office, and a small farm equipment dealer. One new business started in 1995 — In Good Taste Food Service Inc. — has been quite successful, producing high-quality gourmet food products for markets across Canada. Togo is situated in the RM of Cote No. 271.

TOMPKINS, village, pop 173 (2006c), 191 (2001c), is located 23 km west of Gull Lake on Hwy 1, and is reputedly the highest point on the CP main line between Winnipeg and Calgary, at an elevation of just over 801 metres or 2,629 ft. The Cypress Hills are prominent on the southern horizon. The CPR came through in 1883, and shortly thereafter, Tompkins appeared on the company's timetable. It was nothing more than a railway siding until around 1908-09, at which point the townsite began to be built up. The village was incorporated in 1910. In 1912, the CPR constructed a proper station, replacing the boxcar which had previously served the purpose; the first elevator was also erected that year, easing the work of area farmers who, until then, had to shovel their grain straight into the railcars. The village became a busy place as settlers flooded into the area, and in the early 1920s Tompkins' race track drew horse-racing enthusiasts from miles around. The community grew continuously through to the end of the 1950s, and by 1961 the population had reached 453. Since that point, however, Tompkins has steadily declined, with 170 people leaving during the ten years between 1966 and 1976 alone. Yet, today, the community persists. There is a Co-op store, a Co-op gas bar and confectionary on the highway, a grain elevator, and a small number of local businesses and services. There are churches, and curling and skating rinks. Tompkins School was a K-9 institution that had 42 students enrolled in the fall of 2006; due to declining enrollment, however, it was downsized to being a K-5 facility in the summer of 2007. An area attraction, the Tompkins Sod House, was built in 1980 to commemorate Saskatchewan's 75th Anniversary and to pay homage to district pioneers. The regional economy is largely based on oil and gas, and farming and ranching. Tompkins is situated in the RM of Gull Lake No. 139.

TORQUAY, village, pop 184 (2006c), 231 (2001c), is located 38 km west of Estevan on Hwy 18, 16 km north of the Canada-U.S. border. Agriculture is the major industry in the area. Settlers began arriving in the early 1900s, and most of the land in the area was taken up by around 1908. The population grew to include people of Scandinavian (mainly Norwegian), German, and English backgrounds. Before Torquay existed, farmers had to travel to the rail line communities of Estevan and Macoun to deliver their grain or obtain supplies, over what was then a considerable distance. In 1906, however, just across the border in North Dakota, the railway arrived, creating a grain shipping point less than half the distance away. Farmers were then allowed to ship their grain in bond through the United States before it re-entered Canada at Fort William (Thunder Bay), and this arrangement lasted until 1913. In 1912, the CPR purchased a homesteader's land for $2,400 for the townsite of Torquay, and the next year the tracks were laid through. In 1913, the first building, a blacksmith shop, was moved onto the townsite. A general store followed, and a post office in 1914. In the fall of that year, the first grain was loaded into railcars in Torquay, and the first elevator was built. The community grew quickly, and in 1923 Torquay was incorporated as a village. There were 152 people counted during the 1926 Census, and over the next two decades Torquay experienced a slow but stable period of development, as well as the hardships of the 1930s. The years after WWII were boom years. The population of the community doubled and, by 1956, had reached well over 500. Just as rapidly, however, the pattern began to reverse itself. Community

businesses and services slowly began to be supplanted by those in Estevan, and since the early 1960s the population of Torquay has continually fallen. The village today is somewhat of a bedroom community to Estevan, as it is within easy commuting distance. There remains in Torquay a small number of locally-owned businesses including a general store, a café, and a hotel; facilities include a skating arena, a community hall, and a seniors' club. Torquay serves as the administrative centre of the RM of Cambria No. 6.

TRAMPING LAKE, village, pop 60 (2006c), 85 (2001c), is located approximately 40 km northeast of Kerrobert on Hwy 374, west of the lake from which it derives its name. The name of the lake was adapted from a Cree phrase meaning "thundering hooves," referring to the deeply trampled paths made by bison that led to the lake from all directions. The first land seekers came south from the Battlefords in 1905 and filed on homesteads that year, but they returned to the United States for the winter. The next year, in 1906, settlement began. Tramping Lake is situated in the centre of what was known as St. Joseph's Colony, a vast German Catholic settlement (77 townships) peopled by immigrants from the United States and southern Russia. It extended from Landis and Handel in the east, to Kerrobert in the south, the Alberta border and Macklin to the west, and Unity and Wilkie to the north. In 1971, more than 80 per cent of those residing in Tramp-

◄ ▲ **SCENES OF TRAMPING LAKE**, August 27, 2004: the sole remaining grain elevator (top, left), abandoned businesses (above, right) and the former school (bottom, left).

ing Lake still claimed German origins. The parish of St. Michael's was established at Tramping Lake in 1906; the first church was built about a mile and a half southeast of the present community on land donated by homesteader Jacob Reiter (NE28-36-21-W3). The village began to develop between 1911 and 1913, with the construction of the CPR line between Kerrobert and Wilkie. Many businesses were started; the Tramping Lake Post Office was established on April 21, 1914. On April 10, 1917, Tramping Lake attained the status of an incorporated village. In 1922, a new, substantial church was built in the community; the first Ursuline Sisters arrived to teach school in Tramping Lake in 1924. In 1921, the population of the village was 100; by 1931, it was 228. The community's numbers remained fairly stable until the 1950s, when Tramping Lake experienced another period of growth. Its

population was close to 300 by the early 1960s, and remained at close to that level for several years. Businesses operating in Tramping Lake in 1953 included six grain elevators, two cafés, a hotel, three garages and implement dealerships, three general merchants, hardware supplies, lumberyard, oil companies, and a shoe repair service. Beginning in the late 1960s, however, the community entered into a steady decline. By 1976, the population had fallen to 200. It was 178 in 1981, and by 1991, 143. Businesses were closing, and after the end of the school year in June 2000, Tramping Lake School was closed. The Co-op store and farm supply centre in Tramping Lake closed its doors on July 11, 2007; the keylock gas pump was closed at the end of October that year. A branch of the Unity Credit Union and the post office remain; a former Saskatchewan Wheat Pool grain elevator and adjoining annexes

still stand, although now privately owned. On May 22, 2006, Bishop Albert LeGatt of the Roman Catholic Diocese of Saskatoon appointed Rev. Joseph Choji, formerly with the archdiocese of Jos in Northern Nigeria, as the pastor of St. Michael's parish. Tramping Lake is situated in the RM of Mariposa No. 350.

TREVESSA BEACH, organized hamlet, is located north of North Battleford, and is one of several resort communities that circle Jackfish Lake. There were about 40 permanent residents in 2006 (up from 7 in 1996); however, the population varies greatly depending on the sea-

son. Trevessa Beach was established as an organized hamlet in 1982 and is situated in the RM of Meota No. 468.

TRIBUNE, village, pop 35 (2006c), 35 (2001c), is located approximately 47 km south of Weyburn on Hwy 35. The rail line from Estevan came through en route to Radville in 1913, and in 1914 the village was incorporated. Tribune reached a peak population of 166 in 1921; however, other than a decline during the Depression and WWII, the community's numbers remained fairly stable until the early 1970s. But by 1981, the population had fallen to 72. Today, despite its small size,

▲ **OUT OF PLACE.** Although the rail line into Tribune was built by the CPR, this station about a kilometre south of the village was a CN station. Originally situated on their line that had run approximately 20 kilometres to the north, it was moved to its present location from either the village of Goodwater or the former village of Colgate. Photograph taken August 27, 2003.

and because of its fairly remote location, Tribune retains a small core of essential businesses to serve the district. The community has a credit union, a store and a post office, an insurance broker, a church, community hall, and an operational grain elevator. Oungre Memorial Regional Park, located a few kilometres south on Long Creek, provides a venue for recreational and social activities. Agriculture is the major industry in the region. Tribune is situated in the RM of Souris Valley No. 7.

TROSSACHS, organized hamlet, pop 33 (2006c), 30 (2001c), is located west of Weyburn on Hwy 13. Although the area was settled around 1903-04, it was with the arrival of railway construction crews in 1909 that the community began to take shape. Three elevators were erected, a school and church were established, and soon a hotel and a variety of other businesses were in operation. Since the 1960s, however, Trossachs has declined. The population has plummeted, the school long ago closed, and the business community has altogether disappeared. CP abandoned the rail line in 1994. Trossachs had served as the administrative centre of the RM of Brokenshell No. 68 since 1909; however, in January 2001, the office was relocated to Weyburn.

TUFFNELL, organized hamlet, pop 10 (2006c), 15 (2001c), is located east of Foam Lake, just off Hwy 16. The first pioneers to settle in the vicinity came from South Dakota in 1891. They had come because a railway was promised to be built through the area within a year or two. The railway, however, was not to arrive for more than 15 years and, discouraged, many of the early settlers moved on, leaving just a

handful of homesteaders in the district. In the early 1900s, several new contingents of settlers began arriving, a large percentage of them Ukrainian. The first store at the townsite was built in 1905, and a couple of years later the railway finally came through. At first, the chief occupation was ranching; slowly, though, as settlers began felling trees, fencing and breaking their lands, grain farming became the basis of the district economy. Over the years, Tuffnell developed into a lively, active community with several businesses and services including, at one point, a hotel. Tuffnell was established as an organized hamlet in 1948. Since the 1960s, however, the community has been in decline, with the population falling from 100 in 1966 to 42 by 1972. Today, a quiet residential community remains. Tuffnell is situated in the RM of Foam Lake No. 276.

TUGASKE, village, pop 105 (2006c), 116 (2001c), is located northeast of Central Butte on Hwy 367. The Gordon McKenzie Arm of Lake Diefenbaker lies to the northwest, Eyebrow Lake to the northeast. The name Tugaske is derived from a Cree expression meaning "good land." There was some ranching activity along the Qu'Appelle Valley, to the north, as early as 1890 (the local history recounts that a large sheep ranch existed at the north end of Eyebrow Lake early in the decade), but there was little activity in the region until settlers, a good many from Ontario, poured in between 1904 and 1906 in advance of the pending railway, most having travelled by train as far as Craik to the northeast, or Caron or Mortlach to the south. About 80 settlers moved into the Tugaske district in 1904, and over the next two years another 150 arrived. By the time the railway tracks were laid in 1908, much of the available

▲ **BUILT IN 1910.** The Tugaske "Town Hall," perhaps the oldest building in the village, is no longer in use. Photograph taken October 7, 2006.

▼ **DAVID FREEMAN** of Timeless Instruments in Tugaske. Freeman began playing guitar in 1970, and has a background in wood carving, furniture repair, sculpture, pottery, and heavy and fine metal work. After studying guitar repair and design he started his instrument building and repair business in Tugaske in 1980. He sells lutherie supplies, custom-made finished instruments, and offers courses throughout the year in instrument construction. Photograph taken July 30, 2003.

land in the region was occupied. The first businesses were erected on the Tugaske townsite in anticipation of rail service. The Tugaske Post Office was established on January 1, 1908, and the first of five grain elevators were erected that year. The Canadian Bank of Commerce also commenced operations in Tugaske in 1908, and it remained in business until the Depression forced it to close its doors at the beginning of the 1930s. The building

the bank erected a few years after their arrival in the village was sold to the Masons in 1935, and it remains a landmark on Tugaske's main street — Ogema. The community was then without local banking services until 1953, when a meeting was held which resulted in the founding of the Tugaske Credit Union. Tugaske was incorporated as a village on May 7, 1909. In 1910, the original "town hall" was built, housing council chambers, two jail cells, and a section for Tugaske's fire-fighting equipment. Although no longer used for its original purpose, the building remains and is perhaps the oldest standing structure in the village. The first school in the community was also completed in 1910 (classes had been held in the Methodist Church before then); it was a two-storey, two-classroom frame structure that, due to a burgeoning number of school-age children, was replaced in 1929 by a larger brick school, complete with a chemistry lab and a library. The population of Tugaske had settled at 257 in 1926, and in the late 1920s a new wave of settlers entered the district as Mennonite families who had succeeded in fleeing the Soviet Union arrived. Tugaske's first era of growth and prosperity, however, was coming to an end: the Grand Trunk Pacific Railway had built a line south of Tugaske through Mawer into Central Butte by 1914, and in the mid-1920s CN continued a line north from Central Butte through Grainland to Dunblane. The elevator points and communities that developed along these lines drew trade away from Tugaske, and then the Depression hit and the village's population plummeted by almost 100 by the mid-1930s. Tugaske recovered during the post-War period and regained its population in the 1950s. In the 1960s, while the Gardiner Dam and the Qu'Appelle Valley Dam were being built — the latter to prevent Lake Diefenbaker from flowing into the Qu'Appelle Valley — the village's population was greatly supplemented by construction workers and their families: a trailer court was built and filled to capacity, and Tugaske School was packed to overflowing due to the increased number of children. Tugaske's population jumped from 218 in 1956 to 328 by 1966; however, with the completion of the construction projects, the community was down

to 196 residents by 1971. The ensuing decade brought many challenges to the community, many of them the result of the forces of nature. In the spring of 1974, meltwater from snow that had accumulated over the winter in the fields surrounding the village poured over a grid road into the community, when the culverts under the CPR tracks could not handle the volume. Many people's homes were flooded, sewage backed up into a number of basements, and roads were damaged. On May 15, 1974, the village council held a special meeting and declared Tugaske a "Flood Disaster Area." Two years later, on June 7, 1976, council once again had to declare the village a disaster area, after a cyclone ripped through the community, damaging many buildings and uprooting many trees. And during the first week of February 1978, a five-day blizzard buried the village; snow blocked doorways and drifted as high as rooflines. Other challenges the community faced had more of a lasting impact and would ultimately greatly change the physical appearance of the village. Tugaske School, which had stood in a prominent location at the southwest end of Ogema Street since 1929, was closed on June 30, 1970. It became a private residence and was designated a heritage property in 1985. A decade later, the landmark was destroyed by fire. The CPR station buildings, which had stood at the opposite end of Ogema Street, were removed in the summer of 1972. In 1985, two of Tugaske's four remaining grain elevators were torn down; within about a decade none were left standing. On the upside, though, even as the village population has continued to fall, a number of artists and craftspeople have made their home in Tugaske over the past few decades. Among these are musicians, an author, a potter, and a sculptor and carver who works with

soapstone, bone, antlers and horns, creating custom-built knives and jewellery; a woodworker creates miniature vehicles, and people specialize in painting wildlife. A luthier offers courses in the construction of string instruments, and people from 16 different countries have come to Tugaske to study the craft. Other businesses in Tugaske today include a Co-op, a credit union, a general store, the post office, a hotel with a bar and restaurant, and a number of home-based businesses including a catering service, appliance repair, spiritual counselling, and an agricultural consultant who provides disease and weed management services. Tugaske also has a library, a community hall, a seniors' centre, and a community rink/arena. Interestingly, and for reasons unknown, there is a crater on Mars named Tugaske after the village. Tugaske serves as the administrative centre of the RM of Huron No. 223.

TURNOR LAKE is located 90 km north of Buffalo Narrows by road, or 45 km east of La Loche by air, and is situated on the southwest shore of the lake of the same name. Although in essence one community, Turnor Lake is comprised of two legal entities: a northern hamlet that had a population of 155 in 2001, and, immediately adjacent, the Birch Narrows Dene First Nation reserve at Turnor Lake, which has a population of somewhat over 300. Together, the population is comprised of First Nations, Métis, and non-status Indians. The name Turnor Lake dates to 1918 and honours Philip Turnor (c. 1751-c. 1800), a fur trader and surveyor with the Hudson's Bay Company. Turnor was the first Company employee specifically hired to survey its vast empire in the west; he surveyed Lake Athabasca, and, perhaps most notably, was responsible for teaching the principles and art of surveying to both Peter Fidler and David Thompson. It is also believed he may have persuaded Alexander Mackenzie to learn the science. The community at Turnor Lake has a health centre, an RCMP detachment, a community hall, a post office, store, a skating rink, a ball park, a daycare, and Birch Ridge Community School, a K-9 facility with approximately 170 students and

▲ **PLYWOOD SKIFFS** such as the one pictured here in Turnor Lake are common in the western part of northern Saskatchewan. Photograph taken September 19, 2003.

a staff of 20. New homes have been built in Turnor Lake over the past few years.

TURTLE LAKE LODGE, organized hamlet, is an all-season resort area located northeast of Turtleford, halfway up the east side of Turtle Lake. It is one of a number of resorts that encircle both Turtle Lake and nearby Brightsand Lake. Facilities at Turtle Lake Lodge include cabin, boat, canoe, and ice-fishing hut rentals, as well as campgrounds and a store. Fishing, hiking, swimming, hunting, snowmobiling, and riding all-terrain vehicles are popular area activities. There is a nature sanctuary nearby. There are fewer than 20 year-round residents; however, the population varies seasonally. Turtle Lake Lodge is situated within the RM of Parkdale No. 498.

TURTLE LAKE SOUTH BAY, organized hamlet, is one of several resort communities situated northeast of Turtleford on Turtle Lake. There were 28 permanent residents recorded in 2006; however, the population varies greatly depending on the season, reaching approximately 200 during the summer months. Turtle Lake South Bay, originally developed in the late 1960s and 1970s, was established as an organized hamlet in 1987 and lies within the RM of Mervin No. 499.

TURTLEFORD, town, pop 461 (2006c), 465 (2001c), is located approximately 90 km northwest of North Battleford at the junction of Hwys 3, 26, and 303. The first settlers began entering the district in 1907-08. The community is situated in proximity to what was once a ford of the Turtlelake River, and the name

Turtleford was coined by the community's first postmaster, John Bloom. The post office opened in 1913 as the railway approached from North Battleford. Train service into Turtleford began in 1914, and the fledgling community was incorporated as a village in October that year. By the spring of 1915, dozens of places of business had been established, including four general stores, a drug store, two livery and feed stables, and two lumberyards. The railway brought an increasing number of settlers to the district and, over the following decades, the once heavily forested area was cleared and the agricultural production of the region steadily increased. Turtleford became the main supply and service centre for the surrounding farming population. The agricultural output of the district largely consists of cattle and grain. Somewhat ironically, as the land was cleared of the forest, the Turtleford town council of 1931 saw the need to beautify the community, and handed out to residents Maple, Russian Poplar, and Elm trees to plant, many of which are still standing. Today, some logging activity continues in the region to the north of Turtleford. In the 1960s, resort communities began developing at the nearby Brightsand and Turtle Lakes, and the town continues to benefit from a growing seasonal tourist industry. The summer population in the area today is estimated to reach between four and five thousand. Construction workers find much employment building cottages and permanent homes at the lakes, and, more and more, retirees choose to settle permanently in the area. Some Turtleford area residents also find work in outfitting and commercial guiding. In 1983, Turtleford attained town status and, to commemorate the event, an enormous turtle sculpture was constructed at the town's tourist information centre: "Ernie" is

▲ **CANADA'S LARGEST TURTLE.** "Ernie" has welcomed visitors to Turtleford since 1983.

▼ **TURTLEFORD TOWN OFFICE.**

Photographs taken July 24, 2003.

now billed as Canada's largest turtle. Over the past 20 years, the development of the oil and gas industry has come to be significantly important to the Turtleford economy, and several businesses providing oilfield services have developed. The industry provides much off-farm employment. Turtleford's businesses provide a range of goods and services. The town has a health centre with an attached special care home, an RCMP detachment, a fire department, and a veterinary clinic. The community has a number of churches, a library, a museum, and several service clubs and other community-based organizations. Turtleford School is a K-12 facility, which had 259 town and area students enrolled in the fall of 2006. The Turtleford town office is situated in the former 1920 Bank of Commerce building, now a heritage property. The community's premier annual event is the Turtleford Agricultural Fair held at the beginning of August. The event is considered one of the best country fairs in Canada, and in 2005 the 89th annual fair was held. Turtleford serves as the administrative centre of the RM of Mervin No. 499.

TUXFORD, village, pop 88 (2006c), 97 (2001c), is located 22 km north of Moose Jaw at the junction of Hwys 2, 42, and 202. Buffalo Pound Lake lies to the northeast. Settlement of the district began with the advent of the CPR into Moose Jaw, and through 1883-84 there was an influx of people. The first who took up land were largely of British origins, either from eastern Canada or overseas. By 1890, most of the available homestead land was taken, leaving only the CPR or Hudson's Bay Company lands, or homesteads abandoned by those who moved on. With good water, shelter for animals, wood for fuel and building material available in the Qu'Appelle Valley, and good trails leading into Moose Jaw where there were all the supplies and services needed for pioneer living, the "Buffalo Lake District" settlers never quite suffered the extreme privation and isolation as was experienced in other parts of the North-West. Rural post offices, schools, and churches were established, and at the turn of the century there was much talk in the district about the CPR's

▲ **TUXFORD SENTINELS**, above left, and the former village office, above right. Photographs taken July 8, 2003.

proposed line that would run from Moose Jaw into the Outlook area. The route, however, was to run straight northwest of Moose Jaw, several miles south of present-day Tuxford, leaving area farmers with a long haul to market their grain. One homesteader took it upon himself to try to convince the railway to build the planned line straight north of Moose Jaw 12 or 14 miles, closer to Buffalo Pound Lake, before turning northwest. George Stuart Tuxford (1870-1943) spent weeks on horseback circulating a petition among 113 area farmers, feted several notables including high-ranking CPR officials with a successful goose-hunting expedition, and with persistent diplomacy kept the pressure on the railway for four years until he was successful. In late 1905, work on the line began, and when a location for a townsite and railway station was chosen,

◄ **BRIGADIER GENERAL GEORGE STUART TUXFORD.**
Saskatchewan Archives Board R-A10224.

the CPR decided to honour George Tuxford by naming the place after him. Tuxford would later distinguish himself once again, during WWI, when he rose to the rank of Brigadier General. In 1905, the first building was erected on the Tuxford townsite — a real estate and insurance office. By 1906, the rail bed had been graded from Moose Jaw, and two general stores, a lumberyard, and three grain elevators were built before the tracks were laid through the fledgling community the next year. Only seven people evidently lived on the townsite over the winter of 1906-07, but the surrounding countryside by this point was well populated. In 1907, Tuxford experienced a building boom: the post office was established in January, many more businesses were started, and the village was incorporated on July 19 that year. Anglican and Presbyterian churches were soon serving the community. The local history recounts that eight babies were born in the village in 1908, and in 1909 parents of school-aged children decided that Tuxford needed its own school. Until this time, children had been travelling

out to Fairwell School, a few kilometres west of the townsite. A new school district was formed, and Tuxford School opened its doors in 1910. The village had a population of 121 in 1911, and 159 by 1931, but about one-third of the latter number was lost through the 1930s and the subsequent war years. During the post-war period, Tuxford regained its population, but in the 1970s it again began to decline, as did the business community, being superseded by Moose Jaw's commercial sector. Tuxford School was closed in 1974 and students then attended classes in the city. Heading into the 1990s, the community found itself without a post office. Today, most village residents either work in Moose Jaw or are involved in farming or the area's agriculture-related businesses (such as seed-cleaning plants); a local excavating company provides a significant amount of seasonal employment. Tuxford's two remaining grain elevators (formerly Pool and Pioneer) are now in private hands and are used for grain storage. Tuxford is situated in the RM of Marquis No. 191.

▲ **MAIN STREET**, Unity, looking south.

▲ **VICTOR PRYTULA'S GENERAL STORE** in Tway, a family operation with origins dating to 1915, was still in business in 2008. Tway Lake is just visible at the bottom of the hill. Photograph taken August 10, 2004.

TWAY, organized hamlet, pop 10 (2006c), 15 (2001c), is located northeast of Wakaw in a beautiful setting overlooking Tway Lake, which lies just to the north of the community. French settlers were in the area by the late 1800s; Ukrainians began arriving around the turn of the century. The Tway Post Office was established in the district in 1913; the name was derived from the English pronunciation of the last name of the first postmaster, F. Touet. After the railway was built through the area in 1929, and the present townsite began to develop, the post office was relocated to the new locale. The first store in Tway was built by Frank Karasuik; the first elevator agent was a man by the name of Trehearne. Although a rural school had been in existence since early in the century, a school was not built in the hamlet until 1938. The school closed in the mid-1960s. The population of the community was 121 in 1966; however, by 1972 it had fallen to 67. The last grain elevator closed in the late 1970s; the rail line through the area was abandoned in the early 1990s. Tway is located in the RM of Invergordon No. 430.

UHL'S BAY, organized hamlet, is a resort community located west of Bulyea, adjacent to Rowan's Ravine Provincial Park on the east shore of Last Mountain Lake. It is accessed by Hwy 220. There are a small number of permanent residents; however, the population varies depending upon the season. Uhl's Bay was established as an organized hamlet in 1984, and is situated in the RM of McKillop No 220.

UNITY, town, pop 2,147 (2006c), 2,243 (2001c), is located approximately 90 km southwest of the Battlefords at the junction of Hwys 14 and 21. Settlement of the area began in 1904, and Unity began to develop with the arrival of the Grand Trunk Pacific Railway in 1908. Unity was incorporated as a village in 1909, and in 1910 the CPR had a line from Wilkie running just north of the community. In 1919, Unity attained town status, and by the early 1920s Unity's population was over 600 and growing. The community experienced somewhat of a decline during the 1930s, but subsequently recovered,

"A Good Town in a Good District"...
UNITY

Historical Photographs courtesy of the Unity & District Heritage Museum; colour photographs taken August 15, 2003.

▼ **DIGGING OUT.** Main Street after a snowstorm in December 1955.

▲ **THE WILLIAM KUTZ HOMESTEAD** a few miles west of Unity, 1916. Kutz came to the Unity district in 1907 and erected the sod house shortly thereafter.

▲ **UNVEILING THE CENOTAPH** in 1927.

▼ **UNITY CPR STATION**, built in 1909 and originally located just north of the town, now a part of the Unity & District Heritage Museum.

▲ **AN EAST VIEW** of the Unity Townsite in the 1920s.

▲ **THIS LADIES BASEBALL TEAM** were Champions of Western Saskatchewan in the 1920s.

▼ **LARGE INLAND GRAIN HANDLING TERMINALS** dominate the skyline in the Unity area. In the foreground is North West Terminal Ltd. The company was established in 1993 and began accepting grain in 1996. A farmer-owned facility, it is located one mile east of Unity on Hwy 14 and the CN Rail main line. It has a total storage capacity of 2.3 million bushels (63,000 metric tonnes), and can receive up to 30,000 bushels of grain per hour on two driveways. The facility can also load rail cars on its 104-car rail siding at a rate of 30,000 bushels per hour. In the background of the photograph is Viterra's operation (a Saskatchewan Wheat Pool facility at the time the photograph was taken).

particularly after WWII. Much of the community's return to prosperity and future growth was due to oilfield exploration and resultant developments. After natural gas was discovered near Unity, local furnaces and coal stoves were converted to burn the gas, and in 1944 Unity became one of only three communities in Saskatchewan with their own domestic natural gas system, prior to SaskPower being given the authority in the 1950s to establish the provincial utility. (Lloydminster had natural gas in 1934, and Kamsack's system was in place in 1937.) Drilling for oil in the Unity area also revealed a substantial deposit of sodium chloride (common salt) laid down when much of Saskatchewan was covered by inland seas. In the late 1940s, a salt mine was developed. Today, the mine, operated by Sifto Canada, is the community's largest employer with 60 employees. Exploratory drilling also revealed extensive deposits of potash, and the first attempt at potash mining in Saskatchewan, indeed in Canada, was made near Unity in the early 1950s. The industrial activity in the area, combined with modified and more successful agricultural practices after the dry years of the 1930s, caused the town's population to skyrocket. The community's numbers rose from 682 in 1941 to 1,248 in 1951, and between 1955 and 1965 approximately 100 new homes were built in the town. By 1966 the population was 2,154. Yet, despite industrial development, agriculture, a combination of grain and livestock production, remains the major concern in the region, and a number of Unity's businesses either supply or service the industry. There are three large modern inland terminals at the town and substantial farm machinery dealerships. However, the area's oil and gas industry has grown to become very important, and approximately 20 companies in Unity

provide oilfield services. Other significant employers in the town are health care services, educational facilities, financial institutions, a range of service industries, and a diverse retail sector. Over 100 businesses provide a complete range of goods and services. Unity has a hospital that provides acute and long-term care, a seniors' care home, an ambulance service, and an array of additional medical services and practitioners. The community has a local RCMP detachment. The town has public and Catholic elementary schools and a composite high school; combined, the schools provide K-12 education to approximately 550 town and area students. Post-secondary programs, including university classes, are provided by the Northwest Regional College through distance-education broadcasts. Unity has a wide range of recreational facilities and over 70 service clubs, youth organizations, sports associations, and groups involved with artistic and cultural activities. The community's churches accommodate five religious denominations. The Unity Heritage Museum, situated in the regional park adjacent to the community, occupies a large site containing numerous heritage buildings from the district, including the community's CPR station, restored schoolhouses, businesses, homes, and a church. Additionally, two Quonsets house a large collection of restored machinery, including cars, trucks, tractors, a steam engine, and a threshing machine. Unity has been participating in the nationally acclaimed "Communities in Bloom" competitions since 1999. That year they placed first in Saskatchewan in their population category, a feat they repeated the following year. In 2003, the town's floral displays and attractive appearance earned Unity a national Communities in Bloom championship. Unity serves as the admin-

istrative centre of the RM of Round Valley No. 410.

URANIUM CITY, northern settlement, is located at the northern edge of Lake Athabasca, on the north shore of the much smaller Martin Lake. The community lies 725 km northwest of Prince Albert, 725 km northeast of Edmonton, and 48 km south of border between the Northwest Territories and Saskatchewan. High rocky hills dominate the skyline. Uranium City's origins date to 8:15 a.m. on August 6, 1945, when the American B-29 Superfortress bomber, the "Enola Gay," released an atomic bomb over the city of Hiroshima, Japan. The event ushered in the nuclear age and the Cold War. The Canadian Government had established a federal crown corporation in 1943, Eldorado Mining and Refining Limited (later Eldorado Nuclear Ltd.), which was given complete control of all Canadian uranium interests. A ban on private exploration was put in place during the war for reasons of security. In response to the growing demand of the United States for uranium for the nuclear arsenal it intended to amass

following WWII, Eldorado began prospecting for uranium in the Lake Athabasca region, where the radioactive, metallic element had first been discovered in the 1930s. The United States contracted to purchase every last gram of uranium the Saskatchewan mines could produce until 1963, and soon several promising claims were staked in the area. By the late 1940s, Eldorado's monopoly was over, igniting a rush of prospecting and staking in the region. In 1952, the Government of Saskatchewan, with industry input, laid out a townsite to service the area's mining operations. The planned infrastructure was to accommodate a community of 5,000, and within a short period of time there were flourishing businesses, a school, a hospital, and regularly scheduled air services from Prince Albert and Edmonton. A special local government jurisdiction was created in 1956; at the time, Uranium City was the fastest growing community in Saskatchewan. By 1957, the population of Uranium City itself was about 1,500; combined with the communities at the nearby Eldorado and Gunnar mine sites, among others, the total figure for the area reached close to 5,000. Being a single-industry

▼ **URANIUM CITY, 1955.** Saskatchewan Archives Board, Saskatchewan Photographic Services, R-PS55-311-32. Photographer: Gerry Savage.

town, however, meant that Uranium City was subject to boom-and-bust cycles. The community nearly died in the early 1960s, but experienced a brief resurgence later in the decade when the market for uranium somewhat improved. Yet, by decade's end Eldorado was the sole producer left in the area, and a lack of market due to stockpiling almost forced Eldorado to shut down at the beginning of the 1970s. By the mid-1970s, though, things were looking up again: Eldorado planned a major expansion and announced that it was committing to sizable capital expenditures to refurbish existing facilities and the development of new assets. The population of the community, which had fallen to close to 1,000 in the 1960s, climbed back to more

than 2,000 by the end of the seventies. However, in the early 1980s, the demand and price for uranium dropped and the market bottomed out. At the end of 1981, Eldorado announced the pending closure of its operations, and by the early summer of 1982 it permanently shut down. It was a mortal blow. The community experienced economic collapse and immediate depopulation. Within a year, the population of Uranium City was down to 600 and falling. The end of the industry had come so suddenly that houses under construction were simply abandoned unfinished. Due to the community's remote location, homes were left with furnishings in them, and, today, cars dating to the 1960s may still be found parked in the garages of abandoned homes. Many buildings have subsequently been scavenged or vandalized, and existing houses sell for a hundred dollars or less. Within a few years of Eldorado abandoning operations, water and sewer were shut off to the community's outlying neighbourhoods; the services

were provided only to remaining residents who moved into Uranium City's central core area. By 2001, the population was 201. The few remaining businesses were supported by the hospital and the airport, the main employers left in the community. Following the closure of the hospital in 2003 to a new facility in Stony Rapids, the population fell further, to about 70 people. The uranium mining and milling industry did leave a lasting legacy, however — hundreds of thousands of tonnes of radioactive toxic waste: uranium tailings, arsenic, sulphur, and radon gas, blowing and leaching into Lake Athabasca. As of 2007, Saskatchewan's Transwest Air was still flying into the community three times a week from Stony Rapids, and Canada Post continued to serve the community. Ben McIntyre School had 10 students enrolled in grades K-7 in the fall of 2006.

USHERVILLE, organized hamlet, pop 20 (2006c), 15 (2001c), is located north of Preeceville, 2 km west of Hwy 9,

in an area where the northern parklands meet the southern timber zone. Although a few settlers were moving into the region by the time the railway reached Sturgis in 1911, it was after 1928, when the railway was completed through the area north to Hudson Bay, that the hamlet of Usherville developed. The name of Usherville, though, dates to 1911, when George Usher, a sawmill operator, established a post office by that name. It was originally about 13 kilometres (8 miles) south of the present community. In the early 1930s the majority of those who moved into the Usherville area were refugees fleeing the drought on the southern plains. The lumber industry dominated the economy for many years, although, as land was cleared, it supported mixed agriculture. The Searle Grain Company erected an elevator at Usherville in 1932, which operated until the early 1960s and was dismantled in 1974. Usherville, though never very large, grew to consist of a few local businesses, a dance hall, and a school; however, after attendance began to drop at the school in

the 1950s it ran into difficulty and was closed in 1960. There were approximately 50 people living in Usherville in 1970, but that year the post office, too, was closed. Usherville was established as an organized hamlet in 1981; today, there are a few homes and house trailers at the locale, and a gas station/small convenience store is still operating on the corner of Hwy 9. Usherville is situated in the RM of Preeceville No. 334.

VAL MARIE, village, pop 137 (2006c), 134 (2001c), lies roughly 120 km straight south of Swift Current in the Frenchman River Valley, at the junction of Hwys 4 and 18. The Saskatchewan-Montana border is 30 km further south. The Frenchman River passes along the east side of Val Marie and the west block of Grasslands National Park lies just to the southeast. The park's visitor centre is located in the village. The first to settle in the Val Marie area were Métis whose main occupation was hunting. Next came ranchers. In 1910, through the colonizing efforts of Father Louis-Joseph-Pierre Gravel (1868-1926), immigrants from France were brought to the district under the direction of Father Passaplan, a missionary priest who had been working out of Swift Current. French-Canadian families also settled the area, and with reinforcements sent by Fr. Gravel the French-speaking colony began to take shape. Father Passaplan established a post office on January 1, 1912, naming it Val Marie in honour of the Virgin Mary. Louis Denniel, one of the original French settlers, took over the office later in the year and remained the postmaster until 1959. Denniel was also instrumental in the founding of the Val Marie school in 1914. These developments took place only in the general

area of today's community, however; the present townsite itself did not begin to develop until 1924-25, when the railway was built eastward from Climax. A construction boom ensued and the Village of Val Marie was incorporated on September 13, 1926. By this time, grain farming had significantly developed in the region, and the first elevator was erected in Val Marie in 1927. Also that year, a new red-brick school (now a heritage property) opened to accommodate a burgeoning student population. In 1931, the highway from Swift Current was completed and, although it was only a dirt-surfaced route (gravel by 1940), it provided an important transportation link to the rest of the province, as for many years trains ran to Val Marie only on a once-weekly basis and there was no bus service. The customs office on the Canada-U.S. border, on Hwy 4 at Monchy, was established on October 15, 1935. The plan was that the rail line into Val Marie would connect with the track from the east into Mankota (completed in 1929), creating a large loop through the province's southwest. However, the Depression and the war years forever brought an end to this plan, and Val Marie remained at the end of the line. During the 1930s, due to the severe effects of the drought, two dams were constructed on the Frenchman River northwest of Val Marie to facilitate irrigation in the district. The two projects, both Prairie Farm Rehabilitation Administration (PFRA) initiatives, were completed in 1937 and 1940. In 1939, a convent (now a country inn and restaurant) was opened in Val Marie, and it operated until the mid-1960s. The building then remained vacant for years before it was saved from imminent demolition for its current purpose. In the late 1940s, a hospital (18 beds, now long gone) was also built in the village. Major flooding

▲ **PROPERTY OF THE VILLAGE OF VAL MARIE:** former Saskatchewan Wheat Pool grain elevators purchased in January 2001. Photograph taken on September 4, 2007.

VAL MARIE
...gateway to the Grasslands

▼ **THE VAL MARIE HOTEL.** In 1965, when J.A. (Amadee) Vermette was the proprietor of the new hotel in Val Marie he advertised "Modern Rooms, Some with Bath," and that "Your Comfort is Our Pleasure." The hotel was constructed around the late 1950s to replace one built by Ovide Nadeau about 1927. Photograph taken on September 4, 2007.

▲ **THE PARKS CANADA VISITOR CENTRE.** Photograph taken September 5, 2003.

▼ ▶ **GRASSLANDS NATIONAL PARK** encompasses vast tracts of wilderness as well as sparse remains of human habitation, such as this abandoned corral photographed in the park's West Block on September 4, 2003, and this solitary boarded-up ranch house — "Belza's" — photographed four years later to the day, on September 4, 2007.

of the Frenchman River in 1952 caused severe damage to area farmlands and people's homes throughout the region (Eastend was also under water), roads and the railway were submerged, and the dams above Val Marie were in danger of collapsing. For a period, the village could be reached only by boat or plane. It was during this post-war period that Val Marie's population reached its peak, however, and the community was a thriving business centre. From a population of 147 in 1936, the village's numbers had grown to 383 by 1956, and in 1961 the population peaked at 443. From what was originally a

ginning of a decline in population and the resultant slow demise of businesses and services. By the mid-1960s, the hospital was in trouble, and by 1971 the community numbered 307 residents, a drop of more than 25 per cent over 10 years. By 1976, the population was 253; by 1986, it was 204. In 2000, the CPR prepared to abandon and sell four branch lines in the region, including the line into Val Marie, to Westcan Rail Ltd., a railway salvage operation out of Abbotsford, B.C. Producers in the province's southwest intervened, and a deal was struck under which the lines were saved and began operating under the

predominantly French settlement, the village had grown to become home to people of more diverse origins, a fairly significant number of them German. There were new developments in the village in the 1960s — sewer lines were installed at the beginning of the decade, and new skating and curling rinks were built a few years later — but another development was the be-

name of the Great Western Railway. Two years later, however, the stretch from the village of Bracken to Val Marie was abandoned — but not before Val Marie residents had put up a fight. A work crew was charged by police when they tried to tear up the tracks without a permit from local authorities, and the village's mayor stood in front of the wrecking equipment during the process. A remaining elevator in the community, built in 1927, was designated a municipal heritage property in 2003. In 2005, the community was dealt another blow. The village's RCMP detachment, along with those in Consul, Mankota, Climax, and Eastend, was closed. Now, the nearest police service is in Ponteix, 75 kilometres away. And while Val Marie once had its own hospital, today the nearest medical services are health clinics located in Climax and Mankota; the closest hospital is in Swift Current. Val Marie retains its school, though — a K-12 facility that had 54 students enrolled in the fall of 2006. Businesses and services in the community today include a credit union, a grocery store, a hotel, a bulk gas station, a hair salon, the Convent Country Inn, a library, a museum and gift shop, and the Grasslands National Park Visitor Centre. The Crossing Resort, five kilometres south of Val Marie, borders the park, and has guest suites and facilities for camping. Notable one-time residents of Val Marie include former NHL star Bryan Trottier, and the famous traditional Western illustrator, sketch artist, painter, and writer, Will James. Trottier was born in Val Marie on July 17, 1956, and over an NHL career that spanned 18 seasons he was the winner of the Calder, Art Ross, Hart, and Conn Smythe Trophies, as well as six Stanley Cup Championships as a player (four with the New York Islanders and two with Pittsburgh). Trottier won his 7th career Stanley Cup ring in 2001 as an assistant coach with the Colorado Avalanche. Trottier's Métis ancestors had been among the first to settle in the Val Marie area. Will James, born Ernest Dufault in Quebec in 1892, left home for the west at an early age, working the range around Val Marie and manufacturing an identity as a cowboy. He authored and illustrated two dozen

books and numerous magazine articles, and produced scores of drawings and oil paintings depicting cowboy life. Two of his books, *Smoky* and *Lone Cowboy*, were made into movies. Despite acclaim and success, though, James' life was tragic. A short prison term for rustling, a tumultuous marriage, and a devotion to drink contributed to his untimely death in 1942 in the United States at the age of 50. Val Marie serves as the administrative centre of the RM of Val Marie No. 17.

VALPARAISO, village, pop 20 (2006c), 20 (2001c), is located 10 km west of Tisdale, just north of Hwy 3. Settlement of the area began in the early 1900s, and in 1904 the Valparaiso Post Office was established. Its name, selected by the first postmaster, George E. Green, is Spanish for "Valley of Paradise." In 1905 a school was built, and in 1910 the first grain elevator at Valparaiso was constructed. In 1924, the Village of Valparaiso was incorporated. In 1926, the community had a peak popu-

lation of 123, but the community's numbers have since steadily declined through each successive decade. The post office closed in 1970 and fewer than 45 people have lived in the village since the beginning of the 1980s. There were still three grain elevators standing at Valparaiso in 1994; however, these were all dismantled and later replaced by a high-throughput terminal, now owned and operated by Agricore United. The village itself is in an advanced state of decay, with the remains of sidewalks running along vacant lots. Valparaiso, situated in the RM of Star City No. 428, has the appearance of becoming a ghost town.

VANGUARD, village, pop 152 (2006c), 187 (2001c), is located approximately 70 km southeast of Swift Current on Hwy 43. The Notukeu Creek passes just to the south of the community, flowing east to join the Wood River just northeast of Gravelbourg. In the early 1900s, the region was essentially the domain of

ranchers. The Turkey Track Ranch, with headquarters to the north of present-day Vanguard, was a massive operation with more than 30,000 head of cattle and hundreds of horses. However, after the killing winter of 1906-07 dealt a severe blow to Saskatchewan's cattle industry — the Turkey Track alone lost over 10,000 animals — the southwest was increasingly being opened to homesteaders, and soon settlers' shacks were dotting the area around where Vanguard would develop. Land in the region was opened to homesteaders in 1908-09, and in 1908 Latimer Young homesteaded where the village now stands, and it was he who later sold his land to the CPR for the Vanguard townsite. The district became a melting pot of cultures, as settlers of British, French, and Scandinavian origins arrived, along with significant numbers of German-speaking peoples. Many came from eastern Canada, while others came from settlements in the United States founded by earlier emigrants from the Old World; a number came directly from overseas. Once in Sas-

GOOD NEIGHBOURS. Members of the Vanguard Hutterite Colony welcome visitors to their community (top left) — in this case, journalism students from the University of Regina. One of the students, Lee Harding (pictured right with a notebook in hand), entertains an amused crowd with an impromptu rap demonstration. North of Vanguard, toward Hallonquist, lies the Turkey Track Ranch, once one of southern Saskatchewan's most massive ranching operations. The Turkey Track brand was registered in Texas in 1840, and A.J. (Tony) Day began using the brand in southern Texas around the end of the American Civil War in 1865. As the open range in the United States became dotted with homesteads, the Turkey Track began moving northwards, entering Canada from South Dakota in 1902 with 600 horses and 25,000 head of cattle. An additional 8,000 yearling and two-year-old steers were purchased in Manitoba and rebranded with the Turkey Track brand, augmenting the already enormous herd. The range extended from the CPR main line to the Canada-United States border, and from the Wood Mountain Plateau to the Whitemud (Frenchman) River Valley. After the loss of 10,000 head and 600 herd bulls during the catastrophic winter of 1906-07, and the opening of ranch lands to homesteaders, a significantly downsized Turkey Track operation was sold. In 1917, Percy Ostrander purchased the ranch, and it remains in the Ostrander family to this day. Here, a young ranch hand (left) and a young cowgirl (below) demonstrate their roping techniques. Photographs taken October 7, 2003.

◄ **THE VANGUARD FLOOD** (photo on facing page): On July 3, 2000, severe thunderstorms dumped approximately 375 mm of rain (close to 15 inches) on the community and the surrounding area over an eight-hour period. The storm made national news, as the rainfall was the greatest ever recorded on the prairies in such a short period of time; it was also one of the most intense periods of rainfall ever recorded in Canada. The resulting flash flood crushed cars and farm machinery, swept away grain bins, left roads and railway tracks under water, carried away herds of cattle and drowned dozens of deer and antelope in the area. Stranded residents had to be rescued by boat. The village's water-treatment plant was submerged, and contaminated water backed up into people's homes and businesses. The damage to village properties, residences and farms was extensive. Among the first on the scene to help the beleaguered community were members of the Vanguard Hutterite Colony located 10 kilometres south of the village. Eventually, provincial and federal governments contributed much in the way of financial assistance to aid with the clean-up and rebuilding. Photograph courtesy of Mayor Dorothy Saunderson and the Village of Vanguard.

katchewan, settlers detrained at Morse, Herbert, or Swift Current, and purchased supplies before heading south to the Vanguard district. Conversely, these settlers had to haul their first crops back to these points until the railway arrived in their area. CPR surveyors were planning the route into the district from Swift Current in the fall of 1910; track was being laid in 1911; and railway service came to Vanguard in 1912. There followed a great deal of rapid construction at the townsite, and the new village was incorporated on July 8 that year. By early 1913, dozens of businesses, including a bank, general stores, a hotel, lumberyards, and blacksmith and barbers' shops, lined streets where a year earlier there had been nothing. For a year or two, grain from a considerable district was funnelled through Vanguard's newly-constructed elevators. Farmers from Ponteix to Kincaid and even much further south hauled their crops to Vanguard until the rails were laid from Assiniboia to Shaunavon. Farmers from south and west of Hodgeville hauled grain to Vanguard until the early 1920s. In 1914, a two-and-a-half-storey, red-brick school opened in the village, replacing the temporary quarters that had been used to teach classes. In the following years churches were built and, by 1919, a hospital. Vanguard prospered: the population was just under 400 by the end of the 1920s, and the community served hundreds more residing on farms in the countryside. The Depression, the drought, and WWII, however, depleted the village's numbers, as families moved away and young men and women joined the armed services. By 1941 the community had lost well over 100 residents. Five large fires between 1919 and 1937 also took a toll on the community, as each claimed close to an entire block of businesses and residences. The purchase of modern

fire-fighting equipment and the eventual construction of a water supply system, though, mitigated the chance of such disasters recurring. Vanguard recovered its population in the post-war years and it reached a peak of close to 450 between the mid-1950s and the early 1960s; the community was serving a district population of about 1,000 at this time. Beginning in the 1960s, however, the village and area population began to steadily decline, and, as well, the community's businesses began facing challenges as Swift Current was becoming increasingly a regional shopping centre. In the ensuing years and decades, prominent landmarks in the village began to disappear. The 1919 red-brick hospital that was used until the 1960s was demolished; the CPR railway station closed in 1970 and was later moved to a farm north of the village; the original wooden hotel built during Vanguard's first years of existence was torn down in the mid-1990s; and the last grain elevator was demolished in 2002. The village faced one of its biggest challenges, however, when, on July 3, 2000, severe thunderstorms dumped approximately 375 mm of rain (close to 15 inches) on the community and the surrounding area over an eight-hour period. Yet, despite the blows, Vanguard and area residents have demonstrated a tenacious and indomitable spirit in recent years, and, today, in spite of having its lowest-ever population, the village possesses a surprising number and array of businesses and modern facilities. The health care centre had major renovations and an addition built onto it in 1996, as did the school in 1999. A K-12 facility, Vanguard Community School had 82 students enrolled in the fall of 2006. In 2000, as the CPR prepared to abandon and sell four branch lines in the region, including the Vanguard subdivision, to Westcan

Rail Ltd., a railway salvage operation out of Abbotsford, B.C., local producers, along with others in the province's southwest, intervened. A deal was struck under which the lines were saved and began operating under the name of the Great Western Railway. In November of 2004, the crop-dependent short lines were successfully purchased from Westcan by a large group of producers in Saskatchewan's southwest region. Another major development in Vanguard in recent years has been the establishment of Notukeu Processing Inc., which began operations in April 2002. Notukeu Processing is a state-of-the-art facility with the capacity to process 3 million bushels of pulse crops annually. It ships product by either rail cars or semi-trailer trucks. Another new business, a greenhouse, opened in the village in 2003. Vanguard has seniors' and community centres, a playschool, a library and a museum. There are Roman Catholic and United Churches. Recreational facilities include skating and curling rinks (both with artificial ice), sports grounds with four ball diamonds, an outdoor swimming pool, and a playground. There are a number of organized sports programs and clubs operated in the community throughout the year. For close to 40 years, an annual Music Festival has showcased local talent. The village has a volunteer fire department; policing is provided by the RCMP out of Ponteix. A notable Vanguard community landmark, now a municipal heritage property, is the former Bank of Toronto building, constructed in the early 1920s. The two-storey edifice now serves as an office for a local trucking company. Vanguard is the administrative centre of the RM of Whiska Creek No. 106, and its trading area encompasses those living in the western part of the neighbouring RM of Glen Bain No. 105.

VANSCOY, village, pop 339 (2006c), 345 (2001c), is located approximately 25 km southwest of Saskatoon on Hwy 7. Agrium Inc.'s potash operations about 7 km west are clearly visible on the horizon. Settlers began entering the district about 1901; many of the first came up from the mid-western United States or were from England. Area schools and post offices were established within a few years. Vanscoy had its beginnings in 1908 as the Canadian Northern Railway was building its line from Saskatoon to Rosetown. For reasons unknown, the townsite was named Vanscoy after Clinton Verne Vanscoy, who had homesteaded about a mile north of the present community. James Smart erected the first store in Vanscoy in 1908, and became the community's first postmaster when the post office was established on October 1, 1909. A number of other businesses followed after Smart's enterprise — among these were a second general store, an implement agency, the first grain elevator in 1909, and a hotel in 1911. Vanscoy fielded a baseball team by 1913; by 1916, four grain elevators lined the railway tracks. Schoolchildren first attended country schools and then classes in various locations in the hamlet, until a schoolhouse was completed and opened in January of 1916. Vanscoy's Roman Catholic church was built in 1914; Methodists built a new church after the hall they had purchased burned to the ground in 1917. This later became the United Church. On June 17, 1919, the Village of Vanscoy was incorporated; in 1926, the population was 112. While the community's businesses were well-supported by area farmers for many years, Vanscoy remained a fairly small community — its population remained close to its 1926 level until the 1960s (it was 107 in 1956). In the 1960s and 1970s, two developments led to a significant era of growth: the first was the development of two nearby potash mines — one to the west (mentioned above), the other to the northeast, toward Saskatoon. The second factor leading to the village's expansion was that urbanites from Saskatoon were moving into Vanscoy, choosing to live as commuters. In the 1960s, new subdivisions for housing started to be developed and a trailer court was set up; by 1971, the population of Vanscoy had grown to 244 and was climbing. Village infrastructure was improved: in the mid-1970s work began on a new skating arena, a portable classroom had to be added to the school in 1977 due to a burgeoning student population, and in 1979 all unpaved streets were blacktopped. Today, residents are employed at area potash mines, in the area's agricultural industry (including a local pulse crop processing plant), or in Saskatoon. The village has a small core of businesses, its own municipal police service, two churches, seniors' housing, and Vanscoy School, a K-8 institution that had 168 pupils enrolled in the fall of 2006. High school students have been bused to Delisle since 1960. Vanscoy serves as the administrative centre of the RM of Vanscoy No. 345.

VANTAGE, organized hamlet, is located approximately 24 km north of Assiniboia on Hwy 2. Vantage was a creation of the CPR, which built a line to the location in 1914. The community had village status from 1917 to 1951 and the population peaked at close to 100 in the mid-1920s. Vantage was reduced to an organized hamlet in 1952, and although it has virtually disappeared (the last two censuses recorded a population of zero),

it remains a legally established entity within the RM of Sutton No. 103.

VAWN, hamlet, pop 61 (2001c), lies approximately 50 km northwest of North Battleford on Hwy 26 between the villages of Meota, to the southeast, and Edam, to the northwest. Jackfish Lake lies to the east; the North Saskatchewan River, to the south and west. Settlement of the district took place over the late 1880s and the early 1900s and was mainly French. Immigrants from France had joined Québécois in the area by 1907; in 1971, close to half of the population of Vawn still claimed French origins. The name Vawn is an acronym made from the names of early area settlers Vallière, Anderson, Wagner, and Nadon. The community began to develop with the construction of the railway from North Battleford to Edam in 1910-11. Evidently, the line was to have run through the older, already established centre of St. Hippolyte, to the west, which had a church by 1905, a post office by 1907, a store and perhaps a dozen homes. However, unable to procure the necessary lands at the St. Hippolyte site, the railway shifted the route to the east, and the townsite of Vawn was established. Shortly following the completion of the rail line in 1911, J. P. Poulin constructed one of the first stores. A hardware store also went up. The Vawn Post Office was established on July 1, 1912, and Vawn became an incorporated village on December 4, 1912. By that year, two grain elevators had been erected, a barber shop, pool room and real estate business were established, a blacksmith and a butcher were in operation, and a twenty-room hotel had been built. The Vawn School District was set up in 1913, and a railway station was constructed; a doctor arrived in 1914. The village never

▲ **ST. HIPPOLYTE ROMAN CATHOLIC CHURCH, VAWN.** Photograph taken July 23, 2003.

was very large — its population was 78 in 1921, 59 in 1941, 102 in 1961, and 81 in 1981. The Vawn and District Credit Union was incorporated in 1943; the Sisters of the Presentation of Mary arrived to teach school and operate a convent in the mid-1950s; in the late 1950s, the church in St. Hippolyte (built in 1911 to replace the original log structure) was moved into Vawn, where it remains. Despite the community's small numbers, men's baseball and softball teams were fielded, as were hockey teams; notable women's teams played broomball, volleyball, and hockey. In 1965 the CN railway station was closed (it was later sold and moved to Meota for use as a residence); in the 1970s a number of local businesses in Vawn closed; in the early 1970s, Vawn's school began to be downsized as older grades were bused to Edam. By 1980 only classes up to grade 6

were still taught in Vawn — the school was still open in the early 1990s, but was subsequently closed. Today, the credit union, the post office, and a construction company are among the few businesses left in the community; a few residents work in trucking for the area's oil and gas industry; the former convent now houses a hotel and a bar mainly for oil field workers. St. Hippolyte Church closed, other than for special events, in 2003, and no grain elevators remain standing in the community. Vawn relinquished village status on February 16, 2004; the community's peak population was 137 in 1966. Vawn is situated in the RM of Turtle River No. 469.

VEREGIN, hamlet, pop 65 (2006c), 83 (2001c), is a former village located 13 km west of Kamsack on Hwy 5. The community, which once numbered close to 400 persons, is today most notable for being the site of the National Doukhobour Heritage Village. The Doukhobors came to what would become Saskatchewan in 1899, establishing traditional communal villages in four large blocks of land set aside for them by the federal government. But Veregin itself was not a typical Doukhobor village with two rows of structures laid out along a single street. The village of Veregin was a creation of the railway and was surveyed in rectangular blocks

▲ **DOUKHOBOR MEN IN THE VEREGIN AREA, 1899.** Given the unavailability of sufficient oxen and horses, community members were often forced to haul basic necessities such as flour from Yorkton to their villages dozens of miles away.

Historical photographs courtesy of the National Doukhobor Heritage Village, Veregin.

Home of the National Doukhobour Heritage Village...

▼ **THE VILLAGERS OF VEREGIN, MAY 1904.** Pictured just left of centre at the forefront of the men in the photograph are Peter Vasilevich Verigin and James Mavor, the latter a professor of political economy at the University of Toronto who assisted the Doukhobors in negotiations with the Canadian Government.

VEREGIN

▲ **MEALTIME ON THE PRAIRIES**, date unknown.

▲ **WOMEN ON THE PLOUGH.** During their early years in the country the Doukhobors were strapped for cash, unable to afford draft animals and most farm implements. To gain some income, able-bodied men often had to leave their communities to find work building railways, or as farmhands for wealthier settlers. As such, any progress made breaking and seeding their own lands was often left to women and children or the elderly.

▼ **BUILT IN 1917**, this building served as a Prayer Home and the residence of two Doukhobor leaders, Peter Vasilevich Verigin and his son Peter P. Verigin. Photograph taken July 26, 2004.

the same as hundreds of other Saskatchewan communities. And while the Doukhobor role in the village was once very significant, their numbers declined early in the twentieth century, and for most of the community's history the population has been comprised of non-Doukhobor peoples. The other immigrants settling in what became the surrounding RM of Sliding Hills No. 273 were mainly of British, Ukrainian, German, Romanian, and Polish origins. When the Canadian Northern Railway came through the area in 1904-05, the company established the present townsite and the name Veregin was chosen to honour the Doukhobor leader Peter Vasilevich Verigin (1859-1924), who had come to Canada in 1902. Somehow, though, the spelling of the community name ended up being different than the spelling of the name of the man, yet the post office established in 1906 utilized the correct spelling "Verigin" and continues to do so. With the arrival of the railway in the district, Peter Verigin relocated his headquarters to the townsite (previously, the Doukhobor village of Otradnoe to the north of Veregin had been his base), and the village became a market centre with commercial enterprises based in agriculture and industry — a local brickworks produced 1.5 million bricks in 1905. Veregin was incorporated as a village on February 7, 1912. The community grew and prospered throughout much of the first half of the twentieth century — by 1950, there were five grain elevators along the tracks — but by the 1960s it became evident that the village population and the number of businesses were beginning to dwindle. In the mid-1950s the community numbered close to 300 residents; 20 years later the population was down to 140, and in the early 1980s the school was closed. In January 2004, the village suffered major losses when two fires within a week destroyed most of the community's businesses, including the hotel. Veregin relinquished village status on December 31, 2006.

VIBANK, village, pop 361 (2006c), 381 (2001c), is situated approximately 50 km southeast of Regina on Hwy 48. German Catholic settlers, largely from the Odessa region of southern Russia, began arriving in the district in 1891. In 1904, they founded St. Paul's Parish and, that year, the first church was built somewhat north of the present village site. Also in 1904, a school, given the name Elsas, was established in the vicinity of the church. German Lutheran families from Bukovina and the Black Sea area began arriving in the Vibank district in 1898-99, and in 1909 their congregation built Emmanuel Lutheran Church in the village. The village itself began to develop in 1907 with the construction of the Canadian Northern Railway line from Brandon, Manitoba, through Maryfield and Kipling to Regina. Regular train service started in 1908 and, that year, the first grain elevator was erected at Vibank. Over the next few years a number of businesses were established and many homes were built. The Village of Vibank — the origin of the community's name is unknown — was incorporated on June 23, 1911. Both the country church and the school were moved into Vibank in 1912. In 1919, Ursuline Sisters, an order of the Roman Catholic Church, came to Vibank, and in 1923 a mother house and boarding school, the Holy Family Convent, was built. By 1926, the population of Vibank was 365. The drought and the Depression, though, exacted a heavy toll on the community. The village population dropped dramatically — down to

421

229 by 1936 — and businesses closed their doors. The Bank of Toronto folded, the government beer store was closed, the doctor died and was not replaced, and, following this, the druggist was forced to move away. During WWII, the community was committed to the war effort, and one Vibank family, that of John and Regina Leboldus, lost three young sons. Peter, Martin, and John Leboldus all died within 12 months of one another during active service with the RCAF overseas. In 1955, Mrs. Leboldus was chosen by the Royal Canadian Legion as the National Silver Cross Mother, and as such she represented all mothers who lost children during military service by laying the mother's wreath at the National War Memorial in Ottawa on Remembrance Day that year. Following the war, three linked geographic features in northern Saskatchewan — now known as Leboldus Lake, Leboldus Channel, and the Leboldus Islands — were named in memory of the young Vibank men. In recent decades, Vibank has increasingly become home to people who commute to work in Regina, and today approximately 70 per cent of those in the Vibank workforce drive to and from the city during the work week. The population of the village grew from 275 in 1971 as more city workers sought a rural lifestyle. In recent years, there was a shortage of housing in the village, and new housing developments were constructed to address the problem. Today, Vibank businesses include a grocery store and a meat market, a gas station and mechanic's services, a credit union, an insurance agency, the post office, a reflexologist, a massage therapist, tanning and hair salons, and a construction company. A remaining grain elevator is privately owned. Village facilities include skating and curling rinks with artificial ice, sports grounds, a community hall, and a seniors' centre. The community has Roman Catholic and Lutheran churches. The village has a licenced daycare and a K-12 school which had 177 village and district students enrolled in the fall of 2006. The former Holy Family Convent remains a major community landmark. It was run by the Ursuline Sisters until 1977, then taken over by the village in the early 1990s and designated a municipal heritage property in 1992. The Vibank district economy is based in agriculture, mixed grains and cattle, including some dairy production. Vibank is situated in the RM of Francis No. 127.

VICEROY, organized hamlet, pop 29 (2006c), 35 (2001c), is a former village located in south-central Saskatchewan just north of Willow Bunch Lake. Agriculture, consisting of grain and livestock production, forms the basis of the local economy. Settlement of the area began in the early 1900s, and with the arrival of the CPR from Weyburn in 1911 the townsite developed. Viceroy was incorporated as a village on April 1, 1912. One of the first community projects was the beginning of a ferry service across Willow Bunch Lake. With no rail lines south of the lake, grain producers in that region had to either haul their crops north across the ice in winter or travel the long distance overland around the lake to the elevator points on the rail line. Viceroy grain elevator operators subsidized the ferry project, and the service ran until about 1917. Like many early Saskatchewan communities, Viceroy had its fires. Two years after incorporation, a fire claimed the west side of the main street, and, in 1941, history would almost repeat itself when another fire destroyed most of the east side of the same block. The late 1920s and the 1930s were times of great scarcity and hardship for the community, but by the mid-1950s the population of the village was near 300, and Viceroy had developed into an important centre of business and social activity. Rapidly, however, began a brutal downward spiral: rural populations declined, roads and automobiles improved, local businesses were unable to compete with the goods and services offered in larger centres, and within a decade, 100 people were gone. The decline continued and the village's numbers further plummeted from 178 in 1966 to just 88 a decade later, in 1976. By the beginning of the twenty-first century, Viceroy numbered fewer than 40 people, and on May 10, 2002, the village was dissolved. Viceroy serves as the administrative headquarters of the RM of Excel No. 71.

VISCOUNT, village, pop 251 (2006c), 272 (2001c), is located approximately 80 km east of Saskatoon on Hwy 16, the Yellowhead, between the town of Colonsay to the west and the village of Plunkett to the east. Settlers had been in the district only a couple of years when, in May 1907, the first building, a general store, was erected on the Viscount townsite. Construction began in anticipation of the completion of the CPR rail line between Lanigan and Saskatoon. The locale was named after a prominent Irish judge and orator, Viscount Horace Plunkett (1764–1854). The Viscount Post Office was established on January 1, 1908, and on December 17, 1908, with a population of over 50, the Village of Viscount was incorporated. The rail line had become operational in 1908, and, that year, the local public school district was also established. In 1909, the Northern Crown Bank opened its doors and the first grain elevators were erected (there would eventually be five; none remain today). The *Viscount Sun* newspaper began publishing in 1910. In 1911, the population of the village was 72; by 1921 it was 315. By this time a number of religious organizations, reflecting the diversity of people's origins, were active in the community: Methodist services had begun in people's homes in 1907, and construction of their church began in 1911 (it became the United Church in 1925); the first St. Alphonse Roman Catholic Church was built in 1908; St. Paul's Anglican Church was consecrated in 1909; St. John's Lutheran Church, although started a few years earlier, was completed in 1920. A Roman Catholic separate school, St. Alphonse, was started in 1923. The population in 1931 was 342; the Depression, however, reduced the

▲ **THE VISCOUNT FLOUR MILL**, on the northwest corner of Amherst Avenue and Francis Street, was started by Harry "Slim" Carnation in the mid-1920s. It was equipped with a roller mill built in Ontario and a European-built stone mill manufactured in the late 1800s. The mill was purchased by John Ebner in 1956 and then by Alois Koller in 1964. Originally, most of the milling work involved providing grist for farmers, and the commercial sale of flours to the Federated Co-op and the Saskatchewan Wheat Pool; in later years, producing additive-free, stone-ground whole wheat flour for health food stores dominated production as demand increased. When the Viscount mill closed in 2001, it was the smallest operating flour mill in western Canada. Photograph taken August 9, 2004.

community's numbers to 272 by 1941. The 1960s saw new homes being built as the village's population mushroomed when both area farmers and potash workers settled in the community. Three potash mines in the area began to be constructed during the decade — near Allan, Guernsey, and Colonsay — and it was a period of growth, prosperity, and modernization for the entire region. During the 1960s, 150 American elm trees were planted in Viscount, a water and sewer system was constructed, a new community centre was built, and the village received natural gas. By 1976, Viscount reached a peak population of 424. The community's numbers remained close to the 400 mark until the mid-1980s, when they began to decline. Today, many Viscount residents still work at one of the area's potash mines; others find employment related to the district's traditional industry — agriculture. As of 2007, Viscount still retained its two schools: the Catholic separate school, St. Alphonse Elementary, had 11 students

enrolled in the fall of 2006; the public Viscount Central School, a K-12 institution, had 111 students enrolled at the same time. Viscount has a volunteer fire department; the nearest RCMP detachment is in Colonsay; there are hospitals in Watrous, Lanigan, and Humboldt. Viscount serves as the administrative centre of the RM of Viscount No. 341.

VONDA, town, pop 322 (2006c), 322 (2001c), is located approximately 45 km northeast of Saskatoon on Hwy 27. People were settling the district in the 1890s, and with the construction of the Canadian Northern Railway through the area c. 1904-05 the community developed. Vonda was incorporated as a village in 1905 and became a town in 1907. Although the district was extremely multicultural (the region included Mennonite, Ukrainian, Polish, Hungarian, and British settlers), Vonda, along with the communities of Prud'homme and St. Denis, reflected a significant French presence. While English-language education was transferred to the town of Aberdeen in the mid-1960s, the area's French culture is maintained by École Providence in Vonda, a K-10 French-language institution. Developing as a service centre for the

▼ **A THRESHING CREW** poses on a hay wagon on the farm of M.F.X. Loiselle near Vonda in 1914. Saskatchewan Archives Board R-A19745.

surrounding agricultural district, Vonda's population grew to over 400 by the early 1930s; over the following decades, however, the community declined, its numbers falling to close to 200 by the early 1960s. Subsequently, though, the town experienced renewed growth, partially due to commuters working in Saskatoon taking up residence in the town. As well, an agricultural equipment manufacturer, which now operates out of a 75,000-square-foot facility in Vonda, brought many much-needed jobs to the community. Two structures in the town have been designated heritage properties: the former Bank of Commerce, dating to 1906, and the Vonda Rink, housed in an aircraft hangar that was built in the early 1940s at the British Commonwealth Air Training Plan base in Davidson. Vonda serves as the administrative centre of the RM of Grant No. 372.

◀ **WADENA TOWN OFFICE.** Erected in 1938 and situated on the northeast corner of 1st Avenue North and Main Street, this community landmark was originally a federal building, over the years housing the post office, the RCMP barracks, Veteran's Land Administration offices, and the Federal Indian Health office. The Town of Wadena purchased the building from the Canadian Government in 1972, and it was designated a municipal heritage property in 1986.

▶ **AN EARLY PHOTOGRAPH** of Wadena's CNR station with a steam locomotive pulled alongside, date unknown.

WADENA

...on the great wetlands of the Quill Plain

WADENA, town, pop 1,315 (2006c), 1,412 (2001c), is located just northeast of Little Quill Lake at the junction of Hwys 5 and 35. The first settlers in the region were a single Irish family. The Milligans arrived in the early summer of 1882, having travelled north from Fort Qu'Appelle. They settled several miles southeast of present-day Wadena and engaged in ranching. For the next ten years the family lived practically isolated with only the odd white traveller and the region's indigenous inhabitants passing by their home. With the railway arriving at Saltcoats in 1888 and Yorkton a couple of years later, a few more settlers

WADENA HOTEL, 1909.

began trickling into the area; however, before 1900, there were still very few people in the Wadena district. Ranching was still the major activity, and it was not until the early 1900s that substantial tracts of land were broken for the purpose of crop production. Some of the first buildings began to appear on the Wadena townsite in 1904, as the railway was then advancing westward from the Kamsack and Canora areas. With the Canadian Northern Railway running trains through Wadena in 1905, business was booming and the community developed rapidly. Settlers of

▲ **JULY 1ST SPORTS DAY**, circa early 1920s. Photograph taken on Railway Avenue, now Pamela Wallin Drive.

▶ **JUNIOR AND SENIOR STUDENTS** at Wadena High School, June 20, 1922.

Historical photographs courtesy of the Wadena & District Museum; colour photographs taken August 4, 2004.

▼ **WADENA & DISTRICT MUSEUM AND NATURE CENTRE.** The town's 1904 CN railway station (below left) was moved (below, right) to its present site in 1991 to serve as a museum and a tourist information centre.

diverse origins were flooding the district and the Wadena area became a melting pot of a variety of ethnic groups. In 1906, with a population of 141, Wadena was incorporated as a village, being named after Wadena, Minnesota, the home of one of the first families to settle on the townsite in the spring of 1904. In 1912, the community attained town status and by then had become a thriving agricultural service centre. By the early 1920s, the population of Wadena was well over 500. The period following WWII brought another surge of people to the community, although this was less attributable to immigration from beyond Saskatchewan than it was due to the trend toward urbanization within the province. Wadena's population soared from 595 in 1936 to 1,081 in 1951. At this point, Wadena was also substantially rebuilding and modernizing its business sector, as a fire in 1949 had claimed all but three enterprises in the commercial district. The disaster had its upside. Today, Wadena is one of the region's most important distribution and service centres, with a trading area population estimated to be approximately 21,000. Agriculture is the main industry, and Wadena has agricultural implement dealerships, major grain handling facilities, auction services, and manufacturing plants that produce a wide range of farm-related equipment. A substantial retail sector and professional community provide a wide range of goods and services. Additionally, Wadena's elementary and high schools provide K-12 education to over 400 town and area students. Wadena has a hospital, an extended care facility, nursing homes, and an ambulance service, as well as practitioners providing physiotherapy, optometry, and dental and chiropractic services. Wadena has an RCMP detachment and a volunteer fire department. The community's recreational facilities include an outdoor pool, a nine-hole golf course, sports grounds, camping facilities, and rinks for skating, hockey, and curling. Tourism is also becoming an increasing factor in Wadena's economy, and town and area attractions include the Wadena and District Museum, the Wadena Murals (numbering approximately 20 and depicting different aspects of both the community's history and the natural beauty of the surrounding district), and the Wadena Wildlife Wetlands (internationally recognized as important staging grounds for a wide variety of birds including many endangered species). The Quill Lakes attract over 1 million birds annually (Big Quill Lake is Canada's largest saline lake), and a network of boardwalks, nature trails, and viewing towers have been developed throughout the area. Each year, the Wadena district attracts both bird-watchers and hunters from across North America, and each spring the community hosts the Shorebirds and Friends Festival which highlights the ecological importance of the region. Wadena is also the hometown of the widely respected broadcaster and journalist, Pamela Wallin, who in 2002 was appointed Canada's Consul General to New York City. In 1994, Wallin received what she counted as the most precious recognition of her career; she was honoured by the residents of her hometown when they renamed a main street in the community Pamela Wallin Drive. Wadena serves as the administrative centre of the RM of Lakeview No. 337.

WAKAW, town, pop 864 (2006c), 884 (2001c), is located approximately 65 km south of Prince Albert at the junction of Hwys 2, 41, and 312. Beginning in the 1880s a few people came to the area and engaged in ranching. Significant settlement, however, began in the late 1890s, and the Wakaw district would come to be settled by people of Ukrainian, Hungarian, French, and German origins. In 1903, a Presbyterian mission was founded on a point at the west end of Wakaw Lake, followed in 1906 by the construction of a small hospital. The Wakaw Post Office was established at the location in 1905, and stores and a gristmill were also built at the site. Thus, Wakaw had its beginnings on the lakeshore. When the rail line was surveyed, a new townsite was established somewhat less than a kilometre west of the lake, and on December 26, 1911, the Village of Wakaw was incorporated. The name Wakaw is the Cree word for "crooked" and refers to the shape of the lake. After the trains were running through the young community, Wakaw quickly developed into a sizable service and shopping centre for the surrounding agricultural district. In 1919, a young lawyer who had just been called to the Saskatchewan Bar came to the village looking to establish his first practice. Over the next five years, John George Diefenbaker honed skills that would take him far in life. By the 1930s, Wakaw had several hundred residents, and on August 1, 1953, the community attained town status. Today, Wakaw has a wide range of businesses and services, a number of tradespeople, construction companies, and home-

WAKAW

...beginnings at the end of the "crooked lake"

▲ ▼ SCHOOL DAYS: Wakaw School's Grade Elevens, 1942-43 (above), and the Wakaw School Band, 1949-50 (below). Standing in the background at the right is Peter G. Kindrachuk, the band director and a long-time teacher at Wakaw School.

▼ THE ANNUAL PILGRIMAGE to the Shrine of St. Theresa, also known as St. Therese of Lisieux, began in 1925, the very year of her canonization by Pope Pius XI. Special trains once brought pilgrims to Wakaw from Prince Albert, Saskatoon, and Humboldt for the yearly gathering, and since its beginnings the pilgrimage has attracted 2,000 or more people annually. The photograph here was taken circa 1927.

based enterprises. A substantial farmers' market is held weekly during the summer months. Wakaw has a hospital, medical clinics, a special care home, a pharmacy, and home care and ambulance services. A resident doctor, Dr. Fred Cenaiko, has been practicing in Wakaw for well over 40 years. The town has an RCMP detachment and a volunteer fire department. Wakaw School is a K-12 facility, which had 236 town and area students enrolled in the fall of 2006. The town has a number of churches, a library, and a museum with a replica of the Diefenbaker law office. Recreational facilities include an arena, which provides a venue for hockey games, public skating, and the community's figure skating club; a substantial recreation complex houses a curling club, a bowling centre, a seniors' club, a hall for weddings and dances, and a gun club. The Wakaw Gun Club sponsors an annual gun show, which has become one of the most popular in Saskatchewan. The community also has a summer recreation program through which activities are coordinated for all ages, and, additionally, there is a golf course at Wakaw Lake, where there are also opportunities for swimming, boating, fishing, and camping. Wakaw Lake has one of the province's busiest regional parks, as well as a number of resort communities. There are approximately 1,000 cottages in the area. In recent years, the town has developed ambitious plans to develop a canal system to directly link the community to Wakaw Lake: a marina and related tourist facilities would be developed, as well as new residential, commercial, and public spaces. The environmental, physical, and financial feasibility of the project have been assessed, and as of 2007 the community was moving forward with the project. Wakaw is situated in the RM of Hoodoo No. 401.

WAKAW LAKE, resort village, is located approximately 10 km east of Wakaw, off Hwy 41, on the south shore of the lake from which the community derives its name. Originally known as Poplar Beach, the area has been popular for recreational activities since the early twentieth century. By the mid-1920s, there were concessions and a dance pavilion. The resort village, one of several resort communities on the lake, was incorporated in 1959. There are approximately a few dozen permanent residents; however, the population varies greatly depending on the season, and may reach roughly 400 on summer weekends. Wakaw Lake is situated in the RM of Hoodoo No. 401.

WALDECK, village, pop 294 (2006c), 333 (2001c), is located 15 km northeast of Swift Current on Hwy 1. Swift Current Creek, en route to empty into Lake Diefenbaker, passes just north of the community. The CPR arrived in Swift Current toward the end of 1882, and, in the years following, Waldeck was the name of a railway point located about five kilometres east of the present community, near where the Swift Current Creek takes a bend for the northwest. The name Waldeck is German for "wooded corner," and may have been chosen because the willows and other shrubs growing along the creek would have stood in sharp contrast to the surrounding prairie. After the railway company straightened their track in the region in 1905, Waldeck was moved westward and the present community developed, at first south of the CPR tracks, where a large stockyard had been constructed, but by 1909, with a school built on the north side, businesses and

residences shifted to the village's present location. The district, particularly along the creek, was the domain of large-scale ranching enterprises until the first decade of the twentieth century, when the land began to be given over to homesteaders. In the heyday of the ranching era, entire train loads of cattle were shipped out of Waldeck annually. Settlers coming to the region included English-speaking people, many coming from Ontario, and Norwegians, emigrating from the United States (although a good number of these simply unloaded their effects at Waldeck before homesteading in the district to the north). Prominent among those settling in the Waldeck area were Mennonites, and between 1904 and 1910 most of the available land in the area was taken up. On October 1, 1906, the Waldeck Post Office was established. In 1909, area residents petitioned the provincial government for the organization of a rural municipality to replace local improvement districts, and on December 13, 1909, the RM of Waldeck No. 166 legally came into being. In the early years, all bylaws passed by the council were published in both English and German. Within four or five years, though, the RM office was moved to Rush Lake, and in 1916 the name of the RM was changed to the RM of Excelsior No. 166, evidently to avoid confusion with the mail. Waldeck was incorporated as a village on December 23, 1913, and the community flourished during its formative years. The CPR doubled its track through the region over 1912-13 to deal with increasing traffic — primarily the movement of grain — and by 1916 the population of the village had grown to 182. Five grain elevators were built along the tracks at Waldeck and the community grew to boast a wide range of businesses and services. By the early 1920s, however, the village's population

began to steadily drop, and it reached an all-time low of 87 in 1951. According to the local history, consideration was given to reverting back to hamlet status during the Depression, but this did not come to pass. After the completion of the Trans-Canada Highway in the 1950s, Waldeck began again to grow fairly rapidly, its population settling around its current level in the early 1980s. By that time, though, the business sector in Waldeck had disappeared and only the post office remained. Waldeck became a bedroom community to Swift Current, and, today, a sign on the highway advises there are no services in the community. Waldeck retains a school, a K-9 institution that had 158 students enrolled in the fall of 2006.

WALDHEIM, town, pop 868 (2006c), 889 (2001c), is located approximately 50 km north of Saskatoon on Hwy 312. The town of Rosthern lies to the northeast and the Petrofka Bridge across the North Saskatchewan River lies just to the northwest. The origins of the community date to the early 1890s with the settlement of large numbers of Mennonites in the area, a presence which remains strong in Waldheim to this day. The name Waldheim means "forest home" in German and was chosen because the district was well-treed. The Waldheim Post Office was established in 1900, and, with the arrival of the Canadian Northern Railway and the construction of the station in 1909, Waldheim became a railway centre for the developing agricultural community in the rich farmlands of the surrounding area. Waldheim became an incorporated village in 1912. From a population of 230 in 1916, the community has grown steadily over the decades, reaching over 500 by the early 1960s. In Canada's Centennial

▲ **THE OLD AND THE NEW** lined up on Railway Avenue in 1954.

year, 1967, Waldheim attained town status. Today, while Waldheim has a strong business community providing a wide variety of goods and services, residents also benefit from the amenities that the city of Saskatoon has to offer. Waldheim has a range of recreational facilities, including an arena and a regional park with a nine-hole golf course. The community has a number of churches, service clubs, and community-based organizations. Waldheim School provides K-12 education to close to 250 students. Waldheim serves as the administrative centre of the RM of Laird No. 404.

Forest home... # WALDHEIM

The photographs of Railway Avenue in 1954 and John Diefenbaker are courtesy of the Town of Waldheim.

▶ **MR. PRIME MINISTER, START YOUR ENGINE!** During the snowmobile races held at the Waldheim sector of Valley Regional Park in early 1979, the former prime minister, John G. Diefenbaker, then an MP, suited up for this photograph with the race officials. Several months later, on August 16, 1979, Diefenbaker passed away at the age of 83.

◀ **AN ATTRACTIVE FEATURE** of the town is the centrally-located Sam Wendland Heritage Park. The site includes the former Canadian Northern Railway station (the rail line through the community was abandoned in 1992). Now a heritage property, the building serves as the Waldheim library. Photograph taken August 26, 2004.

WALDRON, village, pop 20 (2006c), 15 (2001c), is located southeast of Melville, 3 km west of Hwy 9. The first settlers began arriving in the area in the late 1800s and included British, Scandinavian, and central-European pioneers. The townsite was established shortly after the railway was built through the district in 1906-07, and the village was incorporated in 1909. It was named after Sir Alfred Waldron Smithers, chairman of the Grand Truck Pacific Railway. Within the next few years the community grew rapidly: a post office and a school were established; and two banks, three grain elevators, and a number of stores, livery stables, and lumberyards were opened for business. In its early years, the village was plagued by disasters. The hockey arena built in 1911 was destroyed by a cyclone in 1912, then rebuilt, and destroyed by another cyclone in 1916. Fire claimed a few businesses in 1915, then most of the community's commercial district in 1921. By 1941, Waldron had reached a peak population of 128; however, since the late 1960s, the community has seen its numbers steadily decline. Waldron is situated in the RM of Grayson No. 184, an area of mixed farming.

WAPELLA, town, pop 311 (2006c), 354 (2001c), is located 24 km northwest of Moosomin on Hwy 1. The townsite was developed in 1882 when the CPR was being built through the area, and over the following couple of years a substantial settlement of former Scottish crofters developed over a broad district to the south. The Scots would be joined by English neighbours in 1884 and then, between 1886 and 1907, by about 50 Jewish families, largely from southern Russia, who settled on homesteads just to the north. Canada's famous Bronfman family got its start in this country on a homestead in the Wapella area in 1889. The Wapella Post Office was established in 1883, and over the following years adventurous entrepreneurs set up businesses in the fledgling community. On December 29, 1898, Wapella was incorporated as a village. In 1900, the community suffered something of a setback as a cyclone caused considerable damage; however, on November 20, 1903, Wapella attained town status. By 1911, the population was nearing 500. Germans from Poland arrived in the Wapella district in 1928. Mixed farming developed to become the area's major industry; however, the discovery of oil in the region in 1952 has slowly, but steadily, added diversity and stability to the district economy. Agricultural production consists of livestock and grain, along with some specialty crops, and, today, several oil batteries, oil and gas transmission lines, trucking companies and other oilfield-related services are located in the Wapella area. Wapella also has a small core of local businesses and a volunteer fire department. Nearby Moosomin's substantial commercial sector dominates the regional trading area, providing a wide array of goods and services, as well as policing (RCMP), medical facilities and a variety of medical practitioners. Wapella has a K-9 school, which had 77 students enrolled in the fall of 2005. The community has rinks for skating, hockey, and curling, ball diamonds, and a nine-hole golf course just south of town. A museum is located in the community's former Anglican Church, and the town has several service clubs and community organizations. Wapella is situated in the RM of Martin No. 122.

WARMAN, town, pop 4,764 (2006c), 3,481 (2001c), is one of Saskatchewan's fastest growing municipalities. Since 1966, the year Warman was incorporated as a town, the population has grown from 725. Located roughly 15 minutes north of Saskatoon, the town, like nearby Martensville, Dalmeny and Osler, has in the past 30 years developed essentially into a bedroom community for people working in the city. The origins of Warman date to 1904-05 when the Canadian Northern Railway, being built westward, intersected with the north to south running QLLS railway. The townsite of Warman grew up at the junction, and in 1906 the growing community was incorporated as a village. It was named after Cy Warman, an American journalist who followed and reported on the construction of the Canadian Northern Railway. By 1927, however, the population had dropped to 148 and the village was dissolved, reverting to hamlet status. For the next 35 years its affairs were handled by the surrounding rural municipality. In the 1950s, Warman began to grow again, and in 1962 it was again incorporated as a village. The burgeoning population has led to the development of a large range of local businesses, services and recreational facilities. There is a local RCMP detachment, a fire department, ambulance service, a medical clinic, and a special care home. Warman's elementary and high schools provided K-12 education to more than 1,000 students in 2006-07. The major annual event in the community is the Warman Diamond Rodeo and Family Days. Warman is situated in the RM of Corman Park No. 344.

◄ **WAPELLA, 1977.**
Saskatchewan Archives Board R-B11521. Photograph courtesy of Richard Gustin, Regina, Saskatchewan.

► **WAPELLA, AUGUST 17, 2003.** View from the south.

WASECA, village, pop 144 (2006c), 169 (2001c), is located 40 km southeast of Lloydminster on Hwy 16, the Yellowhead, between the towns of Lashburn, to the west, and Maidstone, to the east. There are conflicting thoughts as to the origins of the community's name; however, there is a small body of water just south of the townsite (a marsh really), and it is possible that the name could be derived from a Cree expression referring to bright or clear water. Although surveyors for the intended trans-continental railway came through the Waseca region in the 1870s, and a cross-country telegraph line was built through the district during the decade, it was not until the late 1890s that the Waseca area had its first permanent settlers. The Barr Colonists passed through in 1903, but it was after the railway was being built from North Battleford to Lloydminster in 1905 that significant numbers of settlers began taking up land in the region. Evidently, however, the Canadian Northern Railway originally intended that the Waseca locale be only a flag stop and a siding for handling grain, as Maidstone and Lashburn were both to be developed short distances away. When William Goodridge arrived in the summer of 1906 there was only a shed that served as a shelter for people waiting for the train. Goodridge set up a tent and proceeded to build the first store; by January of 1907 he had established a post office, and he remained the postmaster until 1936. By the end of 1907, other entrepreneurs had joined Goodridge and several new businesses had been established. A loading platform was built for farmers to load grain, until the first elevator was erected in 1909 (by the early 1930s there would be five). In 1908, the first Waseca School was built, as was an Anglican Church. Waseca became an incorporated village on March 15, 1911, and that year a railway station was built. A Roman Catholic Church was constructed in 1915. Given its proximity to larger centres, however, Waseca's growth was limited; the population was 106 in 1921 and still 115 in 1971. The development of better roads and automobiles diminished its position as a district trading centre. In the 1980s, as the region's oil and gas industry began expanding, the village experienced a period of growth; today, trucking companies and other oilfield services are among Waseca's small core of businesses. The village also has a credit union, post office, and insurance agency. Waseca School was down to a grade one to six facility by the late 1970s and was closed in 1989. Schoolchildren now attend schools in either Lashburn or Maidstone. Waseca has a community hall, an ice rink, and several community-based organizations; it has a volunteer fire department. The nearest hospital and RCMP detachment are located in Maidstone. Waseca is situated in the RM of Eldon No. 471.

WATROUS, town, pop 1,743 (2006c), 1,808 (2001c), is located 110 km southeast of Saskatoon at the junction of Hwys 2 and 365. There were only a few settlers in the district in 1903, but between 1904 and 1906 homesteaders' sod houses and shacks began to dot the country for miles around. A small community developed which the Norwegian Lutheran settlers named Mandal after one homesteader's original hometown, Mandal, Norway. Mandal had a school, a post office, and a number of shops. But when engineers for the Grand Trunk Pacific Railway came through in 1906 and surveyed a townsite somewhat east of Mandal, as the location was more suitable for the development of rail yards, the decision was made to relocate to the site which the railway had named Watrous. The Grand Trunk Pacific was naming all the points along the line in alphabetical order, and the name Watrous, after Frank Watrous Morse, the general manager of the railway, was in keeping with this strategy. Trains were running in 1908. In the period leading up to WWI, there was a great influx of settlers into the area and most of the available homestead land was occupied. Watrous developed rapidly. The community was incorporated as a village on October 15, 1908, and attained town status on December 30, 1909. Very early on, area residents discovered the mineral waters of Little Manitou Lake, about

▼ **WATROUS, CIRCA 1929.** Photograph courtesy of the Lanigan & District Heritage Centre.

5 kilometres north of Watrous, which had long been known to local First Nations peoples. Manitou Beach quickly became a popular resort destination, and the town of Watrous greatly benefitted over the years as throngs of tourists passed through the community en route to the lake. Today, the symbiotic relationship between Watrous and the resort village remains strong. In 1939, Watrous became the location for the Canadian Broadcasting Corporation's only broadcasting outlet between Winnipeg and Vancouver, and the CBK Radio station's 50,000-watt transmitter far exceeded the expectations of providing coverage for the prairie provinces. Reception has been reported from as far away as Australia. Watrous was chosen for the transmitter's location because the same minerals which make Little Manitou Lake unique also make the area's soils highly conductive. Radiating from the base of the 465-foot (142-metre) tower, 120 wires each 500 feet (152 metres) long are buried under the earth, grounding the system. Engineers estimate that to equal the coverage of CBK, an eastern radio station would have to have four times the power. Once a popular tourist attraction with a full-time staff of 14, the CBK transmitter is now remotely operated from Regina. During the 1930s Watrous experienced a slight decline; however, following WWII the community experienced a return to prosperity and renewed growth. Today, the town remains an important service centre for the district and a major shopping centre for area farm families. Major automobile and farm equipment dealerships draw buyers from across Saskatchewan and are significant community employers. One dealership alone has over 80 full and part-time staff, and the stretch of vehicles and machinery lining Hwy 2 has become known locally as the "$35-million mile."

Watrous also benefits from its proximity to three potash mines, which are major employers of town residents. Agriculture, a substantial part of the area economy, includes a diverse array of crops grown, as well as livestock production. Cattle are raised in the area's pastures and marginal lands, and there are intensive hog and dairy operations in the district. Tourism generated by Manitou Beach adds to a diversified economy. Additionally, Watrous has a wide range of health care facilities, including a hospital, medical and dental clinics, and an eye care centre. The community has an ambulance service, a special care home, and seniors' housing. Protection services are provided by a local RCMP detachment and an 18-member volunteer fire department. The community has elementary and high schools that provide K-12 education to over 400 town and area students. Watrous also has a full range of recreational facilities and a strong focus on arts and culture. The town has a number of churches, service clubs, sports clubs, youth groups, and other community-based organizations. A Watrous church may also have what could be the oldest stained glass in window in Canada. The window, located in All Saints Anglican Church on Main Street, was brought to Watrous in 2,000 pieces from England by the first vicar of the church, and dates back to pre-Reformation times. Watrous is situated in the RM of Morris No. 312.

WATSON, town, pop 719 (2006c), 794 (2001c), is located just northwest of Big Quill Lake at the junction of Hwys 5 and 6. Settlement of the area began in the early 1900s, and although people of diverse origins would come to make the district home, a substantial number were German-American Catholics who first

▲ **A WATSON LANDMARK:** This fibreglass Santa Claus statue, which greets visitors entering the town from the south and west, stands 25 feet (7.62 metres) high and weighs 1,500 pounds (680 kilograms). The rotund, white-bearded, red-suited, waving figure commemorates the community's Santa Claus Day, for years held on the first Saturday in December. The origins of the event date to 1932, when Watson's pioneer hardware merchant, Jake Smith, conceived of the idea to have "Santa" visit the community. Santa led the town's children to the Smith brothers' hardware store, where each received a gift. The next year, every business in Watson joined in the fun.

WATSON

Historical photographs courtesy of the Watson & District Heritage Museum; colour photographs taken August 5 and 6, 2004.

▼ **THE KING GEORGE HOTEL** was one of Watson's early businesses. It was still standing in the summer of 2004, although it was no longer in use. It has been subsequently demolished.

WATSON GRAIN GROWERS ASSOCIATION, LTD., circa 1919.

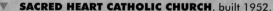

SACRED HEART CATHOLIC CHURCH, built 1952.

◄ **R.P. FINDLAY** was the manager of the Canadian Bank of Commerce in Watson from April 1912 until September 1915. At that time, the bank had a staff of eight to ten people, as the territory served was very large, especially to the north, with customers coming more than 30 miles. When Findlay became the branch manager at Watson he was 27 years old. During their residence in Watson, Mr. and Mrs. Findlay lived in what was known as "the Bank house," still standing at the corner of First Avenue North and First Street East. The highlight of their life at Watson was the birth of their son, Allan. Also important was the purchase of a brand new 1913 Model T Ford for $550, and the building of a garage at "the Bank house." From Watson, Mr. Findlay went on to bank branches in Bassano, Alberta, Owen Sound, Ontario, Sydney, Nova Scotia, and Guelph, Ontario. Mr. Findlay retired in 1944, after nearly 43 years of service to the Bank.

◄ **THE WATSON AND DISTRICT HERITAGE MUSEUM** is located in the town's immaculately preserved 1906 Canadian Bank of Commerce building. A prefabricated structure designed by notable Toronto architects Darling and Pearson (who incidentally were among the seven competitors seeking the contract for Saskatchewan's Legislative Building in 1907), the Watson bank was declared in 1977 by the Historic Sites and Monuments Board of Canada to be representative of a classical bank design which became a familiar western Canadian landmark.

◄ **THE *WATSON WITNESS*** first began production in 1907 with George H. Cameron as the proprietor, editor and publisher. After changing hands a few times, and almost a century in business, the local weekly newspaper ceased publication in about 2003.

began arriving in 1902. They settled in a broad arc ranging from the Watson district north-westward through to the Humboldt, Bruno, and Cudworth areas. With the Canadian Northern Railway progressing westward from Winnipeg toward Edmonton in 1905, the townsite developed and was given the name Watson in honour of Senator Robert Watson of Manitoba, who had owned the land upon which the community sits. Robert Watson was a businessman, an industrialist, and a Liberal MP before he was appointed to the Canadian senate on the advice of Wilfred Laurier in 1900. Watson was incorporated as a village in 1906 and became a town in 1908. In the early 1920s, Watson's status as a transportation hub was significantly bolstered as the CPR pushed through from Lanigan north toward Naicam and on to Melfort, thus making the community the junction of two competing railways. The town had grown steadily since its inception and experienced significant growth in the decades following WWII. The population rose from 444 in 1946 to 718 in 1951, and by the early 1960s the population was over 900. Today, Watson is a well-developed and attractive community whose economic base is agriculture, complemented by a number of industrial and manufacturing firms. The town has a full range of businesses providing a wide array of goods and services to a trading area population numbering several thousand. Additionally, Watson has a health centre, a special care home, an ambulance service, and a fire department shared with the neighbouring community of Englefeld. Policing is provided by the RCMP detachment based in Humboldt. Watson School provides K-12 education to about 150 students. Watson has a range of recreational facilities. McNab Regional Park, at the southern edge of the community, has

a nine-hole golf course, outdoor swimming and paddling pools, tennis courts, and campgrounds; the town also has an arena, a curling rink, a bowling alley, and ball diamonds. Watson is situated in the RM of Lakeside No. 338.

WAWOTA, town, pop 522 (2006c), 538 (2001c), is located just northeast of Moose Mountain Provincial Park and Kenosee Lake on Hwy 48, 46 km west of the Saskatchewan-Manitoba border. Wawota is situated on the edge of the Little Pipestone Valley, which provides the community with an attractive natural setting. Settlers began entering the district around 1882, as the transcontinental railway was being built through the Moosomin area to the north. Some of the first came from eastern Canada, although a substantial number who settled the district over the next couple of years were from Scotland. French settlers came to the district in 1906. The townsite of Wawota was established by the CPR in 1905 as the railway proceeded westward with the construction of their line from Reston, Manitoba, to Wolseley. The track became operational in 1906, and the little mixed train that ran back and forth on the line became affectionately known to local residents as the "Peanut." With the railway came a construction boom, and Wawota was incorporated as a village in 1907 — its name was derived from a First Nations word meaning "deep snow." Developing as an agricultural service centre for the surrounding region, Wawota's population passed the 300 mark by the mid-1920s, but fell somewhat during the 1930s. In 1939, the CPR first started talking about closing the Reston-Wolseley line. In 1960, the railway put forth an application to abandon the line amidst much opposi-

tion from the concerned communities. In 1961, the line was abandoned and the "Peanut" made its last run that August. Wawota lost its two grain elevators, and eight families whose livelihoods were tied to the elevators and the railway left the village. While many believed this was the death knell for the community, Wawota continued to grow, attaining town status in 1975 and reaching a peak population of 676 in 1986. Today, agriculture continues to dominate the area economy, and the community has a number of busi-

nesses which service the industry. There are a large number of livestock producers in the district. Additionally, there is some oilfield activity in the region, and a few related services have been established in the town. Wawota has a health centre with an attached special care home, and a K-12 school, which had 131 students enrolled in the fall of 2006. Wawota's municipal centre houses the offices of the town, the RM of Walpole No. 92, and those of the RM of Wawken No. 93, in which the town is situated. The complex also houses the

▲ **RAILWAY AVENUE, WAWOTA**, from the west, 1910. Saskatchewan Archives Board R-A3293.

▶ **THE ORIGINAL FIRE HALL** in Wawota, built in 1909 by Silas Rogers and Andy Scott. It is now a part of the Wawota & District Museum, located on Main Street in the community. Photograph taken August 21, 2003.

library, an ambulance, a fire truck, and a van for transporting those with special needs. The town's business community provides a variety of services, and Wawota's recreational facilities include an arena and a multi-diamond ball park. The Little Pipestone Valley has trails for hiking, cross-country skiing, and snowmobiling, as well as a natural amphitheatre that has been used for concerts as well as for the RCMP Musical Ride. Additionally, Moose Mountain Provincial Park has a major golf course, beaches, and waterslides, among a wide array of other resort facilities. Wawota hosts an annual music festival and dinner theatre, and an agricultural fair. The community's 1919 Union Bank of Canada building has been designated a heritage property, and situated on the Wawota and District Museum site are a 1905 schoolhouse and a unique fire hall dating to 1909. Murals, and flowers planted in the summer months, adorn Wawota's Main Street and Railway Avenue.

WEBB, village, pop 44 (2006c), 51 (2001c), is located 23 km northeast of Gull Lake about 1.5 km south of Hwy 1. In 1907, Webb consisted of three buildings: a section house for railway crews and a couple of sheds. But at this time settlers were beginning to pour into the area, and in 1908 a store and a post office were established. Two rival real estate developers arrived, one promoting development to the east, the other to the west. An East Webb and a West Webb emerged, both with hotels, stores, blacksmith shops, implement dealers, and livery stables. A bitter feud arose between the factions and, at one point, a barbed-wire fence was erected in the buffer zone between them. The two Webbs existed with the fence for some time until negotiations resulted in

its removal. The community then literally grew together and was incorporated in 1910. The first school opened the same year, and Webb began to develop rapidly. It was a point of disembarkation and support for homesteaders moving into the region. Three churches were built, as well as a dance hall, an increasing number of diverse businesses and, eventually, seven grain elevators. The population of Webb was approaching 300 toward the end of the 1920s, but the Depression hit the community hard. About a third of its residents abandoned the community, and Webb would never recover its population nor the level of commercial activity previously enjoyed. A devastating fire in 1931 also claimed an entire block of businesses, as well as the municipal office which contained the early records of the community. The population hovered at around 160–170 through the 1950s until the mid-1960s, but began to rapidly dwindle thereafter. Webb School was closed in 1974. Today, there are no grain elevators left in the community and its businesses have disappeared. Webb continues, however, to serve as the administrative centre of the RM of Webb No. 138. Agriculture and the oil industry form the basis of the area economy.

WEE TOO BEACH, resort village, is one in a string of resort communities situated on the west side of Last Mountain Lake. The location was originally known as "Fishtown," after an early local commercial whitefish fishery. In the 1950s, cottagers began to develop the beach and resort, and in 1977 Wee Too Beach was set up as an organized hamlet. The community was incorporated as a resort village in 1986, and in 1998 the neighbouring resort of Lipp's Beach amalgamated with

Wee Too Beach, forming a larger legal and political entity. Sixty permanent residents were recorded as living in the community in 2006; however, the population varies greatly depending on the season. Wee Too Beach is situated in the RM of Sarnia No. 221.

WEEKES, village, pop 55 (2006c), 65 (2001c), is located 27 km east of Porcupine Plain and about 62 km southwest of Hudson Bay off Hwy 23. Weekes sits on the southern edge of a swath of what is now agricultural land, just north of the Porcupine Provincial Forest. During the first two decades of the twentieth century, the primary activity in the region north of Weekes — largely along the rail line between Hudson Bay and Tisdale — was that of logging interests. After WWI, land northwest of Weekes was opened up for soldiers returning from overseas, and from 1926 onward a handful of civilian settlers began taking up land in the district. The area immediately surrounding Weekes, however, consisted of little other than dense bush when the Canadian National Railway came through from Crooked River to Reserve in 1928-29. The community had its beginnings in 1934 when a store was established, and in it a post office was set up and given the name of Weekes, after Abel S. Weekes, a surveyor for the Canadian National Railway. However, the area developed slowly during the 1930s, and so Weekes was not much more than a flag stop until 1937, when two more buildings — a hardware store and a community hall — were constructed. In 1938, more businesses were started, and that year the Saskatchewan Wheat Pool built the first grain elevator in the hamlet. Also in 1938, the first school was constructed in the community. As WWII began, the demand

for all types of lumber products was very great and this contributed significantly to the growth of Weekes, as several mills operating in the district greatly boosted the area economy and provided much-needed income for those trying to establish farms. By the end of the war, the population of Weekes was approaching 250, and on January 13, 1947, Weekes was incorporated as a village. Forestry was the primary basis of the district economy for many years, but as the land was cleared it was increasingly developed for the cultivation of crops, and, today, agriculture is the main industry in the region with forestry being second. Cereal grains and oilseeds are the main crops grown, and some farmers also raise livestock. From the mid-1950s through the early 1960s, the population of Weekes hovered around 300, but in the years following, as roads and vehicles were improved and services became increasingly centralized, many businesses in Weekes were no longer viable and closed their doors. The size of the village dwindled, and eventually students in higher grades began to be bused to school in Porcupine Plain. The stretch of railway between Weekes and Reserve was abandoned in 1989, and in the mid-1990s the village faced a significant challenge when CN announced its intention to abandon the remainder of the track that ran west through Porcupine Plain and on to Crooked River. Despite attempts by farmers, municipal officials, and other citizens along the subdivision to negotiate its purchase for a short-line railway, CN refused to debate the issue and the line was abandoned in 1999. The adverse effects for the communities along the line were elevator closures, lost tax revenues, increased pressure on area roads, and changing trading patterns. The newly renovated Saskatchewan Wheat Pool elevator

▲ **THE WEEKES CO-OP STORE**, still in business in 2008, had its beginnings in 1945 after Jim Wallace, Art Fleming, Bernard Rounce, and Alf Smith canvassed people in the district to see how many would be interested in a local co-op store. The first store was purchased from Mike Shawaga in 1945 and George Nelson became the first manager. In 1958, the Co-op purchased the Red & White Store from Mike Siery, and that is the building pictured here. Photograph taken August 11, 2004.

in Weekes was closed, leaving area farmers no choice but to haul their crops the distance to the massive inland terminals in the Tisdale area. Weekes School, which had remained as a K-6 facility, closed at the end of the school year in June 2003, as enrollment had fallen to 25. Today, businesses remaining in Weekes include a hotel, a Co-op, and the post office. The village also has a library, a museum, a curling rink, and a senior citizens centre. Big Sky Farms Inc. began the development of intensive hog operations in the area in 2002. They constructed a nursery and a breeder barn near Weekes, and subsequently established a feed mill and two finishing barns in the Porcupine

Plain area. The total cost of the projects was approximately $31 million, and about 50 full and part-time jobs were created. Weekes is situated in the RM of Porcupine No. 395.

WEIRDALE, village, pop 83 (2006c), 90 (2001c), is located approximately 50 km northeast of Prince Albert on Hwy 55. The first few settlers began making incursions into the district in the years before WWI, and the population would largely come to be comprised of people of Ukrainian, Polish, and British stock. Cordwood was the first crop harvested in the area, but as the land was cleared, wheat and

other cereal crops were increasingly produced. In the early 1930s, the CPR came through, connecting Nipawin and Prince Albert, and communities began to develop at the usual regular intervals along the stretch of rail. Train service began in 1932 — daily, except on Sunday. The first elevator in Weirdale, a Searle, was erected in 1931; the post office was established on February 1, 1932, and toward the end of that year the Weirdale School District was formed, with the school opening in the hamlet in 1933. The community was named after Robert Weir (1882–1939), Conservative member of parliament for the constituency of Melfort and the federal Minister of Agriculture from 1930–1935. By the late 1930s progress in Weirdale was quite evident; unlike in southern Saskatchewan, hamlets, villages, and towns were springing up in this parkland region during the decade, their development to a degree bolstered by the arrival of dust bowl refugees. In its heyday, Weirdale boasted four general stores, two garages, a flour mill, a puffed wheat mill, three machine agencies, a hospital and doctor's office,

a drug store, a lumberyard, the post office, a hotel and barbershop, a poolroom, butcher shop, two blacksmiths, a livery barn, two grain elevators, the school, a church, and a hall. A major fire in 1947 was a substantial blow; however, the Village of Weirdale was incorporated on April 1, 1948. Also in 1948, a new school was built in the community, its opening presided over by Woodrow Stanley Lloyd, then the provincial Minister of Education, later the Premier of Saskatchewan (1961 to 1964). Like most of the communities on the Nipawin–Prince Albert line, Weirdale was its busiest in the years leading up to the end of WWII, when the timber industry dominated the area economy. Decline followed over the ensuing decades, and while improvements such as the construction of water and sewer systems, the planting of trees down the main village thoroughfare, new sidewalks and a playground were undertaken during the 1970s and 1980s, the community's population and number of businesses steadily decreased. In 1983, Weirdale School was closed and students were subsequently bused to Meath Park.

▼ **WEIRDALE**, July 18, 2003.

In early 1998, CP formally abandoned the rail line through the village. Today, Weirdale is essentially a residential community, and its residents largely access the amenities that the city of Prince Albert has to offer. Weirdale is situated in the RM of Garden River No. 490.

WELDON, village, pop 205 (2006c), 219 (2001c), lies about 25 km south of the forks (North and South) of the Saskatchewan River; Peonan Creek passes just north of the community, flowing north-eastward into the Saskatchewan River, and twenty km north of the village the Weldon ferry crosses the South Saskatchewan River. Weldon is located about 14 km northwest of Kinistino, off Hwy 3, and sits surrounded by rich and well-developed farmlands within the boreal transition ecoregion. The village is situated in one of the older settled parts of Saskatchewan: the first settlers began arriving to take up land in the years prior to the North-West Resistance. In 1895, a local post office was established on the homestead of George Ellis, and was named Weldon after one of Ellis's sons, who had died an untimely death. From about 1902 until the outbreak of WWI, there was an influx of settlers into the district; most were Scandinavians, primarily of Norwegian origin, many of whom came to Canada via the United States. The years of the First World War, though, almost brought a complete halt to immigration. A local school, somewhat south of the present community, was opened in the fall of 1905, and that year the railway came through, which would shortly connect Hudson Bay, Tisdale, Melfort, and Prince Albert. Development at the Weldon townsite was initially slow, however. For a number of the years, trains did not make regular stops at Weldon, only coming to a halt if they were flagged down. When farmers petitioned the Canadian Northern Railway for the establishment of a side track to load grain, the railway agreed only if the farmers themselves did the grading and laid the track, which they did. By 1910, a small hamlet which included a general store was emerging, and in 1911 the first grain elevator at Weldon was built. In 1913, the townsite was surveyed, and that year the people of the small community drew up a petition requesting they be granted village status. The request was fulfilled and on January 24, 1914, the Village of Weldon was incorporated. The community grew steadily, and during the 1930s its population was further bolstered as dust bowl refugees pushed their way into the parkland fringes. The area remained productive during the dry years on the southern plains, and in 1932 a grain car loaded in the village of Weldon had the distinction of being the first unloaded at the newly completed Hudson Bay Railway terminal and harbour facilities at Churchill, Manitoba. Before the car had left Weldon, a sign was painted on its side which read, "Hello Churchill, Greetings from Weldon," and, upon its arrival, the elevator attendant at the Hudson Bay seaport wrote back to the village, acknowledging that both the grain shipment and the message had been received. By 1956, Weldon's population had slowly grown to number 220; subsequently, however, it began to swell — through the 1960s and 1970s — reaching a peak of 279 in 1981. Today, the community is rather attractive, as trees planted years ago have reached maturity and line the village's thoroughfares. Weldon has a Co-op, a café, a credit union, an insurance broker, a post office, and a public library. Worship centres accommodate three denominations, the village has a seniors' centre, and recreational facilities include an arena, an auditorium/gymnasium complex, and a sports field. Agriculture remains the basis of the local economy and Weldon is situated in the RM of Kinistino No. 459.

WELWYN, village, pop 142 (2006c), 108 (2001c), is located 17 km southeast of Rocanville on Hwy 308. Three km to the east is the Saskatchewan-Manitoba border, and Moosomin lies 30 km to the southwest. The origins of Welwyn date to 1882 and the establishment of a store and stopping place for travellers southeast of the present community on what was then the Fort Ellice–Wood Mountain Trail. The locale, situated at the Manitoba border, was established by Alexander "Sandy" McArthur, and was known for some time as "Arthur City." When McArthur sought to establish a post office, the name "Arthur City" was rejected by postal authorities, and the name Welwyn, after Welwyn, Hertfordshire, England, was approved in its place. The original Welwyn Post Office was established on January 1, 1884, and it was served by the Moosomin to Birtle, Manitoba, stagecoach until 1888. After this, mail carriers delivered the mail from Moosomin. The Welwyn region was largely settled between 1882 and 1900, with most of the settlers being of British origin. Most of these came from Ontario and Quebec, although some did come from the Maritime provinces, England, and Scotland. In the mid-1880s, the community's first church was built, and in 1887 a school opened a few kilometres south of the present community, a few kilometres west of the McArthur site. Sandy McArthur remained the Welwyn postmaster until 1900, when tragedy struck the family. Shortly after midnight on June 9 of that year, a hired hand, John Morrison, brutally murdered McArthur, his wife and three of their seven children with an axe after McArthur forbade the man from seeing his eldest daughter. Fifteen-year-old Maggie was spared the attack; her three surviving siblings, however, were severely injured, and only one lived beyond childhood. Morrison then attempted suicide, but was taken to Moosomin for treatment before being tried and found guilty of the murders. He was hanged in Regina on January 17, 1901. Today, there is a plaque on the pulpit in the Welwyn United Church placed in memory of the McArthur family. In 1902, the location of the present village was established as the CPR pushed through the district. A post office at the townsite established in 1903 by the storekeeper, C. H. Dumville, was known as Welwyn Station until 1906, when the name was simply shortened to Welwyn, as the post office that had served "Old Welwyn" was closed. The new hamlet developed quickly — businesses, a school, and a church were constructed — and on June 11, 1907, Welwyn was incorporated as a village. By 1926, the population of the community was 263, and it hovered at around the 250 mark until the 1950s, after which it began to drop. In 1986, the population was still 187; but, since then, Welwyn's numbers have declined. Although the 2006 Census figure seems to indicate a significant recovery in population for the village, this increase is considered an anomaly by the village administrator, an inflated figure based upon the counting of a number of temporary residents. Agriculture was and remains the dominant economic base of the community, although no grain elevators are left standing in the village. Beginning in the early 1970s, potash mining became an integral part of the Welwyn area economy, and today the Potash Corporation of Saskatchewan's operation northeast of Rocanville is a major area employer, with approximately 330 full-time employees. Welwyn is served by a volunteer fire department; policing is provided by the RCMP detachment in Moosomin. The nearest hospital is also situated in Moosomin. Community recreation facilities include sports grounds and ball diamonds, and a complex housing skating and curling rinks and a community hall. Welwyn Centennial Regional Park, 2 kilometres north of the village in a well-treed and attractive setting, offers camping, a beach, boating, and fishing. The Welwyn Museum is housed in the former St. Paul's Anglican Church, and municipal heritage properties located in the village are Trinity United Church (originally Presbyterian), built in 1905, and Harper's Store, built in 1910. A two-storey wood-frame structure with a pressed metal façade, the store has served as a general store since its construction, making it one of the oldest continually operated stores in the province. Other businesses active in the village today include the Welwyn Co-op, the post office, a transport company, and construction and repair contractors. Welwyn has seniors' housing units and a seniors' centre. Trinity United Church and Our Lady of Fatima Catholic Church are the active churches in the community. Welwyn is situated in the RM of Moosomin No. 121.

WEST END, resort village, is located in the eastern Qu'Appelle Valley, northeast of Broadview, on the northwest end of Round Lake. It is one of several resort communities whose cottages and permanent residences stretch along much of the lake's northern shore. Some development began as early as the 1920s and, today, the population varies greatly depending on the season. West End, incorporated in 1983,

is accessible via Hwy 247, and is situated in the RM of Fertile Belt No. 183.

WEST CHATFIELD BEACH, organized hamlet, is located north of North Battleford, and is one of several resort communities that circle Jackfish Lake. There are a couple of dozen permanent residents; however, the population varies widely depending on the season. West Chatfield Beach was established as an organized hamlet in 1986, and is situated in the RM of Meota No. 468.

WESTVIEW, organized hamlet, pop 49 (2006c), 53 (2001c), is located a few km west of Melville and is in essence a bedroom community: modern suburban-style homes are situated in a country setting. Westview was established as an organized hamlet in 1968, and is situated in the RM of Stanley No. 215.

WEYAKWIN, northern hamlet, pop 183 (2001c), is located approximately 80 km south of La Ronge on Hwy 2, just west of the north end of Montreal Lake, and just east of Weyakwin Lake, from which the present community derives its name. Originally, the residents of Weyakwin lived at Molanosa, on the east side of Montreal Lake, which was on the old road from Prince Albert to La Ronge. In the early 1970s, the community relocated to its present site as the economic future at Molanosa was uncertain, primarily due to its location. The new Highway 2 was being built up the west side of Montreal Lake, rendering the old route much less travelled; the forest industry was concentrated on the west side of the lake and commercial fishing had proven difficult from the

east; power lines were built along the new highway, whereas there were no plans for power into Molanosa; as well, the location of Molanosa was situated in an area with a high water table and muskeg. Also among the factors behind the community's decision to relocate was the possibility of new homes, a new school, and a sewer and water system. Important as well, the development of a major resort complex at Weyakwin Lake seemed a pending reality. While the name given to the community's new location was Weyakwin, interestingly, the post office retained the name Molanosa for many years. Weyakwin is largely a Métis community of about 50 homes, which includes members of the Montreal Lake Cree Nation. Situated in an area considered at a very high risk for forest fires, the hamlet is the location of a fire-fighting base. In the recent past, fire has, in fact, threatened the community, as well as 400 cottages on the shores of nearby Weyakwin Lake. Weyakwin's school, Kiskahikan, is a K-9 facility, which had 31 students enrolled in the fall of 2005.

WEYBURN, city, pop 9,433 (2006c), 9,534 (2001c), is located on the Souris River 115 km southeast of Regina, 86 km northwest of Estevan, and 75 km north of the Canada–United States border at the junction of Hwys 13, 35, and 39. Settlement of the region was made possible by the completion of two rail lines: in 1892, the CPR completed their line from Brandon, Manitoba, to Estevan, and in 1893 the railway finished the "Soo Line" through North Portal to Moose Jaw, the latter line running through the site of present-day Weyburn. The line from the east brought settlers from eastern Canada, mainly Ontario; the line from the south brought many up from the United States, particu-

larly after 1900. An early homesteader, William Hunt, established the Weyburn Post Office on August 1, 1895; although various theories exist, the origin of the name is unknown. In the spring of 1899, anticipating a land rush, the CPR established a land office at Weyburn, and soon homesteaders were arriving in droves. A local school district was set up in 1899, and at the time businesses were springing up on the townsite. Weyburn was incorporated as a village on October 22, 1900, attained town status on August 5, 1903, and received its city charter on September 1, 1913, becoming the sixth city in the province. The population of Weyburn climbed from 113 in 1901 to 3,050 by 1916. While Weyburn grew steadily throughout the first half of the twentieth century, the development of the area's oil industry in the 1950s was a catalyst for significant growth. Today, the community's economy is based in agricultural shipping and services, oilfield exploration, development, and services, manufacturing and processing, and business and industrial services. The city serves a trading area of approximately 25,000 people. Weyburn has more than 220 stores and services; educational facilities include five elementary schools, two junior high schools, and one high school; post-secondary studies are available through the Southeast Regional College. Weyburn General Hospital is the city's major health care facility; there are municipal police and fire departments. More than 15 church organizations serve the community; the city has two radio stations: AM 1190 and Magic 103.5 FM. The *Weyburn Review*, founded in 1909, is the city's daily newspaper; *Weyburn This Week* is published weekly. The city has a wide range of sports and recreation facilities; the Weyburn Colosseum is home to the Weyburn Red Wings of the Saskatch-

ewan Junior Hockey League. Weyburn has two museums, the Soo Line Historical Museum and the Turner Curling Museum; Weyburn's public library houses the Allie Griffin Art Gallery, which has monthly exhibits featuring the works of local, regional, and provincial artists. The home of the Canadian author and playwright W. O. Mitchell (1914–1998) is one of 18 sites on a historical tour of the city, as is the

▲ **THIRD STREET NORTH IN WEYBURN**, June 1958. Saskatchewan Archives Board R-B6951.

◄ ▼ **WEYBURN LANDMARKS** include this 1909 water tower (left). It is 29 metres (95 feet) high, 7.62 metres (25 feet) in diameter, and has a capacity to hold 682,000 litres (150,000 Imperial gallons). The source of water was local wells, and the tower held the sole supply of water for Weyburn until 1940 when a surface water reservoir was built. Located on a high point of land, the water tower can be seen for miles, and it has been a historic landmark for generations of Weyburnites. The water tower is also featured prominently on the city's coat of arms. Another landmark, situated on ten city lots, is the Weyburn Court House constructed in 1928 (below). Designed by Provincial Architect Maurice Sharon in a distinctive Colonial Revival style, it expressed the confident aspirations of Weyburn in the last good harvest year before the Great Depression. Photographs taken August 26, 2003.

T. C. Douglas Centre, a performing arts centre housed in the former Calvary Baptist Church, built in 1906, where Douglas, a Baptist minister, preached his first sermon. Other community landmarks include the Weyburn water tower, built in 1909, the Signal Hill Arts Centre, situated in a former hospital then nursing home, the Weyburn Court House, designed by Provincial Architect Maurice Sharon and built in 1928, and the Souris Valley Regional Care Centre, which opened as the Saskatchewan Hospital in 1921. The Saskatchewan Hospital was built for the treatment of the mentally ill, and as one of the largest buildings in the province at the time of its completion, it had the capacity for 900 patients and a staff of 120. The later addition of two wings expanded its capacity to accommodate 1,800 patients and staff. Weyburn's city council is comprised of a mayor and six councillors, who are elected for three-year terms. Weyburn serves as the administrative centre of the RM of Weyburn No. 67.

WHITE BEAR, organized hamlet, pop 15 (2006c), 15 (2001c), is located northwest of the town of Kyle on Hwy 342. The district began to be settled around 1906, and within a few years a post office and a school were established. However, it was not until 1925 with the construction of the CNR branch line from Eston that the townsite of White Bear began to take shape. With the arrival of the railway, elevators were built and a number of businesses were started. The community grew over the next few decades, and in 1949 White Bear was established as an organized hamlet. In 1966, the population was 165; however, by the 1970s the population was rapidly decreasing and White Bear was in decline. The rail line

was abandoned in 1980 and the grain elevators were closed. Today, only a few buildings remain. White Bear is situated in the RM of Lacadena No. 228.

WHITE CITY, town, pop 1,113 (2006c), 1,101 (2001c), is located approximately 12 km east of Regina on Hwy 1. It is a bedroom community largely populated by urban professionals escaping the high property taxes of Regina. The community's origins date to the late 1950s, when farmland east of Regina was expropriated for the construction of the Trans-Canada Highway. The landowner chose to subdivide the rest, and White City had its beginnings. In 1958, a committee was organized to discuss the development of community infrastructure and the possibility of formally establishing a hamlet: White City became an organized hamlet in 1959. Since then, the community has grown rapidly. The population was 80 in 1966, 340 in 1976, 783 in 1986, and 907 in 1996. White City became a village in 1967, and a town in 2000. The community is known for its large homes situated on large lots, which, on average, measure 140 x 200 feet. Although many residents work in Regina, White City has a large

manufacturer of steel products, a number of home-based businesses, and a K-8 school, which had 448 students enrolled in the fall of 2006. High school students attend classes in Balgonie. White City and an adjacent residential development, Emerald Park, are bordered by a 27-hole golf course, and, together, the communities have an array of other recreational facilities. White City residents benefit from easy access to the amenities and services that Regina has to offer. According to the 2001 Census, the median income for White City households was $77,368, while Regina's was $46,847. White City is situated in the RM of Edenwold No. 158.

WHITE FOX, village, pop 348 (2006c), 436 (2001c), is located 12 km northwest of Nipawin just off the junction of Hwys 35 and 55. The commu-

nity is named after the White Fox River, which flows just west of the village north into the Torch River. The Torch River, in turn, empties into the Saskatchewan River northeast of Tobin Lake. The first people credited with settling in the White Fox area were a small group of Swedish men who arrived in 1914. After scouting the district and selecting parcels of suitable land, just east of the present community, they travelled to Tisdale to file for their homesteads and obtain supplies. Returning to the White Fox area, they began the construction of homes and, in 1915, began to be joined by additional settlers. A privately operated scow carried people across the Saskatchewan River when it was free of ice until 1918, when the provincial government began a regular ferry service. By 1920, sufficient numbers of people were in the area to warrant the establishment of a post office, and on July

1 that year the White Fox Post Office was officially opened a few kilometres south of today's village. Following WWI, veterans swelled the farming population, and they, with others, claimed most of the available homesteads in the district by the mid-1920s. Until 1921, Tisdale was the closest railway point, but that year the CNR completed a line from Melfort to Ridgedale, significantly reducing the distance that needed to be travelled to reach rail service. A few years later, the CPR reached Nipawin, leaving White Fox residents only several kilometres (and the river crossing) to get to the railway. In 1928, the CPR and government gathered resources, and construction of a combination road and railway bridge began across the Saskatchewan River at Nipawin. In 1929, the railway company established what was to be the townsite of White Fox; lots were surveyed and put up for sale. Shortly af-

▶ **GRAIN ELEVATOR, WHITE FOX.** Formerly operated by the Saskatchewan Wheat Pool, the landmark has been preserved.

▼ **THE WHITE FOX HOTEL**, built in the early 1930s.

Photographs taken July 15, 2006.

ter, a grocery store, a hardware store, a livery barn, and a barbershop appeared; the railway crossed into the country north of the river, and then turned west toward Prince Albert. In 1930, the first child, Bernice Rooen, was born in the new community, and White Fox grew rapidly during the following decade. Elevators were erected, as were a hotel, churches, a school, a small hospital, curling and skating rinks, a tennis court, and a theatre. Lumbering, a key economic activity in the early days, increasingly gave way to agriculture as the forest in the area was cleared. In 1935, the Alfalfa Seed Growers Marketing Association was established, which proved to be a major financial boost for the community; before the decade's end, a Board of Trade was active, managing White Fox's commercial affairs. On July 21, 1941, the Village of White Fox was incorporated, and with the establishment of a village council, electricity was brought to commercial and residential customers, streetlights were installed, streets were gravelled, sidewalks built, and water storage cisterns were placed in strategic locations in the community. Unfortunately, a significant amount of the history of the development of the district surrounding White Fox was lost in 1947 when the Local Improvement District office (the precursor to the RM), and the records therein, went up in flames along with the rest of Main Street. Following WWII, the population of the village increased, creeping toward 400, and, beginning in the 1950s, school enrollment also swelled as country schoolhouses were closed and children were bused into White Fox to attend classes. The seed cleaning plant provided employment and income for many in the district. The population of the community remained stable over the following decades, and the village remained vibrant. However, when the alfalfa

seed plant was destroyed by fire in 1984, it was the end of an era, as it was in 1990 when all but one of the elevators were demolished — the last was preserved only for historical reasons. The construction of the Francois-Finlay Dam, though, a major SaskPower hydroelectric station just south of Nipawin, spanned much of the 1980s, spurring economic growth including a real estate boom, as well as recreational development on the resultant Codette Reservoir. During the 1990s, new facilities were built in White Fox, a new town shop and fire hall among them. A new fire truck was purchased, the sewer and water systems were upgraded, the village office and library computerized. Construction began on a new community centre in 1999. Today, the village has a small, yet varied core of businesses. Nipawin provides White Fox residents with an array of commercial goods, medical services, recreational opportunities, entertainment, and additional employment. White Fox has both curling and skating rinks, and a school, a K-9 facility, which had 120 students enrolled in the fall of 2006. Students in grades 10 through 12 attend classes in Nipawin. Situated on the northern fringe of agricultural settlement in the province, the White Fox area economy depends not only on the production of such crops as cereal grains, canola, and forage seed, as well as the rearing of livestock, but also on tourism. Tobin Lake and the Codette Reservoir on the Saskatchewan River provide for some of the best fishing in North America, and a number of resorts and outfitters operate in the region. White Fox serves as the administrative centre of the RM of Torch River No. 488.

WHITEWOOD, town, pop 869 (2006c), 947 (2001c), is located 21 km

east of Broadview at the junction of Hwys 1 and 9. The Qu'Appelle Valley lies approximately 20 km to the north. The CPR main line was built through the area in 1882, and immediately Whitewood, its name derived from the white poplar trees in the area, became an important supply centre and point of disembarkation for multitudes of settlers of diverse origins. John Hawkes was the editor of the *Whitewood Herald* from 1897 to 1900, and later the first Saskatchewan Legislative Librarian and author of *The Story of Saskatchewan and its People*. He described Whitewood in the 1880s as the most cosmopolitan place in the North-West, and added that to conduct business in the town at the time, one ought to have known eleven languages. Finns, Swedes, Hungarians, Czechs, English, Scottish, and Irish settlers, among others, took up land in the region, and in the years before railway branch lines were built to the north and south of the main line, Whitewood was the nearest significant trading centre for a very large area. One of the more interesting settlements to develop in the Whitewood district in the mid-1880s was that of a group of titled French and Belgian nobility. Much like the British gentry to the south at Cannington Manor, the "French Counts," as they were locally known, tried to build a life on the prairies similar to the aristocratic style to which they had been accustomed in Europe. They brought a retinue of servants along with all the accoutrements of a sophisticated society, built beautiful residences, and initiated a number of optimistic but ultimately unsuccessful business ventures — among them sheep ranching, a sugar beet plantation, a brush manufacturing company, and a cheese factory. For a variety of reasons, all of the business ventures failed, and by the early 1900s all of the

"French Counts" had left, most returning to France. They did leave behind, however, the well-endowed parish of St. Hubert, just southwest of Whitewood, and the descendants of their servants and workers would maintain a unique, French-speaking presence in the area. Whitewood was incorporated on December 31, 1892, and earlier that year, during the first week of April, the first issue of the *Whitewood Herald* rolled off the press. It is now Saskatchewan's oldest continually published weekly newspaper, and its editor, Chris Ashfield, is the fourth consecutive generation of his family involved with the province's weekly newspaper industry. By 1906, the population of Whitewood was over 500, and the town was a well-established trading centre for the surrounding agricultural district. Today, the area industry consists of mixed farms and livestock operations, with cereal grains and oilseeds being the main crops grown. Whitewood has a number of companies catering to the agricultural industry; an array of goods and services are provided by a range of other businesses. Further, the town serves the area with a health centre, an ambulance service, a special care home, and a volunteer fire department. Policing is provided by the Broadview RCMP. Whitewood has a K-12 school, which had 238 town and area students enrolled in the fall of 2006, and the school also facilitates post-secondary programs through the Southeast Regional College. Recreational facilities in the town include a new community arena, which houses rinks for hockey, skating, and curling, as well as a venue for theatrical productions such as those performed by the community's "Not So Famous People Players." Whitewood's Fred J. Hack Park, named in honour of a former mayor, has a golf and country club, a swimming pool, ball diamonds, tennis and beach volley-

▲ **IN FRONT OF THE WHITEWOOD TOWN HALL**, circa 1901. From left to right: James Gallagher, Charlie Bailey, Ned Henry, William Lamont, James Grierson, James Fodor, John A. Hawkes, Richard Street, A.B. Gillis, J.L. Lamont, R.S. Park, J.H. Knowler (mayor), John Scott, Charles E. Baldwin, and William H. Stoddart. The building was demolished in 1983.

▲ **THE WHITEWOOD BAND OF 1901 INCLUDED TITLED NOBILITY.** Back row, left to right: Count de Soras, M. de Wolffe, W.H. Hudson, John Hawkes, W.H. Stoddart, Count Jumilliac, Fred Larry, Mr. Kredbar. Front row, from left to right: Robert Burnie, Count de Langle, Mr. Duffy (tailor), Robert May (Woodbine Hotel proprietor).

◄ **CHARLES WHEELOCK LARRY SR.'S BLACKSMITH SHOP** which he operated with his son, John, on the south side of Third Avenue in Whitewood. The shop was in business for 43 years — from 1903 to 1946.

▲ **THE WHITEWOOD HOCKEY TEAM, 1912 SEASON.** Back row, left to right: F.W. Smallwood (executive committee), W.R. Marshall (goal), W. Shepherd (centre), P. Powell (rover), M. Collins (right wing), R. Carson (supporter). Middle row, left to right: S. Stephens (cover point), J. Ireton (centre), R. Buchan (goal), S. Pidcock (left wing), C.D. Carter (captain / point). Seated in front: G. Armstrong and E. Gillis (mascots).

◄ **ORANGEMEN'S DAY PARADE**, July 12, 1912. The Loyal Orange Lodge in Whitewood was in existence as early as 1892, and ceased to function in 1947.

◄ **A PICNIC AT BIRD'S POINT ON ROUND LAKE**, a popular getaway for Whitewood residents. Although the date of the photograph is unknown, those pictured are Sam Curry, Ethel Armstrong, John Herron, Lucy Curry, Harry Mayhew, Fred Callin, Carrie Callin, Ada Vigar, John Callin, Miss Lobb, Jack Vigar.

► **WHITEWOOD HIGH SCHOOL GRADUATES**, circa 1940s.

WHITEWOOD

...coming of age in "Crossroad Country"

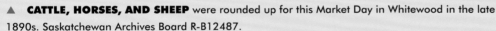

▲ **CATTLE, HORSES, AND SHEEP** were rounded up for this Market Day in Whitewood in the late 1890s. Saskatchewan Archives Board R-B12487.

► ▼ **RECREATING THE SCENE A HUNDRED YEARS LATER:** Working from the original photograph (above), volunteers (right) laboured throughout the summer of 2000 to create the "Whitewood Millennium Mural." Churchbridge artist Rita Swanson spent the first week working with the group, teaching them the art of painting murals. A local Whitewood artist, Janet Blackstock (standing on the scaffold), did much of the detail work and added many of the finishing touches. Located on 3rd Avenue in downtown Whitewood, the mural (left) was unveiled in August 2000 during the community's Homestead Days celebrations.

Black-and-white historical photographs courtesy of the Whitewood Museum; colour photographs courtesy of Janet Blackstock, Whitewood (farm).

ball courts, horseshoe pits, a playground, and campgrounds. Whitewood also has a library, a number of service clubs and community-based organizations, as well as several churches, among them St. Joseph's Church, built in 1959, the first important work of notable Saskatchewan architect Clifford Wiens. Community attractions include three unique museums, the South East Saskatchewan Archives, and a heritage centre housing interpretive displays featuring the story of the French Counts. Whitewood also has a number of heritage properties ranging from residences and commercial buildings to churches, many dating to the 1890s. Annual town events include a trade show and craft fair in the spring, and each August the community holds a week-long fair in conjunction with a rodeo. Whitewood serves as the administrative centre of the RM of Willowdale No. 153 and is also home to the administrative office for the neighbouring RM of Silverwood No. 123.

WILCOX, village, pop 222 (2006c), 322 (2001c), lies about a half-hour's drive south of Regina on Hwy 39 and the CPR's Soo Line. The railway, running from the United States through North Portal, Estevan, and Weyburn to Moose Jaw, was completed in 1893, but there was nothing at the site of what was to become Wilcox for close to a decade. Trains trundled up and down the track through essentially vacant prairie. The first few homesteaders began establishing themselves in the Wilcox district in 1901, and in early 1902 a small group of eight people arrived at the location that would become the present village with all of their worldly possessions. They came from the United States led by a Seward St. John, locally considered as the founder of Wilcox. It is recorded in a vil-

▲ **MAIN STREET, WILCOX, 1935.** Saskatchewan Archives Board R-B4019 (1).

lage history that, as there was no siding at the locale then, orders were given that the group's freight cars were to be placed at the end of a train and moved about 19 kilometres (12 miles) northwest of Milestone (one of the few early stations on the Soo Line) and unhitched at what was then known as "Milepost 35." Spikes were pulled out of a section of the track behind the train, the end rails were then lifted and angled out onto the prairie, the cars were pushed off, the tracks were replaced, and the train rolled on. Thus, Wilcox had its beginnings. Tents were pitched and soon lumber was brought in for construction and the townsite was surveyed. The settlement was to be named after Albert "Bert" Wilcox, a CPR dispatcher in Moose Jaw. Soon a number of businesses opened to provide goods and services to an influx of settlers. The Wilcox Post Office was established on November 1, 1902. Early arrivals in the district came from Ontario and the British Isles, but the majority of those who came to the area arrived via the United States, and they were often continental Europeans or Scandinavians whose families had recently emigrated to the

United States before deciding to come to Canada. A significant number of those who came from south of the border bought land from the Luse Land & Development Company based out of St. Paul, Minnesota. The company purchased large parcels of land, roughly in a triangular area that extended from Yellow Grass to Regina to just east of Moose Jaw, and they ran special excursion trains that brought prospective buyers, most experienced farmers, from the American mid-west to the newly-opened territory on the Canadian plains. A few years later, circa 1908-09, the Luse Land & Development Company began settling large numbers of people in west-central Saskatchewan, and it is for this company that the town of Luseland is named. By 1907, the hamlet of Wilcox had grown significantly, and on April 20 that year the settlement was incorporated as a village. The young community flourished. Its foundations, though, were literally shaken in the late evening of Saturday, May 15, 1909. That night, Wilcox residents, among others, were jarred by what remains as Saskatchewan's largest known earthquake. The

epicentre was judged to be near the Saskatchewan–United States border near where the states of Montana and North Dakota join, and the magnitude is estimated to have been large enough to cause some damage. Vibrations were felt as far away as Winnipeg and Saskatoon, and the event was recorded by Canada's only seismograph at the time, located in Ottawa. Fortunately, there was little development in southern Saskatchewan in 1909, and there were no reports of damage or serious injury. Wilcox, though, was not to be spared a calamity that year. On August 17, a hot air balloon flight was planned for the end of the annual sports day. During the inflation of the balloon there was a miscalculation of the flame volume and the fabric of the balloon was set on fire. It collapsed over a volunteer assistant: Walter Wright, a homesteader from Rouleau, died as a result of the burns he received. In 1910, Wilcox's boxcar station was replaced with a proper stationhouse as traffic on the Soo Line was bustling with passengers and freight coming and going. By 1911, the village population was nearing 300; by 1920, it was nudging toward 400, and the countryside by then was teeming with settlers' families. In 1920, the Sisters of Charity of St. Louis established Notre Dame of the Prairies Academy in Wilcox, and in 1927 a new parish priest, Father Athol (Père) Murray, arrived from Regina with a small group of boys under his tutelage. These, the original "Hounds of Notre Dame," were members of a sports club Murray had founded in Regina to help young boys — some of whom had run afoul of the law — find direction in their lives. Together with the Sisters, Murray established a teaching program that balanced pursuits in spirituality, academics, and athletics. In 1933, Athol Murray succeeded in founding the Notre Dame College of Canada as a liberal arts college affiliated with the University of Ottawa. During these rather lean years, many students' families, not having the money to pay for course fees, were allowed to pay instead with meat, coal, or flour. Additionally, students would also be responsible for the maintenance of the rather rough and Spartan assemblage of near-derelict buildings that then comprised the campus.

Murray believed students should be accepted on the basis of their desire for an education, not their ability to pay for it. Today, 90 per cent of the students graduating from the College continue on to pursue a higher education, many with scholarships. But although noted scholars have come from the ranks of Notre Dame's students over the years (among them a Member of the Order of Canada, historian Olive Dickason, acclaimed for her contributions to our understanding of Aboriginal people's history; and Ray Rajotte, a world leader in promising diabetes research), it is largely for excellence in the field of athletics, especially hockey, that Notre Dame has come to be known far and wide. Murray's teams won 48 provincial and four national championships, and more than 100 Hounds have gone on to the NHL, among them some of the greatest names in the game. Today, Wilcox has the only Olympic-sized ice rink in the province. But Father Murray's interests, reach, and influence went far beyond the realm of hockey. He consorted and corresponded with several Canadian prime ministers

(Mackenzie King, St. Laurent, Diefenbaker, Pearson, and Trudeau), and American leaders (Roosevelt, Eisenhower, and Kennedy), as well as the British prime minister, Winston Churchill. In his 80s, Murray travelled to Rome for an audience with the Pope. And Murray was also a lover of the fine arts, philosophy, and Greek and Latin classics. He was an avid collector of historic artifacts, artworks, and rare books. For his dedication to the development of young people, who were often poor, Father Athol Murray was made an Officer of the Order of Canada in 1968. He was also inducted into both the Saskatchewan and Canadian Sports Halls of Fame. Père Murray died in 1975 and in 1981 the college was renamed the Athol Murray College of Notre Dame in his honour. In 1998, Murray was also posthumously inducted into the Hockey Hall of Fame. Today, the Athol Murray College of Notre Dame accommodates grades 9-12; there were over 200 students enrolled in the fall of 2004. Outside of Wilcox's famous college, however, lies a typical small prairie village where, over the decades, the number of busi-

nesses has declined as village merchants and service providers faced increasing competition from the cities, mainly Regina. Today, only a small handful of businesses remain in the community. Up until the fall of 2005, Wilcox was among the few Saskatchewan communities to still have a row of traditional grain elevators lining its railway tracks; before that year's end, however, the two Pioneer elevators were demolished, leaving only the Patterson standing. So while cereals, pulse crops, and oilseeds remain the basis of the surrounding rural economy, Athol Murray College is the village's economic backbone. It employs about 130 people, the majority of whom reside in the community. Another area company, Canadian Clay Products, Inc., mines and processes sodium bentonite and employs up to 10 people. The village of Wilcox also had a public school, a K-7 facility, which had 46 students registered in the fall of 2006; this, however, was closed in 2007. A former student of the public school, Ralph Goodale, Liberal Member of Parliament for the Saskatchewan riding of Wascana, and

ATHOL MURRAY (1892-1975). Photograph courtesy of M. West, Regina, West's Studio Collection, Saskatchewan Archives Board R-A8006.

Part of Murray's legacy is that the archives and museum on the Notre Dame campus today house an important and fascinating array of art and memorabilia and, most importantly, one of North America's oldest and finest collections of historic rare books and manuscripts. Works date from the thirteenth to the seventeenth century, and some were printed just shortly after Gutenberg invented movable type. Among the literary treasures located in Wilcox are manuscripts hand-written by monks in the 1200s — decrees of Pope Gregory the Tenth written on goatskin and affixed with a chain that was used to attach the manuscripts to walls to protect them from theft. The rare book collection also contains two Martin Luther Bibles, Frankfurt editions in German written around the mid-1500s; a first edition of Erasmus's *Institutio principis Christiani* ("Education of a Christian Prince"), published in 1516; a parchment decree signed by James I of England in 1606; and a priceless copy of the *Nuremberg Chronicle*, published in 1493, written in Latin, and superbly illustrated by 1,809 detailed woodcuts. One of the first comprehensive history books ever written, the *Nuremberg Chronicle* recounts the story of the world from creation until 1492. When Père Murray was at Notre Dame, it was "hands on" with most of these texts, and he would often use the books in his classes while teaching. Today, the collection survives behind glass, housed in a vault where temperature, light, and humidity are regulated with care.

the former federal Minister of Finance, was raised in the Wilcox area, learned to curl in the community, and played baseball for the Wilcox Cardinals. A photograph of Goodale as finance minister in the House of Commons, wearing a Western Red Lily, Saskatchewan's floral emblem, on his lapel, hung in the elementary school foyer. Wilcox serves as the administrative centre of the RM of Bratt's Lake No. 129.

WILKIE, town, pop 1,222 (2006c), 1,282 (2001c), is located approximately 55 km southwest of North Battleford at the junction of Hwys 14 and 29. Settlers began arriving in the fall of 1905, and building at the townsite began in 1907 as construction of the railway approached from the east. Wilkie was established as a divisional point by the CPR in 1908 and, the same year, was incorporated as a village. In 1910, Wilkie became a town and,

interestingly, the first history of the community was published by the *Wilkie Press* that year. The newspaper's printing office, built in 1908, is now at the Wilkie museum site, and is possibly one of the best preserved newspaper offices of its kind remaining in western Canada. The railway came to employ over 100 people in Wilkie, and by the 1920s the town's population was over 1,000. Wilkie grew through to the end of the 1950s, becoming a centre of over 1,600. After 1960, however, the population, regional importance, and economic viability of Wilkie declined.

When the hospital was closed in 1996, community leaders were spurred to action. Proactive and imaginative initiatives to foster economic development were undertaken. Partnerships were formed with the town of Unity and other neighbouring communities, which, by 2001, were proving successful. A number of new agricultural-based businesses were started, creating close to 100 new jobs, revitalizing not only the local economy, but also community spirit. Residents made conscious efforts to shop locally and use as many local services as possible. In 2002, Wilkie

was cited as a community success story by the province's Action Committee on the Rural Economy (ACRE). The town today has a diverse array of businesses, a range of medical services and an RCMP detachment. There are a number of churches, recreational facilities and cultural organizations, and Wilkie's schools provide K-12 education to approximately 360 students (2006-07). Adjacent to the town is Wilkie Regional Park, which has facilities for camping, swimming, baseball and golf. Wilkie serves as the administrative centre of the RM of Buffalo No. 409.

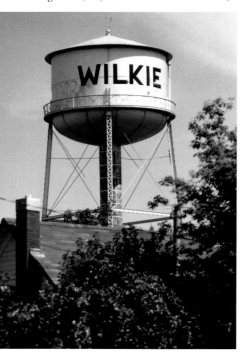

▶ **THE WILKIE POST OFFICE**, built 1930. The first post office in the immediate vicinity of Wilkie was known as Glen Logan, and it was officially established by Charles John Logan in 1907 about a mile east of the present community. There, Logan ran a stopping place and a store. In 1908 Logan built a new store which included the post office within the town limits of Wilkie, and in October that year the name was changed to that of the community, which itself had been named in honour of Daniel Robert Wilkie, president of the Imperial Bank of Canada and a backer of the CPR.

▶ **THE CATHOLIC CHURCH OF ST. JAMES THE APOSTLE** is one of six churches in Wilkie. Construction began in 1953, the first mass was held on Christmas Eve in 1956, and the church was blessed on July 25, 1957. Other churches in the town are the Wilkie United Church, Wilkie Pentecostal Church, Trinity Lutheran Church, St. Paul's Anglican Church, and the Foursquare Gospel Church.

◀ **THE WILKIE WATER TOWER.**

Photographs taken August 15, 2003.

WILLOW BUNCH, town, pop 297 (2001c), 395 (2006c), is one of the oldest settled communities in the province. It is situated southeast of Assiniboia on Hwy 36 amidst a picturesque landscape of alkaline lakes, rolling hills, and wooded coulees. By the 1860s, Red River Métis, pursuing the bison as they retreated southwestward across the plains, began establishing winter camps, or *hivernants*, in the area. In early 1870, as tensions at Red River reached a peak, about 30 families, uncertain of their future in the new province of Manitoba, relocated somewhat west of the present town. Later that year, Jean Louis Legare, who would become recognized as the founder of Willow Bunch, arrived, and today Jean Louis Legare Regional Park, just south of the community, is named in his honour. The first settlement, however, would only be temporary. As the bison began to disappear, many of the Métis moved on, many of these permanently, while others returned to the district to adopt a more sedentary life. Prior to the turn of the century, more Métis families arrived, and a life of herding and ranching replaced the "great buffalo hunts." They would smoke the bark of the abundant willows in the valley, and called the area *talles de saules*, after the "bunches of willows"

WILLOW BUNCH

...talles de saules

▶ **AFTER SUNDAY MASS**, the congregation in Willow Bunch often visited outside of the church. Photograph circa 1916. Saskatchewan Archives Board R-A3468.

▼ **SCHOOL KIDS ON A LUNCH BREAK** enjoy a late summer's day at the start of the school year in 2004, when there were 71 students enrolled in Willow Bunch's K-12 school. Since the school closed in 2007, the village has become a quieter place on school days, as children are bused out of the community in the morning and return late in the day. The building in the background of the photograph is the 1914 convent and boarding school built by the Sisters of the Cross, which today houses the village's museum. Photograph taken August 31, 2004.

WILLOWBUNCH, C. 1916

▼ **THE FINAL RESTING PLACE** of the remains of Edouard Beaupré. Photograph taken August 31, 2004.

À LA MÉMOIRE DE
EDOUARD BEAUPRÉ
9 JANV. 1881 – 3 JUILLET 1904
WILLOW BUNCH – ST-LOUIS, MO.
INHUMATION LE 7 JUILLET 1990
— PAX —

gathered for the purpose. However, the name "Willow Bunch," a translation given later by English-speaking settlers, was the name that would eventually be retained. On January 9, 1881, Willow Bunch's most famous resident was born. Edouard Beaupré, the Willow Bunch Giant, would grow to a height of 2.5 m (8'3") and a weight of 170 kg (375 lbs.). He would be touted as the world's tallest man before his untimely death at age 23 at the St. Louis World's Fair in 1904. His family was unable to afford to have his body returned home, and for years it was put on exhibit, before ending up at McGill University in Montreal to be studied for research purposes. The family fought unsuccessfully for years to recover his body and, finally, in 1989, the university conceded. In 1990, 86 years after Edouard Beaupré's death, he was finally given a memorial service, and his ashes were interred in front of a life-sized statue dedicated to him at the Willow Bunch Museum. Four hundred people attended the ceremony. The museum, formerly a convent and boarding school, and now a heritage property, also honours other notable residents of the town. The pioneering aviator, Charles Skinner, and the musical Campagne family of Hart Rouge fame are featured in the historic building. From around the time of the province's inauguration in 1905 until about the end of the First World War, a wave of French Canadian settlers arrived at Willow Bunch, and increasingly crop production was being combined with ranching. The year 1918 would prove to be a trying one for the community, as more than 35 people died during the Spanish Flu epidemic. Between 1912 and around the end of the War, ferries were operated across Willow Bunch Lake, transporting grain, livestock, and a variety of goods to and from Verwood and Viceroy, which

were the nearest rail points at the time. Then the lake became too shallow, and the options were either to travel across the ice in winter or to take the long way around in the summer months. Then, in 1926, the long-anticipated and much-delayed CNR line finally arrived, and the community's future prospects changed. In 1929 Willow Bunch attained village status. By the mid-1950s the population was approaching 800, and in 1960 Willow Bunch was incorporated as a town. In 1970, the community celebrated its centennial. Today, Willow Bunch retains its heritage through institutions such as the museum, and through Métis and Francophone cultural organizations. The community was dealt a blow in 2007 when its school, which had an intensive French language program, was closed due to declining enrollment. Fifty students had been enrolled in the fall of 2006, down from 81 in the fall of 2003. Agriculture, a combination of grain and livestock production, is the major industry in the area; however, the Poplar River Power Plant, located southeast of Coronach, provides an important source of employment. Willow Bunch serves as the administrative centre of the RM of Willow Bunch No. 42.

WILLOWBROOK, village, pop 46 (2006c), 47 (2001c), is located 22 km west of Yorkton on Hwy 47, just south of the junction with Hwy 52. The community is named after Willow Brook, a small stream that flows in an easterly direction along the community's north side. Settlers began arriving in the region in the 1880s and 1890s, and on June 1, 1901, the Wil-

▶ **THE WILLOWBROOK HOTEL**, now closed. Photograph taken July 14, 2003.

lowbrook Post Office was established at the present village site. In 1903, a school by the same name opened approximately four miles to the northwest. The railway came into Willowbrook from east of Yorkton in 1915 and, until 1928 when track was completed through to Jedburgh and Parkerview, Willowbrook was the western terminus of the line. Willowbrook was incorporated on March 12, 1919. In 1922, villagers decided they needed their own school, and petitioned the rural school to change their name, as they wanted to assume it. In 1923, the country school was renamed Silver Willow and the village school then became Willowbrook. The population of the village was 98 in 1921, it peaked at 120 in 1941, and was 100 in 1966. The community's numbers reached a low of 36 in 1991. The rail line running northwest from the community was abandoned in the late 1970s; the line coming in from the east in 1980. Just outside of Willowbrook on Hwy 52 stands a marker commemorating the achievements of Charles Avery Dunning (1885-1958), the third premier of Saskatchewan (1922-26), who established a homestead approximately four miles north of Willowbrook in the early 1900s. Willowbrook is situated in the RM of Orkney No. 244.

WINDTHORST, village, pop 194 (2006c), 228 (2001c), is located 15 km west of Kipling on Hwy 48. The townsite of Windthorst developed in 1906 as the CPR was building the line that would run from Reston, Manitoba, to Wolseley. The community was named for Ludwig Windthorst (1812-91), a prominent German political leader. A member of the Reichstag from 1867, he was the leader of the Centre Party and an able opponent of Chancellor Otto von Bismarck. Windthorst was also a recognized champion of German Catholicism. A large number of German Catholics emigrated from the United States to the district surrounding what became Windthorst, Saskatchewan, over 1902-03; hence, the choice of the community's name. At first the German settlement was known as the "Stoetzel Colony," evidently after August Stoetzel, the promoter and organizer of the move north. Many English, Scandinavian, Scottish, and Irish also settled in the district — Scots were taking up a good deal of land south of the area between Broadview and Wolseley by the mid-1880s — and in 1909, German Lutherans arrived. In the summer of 1906, the first buildings were erected on

the Windthorst townsite; by winter, about 40 people were living in the fledgling community (the village celebrated its centennial in 2006). The Windthorst Post Office was established on March 18, 1907, and the village was incorporated on August 21 that year. The community's population reached 208 in 1911, and other than a dip during the 1930s Windthorst's numbers have remained fairly stable. The community had a peak population of 254 in 1981. A number of the businesses established in Windthorst in the early 1900s continue to operate to this day. Glover Brothers Hardware, established in 1906, remains, as does the Windthorst Hotel built in 1907 and the Royal Bank which has served the village and district since 1908. The Windthorst Country Club had its beginnings in the mid-1920s when the golf course was built. Other businesses serving the community today include a farm equipment dealership, a grocery store, a café, a gas station and automotive repair shop, a tanning salon, and a hair stylist. Additionally, there are a number of tradespeople including carpenters, an electrician, and a welder based in the village. A museum encapsulates the history of the district and the village has a library. Windthorst also has a seniors' housing complex. Recreational facilities include skating and curling rinks, ball diamonds, a playground, a community hall, and a fully-equipped campground. A hospital, medical clinic, and a special care home are located in Kipling, from where the RCMP serve the district. Windthorst has a volunteer fire department. There are two churches in Windthorst: Roman Catholic and United, the latter built as a Methodist Church over 1910-11. Approximately eight kilometres north of Windthorst stands Zion Lutheran Church, built in 1926 and, today, a designated heritage property. The Windthorst

School, also dating to 1926, is a two-storey structure exhibiting the influence of Collegiate Gothic and Colonial architecture, featuring unique decorative brickwork and a central bell tower; it, too, is a heritage property, designated as such in 2002. Adjoining this structure at the rear is an addition built in 1966. The school was closed at the end of June in 2006, after enrollment had fallen to 31 the previous fall. Local Windthorst organizations include the Lions, the Knights of Columbus, the Legion, a seniors' club, the Windthorst Horticultural Society, and the Windthorst Little Theatre. The foundations of the theatre group were laid in 1939 by Jean Glover, who until 1994 was a driving force in the production of nearly 60 live plays in the community. Monies generated from the productions have gone to a variety of community causes over the years, and in 1992 Glover was awarded the Canada 125 Volunteer Recognition Award. In 2001 she was inducted into Saskatchewan's Margaret Woodward Theatre Hall of Fame. Other Windthorst residents of note have included William John Patterson (1886-1976), MLA, Premier, and Lieutenant Governor of Saskatchewan. Patterson moved to Windthorst following WWI and set up an insurance and financial agency; he served as the secretary-treasurer of the village, the telephone exchange, and the agricultural society. In 1921, he was elected the MLA for the Pipestone constituency, later serving as premier from 1935-44 and as lieutenant governor of the province from 1951-58. Patterson was the first premier born in Saskatchewan, the first bachelor to take the office, and the first to have seen military service. He was also the first lieutenant governor born in the province. Renowned pioneering folk artist Jan Gerrit Wyers (1888-1973) was born in the Netherlands and emigrated to the Windthorst

area from the United States in 1916. A lifelong bachelor, Wyers farmed and engaged in bootlegging before he started painting in 1937. He rose to fame in the 1950s and 1960s following acclaimed exhibitions with the Saskatchewan Arts Board and the National Gallery of Canada. Windthorst is situated within the boundaries of the RM of Chester No. 125.

WISETON, village, pop 96 (2006c), 111 (2001c), is located 32 km northeast of Elrose on Hwy 44. The first homesteaders began arriving the district in 1905, and by about 1911 much of the available land was occupied. Many settlers came to the area via the Old Bone Trail running southwest from Saskatoon, or they disembarked the train at Hanley and crossed the South Saskatchewan River by ferry near present-day Outlook. Others rode the CPR

main line to Moose Jaw or Swift Current, and then crossed the river at either the elbow or Saskatchewan Landing respectively. Settlers mainly came from eastern Canada (primarily Ontario), the United States, or the British Isles. In 1912, work began on the grade for a Canadian Northern Railway line from the Macrorie area to Elrose, and the present Wiseton townsite was established. However, for want of an official name, the locale was originally known as "Sharpe," after Walter Sharp, who had owned the land. In 1913, about the time the track was being laid, the railway decided the new community would be known as Wiseton, after Sir Frederic Wise (1871-1928), a member of the firm Wise, Speke & Company, stockbrokers from Newcastle, England. Wise had been in Canada in 1912 seeking investment opportunities for his clients and, as a guest of the railway, had toured the western

▼ **DAVID CARSWELL DICKSON** standing in front of his sod house on his homestead approximately three miles north of Wiseton in 1909. His "soddy," with its thick walls and recessed windows, was more elaborate than many. Dickson filed on his land (NE32-27-12-W3) in 1906 and received his patent in 1910. That year he also purchased a second quarter-section two miles to the southwest, which was adjacent to his father's. Saskatchewan Archives Board R-A4829.

▲ **THE WISETON VILLAGE OFFICE** (to the right in the photo) and the Pioneer Hotel (left), now known as Micky's Place. The hotel was originally located in Richlea, Saskatchewan, but was moved into Wiseton in 1971.

▼ **THE CANADIAN BANK OF COMMERCE BUILDING** in Wiseton was constructed in 1918 to replace a wooden frame structure built in 1913. When the branch closed to Dinsmore several years ago, the Bank turned the building over to the village for a tax receipt. In recent years, the building, as well as two houses in the village, was bought by an American from Idaho who regularly visits the community.

Photograph taken September 12, 2003.

provinces. Canadian Northern believed the goodwill that came along with naming a community after Wise would prompt him to encourage investment in the company. The Village of Wiseton corresponded with Wise's wife in England after he died, and she sent them a portrait of Sir Frederic that still hangs in the village office. The Wiseton Post Office was established on September 1, 1913; the village was incorporated on September 23. Several businesses had been established by 1913, including a hotel and a branch of the Canadian Bank of Commerce. In 1914, a local school district was set up; schoolchildren had been attending a rural school a few miles to the northeast. Church services were held in various locations for several years; both Pentecostal and United churches were completed in 1926. From a population of 100 that year, Wiseton grew to reach a peak of 246 residents by 1961. For many years the community had men's, women's, and children's baseball teams, as well as men's and women's hockey teams. Curling was competitively played, and for a time, the local tennis courts were a popular diversion. In the 1960s, the community's numbers began to decline, and in 1966 students in grades 9-12 began to be bused to the village of Dinsmore to the east. In 1970, grade 8 followed; by 1980, Wiseton School was down to being a K-6 facility. That year, the railway station was torn down. The village's population was down to 195 in 1981; by 1991 it was 120. The school closed at the end of the school year in 1986. Today, village businesses include a hotel, garage, a concrete and gravel company, the Coteau Co-operative Association, and a small welding company. Wiseton also has a community recreation complex, a community hall, and a United Church. A few abandoned homes, abandoned businesses, and vacant lots dot the townsite. The area economy is based on grain farming, cattle and bison. Barber Lake, north of Wiseton, is a popular destination for bird hunters in the fall. Wiseton is situated in the RM of Milden No. 286.

WISHART, organized hamlet, pop 95 (2006c), 121 (2001c), is located in a rolling parklands setting, southeast of Wynyard, about 8 km west of Hwy 35. The first settlers arrived in the district in the early 1880s; one of the very first was Robert Wishart, for whom the community is named, an Ontarian who took up land about five kilometres southwest of the present-day community. Around his homestead, the nucleus of a settlement developed: the Wishart Post Office, established in 1884, was originally just northwest; Round Plain school, founded in 1885, was to the west; and the "Stone Church," built to serve the district's early Anglicans, Methodists, and Presbyterians, was erected just east of Wishart's homestead in 1888 — it still stands. Qu'Appelle, in 1882, and then Yorkton, in 1890, were the nearest railway points for years. Around 1906-07, significant numbers of Ukrainian and Polish settlers, as well as Hungarians, began settling in the region of present-day Wishart, dramatically changing the cultural fabric of the area; their churches still dot the countryside. Rail lines were completed about 25 kilometres (about 15 miles) to the south and north by 1908-09; however, district farmers still faced long hauls to deliver grain or obtain supplies. It was not until the late 1920s that rail service came to the Wishart area, and the story of its arrival is a classic tale of a fight between rival railway companies. Canadian National began constructing a rail line from Willowbrook in a northwesterly direction, reaching Jedburgh and Parkerview by 1928, and their intention was to continue on through the Wishart district, pushing westward. Immediately, the Canadian Pacific Railway built a line south from Foam Lake to West Bend and then turned westward, effectively cutting off the CNR from continuing through the area. CP reached the area of present-day Wishart in 1928, but had no plans to establish a townsite as was their usual practice. Five grain companies built elevators along the right-of-way, and a railway station was built in a low-lying area to the east. Without surveyed lots or streets, businessmen were forced to build a string of small buildings along the track between the station and the elevators — these were on blocks so they could be moved, since nothing with a permanent foundation could be built until titles to properties could be obtained. Two prominent businessmen took matters into their own hands: they acquired lands and had them surveyed, and the major undertaking of moving buildings onto townsite lots began just as the Depression was starting. The impact of the deteriorating economy was somewhat lessened in the Wishart district, for while much of southern Saskatchewan was turning into a dust bowl, Wishart area farmers harvested some of their best crops in the early 1930s. By 1937, the community had developed substantially enough to warrant incorporation as a village, and Wishart legally attained the standing on June 11 that year. Schoolchildren attended a school about a half-mile east of the community until a school was completed in the village in 1941. From a population of 140 that year, Wishart grew until 1966, when it reached a peak population of 282. By 1981, however, the community's numbers had fallen to 212 and were steadily dropping. In 1982, the rail line into the

community was abandoned — of the five grain elevators that lined the tracks in the late 1970s, none remain. By the beginning of the twenty-first century the village encountered a budgetary crisis — Wishart council considered reducing services to its residents, but resigned themselves to the fact that the community's best interests would be served if the village underwent a voluntary municipal restructuring. As such, Wishart relinquished village status on January 1, 2002. The newly established Organized Hamlet of Wishart and the surrounding RM now share the responsibility for services and administration, and taxes and administrative costs have decreased. The community's relative isolation and distance from major highways have resulted in its retaining a core of essential businesses and services, but the impact of a declining population has nonetheless been felt. Wishart School was a K-12 facility in the fall of 2006, and had an enrollment of 52 students (down from 77 in 2003); in the spring of 2007, however, the decision was taken to terminate grades 10 to 12. The majority of students in those grades are now bused to Wynyard; a small number attend school in Foam Lake. Wishart still retains a strong community spirit, however. Malanka, a Ukrainian folk holiday, is celebrated to coincide with the January 13th New Year's Eve of the Julian calendar, and the Wishart Hopak Dancers, a traditional Ukrainian Dance troupe, is very active, celebrating more than 30 years as an ensemble. Wishart serves as the administrative centre of the RM of Emerald No. 277.

WOLLASTON LAKE is one of Saskatchewan's more remote communities. Situated in the province's northeast on the eastern shore of the lake from

which its name is derived, the community is currently beyond the reach of roads. An all-weather gravel road (Hwy 905) winds north from Lac la Ronge through the Shield, passing the lake's western shore, and from there a barge service operates during the summer months, when many private boats also take advantage of the open water. During winter, when ice thickness permits, an ice road is maintained across Wollaston Lake; year round, a light aircraft service flies into the community, and for a number of months each year, in fact, the community is accessible only by air. Points North Landing, to the west of the lake, is a hub for northern freight and air transport, servicing the communities at Wollaston Lake, Black Lake and Stony Rapids, Fond-du-Lac, and, not least important, the area's uranium mines and processing facilities. The body of water now known as Wollaston Lake was named in 1807 by Peter Fidler to honour George Hyde Wollaston, a member of the governor's committee of the Hudson's Bay Company at the time. The community that has developed on its eastern shore is technically two legal entities: a northern settlement, originally known as "Wollaston Post," that had a population of 129 in 2001; and, just across a small bay (a river's mouth), the much more populous Lac la Hache reserve lands held by the Hatchet Lake Denesuline First Nation. Combined, the population is approximately 1,300. The majority of area residents include members of the Hatchet Lake (Lac la Hache) Denesuline First Nation, non-status First Nations, and Métis people. The Lac la Hache Denesuline signed an adhesion to Treaty 10 in 1907, yet mostly lived a traditional nomadic life until the late 1950s and the 1960s. Children began attending school regularly, necessitating a more sedentary existence,

and a fish plant and a government store were established providing employment and goods. It was at this time that the present community began to develop. The Wollaston Lake Post Office was established in 1958; the reserve was surveyed in 1965 and was formally established as the Lac la Hache Indian Reserve No. 220 in 1970. From the mid-1970s when local area residents numbered a few hundred, the population grew rapidly and today continues to grow and is very young — the average age is just over 17. The people of Wollaston Lake are a people in transition, having settled in the area only 50 years ago after many generations who led an essentially unchanging, traditional way of life over centuries. Thus, the community simultaneously works to retain its language and customs while pursuing economic development and modernity. Addressing the social problems that can accompany such rapid change is one of the priorities for local leaders. Denesuline is the main language spoken, even among children (English is the second language), and the people have retained local traditions and preferences for foods. The annual Carnival features dog mushers, trapping skills competitions, and tournaments of a traditional activity called the "hand game," which is very popular; caribou, fish, and other wildlife continue to be an important part of people's diets. The people have retained close ties to the land, and as many as 75 per cent still engage in traditional activities such as hunting, fishing, berrypicking, trapping, and guiding as a means of self-sufficiency and income. The major area employer is the Hatchet Lake First Nation, which operates elementary and high schools and a number of local businesses and which is responsible for health services, band administration, and economic development. Father Megret Elementary and High Schools provide K-12 education to close to 500 students and employ over 60 staff, who provide curricula promoting Denesuline culture, language, and values. Local businesses and services include two stores, a gas bar, a post office, an insurance broker, a daycare, a theatre, pool halls, air charter companies, snowmobile sales, a restaurant and motel, and a commercial fish plant. Some people work at the region's uranium mines and processing centres, but although the industry does provide some jobs, there are some concerns over the possible contamination of Wollaston Lake (Saskatchewan's third largest lake), which not only provides domestic water for area inhabitants, but also supports commercial and recreational fishing as well. There is seasonal employment in barge operation, ice-road construction and maintenance, and maintenance of the seasonal road to Stony Rapids and Black Lake. The health centre employs four nurses and a dental therapist on a full-time basis; a doctor flies in from La Ronge once or twice a week; dentists and optometrists visit once or twice a year; and mental health services are provided once a month. The community also offers drug and alcohol abuse programs, and the Community Action Plan for Children, which deals with issues such as parenting skills, family violence, and neglect. Wollaston Lake has an RCMP detachment, and a community hall which functions as a courthouse on a monthly basis. The Roman Catholic Church offers services both in Dene and English. Governance and development at Wollaston Lake are overseen by a combination of the northern settlement office, the Hatchet Lake Chief and Council, community elders, and a fully-engaged economic development corporation. In recent years, proposals have been made to federal and provincial

governments to finance the construction of a year-round road into the community, which would reduce isolation and transportation costs, reduce the cost of foods and other essential goods, and improve emergency response efforts as well as access to health services and educational institutions. As of January 2008 the project appears to be moving ahead.

WOLSELEY, town, pop 782 (2006c), 766 (2001c), is one of Saskatchewan's oldest towns, and was listed as one of Canada's 10 prettiest in *Harrowsmith* magazine in 2000. Wolseley is located on the Trans-Canada Hwy and the CP main line approximately 100 km east of Regina. Around 1880, homesteaders began trickling into the area, but with the arrival of the CPR in 1882 they began arriving in significant numbers. The town was incorporated in 1898 and was named after the illustrious Colonel Garnet Joseph Wolseley. The age of the community is reflected in its marvellous streetscapes and architecture. There was a brickworks in Wolseley in the 1880s, and many of the town's stately homes and impressive public buildings are built with brick that was produced locally. A number of buildings have been designated either municipal or provincial heritage properties. One of them, the Wolseley Court House, was constructed during the Territorial period and is the oldest existing court building in the province. When built in 1894-95, it was to serve the judicial district of Eastern Assiniboia. In 1902, the CPR dammed Wolf Creek, which flows north through the town to the Qu'Appelle River, creating a reservoir now known as Fairy Lake, which not only provided water for the railway company's steam engines, but also provided the town with a picturesque

▲ **FARMERS DELIVER BAGS OF GRAIN** to Wolseley's grain elevators during the winter in 1902. Saskatchewan Archives Board R-B2969.

WOLSELEY

... *"the Town around a Lake"*

▼ **WOLSELEY STATION**, date unknown. Photograph courtesy of the Ralph Allen Memorial Museum, Oxbow, Saskatchewan.

▲ **A VIEW ACROSS FAIRY LAKE.** Photograph taken October 16, 2003.

▲ **SHERBROOKE STREET.** Photograph taken October 3, 2003.

◄ **THE WOLSELEY TOWN HALL AND OPERA HOUSE**, designed by prominent Manitoba architect J.H.G. Russell and built in 1906, once housed the town's council chambers, library, fire hall, a jail cell, and an auditorium — the "Opera House." Partially constructed from locally-produced brick, the building was in continuous use from 1906 until structural problems forced its closure in 1989. Restored by the community between 1990 and 1993, the Wolseley Town Hall and Opera House reflects the optimism of the town at the beginning of the twentieth century and is one of the few remaining multi-purpose public buildings of its kind dating to that period in the province. It is used today for weddings, socials, and community events. Photograph taken October 4, 2003.

◄ **THE VIEW** of the Wolseley Town Hall and Opera House as seen from Water Street, to the north. Photograph taken October 3, 2003.

setting. In 1906, a free-standing swinging suspension bridge, a type quite unique in Saskatchewan, was completed across the lake to connect Wolseley's north side residential area with downtown. This first bridge was destroyed by a small cyclone in 1954, and the bridge which replaced it was later damaged while the lake was being dredged. However, in July 2004, amidst a parade and other celebrations, a new suspension bridge was opened. In the early twentieth century Wolseley grew quickly, and many of its businessmen were successful entrepreneurs. The Beaver Lumber Company, which grew to become one of the largest lumber supply companies in Canada, had its beginnings in the town. The original Beaver Lumber Company office building is now at the town's museum. By 1916, the population of Wolseley was over 1,000, and it had become a substantial centre for trade and social and cultural activities. In 1954, Wolseley had Saskatchewan's first drive-in theatre. It was built for 225 cars and, fifty years later, in the summer of 2004, it was still in operation. Although the population of the community has dropped over the past few decades, Wolseley remains an active community, winning in a Communities in Bloom competition in 2002. There is a hospital, a special care home, and a volunteer fire department. Police service is provided by the Indian Head RCMP. There are a variety of businesses, 5 churches, a skating rink, a curling club, and a golf course. Wolseley's two schools provide K-12 education to more than 200 students. Agriculture, and its subsidiary activities, dominates the economy. Wolseley serves as the administrative centre of the RM of Wolseley No. 155.

WOOD MOUNTAIN, village, pop 20 (2006c), 40 (2001c), is located southwest of Assiniboia near the junction of Hwys 18 and 358. The Wood Mountain Plateau consists of flat-topped hills, cut by treed coulees, rising some 400 metres above the surrounding plains. In the 1800s, Red River Métis established wintering camps in the area, calling it *Montagne de Bois* (Mountain of Wood) for the abundance of poplar trees in the otherwise barren region. After 1870 and the uprising at Red River, Métis families settled permanently in the area, and during the 1870s the Hudson's Bay Company and later the NWMP established posts a short distance south of the present village. The International Boundary Commission used the area for a supply depot early in the decade. The police pursued whisky traders and horse thieves in the region, and from 1876 to 1881 they monitored the over 5,000 Sioux and their leader, Sitting Bull, who had sought refuge in Canada after the Battle of the Little Big Horn. Large-scale ranching began in the district in the 1880s, but by 1908 the unfenced range land was gradually being given over to homesteaders. In 1917, the Saskatchewan Provincial Police force was created and the contract with the RNWMP was terminated,

▲ **THE MONUMENT DEDICATED TO SITTING BULL** in Wood Mountain Post Provincial Historic Park, erected by the Department of Natural Resources in 1968. The plaque reads: "Born about 1834 in South Dakota, Sitting Bull, with other noted Sioux Indian Chiefs and several thousand followers, fled into Canada after the Custer Massacre in 1877. For four years he camped in the Wood Mountain district, firmly but fairly treated by the N.W.M.P. and sustained by provisions from the trader Jean Louis Legare. In July 1881, the latter escorted Sitting Bull and the remnants of his band back to the United States, where the famous Chief was killed in December 1890." (Note: a point of clarification — the first Sioux arrived in Canada in 1876; Sitting Bull himself arrived in the spring of the following year.)

▼ **THE LAST GRAIN ELEVATOR** in Wood Mountain. Unused now, it dates to the late 1920s.

Photographs taken September 4, 2003.

resulting in the closing of the Mounties' post at Wood Mountain in 1918. With the arrival of the CPR in 1928 the present Wood Mountain townsite developed, and on March 4, 1930, the Village of Wood Mountain was incorporated. The community has never been particularly large; the population was 127 in 1931, and until the mid-1960s Wood Mountain averaged about 120 residents. Subsequently, however, the village began to decline, facing school closure, elevator closure, and rail line abandonment in the 1990s. Despite its small size, Wood Mountain remains an active community. A horticultural society maintains the regional park south of the village, where an interpretive museum has been established. The site is also the location of Canada's oldest continually running rodeo, which, as of the summer of 2007, will have been running for 117 years. A short walk from the park is the partially restored NWMP post, as well as a hilltop monument dedicated to Sitting Bull. Wood Mountain serves as the administrative centre of the RM of Old Post No. 43.

WOODROW, hamlet, pop 15 (2001c), is located southwest of Gravelbourg on Hwy 13. Settlement of the district began around 1909, and as the CPR arrived on its trek westward from Weyburn to Lethbridge in 1913, the townsite emerged. Woodrow was incorporated as a village the same year, its name honouring Woodrow Wilson, the newly-elected president of the United States. By 1926, the population was 223 and Woodrow was bustling, having, among other businesses, a bowling alley and its own newspaper, *The Woodrow Light*. The village lost its momentum during the Depression, never really recovered, and slowly declined.

Today, three businesses remain to serve the area: the Woodrow Co-op, Agricore United, and the post office. There are also two churches. Woodrow gave up village status March 21, 2002, and now the community's affairs are managed by the RM of Wood River No. 74.

WROXTON, former village, is located approximately 40 km east of Yorkton, just north of the junction of Hwys 8 and 10. This small community, named after Wroxton, England, is dominated by the impressive onion-domed St. Elia Church. Built in 1953, it is one of the last Ukrainian Greek Orthodox Churches built in the traditional design, and for the past half-century, the church has been recognized as a landmark in east-central Saskatchewan. The Wroxton area began to be settled in the 1880s and 1890s. The railway came through in 1911, and in 1912, Wroxton was incorporated. The village reached its peak after WWII, when around 150 people were living in the community. The rail line

▲ **STUDENTS FROM TOPOROUTZ AND CHERNOWKA SCHOOLS** attending July 1 celebrations in Wroxton in 1914. In addition to learning English in school, events such as this furthered the Canadianization of new immigrants. Saskatchewan Archives Board R-B158-4.

▼ **THE UKRAINIAN GREEK ORTHODOX CHURCH OF ST. ELIA, WROXTON.** Photograph taken July 13, 2003.

was abandoned in 1997, and, in the same year, the village was dissolved after the population had fallen below 50. Wroxton serves as the administrative centre of the RM of Calder No. 241.

WYMARK, organized hamlet, pop 144 (2006c), 148 (2001c), is located 20 km south of Swift Current off Hwy 4. Wymark developed in the midst of roughly 20 Mennonite villages that began to be established in the district beginning in 1904-05. With the CPR laying the groundwork for a branch line to run southeast from Swift Current — the route was surveyed in 1910 and track was beginning to be laid in 1911 — the location for a new townsite was chosen and Wymark sprang up. Trains came through in 1912, and the community post office was established on January 1, 1913. In the early 1920s, over the province's insistence that Mennonite children attend public schools instructed in English, there was a large out-migration of Old Colony members from the district to Mexico. Wymark was incorporated as a village from 1928 to 1936, but thereafter reverted to hamlet status under the jurisdiction of the surrounding rural municipality. In 1981, Wymark was established as an organized hamlet, giving it a degree of political and fiscal power within

the RM. The community was once significantly larger — the population was 240 in 1966 — but with its businesses and social activities superseded by those in nearby Swift Current, Wymark became a bedroom community and most residents now commute to the city to work. Today, other than the post office, there are only a handful of home-based enterprises and trucking companies operating out of the hamlet. Wymark does have a large modern school, a K-9 facility, which had 187 community and district students enrolled in the fall of 2006 (older children are bused to Swift Current to complete high school). Emmaus Mennonite Church in the village remains active. The Wymark Evangelical Mennonite Conference Church is situated six and a half kilometres east at the hamlet of Chortitz. Wymark has a community centre with a small surface for skating in the winter months. Residents seek medical services in Swift Current; fire protection is provided by the RM, and policing by the RCMP. Wymark is situated in the RM of Swift Current No. 137.

WYNYARD, town, pop 1,744 (2006c), 1,919 (2001c), is located on Hwy 16, the Yellowhead, immediately south of the Quill Lakes. The first pioneers in the area were Icelanders, who began arriving around 1904-05. They were a part of the Vatnabyggd Icelandic settlement, which stretched south and east of the Quill Lakes, forming several communities. The predominant Icelanders were soon followed by settlers of British, Ukrainian, and Polish origins, among others. The CPR came through Wynyard in 1909, and in 1911 Wynyard was incorporated as a town. The population was then already over 500. The community continued to grow rapidly, reaching the 1,000 mark

WYNYARD

...between the Quills and the Hills

around 1930, and it developed into the largest service centre in the surrounding agricultural district, which currently produces wheat, barley, oats, canola, flax, lentils, and durum. Today, Wynyard serves a trading area population estimated at 15,000 within a radius of approximately 80 kilometres. In addition to shopping and professional services, Wynyard has a hospital, a special care home, and ambulance service. Policing is provided by the local RCMP detachment, and a volunteer fire department with a rescue unit consists of 18 members. The community's two schools provide K-12 education to approximately 450 students, and the town also has a full range of facilities for cultural and recreational activities. Wynyard remains a divisional point on the CPR line and has daily Greyhound bus service and an airport. The town has a diverse economy. It calls itself the "Chicken Capital of the World" because the Wynyard Division of Lilydale Poultry Products supplies chicken to all the Kentucky Fried Chicken outlets across western Canada. Metal fabrication, potassium sulphate, and fertilizer production are additional local industries. Tourism, too, is a factor. The Quill Lakes Interpretive Centre provides information on the significant migratory bird populations which frequent the Quill Lakes' area marshes. The district attracts large numbers of bird watchers, as well as hunters. Wynyard Regional Park offers golfing and fishing for trout. Annual community

▶ **WELCOME TO WYNYARD!** Friendly faces greet the author on one of the town's main thoroughfares.

▶ **OXEN AND HORSES** had the right-of-way on Pacific Avenue in 1909, shortly after the community's founding.

▼ **JACK TESKEY**, pictured here in 1925 with assistant Dia Johannesson on his right, was a reputable shop owner in Wynyard. He started his "Blue Cash" store in the early 1920s and operated it until his retirement. He was known for his kind nature toward needy people and a number of stories about him giving free meals and goods to people who could not afford them have been passed on. Due to this, the Town of Wynyard named one of its streets — Teskey Crescent — in his honour.

▲ **ICELANDIC SETTLERS** stage a play during a Christmas pageant at the Federated Church in Wynyard in 1926. Saskatchewan Archives Board R-B10074-1.

▲ **THE WYNYARD COURT HOUSE**, designed by Provincial Architect Maurice Sharon and built in 1927-28, is prominently situated on 1.45 hectares of landscaped grounds and is a major community landmark. The building continues to serve in its function as a Provincial Court.

▶ **THE EAST SIDE OF BOSWORTH STREET**, looking north.

events include Rodeo Week, the "Famous Chicken Chariot Races," and Thorrablot, an Icelandic Heritage Celebration. A very unique feature of Wynyard is that it has a "twin" town in France. At the invitation of the French town of Martres-De-Veyre, the twinning ceremony took place in 1972. It was to recognize a Wynyard soldier, Peter Dmytruk, who served overseas in WWII. Dmytruk was shot down over France and then served with the French Resistance until he was killed in December 1943 while halting a raid against Martres-De-Veyre. A monument was built on the spot where the young Wynyard man died, and, to this day, he is regarded in France as a national hero. Over the years, residents of the two towns have exchanged a number of visits and have formed lasting friendships. Peter Dmytruk's story is recounted in the award-winning Saskatchewan book, *Their Names Live On*. Wynyard is the administrative centre of the RM of Big Quill No. 308.

YARBO, village, pop 72 (2006c), 93 (2001c), is located northeast of Esterhazy off Hwy 80 and is the site of the world's largest potash mine, K1. Settlement of the region began in the 1880s, and with the construction of the Grand Trunk Pacific Railway line through the area in 1907-08 the hamlet of Yarbo emerged.

Its name was likely chosen to fit the alphabetical sequence of naming locations along the rail line. The Yarbo Post Office was established in 1909. The economy of the district was based on mixed farming until the development of potash mining in the area in the late 1950s and early 1960s. A boom period ensued, and Yarbo grew large enough to be incorporated as a village in 1964. It had a peak population of 208 in 1966. Interestingly, over the years, Yarbo has experienced many small mining-induced earthquakes, the largest in the area registering a magnitude of 3.7 in 1988. Fortunately, however, no one has ever been injured and damage has been negligible. Yarbo is situated in the RM of Langenburg No. 181.

YELLOW CREEK, village, pop 45 (2006c), 55 (2001c), is located approximately halfway between Wakaw and Melfort on Hwy 41. The community derives its name from a small creek that flows through the area; its name is attributed to the reflection in the water of yellow blossoms of willows found along its banks. A rural post office and an area school by the name of Yellow Creek predated the establishment of the present community with the coming of the railway in 1929. Most of the settlers who came to the area were Ukrainian; however, in the surrounding region, there were also people of French, Norwegian, Polish, Hungarian, German, and British origins. The English speakers dominated local power structures; despite the preponderance of Ukrainians, they were long limited in terms of participating in the administration of the rural municipality — it was not until 1937 that the RM of Invergordon No. 430 had its first Slavic reeve: Leon Wojcichowsky. The English-dominated RM council also strongly op-

457

posed the speaking of Ukrainian in area schools, and for many years (up until about WWII) Ukrainian children were strapped if caught speaking their mother tongue in the classroom. Evidently, there finally came a point when it was accepted that having a second language was an asset rather than a liability. With the construction of the Canadian Northern Railway line between Aberdeen and Melfort, the village of Yellow Creek had its beginnings; businessmen moved in as soon as the townsite was surveyed. Joseph Nowak moved his post office in from the country and built a store in 1930 (he was the Yellow Creek postmaster from 1927 until 1961), and, that year, the railway station, section house, and freight shed were constructed, and the first grain elevator, a Searle, also went up. In 1935, the Saskatchewan Wheat Pool built the second elevator; in 1936 St. Paul and Peter Ukrainian Greek Orthodox Church was completed; and in 1937 the Ukrainian Catholic Church was finished. In 1936, a two-room school was built in the community — the original school which had opened in 1921 was a mile or so west of the hamlet. By 1937, the new school boasted a young orchestra of at least 13 members. On May 13, 1943,

the Village of Yellow Creek was incorporated; the population grew from 149 in 1946 to a peak of 191 in 1966. During 1964-65, enrollment at Yellow Creek School peaked at 196 students, as by then all of the rural schools in the region had closed. During its heyday, Yellow Creek had a number of farm equipment dealerships, bulk oil and gas retail operations, hardware stores, a hotel, cafés, lumberyards, general stores, and a poolroom, among other businesses. Duplexes for senior citizens were built in 1979. While the community's population had begun to dwindle somewhat during the second half of the 1960s, it was during the 1970s that its numbers plummeted and the village began to decline. Major blows occurred as Yellow Creek entered the 1980s: the railway station closed in 1979; in 1980 the two grain elevators were closed; and the rail line between Aberdeen and Melfort was abandoned completely by 1981. The population of Yellow Creek had fallen to 131 by 1981, and by this time the congregation at the Greek Orthodox church had dwindled to about 16 members, most in their retirement; the congregation at the Catholic church had fallen to about 25. In 1990, Yellow Creek School closed due to the rapid decrease

in students; schoolchildren then attended either Wakaw or Birch Hills. As Yellow Creek entered the twenty-first century only a handful of businesses remained; as of 2007 most of these had closed. The median age of the village population in 2006 was 58.2; that of all of Saskatchewan was 38.7. Yellow Creek is situated in the RM of Invergordon No. 430.

YELLOW GRASS, town, pop 371 (2006c), 422 (2001c), is located 25 km northwest of Weyburn on Hwy 39. Yellow Grass is also located on the CPR Soo Line, which runs from Moose Jaw through Estevan and down through the United States. It was about the time that the line was built in 1893 that the first settlers began to arrive in the Yellow Grass area; the early population was predominantly German. The Yellow Grass Post Office was established in 1896. Settlement of the district increased after the turn of the century, and on July 22, 1903, Yellow Grass was incorporated as a village. The beautiful two-storey stone schoolhouse built that year is still standing and was designated a heritage property in 1982 (the building currently houses the library). On Febru-

▲ "CANADA'S HOT SPOT" sign in the town of Yellow Grass. Photograph taken August 1, 2003.

▼ YELLOW GRASS, 1906. Photograph courtesy of the Town of Yellow Grass; donated by Don Stephenson, Victoria, British Columbia.

ary 15, 1906, Yellow Grass attained town status. The community developed as the main agricultural service centre between Weyburn and Milestone, and agriculture remains the basis of the area economy today. Grains are the main crops grown, but in recent years there has been an increasing production of pulse crops. Yellow Grass has a small core of essential business and services, indoor rinks for skating and curling, ball diamonds, a bowling alley, a seniors' centre, and three churches. Yellow Grass School is a K-12 facility, which had 115 students enrolled in the fall of 2006. Policing is provided by the Milestone RCMP, and the nearest medical facilities are located in Weyburn. Yellow Grass, along with the town of Midale to the southeast, holds the record for having had the highest temperature ever recorded in Canada: on July 5, 1937, the mercury hit 45 degrees Celsius (113 degrees Fahrenheit). Yellow Grass serves as the administrative centre of the RM of Scott No. 98.

YORKTON, city, pop 15,038 (2006c), 15,107 (2001c) is located 187 km northeast of Regina at the junction of Hwys 9, 10, 16, and 52. Melville lies 43 km to the southwest; Canora, 48 km due north. The origins of Yorkton date to 1882 and the arrival of settlers from York County, Ontario, sponsored by the York Farmers' Colonization Company. They travelled west by train to Whitewood, and headed north from there. The settlers established a hamlet a few kilometres to the northeast of the present city, along the banks of what is now known as the Yorkton Creek. The locale was originally referred to as "York City" — however, with the establishment of a post office in 1884, the name was changed to Yorkton, to clearly distinguish it from post offices back east.

Within a couple of years, a store, gristmill, and sawmill had been established. A school district was set up in 1889. The Manitoba and Northwestern Railway had reached as far as Bredenbury by 1889; about a year later, when it reached the Yorkton area, the line was to the south of the Yorkton hamlet. A move to the present site of the city was necessitated. Yorkton was incorporated as a village on July 11, 1894, and attained town status on April 16, 1900. By this time, the population of the district was becoming more cosmopolitan. Scots had settled to the east in the early 1880s, people of German origins had settled in large numbers to the north by the late 1880s, Doukhobors arrived at Yorkton in 1899, and Ukrainians settled en masse in the region from the late 1890s into the early 1900s. In 1901, the population of Yorkton was 700; by 1921, it was over 5,000. Yorkton received its city charter on February 1, 1928, be-

▲ **MAIN STREET, YORKTON**, looking west, August 1956. Saskatchewan Archives Board, Saskatchewan Photographic Services, R-A11378.

▼ **BETRAYED.** In 1906, Frank Oliver, the new Federal Minister of the Interior, overruled the concessions granted to Doukhobors by his predecessor Clifford Sifton, which had enabled them to live communally while still claiming homestead lands. Change came quickly and 2,500 homesteads were cancelled. While many Doukhobors remained in Saskatchewan, others, such as these pictured here leaving Yorkton in covered wagons circa 1910, headed for British Columbia. Saskatchewan Archives Board R-A21743.

coming Saskatchewan's eighth city. For the next two decades, the population of the city remained virtually unchanged — the city was marking time. Following WWII, however, Yorkton experienced years of rapid growth; its population climbed from 5,714 in 1946 to 12,645 by 1966. In 1986, the city reached a peak population of 15,574. Today, as the largest centre in eastern Saskatchewan, serving one of the largest trading areas in the province, Yorkton plays a vital role in the regional economy. The city's educational facilities include four public elementary schools, four Catholic elementary schools, one public high school, and one Catholic high school. Post-secondary studies are available through the Parkland Regional College. The Yorkton Regional Health Centre is the city's major health care facility, with a total of 87 acute-care beds; the Yorkton Mental Health Centre provides a range of services; the Yorkton and District Nursing Home has 243 long-term-care beds. More than two dozen places of worship serve the community; St. Mary's Ukrainian Catholic Church is a significant city landmark. Yorkton has a wide range of sports and recreation facilities and has a Saskatchewan Junior Hockey League team, the Yorkton Terriers. The Godfrey Dean Art Gallery features local, regional, and national art exhibitions, and the Yorkton Short Film and Video Festival, with beginnings in 1950, is today the longest-running film festival of its kind in North America. The four-day event draws an average of 375 entries annually and features workshops and public showings, culminating in an awards gala and the presentation of Canada's Golden Sheaf Awards. Among the city's major annual events are the Yorkton Summer Fair, the Sunflower Arts and Crafts Show and Sale, and the Threshermen's Show and Seniors' Festival. Major tourist attractions include the Painted Hand Casino and the Western Development Museum. Yorkton's city council is comprised of a mayor and six councillors elected for three-year terms. Yorkton serves as the administrative centre of the RM of Orkney No. 244.

YOUNG, village, pop 263 (2006c), 299 (2001c), is located 25 km northwest of Watrous on Hwy 2. Little Manitou Lake lies a short distance to the east; to the northwest of Young the IMC Potash mine near Colonsay appears on the horizon, one of three potash mines in the region. Intensive settlement of the district began in 1904-05, and in the fall of 1907 the Grand Trunk Pacific Railway surveyed the Young townsite, as the company was building their main line from Winnipeg to Edmonton. The name Young (it is uncertain to what or whom it refers) was chosen to fit the alphabetical sequence of naming communities along the rail line — Watrous, Xena, Young, Zelma, Allan, etc. Trains were running in 1908, and a lumberyard, a store, and a restaurant were among the first businesses established that year. As well, two grain elevators were also erected. A hardware store, and a livery and feed barn followed the year after. The Young Post Office was established on April 1, 1909, by Charles Edward Mattenley in his store, and Mattenley held the position of postmaster until his death in 1944. Also in 1909, the boundaries of the Young School District were set, and by this time all of the available land in the area had been bought up. Young was incorporated on June 7, 1910 — the year the Manitou Hotel was built and a Massey-Harris dealership opened — and by 1912, when the Quebec Bank opened a branch (the Royal Bank after 1917), local businesses could supply most necessary commodities and services. The Young Co-op, organized in 1914, was one of the first established in the province. Visions of the new community becoming a significant railway centre occupied the minds of early residents as the construction of more railway lines progressed through the district. Many found work on these projects. In 1911, the CPR line through Young from Regina to Colonsay was completed; and a few years later the GTP was building north from Young through Cudworth and Wakaw toward Prince Albert. There was talk of other lines passing through Young that never materialized. Although the local history recounts that 10 passenger trains passed through each day, Watrous had become the divisional point on the GTP main line, and Young did not become the railway hub, the possible city once imagined. Yet the village grew from a population of 73 in 1911 to 364 by 1926, the citizenry a combination of people of Norwegian, German, British, and Swedish origins. During the Depression, Young lost close to 12 per cent of its population, but following WWII the community entered a period of expansion and prosperity. In the 1960s, Young became somewhat of a boomtown, as the construction of the region's potash mines was underway. The mine at Allan began production in 1968; the Colonsay mine began production in 1969. Young's population climbed to 500 by the beginning of the 1970s, and it remained at that level for most of the decade. A trailer court accommodated many workers, and the area economy was changing. CN abandoned their line running north of Young in 1977; CP abandoned the Colonsay Subdivision through Young in 1987. In 2001, two grain elevators were left standing in the village, but that year the Saskatchewan Wheat Pool ceased operations in Young and one more elevator was demolished. The remaining elevator was purchased by a private individual. Agriculture remains an important industry in the area; however, today, employment in the region's potash mines is also key to the economy. Businesses in Young today include a store, a service station, the post office, a credit union, an insurance agency, a hotel and café, and a restaurant. Young also has three churches (United, Lutheran, and Roman Catholic), a library, a community hall, a seniors' centre, a curling rink and hockey arena, a swimming pool, a golf course, ball diamonds, and a playground. There is a hospital and an RCMP detachment in Watrous; Young has a volunteer fire department. Young area landmarks include the Bethel Lutheran Church and Cemetery some distance southwest of the village, in an area once known as "Little Norway." Norwegian settlers had established a congregation shortly after their arrival in the district in 1909 and built the existent church in 1916. Regular services were conducted there until 1971. A short distance to the northeast of Young stands Covenant Church, also built in 1916. It was erected by the district's Swedish families, who had established their congregation in 1911. The last weekly services were held at Covenant Church in 1925, although periodic services were held until 1971. Both Bethel Lutheran and Covenant Church were designated heritage properties in the mid-1990s. Young serves as the administrative centre of the RM of Morris No. 312.

ZEALANDIA, town, pop 90 (2006c), 111 (2001c), is located 19 km northeast of Rosetown on Hwy 7. Settlers began arriving in the district around 1904-05, many traversing what was known as the Old Bone Trail, which ran south-westward

▲ **ZEALANDIA, 1910.**
Photograph courtesy of the Harris and District Museum.

▶ **BUSINESSES PAST AND PRESENT:** Zealandia's former hotel (right) and the elevator complex now used for cleaning and processing pulse crops. Photograph taken July 20, 2004.

from Saskatoon. The Zealandia Post Office was established in 1906, and with the construction of the railway from Saskatoon to Zealandia en route to Rosetown in 1908, significant development at the townsite began. The name Zealandia honours the home country of one of the district's early pioneers. In 1909, Zealandia was incorporated as a village, and by 1910 four grain elevators lined the tracks in the community and a good number of businesses had been established. In 1911, Zealandia acquired town status with a population of 264, the largest the community would ever have. The town's numbers significantly declined through the 1920s, and plummeted to 136 by 1936. The town recovered somewhat after WWII, but by the early 1970s it once again was in decline. The school which had been established at the community's inception was closed in 1970. Today, little is left of the once-thriving business community, although there remains a plant which processes lentils,

peas, and chickpeas for export. Zealandia is situated within the RM of St. Andrews No. 287.

ZELMA, village, pop 30 (2006c), 40 (2001c), is located southeast of Saskatoon, between the town of Allan and the village of Young on municipal road No. 763. Settlement of the area began around 1903, and when the Grand Trunk Pacific Railway came through in 1907-08 the townsite was determined. The first places of business appeared in 1908. In 1909, the post office was established, the first elevator was erected, and a hotel was built. Zelma, situated on the railway's alphabet line following Watrous, Xena and Young,

▶ **ZELMA UNITED CHURCH.**
Photograph taken July 22, 2004.

was incorporated on August 10, 1910; the name of the community had been chosen by the area's first doctor, Dr. Nelson Edgar, in honour of his sister-in-law. The railway station was built in 1911, and in 1912 a school district centred on the village was established. The village's peak was between the mid-1920s and the late 1950s, when the population averaged around 100 and the community had a number of businesses. The commercial sector and population subsequently declined, and in 1962 only two students had enrolled in grade 12 at Zelma School. In 1964, all high school students began to be bused to Young, and by the spring of 1969 the doors to Zelma's school were closed to all grades for good. The Zelma Post Office closed in 1985, and today there are no businesses or services left in the community. A feature of the village today is the Zelma United Church. Built in 1909-10 for the community's Presbyterian congregation, the church was designated a heritage property in 1981 and remains meticulously maintained. The last regular service at Zelma United Church, the only church ever built in the village, was held on June 30, 1968. Zelma is situated in an area of mixed agriculture and lies in proximity to three potash mines. The community is situated in the RM of Morris No. 312.

ZENON PARK, village, pop 192 (2006c), 231 (2001c), is located in the eastern parklands, 45 km northeast of Tisdale. In the spring of 1910, French-Canadians who had been working as factory workers in Massachusetts and Rhode Island began arriving in the area. Poverty had driven them to the United States, but the prospect of owning their own land bought them back to Canada, and west. Over the next two years, more families from the United States, Quebec, and Ontario settled the area. Within a couple of years, a school and church were constructed in the district. The townsite of Zenon Park was established in 1929, when the CNR constructed a branch line north from Crooked River. The name of the community pays tribute to Zenon Chamberland, one of the first pioneers and the first postmaster of the new settlement. Within a year of the railway's arrival, four grain elevators, a railway station, and a number of businesses were built adjacent to the tracks. In 1941, the village was incorporated, and from the early 1950s through to the mid-1960s, Zenon Park's population peaked at close to 400. In 1962, the community suffered a disastrous fire, which took several of the buildings on the village's main street. Today, the community remains predominantly French-speaking, although most residents are bilingual. Zenon Park has two schools: École Zenon Park School and École Notre-Dame-des-Vertus. Local businesses include two grocery stores, a credit union, a hotel and restaurant, a post office, and a garage and gas station. A large community hall is used for social occasions, and recreational facilities include curling and skating rinks, and ball diamonds. Our Lady of the Nativity Roman Catholic Church,

constructed in the summer of 1930 with local volunteer labour to replace the original 1913 church that was destroyed by fire earlier that year, has a very active congregation and has been designated a heritage property. The Zenon Park area economy is predominantly agriculture-based, but diverse: it includes honey production, organic seed processing, alfalfa dehydration, seed production, herbs, and spices. Forestry products are also a factor. Zenon Park is situated on the boundary between the RM of Arborfield No. 456 and the RM of Connaught No. 457.

VIEWS OF ZENON PARK: (left) Our Lady of the Nativity Roman Catholic Church / Church Notre Dame de la Nativité; (below) Main Street / Rue Principale, looking east; (bottom) the community with its distinctive water tower as seen from the south. Photographs taken August 13, 2004.

APPENDIX A
Source Materials

Although much of the research conducted during the "Our Towns" project was done by visiting communities and through personal interviews, many other sources were utilized. Sources for population and school enrollment figures are outlined in the Preface. Other sources are listed here.

ATLASES AND MAPS

MapArt Publishing's "Range and Township Road Maps" for southern and central Saskatchewan have proven to be very useful and, in the opinion of the author, are the best general purpose maps of their kind produced. The Government of Canada's 1977 Hall Commission Maps of the then-existing railway network and of the recommended railway network were, as well, invaluable, as was Saskatchewan Highways and Transportation's continuously revised map of the "Saskatchewan Rail Network." The Geological Highway Map of Saskatchewan published by the Saskatchewan Geological Society in 2002 was at times consulted, as were federally-produced 1:50,000 scale and 1:250,000 scale maps dating to the 1940s and as current as the 1990s. Online sources included Statistics Canada's series of maps relating to census geography, and Google Inc.'s Google Earth. The following two excellent atlases were regularly consulted; it should be noted, however, that the 1969 version has the more detailed section on the "Spread of Railways":

Richards, J. Howard, and K.I. Fung, eds. *Atlas of Saskatchewan*. Saskatoon: University of Saskatchewan, 1969.

Fung, K.I., ed. *Atlas of Saskatchewan*. Saskatoon: University of Saskatchewan, 1999.

BOOKS

Hundreds of local history books were consulted during the preparation of *Our Towns*; as such, listing them all here would not be practical. Instead, I refer one to the Saskatchewan local history directory: a locality guide to community and church histories in the Prairie History Room, Regina Public Library, compiled by Sharon Maier of the Regina Public Library. Maier continuously updates the directory as new local histories are produced; copies are available at the Regina Public Library and the province's university libraries. Additionally, a searchable online version (albeit a 1990 version) can be found on the internet at www.ourroots.ca. Other books consulted were:

Acton, Donald F., et al. *The Ecoregions of Saskatchewan*. Regina: Canadian Plains Research Center, 1998.

Archer, John H. *Saskatchewan, a History*. Saskatoon: Western Producer Prairie Books, 1980.

Banting, Meredith Black, comp. and ed. *Early History of Saskatchewan Churches (grass roots)*. 2 vols. Regina: Banting, 1975.

Barnhart, Gordon L. *Building for the Future: A Photo-journal of Saskatchewan's Legislative Building*. Regina: Canadian Plains Research Center, 2002.

Barnhart, Gordon L., ed. *Saskatchewan Premiers of the Twentieth Century*. Regina: Canadian Plains Research Center, 2004.

Barry, Bill. *People Places: Saskatchewan and its Names*. Regina: Canadian Plains Research Center, 1997.

Barry, Bill. *Geographic Names of Saskatchewan*. Regina: People Places Publishing, 2005.

Bocking, D.H., ed. *Pages from the Past: Essays on Saskatchewan History*. Saskatoon: Western Producer Prairie Books, 1979.

Chisholm, Doug. *Their Names Live On: Remembering Saskatchewan's Fallen in WWII*. Regina: Canadian Plains Research Center, 2001.

Clancy, Michael, and Anna Clancy. *A User's Guide to Saskatchewan Parks*. Regina: Canadian Plains Research Center, 2006.

Dale-Burnett, Lisa, ed. *Saskatchewan Agriculture: Lives Past and Present*. Regina: Canadian Plains Research Center, 2006.

Gorman, Jack. *Père Murray and the Hounds: The Story of Saskatchewan's Notre Dame College*. Hanna, Alberta: Gorman Publishers, 1990.

Hahn, Robert H. *None of the Roads Were Paved*. Markham: Fitzhenry and Whiteside, 1985.

Hamilton, Marie Albina, and Zachary Macaulay Hamilton. *These are the Prairies*. Regina: School Aids and Text Book Publishing Co., c1948.

Hawkes, John. *The Story of Saskatchewan and Its People*. Chicago: S.J. Clarke Publishing Co., 1924.

Hodgson, Heather, ed. *Saskatchewan Writers: Lives Past and Present*. Regina: Canadian Plains Research Center, 2004.

Hryniuk, Margaret. *A Tower of Attraction: An Illustrated History of Government House, Regina, Saskatchewan*. Regina: Canadian Plains Research Center, 1991.

Lalonde, Meika, and Elton LaClare. *Discover Saskatchewan: A Guide to Historic Sites*. Regina: Canadian Plains Research Center, 1998.

Marchildon, Greg, and Sid Robinson. *Canoeing the Churchill: A Practical Guide to the Historic Voyageur Highway*. Regina: Canadian Plains Research Center, 2002.

McCourt, Edward. *Saskatchewan*. Toronto: Macmillan of Canada, 1968.

Mortin, Jenni. *The Building of a Province: The Saskatchewan Association of Rural Municipalities — A History*. Saskatoon: Saskatchewan Association of Rural Municipalities, 1995.

Quiring, Brett, ed. *Saskatchewan Politicians: Lives Past and Present*. Regina: Canadian Plains Research Center, 2004.

Ralko, Joe. *Building Our Future: A People's Architectural History of Saskatchewan*. Calgary: Red Deer Press, 2004.

Russell, E.T., ed. *What's in a Name? Travelling through Saskatchewan with the Story behind 1600 Place-names*. 2nd ed. Saskatoon: Western Producer Prairie Books, 1975.

Stegner, Wallace. *Wolf Willow: A History, a Story and a Memory of the Last Prairie Frontier*. 1955; rpt. Toronto: Macmillan of Canada, Laurentian Library ed., 1977.

Stoffel, Holden, ed. *Saskatchewan Sports: Lives Past and Present*. Regina: Canadian Plains Research Center, 2007.

Thompson, Christian, ed. *Saskatchewan First Nations: Lives Past and Present*. Regina: Canadian Plains Research Center, 2004.

Thraves, Bernard, M.L. Lewry, Janis E. Dale, and Hansgeorg Schlichtmann, eds. *Saskatchewan: Geographic Perspectives*. Regina: Canadian Plains Research Center, 2007.

Tracie, Carl J. *"Toil and Peaceful Life": Doukhobor Village Settlement in Saskatchewan, 1899-1918*. Regina: Canadian Plains Research Center, 1996.

Waiser, Bill. *Saskatchewan: A New History*. Calgary: Fifth House, 2005.

Wolvengrey, Arok, comp. *Cree: Words*. 2 vols. Regina: Canadian Plains Research Center, 2001.

Wright, J.C.F. *Saskatchewan: The History of a Province*. Toronto: McClelland and Stewart, 1955.

BUSINESS DIRECTORIES

Henderson's Directories were often quite useful, as were the following:

Business Directory of 117 Northern Saskatchewan Cities, Towns, and Villages. Saskatoon: Saskatchewan Directory Enterprises, 1952.

Business Directory of 140 Southern Saskatchewan Cities, Towns, and Villages. Saskatoon: Prairie Business Directories, 1953.

Golden Jubilee Edition of Saskatchewan Business Directory. Saskatoon: Prairie Business Directories, 1955.

Diamond Jubilee Edition Saskatchewan Business Directory. Saskatoon: Western Canada Directories, 1965.

ENCYCLOPEDIAS

The Encyclopedia of Saskatchewan. David A. Gauthier, general manager. Regina: Canadian Plains Research Center, 2005.

The Canadian Encyclopedia: year 2000 edition. James Marsh, editor in chief. Toronto: McClelland and Stewart, 1999.

Encyclopedia of the Great Plains. David J. Wishart, editor. Lincoln, Nebraska: University of Nebraska Press, c2004.

INTERNET RESOURCES

Note: In addition to the resources listed below, the websites of all cities, most towns, and many villages were consulted. These are easily found by simply searching for the community by name (i.e., "Town of Ituna" or "Ituna, Saskatchewan"). The online resources provided here are not exhaustive; only those most frequently accessed are included. Further, rather than listing all website addresses, which are subject to change, it has been thought that simply describing the resource related to the purpose which it served may be more helpful over the long term.

Community Information (general): see the Government of Saskatchewan's "Saskbiz.ca" website.

Demographics: see Statistics Canada's website.

Genealogy/History, etc.: see the website of the Saskatchewan Genealogical Society or the Saskatchewan GenWeb site at www.rootsweb.com/~cansk/Saskatchewan. Both of these sites have many useful links, relating not only to genealogy, but to many aspects of the province's history as well.

Health Care Facilities: comprehensive listings of facilities and services can be found by going to the provincial government's web site "www.health.gov.sk.ca" and following the links to "Health Regions" or "Regional Health Authorities."

Heritage Properties: see the Saskatchewan Register of Heritage Property online.

Homestead Information: see the Saskatchewan Homestead Index at www.saskhomesteads.com.

Incorporation Dates, information on types of municipalities, restructured villages (dissolutions, etc.), organized hamlets changed to hamlets, rural municipality boundary changes, etc., may be found on the Government of Saskatchewan's Ministry of Municipal Affairs web site. This site contains a link to the province's municipal directory.

Local Histories: a number of federal institutions and Canadian universities have partnered to make local histories available in a digital, searchable format. The site, available in both French and English, is called, "Our Roots: canada's local histories online"; the website address is: www.ourroots.ca.

Manufacturers: see the provincial ministry of Energy and Resources' online Manufacturer's Guide.

Mennonites: see the Global Anabaptist Mennonite Encyclopedia online (www.gameo.org), as well as the Mennonite Church of Saskatchewan's website.

Newspapers (local weeklies): see the Saskatchewan Weekly Newspaper Association's website.

Northern Communities: see the University of Saskatchewan's "Northern Research Portal."

Post offices and Postmasters: the Library and Archives Canada website was used to obtain information on these.

RCMP Detachments: see the online "F" Division detachment list.

MISCELLANEOUS MATERIALS

Directory of Members of Parliament and Federal Elections for the North-West Territories and Saskatchewan, 1887-1966. Regina: Saskatchewan Archives Board, 1984.

Historical Directory of Saskatchewan Newspapers, 1878-1983. Regina: Saskatchewan Archives Board, 1984.

Saskatchewan Executive and Legislative Directory, 1905-1970. Regina: Saskatchewan Archives Board, 1971.

Saskatchewan Executive and Legislative Directory (Supplement), 1964-1977. Regina: Saskatchewan Archives Board, 1978.

Saskatchewan Grain Elevators: A Brief History of the Grain Handling Industry. Regina: Saskatchewan Heritage Foundation, 2006.

Saskatchewan Grain Elevators: An Inventory of Grain Handling Facilities. Regina: Saskatchewan Heritage Foundation, 2006.

Saskatchewan Museums Guide: Your Travelling Companion as You Tour the Province. Regina: Museums Association of Saskatchewan, 2002.

Saskatchewan's Ukrainian Legacy: A Travel Guide to the Cultural and Historical Sites in the Ukrainian Bloc Settlement Communities. [Sask.]: Saskatchewan Ukrainian Historical Society, 2006.

APPENDIX B
List of Saskatchewan Communities in Our Towns by Community Status

273 VILLAGES

Abbey	Canwood	Elbow	Heward	Lucky Lake	North Portal	Sceptre
Abernethy	Carievale	Elfros	Hodgeville	MacNutt	Odessa	Sedley
Albertville	Carmichael	Elstow	Holdfast	Macoun	Osage	Semans
Alida	Caronport	Endeavour	Hubbard	Macrorie	Paddockwood	Senlac
Alsask	Ceylon	Englefeld	Hyas	Major	Pangman	Shackleton
Alvena	Chamberlain	Ernfold	Invermay	Makwa	Paradise Hill	Shamrock
Aneroid	Chaplin	Eyebrow	Jansen	Mankota	Parkside	Sheho
Annaheim	Christopher Lake	Fairlight	Keeler	Manor	Paynton	Shell Lake
Antler	Clavet	Fenwood	Kelliher	Mantario	Pelly	Silton
Archerwill	Climax	Fillmore	Kenaston	Marcelin	Pennant	Simpson
Arran	Coderre	Findlater	Kendal	Marengo	Pense	Smeaton
Atwater	Codette	Flaxcombe	Kennedy	Margo	Penzance	Smiley
Avonlea	Coleville	Forget	Kenosee Lake	Markinch	Perdue	Spalding
Aylesbury	Conquest	Fosston	Killaly	Marquis	Pierceland	Speers
Aylsham	Consul	Fox Valley	Kincaid	Marsden	Pilger	Spy Hill
Bangor	Craven	Frobisher	Kinley	Maryfield	Pleasantdale	St. Benedict
Beatty	Creelman	Frontier	Kisbey	Maymont	Plenty	St. Gregor
Beechy	Dafoe	Gainsborough	Krydor	McLean	Plunkett	St. Louis
Belle Plaine	Debden	Gerald	Laird	McTaggart	Prelate	Stenen
Bethune	Denholm	Gladmar	Lake Alma	Meacham	Primate	Stewart Valley
Bjorkdale	Denzil	Glaslyn	Lake Lenore	Meath Park	Prud'homme	Stockholm
Bladworth	Dilke	Glen Ewen	Lancer	Medstead	Punnichy	Storthoaks
Borden	Dinsmore	Glenavon	Landis	Mendham	Quill Lake	Strongfield
Bracken	Disley	Glenside	Lang	Meota	Quinton	Success
Bradwell	Dodsland	Golden Prairie	Leask	Mervin	Rabbit Lake	Tantallon
Briercrest	Dorintosh	Goodeve	Lebret	Middle Lake	Rama	Tessier
Brock	Drake	Goodsoil	Leoville	Milden	Rhein	Theodore
Broderick	Drinkwater	Goodwater	Leross	Minton	Richard	Togo
Brownlee	Dubuc	Grand Coulee	Lestock	Mistatim	Richmound	Tompkins
Buchanan	Duff	Grayson	Liberty	Montmartre	Ridgedale	Torquay
Buena Vista	Duval	Halbrite	Limerick	Mortlach	Riverhurst	Tramping Lake
Bulyea	Dysart	Harris	Lintlaw	Muenster	Roche Percee	Tribune
Cadillac	Earl Grey	Hawarden	Lipton	Neilburg	Rockhaven	Tugaske
Calder	Ebenezer	Hazenmore	Loon Lake	Netherhill	Ruddell	Tuxford
	Edam	Hazlet	Loreburn	Neudorf	Rush Lake	Val Marie
	Edenwold	Hepburn	Love	Neville	Ruthilda	Valparaiso

Vanguard
Vanscoy
Vibank
Viscount
Waldeck
Waldron
Waseca
Webb
Weekes
Weirdale
Weldon
Welwyn
White Fox
Wilcox
Willowbrook
Windthorst
Wiseton
Wood Mountain
Yarbo
Yellow Creek
Young
Zelma
Zenon Park

172 ORGANIZED HAMLETS

Alta Vista
Amsterdam
Ardill
Arlington Beach
Balone Beach
Bankend
Barrier Ford
Bayard
Bayview Heights
Beaubier
Beaver Creek
Bellegarde
Big Beaver
Blumenthal
Brancepeth
Burgis Beach
Cactus Lake
Candiac

Cannington Lake
Caron
Casa Rio
Cathedral Bluffs
Cedar Villa Estates
Chelan
Chortitz
Claybank
Clemenceau
Colesdale Park
Collingwood Lakeshore
    Estates
Congress
Corning
Courval
Crane Valley
Crawford Estates
Crutwell
Crystal Bay-Sunset
Crystal Lake
Crystal Springs
Cudsaskwa Beach
Darlings Beach
Davin
Day's Beach
Delmas
Demaine
Eagle Ridge Country Estates
Edgeley
Elbow Lake
Eldersley
Erwood
Evergreen Acres
Evergreen Brightsand
Exner's Twin Bays
Fairholme
Fairy Glen
Fife Lake
Fiske
Frenchman Butte
Furdale
Garrick
Good Spirit Acres
Gray
Greenspot

Gronlid
Guernsey
Hagen
Hazel Dell
Hendon
Hitchcock Bay
Hoey
Holbein
Horseshoe Bay
Indian Point-Golden Sands
Jasmin
Kandahar
Kayville
Ketchen
Kopp's Kove
Kronau
Kuroki
Kylemore
Lady Lake
Lakeview
Langbank
Lanz Point
Laporte
Lisieux
Little Fishing Lake
Little Swan River
Livelong
Lone Rock
MacDowall
MacPheat Park
Main Centre
Martinson's Beach
Mayfair
Maymont Beach
McCord
Merrill Hills
Meskanaw
Mikado
Mohr's Beach
Moose Bay
Mowery Beach
Mozart
Mullingar
Nesslin Lake
Neuanlage

Neuhorst
North Colesdale Park
North Shore Fishing Lake
North Weyburn
Northside
Nut Mountain
Okla
Orkney
Ormiston
Otthon
Ottman-Murray Beach
Oungre
Parkland Beach
Parkview
Parry
Pasqua Lake
Peebles
Pelican Cove
Pelican Point
Pelican Shores
Percival
Phillips Grove
Powm Beach
Prairie River
Prince
Riceton
Riversedge
Riverside Estates
Runnymede
Sand Point Beach
Sarnia Beach
Scout Lake
Shipman
Simmie
Sleepy Hollow
Snowden
Sorenson's Beach
South Waterhen Lake
Spring Bay
Spruce Bay
Spruce Lake
St. Isidore-de-Bellevue
St. Joseph's
Summerfield Beach
Sunset Beach

Sunset View Beach
Swan Plain
Sylvania
Tadmore
Taylor Beach
Trevessa Beach
Trossachs
Tuffnell
Turtle Lake Lodge
Turtle Lake South Bay
Tway
Uhl's Bay
Usherville
Vantage
Viceroy
West Chatfield Beach
Westview
White Bear
Wishart
Wymark

147 TOWNS

Aberdeen
Alameda
Allan
Arborfield
Arcola
Asquith
Assiniboia
Balcarres
Balgonie
Battleford
Bengough
Bienfait
Big River
Biggar
Birch Hills
Blaine Lake
Bredenbury
Broadview
Bruno
Burstall
Cabri
Canora

Carlyle
Carnduff
Carrot River
Central Butte
Choiceland
Churchbridge
Colonsay
Coronach
Craik
Cudworth
Cupar
Cut Knife
Dalmeny
Davidson
Delisle
Duck Lake
Dundurn
Eastend
Eatonia
Elrose
Esterhazy
Eston
Fleming
Foam Lake
Fort Qu'Appelle
Francis
Govan
Gravelbourg
Grenfell
Gull Lake
Hafford
Hague
Hanley
Herbert
Hudson Bay
Imperial
Indian Head
Ituna
Kamsack
Kelvington
Kerrobert
Kindersley
Kinistino
Kipling
Kyle

Lafleche
Lampman
Langenburg
Langham
Lanigan
Lashburn
Leader
Lemberg
Leroy
Lumsden
Luseland
Macklin
Maidstone
Maple Creek
Marshall
Martensville
Meadow Lake
Midale
Milestone
Moosomin
Morse
Mossbank
Naicam
Nipawin
Nokomis
Norquay
Ogema
Osler
Outlook
Oxbow
Pilot Butte
Ponteix
Porcupine Plain
Preeceville
Qu'Appelle
Radisson
Radville
Raymore
Redvers
Regina Beach

Rocanville
Rockglen
Rose Valley
Rosetown
Rosthern
Rouleau
Saltcoats
Scott
Shaunavon
Shellbrook
Sintaluta
Southey
Spiritwood
Springside
St. Brieux
St. Walburg
Star City
Stoughton
Strasbourg
Sturgis
Tisdale
Turtleford
Unity
Vonda
Wadena
Wakaw
Waldheim
Wapella
Warman
Watrous
Watson
Wawota
White City
Whitewood
Wilkie
Willow Bunch
Wolseley
Wynyard
Yellow Grass
Zealandia

42 HAMLETS

Admiral
Arelee
Benson
Birsay
Brooksby
Burr
Cando
Crooked River
Dollard
Domremy
Girvin
Glen Bain
Glentworth
Glidden
Griffin
Handel
Herschel
Insinger
Jedburgh
Kelfield
Khedive
Lacadena
Lajord
Leslie
Lockwood
Loverna
Mazenod
Meyronne
Palmer
Piapot
Reward
Robsart
Sovereign
Spring Valley
Springwater
St. Victor
Stalwart

Stornoway
Vawn
Veregin
Woodrow
Wroxton

39 RESORT VILLAGES

Alice Beach
Aquadeo
Beaver Flat
Big Shell
Bird's Point
B-Say-Tah
Candle Lake
Chitek Lake
Chorney Beach
Cochin
Coteau Beach
Echo Bay
Etters Beach
Fort San
Glen Harbour
Grandview Beach
Greig Lake
Island View
Kannata Valley
Kivimaa-Moonlight Bay
Leslie Beach
Lumsden Beach
Manitou Beach
Melville Beach
Metinota
Mistusinne
North Grove
Pebble Baye
Pelican Pointe
Sandy Beach
Shields

South Lake
Sun Valley
Sunset Cove
Thode
Tobin Lake
Wakaw Lake
Wee Too Beach
West End
* Katepwa Beach
* Katepwa South
* Sandy Beach

13 NORTHERN VILLAGES

Air Ronge
Beauval
Buffalo Narrows
Cole Bay
Cumberland House
Denare Beach
Green Lake
Ile-a-la-Crosse
Jans Bay
La Loche
Pelican Narrows
Pinehouse
Sandy Bay

13 CITIES

Estevan
Humboldt
Lloydminster
Melfort
Melville
Moose Jaw
North Battleford
Prince Albert
Regina
Saskatoon

Swift Current
Weyburn
Yorkton

11 NORTHERN SETTLEMENTS

Bear Creek
Black Point
Brabant Lake
Camsell Portage
Descharme Lake
Garson Lake
Sled Lake
Southend
Stanley Mission
Uranium City
Wollaston Lake

9 NORTHERN HAMLETS

Dore Lake
Michel Village
Missinipe
Patuanak
St. George's Hill
Stony Rapids
Timber Bay
Turnor Lake
Weyakwin

2 NORTHERN TOWNS

Creighton
La Ronge

---

* Former resort villages now amalgamated into the Municipal District of Katepwa.

APPENDIX C
Community Status

BEGINNINGS OF LOCAL GOVERNMENT

As the area that is now Saskatchewan slowly began to be settled, the need for local government arose, and in 1883 the Territorial Council passed the Municipal Ordinance providing for town and other municipal organization. Regina was proclaimed a town that year, Moose Jaw followed the next, and in 1885 Prince Albert, too, attained town status. In the late 1880s and in the 1890s legislation was passed pertaining to villages. In 1894 Saltcoats was incorporated as a village, the first community established as such in what is now Saskatchewan. The procedure by which a village might obtain town status was not established until 1901, and until 1908 it needed a population of only 400 to raise itself to the next higher municipal level. Only three cities were incorporated during the Territorial period: Regina and Moose Jaw via special ordinance in 1903, and Prince Albert in 1904. At the time that Saskatchewan became a province in 1905, in addition to the three cities, there legally existed 16 towns and 60 villages. Legislation in 1908-09 further outlined the organization, powers, responsibilities and duties of these local governments. By this time hamlets were recognized, as was how many people could comprise a type of community: hamlets had up to 50 residents; a village up to 500; a town had 500 to 5,000 people; and cities had 5,000 or more.

LEGISLATION TODAY

As the twentieth century progressed and society became more complex, there arose the need for additional community definitions: B-Say-Tah became the first incorporated resort village in 1915; in the late 1940s organized hamlets began to be established. Today, to be incorporated as a village or a resort village, a community must have been an organized hamlet for at least three years, have a population of at least 100 recorded in the most recent census, and contain at least 50 separate dwellings or business premises. Similarly, villages and resort villages may apply to become towns if they have a population of 500 or more. An organized hamlet elects a hamlet board, which acts as an advisory body to the rural municipal council on hamlet matters and receives a portion of municipal taxes and fees collected. To form an organized hamlet, a petition must be signed by 30 people who would be eligible voters within the community. A hamlet, on the other hand, falls completely under the jurisdiction of the rural municipality in which it is situated and is generally legally described as "an unincorporated community with 5 or more occupied dwellings and at least 10 subdivided lots, the majority of which is on average less than an acre."

THE NORTH

Legislation was enacted to accommodate the growing need for local government in the province's north in the latter half of the twentieth century, most notably, *The Northern Municipalities Act* of 1983. Under the *Act*, northern towns, northern villages, and northern hamlets could be incorporated, and northern settlements (unincorporated entities) were legally defined. The latter are a part of the Northern Saskatchewan Administration District and are administered by the Northern Municipal Services Branch. A northern settlement has an advisory committee which works with the Northern Municipal Services Branch, and it may become a northern hamlet if it has a population of at least 50 and contains 25 or more separate dwellings or business premises. Northern hamlets may apply to become northern villages if they have a population of at least 100 and contain 50 or more separate dwellings or business premises. A northern village may seek the status of a northern town if its population is 500 or more.

*****

The above is but a brief history of legislation pertaining to Saskatchewan communities, and the above descriptions of community types are by necessity simplified. Much of the above has been gleaned from *The Municipalities Act, The Cities Act, and The Northern Municipalities Act.* These are available from the Queen's Printer and can be viewed online on their website.